W9-BVF-537

Prentice-Hall Series in Accounting
Charles T. Horngren, Editor

AUDITING: AN INTEGRATED APPROACH, 2/E
Arens/Loebbecke

KOHLER'S DICTIONARY FOR ACCOUNTANTS, 6/E
Cooper/Ijiri

FINANCIAL STATEMENT ANALYSIS
Foster

FINANCIAL ACCOUNTING: PRINCIPLES AND ISSUES, 2/E
Granof

INTRODUCTION TO FINANCIAL ACCOUNTING
Horngren

INTRODUCTION TO MANAGEMENT ACCOUNTING, 5/E
Horngren

COST ACCOUNTING: A MANAGERIAL EMPHASIS, 5/E
Horngren

CPA PROBLEMS AND APPROACHES TO SOLUTIONS, 5/E
VOLUMES I & II
Horngren/Leer

ADVANCED MANAGEMENT ACCOUNTING
Kaplan

FUND ACCOUNTING, 2/E
Lynn/Freeman

A NEW INTRODUCTION TO FINANCIAL ACCOUNTING, 2/E
May/Mueller/Williams

AUDITING PRINCIPLES, 5/E
Stettler

BUDGETING, 4/E
Welsch

Charles T. Horngren
Ph.D., C.P.A., Stanford University

PRENTICE-HALL, INC.
ENGLEWOOD CLIFFS, NEW JERSEY 07632

COST ACCOUNTING

A Managerial Emphasis

Library of Congress Cataloging in Publication Data

HORNGREN, CHARLES T.,
Cost accounting.

Bibliography: p.
Includes index.
1.–Cost accounting. 2.–Costs, Industrial. I.–Title.
HF5686.C8H59–1982 658.1'511 81-17952
ISBN 0-13-179671-2 AACR2

Cost Accounting: A Managerial Emphasis, Fifth Edition *by Charles T. Horngren*

Editorial/production supervision *by Esther S. Koehn*
Interior design/cover design *by Linda Conway, Ass't Art Director*
Cover illustration, Downtown Los Angeles, by *Craig Aurness*
Manufacturing buyer: *Raymond Keating*

Printed in the United States of America

10 9 8 7 6 5 4

ISBN 0-13-179671-2

Prentice-Hall International, Inc., *London*
Prentice-Hall of Australia Pty. Limited, *Sydney*
Prentice-Hall of Canada, Ltd., *Toronto*
Prentice-Hall of India Private Limited, *New Delhi*
Prentice-Hall of Japan, Inc., *Tokyo*
Prentice-Hall of Southeast Asia Pte. Ltd., *Singapore*
Whitehall Books Limited, *Wellington, New Zealand*

TO PROFESSOR WILLIAM J. VATTER

Charles T. Horngren is the Edmund W. Littlefield Professor of Accounting at Stanford University. A graduate of Marquette University, he received his MBA from Harvard University, and his Ph.D. from the University of Chicago. He is also a recipient of an honorary DBA from Marquette University.

A Certified Public Accountant, Horngren served on the Accounting Principles Board for six years, the Financial Accounting Standards Board Advisory Council for five years, and the Council of the American Institute of Certified Public Accountants for three years.

A member of the American Accounting Association, Horngren has been its President and its Director of Research. He received the Outstanding Accounting Educator Award in 1973, when the Association initiated an annual series of such awards.

Professor Horngren is also a member of the National Association of Accountants, where he was on its research planning committee for three years. He is a member of the Board of Regents, Institute of Management Accounting, which administers the Certified Management Accountant examinations.

Horngren is the author of three other Prentice-Hall titles—*Introduction to Financial Accounting,* 1981; *Introduction to Management Accounting,* Fifth Edition, 1981; and *CPA Problems and Approaches to Solutions,* Fifth Edition, 1979 (with J. A. Leer).

In recognition of his outstanding contributions to accounting education, Charles T. Horngren was named the first Consulting Editor for the Prentice-Hall Series in Accounting.

Contents

SECTION TWO

Budgets and Standards as Keys to Planning and Control

5 Master Budget and Responsibility Accounting / 129

6 Flexible Budgets and Standards: Part I / 166

7 Flexible Budgets and Standards: Part II / 200

8 Income Effects of Alternative Product-Costing Methods / 234

SECTION THREE

More on Control

9 Determining How Costs Behave / 285

10 Systems Choice, Discretionary and Nonmanufacturing Costs / 317

SECTION FOUR

Relevant Costs for Nonroutine Decisions

11 Relevance, Pricing, and the Decision Process / 363

12 Capital Budgeting and Cost Analysis / 403

13 Capital Budgeting: A Closer Look / 438

SECTION FIVE
Cost Allocation in a Variety of Roles

14 Cost Allocation: An Introduction / 475

15 Cost Allocation: A Closer Look / 502

SECTION SIX
DECENTRALIZATION AND MANAGEMENT CONTROL

19 DECENTRALIZATION AND TRANSFER PRICING / 629

20 SYSTEMS CHOICE: DIVISION PERFORMANCE MEASUREMENT / 661

SECTION SEVEN

Decision Models and Accounting

25 Variances: Mix, Yield, and Investigation / 856

26 Accounting for Payroll / 891

27 Accounting Systems and Internal Control / 907

28 Cost Accounting in Professional Examinations / 939

SECTION NINE

Appendixes

Cost accounting provides data for three major purposes: (1) planning and controlling routine operations; (2) nonroutine decisions, policy making, and long-range planning; and (3) inventory valuation and income determination. This volume gives abundant consideration to all three of these, but emphasis is placed on the first two. In short, the major theme is "different costs for different purposes."

The topics emphasized from the outset are those that challenge students and spur their curiosity. Because the emphasis is on costs for planning and control, the following topics of prime managerial significance are introduced early: the role of the accountant in the organization; cost-volume-profit relationships; responsibility accounting; standard costs; flexible budgets; cost structures for control and motivation; and relevant costs of nonroutine decisions. The favorable reaction to the format of previous editions is evidence that cost accounting courses can be enriched, relieved of drudgery, and broadened from coverage of procedures alone to a full-fledged treatment of concepts, analyses, and procedures that pays more than lip-service to accounting as a managerial tool.

This flexible treatment of cost accounting and management accounting presupposes just a one-term introduction to basic accounting. Ample text and assignment materials are provided for a two-semester or two-quarter course, especially if they are supplemented with outside readings. The need for supplementation may be diminished with this edition because it has more substance (especially in the latter half) than previously. The first eleven chapters provide the essence of a one-term course. *Because instructors may disagree about what constitutes a proper sequence, this book has been designed to permit a maximum degree of flexibility with a minimum of discontinuity.*

Cost accounting courses now cover a wider range of topics than ever before. Some instructors prefer to concentrate on developing a solid comprehension of the uses and limitations of formal cost accounting systems as they exist. Others prefer a normative approach, focusing on how cost systems should be designed—or on how cost information should be provided for various classes of decisions. This book attempts to satisfy both needs; the order of chapters provided is only one of many possible sequences.

A major objective of this revision has been to promote flexibility by using a modular approach. The material has been arranged to allow instructors—who are working with students having different backgrounds and within curricula having various overlaps—the greatest latitude in picking and choosing chapters. For example, if the courses in finance emphasize capital budgeting, Chapters 12 and 13 might be omitted. If the instructor wishes to cover product-costing systems in depth, Chapters 17 and 18 on process costing (except for the portions on standard costing) and Chapter 26 on payroll accounting might be assigned immediately after Chapter 4. The standard costing in Chapters 17 and 18 might then be assigned immediately after Chapter 8.

changes in this edition

Reviewers of the fourth edition cited its following strengths: inclusion of important topics; good quantity, quality, and range of assignment material; helpful self-study problems; modular, flexible organization; clear, lively presentation; and a helpful solutions manual. These features have been retained and enhanced, but many improvements have been introduced.

Changes have been made in both content and organization. Most chapters have been thoroughly rewritten. In addition, many new problems and cases have been provided.

This edition has been very responsive to the major criticisms of the fourth edition regarding its presentations of process costs, standard cost variances, and mix and yield variances. Major changes include:

1. Introduction of process costing as well as job-order costing in Chapter 4.
2. A thorough revision of process costing in which complete explanations are accompanied by step-by-step exhibits. Operation costing has been added.
3. A complete rewriting and tighter presentation of flexible budgets and standards, which are now covered in two chapters, Chapters 6 and 7, rather than in three, Chapters 7, 8, 9 in the previous edition. This entire subject has been completely rewritten, featuring a major illustration that proceeds from simple to more complicated variance analyses.
4. Chapter 5 stresses operational budgeting, as distinguished from cash budgeting.
5. A new, extensive explanation of the control of discretionary costs, including zero-base budgeting applications in nonmanufacturing and not-for-profit organizations.
6. Updated materials on inflation and the cost of capital are the major changes in the capital budgeting chapters. Inflation is also given ample attention in the material on divisional performance.
7. Another change involves an expanded discussion of uncertainty and the cost of prediction

error in the latter part of this book. Chapters 21 through 25 definitely have clearer and deeper presentations.

8. A completely new, clear, and straightforward presentation of sales mix and production yield variances.
9. Increased attention is given to service industries, nonmanufacturing, and not-for-profit organizations.
10. A Glossary has been added.
11. A chapter-by-chapter description of revisions made is presented at the beginning of the solutions manual.

An important consideration in preparing this revision was the extent to which a quantitative approach should be included. If more quantitative material is added, should it be interwoven with appropriate topics or considered separately? The choice was to add more quantitative material, but to confine it largely to Chapters 21 through 24, again because it allows for maximum flexibility. Those instructors wanting to integrate such material with earlier chapters may do so; suggestions are provided in the solutions manual. Those who prefer to concentrate on other matters will not be hampered by having to omit some quantitative portions of chapters.

Various parts of this book may be packaged to provide a cost accounting course with either a heavy quantitative emphasis (Chapters 1, 21, 3, 4, 9, 24, 11, 22, 23, 12–13, 6–8, 25) or a heavy behavioral emphasis (Chapters 1–11, 19–20). *The front section of the solutions manual contains profuse suggestions regarding various course outlines and choices of problem material.*

comments on organization

The organizational structure of a textbook is a puzzling challenge. After sifting reviews for over twenty years, I have reached the following conclusions:

1. Instructors disagree more markedly about the sequence of chapters in cost/management accounting textbooks than about any other aspect. A tightly integrated sequence may please a segment of instructors, but it narrows a teacher's options. Consequently, I have refrained from *maximizing the satisfaction* of a relatively small fraction of the teacher population; instead, I have tried to *minimize the dissatisfaction* of the teacher population as a whole.
2. If it is impossible to please all of the potential users all of the time, a logical attack is to present a modular, flexible approach that permits jumping around with minimal inconvenience. I have taken great pains to facilitate such hopping and skipping. *In a nutshell, my rationale is to provide a loosely constrained sequence to facilitate diverse approaches to teaching.*
3. As long as deviating from a given structure causes no serious inconvenience, the organization of a text is not a central issue. The content and clarity of the chapters and the quality of the assignment material are far more important than organization. Teaching is highly personal and heavily influenced by the backgrounds and interests of assorted students and faculty in miscellaneous settings. To satisfy this audience, a book must be a pliable tool, not a straitjacket. As one reviewer of the fourth edition stated, "I have never understood the sequencing of chapters in the book, but it has never limited my usage of the book."

acknowledgments

I am indebted to many for their ideas and assistance. The acknowledgments in the four previous editions contain a long list of my creditors. My primary obligation is to Professor William J. Vatter to whom this book is dedicated. For those who know him, no words are necessary; for those who do not know him, no words will suffice.

Professor Dudley W. Curry has aided me immensely with his detailed review of the manuscript of this edition. Moreover, he has revised and expanded his two supplements to the textbook: *Test Bank* (quiz and examination material for instructors) and *Student Guide* (a chapter-by-chapter learning aid for students).

Professor John K. Harris has also been enormously helpful. He reviewed the fourth edition and conducted a detailed review of the manuscript of this edition. He has also prepared a desirable new supplement, *Professional Examination Questions and Answers: A Self-Study Approach,* wherein actual examination materials are aligned with the individual chapters of the textbook.

Another new supplement is Jonathan Schiff's *Instructor's Resource Outlines.* He has my gratitude for writing this guide for preparing day-to-day class schedules and lectures.

My Stanford colleagues have supplied incisive comments. Joel Demski, George Foster, James Patell, and Mark Wolfson have been particularly generous with their reviews and assignment materials.

The following professors influenced this edition by their preparation of reviews of the preceding edition: Joanne A. Collins, Lawrence Gordon, John K. Harris, Ronald Hilton, Bernard K. Loehr, Dee L. Kleespie, Robert Magee, William L. Stephens, Jan Sweeney, Charles J. Weiss, Robert W. Williamson, and Gil Zuckerman.

Incisive comments were received from David Bell, Robert Bickerton, Edward Blocher, Thomas Bollard, Thomas Dyckman, Maurice Hirsch, Jr., Wallace Leese, Frank Mayne, Harvey Segall, Michael Shields, Roy Skinner, and Mary Strecker. In addition, I have received helpful suggestions by mail from many users, too numerous to mention here.

Many students have read the manuscript and worked the new problems to insure that they are as error free as possible. They have also contributed ideas and material for revising chapters and preparing new problems. Particular thanks go to Leslie Burke, Donald Diltz, Sydney Firestone, Richard Hemingway, Pradeep Jotwani, Hal Marshall, and Len Musgrove.

A special note of gratitude is extended to Jackie Keane for her skillful typing of much material in syllabus form.

Also, I thank the people at Prentice-Hall: Ron Ledwith, Elinor Paige, Esther Koehn, Linda Conway, Margaret McAbee, and Marie Lines.

Appreciation also goes to the American Institute of Certified Public Accountants, The National Association of Accountants, The Institute of Management Accounting, the Society of Management Accountants of Canada, the Certified General Accountants' Association of Canada, the Financial Executives Institute of America, and to many other publishers and companies for their generous permission to quote from their publications. Problems from the Uniform CPA Examinations are designated (CPA); problems from the Certificate in Management Accounting examinations are designated (CMA); problems from the Canadian examinations administered by the Society of Management Accountants' Association are designated (SMA); problems from the Certified General Accountants' Association are designated (CGAA). Many of these problems are adapted to highlight particular points.

I am grateful to the professors who contributed assignment material for this edition. Their names are indicated in parentheses at the start of their specific problems; for example (W. Crum) indicates a contribution by William F. Crum.

Comments from users are welcome.

CHARLES T. HORNGREN

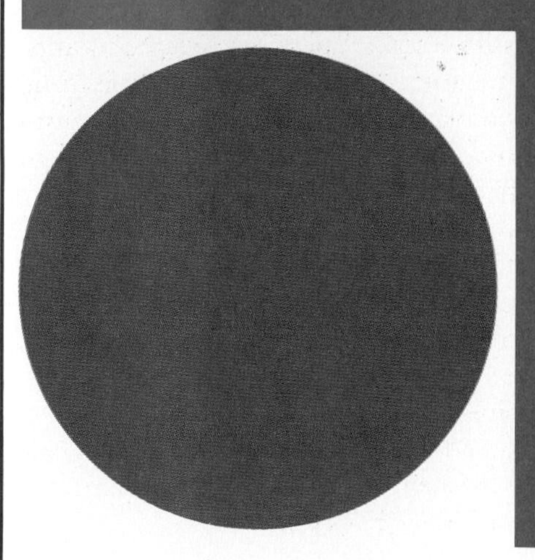

Cost Accounting Fundamentals

SECTION ONE

1 The Accountant's Role in the Organization

As this chapter is being written, former accountants are the top executives in many large companies, including Bethlehem Steel, General Motors, and General Electric. Accounting duties played a key part in their rise to the management summit. Accounting cuts across all facets of the organization; the management accountant's duties are intertwined with executive planning and control.

The study of modern cost accounting yields insight and breadth regarding both the accountant's role and the manager's role in an organization. How are these two roles related? Where may they overlap? How can accounting help managers? This book tries to answer these questions. In this chapter, we[1] shall try to get some perspective on where the accountant should fit in the organization. Then we shall have a framework for studying the rest of the chapters.

[1]Should an author use "I," "we," "the author," or "this writer" in contexts such as these? Each mode of expression has its weaknesses, but I prefer "we." As used in this book, "we" denotes a mutual exploration of the subject by the author and the readers.

Purposes of management accounting and financial accounting

basic distinctions

The accounting system is the major quantitative information system in almost every organization. It should provide information for three broad purposes:

1. Internal reporting to managers, for use in planning and controlling routine operations
2. Internal reporting to managers, for use in making nonroutine decisions and in formulating major plans and policies
3. External reporting to stockholders, government, and other outside parties

Both management and external parties share an interest in all three important purposes, but the emphasis differs. External reporting is mainly concerned with the third purpose: the historical, custodial, and stewardship aspects of accounting. This area is usually called **financial accounting,** which is heavily constrained by generally accepted accounting principles. On the other hand, internal reporting focuses on the first two purposes: management planning and control. This area is usually called **management accounting,** which has looser constraints than financial accounting.

The distinction between financial accounting and management accounting became institutionalized in the United States in 1972 when the **National Association of Accountants (NAA),** the largest association of internal accountants in the United States, established a program leading to the Certificate in Management Accounting (CMA).[2] The **Certified Management Accountant (CMA)** is the internal accountant's counterpart of the CPA (Certified Public Accountant).

boundaries of cost accounting

Where does "cost accounting" fit within the above framework? In its broadest sense, cost accounting has the same three major purposes as those described above. However, its third purpose, costing products for inventory valuation and income determination, simultaneously fulfills the demands of outsiders and those of management for such information. So, when viewed in this way, **cost accounting** *is* management accounting, plus a small part of financial accounting—to the extent that its product-costing function satisfies the requisites of external reporting.

Originally, the label *cost accounting* referred to the ways of accumulating and assigning historical costs to units of product and departments, primarily for purposes of inventory valuation and income determination. Today, cost accounting is generally indistinguishable from management accounting because it serves multiple purposes. Most fundamentally, cost accounting now refers to the gathering and providing of information for decision needs of all sorts, ranging from the management of recurring operations to the making of nonrecurring strategic decisions and the formulation of major organizational policies. As in the past, cost accounting also helps fulfill the legal requirements of reporting to stockholders, creditors, government agencies, and other external parties.

We need not be greatly concerned with the boundaries of cost accounting. The major point is that the focus of a modern cost accounting system is on helping managers deal with both the immediate and the distant future. Its concern with the past is justified only insofar as it helps prediction and satisfies external reporting requirements.

---

[2]The major objective of this program is to establish management accounting as a recognized profession. Information may be obtained from the Institute of Management Accounting, 570 City Center Building, Ann Arbor, Michigan 48104. Also see Chapter 28 in this book, "Cost Accounting in Professional Examinations."

Elements of management control

Is Safeway's management control system better than Kroger's? Unilever's better than Nestlé's? A major purpose of this book is to develop a method for answering such questions. This section provides an overview of the nature of control systems.

planning and control

Consider the following diagram:

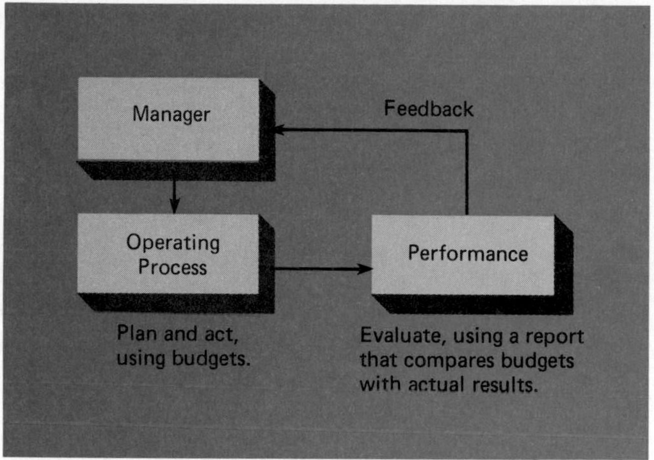

The diagram implies a rhythmic sequence that is sometimes called the management cycle of planning and control. There are countless definitions of planning and control. Here we define **planning** as a delineation of goals, predictions of potential results under various ways of achieving goals, and a decision of how to attain them. *Control* is usually distinguished from planning. **Control** is (a) action that implements the planning decision and (b) performance evaluation that provides feedback of the results.

The Operating Process box in the diagram includes planning plus the action phase of control as just defined. The Performance box and Feedback loops represent the remainder of this definition of control.

Two major accounting tools for helping managers are budgets and performance reports. **Budgets** are the formal quantifications of management's plans. **Performance reports** are measurements of activities. These reports often consist of comparisons of budgets with actual results. The deviations of actual results from budget are called **variances.** The latter help facilitate **management by exception,** which is the practice of concentrating on areas that deserve attention and ignoring areas that are running smoothly.

Planning and control are so strongly interlocked that it seems artificial to draw rigid distinctions between them. Thus, in this book the narrow idea of control will not be used. Unless otherwise stated, control will be employed in its broadest sense to denote the entire management process of *both* planning and control. For example, instead of referring to a *management planning and control system,* we will refer to a *control system.* Similarly, we will refer to the *control purpose* of accounting instead of the more awkward *planning and control purpose* of accounting.

Well-conceived plans include enough flexibility or discretion so that the manager may feel free to seize any unforeseen opportunities. That is, in no case should control mean that managers cling to a preexisting plan when unfolding events indicate the desirability of actions that were not encompassed in the original plan.

EXHIBIT 1-1

Basic Elements of Management Control System*

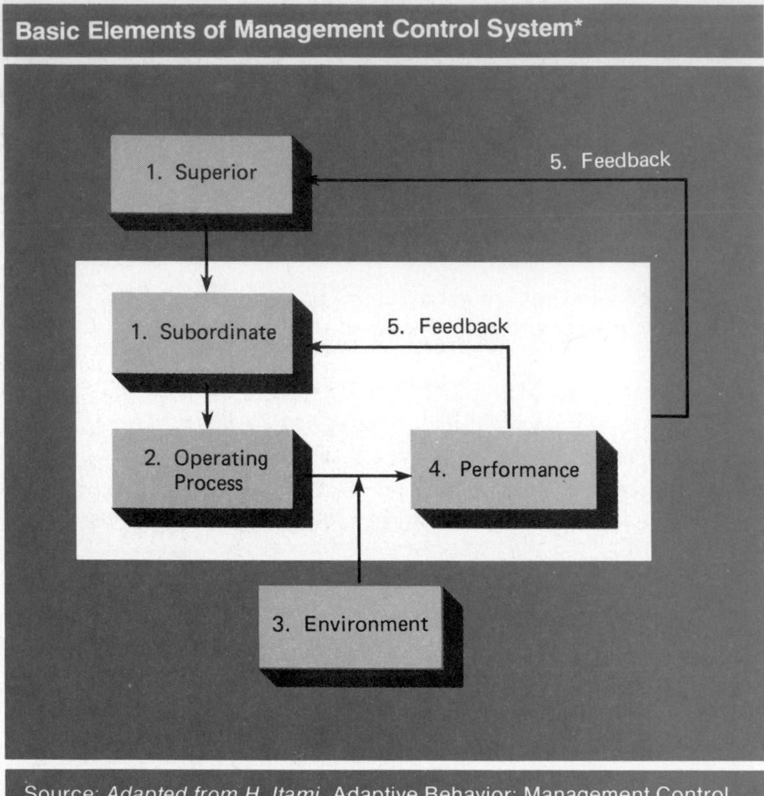

Source: *Adapted from H. Itami,* Adaptive Behavior: Management Control and Information Analysis *(Sarasota, Fla.: American Accounting Association, 1977), p. 9.*

overview of control systems

Exhibit 1-1 demonstrates the basic elements of a **management control system.** Note how our initial diagram is nested within a broader network.

1. There are at least two persons, a superior and a subordinate. The major role of the superior is to oversee the work of subordinates. This control of *human* control is what distinguishes *management control* from *engineering control* (e.g., automatic control of a heating process by a thermostat).

   Visualize hundreds or thousands of these exhibits, all interrelated at both an instant of time and through time. Then you can appreciate the enormity of the problem of management control, which often entails vast numbers of humans making countless decisions in a world of uncertainty.
2. The subordinate, such as a school principal, a train conductor, or a sales manager, supervises an operating process or processes. A **process** is a collection of decisions or activities that should be aimed at some ends. For example, there are processes of teaching, transporting, and selling.
3. The **environment** is the set of uncontrollable factors that affect the success of a process. It is a level of uncertainty or risk as to whether predicted results or outputs will be achieved. Environmental (uncontrollable) variables might include absenteeism, condition of railroad tracks, weather, and competitor reactions. The role of the environment (uncertainty or risk) is explored later, particularly in Chapter 21, which may be studied now if desired.
4. The Performance box highlights the regular evaluation of the results of the operating process. Managers are frequently helped here by various accounting reports regarding inputs or outputs or both.

5. The Feedback loops indicate how managers learn to improve the unending sequence of predictions and decisions that are embedded in the operating process.

feedback: a major key

In control systems, **feedback** often consists of a comparison of the budget with actual results. Feedback may be used for a variety of purposes, including the following:

CHANGING GOALS □ For example, based on an evaluation of past performance, a hospital may decide not to offer major heart surgery services.

SEARCHING FOR ALTERNATIVE MEANS □ For example, a state government may consider alternative ways of issuing drivers' licenses.

CHANGING METHODS FOR MAKING DECISIONS □ For example, a university may have traditionally based its maintenance decisions on how to minimize repair costs for the current year. Feedback may indicate that such a decision method is undoubtedly more expensive over the long run. The university may then base its decisions on a comparison of expected repair costs over a five-year period rather than a one-year period.

MAKING PREDICTIONS □ For example, a bank may use some new economic indicators to predict interest rates or loan demand if its feedback indicates that a poor prediction record influenced past bank budgets. **In particular, note that feedback consists of historical information.** In addition, *other information* is also used in formulating predictions.

CHANGING THE OPERATING PROCESS □ For example, use a different management style by speaking quietly rather than yelling.

CHANGING THE MEASURING AND REWARDING OF PERFORMANCE □ Rewards such as promotions and bonuses are often affected by performance reports. For example, individuals may act differently if their performance is measured by total sales rather than by total profits.

Feedback is obviously important. Yet many control systems are weak, not because the feedback is weak, but because of the managers themselves. *The managers are part of the system.* The feedback is usually available at low cost, but it is often ignored by managers. On the other hand, many successful managers actively support their control system by using feedback in a highly visible way. Both accountants and managers should periodically remind themselves that management control systems are not confined exclusively to technical matters such as data processing. **Management control is primarily a human activity that should focus on how to help other humans in their work.**

Cost-benefit approach

focus on operating decisions

This textbook has a general approach to accounting that will be referred to as a **cost-benefit approach.** That is, the primary criterion for choosing among alternative systems or accounting methods is how well they help achieve management goals in relation to their costs.

Accounting systems are economic goods. They cost money, just like beer and milk. The old adage says that if you build a better mousetrap, people will beat a path to your door. But many sellers of mousetraps will testify that when the buyers get to the door, they say, "What is the price?" Thus, if the price is too high, buyers may be unwilling to pay, and the maker of better mousetraps may face financial ruin.

The costs of buying a new accounting system include the usual clerical and data-processing activities plus educational activities. **The costs of educating users is frequently substantial, particularly when much management time is required and when the users have been reasonably satisfied with existing systems.**

Managers buy a more elaborate management accounting system when its perceived expected benefits exceed its perceived expected costs. Although the benefits may take many forms, they can be summarized as collective sets of operating decisions that will better attain top-management desires.

To illustrate this cost-benefit approach, consider the familiar story of the installation of a company's first budgeting system. Chances are high that the company had been using some historical recordkeeping and little formal planning. A major benefit from purchasing a budgeting system is to compel managers to plan and thus make a *different,* more profitable set of decisions than would have been generated by a historical system.

Admittedly, the measurement of these costs and benefits is seldom easy. Therefore, you may want to call this approach an abstract theory rather than a practical guide. Nevertheless, the cost-benefit approach provides a starting point for analyzing virtually all accounting issues. Moreover, it is directly linked to a vast theoretical structure of information economics (the application of the microeconomic theory of uncertainty to questions of buying information).[3] Furthermore, managers and practicing accountants find its central ideas appealing, probably because they have been using such a "practical" notion for years. After all, a favorite justification for the status quo is that the new system is too costly in light of expected benefits.

needs, wants, and circumstances

We often see opinions about what data are "needed" with little or no reference to the associated costs or benefits. Examples include the need for "more accurate" or "truer" approximations of "economic reality" via the compilation of more-detailed product costs or the use of data adjusted for inflation.

The cost-benefit approach focuses on wants or desires rather than needs. That is, no system or accounting technique is regarded as necessary per se. Instead, the focus is on the collective decisions that will be affected. If the decisions will be unaffected, then the least costly alternative is preferable. If the decisions will be affected differently, then the preferable alternative is that which is expected to produce the greatest benefit after deducting the costs of the system.

A key question asked by the cost-benefit approach is, **How much would we be willing to pay for one system versus another?** For example, the same shirt or blouse at a given price may be a "good buy" for one person but a "bad buy" for another person, whose circumstances may be different. Similarly, a particular cost accounting system or method may be a good buy for General Motors but a bad buy for Ford. Thus, the cost-benefit approach takes a skeptical view of such sweeping generalizations as "This budgeting technique is a vast improvement over other techniques. It is badly needed."

---

[3]For a rigorous description of this *information-evaluation approach,* see J. Demski and G. Feltham, *Cost Determination: A Conceptual Approach* (Ames: Iowa State University Press, 1976). Also see J. Demski, *Information Analysis,* 2nd ed. (Reading, Mass.: Addison-Wesley, 1980); and R. Kaplan, *Advanced Management Accounting* (Englewood Cliffs, N.J.: Prentice-Hall, 1982), Chap. 1.

Omit pg 9-23

The choice of a technique or system is inherently dependent on specific circumstances. Therefore, this book will concentrate on describing alternative techniques and systems and on how to go about making the choices between them. It will not present one cost accounting technique as being innately superior to another.[4] Again, the human element is large. The same system may work well in one organization and not in another because the collective personalities and traditions differ in each. Systems do not exist in a vacuum. Managers and accountants are integral parts of management control systems.

The pervading duties of the management accountant

This section examines how the accountant, particularly the **controller,** fits in modern organizations. Through the years, the "controller has moved from the backroom right to center stage."[5] And "probably the main reason that the controller is getting the ear of top management today is that he or she is virtually the only person familiar with all the working parts of the company."[6]

line and staff relationships

Most entities have the production and sale of goods or services as their basic objectives. Line managers are *directly* responsible for attaining these objectives as efficiently as possible. Staff elements of organizations exist because the scope of the line manager's responsibility and duties expands so that he needs specialized help to operate effectively. When a department's primary task is that of advice and service to other departments, it is a *staff* department.

Except for exerting line authority over his own department, the chief accounting executive generally fills a staff role in his company, as contrasted with the line roles of sales and production executives. This includes advice and help in the areas of budgeting, controlling, pricing, and special decisions. The accounting department does not exercise direct authority over line departments.

Management literature is hazy on these distinctions, and we shall not belabor them here. For example, some writers distinguish among three types of authority: line, staff, and functional. **Line authority** is exerted downward over subordinates. **Staff authority** is the authority to *advise* but not command others; it is exercised laterally or upward. **Functional authority** is the right to *command* action laterally and downward with regard to a specific function or specialty.

Uniformity of accounting and reporting is often acquired through the delegation of authority regarding accounting procedures to the chief management accountant, the controller, by the top line management. Note carefully that when the

---

[4]The cost-benefit way of thinking is widely applicable even if the costs and benefits defy precise measurement. As a motto in the System Analysis Office of the Department of Defense says, "It is better to be roughly right than precisely wrong." For example, if two methods of accomplishing the same disease cure are available, the least costly is preferable. Similarly, if two proposals have equal costs, the proposal that is perceived to yield more benefits is preferable. This judgment can be achieved without a numerical measurement of the levels of benefits. For example, will $100,000 spent on teachers' salaries produce more benefits than $100,000 spent on teaching machines? See R. Anthony and R. Herzlinger, *Management Control in Nonprofit Organizations,* rev. ed. (Homewood, Ill.: Richard D. Irwin, 1980), pp. 242–43, 282–85.

[5]"The Controller: Inflation Gives Him More Clout with Management," *Business Week,* August 15, 1977, p. 84.

[6]Ibid, p. 86.

controller prescribes the line department's role in supplying accounting information, he is speaking for top line management—not as the controller, a staff person. The uniform accounting procedure is authorized by the president and is installed for him by the controller.

Theoretically, the controller's decisions regarding the best accounting procedures to be followed by line people are transmitted to the president. In turn, the president communicates these procedures through a manual of instructions that comes down through the line chain of command to all people affected by the procedures.

Practically, the daily work of the controller is such that his face-to-face relationships with the production manager or foreman may call for directing how production records should be kept or how work tickets should be completed.[7] The controller usually holds delegated authority from top line management over such matters.

Exhibit 1-2 illustrates the general organizational relationships described above. Note the distinction between producing departments and service departments. The primary purpose of a factory is to produce goods. Therefore, the production-line manufacturing departments are usually termed *production* or *operating departments*. To facilitate production, most plants also have *service departments,* which exist to facilitate the tasks of the producing departments.

the controller: the chief management accountant

The word *controller* is applied to various accounting positions. The stature and duties of the controller vary from company to company. In some firms he or she[8] is little more than a glorified bookkeeper who compiles data primarily for conventional balance sheets and income statements. In other firms—for example, General Electric—he is a key executive who aids management planning and control in over 170 subdivisions. In most firms his status is somewhere between these two extremes. For example, his opinion on the tax implications of certain managerial decisions may be carefully weighed, yet his opinion on the other aspects of these decisions may not be sought. Whatever his title, he is viewed in this book as the chief management accounting executive. The point of terminology here is that the modern controller does not do any controlling in terms of line authority except over his own department. Yet the modern concept of controllership maintains that the controller *does* control in a special sense. That is, by reporting and interpreting relevant data, the controller exerts a force or influence that impels management toward logical decisions consistent with objectives.

distinctions between controller and treasurer

Many people confuse the offices of controller and **treasurer.** The position of Vice-President–Finance has evolved in many organizations. This executive typically oversees both the controllership and treasurership functions. The Financial Executives Institute, an association of corporate treasurers and controllers, distinguishes their functions as follows:

[7]According to some writers, this would be exercising the *functional authority* described above.

[8]This book generally uses "he or she" rather than "he" alone. However, as this and the next paragraph illustrate, for conciseness sometimes the masculine gender is used alone. If you prefer, substitute "she" or "her" where appropriate.

CONTROLLERSHIP	TREASURERSHIP
1. Planning and control	1. Provision of capital
2. Reporting and interpreting	2. Investor relations
3. Evaluating and consulting	3. Short-term financing
4. Tax administration	4. Banking and custody
5. Government reporting	5. Credits and collections
6. Protection of assets	6. Investments
7. Economic appraisal	7. Insurance

EXHIBIT 1-2

Partial Organization Chart of A Manufacturing Company

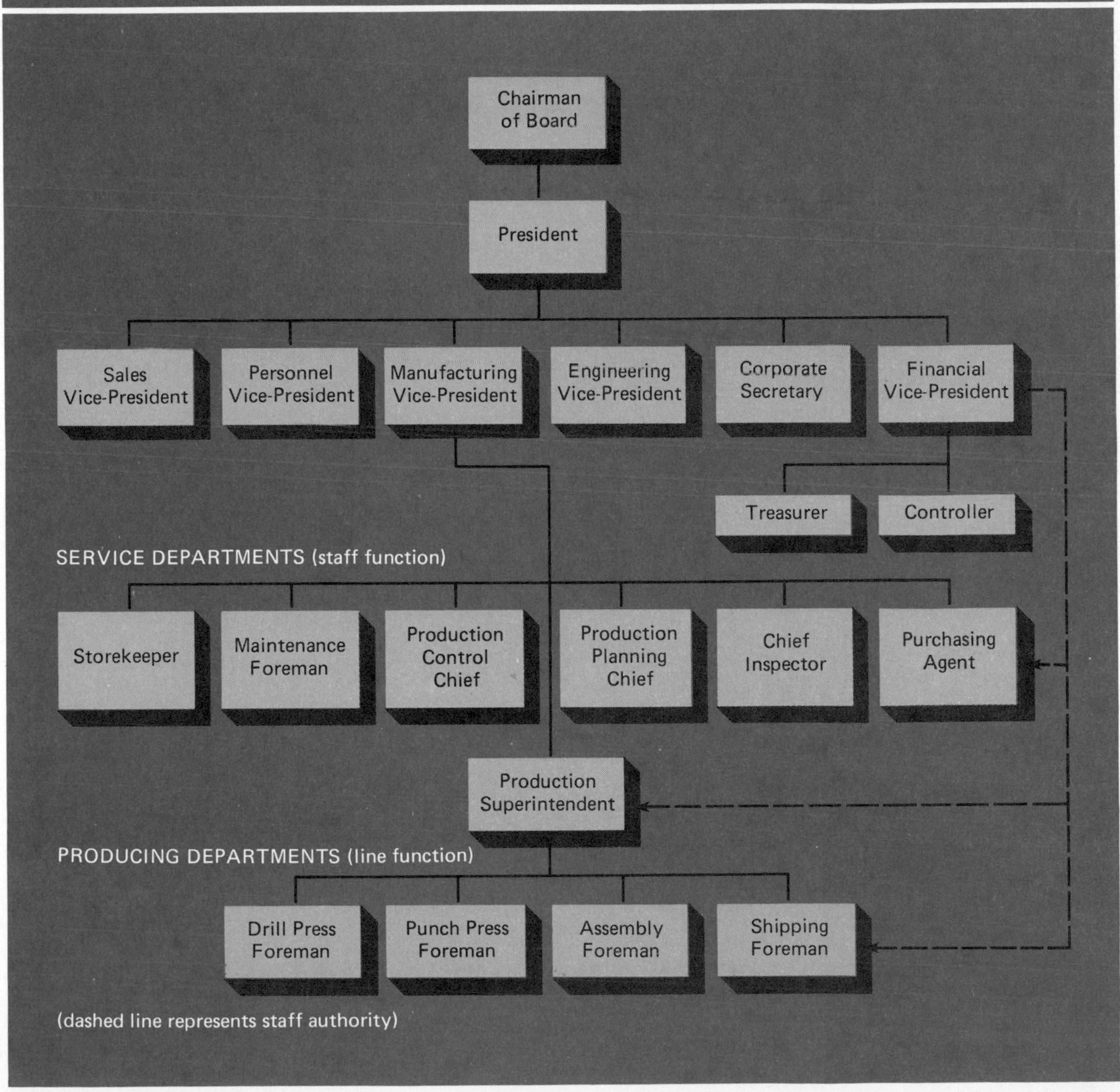

Note how managerial cost accounting is the controller's primary *means* of implementing the first three functions of controllership.

We shall not dwell at length on the treasurer's functions. As the seven points indicate, he is concerned mainly with financial, as distinguished from operating, problems. The exact division of various accounting and financial duties obviously varies from company to company.

The controller has been compared to the ship's navigator. The navigator, with the help of his specialized training, assists the captain. Without the navigator, the ship may founder on reefs or miss its destination entirely, but the captain exerts his right to command. The navigator guides and informs the captain as to how well the ship is being steered. This navigator role is especially evident in points 1 through 3 of the seven functions.

division of duties

Accountants often face a dilemma because they are supposed to fulfill two conflicting roles simultaneously. First, they are seen as watchdogs for top managers. Second, they are seen as helpers for all managers. The "watchdog" role is usually

EXHIBIT 1-3

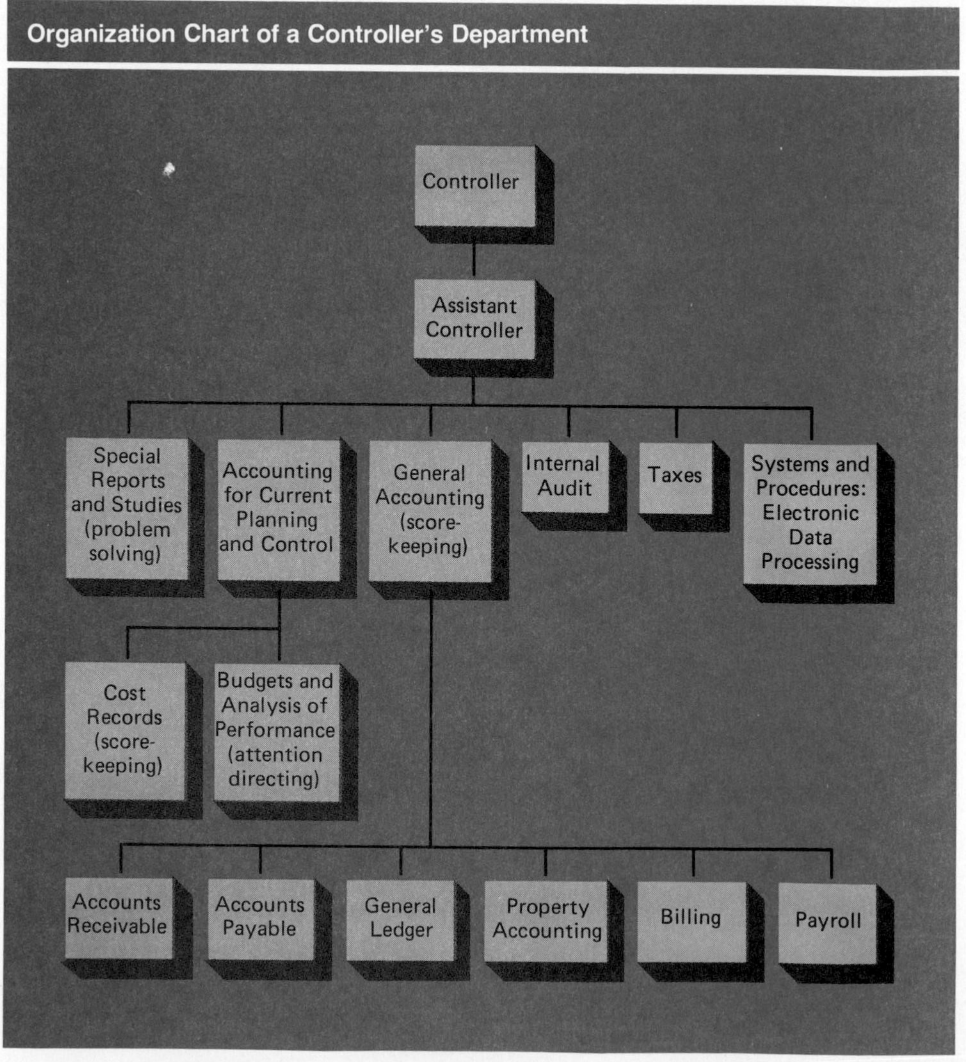

performed via the "scorekeeping" task of accumulating and reporting to all levels of management. The "helper" role is usually performed via the tasks of directing managers' attention to problems and of assisting managers in solving problems.[9]

The sheer volume of the scorekeeping task is often overwhelming; the day-to-day routines and endless deadlines shunt the helper role into the background and often into oblivion. To prevent the helper role from falling by the wayside, many organizations deliberately split the accountants' duties in ways similar to those in Exhibit 1-3.

The attention-directing and problem-solving tasks improve mutual understanding if a member of the controller's staff personally explains and interprets reports as they are presented to line managers. This attention-directing role (for example, explaining the differences between budgeted and actual performance) is often performed by experienced accountants who, at least to some degree, can talk the line manager's language. Indeed, the interpreters are the individuals who will establish the status of the controller's department in the company. Close, direct contacts between accountants and operating managers usually instill confidence in the reliability of the financial reports, which are the measuring devices of performance.

Many companies deliberately rotate their young accountants through scorekeeping, attention-directing, and problem-solving posts. In this way, accountants are more likely to appreciate the decision maker's viewpoint and are thus prone to keep the accounting system tuned to the users.

SUMMARY

This chapter stressed the interrelationship of accounting information and management decisions. The first major part of this chapter provided a conceptual overview. The second major part described how accountants fit into typical organizational settings.

Accounting information is an important input to many decision makers. In turn, the accountant frequently must choose what and how much information to provide. The choices among accounting techniques and systems are aimed at helping the collective operating decisions desired by top management.

The cost-benefit approach is a major theme of this book. In a most fundamental sense, the question of what accounting data, report, or system to buy must focus on how decisions (and resulting benefits) are going to be affected. The method of analysis is to ask what decisions will ensue upon the receipt of each possible set of accounting data (or no accounting data) and what outcomes will follow from these decisions.

problems for self-study

(Try to solve these problems before examining the solutions that follow.)

problem 1

Reexamine the basic elements of a management control system in Exhibit 1-1. Describe how the ideas of planning and controlling and how the major accounting tools mesh with the system.

---

[9]H. A. Simon, H. Guetzkow, G. Kozmetsky, and G. Tyndall, *Centralization vs. Decentralization in Organizing the Controller's Department* (New York: Controllership Foundation, Inc.). This perceptive study is much broader than its title implies.

solution 1

Planning is most obviously linked with the operating process. Planning entails delineation of goals, predictions of potential results, and a decision of how to attain goals. The budget is the principal accounting tool that helps managers plan.

Controlling entails action, which is part of the Operating Process box in Exhibit 1-1. It also includes performance evaluation, often using a report that compares budgets with actual results. **This report provides major feedback, which is the essence of control.**

problem 2

Using the organization charts in this chapter (Exhibits 1-2 and 1-3), answer the following questions:

a. Do the following have line or staff authority over the assembly foreman: maintenance foreman, manufacturing vice-president, production superintendent, purchasing agent, storekeeper, personnel vice-president, president, chief budgetary accountant, chief internal auditor?

b. What is the general role of service departments in an organization? How are they distinguished from operating or producing departments?

c. Does the controller have line or staff authority over the cost accountants? The accounts-receivable clerks?

d. What is probably the *major duty* (scorekeeping, attention directing, or problem solving) of the following?

1. Payroll clerk
2. Accounts-receivable clerk
3. Cost-record clerk
4. Head of general accounting
5. Head of taxes
6. Head of internal auditing
7. Budgetary accountant
8. Cost analyst
9. Head of special reports and studies
10. Head of accounting for planning and control
11. Controller

A sad commentary on many existing accounting systems is that they fulfill their scorekeeping tasks admirably—but they stop there. With minimal additional cost, immense benefit could be generated if the attention-directing and problem-solving functions were also performed.

solution 2

a. The only executives having line authority over the assembly foreman are the president, the manufacturing vice-president, and the production superintendent.

b. A typical company's major purpose is to produce and sell goods or services. Unless a department is directly concerned with producing or selling, it is called a service or staff department. Service departments exist only to help the production and sales departments with their major tasks: the efficient production and sale of goods or services.

c. The controller has line authority over all members of his own department, all of those shown in the controller's organization chart (Exhibit 1-3).

d. The major duty of the first five is typically scorekeeping. Attention directing is probably the major duty of the next three. Problem solving is probably the primary duty of the head of special reports and studies. **The head of accounting for planning and control and the controller should be concerned with all three duties: scorekeeping, attention directing, and problem solving. However, there is a perpetual danger that day-to-day pressures will emphasize scorekeeping. Therefore, accountants and managers should constantly see that attention directing and problem solving are also stressed. Otherwise, the major management benefits of an accounting system may be lost.**

Terms to Learn

Each chapter will include this section. Like all technical subjects, accounting contains many terms with precise meanings. To learn cost accounting with relative ease, pin down the definitions of new terms when you initially encounter them.

Before proceeding to the assignment material or to the next chapter, be sure you understand the following words or terms. Their meaning is explained in the chapter and also in the Glossary at the end of this book.

budgets ***Certified Management Accountant*** ***CMA*** ***control*** ***controller*** ***cost accounting*** ***cost-benefit approach*** ***environment*** ***feedback*** ***financial accounting*** ***functional authority*** ***internal accounting*** ***line authority*** ***management accounting*** ***management by exception*** ***management control system*** ***NAA*** ***National Association of Accountants*** ***performance reports*** ***planning process*** ***staff authority*** ***treasurer*** ***variances***

Special Points and Pitfalls

Many readers tend to skim the first chapter. After all, it contains neither financial statements nor discussions of various cost terms. Nevertheless, the chapter sets an important tone:

1. **Cost accounting is vital to management control, which entails human control of other humans.** Therefore, cost accounting is far more than merely a technical subject. It often has an enormous impact on human behavior.
2. Cost accounting systems come in various shapes and sizes. **Managers buy one system or the other, depending on perceptions of relative costs and benefits.**
3. Cost accounting systems are usually the responsibility of the controller, a staff officer. The controller must worry about the system's technical aspects and its human aspects.

QUESTIONS, PROBLEMS, AND CASES

Special note about the assignment material **No attempt has been made to distinguish among questions, problems, and cases because distinctions among them are so often artificial. Many problems are based on actual business situations. To aid selection, most problems have individual short titles that describe their subject matter.**

1-1 The accounting system should provide information for three broad purposes. Describe the three purposes.

1-2 "Cost accounting *is* management accounting, plus a small part of financial accounting." Explain.

1-3 Identify the basic elements of a management control system.

1-4 Give at least three examples of the environment when it is regarded as a basic element of management control.

1-5 Feedback may be used for a variety of purposes. Identify at least five.

1-6 Why do the controller and his staff have to understand the company organization structure?

1-7 As a new controller, reply to this comment by a factory superintendent: "As I see it, our accountants may be needed to keep records for stockholders and Uncle Sam—but I don't want them sticking their noses in my day-to-day operations. I do the best I know how; no pencil-pusher knows enough about my responsibilities to be of any use to me."

1-8 "The way these modern controllers put themselves on a pedestal, you may as well give them the title of President and be done with it. Look at the first three points in their functions of controllership. With the change of a word or two, these points could be a job description for the company president." Discuss.

1-9 Define *decision making.*

1-10 Define *planning.* Distinguish it from *control.*

1-11 "Planning is really much more vital than control." Do you agree? Why?

1-12 "We need to record replacement costs because they are more accurate approximations of economic reality." How would an advocate of cost-benefit analysis react to this statement?

1-13 "The controller is both a line and a staff executive." Do you agree? Why?

1-14 "The modern concept of controllership maintains that the controller *does* control in a special sense." Explain.

1-15 What are some common causes of friction between line and staff executives?

1-16 How is cost accounting related to the concept of controllership?

1-17 Distinguish among line, staff, and functional authorities.

1-18 Elements of control system. Examine Exhibit 1-1. Consider the operations of a manufacturing department. The department manager is the superior and the foreman is the subordinate. Give at least one example of each of the other elements in the exhibit: operating process, environment, performance, and feedback.

1-19 Uses of feedback. A separate section in the chapter identified six uses of feedback and provided an example of each:

1. Changing goals
2. Searching for alternative means
3. Changing methods for making decisions
4. Making predictions
5. Changing the operating process
6. Changing the measuring and rewarding of performance

Match the numbers with the appropriate following capital letters:

A. The California State University system adopts a WATS (Wide Area Telephone Service) method for making long-distance telephone calls.

B. Sales commissions are to be based on gross profit instead of total revenue.

C. The Ford Motor Company adjusts its elaborate way of forecasting demand for its cars by including the effects of expected changes in the price of crude oil.

D. The hiring of new sales personnel will include an additional step: an interview and evaluation by the company psychiatrist.

E. Quality inspectors at General Motors are now being used in the middle of the process in addition to the end of the process.

F. Procter & Gamble introduces a new soap.

1-20 Role of the accountant in the organization: line and staff functions.

1. Of the following, who have line authority over a cost-record clerk: budgetary accountant; head of accounting for current planning and control; head of general accounting; controller; storekeeper; production superintendent; manufacturing vice-president; president; production-control chief?

2. Of the following, who have line authority over an assembler: stamping foreman; assembly foreman; production superintendent; production-control chief; storekeeper; manufacturing vice-president; engineering vice-president; president; controller; budgetary accountant; cost-record clerk?

1-21 Scorekeeping, attention directing, and problem solving. For each of the following, identify the function the accountant is performing: i.e., scorekeeping, attention directing, or problem solving. *Also* state whether the departments mentioned are service or production departments.

1. Processing the weekly payroll for the maintenance department
2. Explaining the welding foreman's performance report
3. Analyzing the costs of several different ways to blend raw materials in the foundry
4. Tallying sales, by branches, for the sales vice-president
5. Analyzing, for the president, the impact of a contemplated new product on net income
6. Interpreting why a branch did not meet its sales quota
7. Interpreting variances on a machining foreman's performance report
8. Preparing the budget for research and development
9. Preparing adjusting journal entries for depreciation on the personnel manager's office equipment
10. Preparing a customer's monthly statement

1-22 Draw an organization chart. Draw an organization chart for a company that has the following positions:

Vice-president, controller and treasurer
Chief designer
Receiving and stores superintendent
Branch A sales manager
Production superintendent
Chief of finished stockroom
Shipping-room head
Chief of cost accumulation
Maintenance superintendent
Employment manager
Welding and assembly superintendent
Machining superintendent
Vice-president, manufacturing
Finishing-department superintendent
Vice-president, chief engineer
Foundry superintendent
Head of job evaluation
Vice-president, personnel
Head of general accounting
Budget director
Tool-room superintendent
Chief purchasing agent
Head of cost analysis
Inspection superintendent
Stamping superintendent
Head of research
President
Head of production control
Vice-president, sales

1-23 **Responsibility for analysis of performance.** John Phillipson is the new controller of a huge company that has just overhauled its organization structure. The company is now decentralized. Each division is under an operating vice-president who, within wide limits, has responsibilities and authority to run his division like a separate company.

Phillipson has a number of bright staff members, one of whom, Bob Garrett, is in charge of a newly created performance-analysis staff. Garrett and his fellow staff members prepare monthly divisional performance reports for the company president. These reports are divisional income statements, showing budgeted performance and actual performance, and are accompanied by detailed written explanations and appraisals of variances. Each of Garrett's staff members had a major responsibility for analyzing one division; each consulted with divisional line and staff executives and became generally acquainted with the division's operations.

After a few months, Bill Whisler, vice-president in charge of Division C, has stormed into the controller's office. The gist of his complaint follows:

"Your staff is trying to take over part of my responsibilities. They come in, snoop around, ask hundreds of questions, and take up plenty of our time. It's up to me, not you and your detectives, to analyze and explain my division's performance to central headquarters. If you don't stop trying to grab my responsibilities, I'll raise the whole issue with the president."

REQUIRED

1. What events or relationships may have led to Whisler's outburst?
2. As Phillipson, how would you answer Whisler's contentions?
3. What alternative actions can Phillipson take to improve future relationships?

1-24 **Accountant's role in planning and control.** Dick Victor has been president of Sampson Company, a multidivision textile company, for ten months. The company has an industry reputation as being conservative and having average profitability. Previously, Victor was associated with a very successful company that had a heavily formalized accounting system, with elaborate budgets and effective uses of performance reports.

Victor is contemplating the installation of a formal budgetary program. To signify its importance, he wants to hire a new vice-president for planning and control. This person would report directly to Victor and would have complete responsibility for implementing a system for budgeting and reporting performance.

REQUIRED

If you were the controller of Sampson Company, how would you react to Victor's proposed move? What alternatives are available to Victor for installing his budgetary program? In general, should all figure specialists report to one master figure expert, who in turn is responsible to the president?

1-25 **Scorekeeping, attention directing, and problem solving.** Internal (management) accounting tends to emphasize the attention-directing and problem-solving functions of accounting. However, many companies have accounting systems that are oriented almost exclusively to scorekeeping. For example, one critic has stated:

> Very few people in business have had the opportunity to reflect on the way in which the accounting model developed, particularly on how an instrument well adapted to detect fraud and measure tax liability has gradually been used as a general information source. Having become accustomed to information presented in this form, business people have adapted their concepts and patterns of thought and communication to it rather than adapting the information to the job or person. When one suggests the reverse process, as now seems not only logical but well within economic limits, he must expect a real reluctance to abandon a pattern of behavior that has a long history of working apparently quite well.[10]

Considering the introductory material in this chapter, comment on this quotation, particularly on the meaning and implications of the last sentence quoted, for today's and tomorrow's controllers.

1-26 Cost accounting in nonprofit institutions. For many years nonprofit institutions such as school districts, city hospitals, and welfare agencies have prepared budgets. These budgets have usually consisted of a listing of line items like salaries, supplies, maintenance, and so on. During the late 1960s and early 1970s, many of these institutions, particularly hospitals, introduced some cost accounting. For example, hospitals allocated various costs of operating room, X-ray, and laboratories to various classes of patient services. Some hospitals experimented with having nurses trace some of their time to individual patients.

REQUIRED

Why has cost accounting received increasing attention in nonprofit institutions? Why has it taken so long?

1-27 Line and staff, controller (CMA). The Arjohn Corporation is a multidivisional firm. Each division has a manager who is responsible for division operations. The controller for each division is assigned to the division by the corporate controller's office. The division controller manages the division's accounting system and provides analysis of financial information for the division management. The division manager evaluates the performance of the division controller and makes recommendations for salary increases and promotions. However, the final responsibility for promotion evaluation and salary increases rests with the corporate controller.

Each division of Arjohn is responsible for product design, sales, pricing, operating costs and expenses, and profits. However, corporate management exercises very tight control over the financial operations of the divisions. For example, all capital expenditures above a very modest amount must be approved by corporate management. The method of financial reporting from the division to corporate headquarters provides further evidence of the degree of financial control. The division manager and the division controller submit to corporate headquarters separate and independent commentary of the financial results of the division. The corporate management states that the division controller is there to provide an independent view of the division's operations and not as a spy.

REQUIRED

1. Discuss the concept of line, staff, and functional reporting using the facts presented in the question as examples of each.
2. Arjohn Corporation's dual reporting system for divisions may create problems for the division controller.
   a. Identify and discuss the factors that make the division controller's role difficult in this type of situation.
   b. Discuss the effect of the dual reporting relationship on the motivation of the division controller.

1-28 Effectiveness of controller. A research team undertook the task of appraising the relative effectiveness of the controller's department in various organizations. Based on the general descriptions in the chapter, how would you proceed to accomplish this task?

---

[10]William R. Fair, "The Next Step in Management Controls," in *Management Control Systems,* eds. Donald G. Malcom and Alan J. Rowe (New York: John Wiley, 1960), pp. 229–30.

1-29 Organization of accounting department: centralization or decentralization.[11] The following quotation is from an address made by an officer of the Ford Motor Company:

> We can all, I think, take pride in the way cost accounting has kept pace with industrial development in this country. Tremendous strides have been made during the last quarter of a century, and I'm sure that much more progress will be made in the future. In fact, progress will *have* to be made if we are to keep the science of cost accounting abreast of the times. The whole of industry is now operating on a different level than we have known before—a higher plateau, on which cost accounting appears in a new light, becomes more and more significant as a factor in business management.
>
> It is my experience that the function of cost determination is basic to every other function of a modern business. Cost factors thread their way through every phase of a business and to a large extent influence the makeup of the entire enterprise—its products, its markets, and its methods of operation.
>
> We must, of necessity, have rather complex and extensive costing organizations, but the principle according to which they work is the same—finding out what each of the operations costs before it is too late to avoid doing the wrong thing.
>
> I am sure you would be interested in knowing that the accounting office at Ford was formerly almost completely centralized and that we have begun to install a decentralized system. . . .
>
> It is planned that after the decentralized and the local organizations are prepared to assume the responsibilities involved, these accounting offices will be placed under the direct jurisdiction of the managers of the operations which they serve. . . .
>
> Under the decentralized system, each division has its own complete accounting service. . . . Each separate activity, such as each assembly plant, has been provided with an accounting office to compile its own internal operating reports for its own use, and to forward the financial statements required by the central office.

REQUIRED

1. *Decentralization* is frequently defined as the extension of decision-making power to the lowest possible levels of an organization. What accounting functions are the most likely candidates for centralization? For decentralization?
2. Draw three boxes on an organization chart, one each for the corporate controller, the plant controller, and the plant manager. Draw appropriate lines between the boxes that would accord with the system described in the quotation. Use a dashed line to denote "functional" authority and a solid line to denote "line" authority. Describe some major advantages and complications of the new organization arrangements.
3. Assume that accounting's service to management is maximized if it is decentralized as much as feasible, consistent with reasonable costs. Suppose you were to conduct research about the extent of decentralized accounting in a particular organization. What types of evidence would you examine?
4. As a college graduate newly hired by the plant controller's department, would you prefer that the plant controller have line responsibility to the corporate controller or to the plant manager? Explain.
5. "The controller must frequently fulfill two roles simultaneously, as a helper and as a spy." How can accountants' duties be organized to cope with these conflicting roles?

---

[11]From the *N.A.C.A. Bulletin,* Vol. 29, No. 7, Sec. II. This problem is a bit more challenging than the others in this group.

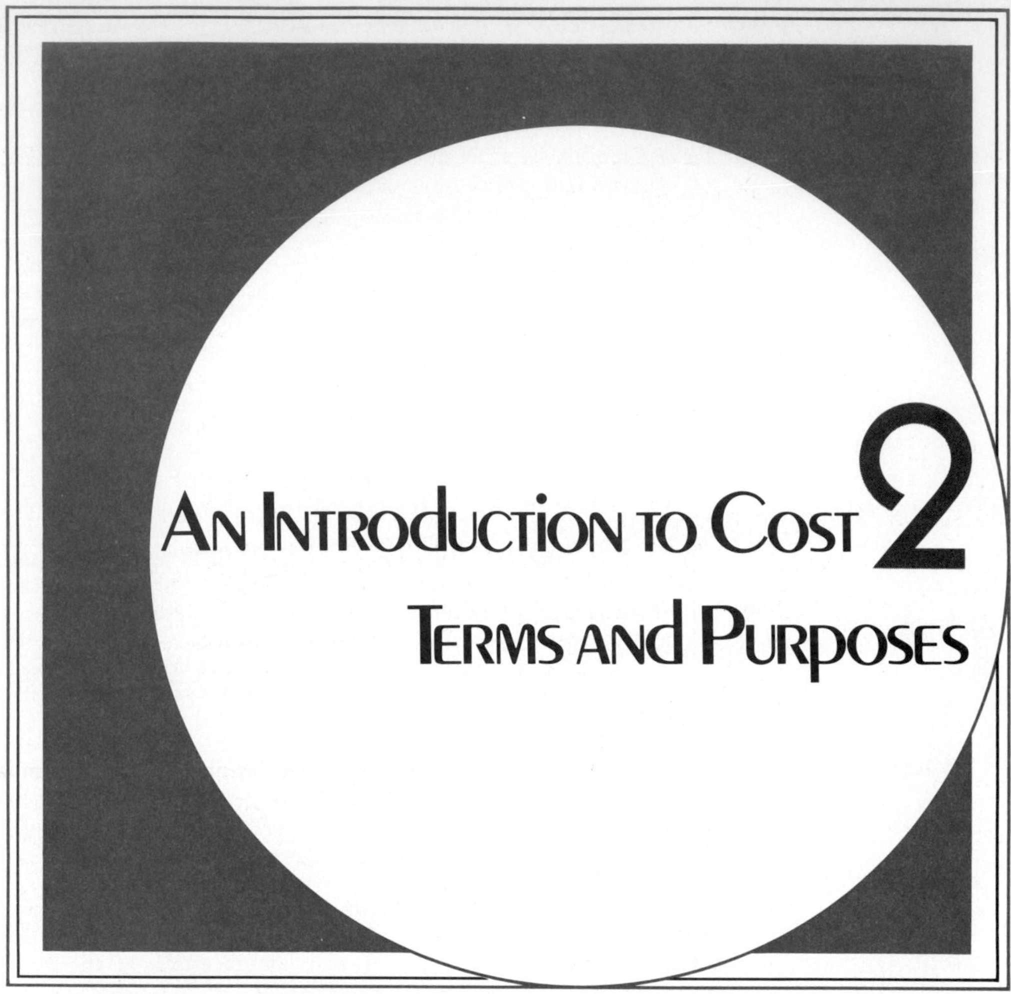

2 An Introduction to Cost Terms and Purposes

Now we turn to the language—what cost means. We usually do not decide to buy a commodity without some idea of its makeup or characteristics. Similarly, if we acquire knowledge of the composition of cost data and systems, we will be in a better position to decide what types to "buy" in what situations. In this chapter we shall learn some basic terminology, the jargon that every technical subject seems to possess. More important, we shall quickly see that there are different costs for different purposes. When it is economically feasible, cost accounting systems are usually designed to serve multiple purposes.

This chapter contains several widely recognized cost concepts and terms. They are sufficient to demonstrate the multiple purposes that will be stressed throughout the book. There are many other types of costs, but you will not be swamped by them in this chapter. It will be more efficient if we ease into the subject matter of cost accounting, and so a discussion of many costs is being deliberately postponed. For example, the idea of controllable and uncontrollable costs is covered at length in Chapter 5, and opportunity cost is covered in Chapter 11.

Costs in general

cost objectives

Accountants usually define *costs* as resources sacrificed or foregone to achieve a specific objective. For now, consider costs as being measured in the conventional accounting way, as monetary units (for example, dollars) that must be paid for goods and services.

To guide decisions, the manager wants data pertaining to a variety of purposes. He or she wants the cost *of something.* This something may be a product, a group of products, a service rendered to a hospital patient or a bank customer, a machine-hour, a social-welfare project, a mile of road, or any conceivable activity. We call this a **cost objective** and define it as *any activity for which a separate measurement of costs is desired.*[1]

cost systems

Cost accumulation is the collection of cost data in an organized way via an accounting system. The word *system* implies regularity—for example, the routine compilation of historical data in an orderly fashion. Other cost data may be gathered on occasion as desired (for example, replacement costs of certain equipment). Of course, continuous compilation is more expensive than occasional compilation; the relative elaborateness of systems is fundamentally a cost-benefit decision as to what data to "buy" on a regular basis.

Cost objectives are chosen not for their own sake but to facilitate decisions. The most economically feasible approach to the design of a cost system is typically to assume some common classes of decisions (for example, inventory control and labor control) and to choose cost objectives (for example, products and departments) that relate to those decisions. Nearly all systems at least accumulate **actual costs,** which are amounts determined on the basis of costs incurred (historical costs), as distinguished from predicted or forecasted costs. The relationships are exemplified as in the chart on the next page.

Years ago many cost accounting systems emphasized one cost objective—product costing for inventory valuation and income determination—as if it were an end in itself. Consequently, many systems failed to collect the data in a form suitable for other purposes. However, modern systems have a more balanced approach; obtaining the inventory cost of finished product units is regarded as only one purpose. Other purposes include getting a reliable basis for predicting the economic consequences of a host of decisions, including:

---

[1]George J. Staubus, *Activity Costing and Input-Output Accounting* (Homewood, Ill.: Richard D. Irwin, (1971), p. 1, stresses that we must recognize that in essence we are determining the cost of an activity or action:

"Costing is the process of determining the cost of doing something, e.g., the cost of manufacturing an article, rendering a service, or performing a function. The article manufactured, service rendered, or function performed is known as the object of costing. . . . Objects of costing are always activities. We want to know the cost of doing something. We may, however, find ourselves speaking of the cost of a product as an abbreviation for the cost of acquiring or manufacturing that product. . . ."

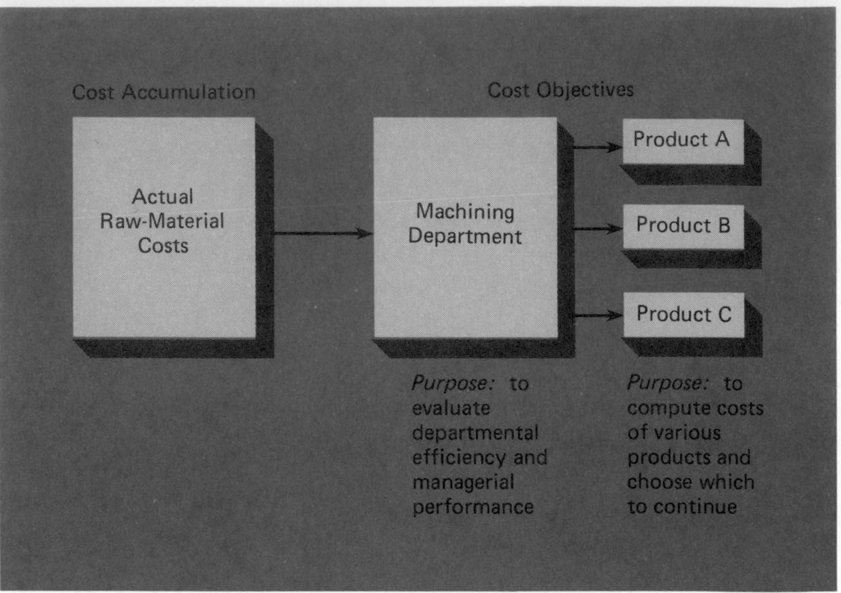

1. Which products should we make? Delete?
2. Should we manufacture a product component or should we acquire it outside?
3. What prices should we charge?
4. Should we buy the proposed equipment?
5. Should we change our manufacturing methods?
6. Should we promote this manager?
7. Should we expand the department?

Variable costs and fixed costs

costs and changes in activity

Variable and **fixed** costs are usually defined in terms of how a *total* cost changes in relation to fluctuations in the activity (often called *volume*) of a chosen cost objective. The activity or volume of the cost objective may be measured in units of product manufactured or sold, hours worked, miles driven, gallons consumed, patients seen, payroll checks processed, lines typed, sales dollars, or any other index of volume. **If a given cost changes in total in direct proportion to changes in activity, it is *variable;* if a total cost remains unchanged for a *given time period* despite *wide fluctuations in activity,* it is *fixed.* Consider two examples:**

1. If Massive Motors Company buys one type of fuel filter at $1 each for its M-1 model car, then the total cost of fuel filters should be $1 times the number of cars produced. This is an example of a variable cost, a cost that is uniform *per unit of volume,* so that it fluctuates in total in direct proportion to changes in the total activity (volume). Examples include most materials and parts, many types of assembly labor, sales commissions, and certain supplies.

   Variable-cost behavior may be plotted graphically. Exhibit 2-1 shows the relationship between direct-material costs and units produced; Exhibit 2-2 shows the relationship between sales commissions and dollar sales.
2. Massive Motors may incur $100 million in a given year for property taxes, executive salaries, rent, insurance, and depreciation. These are examples of fixed costs, costs that do not fluctuate in total over a wide range of volume during a given time span, but that become progressively smaller on a *per unit* basis as production increases.

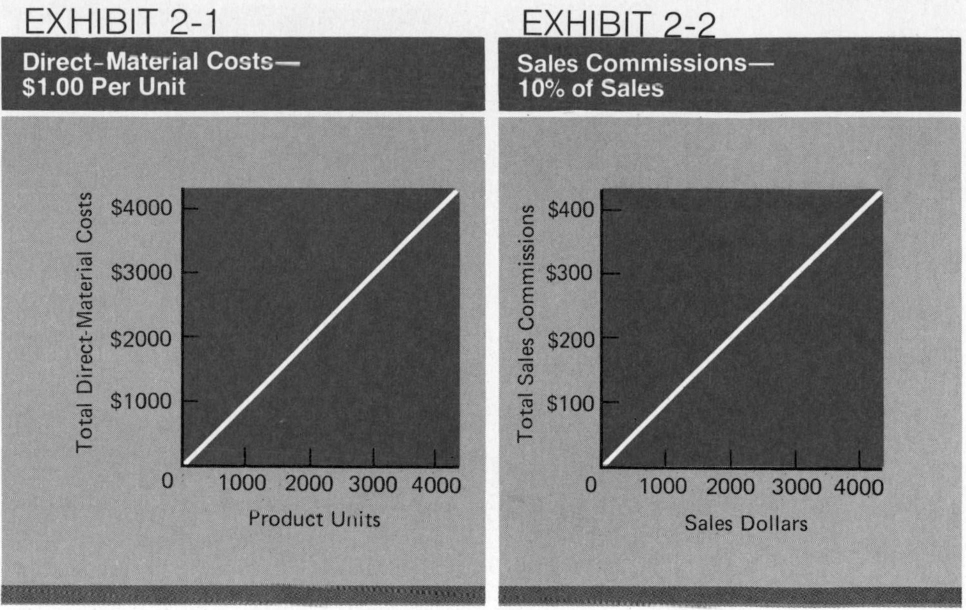

fixed costs and shutdown costs

A fixed cost is fixed only in relationship to a given period of time and a given, though wide, range of activity, called the "relevant range." The **relevant range** may be defined as the band of activity in which budgeted sales and expense relationships will be valid. Thus a company's fixed costs may be unchanged for a given year, although property-tax rates and executive salaries may be higher the next year. In addition, the fixed-cost level may be applicable to, say, a range of 30,000 to 95,000 hours of activity per month. But a prolonged strike or an economic recession may cause executive salary cuts, layoffs, or shutdowns. Therefore, fixed costs may be reduced substantially if activity levels fall drastically. In some cases, an entire plant may be shut down, virtually eliminating the need for executive and service personnel.

These relationships are shown in Exhibit 2-3. The likelihood of activities being outside the relevant range is usually slight, so $50,000 becomes the fixed-cost level. The three-level refinement in Exhibit 2-3 is not usually shown, because the chances are remote that activity will be less than 30,000 hours or more than 95,000 hours. Exhibit 2-4 shows how this $50,000 figure is usually plotted in practice; extending the $50,000 line will cause no particular harm as long as operating decisions are limited to the relevant range.

cost behavior patterns

Nearly every organization has costs that may be classified as either variable or fixed. Throughout this book we shall see why the accountant and the manager find this distinction helpful. Variable and fixed costs are just two of an assortment of cost behavior patterns that are often useful to recognize. For the time being, we shall assume that all costs may be placed in one of these two classifications. In practice, of course, the task of classification is exceedingly difficult and nearly always necessitates some simplifying assumptions.

One basic simplification is the widespread assumption that cost behavior patterns are linear rather than curvilinear; that is, when plotted on simple graph paper they appear as unbroken straight lines instead of steps or curves. Moreover, in practice,

EXHIBIT 2-3

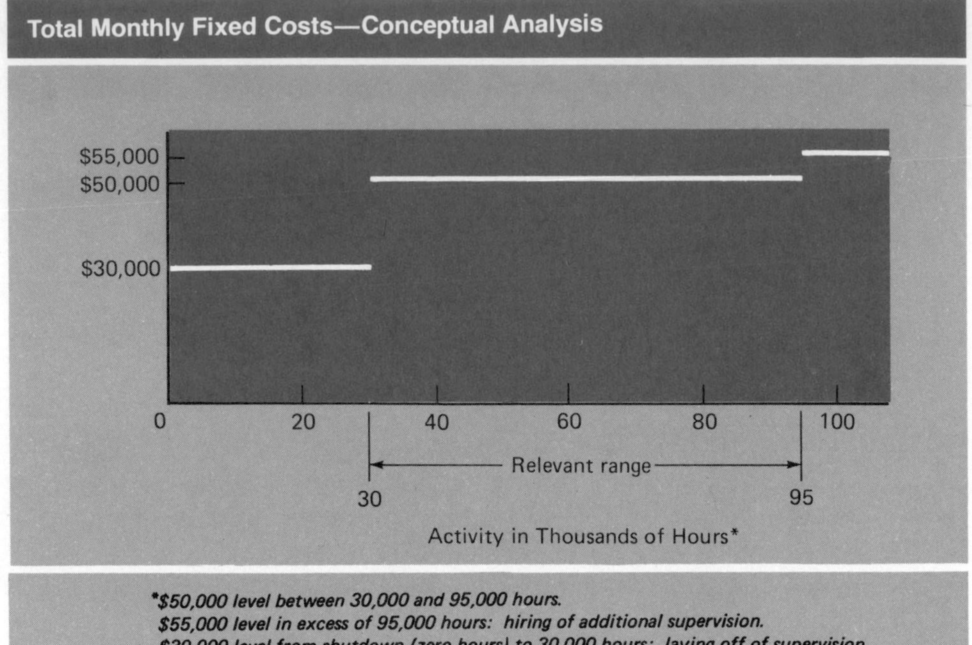

activity is inevitably assumed to be unidimensional: only units of product, only labor-hours, only machine-hours, only sales dollars, and so on. The relationships between a given cost incurrence and changes in a single related activity level may be vastly oversimplified and misleading because many costs are clearly affected by more than

EXHIBIT 2-4

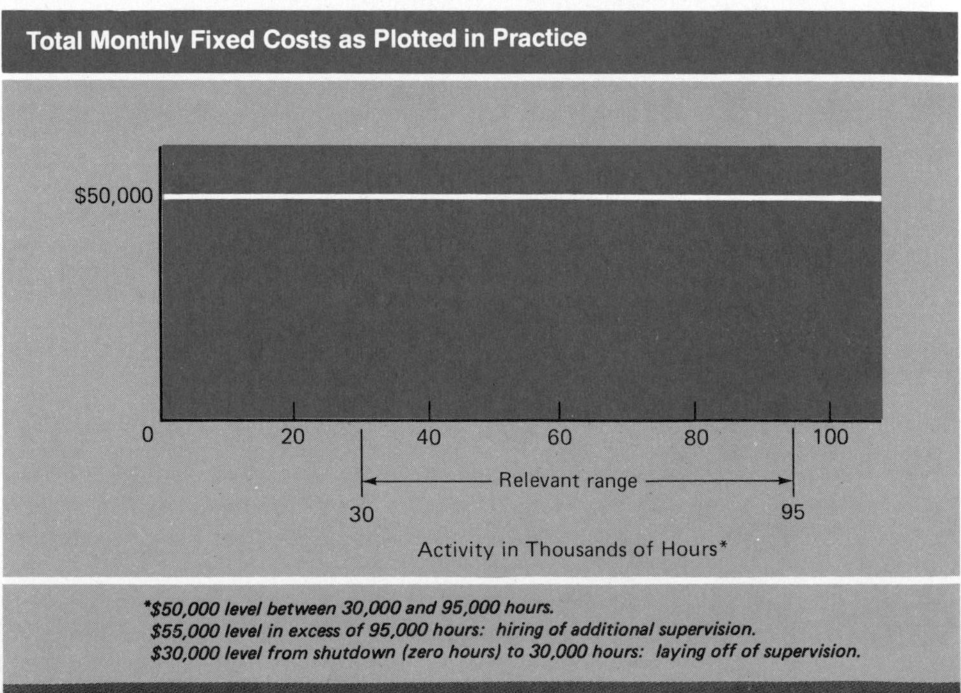

one factor. For example, the cost of fuel is affected by both the weight of the vehicle and distance traveled. These ideas are explored more fully in Chapters 9 and 24.

Average costs and total costs

helping understanding

The preceding section concentrated on the behavior patterns of total costs in relation to chosen activity levels of the cost objective. Generally, the decision maker should take a straightforward analytical approach by thinking in terms of total costs rather than average costs. As we shall see momentarily, average costs must be interpreted cautiously. Nevertheless, their use is essential in many decision contexts. For example, the chairman of the social committee of a fraternity may be trying to decide whether to hire a musical group for a forthcoming party. The total fee may be predicted with certainty at $1,000. This knowledge is helpful for the decision, but it may not be enough.

Before a decision can be reached, the decision maker must predict both the total cost and the probable number of persons who will attend. Without knowledge of both, he cannot decide intelligently on a possible admission price or even on whether to have a party at all. So he computes an average cost by dividing the total cost by the expected number of persons who will attend. If 1,000 people attend, the average cost is $1; if 100 attend, the average cost soars to $10 per person.

Unless the total cost is averaged (that is, "unitized"), the $1,000 cost is difficult to interpret; so the average cost (or unit cost) combines the total cost and the number of persons in a handy communicative way.

meaning of average costs

An **average cost** is computed by dividing some total cost (the numerator) by some denominator. Often the denominator is a measure of activity that is most closely related with the total cost incurred. Examples of denominators include units of product, hours of service, student credit hours, pounds handled in a shipping department, and number of invoices processed or lines billed in a billing department. Generally, average costs are expressed in terms most meaningful to the people who are responsible for incurring the costs.

The average cost of making a finished good is frequently computed by accumulating manufacturing costs and then dividing the total by the number of units produced. For example:

Total costs of manufacturing 1,000 units (numerator)		$3,800
Divided by the number of units produced (denominator)	÷	1,000
Equals a cost per unit (average cost)	=	$3.80

Suppose that 800 units are sold and 200 units remain in ending inventory. The average-cost idea facilitates the assignment of a total cost to various accounts:

Cost of goods sold, 800 units × $3.80	= $3,040
Ending inventory of finished goods, 200 units × $3.80 =	760

Unit costs are averages, and they must be interpreted with caution. For example, what does it mean to say that the unit cost for the musicians is $1 if 1,000 persons attend? In this case of fixed costs, the *total* cost of $1,000 is unaffected by the activity level, the size of the denominator. But the *unit* cost is strictly a function of the size of the denominator; it would be $1,000 per unit if one person attended, $1.00 per unit if 1,000 persons attended, and $.10 per unit if 10,000 persons attended.

In contrast, assume that the musicians agreed to perform for $1.00 per person. Then we would have a variable-cost situation. If one person attended, the *total* cost would be $1.00; if 1,000 attended, $1,000; if 10,000 attended, $10,000.

Note that for decision purposes the fixed cost per unit must be distinguished from the variable cost per unit. A common mistake is to regard all average costs indiscriminately—as if all costs were variable costs. **Changes in activity will affect *total* variable costs but not *total* fixed costs.** In our first example, the committee chairman could use the $1.00 unit variable cost to predict the total costs. But using a $1.00 unit fixed cost to predict the total costs would be perilous. His prediction would be correct if, and only if, 1,000 persons attended—total fixed costs would be $1,000 regardless of the number attending. The moral is: Average costs are often useful, but they should be interpreted with extreme caution, especially if they are in the form of fixed costs per unit.

These relationships are summarized below:

Behavior as Volume Fluctuates

	TOTAL COST	AVERAGE COST PER UNIT
Variable cost	Change	No change
Fixed cost	No change	Change

Product costs and period costs

manufacturing and nonmanufacturing activities

Some form of cost accounting is applicable to any entity that has a goal, including manufacturing companies, railroads, retail stores, insurance companies, advertising agencies, government units, hospitals, and nearly all other organizations, whether or not they are operated for a profit goal. We shall consider both manufacturing and nonmanufacturing companies throughout this book, but we shall begin with the manufacturing company because it provides the most general case—embracing production, marketing, and general administration functions. This will develop a completely general framework of cost accounting for ready application to any organization.

Historically, accounting techniques for planning and control arose in conjunction with manufacturing rather than nonmanufacturing because the measurement problems were less imposing and environmental factors such as economic conditions, customer reactions, and competitor activity were generally less influential. However, the basic concepts of planning and control are equally applicable to both manufacturing and nonmanufacturing activities. At the moment, we shall examine manufacturing and nonmanufacturing from the viewpoint of inventory costing and income determination—the product-costing purpose when the cost objective is the unit of product.

Manufacturing is the transformation of materials into other goods through the use of labor and factory facilities. Merchandising is the selling of goods without changing their basic form. For example, assume that Jane Nentlaw wants to make hairdressing and sell it directly to retailers. She may buy certain oils and fancy containers, purchase a factory and equipment, hire some workers, and manufacture thousands of units of finished product. This is her manufacturing function. But in order to persuade retailers to buy her hairdressing, Nentlaw will have to convince the ultimate consumer that this product is desirable. This means advertising, including the development of a sales appeal, the selection of a brand name, the choice of media, and so forth. To maximize her success, Nentlaw must effectively manage both manufacturing and merchandising functions.

three manufacturing-cost elements

Note the basic difference between the conventional income statements of Nentlaw's business and Crump's Department Store in Exhibit 2-5. In the cost-of-goods-sold section, the Nentlaw statement has a "cost of goods manufactured" line instead of the "purchases" line found in the Crump statement. The details of the cost of goods manufactured appear in the separate supporting schedule.

There are three major elements in the cost of a manufactured product:

1. **Direct materials.** All materials that are physically observable as being identified with the finished good and that may be traced to the finished good in an economically feasible manner. Examples are sheet steel and subassemblies for an automobile company. Direct materials often do *not* include minor items such as glue or nails because the costs of tracing insignificant items do not seem worth the possible benefits of having more accurate product costs. Such items are considered *supplies* or *indirect materials.*
2. **Direct labor.** All labor that is physically traceable to the finished good in an economically feasible manner. Examples are the labor of machine operators and assemblers. Much labor, such as that of material handlers, janitors, and plant guards, is considered **indirect labor** because of the impossibility or economic infeasibility of tracing such activity to specific products via physical observation.
3. **Indirect manufacturing costs.** All costs other than direct materials and direct labor that are associated with the manufacturing process. Other terms describing this category include **factory overhead, factory burden, manufacturing overhead,** and **manufacturing expenses.** The term *indirect manufacturing costs* is a clearer descriptor than *factory overhead,*[2] but the latter will be used throughout this book because it is briefer. Two subclassifications of factory overhead are
   a. *Variable factory overhead.* Examples are power, supplies, and most indirect labor. Whether the cost of a specific subcategory of indirect labor is variable or fixed depends on its behavior pattern in a given company. In this book, unless we specify otherwise, indirect labor will be considered a variable rather than a fixed cost.
   b. *Fixed factory overhead.* Examples are rent, insurance, property taxes, depreciation, and supervisory salaries.

Two of the three major elements are sometimes combined in cost terminology as follows: **Prime cost** consists of (1) + (2), direct materials plus direct labor. **Conversion cost** consists of (2) + (3), direct labor plus factory overhead.

inventoriable costs

Accountants often distinguish between *product costs* and *period costs.* **Product costs** are those identified with goods purchased or produced for resale; they are also called **inventoriable costs** because they are initially identified as a part of the inventory on hand. In turn, these inventoriable costs become expenses in the form of *cost of goods sold* only when the inventory is sold. In contrast, **period costs** are noninventoriable costs; they are deducted as expenses during the current period without having been previously classified as costs of inventory.

---

[2]The term *overhead* is peculiar; its origins are unclear. Some accountants have wondered why such costs are not called "underfoot" rather than "overhead" costs. The answer probably lies in the organization chart. Lower departments ultimately bear all costs, including those coming from over their heads.

EXHIBIT 2-5 *(Place a clip on this page for easy reference.)*

Comparison of Income Statements

NENTLAW (A MANUFACTURER)

income statement
for the year ended December 31, 19_2

Sales		$210,000
Less cost of goods sold:		
Finished goods, December 31, 19_1	$ 22,000	
Cost of goods manufactured (see schedule)	104,000	
Cost of goods available for sale	$126,000	
Finished goods, December 31, 19_2	18,000	
Cost of goods sold		108,000
Gross margin (or gross profit)		$102,000
Less selling and administrative expenses (detailed)		80,000
Net income*		$ 22,000

CRUMP'S (A RETAILER)

income statement
for the year ended December 31, 19_2

Sales		$1,500,000
Less cost of goods sold:		
Merchandise inventory, December 31, 19_1	$ 95,000	
Purchases	1,100,000	
Cost of goods available for sale	$1,195,000	
Merchandise inventory, December 31, 19_2	130,000	
Cost of goods sold		1,065,000
Gross margin (or gross profit)		$ 435,000
Less selling and administrative expenses (detailed)		315,000
Net income		$ 120,000

NENTLAW

schedule of cost of goods manufactured†

Direct materials:		
Inventory, December 31, 19_1	$11,000	
Purchases of direct materials	73,000	
Cost of direct materials available for use	$84,000	
Inventory, December 31, 19_2	8,000	
Direct materials used		$ 76,000
Direct labor		18,000
Factory overhead:		
Indirect labor	$ 4,000	
Supplies	1,000	
Heat, light, and power	1,500	
Depreciation—plant building	1,500	
Depreciation—equipment	2,500	
Miscellaneous	500	11,000
Manufacturing costs incurred during 19_2		$105,000
Add work-in-process inventory, December 31, 19_1		6,000
Manufacturing costs to account for		$111,000
Less work-in-process inventory, December 31, 19_2		7,000
Cost of goods manufactured† (to Income Statement)		$104,000

**In practice, the term* net income *is usually used to describe the final residual after deducting all expenses, including income taxes, from all revenue of any kind. The term* operating income *is usually used to describe the result after deducting "operating" expenses from the normal major sources of revenue. In situations like this example, the term* net income *is used frequently in place of* operating income, *because for convenience other income and other expenses, including income taxes, are ignored. In short, in this text you will sometimes encounter the terms* operating income *and* net income *being used interchangeably because it is either expressed or implied that their amounts are identical.*

†Note that the term cost of goods manufactured *refers to the cost of goods brought to completion (finished) during the year, whether they were started before or during the current year. Some of the manufacturing costs incurred are held back as costs of the ending work in process; similarly, the costs of the beginning work in process become a part of the cost of goods manufactured for 19_2.*

Note too that this schedule can become a Schedule of Cost of Goods Manufactured and Sold simply by including the opening and closing finished-goods inventory figures in the supporting schedule rather than directly in the body of the income statement.

Exhibit 2-6 should help clarify the differences between product (inventoriable) and period (noninventoriable) costs. Study the top of the exhibit. A retailer or wholesaler buys goods for resale without changing their basic form. The *only* inventoriable cost is the cost of merchandise. Unsold goods are held as merchandise inventory whose cost is shown as an asset on the balance sheet. As the goods are sold, their costs become expenses in the form of "cost of goods sold."

A retailer or wholesaler also has a variety of selling and administrative expenses, which are the main examples of period costs (noninventoriable costs). These are called period costs because in the income statement they are deducted from revenue as expenses without ever having been regarded as a part of inventory.

A manufacturer, as the bottom half of Exhibit 2-6 shows, transforms direct materials into salable form with the help of direct labor and factory overhead. All these costs are product costs because they are allocated to inventory until the goods are sold. As in accounting for retailers and wholesalers, the selling and administrative expenses are regarded as period costs.

effect on the balance sheet

As Exhibit 2-6 shows, balance sheets of manufacturers and merchandisers differ with respect to inventories. The merchandise inventory account is supplanted in a manufacturing company by three inventory classes, each depicting a stage in the production process:

1. **Direct-materials inventory.** Materials on hand and awaiting entry into the production process.
2. **Work-in-process inventory.** Also sometimes called **work in progress** or **goods in process.** Goods undergoing the production process not fully completed. Costs include the three major manufacturing costs (direct material, direct labor, and factory overhead).
3. **Finished-goods inventory.** Goods fully completed but not yet sold.

The only essential difference between the structure of the balance sheet of a manufacturer and that of the balance sheet of a retailer or wholesaler would appear in their respective current-asset sections (numbers are assumed):

Current-asset Sections of Balance Sheets

MANUFACTURER			RETAILER OR WHOLESALER	
Cash		$ 4,000	Cash	$ 30,000
Receivables		5,000	Receivables	70,000
Finished goods	$12,000			
Work in process	2,000			
Materials and supplies	3,000			
Total inventories		17,000	Merchandise inventories	100,000
Prepaid expenses		1,000	Prepaid expenses	3,000
Total current assets		$27,000	Total current assets	$203,000

perpetual and periodic inventories

There are two fundamental ways of accounting for inventories: perpetual and periodic. The **perpetual inventory method** requires a continuous record of additions to or reductions in materials, work in process, and cost of goods sold on a day-to-day basis. Such a record facilitates managerial control and preparation of interim financial

EXHIBIT 2-6

Relationships of Product Costs and Period Costs

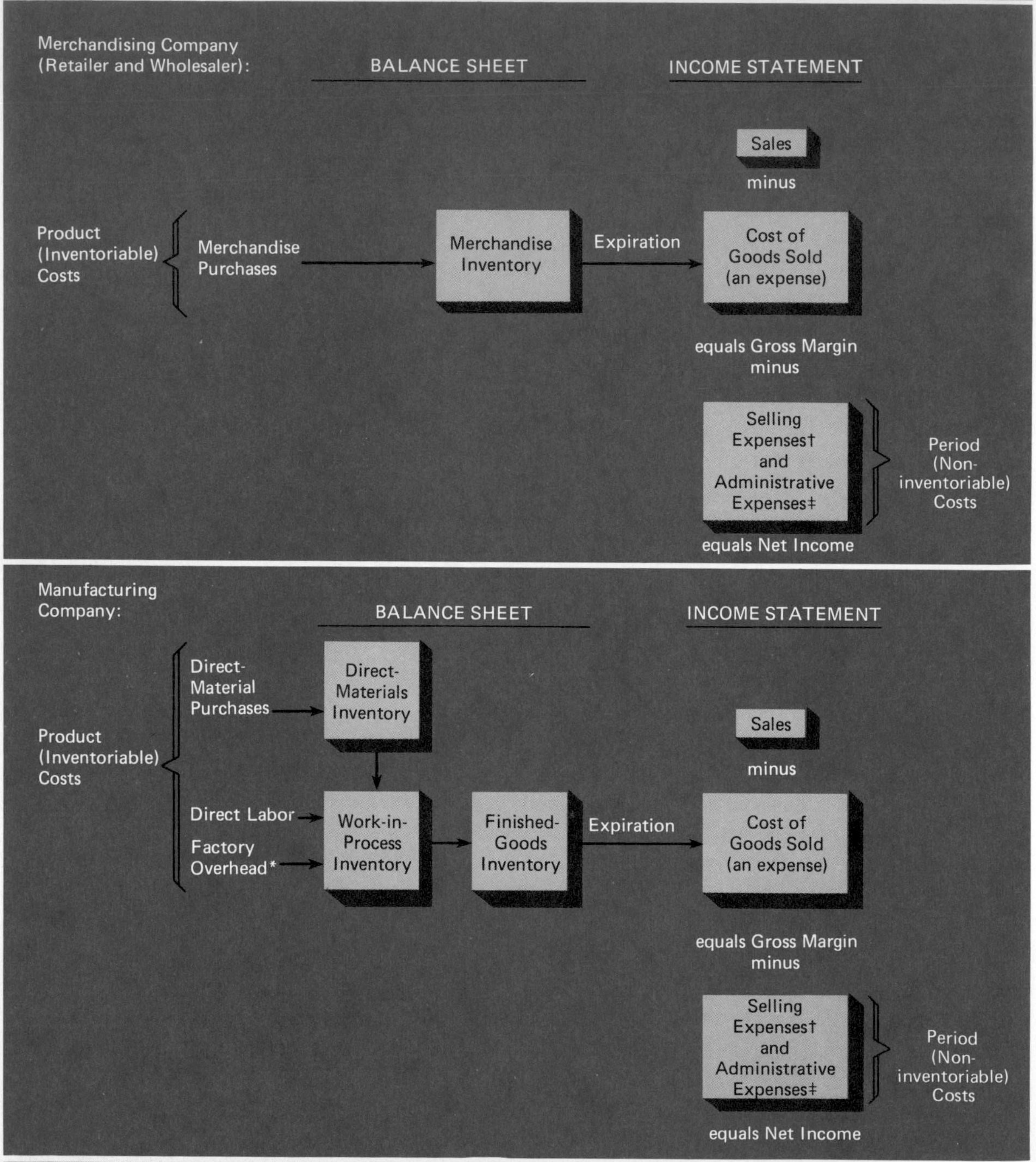

**Examples:* *indirect labor, factory supplies, insurance and depreciation on plant. (Note particularly that where insurance and depreciation relate to the manufacturing function, they are inventoriable; but where they relate to selling and administration, they are not inventoriable.)*

†Examples: insurance on salesmen's cars, depreciation on salesmen's cars, salesmen's salaries.

‡Examples: insurance on corporate headquarters building, depreciation on office equipment, clerical salaries.

EXHIBIT 2-7

Summary Comparison of Periodic and Perpetual Inventory Methods
(Figures from Exhibit 2-5)

PERIODIC METHOD		PERPETUAL METHOD	
Beginning inventories (by physical count)	$ 22,000	Cost of goods sold (kept on a day-to-day basis rather than being determined periodically)*	$108,000
Add: Manufacturing costs (direct materials used, direct labor, factory overhead)	104,000		
Cost of goods available for sale	126,000		
Less ending inventories (by physical count)	18,000		
Cost of goods sold	$108,000		

**Such a condensed figure does not preclude the presentation of a supplementary schedule showing details of production costs similar to that in Exhibit 2-5.*

statements. Physical inventory counts are usually taken at least once a year in order to check on the validity of the clerical records.

The **periodic inventory method** does not require a day-to-day record of inventory changes. Instead, costs are recorded by natural classifications, such as Material Purchases, Freight In, and Purchase Discounts. Costs of materials used or costs of goods sold cannot be computed accurately until ending inventories, determined by physical count, are subtracted from the sum of the opening inventory, purchases, and other operating costs. See Exhibit 2-7 for a comparison of perpetual and periodic inventory methods.

Some cost accounting language

troublesome terminology

There are many terms that have very special meanings in accounting. The meanings often differ from company to company; each organization seems to develop its own distinctive and extensive accounting language. This is why you will save much confusion and wasted time if you always find out the exact meaning of any strange jargon that you encounter.

Before proceeding, reflect on some commonly misunderstood terms that are displayed in Exhibits 2-5 and 2-6. Consider the misnomer *manufacturing expenses,* which is often used to describe the factory overhead shown in Exhibit 2-5. **Factory overhead is not an expense. It is part of product cost and will funnel into the expense stream only when the product costs are released as cost of goods sold.**

Also, *cost of goods sold* is a widely used term that is somewhat misleading when you try to pin down the meaning of *cost.* Cost of goods sold is every bit as much an *expense* as salesmen's commissions. Cost of goods sold is also often called *cost of sales.*

Distinguish clearly between the merchandising accounting and the manufacturing accounting for such costs as wages, depreciation, and insurance. As Exhibit 2-6 demonstrates, in merchandising accounting all such items are period costs (expenses of the current period). **In manufacturing accounting, many of such items are related to production activities and thus, as factory overhead, are inventoriable costs (and become expenses as the inventory is sold).**

Both merchandising accounting and manufacturing accounting regard selling and general administrative costs as period costs. Therefore, the inventory cost of a manufactured product excludes sales salaries, sales commissions, advertising, legal, public relations, and the president's salary. **Manufacturing overhead is traditionally regarded as a part of the cost of finished goods inventory, whereas selling expenses and general administrative expenses are not.** The underlying idea is that the finished goods inventory should *include* all costs of factory functions necessary to get the product to a completed state but should *exclude* all nonmanufacturing costs.

Pause and ponder Exhibit 2-5, page 28, in its entirety. The following T-accounts for a perpetual inventory system may help clarify some key terms (in thousands):

WORK-IN-PROCESS INVENTORY

Bal. Dec. 31, 19_1	6	Cost of goods manufactured	104
Direct materials used	76		
Direct labor	18		
Factory overhead	11		
To account for	111		
Bal. Dec. 31, 19_2	7		

FINISHED-GOODS INVENTORY

Bal. Dec. 31, 19_1	22	Cost of goods sold	108
→	104		
Available for sale	126		
Bal. Dec. 31, 19_2	18		

COST OF GOODS SOLD

→108	

In particular, the cost of goods manufactured is the cost of all goods completed during the reporting period. Such goods are usually transferred to finished-goods inventory. They become cost of goods sold either quickly or slowly, depending on the nature of the product, types of customers, and business conditions.

subdivisions of labor costs

The terminology for labor costs is usually the most confusing because each organization has seemingly developed its own interpretation of various labor-cost classifications. Let us consider some commonly encountered labor terminology.

All factory-labor costs other than direct labor are usually classified as *indirect labor,* a major component of indirect manufacturing costs. The term has many subsidiary classifications to facilitate appraisal of these costs. Thus, wages of forklift truck operators are generally not commingled with janitors' salaries, although both are regarded as indirect labor.

Costs are classified in a detailed fashion primarily in the attempt to associate a specific cost with its specific cause or reason for incurrence. Two classes of indirect labor need special mention. **Overtime premium** paid to factory workers is usually considered a part of overhead. If a lathe operator, George Flexner, gets $12 per hour for regular time, and time and one-half for overtime, his *premium* would be $6 per overtime hour. If he works forty-four hours, including four overtime hours, in one week, his gross earnings would be classified as follows:

Direct labor	44 hours × $12	$528
Overtime premium (factory overhead):		
	4 hours × $6	24
Total earnings		$552

Another subsidiary classification of indirect labor is **idle time.** This typically represents wages paid for unproductive time caused by machine breakdowns, material shortages, sloppy production scheduling, and the like. For example, if the lathe operator's machine broke down for three hours, his earnings would be classified as follows:

Direct labor:	41 hours × $12	$492
Overtime premium (factory overhead):		
	4 hours × $6	24
Idle time (factory overhead):		
	3 hours × $12	36
Total earnings		$552

Why is overtime premium usually considered an indirect cost rather than direct? After all, it can usually be traced to specific batches of work. It is usually not considered a direct charge because the scheduling of production jobs is generally *random*. For example, assume that Jobs 1 through 5 are scheduled for a specific workday of ten hours, including two overtime hours. Each job requires two hours. Should the job scheduled during hours 9 and 10 be assigned the overtime premium? Or should the premium be prorated over all the jobs? The latter approach does not penalize a particular batch of work solely because it happened to be worked on during the overtime hours. **Instead, the overtime premium is considered to be attributable to the heavy overall volume of work, and its cost is thus regarded as part of factory overhead, which is borne by all units produced.**

Sometimes overtime premium is not random. For example, a special or rush job may clearly be the sole source of the overtime. In such instances, the premium is regarded as a direct cost of the products made for that job.

payroll fringe costs

The classification of factory-payroll fringe costs, such as employer contributions to Social Security, life insurance, health, pension, and miscellaneous other employee benefits, differs from company to company. In most companies, these are classified as factory overhead. For instance, a direct laborer such as a lathe operator, whose gross paycheck is computed on the basis of a $12 regular-time hourly rate, may enjoy payroll fringe benefits totaling, say, $2 per hour. Most companies tend to classify the $12 as direct labor and the $2 as factory overhead. In some companies, however, the fringe benefits related to direct labor are charged as an additional direct-labor cost; these companies would classify the entire $14 as direct labor. The latter approach is conceptually preferable because these costs are also a fundamental part of acquiring labor services.

Classifications of cost

This chapter has merely hinted at the vast number of classifications of cost that have proven useful for various purposes. Among other categories, classifications can be made by:

1. Time when computed
   a. Historical costs
   b. Budgeted or predetermined costs (via cost "prediction")
2. Behavior in relation to fluctuations in activity
   a. Variable costs
   b. Fixed costs
   c. Other costs

3. Degree of averaging
    a. Total costs
    b. Average costs per unit (e.g., per student, per hour, per pound)
4. Management function
    a. Manufacturing costs
    b. Selling costs
    c. Administrative costs
5. Ease of traceability to cost objective
    a. Direct costs
    b. Indirect costs
6. Timing of charges against revenue
    a. Product costs
    b. Period costs

SUMMARY

Accounting systems should serve multiple decision purposes, and there are different measures of cost for different purposes. A frequent distinction that is made concerning cost accounting systems is between the purposes of providing costs for inventory valuation and providing costs for planning and control.

The most economically feasible approach to designing a management accounting system is to assume some common wants for a variety of decisions and choose cost objectives for routine data accumulation in light of these wants.

problem for self-study

(Try to solve this problem before examining the solution that follows.)

problem

Consider the following data of the Laimon Company for the year 19_1:

Sandpaper	$ 2,000	Depreciation—equipment	$ 40,000
Material handling	40,000	Factory rent	50,000
Lubricants and coolants	5,000	Property taxes on equipment	4,000
Overtime premium	20,000	Fire insurance on equipment	3,000
Idle time	10,000	Direct materials purchased	400,000
Miscellaneous indirect labor	40,000	Direct materials, 12/31/_1	50,000
Direct labor	300,000	Sales	1,200,000
Direct materials, 12/31_0	40,000	Sales commissions	60,000
Finished goods, 12/31/_1	150,000	Sales salaries	100,000
Finished goods, 12/31/_0	100,000	Shipping expenses	70,000
Work in process, 12/31/_0	10,000	Administrative expenses	100,000
Work in process, 12/31/_1	14,000		

REQUIRED

1. Prepare an income statement with a separate supporting schedule of cost of goods manufactured. For all items except sales, purchases of direct materials, and inventories, indicate by "V" or "F" whether each is basically a variable or a fixed cost. If in doubt, decide on the basis of whether the total cost will fluctuate substantially over a wide range of volume.
2. Suppose that both the direct-material and rent costs were related to the manufacturing of the equivalent of 900,000 units. What is the average cost per unit for the direct materials assigned to those units? What is the average cost per unit of the factory rent? Assume that the rent is a fixed cost.

3. Repeat the computation in requirement 2 for direct materials and factory rent, assuming that the costs are being predicted for the manufacturing of the equivalent of 1,000,000 units next year. Assume that the implied cost behavior patterns persist.
4. As a management consultant, explain concisely to the president why the unit costs for materials and rent differed in requirements 2 and 3.

solution

1. Laimon Company

Income Statement
For the Year Ended December 31, 19_1

Sales		$1,200,000
Less cost of goods sold:		
Finished goods, December 31, 19_0	$ 100,000	
Cost of goods manufactured (see schedule below)	900,000	
Cost of goods available for sale	$1,000,000	
Finished goods, December 31, 19_1	150,000	
Cost of goods sold		850,000
Gross margin		$ 350,000
Less selling and administrative expenses:		
Sales commissions	$ 60,000 (V)	
Sales salaries	100,000 (F)	
Shipping expenses	70,000 (V)	
Administrative expenses	100,000*	330,000
Operating income		$ 20,000

**Probably a mixture of fixed and variable items.*

Laimon Company

Schedule of Cost of Goods Manufactured
For the Year Ended December 31, 19_1

Direct materials:		
Inventory, December 31, 19_0		$ 40,000
Purchases of direct materials		400,000
Cost of direct materials available for use		$440,000
Inventory, December 31, 19_1		50,000
Direct materials used		$390,000 (V)
Direct labor		300,000 (V)
Indirect manufacturing costs:		
Sandpaper	$ 2,000 (V)	
Lubricants and coolants	5,000 (V)	
Material handling (example: wages of forklift truck operators)	40,000 (V)	
Overtime premium	20,000 (V)	
Idle time	10,000 (V)	
Miscellaneous indirect labor	40,000 (V)	
Factory rent	50,000 (F)	
Depreciation—equipment	40,000 (F)	
Property taxes on equipment	4,000 (F)	
Fire insurance on equipment	3,000 (F)	214,000
Manufacturing costs incurred during 19_1		$904,000
Add work in process, December 31, 19_0		10,000
Manufacturing costs to account for		$914,000
Less work in process, December 31, 19_1		14,000
Cost of goods manufactured (to Income Statement)		$900,000

2. Direct-material unit cost = Direct materials used ÷ Units produced
= $390,000 ÷ 900,000 = $.4333

Factory-rent unit cost = Factory rent ÷ Units produced
= \$50,000 ÷ 900,000 = \$.0556

3. The material costs are variable, so they would increase in total. However, their unit costs would be unaffected:

Direct materials = \$433,333 ÷ 1,000,000 units = \$.4333

In contrast, the factory rent is fixed, so it would not increase in total. However, if the rent is assigned to units produced, the unit costs would decline from \$0.556 to \$.05:

Factory-rent unit cost = \$50,000 ÷ 1,000,000 = \$.05

4. The explanation would begin with the answer to part 3. The accountant should stress that the averaging (unitization) of costs having different behavior patterns can be misleading. A common error is to assume that a total unit cost, which is often a sum of some variable unit costs and some fixed unit costs, is an indicator that *total* costs change in a wholly variable way as activity fluctuates. The next chapter demonstrates the necessity for distinguishing between cost behavior patterns.

As already mentioned, in information gathering the basic want is for a set of signals that will facilitate the prediction of how the costs of the total organization will be affected under each decision alternative. The total costs assigned to a cost objective are essentially an estimate of how the total costs of the organization have been affected by a particular action. That is, if the cost objective (e.g., unit of product) had not been present, the total costs assigned thereto would not have been incurred. In practice, this ideal is rarely attainable. Above all, the user must be wary about unit fixed costs. Too often, unit fixed costs are erroneously regarded as being indistinguishable from variable costs.

Terms to Learn

This chapter contains more basic terms than any other in this book. Do not proceed before you check your understanding of the following terms. Both the chapter and the Glossary contain definitions.

actual costs ***average costs*** ***conversion costs*** ***cost accumulation***
cost objective ***direct labor*** ***direct-materials inventory***
direct materials ***factory burden*** ***factory overhead***
finished-goods inventory ***fixed costs*** ***goods in process*** ***idle time***
indirect labor ***indirect manufacturing costs*** ***inventoriable costs***
manufacturing expenses ***manufacturing overhead*** ***overtime premium***
period costs ***periodic inventory method*** ***perpetual inventory method***
prime costs ***product costs*** ***relevant range*** ***variable costs***
work-in-process inventory ***work in progress***

Special Points and Pitfalls

At this point, your biggest task is to learn the meaning of the block of new terms introduced in this chapter. In particular, see the "Troublesome Terminology" section in this chapter.

Be sure you understand Exhibit 2-5, including the footnotes and the new terms. Newcomers to cost accounting are used to assuming that such costs as power, telephone, and depreciation are expenses unconnected with inventories. However, if these costs are related to manufacturing, they are overhead costs that most cost accounting systems regard as inventoriable.

QUESTIONS, PROBLEMS, AND CASES

2-1 "For purposes of income determination, insurance, depreciation, and wages should always be treated alike." Comment.

2-2 Why is the term *manufacturing expenses* a misnomer?

2-3 "Cost of goods sold is an expense." Do you agree? Explain.

2-4 Why is the unit-cost concept helpful in accounting?

2-5 Define *variable cost, fixed cost, relevant range.*

2-6 Give three examples of variable factory overhead.

2-7 Distinguish between *costing for inventory valuation* and other purposes.

2-8 Give three examples of fixed factory overhead.

2-9 "Fixed costs are really variable. The more you produce, the less they become." Do you agree? Explain.

2-10 "An action once taken cannot be changed by subsequent events." What implications does this have for the cost accountant?

2-11 Why is overtime premium usually considered an indirect cost rather than direct?

2-12 What two major purposes of cost accounting were stressed in this chapter?

2-13 Distinguish between *manufacturing* and *merchandising.*

2-14 What are the three major elements in the cost of a manufactured product?

2-15 Define the following: *direct materials, direct labor, indirect materials, indirect labor, factory overhead, prime cost, conversion cost.*

2-16 Give at least four terms that may be substituted for the term *factory overhead.*

2-17 Distinguish among *direct labor, indirect labor, overtime premium,* and *idle time.*

2-18 What is the major difference between the balance sheets of manufacturers and merchandisers?

2-19 "Fixed costs decline as production increases." Do you agree? Explain.

2-20 ***Periodic or perpetual inventory methods.*** (SMA) The terms *periodic* and *perpetual inventories* are referred to frequently in presenting the accounting procedures that are followed by businesses in recording their business transactions in any given period of their operations. Discuss the difference between periodic and perpetual inventory procedures and indicate the advantages and disadvantages of each method.

2-21 ***Average costs and total costs.*** Reconsider the example in this chapter regarding the fraternity party, where the cost of the music was to be a fixed sum of $1,000.

REQUIRED

1. Suppose 500 persons attend the party. What will be the total cost of the musical group? The cost per person?
2. Suppose 2,000 persons attend. What will be the total cost of the musical group? The cost per person?
3. For prediction of total costs, should the manager of the party use the unit costs in requirement 1? In requirement 2? What is the major lesson of this problem?

2-22 ***Straightforward manufacturing statement.*** Use the data found on the following page to answer the following questions on the XY Company (in millions):

REQUIRED

1. Prepare a statement of cost of goods manufactured and sold.
2. Compare your statement with those in Exhibit 2-5. How does your statement differ from the Schedule of Cost of Goods Manufactured in Exhibit 2-5?
3. Compute the prime costs incurred during 19_4. Compute the conversion costs incurred during 19_4.
4. What is the difference in meaning between the terms "total manufacturing costs incurred in 19_4" and "cost of goods manufactured in 19_4"?
5. Draw a T-account for Work in Process. Enter the amounts shown on your financial statement into the T-account as you think they might logically affect Work in

	INVENTORIES	
	12/31/_3	12/31/_4
Direct materials	$ 9	$ 7
Work in process	4	3
Finished goods	10	13

Manufacturing Costs Incurred During 19_4

Direct materials used		$20
Direct labor		13
Indirect manufacturing costs:		
Indirect labor	$ 5	
Utilities	2	
Depreciation—plant and equipment	3	
Other	6	16
Total		$49

Process, assuming that the account was kept on a perpetual inventory basis. Use a single summary number of $16 million for entering any effects of the indirect manufacturing costs rather than entering the four individual amounts.

2-23 ***Statement of cost of goods manufactured.*** The following items pertain to the Engle Corporation:

		FOR YEAR 19_2	
Work in process, Dec. 31, 19_2	$ 2,000	Selling and administrative expenses (total)	$ 70,000
Finished goods, Dec. 31, 19_1	40,000	Direct materials purchased	80,000
Accounts receivable, Dec. 31, 19_2	30,000	Direct labor	70,000
Accounts payable, Dec. 31, 19_1	40,000	Factory supplies	6,000
Direct materials, Dec. 31, 19_1	30,000	Property taxes on factory	1,000
Work in process, Dec. 31, 19_1	10,000	Factory utilities	5,000
Direct materials, Dec. 31, 19_2	5,000	Indirect labor	20,000
Finished goods, Dec. 31, 19_2	12,000	Depreciation—plant and equipment	21,000
Accounts payable, Dec. 31, 19_2	20,000	Sales	350,000
Accounts receivable, Dec. 31, 19_1	50,000	Miscellaneous factory overhead	10,000

REQUIRED

Prepare an income statement and a supporting schedule of cost of goods manufactured. (For additional questions regarding these facts, see the next problem.)

2-24 ***Interpretation of statements.*** Refer to the preceding problem.

REQUIRED

1. How would the answer to the preceding problem be modified if you were asked for a schedule of cost of goods manufactured and sold instead of a schedule of cost of goods manufactured? Be specific.
2. Examine Exhibit 2-6. Would the sales manager's salary be accounted for any differently if the Engle Corporation were a merchandising company instead of a manufacturing company? Using the boxes in the exhibit, describe how an assembler's wages would be accounted for in this manufacturing company.
3. Factory supervisory salaries are usually regarded as indirect manufacturing costs. When might some of these costs be regarded as direct costs? Give an example.
4. Suppose that both the direct materials and the depreciation were related to the manufacture of the equivalent of 105,000 units of product. What is the unit cost for the direct materials assigned to those units? For depreciation? Assume that yearly depreciation is computed on a straight-line basis.
5. Assume that the implied cost behavior patterns in requirement 4 persist. That is, direct material costs behave as a variable cost and depreciation behaves as a fixed

cost. Repeat the computations in requirement 4, assuming that the costs are being predicted for the manufacture of the equivalent of 126,000 units of product. How would the total costs be affected?

6. As a management accountant, explain concisely to the president why the unit costs differed in requirements 4 and 5.

2-25 ***Statement of cost of goods manufactured and sold.*** From the Younger Manufacturing Company's adjusted trial balance of December 31, 19_1, the following account balances have been obtained:

Raw materials, January 1, 19_1	$ 75,000
Work in process, January 1, 19_1	21,200
Finished goods, January 1, 19_1	50,000
Purchases	198,000
Purchase returns and allowances	3,000
Direct labor	125,000
Indirect labor	40,000
Heat, light, and power	35,000
Insurance on factory	6,000
Factory and machine maintenance	8,000
Factory supplies	6,000
Depreciation—factory building	9,000
Depreciation—equipment	39,000
Property taxes on factory	3,600

In addition, raw materials costing $187,000 were used, the cost of goods manufactured for the year 19_1 was $440,000, and the cost of goods sold was $430,000.

REQUIRED

1. A statement of cost of goods manufactured and sold for the year 19_1.
2. Suppose that both the direct materials and the depreciation were related to the production of the equivalent of 200,000 units. What is the unit cost for the direct materials assigned to those units? What is the unit cost of the depreciation on the factory building and on the machinery? Assume that depreciation is a straight-line, fixed cost.
3. Repeat the computations in requirement 2 for direct materials and depreciation, assuming that costs are being predicted for the manufacture of 160,000 units next year. Assume that the implied cost behavior patterns persist.
4. As the controller, explain concisely to the president why the unit costs differed in requirements 2 and 3.

2-26 ***Compute cost of goods sold.*** (SMA) A manufacturing company had inventories at the beginning and end of its most recent fiscal period as follows:

	BEGINNING	END
Raw materials	$22,000	$30,000
Work in process	40,000	48,000
Finished goods	25,000	18,000

During this period, the following costs and expenses were incurred:

Raw materials purchased	$300,000
Direct-labor cost	120,000
Indirect-labor cost (factory)	60,000
Taxes, utilities, and depreciation on factory building	50,000
Sales and office salaries	64,000

Cost of goods sold during the period was (choose one): (1) $514,000, (2) $521,000, (3) $522,000, (4) $539,000.

2-27 ***Finding unknown balances.*** For each of the cases in the accompanying list, find the unknowns designated by a capital letter.

	CASE 1	CASE 2
Gross profit or gross margin	$11,300	C
Work in process, 1/1	-0-	$ 800
Work in process, 12/31	-0-	3,000
Finished-goods inventory, 1/1	5,000	4,000
Direct materials used	8,000	6,000
Direct labor	13,000	12,000
Factory overhead	7,000	D
Purchases of direct materials	9,000	7,000
Sales	44,000	33,800
Accounts receivable, 1/1	2,000	1,400
Accounts receivable, 12/31	6,000	2,100
Cost of goods sold	A	22,000
Accounts payable, 1/1	3,000	1,700
Accounts payable, 12/31	1,800	1,500
Finished-goods inventory, 12/31	B	5,300

2-28 ***Finding unknown balance.*** You have been trying to reconstruct the records of the Goldberg Company. Some employees are suspected of having taken some inventory. Many records are missing. Nevertheless, you have gathered the following data regarding the current year (in thousands):

Work in process, beginning	$ 2,000	Accounts payable, 1/1	$ 300
Work in process, end	2,500	Accounts payable, 12/31	1,200
Gross margin	25,000	Purchases of direct materials	8,000
Accounts receivable, 12/31	2,800	Factory overhead	7,000
Finished-goods inventory, end	7,600	Sales	41,000
Cost of goods sold	16,000	Direct labor	6,000
Selling expenses	4,000	Direct materials used	5,000
Administrative expenses	3,000		

REQUIRED | Compute the beginning finished-goods inventory.

2-29 ***Fire loss; computing inventory costs.*** A distraught employee, Fang W. Arson, put a torch to a factory on a blustery February 26. The resulting blaze completely destroyed the plant and its contents. Fortunately, certain accounting records were kept in another building. They revealed the following for the period December 31, 19_1–February 26, 19_2:

Prime costs, $301,000
Gross profit percentage based on net sales, 20 percent
Cost of goods available for sale, $460,000
Direct materials purchased, $170,000
Work in process, 12/31/_1, $34,000
Direct materials, 12/31/_1, $16,000
Finished goods, 12/31/_1, $30,000
Factory overhead, 40 percent of conversion costs
Sales, $500,000
Direct labor, $180,000

The loss was fully covered by insurance. The insurance company wants to know the approximate cost of the inventories as a basis for negotiating a settlement, which is really to be based on replacement costs, not historical cost.

REQUIRED | Calculate the cost of

1. Finished-goods inventory, 2/26/_2
2. Work-in-process inventory, 2/26/_2
3. Direct-materials inventory, 2/26/_2

2-30 ***Classification of costs.*** Classify each of the following as direct or indirect (D or I) with respect to product, and as variable or fixed (V or F) with respect to whether the cost fluctuates in total as activity or volume changes.[3] You will have two answers, D or I and V or F, for *each* of the ten items:

1. Cutting bits in a machinery department
2. Workmen's compensation insurance in a factory
3. Cement for a roadbuilder
4. Iron ore for a blast furnace
5. Paper towels for a factory washroom
6. Food for a factory cafeteria
7. Factory rent
8. Salary of a factory storeroom clerk
9. Foreman training program
10. Abrasives (sandpaper, etc.)

2-31 ***Overtime and fringe costs.*** A city planning department had a flurry of work during a particular week. The printers' labor contract provided for payment to workers at a rate of 150 percent of the regular hourly wage rate for all hours worked in excess of 8 per day. Anthony Bardo worked 8 hours on Monday through Wednesday, 10 hours on Thursday, and 9 hours on Friday. His regular pay rate is $12 per hour.

REQUIRED

1. Suppose that the printing department works on various jobs. All costs of the jobs are eventually allocated to the users, whether the consumers be the property-tax department, the city hospital, the city schools, or individual citizens who purchase some publications processed by the department. Compute Bardo's wages for the week. How much, if any, of Bardo's wages should be classified as indirect costs of particular printing jobs. Why?
2. The city pension plan provides for the city to contribute to an employee pension fund for all employees at a rate of 20 percent of gross wages (not considering pension benefits). How much, if any, of Bardo's retirement benefits should be classified as direct costs of particular printing jobs? Why?

For an expansion of this problem, see Problem 4-19.

2-32 ***Comprehensive problem on unit costs, product costs, variable and fixed costs.*** The Morrow Company makes a single product. Costs are as follows (V stands for variable, F for fixed):

Production in units	100,000
Costs incurred:	
Direct materials used	$100,000 V
Direct labor	70,000 V
Power	5,000 V
Indirect labor	10,000 V
Indirect labor	20,000 F
Other factory overhead	8,000 V
Other factory overhead	20,000 F
Selling expenses	30,000 V
Selling expenses	20,000 F
Administrative expenses	50,000 F
Work-in-process inventory, December 31, 19_1	0
Direct-materials inventory, December 31, 19_1	2,000 lbs.
Finished-goods inventory, December 31, 19_1	$ 20,970

Dollar sales were $364,000 in 19_1. There were no beginning inventories in 19_1. The company's ending inventory of finished goods was carried at the average unit cost of production for 19_1. Direct-material prices have been stable throughout the year. Two pounds of direct materials are used to make a unit of finished product.

[3]If in doubt, select on the basis of whether the item will vary over wide ranges of activity.

REQUIRED

1. Direct-materials inventory, total cost, December 31, 19_1.
2. Finished-goods inventory, total units, December 31, 19_1.
3. Unit sales price, 19_1.
4. Net income, 19_1. Show computations.

2-33 ***Budgeted income statement.*** This problem is more difficult than previous problems. Refer to Problem 2-32.

Management has asked that you prepare a budgeted income statement for 19_2, assuming that all unit prices for sales and variable costs will not change. Assume that sales will be 102,000 units and that ending inventory of finished goods, December 31, 19_2, will be 12,000 units. Assume that fixed costs will remain the same. Show supporting computations, and include a schedule of cost of goods manufactured. The ending inventory of finished goods is to be carried at the average unit cost of production for 19_2.

The preceding chapter distinguished sharply between two major purposes of cost accounting systems: (a) decision making for planning and control, and (b) product costing for inventory valuation and income determination. This chapter and the next will examine these two purposes in more depth. Cost-volume-profit analysis is a subject inherently appealing to most students of management because it gives a sweeping overview of the planning process and because it provides a concrete example of the importance of understanding cost behavior—the response of costs to a variety of influences. That is why we consider this subject now, even though it could just as easily be studied later.

Managers are constantly faced with decisions about selling prices, variable costs, and fixed costs. Basically, managers must decide how to acquire and utilize economic resources in light of some objective. Unless they can make reasonably accurate predictions about cost and revenue levels, their decisions may yield undesirable or even disastrous results. These decisions are usually short run: How many units should we manufacture? How many nurses should we hire? Should we change our price? Should we spend more on advertising? However, long-run decisions such as the purchase of plant and equipment also hinge on predictions of the resulting cost-volume-profit relationships.

At the outset, remember that we will be considering simplified versions of the real world. Are these simplifications justifiable? The answer depends on the facts in a particular organization. The manager has a method for deciding among courses of action, often called a *decision model.* Models of cost-volume-profit relationships are examples of decision models. The simpler model is always preferable provided that the management decisions will be unaffected by the buying of a more complicated model. That is, a more complicated model is attractive only when the resulting decisions will be improved in a net benefit sense.

The breakeven point

We obtain an overview of decision models by examining the interrelationships of changes in costs, volume, and profits—sometimes too narrowly described as breakeven analysis. The breakeven point is often only incidental in these studies. **Instead, the focus is on the impact upon operating income or net income of various decisions that affect sales and costs.** The **breakeven point** is that point of activity (sales volume) where total revenues and total expenses are equal; that is, there is neither profit nor loss. The terms *net income* and *net profit* are used interchangeably.

Consider the following example:

» ***EXAMPLE***

George plans to sell a toy rocket at the state fair. He may purchase these rockets at 50¢ each with the privilege of returning all unsold rockets. The booth rental is $200, payable in advance. The rockets will be sold at 90¢ each. How many rockets must be sold to break even? (Ignore income taxes, which we consider later in the chapter.)

equation method

The first solution method for computing the breakeven point is the *equation method.* Every income statement may be expressed in equation form, as follows:

Sales − Variable expenses − Fixed expenses = Net income

or

Sales = Variable expenses + Fixed expenses + Net income

This equation provides the most general and easy-to-remember approach to any breakeven or profit-estimate situation. For the example above:

Let X = Number of units to be sold to break even, where the breakeven point is determined by zero net income

$$\$.90X = \$.50X + \$200 + 0$$

$$\$.40X = \$200 + 0$$

$$X = \frac{\$200 + 0}{\$.40}$$

$$X = 500 \text{ units (or \$450 total sales at 90¢ per unit)}$$

contribution-margin method A second solution method emphasizes a formula. It is the *contribution-margin* or *marginal-income* method. **Contribution margin** is equal to sales minus *variable* expenses. Sales and expenses are analyzed as follows:

1. *Unit contribution margin* to cover fixed expenses and desired net income

$$= \textbf{Unit sales price} - \textbf{Unit variable expense} = \$.90 - \$.50 = \$.40$$

2. *Breakeven point* in terms of units sold

$$= \frac{\textbf{Fixed expenses + Desired net income}}{\textbf{Unit contribution margin}} = \frac{\$200 + 0}{\$.40} = 500 \textbf{ units}$$

Stop a moment and relate the contribution-margin method to the equation method. The key calculation was dividing \$200 by \$.40. Look at the third line in the equation solution. It reads:

$$\$.40X = \$200 + 0$$

$$X = \frac{\$200 + 0}{\$.40}$$

giving us a general formula:

$$\textbf{Breakeven point in units} = \frac{\textbf{Fixed expenses + Desired net income}}{\textbf{Contribution margin per unit}}$$

The *contribution-margin* method is merely a restatement of the *equation* in different form. Use either technique; the choice is a matter of personal preference.

graphic approach The relationships in this example are graphed in Exhibit 3-1. The graph in Exhibit 3-1 used the following building blocks:

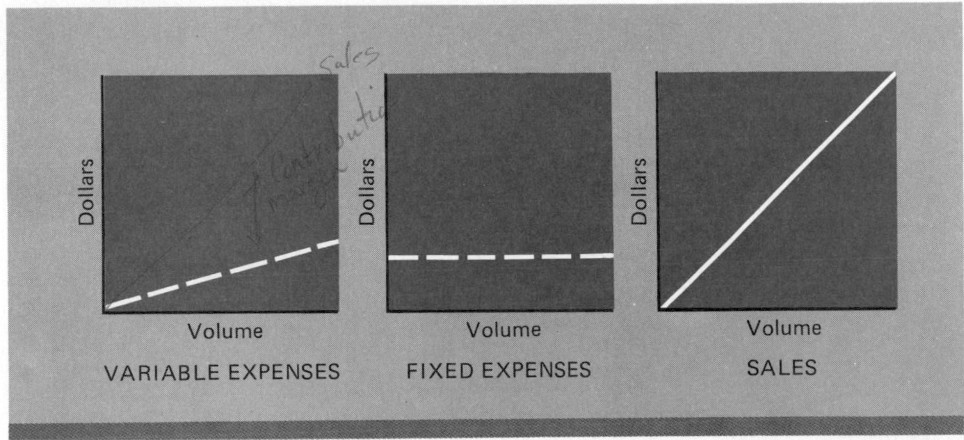

Note that total sales and total variable expenses fluctuate in direct proportion to changes in physical volume, whereas fixed expenses are the same in total over the entire volume range.

Now combine the fixed and variable expenses in a single graph:

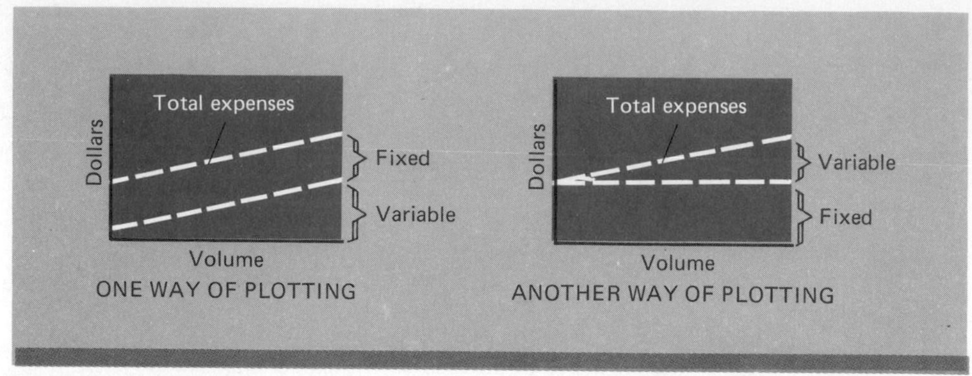

Note that the "total expenses" line is the same under either method. The graph that plots fixed expenses above the variable expenses is preferred by many accountants because it emphasizes the contribution-margin notion. (See Exhibit 3-1.) Both the sales and variable-cost lines start at the origin; the vertical distance between them is the contribution margin. Whether operations are above or below the breakeven point, the vertical distance between the sales line and the variable-cost line always measures the total amount of the "contribution" that sales volume is making toward coverage of the fixed expenses.

Finally, introduce the sales line:

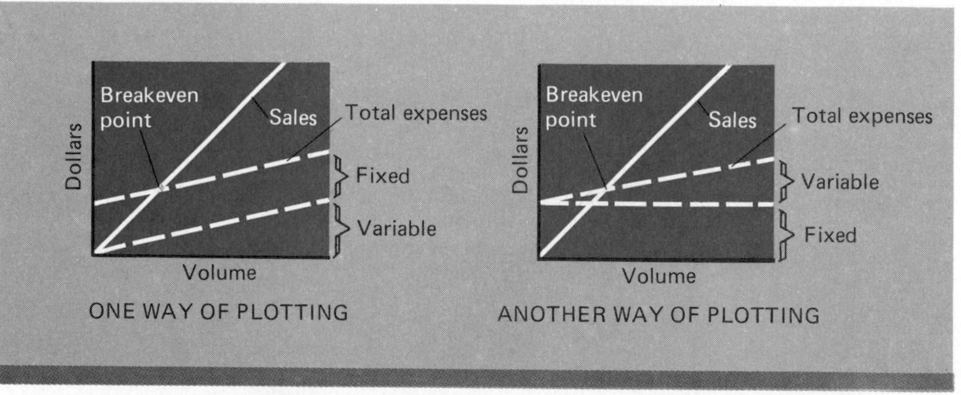

Exhibit 3-1 shows the complete breakeven chart. The *breakeven point* is the point where the total-sales line and total-expense line intersect. But note further that this graph shows the profit or loss outlook for a wide range of volume. The confidence we place in any particular breakeven chart is naturally a consequence of the relative accuracy of the cost-volume-profit relationships depicted.

EXHIBIT 3-1

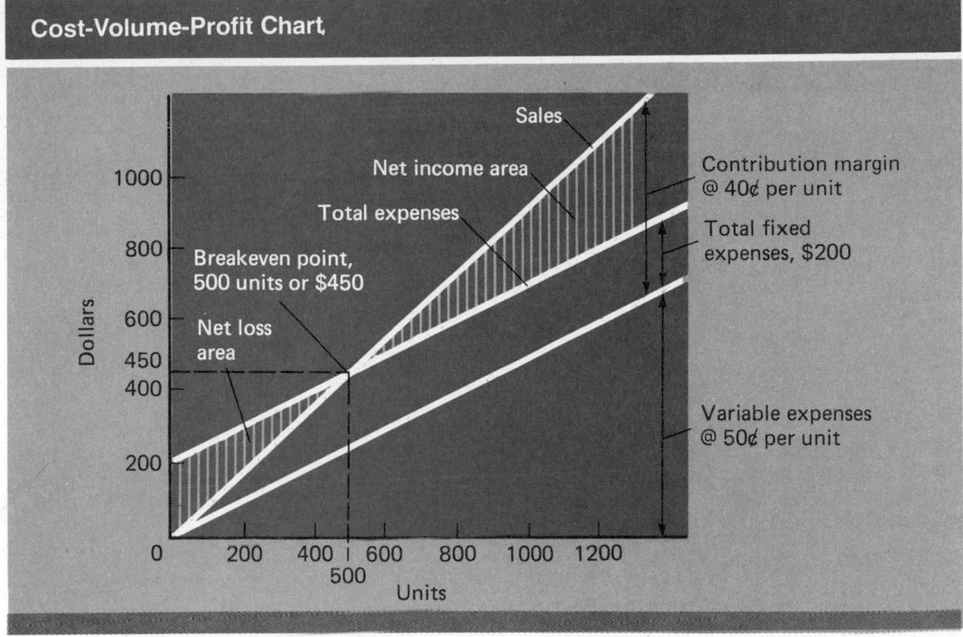

The use of the chart in Exhibit 3-1 may also be depicted as follows:

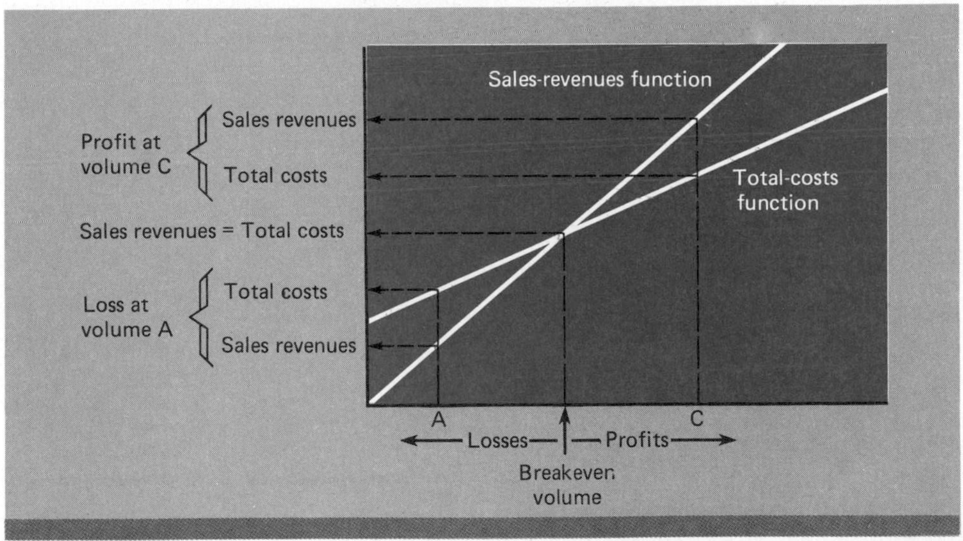

ASSUMED VOLUME LEVEL	SALES	TOTAL COSTS (variable + fixed)	NET INCOME
A (200 units)	$.90 × 200 = $180	($.50 × 200) + $200 = $300	$−120
Breakeven (500 units)	$.90 × 500 = $450	($.50 × 500) + $200 = $450	0
C (800 units)	$.90 × 800 = $720	($.50 × 800) + $200 = $600	120

The chart on page 47 uses total *costs* rather than total *expenses.* To confuse you? No, but to underscore the widespread tendency to use *costs* and *expenses* interchangeably. In this context, costs refer to the costs expiring and thus becoming expenses during the period in question.

target net income

Let us introduce a profit element by asking, *How many rockets must be sold to yield a net income of 20 percent of sales?* The same basic approach may be used. The equation method follows:

Let X = Number of units to be sold to yield desired net income
Sales = Variable expenses + Fixed expenses + Desired net income

$$\$.90X = \$.50X + \$200 + .20(\$.90X)$$
$$\$.90X = \$.50X + \$200 + \$.18X$$
$$\$.22X = \$200$$
$$X = 909 \text{ units}$$

Proof:			
	Sales = 909 × \$.90	\$818.10	100.00%
	Variable expenses = 909 × \$.50	454.50	55.56
	Contribution margin	\$363.60	44.44%
	Fixed expenses	200.00	24.44
	Net income	\$163.60	20.00%

Find the 909-unit volume on the graph in Exhibit 3-1. The difference between sales and total expenses at that volume is the \$164 net income.

Alternatively, the contribution-margin method could be used:

$$X = \frac{\text{Fixed expenses} + \text{Desired net income}}{\text{Unit contribution margin}}$$
$$X = \frac{\$200 + .20(\$.90X)}{\$.40}$$
$$\$.40X = \$200 + \$.18X$$
$$\$.22X = \$200$$
$$X = 909 \text{ units}$$

Cost-volume-profit assumptions

relevant range

In a real-world company situation, the breakeven chart may be drawn as shown in Exhibit 3-1. However, the many assumptions that underlie the chart are subject to change if actual volume falls outside the relevant range that was the basis for drawing the chart. It would be more realistic if the lines on these charts were not extended back to the origin, as shown on page 49.

The modified chart highlights the fact that tenuous, static assumptions underlie a graph of cost-volume-profit relationships. **The sales and expense relationships may be valid only within a band of activity called the *relevant range*.** The relevant range is usually a range in which the firm has had some recent experience. But the same

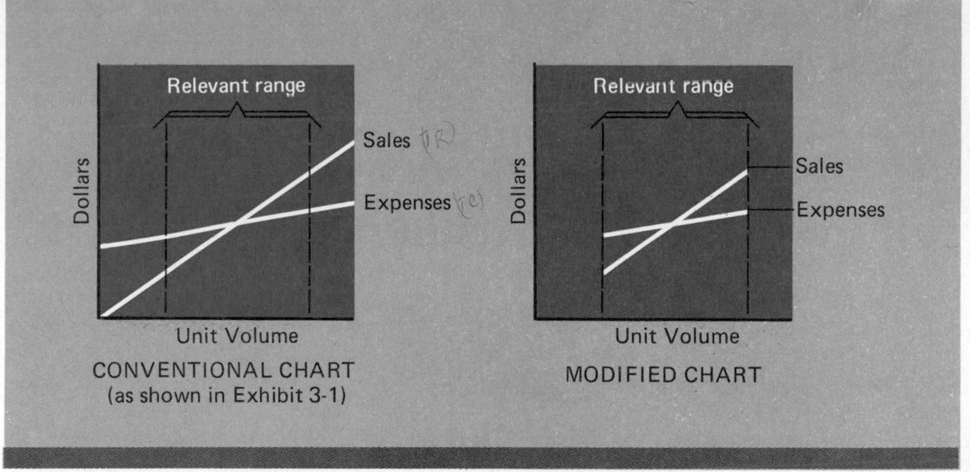

relationships are unlikely to persist if volume falls outside the limits of the relevant range. For example, as shown in the preceding chapter, some fixed costs may be avoided at low-volume levels.

the economist's breakeven chart

Two principal differences between the accountant's and the economist's breakeven charts are:

1. The accountant usually assumes a constant *unit* variable cost instead of a unit variable cost that changes with the level of production. In other words, the accountant assumes linearity, but the economist does not.
2. The accountant's sales line is drawn under the assumption that price does not change with the level of production or sales, but the economist assumes that price changes may be needed to spur sales volume. Therefore, the economist's chart is nonlinear.[1]

The differences can be graphed as shown on page 50.

The economist's assumptions are undoubtedly more valid; the accountant's simplifications may or may not lead to less-profitable decisions. The point is that obtaining more accurate cost functions is often difficult and expensive. Managers and accountants are aware of the simplifications introduced by the assumptions of linearity, but generally they have decided that the value of any additional information that might be gained from more accurate data would not exceed the additional costs of obtaining the data. They also take comfort in knowing that most of their decisions

[1]An extension of the economist's curves in the accompanying graph would show a second breakeven point at a high-volume level. Total revenue would begin to fall as unit prices fall. Extension beyond the second breakeven volume would generate net losses. In contrast, extension of the accountant's lines would add to net profit until the maximum attainable volume is reached. For additional discussion, see R. Kaplan, *Advanced Management Accounting* (Englewood Cliffs, N.J.: Prentice-Hall, 1982), Chap. 5. K. Middleton, "A Critical Look at Breakeven Analysis," *Australian Accountant,* May 1980, pp. 264–68, compares the accountant's and the economist's assumptions. He is unsympathetic to using the idea of a relevant range to justify linear rather than nonlinear cost patterns. However, he concludes that "a linear expression of total cost may often be a reasonable reflection of reality."

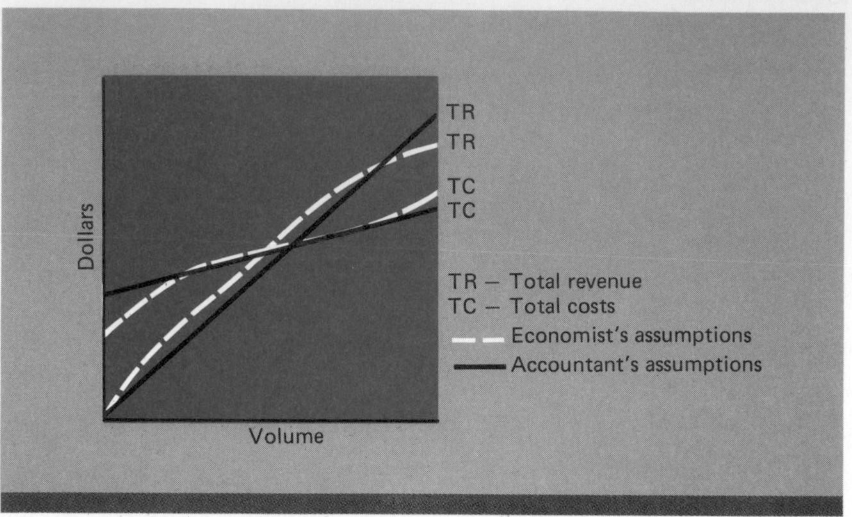

are made within the relevant range of volume, where the linearity assumptions is likely to be more accurate.

limitations of assumptions

Cost behavior is affected by the interplay of a number of factors. Physical volume is only one of these factors; others include unit prices of inputs, efficiency, changes in production technology, wars, strikes, legislation, and so forth. Any breakeven analysis is based on assumptions made about the behavior of revenue, costs, and volume. A change in expected behavior will alter the breakeven point; in other words, profits are affected by changes in other factors *besides volume.* A breakeven chart must be interpreted in the light of the limitations imposed by its underlying assumptions. **The real benefit of preparing breakeven charts is in the enrichment of understanding of the interrelationships of all factors affecting profits, especially cost behavior patterns over ranges of volume.**

In summary, the following typical underlying assumptions will limit the precision and reliability of a given breakeven analysis:

1. The behavior of total costs and total revenues has been reliably determined and is linear over the relevant range.
2. All costs may be divided into fixed and variable elements.
3. Total fixed costs remain constant over the relevant volume range of the breakeven analysis.
4. Total variable costs are directly proportional to volume.
5. Selling prices are to be unchanged.
6. Prices of the factors of production are to be unchanged (for example, material prices, wage rates).
7. Efficiency and productivity are to be unchanged.
8. The analysis either covers a single product or assumes that a given sales mix will be maintained as total volume changes. (This assumption will be discussed later in this chapter.)
9. Revenue and costs are being compared on a single activity base (for example, sales value of production or units produced).

10. Perhaps the most basic assumption of all is that volume is the only relevant factor affecting cost. Of course, other factors also affect costs and sales. Ordinary cost-volume-profit analysis is a crude oversimplification when these factors are unjustifiably ignored.

11. Changes in beginning and ending inventory levels are insignificant in amount. (The impact of inventory changes on cost-volume-profit analysis depends on what inventory valuation method is used. This complexity is discussed in Chapter 8.)

Business is dynamic, not static. The user of cost-volume-profit analysis must constantly challenge and reexamine assumptions in the light of changes in business conditions, prices, factors of production, sales mixes, factor mixes, and the like. Moreover, cost-volume-profit analysis need not adhere rigidly to the traditional assumptions of linearity and unchanging prices.

Interrelationships of cost, volume, and profits

uncertainty and sensitivity analysis

Throughout this book we almost always work with single-number "best estimates" in order to emphasize and simplify various important points. For example, our cost-volume-profit models, budget models, and capital-investment models make strong assumptions regarding such critical items as the levels of variable costs, fixed costs, volume attainable, and so on. In short, for purposes of introducing and using many decision models, we often conveniently assume a world of certainty.

Obviously, our estimates and predictions are subject to varying degrees of uncertainty, which is defined here as the possibility that the actual amount will deviate from the expected amount. How do we cope with uncertainty? There are many complex models available that formally analyze expected values in conjunction with probability distributions. But the application of *sensitivity analysis* to the certainty model is the most widely used approach.

Sensitivity analysis is a "what-if" technique that essentially asks how a result will be changed if the original predicted data are not achieved. In the context of cost-volume-profit analysis, sensitivity analysis answers such questions as "What will net income be if volume changes from that originally predicted?" Such sensitivity analysis can be conducted in informal ways or in more formal ways, as described in Chapter 21.

changes in variable costs

Both the unit contribution margin and the breakeven point are altered by changes in unit variable costs. Thus, in the toy-rocket example, if the cost of a toy rocket increases from 50¢ to 70¢ and the sales price is unchanged at 90¢, the unit contribution decreases from 40¢ to 20¢, and the breakeven point increases from 500 to 1,000 units ($200 fixed expenses divided by $.20). A decrease in rocket cost from 50¢ to 30¢ would change the unit contribution from 40¢ to 60¢. The new breakeven point would become 333 units ($200 fixed expenses divided by $.60).

Variable costs are subject to various degrees of control at different volumes because of psychological as well as other factors. When business is booming, management tends to be preoccupied with the generation of volume "at all costs." When business is slack, management tends to ride herd on costs. Decreases in volume are often accompanied by increases in selling expenses and lower selling prices; at the same time labor turnover falls, labor productivity changes, and raw-material prices change. This is another illustration of the limitations of a breakeven chart; conventional breakeven charts assume directly proportional fluctuations of variable costs with volume. This implies adequate and uniform control over costs, whereas in practice such control is often erratic.

changes in fixed costs

Fixed costs are not static year after year. They may be deliberately increased in order to obtain more profitable combinations of production and distribution; these affect the three major profit determinants: revenue, variable costs, and fixed costs. For example, a sales force may be established to reach markets directly instead of through wholesalers, thereby obtaining increased unit sales prices. More-complicated machinery may be bought so as to reduce unit variable costs. Increases in labor rates are likely to make it desirable for a firm to invest in labor-saving equipment. In some cases, on the other hand, it may be wise to reduce fixed costs in order to obtain a more favorable combination. Thus, direct selling may be supplanted by the use of manufacturers' agents. A company producing stoves may find it desirable to dispose of its foundry if the resulting reduction in fixed costs would more than counterbalance increases in the variable costs of purchased castings over the expected volume range.

When a major change in fixed costs is proposed, management uses forecasts of the effect on the targeted net income and the unit contribution margin as a guide toward a wise decision. The management accountant makes continuing analyses of cost behavior and redetermines breakeven points periodically. He keeps management informed of the cumulative effect of major and minor changes in the company's cost and revenue patterns.

Fixed costs are constant only over a contemplated range of activity for a given time period. The volume range rarely extends from shutdown levels to 100 percent capacity. Thus, when a radical reduction in volume is foreseen, many fixed costs are "jarred loose" by managerial action. The slashing of fixed costs lowers the breakeven point and enables the firm to endure a greater decrease in volume before losses appear. The president of Emery Air Freight commented (*Business Week,* March 31, 1980, p. 111):

> We would prefer to keep out of the airline business and buy space from the existing airlines because that's a variable cost. If we don't have the need for capacity, we don't buy it, but if we have to own or charter airplanes, the costs become fixed and we're stuck with excess capacity sometimes.

Introduction to variable costing

absorption and variable costing

Two major methods of product costing will be emphasized in this book: **absorption costing** and **variable costing.** These methods differ in only one conceptual respect: **Fixed manufacturing overhead is included in the inventoriable costs under absorption costing, but it is excluded from the inventoriable costs under variable costing.**

Exhibit 3-2 compares the flow of costs under absorption costing and variable costing. The top part of the exhibit should be familiar because **it is the same approach to inventory that was discussed in Chapter 2;** nevertheless, the term *absorption costing* has not been used until now. Both absorption costing and variable costing apply variable manufacturing costs to products. However, as the bottom half of Exhibit 3-2 indicates, **variable costing regards fixed manufacturing overhead as a period cost to be immediately charged against sales** rather than as a product cost to be held back as inventory and charged against sales later as a part of cost of goods sold.

The term **variable costing** is an accurate description, but **direct costing** and **marginal costing** are also widely used to signify the exclusion of factory-fixed overhead

EXHIBIT 3-2

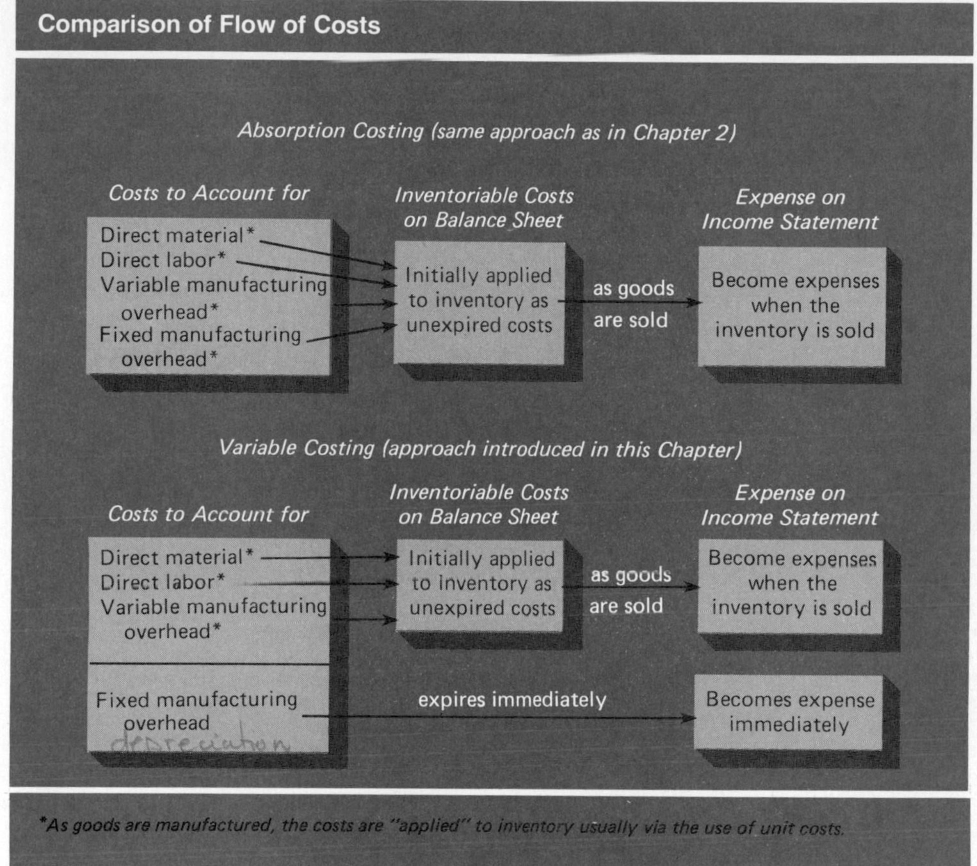

from inventories. *Direct costing* is an especially unfortunate choice of terms; after all, the approach includes in inventory not only direct material and direct labor but also *variable indirect* manufacturing costs.

Variable costing has been a controversial subject among accountants—not so much because there is disagreement about the need for delineating between variable- and fixed-cost behavior patterns for management planning and control, but because there is a question about its theoretical propriety for *external* reporting. Proponents of variable costing maintain that the fixed part of factory overhead is more closely related to the *capacity* to produce than to the production of specific units. Opponents of variable costing maintain that inventories should carry a fixed-cost component because both variable and fixed costs are necessary to produce goods; both these costs should be inventoriable, regardless of their differences in behavior patterns. Neither the public accounting profession nor the Internal Revenue Service has approved of variable costing as a generally acceptable method of inventory valuation.

contribution approach

The traditional income statement uses absorption costing and classifies expenses primarily by *management function,* such as manufacturing, selling, and administrative expenses (numbers assumed in thousands):

Sales	$1,000
Less manufacturing cost of goods sold (including fixed manufacturing overhead)	600
Gross profit or gross margin	400
Less selling and administrative expenses	300
Net income	$ 100

In contrast, the variable costing income statement features *cost behavior* as the primary classification scheme. **Indeed, the income statement is often called a *contribution* income statement instead of a *variable costing* income statement:**

Sales		$1,000
Less variable expenses:		
Manufacturing	$360	
Selling	100	
Administrative	20	480
Contribution margin		520
Less fixed expenses:		
Manufacturing	$240	
Selling	120	
Administrative	60	420
Net income		$ 100

These two income statements represent differing basic approaches to presenting the results of operations. However, there are halfway approaches too. For example, some companies use absorption costing but include a few distinctions between variable and fixed costs. That is, these income statements retain the primary classifications by management function, but manufacturing overhead, selling, and administrative expenses are subclassified into variable and fixed categories.

The typical discussions of cost-volume-profit analysis assume that the units produced are equal to the units sold. That is, as assumed in this chapter, there are no changes in inventory levels. The implications of inventory changes regarding absorption costing and variable costing are explored more fully in Chapter 8, but for our immediate purposes they are unimportant.

Note that the absorption costing statement does not show any contribution margin. This raises analytical difficulties in the computation of the impact on net income of changes in sales. Fixed manufacturing overhead, under absorption costing procedures, is averaged (unitized) and assigned to products. Hence, as we will often see in later chapters, unit costs and gross-profit figures include fixed overhead that must be removed for a short-run cost-volume-profit analysis.

The contribution approach stresses the lump-sum amount of fixed costs to be recouped before net income emerges. This highlighting of total fixed costs helps to attract management attention to fixed-cost behavior and control when both short-run and long-run plans are being made. Keep in mind that advocates of this contribution approach **do not maintain that fixed costs are unimportant or irrelevant,** but they do stress that the distinctions between behaviors of variable and fixed costs are crucial for certain decisions.

comparison of contribution margin and gross margin

Avoid confusing the terms **contribution margin** and **gross margin** (which is often also called **gross profit**). As the preceding financial statements show, *contribution margin* is the excess of sales over *all* variable expenses, including variable manufacturing, selling, and administrative categories.

Even in retailing, the gross margin is not necessarily the same as the contribution margin. For example, a retail salesperson may earn, say, a 10 percent commission on sales (numbers assumed in thousands):

Sales	$100	Sales		$100
Cost of goods sold	55	Cost of goods sold	$55	
Gross margin	$ 45	Sales commissions	10	
		Total variable costs		65
		Contribution margin		$ 35

In contrast, *gross margin* or *gross profit* is the excess of sales over the inventory cost of the goods sold. Therefore, in a manufacturing company, the manufacturing cost of goods sold (including *fixed* indirect manufacturing costs) is deducted from sales to obtain the gross margin.

Both the contribution margin and the gross margin may be expressed as *totals,* as amounts *per unit,* or as *percentages of sales* in the form of ratios. For example, a **contribution-margin ratio** is the total contribution margin divided by the total sales. Similarly, the **variable-cost ratio** is the total variable costs divided by the total sales.

advantages of contribution margins and ratios

The advantages of knowing the contribution margins and ratios of divisions and product lines include:

1. *Contribution-margin ratios* often help management decide on which products to push and which to de-emphasize or to tolerate only because of the sales benefits that relate to other products.

2. *Contribution margins* are essential for helping management to decide whether a product line should be dropped. In the short run, if a product recovers more than its variable costs, it is making a contribution to overall profits. This information is provided promptly by the contribution approach. Under the traditional approach, the relevant information not only is difficult to gather but there is a danger that management may be misled by reliance on unit costs that contain an element of fixed cost.

3. Contribution margins may be used to appraise alternatives that arise with respect to price reductions, special discounts, special advertising campaigns, and the use of premiums to spur sales volume. Decisions such as these are really determined by a comparison of the added costs with the prospective additions in sales revenue. Ordinarily, the higher the contribution-margin ratio, the better the potential net benefit from sales promotion; the lower the ratio, the greater the increase in volume that is necessary to recover additional sales-promotion costs.

4. When desired profits are agreed upon, their attainability may be quickly appraised by computing the number of units that must be sold to secure the wanted profits. The computation is easily made by dividing the fixed costs plus desired profits by the contribution margin per unit.

5. Decisions must often be made as to how to utilize a given set of resources (for example, machines or materials) most profitably. The contribution approach furnishes the data for a proper decision, because the latter is determined by the product that makes the largest total contribution to profits. (However, the solution to the problem of calculating the maximum contribution is not always intuitively obvious. This point is amplified in Chapters 11 and 23.)

6. The contribution approach is helpful where selling prices are firmly established in the industry, because the principal problem for the individual company is how much variable cost is allowable (a matter most heavily affected in many companies by design of products) and how much volume can be obtained.

7. Advocates of a contribution approach maintain that the compilation of unit costs for products on a contribution basis helps managers understand the relationships among costs, volume, prices, and profits and hence leads to wiser pricing decisions. Ultimately, maximum prices are set by customer demand. Minimum short-run prices are sometimes determined by the variable costs of producing and selling. Pricing is discussed at greater length in Chapter 11.

The P/V chart

Exhibit 3-1 can be recast in simpler form as a so-called **P/V chart** (a profit-volume graph). This form is preferred by many managers who are interested mainly in the impact of changes in volume on net income. The first graph in Exhibit 3-3 illustrates the chart, using the data in our example. The chart is constructed as follows:

1. The vertical axis is net income in dollars. The horizontal axis is volume, which may be expressed in units or in sales dollars.
2. At zero volume, the net loss would be approximated by the total fixed costs: $200 in this example.
3. A net-income line will slope upward from the −$200 intercept at the rate of the unit contribution margin of 40¢. The line will intersect the volume axis at the breakeven point of 500 units. Each unit sold beyond the breakeven point will add 40¢ to net income.

The P/V chart provides a quick condensed comparison of how alternatives on pricing, variable costs, or fixed costs may affect net income as volume changes. For example, the second graph in Exhibit 3-3 shows how net income and the breakeven point would be affected by a decrease in rocket cost from 50¢ to 30¢ and an increase in rent from $200 to $240. The unit contribution margin would become 60¢, and the breakeven point would fall from 500 units to 400 units:

New breakeven point = $240 ÷ $.60
= 400 units

Note also the steeper slope of the new net-income line, which means that the net income will increase at a faster rate as volume increases.

Measuring volume

In our examples so far, we have used units of product as a measure of volume. But "volume" is a general term for activity levels that may be measured in several ways. For example, the volume of a hospital is often expressed in patient-days (number of

EXHIBIT 3-3

P/V Chart

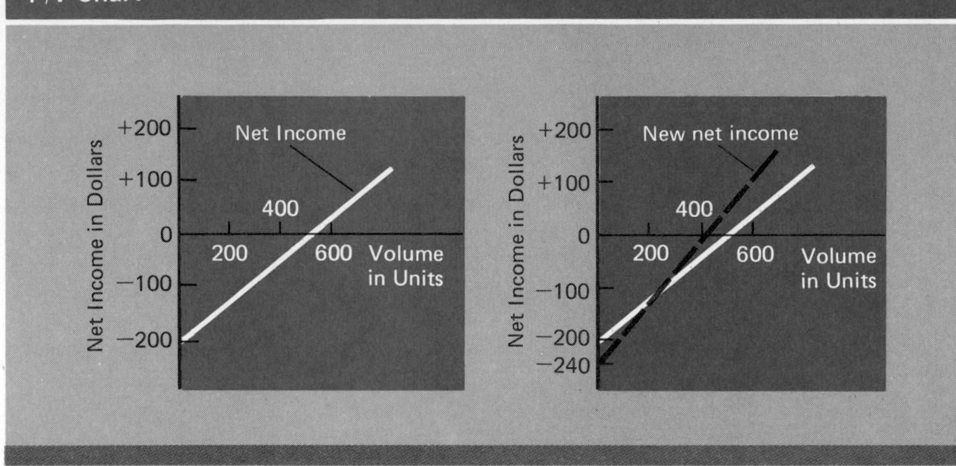

patients multiplied by the average number of days each patient remained in the hospital). As another example, the volume of the teaching activity of a university is often expressed in terms of total student credit hours taken, not number of students enrolled.

Moreover, the breakeven point is frequently expressed in different forms in different industries. For example, a letter to the shareholders of Ozark Air Lines stated that personnel reductions and improved scheduling had lowered the company's "breakeven load factor from 52 percent to 50 percent." The latter is the percentage of seats occupied. Essentially, Ozark had improved its breakeven point by lowering fixed costs via personnel reductions and by running the airplanes more intensively each day.

The most widely encountered aggregate measure of the volume of activity is sales dollars, a monetary rather than a physical calibration of activity. Nearly all companies have more than one product. Although apples and oranges can be aggregated in physical units, such a sum is harder to interpret than their sales values in *dollars.* Similarly, it would be nonsense to aggregate in *units* for a company such as Sears that sells thousands of different products.

Reconsider our initial toy-rocket example. Suppose the data in units are unavailable. However, we do know that fixed costs are \$200. We also know that when total sales are \$900, total variable costs are \$500. The *variable-cost ratio* is \$500 ÷ \$900 = .5556, and the *contribution-margin ratio* is \$400 ÷ \$900 = .4444. Using the variable-cost ratio, the breakeven point could be calculated as follows:

$$\text{Let } X = \text{Total sales dollars to break even}$$
$$X = \text{Variable cost ratio times } X + \text{Fixed costs} + \text{Net income}$$
$$X = \frac{\$500}{\$900}X + \$200 + 0$$
$$X = .5556X + \$200 + 0$$
$$X - .5556X = \$200 + 0$$
$$.4444X = \$200 + 0$$
$$X = \frac{\$200 + 0}{.4444} = \$450$$

or using the contribution-margin ratio in a formula:

$$X = \frac{\textbf{Fixed expenses} + \textbf{Desired net income}}{\textbf{Contribution-margin ratio}}$$

$$X = \frac{\$200 + 0}{.4444} = \$450$$

Sales mix and P/V charts

Sales mix may be defined as the relative combination of quantities of a variety of company products that compose total sales. If the mix changes, overall sales targets may be achieved, but the effects on profits depend on whether low-margin or high-margin goods predominate in the sales mix. When managers plan a sales mix, it can be depicted on a breakeven chart or P/V chart by assuming average revenues and average costs for a given mix.

For example, suppose that a two-product company had the following budget:

	A	B	TOTAL
Sales in units	120,000	40,000	160,000
Sales @ \$5 and \$10	\$600,000	\$400,000	\$1,000,000
Variable costs @ \$4 and \$3	480,000	120,000	600,000
Contribution margins @ \$1 and \$7	\$120,000	\$280,000	\$ 400,000
Fixed costs			300,000
Net income			\$ 100,000

For simplicity, ignore income taxes. What would be the breakeven point? The usual answer assumes that the budgeted mix will not change—that is, that volume is measured in units that consist of a combination of $\frac{120}{160}$ of A and $\frac{40}{160}$ of B, or 3 A for every 1 B. As the last column of the table shows, the contribution to income of each composite unit averages \$400,000 ÷ 160,000, or \$2.50. Therefore, the breakeven point is:

\$300,000 ÷ \$2.50 = 120,000 units (consisting of 90,000 A and 30,000 B)

But the breakeven point is not a unique number. It obviously depends on the composition of sales volume. For example, suppose only A (its unit contribution margin is \$1) were sold:

\$300,000 ÷ \$1.00 = 300,000 units (consisting exclusively of A)

Similarly, if only B (its contribution margin is \$7) were sold:

\$300,000 ÷ \$7.00 = 42,857 units (consisting exclusively of B)

These breakeven relationships are shown in Exhibit 3-4:

1. At zero volume, the net loss is \$300,000, the total fixed costs.
2. A net-income line will slope upward from the −\$300,000 intercept at the rate of how many dollars are contributed to income by each unit increase in volume.

EXHIBIT 3-4 **P/V Charts, Product Combinations**

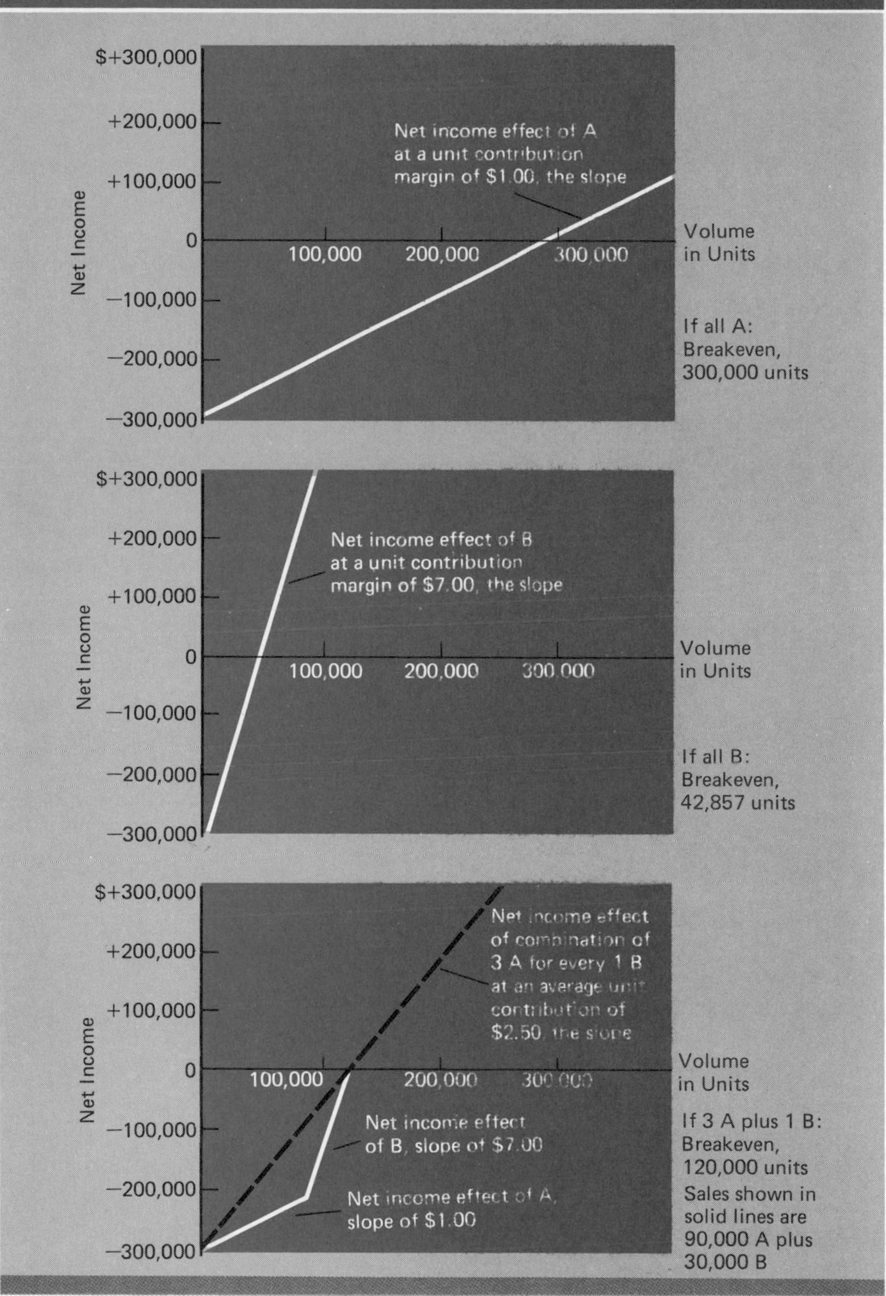

The top graph shows the income effects of A, sold alone, with its contribution to income of $1.00 per unit and a breakeven point of 300,000 units. The middle graph shows the similar effects of B, taken alone. The bottom graph highlights the basic assumption of what "volume" means when plans are based on a specified combination of products. **Then volume, whether expressed as units or as sales dollars, is assumed to fluctuate without changing the assumed combination or mix of the components.**

The dashed line is based on a contribution margin for each "package" of product (3 A plus 1 B), which provides 3($1) + 1($7), or $10. The average contribution margin per unit of product would be $10 ÷ 4 units in each package = $2.50.

In sum, cost-volume-profit analysis must be done carefully because so many initial assumptions may not hold. When the assumed combinations change, the breakeven point and the expected net incomes at various volume levels also change. Of course, the breakeven points are frequently incidental data. Instead, the focus is on the effects on net income under various production and sales strategies.

Role of income taxes

Income taxes are most often computed as some percentage of income before income taxes. Therefore, the breakeven equation in our basic example would have to be modified accordingly. Suppose we are asked to compute the number of rockets that must be sold to yield a net income after taxes of $164, the same amount calculated earlier in the "Target Net Income" section of this chapter. Assume an income tax rate of 30 percent. The equation would be:

$$\$.90X = \$.50X + \$200 + \frac{\text{Target after-tax net income}}{1 - \text{Tax rate}}$$

$$\$.90X = \$.50X + \$200 + \frac{\$164}{1 - .30}$$

$$\$.90X = \$.50X + \$200 + \$234$$

$$\$.40X = \$434$$

$$X = 1{,}085 \text{ units}$$

Proof:		
	Sales = 1,085 × $.90 =	$976.50
	Variable expenses = 1,085 × $.50 =	542.50
	Contribution margin	$434.00
	Fixed expenses	200.00
	Income before income taxes	$234.00
	Income taxes @ 30%	70.20
	Net income	$163.80, or $164

Note that the only change in the general equation approach is to modify the target net income to allow for the impact of income taxes. Our previous equation approach was:

Sales = Variable expenses + Fixed expenses + Income before taxes

We now have to introduce income tax effects:

$$\text{Let } y = \text{Income before taxes}$$
$$.3 = \text{Income tax rate}$$
$$z = \text{Income after taxes}$$

Then

$$z = y - .3y$$
$$z = y(1 - .3)$$
$$y = \frac{z}{1 - .3} = \frac{\text{Target after-tax net income}}{1 - \text{Tax rate}}$$

Reexamine our solution. Using those numbers, a recapitulation of the relationships follows:

Income before taxes	$234	100%
Income taxes	70	30
Net income	$164	70%

Note that

$$\text{Income before taxes} = \frac{\text{Target after-tax net income}}{1 - \text{Tax rate}}$$

$$\$234 = \frac{\$164}{1 - .30}$$

SUMMARY

The modern multiproduct company's performance is influenced by so many factors that the attempt to portray all of them on a breakeven chart by making assumptions is an ambitious one. The breakeven chart may be compared to the use of a meat-ax, not a scalpel. The chart is useful as a frame of reference for analysis, as a vehicle for expressing overall performance, and as a planning device.

Whenever the underlying assumptions of cost-volume-profit analysis do not correspond to a given situation, the limitations of the analysis must be clearly recognized. **A single breakeven graph is static because it is a picture of relationships that prevail under only one set of assumptions. If conditions change, a different set of cost-volume-profit relationships is likely to appear. The fluid nature of these relationships must be kept uppermost in the minds of executives and accountants if the breakeven tool is to be useful and educational.**

Properly used, cost-volume-profit analysis offers essential background for important management decisions regarding distribution channels, outside contracting, sales-promotion expenditures, and pricing strategies. It offers an overall view of costs and sales in relation to profit planning, and it provides clues to possible changes in management strategy. It is also the springboard for a different type of income statement, which emphasizes cost behavior patterns. This is often called the "contribution" income statement or the "variable costing" income statement. Such a statement differs from the traditional "absorption costing" statement because it excludes fixed factory overhead from inventories and it includes a contribution margin. Solution 3 in the "Problems for Self-Study" displays these latter distinctions.

problems for self-study

problem 1

Reconsider the toy-rocket problem in the chapter. Suppose you want to obtain a net income of $250. How many rockets must be sold?

solution 1

The equation method follows:

$$\text{Let } X = \text{Number of units to be sold to yield desired net income}$$
$$\$.90X = \$.50X + \$200 + \$250$$
$$\$.40X = \$450$$
$$X = 1{,}125 \text{ units}$$

problem 2

Here is the income statement of C Company:

Net sales		$500,000
Less expenses:		
Variable	$350,000	
Fixed	250,000	600,000
Net loss		($100,000)

Assume that variable expenses will always remain the same percentage of sales.

a. If fixed expenses are increased by $100,000, what amount of sales will cause the firm to break even?

b. With the proposed increase in fixed expenses, what amount of sales will yield a net income of $50,000?

solution 2

This problem differs from the example in the text because all data are expressed in dollars; no information is given on the number of units:

a.

$$\text{Let } S = \text{Breakeven sales in dollars}$$
$$S = \text{Variable expenses} + \text{Fixed expenses} + \text{Desired net income}$$
$$S = \frac{\$350{,}000}{\$500{,}000}S + (\$250{,}000 + \$100{,}000)$$
$$S = .70S + \$350{,}000$$
$$.30S = \$350{,}000$$
$$S = \$1{,}166{,}667$$

b.

$$\text{Let } S = \text{Sales needed to earn } \$50{,}000$$
$$S = .70S + \$350{,}000 + \$50{,}000$$
$$.30S = \$400{,}000$$
$$S = \$1{,}333{,}333$$

Note that 30 percent of each sales dollar is available for the coverage of fixed expenses and the making of *net income.* This *contribution-margin ratio* (*variable income ratio* or *contribution percentage*) is computed by subtracting the variable expense percentage, 70 percent, from 100 percent. This relationship is the foundation for the following commonly used formulas:

a.

$$\text{B.E.} = \frac{\text{Fixed expenses} + \text{Desired net income}}{1 - \dfrac{\text{Variable expenses}}{\text{Sales}}}$$

$$\text{or} \quad \frac{\text{Fixed expenses} + \text{Desired net income}}{\text{Contribution-margin ratio}}$$

$$\text{B.E.} = \frac{\$350{,}000}{1 - \dfrac{\$350{,}000}{\$500{,}000}}, \quad \text{or} \quad \frac{\$350{,}000}{.30}$$

$$\text{B.E.} = \$1{,}166{,}667$$

b.

$$\text{Required Sales } (RS) = \frac{\text{Fixed expenses} + \text{Desired net income}}{\text{Contribution-margin ratio}}$$

$$RS = \frac{\$400{,}000}{.30}$$

$$RS = \$1{,}333{,}333$$

problem 3

Using the following data (in millions) for 19_3 for the Sprouse Company, prepare a variable-costing income statement and an absorption-costing income statement. Assume that there are no beginning or ending inventories. (The problem of changes in inventory levels and how they affect these statements is discussed in Chapter 8.)

Sales	$150	Variable factory overhead	$ 5
Variable selling expenses*	15	Direct labor	20
Variable administrative expenses	12	Direct materials used	50
Fixed selling expenses	20	Fixed administrative expenses	5
Fixed factory overhead	10		

These and other expenses would be detailed.

solution 3

Sprouse Co.

*Variable-costing Income Statement**
For the Year Ended Dec. 31, 19_3
(In millions of dollars)

Sales		$150
Less variable expenses:		
Direct materials used	$50	
Direct labor	20	
Variable factory overhead	5	
Total variable manufacturing costs	$75	
Variable selling expenses	15	
Variable administrative expenses	12	
Total variable expenses		102
Contribution margin		$ 48
Less fixed expenses:		
Fixed factory overhead	$10	
Fixed selling expenses	20	
Fixed administrative expenses	5	
Total fixed expenses		35
Net income		$ 13

Sprouse Co.

Absorption-Costing Income Statement†
For the Year Ended Dec. 31, 19_3
(in millions of dollars)

Sales			$150
Less manufacturing cost of goods sold:			
Direct materials used		$50	
Direct labor		20	
Variable factory overhead		5	
Fixed factory overhead		10	85
Gross profit or gross margin			$ 65
Selling expenses:			
Variable	$15		
Fixed	20	$35	
Administrative expenses:			
Variable	$12		
Fixed	5	17	
Total selling and administrative expenses			52
Net income			$ 13

**Often called a "contribution" income statement.*
†*Often called a "traditional" or "functional" income statement. This type is described more fully in the preceding chapter.*

Terms to Learn

This chapter and the Glossary contain definitions of the following important terms:

absorption costing ***breakeven point*** ***contribution margin*** ***contribution-margin ratio*** ***direct costing*** ***gross margin*** ***gross profit*** ***marginal costing*** ***P/V chart*** ***sales mix*** ***sensitivity analysis*** ***variable costing*** ***variable-cost ratio***

Special Points and Pitfalls

Do not confuse the distinction between *absorption costing,* which was introduced in Chapter 2, and *variable costing,* which was introduced in this chapter. As Exhibit 3-2 shows:

	INVENTORIABLE COST?	
	absorption costing	**variable costing**
Direct materials	yes	yes
Direct labor	yes	yes
Variable factory overhead	yes	yes
Fixed factory overhead	yes	no

Also see Solution 3 of the "Problems for Self-Study." Note especially that the contribution margin is the difference between sales and *all variable* expenses, including *variable* selling and *variable* administrative expenses. In contrast, gross profit or gross margin is the difference between sales and *all manufacturing* costs of goods sold, including the *fixed* factory overhead.

Appendix 3: nonprofit institutions and cost-volume analysis

Cost-volume analysis is not confined to profit-seeking institutions. For example, many private colleges in the United States are facing severe financial difficulties. Breakeven analysis helps trustees and administrators to understand the potential economic consequences of their decisions.

Some institutions use cost-volume-revenue models for budget planning. Exhibit 3-5 displays the current budget of a college's costs and revenues. Most of the costs are fixed in the short run; for example, faculty and staff costs. Revenue is of two kinds, variable and fixed. For example, tuition and fees are variable in relation to the number of students, whereas gifts, grants, and contracts have no relationship to enrollment. Using assumed figures, Exhibit 3-5 indicates that the college will break even at a level of 2,300 students.

Exhibit 3-6 shows the effect of a decision to raise maintenance costs by $200,000. The breakeven point would increase to 2,350 students.

Similarly, suppose the tuition per student were increased. If all other costs and revenues were unchanged, Exhibit 3-7 shows that the breakeven point would decrease to 2,150 students.

EXHIBIT 3-5

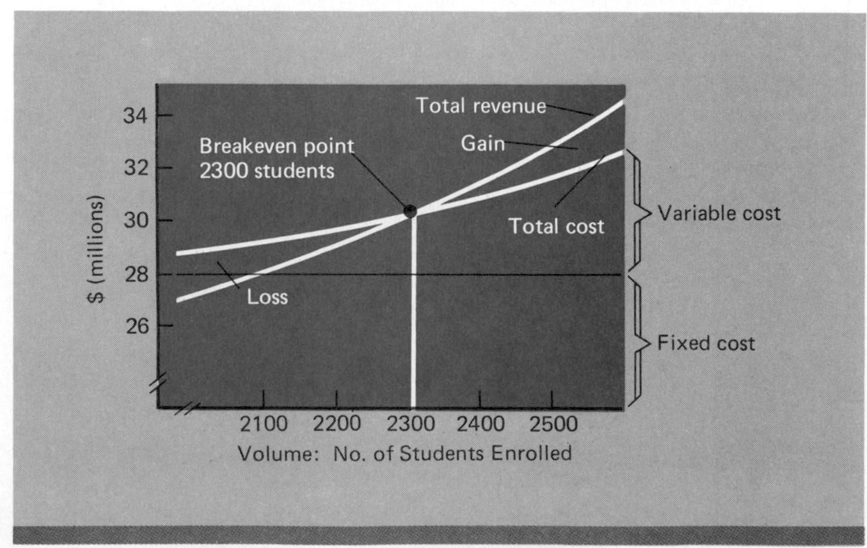

EXHIBIT 3-6

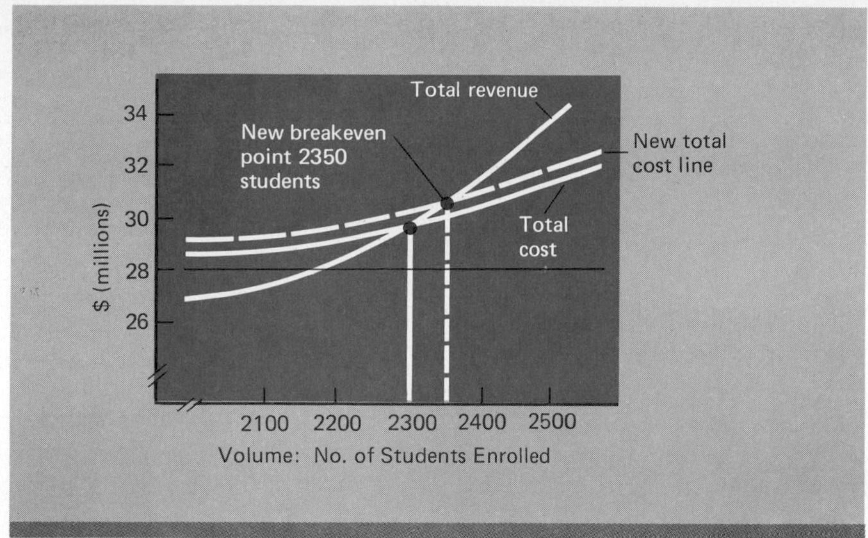

EXHIBIT 3-7

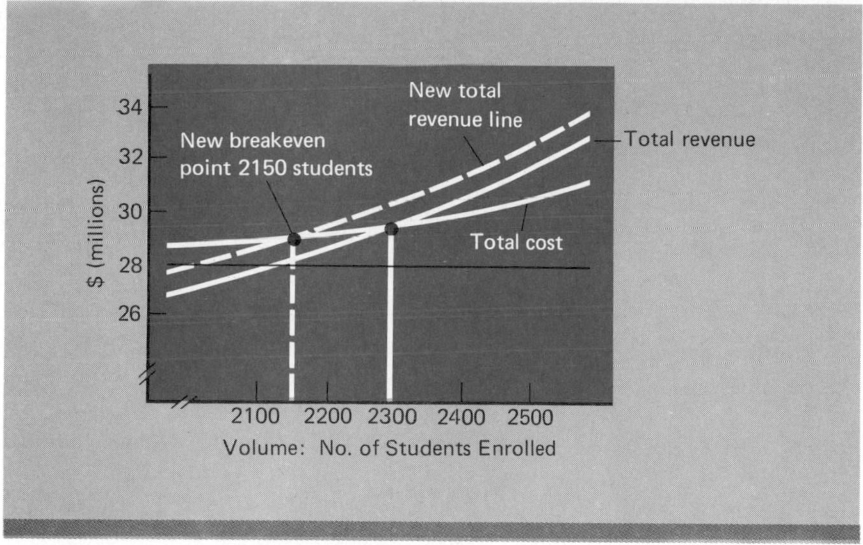

Source: F. Turk, "A Tool for Planning and Decision Making," *Management Focus,* March–April 1980, pp. 10–12.

The cost-volume-revenue model can be used for many potential decisions, such as solicitations of annual gifts or increases in student aid. If several possible interactive changes are to be analyzed simultaneously, a computerized planning model will undoubtedly be useful. Such models are based on assumptions regarding how various revenues and costs behave in relation to changes in the volume of students or programs.

QUESTIONS, PROBLEMS, AND CASES

3-1 Why is it more accurate to describe the subject matter of this chapter as *cost-volume-profit relationships* rather than as *breakeven analysis?*

3-2 Why is it often more desirable to plot fixed costs above the variable costs on a breakeven chart?

3-3 What are the principal differences between the accountant's and the economist's breakeven charts?

3-4 Define *contribution margin, variable-cost ratio, contribution-margin ratio.*

3-5 "This breakeven approach is great stuff. All you need to do is worry about variable costs. The fixed costs will take care of themselves." Discuss.

3-6 A lithographic company follows a policy of high pricing each month until it reaches its monthly breakeven point. After this point is reached, the company tends to quote low prices on jobs for the rest of the month. What is your opinion of this policy? As a regular customer, and suspecting this policy, what would you do?

3-7 ***Relationships in chapter illustration.*** Refer to the initial toy-rocket example in the chapter.

REQUIRED

1. Suppose the unit purchase cost of rockets rises from 50¢ to 60¢, but the sales price is unchanged. What is the new breakeven point in units?
2. Suppose the unit purchase cost of rockets declines from 50¢ to 40¢, but the sales price is unchanged. What is the new breakeven point in units?

3-8 ***Fill in blanks.*** In the data presented below, fill in the information that belongs in the blank spaces for each of the four unrelated cases:

	SALES	VARIABLE EXPENSES	FIXED EXPENSES	TOTAL COSTS	NET PROFIT	CONTRIBUTION-MARGIN RATIO
a.	$1,000	$700	$___	$1,000	$___	___
b.	1,500	___	300	___	___	.30
c.	___	500	___	800	1,200	___
d.	2,000	___	300	___	200	___

3-9 ***Exercises in cost-volume-profit relationships.*** The Best Buy Grocers Corporation owns and operates twelve supermarkets in and around Detroit. You are given the following corporate budget data for next year:

Sales	$10,000,000
Fixed expenses	1,650,000
Variable expenses	8,200,000

REQUIRED

Compute expected profit for each of the following deviations from budgeted data. (Consider each case independently.)

a. 10 percent increase in total contribution margin, holding sales constant
b. 10 percent decrease in total contribution margin, holding sales constant
c. 5 percent increase in fixed costs
d. 5 percent decrease in fixed costs
e. 8 percent increase in sales volume
f. 8 percent decrease in sales volume
g. 10 percent increase in fixed costs and 10 percent increase in sales volume
h. 5 percent increase in fixed costs and 5 percent decrease in variable costs

3-10 ***Cost-volume-profits and shoe stores.*** The Walk Rite Shoe Company operates a chain of rented shoe stores. The stores sell ten different styles of relatively inexpensive men's shoes with identical purchase costs and selling prices. Walk Rite is trying to determine the desirability of opening another store, which would have the following expense and revenue relationships:

	PER PAIR
Variable data:	
Selling price	$ 30.00
Cost of shoes	$ 19.50
Salesmen's commissions	1.50
Total variable expenses	$ 21.00

Annual fixed expenses:	
Rent	$ 60,000
Salaries	200,000
Advertising	80,000
Other fixed expenses	20,000
	$360,000

REQUIRED

(Consider each question independently.)

1. What is the annual breakeven point in dollar sales and in unit sales?
2. If 35,000 pairs of shoes are sold, what would be the store's net income (loss)?
3. If the store manager were paid 30¢ per pair as commission, what would be the annual breakeven point in dollar sales and in unit sales?
4. Refer to the original data. If sales commissions were discontinued in favor of an $81,000 increase in fixed salaries, what would be the annual breakeven point in dollars and in unit sales?
5. Refer to the original data. If the store manager were paid 30¢ per pair as commission on each pair sold in excess of the breakeven point, what would be the store's net income if 50,000 pairs were sold?

3-11 ***Extension of preceding problem.*** Refer to requirement 4 of the preceding problem.

1. Compute the point of indifference between a fixed salary plan and a commission plan. That is, calculate the volume level in units where the profit under each plan would be equal. Above that volume level, one plan would be more profitable than the other; below that level, the reverse would occur.

2. Compute the net income or loss under each plan at volume levels of 50,000 units and 60,000 units.

3. Suppose the target net income is $168,000. How many units must be sold to reach the target under (a) the commission plan and (b) the salary plan?

3-12 ***Sensitivity and inflation.*** Refer to Problem 3-10. As president of Walk Rite, you are concerned that inflation may squeeze your profits. Specifically, you feel committed to the thirty-dollar selling price and fear that diluting the quality of the shoes in the face of rising costs would be an unwise marketing move. You expect cost prices of the shoes to rise by 10 percent during the forthcoming year. Therefore, you are tempted to avoid the price rise by placing a noncancelable order with a large supplier that would provide 50,000 pairs of a specified quality for each store at $19.50 per pair. (To simplify this analysis, assume that all stores will face identical demands.)

These shoes could be acquired and paid for as delivered throughout the year. However, all shoes must be delivered to the stores by the end of the year.

As a shrewd merchandiser, you can foresee some risks in the sense that you deal exclusively in high-fashion goods that are subject to rapid obsolescence. If sales were less than 50,000 pairs, you feel that markdowns of the unsold merchandise would be necessary to move the goods. You predict that the average selling price of the leftover pairs would be $18.00 each. The regular sales commission of 5 percent of sales would be paid.

REQUIRED

1. Suppose that the actual demand for the year is 48,000 pairs and that you contracted for 50,000 pairs. What is the net profit for the store?
2. If you had had perfect knowledge, you would have contracted for 48,000 rather than 50,000 pairs. What would the net profit have been if you had ordered 48,000 pairs?
3. Given an actual volume of 48,000 pairs, by how much would the average purchase cost of a pair have had to rise before you would have been indifferent between having the contract for 50,000 pairs and not having the contract?

3-13 ***Cost-volume-profit relationships.*** The Dowell Company makes and sells pens. Some pertinent facts follow:

Present sales volume, 500,000 units per year at a selling price of 50¢ per unit. Fixed expenses, $80,000 per year. Variable expenses are 30¢ per unit.

REQUIRED

(Consider each case separately.)

1. a. What is the present total profit for a year?
   b. What is the present breakeven point in dollars?

Compute the new profit for each of the following changes:

2. A 4¢-per-unit increase in variable expenses.
3. A 10 percent increase in fixed expenses and a 10 percent increase in sales volume.
4. A 20 percent decrease in fixed expenses, a 20 percent decrease in selling price, a 10 percent decrease in variable expenses per unit, and a 40 percent increase in units sold.

Compute the new breakeven point in units for each of the following changes:

5. A 10 percent increase in fixed expenses.
6. A 10 percent increase in selling price and a $20,000 increase in fixed expenses.

3-14 ***Choosing most profitable volume level.***

1. Company B manufactures and sells pens at a variable cost of $3 each and a fixed cost of x. It can sell 6,000 pens at $5 and net $2,000 profit, or it can sell 3,500 at $6 and another 2,000 at $4 each. Which alternative should Company B choose?
2. Company C manufactures and sells a consumer item. It can produce and sell up to 3,000 units at a variable cost of $1.50 per unit and fixed costs of $5,000; from 3,001 to 6,000 units at a variable cost of $1 per unit and fixed costs of $7,000; and from 6,001 to 10,000 units at a variable cost of $.50 per unit and fixed costs of $15,000. The president of Company C has discovered that 2,500 units can be sold at a price of $6 each, or 5,000 at a price of $4 each. Eight thousand units could probably be sold at $3.50 per unit if advertising were increased by $1,000 and selling costs by $.10 per unit. The latter costs are in addition to those already stated for the 6,001-to-10,000-unit range. How many units should Company C plan to produce and sell: 2,500, 5,000, or 8,000?

3-15 ***Target net incomes and contribution margins.*** The Blair Company has a maximum capacity of 200,000 units per year. Variable manufacturing costs are $12 per unit. Fixed factory overhead is $600,000 per year. Variable selling and administrative costs are $5 per unit, whereas fixed selling and administrative costs are $300,000 per year. Current sales price is $23 per unit.

REQUIRED

(Consider each situation independently.)

1. What is the breakeven point in (a) units? (b) dollar sales?
2. How many *units* must be sold to earn a target net income of $240,000 per year?
3. Assume that the company's sales for the year just ended totaled 185,000 units. A strike at a major supplier has caused a materials shortage, so that the current year's sales will reach only 160,000 units. Top management is planning to slash fixed costs so that the total for the current year will be $59,000 less than last year. Management is also thinking of either increasing the selling price or reducing variable costs, or both, in order to earn a target net income that will be the same dollar amount as last year's. The company has already sold 30,000 units this year at a sales price of $23 per unit with variable costs per unit unchanged. What contribution margin per unit is needed on the remaining 130,000 units in order to reach the target net income?

3-16 ***Target prices and profits.*** (SMA) The Martell Company has recently established operations in a very competitive market. Management has been very aggressive in its attempt to establish a market share.

The price of its product was set at $5 per unit, well below the major competition's selling price. Variable costs were $4.50 per unit, and total fixed costs were $600,000 during the first year.

REQUIRED

1. Assume that the firm was able to sell 1,000,000 units in the first year. What was the profit (loss) for the year?
2. Assume that variable costs per unit and total fixed costs do not increase in the second year. Management has been successful in establishing its position in the

market. What price must be set to achieve a profit of $25,000? Assume that output cannot be increased over the first-year level.

3-17 ***Margin of safety.*** The *margin of safety* is the excess of budgeted or actual sales over the breakeven sales volume. It shows the amount by which sales may decrease before losses occur. This concept may be expressed as a percentage through dividing the dollar margin of safety by budgeted or actual sales (M/S). The validity of such a margin depends on the accuracy of cost estimates at the contemplated breakeven point. Often any drastic decrease in sales is accompanied by severe slashes in costs; the margin of safety is an approximation that presupposes given cost relationships.

The Axel Swang Company has the following data:

Budget (300,000 Units)

Sales	$930,000	(100%)
Variable costs	325,500	(35%)
Contribution margin	$604,500	(65%)
Fixed costs	520,000	
Net income	$ 84,500	

Since management is not satisfied with the projected net income, it is considering four independent possibilities: (1) increase unit volume 10 percent; (2) increase unit selling price 10 percent; (3) decrease unit variable costs 10 percent; or (4) decrease fixed costs 10 percent.

REQUIRED

1. Compute the breakeven sales and the margin of safety as a percentage of sales.
2. Rank the four action possibilities in terms of net income. Show computations. Are the four possibilities likely to be independent? Why?

3-18 ***Channels of distribution.*** Munez Co., a manufacturer of stationery supplies, has always sold its products through wholesalers. Last year its sales were $2 million and its net profit was 10 percent of sales.

As a result of the increase in stationery sales in department stores and discount houses, Munez is considering eliminating its wholesalers and selling directly to retailers. It is estimated that this would result in a 40 percent drop in sales, but net profit would be $180,000 as a result of elimination of the middleman. Fixed expenses would increase from the present figure of $200,000 to $300,000, owing to the additional warehouses and distribution facilities required.

REQUIRED

1. Would the proposed change raise or lower the breakeven point in dollars? By how much?
2. What dollar sales volume must Munez obtain under the proposed plan to make as much profit as it made last year?

3-19 ***Effects of size of machines.*** Verne Pastries, Inc., is planning to manufacture doughnuts for its chain of pastry shops throughout the city. Two alternatives have been proposed for the production of the doughnuts—use of a semiautomatic machine or a fully automatic machine.

The shops now purchase their doughnuts from an outside supplier at a cost of 10¢ per doughnut.

	SEMIAUTOMATIC	AUTOMATIC
Annual fixed cost	$7,000	$13,000
Variable cost per doughnut	$ .05	$ .035

Outside 10¢ doughnut

REQUIRED

The president has asked for the following information:

1. For each machine, the minimum annual number of doughnuts that must be sold in order to have the total annual costs equal to outside purchase costs
2. The most profitable alternative for 250,000 doughnuts annually
3. The most profitable alternative for 500,000 doughnuts annually

4. The volume level that would produce the same net income regardless of the type of machine owned

3-20 ***Effects of sales forecast.*** The Fragile Company has just been incorporated and plans to produce a product that will sell for $10 per unit. Preliminary market surveys show that demand will be less than 10,000 units per year, but it is not as yet clear how much less.

The company has the choice of buying one of two machines, each of which has a capacity of 10,000 units per year. Machine A would have fixed costs of $30,000 per year and would yield a profit of $30,000 per year if sales were 10,000 units. Machine B has a fixed cost of $16,000 per year and would yield a profit of $24,000 per year with sales of 10,000 units. Variable costs behave linearly for both machines.

REQUIRED

1. Breakeven sales for each machine
2. The sales level where both machines are equally profitable
3. The range of sales where one machine is more profitable than the other

3-21 ***Comparison of two businesses.*** Consider two businesses with the following unit prices and fixed and variable costs:

BUSINESS A	
Selling price per unit	$1.00
Variable cost per unit	$ .20
Fixed cost of operations per year	$5,000
BUSINESS B	
Selling price per unit	$1.00
Variable cost per unit	$ .60
Fixed cost of operations per year	$2,500

REQUIRED

1. Calculate the breakeven point of each business in units.
2. Compute the profits of each business if sales in units are 10 percent above the breakeven point.
3. Which business would fare better if sales dropped to 5,000 units? Why?
4. Which business would fare better if the market collapsed and the price per unit fell to 50¢? Why?

3-22 ***Promotion of entertainment.*** George Florene, a theatrical promoter, is trying to decide whether to engage The Bugs, a very popular singing group, for a one-night appearance at the local arena, which has a salable capacity of 5,000 seats. He has gathered the following data:

Rental, including ushering and cleanup service	$ 4,000
Advertising	3,000
Ticket service and ticket printing	1,000
Miscellaneous expenses	2,000
Entertainers' fee	10,000
Total	$20,000

Sales and entertainment taxes are 10 percent of the price (excluding the tax) on each ticket, and ticket prices include this tax. That is, if the price of the ticket is $5 (excluding taxes), the total price is $5.50. Therefore, the tax is one-eleventh of the total price of the ticket.

REQUIRED

All prices include the sales and entertainment taxes.

1. What is the average price for each ticket that is needed for Florene to break even, assuming that the arena can be filled to capacity?
2. Suppose Florene thinks that he can maximize his return by pricing as follows: 1,000 seats @ $10; 1,000 @ $8; 1,000 @ $6; and 2,000 @ $4. If the house were sold out, how much net income would be produced for Florene at such prices?
3. Suppose that The Bugs appeal mainly to young people who are unlikely to pay high prices. Suppose 300 seats are sold @ $10; 700 @ $8; 900 @ $6; and 2,000 @ $4.

(a) How much net income would Florene make? (b) What is the average price of the sold tickets? How does it compare with your answer in requirement 1? In your own words, explain the difference.

4. a. The Bugs' agent phoned Florene and offered an alternative arrangement for compensation: $5,000 plus $1 per ticket sold, regardless of the ticket price. How would this arrangement affect your answers to requirements 1, 2, and 3a? Show computations.
   b. If you were Florene, which arrangement would you prefer? Why?
   c. Would your answer to requirement 4b change if the compensation were based on $1.20 per ticket rather than $1.00? Why?

3-23 ***Cost-volume-profit relationships.*** The McCovey Company has a maximum production capacity of 20,000 units per year. At that level, fixed costs are $280,000 annually. Variable costs per unit are $30 at all production levels.

For the ensuing year, the company has orders of 24,000 units at $50. If the company desires to make a minimum overall net income of $148,000 on these 24,000 units, what maximum unit purchase price would it be willing to pay to a subcontractor for 4,000 units? Assume that the subcontractor would act as McCovey's agent and deliver the units to customers directly and bear all related costs of manufacture, delivery, and so on. The customers, however, would pay McCovey directly as goods are delivered.

3-24 ***Breakeven for multiple products.*** (CPA) The Dooley Co. manufactures two products, baubles and trinkets. The following are projections for the coming year:

	BAUBLES		TRINKETS		
	units	**amount**	**units**	**amount**	**totals**
Sales	10,000	$10,000	7,500	$10,000	$20,000
Costs:					
Fixed		$ 2,000		$ 5,600	$ 7,600
Variable		6,000		3,000	9,000
		$ 8,000		$ 8,600	$16,600
Income before taxes		$ 2,000		$ 1,400	$ 3,400

Choose the best answer for each question:

1. Assuming that the facilities are not jointly used, the breakeven output (in units) for baubles would be (a) 8,000; (b) 7,000; (c) 6,000; (d) 5,000.

2. The breakeven volume (dollars) for trinkets would be (a) $8,000; (b) $7,000; (c) $6,000; (d) $5,000.

3. Assuming that consumers purchase composite units of four baubles and three trinkets, the composite unit contribution margin would be (a) $4.40; (b) $4.00; (c) $1.33; (d) $1.10.

4. If consumers purchase composite units of four baubles and three trinkets, the breakeven output for the two products would be
   a. 6,909 baubles; 6,909 trinkets
   b. 6,909 baubles; 5,182 trinkets
   c. 5,000 baubles; 8,000 trinkets
   d. 5,000 baubles; 6,000 trinkets

5. If baubles and trinkets become one-to-one complements and there is no change in the Dooley Co.'s cost function, the breakeven volume would be (a) $22,500; (b) $15,750; (c) $13,300; (d) $10,858.

6. If a composite unit is defined as one bauble and one trinket, the composite contribution-margin ratio would be (a) 7/10; (b) 4/7; (c) 2/5; (d) 19/50.

3-25 ***Breakeven and sales-mix assumption.*** Refer to Exhibit 3-4. Fixed costs are $300,000. The chapter showed three possible breakeven points, one for all A, one for all B, and one for a combination of 3 A and 1 B. Suppose that plans changed so that the budget was going to be 100,000 A and 60,000 B. Compute the new budgeted income and the new breakeven point. Are they better than the original combination of 120,000 A and 40,000 B?

3-26 ***Basic product mix and breakeven.*** The multiplicity of products is exemplified by women's (or men's) clothing stores. Consider an oversimplified illustration in Exhibit 3-8, where there are only three product lines and the variable expenses consist only of the costs of the products plus sales commissions.

EXHIBIT 3-8

Multiple-Product Analysis

FOR THE MONTH ENDED MAY 31, 19_1

	BUDGET FOR MAY			ACTUAL FOR MAY		
	sales	**contribution margin**	**contribution-margin percentage**	**sales**	**contribution margin**	**contribution-margin percentage**
Dresses	$20,000	$ 8,000	40.0%	$10,000	$4,000	40.0%
Shoes	10,000	3,000	30.0	10,000	3,000	30.0
Blouses	10,000	2,000	20.0	10,000	2,000	20.0
Total	$40,000	$13,000	32.5%	$30,000	$9,000	30.0%

Budget variances (the differences between budgeted and actual outcomes):

Variance in sales	$10,000 U
Variance in total contribution margin	4,000 U
Variance in total contribution-margin percentage	2.5% U

U = Unfavorable.

REQUIRED

1. Suppose the fixed costs applicable to the store were $7,000 per month. What would be the breakeven point in dollar sales based on the budgeted mix? Based on the actual mix?
2. Suppose that actual sales for May were $40,000, consisting of dresses, $25,000; shoes, $8,000; and blouses, $7,000. There have been no changes in unit prices, unit variable costs, or the mix within each of the three product lines. Compute the variance in total contribution margin and total contribution-margin percentage. If this mix persists, what is the new breakeven point?
3. Breakeven points are often incidental to the study of cost-volume-profit relationships. As the manager of this store, how would you react to the analysis in requirement 2?

3-27 ***P/V chart and sales mix.*** The Bannister Company has three products—A, B, and C—having contribution margins of $3, $2, and $1, respectively. The president is planning to sell 200,000 units in the forthcoming period, consisting of 20,000 A, 100,000 B, and 80,000 C. The company's fixed costs for the period are $255,000.

REQUIRED

1. What is the company breakeven point in units, assuming that the given sales mix is maintained?
2. Prepare a P/V chart for a volume of 200,000 units: Have a broken line represent the average contribution margin per unit and have solid lines represent the net income effects of each product by showing their unit contribution margins as the slopes of each line. What is the total contribution margin at a volume of 200,000 units? Net income?
3. What would net income become if 20,000 units of A, 80,000 units of B, and 100,000 units of C were sold? What is the new breakeven point if these relationships persist in the next period?

3-28 ***Breakeven analysis and the product-mix assumption.*** Suppose that the Blanton Company has the following budget data for 19_1:

	PRODUCT		
	X	Y	TOTAL
Selling price	$3	$6	
Variable expenses	1	2	
Contribution margin	$2	$4	
Total fixed expenses	$100,000	$120,000	
Number of units to be sold to break even	?	?	?
Number of units expected to be sold	30,000	50,000	80,000

REQUIRED

1. Compute the breakeven point for each product.
2. Suppose that Products X and Y were made in the same plant. Assume that a prolonged strike at the factory of the sole supplier of raw materials prevented the production of X for all of 19_1. Suppose also that the Blanton fixed costs were unaffected.
   a. What is the breakeven point for the company as a whole, assuming that no X is produced?
   b. Suppose instead that the shortage applied so that only X and no Y could be produced. Then what is the breakeven point for the company as a whole?
3. Draw a breakeven chart for the company as a whole, using an average selling price and an average variable expense per unit. What is the breakeven point under this aggregate approach? What is the breakeven point if you add together the individual breakeven points that you computed in requirement 1? Why is the aggregate breakeven point different from the sum of the individual breakeven points?

3-29 ***Multiple choice; income taxes.*** (CMA) The Maxwell Company manufactures and sells a single product. Price and cost data regarding Maxwell's product and operations are as follows:

Selling price per unit	$25.00
Variable costs per unit:	
Raw materials	$11.00
Direct labor	5.00
Manufacturing overhead	2.50
Selling expenses	1.30
Total variable costs per unit	$19.80
Annual fixed costs:	
Manufacturing overhead	$192,000
Selling and administrative	276,000
Total fixed costs	$468,000
Forecasted annual sales volume (120,000 units)	$3,000,000
Income tax rate	40%

Choose the best answer:

1. Maxwell's breakeven point in units is
(a) 76,667 (b) 90,000 (c) 130,000 (d) 72,000
(e) Some amount other than those shown above.

2. How many units would Maxwell Company have to sell in order to earn $156,000 after taxes?
(a) 120,000 units (b) 165,000 units (c) 140,000 units (d) 148,889 units
(e) None of the above responses is correct.

3. Maxwell Company estimates that its direct-labor costs will increase 8 percent next year. How many units will Maxwell have to sell next year to reach breakeven?

(a) 97,500 units (b) 101,740 units (c) 83,572 units (d) 86,250 units
(e) None of the above responses is correct.

4. If Maxwell Company's direct-labor costs do increase 8 percent, what selling price per unit of product must it charge to maintain the same contribution-margin ratio?
(a) $25.51 (b) $27.00 (c) $25.40 (d) $26.64 (e) None of the above responses is correct.

3-30 ***Role of income taxes.*** Reconsider the toy-rocket problem as described in Problem 1 for Self-Study at the end of the chapter. Suppose you want to obtain a net income of $250 after taxes. How many rockets must be sold? Assume an income-tax rate of 40 percent.

3-31 ***Role of income taxes.*** Reconsider Problem 2 for Self-Study at the end of the chapter. With the proposed increase in fixed expenses, what amount of sales will yield a net income of $50,000 after taxes? The income tax rate is 40 percent.

✓ 3-32 ***Cost-volume relationships, income taxes.*** (CMA) R. A. Ro and Company, maker of quality handmade pipes, has experienced a steady growth in sales for the past five years. However, increased competition has led Mr. Ro, the president, to believe that an aggressive advertising campaign will be necessary next year to maintain the company's present growth.

To prepare for next year's advertising campaign, the company's accountant has prepared and presented Mr. Ro with the following data for the current year, 19_2:

Variable costs (per pipe):	
Direct labor	$ 8.00
Direct materials	3.25
Variable overhead	2.50
Total variable costs	$13.75
Fixed costs:	
Manufacturing	$ 25,000
Selling	40,000
Administrative	70,000
Total fixed costs	$135,000
Selling price, per pipe	$25.00
Expected sales, 19_2 (20,000 units)	$500,000
Tax Rate: 40%	

REQUIRED

1. What is the projected after-tax net income for 19_2?
2. What is the breakeven point in units for 19_2?
3. Mr. Ro has set the sales target for 19_3 at a level of $550,000 (or 22,000 pipes). He believes an additional selling expense of $11,250 for advertising in 19_3, with all other costs remaining constant, will be necessary to attain the sales target. What will be the after-tax net income for 19_3 if the additional $11,250 is spent?
4. What will be the breakeven point in dollar sales for 19_3 if the additional $11,250 is spent for advertising?
5. If the additional $11,250 is spent for advertising in 19_3, what is the required sales level in dollar sales to equal 19_2's after-tax net income?
6. At a sales level of 22,000 units, what maximum amount can be spent on advertising if an after-tax net income of $60,000 is desired?

3-33 ***Change in sales mix; income taxes.*** (CMA) Hewtex Electronics manufactures two products—tape recorders and electronic calculators—and sells them nationally to wholesalers and retailers. The Hewtex management is very pleased with the company's performance for the current fiscal year. Projected sales through December 31, 19_7, indicate that 70,000 tape recorders and 140,000 electronic calculators will be sold this year. The projected earnings statement, which appears below, shows that Hewtex will exceed its earnings goal of 9 percent on sales after taxes.

The tape recorder business has been fairly stable the last few years, and the company does not intend to change the tape recorder price. However, the competition among manufacturers of electronic calculators has been increasing. Hewtex's calculators have been very popular with consumers. In order to sustain this interest in its calculators and to meet the

Hewtex Electronics

Projected Earnings Statement For the Year Ended December 31, 19_7

	TAPE RECORDERS		ELECTRONIC CALCULATORS		
	total amount (000 omitted)	**per unit**	**total amount (000 omitted)**	**per unit**	**total (000 omitted)**
Sales	$1,050	$15.00	$3,150	$22.50	$4,200.0
Production costs:					
Materials	$ 280	$ 4.00	$ 630	$ 4.50	$ 910.0
Direct labor	140	2.00	420	3.00	560.0
Variable overhead	140	2.00	280	2.00	420.0
Fixed overhead	70	1.00	210	1.50	280.0
Total production costs	$ 630	$ 9.00	$1,540	$11.00	$2,170.0
Gross margin	$ 420	$ 6.00	$1,610	$11.50	$2,030.0
Fixed selling and administrative					1,040.0
Net income before income taxes					$ 990.0
Income taxes (55%)					544.5
Net income					$ 445.5

price reductions expected from competitors, management has decided to reduce the wholesale price of its calculator from $22.50 to $20.00 per unit effective January 1, 19_8. At the same time the company plans to spend an additional $57,000 on advertising during fiscal year 19_8. As a consequence of these actions, management estimates that 80 percent of its total revenue will be derived from calculator sales as compared with 75 percent in 19_7. As in prior years, the sales mix is assumed to be the same at all volume levels.

The total fixed overhead costs will not change in 19_8, nor will the variable overhead cost rates (applied on a direct-labor-hour base). However, the cost of materials and direct labor is expected to change. The cost of solid state electronic components will be cheaper in 19_8. Hewtex estimates that material costs will drop 10 percent for the tape recorders and 20 percent for the calculators in 19_8. However, direct labor costs for both products will increase 10 percent in the coming year.

REQUIRED

1. How many tape recorder and electronic calculator units did Hewtex Electronics have to sell in 19_7 to break even?
2. What volume of sales is required if Hewtex Electronics is to earn a profit in 19_8 equal to 9 percent on sales after taxes?
3. How many tape recorder and electronic calculator units will Hewtex have to sell in 19_8 to break even?

3-34 ***Review of chapters 2 and 3.*** For each of the following independent cases, find the unknowns designated by the capital letters.

	CASE 1	CASE 2
Sales	$100,000	$100,000
Direct materials used	H	40,000
Direct labor	30,000	15,000
Variable selling and administrative expenses	K	T
Fixed manufacturing overhead	I	20,000
Fixed selling and administrative expenses	J	10,000
Gross profit	25,000	20,000
Finished-goods inventory, 1/1	0	5,000
Finished-goods inventory, 12/31	0	5,000
Contribution margin (dollars)	30,000	V
Direct-materials inventory, 1/1	12,000	20,000

Direct-materials inventory, 12/31	5,000	W
Variable manufacturing overhead	5,000	X
Work in process, 1/1	0	9,000
Work in process, 12/31	0	9,000
Purchases of direct materials	15,000	50,000
Breakeven point (in dollars)	66,667	Y
Cost of goods manufactured	G	U
Net income (loss)	L	(5,000)

3-35 ***Review of chapters 2 and 3.*** The Reader Co. makes deluxe bookcases to special order. The controller has given you, his newly hired assistant, the task of constructing a so-called contribution income statement for the year ended December 31, 19_5. You are troubled because all the data produced by the routine accounting system do not distinguish between variable and fixed costs.

After laboring with statistical regressions, you have identified various cost behavior patterns to your satisfaction. You have determined a breakeven point of $360,000; your computations were relatively easy because Reader's policy is not to carry any inventories. Instead, the company finishes pending orders sometime in December and gives all employees vacations that end in early January.

The traditional income statement included a gross profit of $130,000, sales of $600,000, direct labor of $170,000, and direct materials used of $220,000.

The contribution margin was $150,000, and the variable manufacturing overhead was $20,000.

REQUIRED

You need not work these in sequence:

1. Fixed manufacturing overhead.
2. Variable selling and administrative expenses
3. Fixed selling and administrative expenses

3-36 ***Hospital breakeven.*** (CPA) The Columbus Hospital operates a general hospital but rents space and beds to separate entities for specialized areas such as pediatrics, maternity, and psychiatric. Columbus charges each separate entity for common services to its patients such as meals and laundry and for administrative services such as billings and collections. All uncollectible accounts are charged directly to the entity. Space and bed rentals are fixed for the year.

For the entire year ended June 30, 19_3, the Pediatrics Department at Columbus Hospital charged each patient an average of $65 per day, had a capacity of 60 beds, operated 24 hours per day for 365 days, and had revenue of $1,138,800.

Expenses charged by the hospital to the Pediatrics Department for the year ended June 30, 19_3, were as follows:

	BASIS OF ALLOCATION	
	patient-days	**bed capacity**
Dietary	$ 42,952	
Janitorial		$ 12,800
Laundry	28,000	
Laboratory, other than direct charges to patients	47,800	
Pharmacy	33,800	
Repairs and maintenance	5,200	7,140
General administrative services		131,760
Rent		275,320
Billings and collections	40,000	
Bad-debt expense	47,000	
Other	18,048	25,980
	$262,800	$453,000

The only personnel directly employed by the Pediatrics Department are supervising nurses, nurses, and aides. The hospital has minimum personnel requirements based on total annual patient-days. Hospital requirements beginning at the minimum expected level of operation follow.

ANNUAL PATIENT-DAYS	AIDES	NURSES	SUPERVISING NURSES
10,000–14,000	21	11	4
14,001–17,000	22	12	4
17,001–23,725	22	13	4
23,726–25,550	25	14	5
25,551–27,375	26	14	5
27,376–29,200	29	16	6

The staffing levels above represent full-time equivalents, and it should be assumed that the Pediatrics Department always employs only the minimum number of required full-time equivalent personnel.

Annual salaries for each class of employees follows: supervising nurses—$18,000, nurses—$13,000, and aides—$5,000. Salary expense for the year ended June 30, 19_3, for supervising nurses, nurses, and aides was $72,000, $169,000, and $110,000, respectively.

The Pediatrics Department operated at 100 percent capacity during 111 days for the past year. It is estimated that during 90 of these capacity days, the demand averaged 17 patients more than capacity and even went as high as 20 patients more on some days. The hospital has an additional 20 beds available for rent for the year ending June 30, 19_4.

REQUIRED

1. Calculate the **minimum** number of patient days required for the Pediatrics Department to break even for the year ending June 30, 19_4, if the additional 20 beds are not rented. Patient demand is unknown, but assume that revenue per patient-day, cost per patient-day, cost per bed, and employee salary rates will remain the same as for the year ended June 30, 19_3. Present calculations in good form.
2. Assuming for purposes of this problem that patient demand, revenue per patient-day, cost per patient-day, cost per bed, and employee salary rates for the year ending June 30, 19_4 remain the same as for the year ended June 30, 19_3, should the Pediatrics Department rent the additional 20 beds? Show the annual gain or loss from the additional beds. Present calculations in good form.

3-37 ***Miscellaneous alternatives; contribution income statement.*** The income statement of the Hall Company appears on page 78. Commissions are based on sales dollars; all other variable expenses vary in terms of units sold.

The factory has a capacity of 150,000 units per year. The results for 19_1 have been disappointing. Top management is sifting a number of possible ways to make operations profitable in 19_2.

REQUIRED

(Consider each situation independently.)

1. Recast the income statement into a contribution format. There will be three major sections: sales, variable expenses, and fixed expenses. Show costs per unit in an adjacent column. Allow adjacent space for entering your answers to requirement 2.
2. The sales manager is torn between two courses of action:
   a. He has studied the market potential and believes that a 15 percent slash in price would fill the plant to capacity.
   b. He wants to increase prices by 25 percent, to increase advertising by $150,000, and to boost commissions to 10 percent of sales. Under these circumstances, he thinks that unit volume will increase by 50 percent.

   Prepare the budgeted income statements, using a contribution margin format and two columns. What would be the new net income or loss under each alternative? Assume that there are no changes in fixed costs other than advertising.

Hall Company

Income Statement For the Year Ended December 31, 19_1

Sales (90,000 units @ $4.00)				$360,000
Cost of goods sold:				
Direct materials			$90,000	
Direct labor			90,000	
Factory overhead:				
Variable		$18,000		
Fixed		80,000	98,000	278,000
Gross margin				$ 82,000
Selling expenses:				
Variable:				
Sales commissions*	$18,000			
Shipping	3,600	$21,600		
Fixed:				
Advertising, salaries, etc.		40,000	$61,600	
Administrative expenses:				
Variable		$ 4,500		
Fixed		20,400	24,900	86,500
Net loss				$ (4,500)

**Based on sales dollars, not physical units.*

3. The president does not want to tinker with the price. How much may advertising be increased to bring production and sales up to 130,000 units and still earn a target profit of 5 percent of sales?
4. A mail-order firm is willing to buy 60,000 units of product "if the price is right." Assume that the present market of 90,000 units at $4 each will not be disturbed. Hall Company will not pay any sales commission on these 60,000 units. The mail-order firm will pick up the units directly at the Hall factory. However, Hall must refund $24,000 of the total sales price as a promotional and advertising allowance for the mail-order firm. In addition, special packaging will increase manufacturing costs on these 60,000 units by 10¢ per unit. At what unit price must the mail-order chain business be quoted for Hall to break even on total operations in 19_2?
5. The president suspects that a fancy new package will aid consumer sales and ultimately Hall's sales. Present packaging costs per unit are all variable and consist of 5¢ direct materials and 4¢ direct labor; new packaging costs will be 30¢ and 13¢, respectively. Assuming no other changes in cost behavior, how many units must be sold to earn a net profit of $20,000?

Note: See Chapter 21 for a discussion of cost-volume-profit analysis under uncertainty. Also see problems 21-18 through 21-23 and 21-29 through 21-31.

Job, Process, and Operation Systems 4

This chapter examines a general approach to accounting for costs in a multiple-purpose accounting system. Two major cost objectives are discussed: departments and units of product. The former illustrates the control purpose of the system; the latter illustrates the product-costing purpose.

Here we must dwell heavily on techniques because they are an essential part of the accounting function. Equally important, there is an opportunity to become familiar with many terms and fundamental ledger relationships that will aid visualization and comprehension of the key subjects covered in Chapters 5 through 11.

If you have never worked in a factory, you will need to study this chapter and its Appendix with care. The chapter was written to be understood by the student with little business background. If you have had some business experience, you will probably be able to skip the Appendix to this chapter. If you want a more complete study of the bookkeeping aspects of cost accounting, refer to Chapter 26 and the Appendix to Chapter 27.

In any event, you should study the section on overhead accounting carefully.

Product-costing and control purposes

Ultimately, all costs are accumulated to facilitate someone's decisions. But all these decisions cannot be foreseen, so systems are designed to fulfill predetermined general desires that are commonplace among managers. **We will frequently distinguish between the *product-costing* purpose of a system and all other purposes. For convenience, we will sometimes refer to all other purposes as *planning and control purposes, budgetary-control purposes,* or, for brevity, as the *control purpose.***

Aside from meeting the obvious external reporting demands for inventory valuation and income determination, managers want product costs for guiding their decisions regarding pricing and product strategies. In addition, managers want departmental costs (or costs of other parts of the organization) for judging the performance of their subordinates and the parts of the organization as economic investments.

Management accounting systems fulfill these general planning and control purposes by choosing parts of the organization as cost objectives. The aim is to compile costs by **responsibility** or **accountability center.** For example, costs are often routinely traced to a **cost center,** the smallest segment of activity or area of responsibility for which costs are accumulated. Typically, cost centers are departments, but in some instances a department may contain several cost centers. For example, although a machining department may be under one foreman, it may contain various groups of machines, such as lathes, punch presses, and milling machines. Each group of machines is sometimes regarded as a separate cost center with its own assistant foreman.

Another major cost objective is product costing for purposes of inventory valuation and income determination. **Therefore, the system must trace costs to these two major cost objectives: departments and products. This tracing is frequently accomplished in two steps: (1) *accumulation* of costs by departments and (2) *application* of the department costs to the physical units (or other measures of output) that pass through the departments. This second step is sometimes called cost *absorption* rather than cost *application.***

The following tabulation summarizes the main ideas of this chapter:

control purpose	product costing purpose
Accumulate costs by:	Apply costs by:
1. Responsibility center	Job-order costing
2. Responsibility center	Process costing
3. Responsibility center	Operation costing

Note especially that no matter what label is used to describe how costs are applied for product costing, **the costs are always accumulated by responsibility center for control purposes.** The three major ways of achieving product costing will be described in sequence.

Job-order costing

Job-order (or *job-cost* or *production-order* or *job*) **costing** systems are used by organizations whose products or services are readily identified by individual units or batches, each of which receives varying inputs of direct materials, direct labor, and factory overhead. Industries that commonly use job-order methods include construction, printing, aircraft, furniture, and machinery.

Although a manufacturing situation is illustrated in this chapter, the job-costing approach is used in nonmanufacturing organizations too. Examples include auto repair, auditing and consulting engagements, hospital cases, social-welfare cases, and research projects.[1]

source documents

The basic document used by a job-order system to accumulate *product costs* is called the **job-order** or **job-cost sheet.** The file of job-cost sheets for the uncompleted jobs makes up the subsidiary ledger for Work-in-Process Control, the major product-costing account. Exhibit 4-1 illustrates a job-cost sheet.

EXHIBIT 4-1

Job-Cost Sheet

SAMPLE COMPANY Job Order No.________

For stock________ Customer________

Product________ Date started________ Date completed________

Department A							
Direct Material			Direct Labor			Overhead	
Date	Reference (stores requisition number)	Amount	Date	Reference (work ticket number)	Amount	Date	Amount (based on predetermined overhead rate)

Department B							
Direct Material			Direct Labor			Overhead	
Date	Reference	Amount	Date	Reference	Amount	Date	Amount

Summary of Costs

	Dept. A	Dept. B	Total
Direct material	xx	xx	xxx
Direct labor	xx	xx	xxx
Factory overhead applied	xx	xx	xxx
Total	xxx	xxx	xxx

[1]In nonprofit organizations the "job order" or class of services is often called a *program,* an identifiable segment of activities that often results in output in the form of services rather than goods. Examples are an alcoholic rehabilitation program, a drug-addict rehabilitation program, a safety program, and so on. Often various departments work on a multitude of programs, so the cost accounting challenge is to apply intelligently the various departmental costs to the various programs. Then more knowledgeable management decisions can be made regarding how to allocate limited resources among competing programs.

The evaluation of nonprofit programs entails special difficulties. The problem of cost measurement is similar to that in commercial enterprises. But there are only scattered messages from the marketplace to help managers estimate benefits, particularly for such activities as saving lives, curing the ill, and educating the handicapped. Because market prices are seldom available, indirect measurements of value are employed. See R. Anthony and R. Herzlinger, *Management Control in Nonprofit Organizations,* rev. ed. (Homewood, Ill.: Richard D. Irwin, 1980).

EXHIBIT 4-2

Stores Requisition

Job No. 41

Department B

Date 2/22

Debit Account WORK IN PROCESS

Authorized by GL

Description	Quantity	Unit Cost	Amount
AT 462 BRACKETS	80	$2.50	$200.00

Job shops usually have several jobs passing through the plant simultaneously. Each job typically requires different kinds of materials and department effort. Thus, jobs may have different routings, different operations, and different times required for completion. **Stores requisitions** (Exhibit 4-2) are used to charge job-cost sheets for direct materials used. **Work tickets** (Exhibit 4-3) are used to charge jobs for direct labor used. This work ticket (sometimes called *time ticket* or *time card*) indicates the time spent on a specific job. An employee who is paid an hourly wage and who operates a lathe will have one **clock card** (Exhibit 4-4), which is used as a basis for determining individual earnings; but the worker will also fill out or punch several *work tickets* each day as he or she starts and stops work on particular jobs or operations. Many auto mechanics must account for their time in a similar way. (Of course, all the illustrated source documents might be in the form of punched cards to facilitate data processing.)

responsibility and control

The department responsibility for usage of direct materials and direct labor is clearly drawn. Copies of direct-material requisitions and direct-labor work tickets are used for two purposes. One copy is used to post to job-cost sheets; another copy is used for fixing responsibility by departments. The department heads are usually kept informed

EXHIBIT 4-3

Work Ticket

Employee No. 741 Date 2/22 Job No. 41

Operation drill Account Work in Process Dept. A

Pieces:

Stop 4:45 P.M. Rate $12.00 Worked 15

Rejected —

Start 4:00 P.M. Amount $ 9.00 Completed 15

EXHIBIT 4-4

Clock Card

Name FRANK YOUNG Employee Number 741

Department A Week ending 2/26

Date	AM In	AM Out	PM In	PM Out	Excess Hours In	Excess Hours Out	Total Hours
2/22	7:58	12:01	1:00	5:01			8
2/23	7:55	12:00	1:00	5:02			8
2/24	8:00	12:02	12:58	5:00	6:00	9:00	11
2/25	7:58	12:02	12:59	5:03			8
2/26	7:56	12:01	12:59	5:01			8

Regular Time 43 hrs. @ $12.00 $516.00

Overtime Premium 3 hrs. @ $6.00 $18.00

Gross Earnings $534.00

of their direct-material and direct-labor performance by daily or weekly classified summaries of requisitions and work tickets charged to their departments.

The job-cost sheets also serve a control function. Comparisons are often made between predictions of job costs and the costs finally applied to the job. Deviations are investigated so that their underlying causes may be discovered.

Illustration of job-order accounting

Because each job order often contains different materials and gets a different routing through departments, the time, costs, and attention devoted by departments to any given job may vary considerably. It is desirable, therefore, to keep a separate account for inventory purposes and another account, or other accounts, for department responsibility purposes. In practice, a Work-in-Process Control account, supported by a subsidiary ledger of individual job orders, is widely used for product-costing purposes. However, practice differs greatly as to the general-ledger accumulation of costs for department responsibility purposes.

Consider a specific example. Assume that a factory has two departments and uses the job-cost system. Department A is the machining department; Department B is the assembly department. Exhibit 4-5 shows T-account relationships and relationships between the general and subsidiary ledgers. Typical general-journal entries for a job-cost system follow. **(Please be sure to trace each entry, step by step, to the accounts in Exhibit 4-5.)** Special points are included in the explanation for each entry.

EXHIBIT 4-5 *(Place a clip on this page for easy reference.)*

Job-Cost System, Diagram of Ledger Relationships

(Circled numbers refer to journal entries described more thoroughly in text.)

General Ledger

① Purchases

② Usage of direct materials ($48,000) and supplies ($4,000)

③ Incurrence of direct labor ($39,000) and indirect labor ($5,000)

④ Payment of payroll liability

⑤ Incurrence of other factory overhead

⑥ Application of factory overhead

⑦ Completion of goods

⑧ Cost of goods sold

STORES CONTROL

Debit		Credit	
①	60,000	②	52,000

ACCRUED PAYROLL

Debit		Credit	
④	44,000	③	44,000

ACCOUNTS PAYABLE

Debit		Credit	
		①	60,000
		⑤	11,000

ALLOWANCE FOR DEPRECIATION

Debit		Credit	
		⑤	6,000

FACTORY DEPARTMENT OVERHEAD CONTROL

Debit		Credit	
②	4,000		
③	5,000		
⑤	18,000		

FACTORY OVERHEAD APPLIED

Debit		Credit	
		⑥	26,460

UNEXPIRED INSURANCE

Debit		Credit	
		⑤	1,000

WORK-IN-PROCESS CONTROL

Debit		Credit	
②	48,000	⑦	108,800
③	39,000		
⑥	26,460		

CASH

Debit		Credit	
		④	44,000

FINISHED-GOODS CONTROL

Debit		Credit	
⑦	108,800	⑧	102,000

COST OF GOODS SOLD

Debit		Credit	
⑧	102,000		

EXHIBIT 4-5 *(Cont.)*

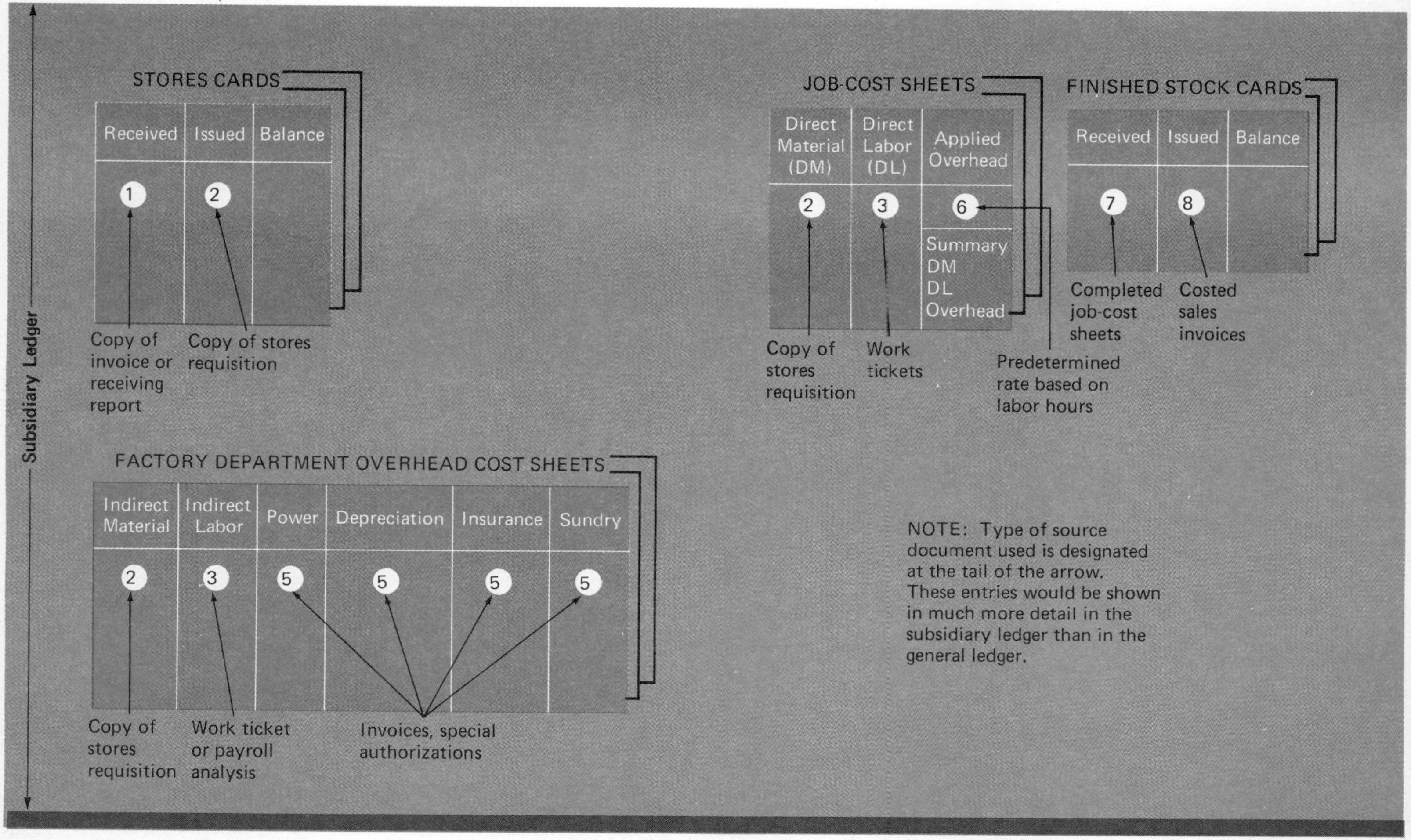

Subsidiary Ledger

STORES CARDS

Received	Issued	Balance
1	2	

1 — Copy of invoice or receiving report
2 — Copy of stores requisition

JOB-COST SHEETS

Direct Material (DM)	Direct Labor (DL)	Applied Overhead
2	3	6
		Summary DM DL Overhead

2 — Copy of stores requisition
3 — Work tickets
6 — Predetermined rate based on labor hours

FINISHED STOCK CARDS

Received	Issued	Balance
7	8	

7 — Completed job-cost sheets
8 — Costed sales invoices

FACTORY DEPARTMENT OVERHEAD COST SHEETS

Indirect Material	Indirect Labor	Power	Depreciation	Insurance	Sundry
2	3	5	5	5	5

2 — Copy of stores requisition
3 — Work ticket or payroll analysis
5 — Invoices, special authorizations

NOTE: Type of source document used is designated at the tail of the arrow. These entries would be shown in much more detail in the subsidiary ledger than in the general ledger.

1. **Stores control*** 60,000
   Accounts (or vouchers) payable 60,000
   To record purchases of materials and supplies.

**The word "control," as used in journal entries and general-ledger accounts, has a narrow bookkeeping meaning. As contrasted with "control" in the management sense, "control" here means that the control account in question is supported by an underlying subsidiary ledger. To illustrate: In financial accounting, Accounts Receivable Control is supported by a subsidiary customers' ledger, with one account for each customer. The same meaning applies to the "Stores" account here; the stores subsidiary ledger consists of individual accounts for the various materials in inventory.*

All purchases of materials and supplies are charged to Stores Control as purchased because the storekeeper is accountable for them. The subsidiary records for Stores Control would be perpetual-inventory records called *stores cards.* As a minimum, these cards would contain quantity columns for receipts, issues, and balance. Exhibit 4-6 is an illustration of a stores card.

2. **Work-in-process control** 48,000
   Factory department overhead control (supplies) 4,000
   Stores control 52,000
   To record materials and supplies issued.

Responsibility is fixed by using *stores requisitions* (sometimes called **material requisitions**) as a basis for charging departments. A stores requisition was shown in Exhibit 4-2.

Direct materials are charged to job orders; indirect materials (supplies) are charged to individual department-overhead cost sheets, which form a subsidiary ledger for Factory Department Overhead Control. In job-cost accounting, a single Factory Department Overhead Control account may be kept in the general ledger. The detail of factory overhead is charged to departments and recorded in subsidiary department-overhead ledgers (department-overhead cost sheets). (See Exhibit 4-7.) In turn, the overhead is applied to jobs, as will be described later in this illustration.

EXHIBIT 4-6

Stores Card

Item AT 462 Brackets

		Received			Issued			Balance		
Date	Reference	Quantity	Unit Cost	Total Cost	Quantity	Unit Cost	Total Cost	Quantity	Unit Cost	Total Cost
2/10	V1014	300	2.50	750				300	2.50	750
2/22	R41				80	2.50	200	220	2.50	550

EXHIBIT 4-7

Factory Department Overhead Cost Sheet

Date	Source Document	Lubricants	Other Supplies	Material Handling	Idle Time	Overtime Premium	Other Labor	Utilities	Insurance	Depr.
	Requisitions	xx	xx							
	Labor recap.			xx	xx	xx	xx			
	Invoices							xx		
	Special memos from chief accountant on accruals, prepayments, etc.							xx	xx	xx

3. Work-in-process control (direct labor) 39,000
Factory department overhead control (indirect labor) 5,000
Accrued payroll 44,000
To record incurrence of factory payroll costs.

Payroll withholdings from employees are ignored in this example. Responsibility is fixed by using work tickets (Exhibit 4-3) or individual time summaries as a basis for tracing direct labor to jobs and direct and indirect labor to departments. Clock cards (Exhibit 4-4) are widely used as attendance records and as the basis for computation of payroll.

4. Accrued payroll 44,000
Cash 44,000
To record payment of payroll for the month.

Actual payments and entries may be made weekly, even though payroll costs incurred (entry 3) are recorded monthly. The reason for this is that paydays seldom coincide with the conventional accounting period (the month) for which costs are accumulated in the general ledger.[2] Thus, the Accrued Payroll account typically appears as follows:

ACCRUED PAYROLL

Payments:		Gross Earnings:	
	x		x
	x		
	x		
	x		
		Balance represents wages earned but unpaid	x

[2]For a detailed treatment of the mechanics of payroll accounting, see Chapter 26, which may be studied now if desired without losing continuity.

5. Factory department overhead control	18,000	
Accounts payable		11,000
Unexpired insurance		1,000
Allowance for depreciation—Equipment		6,000

To record incurrence of other factory-overhead costs:

Utilities, repairs, etc.	$11,000
Depreciation	6,000
Insurance	1,000
	$18,000

The detail of these costs is distributed to the appropriate columns of the individual department-overhead cost sheets that make up the subsidiary ledger for Factory Department Overhead Control. The basic documents for these distributions may be vouchers, invoices, or special memos from the responsible accounting officer.

6. Work-in-process control	26,460	
Factory overhead applied*		26,460

To record application of factory overhead to job orders.

***Absorption costing is used. As was explained in the preceding chapter, absorption costing is the common practice of applying both variable and fixed manufacturing overhead to products.**

The predetermined overhead rate used here is $2.70 per direct-labor hour. Thus, the amount of overhead applied to a particular job is dependent on the amount of direct-labor hours used on that job. It is assumed here that 9,800 direct-labor hours were used for all jobs, resulting in a total overhead application of $26,460. This entry is explained further in a subsequent section of this chapter.

7. Finished-goods control	108,800	
Work-in-process control		108,800

To record completion of Job Nos. 101–108.

As job orders are completed, the job-cost sheets are totaled. Note especially that the totals consist of *actual* direct material, *actual* direct labor, and *applied* factory overhead. Some companies use the completed job-cost sheets as their subsidiary ledger for finished goods. Other companies use separate finished-stock cards to form a subsidiary ledger.

8. Cost of goods sold (sometimes called cost of sales)	102,000	
Finished-goods control		102,000

To record cost of goods sold.

The eight summary entries are usually made monthly. The biggest share of clerical time is devoted to compiling the day-to-day details that are recorded in subsidiary ledgers. There is a mass of daily detail that finds its way to subsidiary ledgers, in contrast to the summaries of the detail that are posted monthly to the general ledger. Incidentally, these "ledgers" are increasingly being stored on a computer rather than on loose-leaf pages.

At this point please pause and reexamine this entire illustration, step by step.

The conceptual approach to accounting for prime costs

The general-ledger treatment of prime costs—direct materials and direct labor—differs extensively among companies. The method illustrated in our example is probably the easiest to learn because it uses the fewest journal entries and accounts. However, the conceptual treatment ought to be examined so that the short-cut treatment may be viewed as a less costly expedient rather than as the best theoretical design. See Exhibit 4-8 for a comparison of the conceptual notion with a treatment common in practice.

Exhibit 4-8 shows that direct materials and direct labor conceptually are (a) charged to departments and (b) then applied to jobs. But note that the department account becomes a clearing account for direct materials and direct labor. For example, the debit to Department-Responsibility Cost Control in 2(a) is immediately offset by the credit in 2(b). A common practical treatment is to charge these items directly to the Work-in-Process account and not use the Department Responsibility account for either direct materials or direct labor.

This simplifies the general ledger and, as we shall see, highlights the intricate problem of overhead accounting. Make no mistake—accounting records are kept by department responsibility for direct materials and direct labor, but they are material- and labor-usage summaries and reports, which are maintained apart from the general ledger itself.

These reports, plus the report on department-overhead costs, may easily have different timing. Depending on their relative importance, direct-material usage may be reported daily; direct-labor usage, weekly; and department-overhead incurrence,

EXHIBIT 4-8 *(amounts are from Exhibit 4-5)*

Journal Entries For Direct Materials and Direct Labor—Job-order System

CONCEPTUAL TREATMENT			PRACTICAL TREATMENT		
Direct materials and direct labor are (a) charged to the department and (b) applied to product.			Direct materials and direct labor are charged directly to product. Accounting records are kept outside the general ledger to fix department responsibility for material and labor usage. Analysis sheets that summarize material usage and labor usage by departments are used for performance reports. These reports may be made weekly, daily, or sometimes even hourly. Furthermore, the direct-material usage and labor usage may be reported separately.		
DIRECT-MATERIAL USAGE					
2(a). Department-responsibility cost control	48,000		2. Work-in-process control	48,000	
Stores control		48,000	Stores control		48,000
2(b). Work-in-process control	48,000				
Department-responsibility cost control		48,000			
DIRECT-LABOR USAGE					
3(a). Department-responsibility cost control	39,000		3. Work-in-process control	39,000	
Accrued payroll		39,000	Accrued payroll		39,000
3(b). Work-in-process control	39,000				
Department-responsibility cost control		39,000			

monthly. In such cases, there is little need for keeping a subsidiary multicolumn department-cost sheet for direct-material, direct-labor, and overhead items. **Instead, the department cost sheet is usually kept only for overhead items, whereas direct-material-usage and direct-labor-usage reports are automatically produced in summaries of requisitions and work tickets. Thus, source documents for direct materials and direct labor are used directly as a basis for control without necessarily having them formally summarized by department in either the subsidiary ledgers or the general ledger.**

Limitations of general ledger

We cannot overemphasize the fact that many appropriate accumulations of costs for planning and control are too broad and too deep to be fitted into a general ledger. The scope of management accounting extends far beyond ledger bookkeeping. Because most general ledgers are traditionally oriented toward product costing, especially in accounting for materials and labor, be on guard to avoid being preoccupied with the product-costing purpose while losing sight of the major purpose of management accounting: that of aiding decisions for planning and control. **The position here is that costing for control is a day-to-day task that is primarily accomplished by source documents and daily or weekly summaries.** Although the control devices can be fully integrated into the general ledger, the resulting complexities are more cumbersome and costly than the benefits derived.

Overhead application

tracing overhead to product

Entry 6 (see page 88) in our master illustration used a predetermined overhead rate to apply factory overhead to product. Direct materials and direct labor may be traced to physical units worked on through requisitions and work tickets. But, by its very nature, factory overhead cannot be specifically identified with physical units. Yet the making of goods would be impossible without the incurrence of such overhead costs as depreciation, material handling, janitorial services, repairs, property taxes, heat, and light.

Overhead is *applied to* (*absorbed by*) products because of management's desire for a close approximation of costs of different products. If such product costs are to be helpful to management for product pricing, income determination, and inventory valuation, they must be timely as well as accurate. If the purpose were to apply all actual overhead to actual production for the year, the most accurate application of overhead could be made only at the end of the year, after actual results were determined. However, this would be too late. Managers want product-cost information throughout the year. Therefore, overhead application rates are usually computed in advance of production.

Accountants have chosen an averaging process for identifying overhead with product. Overhead items are often classified into variable and fixed categories. The behavior of individual overhead items is forecast for the forthcoming year. The total forecasted overhead is related to some common denominator or base, such as expected total machine-hours, direct-labor hours, or direct-labor dollars for the ensuing year. A predetermined overhead rate is obtained by dividing the expected overhead costs by the chosen base. This rate is used to apply overhead to specific jobs as they are manufactured.

To illustrate, a company may budget its factory overhead for a forthcoming year as shown in Exhibit 4-9. Assume that the forecast is based on a volume of

EXHIBIT 4-9

Budget of Factory Overhead for the Year Ending 19_1

Overhead predicted:	
Variable items:	
Lubricants	$ 8,000
Other supplies	40,000
Material handling*	21,000
Idle time†	4,000
Overtime premium	8,000
Other labor	65,000
Utilities and other variable overhead	58,000
Total variable overhead	$204,000
Fixed items:	
Insurance	$ 5,000
Depreciation	65,000
Supervision	31,000
Other fixed overhead	19,000
Total fixed overhead	$120,000
Total budgeted overhead	$324,000
Divided by:	
Budgeted direct-labor hours	120,000
Predetermined overhead rate per hour	$ 2.70

**Labor costs of moving materials and supplies.*
†Labor costs incurred for employee time not devoted to production. Causes include equipment failure, poor scheduling, material shortages, and the like.

activity expressed in direct-labor hours, Then, if detailed forecasts result in a prediction of total overhead of $324,000 for the forthcoming year at an anticipated 120,000-direct-labor-hour level of activity, the predetermined overhead rate would be:

$$\frac{\textbf{Total budgeted overhead}}{\textbf{Total budgeted volume}} = \frac{\$324{,}000}{120{,}000} = \textbf{\$2.70 per hour}$$

(This example assumes that a single plantwide overhead rate is appropriate. This is an oversimplification. There are usually different overhead rates for different departments. These are illustrated and explained in Chapter 14, which can be studied now if desired.)

The $2.70 rate would be used for costing job orders. For example, a job-cost sheet for Job 323 included the following information:

Direct-material cost	$100
Direct-labor cost	$280
Direct-labor hours	40

The overhead to be applied to Job 323 would be: 40 hours times $2.70, or $108. The total cost of Job 323 would be: $100 plus $280 plus $108, or $488. If four units were produced, their unit cost would be $488 ÷ 4 = $122 each.

If actual results for the year conform to the prediction of the $324,000 overhead cost and the 120,000-direct-labor-hour level of volume, total overhead costs will have been exactly applied to products worked on during the year. The basic idea of this approach is to use an annual average overhead cost per hour without changing this annual overhead rate in costing jobs from day to day and from month to month. The resultant product costs are more properly called **normal costs** rather than *actual costs,* because they include an average or normalized chunk of overhead. (Indeed, perhaps *normalized costs* is a more accurate description than *normal costs.*)

annualized rates Should overhead rates be set on the basis of weekly, or monthly, or yearly activity? Two major conditions have prompted the use of an annualized basis for predetermined rates:

1. To overcome volatility in computed unit costs that would result because of fluctuations in the level of volume (the denominator reason) from month to month. This is the dominant reason.
2. To overcome the volatility in computed unit costs that would result because of seasonal, calendar, and other peculiar variations in the total level of overhead costs (the numerator reason) incurred each month.

THE DENOMINATOR REASON: FLUCTUATIONS IN MONTHLY ACTIVITY ☐ Some overhead costs are variable (for example, supplies and indirect labor), whereas others are fixed (for example, property taxes, rent, and depreciation). If production fluctuates from month to month, total variable overhead cost incurrence should change in close proportion to variations in production, whereas total fixed

EXHIBIT 4-10

Monthly Versus Annual Overhead Rates

MONTH	TOTAL FACTORY OVERHEAD BUDGETED (**$50,000 per month plus $1 per hour)**	DIRECT-LABOR HOURS	MONTHLY RATE PER HOUR*	ANNUAL RATE PER HOUR†
January	$ 70,000	20,000	$ 3.50	$3.715
February	80,000	30,000	2.67	3.715
March	90,000	40,000	2.25	3.715
April	100,000	50,000	2.00	3.715
May	65,000	15,000	4.33	3.715
June	60,000	10,000	6.00	3.715
July	55,000	5,000	11.00	3.715
August	51,000	1,000	51.00	3.715
September	55,000	5,000	11.00	3.715
October	60,000	10,000	6.00	3.715
November	65,000	15,000	4.33	3.715
December	70,000	20,000	3.50	3.715
	$821,000	221,000	—	3.715

**Note that the fluctuation here is based solely on the presence of fixed overhead. By definition, variable overhead rates would be $1.00 regardless of whether monthly or annual rates were used.*

†Can be subdivided as follows:

$$\text{Variable-overhead portion} = \frac{\$821{,}000 - (\$50{,}000 \times 12)}{221{,}000} = \$1.000$$

$$\text{Fixed-overhead portion} = \frac{\$600{,}000}{221{,}000} = 2.715$$

$$\text{Combined-overhead rate} = \$3.715$$

overhead will remain unchanged. This means that overhead rates based on monthly volume may differ greatly from month to month ***solely because of fluctuations in the volume over which fixed overhead is spread.***

Exhibit 4-10 gives an example of a company that gears production of its single product to a highly seasonal sales pattern. Few people support the contention that an identical product should be inventoried with an $11.00 or $51.00 overhead rate at the end of July or August and only a $2.25 or $2.00 overhead rate at the end of March or April. These different overhead rates are not representative of typical, normal production conditions. Management has committed itself to a specific level of fixed costs in the light of foreseeable needs far beyond a mere thirty days. Thus, where production fluctuates, monthly overhead rates may be volatile. An average, annualized rate based on the relationship of total annual overhead to total annual volume is more representative of typical relationships between total costs and volume than a monthly rate.

THE NUMERATOR REASON: PECULIARITIES OF SPECIFIC OVERHEAD ITEMS ☐ Fluctuation in monthly volume rather than fluctuation in monthly costs incurred is the dominant reason for using an annualized overhead rate. Still, certain costs are incurred in different amounts at various times of the year. If a month's costs alone were considered, the heating cost, for example, would be charged only to winter production and the air-conditioning cost only to summer production.

Typical examples of erratic behavior include repairs, maintenance, and certain supplies requisitioned in one month that will be consumed over two or more months. These items may be charged to a department on the basis of monthly repair orders or requisitions. Yet the benefits of such charges may easily extend over a number of months' production. It would be illogical to load any single month with costs that are caused by several months' operations.

The calendar itself has an unbusinesslike design; some months have twenty workdays, while others have twenty-two or more. Is it sensible to say that a product made in February should bear a greater share of overhead like depreciation and property taxes than it would if it were produced in March?

Other erratic items that distort monthly overhead rates are vacation and holiday pay, professional fees, subscriptions that may fall due in one month, extra costs of learning, idle time related to the installation of a new machine or product line, and the employer's share of Social Security taxes—which is smallest late in the year, when many employee wages exceed the taxable maximum.

All the costs and peculiarities mentioned above are collected in the annual-overhead pool along with the kinds of overhead that do have uniform behavior patterns (for example, many supplies and indirect labor). In other words, accountants throw up their hands and say, "We have to start somewhere, so let's pool the year's overhead and develop an annual overhead rate regardless of month-to-month peculiarities of specific overhead costs." **Such an approach provides a *normal* product cost that is based on an annual average instead of a so-called actual product cost that is affected by month-to-month fluctuations in production volume and by erratic or seasonal behavior of many overhead costs.** Such a normal cost is often used as a point of departure for setting and appraising the selling prices of products.

ledger procedure for overhead

Let us see how the notions above affect general-ledger procedure. For some reason, students have great trouble in understanding this phase of product costing; therefore, **special study of this section is warranted.**

As overhead costs are incurred by departments from month to month, these "actual" costs are charged in detail to department-overhead cost sheets (the subsidiary ledger) and in summary to Factory Department Overhead Control. These costs are accumulated weekly or monthly without regard to how factory overhead is applied to specific jobs. This ledger procedure serves the purpose of managerial control of overhead. These actual costs are compared with budgeted amounts in performance reports.

Because a predetermined overhead rate (such as $2.70 per direct-labor hour) is an average used to apply costs to products, the daily, weekly, or monthly costing of *inventory* is independent of the actual incurrence of overhead costs by *departments.* For this reason, at any given time during the year, the balance in Factory Department Overhead Control is unlikely to coincide with the amount applied to product. Thus, managerial control can be exercised by comparing, say, actual lubricants used with the budget for lubricants. The actual lubricants used are accumulated on the department-overhead cost sheet. For product costing, all overhead items are pooled together, a predetermined overhead rate is computed, and this average rate is used on job orders for costing Work in Process. The use of an annual average results in inventories bearing a normalized share of factory overhead.

Most accountants stress this peculiarity of overhead accounting by confining Factory Department Overhead Control to the accumulation of "actual" overhead charges incurred and by setting up the credit side in a separate account called *Factory Overhead Applied* (sometimes called Factory Overhead *Absorbed*), much as Allowance for Depreciation is the separate credit side of, say, a Machinery account. To illustrate:

ACCOUNTS PAYABLE, UNEXPIRED INSURANCE, ETC.	
	A ------→ Liabilities or Reductions of Asset Balances

FACTORY DEPARTMENT OVERHEAD CONTROL	
A "Actual" Overhead	

FACTORY OVERHEAD APPLIED	
	B ------→ Applied Overhead

WORK-IN-PROCESS CONTROL	
B Applied Overhead	

underapplied or overapplied overhead

The workings of the ledger accounts for overhead may be more clearly understood if we pursue our master illustration. Let us assume that the month's entries are for January, the first month of the company's year. Postings would appear as follows:

FACTORY DEPARTMENT OVERHEAD CONTROL	
Jan. 31(2) 4,000	
Jan. 31(3) 5,000	
Jan. 31(5) 18,000	
Jan. 31 Balance 27,000	

FACTORY OVERHEAD APPLIED	
	Jan. 31(6) 26,460

The monthly debits to Factory Department Overhead will never equal the monthly credits to Factory Overhead Applied except by coincidence. In January, for example, there is a $540 difference between the two balances. This $540 amount is commonly referred to as *underapplied* (or *underabsorbed*) *overhead*. **Overhead is underapplied when the applied balance is less than the incurred (actual) balance; it is overapplied when the applied balance exceeds the incurred balance.**

Although the month-end balances seldom coincide, the final year-end balances should be nearly equal. Experienced budgetary accountants can predetermine rates with astounding accuracy (with 1 percent error). Of course, the accuracy of predetermined overhead rates depends largely on the skill of those who do the predicting and on the nature of the business. Assume that the year's overhead costs incurred are $326,000, while only $324,000 has been applied to product. The year-end balances are closed out against one another; any insignificant difference between the final balances is generally carried to Cost of Goods Sold as an adjustment of that figure. Several bookkeeping techniques may be used. One simple way is:

Cost of goods sold	2,000	
Factory overhead applied	324,000	
Factory department overhead control		326,000
To close the overhead accounts and to charge underapplied overhead to Cost of Goods Sold. (If overhead is overapplied, the overapplication would be credited to Cost of Goods Sold.)		

Conceptually, the disposition of underapplied or overapplied overhead should require correction of the costs of jobs worked on during the year. These jobs were costed by using a predetermined overhead rate instead of the actual overhead rate, which can be determined only at year-end. Ideally, a clerk would get all the job orders worked on during the year and would adjust their final costs. Thus, the most defensible way to convert job orders to "actual" costs would appear as in Exhibit 4-11.

EXHIBIT 4-11

Analysis for Proration of Underapplied Overhead

		ENDING BALANCE IN ACCOUNTS					CORRECTION FOR UNDERAPPLIED OVERHEAD	
		overhead	%	total product cost	%	account	BASED ON OVERHEAD APPLIED	BASED ON TOTAL COSTS IN ACCOUNTS
Jobs worked on:	101 – 150						(first choice)	(second choice)
Sold:	101 – 140	$275,400	85	$ 900,000	90	Cost of goods sold	$1,700	$1,800
Finished:	141 – 146	32,400	10	70,000	7	Finished goods	200	140
In process:	147 – 150	16,200	5	30,000	3	Work in process	100	60
		$324,000	100%	$1,000,000	100%		$2,000	$2,000

Assume that the year-end analysis is as shown in Exhibit 4-11. Ideally, the $2,000 underapplied overhead should be spread over the three accounts that contain the job costs. **This proration should theoretically be in proportion to the unadjusted overhead component in each account.** The journal entry would appear as follows:

Cost of goods sold	1,700	
Finished-goods control	200	
Work-in-process control	100	
Factory overhead applied	324,000	
Factory department overhead control		326,000

To close the overhead accounts and to prorate underapplied overhead among the three relevant accounts.

Some companies will prorate in proportion to total product costs. This method is theoretically valid only when the proportions of direct material, direct labor, and overhead costs are constant among jobs. To illustrate, if leather is used for making 100 purses (Job A) and imitation fine leather is used for making 100 identical purses (Job B), the respective total job costs will differ markedly because of the large difference in material costs; yet their overhead components are unlikely to differ, because the labor-hours on each job should be approximately the same. In this case, to adjust for underapplied overhead on the basis of total product costs would be misleading because conceptually a different base is used for year-end adjustments from what was used for overhead application during the year. Despite these objections, many companies will prorate on the basis of total product costs because the increase in accuracy is not significant enough to warrant the additional effort. For example, examine the small difference in the results of the two methods as shown in Exhibit 4-11.

Despite the theoretical superiority of the foregoing kinds of adjustments, ***adjusting Cost of Goods Sold for all the underapplied or overapplied overhead is the most widely practiced treatment.*** It is valid as long as final results are not misleading. Exhibit 4-11 shows that more refined calculations that result in proration may not affect final costs enough to be significant. However, if underapplied or overapplied overhead is large enough to indicate some significant error in the overhead rate, the underapplied or overapplied overhead should be spread over the three accounts that contain the jobs bearing the faulty rate.

actual and normal absorption costing

The most difficult aspects of these early chapters are probably the flock of new terms and the accounting for overhead. This chapter illustrates *normal absorption costing,* which can be distinguished from *actual absorption* costing:

	CHAPTER 2 APPROACH, CALLED ACTUAL ABSORPTION COSTING: WORK-IN-PROCESS INVENTORY	CHAPTER 4 APPROACH, CALLED NORMAL ABSORPTION COSTING: WORK-IN-PROCESS INVENTORY
Direct materials	actual costs	actual costs
Direct labor	actual costs	actual costs
Variable factory overhead	actual costs	actual inputs × predetermined overhead rates
Fixed factory overhead	actual costs	(same: actual inputs × predetermined overhead rates)

The job-order system described in this chapter should be called a *normal* costing system, not an *actual* costing system, because the overhead is applied to products on an average or "normalized" basis in order to get representative inventory valuations. Hence, the *normal cost* (perhaps more accurately called *normalized cost*) of the manufactured products is composed of *actual* direct material, *actual* direct labor, and *normal* applied overhead.

The Chapter 2 approach would not apply overhead to the products until the end of a fiscal period. Then the actual overhead would be used for computing the costs of the products worked on. Reconsider the factory overhead cost in Exhibit 4-5 (page 84). Under actual costing, the Factory Overhead Applied would be $27,000 instead of the $26,460 used under normal costing. All costs actually incurred would be precisely offset by costs applied to Work in Process.

Normal costing has replaced actual costing in many companies because the latter fails to provide costs of products when they are manufactured. Of course, it is possible to use a normal costing system plus year-end adjustments to obtain final results that closely approximate the results under actual costing, as shown earlier in the proration of underapplied overhead (Exhibit 4-11). Thus, because of the desire for yearly "actual" costing results, year-end prorations are used in conjunction with the normal costing that exists throughout the year.

Process and operation costing

The two polar extremes of product costing are *job-order costing* and **process costing.** The latter is a system for applying costs to like products that are mass produced in continuous fashion through a series of production steps called *processes.* Process costing is most often found in such industries as chemicals, oil, textiles, paints, flour, canneries, rubber, steel, glass, food processing, mining, and cement.

The process-costing system is used in nonmanufacturing too. Examples include check clearing in banks, mail sorting in post offices, food preparation in fast-food outlets, and premium handling in insurance companies. In practice, there are often no clear lines between job-order and process costing. Instead, many hybrid systems are found.

product costing is averaging

The major illustration in this chapter has featured job-order costing. Whether a process-cost or a job-cost system is used, costs are accumulated for *control* in a similar way. However, the application of costs for *product costing* is typically much easier because individual jobs do not exist. **The most important point is that product costing under both cost systems is an *averaging* process. The unit cost used for inventory purposes is the result of taking some accumulated cost and dividing it by some measure of production. The basic distinction between job-order costing and process costing is the size of the denominator: In job-order costing, it is small (for example, one painting, one hundred advertising circulars, or one special packaging machine); but in process costing, it is large (for example, thousands of pounds, gallons, or board feet).**

equivalent units

Assume that our sample company produced hand-held calculators in large quantities. Suppose it completed 10,000 units during January. Then the unit cost of goods completed would simply be $108,800 (from the Work-in-Process account in Exhibit 4-5, page 84) ÷ 10,000 = $10.88.

The major difficulty in process costing is in applying costs to uncompleted products, goods still in process at the end of the accounting period. For instance, suppose 1,000 calculators were in process at the end of the month; therefore, 10,000 units were started, but only 9,000 were fully completed during January. All the parts had been made or requisitioned, but only half of the labor had been completed for each of the 1,000 calculators. What was the output for January?

An obvious answer would be 9,000 completed units plus 1,000 half-completed units. But we should hesitate to express the sum of the output as 10,000 units. Why? Because each of the partially completed units is not a perfect substitute for a completed unit. Therefore, we express output not as *physical* units, but as *equivalent* units.

Equivalent units is the expression of output in terms of *doses* or *amounts* of resources applied thereto. That is, an equivalent unit is viewed as a collection of work applications necessary to produce one complete physical unit of output. In other words, an equivalent unit is a measure of the factors of production—direct materials, direct labor, and factory overhead.

Recall that direct labor plus factory overhead is called conversion costs. In terms of equivalent units of conversion costs, the ending work in process of 1,000 units half completed is equivalent to 500 units of work accomplished. In a like manner, an ending work in process of 750 units two-thirds completed is equivalent to 500 units of work accomplished.

The concept of equivalent units is not restricted to the task of applying costs to products. More fundamentally, it is a means of measuring activities or workload in terms of a common denominator. Equivalent units are all around us in all types of organizations, although perhaps not in the usual form portrayed by cost accounting texts. Examples are "full time equivalents" for measuring faculty positions and student enrollments. Breweries express their production in equivalent barrels even though most of their actual products may come in small cans and bottles.

illustration of process costing

To illustrate basic process costing, for simplicity assume that all the costs in work in process in Exhibit 4-5 pertain to a one-department company:

		EQUIVALENT UNITS	
FLOW OF PRODUCTION	PHYSICAL UNITS	**direct materials**	**conversion costs**
Started and completed	9,000	9,000	9,000
Work in process, ending inventory:	1,000		
Direct materials added: 1,000 × 1		1,000	
Conversion costs added: 1,000 × ½			500
Total accounted for	10,000		
Total work done		10,000	9,500
Total costs to account for:	$113,460		
Direct materials added		$48,000	
Conversion costs added ($39,000 labor + $26,460 applied overhead)			$65,460
Divide by equivalent units		10,000	9,500
Unit costs		$4.80	$6.89053

Costs are transferred from Work in Process to Finished Goods on the basis of costs per equivalent unit. Therefore, the cost of the ending Work in Process could be analyzed accordingly:

Total costs applied:

To units completed and transferred to Finished Goods, 9,000 × ($4.80 + $6.89053) =		$105,215
To units still in Work in Process:		
Materials, 1,000 equivalent units × $4.80 =	$4,800	
Conversion costs, 500 equivalent units × $6.89053 =	3,445	
Ending work-in-process inventory		8,245
Total costs accounted for		$113,460

Using these data, the earlier journal entry (Number 7, page 88) would be revised because the cost of goods transferred would no longer be $108,800, as shown in Exhibit 4-5. The pertinent T-accounts would show:

WORK-IN-PROCESS CONTROL				*FINISHED-GOODS CONTROL*		
(2)	48,000	(7)	105,215 →	(7)	105,215	
(3)	39,000					
(6)	26,460					
	113,460					
Bal.	8,245					

As you might expect, each manufacturing company develops its own hybrid accounting system to suit its own desires. For example, many companies have so-called **operation costing** systems. In these systems, distinctions are made between batches of product, such as Model A calculators and Model B calculators. Materials are specifically allocated to the batches. Conversion costs are computed for each operation. The final costs of Model A and Model B depend on their particular material components plus what operations were conducted in their manufacture. Obviously, the more materials and the more operations undergone, the more costs are applied to the specific product.

CHAPTER 17 DESCRIBES PROCESS COSTING AND OPERATION COSTING IN MORE DETAIL. IT CAN BE STUDIED NOW, IF DESIRED, WITHOUT BREAKING CONTINUITY.

SUMMARY

The job-cost system described in this chapter illustrates how historical costs are compiled for evaluation of performance and for facilitating predictions of how various departments and managers will perform in forthcoming periods and of how various future jobs should be priced. Job-order costing is an expensive accounting system because of the detailed underlying recordkeeping required for each job. The number of departments and the number of overhead application rates utilized in this system depend on the perceived improvements in decisions in relation to the extra costs of more elaborate recordkeeping.

Scorekeeping for the purpose of planning and control consists largely of *accumulating* costs by departments; for the product-costing purpose, it consists largely of *applying* costs to products in order to obtain a representative

indication of the relative costs of resources devoted to various physical units of product. As in most phases of accounting, the bulk of clerical time is spent on basic source documents and subsidiary ledgers rather than on the general ledger itself. However, the general-ledger relationships of job costing offer a bird's-eye view of an entire system.

The two extremes of product costing are job-order costing and process costing. Many companies use some sort of hybrid, notably operation costing. Job-order costing was discussed at length in this chapter.

Many companies apply overhead at predetermined rates. The resultant product cost consists of "actual" direct materials, "actual" direct labor, and overhead applied using "predetermined" rates. Thus, this total product cost should be called a ***normal*** cost rather than an ***actual*** cost. Therefore, a given product-costing system can properly be called an ***actual-cost*** system (where no costs are predetermined) or a ***normal-cost*** system (where predetermined rates are used to apply overhead). Within a given system, either a job-order-costing approach or a process-costing approach or some hybrid approach, such as *operation costing,* is tailored to needs.

Some thoughtful solving of homework at this stage will strengthen your understanding of basic relationships and terminology.

problems for self-study

Restudy the illustration of job-order accounting in this chapter. Then try to solve one or two straightforward job-order problems such as Problems 4-8 and 4-11. Then try to solve the following problem, which requires consideration of most of this chapter's important points.

problem 1

You are asked to bring the following incomplete accounts of a plant in a foreign country up to date through January 31, 19_2. Also consider the data that appear after the T-accounts.

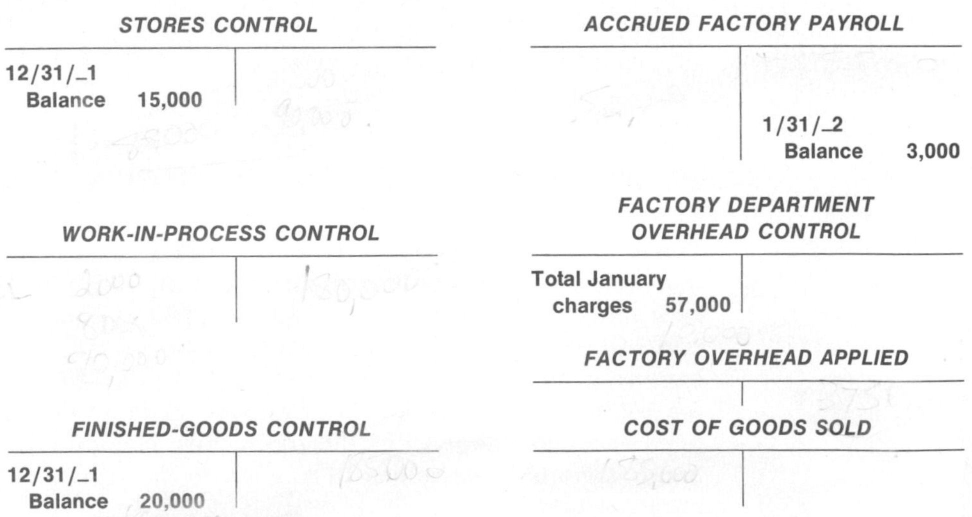

STORES CONTROL

12/31/_1 Balance 15,000	

ACCRUED FACTORY PAYROLL

	1/31/_2 Balance 3,000

WORK-IN-PROCESS CONTROL

FACTORY DEPARTMENT OVERHEAD CONTROL

Total January charges 57,000	

FACTORY OVERHEAD APPLIED

FINISHED-GOODS CONTROL

12/31/_1 Balance 20,000	

COST OF GOODS SOLD

ADDITIONAL INFORMATION

1. The overhead is applied using a predetermined rate that is set every December by forecasting the following year's overhead and relating it to forecast direct-labor costs. The budget for 19_2 called for $400,000 of direct labor and $600,000 of factory overhead.

2. The only job unfinished on January 31, 19_2, was No. 419, on which total labor charges were $2,000 (125 direct-labor hours) and total direct-material charges were $8,000.

3. Total materials placed into production during January totaled $90,000.

4. Cost of goods completed during January was $180,000.

5. January 31 balances on stores cards totaled $20,000.

6. Finished-goods inventory as of January 31 was $15,000.

7. All factory workers earn the same rate of pay. Direct labor hours for January totaled 2,500. Indirect labor and supervision totaled $10,000.

8. The gross factory payroll paid on January paydays totaled $52,000. Ignore withholdings.

9. All "actual" factory overhead incurred during January has already been posted.

REQUIRED

a. Materials purchased during January
b. Cost of goods sold during January
c. Direct-labor costs incurred during January
d. Overhead applied during January
e. Balance, Accrued Factory Payroll, December 31, 19_1
f. Balance, Work in Process, December 31, 19_1
g. Balance, Work in Process, January 31, 19_2
h. Overapplied or underapplied overhead for January

solution 1

a. Materials purchased: $90,000 + $20,000 – $15,000 = $95,000.
b. Cost of goods sold: $20,000 + $180,000 – $15,000 = $185,000.
c. Direct-labor rate: $2,000 ÷ 125 hours = $16 per hour (see 2). Direct-labor cost: 2,500 hours × $16 = $40,000 (see 7).
d. Overhead rate: $600,000 ÷ $400,000 = 150%. Overhead applied: 150% × $40,000 = $60,000.
e. Accrued factory payroll, Dec. 31: $52,000 + $3,000 – $40,000 – $10,000 = $5,000.
f. Work in process, Dec. 31: $180,000 + $13,000 – $90,000 – $40,000 – $60,000 = $3,000.
g. Work in process, Jan. 31: $8,000 + $2,000 + 150% of $2,000 = $13,000.
h. Overapplied overhead: $60,000 – $57,000 = $3,000.

Entries in T-accounts are numbered in accordance with the "additional information" in the problem and are lettered in accordance with the amounts required to be determined.

STORES CONTROL

(given)	12/31/_1 Bal.	15,000		
	(a)	95,000*	(3)	90,000
1/31/_2 Bal.	(5)	20,000		

WORK-IN-PROCESS CONTROL

12/31/_1 Bal.	(f)	3,000*	(4)	180,000
Direct materials	(3)	90,000		
Direct labor	(2) (7) (c)	40,000		
Overhead	(7) (1) (d)	60,000		
1/31/_2 Bal.	(2) (g)	13,000		

FINISHED-GOODS CONTROL

(given)	12/31/_1 Bal.	20,000		
	(4)	180,000	(6) (b)	185,000
1/31/_2 Bal.	(6)	15,000		

ACCRUED FACTORY PAYROLL

(8)	52,000	12/31/_1	(e)	5,000*
		(7)		40,000 10,000
		1/31/_2 Bal. (given)		3,000

FACTORY DEPARTMENT OVERHEAD CONTROL

January charges (given)	57,000		

FACTORY OVERHEAD APPLIED

		(7) (1) (d)	60,000

COST OF GOODS SOLD

(6) (b)	185,000		

Can be computed only after all other postings in the account have been found, so (g) must be computed before (f).

problem 2

A letter to the shareholders of Superscope, Inc., October 24, 1980, described many competitive troubles, including the following: "The reduced level of orders . . . resulted in increased unabsorbed costs . . . which further adversely affected the Company's overall competitive position."

REQUIRED | Using the terms introduced in this book, prepare a precise explanation of the quotation.

solution 2

"Increased unabsorbed costs" means that the *applied* or *absorbed* factory overhead was less than the *actual* factory overhead. In other words, the underapplied or underabsorbed overhead becomes greater and greater if the company falls shorter and shorter of the volume level originally budgeted.

Superscope was confronted with a common difficulty. If sales drop precipitously, production must be cut back. At the same time, the fixed costs of factory facilities, such as rent, depreciation, and property taxes, are not easily reduced. These costs tend to be the bulk of the unabsorbed costs referred to in the quotation.

Terms to Learn

This chapter and the Glossary contain definitions of the following important terms:

accountability center ***applied overhead*** ***clock card***
cost center ***equivalent units*** ***job-cost sheet*** ***job-order costing***
material requisition ***normal costing*** ***operation costing***
overapplied overhead ***process costing*** ***proration***
responsibility center ***stores requisition*** ***underapplied overhead***
work ticket

Special Points and Pitfalls

This chapter focused on product costing, as distinguished from control. It introduced normal costing, which means that overhead is applied to product by multiplying a *predetermined* overhead rate by the *actual* amount of the application base. For example, a budgeted overhead rate would be multiplied by the actual number of direct-labor hours of input on a job.

In normal costing, throughout the fiscal year, Work in Process, Finished Goods, and Cost of Goods Sold are carried at actual direct materials, actual direct labor, and applied factory overhead. Underapplied or overapplied overhead usually accumulates in the accounts from month to month; its final amount is typically added to or subtracted from the Cost of Goods Sold at the end of the year. However, if the amount of underapplied or overapplied overhead is significant, it is prorated over Work in Process, Finished Goods, and Cost of Goods Sold.

Appendix 4: supplementary description of ledger relationships

This Appendix explains some of the paper work that underlies the general-ledger relationships described in this chapter. A factory setting is used to illustrate some of the basic manufacturing transactions and to show how source documents and auxiliary records can be used to facilitate the accumulation of data. Also included is an exhibit that summarizes sample accounting entries for job costing.

subsidiary ledgers and general ledger

The general ledger is a summary device. Postings are made to it from totals and subtotals of underlying transactions. For example, the balance of the Stores Control may be supported by a voluminous file of stores cards. Postings to the debit side of the Stores Control may be made from the Stores column in a special journal, such as a purchases journal or a voucher register. But the specific stores card in the subsidiary ledger is posted from a copy of a voucher or an invoice.

The general ledger gives a bird's-eye view of cost accounting relationships; the subsidiary ledgers contain the underlying details—the worm's-eye view. In turn, source documents, such as voucher copies, stores requisitions, work tickets, clock cards, and other memoranda, are the primary means of recording business events. In a sense, the source documents are the everyday tools for systematically recording operating activities. They are vital because all subsequent accounting classifications and reports are dependent on source documents.

direct-material-usage reports

A multicopy stores requisition may be made out by a foreman. For example, separate copies may serve as follows:

Copy 1—Kept by storekeeper
Copy 2—Used by job-order cost clerk to post to job-cost sheet
Copy 3—Used by accounting department as a basis for a summary of requisitions

This summary is the support for the general-ledger entry:

Work-in-process control	**xx**	
Stores control		**xx**
This entry is usually made monthly, although it can be made more frequently if desired.		

Copy 4—Used by department cost clerk as a basis for departmental material-usage reports. If these reports are to prove useful for control, they must typically be prepared more often than once a month. Stale, month-old reports concerning major costs are not helpful. Daily or weekly reports are common. This is another reason why the

general ledger is oriented toward product costing rather than toward costing for control. The reports for control are needed before formal postings can be made.
Copy 5—Retained by foreman. Used as a cross-check against the usage reports sent by the accounting department.

The accounting department may use punched cards as requisitions. These may be sorted in many ways. For example:

Direct-Material Requisition Summary

REQUISITION NUMBER	JOB ORDER	DEPARTMENT	AMOUNT	JOB-ORDER SUBTOTALS	DEPARTMENT SUBTOTALS
501	1415	26	$ 32.00		
502	1415	27	51.00	$83.00	
503	1408	26	204.00		
504	1414	26	19.00		$255.00
505	1409	28	101.00		

Machine or computer accounting facilitates the accumulation and tabulation of data so that they may be classified, reclassified, summarized, and resummarized to provide the specific information needed by management. Thus, a material-usage report may be submitted to the foreman of Department 26 on a daily, weekly, or monthly basis:

Department 26
Direct-Material Usage
For the week ending ________

REQUISITION NUMBER	JOB ORDER	AMOUNT
501	1415	$ 32.00
503	1408	204.00
504	1414	19.00
510	1408	55.00
511	1412	122.00

direct-labor-cost recapitulation

Similar analysis can be applied to the sorting of direct-labor costs, using the work ticket as the source document. Producing departments may have their labor classified by operations as well as by jobs. For example, the machining department may perform one or more of the following operations: milling, cleaning, grinding, and facing. Thus, work tickets may be recapitulated as shown on the next page.

This labor recapitulation can be used as a basis for the general-ledger entry that charges direct labor to product:

Work in process	xx	
Accrued payroll		xx

This entry is usually made monthly, although it can be made more frequently if desired.

Direct-Labor-Cost Recapitulation

WORK TICKET NUMBER	EMPLOYEE ID NUMBER	JOB NUMBER	DEPT. NUMBER	OPERATION NUMBER	AMOUNT	JOB SUB-TOTALS	OPERATION SUBTOTALS	DEPT. SUB-TOTALS
14	49	1410	26	6500	$20.00		$20.00	
15	49	1410	26	6501	6.00		6.00	$26.00
16	52	1410	27	7520	19.00		19.00	
17	53	1410	27	7522	16.00	$61.00		
18	30	1411	25	5298	30.00	30.00	30.00	30.00
19	61	1409	28	8414	24.60		24.60	24.60
20	52	1409	27	7522	9.75	34.35	25.75	44.75

The recapitulation also supplies the information for daily, weekly, or monthly usage reports to the department foreman. These reports may be broken down by jobs or operations to suit the foreman.

Work tickets may also be used for idle time (for example, caused by machine breakdowns or shortages of material), overtime premium, material handling, and so forth. A clerk or timekeeper may have the duty of preparing a daily reconciliation of employee clock cards with individual work tickets to see that all clock-card time is accounted for as direct labor, idle time, overtime premium, and so forth.

sample entries Exhibit 4-12 on pages 106–107 summarizes the accounting entries for job costing.

QUESTIONS, PROBLEMS, AND CASES

4-1 Distinguish between a *clock card* and a *work ticket.*

4-2 What are the limitations of the general ledger as a cost accounting device?

4-3 What is a *normal product cost?*

4-4 Distinguish between *producing departments* and *service departments.*

4-5 Give two definitions of *control* as the word may be used by an accountant.

4-6 What is the purpose of a *department cost sheet?*

4-7 What is the principal difference between *job-cost* and *process-cost* accounting systems?

4-8 ***Basic entries.*** The University of Chicago Press is wholly owned by the university. A job-order system is used for printing. The bulk of the work is done for other university departments, which pay as though the Press were an outside business enterprise. The Press also publishes and maintains a stock of books for general sale.

The following data pertain to 19_2 (in thousands):

Direct materials and supplies purchased on account	$ 800
Direct materials issued to the producing departments for production	710
Supplies issued to various producing departments	100
Labor used directly on production	2,600
Indirect labor incurred by various departments	900
Depreciation, buildings and equipment	400
Miscellaneous factory overhead* incurred by various departments (ordinarily would be detailed as repairs, photocopying, utilities, etc.)	550

**The term* factory overhead *is not used uniformly. Other terms that are often encountered in printing companies include* job overhead *and* shop overhead.

EXHIBIT 4-12

Job-Order-System Sample Entries

TRANSACTION	GENERAL-LEDGER EFFECTS	SUBSIDIARY LEDGERS	SOURCE DOCUMENTS	EXPLANATORY COMMENTS
1. Purchases of materials or supplies	Stores control Accounts payable	Dr. Stores card, "Received" column	Approved invoice	
2. Issuance of direct materials	Work-in-process control Stores control	Dr. Job order Cr. Stores card, "Issued" column	Stores requisition	Requisitions are summarized and classified by department for hourly, daily, weekly, or monthly, direct-material-usage reports
3. Issuance of supplies	Factory department overhead control Stores control	Dr. Department overhead cost sheets, appropriate columns Cr. Stores card, "Issued" column	Stores requisition	
4. Distribution of labor costs	Work-in-process control Factory department overhead control Accrued payroll	Dr. Job orders Dr. Department overhead cost sheets, appropriate columns for various classes of of indirect labor	Summary of work tickets or daily time analyses. This summary is sometimes called a labor cost distribution summary or a payroll recapitulation	
5. Payment of payroll (for a complete description, see Chapter 26)	Accrued payroll Withholdings payable Cash		Summary of clock cards and individual withholdings as shown on payroll sheets	This entry is usually made weekly, while the cost distribution (the prior entry) is not necessarily made at the same time
6. Payment of withholdings	Withholdings payable Cash			Withholdings are usually broken down by type rather than lumped in one account
7. Employer payroll taxes	Factory department overhead control Employer payroll taxes payable	Dr. Department overhead costs sheets, appropriate columns	Accrual memoranda from accounting officer	

(Continued on next page)

TRANSACTION	GENERAL-LEDGER EFFECTS	SUBSIDIARY LEDGERS	SOURCE DOCUMENTS	EXPLANATORY COMMENTS
8. Utilities	Factory department overhead control Accounts payable or Accrued utilities	Dr. Department overhead cost sheets, appropriate columns	Approved invoices or accrual memoranda	
9. Depreciation on factory equipment	Factory department overhead control Allowance for depreciation—Equipment	Dr. Department overhead cost sheets, appropriate columns	Depreciation schedule	
10. Factory insurance write-off	Factory department overhead control Unexpired insurance	Dr. Department overhead cost sheets, appropriate columns	Insurance register or memoranda from accounting officer	
11. Application of overhead to product	Work-in-process control Factory overhead applied	Dr. Job order	Predetermined overhead rate computed by using overhead budget	
12. Transfer completed goods to finished stock	Finished-goods control Work-in-process control	Dr. Finished stock card, "Received" column Cr. Job order	Production report	Sometimes the completed job order serves as a finished stock card
13. Sales	Accounts-receivable control Sales	Dr. Customers' accounts	Copy of sales invoice	
14. Cost of goods sold	Cost of goods sold Finished-goods control	Dr. Cost of goods sold record (optional) Cr. Finished stock cards	Copy of sales invoice plus costs as shown on finished stock cards	
15. Yearly closing of overhead accounts	Factory overhead applied Factory department overhead control Cost of goods sold (cr. if overhead is overapplied; dr. if overhead is underapplied)		General ledger balances	

Dr. = debit; Cr. = credit

Factory overhead applied at 80 percent of direct-labor cost	?
Cost of goods manufactured and transferred to finished goods	5,420
Sales	8,000
Cost of goods sold	5,320
Inventories, December 31, 19_1 (not 19_2):	
Stores control	100
Work-in-process control	60
Finished-goods control	500

REQUIRED

1. Prepare general journal entries to summarize 19_2 transactions. As your final entry, dispose of the year-end overapplied or underapplied factory overhead as a direct adjustment to Cost of Goods Sold. Number your entries. Explanations for each entry may be omitted.
2. Show posted T-accounts for all inventories, Cost of Goods Sold, Factory Department Overhead Control, and Factory Overhead Applied.
3. Sketch how the subsidiary ledger would appear for Factory Department Overhead Control. Assume that there are three departments: art, photo, and printing. You need not show any numbers.

4-9 ***Journal entries and source documents.*** Refer to Problem 4-8. For each journal entry, (a) indicate the most likely name of the source documents that would authorize the entry, and (b) give a description of the entry into the subsidiary ledgers affected, if any.

4-10 ***Journal entries.*** The N Company uses a job-order cost system. The following relate to the month of March:

1. Raw materials issued to production, $96,000.

2. Direct-labor analysis, $78,000.

3. Manufacturing overhead is applied to production on the basis of $4 per direct-labor hour. There were 13,000 direct-labor hours incurred.

4. Total manufacturing overhead for the month was $54,000.

5. Production orders that cost $200,000 were completed during the month.

6. Production orders that cost $190,000 were shipped and invoiced to customers during the month at a profit of 20 percent based on cost.

REQUIRED

The beginning inventory of work in process was $20,000. Prepare the general-journal entries required to record this information. What is the ending balance of work in process?

4-11 ***Accounting for overhead; predetermined rates.*** The Aaron Company uses a predetermined overhead rate in applying overhead to production orders on a *labor-cost* basis for Department A and on a machine-hour basis for Department B. At the beginning of 19_1, the company made the following predictions:

	DEPT. A	DEPT. B
Direct-labor cost	$128,000	$ 35,000
Factory overhead	144,000	150,000
Direct-labor hours	16,000	5,000
Machine-hours	1,000	20,000

REQUIRED

1. What is the predetermined overhead *rate* that should be used in Department A? In Department B?
2. During the month of January, the cost sheet for production order No. 200 shows the following:

	DEPT. A	DEPT. B
Materials requisitioned	$20	$40
Direct-labor cost	$32	$21
Direct-labor hours	4	3
Machine-hours	1	13

What is the *total overhead* cost of production order No. 200?

3. Assuming that Job No. 200 consisted of 20 units of product, what is the *unit cost* of Job No. 200?
4. At the *end* of 19_1, it was found that *actual* factory-overhead costs amounted to $160,000 in Department A and $138,000 in Department B.

   Give the overapplied or underapplied overhead amount for each department and for the factory as a whole. Assume that total actual direct-labor costs and machine-hours conformed with the original predictions.
5. Assume the same facts as in requirement 4 regarding actual factory overhead. Suppose that the actual direct-labor cost was $148,000 in Department A and the actual machine-hours were 18,000 in Department B. Compute the overapplied or underapplied overhead amount for each department and for the factory as a whole.

4-12 ***Overhead balances.*** (SMA) Budgeted overhead, based on a budgeted volume of 100,000 direct-labor hours, was $255,000. Actual overhead costs amounted to $270,000, and actual direct-labor hours were 105,000. Overhead overapplied (underapplied) amounted to (choose one): (1) $2,250 overapplied, (2) ($2,250) underapplied, (3) $15,000 overapplied, or (4) ($15,000) underapplied.

4-13 ***Statement of cost of goods manufactured.*** (CPA) The Rebecca Corporation is a manufacturer that produces special machines made to customer specifications. All production costs are accumulated by means of a job-order costing system. The following information is available at the beginning of the month of October 19_1.

Direct-materials inventory, October 1	$16,200
Work-in-process, October 1	3,600

A review of the job-order cost sheets revealed the composition of the work-in-process inventory on October 1 as follows:

Direct materials	$1,320
Direct labor (300 hours)	1,500
Factory overhead applied	780
	$3,600

Activity during the month of October was as follows:

Direct materials costing $20,000 were purchased.
Direct labor for job orders totaled 3,300 hours at $5 per hour.
Factory overhead was applied to production at the rate of $2.60 per direct-labor hour.

On October 31, inventories consisted of the following components:

Direct-materials inventory	$17,000
Work-in-process inventory:	
Direct materials	$ 4,320
Direct labor (500 hours)	2,500
Factory overhead applied	1,300
	$ 8,120

REQUIRED

Prepare in good form a detailed statement of the cost of goods manufactured for the month of October.

4-14 ***Meaning of overapplied overhead.*** The Walgenbach Company had budgeted the following performance for 19_3:

Units	100,000
Sales	$110,000
Total variable expenses	$ 65,000

Total fixed expenses	$ 40,000
Net income	$ 5,000
Factory overhead:	
Variable	$ 5,000
Fixed	$ 30,000
Beginning inventories	None

It is now the end of 19_3. A factory-overhead rate of 35¢ per unit was used throughout the year for costing product. Total factory overhead incurred was $35,000. Overapplied factory overhead was $2,100. There is no work in process. How many units were produced during 19_3?

4-15 ***Applying overhead, job costing.*** (CMA, adapted) Baehr Company is a manufacturing company with a fiscal year that runs from July 1 to June 30. The company uses a job-order accounting system for its production costs.

A predetermined overhead rate based upon direct-labor hours is used to apply overhead to individual jobs. A flexible budget of overhead costs was prepared for the 19_7–_8 fiscal year as follows:

Direct-labor hours	100,000	120,000	140,000
Variable overhead costs	$325,000	$390,000	$455,000
Fixed overhead costs	216,000	216,000	216,000
Total overhead	$541,000	$606,000	$671,000

Company officials have determined 120,000 direct-labor hours as the expected volume for the year. The following information is for November, 19_7. Jobs 77-50 and 77-51 were completed during November.

Inventories November 1, 19_7:	
Raw materials and supplies	$ 10,500
Work-in-process (Job 77-50)	54,000
Finished goods	112,500
Purchases of raw materials and supplies:	
Raw materials	$135,000
Supplies	15,000
Materials and supplies requisitioned for production:	
Job 77-50	$ 45,000
Job 77-51	37,500
Job 77-52	25,500
Supplies	12,000
	$120,000
Factory direct-labor hours:	
Job 77-50	3,500 DLH
Job 77-51	3,000 DLH
Job 77-52	2,000 DLH
Labor costs:	
Direct-labor wages	$ 51,000
Indirect-labor wages (4,000 hours)	15,000
Supervisory salaries	6,000
Building occupancy costs (heat, light, depreciation, etc.):	
Factory facilities	$ 6,500
Sales offices	1,500
Administrative offices	1,000
	$ 9,000
Factory equipment costs:	
Power	$ 4,000
Repairs and maintenance	1,500
Depreciation	1,500
Other	1,000
	$ 8,000

REQUIRED

Answer the following multiple-choice questions.

1. The predetermined overhead rate to be used to apply overhead to individual jobs during the 19_7–_8 fiscal year is
   (a) $3.25 per DLH (b) $4.69 per DLH (c) $5.05 per DLH
   (d) $5.41 per DLH (e) None of these.

Note: Without prejudice to your answer to Item 1, assume that the predetermined overhead rate is $4.50 per direct-labor hour. Use this amount in answering items 2 through 6.

2. The total cost of job 77-50 is
   (a) $81,750 (b) $135,750 (c) $142,750 (d) $146,750 or
   (e) None of these.
3. The factory-overhead costs applied to job 77-52 during November were
   (a) $9,000 (b) $47,500 (c) $46,500 (d) $8,000 or
   (e) None of these.
4. The total amount of overhead applied to jobs during November was
   (a) $29,250 (b) $38,250 (c) $47,250 (d) $56,250 or
   (e) None of these.
5. Actual factory overhead incurred during November 19_7 was
   (a) $38,000 (b) $41,500 (c) $47,500 (d) $50,500 or
   (e) None of these.
6. At the end of the last fiscal year (June 30, 19_7), Baehr Company had the fol- account balances:

Overapplied overhead	$ 1,000
Cost of goods sold	980,000
Work-in-process inventory	38,000
Finished-goods inventory	82,000

The most common treatment of the overapplied overhead would be to
(a) Prorate it between work-in-process inventory and finished-goods inventory
(b) Prorate it between work-in-process inventory, finished-goods inventory and cost of goods sold (c) Carry it as a deferred credit on the balance sheet (d) Carry it as miscellaneous operating revenue on the income statement or (e) Credit it to cost of goods sold.

4-16 ***Application and proration of overhead.*** (SMA, heavily adapted) Nicole Limited is a company that produces machinery to customer orders, using a job-order cost system. Manufacturing overhead is applied to production using a predetermined rate. This overhead rate is set at the beginning of each fiscal year by forecasting the following year's overhead and relating it to direct-labor dollars. The budget for the company's last fiscal year was:

Direct labor	$280,000
Manufacturing overhead	$168,000

As of the end of the year, two jobs were incomplete. These were No. 1768B—total direct-labor charges were $11,000; and No. 1819C—total direct-labor charges were $39,000. On these jobs, machine-hours were 287 for No. 1768B, and 647 for No. 1819C. Direct materials issued to No. 1768B amounted to $22,000, and $42,000 to No. 1819C.

Total charges to the manufacturing-overhead control account for the year were $186,840; while direct-labor charges made to all jobs were $400,000, representing 20,000 direct-labor hours.

There were no beginning inventories. In addition to the ending work in process described above, the ending finished goods showed a balance of $72,000.

Sales for the year totaled $2,700,680; cost of goods sold totaled $648,000; and selling, general, and administrative expenses were $1,857,870.

The amounts for inventories and cost of goods sold were not adjusted for any overapplication or underapplication of manufacturing overhead to production. It is the company's practice to prorate any overapplied or underapplied overhead to inventories and cost of goods sold.

REQUIRED

1. Prepare a detailed schedule showing the ending balances in the inventories and cost of goods sold (before considering any underapplied or overapplied manufacturing overhead).
2. Assume that underapplied or overapplied manufacturing overhead is prorated in proportion to the ending balances (before the proration) in Work in Progress, Finished Goods, and Cost of Goods Sold. Prepare a detailed schedule showing the proration and the final balances after proration.
3. Assume that all the underapplied or overapplied manufacturing overhead was added to or subtracted from Cost of Goods Sold. Would operating income be higher or lower than the operating income that would result from the prorations in requirement 2 above? By what amount?

4-17 ***Overhead application and year-end disposition.*** (D. Jacque Grinnell) A manufacturing company is divided into three producing departments, A, B, and C. All production is to customer's order. Budgeted manufacturing costs for 19_1 are as follows:

	DEPT. A	DEPT. B	DEPT. C	TOTAL
Direct material				$170,000
Direct labor	$40,000	$20,000	$60,000	120,000
Manufacturing overhead	10,000	40,000	30,000	80,000

The actual material and labor cost of producing a particular order (order #162) during 19_1 was as follows:

Direct material			$1,500
Direct labor:			
	Dept. A	$200	
	Dept. B	190	
	Dept. C	240	630

Manufacturing overhead is applied to product on the basis of direct-labor cost. Overhead rates are predetermined at the beginning of the year using annual budget data.

REQUIRED

1. Determine the total manufacturing cost associated with order #162 assuming that (a) a factorywide manufacturing overhead rate is used to apply cost to product, and (b) departmental rates are used to apply cost to product.
2. *Actual* manufacturing costs for 19_1 were as follows:

	DEPT. A	DEPT. B	DEPT. C	TOTAL
Direct material				$180,000
Direct labor	$44,000	$19,000	$72,000	135,000
Manufacturing overhead	12,000	36,000	39,000	87,000

Determine the underapplied or overapplied overhead for the year assuming
a. The use of the factorywide overhead rate
b. The use of the departmental overhead rates
3. Consider the information provided in requirement 2 above. Assume that the firm chose to use departmental rates to apply overhead to product. Also assume that at the beginning of 19_1 there were no work-in-process or finished-goods inventories. At the end of 19_1 the work-in-process and finished-goods inventories were represented by the following balances:

Work in process	$19,500
Finished goods	60,500

The balances include actual direct-material costs, actual direct-labor costs, and applied overhead costs; that is, no year-end adjustments have been made for underapplied or overapplied overhead. Assuming the company desires to prorate underapplied or overapplied overhead between ending inventories and cost of goods sold in proportion to their unadjusted balances, compute the correct prorated amount to be assigned to cost of goods sold.

4-18 ***Proration of overhead.*** The Invincible Company has commercial and defense contracting business. A contracting officer for the United States Air Force has insisted that underapplied overhead should no longer be written off directly as an adjustment of Cost of Defense Goods Sold for a given year. His insistence was prompted by the fact that $40 million of underapplied overhead was added to the $400 million of unadjusted Cost of Goods Sold in 19_4. There were no beginning inventories.

Overhead is applied as a percentage of direct labor as contracts are produced. The air force had a large cost-plus-fixed-fee contract representing $300 million of the $400 million of defense production started and sold during 19_4; it had no other contracts pending with Invincible. An analysis of costs showed (in millions):

DEFENSE BUSINESS

	Contracts in progress	Finished goods inventory	Cost of goods sold
Direct material used	$380	$20	$200
Direct-labor cost	90	10	100
Factory overhead applied	90	10	100
Total before adjustment	560	40	400*
Add: Underapplied overhead	—	—	40
Total after adjustment	$560	$40	$440

**Includes $300 million attributable to air force contract.*

REQUIRED

1. As a judge trying to settle a dispute on the disposition of the overhead, what position would you favor? Why? Show computations and, assuming your answer would be formally recorded in the books of account, show a journal entry for the proration.
2. As the contracting officer, what proration of the underapplied overhead would you favor? Why? Show computations.

4-19 ***Classification of overtime costs.*** This is an expansion of Problem 2-31. Suppose that the printing department gathers all of its indirect costs and applies them via a single overhead rate on the basis of, say, 300 percent of the direct-labor cost of individual jobs. If overtime premium and some pension costs were regarded as direct-labor costs rather than overhead, would the overhead rate be higher or lower than 300 percent? Why?

4-20 ***Incomplete data; journal entries.*** The following account balances were selected from the general ledger of the Cepeda Manufacturing Company at the start of business on January 1, 19_1, and the close of business on December 31, 19_1. The company uses perpetual inventories.

	BALANCES, JANUARY 1, 19_1	BALANCES, DECEMBER 31, 19_1
Stores	$ 5,000	$ 20,000
Manufacturing overhead	—	22,000
Manufacturing overhead applied (at a rate of ⅔ of the direct-labor cost)	—	20,000
Work in process	35,000	15,000
Finished goods	20,000	30,000
Cost of goods sold	—	100,000

REQUIRED

Entries in general-journal form summarizing the operating activities of the year 19_1, which were recorded in the above accounts. Present T-accounts also.

4-21 ***Overview of general-ledger relationships.*** The Blakely Company uses a job-order cost system. The total debits and credits in certain accounts at year-end are:

	DECEMBER 30, 19_6	
	total debits	**total credits**
Direct-material control	$100,000	$ 70,000
Work-in-process control	320,000	305,000
Factory department overhead control	85,000	—
Finished-goods control	325,000	300,000
Cost of goods sold	300,000	—
Factory department overhead applied	—	90,000

Note that "total debits" in the inventory accounts would include beginning inventory balances, if any.

The above accounts *do not* include the following:

a. The labor-cost recapitulation for the December 31 working day: direct labor, $5,000; and indirect labor, $1,000

b. Miscellaneous factory overhead incurred on December 30 and December 31: $1,000

ADDITIONAL INFORMATION

Factory overhead has been applied as a percentage of direct labor through December 30.
Direct-material purchases during 19_6 were $90,000.
There were no returns to suppliers.
Direct-labor costs during 19_6 totaled $150,000, not including the December 31 working day described above.

REQUIRED

1. Beginning inventories of direct material, work in process, and finished goods. Show T-accounts.
2. Prepare all adjusting and closing journal entries for the above accounts. Assume that all underapplied or overapplied overhead is closed directly to Cost of Goods Sold.
3. Ending inventories, after adjustments and closing, of direct material, work in process, and finished goods.

4-22 ***Multiple choice; incomplete data.*** Some of the general-ledger accounts of the Sharman Manufacturing Company appear as follows on January 31, 19_1.

The accounts are incomplete because the accountant had an emergency operation for ulcers after he ate lunch in the company cafeteria on January 31. The treasurer, an old friend of yours, supplied you with the following incomplete accounts and three bits of additional information.

DIRECT-MATERIAL STORES CONTROL

Bal. Jan. 1	**15,000**	
	35,000	

WORK-IN-PROCESS CONTROL

Bal. Jan. 1	**1,000**	**40,000**
Direct materials requisitioned	**20,000**	

FINISHED-GOODS CONTROL

Bal. Jan. 1	**10,000**	**20,000**

COST OF GOODS SOLD

ACCRUED FACTORY PAYROLL

	Bal. Jan. 1	**1,000**
	Gross earnings of all factory workers	**40,000**

ADDITIONAL INFORMATION

a. Factory Overhead Applied is credited for all indirect costs that are applied to production orders.

b. Work tickets for the month totaled 5,500 direct labor-hours. All factory workers received $6 per hour.
c. Indirect costs are applied at a rate of $4 per direct labor-hour.

After giving you a few minutes to look over the data given, your old friend asks you the following (place all answers on an answer sheet; indicate your answer by letter):

REQUIRED

1. The January 31 balance of Direct-Material Stores Control should be
(a) $50,000 (b) $25,000 (c) $30,000 (d) $20,000 (e) $35,000 or
(f) None of these.
2. The amount of total direct-labor cost that should have been charged to all the individual production orders worked on during January should be
(a) $40,000 (b) $41,000 (c) $55,000 (d) $30,000 (e) $33,000 or
(f) None of these.
3. The *total* factory-labor cost for the month of January (ignoring employer's Social Security contributions) is
(a) $41,000 (b) $40,000 (c) $55,000 (d) $33,000 (e) $56,000 or
(f) None of these.
4. The total *indirect* cost that should have been applied to production is
(a) $17,000 (b) $75,000 (c) $40,000 (d) $33,000 (e) $24,000 or
(f) None of these.
5. The January 31 balance of Work-in-Process Control should be
(a) $75,000 (b) $77,000 (c) $76,000 (d) $36,000 (e) $35,000 or
(f) None of these.
6. The January 31 balance of Finished-Goods Control should be
(a) $5,000 (b) $10,000 (c) $20,000 (d) $25,000 (e) $30,000 or
(f) None of these.
7. *Total* indirect costs actually incurred during the month amount to $24,000. The balance in Factory-Overhead Control at the end of January should be
(a) $24,000 (b) $17,000 (c) $26,000 (d) $41,000 (e) $22,000 (f) $2,000 or (g) None of these.
8. The Cost of Goods Sold during January was
(a) $40,000 (b) $10,000 (c) $20,000 (d) $30,000 (e) $50,000 or
(f) None of these.
9. The January 31 balance of Factory Overhead Applied should be
(a) $33,000 (b) $40,000 (c) $24,000 (d) $22,000 (e) $26,000
(f) $30,000 or (g) None of these.
10. The amount of underapplied (or overapplied) costs for January is
(a) Underapplied by $1,000 (b) Underapplied by $2,000
(c) Overapplied by $1,000 (d) Overapplied by $2,000
(e) Overapplied by $3,000 (f) Neither overapplied nor underapplied or
(g) None of these.

4-23 ***Review of job costing: general ledger relationships.*** The Weismer Co.'s job-order accounting system is on a calendar-year basis. As of January 31, 19_2, the following information is available:

a. Direct-materials stores requisitions for January totaled $200,000.
b. The cost of goods sold during January was $500,000.
c. Stores (i.e., direct-materials inventory), on January 31, 19_2, were $9,000.
d. The cost of goods completed and transferred to finished goods during January was $600,000.
e. The predetermined factory overhead application rate for 19_2 is 180 percent of direct-labor costs.
f. The finished-goods inventory, on December 31, 19_1, was $42,000.
g. Gross factory wages paid in January totaled $195,000. (Ignore withholdings.)

h. All employees performing direct labor get the same rate of pay. Direct labor hours for January totaled 10,000. Indirect labor, supervision, and miscellaneous factory overhead payroll totaled $30,000.

i. Jobs No. 480 and No. 482 were uncompleted on January 31, 19_2. Together, their total labor charges were $6,000 (400 direct-labor hours). Their total direct-material charges were $13,200.

j. The overapplied factory overhead, as of January 31, was $14,000.

k. Direct materials purchased during January totaled $207,000.

l. Balance, Accrued Factory Payroll, as of January 31, 19_2, was $4,000.

REQUIRED

Compute, showing your work:

1. Balance, Stores (direct-materials inventory), on December 31, 19_1
2. Balance, Finished Goods, on January 31, 19_2
3. Direct-labor costs incurred during January
4. Actual overhead incurred during January
5. Balance, Accrued Factory Payroll, on December 31, 19_1
6. Balance, Work in Process, on January 31, 19_2
7. Balance, Work in Process, on December 31, 19_1

4-24 ***Process costing: material introduced at start of process.*** A certain process incurred $40,000 of production costs during a month. Materials costing $22,000 were introduced at the start of processing, while conversion costs of $18,000 were incurred at a uniform rate throughout the production cycle. Of the 40,000 units of product started, 38,000 were completed; 2,000 were still in process at the end of the month, averaging one-half complete.

REQUIRED

In step-by-step fashion, prepare a production-cost report showing cost of goods completed and cost of ending work in process.

4-25 ***Process costs; single department.*** The following data pertain to the mixing department for July:

Units:	
Work in process, July 1	0
Units started	50,000
Completed and transferred to finishing department	35,000
Costs:	
Material P	$200,000
Material Q	$ 70,000
Direct labor and overhead	$135,000

Material P is introduced at the start of the process, while Material Q is added when the product reaches a three-fourths stage of completion. Conversion costs are incurred uniformly throughout the process.

REQUIRED

Cost of goods transferred during July. Cost of work in process as of July 31. Assume that ending work in process is two-thirds completed.

4-26 ***Process—operation cost accumulation.*** The Zarno Co. produces a single product, a mechanical device called Zarno. The company maintains an "operation-process-cost" accounting system.

The process starts with Material A, a metal, which is stamped and assembled with a purchased part "B." The resulting unit is enameled in the final operation.

Time and motion studies indicate that, of the total time needed for the manufacture of a complete unit, the first operation requires 40 percent of the labor cost; the assembly requires 50 percent; and the enameling, 10 percent. Factory overhead is considered to follow the same pattern by operations as does labor.

The following data are presented to you as of March 31, the end of the first month of operation:

Material A purchased—200,000 square feet	$60,000
Part B purchased—24,000 units	24,000
Enamel used	1,200
Direct labor and factory overhead	60,000

	UNIT QUANTITY
Units completed and sent to finished-goods warehouse	12,000
Inventories at end of the month:	
Units stamped but not assembled	3,000
Units assembled but not enameled	2,000
Material A (in square feet)	30,000
Part B	10,000
Total units in process	5,000

There was no spoilage or shrinkage.

REQUIRED

1. Equivalent units of work performed for (a) Material A; (b) Material B; (c) enamel; (d) conversion costs
2. Cost of goods completed and transferred, divided into the four components: three materials plus conversion costs
3. Cost of goods stamped but not assembled
4. Cost of goods assembled but not enameled

4-27 ***Program budgeting and job costing.*** Nonprofit institutions such as health centers and colleges continually face decisions concerning how to allocate their limited resources. A technique called program budgeting has been developed to help in the making of these decisions. The "program" is an activity or set of activities with a particular goal such as placing children for adoption, helping ex-convicts on parole, aiding disabled veterans, or educating students of management.

Program budgeting is a philosophy or state of mind rather than a rigid set of procedures. Questions such as the following are raised: (1) What are the organization's objectives or goals? Program categories sometimes cut across organizational lines so that two or more departments work together toward a common goal. (2) How much does each program cost? Costs typically include specifically traceable costs such as direct labor plus applied overhead. (3) How is each program funded? Are cash receipts from donations, tuition, or government grants earmarked specifically for one purpose? Sometimes raising money for a specific program can dislodge general funds for other purposes.

As 19_5 began, Muriel Clayton, director of the Uppervale Health Center, faced a decision. She had talked recently with Theodore Rosenberg, an administrator in the State Health Department. He told her that the state might be able to increase its support to the center by $30,000. Ms. Clayton had to determine which of two activities, drug-addict rehabilitation or alcoholic rehabilitation, was more effective so she could write a formal request for the additional funds.

For purposes of cost analysis, the center's activities were divided into four programs: (1) alcoholic rehabilitation, (2) drug-addict rehabilitation, (3) children's clinical services, and (4) after-care (counseling and support of patients after release from a mental hospital).

Ms. Clayton felt that costs per program would help her decide where to invest additional funds. Of course, such costs would give her some idea of the inputs devoted to each program. The measure of outputs is far more troublesome. Should it be patients treated, patients cured, patients not requiring further treatment for two years, or what measure? Ms. Clayton decided that cost per patient per year would be a helpful statistic for making her decision. She felt that it would be too expensive and too difficult to develop a more elegant measure of effectiveness. The center's board and staff agreed that if the cost per drug patient per year was not more than 20 percent higher than for the alcoholic patient, the drug program would receive the additional funds.

The center's simplified budget was typical for a nonprofit institution in the sense that it was a line-item budget, a mere listing of various costs classified by so-called natural descriptions:

Professional salaries:		
6 physicians @ $37,500	$225,000	
19 psychologists @ $25,000	475,000	
24 nurses @ $12,500	300,000	$1,000,000
Medical supplies		150,000
General overhead (administrative salaries, rent, utilities, etc.)		500,000
		$1,650,000

The budget and the accounting system did not show how the costs related to the four programs. Ms. Clayton decided to ask the professional staff to fill out a form indicating what percentage of time each devoted to the four programs. This was a critical form, and Clayton, who had earned uniformly high respect from the professional staff, stressed that it be filled out conscientiously.

Costs of medical supplies were to be allocated on the basis of physician-hours spent in each program. General overhead would be allocated on the basis of direct-labor cost (where direct labor is defined to include the time of doctors, psychologists, and nurses multiplied by the salary rate of each).

Clayton compiled the following data concerning allocations from individual time allocation forms:

		DRUG				
	alcohol	**counseling**	**clinical**	**children**	**after-care**	**total**
Physicians			2	4		6
Psychologists	6	4			9	19
Nurses	4	4	2	4	10	24

At any point in time, an average of 30 patients are in residence in the alcohol program, each staying about a half-year. Thus, the clinic processed 60 patients but provided only 30 patient-years of service. Similarly, an average of 40 patients were involved in the drug program for about a half-year each; they received both counseling and clinical services.

REQUIRED

What is the cost of the alcohol and drug programs, using the Clayton approach to cost analysis? What action should be taken?

4-28 ***Job costing in a service industry.*** Howe and Halling, Certified Public Accountants, use a form of job-costing system. In this respect they are similar to many professional service firms, such as management counsulting firms, law firms, and professional engineering firms.

An auditing client may be served by various staff who hold professional positions in the hierarchy from partners to managers to senior accountants to assistants. In addition, there are secretaries and other employees.

Suppose that Howe and Halling have the following budget for 19_2:

Compensation of professional staff	$4,000,000
Other costs	2,400,000
Total budgeted costs	$6,400,000

Each professional staff member must submit a weekly time report, which is used to assign costs to jobs. An example is the time report of a senior accountant:

WEEK OF JANUARY 8	S	M	T	W	T	F	S	TOTAL
CHARGEABLE HOURS								
Client A		8	8	5				21
Client B				3		4		7
Etc.								

WEEK OF JANUARY 8	S	M	T	W	T	F	S	TOTAL
NONCHARGEABLE HOURS								
Professional development (attending seminar on computer auditing)					8			8
Unassigned time						4		4
Total	0	8	8	8	8	8	0	40

In turn, these time reports are used for charging hours to a client job-order sheet, summarized as follows for Client A:

	WEEK OF				
EMPLOYEES CHARGED	**Jan. 8**	**Jan. 15**	TOTAL HOURS	BILLING RATES	TOTAL BILLED
Partners	4	4	8	$100	$ 800
Managers	4	4	8	60	480
Seniors	21	30	51	40	2,040
Assistants	48	70	118	20	2,360
Total hours	77	108	185		$5,680

In many cases, these job-cost sheets bear only a summary of the *hours* charged. Each class of labor is billed at an appropriate hourly rate, so that the job-cost sheet is the central basis for billing the client.

REQUIRED

1. Suppose that this firm had a policy of charging overhead to jobs at a predetermined percentage of the salaries charged to the job. The experience of the firm has been that chargeable hours average 80 percent of available hours for all categories of professional personnel. The nonchargeable hours are regarded as additional overhead. What is the overhead rate as a percentage of the "direct labor," the chargeable professional compensation cost?
2. Compute the *total cost* of the Client A job for the two weeks that began January 8. Be as specific as possible. Assume that the average weekly compensation (based on a 40-hour week) of the personnel working on this job is: partners, $2,000; managers, $1,200; seniors, $800; assistants, $400.
3. As the tabulation for Client A implies, the job order often consists of only the time and no costs. Instead, the revenue is computed via multiplying the time by the billing rates. Suppose the partners' profit object is 20 percent of the total costs budgeted. What predetermined percentage of the salaries charged to the jobs would be necessary to achieve a total billing that would ultimately provide the profit objective? That is, what is the billing rate as a percentage of "direct labor"?
4. In addition to billing, what use might you make of the data compiled on the job orders?

4-29 ***Government contracts and incentives.*** (David Ng, adapted) The Department of Defense (DOD) wishes to develop the MX-missile system and has obtained bids from various defense contractors to develop a subsystem for the MX-missile project. Because it is somewhat technologically uncertain whether a successful subsystem can be developed, contract negotiators in the Department of Defense feel that CPIF (cost plus incentive fee) contracts would be the most appropriate.

One of the most attractive bids is from a company that claims it will take 50,000 engineering hours and 30,000 direct-labor hours to develop the subsystem. Wage rate for engineering design is $25 per hour, and wage rate for direct labor is $10 per hour. Allowable overhead and general and administrative expenses are approximately related with engineering hours and direct-labor hours as follows:

Allowable overhead & general & administrative expenses
= ($6 × Engineering hours) + ($8 × Direct-labor hours)

"Allowable" overhead is that portion of overhead that will be reimbursed by the DOD.

Analysis of the hours by the DOD leads to the conclusion that the work could be done for 35,000 engineering hours and 20,000 direct-labor hours or might take as many as 60,000 engineering hours and 35,000 direct-labor hours. However, the most likely estimates are 45,000 hours and 27,000 hours for engineering and direct labor, respectively. These conclusions were arrived at in fact-finding sessions with the contractor.

In addition to the engineering and direct labor, costs for parts and subcontracts are also necessary. The low, likely, and high estimates of these costs are:

	LOW	LIKELY	HIGH
Parts	$240,000	$300,000	$350,000
Subcontracts	440,000	500,000	600,000

The DOD usually stipulates that the target cost must be set at the most likely estimated cost. At this cost level, the profit allowable under current regulations for the contractor is $250,000. The profit ceiling that the DOD is willing to pay is $310,000. This will be paid if the contractor can control its costs at or below the original low-cost estimate established by the department. On the other hand, if the contractor's cost is at or above the original high estimate established by the department, then the department is only willing to pay a profit of $200,000 to the contractor.

REQUIRED

1. Calculate the target cost for the CPIF contract that is going to be offered by the Department of Defense.
2. What is the target fee? The maximum fee? The minimum fee?
3. Calculate the share ratio. (Round your computations to the nearest whole percent.) A *share ratio* is a measure of how the government and the defense contractor will split the increase or decrease in fee if the total costs do not equal the target but fall between the high and low estimated costs. The defense contractor's share is dependent on whether the final cost is

   Below the target cost:

   $$\text{Defense contractor's share} = \frac{\text{Maximum fee} - \text{Target fee}}{\text{Target cost} - \text{Low-cost estimate}}$$

   or

   Above the target cost:

   $$\text{Defense contractor's share} = \frac{\text{Target fee} - \text{Minimum fee}}{\text{High-cost estimate} - \text{Target cost}}$$

   If the final costs are outside the range of high and low estimated costs, the share ratio does not apply. Instead, the minimum fee applies to costs in excess of the high-cost estimate; similarly, the maximum fee applies to costs below the low-cost estimate.
4. If the final cost at the completion of the project turns out to be $4.5 million, how much is the contractor's profit?
5. If the final cost turns out to be $2.3 million, how much will the Department of Defense pay? How much is the contractor's profit?
6. If the final cost turns out to be $1 million, how much will the Department of Defense pay? How much is the contractor's profit?

4-30 ***Comprehensive review problem—job-order costs.*** This problem is intended to provide a summary of general-ledger and subsidiary-ledger relationships for factory costs under a job-order cost system. The facts are unrealistic because, in order to save student time, the tremendous detail and number of accounts in a real situation are not reproduced here. However, the solving of this problem should provide the student with a comprehensive view of the basic ledger framework.

Assume that the Mafco Company has been in business in Hong Kong for many years. The company rents its factory building. It also uses a job-order cost system because it has a wide variety of products that receive varying attention and effort in the two factory departments, Machining and Assembly.

Mafco has the following trial balance as of December 31, 19_0:

Cash	$ 15,000	
Accounts receivable	40,000	
Stores control	29,600	
Work-in-process control	4,000	
Finished-goods control	20,000	
Unexpired insurance	12,000	
Office equipment	15,000	
Accumulated depreciation—office equipment		$ 5,000
Factory equipment	950,000	
Accumulated depreciation—factory equipment		220,000
Accounts payable		23,000
Accrued payroll		1,000
Accrued utilities		2,000
Accrued property taxes		3,000
Capital stock		100,000
Retained earnings		731,600
	$1,085,600	$1,085,600

Detail on Subsidiary Records as of December 31, 19_0

STORES:

CODE	QUANTITY	UNIT COST	AMOUNT
A	5,000	$2.00	$10,000
B	10,000	1.50	15,000
C	400	8.00	3,200
Supplies	Various	—	1,400
			$29,600

WORK IN PROCESS:

JOB-ORDER NUMBER	DEPARTMENT	DIRECT MATERIALS	DIRECT LABOR	FACTORY OVERHEAD	TOTAL
100	Machining	$1,800	$800	$900	$3,500
	Assembly	200	200	100	500
					$4,000

FINISHED GOODS:

STOCK NO.	REFERENCE	QUANTITY	UNIT COST	AMOUNT
X-1	Job 97	100	$80	$ 8,000
X-2	Job 99	1,000	12	12,000
				$20,000

The factory-overhead budget at the top of page 122 has been prepared for the coming year, 19_1. This budget has been prepared after careful consideration of the sales outlook for the coming year. The production schedules are geared to the forecast sales pattern.

	machining	assembly	total
FACTORY OVERHEAD BUDGET FOR YEAR ENDING DECEMBER 31, 19_1			
FACTORY OVERHEAD:			
CONTROLLABLE:			
Supplies	$ 14,400	$ 5,400	$ 19,800
Indirect labor	22,800	16,800	39,600
Utilities	30,000	9,000	39,000
Repairs	24,000	6,000	30,000
Miscellaneous	22,800	12,000	34,800
	$114,000	$ 49,200	$163,200
UNCONTROLLABLE:			
Insurance	$ 7,200	$ 2,400	$ 9,600
Depreciation	114,000	14,400	128,400
Rent	24,000	16,800	40,800
Property taxes	4,200	1,200	5,400
Supervision	14,400	19,200	33,600
	$163,800	$ 54,000	$217,800
Total factory overhead	$277,800	$103,200	$381,000

In order to cost jobs as they are worked on, a predetermined overhead rate is computed as follows:

	YEAR 19_1	
	machining	**assembly**
Factory overhead	$277,800	$103,200
Machine-hours	69,450	
Direct-labor cost		$206,400
Rate per machine-hour	$ 4.00	
Rate per direct-labor dollar		50%

These overhead rates will be used throughout the year to cost various jobs as they are worked on by each department. All overhead will be applied to all jobs worked on during the year in proportion to the machine-hour or direct-labor cost factor devoted to each job. If management predictions are accurate, total overhead applied to the year's jobs through the use of predetermined rates should be equal to the total overhead costs actually incurred.

January data:

1. Purchases for stores (credit Accounts Payable):

	QUANTITY	UNIT COST	JANUARY
A	7,500	$2.00	$15,000
B	14,000	1.50	21,000
C	2,125	8.00	17,000
Supplies			2,000
			$55,000

2. Returns (debit Accounts Payable): 50 units of Material B.
3. The direct-material requisitions were summarized, and the following data were shown on a material-usage report. These reports were submitted weekly to department foremen, although monthly data are shown here.

Machining Department

Direct-Material Usage
For the Month Ending January 31, 19_1

REQUISITION	TYPE	JOB ORDER	QUANTITY	UNIT COST	AMOUNT
M90	A	102	3,000	2.00	6,000
M91	A	103	1,000	2.00	2,000

REQUISITION	TYPE	JOB ORDER	QUANTITY	UNIT COST	AMOUNT
M89	B	101	1,500	1.50	2,250
M92	B	103	1,000	1.50	1,500
M93	B	102	3,000	1.50	4,500
M94	B	101	200	1.50	300
M95	A	104	2,000	2.00	4,000
					$20,550

Assembly Department

Direct-Material Usage
For the Month Ending January 31, 19_1

REQUISITION	TYPE	JOB ORDER	QUANTITY	UNIT COST	AMOUNT
A301	C	100	5	$8.00	$ 40
A302	C	103	200	8.00	1,600
A303	C	101	800	8.00	6,400
A304	C	102	1,500	8.00	12,000
A305	C	103	20	8.00	160
					$20,200

4. A summary of payroll costs incurred follows. Compare with item (7) below. Payments (settlements) are independent of recognition of cost incurrence. In other words, costs may be summarized monthly while settlements are made weekly.

		LABOR HOURS		COST		
work ticket*	**job order**	**machining**	**assembly**	**machining**	**assembly**	**total**
ML480	101	20		$ 50	$	$ 50
ML481	101	1,500		3,750		3,750
ML482	103	1,000		2,500		2,500
ML483	102	1,200		3,000		3,000
ML484	104	500		1,250		1,250
ML485	103	100		250		250
AL60	100		20		40	40
AL61	102		7,000		14,000	14,000
AL62	101		500		1,000	1,000
AL63	103		1,000		2,000	2,000
AL64	102		200		400	400
Total direct labor		4,320	8,720	$10,800	$17,440	$28,240
Indirect labor				2,000	1,500	3,500
Supervision				1,200	1,600	2,800
Total factory labor				$14,000	$20,540	$34,540
Selling and administrative wages						6,000
Total payroll costs						$40,540

**In practice, there would be many more of these. Often they are recapitulated daily and posted to each job in groups rather than as individual tickets.*

5. Apply overhead to jobs. Rates as calculated when overhead budget was prepared: Machining, $4.00 per machine-hour; Assembly, 50 percent of direct-labor cost. See data for item 6 to obtain machine-hours worked.

6. Production and sales data:

JOB	UNITS COMPLETED	FINISHED	FINISHED STOCK NO.	UNITS SOLD	SOLD FOR	JANUARY MACHINE-HOURS WORKED IN MACHINING DEPT.
97	100	19_0	X-1	100	$ 9,000	
98	—	—	—	—	—	
99	1000	19_0	X-2	1000	16,000	
100	50	Jan. 5, 19_1	X-1	20	1,800	
101	1750	Jan. 12, 19_1	X-2	900	14,400	3,000
102	1000	Jan. 19, 19_1	X-3	950	55,000	2,000
103	100	Jan. 30, 19_1	X-4	50	6,500	150
104	Unfinished					800
					$102,700	5,950

7. Gross payroll paid in cash during month, $39,000.
8. The following additional overhead costs were incurred during January:

ITEM	TOTAL	DEPARTMENT machining	DEPARTMENT assembly	SELLING AND ADMINISTRATIVE	GENERAL-LEDGER ACCOUNT TO BE CREDITED
Supplies requisitioned	$ 2,000	$ 1,500	$ 400	$ 100	?
Utilities (cost recognized on basis of usage estimates for month rather than on basis of invoices, which may cover other dates than a current calendar month)	4,000	2,700	800	500	Accrued Utilities Payable
Repairs by outsiders (parts and labor)	3,000	2,350	600	50	Accounts Payable
Miscellaneous	3,000	2,000	900	100	Accounts Payable
Insurance	1,000	600	200	200	?
Depreciation on equipment	11,000	9,500	1,200	300	?
Rent	4,000	2,000	1,400	600	Accounts Payable
Property taxes	500	350	100	50	Accrued Property Taxes
	$28,500	$21,000	$5,600	$1,900	

9. Utility bills received, $2,900 (dr. Accrued Utilities).
10. Utility bills paid, $2,525 (dr. Accounts Payable).
11. Other selling and administrative expenses, $15,000 (cr. Accounts Payable).
12. Payments on accounts payable, other than the $2,525 in (10), $65,300.
13. Collections on accounts receivable, $99,000.

REQUIRED

1. Enter beginning balances in general-ledger T-accounts.
2. Draw up stores cards, job-cost sheets, and finished-goods stock cards. Be sure to put in "reference" columns so that appropriate requisitions and work tickets, as well as dollar amounts, may be entered in the subsidiary ledger. See the accompanying sample stores card and job-cost sheet.

   Finished-stock cards would be similar in design to stores cards.

   The factory-overhead cost sheets have columns for: date, reference, supplies, indirect labor, utilities, repairs, miscellaneous, insurance, depreciation on equipment, rent, property taxes, and supervision.

   Post beginning balances to subsidiary records.
3. Journalize and post entries for January.

4. Prepare a trial balance as of January 31, 19_1. Also prepare schedules of subsidiary-ledger balances.
5. Prepare an income statement for January and a balance sheet as of January 31, 19_1. Underapplied overhead is treated as an addition to cost of goods sold on interim financial statements.
6. Prepare factory-overhead performance reports for January, one for Machining and one for Assembly. Show actual overhead, budgeted overhead, and variances. Assume arbitrarily that budget figures for January are one-twelfth of those shown in the annual overhead budget.

Stores Card

material A

REFERENCE	RECEIVED			ISSUED			BALANCE			
	quantity	unit cost	amount	quantity	unit cost	amount	date	quantity	unit cost	amount
Vouchers, Invoices, or Requisitions							12/31/_0	5,000	$2.00	$10,000

job order no. 100

Machining Department

DIRECT MATERIAL				DIRECT LABOR				OVERHEAD	
reference	quantity	unit cost	amount	reference	quantity	unit cost	amount	machine-hours worked	amount
Req. A88	900	$2.00	$1800	work tickets	320 hrs	$2.50	$800	225	$900

Assembly Department

DIRECT MATERIAL				DIRECT LABOR				OVERHEAD	
reference	quantity	unit cost	amount	reference	quantity	unit cost	amount	reference	amount
Req. #A300	25	$8.00	$200	Work tickets	100 hrs	$2.00	$200	50% of direct labor	$100

Summary

	Machining	Assembly	Total
Direct material	$____	$____	$____
Direct labor			
Factory overhead applied			
Total cost	$____	$____	$____

7. Assume that operations continue for the remainder of 19_1. Certain balances at December 31, 19_1 follow:

Stores	$ 30,000	
Work in process	10,000	
Finished goods	30,000	
Cost of goods sold	960,000	
Factory-overhead control	400,000	
Factory overhead applied		$385,000

Prepare journal entries to close the factory-overhead accounts, assuming that

a. Underapplied overhead is treated as a direct adjustment of Cost of Goods Sold.
b. Underapplied overhead is spread over appropriate accounts in proportion to their unadjusted ending balances.

Budgets and Standards as Keys to Planning and Control

SECTION TWO

Master Budget and Responsibility Accounting 5

What is the most widely used type of accounting system among well-managed organizations today? Is it a historical cost system? No, although it is often referred to as such. Instead, it is better described as a budgeting system, a system that includes *both* expected results and historical or actual results.

Budgeting has come of age. It is becoming increasingly important, and it is all around us. For some reason, however, accountants and managers seem reluctant to give it the respect it deserves. Still, there has been a steady increase in the prominence of budgeting in both nonprofit and profit-seeking organizations.

This chapter examines the master, or comprehensive, budget as a planning and coordinating device. The succeeding chapters, especially Chapters 6, 7, and 8, will examine various aspects of the budgeting decisions and their implementation.

Evolution of systems

Reflect on the evolution of control systems. As small organizations begin, there is usually a dominant means of control—physical observation. A manager sees, touches and hears the relationships between inputs and outputs; he or she oversees the behavior of various personnel.

The next step is historical records. No fancy cost-benefit analysis is necessary to justify keeping some historical records for internal purposes. These records help answer essential operating questions such as what are the amounts of sales, purchases, cash, inventories, receivables and payables. Historical records also help answer other questions, for example, how an employee performed in 19_3 versus 19_2. Employees' analyses of past performance may help them improve their future performances. Managers must deal with a series of periods, not just one.

The next step is budgets. A manager would find it more helpful to compare *performance* in 19_3 with *plans* for 19_3. Budgeting systems evidently meet the cost-benefit test. Typically, they are purchased voluntarily rather than as a result of outside forces. Why? Because budgeting systems are looked at as good investments. They change human behavior (and decisions) in the ways sought by top management. For example, budgeting may prompt managers to extend their planning horizons much further. Therefore, many prospective difficulties are foreseen and avoided. Without a budgeting system, many managers may veer from one crisis to another.

Do budgeting systems meet the cost-benefit test? Let's hypothesize: suppose we took a poll of 1,000 executives, asking them to rank their favorite operating activities (e.g., talking with customers, designing a product, bargaining with suppliers, training subordinates, planning a new production system, etc.). The chances are good that budgeting would rank very low on the managers' lists. Nevertheless, the poll would also probably show that few managers would be willing to discard their budgeting systems. Improve them? Yes. Abolish them? No.

Major features of budgets

definition and role of budgets

A *budget* is a quantitative expression of a plan of action and an aid to coordination and implementation. Budgets may be formulated for the organization as a whole or for any subunit. The **master budget** summarizes the objectives of all subunits of an organization—sales, production, distribution, and finance. It quantifies the expectations regarding future income, cash flows, financial position, and supporting plans. These are the culmination of a series of decisions resulting from a careful look at the organization's future. In most cases, the master budget is the best practical approximation to a formal model of the total organization: its objectives, its inputs, and its outputs.

Chapter 1 used the diagram on page 131 to show how budgets and performance reports help managers. Note how budgets can play a key part in the entire work of the manager. Our focus in this chapter will be on the planning function. However, budgets serve a variety of functions: planning, evaluating performance, coordinating activities, implementing plans, communicating, motivating, and authorizing actions. The last-named function seems to predominate in government budgeting and not-for-profit budgeting, where budget appropriations serve as authorizations and ceilings for management actions.

This book emphasizes how accounting helps the manager make *operating decisions,* those concerning the acquisition and utilization of scarce resources. However, we cannot ignore the importance of *financing decisions,* which concern the obtaining of

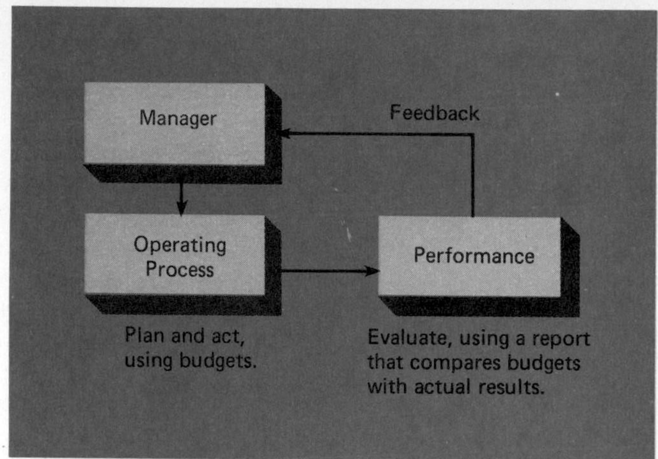

funds for acquisition of resources. The master budget embraces the impact of both kinds of decisions; that is why this chapter examines cash budgets as well as operating budgets. However, because cash budgeting is usually covered in detail in introductory finance courses, this chapter's emphasis is on operating budgets, with a review of cash budgets in Appendix 5A. Incidentally, the leading organizations are usually marked by both impressive operating management and excellent financial management. Business failures are often attributable to weaknesses in one or the other of these responsibilities.

wide use of budgets

Budgetary systems are more common in larger companies, where formalized and sophisticated techniques are developed to serve management. Still, the usefulness of budgeting to very small concerns should not be overlooked. Many deaths (and unwarranted creations) of small businesses could have been circumvented by an early attempt to quantify the dreams of headstrong but sloppy-thinking entrepreneurs who never directly faced the uncertainties of their venture.

For example, a small business with lofty hopes moved into a lush market for school equipment. However, failure to quantify the long collection periods, to forecast a maximum sales potential, and to control costs from the outset resulted in disaster within a year. Budgets for small businesses need not be as elaborate as those outlined in budgeting textbooks, but some budgeting is useful to an enterprise of any size. In fact, many companies have implicit budgets without even realizing their existence; that is, every manager considers the future as decisions are being made.

Many managers claim that the uncertainties peculiar to their business make budgets impractical for them. Yet one can nearly always find at least some companies in the same industry that use budgets. Such companies are usually among the industry leaders, and they regard budgets as indispensable aids. The point is that managers must grapple with uncertainties, either with a budget or without one. The advocates of budgeting maintain that the benefits from budgeting nearly always exceed the costs. Some budget program, at least, will be helpful in almost every organization.

Advantages of budgets

Budgets are a major feature of most control systems. When administered intelligently, budgets (a) compel planning, (b) provide performance criteria, and (c) promote communication and coordination.

compelled planning

"Plan ahead" is a redundant watchword for business managers and for any individual as well. Yet too often, everyday problems interfere with such planning; operations drift along until the passage of time catches the firms or individuals in undesirable situations that should have been anticipated and avoided.

Budgets formulate expected performance; they express managerial targets. Without such targets, operations lack direction, problems are not foreseen, results lack meaning, and the implications for future policies are dwarfed by the pressure of the present. The planning role of all levels of management should be accentuated and enlarged by a budgetary system. Managers will be compelled to look ahead and will be ready for changing conditions. **This forced planning is by far the greatest contribution of budgeting to management.**

Budgets have direct or indirect influence on strategies. *Strategies* are the relatively general and permanent plans that change as conditions or objectives change—for example, when new products are added, old products are dropped, organizations are revamped, or production methods are changed. Budgets affect the formulation of overall organization strategies and then help to implement such strategies. Thus, strategic planning (long-range planning) is often affected either directly by budgetary information or indirectly by the thinking that has evolved from dealing with budgets. According to *Business Week* (February 19, 1979, p. 55), Boise Cascade Corporation uses detailed planning in many ways: "Five-year and ten-year blueprints, 'comprehensive business review,' 'key budgets,' and elaborate income and expense projections are the starting point for the strategic discussions at Boise headquarters."

framework for judging performance

Despite the existence of complex computers and automation, individuals still run organizations, from the president down to the supervisor of the smallest department. Employees do not like to fumble along not really knowing what their superiors anticipate or to see such expectations vary with, for example, the conditions of the superior's sinus trouble. The budget helps meet this difficulty by letting employees know what is expected of them.

As a basis for judging actual results, budgeted performance is generally viewed as being a better criterion than past performance. The fact that sales are better than last year's, or that direct-labor costs are lower than last year's, may be encouraging—but it is by no means conclusive as a measure of success. For example, the news that a company sold 100,000 units this year as compared with 90,000 units in the previous year may not necessarily be greeted with joy. Perhaps sales should have been 112,000 units this year. A major weakness of using historical data for judging performance is that inefficiencies may be buried in the past performance. Furthermore, the usefulness of comparisons with the past may be hampered by intervening changes in technology, personnel, products, competition, and general economic conditions.

communication and coordination

Coordination is the meshing and balancing of all factors of production and of all the departments and functions of the organization so that its objectives are attained—that is, the interests of the individual managers are subordinated for the benefit of the organization as a whole.

The concept of coordination implies, for example, that purchasing officers integrate their plans with production requirements, and that production officers use the sales budget as a basis for planning personnel needs and utilization of machinery.

Budgets help management to coordinate in several ways:

1. The existence of a well-laid plan is the major step toward achieving coordination. Executives are forced to think of the relationships among individual operations, and the company as a whole.
2. Budgets help to restrain the empire-building efforts of executives. Budgets broaden individual thinking by helping to remove unconscious biases on the part of engineers, sales managers, and production officers.
3. Budgets help to search out weaknesses in the organizational structure. The formulation and administration of budgets isolate problems of communication, of fixing responsibility, and of working relationships.

The idea that budgets improve coordination and communication may look promising on paper, but it takes plenty of intelligent administration to achieve in practice. For instance, the use of budgets to judge performance may cause managers to wear blinders and concentrate more than ever on their individual worlds. We shall examine this problem in more detail later in the chapter.

The cost-conscious, cooperative attitudes toward budgetary control must permeate all levels of management. A skeptical top-management attitude will trickle down to the detriment of the entire company. **Top management must understand and enthusiastically support the budget and all aspects of the control system.**

Administration of budgets must not be rigid. Changed conditions call for changes in plans. The budget must receive respect, but it does not have to be so revered that it prevents a manager from taking prudent action. A department head prepares and accepts his budget; he commits himself to the outlined performance. But if matters develop so that some special repairs or a special advertising outlay will best serve the interests of the firm, the manager should feel free to request permission for such outlays, or the budget itself should provide enough flexibility to permit a manager reasonable discretion in deciding how best to get his job done.

Types of budgets

time coverage

Budgets may span a period of one year or less—or, in cases of plant and product changes, up to ten or more years. More and more companies are using budgets as essential tools for long-range planning. The usual planning-and-control budget period is one year. The annual budget is often broken down by months for the first quarter and by quarters for the remainder of the year. The budgeted data for a year are often revised as the year unfolds. For example, at the end of the first quarter, the budget for the next three quarters is changed in light of new information. *Continuous budgets* are increasingly used, whereby a twelve-month forecast is always available by adding a month or quarter in the future as the month or quarter just ended is dropped. Continuous budgets are desirable because they force management constantly to think concretely about the forthcoming twelve months, irrespective of whether the month at hand is May or October. Arizona Public Service Co. has a budget that looks ahead two years but is updated every month. The choice of budget periods largely flows from the objectives, uses, and dependability of the budget data.

classification of budgets

Various descriptive terms for budgets have arisen. Terminology varies among organizations. For example, budgeted financial statements are sometimes called **pro forma statements.** Some organizations, such as Hewlett-Packard, refer to *targeting* rather than budgeting. Indeed, to give a more positive thrust to the entire area, many organizations do not use the term *budget* at all. Instead, they use the term *profit planning.*

There are countless forms of budgets. Many special budgets and related reports are prepared, including

Comparisons of budgets with actual performance (performance reports)

Reports for specific managerial needs—for example, cost-volume-profit projections

Long-term budgets, often called "capital" or "facilities" or "project" budgets (see Chapter 12)

Flexible overhead budget (see Chapter 6)

EXHIBIT 5-1

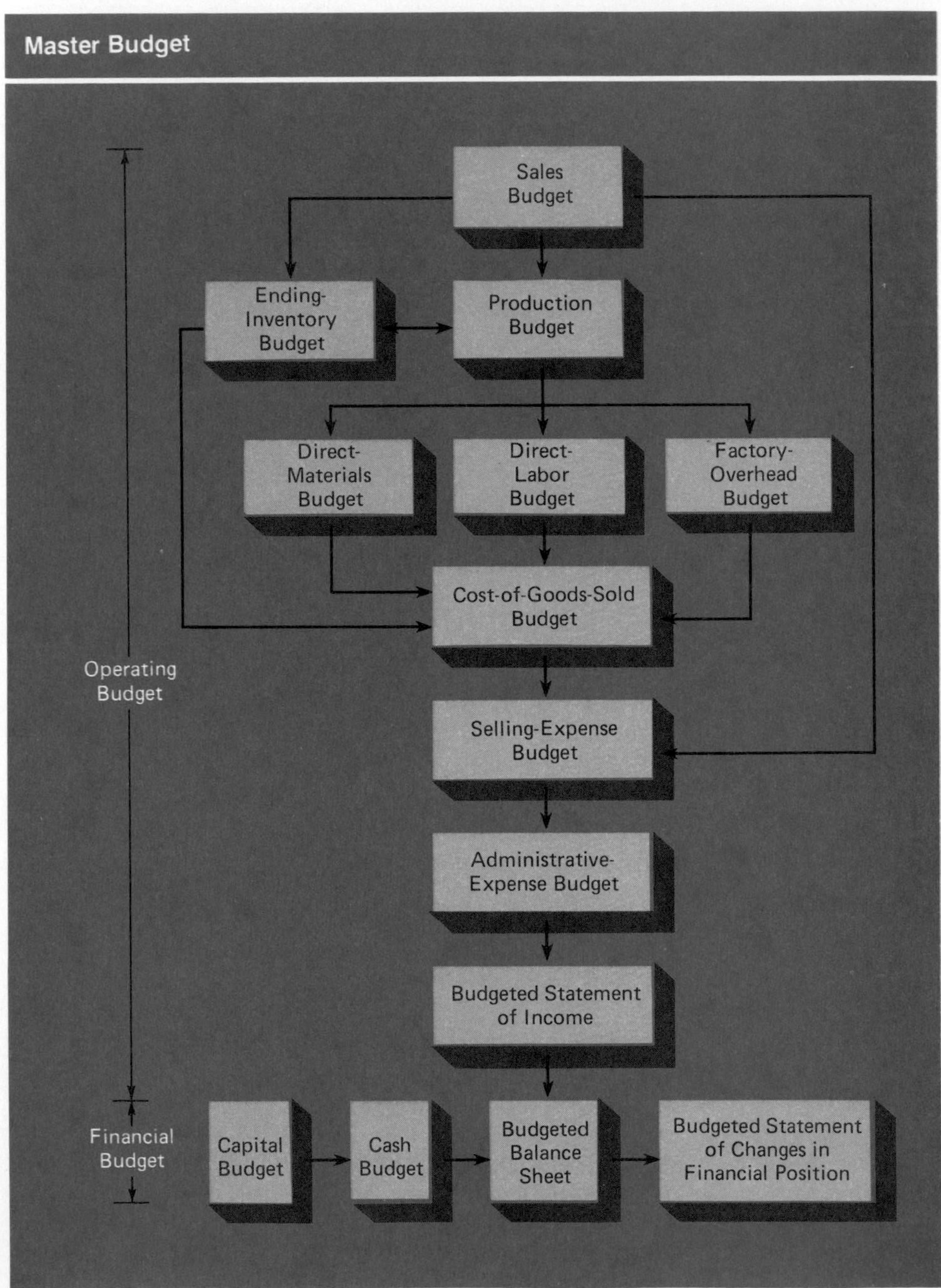

Exhibit 5-1 shows a simplified diagram of the various parts of the *master budget,* the comprehensive plan. As the diagram indicates, many subsidiary budget schedules are necessary in actual practice. The bulk of the diagram presents various elements that together are often called the **operating budget.** They focus on the income statement and its supporting schedules. In contrast, the **financial budget** focuses on the impact on cash of operations and other factors, such as planned capital outlays for equipment.

Illustration of master budget

This illustration is largely mechanical, but remember that the master-budget process generates key top-management decisions regarding pricing, product lines, production scheduling, capital expenditures, research and development, management assignments, and so on. For instance, the first draft of the budget almost always leads to decisions that prompt further drafts before a final budget is chosen.

basic data and requirements

The M Company in Hong Kong uses a normal absorption-costing system. The company is ready to prepare its master budget for the year 19_2. Having carefully examined all relevant factors, the executives expect the following for 19_2:

Direct materials:		
Material 111	$1.20 per kilogram	
Material 112	$2.60 per kilogram	
Direct labor	$2.05 per hour	
Factory overhead is applied on the basis of direct-labor hours.		
	PRODUCT F SPECIAL WIDGETS	PRODUCT G DELUXE WIDGETS
Finished goods:		
(content of each unit)		
Direct material 111	12 kilograms	12 kilograms
Direct material 112	6 kilograms	8 kilograms
Direct labor	14 hours	20 hours

Additional information regarding the year 19_2:

	FINISHED GOODS	
	F	**G**
Expected sales in units	5,000	1,000
Selling price per unit	$ 105.40	$ 164.00
Desired ending inventory in units	1,100	50
Beginning inventory in units	100	50
	DIRECT MATERIALS	
	111	**112**
Beginning inventory in kilograms	5,000	5,000
Desired ending inventory in kilograms	6,000	1,000

(Work in process is negligible and may be ignored.)

At anticipated volume levels, the following costs will be incurred:

Factory overhead:	
Supplies	$ 30,000
Indirect labor	70,000
Payroll fringe costs	25,000
Power—variable portion	8,000
Maintenance—variable portion	20,000
Depreciation	25,000
Property taxes	4,000
Property insurance	500
Supervision	20,000
Power—fixed portion	1,000
Maintenance—fixed portion	4,500
	$208,000
Selling and administrative expenses:	
Sales commissions	$ 20,000
Advertising	3,000
Sales salaries	10,000
Travel	5,000
Clerical wages	10,000
Supplies	1,000
Executive salaries	21,000
Miscellaneous	5,000
	$ 75,000

REQUIRED

Prepare a budgeted income statement (through operating income) for the year 19_2. Include the following detailed schedules:

1. Sales budget
2. Production budget, in units
3. Direct-material-purchases budget
4. Direct-labor budget
5. Factory-overhead budget
6. Ending-inventory budget
7. Cost-of-goods-sold budget
8. Selling and administrative-expense budget

formulating the master budget

The master budget is basically nothing more than the preparation of familiar financial statements. The major difference is in dealing with expected future data rather than with historical data. Therefore, this illustration provides a review of the technical material covered in the previous chapters and culminates with a major part of the master budget, the income statement. Thus, we concentrate on the operating budget. The financial budget, notably the ending balance sheet and the cash budget, is discussed in Appendix 5A.

The basic steps in preparing budgeted statements are presented in conjunction with the specific solution. Try to prepare your own budget schedules, step by step, before looking at the solution. Check each detailed schedule, one by one, before proceeding to the next step.

steps in preparing operating budget

1. **The sales forecast is the starting point for budgeting,** because inventory levels and production (and hence costs) are generally geared to the rate of sales activity.[1] The sales budget (Schedule 1 in the solution) is the result of a series of management decisions reached through a process that is described more fully in a separate section near the end of this chapter.

2. After sales are budgeted, the production budget (Schedule 2) may be prepared. The total units needed will be the sum of the desired ending inventory plus the amount needed to fulfill budgeted sales. The total need will be partially met by the beginning inventory; the remainder must come from planned production. Therefore, production is computed as follows:

$$\begin{pmatrix}\textbf{Units to be}\\ \textbf{produced}\end{pmatrix} = \begin{array}{l}\textbf{Desired ending inventory of finished goods in units}\\ + \textbf{ Budgeted sales in units}\\ - \textbf{ Beginning inventory of finished goods in units}\end{array}$$

Note that the production budget is stated in finished physical units. As the calculation indicates, production is affected by both inventory levels and the sales budget. Frequently, production is stabilized throughout the year despite seasonal fluctuations in sales. Therefore, inventory serves as a coordinating link between manufacturing and sales by providing a cushion that satisfies not only the marketing need for goods when demand is unusually heavy but also a production aim of stable utilization of personnel and facilities.

3. When the level of production activity has been determined, the following budget schedules may be constructed:

a. Direct-material usage and purchases (Schedule 3). Usage will depend upon the level of production activity determined in step 2 above (Note A to Schedule 3). The purchases are influenced by both expected usage and inventory levels. The computation is Purchases in units = Desired ending direct-material inventory quantities + Usage − Beginning inventory quantities.

b. Direct-labor costs (Schedule 4). These depend upon the types of products produced and the labor rates and methods that must be used to obtain desired production.

c. Factory-overhead costs (Schedule 5). These depend upon the behavior of costs of the individual overhead items in relation to the anticipated level of production.

d. Inventory levels (Schedule 6). These are the desired ending inventories. This information is required not only for the production budget and the direct-material purchases budget, but also for the construction of budgeted financial statements.

4. Cost-of-goods-sold budget (Schedule 7). This budget depends upon the information gathered in step 3.

5. Budget of selling, administrative, and other expenses (Schedule 8).

6. Budgeted income statement (Exhibit I). Steps 1 through 5 will provide enough information for this statement.

---

[1]Occasionally, limits to productive capacity result in sales being geared to production rather than vice versa. Examples are shortages of machinery, personnel, or materials because of wars, strikes, or other imbalances in supply and demand.

solution

M Company

Sales Budget
For the Year Ending December 31, 19_2

SCHEDULE 1	UNITS	SELLING PRICE	TOTAL SALES
Product F (special)	5,000	$105.40	$527,000
Product G (deluxe)	1,000	164.00	164,000
Total			$691,000

M Company

Production Budget, In Units*
For the Year Ending December 31, 19_2

	PRODUCTS	
SCHEDULE 2	F	G
Planned sales (Schedule 1)	5,000	1,000
Desired ending finished-goods inventory	1,100	50
Total needs	6,100	1,050
Less beginning finished-goods inventory	100	50
Units to be produced	6,000	1,000

**Work in process is negligible and is ignored.*

M Company

Direct-Material-Purchases Budget
For the Year Ending December 31, 19_2

SCHEDULE 3	MATERIAL 111	MATERIAL 112	TOTAL
Desired ending direct-material inventory in kilograms	6,000	1,000	
Kilograms needed for production (Note A)	84,000	44,000	
Total needs	90,000	45,000	
Less beginning direct-material inventory in kilograms	5,000	5,000	
Kilograms to be purchased	85,000	40,000	
Price per kilogram	$ 1.20	$ 2.60	
Purchase cost	$102,000	$104,000	$206,000

Note A to Schedule 3—Usage of Direct Materials in Kilograms and Dollars

	PRODUCTION				
DIRECT MATERIALS	**product F (6,000 units)**	**product G (1,000 units)**	TOTAL DIRECT-MATERIAL USAGE	MATERIAL PRICE PER KILOGRAM	COST OF DIRECT MATERIALS USED
111 (12 kilograms per finished product)	72,000	12,000	84,000	$1.20	$100,800
112 (6 kilograms per Product F, 8 kilograms per Product G)	36,000	8,000	44,000	2.60	114,400
					$215,200

M Company

Direct-Labor Budget
For the Year Ending December 31, 19_2

SCHEDULE 4	UNITS PRODUCED	DIRECT-LABOR HOURS PER UNIT	TOTAL HOURS	TOTAL BUDGET @ $2.05 PER HOUR
Product F	6,000	14	84,000	$172,200
Product G	1,000	20	20,000	41,000
Total			104.000	$213,200

M Company

Factory-Overhead Budget
For the Year Ending December 31, 19_2

SCHEDULE 5	*At Anticipated Activity of 104,000 Direct-Labor Hours:*	
Supplies	$30,000	
Indirect labor	70,000	
Payroll fringe costs	25,000	
Power—variable portion	8,000	
Maintenance—variable portion	20,000	
Total variable overhead		$153,000
Depreciation	$25,000	
Property taxes	4,000	
Property insurance	500	
Supervision	20,000	
Power—fixed portion	1,000	
Maintenance—fixed portion	4,500	
Total fixed overhead		55,000
Total factory overhead: ($208,000 ÷ 104,000 is $2.00 per direct-labor hour)		$208,000

M Company

Ending-Inventory Budget
December 31, 19_2

SCHEDULE 6	KILOGRAMS	PRICE PER KILOGRAM	TOTAL AMOUNT	
Direct materials:				
111	6,000*	$ 1.20	$ 7,200	
112	1,000*	2.60	2,600	$ 9,800
	UNITS	COST PER UNIT		
Finished goods:				
F	1,100[†]	$ 86.70[‡]	$95,370	
G	50[†]	116.20[‡]	5,810	101,180
Total				$110,980

**From top line in Schedule 3.*
[†]From second line in Schedule 2.
[‡]Computation of unit costs:

	COST PER KILOGRAM OR HOUR OF INPUT	PRODUCT F inputs	PRODUCT F amount	PRODUCT G inputs	PRODUCT G amount
Material 111	$1.20	12	$14.40	12	$ 14.40
Material 112	2.60	6	15.60	8	20.80
Direct labor	2.05	14	28.70	20	41.00
Factory overhead	2.00	14	28.00	20	40.00
Total			$86.70		$116.20

M Company

Cost-of-Goods-Sold Budget
For the Year Ending December 31, 19_2

SCHEDULE 7	FROM SCHEDULE		
Direct materials used	3		$215,200
Direct labor	4		213,200
Factory overhead	5		208,000
Total manufacturing costs			$636,400
Less inventory increase for year			
Finished goods, December 31, 19_1	Given*	$ 14,480	
Finished goods, December 31, 19_2	6	101,180	(86,700)
Cost of goods sold			$549,700

**Given quantities times unit costs from Schedule 6: (100 units F × $86.70) + (50 units G × $116.20)*

M Company

Selling-and-Administrative-Expense Budget
For the Year Ending December 31, 19_2

SCHEDULE 8		
Sales commissions	$20,000	
Advertising	3,000	
Sales salaries	10,000	
Travel	5,000	
Total selling expenses		$38,000
Clerical wages	$10,000	
Supplies	1,000	
Executive salaries	21,000	
Miscellaneous	5,000	
Total administrative expenses		37,000
Total selling and administrative expenses		$75,000

M Company

Budgeted Income Statement
For the Year Ending December 31, 19_2

EXHIBIT I	SOURCE	
Sales	Schedule 1	$691,000
Cost of goods sold	Schedule 7	549,700
Gross margin		$141,300
Selling and administrative expenses	Schedule 8	75,000
Operating income		$ 66,300

Sales forecasting— a difficult task

Incurrence of cost is necessarily keyed to production activity. Activity, in turn, depends on predicted sales. The sales prediction is the foundation for the quantification of the entire business plan.[2]

factors in sales forecasting

The chief sales officer has direct responsibility for the preparation of the sales budget. The task of preparation forces the crystallization of plans.

The sales forecast is made after consideration of the following factors:

1. Past sales volume
2. General economic and industry conditions
3. Relationship of sales to economic indicators such as gross national product, personal income, employment, prices, and industrial production
4. Relative product profitability
5. Market research studies
6. Pricing policies
7. Advertising and other promotion
8. Quality of sales force
9. Competition
10. Seasonal variations
11. Production capacity
12. Long-term sales trends for various products

forecasting procedures

An effective aid to accurate forecasting is to approach the same goal by several methods; each forecast acts as a check on the others. The three methods described below are usually combined in some fashion that is suitable for a specific company.

SALES STAFF PROCEDURES ☐ As is the case for all budgets, those responsible should have an active role in sales-budget formulation. If possible, the budget data should flow from individual sales personnel or district sales managers upward to the chief sales officer. A valuable benefit from the budgeting process is the holding of discussions, which generally result in adjustments and which tend to broaden participants' thinking.

Previous sales volumes are usually the springboard for sales predictions. Sales executives examine historical sales behavior and relate it to other historical data such as economic indicators, advertising, pricing policies, and competitive conditions. Current information is assembled, production capacity is considered, and then the outlook is derived for the ensuing months (years, in long-run sales budgets).

One of the common difficulties in budgeting sales is the widespread aversion of sales executives to figures. The usefulness of budgeting must be sold to sales personnel. The best sales executives may not particularly enjoy working with figures, but they realize that intelligent decisions cannot be made without concrete information. Market research is a sales executive's tool that helps to eliminate hunches and guessing. The market research group is a major staff department in many corporations.

---

[2]The term *sales forecast* is sometimes distinguished from *sales budget* as follows: The forecast is the estimate—the prediction—that may or may not become the sales budget. The forecast becomes the budget only if management accepts it as an objective. Often, the forecast leads to adjustments of managerial plans, so that the final sales budget differs from the original sales forecast.

STATISTICAL APPROACHES □ Trend, cycle projection, and correlation analysis are useful supplementary techniques. Correlations between sales and economic indicators help make sales forecasts more reliable, especially if fluctuations in certain economic indicators precede fluctuations in company sales. However, no firm should rely entirely on this approach. Too much reliance on statistical evidence is dangerous because chance variations in statistical data may completely upset a program. As always, statistical analysis can provide help but not outright answers.

GROUP EXECUTIVE JUDGMENT □ All top officers, including production, purchasing, finance, and administrative officers, may use their experience and knowledge to project sales on the basis of group opinion. This quick method dispenses with intricate statistical accumulations; however, it muddles responsibility for sales predictions and ignores the need for a tough-minded approach to this important task.

It is beyond the scope of this book to give a detailed description of all phases of sales-budget preparation, but its key importance should be kept in mind. The "Suggested Readings" at the end of this chapter list some references on sales forecasting.

Planning models

A master budget can be regarded as a comprehensive planning model for the organization. As the budget is formulated, it is frequently altered via a step-by-step process as executives exchange views on miscellaneous aspects of expected activities and ask "what-if" questions. Such alterations are cumbersome by hand, but they are facilitated by the computer.

Computer-based **financial planning models** often use the master budget as their structural base. They are mathematical statements of the relationships among all operating and financial activities, as well as other major internal and external factors that may affect decisions.[3] The models are used for budgeting, for revising budgets with little incremental effort, for conducting "what-if?" analysis, and for comparing a variety of decision alternatives as they affect the entire organization. Examples include Ralston Purina Co., where a 1 percent change in the price of a prime commodity causes a change in company's cost models and a possible change in the whole corporate plan. At Dow Chemical Co., 140 separate cost inputs, constantly revised, are fed into the model. Such factors as major raw-material costs and prices by country and region are monitored weekly. Multiple contingency plans, rather than a single, master plan, are used more widely than before.

Computer models have various degrees of sophistication and usefulness, depending on how much an organization is willing to pay.[4] Rudimentary general-purpose models can be rented from consultants or software firms. These usually entail gathering specific firm data as input; the output consists of the conventional financial statements and supporting schedules. At the other extreme, management can have a special-purpose model designed that includes interactive capabilities, integrates de-

[3]See Thomas J. Gorman, "Corporate Financial Models in Planning and Control," *Price Waterhouse Review,* XV, No. 2, 41–53. Also see "'What If' Help for Management," *Business Week,* January 21, 1980.

[4]George W. Gershefski, "Building a Corporate Financial Model," *Harvard Business Review,* 47, No. 4, 61–72. Also see R. C. Murphy, "A Computer Model Approach to Budgeting," *Management Accounting,* LVI, No. 12, 34–38.

tailed activities of all subunits of an organization, encompasses internal and external data, and permits probabilistic analyses.

As in all aspects of systems design, cost-benefit approaches must be applied in deciding whether to use computer-based models. Some benefits were enumerated above, and the costs of using general-purpose models continue to decline. For example, some credit departments of banks now find it worthwhile to use a general-purpose model to monitor the progress of their borrowers. The borrowers' data are the input, which is updated periodically. The prospects of more widespread use of simple general-purpose models are excellent, but the costs of complex models are still too imposing to warrant predictions of their rapid adoption. Most corporations concentrate their attention on the eight to twelve variables most crucial to their industry—rate of inflation, consumer spending on nondurables, interest rates, and so on.

Responsibility accounting

This section emphasizes that management is essentially a human activity and that budgets exist, not for their own sake, but to help managers.

Managers supervise subordinates. To improve performance, top managers subdivide operating processes. Top managers also design an **organization structure,** which can be defined as an arrangement of lines of responsibility within an entity. For example, one company may be organized primarily by business functions, such as manufacturing and marketing. Another company, such as General Foods, may be organized by product lines. If so, the managers of the individual coffee and cereal divisions would each have decision-making authority concerning both the manufacturing and the marketing functions of their divisions.

The organization structure is typically hierarchical. Each manager is expected to oversee a sphere of responsibiity and ordinarily has some degree of latitude to make decisions within that sphere. The sphere of responsibility usually bears one of three basic labels:

1. **Cost center**—formal reporting of costs only
2. **Profit center**—formal reporting of revenues and costs
3. **Investment center**—formal reporting of revenues, costs, and investment

definition of responsibility accounting

As a minimum, **responsibility accounting, profitability accounting,** or **activity accounting** systems recognize various decision centers throughout an organization and trace costs (and revenues, assets, and liabilities, where pertinent) to the individual managers who are primarily responsible for making decisions about the costs in question.

The impact of the responsibility accounting approach is described in the following:

> The sales department requests a rush production. The plant scheduler argues that it will disrupt his production and cost a substantial though not clearly determined amount of money. The answer coming from sales is: "Do you want to take the responsibility of losing the X Company as a customer?" Of course the production scheduler does not want to take such a responsibility, and he gives up, but not before a heavy exchange of arguments and the accumulation of a substantial backlog of ill feeling. Analysis of the payroll in the assembly department, determining the costs involved in getting out rush orders, eliminated the cause for argument. Henceforth, any rush order was accepted with a smile by the production scheduler, who made sure that the extra cost would be duly recorded and charged to the sales department—"no questions asked."

> As a result, the tension created by rush orders disappeared completely; and, somehow, the number of rush orders requested by the sales department was progressively reduced to an insignificant level.[5]

Ideally, revenues and costs are recorded and automatically traced to the individual at the lowest level of the organization who shoulders primary day-to-day decision responsibility for the item. He or she is in the best position to evaluate and to influence a situation—to implement decisions.

Note the philosophy implied in the above quotation. Top management has delegated the freedom to make decisions to a lower level. Instead of having to check with somebody before accepting a rush order, the manager has full discretion. Thus, the manager is not subject to day-to-day monitoring of his or her behavior (decisions). However, the manager is accountable for the results via responsibility accounting. So responsibility accounting is a mechanism that supplies the desired balance to the greater freedom of action that individual executives are given.

illustration of responsibility accounting

The simplified organization chart in Exhibit 5-2 will be the basis for our illustration. We will concentrate on the manufacturing phase of the business. The lines of responsibility are easily seen in Exhibit 5-3, which is an overall view of responsibility reporting. Starting with the supervisor of the machining department, George Phelan, and working toward the top, we shall see how these reports may be integrated through three levels of responsibility.

Note that each of three responsibility reports furnishes the department head with figures on only those items subject to his control. Items not subject to his control are removed from these performance reports; he should not receive data that may clutter and confuse his decision making. For example, a fixed cost such as depreciation on the factory building is excluded.

Trace the $72,000 total from the machining department report in Exhibit 5-3 to the production vice-president's report. The vice-president's report merely summarizes the reports of the three individuals under her jurisdiction. She may also want copies of the detailed statements of each supervisor responsible to her.

Also trace the $116,000 total from the production vice-president's report to the report of Dudley Curry, the president. Curry's summary report includes data for his own office plus a summarization of the entire company's current cost-control performance.

format of feedback reports

This set of illustrative reports shows only the budgeted amount and the variance, which is defined as the difference between the budgeted and the actual amounts. This places the focus on the variances and illustrates *management by exception,* which means that the executive's attention is concentrated on the important deviations from budgeted items. In this way, managers do not waste time on those parts of the reports that reflect the smoothly running phases of operations.

---

[5]Raymond Villers "Control and Freedom in a Decentralized Company," *Harvard Business Review,* XXXII, No. 2, 95. Another example is National City Bank's responsibility accounting system for a check-processing department. On any given day, for every $1 million that is not delivered to the Federal Reserve Bank on time, the department is "fined" $167, the amount the parent company loses in potential interest. See *Wall Street Journal,* June 6, 1975, p. 17.

EXHIBIT 5-2

Curry Co.: Simplified Organization Chart

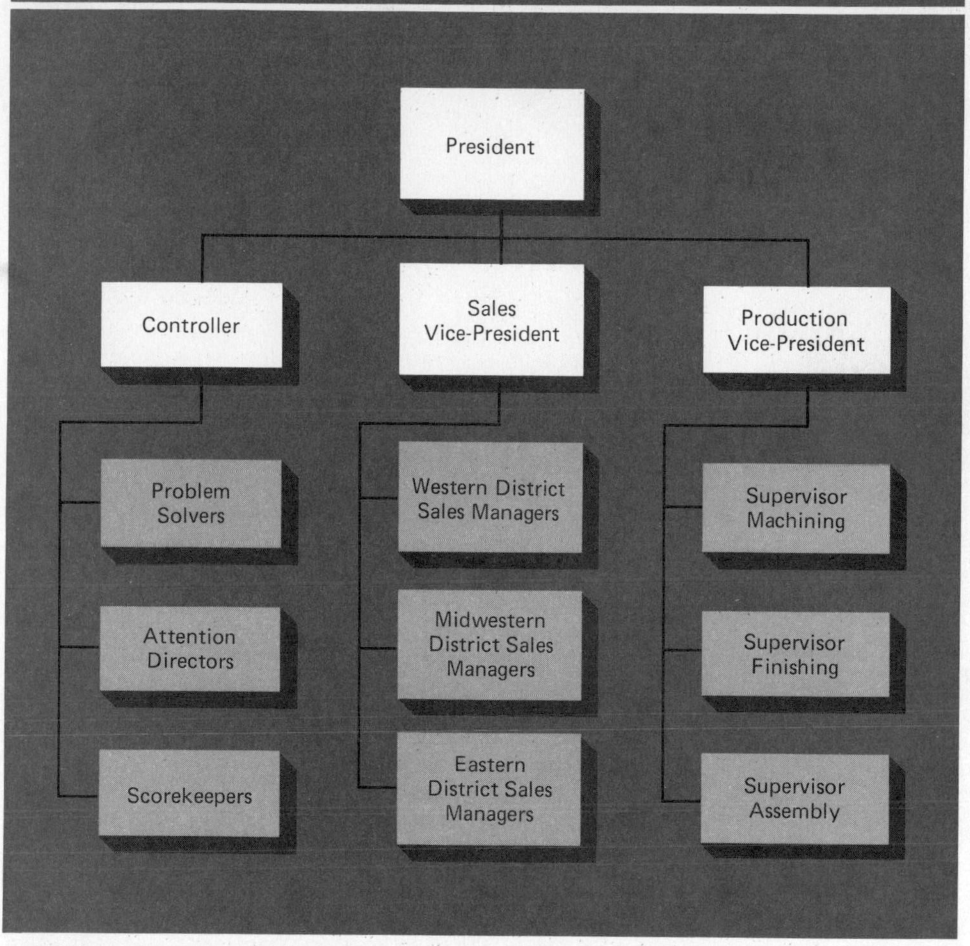

Exhibit 5-3 on page 146 is only one possible means of presenting a report of performance. Another common reporting method shows three sets of dollar figures instead of two sets. Moreover, the variances could also be expressed in terms of percentages of budgeted amounts. For example, direct labor in the machining department could appear as follows:

	BUDGET		ACTUAL RESULTS		VARIANCE: FAVORABLE, (UNFAVORABLE)		VARIANCE: PERCENT OF BUDGETED AMOUNT	
	this month	year to date	this month	year to date	this month	year to date	this month	year to date
Direct labor	$25,000	$75,000	$27,000	$82,000	$(2,000)	$(7,000)	(8.0%)	(9.4%)

The full performance report would contain a similar line-by-line analysis of all items. The exact format adopted in a particular organization depends heavily on user preferences.

EXHIBIT 5-3

Curry Co.

President's Monthly Responsibility Performance Report	BUDGET		VARIANCE: FAVORABLE, (UNFAVORABLE)	
	this month	**year to date**	**this month**	**year to date**
President's office	$ 6,000	$ 20,000	$ 100	$ 400
Controller	4,000	13,000	(200)	(1,000)
Production vice-president	116,000	377,000	(8,950)	(20,600)
Sales vice-president	40,000	130,000	(1,000)	(4,000)
Total controllable costs	$166,000	$540,000	$(10,050)	$(25,200)

Production Vice-President's Monthly Responsibility Performance Report	BUDGET		VARIANCE: FAVORABLE, (UNFAVORABLE)	
	this month	**year to date**	**this month**	**year to date**
Vice-president's office	$ 9,000	$ 29,000	$ (1,000)	$ (1,000)
Machining department	72,000	236,000	(2,950)	(11,600)
Finishing department	15,000	50,000	(2,000)	(3,000)
Assembly department	20,000	62,000	(3,000)	(5,000)
Total controllable costs	$116,000	$377,000	$ (8,950)	$(20,600)

*Machining Department Supervisor's Monthly Responsibility Performance Report**	BUDGET		VARIANCE: FAVORABLE, (UNFAVORABLE)	
	this month	**year to date**	**this month**	**year to date**
Direct materials	$ 40,000	$140,000	$ (1,000)	$ (4,000)
Direct labor	25,000	75,000	(2,000)	(7,000)
Setup	4,000	12,000	400	100
Rework	2,000	6,000	(200)	(300)
Supplies	200	600	(40)	(100)
Small tools	300	900	(50)	(100)
Other	500	1,500	(60)	(200)
Total controllable costs	$ 72,000	$236,000	$ (2,950)	$(11,600)

**He receives an itemized report of his performance. Totals are carried to the report of his immediate superior, whose results are, in turn, reported upward.*

feedback and fixing blame

Budgets coupled with responsibility accounting provide systematic help for managers, particularly if the feedback is interpreted carefully. **Discussions among managers, accountants, and students have repeatedly disclosed a tendency to "fix the blame"—as if the variance arising from a responsibility accounting system should pinpoint misbehavior and provide answers.** However, no accounting system or variances can provide answers, ipso facto. But variances can suggest questions about possible causes of the variances or can direct attention to persons who should be asked to explain the variances. **In associating costs or variances with individuals, we should inquire *who should be asked* in a specific situation—*not* who should be blamed.**

human aspect Budgeting is too often looked upon from a purely mechanistic viewpoint. The human factors in budgeting are more important than the accounting techniques. The success of a budgetary system depends upon its acceptance by the company members who are affected by the budgets.

Budgets place managers in the spotlight. The natural reaction to restriction, to criticism, and to control is resistance and self-defense. *The job of education and selling is overwhelmingly important here.* Too many department heads think that budgets represent a penny-pinching, negative brand of managerial pressure.[6] To them, the word *budget* is about as popular as, say, *layoff, strike,* or *pay decrease.* Ideally, company personnel should understand and accept the role of budgets as positive vehicles for company improvement, department improvement, and individual improvement. The budget is not a heinous means of squeezing the last drop of sweat out of employees. Properly used, it is simply a systematic tool for establishing standards of performance, for providing motivation, for gauging results, and for helping management advance toward its objectives. The budget technique in itself is free of emotion; its administration, however, is often packed with trouble. The budget's major role is to communicate the various motivations that basically already exist among the management personnel, so that everybody sees, understands, and coordinates the goals, means, and drives of the organization.

The importance of these human aspects cannot be overemphasized. Without a thoroughly educated and cooperative management group at all levels of responsibility, budgets are a drain on the funds of the business and are a hindrance instead of a help to efficient operations. A budgetary program per se is not a remedy for weak managerial talent, faulty organization, or a poor information system.

Responsibility and controllability

definition of controllability Responsibility accounting is often focused primarily on the lowest-level managers who have the most day-to-day influence on the operations in question. These managers, however, frequently complain about this situation as follows: "It is unfair to allocate revenues or costs to me unless I can control them," or "There should be no responsibility without control."

Controllable costs are those that are definitely influenced by a *given manager* within a *given time span.* A major problem with this definition is that few costs are clearly under the sole influence of one person. For example, *prices* of direct materials may be heavily influenced by the purchasing manager, while *quantities* may be heavily influenced by the production manager.

Another major problem is the time period. With enough time, virtually all costs will be controllable by somebody in the organization. As the time period shortens, fewer and fewer costs can be considered controllable. For example, the cost of a one-year insurance policy may be controllable by the insurance manager. But it might not be deemed controllable if the time period were a week or a month.

Beware of overemphasis on controllability. Responsibility accounting is more far-reaching. The basic focus should be on *knowledge* or *information,* not control. The key question is, Who is the best informed? Put another way: Who is the one person in the organization who can tell us the most about the specific item, regardless of his or her ability to exert personal control? For instance, responsibility for the prices and total

[6]Pressure, in varying amounts, is a part of almost every job responsibility. Used with care, pressure motivates toward goals and is thus desirable. However, the word *pressure* has unpleasant connotations and usually indicates unreasonable, unbearable stress.

costs of various drugs may be assigned to the manager of the purchasing department of a hospital because, while the manager has minimal influence over prices and quantities, he is usually in the best position to predict prices and to explain any deviations from budget.

importance of budget and MBO

The message given to managers is frequently *not* to *maximize* a single measure such as operating income. Instead, the message is to *attain* a *budgeted* operating income of, say, $1 million, subject to simultaneously achieving additional goals such as a target share of a market. Budgets can be enormously helpful, versatile tools.

Intelligent budgeting can overcome many of the problems of human behavior that are inherent in commonly used performance measures such as income or return on investment. For example, many organizations have successfully used some form of *management by objectives* (MBO). Under this procedure a subordinate and his or her superior jointly formulate the subordinate's set of goals and plans for attaining those goals for a subsequent period. For our purposes, *goals* and *objectives* are synonymous.

The plans are frequently crystallized in a responsibility accounting budget. In addition, various subgoals may be measured, such as levels of product innovation, share of the market, and management training. The subordinate's performance is then evaluated in relation to these agreed-upon budgeted goals.

controllability and risks

A favorite theme in the management accounting literature is that a manager's performance should be judged on the basis of controllable items only. Unfortunately, managers live in an uncertain, interdependent world; controllability is difficult to pinpoint. **Managers are expected to take risks even though they have limited control over many outcomes.**[7]

In sum, distinctions between controllable and uncontrollable items should be made whenever feasible. However, financial responsibility may be assigned to managers even though controllability may be minimal. The final test is what behavior will be sparked by the measurement system. Put another way:

1. What do you want a profit center manager to worry about? (he can't pay attention to costs that are not assigned) and
2. How much do you want him to worry? (the method of cost assignment may give him more or less direct control over the amount of costs charged to him)[8]

An MBO approach can help overcome the problems and complaints regarding risk responsibility and lack of control. The focus is on *budgeted results,* given the degree of risks. That is, a budget for a subordinate is negotiated between the subordinate and his or her superior for a *specific* time period and a *specific* set of expected inside and outside influences, even though many of these influences may be beyond the subordinate's direct control.

The wise use of budgets can provide more credibility to the management control system. Budgets are often preferable to a system that emphasizes maximizing some profitability measure for its own sake. Managers may be more willing to under-

---

[7]Also see Appendix 20B. For additional discussion, see J. Demski, *Information Analysis,* 2nd ed. (Reading, Mass.: Addison-Wesley, 1980), Chap. 6. Also see R. Kaplan, *Advanced Management Accounting* (Englewood Cliffs, N.J.: Prentice-Hall, 1982), Chaps. 16 and 17.

[8]R. Vancil, *Decentralization: Managerial Ambiguity by Design* (New York: Financial Executives Research Foundation, 1979), p. 21.

take risks. For instance, a manager may more readily accept an assignment to a less-successful subunit. Unless focus is placed on currently attainable results, able managers are less likely to accept responsibility for weak subunits.

SUMMARY

Comprehensive budgeting is the expression of management's master operating and financing plan—the formalized outlining of company objectives and their means of attainment. When administered wisely, budgets (a) compel management planning, (b) provide definite expectations that are the best framework for judging subsequent performance, and (c) promote communication and coordination among the various segments of the business.

The foundation for budgeting is the sales forecast. Inventory, production, and cost incurrence are generally geared to the rate of sales activity.

Responsibility accounting systems identify various decision centers and trace financial data to the individual managers who are primarily responsible for the data in question.

A budgeting system includes performance evaluation, which usually compares the planned data with the actual results. More will be said about budgeting systems in succeeding chapters.

SUGGESTED READINGS

CONFERENCE BOARD, **Sales Forecasting.** New York: Conference Board, 1978.

EBY, FRANK H., JR., and WILLIAM J. O'NEILL, **The Management of Sales Forecasting.** Lexington, Mass.: Heath, 1977.

WELSCH, G., **Budgeting: Profit Planning and Control,** 4th ed. Englewood Cliffs, N.J.: Prentice-Hall, 1976.

WHEELWRIGHT, STEVEN C., and SPYROS MAKRIDAKIS, **Forecasting Methods for Management,** 3rd ed. New York: Wiley-Interscience, 1980.

PROBLEM FOR SELF-STUDY

Before trying to solve the homework problems, review the illustrations in this chapter.

Terms to Learn

The chapter and the Glossary contain definitions of the following important terms:

activity accounting ***cash budget*** ***cash cycle***
comprehensive budget ***cost center*** ***financial budget***
financial planning model ***investment center*** ***master budget***
operating budget ***organization structure*** ***profitability accounting***
profit center ***pro forma statements*** ***responsibility accounting***
self-liquidating cycle ***working-capital cycle***

Special Points and Pitfalls

This chapter began with a section on the evolution of control systems. Ponder the steps:

1. Physical observation
2. Historical records
3. Budgets

Budgeting systems are costly. They are bought because managers believe that the systems will help subordinates make better collective operating decisions.

Students are frequently overwhelmed by the variety of data required for preparing a master budget. The prediction of sales is almost always the best place to begin.

Because budgeting is loaded with technical trappings, accountants often forget the human aspects. The budget is usually a major tool for judging actual performance. Hence, it often has an enormous influence on managers' behavior.

Some organizations mistakenly tend to use budgets and performance reports to pinpoint blame. The important question is who should be asked, *not* who should be blamed.

Appendix 5a: the cash budget

The major illustration in the chapter featured the operating budget. The other major part of the master budget is the financial budget, which includes the capital budget, cash budget, ending balance sheet, and statement of changes in financial position. This Appendix focuses on the cash budget and the ending balance sheet. Capital budgeting is covered in Chapter 12; coverage of the statement of changes in financial position is beyond the scope of this book.

problem

The balance sheet for the year just ended is as follows:

M Company

Balance Sheet
December 31, 19_1

ASSETS		
Current assets:		
Cash	$ 10,000	
Accounts receivable	25,000	
Direct materials	19,000	
Finished goods	14,480	
		$ 68,480
Fixed assets:		
Land	$ 50,000	
Building and equipment	380,000	
Accumulated depreciation	(75,000)	355,000
Total assets		$423,480
EQUITIES		
Current liabilities:		
Accounts payable	$ 8,200	
Income taxes payable	5,000	$ 13,200
Stockholders' equity:		
Common stock, no-par—25,000 shares outstanding	$350,000	
Retained income	60,280	410,280
Total equities		$423,480

Budgeted cash flows are:

	QUARTERS			
	1	2	3	4
Collections from customers	$125,000	$150,000	$160,000	$221,000
Disbursements:				
For direct materials	20,000	35,000	35,000	54,200
For other costs and expenses	25,000	20,000	20,000	17,000
For payroll	90,000	95,000	95,000	109,200
For income taxes	5,000	—	—	—
For machinery purchase	—	—	—	20,000

(The quarterly data are given for convenience. The figures are based on the cash effects of the operations formulated in Schedules 1 through 8 in the solution.)

The company desires to maintain a $15,000 minimum cash balance at the end of each quarter. Money can be borrowed or repaid in multiples of $500 at an interest rate of 10 percent per annum. Management does not want to borrow any more cash than is necessary and wants to repay as promptly as possible. In any event, loans may not extend beyond four quarters. Interest is computed and paid when the principal is repaid. Assume that borrowings take place at the beginning and repayments at the end of the quarters in question. Compute interest to the nearest dollar.

Use the above data and the other data contained in the solution in the chapter (pages 138–40). Try to solve this problem on your own. As you proceed, you may wish to check your work, step by step, against the solution that follows.

REQUIRED

1. Prepare a cash budget. That is, prepare a statement of cash receipts and disbursements by quarters, including details of borrowings, repayments, and interest.
2. Prepare a budgeted balance sheet.
3. Prepare a budgeted income statement, including the effects of interest expense and assumed income taxes for 19_2 of $20,000.

solution

1. The cash budget (Exhibit II) predicts the effects on cash position of the levels of operation above. The illustrative cash budget is presented by quarters to show the impact of cash-flow timing on bank loan schedules. In practice, monthly—and sometimes weekly—cash budgets are very helpful for cash planning and control. Cash budgets aid in avoiding unnecessary idle cash and unnecessary cash deficiencies. The astute mapping of a financing program keeps cash balances in reasonable relation to needs. Ordinarily, the cash budget has the following main sections:

a. The beginning cash balance plus cash receipts yields the total cash available for needs, before financing. Cash receipts depend on collections of accounts receivable, cash sales, and miscellaneous recurring sources such as rental or royalty receipts. Studies of the prospective collectibility of accounts receivable are needed for accurate predictions. Key factors include bad-debt experience and average time lag between sales and collections.

b. Cash disbursements:

(1) Direct-material purchases—depends on credit terms extended by suppliers and bill-paying habits of the buyer.

(2) Direct labor and other wage outlays—depends on payroll dates.

(3) Other costs and expenses—depends on timing and credit terms. **Note that depreciation does not entail a cash outlay.**

(4) Other disbursements—outlays for fixed assets, long-term investments.

c. Financing requirements depend on how the total cash available for needs, keyed as (a) in Exhibit II, compares with the total cash needed. Needs include disbursements, keyed as (b), plus the ending cash balance desired, keyed as (d). The financing plans will depend on the relationship of cash available to cash required. If there is an excess, loans may be repaid or temporary investments made. The pertinent outlays for interest expenses are usually shown in this section of the cash budget.

d. The ending cash balance. The effect of the financing decisions on the cash budget, keyed as (c) in Exhibit II, may be positive (borrowing) or negative (repayment), and the ending cash balance, (d), equals (a) + (c) − (b).

The cash budget in Exhibit II shows the pattern of short-term "self-liquidating cash loans." Seasonal peaks of production or sales often result in heavy cash disbursements for purchases, payroll, and other operating outlays as the products are produced and sold. Cash receipts from customers typically lag behind sales. The loan is **self-liquidating** in the sense that the borrowed money is used to acquire resources that are combined for sale, and the proceeds from the sale are used to repay the loan. This cycle (sometimes called the **working-capital, cash,** or **operating cycle**) moves from cash to inventories to receivables and back to cash.

Cash budgets help managers avoid having unnecessary idle cash, on the one hand, and unnecessary nerve-racking cash deficiences on the other.

2. Budgeted balance sheet (Exhibit III). Each item is projected in the light of the details of the business plan as expressed in the previous schedules. For example, the ending balance of Accounts Receivable would be computed by adding the budgeted sales (from Schedule 1) to the beginning balance (given) and subtracting cash receipts (given and in Exhibit II).
3. The budgeted income statement is in Exhibit IV. It is merely the income statement in Exhibit I page 140, but now includes interest and income taxes.

M Company

Budgeted Statement of Cash Receipts and Disbursements
For the Year Ending December 31, 19_2

EXHIBIT II	QUARTERS				FOR THE YEAR AS A WHOLE
	1	2	3	4	
Cash balance, beginning	10,000	$ 15,000	$ 15,000	$ 15,325	$ 10,000
Add receipts:					
Collections from customers	125,000	150,000	160,000	221,000	656,000
(a) Total available before current financing	$135,000	$165,000	$175,000	$236,325	$666,000
Less disbursements:					
For direct materials	$ 20,000	$ 35,000	$ 35,000	$ 54,200	$144,200
For other costs and expenses	25,000	20,000	20,000	17,000	82,000
For payroll	90,000	95,000	95,000	109,200	389,200
For income taxes	5,000	—	—	—	5,000
For machinery purchase	—	—	—	20,000	20,000
(b) Total disbursements	$140,000	$150,000	$150,000	$200,400	$640,400
Minimum cash balance desired	15,000	15,000	15,000	15,000	15,000
Total cash needed	$155,000	$165,000	$165,000	$215,400	$655,400
Excess of total cash available over total cash needed before current financing (deficiency)	$ (20,000)	$ —	$ 10,000	$ 20,925	$ 10,600
Financing:					
Borrowings (at beginning)	$ 20,000	$ —	$ —	$ —	$ 20,000
Repayments (at end)	—	—	(9,000)	(11,000)	(20,000)
*Interest (at 10% per annum)	—	—	(675)	(1,100)	(1,775)
(c) Total effects of financing	$ 20,000	$ —	$ (9,675)	$ (12,100)	$ (1,775)
(d) Cash balance, end (a + c − b)	$ 15,000	$ 15,000	$ 15,325	$ 23,825	$ 23,825

**The interest payments pertain only to the amount of principal being repaid at the end of a given quarter. Note that the remainder of the $20,000 loan must be repaid by the end of the fourth quarter. Also note that depreciation does not necessitate a cash outlay. The specific computations regarding interest are: $9,000 × .10 × 3/4 = $675 and $11,000 × .10 = $1,100.*

M Company

Budgeted Balance Sheet
December 31, 19_2

EXHIBIT III	ASSETS		
Current assets:			
Cash (from Exhibit II)		$ 23,825	
Accounts receivable (1)		60,000	
Direct materials (2)		9,800	
Finished goods (2)		101,180	$194,805
Fixed assets:			
Land (3)		$ 50,000	
Building and equipment (4)	$400,000		
Accumulated depreciation (5)	100,000	300,000	350,000
Total assets			$544,805
	EQUITIES		
Current liabilities:			
Accounts payable (6)		$ 70,000	
Income taxes payable (7)		20,000	90,000
Stockholders' equity:			
Common stock, no-par, 25,000 shares outstanding (8)		$350,000	
Retained income (9)		104,805	454,805
Total equities			$544,805

Notes:

Beginning balances are used as a start for most of the following computations:

(1) $25,000 + $691,000 sales − $656,000 receipts = $60,000.
(2) From Schedule 6.
(3) From beginning balance sheet.
(4) $380,000 + $20,000 purchases.
(5) $75,000 + $25,000 depreciation.
(6) $8,200 + ($206,000 direct-materials purchases, $213,200 direct labor, $183,000 factory overhead, $75,000 selling and administrative expenses) − ($144,200 direct materials, $82,000 other costs and expenses, and $389,200 payroll) = $70,000.*
(7) $5,000 + $20,000 current year − $5,000 payment.
(8) From beginning balance sheet.
(9) $60,280 + $44,525 net income.

**$208,000 from Schedule 5 minus depreciation of $25,000.*

M Company

Budgeted Income Statement
For the Year Ending December 31, 19_2

EXHIBIT IV	SOURCE	
Sales	Schedule 1	$691,000
Cost of goods sold	Schedule 7	549,700
Gross margin		$141,300
Selling and administrative expenses	Schedule 8	75,000
Operating income		$ 66,300
Interest expense	Exhibit II	1,775
Income before income taxes		$ 64,525
Income taxes	Assumed	20,000
Net income		$ 44,525

Appendix 5b: installing and administering the budget

The accounting system and the budgetary system should be synchronized with the organizational structure. Although budgets may be used for *planning* without being integrated with the accounting system, they may rarely be used for comprehensive *control* without being so integrated. Progressive firms link a budget with an accounting

budgeting and the accounting system

system that accumulates homogeneous information from the lowest levels of responsibility to the highest. Thus, careful attention should be given to the overall design of the budget system, and its operation should always be strongly supported by top management.

budget director

Although line management has the ultimate responsibility for the preparation of individual budgets, there is also an evident need for technical, unbiased help and overall responsibility for the budget program. This need is usually satisfied by assigning responsibility to a budget director for establishing preparatory procedures, designing forms, *effective educating and selling,* collecting and coordinating data, verifying information, and reporting performance. The budget director is usually the controller or somebody who is responsible to the controller. The budget director serves as the staff expert, the person upon whom line management depends for technical guidance. He or she may also be a valuable communications official between line and staff departments.

The able budget director typically has warm rapport with line management. He or she particularly avoids grabbing line authority—an easy trap to fall into when a person has the position of company expert on budgetary matters.

budget committee

A budget committee usually serves as a consulting body to the budget officer. Members generally include the budget director and the top-level line executives. However, very large businesses often exclude line executives other than the president from their budget committees; membership is confined to the budget director, the treasurer, the economist, and the president. Special budget committees are formed also—for example, a sales-budget committee and a production-budget committee.

The budget committee is concerned with developing and scrutinizing long-term operating and financial plans, offering advice, reconciling divergent views, and coordinating budgetary activities. The committee's very existence lends an aura of formality and prestige to the budget program.

The budget committee generally has an advisory role only; yet its advice is usually very influential. Initially, the committee usually assembles, reviews, and transmits underlying economic conditions and assumptions in relation to the ensuing budget period. It reviews departmental budgets and makes recommendations. It scrutinizes periodic reports comparing actual performance with the budget. As a result, it submits a variety of recommendations for top-management decision making.

budget manual

It is usually desirable to have policies, organizational structure, and designations of responsibility and authority expressed in writing. The budget manual is a written set of instructions and pertinent information that serves as a rule book and a reference for the implementation of a budget program. It tells what to do, how to do it, when to do it, and which form to do it on. The effort and time needed for the manual's preparation are justified by its long-run usefulness, its tendency to crystallize all aspects of a budget program, and its documentation of procedures that otherwise are carried around in the heads of individuals who will not have the same job forever.

follow-up is important

The investigation of budget deviations is the line manager's responsibility. The controller may assist to a very great extent, but the actual preparation of individual department budgets and decisions on deviations should be the responsibility of line management.

Ineffective budgetary systems are marked by failure to develop and use budgets to their fullest potential. That is, budgets are often used as tools for *planning* only. Great benefits from budgeting lie in the quick investigation of deviations and in the subsequent corrective action. Budgets should not be prepared in the first place if they are ignored, buried in files, or improperly interpreted. Abuses in this area of control probably outnumber the good uses. Again this points up the dire need for the education of company personnel.

QUESTIONS, PROBLEMS, AND CASES

5-1 What are the two major features of a budgetary program? Which feature is more important? Why?

5-2 What are the elements of the budgetary cycle?

5-3 Define *continuous budget, pro forma statements.*

5-4 "The sales forecast is the cornerstone for budgeting." Why?

5-5 Enumerate four common duties of a budget director.

5-6 What is the function of a *budget committee?* A *budget manual?*

5-7 "Budgets are half-used if they serve only as a planning device." Explain.

5-8 Define *responsibility accounting.*

5-9 Define *controllable cost.* What two major factors help an evaluation of whether a given cost is controllable?

5-10 "An action once taken cannot be changed by subsequent events." What implications does this have for the cost accountant?

5-11 "Budgets are wonderful vehicles for communication." Comment.

5-12 ***Responsibility for downtime.*** Two of several departments performed successive operations in the manufacture of automobile frames. The frames were transported from department to department via an overhead conveyor system that was paced in accordance with budgeted time allowances. Each department manager had responsibility for the budgeted costs and budgeted output of his department.

On Tuesday morning Department D had some equipment failure that caused the manager to ask the manager of Department C to stop the conveyor system. The Department C manager refused, so workers in Department D had to remove the frames, stack them, and return the frames to the conveyor later when production resumed.

The manager of Department D was bitter about the incident and insisted that the manager of Department C should bear the related labor and overhead costs of $1,770. In contrast, the manager of Department C said, "I was just doing my job as specified in the budget."

REQUIRED | As the controller, how would you account for the $1,770? Why?

5-13 ***Responsibility of purchasing agent***[9]. Richards is the purchasing agent for the Hart Manufacturing Company. Sampson is head of the production planning and control department. Every six months, Sampson gives Richards a general purchasing program. Richards gets specifications from the engineering department. He then selects suppliers and negotiates prices.

When he took this job, Richards was informed very clearly that he bore responsibility for meeting the general purchasing program once he accepted it from Sampson.

During Week No. 24, Richards was advised that Part No. 1234—a critical part—would be needed for assembly on Tuesday morning, Week No. 32. He found that the regular

[9]Adapted from Raymond Villers, "Control and Freedom in a Decentralized Company," *Harvard Business Review,* XXXII, No. 2, 89–96.

supplier could not deliver. He called everywhere, finally found a supplier in the Middle West, and accepted the commitment.

He followed up by mail. Yes, the supplier assured him, the part would be ready. The matter was so important that on Thursday of Week No. 31, Richards checked by phone. Yes, the shipment had left in time. Richards was reassured and did not check further. But on Tuesday of Week No. 32, the part was not in the warehouse. Inquiry revealed that the shipment had been misdirected by the railroad company and was still in Chicago.

REQUIRED

What department should bear the costs of time lost in the plant? Why? As purchasing agent, do you think it fair that such costs be charged to your department?

5-14 ***A study in responsibility accounting.*** The David Machine Tool Company is in the doldrums. Production volume has fallen to a ten-year low. The company has a nucleus of skilled tool-and-die workers who could find employment elsewhere if they were laid off. Three of these workers have been transferred temporarily to the building and grounds department, where they have been doing menial tasks such as washing walls and sweeping for the past month. They have earned their regular rate of $13 per hour. Their wages have been charged to the building and grounds department. The supervisor of building and grounds has just confronted the controller as follows: "Look at the cockeyed performance report you pencil pushers have given me." The helpers' line reads:

	BUDGET	ACTUAL	DEVIATION	
Wages of helpers	$4,704	$7,644	$2,940	Unfavorable

"This is just another example of how unrealistic you bookkeepers are! Those tool-and-die people are loafing on the job because they know we won't lay them off. The regular hourly rate for my three helpers is $8. Now that my regular helpers are laid off, my work is piling up, so that when they return they'll either have to put in overtime or I'll have to get part-time help to catch up with things. Instead of charging me at $13 per hour, you should charge about $6—that's all those tool-and-die slobs are worth at their best."

REQUIRED

As the controller, what would you do *now?* Would you handle the accounting for these wages any differently?

5-15 ***Fixing responsibility.*** (Adapted from a description by Harold Bierman, Jr.) The city of Mountainvale had hired its first city manager four years ago. She favored a "management by objectives" philosophy and accordingly had set up many profit responsibility centers, including a sanitation department, a city utility, and a repair shop.

For many months, the sanitation manager had been complaining to the utility manager about wires being too low at one point in the road. There was barely clearance for large trucks. The sanitation manager asked the repair shop to make changes in the clearance. The repair shop manager asked, "Whom should I charge for the $2,000 cost of making the adjustment, the sanitation or the utility department?" Both departments refused to accept the charge, so the repair department refused to do the work.

Late one day the top of a truck caught the wires and ripped them down. The repair department made an emergency repair at a cost of $2,600. Moreover, the city lost $1,000 of utility revenue (less variable costs) because of the disruption of service.

Investigation disclosed that the truck had failed to clamp down its top properly. The extra two inches of height caused the catching of the wire.

Both the sanitation and utility managers argued strenuously about whether they should bear the $3,000 cost. Moreover, the utility manager demanded reimbursement from the sanitation department of the $1,000 of lost contribution.

REQUIRED

As the city controller in charge of the responsibility accounting system, how would you favor accounting for these costs? Specifically, what would you do next? What is the proper role of responsibility accounting in determining the blame for this situation?

5-16 ***Interdepartmental conflict and budgets.*** Professor Argyris and others have pointed out that budgets help foster a *departmental* orientation rather than a *plantwide* orientation. This causes trouble because departmental executives concentrate on the correct functioning of their individual departments but pay no attention to the functioning of individual departments in relation to one another.

For example, Argyris cites the example of the plant in which a mistake was made on a customer order. The goods were returned and a correction was made at a cost of $3,000, a large amount. Some department had to be charged with the error. But which department?

After two months of battling among the supervisors as to who was guilty, emotions became so heated that two supervisors stopped talking to each other.

The plant manager finally gave up; he decided to charge the error to no department. He explained, "I thought it might be best to put the whole thing under general factory loss. Or else someone would be hurt."

REQUIRED

Do you agree that budgets foster too narrow an orientation? Do you agree with the action of the plant manager? Did the budget and departmental accounting system cause the trouble? Explain fully.

5-17 ***Budgeted manufacturing costs.*** The Bridget Company has budgeted sales for 100,000 units of its product for 19_1. Expected unit costs, based on past experience, should be $60 for direct materials, $40 for direct labor, and $30 for manufacturing overhead. Assume no beginning or ending inventory in process. Bridget begins the year with 40,000 finished units on hand but budgets the ending finished-goods inventory at only 10,000 units. Compute the budgeted costs of production for 19_1.

5-18 ***Budgeting material purchases.*** The X Company has prepared a sales budget of 42,000 finished units for a three-month period. The company has an inventory of finished goods on hand at December 31 and desires a finished-goods inventory at the end of the succeeding quarter as follows:

	UNITS	
	Dec. 31	**March 31**
Finished product	22,000	24,000

It takes three units of direct materials to make one unit of finished product. The company has an inventory of units of raw material at December 31 and desires an ending raw-material inventory as follows:

	UNITS	
	Dec. 31	**March 31**
Direct materials	100,000	110,000

How many units of direct materials should be purchased during the three months ending March 31?

5-19 ***Budgeting material costs.*** The Maxwell Company uses a single raw material to make its product; for each unit of product, three pounds of this material are required. The price of this material is $10 per pound. The company follows a purchasing policy of placing orders on or before the fifth of each month to cover that month's requirements. It plans its inventory position in advance, to cover expected situations.

The inventory of material at June 30, 19_1 was	9,000 pounds
The inventory level planned for July 31 was	15,000 pounds
The inventory level planned for August 31 was	35,000 pounds
The inventory level planned for September 30 was	20,000 pounds

Production scheduled for the three-month period was:

During July,	10,000 units of product
During August,	12,000 units of product
During September,	15,000 units of product

Suppose that this set of plans is carried out. What will be the total cost of materials purchased for the month of July? August? September?

5-20 ***Production budget.*** (W. Crum) Hobby Company manufactures and sells precut packaged sets of wooden birdhouses, together with the requisite small hardware. The buyer then assembles the birdhouse.

Complete sets have: 2 units of piece A (roof sections), 2 units of piece B (side sections), 1 front section (with hole), 1 back section, 1 bottom section, and 1 package containing the small hardware pieces needed.

The budgeted sales of birdhouses for April–June are 20,000. Inventory at April 1 is expected to be 600. Desired inventory at June 30 is 900. Piece A's (roof sections) on hand April 1 are 250; desired inventory at June 30 is 140.

REQUIRED

Compute, by means of a neat concise schedule, the budgeted production of birdhouse sets for this three-month period, and the budgeted number of piece A's to be produced.

5-21 ***Sales and production budgets.*** (CPA) The Scarborough Corporation in Singapore manufactures and sells two products. Thingone and Thingtwo. In July 19_7, Scarborough's budget department gathered the following data in order to project sales and budget requirements for 19_8:

19_8 Projected Sales:

PRODUCT	UNITS	PRICE
Thingone	60,000	$ 70
Thingtwo	40,000	$100

19_8 Inventories—in units:

PRODUCT	EXPECTED JANUARY 1, 19_8	DESIRED DECEMBER 31, 19_8
Thingone	20,000	25,000
Thingtwo	8,000	9,000

In order to produce one unit of Thingone and Thingtwo, the following raw materials are used:

		AMOUNT USED PER UNIT	
RAW MATERIAL	UNIT	**thingone**	**thingtwo**
A	lbs.	4	5
B	lbs.	2	3
C	each		1

Projected data for 19_8 with respect to raw materials are as follows:

RAW MATERIAL	ANTICIPATED PURCHASE PRICE	EXPECTED INVENTORIES JANUARY 1, 19_8	DESIRED INVENTORIES DECEMBER 31, 19_8
A	$8	32,000 lbs.	36,000 lbs.
B	$5	29,000 lbs.	32,000 lbs.
C	$3	6,000 each	7,000 each

Projected direct-labor requirements for 19_8 and rates are as follows:

PRODUCT	HOURS PER UNIT	RATE PER HOUR
Thingone	2	$3
Thingtwo	3	$4

Overhead is applied at the rate of $2 per direct-labor hour.

REQUIRED

Based upon the above projections and budget requirements for 19_8 for Thingone and Thingtwo, prepare the following budgets for 19_8:

1. Sales budget (in dollars)
2. Production budget (in units)
3. Raw-materials purchase budget (in quantities)

4. Raw-materials purchase budget (in dollars)
5. Direct-labor budget (in dollars)
6. Budgeted finished-goods inventory at December 31, 19_8 (in dollars)

5-22 ***Predicting raw-material quantities.*** (CMA) The Press Company manufactures and sells industrial components. The Whitmore Plant is responsible for producing two components referred to as AD-5 and FX-3. Plastic, brass, and aluminum are used in the production of these two products.

Press Company has adopted a thirteen-period reporting cycle in all of its plants for budgeting purposes. Each period is four weeks long and has twenty working days. The projected inventory levels for AD-5 and FX-3 at the end of the current (seventh) period and the projected sales for these two products for the next three four-week periods are as follows:

	PROJECTED INVENTORY LEVEL (IN UNITS)	PROJECTED SALES (IN UNITS)		
	end of seventh period	**eighth period**	**ninth period**	**tenth period**
AD-5	3,000	7,500	8,750	9,500
FX-3	2,800	7,000	4,500	4,000

Past experience has shown that adequate inventory levels for AD-5 and FX-3 can be maintained if 40 percent of the next period's projected sales are on hand at the end of a reporting period. Based on this experience and the projected sales, the Whitmore Plant has budgeted production of 8,000 AD-5 and 6,000 FX-3 in the eighth period. Production is assumed to be uniform for both products within each four-week period.

The raw-material specifications for AD-5 and FX-3 are as follows:

	AD-5	FX-3
Plastic	2.0 lb.	1.0 lb.
Brass	0.5 lb.	—
Aluminum	—	1.5 lb.

Data relating to the purchase of raw materials are as follows:

	PURCHASE PRICE PER POUND	STANDARD PURCHASE LOT (IN POUNDS)	REORDER POINT (IN POUNDS)	PROJECTED INVENTORY STATUS AT THE END OF THE SEVENTH PERIOD (IN POUNDS)		LEAD TIME IN WORKING DAYS
				on hand	**on order**	
Plastic	$.40	15,000	12,000	16,000	15,000	10
Brass	.95	5,000	7,500	9,000	—	30
Aluminum	.55	10,000	10,000	14,000	10,000	20

The sales of AD-5 and FX-3 do not vary significantly from month to month. Consequently, the safety stock incorporated into the reorder point for each of the raw materials is adequate to compensate for variations in the sales of the finished products.

Raw-material orders are placed the day the quantity on hand falls below the reorder point. Whitmore Plant's suppliers are very dependable, so that the given lead times are reliable. The outstanding orders for plastic and aluminum are due to arrive on the tenth and fourth working days of the eighth period, respectively. Payments for all raw-material orders are remitted in the period of delivery.

REQUIRED

Whitmore Plant is required to submit a report to corporate headquarters of Press Company summarizing the projected raw-material activities before each period commences. The data for the eighth-period report are being assembled. Determine the following items for plastic, brass, and aluminum for inclusion in the eighth-period report:

1. Projected quantities (in pounds) of each raw material to be issued to production
2. Projected quantities (in pounds) of each raw material ordered and the date (in terms of working days) the order is to be placed
3. The projected inventory balance (in pounds) of each raw material at the end of the period
4. The payments for purchases of each raw material

5-23 ***Production budget.*** (CMA) The Wyoming Division of Reid Corporation produces an intricate component part used in Reid's major product line. The division manager has recently been concerned about a lack of coordination between purchasing and production personnel and believes that a monthly budgeting system would be better than the present system.

Wyoming's division manager has decided to develop budget information for the third quarter of the current year as a trial before the budget system is implemented for an entire fiscal year. In response to the division manager's request for data that could be used to develop budget information, the division controller accumulated the following data.

SALES

Sales through June 30, 19_7, the first six months of the current year, are 24,000 units. Actual sales in units for May and June and estimated unit sales for the next four months are detailed as follows:

May (actual)	4,000
June (actual)	4,000
July (estimated)	5,000
August (estimated)	6,000
September (estimated)	7,000
October (estimated)	7,000

Wyoming Division expects to sell 60,000 units during the year ending December 31, 19_7.

DIRECT MATERIAL

Data regarding the materials used in the component are shown in the following schedule. The desired monthly ending inventory for all direct materials is to have sufficient materials on hand to produce the next month's estimated sales.

DIRECT MATERIAL	UNITS OF DIRECT MATERIALS PER FINISHED COMPONENT	COST PER UNIT	INVENTORY LEVEL 6/30/_7
#101	6	$2.40	35,000 units
#211	4	3.60	30,000 units
#242	2	1.20	14,000 units

DIRECT LABOR

Each component must pass through three different processes to be completed. Data regarding the direct labor are as follows:

PROCESS	DIRECT-LABOR HOURS PER FINISHED COMPONENT	COST PER DIRECT-LABOR HOUR
Forming	0.80	$8.00
Assembly	2.00	5.50
Finishing	0.25	6.00

FACTORY OVERHEAD

The division produced 27,000 components during this six-month period through June 30, 19_7. The actual variable overhead costs incurred during this six-month period are shown below. The division controller believes the variable overhead costs will be incurred at the same rate during the last six months of 19_7.

Supplies	$ 59,400
Electricity	27,000
Indirect labor	54,000
Other	8,100
Total variable overhead	$148,500

The fixed-overhead costs incurred during the first six months of 19_7 amounted to $93,500. Fixed-overhead costs are budgeted for the full year as follows:

Supervision	$ 60,000
Taxes	7,200
Depreciation	86,400
Other	32,400
Total fixed overhead	$186,000

FINISHED-GOODS INVENTORY

The desired monthly ending inventory in units of completed components is 80 percent of the next month's estimated sales. There are 5,000 finished units in the inventory on June 30, 19_7.

REQUIRED

1. Prepare a production budget in units for the Wyoming Division for the third quarter ending September 30, 19_7.
2. Without prejudice to your answer in requirement 1, assume that the Wyoming Division plans to produce 18,000 units during the third quarter ending September 30, 19_7, and 60,000 units for the year ending December 31, 19_7.
   a. Prepare a Direct-Materials Purchase Budget in units and dollars for the third quarter ending September 30, 19_7.
   b. Prepare a Direct-Labor Budget in hours and dollars for the third quarter ending September 30, 19_7.
   c. Prepare a Factory-Overhead Budget for the six-month period ending December 31, 19_7.
3. Assume that Wyoming Division actually produced 38,000 components during the six-month period of July 1–December 31, 19_7, and incurred variable overhead of $203,300 and fixed overhead of $95,000. Evaluate Wyoming Division's performance for the last six months of 19_7 with respect to its control of factory overhead costs. Show and explain briefly any supporting calculations used in your evaluation.

5-24 ***Cash budget.*** (W. Crum) Read Appendix 5A. Jack's Radio Emporium expects to have these balances at June 1:

Cash	$ 6,000	Accounts payable—trade	$ 20,000
Receivables	38,000	Notes payable—bank	90,000
Inventory	40,000	Common stock	40,000
Fixed assets	100,000	Retained income	34,000
	$184,000		$184,000

June sales are budgeted at $90,000. June purchases of parts and supplies are planned at $50,000. Past patterns indicate that 20 percent of purchases are paid in month of purchase, with remainder paid for in next month. Of the Accounts Receivable, $30,000 is due from sales made in May, and $8,000 from sales made in April. Customers generally pay 40 percent of their bills in the month of credit sale, 40 percent in the next month, and 20 percent in the third month. Budgeted items for June include wages, $6,000; advertising, $500; utilities, $400; depreciation, $1,000; postage and supplies, $700; taxes due in December, $1,100; insurance due in July, $300; interest and payment on note due bank on June 14, $10,300; other expenses requiring cash, $2,000; purchase of new equipment to be bought in June, to be paid for in July, $12,000. All expenses payable in cash are paid in month of recognition unless otherwise indicated.

REQUIRED Prepare a cash budget for June.

5-25 ***Predicting cash balance.*** (SMA) Read Appendix 5A. Alex Ltd., a wholesaler, budgeted the following sales for the first four months of the year:

	CREDIT	CASH	TOTAL
January	$ 3,000,000	$ 400,000	$ 3,400,000
February	3,200,000	420,000	3,620,000
March	3,400,000	440,000	3,840,000
April	3,100,000	390,000	3,490,000
	$12,700,000	$1,650,000	$14,350,000

The company's collections have been excellent, with negligible bad-debt experience. Credit sales are usually paid 70 percent during the month of sale and the balance during the subsequent month. Suppliers are paid cash on delivery.

On January 1, cash and accounts receivable balances were $685,000 and $750,000, respectively. Cash-expense outlays during the year other than for purchases are expected to average $546,000 per month. A cash dividend was declared in December in the amount of $15,000 and is payable on February 15.

The company has an average markup on inventory of 25 percent over costs, and inventories at the beginning of each month are 30 percent of the month's projected cost of sales.

REQUIRED | Prepare a statement showing calculations of the projected cash balance as of April 1.

5-26 ***Comprehensive budget; fill in schedules.*** Read Appendix 5A. Ignore income taxes. Following is certain information relative to the position and business of the Newport Stores Company.

Current assets as of Sept. 30:	
Cash on deposit	$ 12,000
Inventory	63,600
Accounts receivable	10,000
Fixed assets—net	100,000
Current liabilities as of Sept. 30	None
Recent and anticipated sales:	
September	$ 40,000
October	48,000
November	60,000
December	80,000
January	36,000

Credit sales: Sales are 75 percent for cash, and 25 percent on credit. Assume that credit accounts are all collected within 30 days from sale. The accounts receivable on September 30 are the result of the credit sales for September (25 percent of $40,000).

Gross profit averages 30 percent of sales. Purchase discounts are treated on the income statement as "other income" by this company.

Expenses: Salaries and wages average 15 percent of monthly sales; rent, 5 percent; all other expenses, excluding depreciation, 4 percent. Assume that these expenses are disbursed each month. Depreciation is $750 per month.

Purchases: There is a basic inventory of $30,000. The policy is to purchase each month additional inventory in the amount necessary to provide for the following month's sales. Terms on purchases are 2/10, n/30. Assume that payments are made in the month of purchase, and that all discounts are taken.

Fixtures: In October, $600 is spent for fixtures, and in November, $400 is to be expended for this purpose.

Assume that a minimum cash balance of $8,000 is to be maintained. Assume that all borrowings are effective at the beginning of the month and all repayments are made at the end of the month of repayment. Loans are repaid when sufficient cash is available. Interest is paid only at the time of repaying principal. Interest rate is 18 percent per annum.

REQUIRED | On the basis of the facts as given above:

1. Complete Schedule A.

Schedule A
Budgeted Monthly Dollar Receipts

ITEM	SEPTEMBER	OCTOBER	NOVEMBER	DECEMBER
Total sales	$40,000	$48,000	$60,000	$80,000
Credit sales	10,000	12,000		
Cash sales				
Receipts:				
Cash sales		$36,000		
Collections on accounts receivable		10,000		
Total		$46,000		

2. Complete Schedule B. Note that purchases are 70 percent of next month's sales.

Schedule B
Budgeted Monthly Cash Disbursements for Purchases

ITEM	OCTOBER	NOVEMBER	DECEMBER	TOTAL
Purchases	$42,000			
Less 2% cash discount	840			
Disbursements	$41,160			

3. Complete Schedule C.

Schedule C
Budgeted Monthly Cash Disbursements for Operating Expenses

ITEM	OCTOBER	NOVEMBER	DECEMBER	TOTAL
Salaries and wages	$ 7,200			
Rent	2,400			
Other expenses	1,920			
Total	$11,520			

4. Complete Schedule D.

Schedule D
Budgeted Total Monthly Disbursements

ITEM	OCTOBER	NOVEMBER	DECEMBER	TOTAL
Purchases	$41,160			
Operating expenses	11,520			
Fixtures	600			
Total	$53,280			

5. Complete Schedule E.

Schedule E
Budgeted Cash Receipts and Disbursements

ITEM	OCTOBER	NOVEMBER	DECEMBER	TOTAL
Receipts	$46,000			
Disbursements	53,280			
Net cash increase				
Net cash decrease	$ 7,280			

6. Complete Schedule F (assume that borrowings must be made in multiples of $1,000).

Schedule F
Financing Required by Newport Stores Company

ITEM	OCTOBER	NOVEMBER	DECEMBER	TOTAL
Opening cash	$12,000	$ 8,720		
Net cash increase				
Net cash decrease	7,280			
Cash position before financing	4,720			
Financing required	4,000			
Interest payments				
Financing retired				
Closing balance	$ 8,720			

7. What do you think is the most logical means of arranging the financing needed by Newport Stores Company?
8. Prepare a budgeted (pro forma) income statement for the fourth quarter and a balance sheet as of December 31. Ignore income taxes.
9. Certain simplifications have been introduced in this problem. What complicating factors would be met in a typical business situation?

5-27 ***Cash budgeting.*** Read Appendix 5A. On December 1, 19_1, the XYZ Wholesale Co. is attempting to project cash receipts and disbursements through January 31, 19_2. On this latter date, a note will be payable in the amount of $10,000. This amount was borrowed in September to carry the company through the seasonal peak in November and December.

The trial balance on December 1 shows in part:

Cash	$ 1,000	
Accounts receivable	28,000	
Allowance for bad debts		$1,580
Inventory	8,750	
Accounts payable		9,200

Sales terms call for a 2 percent discount if paid within the first ten days of the month after purchase, with the balance due by the end of the month after purchase. Experience has shown that 70 percent of the billings will be collected within the discount period, 20 percent by the end of the month after purchase, and 8 percent in the following month, and that 2 percent will be uncollectible. There are no sales for cash.

The unit sales price of the company's one product is $10. Actual and projected sales are:

October actual	$ 18,000
November actual	25,000
December estimated	30,000
January estimated	15,000
February estimated	12,000
Total estimated for year ending June 30	150,000

All purchases are payable within fifteen days. Thus, approximately 50 percent of the purchases in a month are due and payable in the next month. The unit purchase cost is $7. Target ending inventories are 500 units plus 25 percent of the next month's unit sales.

Total budgeted selling and administrative expenses for the year are $40,000. Of this amount, $15,000 is considered fixed (includes depreciation of $3,000). The remainder varies with sales. Both fixed and variable selling and administrative expenses are paid as incurred.

REQUIRED

Prepare a columnar statement of budgeted cash receipts and disbursements for December and January.

5-28 ***Review of Chapters 4 and 5; control in consulting firms.*** The definitions of *direct labor* differ among and within industries. For example, some accounting, law, and consulting firms have secretaries and bookkeepers tabulate their time as worked for various clients. Other firms regard such work as general overhead. They confine their classification of direct labor to the time worked by their "professional staff." Similarly, some firms trace photocopying and phone calls to individual clients. If clients are billed by applying some multiple to direct-labor and other direct costs, differences in cost classifications obviously might affect the total charges to individual clients.

Exhibit A displays the budgeting of 19_2 revenue for the San Francisco office of Lansing and Company, a consulting firm. The target billing rates are usually somewhere between two and three times the "direct-labor" costs. A partner's services are frequently quoted at the lower multiple or less because he or she will also get a partner's share of the profits generated by the work of all members of the professional staff.

REQUIRED

Label your supporting computations.

1. Fill in the blanks indicated by the question marks in the accompanying exhibit.
2. Suppose that overhead costs (all fixed), including the secretarial salaries but excluding any professional salaries, were $285,000. Fill in the blanks of the following budgeted income statement:

Fees earned for professional services	$?
Direct labor	?
Contribution to overhead and profit	?
Overhead, including professional salaries other than direct labor	?
Operating profit (after deducting base salary of partner)	$?

Exhibit A
Summary Operating Revenue Budget

POSITION	NUMBER OF PEOPLE	TOTAL SALARIES	HOURS TO ACCOUNT FOR	BILLABLE PERCENTAGE	BILLABLE (CHARGEABLE) HOURS	DIRECT-LABOR COST	HOURLY COST	BILLING RATE	BUDGETED BILLINGS
Partner	1	$140,000	2,080	50%	1,040	$ 70,000	$67.31	$130	$135,200
Manager	1	60,000	2,080	75	?	?	?	75	?
Senior	2	80,000	?	85	3,536	?	19.23	50	176,800
Associate	6	?	12,480	90	?	162,000	?	30	?
		?	?		?	?			?

3. Consider *each* of the following effects *independently*. That is, all the basic facts in requirements 1 and 2 would be unchanged with the exception of the new information given. Compute the new operating profit if:
   a. The associates have a billable percentage of 85 percent instead of 90 percent.
   b. The partner has a billable percentage of 45 percent instead of 50 percent. Refer to the original data. Compare the results in 3a and 3b. What are their implications for management control?
   c. The budget should have provided for "write-downs" of 3 percent of gross revenue for billings not collectible. These usually take the form of "adjustments" when the client balks at paying too high a fee. They are typically accounted for as deductions from gross revenue to arrive at a net revenue amount. Refer to the original data. What is the implication of write-downs for management control?
4. As the partner in charge of the office, what detailed records and ratios would you want maintained to assist your planning and control? Be as specific as possible.

5-29 ***Cash budgeting.*** For a problem dealing with cash budgeting under uncertainty, see Problem 24-20; under linear programming, see Problem 23-18.

6 Flexible Budgets and Standards: Part I

The preceding chapter focused on the general ideas of budgeting and the use of responsibility accounting to help plan performance. A key element of the control system is feedback—the comparison of actual performance with planned performance. Now we focus on how managers use flexible budgets and standard costs as helpful tools for planning and controlling.

The bulk of the chapter deals with standard costs, which are predetermined measures of what costs should be under specified conditions. The analysis of the variances of actual costs from standard costs can aid managers in judging and improving performance. The basic analysis is illustrated for the price and efficiency variances of direct-material costs and direct-labor costs.

Throughout this chapter, to stress some fundamental ideas we assume that production is equal to sales; indeed, there are no beginning or ending inventories of work in process or finished goods. Chapter 8 will explore the implications of inventories for the measurement of performance.

Analysis levels 0 and 1: static budget

When managers evaluate performance, they seek various levels of detail. For example, consider the Webb Company. Suppose for simplicity that the company manufactures a single product, a finely crafted, heavy ashtray made of a special alloy having a unique color and luster. Webb has a budgeting system, basing its budget on last year's performance, general economic conditions, and its expected share of predicted industry sales.

Exhibit 6-1 begins the variance analysis that will be covered throughout this and the next chapter. The exhibit presents two successive depths of detail of variance analysis. *Level 0* has the least depth, and *Level 1* has more depth.[1]

The top of Exhibit 6-1 presents a *Level 0* analysis of variances. Most observers, unless they are totally passive, would not be satisfied with such a skimpy report. Merely knowing that a relatively huge variance exists ($110,600, or 98.7 percent of budgeted operating income) is not enough. Instead, as a minimum, managers would seek the *Level 1* analysis shown in Exhibit 6-1. That is, actual results are compared with the original budget for at least the total revenues, variable costs, contribution margins, fixed costs, and operating income. If desired, a detailed analysis could be conducted for subclassifications of variable and fixed costs.

EXHIBIT 6-1

(Place a clip on this page for easy reference.)

Webb Company

Overview of Variance Analysis
For the Month Ended April 30, 19_1

ANALYSIS LEVEL 0

		%
Actual operating income	$ 1,400	1.3
Budgeted operating income	112,000	100.0
Operating income variance	$110,600 U	98.7

ANALYSIS LEVEL 1

	(1) ACTUAL	%	(2) STATIC (MASTER) BUDGET	%	(3) (1) − (2) VARIANCE
Units	10,000	—	12,000	—	2,000 U
Revenues (sales)	$720,000	100.0	$840,000	100.0	$120,000 U
Variable costs	546,600	75.9	552,000	65.7	5,400 F
Contribution margin	173,400	24.1	288,000	34.3	114,600 U
Fixed costs	172,000	23.9	176,000	21.0	4,000 F
Operating income	$ 1,400	0.2	$112,000	13.3	$110,600 U

↑ Operating income variance ↑
$110,600 U

F = Favorable; U = Unfavorable effect on operating income.

[1] J. Shank and N. Churchill, "Variance Analysis: A Management-oriented Approach," *Accounting Review*, October 1977, pp. 950–57.

The *Level 1* analysis indicates that the *Level 0* analysis stops too soon. A total variance of $110,600 in operating income may be the result of many factors that are frequently offsetting. Percentages are often used to highlight relationships, as is illustrated by both the *Level 0* and the *Level 1* analysis. In this instance, only 10,000 units were sold instead of the original target of 12,000. But the shortfall in sales was not accompanied by a corresponding fall in variable costs, which decreased by only $5,400 and became 75.9 percent of sales instead of the 65.7 percent that was budgeted.[2] Thus, the contribution margin percentage was only 24.1 percent instead of the budgeted 34.3 percent.

The *Level 1* analysis assumes that the budgeted amounts were those originally formulated in the master budget for April. That is, the master budget is *static* because it has a single planned volume level for the organization. By definition, a **static budget** **is not adjusted or altered, regardless of changes in volume or other conditions during the fiscal period.** For example, the *Level 1* comparison aligns the originally budgeted sales volume of 12,000 units against the 10,000 units actually sold.

The *Level 1* combination of percentage analyses and absolute dollar amounts of variances tells the manager much more about underlying performance than the *Level 0* analysis. But most managers would consider *Level 1* as not being sufficiently informative.

Analysis level 2: flexible budget

adjusting for changes in volume

As the chief executive of the Webb Company, you would probably want a flexible budget to help provide an explanatory trail between the static budget and the actual results. **A flexible budget (also called a variable budget) is a master budget that is adjusted for changes in volume.** It is essentially a budget that may be tailored to any volume level. Thus, the flexible budget is based on a knowledge of how revenue and costs should behave over a range of activity.

Exhibit 6-2 shows how the flexible-budget data might appear for the Webb Company. The costs in Exhibit 6-2 may be graphed as in Exhibit 6-3. These exhibits are based on a study of cost behavior patterns that lead to a mathematical function or formula: $176,000 fixed cost per month plus $46 variable cost per unit of product. Note especially that the graph in Exhibit 6-3 can be transformed to become the familiar cost-volume-profit graph by merely drawing the sales line, which is not shown there. Thus, in its fullest form the flexible budget is an expression of the cost-volume-profit relationships already described in Chapter 3.

Flexible budgets may be useful either before or after a specific period in question. They may be helpful when managers are trying to choose a level of volume for planning purposes. They may also be helpful at the end of the period when managers are trying to analyze actual results.

To recapitulate, the flexible budget is the master budget that *would have been* formulated if all the managers were perfect forecasters of the activity volume; there would never be any difference between the budgeted volume and the actual volume

[2]Managers and others tend to watch these percentages regularly. Comparisons are made from period to period and from company to company. For example, during the 1970s Northwest and National Airlines consistently challenged union demands. As a result, these two airlines suffered 86 percent of the industry's strike days. However, in 1980 Northwest's labor costs were 27 percent of revenues; National's, 37 percent. In contrast, the labor costs of United, Eastern, and American Airlines were 42 to 43 percent of their revenues.

EXHIBIT 6-2

(Place a clip on this page for easy reference.)

Webb Company
Flexible-Budget Data
Relevant Range of Activity (Volume)
For the Month Ended April 30, 19_1

	BUDGETED AMOUNT PER UNIT	VARIOUS LEVELS OF VOLUME		
Units		10,000	12,000	14,000
Revenues (sales)	$70	$700,000	$840,000	$980,000
Variable costs:				
Direct material	20	200,000	240,000	280,000
Direct labor	16	160,000	192,000	224,000
Variable factory overhead	3	30,000	36,000	42,000
Variable manufacturing costs	39	390,000	468,000	546,000
Variable selling and administrative costs*	7	70,000	84,000	98,000
Total variable costs	46	460,000	552,000	644,000
Contribution margin	$24	240,000	288,000	336,000
Fixed costs:				
Manufacturing†		96,000	96,000	96,000
Selling and administrative‡		80,000	80,000	80,000
Total fixed costs		176,000	176,000	176,000
Total costs		636,000	728,000	820,000
Operating income		$ 64,000	$112,000	$160,000

**Examples: Sales commissions, shipping, photocopying.*
†Examples: Supervision, depreciation, property taxes.
‡Examples: Advertising, supervision, accounting.

achieved. In our example, if the managers could have foreseen that actual volume would be 10,000 units, a master budget would have been geared to that level.

The flexible budget is the path to the more-penetrating *Level 2* variance analysis in Exhibit 6-4. The $110,600 operating income variance is split into two major categories: (a) sales volume variances and (b) flexible-budget variances. Brief definitions follow:

> **Sales volume variance**—the difference between the flexible-budget amounts and the static (master) budget amounts. Unit prices are held constant.
>
> **Flexible-budget variance**—the difference between actual amounts and the flexible-budget amounts for the actual output achieved.

sales volume variances

Exhibit 6-4 clearly shows how the variances due to the level of *sales volume* ($48,000 U) are unaffected by any changes in unit prices. Why? Because both the flexible budget and the static budget are constructed using budgeted prices. Thus, the final three columns in Exhibit 6-4 focus on effects of volume changes while holding unit prices constant.

EXHIBIT 6-3 **Webb Company**
Graph of Flexible Budget of Costs

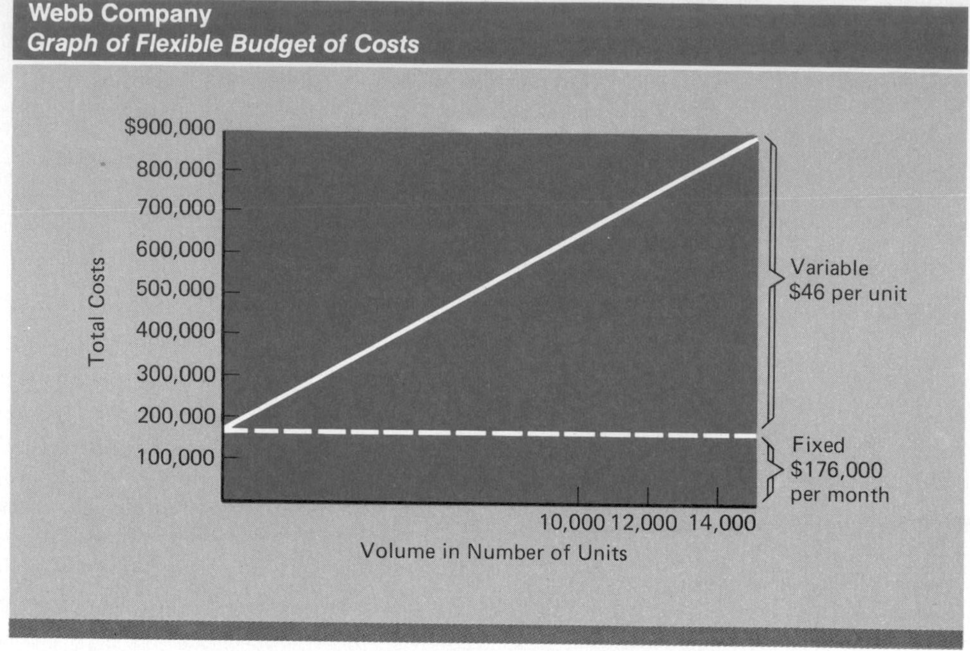

The total of the sales volume variances in *Level 2* tells the manager that operating income would be expected to be $48,000 lower ($64,000 instead of $112,000). The tabulation in Exhibit 6-4, column 4, shows that the underachievement of sales by

EXHIBIT 6-4 *(Place a clip on this page for easy reference.)*

Webb Company
Summary of Performance
For the Month Ended April 30, 19_1

ANALYSIS LEVEL 2	(1) ACTUAL	(2) (1) – (3) FLEXIBLE-BUDGET VARIANCES	(3) FLEXIBLE BUDGET	(4) (3) – (5) SALES VOLUME VARIANCES	(5) STATIC (MASTER) BUDGET
Physical units of output	10,000	—	10,000	2,000 U	12,000
Revenues (sales)	$720,000	$20,000 F	$700,000	$140,000 U	$840,000
Variable costs	546,600	86,600 U	460,000	92,000 F	552,000
Contribution margin	173,400	66,600 U	240,000	48,000 U	288,000
Fixed costs	172,000	4,000 F	176,000	—	176,000
Operating income	$ 1,400	$62,600 U	$ 64,000	$ 48,000 U	$112,000

↑ Flexible-budget variances, $62,600 U ↑ Sales volume variances, $48,000 U ↑

↑ Operating income variance, $110,600 U ↑

2,000 units and $140,000 would decrease contribution margin by $48,000 and hence decrease operating income by $48,000.

In summary, the following explanation is offered by *Level 2* analysis. The budgeted unit contribution margin as indicated in Exhibit 6-2 is $70 − $46 = $24:

$$\text{Sales volume variance} = \begin{pmatrix}\text{Flexible-budget units} \\ - \text{Static budget units}\end{pmatrix} \times \begin{pmatrix}\text{Budgeted unit} \\ \text{contribution margin}\end{pmatrix}$$
$$= (10{,}000 - 12{,}000) \times \$24$$
$$= \$48{,}000 \text{ U}$$

For now, we stop at *Level 2* for the sales volume variances. Such variances can be analyzed in much more detail. For example, Chapter 25 explores how variances can be compiled for intervening changes in market size, market share, and sales mix.

Who has responsibility for the sales volume variance? Fluctuations in sales are attributable to many factors, but the executive in charge of marketing is usually in the best position to explain why the volume achieved differs from the volume in the static budget.

flexible-budget variances

The first three columns of Exhibit 6-4 compare the actual results (that is, actual total revenue and actual total costs) with the flexible-budget amounts. The flexible-budget variances are the differences between columns 1 and 3. The following summary explanation is offered by *Level 2* analysis:

$$\begin{matrix}\text{Flexible-budget variance} \\ \text{in operating income}\end{matrix} = \begin{pmatrix}\text{Actual operating} \\ \text{income}\end{pmatrix} - \begin{pmatrix}\text{Flexible-budget} \\ \text{operating income}\end{pmatrix}$$
$$= \$1{,}400 - \$64{,}000$$
$$= \$62{,}600 \text{ U}$$

Most managers are not satisfied with such a sparse summary. They want at least a line-by-line listing of revenues, costs, and their flexible-budget variances.

The variances in revenues of a single-product firm are attributable to two causes, volume and price. The sales volume variance has already been discussed. A **price variance** is defined as **the difference between actual unit prices and budgeted unit prices multiplied by the quantity of goods or services in question.** To illustrate, the flexible-budget revenue variance is wholly explained by changes in unit prices. The *Level 2* analysis indicates that sales prices were raised by an average $2 per unit (from $70 to $72) after the original budget was formulated:

$$\text{Price variance} = (\text{Difference in price}) \times (\text{Actual quantity of units affected})$$
$$= (\text{Actual price} - \text{Budgeted price}) \times (\text{Actual quantity of units affected})$$
$$V_p = (AP - SP) \times AQ$$
$$V_p = (\$72 - \$70) \times 10{,}000 \text{ units}$$
$$V_p = \$20{,}000 \text{ F, where } F \text{ means a favorable effect on operating income}$$

A *Level 2* analysis of costs can be conducted at increasing levels of detail. For instance, Exhibit 6-5 shows an analysis of variable and fixed costs on a line-by-line basis. If desired, even more details could be gathered. For example, the actual costs

EXHIBIT 6-5 *(Place a clip on this page for easy reference.)*

Webb Company

Cost Control Performance Report
For the Month Ended April 30, 19_1

	ACTUAL	FLEXIBLE BUDGET*	FLEXIBLE-BUDGET VARIANCES†	EXPLANATORY COMMENTS
Units	10,000	10,000	—	
Variable costs:				
Direct material	$270,000	$200,000	$ 70,000 U	Excess price and usage‡
Direct labor	171,600	160,000	11,600 U	Lower price but excess usage‡
Variable factory overhead	32,000	30,000	2,000 U	Miscellaneous reasons
Total variable manufacturing costs	473,600	390,000	83,600 U	
Variable selling and administrative costs	73,000	70,000	3,000 U	Use of air freight
Total variable costs	546,600	460,000	86,600 U	
Fixed costs:				
Fixed manufacturing costs	92,000	96,000	4,000 F	Fewer pay raises
Fixed selling and administrative costs	80,000	80,000	—	
Total fixed costs	172,000	176,000	4,000 F	
Total variable and fixed costs	$718,600	$636,000	$ 82,600 U	

F = Favorable; U = Unfavorable
**From Exhibit 6-2, 10,000-unit column.*
†This represents a line-by-line breakdown of the variances in column 2 of Exhibit 6-4.
‡This type of analysis is described later in this chapter.

and the flexible budgeted amounts of subclassifications of direct material and direct labor might be routinely reported.

Compare the *Level 1* analysis with the *Level 2* analysis. Note how the variable costs had favorable variances when a static budget was used as a basis for comparison. Exhibit 6-1, *Level 1,* shows a favorable variance of $5,400. But the flexible budget provides a more revealing picture. Exhibits 6-4 and 6-5 pinpoint unfavorable variable-cost variances of $86,600, which were partially offset by favorable fixed-cost variances of $4,000.

Analysis level 3: detailed variances

In most organizations, top management tends to be satisfied with a *Level 2* depth of variance analysis. Subordinate managers, however, tend to seek more detail. For example, marketing executives may not know revenue price variances by sales territory. In our Webb Company illustration, a *Level 3* analysis might indicate that half the sales price variances were attributable to each of two territories. However, the price might also have been raised in one territory and not in the other. For example, if half the unit sales were in each territory, a price of $74 in Territory A and $70 in Territory B would produce the same total variance. The *Level 2* sales price variance would be unchanged, but the *Level 3* sales price variances would change:

ANALYSIS LEVEL 3	DETAILED REVENUE PRICE VARIANCES	
	if uniform price changes	**if price change in territory A only**
Territory A	$10,000 F	$20,000 F
Territory B	10,000 F	—
Total sales price variances	$20,000 F	$20,000 F

For perspective, you may wish to refer to Exhibit 6-6 occasionally. It provides an overall road map of where you have been and where you are going. *Level 0* and *Level 1* are reproductions of Exhibit 6-1. *Level 2* is a reproduction of Exhibit 6-4. *Level 3* was just discussed regarding revenues.

Please do not attach too much importance to the labels *Level 0, Level 1,* and so forth. By themselves such labels have no universal meaning in the field of cost accounting. They merely represent increasingly detailed analysis. We will not probe beyond *Level 3;* however, many more levels of detail could be specified. For example, sales price variances might be subdivided within territories by customer, by sales personnel, by product color, by week, and by season of the year.

The flexible-budget variances for costs are also candidates for further analysis. The remainder of this chapter will show how a *Level 3* analysis uses standards to subdivide these variances into price and efficiency components. Two major categories of costs will be explored, direct materials and direct labor. The next chapter will study factory overhead.

Standards for materials and labor

distinction between budgets and standards

Many organizations have budgeting systems that are confined to a static budget. That is, a master budget is prepared and performance is not evaluated beyond the *Level 1* analysis in Exhibit 6-6. However, when an organization invests in a flexible budgeting system, it typically develops standards for major costs.

Standard costs are carefully predetermined costs; they are target costs, costs that should be attained. Standard costs help to build budgets, gauge performance, obtain product costs, and save bookkeeping costs. Standard costs are the building blocks of a flexible budgeting and feedback system.

A set of standards outlines how a task should be accomplished and how much it should cost. As work is done, actual costs incurred are compared with standard costs to reveal variances. This feedback helps discover better ways of adhering to standards, of altering standards, and of accomplishing objectives.

What is the difference between a standard amount and a budgeted amount? **As they are most widely used, the term *standard cost* is a *unit* concept and the term *budgeted cost* is a *total* concept.** It may be helpful to think of a standard as a budget for the production of a single unit of output. However, keep in mind that in practice the terms *budgets* and *standards* are used loosely and often interchangeably.

inputs, outputs, and efficiency

Consider the following standards for the manufacture of the units in our Webb Company illustration:

EXHIBIT 6-6 *(Place a clip on this page for easy reference.)*

Webb Company
Overview of Variance Analysis
For the Month Ended April 30, 19_1

ANALYSIS LEVEL 0

		%
Actual operating income	$ 1,400	1.3
Budgeted operating income	112,000	100.0
Operating income variance	$110,600 U	98.7

ANALYSIS LEVEL 1

	(1) ACTUAL	%	(2) STATIC (MASTER) BUDGET	%	(3) (1) − (2) VARIANCE
Units	10,000	—	12,000	%	2,000 U
Revenues (sales)	$720,000	100.0	$840,000	100.0	$120,000 U
Variable costs	546,600	75.9	552,000	65.7	5,400 F
Contribution margin	173,400	24.1	288,000	34.3	114,600 U
Fixed costs	172,000	23.9	176,000	21.0	4,000 F
Operating income	$ 1,400	0.2	$112,000	13.3	$110,600 U

↑ Operating income variance ↑
$110,600 U

ANALYSIS LEVEL 2

	(1) ACTUAL	(2) (1) − (3) FLEXIBLE-BUDGET VARIANCES	(3) FLEXIBLE BUDGET	(4) (3) − (5) SALES VOLUME VARIANCES	(5) STATIC (MASTER) BUDGET
Physical units of output	10,000	—	10,000	2,000 U	12,000
Revenues (sales)	$720,000	$20,000 F*	$700,000	$140,000 U‡	$840,000
Variable costs	546,600	86,600 U†	460,000	92,000 F	552,000
Contribution margin	173,400	66,600 U	240,000	48,000 U	288,000
Fixed costs	172,000	4,000 F†	176,000	—	176,000
Operating income	$ 1,400	$62,600 U	$ 64,000	$ 48,000 U	$112,000

↑ Flexible-budget variances, $62,600 U ↑ Sales volume variances, $48,000 U ↑

↑ Operating income variance, $110,600 U ↑

ANALYSIS LEVEL 3

***DETAILED SALES PRICE VARIANCES**

Territory A	*$ 10,000 F*
Territory B	*10,000 F*
Sales price variances	*$ 20,000 F*

†DETAILED COST VARIANCES

Price and efficiency variances for materials, labor, and other costs (See text.)

‡DETAILED SALES VOLUME VARIANCES

Sales quantity variances
Sales mix variances
(These aspects are covered in Chapter 25.)

F = Favorable, U = Unfavorable effect on operating income.

Direct materials	Four pounds of input allowed @ $5 = $20 per unit of output
Direct labor	Two hours of input allowed @ $8 = $16 per unit of output

In addition to the preceding data, the following data were compiled regarding *actual* performance:

Good units produced	10,000	Direct-labor costs	$171,600
Direct-material costs	$270,000	Hours of input	22,000
Pounds of input	50,000	Labor price per hour	$7.80
Price per pound	$5.40		

These additional data permit the subdivision of the flexible-budget variances in Exhibit 6-5 into separate price and efficiency variances:

	ACTUAL COSTS	FLEXIBLE BUDGET	FLEXIBLE-BUDGET VARIANCE	PRICE VARIANCE*	EFFICIENCY VARIANCE*
Direct material	$270,000	$200,000	$70,000 U	$20,000 U	$50,000 U
Direct labor	171,600	160,000	11,600 U	$ 4,400 F	$16,000 U

Computations to be explained shortly.

The flexible budget totals for variable costs such as direct materials and direct labor are also sometimes expressed as *total standard costs allowed.* They are computed as follows:

$$\begin{pmatrix}\textbf{Actual}\\ \textbf{good}\\ \textbf{output}\end{pmatrix} \times \begin{pmatrix}\textbf{Input allowed}\\ \textbf{per unit of}\\ \textbf{output}\end{pmatrix} \times \begin{pmatrix}\textbf{Standard}\\ \textbf{unit price}\\ \textbf{of input}\end{pmatrix} = \begin{pmatrix}\textbf{Total standard}\\ \textbf{cost allowed}\end{pmatrix}$$

Direct materials: 10,000 units × 4 pounds × $5 per pound = $200,000
Direct labor: 10,000 units × 2 hours × $8 per hour = $160,000

Before proceeding, note especially that the flexible-budget amounts (that is, the standard costs allowed) are keyed to an initial question: What was the *output* achieved? No isolation of efficiency variances in a standard-cost system can occur without the measurement of *outputs* as well as *inputs*.

definitions of price and efficiency variances

Price variance was defined and discussed earlier in conjunction with revenue variance. Its definition also holds with respect to cost variances. Definitions follow:

Price variance—the difference between actual unit prices and budgeted unit prices multiplied by the quantity of goods or services in question.

Efficiency variance—the difference between the quantity of actual inputs (such as pounds of materials) and the quantity of inputs that should have been allowed (the flexible budget) *for any actual output achieved* (such as finished goods), multiplied by some budgeted price.

A major purpose of computing price variances is to exclude the often confusing effects of price fluctuations from other variances. The definition of the efficiency variance has an important underlying assumption. **All unit prices are budgeted prices,** which are also called *predetermined, estimated,* or *standard prices,* depending on the specific context.

The evaluation of performance is eased by isolating the items that are more likely to be under the manager's influence. The usual approach is to separate *price* factors from *efficiency* factors. Price factors tend to be less subject to immediate control, principally because price is more affected by external forces. **Price variances are computed not only for their own sake *but to obtain a sharper focus on efficiency.*** In this way, efficiency can be measured by holding unit prices constant. After all, managers do not like uncontrollable price fluctuations to affect judgments about whether their operating performance is efficient.

price and efficiency variance computations

The detailed computations of price and efficiency variances follow:

Price variance: difference between actual unit prices of inputs and standard unit prices *multiplied by the actual inputs:*

$$\begin{pmatrix}\text{Difference in}\\ \text{unit price}\\ \text{of inputs}\end{pmatrix} \times \begin{pmatrix}\text{Actual}\\ \text{inputs}\\ \text{used}\end{pmatrix} = \begin{pmatrix}\text{Price}\\ \text{variance}\end{pmatrix}$$

Direct materials: (\$5.40 − \$5.00) × 50,000 = \$20,000 Unfavorable (U)
Direct labor: (\$7.80 − \$8.00) × 22,000 = \$4,400 Favorable (F)

Efficiency variance: For any given level of output (e.g., units produced) the efficiency variance is the difference between the inputs that should have been used and the inputs that were actually used—holding unit prices of inputs constant at the standard unit price:[3]

$$\begin{pmatrix}\text{Inputs} & & \text{Inputs that}\\ \text{actually} & - & \text{should have}\\ \text{used} & & \text{been used}\end{pmatrix} \times \begin{pmatrix}\text{Standard}\\ \text{unit}\\ \text{price of inputs}\end{pmatrix} = \begin{pmatrix}\text{Efficiency}\\ \text{variance}\end{pmatrix}$$

$$\begin{pmatrix}\text{Actual} & & \text{Standard allowed}\\ \text{pounds or} & - & \text{pounds or hours}\\ \text{hours used} & & \text{for good output}\end{pmatrix} \times \begin{pmatrix}\text{Standard}\\ \text{unit}\\ \text{price of inputs}\end{pmatrix} = \begin{pmatrix}\text{Efficiency}\\ \text{variance}\end{pmatrix}$$

Direct materials: (50,000 − 40,000) × \$5.00 = \$50,000 U
Direct labor: (22,000 − 20,000) × \$8.00 = \$16,000 U

efficiency and effectiveness

Efficiency and effectiveness are often distinguished as separate concepts. **Efficiency** is defined as the relationship between inputs and outputs. The fewer inputs used to obtain a given output, the greater the efficiency. **Effectiveness** is defined as the attainment of a predetermined goal.

[3]Expressed algebraically, these variances are $V_p = (AP - SP) \times AQ$ and $V_e = (AQ - SQ) \times SP$. V_p = price variance, V_e = efficiency variance, AP = actual unit price of inputs, SP = standard unit price of inputs, AQ = actual quantity of inputs, SQ = standard quantity of inputs allowed for good output.

Performance may be both efficient and effective, but either condition can occur without the other. For example, Webb Company set a static budget goal of producing and selling 12,000 units. Subsequently, only 10,000 units were produced and sold. Performance would be judged ineffective. Whether performance was efficient is a separate question. The degree of efficiency is measured by comparing actual outputs achieved (10,000 units) with actual inputs. In Webb's case, performance was both ineffective and inefficient.

measuring and expressing output

Exhibit 6-7 is a graphical representation of the analysis of direct labor. The cost function is linear, sloping upward at a standard price of $8.00 per hour. At any quantity of output you can read the total standard costs that would be allowed for any given output. Note that quantity is expressed in hours rather than in physical units of product. *This is commonly done because most departments have an assortment of products; hours become a useful common denominator for measuring the total level of all production.*

Standard-cost systems frequently do not express output as, say, 10,000 ash-trays. Instead, output is expressed as 20,000 **standard hours allowed** (also called **standard hours earned, standard hours worked.** or, most accurately, **standard hours of input allowed for good output produced).** This is another key concept in standard costs, so be sure you grasp it before reading on.

substitute terminology

To underscore their basic similarity, the two primary variances are designated here as price and efficiency variances for both direct material and direct labor. In practice, however, be alert for a variety of terms that are sometimes used to designate these variances. For example, the price variance is often called a *rate* variance when it is used in conjunction with direct labor. The efficiency variance is often called a *usage* or *quantity* variance when it is used in conjunction with either direct materials or direct labor.

In standard-cost systems, the concept of flexible budget, in contrast to static budget, is pivotal to the analysis of variances. **For brevity, the terms *budget* and *budget variance* will frequently be used henceforth instead of *flexible budget* and *flexible-budget variance*.** For example, Exhibit 6-7 might have used *budget* and *budgeted* without the *flexible* adjective.

cost-benefit approach to variances

In practice, direct material and direct labor are often said to be controlled with the aid of *standard costs,* whereas all other costs are said to be controlled with the aid of *departmental overhead budgets.* This distinction probably arose, because, as Exhibit 6-6 indicates, there may be different levels of analysis desired for different costs. Indeed, direct material and direct labor are relatively costly and easily identifiable for control purposes. Therefore, managers may seek highly refined methods for monitoring such costs.[4] In contrast, overhead costs are usually collections of many individual costs, none of which justifies an elaborate control system. Consequently, some companies

[4]The pace of production is often watched closely. For example, at a General Motors factory, X-Model cars are supposed to be produced at the rate of 1 every 51.3 seconds, 70 cars per hour, 1,400 cars per day. Some organizations use a Performance Achievement Monitor (PAM) made by Pammac Corp. of Scotland. A worker using a PAM gets constant feedback by watching a digital screen. Effort and methods are adjusted accordingly, often with dramatic improvements in productivity.

EXHIBIT 6-7 *(Place a clip in this page for easy reference.)*

Graphical Analysis of Direct Labor

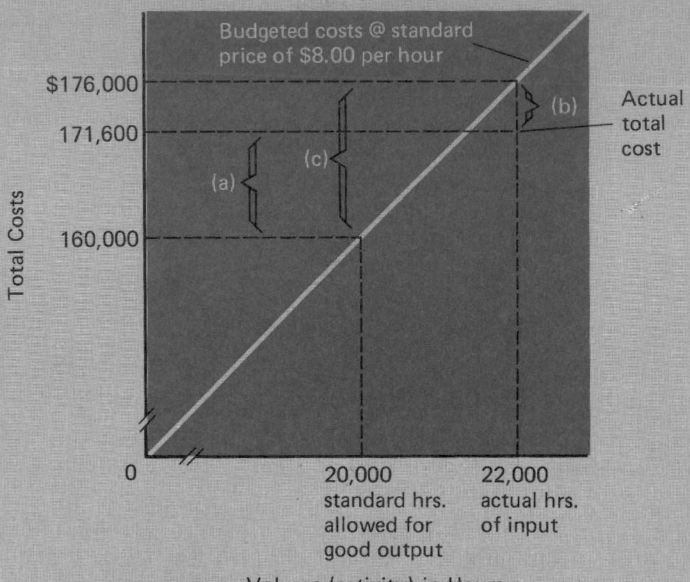

(a) Budget variance = Actual costs − Budgeted costs
= $11,600 U, as subdivided in (b) and (c)

(b) Price variance = Difference in price X Actual hours
= $4,400 F

(c) Efficiency variance = Difference in hours X Standard price
= $16,000 U

The graphic relationships can also be analyzed as follows:

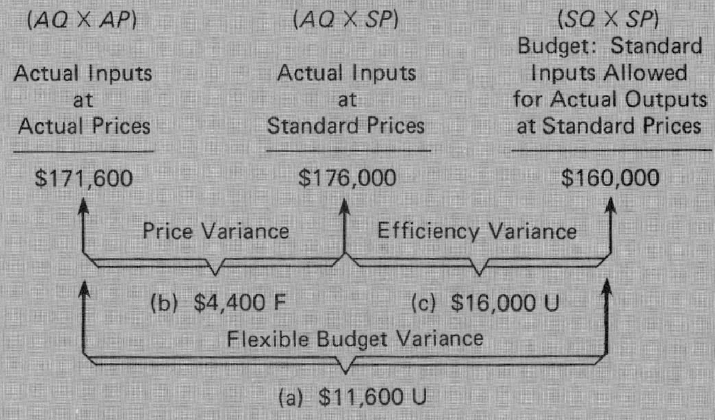

U = Unfavorable; F = Favorable

may analyze material on a daily basis, labor on a weekly basis, and overhead on a monthly basis.

Exhibits 6-5 and 6-6 underscore the cost-benefit approach to management accounting systems. Some costs may receive heavy analysis; others, almost no analysis. For example, the direct-material and direct-labor variances in Exhibit 6-5 may be subdivided into price and efficiency variances, as just shown. However, regarding other costs, the Webb managers may decide not to have subdivisions beyond the flexible-budget variances in Exhibit 6-5, page 172.

General-ledger entries

illustrative entries

General-ledger accounting for direct material and direct labor has been straightforward until this chapter. Two major inventory accounts have included:

STORES	
Actual costs of direct material purchased	

WORK IN PROCESS	
Actual costs of direct material and direct labor used	

The general-ledger accounting in standard-costing systems introduces some separate accounts for variances.

General-ledger entries for standard-cost systems are usually *monthly* summaries of detailed variance analyses that were computed from day to day. Using the data of our earlier illustration, suppose materials are carried in Stores at *actual* prices in contrast to *standard* prices. All direct-material variances are isolated (that is, separately identified) when Work in Process is charged at standard quantities of inputs allowed times standard unit prices:

1. Work in process	200,000	
Direct-material price variance	20,000	
Direct-material efficiency variance	50,000	
Stores		270,000
To record direct materials used. (Note that unfavorable variances are always debits and favorable variances are always credits.)		

Accrued Payroll is accounted for at *actual* wage rates. Work in Process is charged at standard quantities allowed times *standard rates,* and the direct-labor variances are recognized:

2. Work in process	160,000	
Direct-labor efficiency variance	16,000	
Direct-labor price variance		4,400
Accrued payroll		171,600
To record liability for and allocation of direct-labor costs.		

early warning systems

Our chapter illustration has shown how the price and efficiency variances for materials were computed simultaneously as production occurred. This approach is adequate where material prices are not too volatile, or where large raw-material inventories are not carried, or where the purpose is solely to remove influences of price from efficiency reports. **However, when current control of purchasing activities is also a major objective of isolating price variances, the approach should be modified so that price variances are reported at the time of *purchase* by taking the difference between actual and standard unit price times the actual quantity acquired.** To delay the computation of the price variance until the time the quantity is *issued* (as we did in our illustration) usually defeats the usefulness of the information for control, because corrective action is then seldom possible.

Reconsider our illustration by assuming that 90,000 pounds were purchased during the month, although only 50,000 pounds were requisitioned by the production department:

1a. Stores (90,000 lbs. @ $5.00)	450,000	
Direct-material price variance (90,000 lbs. @ $.40)	36,000	
Accounts payable (90,000 lbs. @ $5.40)		486,000
To record direct-material purchases.		
1b. Work in process (40,000 lbs. @ $5.00)	200,000	
Direct-material efficiency variance (10,000 lbs. @ $5.00)	50,000	
Stores (50,000 lbs. @ $5.00)		250,000
To record direct materials used.		

T-accounts would appear as follows:

STORES	
1a. Actual quantity purchased × standard unit price, 450,000	1b. Actual quantity requisitioned × standard price, 250,000

DIRECT-MATERIAL PRICE VARIANCE	
1a. Actual quantity purchased × difference in unit price, 36,000	

WORK IN PROCESS	
1b. Standard quantity requisitioned × standard unit price, 200,000	

DIRECT-MATERIAL EFFICIENCY VARIANCE	
1b. Difference in quantity used × standard unit price, 50,000	

The major advantage of this system is its stress on the control feature of standard costs, whereby all variances are isolated as early as is economically feasible. Another advantage is the economical simplicity of carrying all inventories at standard unit prices. Thus, it avoids the problems and extra clerical costs of making cost-flow assumptions such as first-in, first-out, or last-in, first-out.

disposition of variances

Like the disposition of underapplied or overapplied overhead discussed in Chapter 4, price and efficiency variances are either written off immediately or prorated among the inventories and cost of goods sold. A full discussion is found in Chapter 8.

costs of data gathering

At first glance, it might appear that standard-cost systems would always be more costly to operate than other systems. Obviously, a startup investment must be made to develop the standards; but the ongoing costs can be even less than so-called actual-cost systems.

Of course, standard-cost systems will be more costly if they are run in complete parallel with an actual-cost system (see Chapter 2) or normal-cost system (see Chapter 4). For instance, if actual direct-material costs and direct-labor costs continue to be traced to individual products even though a standard-cost system is in use, the costs of recordkeeping will increase.

On the other hand, **many standard-cost systems have been adopted for the *major* purpose of saving recordkeeping costs.** A standard-cost system can be designed so that

1. No "actual" costs of stores, work in process, and finished goods are traced to batches of product on a day-to-day basis. Only records of physical counts are kept.
2. Actual consumption of material and labor can be totaled by operation or department for, say, a month without tracing such consumption to jobs. Feedback on performance can be based on these actual totals of input compared with the total standard allowed inputs for the physical output during the month. However, the major advantage of this procedure is its clerical simplicity.

Standards for control

How demanding should standards be? Should they express perfection, or should they allow for the various factors that prevent perfect performance?

current attainability

Perfection, ideal, maximum efficiency, or theoretical standard costs reflect industrial engineers' dreams of a "factory heaven." Perfection standard costs are the absolute minimum costs that are possible under the best conceivable operating conditions, using existing specifications and equipment. Ideal standards, like other standards, are used where the management feels that they provide psychologically productive goals.

Currently attainable standard costs are the costs that should be incurred under very efficient operating conditions. They are difficult but possible to achieve. Attainable standards are looser than ideal standards because of allowance for normal spoilage, ordinary machine breakdowns, and lost time. However, attainable standards are usually set tight enough so that the operating people will consider the achievement of standard performance to be a satisfying accomplishment. In other words, variances are more likely to be slightly unfavorable than favorable—but favorable variances may be attained by a little more than expected efficiency.

Currently attainable standards are the most widely used because the resulting standard costs can serve many purposes simultaneously and because they have the most appealing motivational impact on employees.[5]

presence of expected variances

Currently attainable standards may be used simultaneously for product costing, master budgets, and motivation. Throughout the illustrations and problems in this book, unless otherwise stated, currently attainable standards are assumed to be in use.

If standards are not currently attainable because they are perfection standards, the amount budgeted for financial (cash) planning purposes has to differ from the standard. Otherwise, projected income and cash disbursements will be forecast incorrectly. In such cases, perfection standards may be used for compiling performance reports, but expected variances are stipulated in the budget for cash planning. For example, if unusually strict labor standards are used, the standard cost per finished

[5]For a discussion of budgets as targets, see Anthony Hopwood, *Accounting and Human Behavior* (London: Prentice-Hall International, 1974), pp. 57–69.

unit may be $16 even though top management anticipates an unfavorable performance variance of, say, $1.60 per unit. In the master budget the total labor costs allowed would be $17.60 per unit: $16.00 plus an expected variance of $1.60. In our example, a master budget could conceivably include the following item:

Direct labor:	
Budget allowance shown on departmental performance report	$160,000
Expected variance that will appear in cash budget	16,000
Total budget allowance for cash planning	$176,000

developing the standards

The standard-setting and budget-setting process in an organization often is primarily the responsibility of the line personnel directly involved. The relative tightness of the budget is the result of face-to-face discussion and bargaining between the manager and his or her immediate superior. The budgetary accountants, the industrial engineers, and the market researchers should extend all desired technical assistance and advice, but the final decisions ordinarily should not be theirs. The line manager is the person who is supposed to accept and live with the budget or standard.

The job of the accounting department is (a) to price the physical standards—that is, to express the physical standards in the form of dollars and cents; and (b) to report operating performance in comparison with standards.

Textbooks generally give the impression that standard costs are always based on technical engineering studies and rigorous specifications. Accurate measurement is indeed the foundation for control. However, although a rigorous approach is desirable, it should be remembered that less-scientific standards may still provide a useful way of presenting information in order to stimulate corrective action.

trade-offs among variances

Managers often have opportunities to take advantage of bargain purchases or to combine available resources in a way that will save overall costs. For example, a quantity of a raw material having a few inferior characteristics (perhaps a different grade of lumber or shade of color) might be consciously acquired at an unusually low price. This material might lead to unusually heavy spoilage or excessive labor times in order to produce a finished product that will meet the standard quality specifications. Nevertheless, the manager may have enough discretion to proceed. The aim would be to reduce the total costs of manufacturing by trading off favorable price variances against expected unfavorable efficiency variances.

A standard-cost system should not be a straitjacket that prevents the manager from looking at the overall company objectives. Too often, each unfavorable variance is regarded as, ipso facto, bad; and each favorable variance is regarded as, ipso facto, good. If the manager guesses wrong, and the unfavorable efficiency variances exceed the favorable price variance, the decision to make the bargain purchase was unfavorable despite the favorable label pinned on the price variance. Similarly, if the manager guesses correctly, so that the favorable price variance exceeds the unfavorable efficiency variances, the decision was favorable despite the unfavorable label pinned on the efficiency variances. The point is that there are too many interdependencies among activities; an "unfavorable" or a "favorable" label should not lead the manager to jump to conclusions about what happened. By themselves, such labels merely raise questions and provide clues. They are attention directors, not answer givers.

Controllability and variances

responsibility for material variances

In most companies, the *acquisition* of materials or merchandise entails different control decisions than their *use.* Thus, the responsibility for price variances usually rests with the purchasing officer, and the responsibility for efficiency variances usually rests with the production manager or sales manager.

Price variances are often regarded as measures of forecasting ability rather than of failure to buy at specified prices. Some control over the price variance is obtainable by getting many quotations, buying in economical lots, taking advantage of cash discounts, and selecting the most economical means of delivery. Price variances may lead to improvements in methods of forecasting and decisions to change suppliers or freight carriers.

However, failure to meet price standards may result from a sudden rush of sales orders or from unanticipated changes in production schedules, which in turn may require the purchasing officer to buy at uneconomical prices or to request delivery by air freight. In such cases, the responsibility may rest with the sales manager or the head of production scheduling, rather than with the purchasing officer.

responsibility for labor variances

In most companies, because of union contracts or other predictable factors, labor prices can be foreseen with much greater accuracy than can prices of materials. Therefore, labor price variances tend to be relatively insignificant.

Labor, unlike material and supplies, cannot ordinarily be stored for later use. The acquisition and use of labor occur simultaneously. For these reasons, labor rate variances are usually charged to the same manager who is responsible for labor usage.

Labor price variances may be traceable to faulty predictions of the labor rates. However, the more likely causes include (1) the use of a single average standard labor price for a given operation that is, in fact, performed by individuals earning different rates because of seniority; (2) the assignment of a worker earning, perhaps, \$12 per hour to a given operation that should be assigned to a less-skilled worker earning, say, \$10 per hour; and (3) the payment of hourly rates, instead of prescribed piece rates, because of low productivity.[6]

material efficiency

The physical "engineered" relationship of inputs to outputs is central to the development of standards for direct material, direct labor, or any other factor of production. Therefore, daily and weekly reports to first-line supervisors are often expressed in physical terms only—gallons used, pounds consumed, hours of input, and so on. An efficiency variance may be expressed in dollars by multiplying the standard unit price by the physical quantity variance.

Exhibit 6-8 is a **standard bill of materials.** It specifies the physical quantities allowed for manufacturing a specified number of acceptable finished units. In many companies, when production of a product is about to begin, the standard bill becomes the stores requisition. The storekeeper then issues the standard amount of materials allowed. As production occurs, any *additional* materials needed may be withdrawn from stores only by submitting an **excess materials requisition.** The latter usually bears a distinct color. The supervisor must sign the requisition, so he or she is immediately informed of excess usage.

[6]See Chapter 26 for an explanation of piecework incentive plans.

EXHIBIT 6-8

Standard Bill of Materials

Assembly No. b   Description TV Table

Part Number		Number Required	Description
A	1426	4 sq. ft.	Plastic sheet — Pearl grey
	455	1/8 lb.	Adhesive
	642	1	Table top
	714	4	Steel legs
	961	1	Nut and bolt kit

A periodic summary of excess materials requisitions provides the total unfavorable efficiency variance (often called *usage* or *quantity* variance). If performance is better than standard, special returned-materials forms are used to calculate favorable efficiency variances. Many possible reasons for efficiency variances include quality, workmanship, choice of materials, mix of materials, and faulty standards.

mutual effects Exhibit 6-9 shows how the $20,000 original price variance for materials could be subdivided:

1. Pure price variance = Difference in price × Standard quantity (instead of Actual quantity)
2. Combined or joint price-efficiency variance = Difference in price × Difference in quantity

EXHIBIT 6-9

Graphic Analysis of Variances

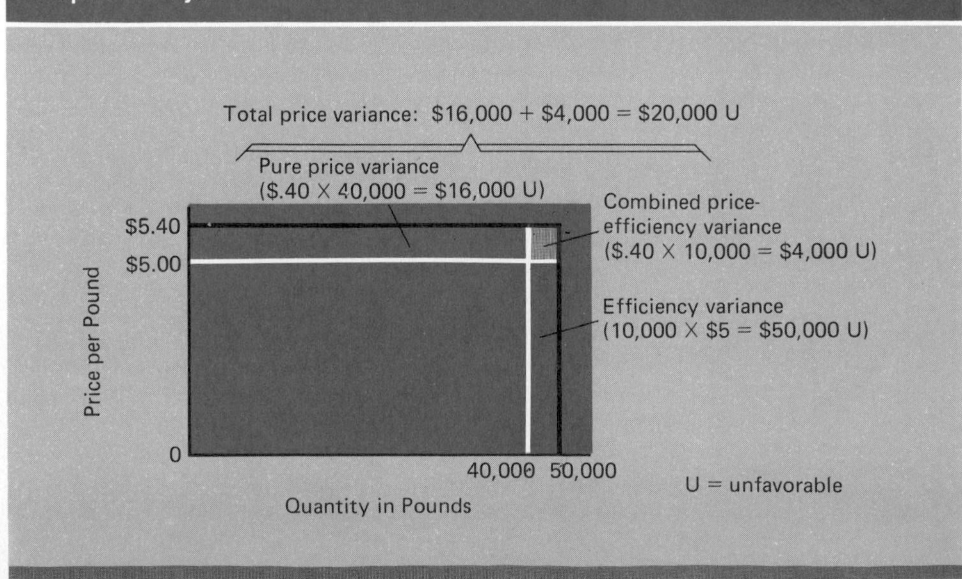

1. Pure price variance = $.40 × 40,000 =		$16,000 U
2. Combined variance = $.40 × 10,000 =		4,000 U
Price variance as originally calculated	=	$20,000 U

The importance of this refinement depends on the significance and usefulness of isolating the joint variance. Where executive bonuses depend on variances, this refinement may be necessary. For example, an unfavorable total-price variance, as ordinarily computed, could be partially attributable to inefficient usage. Thus, a part of the price variance in our example would not have arisen if quantities used had not exceeded standard: (50,000 lbs. − 40,000 lbs.) ($5.40 − $5.00) = $4,000. In this book, we shall not refine our analysis this far; all of the $20,000 is called price variance. That is, we shall consider the price variance to be the sum of the pure price variance and the combined price-efficiency variance. The philosophy of responsibility accounting supports this practice. Why? Because the responsibility of the purchasing manager is usually deemed to include buying for *all* needs regardless of whether the materials are used efficiently.

labor efficiency

The human element makes the setting of labor efficiency standards (also called *time, usage, quantity,* or *performance* standards) a complicated task. As may be expected, disputes over proper standards are much more likely to arise over labor efficiency standards than over material efficiency standards.

Time standards are usually set for each operation. In turn, **master operations lists,** such as the one in Exhibit 6-10, may be compiled for routing and scheduling a variety of products.

The source documents for variance reports are usually some form of work ticket showing the actual time used. These work tickets are analyzed and variances are coded and classified. The classifications are almost always by responsibility (that is, by cost center), and often by operations, products, orders, and causes. Thus, a work ticket may have a number designating departmental responsibility and another number designating the cause of the variance. Causes may include machinery breakdowns, rework, faulty material, use of nonpreferred equipment, and so forth.

Absenteeism can dramatically affect efficiency. A General Motors executive has commented:

> When deer season opens, production drops from 70 to 35 cars per hour. Workers are shifted around to handle unfamiliar jobs. Quality declines. And the workers get paid overtime. . . . We have begun computerizing medical excuses signed by local doctors to determine if any definitive pattern exists among the chronic absentees.

setup time

Machines and accessory equipment often must be adjusted and "made ready" before a particular operation or job can commence. This **setup time** is easily traceable to an operation or a job, yet its total cost is seldom affected by whether 100 pieces or 2,000 pieces are subsequently processed. The question then is whether setup costs should be treated as direct labor or as a part of factory overhead. No categorical answer can be given. It seems clear that if production runs fluctuate wildly, setup costs should not ordinarily be regarded as direct labor, because the cost *per unit* of product would fluctuate solely because of the length of production run.

For analytical purposes and for cost-control follow-up, setup costs should not be commingled and averaged with the regular direct-labor costs even if it appears

EXHIBIT 6-10

Operations Routing Sheet

MASTER OPERATIONS LIST

Part Name Fuel pump body with bushings Part Number B-489

Stock Specifications Grey iron casting Standard Quantity 200

Operation Number	Department Number	Standard Time Allowed in Minutes		Description of Operation
		Setup	Operation Per Unit	
20	27	90	10.2	Drill, bore, face, chamfer and ream
25	29	18	.7	Face and chamfer hub
30	29	12	1.5	Mill eng. fit pad
35	31	18	8.0	Drill and tap complete
40	29	12	1.5	Mill clearance
45	29	—	1.8	Clean and grind hose connection
50	29	12	2.3	Press in 2 bushings G-98 and face flange on mandrel
	13			Inspect
	21			To stockroom

desirable to trace setup costs to specific jobs or operations. Most standard-cost systems have standard lot sizes for production runs. Often setup costs are allowed for in the standard direct-labor cost per unit by allocating the setup labor for each operation over the quantity in the standard lot. This practice may be suitable for product-costing purposes; but it has drawbacks for cost-control purposes, especially where standard lot sizes are seldom adhered to, because it mixes together two dissimilar elements that are subject to different control features. As a minimum, then, setup costs should always be coded so that they may be sharply distinguished from operating-labor costs. In this book, we shall assume that setup costs are classified as a part of overhead.

When to investigate variances

When should variances be investigated? Frequently the answer is based on subjective judgments, hunches, guesses, and rules of thumb. **The most troublesome aspect of feedback is deciding when a variance is significant enough to warrant management's attention.** For some items, a small deviation may prompt follow-up. For other items, a minimum dollar amount or 5, 10, or 25 percent deviations from budget may be necessary before investigations commence. Of course, a 4 percent variance in a $1 million material cost may deserve more attention than a 20 percent variance in a $10,000 repair cost. Therefore, rules such as "Investigate all variances exceeding $5,000, or 25 percent of standard cost, whichever is lower" are common.

Variance analysis is subject to the same cost-benefit test as other phases of an information system. The trouble with the foregoing rules of thumb is that they are too frequently based on subjective assessments, guesses, or hunches. The field of statistics offers tools to help reduce these subjective features of variance analysis. These tools help answer the cost-benefit question, and they help separate variances caused by random events from variances that are controllable.

Accounting systems have traditionally implied that a standard is a single acceptable measure. Practically, the accountant (and everybody else) realizes that the standard is a *band* or *range* of possible acceptable outcomes. Consequently, the accountant expects variances to fluctuate randomly within some normal limits.

By definition, a random variance per se is within this band or range. It calls for no corrective action to an existing process; random variances are attributable to chance rather than to management's implementation decisions. For a further discussion, see Chapter 25.

SUMMARY

Variance analysis can be conducted in various levels of detail, depending on managers' preferences. The concepts of a flexible budget and the measurements of both inputs and outputs are the keys to isolating separate effects of prices, efficiency, and sales volume.

Standard costs are used for building a budgeting and feedback system. They aid management predictions and provide a framework for judging performance. Actual costs are compared with standard costs to obtain variances. Variances raise questions; they do not provide answers. The variances are investigated to decide (a) how to improve the implementation of a given decision model or set of plans, or (b) how to change objectives, methods, or standards.

Currently attainable standards are the most widely used because they usually have the most desirable motivational impact and because they may be used for a variety of accounting purposes, including financial planning, as well as for monitoring departmental performance.

When standards are currently attainable, there is no real difference between standards and budgets. A standard is a *unit* concept, whereas a budget is a *total* concept. In a sense, the standard is the budget for one unit.

Material and labor variances are primarily divided into two categories: (a) price or rate, and (b) efficiency or usage. Price or rate variances are computed by multiplying differences in price by actual quantities. Efficiency or usage variances remove influences of price changes; they are computed by multiplying differences in quantities by a standard price.

General-ledger treatments for standard costs vary considerably. The method advocated in this book stresses isolation of variances as quickly as possible.

It is extremely important to personalize variances so that each variance is assignable to the person primarily responsible. Otherwise, the investigative follow-ups of reported variances—where the real payoff lies—will be fruitless. There is also a need to have some objective way to decide when a given variance is significant enough to warrant investigation.

problems for self-study

problem 1

Consider some changed data in the Webb Company illustration in the chapter. All the necessary original and changed data follow:

Actual unit selling price for all units sold, $75
Unit sales, 10,800
Budgeted or standard amounts per unit:

Selling price	$70
Direct material (4 pounds @ $5.00)	20
Direct labor (2 hours @ $8.00)	16
Variable factory overhead (2 hours @ $1.50)	3
Variable selling and administrative costs	7

Budgeted fixed factory overhead, $96,000
Actual fixed factory overhead, $92,000
Budget and actual fixed selling and administrative costs, $80,000
Actual variable selling and administrative costs, $73,000
Other actual data:

Direct-material costs	$270,000	Direct-labor costs	$171,600
Pounds of input	50,000	Hours of input	22,000
Price per pound	$ 5.40	Labor price per hour	$ 7.80
		Variable factory overhead	$ 32,000

REQUIRED

1. Prepare an exhibit similar to Exhibit 6-4.
2. Compute (a) price and efficiency variances for direct material and (b) price and efficiency variances for direct labor. Present your answer in a format similar to the analysis that appears at the bottom of Exhibit 6-7.
3. Suppose that the Webb Company control system were designed to isolate material price variances upon purchases rather than upon usage of the materials. Suppose further that 60,000 pounds of material were purchased during April, but only 50,000 pounds were issued to production. Compute the purchase-price variance that would be reported by the control system.

solution 1

1. The solution is in Exhibit 6-11. Note that the dramatic effect of the price increase is ($75 − $70) × 10,800 units = $54,000, favorable. Thus, the expected operating income of $83,200 at the achieved volume level was exceeded despite the $49,800 of unfavorable variable-cost variances.

EXHIBIT 6-11

Summary of Performance

For the Month Ended April 30, 19_1

	(1) ACTUAL	(2) (1) − (3) FLEXIBLE-BUDGET VARIANCES	(3) FLEXIBLE BUDGET	(4) (3) − (5) SALES VOLUME VARIANCES	(5) STATIC BUDGET
Physical units of output	10,800	—	10,800	1,200 U	12,000
Revenue (sales)	$810,000	$54,000 F	$756,000	$84,000 U	$840,000
Variable costs	546,600*	49,800 U	496,800‡	55,200 F	552,000
Contribution margin	263,400	4,200 F	259,200	28,800 U	288,000
Fixed costs	172,000†	4,000 F	176,000	—	176,000
Operating income	$ 91,400	$ 8,200 F	$ 83,200	$28,800 U	$112,000

**Direct material*	*$270,000*
Direct labor	*171,600*
Variable factory overhead	*32,000*
Selling and administrative costs	*73,000*
Total variable costs	*$546,600*

†Fixed factory overhead	*$ 92,000*
Fixed selling and administrative costs	*80,000*
Total fixed costs	*$172,000*

‡10,800 × ($20 + $16 + $3 + $7) = $496,800

2. Exhibit 6-12 presents a general framework for analyzing variances. It may seem awkward at first, but upon review you will discover that it provides perspective and insight.

EXHIBIT 6-12 *(Place a clip on this page for easy reference.)*

Framework for Analysis of Variances

	(AQ × AP)*	(AQ × SP)†	(SQ × SP)‡
Direct materials	50,000 × $5.40 = $270,000	50,000 × $5.00 = $250,000	10,800 × 4 lbs. × $5.00 = $216,000
	50,000 × (5.40 − $5.00)		(50,000 − 43,200) × $5.00
	Price variance, $20,000 U		Efficiency variance, $34,000 U
	Flexible-budget variance, $54,000 U		
Direct labor	22,000 × $7.80 = $171,600	22,000 × $8.00 = $176,000	10,800 × 2 hrs. × $8.00 = $172,800
	22,000 × ($7.80 − $8.00)		(22,000 − 21,600) × $8.00
	Price variance, $4,400 F		Efficiency variance, $3,200 U
	Flexible-budget variance, $1,200 F		

**Actual costs incurred: actual inputs × actual prices.*
†Actual inputs × standard prices.
‡Flexible-budget amount: standard inputs allowed for actual outputs achieved × standard prices.

3. The purchase-price variance would be the full 60,000 pounds × $.40 = $24,000, unfavorable. In most accounting systems, the variance would reduce operating income by $24,000 instead of 50,000 pounds × $.40 = $20,000. For further discussion of the effects of variances on operating income, see the next two chapters.

problem 2

Consider the following for the Maher Company for April, when 2,000 finished units were produced:

Direct materials used, 4,400 pounds. The standard allowance per finished unit is two pounds at $5 per pound. Six thousand pounds were purchased at $5.50 per pound, a total of $33,000.

Actual direct-labor hours were 6,500 at a total cost of $40,300. The standard labor cost per finished unit was $18. Standard labor time allowed is three hours per unit.

REQUIRED

1. Journal entries for a "normal"-cost system as described in Chapter 4. That is, "actual" charges for direct materials and direct labor are charged to Work in Process.
2. Journal entries for a "standard"-cost system.
3. Show an alternative approach, including journal entries, to the way you quantified the material-price variance in requirement 2. Which way is better? Explain.

solution 2

1. ***NORMAL-COST SYSTEM***

Stores or direct-material inventory	**$33,000**	
Accounts payable		**$33,000**
Work in process (4,400 @ $5.50)	**24,200**	
Stores		**24,200**
Work in process (6,500 @ $6.20)	**40,300**	
Accrued payroll		**40,300**

2. *STANDARD-COST SYSTEM*

Stores or direct-material inventory (6,000 @ $5.00)	$30,000	
Direct-material purchase-price variance	3,000	
Accounts payable		$33,000
Work in process (4,000 @ $5.00)	20,000	
Direct-material efficiency variance	2,000	
Stores (4,400 @ $5.00)		22,000
Work in process (2,000 @ $18.00)	36,000	
Direct-labor price variance	1,300	
Direct-labor efficiency variance	3,000	
Accrued payroll		40,300

($AQ \times AP$) Actual Inputs × Actual Prices	($AQ \times SP$) Actual Inputs × Standard Prices	($SQ \times SP$) Flexible Budget: Standard Inputs Allowed for Actual Outputs × Standard Prices
(6,500 × $6.20) $40,300	(6,500 × $6.00) $39,000	(2,000 × $18.00) or (6,000 × $ 6.00) $36,000

6,500 × $.20 — Price variance, $1,300 U

500 @ $6.00 — Efficiency variance, $3,000 U

Flexible-budget variance, $4,300 U

3. An alternative standard-cost approach to that shown in 2 (Approach in 2 is better *for control purposes* because it isolates variances earlier, when something is more likely to be done about the variances):

Stores	$33,000	
Accounts payable		$33,000
Work in process (4,000 @ $5.00)	20,000	
Direct-material price variance (4,400 @ $.50)	2,200	
Direct-material efficiency variance	2,000	
Stores (4,400 @ $5.50)		24,200

The direct-labor entries would be the same as under requirement 2.

Terms to Learn

currently attainable standards *effectiveness* *efficiency*
efficiency variance *excess materials requisition*
expected variance *flexible budget* *flexible-budget variance*
master operations lists *price variance* *sales volume variance*
setup time *standard bill of materials* *standard costs*
standard hours allowed *standard hours earned*
standard hours of input allowed for good output produced
standard hours worked *static budget* *variable budget*

Special Points and Pitfalls

Some important relationships deserve emphasis:

ACTUAL RESULTS		ACTUAL INPUTS × STANDARD PRICES		FLEXIBLE BUDGET		STATIC (MASTER) BUDGET
XXX		XXX		XXX		XXX
↑	Price variance	↑	Efficiency variance	↑	Sales volume variance	↑
↑		Flexible-budget variance		↑	Sales volume variance	↑

The flexible-budget variance enables the manager to separate the effects of sales volume from other explanations of why the original (static) budget was not achieved.

In turn, the flexible-budget variance is often subdivided into its price and efficiency components. Efficiency is measured by comparing inputs with outputs. Therefore, some measures of inputs and outputs are necessary to obtain an efficiency variance.

Price variances enhance understanding of the influence of prices on actual results. In addition, price variances permit the exclusion of price effects from *other* variances. The definitions of efficiency *and* sales volume variances have a noteworthy common assumption: All unit prices are *standard* or *budgeted* prices.

As a minimum, be sure to solve the problems for self-study before proceeding to the next chapter. Inevitably, the first question to ask in solving standard-cost problems is, What was the good output achieved? The second question frequently asked is, What were the standard direct-labor hours allowed for the good output achieved? Because more than one product is frequently produced, output is usually expressed in terms of standard hours allowed which is also called standard hours earned.

QUESTIONS, PROBLEMS, AND CASES

6-1 Why do techniques for overhead control differ from techniques for control of direct materials and direct labor?

6-2 When can't the terms *budgeted performance* and *standard performance* be used interchangeably?

6-3 "The idea of comparing performance at one activity level with a plan that was developed at some other activity level must be pertinent in judging the effectiveness of planning and control." Comment.

6-4 What are standard costs? Why is their use superior to comparisons of actual data with past data?

6-5 What are the key questions in deciding how variances should be collected and analyzed?

6-6 List and briefly describe two different types of standards.

6-7 "Cost control means cost reduction." Do you agree? Why?

6-8 List four common causes of material-price variances.

6-9 List the major factors that affect control procedures for material quantities.

6-10 Define *standard bill of materials, excess materials requisition, operations list.*

6-11 "Setup costs are easily traceable to specific jobs. Therefore, they should be classified as direct-labor costs." Do you agree? Why?

6-12 "Standard costing is OK for big companies that can afford such an elaborate system. But our company relies on an 'actual' system because it saves clerical costs." Comment.

6-13 How does management decide when a variance is large enough to warrant investigation?

6-14 List five purposes of standard costs.

6-15 Who is responsible for developing standards?

6-16 Why do budgeted variances arise?

6-17 When will budgets differ from standards? When will they be the same?

6-18 ***Material variances.*** Assume that a table manufacturer uses plastic tops. Plastic is purchased in large sizes, cut down as needed, and then glued to the tables. A given-sized table will require a specified amount of plastic. If the amount of plastic needed per Type-F TV table is 4 square feet and the cost per square foot is 65¢, then the standard cost of plastic for a single TV table would be $2.60. But a certain production run of 1,000 tables results in usage of 4,300 square feet at 70¢ per square foot, a total cost of $3,010.

REQUIRED Compute the price variance and the efficiency variance.

6-19 ***General journal entries for materials.*** Consider the following data compiled by the manufacturer of 1,000 television tables:

Standard price per square foot	$.65
Actual price per square foot	$.62
Standard quantity allowed	4,000 square feet
Actual quantity used	4,300 square feet
Actual quantity purchased	5,000 square feet

REQUIRED

1. The manager of purchasing wants early monitoring of price variances, and the manager of production wants early detection of efficiency variances. Prepare journal entries that would most closely reflect the timing of the isolation of each variance. Price variances are isolated upon purchase of direct materials, and efficiency variances upon the use of excess-materials requisitions.
2. Another company has the same process, but its managers are less concerned about early isolation of variances. Instead, price variances are isolated upon issuance of direct material to the producing departments. In this way, the production department's efficiency can still be measured because price volatility will not affect the efficiency variance. This company does not isolate efficiency variances until after production is completed. Prepare journal entries that would most closely reflect the timing of the isolation of each variance. Show T-accounts.

6-20 ***Journal entries for direct labor.*** The AB Company had a standard rate (price) of $16.00 per direct-labor hour. Actual hours in July were 10,263 at an actual price of $15.80 per hour. The standard direct-labor hours allowed for the output achieved were 10,000.

REQUIRED Prepare general-journal entries that isolate price and efficiency variances. Prepare one entry whereby Work in Process is carried at standard hours allowed times standard prices. Then prepare a second set of entries whereby (a) price variances are isolated as labor costs are originally journalized, and (b) efficiency variances are isolated as units are transferred from Work in Process to Finished Goods.

6-21 ***Analysis of variances.*** Chemical, Inc., has set up the following standards for materials and direct labor:

	PER FINISHED BATCH
Materials: 10 lbs. @ $3.00	$30.00
Direct labor: .5 hours @ $20.00	10.00

The number of finished units budgeted for the period was 10,000; 9,810 units were actually produced.

Actual results were:

Materials: 98,073 lbs. used	
Direct labor: 4,900 hrs.	$102,900

REQUIRED

During the month, purchases amounted to 100,000 lbs. at a total cost of $310,000. Price variances are isolated upon purchase.

1. Give journal entries to record the data above.
2. Show computations of all material and labor variances.
3. Comment on each of the variances.

6-22 ***Comparison of general-ledger entries for direct materials and direct labor.*** The Sweeney Co. has the following data for the month of March, when 1,100 finished units were produced:

Direct materials used, 3,600 pounds. The standard allowance per finished unit is 3 pounds at $3.00 per pound. Five thousand pounds were purchased at $3.25 per pound, a total of $16,250.

Direct labor, actual hours, was 2,450 hours at a total cost of $9,800. The standard labor cost per finished unit was $7.60. Standard time allowed is 2 hours per unit.

REQUIRED

1. Prepare journal entries for a "normal"-cost system.
2. Prepare journal entries for a "standard"-cost system. Support your entries with a detailed variance analysis, using the columnar analytical format illustrated in the chapter.
3. Show an alternative approach, including journal entries, to the way you quantified the material price variance in requirement 2. Which way is better, and why?

6-23 ***Budgets and expected variances.*** The Werelius Manufacturing Company uses standard costs and budgets for planning and controlling current production of its two products, F and G. Schedules for the year ending December 19_1 call for the production of 6,000 units of F and 1,000 units of G.

The standards set for direct labor call for 14 direct-labor hours per unit for F and 20 direct-labor hours for G. However, these standards have been deliberately made tight so as to encourage better performance. Management expects that direct-labor performance will fall short of these goals by one direct-labor hour per unit for each product.

The standard rate for direct labor is $16 per hour. However, negotiations are under way with the union for a new contract. Although the results of these negotiations are uncertain, management expects the rate for direct labor to rise to $16.30 per hour.

Develop the budget for direct labor, showing both standard cost and expected cost, and show any expected or budgeted variances.

6-24 ***Direct material and labor variances.*** (CMA) The Lonn Manufacturing Co. produces two primary chemical products to be used as base ingredients for a variety of products. The 19_8 budget for the two products was (000 omitted):

	X-4	Z-8	TOTAL
Production output in gallons	600	600	1,200
Direct material	$1,500	$1,875	$3,375
Direct labor	900	900	1,800
Total prime manufacturing cost	$2,400	$2,775	$5,175

The following planning assumptions were used for the budget:

Direct-material yield of 96 percent

Direct-labor rate of $6 per hour

The actual direct production cost for 19_8 was (000 omitted):

	X-4	Z-8	TOTAL
Production output in gallons	570.0	658.0	1,228.0
Direct material	$1,368.0	$2,138.5	$3,506.5
Direct labor	936.0	1,092.0	2,028.0
Total prime manufacturing cost	$2,304.0	$3,230.5	$5,534.5

The actual production yield was 95 percent for X-4 and 94 percent for Z-8. The direct-labor cost per hour for both products was $6.50.

REQUIRED

1. Calculate for product X-4:
   a. The direct-material price variance
   b. The direct-material efficiency (yield) variance
2. Calculate for product Z-8.
   a. The direct-labor price variance
   b. The direct-labor efficiency variance

6-25 ***Responsibility for purchase-price variances.*** The Chester Company uses standard costs. The purchasing manager, Amy Strotz, is responsible for material-price variances, and the production manager, Juan Morales, is responsible for material-efficiency variances and direct-labor price and efficiency variances.

The standard price for metal used as a principal raw material was $2 per pound. The standard allowance was six pounds per finished unit of product.

The standard rate for direct labor was $14 per hour. The standard allowance was one-half hour per finished unit of product.

During the past week, 10,000 good finished units were produced. However, labor trouble caused the production manager to use much nonpreferred personnel. Actual labor costs were $78,000 for 6,500 actual hours; 80,000 pounds of metal were acquired for $1.80 per pound; and 71,000 pounds of metal were consumed during production.

REQUIRED

1. Compute the material purchase-price variance, material-efficiency variance, direct-labor price variance, and direct-labor efficiency variance.
2. As a supervisor of both the purchasing manager and the production manager, how would you interpret the feedback provided by the computed variances?
3. What are the budget allowances for the production manager for direct materials and direct labor? Would they be different if production were 7,000 good finished units?
4. Prepare a condensed responsibility performance report for the production manager for the 10,000 units produced. Show three columns: charges to department, budget, and variance.

6-26 ***Flexible-budget preparation.*** The managing partner of Olde Music Box Fabricators has become aware of the disadvantages of static budgets and has asked you to prepare a flexible budget for October for its main style of music box. The following partial data are available for the actual operations in a recent typical month:

Boxes produced and sold	4,500
Direct-material costs	$45,000
Direct-labor costs	$67,500
Depreciation and other fixed manufacturing costs	$50,700
Average selling price per box	$ 50
Fixed selling and administrative expenses	$31,350

A 20 percent increase in the selling price is expected. The only variable selling expense is a 10 percent commission paid to the manufacturer's representatives, who bear all their own expenses of traveling, entertaining customers, and so on. The only variable overhead is a patent royalty of $2 per box manufactured. Salary increases that will become effective in October are $12,000 per year for the production superintendent and $15,000 per year for the sales manager. A 10 percent increase in direct-material prices is expected to become effective in October. No changes are expected in direct-labor wage rates or in the productivity of the direct-labor personnel.

REQUIRED

1. Prepare a flexible budget for October, showing expected results at each of three levels of volume: 4,000 units, 5,000 units, 6,000 units.
2. Draw a freehand sketch of a graph for your flexible-budget costs. *Hint:* See Exhibits 6-2 and 6-3.

6-27 ***Cost control performance.*** You have just received a long-distance telephone call from a client in Calcutta who is in a near panic concerning the operating costs of his company for the month just ended. He insists that a cost control performance report be sent immediately by special air courier. Because of a poor telephone connection, the data he provided you are incomplete, but you must nevertheless prepare the report now without being able to obtain any additional information.

Here are the notes you made during the telephone conversation:

a. Product units actually produced and sold last month 6,000

b. Actual total costs:

Direct materials	$150,000
Fixed selling and administrative costs	23,600
Variable and fixed costs (total)	635,300

c. Flexible-budget total costs:

Direct labor	$249,000
Fixed manufacturing costs	110,800
Total fixed costs	135,200
Total variable costs	474,400

d. Costs per product unit:

Direct materials, budgeted	$ 23
Variable factory overhead, budgeted	7
Direct labor, actual	42

e. The only difference between actual and budgeted fixed manufacturing costs was an extra termination payment of $4,300 made to a supervisor during the month.

f. The only difference between actual and budgeted fixed selling and administrative costs was the replacement of two clerks at a total decrease in compensation of $800 for the month.

g. Higher electricity rates caused variable overhead costs to go over the budget by 15 percent.

h. The change in variable selling and administrative costs was caused by changes in sales commission rates. (The direction and amount of these is not known because of garbled communication.)

i. The increased speed of better-trained direct-labor workers did not justify their higher wage rates.

REQUIRED

Prepare the cost control performance report as completely as you can, showing all supporting computations clearly. *Hint:* See Exhibit 6-5.

6-28 ***Basic variance analysis.*** Cash Management Printers, Inc., produces luxury checkbooks with three checks and stubs on each page. Each checkbook is designed for an individual customer and is ordered through the customer's bank. The company's operating budget for September included these data:

Number of checkbooks	15,000
Selling price, each	$ 20
Variable costs per book	$ 8
Total fixed costs for the month	$145,000

The actual results for September were:

Number of checkbooks produced and sold	12,000
Average selling price, each	$ 21
Variable costs per book	$ 7
Total fixed costs for the month	$150,000

The executive vice-president of the company observed that the operating income for September was much less than anticipated, despite a higher-than-budgeted selling price and a lower-than-budgeted variable cost per unit. You have been asked to provide explanations for the disappointing results in September.

REQUIRED

1. Prepare analyses of September performance. Prepare a *Level 1* and a *Level 2* analysis.
2. Comment briefly on your findings.

6-29 ***Overview of variance analysis.*** You have been hired as a consultant by Mary Flanagan, the president of a small manufacturing company that makes automobile parts. Flanagan is an excellent engineer, but she has been frustrated by not having adequate cost data.

You helped install flexible budgeting and standard costs. Flanagan has asked you to consider the following May data and recommend how variances might be computed and presented in performance reports:

Budgeted selling price per unit	$ 40
Budgeted variable costs per unit	$ 25
Budgeted total fixed costs per month	$200,000
Static budget in units	20,000
Actual units produced and sold	23,000
Actual revenue	$874,000
Actual variable costs	$630,000
Favorable variance in fixed costs	$ 3,000

Flanagan was disappointed that, although volume exceeded expectations, operating income had not.

Assume that there were no beginning or ending inventories.

REQUIRED

1. You decide to present Flanagan with alternative ways to analyze variances so that she can decide what level of detail she prefers. The reporting system can then be designed accordingly. Prepare an analysis similiar to Levels 0, 1, and 2 in Exhibit 6-6.
2. What are some likely causes for the variances?

6-30 ***Analysis of airline operations.*** The Carruthers Airline had the data at the top of page 197 for 19_2 (in thousands of dollars).

You discover that a midyear airfare increase of 9 percent had resulted in a 5 percent increase in average revenue per passenger mile flown for the year. Wage, meal, and fuel increases and various inefficiencies had exceeded the pace of the fare increases and averaged 10 percent for the year. Other price and efficiency effects were minor and can be ignored.

	MASTER BUDGET	RESULTS AT ACTUAL PRICES	VARIANCE
Revenue	100,000	84,000	16,000 U
Variable expenses	60,000*	51,600	8,400 F
Contribution margin	40,000	32,400	7,600 U
Fixed expenses	35,000	35,000	0
Operating income	5,000	(2,600)	7,600 U

*Includes $45 million of wages, meals, and fuel.

REQUIRED

Prepare an analytical tabulation as an explanation for the president. Begin with actual results at actual prices and end with the master budget. Show the variances attributable to (a) combined price and efficiency and (b) volume effects.

6-31 ***Elementary variance analysis and graph.*** Consider the following data regarding the manufacture of units (pairs) of boots:

	STANDARDS
Direct materials	Two pounds of input at $4 per pound, or $8 per unit of output
Direct labor	One-half hour of input at $10 per hour, or $5 per unit of output

The following data were compiled regarding actual performance: good units produced, 20,000; pounds of input acquired and used, 37,000; price per pound, $4.10; direct-labor costs, $88,200; actual hours of input, 9,000; labor rate per hour, $9.80.

REQUIRED

1. Show computations of price and efficiency variances for direct materials and for direct labor. Prepare a plausible explanation of why the variances arose.
2. Sketch a graphical analysis of the direct-labor variance, using the vertical axis for total costs and the horizontal axis for volume or activity in hours. Indicate what vertical distances represent the flexible-budget variance, price variance, and efficiency variance.
3. Suppose 60,000 pounds of materials were purchased even though only 37,000 pounds were used. Suppose further that variances are identified with their most likely control point; accordingly, direct-material purchase-price variances are isolated and traced to the purchasing department rather than to the production department. Compute the price and efficiency variances under this approach.

6-32 ***Flexibility in budgets.*** Refer to Problem 6-31. Suppose that the original budget was for 24,000 units of output. The general manager is gleeful about the following report:

	ACTUAL COSTS	ORIGINAL BUDGET	VARIANCE
Direct materials	$151,700	$192,000	$40,300 F
Direct labor	$ 88,200	$120,000	$31,800 F

REQUIRED

Is the manager's glee warranted? Prepare a report that might provide a more detailed explanation of why the original budget was not achieved. Good output was 20,000 units.

6-33 ***Journal entries and T-accounts.*** Prepare journal entries and T-accounts for all transactions in Problem 6-31, including requirement 3. Summarize how these journal entries differ from the normal costing entries as described in Chapter 4.

6-34 ***Analysis of labor.*** The city of San Francisco has a maintenance shop where all kinds of truck repairs are performed. Through the years, various labor standards have been developed to judge performance. However, during a March strike, some labor records vanished. The actual hours of input were 1,000. The direct-labor flexible-budget variance was $1,800, favorable. The standard labor price was $14.00 per hour; however, a recent labor shortage had necessitated using higher-paid workers for some jobs and had produced a labor-price variance for March of $300, unfavorable.

REQUIRED

1. Actual labor price per hour.
2. Standard hours allowed for output achieved.

6-35 ***Solving for unknowns.*** The Kessler Company has the following data that pertain to the month of March:

Physical units of output, actual	21,000
Fixed costs, actual	$497,000
Operating income, static budget	$220,000
Sales price variance	$ 84,000 U
Beginning and ending inventories	None
Sales volume variance, revenue	$300,000 U
Budgeted selling price per unit	$100
Variable costs, static budget	$1,680,000
Contribution margin, actual	$516,000

REQUIRED

Prepare a summary of performance, using the same format as in Exhibit 6-4. *Hint:* To do so, you will have to compute the sales volume variance in units and the static budgeted revenue. Place the given numbers in the format and then work from the knowns to the unknowns.

6-36 ***Solving for unknowns.*** (SMA, adopted) King Corporation manufactures a special type of metal alloy. Budgeted sales for 19_8 were 10,000 kilos at $50 per kilo. Standard variable production and selling costs were $30 per kilo. Fixed costs were budgeted at $50,000 for 19_8.

Actual fixed costs in 19_8 were $50,000, but the market price realized was $55 per kilo due to an international shortage. Operating income was below the static budget figure amount by $50,000. The sales-volume variance for revenue for 19_8 was $100,000, unfavorable. Contribution margin price variance was $20,000, unfavorable.

REQUIRED

Determine the following:

1. Revenue price variance
2. Variable-cost price variance
3. Variable-cost efficiency variance
4. Contribution-margin efficiency variance
5. Variable-cost sales-volume variance
6. Contribution-margin sales-volume variance
7. Operating income sales-volume variance.

6-37 ***Journal entries for standard operation costing.*** A machining department in Singapore works on three varieties of a basic product. The product contains two raw materials and entails a sequence of from two to four operations, depending on the model type.

Standard Usage per Finished Unit

	UNITS OF RAW MATERIALS		STANDARD TIME PER LABOR OPERATION IN HOURS			
FINISHED PRODUCT	**A**	**B**	**1**	**2**	**3**	**4**
X	3	1	1	2	—	—
Y	3	2	1	—	3	—
Z	3	3	1	2	3	1

Standard Prices and Labor Rates

Raw material A, $5 per unit
Raw material B, $1 per unit
Labor rates, which are typical in Singapore, are $2.40, $3.00, $3.20, and $4.00, respectively, in the four successive operations.

Operating Data

Purchases:

Material A	120,000 units	$612,000
Material B	65,000 units	61,750

Material requisitions:

Issued from stores:	A	B
Standard quantity	105,000	61,000
Over standard	5,000	3,000
Returned to stores		400

Direct labor:

OPERATION	ACTUAL HOURS	TOTAL ACTUAL COST
1	36,000	$ 90,000
2	48,000	144,960
3	58,000	174,000
4	6,900	28,980
		$437,940

There are no beginning or ending work-in-process inventories. Units produced were X, 16,000; Y, 12,000; and Z, 7,000.

REQUIRED

1. Journal entries, assuming that material-price variances are isolated upon purchase. Accompany each journal entry with a detailed analysis of variances as far as the data permit.
2. Prime standard costs per unit for Products X, Y, and Z. Show computations.
3. What are some of the frequent causes for the variances computed in requirement 1?
4. What is the merit of isolating price variances as materials are purchased rather than as they are issued?

6-38 ***Combined or joint price-efficiency variances and incentives.*** The MTT Company had a long history of using bonuses that were specifically tied to performance. Minimal inventories of any kind were kept. The purchasing manager was given a bonus of 5 percent of the favorable purchase-price variance for the year. The production manager was given a bonus of 5 percent of the favorable direct-material efficiency variance for the year plus additional bonuses regarding labor and overhead variances.

In 19_4, the performance regarding Material A, an important chemical ingredient, was:

Standard pounds allowed @ $1.00, one per finished unit
Actual pounds consumed, 500,000
Actual production, 520,000 finished units
Actual unit purchase price, $.90

REQUIRED

1. Compute the material price and efficiency variances.
2. Split the price variance into a "pure" price variance and a combined price-efficiency variance. As the purchasing manager, would you be pleased by the favorable efficiency variance? Why? Would your attitude change if the actual unit price were $1.10?
3. As the production manager, what would be your attitude toward the bonus system?
4. Given that top management is committed to a bonus system based on variances, what modifications in the bonus system would you favor? Why?

This chapter continues the *Level 3* analysis of manufacturing costs introduced in the preceding chapter. We analyze variable and fixed factory overhead. We also compare the effects of the *budgetary control* purpose and the *product-costing* purpose on accounting for overhead.

In addition this chapter covers some widely used methods of budgeting overhead, applying overhead, and analyzing overhead variances. Practices vary, depending on the preferences of the individual managers concerned.

Please proceed slowly as you study this chapter. Pause frequently. Trace the data to the graphs in a systematic manner. In particular, ponder on how fixed factory overhead is accounted for in one way for budgetary control purposes and in a different way for product costing purposes. The accounting for fixed factory overhead tends to be the most puzzling aspect of the study of flexible budgets and standards.

Variable factory overhead: control and product costing

The Webb Company illustration in the preceding chapter provides the following data concerning variable factory overhead:

Rate per direct-labor hour	$1.50
Standard direct-labor hours allowed per unit of finished product	2
Rate per unit of finished product	$3.00
Flexible budget for 20,000 hours or 10,000 units	$30,000

the control purpose

Variable factory overhead typically consists of many items, including power, repairs, indirect labor, idle time, and fringe benefits such as employer payroll taxes. The most convincing way to discover why overhead performance did not agree with a budget is to investigate possible causes, line item by line item.

The price-efficiency distinctions provide a starting point for analysis. However, the two tidy categories of "price" and "efficiency" are a crude split for variable factory overhead. Keep their limitations in mind. In practice, a fragile assumption frequently underlines the efficiency variance computation for variable overhead items: Variable overhead fluctuates in direct proportion to some measure of direct labor, such as direct-labor hours or direct-labor costs. Webb Company uses direct-labor hours.

Recall that in April the company had good output achieved of 10,000 finished units of product. Standard direct-labor hours allowed were 10,000 × 2 = 20,000. However, actual direct-labor hours of input were 22,000. Using a format similar to that at the bottom of Exhibit 6-7 (page 178):

INCURRED	ACTUAL INPUTS × STANDARD PRICES $AQ \times SP$	FLEXIBLE BUDGET: $SQ \times SP$
Given $32,000	22,000 × $1.50 = $33,000	20,000 × $1.50 = $30,000
Price variance, $1,000 F	Efficiency variance, $3,000 U	
Flexible budget variance, $2,000 U		

The efficiency variance for variable overhead is a measure of the extra overhead (or savings) incurred *solely* because the *actual direct-labor hours* of input differed from the standard hours allowed:

$$\textbf{Variable-overhead efficiency variance} = \left(\begin{array}{c}\textbf{Actual}\\ \textbf{direct-labor}\\ \textbf{hours used}\end{array} - \begin{array}{c}\textbf{Standard}\\ \textbf{allowed}\\ \textbf{hours}\end{array}\right) \times \left(\begin{array}{c}\textbf{Standard}\\ \textbf{price per}\\ \textbf{hour}\end{array}\right)$$

$$\begin{aligned} V_e &= (AQ - SQ) \times SP \\ &= (22{,}000 - 20{,}000) \times \$1.50 \\ &= \$3{,}000 \text{ U} \end{aligned}$$

To be more specific, suppose the variable overhead consisted wholly of supplies such as polishing cloths. The above analysis shows that, **because direct labor was inefficiently used,** the related usage of supplies would be expected to be proportionately excessive. Whether in fact this clear-cut relationship exists depends on particular circumstances.

To review, the $3,000 unfavorable efficiency variance is the amount that would be expected because of *labor* inefficiency. The "price" variance is deceptive because it is really a glob. It is that remaining part of the budget variance that is unexplained by the efficiency variance:

Price variance = Budget variance − Efficiency variance

$1,000 F = $2,000 U − $3,000 U

The point here is that the variance could result from favorable unit price changes for polishing cloths. But it could also arise from careful use of these supplies. In brief, this "price" variance could be partially or completely traceable to the *efficient use* of supplies, even though it is labeled as a price variance. **For this reason, most practitioners call this type of overhead variance a spending variance rather than merely a price variance.** A *variable-overhead spending variance* is defined as the actual amount of overhead incurred minus the amount expected to be incurred based on actual inputs. The latter amount is the variable-overhead rate multiplied by the actual inputs.

the product-costing purpose

Consider some graphical displays of how variable factory overhead relates to (1) responsibility budgeting for planning and control purposes, and (2) product-costing purposes. The graphs for variable factory overhead are:

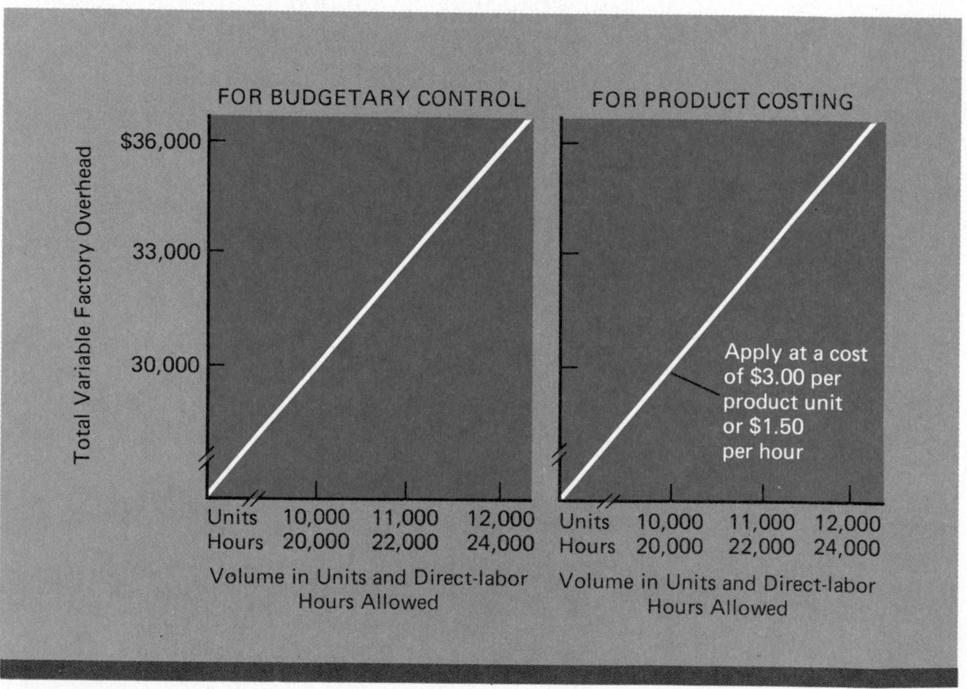

The lines on the two graphs are identical. Either graph may be used as a basis for predicting how total costs will behave. Variable factory overhead will increase at a rate of:

$30,000 ÷ 10,000 = $3.00 per unit

$33,000 ÷ 11,000 = $3.00 per unit

$36,000 ÷ 12,000 = $3.00 per unit

Thinking in terms of *total costs* is the most popular way to exert budgetary control over operations at various levels of volume. In contrast, thinking in terms of *unit costs* is the most popular way to apply costs for product-costing purposes. For example, managers tend to say that their budget for 10,000 units is $30,000, and their cost per unit is $3.00.

Fixed factory overhead: control and product costing

the control purpose

The Webb Company illustration indicates that budgeted fixed factory overhead was $96,000. By definition, this is a lump sum that is not expected to vary as volume fluctuates. Fixed costs are frequently a component of a flexible budget, as shown in Exhibit 6-2 (page 169). However, the "flex" in the flexible budget is attributable to the variable costs, not the fixed costs. Indeed, a flexible-budget formula for Webb Company factory can be depicted as follows:

Flexible budget for factory overhead	=	**Fixed factory overhead**	+	**Variable factory overhead**
	=	**$96,000 per month**	+	**$1.50 per direct labor hour or $3.00 per unit of output**
For 10,000 units	=	**$96,000**	+	**$3.00 (10,000) = $126,000**
For 12,000 units	=	**$96,000**	+	**$3.00 (12,000) = $132,000**

Budgetary control of fixed factory overhead concentrates on line-by-line plans for such typical items as supervision, depreciation, insurance, property taxes, and rentals. Chapter 10 discusses these aspects in more detail. Fixed factory overhead is generally not subject to as much day-to-day (or month-to-month) influence as variable overhead. The variances of actual costs from fixed overhead budgets tend to be relatively small.

the product-costing purpose

This chapter assumes that Webb Company uses absorption costing. Recall that absorption costing applies both variable and fixed factory overhead to products.[1] The basic procedure is the same as that introduced in Chapter 4. The budgeting and choice

[1]About 65 percent of the American companies that use standard costing systems use absorption costing. The other 35 percent use variable costing, which is discussed in the next chapter. See J. Chiu and Y. Lee, "A Survey of Current Practice in Overhead Accounting and Analysis," *Proceedings of the 1980 Western Regional Meeting of the American Accounting Association* (O. R. Whittington, San Diego State University, School of Accounting, 1980). The survey received usable responses from 327 of the Fortune 500 American industrial firms. Of these, 75 percent either did not use standard costs or did not have factory operations. Of the companies that use standard costs, 70 percent maintained accounts that separated factory overhead into variable and fixed elements. Similar but less-definitive data regarding the separation of costs were collected in another survey (Unpublished staff research study, "Management Uses of Fixed and Variable Expense Analysis" [New York: National Association of Accountants, April 1, 1980]).

of overhead rate are usually done annually. The predetermined rate for applying fixed factory overhead is computed as follows:

$$\text{Predetermined fixed-factory-overhead rate for applying costs to product} = \frac{\text{Budgeted total fixed factory overhead}}{\text{Some preselected volume level for the year}}$$

$$= \frac{\$96{,}000 \times 12 \text{ months}}{12{,}000 \text{ units} \times 12 \text{ months}}$$

$$= \frac{\$1{,}152{,}000}{144{,}000 \text{ units}} = \$8 \text{ per unit}$$

$$\text{or} = \frac{\$1{,}152{,}000}{144{,}000 \text{ units} \times 2 \text{ hours}} = \frac{\$1{,}152{,}000}{288{,}000 \text{ hours}} = \$4 \text{ per hour}$$

The preselected volume level is based on the originally expected volume for the year. It may be expressed as either 144,000 units or 288,000 hours per year or 12,000 units or 24,000 hours per month. **This prechosen volume level will be referred to as the denominator level.**

For inventory purposes, as each unit is produced, an $8 fixed-factory-overhead cost will be applied thereto. Thus, the first 5,000 units would bear a total *product cost* of $40,000. The next 5,000 units would bear an additional $40,000, as the next graphs demonstrate:

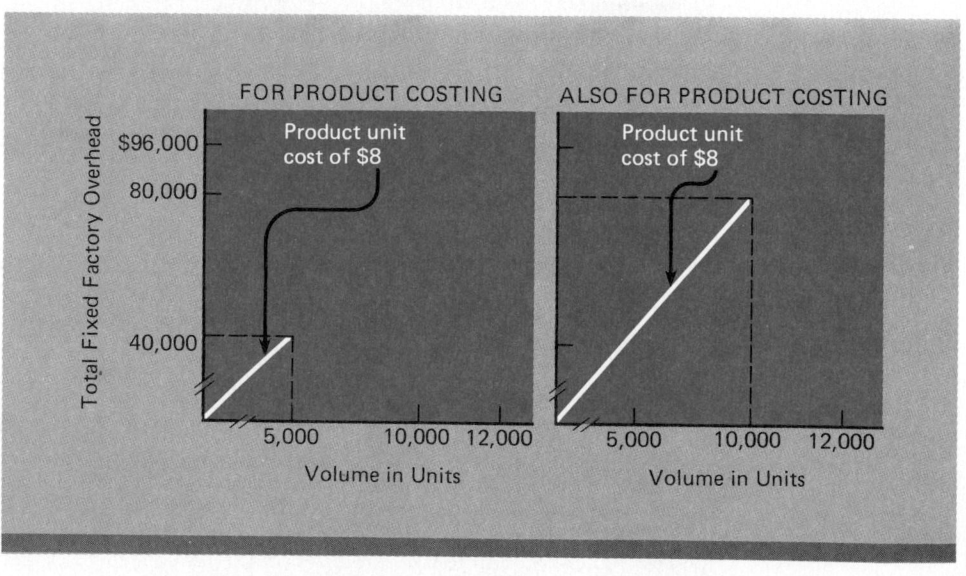

To recapitulate, the first of the following graphs shows that the focus for budgetary *control* is on the $96,000 lump-sum total of fixed factory overhead. However, the second graph shows how, for *product-costing* purposes, **the total costs in the first graph are typically "unitized" by using some predicted volume as the denominator:**

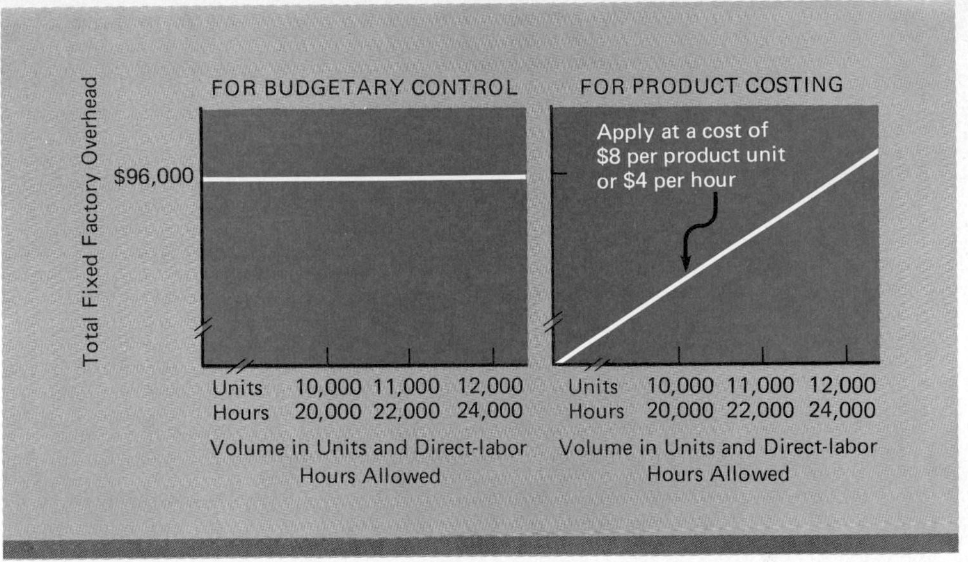

variety of unit costs

The *total* fixed cost for budgetary control is unaffected by the specific predicted volume used as a denominator. However, if fixed costs are important, the choice of a denominator level can have a significant effect on unit product costs:

(1) TOTAL ANNUAL COSTS	(2) TOTAL VOLUME LEVEL FOR YEAR	(1) ÷ (2) PREDETERMINED FIXED-OVERHEAD RATE FOR PRODUCT COSTING
$1,152,000	10,000 × 12 = 120,000	$9.60
1,152,000	11,000 × 12 = 132,000	8.73
1,152,000	12,000 × 12 = 144,000	8.00

A graphical depiction of these data on a monthly basis follows:

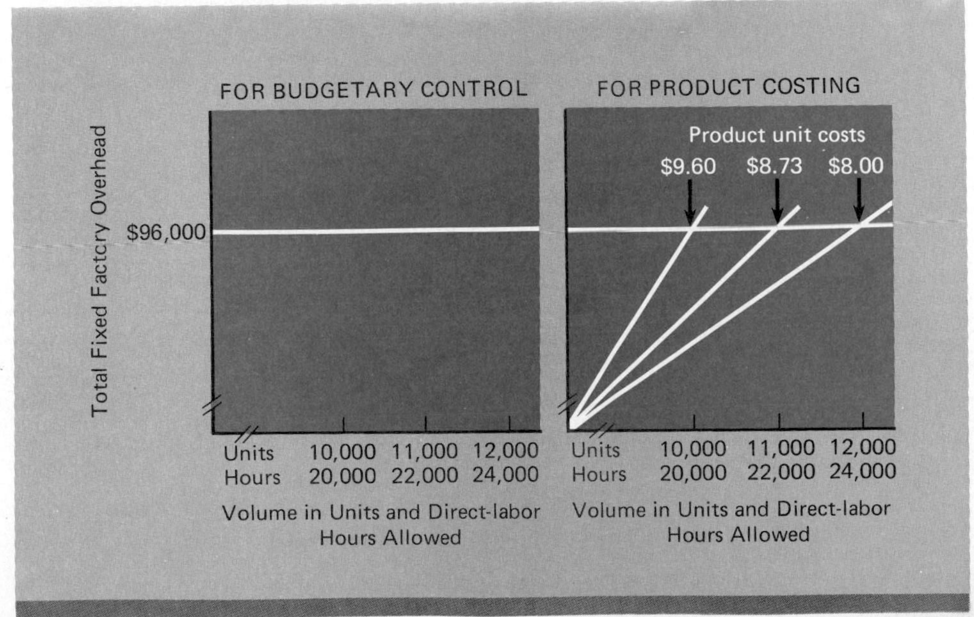

choosing the denominator level

The right-hand graph clearly demonstrates that the unit cost depends on the volume level chosen as the denominator in the computation; the higher the volume level, the lower the product unit cost. The costing difficulty is troublesome because managers usually want a single representative unit fixed cost despite month-to-month fluctuations in production volume.

The two graphs underscore how the two purposes differ. The budgetary-control purpose regards fixed costs in accordance with their actual cost behavior pattern, costs that arise in chunks rather than in finely granulated portions. **In contrast, absorption product costing views these *fixed* costs *as though* they had a *variable* cost behavior pattern.** Therefore, absorption costing seemingly transforms a fixed cost into a variable cost, and for product-costing purposes, *all manufacturing costs* are routinely regarded as variable.

The choice of an appropriate denominator level for the predetermination of fixed-overhead rates is a matter of judgment rather than science. Given the same set of facts independently, ten accountants or engineers would probably select ten different denominator levels. The most widely used denominator level is the budgeted volume for the year. The choice of the denominator is discussed more fully in the next chapter.

Journal entries for overhead

The only change in general-ledger procedure in this chapter is the replacement of a single Department Factory–Overhead Control account with two new accounts, one for variable overhead and another for fixed overhead. Also, there will be two Applied accounts instead of the single Applied account used in Chapter 4.

Consider the journal entries for the Webb Company. Recall that the April actual variable factory overhead was $32,000; fixed factory overhead, $92,000.

As described in Chapter 4, the accounting for overhead during the fiscal period does not isolate overhead variances in separate accounts. Instead, actual overhead is accumulated in one account and overhead is applied via a separate account:

a. Variable factory overhead control	32,000	
Accounts payable and other accounts		32,000
To record actual variable factory overhead incurred.		
b. Work in process	30,000	
Variable factory overhead applied		30,000
To record application of variable factory overhead.		

Note that the total variable-overhead variance is not shown in a separate variance account, whereas direct-material and direct-labor variances are commonly isolated in separate accounts as general-ledger entries are made. However, the total variable-overhead variance may be readily computed by taking the difference between the debit balance of the Variable Factory–Overhead Control account and the credit balance of the Variable Factory–Overhead Applied account.

Budgeted fixed factory overhead was $96,000. Assume that the denominator volume was 12,000 units. Therefore, the fixed factory overhead would be applied at $8 per unit or $4 per hour. Recall that the actual April volume was 10,000 units.

The journal entries would be:

a. Fixed factory overhead control		92,000
a. Fixed factory overhead control	92,000	
Accrued payroll, accumulated depreciation, etc.		92,000
To record actual fixed overhead incurred. (Detailed postings of fixed-overhead items such as salaries, depreciation, property taxes, and insurance would be made to the department overhead sheets in the subsidiary ledger for Fixed Factory Overhead Control.)		
b. Work in process	80,000	
Fixed factory overhead applied		80,000
To apply overhead at the predetermined rate of $8 per unit or $4 per standard hour allowed for the output achieved. (Note how this total differs from the fixed-overhead budget for this level of volume. The budget is $96,000 for *any* level of volume.)		

Again, note that the total fixed-factory overhead variance (that is, the underapplied fixed factory overhead) is not shown in a separate variance account.

The general-ledger treatment practiced in standard-cost systems is not at all uniform. However, the reader who really understands the features of standard costs can easily adapt to any given bookkeeping system. Differences in general-ledger treatment usually center on (a) the number of detailed variance accounts desired, and (b) the timing of isolation of variances in the ledger.

Standard, normal, and actual costing

The cost accounting literature often mistakenly divides product cost accounting systems into three systems, as if they were mutually exclusive: job costing, process costing, and standard costing. Such a three-way classification is erroneous because standard costs can be used in a wide variety of organizations and in conjunction with any kind of product costing, whether it be job-order costing, process costing, or some hybrid product costing.

There is a major difference in absorption costing between standard-costing and other product-costing systems. Under standard costing, Work in Process is usually carried at what the products *should* cost, rather than on the basis of the actual costs:

	CHAPTER 2 APPROACH, CALLED ACTUAL ABSORPTION COSTING: *WORK-IN-PROCESS INVENTORY*	*CHAPTER 4 APPROACH, CALLED* NORMAL ABSORPTION COSTING: *WORK-IN-PROCESS INVENTORY*	*CHAPTER 7 APPROACH, CALLED* STANDARD ABSORPTION COSTING: *WORK-IN-PROCESS INVENTORY*
Direct materials	actual costs	actual costs	standard inputs allowed for actual output achieved × standard prices (all four cost elements)
Direct labor	actual costs	actual costs	
Variable factory overhead	actual costs	actual inputs × predetermined overhead rates (overhead items)	
Fixed factory overhead	actual costs		

Ponder the major difference in overhead application in *normal* absorption costing and *standard* absorption costing. In normal costing, a predetermined rate (that is, a budgeted rate) is multiplied by *actual* inputs such as direct-labor hours. In standard costing, a predetermined rate (that is, a budgeted or standard rate) is multiplied by *standard inputs allowed for the actual outputs achieved.* In normal costing, data regarding only *actual inputs* are generated. In standard costing, data regarding both *actual inputs* and *standard inputs allowed* are generated.

Analysis of fixed-factory-overhead variances

The most perplexing and controversial variance in standard absorption cost accounting arises from the inevitable failure to achieve a production volume exactly equal to the denominator volume. Consider the Webb Company facts:

general framework

Production originally budgeted	12,000 units
Standard inputs of direct labor allowed, 12,000 × 2 =	24,000 hours
Production actually achieved	10,000 units
Standard inputs of direct labor allowed, 10,000 × 2 =	20,000 hours
Actual hours of input	22,000

The framework that was used at the beginning of this chapter to analyze variable overhead is repeated here so that it may easily be compared with the framework for fixed overhead:

INCURRED	ACTUAL INPUTS × STANDARD PRICES ($AQ \times SP$)	FLEXIBLE BUDGET AND APPLIED: ($SQ \times SP$)
Given $32,000	22,000 × $1.50 = $33,000	20,000 × $1.50 = $30,000

Price (spending) variance, $1,000 F

Efficiency variance, $3,000 U

Budget variance and underapplied overhead, $2,000 U

Compare this with how fixed overhead may be analyzed:

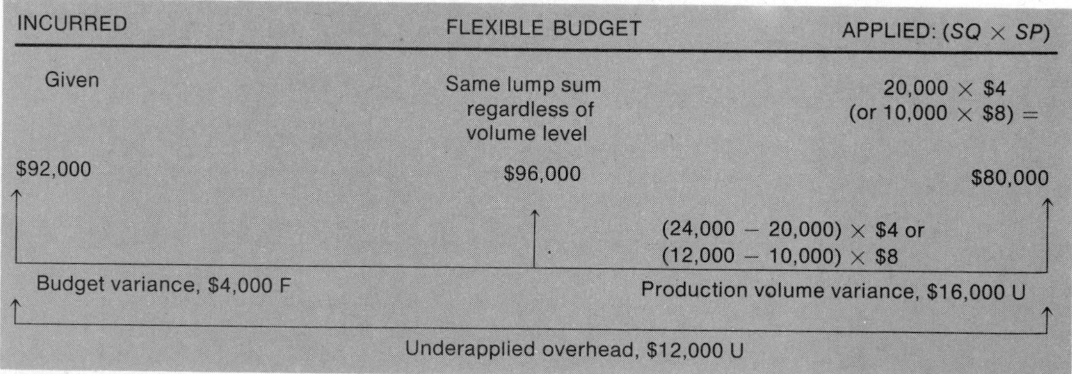

Ponder the differences. For all variable costs, the flexible-*budget* allowance will *always* equal the amounts *applied* to products. Thus, the amount of the budget variance for variable overhead will always be identical to underapplied (or overapplied) overhead, $2,000 U in this example. In contrast, except when actual output achieved equals the denominator level, the flexible *budget* for fixed factory overhead will *never* equal the amount *applied* to products. Thus, the amount of the flexible-budget variance for fixed overhead will rarely be identical to underapplied (or overapplied) overhead, \$4,000 F versus \$12,000 U in this example.

Finally, note that an efficiency variance is computed for variable but not fixed overhead. Why? Because variances are measures to help the short-run control of performance. Efficient use of direct materials, direct labor, and variable factory overhead can affect actual costs, but short-run fixed overhead is unaffected by efficiency.

production volume variance In an absorption-costing system, the first step in analyzing fixed overhead is to calculate the underapplied or overapplied overhead:

Actual of \$92,000 − Applied of \$80,000 = Underapplied overhead of \$12,000 U

This \$12,000 may be subdivided into two variances, the same budget variance as before, \$4,000 F, plus a *production volume variance* of \$16,000 U. **A production volume variance arises only in an absorption-costing system.** It is a measure of the cost of departing from the level of volume (activity) originally used to set the fixed-overhead rate.

EXHIBIT 7-1

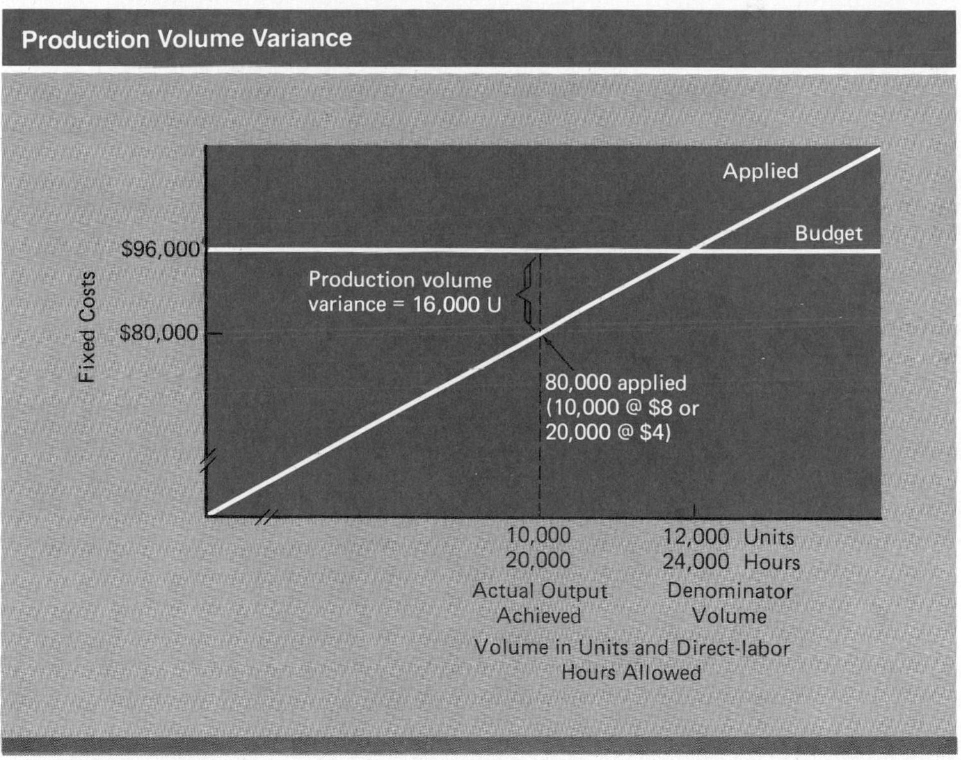

Exhibit 7-1 is a graph of the \$16,000 production volume variance. **When actual activity achieved is less than denominator activity, the production volume variance is unfavorable.** It is viewed as a cost of idle capacity and is measured in Exhibit 7-1. Computations may be expressed in product units or in hours. Using hours:

$$\textbf{Production volume variance} = \textbf{(Denominator volume − Actual volume of output achieved)} \times \textbf{Predetermined fixed-overhead rate}$$
$$= (24,000 - 20,000) \times \$4$$
$$= \$16,000\ U$$

or

Production volume variance = Budget − Applied
= $96,000 − (20,000 × $4)
= $96,000 − $80,000
= $16,000 U

When actual volume exceeds denominator volume, the production volume variance is favorable. It is viewed as a benefit of better-than-expected utilization of facilities.

There is no production volume variance for variable overhead. The concept of production volume variance arises for fixed overhead because of the conflict between accounting for control (by budgets) and accounting for product costing (by application rates). Note again that the fixed-overhead budget serves the control purpose, **whereas the development of a product-costing rate results in the treatment of fixed overhead as if it were a variable cost.** In other words, the applied line in Exhibit 7-1 is artificial in the sense that, for product-costing purposes, it seemingly transforms a fixed cost into a variable cost. This bit of magic forcefully illustrates the distinction between accounting for control and accounting for product costing.

To summarize, the production volume variance arises because the actual production activity level achieved frequently does not coincide with the activity level used as a denominator for selecting a predetermined product-costing rate for fixed factory overhead.

no efficiency variance for fixed overhead

The position in this chapter has been to distinguish between fixed and variable overhead as separate management problems. This contrasts with the tendency among many accountants to analyze variable costs and fixed costs in a parallel manner. For instance, an efficiency variance for fixed overhead is often computed, just as it is for the other variable costs:[2]

Efficiency variance = (Actual hours − Standard hours allowed)
× Hourly fixed-overhead rate

However, the resulting variance is very different from the efficiency variances for materials, labor, and variable overhead. Efficient usage of these three factors

---

[2]Some accountants favor computing production volume variance on the basis of the difference between the fixed-overhead budget ($96,000) and (actual hours worked × fixed-overhead rate). In this example, the production volume variance would then become $96,000—(22,000 × $4), or $8,000 unfavorable instead of $16,000 unfavorable. The remaining variance of $8,000 unfavorable [(*actual* hours − standard hours) × $4 overhead rate] is sometimes called the fixed-overhead *efficiency* or *effectiveness* variance—the measure of the ineffective use or waste of facilities because of off-standard labor performance. This breakdown of the production volume variance really attempts to separate the cost of *misused* facilities from the cost of *unused* facilities.

The author thinks this refinement is unnecessary in most cases because (a) in the short run, total fixed costs incurred are *not* changed by efficiency changes, and (b) if the budget uses standard hours as a base, the production volume variance is more logically calculated by comparing standard hours achieved with the denominator volume that was used as a basis for setting the predetermined overhead rate. For an elaboration, see Chapter 28.

The Chiu and Lee survey, op. cit., indicated that 23 percent of their relevant respondents calculate an efficiency variance for fixed factory overhead.

can affect actual cost, **but short-run fixed-overhead cost is not affected by efficiency.** Furthermore, the managers responsible for inefficiency will be aware of its existence through reports on variable-cost control, so there is little to gain from expressing ineffective utilization of facilities in historical dollar terms.

economic meaning of production volume variance

The economic meaning of the flexible-budget variances for fixed factory overhead is relatively straightforward. The amounts actually incurred are compared with the lump-sum amounts budgeted.

In contrast, the economic meaning of the production volume variance is less clear. The Webb Company April variance is (12,000 − 10,000) × $8 = $16,000. Remember that the variance is a creature of the "unitizing" of fixed costs. Does the production volume variance measure the economic cost to Webb Company of producing and selling 10,000 rather than 12,000 units in April? The presence of idle facilities has no bearing on the amount of fixed costs currently incurred.

How should the costs of idle capacity be measured? **The economic impacts of the inability to reach a target denominator volume level are often directly measured by lost contribution margins, even if they must be approximated.** In the Webb Company example, Exhibit 6-4 (page 170) revealed that the lost contribution margin was 2,000 units × $24 = $48,000. Managers tend to understand the meaning of the latter, but they find the production volume variance less informative.[3]

The use of unit historical fixed-overhead costs might be justified in an economic sense on the following grounds: "We cannot regularly maintain measurements of lost contribution margins per unit. Therefore, as a practical but crude substitute, we use unit historical fixed-overhead costs instead."

impact of choice of denominator volume

The economic meaning of the production volume variance is also clouded because its amount is affected by the choice of the denominator level. For example, consider Webb's April operations:

(1) Budgeted fixed factory overhead	$96,000	$96,000	$96,000
(2) Denominator volume	10,000	11,000	12,000
(3) Overhead rate per unit of product	$9.60	$8.73	$8.00
(4) Applied (10,000 units of output × $9.60, $8.73, $8.00)	$96,000	$87,300	$80,000
(5) Production volume variance (1 − 4)	0	$8,700	$16,000

Thus, the choice of denominator level can affect inventory valuations and, if inventory levels change, operating profits—even if all other facts and conditions are the same.

different terminology

Production volume variances have a number of widely used synonyms: **capacity variance, idle capacity variance, activity variance, denominator variance,** and just plain **volume variance.** The last term is particularly popular, but we use *production volume variance* here. Why? To distinguish *production* volume variances, which are unique to absorption costing, from *sales* volume variances. The latter were explained in the preceding chapter. Sales volume variances are encountered in *all* accounting systems and in *all* types of organizations, including service industries and nonprofit entities.

---

[3]For an elaboration of these ideas, see Charles T. Horngren, "A Contribution Margin Approach to the Analysis of Capacity Utilization," *Accounting Review,* XLII, No. 2, 254–64.

problems for self-study

problem 1

Exhibit 7-2 shows a flexible budget for variable and fixed factory overhead for a machining department. Note how the "flex" in the flexible budget is confined to variable costs. The budget for fixed costs is the same regardless of the volume level.

The variable-overhead rate is $1.70 per standard direct-labor hour. The denominator level used to set the fixed-overhead rate for product costing is 10,000 hours.

The actual hours of input were 7,900. Four standard hours are allowed per unit of product. There were 2,000 units of product produced, which are often expressed as 8,000 standard hours allowed or standard hours earned. Exhibit 7-3 lists the actual costs incurred.

REQUIRED

1. Compute in summary form the variable-factory-overhead budget variance, price (spending) variance, and efficiency variance. "Summary form" means to analyze all of the variable overhead as a single-line item. Thus, the actual variable costs incurred are $14,250.
2. Compute in summary form the fixed-factory-overhead budget variance and the production volume variance.

EXHIBIT 7-2

M Company
Machining Department

Simplified Flexible Factory-Overhead Budget for Anticipated Monthly Activity Range

Standard direct-labor hours allowed	8,000	9,000	10,000	11,000
Variable factory overhead:				
Material handling	$ 8,000	$ 9,000	$10,000	$11,000
Idle time	800	900	1,000	1,100
Rework	800	900	1,000	1,100
Overtime premium	400	450	500	550
Supplies	3,600	4,050	4,500	4,950
Total	$13,600	$15,300	$17,000	$18,700
Variable-overhead rate, $1.70 per DLH				
Fixed factory overhead:				
Supervision	$ 2,700	$ 2,700	$ 2,700	$ 2,700
Depreciation—plant	1,000	1,000	1,000	1,000
Depreciation—equipment	5,000	5,000	5,000	5,000
Property taxes	1,000	1,000	1,000	1,000
Insurance—factory	300	300	300	300
Total	$10,000	$10,000	$10,000	$10,000

EXHIBIT 7-3

M Company
Machining Department

Actual Factory Overhead Costs For the Month Ended March 31, 19_1

Variable overhead:		Fixed overhead:	
Material handling	$ 8,200	Supervision	$ 2,700
Idle time	600	Depreciation—plant	1,000
Rework	850	Depreciation—equipment	5,000
Overtime premium	600	Property taxes	1,150
Supplies	4,000	Insurance—factory	350
Total	$14,250	Total	$10,200

solution 1

This analysis uses the analytical framework introduced earlier in this chapter.

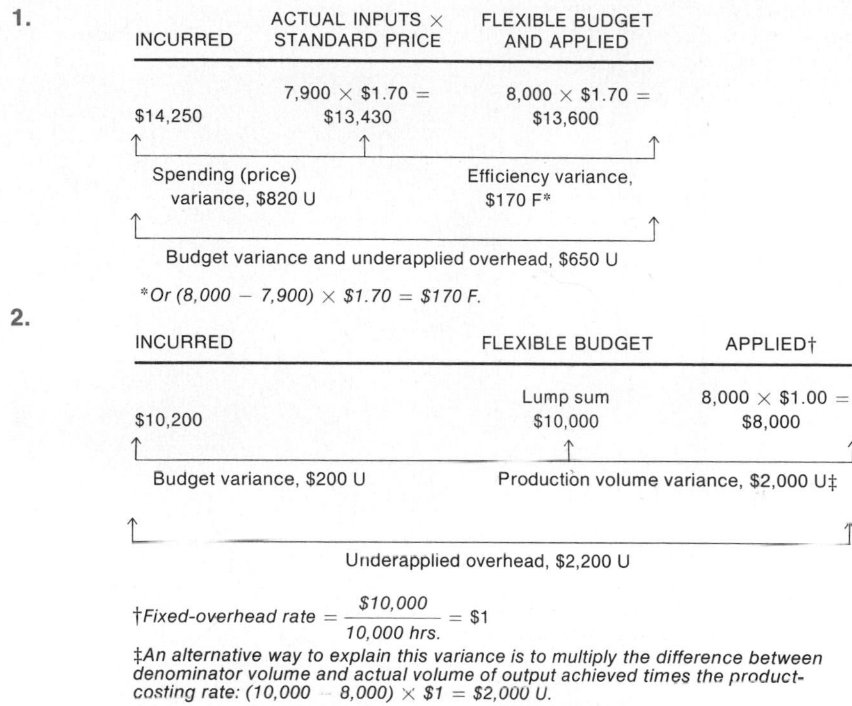

Some additional aspects of this problem are explored in subsequent sections.

Combined-overhead rate and two-way and three-way analysis

combined rate

Many companies, while separating variable overhead and fixed overhead for control purposes, combine them for product-costing purposes and use a single predetermined overhead rate. In the preceding example, such a rate would be $2.70, which is the variable-overhead rate of $1.70 plus the fixed-overhead rate of $1.00. In such cases, the overhead-variance analysis would merely be sums of what we computed earlier. Do not attempt the study of this section until you are thoroughly familiar with the earlier material in this chapter.

The easiest way to grasp these relationships is to examine Exhibit 7-4, which is really a combination of two separate graphs that might be drawn for variable and fixed overhead. You can readily see that what we are about to study is **nothing more than a simultaneous consideration of the variable and fixed components, where the flexible-budget formula is expressed as $10,000 per month plus $1.70 per hour.**

two-way and three-way analysis

Exhibit 7-5 provides a comprehensive analysis of all relationships among the combined-overhead analysis and its variable and fixed parts. Study it slowly, step by step. Begin at the bottom with the one-way analysis. Then move up.

Even when the actual overhead costs cannot be separated into variable and fixed components, it is still possible to generate almost all of the flexible-budget analysis illustrated in the chapter. The only variances that could not be derived are the separate variable-overhead spending variance and the separate fixed-overhead budget variance.

EXHIBIT 7-4

Combined Variable- and Fixed-Overhead Budget and Application at Various Monthly Production Volumes

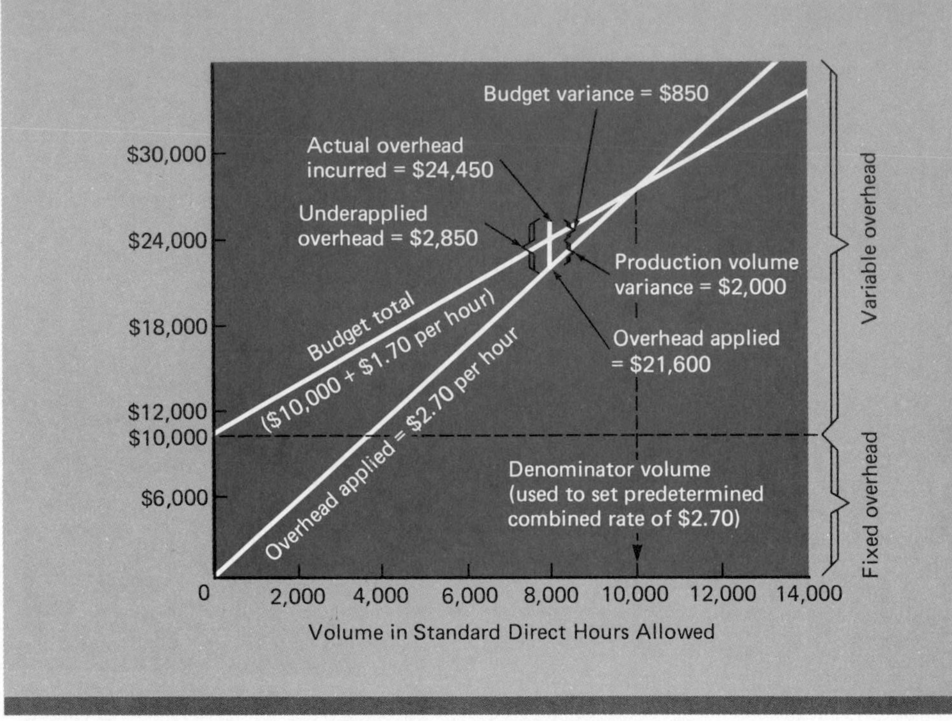

Distinguish between the so-called two-way and three-way overhead analysis. The three-way analysis is the method that was used earlier in the chapter, where three different variances were computed: spending, efficiency, and production volume variances. The two-way analysis computes only two: budget (sometimes called the *controllable variance*) and production volume variances. The budget variance, as is clear in Exhibit 7-5, is simply the difference between actual costs and the budget allowance based on standard hours allowed. The two-way analysis stops there; it does not subdivide the budget variance into spending and efficiency variances.[4]

Overhead variances in the ledger

There are several ways of accounting for overhead variances. The easiest way is probably to allow the department-overhead control accounts and applied accounts to cumulate month-to-month postings until the end of the year. Monthly variances would not be isolated formally in the accounts, although monthly variance reports would be prepared. Assume that the data in Exhibit 7-5 are for the *year* rather than for the *month*. At the year-end, isolating (that is, separately identifying) and closing entries could be made as follows:

[4]The respondents to the Chiu and Lee survey, op. cit., indicated that 40 percent used the two-way analysis; 37 percent, the three-way; and 23 percent, some other way.

EXHIBIT 7-5 *(Place a clip on this page for easy reference.)*

Worksheet Summary of Relationships of Combined-overhead Analysis and its Variable and Fixed Parts

	(1) INCURRED	(2) FLEXIBLE BUDGET* BASED ON ACTUAL INPUTS		(3) FLEXIBLE BUDGET* BASED ON ACTUAL OUTPUTS ACHIEVED		(4) APPLIED	
V	14,250	(7,900 × $1.70)	13,430	(8,000 × $1.70)	13,600	(8,000 × $1.70) =	13,600
F	10,200	Lump sum	10,000	Lump sum	10,000	(8,000 × $1.00) =	8,000
Combined	24,450		23,430		23,600	(8,000 × $2.70) =	21,600

3-way Analysis

	Spending Variance (1) − (2)	Efficiency Variance (2) − (3)	Production volume variance (3) − (4)
V	820 U	170 Fav.	(not applicable)
F	200 U	(not applicable)	2,000 U
Combined	1,020 U	170 Fav.	2,000 U

2-way Analysis

	Flexible-Budget Variance (1) − (3)	Production volume variance (3) − (4)
V	650 U	(not applicable)
F	200 U	2,000 U
Combined	850 U	2,000 U

1-way Analysis

	Underapplied Overhead (1) − (4)
V	650 U
F	2,200 U
Combined	2,850 U

U = Unfavorable   Fav. = Favorable   V = Variable   F = Fixed

Note: See footnote 2 in this chapter for a discussion of an alternative way to compute the denominator variance.

**Budget Formula: $10,000 per month + $1.70 per hour. A lump-sum component of $10,000 is included in column (2). Therefore, that column may also be accurately depicted as a flexible-budget column—based on actual inputs rather than the actual outputs in column (3). Indeed, if preferred, that label may properly be used elsewhere (instead of actual inputs × standard price) for the analysis of all variable costs.*

1. Variable factory overhead applied	**$13,600**	
Variable-overhead spending variance	**820**	
Variable-overhead efficiency variance		**$ 170**
Variable factory-overhead control		**14,250**
To isolate variances for the year.		
2. Fixed factory overhead applied	**8,000**	
Fixed-overhead budget variance	**200**	
Fixed-overhead production volume variance	**2,000**	
Fixed factory-overhead control		**10,200**
To isolate variances for the year.		

3. Income summary (or Cost of goods sold)	650	
Variable-overhead efficiency variance	170	
Variable-overhead spending variance		820
To close.		
4. Income summary (or Cost of goods sold)	2,200	
Fixed-overhead budget variance		200
Fixed-overhead production volume variance		2,000
To close.		

If desired, the isolation entries for the monthly variances could be made monthly, although the closing entries are usually confined to the year-end.

Of course, rather than being closed directly to the Income Summary or Cost of Goods Sold, in certain cases the overhead variances may be prorated at the year-end, as is shown in the next chapter.

SUMMARY

Thorough study of the contents of this chapter should be rewarding, because analysis of overhead variances must consider two major frames of reference: the flexible budget for control and the use of predetermined overhead rates for product costing. The budget variance is considered to be controllable, at least to some degree. The production volume variance is considered uncontrollable in most instances. Thus, this chapter has highlighted and contrasted the many purposes that must be served in accounting for overhead. The general ledger is designed mainly to serve purposes of product costing. Yet management's major purpose, that of control, is aided by using flexible-budget figures, which are not highlighted in general-ledger balances. As is often the case, conventional general-ledger bookkeeping for overhead often provides only minimal information for control.

Note that the general-ledger entries in this chapter sharply distinguish between fixed and variable overhead. This treatment is more effective for management than combining the two because it emphasizes the basic differences in cost behavior of these two kinds of overhead. Such basic differences are often important in influencing managerial decisions. The final section demonstrates that these distinctions can be maintained even if a combined overhead rate is used for product costing.

The worksheet analysis illustrated in Exhibit 7-5 provides a useful approach to the analysis of overhead variances. The first step is to obtain the underapplied or overapplied overhead—the difference between overhead incurred and overhead applied. Then any further variance breakdowns can be added algebraically and checked against the total variance.

problems for self-study

The first problem appears earlier in this chapter. The following problem reviews both this and the preceding chapter. The numbers have deliberately been kept low to simplify the computations.

problem 2

The McDermott Furniture Company has established standard costs for the cabinet department, in which one size of a single four-drawer style of dresser is produced. The standard costs are used in evaluating actual performance. The standard costs of producing one of these dressers are shown below:

STANDARD-COST CARD

Dresser, Style AAA	
Materials: Lumber—50 board feet @ $.20	$10.00
Direct labor: 3 hours @ $6.00	18.00
Indirect costs:	
Variable charges—3 hours @ $1.00	3.00
Fixed charges—3 hours @ $.50	1.50
Total per dresser	$32.50

The costs of operations to produce 400 of these dressers during January are stated below (there were no initial inventories):

Materials purchased:	25,000 board feet @ $.21	$5,250.00
Materials used:	19,000 board feet	
Direct labor:	1,100 hours at $5.90	6,490.00
Indirect costs:		
Variable charges		1,300.00
Fixed charges		710.00

The flexible budget for this department at the monthly volume level used to set the fixed-overhead rate called for 1,400 direct-labor hours of operation. At this level, the variable indirect cost was budgeted at $1,400, and the fixed indirect cost at $700.

REQUIRED

All journal entries. Compute the following variations from standard cost. Label your answers as *favorable* (F) or *unfavorable* (U).

1. Material purchase price, isolated at time of purchase.
2. Material efficiency.
3. (a) Direct-labor price;
   (b) Direct-labor efficiency.
4. (a) Variable-overhead budget variance;
   (b) Fixed-overhead budget variance;
   (c) Fixed-overhead production volume variance.
5. (a) Variable-overhead spending variance;
   (b) Variable-overhead efficiency variance.

solution 2

Journal entries are supported by pertinent variance analysis.

1. Stores control (25,000 @ $.20)	**5,000**	
Material purchase-price variance (25,000 @ $.01)	**250**	
Accounts payable (25,000 @ $.21)		**5,250**
2. Work-in-process control (400 units × 50 board feet × $.20)	**4,000**	
Material-efficiency variance (1,000 × $.20)		**200**
Stores control (19,000 × $.20)		**3,800**
3. Work-in-process control (400 units × $18.00)	**7,200**	
Direct-labor price variance (1,100 hrs. × $.10)		**110**
Direct-labor efficiency variance (100 hrs. × $6.00)		**600**
Accrued payroll (1,100 hrs. × $5.90)		**6,490**

For analysis of variances, see Exhibit 7-6.

4. Variable-overhead control	1,300	
Acounts payable and other accounts		1,300
Work-in-process control	1,200	
Variable overhead applied (400 × 3 × $1.00)		1,200
5. Fixed-overhead control	710	
Accounts payable and other accounts		710
Work-in-process control	600	
Fixed overhead applied (400 × 3 × $.50)		600

The analysis of variances in Exhibit 7-6 summarizes the characteristics of different cost behavior patterns. The approaches to direct labor and variable overhead are basically the same. Furthermore, there is no fundamental conflict between the budgetary-control and product-costing purposes; that is, the applied amounts in column (4) also equal the flexible-budget

EXHIBIT 7-6 *(Place a clip on this page for easy reference.)*

McDermott Furniture Company

Analysis of Manufacturing Costs

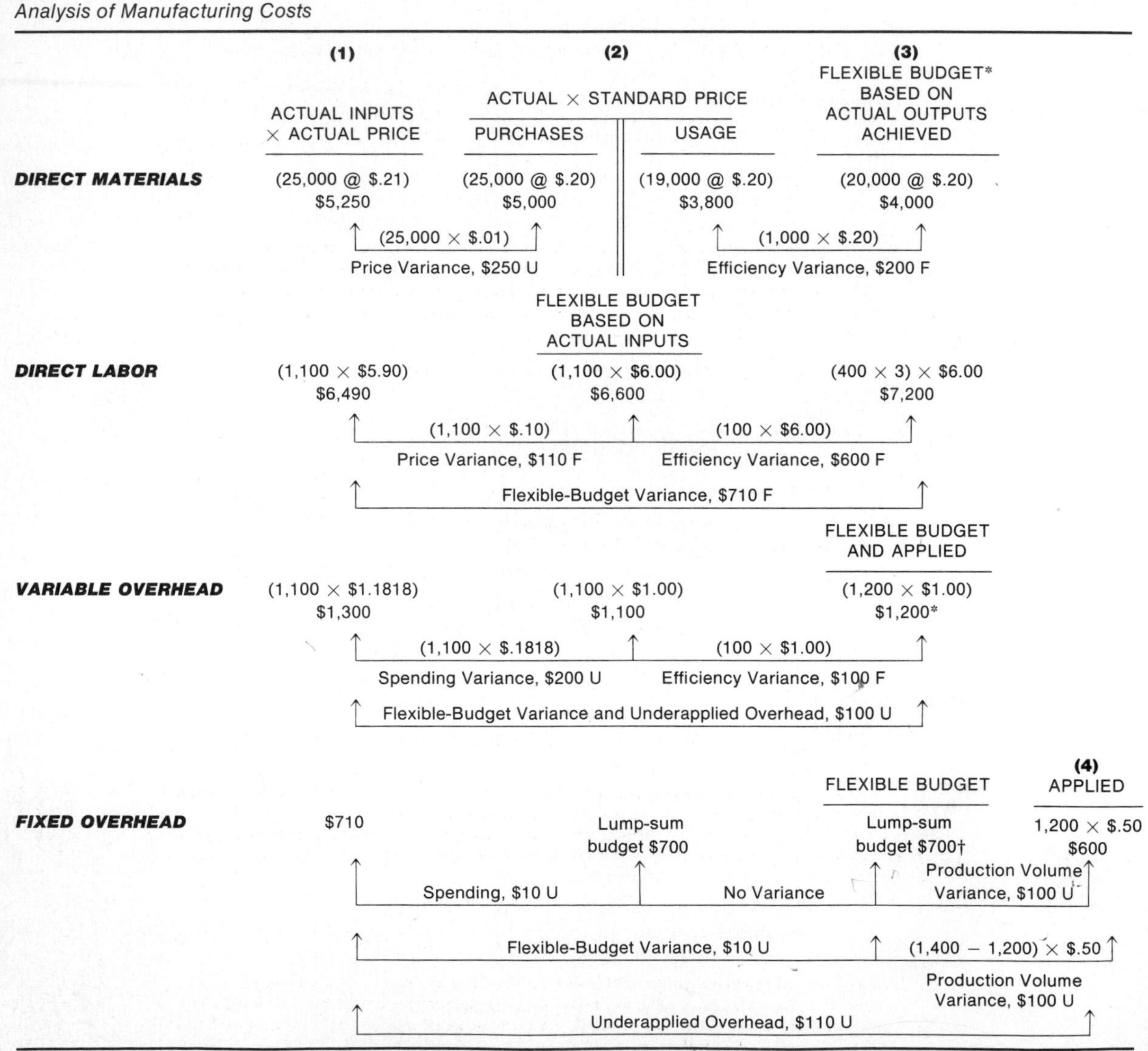

*U = Unfavorable   F = Favorable   *See next page.   †See next page.*

allowances. In contrast, the behavior patterns and control features of fixed overhead require a different analytical approach. The budget is a lump sum. There is no efficiency variance for fixed factory overhead because short-run performance cannot ordinarily affect incurrence of fixed factory overhead. Finally, there will nearly always be a conflict between the budgetary-control and product-costing purposes because the applied amount in column (4) for fixed overhead will differ from the lump-sum budget allowance. The latter conflict is highlighted by the production volume variance, which measures the effects of working at other than the denominator volume used to set the product-costing rate.

**Graphically, the flexible budget line for variable costs and the applied line for variable costs are identical. The example above for variable overhead would appear as follows:*

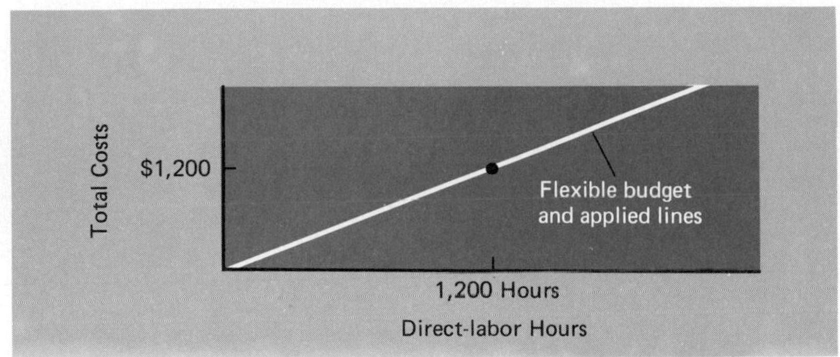

†Graphically, the flexible-budget line for fixed costs is not really flexible because it is horizontal (the total budgeted fixed overhead is the same over a wide range of volume). Hence the budget amount will differ from the applied amount when activity is not at the level (hence called denominator activity) used to set the fixed overhead rate for product costing:

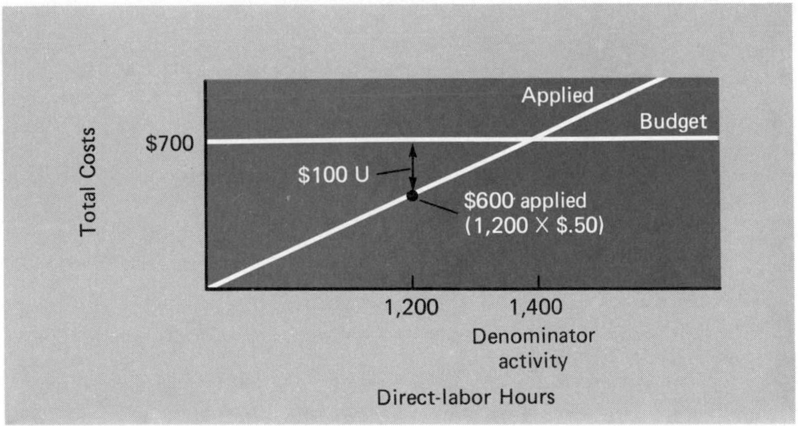

In sum, the accountant is faced with a special problem with regard to fixed overhead, which has very different cost behavior characteristics and cost control features than variable overhead. In trying to apply fixed overhead to product, he must develop a predetermined costing rate. In so doing, the accountant must select a level of activity as the denominator in the formula:

$$\text{Fixed overhead rate} = \frac{\text{Budget}}{\text{Denominator activity}} = \frac{\$700}{1{,}400 \text{ hours}} = \$.50 \text{ per hour}$$

Therefore a production volume variance will arise when ensuing activity differs from denominator activity. Production volume variance arises only in connection with fixed overhead. There is no production volume variance for variable overhead. The budget and the applied amounts for fixed overhead will usually not be equal, in contrast to the equality of the amounts for variable costs.

The following is a summary of variances:

1. Material purchase price	$250 U
2. Material efficiency	200 F
3. (a) Direct-labor price	110 F
(b) Direct-labor efficiency	600 F
4. (a) Variable-overhead budget variance	100 U
(b) Fixed-overhead budget variance	10 U
(c) Fixed-overhead production volume variance	100 U
5. (a) Variable-overhead spending variance	200 U
(b) Variable-overhead efficiency variance	100 F

Terms to Learn

activity variance ***capacity variance*** ***denominator level*** ***denominator variance*** ***idle capacity variance*** ***production volume variance*** ***spending variance*** ***volume variance***

Special Points and Pitfalls

This chapter is probably the most technically demanding so far. The solving of a few homework problems is necessary for understanding. Review the graphs, the Problem for Self-study, and the final exhibit showing the worksheet summary before beginning any assigned problems. Students tend to become especially confused if they fail to:

1. Compute the actual output achieved and the standard hours allowed for that output before proceeding with any other part of their solution. The Applied column in the analytical framework is based on outputs, not inputs.
2. Clearly distinguish between variable factory overhead, which has an efficiency variance but no production volume variance, and fixed factory overhead, which has a production volume variance but no efficiency variance.
3. Remember that a production volume variance may be computed in either of two main ways: (a) Budget − Applied or (b) Fixed-overhead rate × (Denominator volume − Actual volume achieved).
4. Remember that the flexible budget for fixed factory overhead is a lump sum that is unaffected by either actual hours of input or standard hours of input allowed for actual output achieved.

The following tabulation is a capsule review of the key variances presented in this and the preceding chapter.

	DIRECT MATERIALS	DIRECT LABOR	VARIABLE FACTORY OVERHEAD	FIXED FACTORY OVERHEAD
Denominator volume concept?	No	No	No	Yes
Flexible-budget variance?	Yes	Yes	Yes	Yes
Price variance?	Yes	Yes	No	No
Spending variance?	No	No	Yes	Yes*
Efficiency variance?	Yes	Yes	Yes	No
Production volume variance?	No	No	No	Yes

**Exhibit 7-5 shows that the* flexible-budget *variance and the* spending *variance for* fixed *overhead are always equal.*

QUESTIONS, PROBLEMS, AND CASES

7-1 What is the essential difficulty in applying fixed overhead to product?

7-2 "There should be an efficiency variance for fixed overhead. A foreman can inefficiently use his fixed resources." Comment.

7-3 Why is the title "flexible budget" a misnomer?

7-4 What two basic questions should be asked in approaching the control of overhead?

7-5 ***Price and spending variances.*** The GH Company used a flexible budget and standard costs. In March, the company produced 7,000 units of its finished product. Assume that 15,000 actual hours were used at an actual hourly rate of $4.10. Two direct-labor hours is the standard allowance for producing one unit. The standard-labor rate is $4 per hour. The flexible budget for miscellaneous supplies is based on a formula of 60¢ per unit, which can also be expressed as 30¢ per direct-labor hour. The actual cost of supplies was $4,700.

REQUIRED

1. Compute the "price" and "efficiency" variances for direct labor and for supplies.
2. The "price" variance for supplies is rarely labeled as such. Instead, it is often called a spending variance. The plant manager has made the following comments: "I have been troubled by the waste of supplies for months. I know that the prices are exactly equal to the budgeted prices for every supply item, because a two-year stock of supplies was bought a year ago in anticipation of prolonged inflation. Consequently, we used known prices for preparing our budgets. Given these facts, please explain how a price or spending variance can arise for miscellaneous supplies. Why doesn't all waste appear as an efficiency variance?" Respond to the manager's comments. Be clear and specific; the manager is impatient with muddled explanations, and your next pay raise will be affected by her appraisal of your explanation.

7-6 ***Fundamentals of flexible budgets.*** The Carey Company produces one uniform product. The assembly department encounters wide fluctuations in volume (activity) levels from month to month. However, the following department-overhead budget depicts expectations of currently attainable efficiency for an "average" or "normal" level of activity of 20,000 units of production per month:

	BUDGET—NORMAL MONTH	INCURRED "ACTUAL" COSTS IN JUNE
Indirect labor—variable	$20,000	$19,540
Supplies—variable	1,000	1,000
Power—variable	1,000	980
Repairs—variable	1,000	880
Other variable overhead	2,000	1,800
Depreciation—fixed	10,000	10,000
Other fixed overhead	5,000	5,000
	$40,000	$39,200

REQUIRED

1. Prepare a columnar flexible budget at 16,000-, 20,000-, and 24,000-unit levels of volume. For an example of the format, see Exhibit 6-2, page 169.
2. Express requirement 1 in formula form.
3. In June, the department operated at a 17,600-unit level of volume. Prepare two performance reports, comparing actual performance with (a) budget at normal volume and (b) budget at a 17,600-unit level of volume.
4. Which comparison, 3(a) or 3(b), would be more helpful in judging the foreman's efficiency? Why?
5. Sketch a graph (not necessarily to exact scale) of how the flexible-budget total behaves over the 16,000- to 24,000-unit range of volume. Sketch a graph of how the variable-overhead items behave and of how the fixed-overhead items behave. Why is the "flex" in the flexible budget confined to variable overhead?

7-7 ***Spending and efficiency variances.*** Refer to Problem 7-6. Suppose that it actually took 9,500 hours of input to obtain the 17,600 units of output achieved. The standard direct-labor allowance is one-half hour per unit of product manufactured.

REQUIRED

1. Prepare a performance report showing five columns: (a) actual costs incurred, (b) spending variance, (c) flexible budget based on actual hours of input, (d) efficiency variance, and (e) flexible budget based on standard hours allowed for the actual output achieved.
2. Sketch a graph of how the total overhead behaves. Indicate where the total spending variance and the total efficiency variance would appear on the graph.
3. Suppose that a new worker wasted an extra $300 of supplies during the month, so that the actual cost of supplies was $1,300. The unit cost of supplies was unaffected. Would the $300 appear as an additional efficiency variance or as an additional spending variance? Explain fully.

7-8 ***Detailed analysis of variable overhead.*** A department is scheduled to produce 10,000 units of product in 5,000 standard direct-labor hours. However, it has taken 6,000 actual direct-labor hours to produce the 10,000 units. The variable-factory-overhead items are as follows:

	BUDGET FORMULA PER STANDARD DIRECT-LABOR HOUR ALLOWED	ACTUAL COSTS INCURRED
Indirect labor	$2.00	$11,700
Maintenance	.20	1,150
Lubricants	.10	600
Cutting tools	.16	1,500
	$2.46	$14,950

The actual direct-labor rate is $16.20 per hour; the standard rate is $16.00.

REQUIRED

1. Prepare a performance report with separate lines for direct labor, indirect labor, maintenance, lubricants, and cutting tools. Show three columns: actual costs incurred, flexible budget, and flexible-budget variance.
2. Prepare a more detailed version of your answer to requirement 2, showing six columns: actual costs incurred, actual quantities × standard prices, flexible budget, flexible-budget variance, price or spending variance, and efficiency variance.
3. Explain the similarities and differences between the direct-labor and the variable-overhead variances.

7-9 ***Fundamentals of flexible budgets.*** Joan Eastman, the manager of a medical testing laboratory, has been under pressure from the director of a large clinic, Dr. Elvira Coleman, to get more productivity from her employees. New government rules for reimbursement of medical charges had resulted in the disallowance of many costs in the clinic as being too high in relation to standard fees charged elsewhere. In particular, the costs of various blood tests were deemed "outrageous" by one government auditor.

Eastman had been provided with some industry standards for various tests and had compiled a budgeted cost behavior pattern for direct labor and indirect costs. Some selected variable-cost items for a recent four-week period were:

	BUDGETED COST BEHAVIOR PATTERN PER DIRECT-LABOR HOUR	BUDGET BASED ON 4,000 ACTUAL LABOR HOURS	ACTUAL COSTS INCURRED	VARIANCE	
				amount	**percentage of budget**
Direct labor	$8.00	$32,000	$32,000	—	—
Supplies	2.00	8,000	6,400	1,600	20%
Indirect labor	1.00	4,000	3,000	1,000	25
Miscellaneous	2.00	8,000	6,000	2,000	25

Eastman was pleased with her budgetary performance, but Coleman was not happy. She asked you to reconstruct the performance report, saying, "This report seems incomplete. I want a better pinpointing of the degree of basic efficiency in that department."

Your investigation of the industry literature and your discussion with a management consultant in health care revealed that standard times have been developed for these clinical procedures. Although the standard times were open to criticism if examined on an hour-by-hour or day-by-day basis, in the aggregate over a week they provided a fairly reliable benchmark for measuring outputs against inputs. Your study of the output showed that about 2,600 standard direct-labor hours should have been allowed for the output actually achieved by the laboratory.

REQUIRED

For the chosen items, prepare a better performance report for Dr. Coleman. Why is your report better? Be specific.

7-10 ***Material, labor, variable-overhead variance.*** Flanagan Company had the following standards:

Direct material. Three pounds of input allowed at $3 per pound, or $9 per unit of output.
Direct labor. Thirty minutes of input allowed at $12 per hour, or $6 per unit of output.
Variable factory overhead. Fluctuates at a rate of 66⅔ percent of direct labor, or $8 per hour.
Actual costs and quantities of inputs were:

DIRECT MATERIALS		DIRECT LABOR	
Total actual costs	$210,000	Total actual costs	$166,050
Pounds of input	75,000	Hours of input	13,500
Price per pound	$2.80	Price (rate) per hour	$12.30

Actual variable factory overhead was $112,000. Actual units produced and sold were 23,000.

REQUIRED

1. Compute the price and efficiency variances for direct material and direct labor. Also compute the "spending" and efficiency variances for variable factory overhead. Use the format displayed at the beginning of this chapter.
2. Suppose that the variable factory overhead consisted solely of factory supplies having prices exactly as budgeted. Explain how the variance probably arose.
3. Control systems are often designed to pinpoint material price variances as soon as feasible. Thus, when there are delays between the acquisition and the use of materials, price variances are isolated upon acquisition. Suppose 100,000 pounds of material were acquired in May, even though only 75,000 pounds were used. Compute the price variance for direct materials.

7-11 ***Graphs and overhead variances.*** The Duglio Company is a manufacturer of footwear. The company uses a standard absorption-costing system. The budget for 19_2 included:

Variable factory overhead	$9 per direct-labor hour
Fixed factory overhead	$12,000,000
Denominator volume based on expected direct-labor hours allowed for budgeted output	4,000,000 hours

REQUIRED

1. Prepare four freehand graphs, two for variable overhead and two for fixed overhead. Each pair should display how total costs will fluctuate for (a) budgetary-control purposes and (b) product-costing purposes.
2. Suppose 3,500,000 standard direct-labor hours were allowed for the production actually achieved in 19_2. However, 3,800,000 actual hours of input were used. Actual factory overhead was: variable, $36,100,000; fixed, $12,200,000. Compute (a) variable-overhead spending and efficiency variances and (b) fixed-overhead budget variance and production volume variance. Use the analytical framework illustrated in the Problem for Self-Study.
3. Prepare a graph for fixed factory overhead that shows a budget line and an applied line. Indicate the production volume variance on the graph.

4. What is the amount of the underapplied variable overhead? Fixed overhead? Why are the budget variance and the underapplied overhead always the same amount for variable factory overhead but rarely the same amount for fixed factory overhead?
5. Suppose the denominator volume level was 3,000,000 rather than 4,000,000 hours. What variances in requirement 2 would be affected? What would be their new amounts?

7-12 ***Journal entries.*** Refer to the preceding problem, requirement 2. Consider variable factory overhead and then fixed factory overhead. Prepare the journal entries for (a) the incurrence of overhead, (b) the application of overhead, and (c) the isolation and closing of overhead variances for the year.

7-13 ***Comprehensive, straightforward problem on a standard-cost system.*** The Korean Company uses a standard-cost system. The month's data regarding its lone product follow:

Fixed-overhead costs incurred, $6,150
Variable overhead applied at $.90 per hour
Standard direct-labor cost, $4.00 per hour
Standard material cost, $1.00 per pound
Standard pounds of material in a finished unit, 3
Denominator volume per month, 2,500 units
Standard direct-labor hours per finished unit, 5
Materials purchased, 10,000 lbs., $9,500
Materials used, 6,700 lbs.
Direct-labor costs incurred, 11,000 hours, $41,800
Variable-overhead costs incurred, $9,500
Fixed-overhead budget variance, $100, favorable
Finished units produced, 2,000

REQUIRED

Prepare journal entries. Prepare schedules of all variances, using the worksheet approach described in this chapter. Material price variances are isolated as materials are purchased.

7-14 ***Straightforward overhead analysis.*** The Crum Company uses a standard-cost system. Its standard cost of Product Y, based on a denominator activity of 40,000 units per year, included six hours of variable overhead at $.80 per hour and six hours of fixed overhead at $1.50 per hour. Actual output achieved was 44,000 units. Actual variable factory overhead was $240,000. Actual hours of input were 284,000. Actual fixed overhead was $368,000.

Prepare journal entries. Prepare a worksheet analysis for all variable-overhead and fixed-overhead variances, using the approach illustrated in the chapter.

7-15 ***Characteristics of fixed-overhead variances.*** Fox Company executives have studied their operations carefully and have been using a standard-cost system for years. They are now formulating standards for 19_1. They agree that the standards for direct materials will amount to $10 per finished unit produced and that the standards for direct labor and variable overhead are to be $9 and $1 per direct-labor hour, respectively. Total fixed overhead is expected to be $600,000. Two hours of direct labor is the standard time for finishing one unit of finished product.

REQUIRED

1. Graph the budgeted fixed overhead for 400,000 to 800,000 standard allowed direct-labor hours of activity, assuming that the total budget will not change over that activity level. What would be the appropriate product-costing rate per standard direct-labor hour for fixed overhead if denominator activity is 500,000 hours? Graph the applied fixed-overhead line.
2. Assume that 250,000 units of product were produced. How much fixed overhead would be applied to product? Would there be a production volume variance? Why? Assume that 200,000 units were produced. Would there be a volume variance? Why? Show the latter volume variance on a graph. In your own words, define *volume variance.* Why does it arise? Can a volume variance exist for variable overhead? Why?
3. Assume that 220,000 units are produced. Fixed-overhead costs incurred were $617,000. What is the total fixed-overhead variance? Budget variance? Volume variance? Use the analytical technique illustrated in the chapter.

4. In requirement 1 (ignoring requirements 2 and 3), what would be the appropriate product-costing rate per standard direct-labor hour for fixed overhead if denominator activity is estimated at 400,000 hours? At 600,000 hours? At 800,000 hours? Draw a graph showing budgeted fixed overhead and three "applied" lines, using the three rates just calculated. If 200,000 units are produced, and the denominator activity is 600,000 standard direct-labor hours, what is the volume variance? Now compare this with the volume variance in your answer to requirement 2; explain the difference.
5. Specifically, what are the implications in requirements 1 and 4 regarding (a) the setting of product-costing rates for fixed overhead, (b) the meaning of budget and volume variances, and (c) the major differences in planning and control techniques for variable and fixed costs?

7-16 ***Find the unknowns.*** Consider each of the following situations independently. Data refer to operations for a week in April. For each situation assume a standard product-cost system. Also assume the use of a flexible budget for control of variable and fixed overhead based on standard direct-labor hours.

	CASES		
	A	B	C
(1) Actual fixed overhead	—	$12,000	$10,600
(2) Actual variable overhead	—	—	7,000
(3) Denominator activity in hours	—	11,000	5,000
(4) Standard hours allowed for good output	6,500	—	—
Flexible-budget data:			
(5) Fixed factory overhead	—	—	—
(6) Variable factory overhead (per standard hour)	85¢	50¢	—
(7) Budgeted fixed factory overhead	—	11,000	10,000
(8) Budgeted variable factory overhead*	—	—	—
(9) Total budgeted factory overhead*	12,525	—	—
(10) Standard variable overhead applied	—	—	7,500
(11) Standard fixed overhead applied	—	—	10,000
(12) Production volume variance	500 U	500 F	—
(13) Variable-overhead spending variance	-0-	250 U	950 F
(14) Variable-overhead efficiency variance	-0-	100 U	—
(15) Fixed-overhead budget variance	300 F	—	—
(16) Actual hours of input	—	—	—

**For standard hours allowed for output achieved.*

REQUIRED

Fill in the blanks under each case. Prepare your answer by (a) listing the numbers that are blank for each case and (b) putting the final answers next to the numbers. Prepare supporting computations on a separate sheet. For example, your answer to Case A would contain a vertical listing of the numbers 1, 2, 3, 5, 7, 8, 10, 11, and 16, with answers next to the appropriate numbers. *Hint:* Prepare a worksheet similar to that in Exhibit 7-6. Fill in the knowns and then solve for the unknowns.

7-17 ***Two-way and three-way analysis.*** The Harrison Company has a standard absorption-costing system. A single hourly rate is used to apply factory overhead to product. However, a flexible-budget formula is used for budgetary-control purposes: $8,000,000 per year plus $7 per direct-labor hour.

For 19_1, the denominator volume for developing a product-costing rate was the expected activity of 1,600,000 direct-labor hours. The actual factory overhead was $18,100,000. Direct-labor hours were: standard allowed for actual output achieved, 1,300,000; actual hours of input, 1,500,000.

REQUIRED

Prepare an analysis of all overhead variances. Use the format of Exhibit 7-5 to display a two-way analysis and a three-way analysis. See page 215.

7-18 ***Multiple choice.*** (CMA, adapted). The Organet Stamping Company manufactures a variety of products made of plastic and aluminum components. During the winter months substantially all of the production capacity is devoted to the production of lawn sprinklers for the following spring and summer season. Other products are manufactured during the remainder of the year. Because a variety of products are manufactured throughout the year, factory volume is measured by production labor-hours rather than units of product.

Production and sales volume have grown steadily during the past several years, as can be seen from the following schedule of standard production labor content of annual output expressed in hours:

19_3	16,000
19_2	15,000
19_1	13,500
19_0	14,000
19_9	13,000

The company has developed standard costs for its several products. Standard costs for each year are set in the preceding October. The standard cost of a sprinkler for 19_4 was $2.50, computed as follows:

Direct materials:			
Aluminum	.2 lbs.	@ $ .40 per lb.	$ .08
Plastic	1.0 lbs.	@ .38 per lb.	.38
Production labor	.15 hrs.	@ 8.00 per hr.	1.20
Overhead (calculated using 15,000 production labor-hours as denominator volume):			
Variable	.15 hrs.	@ 3.20 per hr.	.48
Fixed	.15 hrs.	@ 2.40 per hr.	.36
Total			$2.50

During February 19_4, 8,500 good sprinklers were manufactured. The following costs were incurred:

Materials requisitioned for production:			
Aluminum	1,900 lbs.	@ $ .40 per lb.	$ 760
Plastic:			
Regular grade	6,000 lbs.	@ .38 per lb.	2,280
Low grade*	3,500 lbs.	@ .38 per lb.	1,330
Production labor:			
Straight time	1,150 hrs.	@ 8.00 per hr.	9,200
Overtime	200 hrs.	@ 12.00 per hr.	2,400†
Overhead:			
Variable			5,200
Fixed			3,100
Total costs charged to manufacturing departments			$24,270

**Owing to plastic shortages, the company was forced to purchase lower-grade plastic than called for in the standards. This increased the number of sprinklers rejected on inspection.*

†Unlike most companies, Organet did not classify overtime premium as overhead.

Material-price variations are not charged to production but to a material-price-variation account at the time the invoice is entered. All materials are carried in inventory at standard prices. Material purchases for February were:

Aluminum	1,800 lbs.	@ $ .48 per lb.	$ 864
Plastic:			
Regular grade	3,000 lbs.	@ .50	1,500
Low grade	6,000 lbs.	@ .29	1,740

Every item below is related to the above facts and should be answered on the basis of those facts. Show your computations. Choose the best answer:

REQUIRED

1. The total variation from "standard cost applied" of the costs charged to manufacturing departments from February 19_4 is (a) $3,080 unfavorable, (b) $3,020 unfavorable, (c) $3,140 favorable, (d) $3,020 favorable, (e) some other amount.
2. The standard material quantities already include an allowance for acceptable material scrap loss. In this situation the material efficiency variations would most likely be caused by (a) defective aluminum, (b) improper processing by labor, (c) inadequate allowance for scrap loss, (d) substitute plastic, (e) none of these reasons.
3. The spending or budget variation for the fixed portion of the overhead costs is (a) $100 unfavorable, (b) $60 favorable, (c) zero, (d) not calculable from the problem, (e) not listed above.
4. The labor-efficiency variation is the difference between standard labor-hours allowed for output achieved and (a) 1,150 hours, (b) 1,350 hours, (c) 1,450 hours, (d) 1,250 hours, (e) some other amount.
5. The production labor-price variation is (a) $0, (b) $600 unfavorable, (c) $800 unfavorable, (d) $1,400 unfavorable, (e) $2,400 unfavorable.
6. The manufacturing-overhead production volume variation is (a) the result of inadequate cost-control effort, (b) the result of sales volume exceeding production volume, (c) the result of actual production hours exceeding standard production hours of output, (d) the result of the overapplication of fixed cost to output, (e) not the result of any of these reasons.
7. The variable-overhead-budget variation is (a) $1,120 unfavorable, (b) $1,220 unfavorable, (c) $1,160 unfavorable, (d) $1,280 unfavorable, (e) none of these.
8. The variations of material prices from standard would (a) best be reported as materials-price variations—$36 favorable, (b) best be reported as materials-price variations—aluminum, $144 unfavorable; plastic, $180 favorable, (c) best be reported as materials-price variations— aluminum, $144 unfavorable; plastic, $360 unfavorable; material substitution $540 favorable, (d) best be reported as materials-price variations—aluminum, $144 unfavorable; plastic, $360 unfavorable; price difference due to plastic substitution not reported, (e) not be reported because material prices are uncontrollable.

7-19 ***Normal costing and overhead analysis.*** The Blaney Company had *budgeted* the following performance for 19_4:

Units	10,000
Sales	$120,000
Total variable production costs, including variable factory overhead of $5,000	60,000
Total fixed production costs	25,000
Gross margin	35,000
Beginning inventories	None

It is now December 31, 19_4. The factory-overhead rate that was used throughout the year was $3 per unit. Total factory overhead incurred was $30,000. Underapplied factory overhead was $900. There is no work in process.

REQUIRED

1. How many units were produced during 19_4?
2. Nine thousand units were sold at regular prices during 19_4. Assuming that the predicted cost behavior patterns implicit in the budget above have conformed to the plan (except for variable factory overhead), and that underapplied factory overhead is written off directly as an adjustment of cost of goods sold, what is the gross margin for 19_4? How much factory overhead should be assigned to the ending inventory if it is to be carried at "normal" cost?
3. Explain *why* overhead was underapplied by $900. In other words, analyze the variable- and fixed-overhead variances as far as the data permit.

7-20 ***Combined overhead rate.*** The Wright-Peterson Air Force Base contained an extensive repair facility for jet engines. It had developed standard costing and flexible budgets for this activity. Budgeted *variable* overhead at a 16,000 standard monthly direct-labor-hour level was $64,000; budgeted *total* overhead at a 20,000 standard direct-labor-hour level was $197,600. The standard cost applied to repair output included a combined overhead rate of 120 percent of standard direct-labor cost.

Total actual overhead for October was $250,000. Direct-labor costs actually incurred were $202,440. The direct-labor price variance was $9,640, unfavorable. The direct-labor budget variance was $14,440, unfavorable. The standard labor price was $8.00 per hour. The denominator variance was $14,000, favorable.

REQUIRED

Direct-labor efficiency variance. Combined overhead spending, efficiency, and denominator variances. Also compute the denominator volume. (*Hint:* See Exhibit 7-5.)

7-21 ***Combined overhead variances.*** (SMA, adapted). The Weser Company uses a predetermined total overhead rate of $4 per unit based on a denominator capacity of 600,000 units a year or 50,000 units a month.

During October, the company produced 52,000 units and experienced the following combined overhead variances:

Overhead budget variance	$1,500 unfavorable
Overhead denominator variance	$5,000 favorable

During November, unit production was 49,000 units and the actual overhead cost incurred was $2,000 less than October's overhead.

Determine the overhead budget and production volume variances for the month of November.

7-22 ***Hospital cost control.*** The Sharon Hospital, a large metropolitan health-care complex, has had much trouble in controlling its accounts receivable. Bills for patients, for various government agencies, and for private insurance companies have frequently been inaccurate and late. This has led to intolerable levels of bad debts and investments in receivables.

You were employed by the hospital as a consultant on this matter. After conducting a careful study of the billing operation, you developed some currently attainable standards that were implemented in conjunction with a flexible budget four weeks ago. You had divided costs into fixed and variable categories. You regarded the bill as the product, the unit of output.

You have reasonable confidence that the underlying source documents for compiling the results have been accurately tallied. However, the bookkeeper has had some trouble summarizing the data and has provided the following:

Variable costs, including all billing operators, whose compensation is regarded as variable, allowance per standard hour	$ 10
Fixed-overhead budget variance, favorable	200
Combined budgeted costs for the bills produced	22,500
Production volume variance, favorable	900
Variable-cost "spending" variance, unfavorable	2,000
Variable-cost efficiency variance, favorable	2,000
Standard hours allowed for the bills produced, 1,800	

REQUIRED

1. Actual hours of input
2. Fixed-overhead budget
3. Standard fixed overhead applied
4. Denominator activity in hours

special review material for chapters 6 and 7

7-23 ***Miscellaneous aspects of standard costing.*** (D. Kleespie). The J/M Company manufactures a single product in a single department and utilizes a standard-cost system. Standard costs per unit of finished product include a total direct-materials cost of $20, which consists of 4 pounds of direct material at $5 per pound. Two hours of direct labor are required per unit of finished product. The standard direct-labor-hour rate is $5 per hour. The following represents a condensed monthly flexible factory-overhead budget for the firm:

Standard direct-labor hours allowed	30,000 HRS.	40,000 HRS.	50,000 HRS.
Variable manufacturing overhead:			
Supplies	$ 9,000	$ 12,000	$ 15,000
Indirect labor	22,000	33,000	44,000
Other variable overhead	17,000	19,000	21,000
	$ 48,000	$ 64,000	$ 80,000
Fixed manufacturing overhead:			
Supervision	$ 48,000	$ 48,000	$ 48,000
Depreciation	40,000	40,000	40,000
Other fixed overhead	17,000	17,000	17,000
	$105,000	$105,000	$105,000
Total budgeted manufacturing overhead	$153,000	$169,000	$185,000

The company uses a combined manufacturing-overhead rate (fixed and variable) of $8.20 per finished unit for product-costing purposes. Data for a certain month's production follow:

20,000 units produced (there were no units in process at either the beginning or the end of the month);
Direct labor, 41,000 actual direct-labor hours at $5.50 per hour;
Direct material purchased, 96,000 pounds at $5.20 per pound;
Direct material used in production, 90,000 pounds;
Total actual manufacturing-overhead costs incurred, $176,000, of which $104,000 were fixed-overhead costs.

REQUIRED

(Show supporting computations for your answers.)

For items 1 through 3 you are to determine the total dollar amounts of the indicated variances. Use *F* or *U* to designate favorable or unfavorable.

1. Labor efficiency variance.
2. Variable-overhead spending variance.
3. Fixed-overhead production volume variance.
4. Amount that should be debited to Work in Process for *total* factory overhead applied for this month.
5. Total amount that should be debited to Work in Process for direct labor used during this month.
6. Monthly denominator activity expressed in standard direct-labor hours.
7. Total amount of manufacturing overhead that would be *budgeted* for a month in which 22,000 *units of product* were expected to be produced.
8. Total dollar amount debited to the finished-goods inventory for the units produced this month. (Assume that all variances are closed directly to cost of goods sold, i.e., reported on the monthly income statement.)

7-24 ***Normal costing.*** Refer to the preceding problem.

What is the total dollar amount debited to the finished-goods inventory for the units produced this month if a "normal" costing system had been used instead of the standard cost system described in requirement 8 above? (You may assume that any overhead that was over-applied or underapplied would be closed to cost of goods sold.)

7-25 ***Working backward from given variances.*** The Mancuso Company uses a flexible budget and standard costs to aid planning and control. At a 60,000-direct-labor-hour level, budgeted variable overhead is $30,000 and budgeted direct labor is $480,000.

The following are some results for August:

Variable-overhead budget variance	$ 10,500 U
Variable-overhead efficiency variance	9,500 U

Actual direct-labor costs incurred	574,000
Material purchase-price variance (based on goods purchased)	16,000 F
Material-efficiency variance	9,000 U
Fixed overhead incurred	50,000
Fixed-overhead budget variance	2,000 U

The standard cost per pound of direct materials is $1.50. The standard allowance is one pound of direct materials for each unit of finished product. Ninety thousand units of product were made during August. There was no beginning or ending work in process. In July, the material-efficiency variance was $1,000, favorable, and the purchase-price variance was $.20 per pound, unfavorable. In August, the purchase-price variance was $.10 per pound.

In July, labor troubles caused an immense slowdown in the pace of production. There had been an unfavorable direct-labor efficiency variance of $60,000; there was no labor-price variance. These troubles had persisted in August. Some workers quit. Their replacements had to be hired at higher rates, which had to be extended to all workers. The actual average wage rate in August exceeded the standard average wage rate by $.20 per hour.

REQUIRED

For August:

1. Total pounds of direct materials purchased during August
2. Total number of pounds of excess material usage
3. Variable-overhead spending variance
4. Total number of actual hours of input
5. Total number of standard hours allowed for the finished units produced

7-26 ***Working backward from given variances.*** The Vanguard Company manufactures one product. Its standard-cost system incorporates flexible budgets and assigns indirect costs on the basis of standard direct-labor hours.

At denominator activity, the standard cost per unit is as follows:

Direct materials, 3 lbs. @ $5.00	$15.00
Direct labor, .4 hr. @ $20.00	8.00
Variable indirect costs, .4 hr. @ $6.00	2.40
Fixed indirect costs, .4 hr. @ $4.00	1.60
Total	$27.00

For the month of October 19_2, the performance report included the following information (in dollars):

	INCURRED AT ACTUAL PRICE	STANDARD COSTS APPLIED	TOTAL VARIANCE	VARIANCE ANALYSIS		
				price or spending	**efficiency**	**production volume**
Direct materials used	$134,400	$135,000	$ 600 F	$5,600 F	$ 5,000 U	—
Direct labor	77,900	72,000	5,900 U	1,900 U	4,000 U	—
Variable indirect costs	21,500	21,600	100 F	1,300 F	1,200 U	—
Fixed indirect costs	15,800	14,400	1,400 U	200 F*	—	$1,600 U
	$249,600	$243,000	$6,600 U	$5,200 F	$10,200 U	$1,600 U

**Budget variance.*

Direct materials were quoted at $5.50 per pound throughout September and October by all suppliers. There was no *purchase*-price variance for materials in October; the price variance shown relates solely to the materials *used* during October.

Wage standards were set in accordance with an annual union contract, but a shortage of workers in the local area has resulted in rates higher than standard.

There were no beginning or ending inventories of work in process.

REQUIRED

For the month of October.

1. Number of units produced. Triple-check your computations here before proceeding.
2. Actual number of direct-labor hours.
3. Actual wage rate.
4. Budget for fixed indirect costs.
5. Denominator activity expressed in direct-labor hours.
6. Pounds of direct materials used.
7. Pounds of direct materials purchased.

7-27 ***Variance analysis from fragmentary evidence.*** Being a bright young person, you have just landed a wonderful job as assistant controller of Gyp-Clip, a new and promising Singapore division of Croding Metals Corporation. The Gyp-Clip Division has been formed to produce a single product, a new-model paper clip. Croding Laboratories has developed an extremely springy and lightweight new alloy, Clypton, which is expected to revolutionize the paper-clip industry.

Gyp-Clip has been in business one month; it is your first day on the job. The controller takes you on a tour of the plant and explains the operation in detail: Clypton wire is received on two-mile spools from the Croding mill at a fixed price of $40 a spool, which is not subject to change. Clips are bent, cut, and shipped in bulk to the Croding packaging plant. Factory rent, depreciation, and all other items of fixed factory overhead are handled by the home office at a set rate of $100,000 per month. Ten thousand tons of paper clips have been produced, but this is only 75 percent of denominator activity, since demand for the product must be built up.

The controller has just figured out the month's variances; she is looking for a method of presenting them in clear, logical form to top management at the home office. You say that you know of just the method, and promise to have the analysis ready the next morning.

Filled with zeal and enthusiasm, feeling that your future as a rising star in this growing company is secure, you decide to take your spouse out to dinner to celebrate the trust and confidence that your superior has placed in you.

Upon returning home, with the flush of four martinis still upon you, you are horrified to discover your dog happily devouring the controller's figure sheet. You manage to salvage only the following fragments:

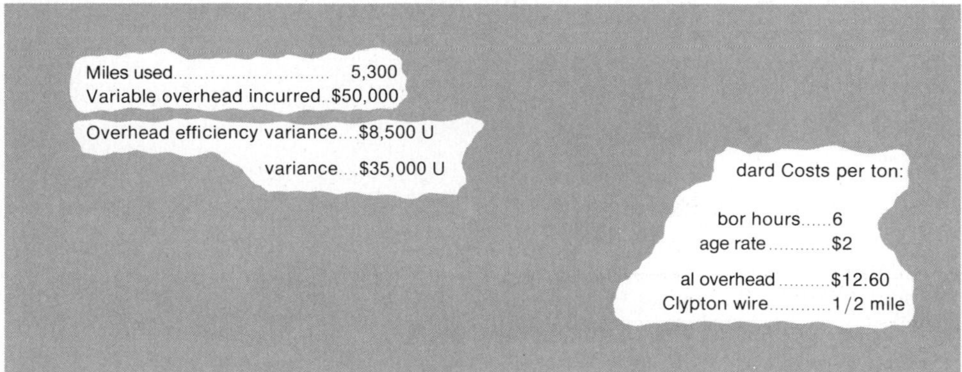

You remember that the $35,000 variance did not represent the grand total of all variances. You also recall that variance analysis was easier to tackle by expressing items in terms of inputs (such as hours) rather than outputs.

REQUIRED

Don't let the controller think you're a knucklehead; go ahead and make up your analysis of all variances.

7-28 ***Variance analysis.*** (J. Patell). During 19_6 the T-M Division of Acro-Cel Tool and Machine had specialized in the production of a single heavy-duty motorcycle component. Original engineering estimates and the use of Acro-Cel's *Total Overhead* Flexible Budget had yielded the following standard cost per unit:

Standard Cost		
Materials	10 lbs. @ $1.50 per lb. =	$15.00
Labor	2 hours @ $6.00 per hr. =	12.00
Variable overhead	2 hours @ $1.00 per hr. =	2.00
Fixed overhead	2 hours @ $4.00 per hr. =	8.00
Total standard cost		$37.00

Flexible Budget—Total Overhead	
LABOR HOURS	EXPECTED COST
16,000	$ 96,000
18,000	$ 98,000
20,000	$100,000
22,000	$102,000

Tom, the T-M Division shop foreman, tends to communicate in brief, blunt reports. His analysis of 19_6 is reproduced below:

> As usual, the yo-yos in Purchasing and Personnel goofed and are trying to pass the buck to us. Your hotshot planners predicted an average wage rate of $6.00, and then your bleeding heart labor negotiators conceded to $6.60 an hour, for a 10 percent overrun. On top of that, Purchasing paid $1.80 per pound for materials they should have gotten for $1.50, or a whopping 20 percent overexpenditure. Given that kind of incompetence, I feel the T-M production line deserves a big thank-you for holding actual total costs per unit down to $41.58, which works out to 12.4 percent over standard.
>
> Actual Expenditures:

Materials	$226,800	Total cost	$498,920
Labor	166,320	Actual output	12,000 units
Variable overhead	24,800	Actual cost per unit	$41.58
Fixed overhead	81,000		
Total costs	$498,920		

REQUIRED

For ease of computation, assume that both the beginning and ending material inventory balances were zero.

1. Rework Tom's report into a complete variance analysis. Compute and *label* price, spending, and efficiency variances for direct material, direct labor, and variable overhead, as well as budget and production volume variances for fixed overhead.
2. Tom's report is also difficult to reconcile with a complaint from the controller's office that the T-M Division's cash expenditures were almost 35 percent higher than originally budgeted and had placed a severe strain on Acro-Cel's relationships with the bank. What was the original (static) budget figure for the T-M Division's total costs?

7-29 ***Interpretation of variances.*** Refer to the preceding problem. Analyze the quotation therein. Is Tom correct? Be specific, supplying as many numbers as possible. *Hint:* Remember the display in Exhibit 6-4, p. 170.

7-30 ***Xerox Corporation variance analysis.*** The following memorandum was prepared by a financial analyst for distribution by the research department of a New York brokerage house.

Summary

In determining the cost of rental equipment capitalized, Xerox utilizes a standard manufacturing cost system. When actual production falls below that forecasted, this results in a portion of manufacturing overhead not being absorbed (capitalized) in production. This unabsorbed manufacturing overhead is expensed through the income statement as incurred. This situation has been a major earnings depressant this year. Management will go only so far as to say that *this 1975 expense item will be tens of millions of dollars.* Given the normal adjustment which would occur to manufacturing standards because of the most recent experience (1975), coupled with a new marketing strategy that deemphasizes net additions to the installed population of traditional rental machines and the expected pressure on 1976 earnings, we think there is a reasonable possibility that the projection of 1976 unit production for traditional copying products may be low enough that unabsorbed manufacturing overhead expense may be importantly reduced in 1976. In effect, in 1976 Xerox would then be capitalizing a portion of a cost item that was expensed in 1975, providing a significant stimulus to earnings. In a recent conversation with management, it was indicated that Xerox does intend to alter to some degree its standard cost of manufacture in 1976.

Analysis of Unabsorbed Manufacturing Overhead

Over a period of time, management responses to our questions would appear to allow a calculation of the components of manufacturing costs. The computation suggests the following breakdown of manufacturing costs: materials, 35%; direct labor, 13%; and overhead, 52%. However, our knowledge and observations of the Xerox production process lead us to question the results of this mathematical exercise. Our judgment would indicate that the direct labor component is reasonable, but material should be higher and overhead lower. Our view is that a breakdown of 50% material, 15% labor, and 35% overhead appears more realistic.

The following table is constructed based on comments made to us recently by management and our own estimates:

Components of Gross Additions to Rental Equipment and Related Inventories

(Millions)

	1974	1975E
Gross additions to rental equipment and related inventory	$865	$625
Accounted for by:		
Gross additions to rental equipment	765	665
Additions to inventory	100	(40)

Additions to inventory relate primarily to materials, and to a lesser extent to work-in-process. Any attempt to quantify unabsorbed manufacturing overhead should use the estimated figure for gross additions to rental equipment (excluding additions to inventory). Applying the range of 35% to 52% for overhead to 1974 estimated gross additions of $765 results in a manufacturing overhead component of $268 to $398 million. If 1975 *gross* additions decline by 13% ($765 million to $665 million) and the same standard cost of manufacture applies to both years, then unabsorbed manufacturing overhead would range between $35 million and $52 million or roughly $0.20–0.30 per share (assuming Rank Xerox accounted for one quarter of the decline in production).

If, as appears possible, management changes its standard cost of manufacture in 1976, there would then be greater absorption of manufacturing overhead in unit production and a welcome favorable earnings swing of some significance. It should be noted that a change in standard cost of manufacture is a normal procedure at any corporation and since it does not represent an alteration in the accounting *method,* its change and effect would not have to be reported. Nonetheless, such a change would benefit earnings in the short run but increase the cost of gross additions to rental equipment and, consequently, depreciation expense in future years.

In light of the 1975 production experience, as well as the implication to future production of the change in marketing strategy toward emphasis on increasing usage of the installed base of traditional copying equipment rather than net machine additions, management is making an effort to reduce the actual level of manufacturing overhead. Manufacturing overhead should show an outright decline in 1976. Xerox is essentially a non-integrated assembler of components, and therefore the magnitude of the fixed investment in production is relatively low (in 1974, the cost of plant machinery installed totaled $359 million out of total assets of over $4 billion). According to management, a major source of manufacturing overhead is indirect labor. It would seem that this represents an area that can be reduced at Xerox's discretion.

REQUIRED

Prepare a summary translation of the memorandum that your fellow students can understand.

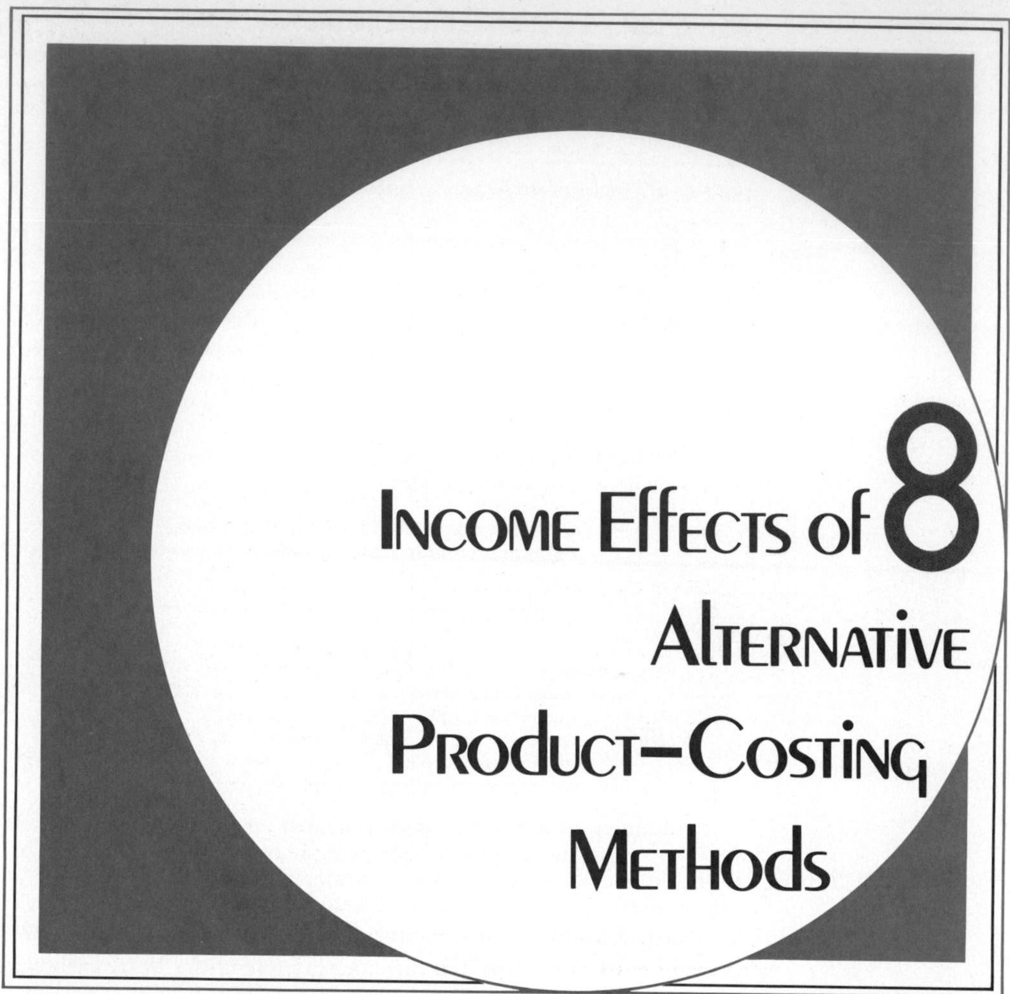

8 Income Effects of Alternative Product-Costing Methods

When an accounting system is designed, managers and accountants must choose an inventory-costing method. This decision is vital for many reasons, including its effects on reported income in any given fiscal period, on the evaluation of a manager's performance, and on pricing decisions.

The major purposes of this chapter are to **examine and compare the effects of some costing alternatives on the measurements of product costs and income.** Other decision implications of these alternatives are also mentioned, but they are discussed more fully in subsequent chapters.

We consider three major topics: (a) variable and absorption costing, (b) the role of various denominator levels in absorption costing, and (c) standard-cost variances and the income statement. Chapter Appendixes cover (a) additional discussions of prorations of variances and (b) interim reporting. These topics are related sufficiently to warrant their being considered in a single chapter. *However, they may be studied indepen-*

dently. Consequently, each of the Problems for Self-Study in this chapter is placed at the end of the appropriate major section. Pause at the end of each section and solve the pertinent Problem for Self-Study.

Variable and absorption costing

The rudiments of **variable costing** (also called **direct costing**) were introduced in Chapter 3, pages 52–54 and 63. You may wish to refresh your memory by rereading that discussion.

impact of fixed factory overhead

The basic impact of variable and absorption costing on income is deceptively simple. Differences arise because fixed factory overhead is not inventoried under variable costing and is inventoried under absorption costing. Using simple numbers, assume that fixed factory overhead incurred was $2,200 for the year 19_1. Also assume that 1,100 units were produced, that the denominator volume for absorption costing was also 1,100 units, but that only 1,000 units were sold:

COST TO ACCOUNT FOR	VARIABLE COSTING—INVENTORIED COSTS	EXPENSE IN 19_1
$2,200 →	expires immediately as a period cost →	$2,200

COST TO ACCOUNT FOR	ABSORPTION COSTING—INVENTORIED COSTS	EXPENSE IN 19_1
$2,200 →	Additions to inventory: 1,100 × $2.00 = $2,200	
	Cost of goods sold: 1,000 × $2.00 = $2,000 →	$2,000
	Ending inventory: 100 × $2.00 $ 200	

The chart contains only one item, fixed factory overhead, because *all* other manufacturing costs are accounted for exactly alike under both variable and absorption costing. That is, direct material, direct labor, and variable factory overhead are always inventoriable.

Trace the $2,200 to Exhibit 8-1 where additional information is presented. The variable-costing statement deducts the lump sum as an expense in 19_1. In contrast, the absorption-costing statement regards each finished unit as bearing $2,200 ÷ 1,100 = $2 fixed factory overhead. The variable manufacturing costs are accounted for no differently in either statement.

The general format of these income statements should be familiar. The new feature is explained in the final footnote in Exhibit 8-1. If inventory levels change, income will differ because of the different accounting for fixed factory overhead.

generality of variable costing

Exhibit 8-1 presents the general features of variable and absorption costing. Using a Work-in-Process account, a capsule comparison of six alternative product-costing systems is presented on the top of page 237.

The boxes represent the debits to Work in Process (that is, the amounts applied to product) under alternative cost systems. The major systems in use are the standard-costing systems, which were introduced in the preceding two chapters, and the normal-costing systems, which were introduced in Chapter 4. As the boxes indicate, variable

EXHIBIT 8-1

Comparison of Variable and Absorption Costing

B Company

Income Statements for the Year Ending Dec. 31, 19_1

(Data assumed; there is no beginning inventory; the unit *variable* manufacturing cost is $6.00.)

VARIABLE (DIRECT) COSTING

Sales: 1,000 units @ $10.00		$10,000
Variable manufacturing cost of goods available for sale: 1,100 units @ $6.00	$6,600*	
Less ending inventory: 100 units @ $6.00	600	
Variable manufacturing cost of goods sold	$6,000	
Add variable selling and administrative expenses	400	
Total variable costs charged against sales		6,400
Contribution margin		$ 3,600
Less fixed costs:		
Fixed manufacturing costs	$2,200	
Fixed selling and administrative expenses	500	$ 2,700
Operating income		$ 900†

ABSORPTION COSTING

	UNIT COST	TOTAL	
Sales,			$10,000
Cost of goods sold:			
Variable manufacturing costs: 1,100 units	$6.00	$6,600*	
Fixed manufacturing costs	2.00	2,200	
Cost of goods available for sale	$8.00	$8,800	
Less ending inventory: 100 units	8.00	800	$ 8,000
Gross margin			$ 2,000
Less total selling and administrative expenses, including $400 of variable expenses			900
Operating income			$ 1,100†

Composed of

	UNIT COST	*TOTAL*
Direct materials	*$3.00*	*$3,300*
Direct labor	*2.00*	*2,200*
Variable overhead	*1.00*	*1,100*
Variable manufacturing costs	*$6.00*	*$6,600*

†*The $200 difference in operating income is caused by the $200 ($800 − $600) difference in ending inventories. Under absorption costing, $200 of the $2,200 fixed manufacturing costs is held back in inventory, whereas under variable costing the $200 is released immediately as a charge against sales.*

WORK-IN-PROCESS INVENTORY

	ACTUAL COSTING	NORMAL COSTING	STANDARD COSTING
Direct materials and direct labor	Actual inputs × Actual prices	Actual inputs × Actual prices	Standard inputs allowed × Standard prices
Variable factory overhead	Actual inputs × Actual overhead rates	Actual inputs × Predetermined overhead rates	Standard inputs allowed × Standard prices
Fixed factory overhead	Actual inputs × Actual overhead rates	Actual inputs × Predetermined overhead rates	Standard inputs allowed × Standard prices

(1) Absorption Costing—Includes All Boxes
(2) Variable (Direct) Costing—Excludes Bottom Boxes

costing or absorption costing may be combined with actual, normal, or standard costing. **Variable costing signifies that fixed factory overhead is *not* inventoried.**

Variable (direct) costing has been a controversial subject among accountants—not so much because there is disagreement about the need for delineating between variable- and fixed-cost behavior patterns for management planning and control, but because there is a question about its theoretical propriety for *external* reporting. Proponents of direct costing maintain that the fixed part of factory overhead is more closely related to the *capacity* to produce than to the production of specific units. Opponents of direct costing maintain that inventories should carry a fixed-cost component, because both variable and fixed costs are necessary to produce goods; both these costs should be inventoriable, regardless of their differences in behavior patterns. Neither the public accounting profession nor the Internal Revenue Service has approved of direct costing as a generally acceptable method of inventory valuation.

Absorption costing is much more widely used than variable costing, although the growing use of the contribution approach in performance measurement and cost analysis has led to increasing use of variable costing for *internal* purposes. A survey of *Fortune 500* industrial corporations indicated that 35 percent of the companies that use standard costing have adopted standard variable costing.[1]

illustration of standard variable costing

Let us consider the implications of accounting for fixed factory overhead in more depth. We will pursue the Webb Company illustration that was discussed in the preceding two chapters. The illustration focused on the month of April. Now consider both March and April.

The basic production data at standard costs were:

Direct material	$20
Direct labor	16
Variable factory overhead	3
Standard variable manufacturing costs per unit	$39

[1] J. Chiu and Y. Lee, "A Survey of Current Practice in Overhead Accounting and Analysis," *Proceedings of the 1980 Western Regional Meeting of the American Accounting Association* (O. R. Whittington, San Diego State University, School of Accounting, 1980), p. 239. Also see E. Imhoff, "Management Accounting Techniques: A Survey," *Management Accounting,* LX, No. 5 (Nov. 1978), which summarizes 53 responses from a survey of 105 publicly-traded companies.

Fixed factory overhead was budgeted at $96,000 per month. The budgeted monthly production volume is 12,000 units, so for absorption costing the fixed overhead rate is $96,000 ÷ 12,000 = $8 per unit.

Budgeted sales price is $70 per unit. Selling and administrative expenses are budgeted at: variable, $7 per unit sold; and fixed, $80,000 per month.

The following actually occurred in March and April:

	MARCH	APRIL
In units of finished goods:		
Opening inventory	—	3,000
Production	13,000	10,000
Sales	10,000	11,000
Ending inventory	3,000	2,000

There were no variances from any standard variable costs or budgeted selling prices or budgeted fixed costs in March.

The following absorption-costing results occurred in April for the production of 10,000 units:

	ACTUAL	FLEXIBLE BUDGET*	FLEXIBLE-BUDGET VARIANCE‡
Direct materials	$270,000	$200,000	$70,000 U
Direct labor	171,600	160,000	11,600 U
Variable factory overhead	32,000	30,000	2,000 U
Total variable manufacturing costs	473,600	390,000	83,600 U
Fixed factory overhead:			
Applied		80,000	
Production volume variance		16,000†	
Total	92,000	96,000	4,000 F
Absorption cost of goods manufactured	$565,600	$486,000	$79,600 U

*For 10,000 units: 10,000 × $20 = $200,000, etc.
†(12,000 − 10,000) × $8 = $16,000.
‡Identical under absorption costing and variable costing.*

Before proceeding, note that all flexible-budget variances, including any subdivisions thereof into price, spending, and efficiency variances, are identical under both variable costing and absorption costing. The only difference is the special handling given by absorption costing to the budgeted fixed factory overhead, which distinguishes between the $80,000 applied to product and the $16,000 unfavorable production volume variance attributable to idle capacity.

Production fell short of denominator volume by 2,000 units, resulting in only $80,000 of the total budgeted amount of $96,000 being applied to product. This presentation underscores the fact that the production volume variance is tied only to the *budget* and the *applied* amounts. The amount of *actual* fixed overhead will affect the budget variance; it will not affect the production volume variance.

The final line, absorption cost of goods manufactured, may be analyzed as follows:

Standard variable cost of goods manufactured, 10,000 × $39	$390,000
Fixed factory overhead applied, 10,000 × $8	80,000
Standard absorption cost of goods manufactured, 10,000 × $47	$470,000
Add unfavorable manufacturing variances:	
Production volume variance	16,000
Subtotal, which is the flexible budget	$486,000
Flexible-budget variances	79,600
Actual absorption cost of goods manufactured	$565,600

The production is the same as that presented for April in the preceding chapter. **However, now we assume that sales and production are no longer equal.** Sales exceeded production by 1,000 units. We assume actual sales of $790,000 and actual variable selling and administrative costs of $80,800. Therefore, the following results occurred:

	ACTUAL	FLEXIBLE BUDGET	FLEXIBLE-BUDGET VARIANCE
Sales	$790,000	$770,000*	$20,000 F
Selling and administrative costs:			
Variable	80,800	77,000†	3,800 U
Fixed, as before	80,000	80,000	

**11,000 units × $70.*
†11,000 units × $7.

Assume that there is no beginning or ending work in process.

income effects of variable costing

Exhibit 8-2 shows how *variable costing* affects income measurement. The format is different from that shown previously. Here the statement begins with all items valued at standard. The variances are then grouped and deducted to show actual operating income.

Before reading on, trace the facts from the illustration to the presentation in Exhibit 8-2, step by step. In particular, note that fixed manufacturing costs of $96,000 were deducted as period costs. **Note also that variable selling and administrative costs are more logically assumed to be related to fluctuations in *sales* rather than *production*.**

income effects of absorption costing

Exhibit 8-3 shows the impact of *absorption costing* on operating income. Again, before reading on trace the facts from the illustration to the exhibit, step by step. In particular, note the following:

1. The unit product cost is $47, not $39, because variable manufacturing costs ($39) plus fixed factory overhead ($8) are applied to product.
2. The $8 application rate was based on a denominator volume of 12,000 units. Whenever *production* (not sales) deviates from the denominator volume, a production volume variance arises. The measure of the variance is $8 multiplied by the difference between the actual volume of production and the denominator volume.

EXHIBIT 8-2

Standard Variable Costing
Webb Company
Income Statements
For the Months of March and April, 19_1

		MARCH	APRIL
(1)	Sales—at standard prices (10,000 × $70) and (11,000 × $70)	$700,000	$770,000
	Opening inventory—at standard variable cost: 3,000 × $39	—	117,000
	Add variable cost of goods manufactured at standard*	507,000	390,000
	Variable cost of goods available for sale	507,000	507,000
	Deduct ending inventory at standard variable cost: 3,000 × $39 and 2,000 × $39	117,000	78,000
	Variable manufacturing cost of goods sold	390,000	429,000
	Variable selling and administrative costs at budget of $7 per unit sold	70,000	77,000
(2)	Total variable costs	460,000	506,000
(1) − (2)	Contribution margin at standard	240,000	264,000
	Fixed factory overhead at budget	96,000	96,000
	Fixed selling and administrative costs	80,000	80,000
	Total fixed costs	176,000	176,000
	Operating income before variances	64,000	88,000
	Variances:		
	Selling prices	—	20,000 F
	Variable manufacturing costs	—	83,600 U
	Variable selling and administrative costs	—	3,800 U
	Fixed factory overhead	—	4,000 F
	Total variances	—	63,400 U
	Operating income	$ 64,000	$ 24,600

**13,000 × $39 = $507,000, and 10,000 × $39 = $390,000.*

3. The variances are shown as adjustments that convert the operating income "at standard" to operating income "at actual." All variances, including the production volume variances, are usually accounted for as deductions from (or additions to) income of the current fiscal period.

4. The absorption-costing statement in Exhibit 8-3 differentiates between the variable and fixed costs only to aid your comparison. Costs are often not classified as fixed or variable in absorption-costing statements, although such a classification is possible. Managers who are accustomed to looking at operations from a breakeven-analysis and flexible-budget viewpoint find that the absorption income statement fails to dovetail with cost-volume-profit relationships. They are then forced to take time for an attempt to reconcile and interpret two or more sets of figures that portray a single operating situation. Variable-costing proponents say that it is more efficient to present important cost-volume-profit relationships as integral parts of the major financial statements.

5. If inventories increase during a period, the variable-costing method will generally report less operating income than absorption costing; when inventories decrease, variable costing will report more operating income than absorption costing. These differences in operating income are due *solely* to the moving of fixed factory overhead in and out of

EXHIBIT 8-3 *(Place a clip on this page for easy reference.)*

Standard Absorption Costing
Webb Company
Income Statements
For the months of March and April, 19_1

	MARCH	APRIL
Sales—at standard prices (10,000 × $70) and (11,000 × $70)	$700,000	$770,000
Opening inventory—at standard absorption cost: 3,000 × $47*	—	141,000
Add cost of goods manufactured at standard†	611,000	470,000
Absorption cost of goods available for sale	611,000	611,000
Deduct ending inventory at standard absorption cost: 3,000 × $47 and 2,000 × $47*	141,000	94,000
Absorption cost of goods sold at standard	470,000	517,000
Gross profit at standard	230,000	253,000
Deduct selling and administrative costs:		
Variable at standard (10,000 × $7) and (11,000 × $7)	70,000	77,000
Fixed at budget	80,000	80,000
Total selling and administrative costs	150,000	157,000
Operating income before variances	80,000	96,000
Variances:		
Selling prices	—	20,000 F
Variable manufacturing costs	—	83,600 U
Variable selling and administrative costs	—	3,800 U
Fixed factory overhead:		
Budget variance	—	4,000 F
Production volume variance‡	8,000 F	16,000 U
Total variances	8,000 F	79,400 U
Operating income	$ 88,000	$ 16,600

**Variable cost of $39 + fixed factory overhead of $8 = $47.*
†13,000 × $47 = $611,000, and 10,000 × $47 = $470,000.
‡(13,000 − 12,000 denominator volume) × $8 = $8,000 F, and (12,000 − 10,000) × $8 = $16,000 U.

inventories as they increase and decrease, respectively.[2]

To illustrate this important point, assume that all variances are written off completely as period costs, no change occurs in work-in-process inventory, and no change occurs in the predetermined rate (budgeted fixed overhead divided by the units of denominator volume). Then, the difference between the operating incomes under absorption and variable costing may be shown by formulas:

(1)
$$\left(\begin{array}{c}\textbf{Absorption-}\\\textbf{costing}\\\textbf{operating}\\\textbf{income}\end{array}\right) - \left(\begin{array}{c}\textbf{Variable-}\\\textbf{costing}\\\textbf{operating}\\\textbf{income}\end{array}\right) = \left(\begin{array}{c}\textbf{Units}\\\textbf{produced}\\\textbf{minus}\\\textbf{units}\\\textbf{sold}\end{array}\right) \times \left(\begin{array}{c}\textbf{Predetermined}\\\textbf{fixed overhead}\\\textbf{rate}\end{array}\right)$$

[2]Also see Yuji Ijiri, Robert K. Jaedicke, and John L. Livingstone, "The Effect of Inventory Costing Methods on Full and Direct Costing," *Journal of Accounting Research*, III, No. 1, 63–74.

EXHIBIT 8-4

Webb Company

Detailed Analysis of Fixed Overhead Charged Off Against Current Income

VARIABLE COSTING: FIXED FACTORY OVERHEAD CHARGED OFF

$$\begin{pmatrix}\text{Budgeted}\\ \text{costs}\end{pmatrix} + \begin{pmatrix}\text{Budget}\\ \text{variance U}\end{pmatrix}$$

March $96,000 + 0 = $96,000, which is $24,000 higher than $72,000 for absorption costing (see below)

April $96,000 − $4,000 F = $92,000, which is $8,000 lower than $100,000 for absorption costing (see below)

ABSORPTION COSTING: FIXED FACTORY OVERHEAD CHARGED OFF

(1)

$$\begin{pmatrix}\text{Budget}\\ \text{variance U}\end{pmatrix} + \begin{pmatrix}\text{Production}\\ \text{volume}\\ \text{variance U}\end{pmatrix} + \begin{pmatrix}\text{Units}\\ \text{sold}\end{pmatrix} \times \begin{pmatrix}\text{Predetermined}\\ \text{rate}\end{pmatrix}$$

March	0	−	$ 8,000 F	+ (10,000	×	$8) =	$ 72,000
April	−$4,000 F	+	$16,000 U	+ (11,000	×	$8) =	$100,000

or **(2)** To rearrange the left side of the equation for easier comparison with the variable-costing formula above:

$$\begin{pmatrix}\text{Budget}\\ \text{variance U}\end{pmatrix} + \left[\begin{pmatrix}\text{Denominator}\\ \text{units}\end{pmatrix} - \begin{pmatrix}\text{Units}\\ \text{produced}\end{pmatrix} \times \begin{pmatrix}\text{Predetermined}\\ \text{rate}\end{pmatrix}\right] + \begin{pmatrix}\text{Units}\\ \text{sold}\end{pmatrix} \times \begin{pmatrix}\text{Predetermined}\\ \text{rate}\end{pmatrix}$$

$$\begin{pmatrix}\text{Budget}\\ \text{variance U}\end{pmatrix} + \begin{pmatrix}\text{Denominator}\\ \text{units}\end{pmatrix} \times \begin{pmatrix}\text{Predetermined}\\ \text{rate}\end{pmatrix} + \left[\begin{pmatrix}\text{Units}\\ \text{sold}\end{pmatrix} - \begin{pmatrix}\text{Units}\\ \text{produced}\end{pmatrix} \times \begin{pmatrix}\text{Predetermined}\\ \text{rate}\end{pmatrix}\right]$$

$$\begin{pmatrix}\text{Budget}\\ \text{variance U}\end{pmatrix} + \begin{pmatrix}\text{Budgeted}\\ \text{costs}\end{pmatrix} + \left[\begin{pmatrix}\text{Increase or}\\ \text{decrease in}\\ \text{inventory units}\end{pmatrix} \times \begin{pmatrix}\text{Predetermined}\\ \text{fixed overhead}\\ \text{rate}\end{pmatrix}\right]$$

These two elements are the same as the two elements in the variable-costing formula above.

This is the difference between the factory overhead amounts charged off, which is the difference between operating incomes.

March	0	+ $96,000	+	(10,000 − 13,000) × $8	= $ 72,000
April	−$4,000 F	+ $96,000	+	(11,000 − 10,000) × $8	= $100,000

or

(2)

$$\begin{pmatrix}\textbf{Difference in}\\ \textbf{operating income}\end{pmatrix} = \begin{pmatrix}\textbf{Increase or}\\ \textbf{decrease in}\\ \textbf{inventory units}\end{pmatrix} \times \begin{pmatrix}\textbf{Predetermined}\\ \textbf{fixed overhead}\\ \textbf{rate}\end{pmatrix}$$

The use of these formulas is illustrated by the data from Exhibits 8-2 and 8-3:

USING THE FIRST FORMULA

March $88,000 − $64,000 = (13,000 − 10,000 units) × $8
$24,000 = $24,000

April $16,600 − $24,600 = (10,000 − 11,000 units) × $8
$−8,000 = $−8,000

USING THE SECOND FORMULA

March $24,000 = (Increase in inventory of 3,000 units) × $8

April $−8,000 = (Decrease in inventory of 1,000 units) × $8

Fixed factory overhead charged off against current income can also be analyzed as shown in Exhibit 8-4. The exhibit shows why the formulas are correct. It deserves careful study.

EXHIBIT 8-5

Comparative Income Effects

	VARIABLE COSTING	ABSORPTION COSTING	COMMENTS
1. Fixed factory overhead inventoried?	No	Yes	Basic theoretical question of when a cost should become an expense.
2. Production volume variance?	No	Yes	Choice of denominator volume affects measurement of operating income under absorption costing.
3. Treatment of other variances?	Same	Same	Underscores the fact that the basic difference is the accounting for fixed factory overhead, not the accounting for variable factory overhead.
4. Classifications between variable and fixed costs are routinely made?	Yes	No	However, absorption cost can be modified to obtain subclassifications of variable and fixed costs, if desired.
5. Usual effects of changes in inventory levels on operating income: Production = sales Production > sales Production < sales	 Equal Lower* Higher	 Equal Higher† Lower	Differences are attributable to timing of the transformation of fixed factory overhead into expense.
6. Cost-volume-profit relationships	Tied to sales	Tied to production *and* sales	Management control benefit: Effects of changes in volume on operating income are easier to understand under variable costing.

**That is, lower than absorption costing.*
†That is, higher than variable costing.

6. As these formulas imply, under variable costing, budgeted operating income is a function of sales. That is, if sales rise, operating income also rises, and vice versa. In contrast, under absorption costing, income is a function of sales *and* production. Under some circumstances, sales could rise, but budgeted operating income could fall. For instance, see the Problem for Self-Study that follows. Heavy reductions of beginning inventory levels might combine with low production and a large production volume variance. This could result in unusually large amounts of fixed overhead being charged to a single period. Thus, under absorption costing, an increase in sales could be accompanied by a lower reported income, which could result in a confusing and misleading portrayal of operating results.

Exhibit 8-5 is a concise presentation of the preceding six points regarding variable and absorption costing.

the central issue: a question of timing

Nearly all accountants agree that distinctions between variable and fixed costs are helpful for a wide variety of managerial decisions. The traditional view recognizes this possibility but takes the position that such information may be supplied without changing the conventional methods of income determination. Adherents of variable costing maintain that the importance of variable- and fixed-cost behavior should be spotlighted not only by changing the format of the financial statements but also by changing the basic principles or concepts, whereby fixed factory overhead would be written off in the period incurred rather than funneled into inventory as an integral part of inventory costs. Thus, the central question becomes, What is the proper *timing* for expensing of fixed factory overhead as expense: at the time of incurrence, or at the time that the finished units to which the fixed overhead relates are sold? The focus must be upon relating fixed overhead to the definition of an asset.[3]

Absorption costing is far from uniform in its application. There are different inventory methods, such as first-in, first-out; last-in, first-out; and weighted average.[4] There are different assumptions as to overhead application, such as the inclusion of some administrative costs in inventory and the classification of packaging costs. However, these problems remain, whether variable costing or absorption costing is used. **The issue thus narrows to the propriety of excluding fixed factory overhead from inventory.**

problem for self-study

problem

Suppose Stassen Company began business on January 1, 19_1. It is now the end of 19_2. The company uses standard absorption costing. The president is trying to decide whether to adopt variable costing for measuring management performance. She has asked you to prepare comparisons of income statements for 19_1 and 19_2 under absorption and variable costing.

The following simplified data are available:

	19_1	19_2
Beginning inventory	—	4,000
Production	6,000	900
Sales	2,000	3,000
Ending inventory	4,000	1,900

Other data:

Variable manufacturing costs per unit	$2
Fixed manufacturing costs	$10,000
Denominator volume in units	10,000
Fixed manufacturing costs per unit	$1
Selling and administrative costs (all fixed)	$ 1,400
Selling price per unit	$8

There were no inventories of work in process or raw materials. Production was far below expected volume in 19_2 because of persistent shortages of raw materials.

REQUIRED

1. Prepare the requested comparative income statements.
2. Explain the difference in operating income between absorption costing and variable costing in each of the two years.
3. Sales rose in 19_2. Did operating income rise? Explain.

[3]See G. H. Sorter and C. T. Horngren, "Asset Recognition and Economic Attributes—The Relevant Costing Approach," *Accounting Review*, Vol. XXXVII, No. 3, for a discussion of the role of fixed overhead in the valuation of inventory.

[4]For a discussion, see Appendix 22 (page 772).

solution

1. Exhibit 8-6 shows the income statements.

EXHIBIT 8-6 *(Place a clip on this page for easy reference.)*

Stassen Company

Comparative Income Statements
For the Years 19_1 and 19_2

VARIABLE COSTING:	19_1	19_2
Sales at $8	$16,000	$24,000
Beginning inventory at $2	—	$ 8,000
Add variable cost of goods manufactured	12,000	1,800
Available for sale	12,000	9,800
Deduct ending inventory	8,000	3,800
Variable manufacturing cost of goods sold	4,000	6,000
Contribution margin	12,000	18,000
Fixed factory overhead	10,000	10,000
Fixed selling and administrative costs	1,400	1,400
Total fixed costs	11,400	11,400
Operating income	$ 600	$ 6,600
ABSORPTION COSTING:		
Sales	$16,000	$24,000
Beginning inventory at $3	—	12,000
Add absorption cost of goods manufactured	18,000	2,700
Available for sale	18,000	14,700
Deduct ending inventory	12,000	5,700
Cost of goods sold—at standard	6,000	9,000
Production volume variance*	4,000 U	9,100 U
Adjusted cost of goods sold	10,000	18,100
Gross margin or gross profit—at "actual"	6,000	5,900
Selling and administrative costs	1,400	1,400
Operating income	$ 4,600	$ 4,500

**Computation of production volume variance based on denominator volume of 10,000 units:*

19_1	*$ 4,000 underapplied (10,000 − 6,000) × $1*
19_2	*9,100 underapplied (10,000 − 900) × $1*
Two years together	*$13,100 underapplied (20,000 − 6,900) × $1*

2. Reconciliation of differences in operating income:

	19_1	19_2	TOGETHER
Operating income under:			
Absorption costing	$4,600	$ 4,500	$9,100
Variable costing	600	6,600	7,200
Difference to be explained	$4,000	$−2,100	$1,900

The difference can be reconciled by multiplying the fixed overhead rate by the *change* in the total inventory units

Fixed overhead rate	$1	$1	$1
Change in inventory units			
Beginning inventory	—	4,000	—
Ending inventory	4,000	1,900	1,900
Change	4,000	−2,100	1,900
Difference in operating income explained	$4,000	−$2,100	$1,900

3. Under variable costing, operating income is tied directly to fluctuations in sales. Operating income should rise as sales rise, and vice versa, at the rate of the contribution margin per unit:

Increase in operating income from 19_1 to 19_2 = Contribution margin of ($8 − $2) × (3,000 units sold in 19_2 − 2,000 units sold in 19_1) = $6,000

Under absorption costing, operating income is tied to both sales *and* production. For example, in 19_1 income is higher than under variable costing because production exceeded sales. The opposite effect occurred in 19_2. Moreover, in 19_2 sales rose over the 19_1 level. Nevertheless, under absorption costing, operating income fell from $4,600 to $4,500. Why? Because 19_2 had to bear some of the fixed overhead carried over in inventory from 19_1. In addition, 19_2 bore the effects of a lower-than-denominator production volume. Thus, *production* schedules affect income under absorption costing but not under variable costing. The detailed effects of fixed factory overhead on 19_2 operations are shown in Exhibit 8-7.

EXHIBIT 8-7

Stassen Company

Analysis of Application of Fixed Factory Overhead in 19_2

		INVENTORY		EXPENSE
VARIABLE COSTING				
No fixed factory overhead carried over from 19_1				
Fixed factory overhead incurred in 19_2	$10,000	→		$10,000
ABSORPTION COSTING		UNITS	DOLLARS	
Fixed factory overhead in beginning inventory	$ 4,000	4,000	$4,000	
Fixed factory overhead incurred in 19_2	10,000			
To account for:	$14,000			
Applied to product, 900 × $1 =		900	900	
Available for sale		4,900	$4,900	
Contained in standard cost of goods sold	$ 3,000	3,000	3,000 →	3,000
In ending inventory	1,900	1,900	$1,900	
Not applied, so becomes production volume variance	9,100	→		9,100
Fixed factory overhead charged against 19_2 operations				$12,100
Fixed factory overhead accounted for in 19_2, as above	$14,000			
Difference in 19_2 operating income, $12,100 − $10,000				$ 2,100

Breakeven points and absorption costing

Cost-volume-profit analysis was introduced in Chapter 3. The typical discussion assumes (a) the use of variable costing or (b) the use of absorption costing with no changes in beginning or ending inventory levels.

If variable costing is used, the breakeven point is computed in the usual manner. It is unique; there is no more than one breakeven point. Moreover, income is a function of sales. As sales rise, income rises, and vice versa.

In contrast, if absorption costing is used, income is a function of *both* sales and production. Therefore, changes in inventory levels can dramatically affect income, as

demonstrated by the Problem for Self-Study. The breakeven point is not unique. There may be several combinations of sales and production that produce an income of zero.

Thus, variable costing dovetails precisely with cost-volume-profit analysis. The user of variable costing can easily compute the breakeven point or any effects that changes in sales volume may have on income. In contrast, the user of absorption costing must consider both sales volume and production volume before making such computations.

Suppose in the Problem for Self-Study that actual production in 19_2 were equal to denominator volume, 10,000 units. Also suppose that there were no sales and no selling costs. All the production would be placed in inventory. Then all the fixed factory overhead would be lodged in inventory. There would be no production volume variance. Thus, the company could break even if it sold nothing at all![5] In contrast, under variable costing the operating loss would be equal to the fixed costs.

Role of various denominator levels in absorption costing

Chapter 7 pointed out that product costs and income can be significantly affected by the choice of a particular volume level (also called *activity* level) as a denominator in the computation of fixed-overhead rates. We now study how various alternative levels of activity can affect operating income under absorption costing. As fixed manufacturing costs become a more prominent part of an organization's total costs, the importance of this choice becomes greater.

characteristics of capacity

The choice of a capacity size is usually the result of capital-budgeting decisions, which are reached after studying the expected impact of these capital outlays on operations over a number of years. The choice may be influenced by a combination of two major factors, each involving trade-off decisions and each heavily depending on long-range forecasts of demand, material costs, and labor costs:

1. Provision for *seasonal* and *cyclical fluctuations* in demand. The trade-off is between (a) additional costs of physical capacity and (b) the costs of inventory stockouts and/or the carrying costs of inventory safety stocks of such magnitude to compensate for seasonal and cyclical variations, the costs of overtime premium, subcontracting, and so on.
2. Provision for upward *trends* in demand. The trade-off is between (a) the costs of constructing too much capacity for initial needs and (b) the later extra costs of satisfying demand by alternative means. For example, should a factory designed to make color television tubes have an area of 100,000, 150,000, or 200,000 square feet?

Although it can be defined and measured in a particular situation, capacity is an illusive concept. Consider, for example, the following:

> Capacity planning requires definition and measurement of capacity in a manner relevant to questions which arise in the planning process. This problem has two aspects. First, it is necessary to specify capacity in terms of how much the company should be prepared to make and to sell. Second, the capacity of specific facilities available or to be acquired must be determined. . . . A variety of alternative combinations of capacity and operating patterns is usually possible.[6]

---

[5]For an expanded discussion, see David Solomons, "Breakeven Analysis under Absorption Costing," *Accounting Review,* XLIII, No. 3, pp. 447–52.

[6]"Accounting for Costs of Capacity," *N.A.A. Research Series Report No. 39* (New York: National Association of Accountants), p. 10.

There is much fluidity in the quotation above. To most people, the term *capacity* implies a constraint, an upper limit. We sometimes hear, "I'm working at capacity now. I simply can't do more." This same notion of capacity as a constraint is commonly held in industry.

Although the term *capacity* is usually applied to plant and equipment, it is equally applicable to other resources, such as people and materials. A shortage of direct labor, executive time, or materials may be critical in limiting company production or sales.

The upper limit of capacity is seldom absolutely rigid, at least from an engineering viewpoint. That is, ways—such as overtime, subcontracting, or paying premium prices for additional materials—can usually be found to expand production. But these ways may be totally unattractive from an economic viewpoint. **Hence, the upper limit of capacity is *specified* by management for current planning and control purposes after considering engineering *and* economic factors.** In this way, the upper limit is usually imposed by management, not by external forces.

Measurement of capacity usually begins with **theoretical capacity** (also called *maximum* or *ideal* capacity) that assumes the production of output 100 percent of the time. Then deductions are made for Sundays, holidays, downtime, changeover time, and similar items to attain a measure of **practical capacity.** The latter is defined as the maximum level at which the plant or department can operate efficiently. Practical capacity often allows for unavoidable operating interruptions such as repair time or waiting time (downtime).[7]

Two other commonly used levels of capacity utilization are

1. **Normal volume,** which is the level of capacity utilization (which is less than 100 percent of practical capacity) that will satisfy average consumer demand over a span of time (often five years) that includes seasonal, cyclical, and trend factors; and
2. **Master-budget volume,** which is usually the anticipated level of capacity utilization for the coming year.

A survey of *Fortune 500* companies disclosed that the denominator volume bases shown at the top of the next page were used among 247 respondents.[8] Please study that presentation.

There are apt to be differences in terms used between companies, so be sure to obtain their exact meaning in a given situation. For example, *master-budget volume* is often called **expected annual volume** or **expected annual capacity** or **expected annual activity** or **master-budget activity.**

normal volume versus master-budget volume

Master-budget volume is the denominator for applying all fixed overhead to products on a year-to-year basis, while the denominator based on *normal* volume attempts to apply fixed overhead by using a *longer-run* average expected activity. **Conceptually, the *normal rate* results in overapplications in some years that are offset by underapplications in other years.**

We shall deal with fixed overhead only, because variable overhead fluctuates with changes in activity and fixed overhead does not. ***Thus, the entire problem***

---

[7]See S. Goodman and J. Reece, eds., *Controller's Handbook* (Homewood, Ill.: Dow-Jones-Irwin, 1978), Chap. 11.

[8]Chin and Lee, op. cit. Percentages are from their Table 3, p. 242. The sketch was added here. Also see various publications of the Cost Accounting Standards Board (Washington, D.C.) for descriptions of overhead practices.

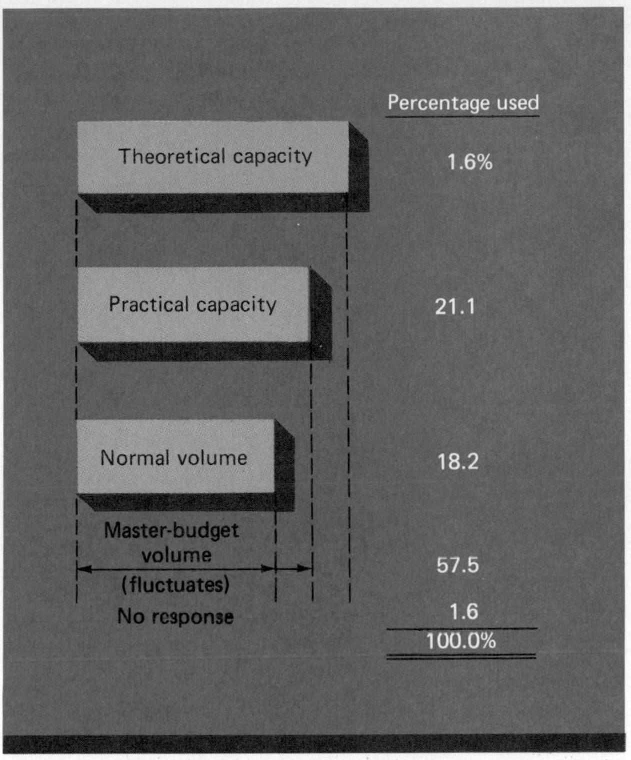

of using master-budget volume or normal volume is raised by the presence of fixed overhead. Recall that the production volume variance in Chapter 7 was confined to fixed overhead. Consider the following data:

Fixed factory overhead	$499,500
Practical capacity per year	100,000 standard direct-labor hours
Normal volume per year	90,000 standard direct-labor hours
Master-budget volume for specific year	(Fluctuates from year to year)
Normal overhead rate	
$499,500 ÷ 90,000 hours	$5.55
Master-budget volume overhead rate	(Varies from year to year)

Exhibit 8-8 shows that if normal volume is the denominator, the overhead rate of $5.55 would be used for costing inventory. In the second year, there would be an underapplied fixed-overhead balance of $5.55 times 20,000 hours, or $111,000. This unfavorable production volume variance would be considered the measure of the cost of *not* producing—the loss from idle capacity. Inventories would be costed with a $5.55 rate instead of a $7.14 rate. Under the master-budget volume method, if volume fluctuates from year to year, product and inventory costs will vary solely because of differences in utilization of facilities. Using a normal rate will avoid changes in unit costs and will also provide a yearly and monthly measure of the cost of idle capacity.

Note carefully that Exhibit 8-8 is designed to stress only the computation of overhead rates under different denominator volumes. It deliberately avoids introducing changes in budgeted fixed-overhead costs; instead, it assumes that total fixed overhead is constant from year to year. Actually, year-to-year changes in the prices

EXHIBIT 8-8 **Comparison of Master-Budget Volume and Normal Volume for Overhead Application**

		MASTER-BUDGET VOLUME			NORMAL VOLUME BASIS		
YEAR	STANDARD LABOR-HOURS ALLOWED*	**over-head rate†**	**total applied†**	**under-(over-) applied***	**over-head rate**	**total applied‡**	**under-(over-) applied†**
1	90,000	$5.55	$499,500	$—	$5.55	$499,500	$ —
2	70,000	7.14	499,500	—	5.55	388,500	111,000
3	100,000	5.00	499,500	—	5.55	555,000	(55,500)
4	80,000	6.24	499,500	—	5.55	444,000	55,500
5	100,000	5.00	499,500	—	5.55	555,000	(55,500)
6	100,000	5.00	499,500	—	5.55	555,000	(55,500)
				$—			$ -0-

For illustrative purposes, we assume that master-budget volume in terms of standard labor-hours allowed is equal to actual output achieved.

†*Debit underapplied or credit overapplied overhead directly to Income Summary as a measure of loss or gain from underutilization or overutilization of capacity. Note that this is simply the production volume variance.*

‡*Rounded in years 2 and 4.*

paid for fixed-overhead items can affect the overhead rate, regardless of the denominator used to set the rate.

characteristics of normal volume

Many accountants reject the normal-volume notion and maintain that each year must stand by itself; that is, each year's overhead must be applied to each year's production, written off as a loss, or both. This attitude arises from (a) the widespread conviction that the year is the key time period, and (b) adherence to the idea that overhead costs for a given year generally must cling or attach to the units produced during that year regardless of the relationship of that year's activity to average long-run activity.

A more convincing reason for using master-budget volume as a denominator is the overwhelming forecasting problem that accompanies the determination of normal volume. Sales not only fluctuate cyclically but have trends over the long run. In effect, the use of normal volume implies an unusual talent for accurate long-run forecasting. Many accountants and executives who reject the normal volume as a denominator claim that the nature of their company's business precludes accurate forecasts beyond one year.

Where companies use normal volume, the objective is to choose a period long enough to average out sizable fluctuations in volume and to allow for trends in sales. The uniform rate for applying fixed overhead supposedly provides for "recovery" of fixed costs over the long run. Companies expect that overapplications in some years will be offset by underapplications in other years.

Conceptually, when normal volume is the denominator, the yearly overapplied or underapplied overhead should be carried forward on the balance sheet. Practically, however, year-end balances are closed directly to Income Summary, because the accounting profession (and the Internal Revenue Service) generally views the year as being the terminal time span for allocation of underapplied or overapplied overhead.

In year 2 in Exhibit 8-8, the year-end journal entry for closing the Fixed Factory Overhead accounts may appear as follows:

Fixed factory overhead applied	**388,500**	
Production volume variance (to be closed to income summary)	**111,000**	
Fixed factory overhead control		**499,500**

The journal entry for the end of year 3 would appear as follows:

Fixed factory overhead applied	**555,000**	
Production volume variance		**55,500**
Fixed factory overhead control		**499,500**

The logical question that should arise at this point is, Why use normal volume at all if the yearly overapplications or underapplications are written off at year-end anyway? Are the yearly results not the same, whether master-budget or normal volume is used? The Problem for Self-Study shows the fundamental answer: "There is still a difference, because inventory costs are different."

practical capacity

Many managements want to keep running at full capacity, which really means practical capacity. Their "normal volume" for applying fixed costs is "practical capacity"; anything less reduces profits and is undesirable. Where product costs are used as guides for pricing, some managers say that this policy results in more competitive pricing, which maximizes both volume and profits in good times and bad. Of course, profits also depend on factors other than physical volume—for example, the elasticity of demand. The accounting effects of such a policy are lower unit costs for inventory purposes and the almost perpetual appearance of an unfavorable production volume variance, sometimes described on the income statements as loss from idle capacity.

Using practical capacity as a denominator volume has become increasingly popular with American businesses. As indicated earlier, over 21 percent of the surveyed companies prefer to use practical capacity. A major reason is probably the position of the Internal Revenue Service, which forbids variable costing but permits using practical capacity as a denominator volume in conjunction with absorption costing. As compared with normal volume or master-budget volume, the practical-capacity denominator volume results in the faster write-offs of fixed factory overhead as a tax deduction.

There is no requirement that American companies use the same denominator volumes for internal management purposes and for income-tax purposes. Nevertheless, the economies of recordkeeping often lead to the same accounting for management and tax purposes.

significance of denominator volume for product costing and control

Obviously the denominator volume for product costing is largely a matter of opinion. The selection of a denominator probably becomes crucial where product costs heavily influence managerial decisions. For example, in a cyclical industry, the use of master-budgeted rather than normal volume as a denominator would tend to cause a company to quote low prices in boom years and high prices in recession years—in obvious conflict with good business judgment. That is why normal volume may make more sense as a denominator when there are wide swings in business volume through the years, even though the yearly overapplied and underapplied overhead is not carried forward in the balance sheet from year to year.

In the realm of current planning and control, however, normal volume is an empty concept. Normal volume is used as a basis for long-range plans. It depends on the time span selected, the forecasts made for each year, and the weighting of these forecasts. In Exhibit 8-8, a comparison in year 2 of the 70,000-hour master-budget volume with the 90,000-hour normal volume might be suggested as the best basis for auditing long-range planning. **However, normal volume is an average that has no particular significance with respect to a follow-up for a particular year.** The pertinent comparison is a particular year's master-budget volume with that year's volume level used in the authorization for the acquisition of facilities. This comparison may be done project by project. It need not be integrated in the accounting system on a routine basis. Furthermore, attempting to use normal volume as a reference point for judging current performance is an example of misusing a long-range measure for a short-range purpose.

The master-budget volume, rather than normal volume or practical capacity, is more germane to the evaluation of current results. The master budget is the principal short-run planning and control tool. Managers feel much more obligated to reach the levels stipulated in the master budget, which should have been carefully set in relation to the maximum opportunities for sales in the current period. In contrast, normal volume and practical capacity are not so pertinent to current operating problems, because they are not usually incorporated in the comprehensive or master budget—the focus of attention.[9]

PROBLEM FOR SELF-STUDY

problem

The Shane Co. incurs fixed manufacturing overhead of $499,500 annually. Practical capacity is 100,000 standard direct-labor hours allowed; normal volume, 90,000 hours; and master-budget volume, 70,000 hours. In 19_1, 70,000 units were produced (in 70,000 standard hours) and 60,000 units were sold. Standard hours allowed were 70,000. There was no beginning inventory.

REQUIRED

1. Prepare a three-column comparison of the various methods of applying fixed overhead to product. Designate which methods would result in the highest and the lowest net income. For each method, show the amounts that would be charged to:

   Cost of sales (expense)
   Loss from idle capacity, production volume variance (loss)
   Ending inventory

2. Why is master-budget volume better than either practical capacity or normal volume for judging current operating performance?

solution

1. Exhibit 8-9 shows that the use of different denominator volumes for developing product-costing overhead rates results in different *inventory valuations* and different operating incomes. Further, the measure of utilization of facilities, the production volume variance, will differ markedly. In Exhibit 8-9, income is lowest where practical capacity is the denominator volume and highest when master-budget volume is the denominator volume, because a smaller portion of overhead is held back as an asset in inventory when a lower overhead rate is used.

   The exhibit also indicates that the accounting effects of using practical capacity are lower unit costs for inventory purposes and the steady appearance of "Loss from idle capacity" on the income statement.

[9]Also see Charles T. Horngren, "A Contribution Margin Approach to the Analysis of Capacity Utilization," *Accounting Review,* XLII, No. 2, pp. 254–64.

EXHIBIT 8-9

Solution to Self-Study Problem, Part 1

Income-Statement Effects of Using Various Activity Bases for Overhead Application

	MASTER-BUDGET VOLUME*		NORMAL VOLUME†		PRACTICAL CAPACITY‡	
	using a $7.14 overhead rate		**using a $5.55 overhead rate**		**using a $4.995 overhead rate**	
Sales		$ xxx		$ xxx		$ xxx
Production costs:						
Direct materials, direct labor, variable overhead	$ xxx		$ xxx		$ xxx	
Fixed overhead applied to product	499,500		388,500		349,650	
Total production costs—70,000 units	$ xxx		$ xxx		$ xxx	
Ending inventory—fixed-overhead component—10,000 units	71,400		55,500		49,950	
Total fixed-overhead component of cost of sales		428,100		333,000		299,700
Loss from idle capacity (shown separately on income statements)—the production volume variance, unfavorable		None		111,000		149,850
Total fixed overhead charged to the period's sales		$428,100		$444,000		$449,550
Operating income		Highest		Middle		Lowest
Recapitulation:						
Total overhead to account for		$499,500		$499,500		$499,500
Accounted for as follows:						
Charged to Cost of Sales (expense)		$428,100		$333,000		$299,700
Charged to Loss from Idle Capacity, production volume variance		None		111,000		149,850
Charged to Ending Inventory (asset)		71,400		55,000		49,950
Overhead accounted for		$499,500		$499,500		$499,500

**499,500 ÷ 70,000 hours allowed = $7.14 (rounded).*
†499,500 ÷ 90,000 hours normal activity = $5.55.
‡499,500 ÷ 100,000 hours practical capacity = $4.995.

2. **As is explained more fully in the chapter, master-budget volume is more pertinent to current operating problems because it is usually the volume that is incorporated in the master budget.** Therefore, it has more current meaning to the department managers who must live with the budget.

Standard-cost variances and the income statement

proration to achieve actual costs

Managers and accountants tend to think of "actual" costs as somehow representing absolute truths. Therefore, "normal" or "standard costs" produce valuations that are somehow untrue unless month-end or year-end variances are prorated among the affected accounts to get corrected valuations that better approximate "actual" costs.[10] Of course, in all cases immaterial variances (however defined) can be written off immediately as adjustments to cost of goods sold.

How do companies dispose of their variances at year-end? A survey of 247 large companies regarding overhead variances showed:[11]

[10]For example, see Standard #407, "Use of Standard Costs for Direct Material and Direct Labor," of the Cost Accounting Standards Board, Washington, D.C. Also see Appendix 8b for a discussion of interim reporting.

[11]Chiu and Lee, op. cit., Table 4, p. 242.

Closed to cost of goods sold	53.1%
Closed to income account	10.5
Subtotal affecting current income	63.6
Prorated (apportioned) among Work in Process, Finished Goods, and Cost of Goods Sold	33.6
Carried forward to next year	1.2
No response	1.6
Total	100.0%

The disposition of overhead variances at year-end was initially discussed in Chapter 4. The same concepts apply to all variances. First, decide whether **proration** should occur. This decision usually depends on judgments about whether the variances are significant. Second, if proration is desired, find out where the related "normal" or "standard" costs are now lodged. Use these balances as bases for apportioning the variances. For example, suppose underapplied factory overhead (that is, the unfavorable overhead variance) is $120,000 at year-end. The proration would be in proportion to the balances (assumed) in the accounts where the related applied overhead now exists:

	WORK IN PROCESS	FINISHED GOODS	COST OF GOODS SOLD
Unadjusted balances (before proration), $1,000,000	$100,000	$300,000	$600,000
Overhead variance, $120,000	12,000*	36,000*	72,000*
Adjusted balances (after proration), $1,120,000	$112,000	$336,000	$672,000

$120,000 ÷ $1,000,000 = 12%; 12% × $100,000 = $12,000; or $100,000 ÷ $1,000,000 = 10%; 10% × $120,000 = $12,000; etc.

illustration of proration problem

The following facts will be used for an extended discussion of the general approach to proration. To keep the calculations manageable, the numbers are relatively small.

Star Company uses absorption costing. It has the following results for the year:

Purchases of direct materials (charged to Stores at standard prices), 200,000 lbs. @ $.50	$100,000
Purchase-price variance, 200,000 lbs. @ $.05	10,000
Direct labor—applied at standard rate, 2,000 hrs. @ $20	40,000
Direct-labor price variance, 2,200 hrs. @ $.4545	1,000
Direct-labor efficiency variance, 200 hrs. @ $20	4,000
Direct-material efficiency variance, 8,000 lbs. @ $.50	4,000
Direct materials—applied at standard prices, 160,000 lbs. @ $.50	80,000
Manufacturing overhead applied—at standard rate per labor hour	40,000
Manufacturing overhead incurred	45,000
Underapplied manufacturing overhead	5,000
Sales	135,000
Selling and administrative expenses	20,000

Assume that there is no ending work in process. Assume that one uniform product is made, that 40 percent of the production is in the ending inventory of finished goods, and that 60 percent of the production has been sold. All variances are unfavorable.

There were no beginning inventories. The unadjusted balances (before proration) at the end of the year are based on the data given above:

		PERCENT
Work in process	$ 0	0%
Finished goods, 40% of the total standard costs applied for material, labor, and overhead ($80,000 + $40,000 + $40,000): 40% of $160,000	64,000	40
Cost of goods sold, 60% of $160,000	96,000	60
Total	$160,000	100%

An analysis of the data regarding direct materials follows:

	POUNDS	TOTAL COSTS AT $.50 STANDARD PRICE PER POUND	PERCENTAGE
To account for	200,000	$100,000	100%
Now present in:			
Direct-material efficiency variance	8,000	$ 4,000	4%
Finished goods	64,000	32,000	32
Cost of goods sold	96,000	48,000	48
Remainder, in stores	32,000	16,000	16
Accounted for	200,000	$100,000	100%

REQUIRED

A comparative analysis of the effects on operating income (1) without proration of any variances and (2) with proration of all variances.

solution

The solution is in Exhibit 8-10, which appears at the end of the following discussion.

general guidelines for proration

The following general guidelines will be illustrated:

1. The assumption is often made that standard costs are present in uniform proportions in Work in Process, Finished Goods, and Cost of Goods Sold. If the assumption is invalid and significant, then the direct materials, direct labor, and factory-overhead components should be separately identified; the related variances should then be prorated in proportion thereto.

In our example, there is no work in process. Finished goods represents 40 percent of total manufacturing costs; cost of goods sold, 60 percent. Therefore, all direct-labor and factory-overhead variances may be prorated accordingly:

	TOTAL VARIANCE	FINISHED GOODS **40%**	COST OF GOODS SOLD **60%**
Direct-labor price variance	$1,000	$ 400	$ 600
Direct-labor efficiency variance	4,000	1,600	2,400
Manufacturing-overhead variance	5,000	2,000	3,000

For simplicity, the manufacturing-overhead variance of $5,000 has not been subdivided into components such as spending, efficiency, or production volume variances.

2. The direct-material variances should be prorated slightly differently from direct labor and factory overhead. Why? Because direct material may be inventoried before use, whereas the other elements of production cannot.

The most critical proration is the material price variance. To be most accurate, its proration in our illustration should be traced at 5 cents per pound to wherever the 200,000 pounds have been charged at standard prices. As the analysis in the body of the problem indicates, the pounds are not only in Finished Goods and Cost of Goods Sold. **They are also in Stores and in the Direct-Material Efficiency Variance account.** Hence, we begin with a proration of the material price variance to four accounts, using the percentages shown for direct materials in the problem data:

Direct-material price variance	$10,000
Allocated to:	
Stores, 16%	$ 1,600
Direct-material efficiency variance, 4%	400
Finished-goods inventory, 32%	3,200
Cost of goods sold, 48%	4,800
Total allocated	$10,000

In turn, the adjusted balance of the direct-material efficiency variance is prorated to Finished Goods and Cost of Goods Sold in the same manner as direct labor and manufacturing overhead, 40 percent and 60 percent:

Direct-material efficiency variance, unadjusted	$4,000
Add allocation of material price variance (above)	400
Adjusted material efficiency variance to be allocated	$4,400
Allocated to:	
Finished-goods inventory, 40%	$1,760
Cost of goods sold, 60%	2,640
Total allocated	$4,400*

**In practice, the proration is often done less accurately. That is, the impact of the price variance on the efficiency variance is ignored. In our illustration, such an error would entail proration as follows:*

	TOTAL VARIANCE	TO STORES	TO FINISHED GOODS	TO COST OF GOODS SOLD
Direct-material purchase price	*$10,000[a]*	*$1,667*	*$3,333*	*$5,000*
Direct-material efficiency	*$ 4,000[b]*		*$1,600*	*$2,400*
[a]Percentages used for proration	*100%*	*16⅔%*	*33⅓%*	*50%*
[b]Percentages used for proration	*100%*		*40%*	*60%*

This proration produces an erroneous "actual" unit cost for stores. The total balance in stores is $16,000 + $1,667 = $17,667. The unit price is $17,667 ÷ 32,000 pounds = $.5521. In contrast, as Exhibit 8-10 shows, the correct proration is $1,600. The total balance in stores should be $16,000 + $1,600 = $17,600. The correct unit price is $17,600 ÷ 32,000 pounds = $.55, which is the 50¢ standard price plus the 5¢ price variance.

EXHIBIT 8-10 *(Place a clip on this page for easy reference.)*

Star Company

Comprehensive Schedule of Proration of Variances
(All Variances Are Unfavorable)

TYPE OF VARIANCE	(1) TOTAL VARIANCE	(2) TO STORES	(3) TO DIRECT-MATERIAL EFFICIENCY	(4) TO FINISHED GOODS	(5) TO COST OF GOODS SOLD
Direct-material purchase price	$10,000[a]	$1,600	$ 400	$3,200	$ 4,800
Direct-material efficiency					
Unadjusted balance	4,000		4,000		
Adjusted balance			$4,400[b]	1,760	2,640
Direct-labor price	1,000[b]			400	600
Direct-labor efficiency	4,000[b]			1,600	2,400
Manufacturing overhead	5,000[b]			2,000	3,000
Total variances prorated	$24,000	$1,600		$8,960	$13,440
[a]Percentages used for proration	*100%*	*16%*	*4%*	*32%*	*48%*
[b]Percentages used for proration	*100%*			*40%*	*60%*

All of the variance prorations explained here are summarized in a comprehensive schedule, Exhibit 8-10.

Exhibit 8-11 shows how proration affects operating income. The lack of proration hurts income by $24,000 instead of $13,440, a difference of $10,560. Hence, operating income without proration is a negative $5,000; with proration, a positive $5,560, a relatively significant difference indeed.

the case against proration Some accountants, industrial engineers, and managers reject the idea that actual costs represent absolute truth. Instead, they claim that currently attainable standard costs are the "true costs" in the sense that such costs are the only costs that may be carried forward as assets or unexpired costs. They contend that variances are measures

EXHIBIT 8-11

Star Company

Effects of Prorations of Variances on Operating Income

	STANDARD ABSORPTION COSTING without proration	STANDARD ABSORPTION COSTING with proration
Sales	$135,000	$135,000
Cost of goods sold—at standard	96,000	96,000
Total variances (from column 1, Exhibit 8-10)	24,000	
Prorated variances (from column 5, Exhibit 8-10)		13,440
Cost of goods sold—adjusted for variances	120,000	109,440
Selling and administrative expenses	20,000	20,000
Total charges against revenue	140,000	129,440
Operating income (loss)	$ (5,000)	$ 5,560

of inefficiency or abnormal efficiency. Therefore, variances are not inventoriable and should be completely charged or credited against revenue of the period instead of being prorated among inventories and cost of sales. In this way, inventory valuations will be more representative of desirable and attainable costs. **In particular, there is no justification for carrying costs of inefficiency as assets, which is what proration accomplishes.**

varieties of proration

Variations of these proration methods may be desirable under certain conditions. For instance, efficiency variances may be viewed as being currently avoidable and price variances as being unavoidable and therefore proratable. Conceptually, this is superior to the other methods because the costs of avoidable inefficiency are written off, whereas unavoidable costs are not. This treatment is correct because the costs of avoidable inefficiency do not qualify as assets under any economic test.

The author believes that unfavorable variances do not have to be inventoried as long as standards are currently attainable. However, if standards are not up to date, or if they reflect perfection performance rather than expected performance under reasonably efficient conditions, then conceptually the variances should be split between the portion that reflects departures from currently attainable standards and the portion that does not. The former should be written off as period charges; the latter should be prorated to inventories and cost of sales. For example, assume that an operation has a perfection standard time allowed of 50 minutes, which is reflected in a formal standard-cost system. The currently attainable standard is 60 minutes. Now if it takes, say, 75 actual minutes to perform the operation, the conceptual adjustment would call for writing off the cost of 15 minutes of the 25-minute variance as a period cost and for treating the cost of the remaining 10-minute variance as a product cost.

The prorations of variances can have significant effects on the measurement of operating income, particularly where inventories have increased or decreased substantially and where the variances are relatively large. The Problem for Self-Study demonstrates these effects, using a variety of costing assumptions.

Adjusting inventories for external reporting

To satisfy external reporting requirements, companies often make adjustments to inventory accounts. Examples include (a) converting a variable-costing inventory valuation to absorption costing and (b) prorating variances. Typically, these companies do *not* alter their ongoing inventory records. Instead, they create a separate but related "inventory adjustment" valuation account that bears a host of labels, some short, some long.

To illustrate the working of such an account, assume that a company adjusts its Finished-Goods Inventory of $700,000 upward by $100,000. The adjustment may be (a) to convert the inventory from variable costing to absorption costing or (b) to restate the inventory because of a proration of variances. The journal entry would be:

a. Finished-goods inventory adjustment account	100,000	
Fixed factory overhead		100,000

or

b. Finished-goods inventory adjustment account	100,000	
Cost variances		100,000

Under first-in, first-out assumptions, the adjustment account would disappear in the subsequent period when the related inventories are sold. For example:

Cost of goods sold (from inventory adjustment account)	**100,000**	
Finished-goods inventory adjustment account		**100,000**

PROBLEM FOR SELF-STUDY

problem

Review the Star Company illustration, which begins on p. 254.

Column 2 in Exhibit 8-11 showed operating income of $5,560 under standard absorption costing with proration of all variances. Suppose the purchase-price variance had been $15,000, favorable, instead of $10,000, unfavorable. Compute the new operating income under standard absorption costing with proration of all variances.

solution

Material variances prorated to Cost of Goods Sold in original solution (from column 5 of Exhibit 8-10):

Material price	$4,800 U
Material efficiency	2,640 U
Unfavorable effect on income	$7,440 U

Material variances prorated to Cost of Goods Sold in revised solution:

	(1) TOTAL VARIANCE	(2) TO STORES	(3) TO DIRECT-MATERIAL EFFICIENCY VARIANCE	(4) TO FINISHED GOODS	(5) TO COST OF GOODS SOLD
Material price variance, favorable	$15,000[a]	$2,400	$ 600	$4,800	$ 7,200
Material efficiency variance:					
Unadjusted balance, unfavorable	$ 4,000		4,000		
Adjusted balance, unfavorable			$3,400[b]	1,360	2,040
Favorable effect on income					$ 5,160
[a]Percentages used for proration	100%	16%	4%	32%	48%
[b]Percentages used for proration	100%			40%	60%
Original, unfavorable effect on income					$ 7,440
Revised, favorable effect on income					5,160
Difference, improvement in income					$12,600
Operating income in original solution					5,560
Operating income as revised					$18,160

SUMMARY

Absorption costing and variable costing have different effects on income when inventory levels fluctuate. Differences occur because fixed factory overhead is inventoried only under absorption costing. Income is influenced by sales under variable costing, but by sales *and* production under absorption costing.

Three commonly used denominator volumes for developing product-costing fixed-overhead rates are (a) master-budget volume for the year,

(b) normal volume over three to five years, and (c) practical capacity. The selection is essentially a matter of opinion. The choice will influence inventory valuations and resultant timing of income recognition.

If they are significant, standard-cost variances are usually prorated among various inventory accounts and cost of goods sold. In this way, better approximations of "actual" costs are achieved.

The advocates of currently attainable standard costs for product costing maintain that the results are conceptually superior to the results under "actual" or "normal" product-costing systems. They contend that the costs of inefficiency are not inventoriable.

SUGGESTED READINGS

BOER, GERMAIN, ***Direct Cost and Contribution Accounting: An Integrated Management Accounting System.*** New York: John Wiley, 1974.

MCFARLAND, W. B., ***Concepts for Management Accounting.*** (New York: National Association of Accountants, 1966.

STANDARD NO. 407, **"Use of Standard Costs for Direct Material and Direct Labor."** Cost Accounting Standards Board, Washington, D.C.

There are literally hundreds of articles on variable (direct) costing or the contribution approach in accounting periodicals, most notably *Management Accounting.*

Terms to Learn

direct costing ***expected annual activity*** ***expected annual capacity*** ***expected annual volume*** ***master-budget activity*** ***master-budget volume*** ***normal volume*** ***practical capacity*** ***proration*** ***theoretical capacity*** ***variable costing***

Special Points and Pitfalls

Variable costing and absorption costing are completely general in the sense that there may be:

actual variable costing	actual absorption costing
normal variable costing	normal absorption costing
standard variable costing	standard absorption costing

Standard-costing systems have the same cost variances regardless of whether variable costing or absorption costing is used. There is one exception: Production volume variances are not present when variable costing is used because all fixed factory overhead is regarded as a period cost rather than an inventoriable cost.

Master-budget volume is the most popular denominator volume, followed by practical capacity and normal volume, respectively.

Proration of variances occurs when they are judged to be significant. Most managers and accountants seek prorations so that standard or normal costs are adjusted to approximate "actual" costs.

Appendix 8a: comparison of variance prorations, normal and standard costing

The main goal of this Appendix is to provide a comparative review of standard, normal, and actual cost systems. The principal vehicle for this review is regarded as the Star Company illustration of how variances are prorated (begins on p. 254).

Exhibit 8-11 shows the effects of standard absorption costing on operating income, without and with variance prorations. We now compare these effects with those that would result using normal costing and actual costing. Exhibit 8-12 presents these comparisons. Columns 1 and 2 are the same columns as those in the body of Exhibit 8-11, p. 257.

Consider Exhibit 8-12, column by column. Column 1 shows standard costing without proration of any variances. All the variances, $24,000, are added as an adjustment to the standard cost of goods sold.

Column 2 adds only $13,440, the results of the proration of standard-cost variances in the supporting comprehensive schedule (Exhibit 8-10).

EXHIBIT 8-12

Star Company

Comparative Effects of Variance Prorations, Absorption Costing

	STANDARD COSTING		NORMAL COSTING		ACTUAL HISTORICAL COSTING
	without proration	**with proration**	**without proration**	**with proration of underapplied overhead**	**with proration**
	(1)	(2)	(3)	(4)	(5)
Sales	$135,000	$135,000	$135,000	$135,000	$135,000
Cost of goods sold—at standard	96,000	96,000	96,000	96,000	96,000
Total variances (from column 1, Exhibit 8-10)	24,000				
Prorated variances (from column 5, Exhibit 8-10)		13,440		13,440	13,440
Prorated variances, $13,440 + $400 from schedule below			13,840		
Cost of goods sold—adjusted for variances	120,000	109,440	109,840	109,440	109,440
Selling and administrative expenses	20,000	20,000	20,000	20,000	20,000
Total charges to revenue	$140,000	$129,440	$129,840	$129,440	$129,440

Schedule Analyzing Overhead Application

	STANDARD COSTING	NORMAL COSTING
Overhead incurred	$45,000	$45,000
Overhead applied under standard costing, based on 2,000 standard hours allowed for output achieved	40,000	
Overhead applied under normal costing, based on 2,000 hours of input, which is 10% higher		44,000
Underapplied overhead	$ 5,000	$ 1,000
Proration—40% to Finished-Goods Inventory	$ 2,000	$ 400

The $400 charged to Finished Goods under alternatives 4 and 5 would be charged to Cost of Goods Sold in alternative 3.

Column 3 presents the results under normal costing without proration of underapplied overhead. The results in this and the next two columns hinge on a key assumption. Any unfavorable variances affect Finished Goods and Cost of Goods Sold in the same proportions regardless of whether actual, normal, or standard costing is used. For example, direct-labor hours were overused by 10 percent. Under normal costing, Finished Goods and Cost of Goods Sold would already have direct-labor price and efficiency variances (though not identified as such) therein as part of the actual direct costs:

	FINISHED GOODS	COST OF GOODS SOLD
Standard Costing:		
Direct labor—at standard, $40,000	$16,000	$24,000
Direct-labor price variance, $1,000	400	600
Direct-labor efficiency variance, $4,000	1,600	2,400
Total direct-labor costs after proration	$18,000	$27,000
Normal Costing:		
Direct-labor costs, actual	$18,000	$27,000

The results would differ between standard costing and other costing systems only if the prorations under standard costing made wrong assumptions about the actual proportions of labor in Finished Goods and Cost of Goods Sold.

The only difference between columns 3 and 4 is that the overhead prorated to Finished Goods in column 3 is charged to Cost of Goods Sold in column 4.

Columns 4 and 5 have full prorations under normal and actual costing, respectively. They have identical final results. Thus, full prorations generally yield accurate approximations of "actual" costs.

A careful study of Exhibit 8-12 shows that differences in operating income and inventories could become especially significant if the variances are relatively large.

Appendix 8b: variances and interim reporting

effects of objectives

Interim reporting is far from uniform. Some companies write off all variances monthly or quarterly as additions to or subtractions from Cost of Goods Sold. Others prorate the variances among inventories and Cost of Goods Sold. For example, consider the practices of 247 companies in a survey concerning interim accounting for overhead variances (underapplied or overapplied overhead):[12]

Closed to cost of goods sold	60.3%
Closed to income account	11.3
Subtotal affecting current income	71.6%
Prorated (apportioned) among Work in Process, Finished Goods, and Cost of Goods Sold	23.1
Carried forward to next period	4.1
No response	1.2
Total	100.0%

[12]Chiu and Lee, op. cit., p. 242.

Most companies follow the same practices for both interim and annual financial statements. They apparently favor the first of two major conflicting objectives of interim reporting.

> *Objective 1:* The results for each interim period should be computed in the same way as if the interim period were an annual accounting period. For example, the interim underapplied overhead would be written off or prorated just like the annual underapplied overhead.
>
> *Objective 2:* Each interim period is an integral part of the annual period. For example, a February repair cost may be regarded as benefiting the entire year's operations. Suppose the repair is the major cause of the underapplied overhead. Then the underapplied overhead should be deferred and spread over the entire fiscal year.

The author believes that the second objective has merit, even though few companies seem to favor it. The central idea of overhead application is the use of a predetermined annual average rate. There are bound to be random month-to-month underapplications or overapplications that should come near to offsetting one another by the end of the year. The most frequent causes of these month-to-month deviations are (a) operations at different levels of volume; and (b) the presence of seasonal costs, such as heating, that are averaged in with other overhead items in setting an annual overhead rate.

If underapplied manufacturing overhead is carried forward during the year, it would appear on an interim balance sheet as a current asset, a "prepaid expense." Similarly, overapplied overhead would be a current liability, a "deferred credit."

external reporting

The rules for external reporting distinguish among the types of standard-cost variances. In general, the same reporting procedures should be used for interim and annual statements. However, Accounting Principles Board Opinion No. 28 pinpoints direct-material price variances and factory-overhead production volume variances for special treatment. If these interim variances are expected to be offset by the end of the annual period, they should "ordinarily be deferred at interim reporting dates."

The latter overhead variances are often called *planned variances.* They are especially common in seasonal businesses. Deferral is favored because such amounts are expected to disappear by the end of the year via the use of averaging as costs are applied to product. However, "unplanned" or unanticipated underapplied or overapplied overhead should be reported "at the end of an interim period following the same procedures used at the end of a fiscal year."[13]

This approach of Opinion 28 represents a compromise between Objectives 1 and 2 above. Why? Because "unplanned" and "planned" overhead variances are accounted for differently.

---

[13]Accounting Principles Board Opinion No. 28, *Interim Financial Reporting,* Paragraph 14(d). Also see the latest pronouncements of the Financial Accounting Standards Board and Alfred Rappaport, "Towards a Theory of Interim Reports: A Modification and an Extension," *Journal of Accounting Research,* 4, No. 1, pp. 121–26.

QUESTIONS, PROBLEMS, AND CASES

8-1 Why is *direct costing* a misnomer?

8-2 List three different types of denominator volumes.

8-3 "The central issue in variable costing is *timing*." Explain.

8-4 "The main trouble with variable costing is that it ignores the increasing importance of fixed costs in modern business." Do you agree? Why?

8-5 "The depreciation on the paper machine is every bit as much a part of the cost of the manufactured paper as the cost of the raw pulp." Do you agree? Why?

8-6 ***Comparison of unit costs.*** (W. Crum) Summarized total costs for the Hilo Company for 19_0 are as follows for an output of 10,000 units:

Fixed selling and administrative expense	$ 900,000
Financial expenses	300,000
Fixed manufacturing overhead	1,000,000
Variable selling and administrative expense	240,000
Variable manufacturing overhead	800,000
Direct materials used	2,000,000
Direct labor used	1,600,000

1. Using absorption costing, what is the manufacturing cost of one unit of the product?
2. Using variable costing, what is the manufacturing cost of one unit of the product?

8-7 ***Variable costing statement.*** (W. Crum) Prepare an income statement for 19_5 for the Andes Company. Use variable costing. Prepare such a statement in good form, marking your answer carefully for the contribution margin.

Direct material used	$4,100,000	Beginning finished goods	None
Direct labor incurred	3,300,000	Ending finished goods	10,000 units
Current liabilities	3,500,000	Total production for year	100,000 units
Net sales (90,000 units)	10,000,000	Retained earnings	$4,000,000
Variable manufacturing overhead	400,000	Current assets	6,000,000
Fixed manufacturing overhead	1,000,000	Variable selling and administrative expense	180,000
Fixed selling and administrative expense	900,000	Cash	950,000

8-8 ***Comparison of actual costing methods.*** The AX Company sells its product at $2 per unit. The company uses a first-in, first-out, actual costing system. That is, a new fixed-factory-overhead application rate is computed each year by dividing the actual fixed factory overhead by the actual production. The following data relate to its first two years of operation:

	YEAR 1	YEAR 2
Sales	1,000 units	1,200 units
Production	1,400 units	1,000 units
Costs:		
Factory—variable	$700	$500
—fixed	700	700
Selling—variable	100	120
Administrative—fixed	400	400

REQUIRED

1. Income statements for each of the years based on absorption costing.
2. Income statements for each of the years based on direct or variable costing.
3. A reconciliation or explanation of the differences in the operating income for each year resulting from the use of the methods required above.

8-9 ***Standard variable and absorption costing.*** The Blazek Company had the following operating characteristics in 19_4 and 19_5:

Basic production data at standard cost:		
Direct materials	$1.30	
Direct labor	1.50	
Variable overhead	.20	$3.00
Fixed overhead ($150,000 ÷ 150,000 units of denominator volume)		1.00
Total factory cost at standard		$4.00

Sales price, $5.00 per unit.
Selling and administrative expense is assumed for simplicity as being all fixed at $65,000 yearly, except for sales commissions at 5% of dollar sales.

	19_4	19_5
In units:		
Opening inventory	—	30,000
Production	170,000	140,000
Sales	140,000	160,000
Closing inventory	30,000	10,000

There were no variances from the standard variable costs, and fixed overhead incurred was exactly $150,000 per year. Any production volume variance is written off directly at year-end as an adjustment to Cost of Goods Sold.

REQUIRED

1. Income statements for 19_4 and 19_5 under variable costing and absorption costing.
2. A reconciliation of the difference in operating income for 19_4, 19_5, and the two years as a whole.

8-10 ***Variable and absorption costing.*** The Mears Company had operating income of $200,000 for the first ten months of 19_2. There were no variances of any kind through October 31. One hundred thousand units were manufactured and sold during the ten-month period. Fixed manufacturing overhead was $2,000,000 through October 31. The company uses a standard-costing system. All variances are disposed of at year-end as an adjustment to Standard Cost of Goods Sold. Both variable and fixed costs are expected to continue at the same rates for the balance of the year.

There were 10,000 units in the beginning inventory. During the remainder of the year, 13,000 units are to be produced and 14,000 units are to be sold.

REQUIRED

If operations proceed as described, what is the operating income for 19_2 likely to be under (a) variable costing; (b) absorption costing? Ignore all selling and administrative expenses.

8-11 ***Variable versus absorption costing.*** The Mavis Company uses an absorption-costing system based on standard costs. Variable manufacturing costs, including material costs, were $3 per unit; the standard production rate was ten units per hour. Total budgeted and actual fixed factory overhead were $420,000. Fixed factory overhead was applied at $7 per hour ($420,000 ÷ 60,000 hours of denominator activity). Sales price is $5 per unit. Variable selling and administrative costs, which are related to units sold, were $1 per unit. Fixed selling and administrative costs were $120,000. Beginning inventory in 19_2 was 30,000 units; ending inventory was 40,000 units. Sales in 19_2 were 540,000 units. The same standard unit costs persisted throughout 19_1 and 19_2. For simplicity, assume that there were no price, spending, or efficiency variances.

REQUIRED

1. Prepare an income statement for 19_2 assuming that all underapplied or overapplied overhead is written off directly at year-end as an adjustment to Cost of Goods Sold.
2. The president has heard about variable (direct) costing. She asks you to recast the 19_2 statement as it should appear under variable costing.

3. Explain the difference in operating income as calculated in requirements 1 and 2.
4. Prepare a freehand graph of how *fixed factory* overhead was accounted for under absorption costing. That is, there will be two lines—one for the budgeted fixed overhead (which also happens to be the actual fixed factory overhead) and one for the product application rate. Show how the overapplied or underapplied overhead might be indicated on the graph.

8-12 ***Breakeven under absorption costing.*** Refer to the preceding problem.

REQUIRED

1. What is the breakeven point (in units) under variable costing? Explain.
2. What is the breakeven point (in units) under absorption costing? Explain.
3. Suppose production were exactly equal to the denominator activity, but no units were sold. Fixed factory costs are unaffected. However, assume that *all* selling and administrative costs were avoided. Compute operating income under (a) variable costing and (b) absorption costing. Explain the difference in your answers.

8-13 ***The all-fixed company in 1996.*** (R. Marple, adapted) It is the end of 1996. The All-Fixed Company began operations in January 1995. The company is so named because it has no variable costs. All its costs are fixed; they do not vary with output.

The All-Fixed Company is located on the bank of a river and has its own hydroelectric plant to supply power, light, and heat. The company manufactures a synthetic fertilizer from air and river water and sells its product at a price that is not expected to change. It has a small staff of employees, all hired on an annual-salary basis. The output of the plant can be increased or decreased by adjusting a few dials on a control panel.

The following are data regarding the operations of the All-Fixed Company:

	1995	1996*
Sales	10,000 tons	10,000 tons
Production	20,000 tons	—
Selling price	$30 per ton	$30 per ton
Costs (all fixed):		
Production	$280,000	$280,000
General and administrative	$ 40,000	$ 40,000

**Management adopted the policy, effective January 1, 1996, of producing only as the product was needed to fill sales. During 1996, sales were the same as for 1995 and were filled entirely from inventory at the start of 1996.*

REQUIRED

1. Prepare three-column income statements for 1995, 1996, and the two years together, using
   a. Variable (direct) costing
   b. Absorption costing
2. What is the breakeven point under (a) variable costing and (b) absorption costing?
3. What inventory costs would be carried on the balance sheets at December 31, 1995 and 1996, under each method?
4. Comment on the results in requirements 1 and 2. Which costing method appears more useful?

8-14 ***The semi-fixed company in 1996.*** The Semi-Fixed Company began operations in 1995 and differs from the All-Fixed Company (described in Problem 8-13) in only one respect: It has both fixed and variable production costs. Its variable costs are $7 per ton and its fixed production costs $140,000 a year. Normal activity is 20,000 tons per year.

REQUIRED

1. Using the same data as in Problem 8-13, except for the change in production-cost behavior, prepare three-column income statements for 1995, 1996, and the two years together, under
   a. Variable costing
   b. Absorption costing

2. Why did the Semi-Fixed Company earn a profit for the two-year period while the All-Fixed Company in Problem 8-13 suffered a loss?
3. What inventory costs would be carried on the balance sheets at December 31, 1995 and 1996, under each method?
4. How may the variable-costing approach be reconciled with the definition of an asset as being "economic service potential"?

8-15 ***Absorption and variable costing.*** (D. Kleespie) The Estevan Mfg. Co. produces a product that has a selling price of $5 per unit; the firm uses a standard-cost system and allocates the fixed factory costs based on a denominator activity of 50,000 units. During 19_1, production amounted to 46,000 units while sales for this period were 56,000 units; the "net" variance for variable manufacturing costs in 19_1 was $4,000, favorable, and fixed factory costs amounted to $60,000 (there was no budget variance for fixed factory costs). Variable manufacturing costs (materials, labor, and variable manufacturing overhead) at standard are $2 per unit. Fixed selling and administrative expenses in 19_1 were $10,000, and variable selling and administrative expenses are $1 per unit. There were no inventories of work in process at either the beginning or the end of 19_1; the finished-goods inventory at the beginning of 19_1 was 18,000 units, and it was valued at standard cost. All manufacturing-cost variances are to be written off as additions to (or deductions from) Cost of Goods Sold.

REQUIRED

1. The "actual" contribution margin for 19_1 was? $______
2. The inventory of finished goods at December 31, 19_1, was:
   a. If absorption costing is used? $______
   b. If variable costing is used? $______
3. The total amount of fixed manufacturing costs deducted on the 19_1 absorption-costing income statement was? $______
4. Absorption-costing operating profit for 19_1 differed from variable-costing operating profit by $______ (indicate direction of difference).

8-16 ***Variable costing and cost-volume-profit relationships.*** (Prepared by the author and adapted for use in a CPA examination.) The Fleer Company has a maximum capacity of 210,000 units per year. Denominator volume is regarded as 180,000 units per year. Standard variable manufacturing costs are $11 per unit. Fixed factory overhead is $540,000 per year. Variable selling costs are $3 per unit, while fixed selling costs are $252,000 per year. Sales price is $20 per unit.

REQUIRED

(Assume no variances from standard variable manufacturing costs in requirements 1 through 3)

1. What is the breakeven point expressed in *dollar* sales?
2. How many *units* must be sold to earn a target net income of $60,000 per year?
3. How many units must be sold to earn a net income of 10 percent of sales?
4. Assume the following results for a given year:

   Sales, 150,000 units. Net variance for standard variable manufacturing costs, $40,000, unfavorable. Production, 160,000 units. Beginning inventory, 10,000 units.

   All variances are written off as additions to (or deductions from) Standard Cost of Sales.

   a. Prepare income statements for the year under:
      (1) Absorption costing
      (2) Variable costing
   b. In fifty words or less, explain the difference in net income between the two statements.

8-17 ***Inventory techniques and management planning.*** It is November 30, 19_4. Given the following for a company division's operations for January through November, 19_4:

Division G

Income Statement for Eleven Months Ending November 30, 19_4

	UNITS	DOLLARS	
Sales @ $1,000	1,000		1,000,000
Less cost of goods sold:			
Beginning inventory, December 31, 19_3, @ $800	50	40,000	
Manufacturing costs @ $800, including $600 per unit for fixed overhead	1,100	880,000	
Total standard cost of goods available for sale	1,150	920,000	
Ending inventory, November 30, 19_4, @ $800	150	120,000	
Standard cost of goods sold*	1,000		800,000
Gross margin			200,000
Other expenses:			
Variable, 1,000 units @ $50		50,000	
Fixed, @ $10,000 monthly		110,000	160,000
Operating income			40,000

**There are absolutely no variances for the eleven-month period considered as a whole.*

Production in the past three months has been 100 units monthly. Practical capacity is 125 units monthly. In order to retain a stable nucleus of key employees, monthly production is never scheduled at less than 40 units.

Maximum available storage space for inventory is regarded as 200 units. The sales outlook for the next four months is 70 units monthly. Inventory is never to be less than 50 units.

The company uses a standard absorption-costing system. Denominator production activity is 1,200 units annually. All variances are disposed of at year-end as an adjustment to Standard Cost of Goods Sold.

REQUIRED

1. The division manager is given an annual bonus that is geared to operating income. Given the data above, assume that the manager wants to maximize the company's operating income for 19_4. How many units should he schedule for production in December? Note carefully that you do not have to (*nor should you*) compute the exact income for 19_4 in this or in subsequent parts of this question.
2. Assume that standard variable costing is in use rather than standard absorption costing. Would variable-costing operating income for 19_4 be higher, lower, or the same as standard absorption-costing income, assuming that production for December is 80 units and sales are 70 units? Why?
3. If standard direct costing were used, what production schedule should the division manager set? Why?
4. Assume that the manager is interested in maximizing his performance over the long run, and that his performance is being judged on an after-income-tax basis. Given the data in the beginning of the problem, assume that income-tax rates will be halved in 19_5, and assume that the year-end write-offs of variances are acceptable for income-tax purposes. Assume that standard absorption costing is used. How many units should be scheduled for production in December? Why?

8-18 ***Some additional requirements to problem 8-17; absorption costing and production volume variances.*** Refer to Problem 8-17.

1. What operating income will be reported for 19_4 as a whole, assuming that the implied cost behavior patterns will continue in December as they did in January through November, and assuming—without regard to your answer to requirement 1 in Problem 8-17—that production for December is 80 units and sales are 70 units?

2. Assume the same conditions as in requirement 1, except that practical capacity was used in setting fixed-overhead rates for product costing throughout 19_4. What production volume variance would be reported for 19_4?

8-19 ***Executive incentives; relevant costing.*** The data below pertain to the B. E. Company:

	YEAR 19_1
Selling price per unit	$ 2.00
Total fixed costs—production	$ 8,400,000.00
Total fixed costs—selling and administrative	$ 600,000.00
Variable cost per unit—selling and administrative	$ .50
Sales in units	17,000,000
Production in units	17,000,000
Normal activity in units (based on three- to five-year demand)	30,000,000
Operating loss	$ 500,000.00
No opening or closing inventories.	

The board of directors has approached a competent outside executive to take over the company. He is an optimistic soul and he agrees to become president at a token salary, but his contract provides for a year-end bonus amounting to 10 percent of operating profit (before considering the bonus or income taxes). The annual profit was to be certified by a huge public accounting firm.

The new president, filled with rosy expectations, promptly raised the advertising budget by $3,500,000, stepped up production to an annual rate of 30,000,000 units ("to fill the pipelines," the president said). As soon as all outlets had sufficient stock, the advertising campaign was launched, and sales for 19_2 increased—but only to a level of 25,000,000 units.

The certified income statement for 19_2 contained the following data:

Sales, 25,000,000 × 2		$50,000,000
Production costs:		
Variable, 30,000,000 × $1	$30,000,000	
Fixed	8,400,000	
Total	$38,400,000	
Inventory, 5,000,000 units (1/6)	6,400,000	
Cost of goods sold		32,000,000
Gross margin		$18,000,000
Selling and administrative expenses:		
Variable	$12,500,000	
Fixed	4,100,000	
		16,600,000
Operating profit		$ 1,400,000

The day after the statement was certified, the president resigned to take a job with another corporation having difficulties similar to those that B. E. Company had a year ago. The president remarked, "I enjoy challenges. Now that B. E. Company is in the black, I'd prefer tackling another knotty difficulty." His contract with his new employer is similar to the one he had with B. E. Company.

REQUIRED

1. As a member of the board, what comments would you make at the next meeting regarding the most recent income statement? Maximum production capacity is 40,000,000 units per year.
2. Would you change your remarks in requirement 1 if (consider each part independently):
   a. Sales outlook for the coming three years is 20,000,000 units per year?
   b. Sales outlook for the coming three years is 30,000,000 units per year?
   c. Sales outlook for the coming three years is 40,000,000 units per year?

d. The company is to be liquidated immediately, so that the only sales in 19_3 will be the 5,000,000 units still in inventory?
e. The sales outlook for 19_3 is 45,000,000 units?

3. Assuming that the $140,000 bonus is paid, would you favor a similar arrangement for the next president? If not, and you were outvoted, what changes in a bonus contract would you try to have adopted?

8-20 ***Overhead rates and cyclical business.*** It is a time of severe business depression throughout the capital-goods industries. A division manager for a large corporation in a heavy-machinery industry is confused and unhappy. He is distressed with the controller, whose cost department keeps feeding the manager costs that are of little use because they are higher than ever before. At the same time, the manager has to quote lower prices than before in order to get any business.

REQUIRED

1. What activity base is probably being used for application of overhead?
2. How might the overhead be applied in order to make the cost data more useful in making price quotations?
3. Would the product costs furnished by the cost department be satisfactory for the costing of the annual inventory?

8-21 ***Income taxes and practical capacity.*** In the United States there is nothing illegal or immoral about keeping multiple sets of accounting records, one to satisfy income-tax reporting requirements, one to satisfy invester reporting requirements, one to satisfy manager decision requirements, and so on. Nevertheless, real or imagined costs versus benefits lead most companies to have one or, at most, two sets of records. Income-tax regulations have heavy effects on accounting systems because records must be kept to satisfy tax laws.

For years the Internal Revenue Service was liberal regarding the tendency of companies to write off many indirect manufacturing costs, particularly depreciation on equipment, as charges against income immediately. However, in 1975 new income-tax regulations (see the Regulations 1.471-11) forced industry to hold back more indirect costs as "inventoriable" costs. In short, the regulations came down hard against the variable- or direct-costing approach to inventory valuation and in favor of absorption costing.

The regulations insist that any significant underapplied or overapplied overhead be prorated among the appropriate inventory accounts and cost of goods sold. However, the regulations explicitly approve a "practical capacity concept." This permits the immediate write-off (rather than proration) of the production volume variance that results from using a fixed overhead rate based on a practical capacity denominator volume level.

Corporation X operates a stamping plant with a theoretical capacity of 50 units per hour. The plant is actually open 1,960 hours per year based on an 8-hour day, 5-day week and 15 shutdown days for vacations and holidays. A reasonable allowance for downtime (the time allowed for ordinary and necessary repairs and maintenance) is 5 percent of theoretical capacity. The latter is defined as the level of production that the manufacturer could reach if all machines and departments were operated continuously for the 1,960 hours at peak efficiency.

REQUIRED

1. Compute practical capacity in units per year. Assume no loss of production during starting up, closing down, or employee work breaks.
2. Assume that 74,480 units are produced for the year and that budgeted and actual fixed indirect production costs totaled $9,310,000. Also assume that 7,448 units are on hand at the end of the taxable year and that there were no beginning inventories. Compute the amount of fixed indirect costs that would have been applied to production during the year. What amount will be allowed as a deduction in the computation of income taxes for the year? Label your computations.

8-22 ***Effects of denominator choice.*** The Armstrong Company installed standard costs and a flexible budget on January 1, 19_3. The president had been pondering on how fixed manufacturing overhead should be applied to product. He decided to wait for the first month's results before making a final choice of what denominator volume should be used from that day forward.

In January, the company operated at an activity of 70,000 standard hours allowed for the good units actually produced. If the company had used practical capacity as a denominator volume, the budget variance would have been $10,000, unfavorable, and the production volume variance would have been $36,000, unfavorable. If the company had used "normal" activity as a denominator volume, the production volume variance would have been $20,000, favorable. Budgeted fixed overhead was $120,000 for the month.

REQUIRED

1. Denominator volume, assuming "normal" activity as the denominator.
2. Denominator volume, assuming practical capacity as the denominator.

8-23 ***Proration of variances, multiple choice.*** (CPA, adapted) Tolbert Manufacturing Company uses a standard-cost system in accounting for the cost of production of its only product, Product A. The standards for the production of one unit of Product A are as follows:

Direct materials: 10 feet of item 1 at $.75 per foot and 3 feet of item 2 at $1.00 per foot.
Direct labor: 4 hours at $15.00 per hour.
Manufacturing overhead: applied at 150 percent of standard direct-labor costs.

There was no inventory on hand at July 1, 19_2. Following is a summary of costs and related data for the production of Product A during the year ended June 30, 19_3.

100,000 feet of item 1 were purchased at $.78 per foot.
30,000 feet of item 2 were purchased at $.90 per foot.
8,000 units of Product A were produced, which required 78,000 feet of item 1; 26,000 feet of item 2; and 31,000 hours of direct labor at $16.00 per hour.
6,000 units of Product A were sold.

At June 30, 19_3, there are 22,000 feet of item 1, 4,000 feet of item 2, and 2,000 completed units of Product A on hand. All purchases and transfers are "charged in" at standard.

REQUIRED

Choose the best answers:

1. For the year ended June 30, 19_3, the total debits to the raw-materials account for the purchase of item 1 would be (a) $75,000, (b) $78,000, (c) $58,500, (d) $60,000.
2. For the year ended June 30, 19_3, the total debits to the work-in-process account for direct labor would be (a) $496,000, (b) $465,000, (c) $480,000, (d) $512,000.
3. Before allocation of standard variances, the balance in the material-efficiency-variance account for item 2 was (a) $1,000 credit, (b) $2,600 debit, (c) $600 debit, (d) $2,000 debit.
4. If all standard variances were prorated to inventories and cost of goods sold, the amount of material-efficiency variance for item 2 to be prorated to raw-materials inventory would be (a) $0, (b) $333 credit, (c) $333 debit, (d) $500 debit.
5. If all standard variances were prorated to inventories and cost of goods sold, the amount of material-price variance for item 1 to be prorated to raw-materials inventory would be (a) $0, (b) $647 debit, (c) $600 debit, (d) $660 debit.

8-24 ***Proration of variances, beginning inventory.*** (CMA, adapted) Nanron Company has a process standard-cost system for all its products. All inventories are carried at standard during the year. The inventories and cost of goods sold are adjusted for all variances considered material in amount at the end of the fiscal year for financial statement purposes. All products are considered to flow through the manufacturing process to finished goods and ultimate sale in a first-in, first-out pattern.

The standard cost of one of Nanron's products manufactured in the Dixon Plant, unchanged from the prior year, is as follows:

Raw materials	$2.00
Direct labor (.25 DLH @ $16.00)	4.00
Manufacturing overhead	3.00
Total standard cost	$9.00

There is no work-in-process inventory of this product due to the nature of the product and the manufacturing process.

The following schedule reports the manufacturing and sales activity measured at standard cost for the current fiscal year:

	UNITS	DOLLARS
Product manufactured	95,000	$855,000
Beginning finished-goods inventory	15,000	135,000
Goods available for sale	110,000	$990,000
Ending finished-goods inventory	19,000	171,000
Cost of goods sold	91,000	$819,000

The manufacturing performance relative to standard costs both this year and last year was not good. The balance of the finished-goods inventory, $140,800, reported on the balance sheet at the beginning of the year included a $5,800 adjustment for variances from standard cost. The unfavorable standard-cost variances for labor for the current fiscal year consisted of a wage-price variance of $32,000 and a labor-efficiency variance of $20,000 (1,250 hours @ $16.00). There were no other variances from standard cost for this year.

REQUIRED

Assume that the unfavorable labor variances totaling $52,000 are considered material in amount by management and are to be prorated to finished-goods inventory and to cost of goods sold. Determine the amount that will be shown on the year-end balance sheet for finished-goods inventory, and the amount that will be shown for cost of goods sold on the income statement prepared for the fiscal year.

8-25 ***Prorations of variances using variable costing.*** Reconsider the Star Company illustration on page 257.

Suppose that all manufacturing overhead is fixed and that the company uses variable (direct) costing. Compute the operating income under standard variable costing (a) without proration of any variances and (b) with proration of all variances.

8-26 ***Proration of variances and income effects of standard costs.*** The Pearson Company uses a standard absorption-costing system, which shows the following unadjusted accounts at December 31, 19_2:

Stores (direct materials only), ending inventory	$175,000
Work in process, ending inventory	100,000
Finished goods, ending inventory	300,000
Cost of goods sold	600,000
Direct-materials price variance	64,000
Direct-materials efficiency variance	25,000
Direct-labor price variance	5,000
Direct-labor efficiency variance	25,000
Factory overhead incurred	210,000
Factory overhead applied, at standard rate	170,000
Sales	900,000
Selling and administrative expenses	180,000

Materials price variances are measured when the material is purchased rather than when it is used. Assume that Work in Process, Finished Goods, and Cost of Goods Sold contain standard costs in uniform proportions of direct material, direct labor, and factory overhead. The direct-material component represented 60 percent of the ending balance in Work in Process, Finished Goods, and Cost of Goods Sold. All variances are unfavorable. There are no beginning inventories.

REQUIRED

1. Prepare a comprehensive schedule of proration of all variances.
2. Prepare comparative summary income statements based on a standard absorption-costing system:
   a. Without proration of any variances
   b. With proration of all variances

8-27 ***Comparative income effects of variance prorations.*** Study Appendix 8A. Refer to the preceding problem for Pearson Company.

REQUIRED

Prepare comparative income statements for each of the five systems listed below, assuming the use of absorption costing as opposed to direct (variable) costing:

1. Standard costing without proration of any variances
2. Standard costing with proration of all variances
3. Normal costing without proration of underapplied overhead
4. Normal costing with proration of underapplied overhead
5. Actual historical costing—that is, no predetermined cost used

Hint: Make use of the appropriate data from the comprehensive proration schedule that you prepared in solving the preceding problem.

8-28 ***Proration of variances and income effects of standard costs.*** The Drake Company began business on January 1, 19_1. A standard absorption-costing system has been in use. Balances in certain accounts at December 31, 19_1, are as follows:

At standard unit prices:	
Stores	$ 20,000
Work in process	10,000
Finished goods	30,000
Cost of goods sold	60,000
Total	$120,000
Variances (unfavorable):	
Direct-material usage	$ 10,000
Direct-material purchase price	12,000
Direct-labor rate	2,000
Direct-labor efficiency	10,000
Underapplied overhead	5,000
Total	$ 39,000
Sales	$150,000

The executives have asked you to compute the gross margin (after deductions for variances, if any), assuming first that no variances are prorated, and second that all variances are prorated.

Assume that all variances that are not prorated are considered direct adjustments of standard cost of goods sold. Assume that prorations are based on the ending balances of the applicable accounts affected, even though more refined methods would be possible if additional data were available. There are not enough data about the direct-material components in the various accounts to warrant the proration of some of the direct-material purchase-price variance to the direct-material usage variance; therefore, prorate the price variance directly to Stores, Work in Process, Finished Goods, and Cost of Goods sold.

REQUIRED

1. Prepare a comprehensive schedule of proration of all variances.
2. Prepare comparative summary statements of gross margin under each of the two assumptions specified by the company's executives.

8-29 ***Income effects of standard costs and normal costs.*** Study Appendix 8A. Refer to the preceding problem for the Drake Company.

REQUIRED

1. The executives have asked you to compute the gross margin (after deductions for variances, if any) had the company followed these assumptions:
   (a) Standard costing without proration of variances
   (b) Standard costing with proration of all variances
   (c) Normal costing without proration of underapplied overhead
   (d) Normal costing with proration of underapplied overhead
   (e) Actual historical costing—that is, no predetermined costs used
   Hint: Make use of the appropriate data from the comprehensive proration schedule you prepared in solving the preceding problem.
2. Analyze the results in requirement 1. Which assumption writes costs off to expense most quickly? What other generalizations about the five assumptions can be made? Do you think Drake's standards were currently attainable? Why, or why not?

3. What approach would you take if you had more data and wanted to obtain a more accurate proration of variances?

8-30 ***Multiple-choice interim reporting.*** (CPA) Read Appendix 8B. The following annual flexible budget has been prepared for use in making decisions relating to Product X.

	100,000 UNITS	150,000 UNITS	200,000 UNITS
Sales volume	$800,000	$1,200,000	$1,600,000
Manufacturing costs:			
Variable	$300,000	$ 450,000	$ 600,000
Fixed	200,000	200,000	200,000
	$500,000	$ 650,000	$ 800,000
Selling and other expenses:			
Variable	$200,000	$ 300,000	$ 400,000
Fixed	160,000	160,000	160,000
	$360,000	$ 460,000	$ 560,000
Income (or loss)	$(60,000)	$ 90,000	$ 240,000

The 200,000-unit budget has been adopted and will be used for allocating fixed manufacturing costs to units of Product X; at the end of the first six months the following information is available:

	UNITS
Production completed	120,000
Sales	60,000

All fixed costs are budgeted and incurred uniformly throughout the year, and all costs incurred coincide with the budget.

Overapplied and underapplied fixed manufacturing costs are deferred until year-end. Annual sales have the following seasonal pattern:

	PORTION OF ANNUAL SALES
First quarter	10%
Second quarter	20
Third quarter	30
Fourth quarter	40
	100%

REQUIRED

1. The amount of fixed factory costs applied to product during the first six months under absorption costing would be (a) overapplied by $20,000, (b) equal to the fixed costs incurred, (c) underapplied by $40,000, (d) underapplied by $80,000, (e) none of the above.
2. Reported net income (or loss) for the first six months under absorption costing would be (a) $160,000, (b) $80,000, (c) $40,000, (d) ($40,000), (e) none of the above.
3. Reported net income (or loss) for the first six months under direct costing would be (a) $144,000, (b) $72,000, (c) $0, (d) ($36,000), (e) none of the above.
4. Assuming that 90,000 units of Product X were sold during the first six months and that this is to be used as a basis, the revised budget estimate for the total number of units to be sold during this year would be (a) 360,000, (b) 240,000, (c) 200,000, (d) 120,000, (e) none of the above.

8-31 ***Interim reporting.*** Read Appendix 8B. Munoz Company had the following data for the quarter ended March 31, 19_1:

	ACTUAL	FLEXIBLE BUDGET	FLEXIBLE-BUDGET VARIANCES
Variable factory overhead	$200,000	$178,000	$22,000 U
Fixed factory overhead:			
Applied		300,000	
Production volume variance		50,000	
Total	355,000	350,000	5,000 U
Total factory overhead	$555,000	$528,000	$27,000 U
Operating income	$100,000	$180,000	$80,000 U

For simplicity, assume that there are no beginning or ending inventories.

REQUIRED

1. Does the company use variable or absorption costing? Explain your answer.
2. Suppose the company had "planned" production volume variances. That is, volume fluctuated from month to month, but by the end of the year the total production volume variance was expected to be negligible. Under this approach, what "actual" operating income would be shown for the quarter? Explain your answer.
3. If variable costing is used, what "actual" operating income would be reported? Explain.

special review material for chapters 6 through 8

8-32 ***Difficult comparison of absorption and direct costing.*** Goodwill Industries, a not-for-profit charity, has an extensive profit-seeking activity that repairs old furniture and appliances for resale. Through the years, experience has led to the development of a standard absorption-costing system for controlling activities. As donated goods are received, decisions are made regarding which items to repair, which items to sell untouched, and which items to discard altogether. The profit from the repair activity is used to help cover other organizational overhead.

The manager of a centralized Chicago repair center, Susan Zingler, decides what items should be repaired and uses a form of standard-cost analysis. She tries to maximize profit in relation to total available hours. However, despite her contribution approach to work scheduling, she has been forced to use an absorption-costing system that was installed with the help of a CPA firm in 1923.

For the year 19_4, the budgeted and actual fixed costs were both equal in the manufacturing ($135,000) and nonmanufacturing ($10,000) phases of the activity. The sum of the spending, price, and efficiency variances was $30,000, unfavorable. On an absorption-costing basis, the fixed manufacturing overhead had been applied to various products on the basis of the denominator volume level in hours used in the master budget. There was an unfavorable production volume variance for fixed manufacturing overhead of $15,000. Production and sales were expressed in terms of equivalent standard hours earned; 40,000 standard hours were produced and sold at an average selling price of $30 per hour during 19_4. The budgeted average selling price was also $30 per hour.

REQUIRED

You have been asked to prepare a comparative statement of the original budgeted income statement for the year and the actual results. No variances were anticipated in the original budget. Even though the organization has kept records on an absorption-costing basis, you have decided to prepare a statement on the direct-costing basis. You have determined that the standard contribution margin was $10 per hour. Please present a neat, fully labeled statement.

8-33 ***Review of standard absorption and variable costing.*** (D. Kleespie) The Mlima Company produces a top-quality product called "Mbege" at its Kilimanjaro factory. Sales for the current period amounted to 1,800 barrels at a sale price of $50 per barrel for total revenue of $90,000. Selling and administrative expenses for the period were $22,000, of which $13,000 were fixed and the remainder were variable expenses. There were 300 barrels of "Mbege" on hand at the beginning of the period, and 1,900 barrels were produced during the period. There were no beginning or ending inventories of Work in Process.

The company uses a standard-cost system in accounting for manufacturing costs. The standard-cost sheet (which has remained unchanged for recent periods) shows the following details:

Direct materials (4 pounds at $3 per pound)	$12
Direct labor (1 hour at $8 per hour)	8
Manufacturing overhead:	
Variable ($2 per direct-labor hour)	2
Fixed ($4 per direct-labor hour)	4
Total cost per barrel	$26

During the current period, purchases of direct materials amounted to $27,000 for 9,000 pounds. There was a favorable direct-materials efficiency variance of $1,200. The direct-labor price variance was $760, unfavorable, while the direct-labor efficiency variance was $800, favorable. The variable-overhead variances totaled $1,500, unfavorable. The only fixed-overhead variance was an $800 unfavorable production volume variance. All variances are written off to Cost of Goods Sold.

REQUIRED

(Show supporting computations in good form)

1. Standard hours allowed for output during the current period.
2. Actual hours of input.
3. Actual direct-labor rate.
4. Standard pounds of direct materials allowed.
5. Actual pounds of direct materials used.
6. Total actual manufacturing-overhead costs.
7. a. Budgeted fixed overhead for the period.
   b. Denominator volume in hours.
8. Determine the value of the ending inventory assuming the company uses:
   a. Absorption costing
   b. Direct (variable) costing
9. Determine the amount of "actual" contribution margin reported on the variable (direct) costing income statement for the current period. To compute this amount, adjust for all pertinent variances.
10. Determine the *total* fixed manufacturing costs charged against revenue on the income statement for the current period (assume absorption costing).
11. What is the amount of the net income reported using variable (direct) costing? Using absorption costing?

(*Note:* An income statement is not required)

8-34 ***Comparison of alternative income statements.*** (By J. March and adapted for use in SMA examination) By applying a variety of cost accounting methods to the operating data of a given year, the controller of a manufacturing company prepares the following alternative income statements:

	A	B	C	D
Sales	$1,000,000	$1,000,000	$1,000,000	$1,000,000
Cost of goods sold	$ 375,000	$ 250,000	$ 420,000	$ 395,000
Variances:				
Direct materials	15,000	15,000	—	—
Direct labor	5,000	5,000	—	—
Manufacturing overhead	25,000	—	—	25,000
Other expenses (all fixed)	350,000	475,000	350,000	350,000
	$ 770,000	$ 745,000	$ 770,000	$ 770,000
Income before tax	$ 230,000	$ 255,000	$ 230,000	$ 230,000

REQUIRED

1. The controller used the following costing methods: (a) actual cost, (b) actual materials and labor, predetermined overhead, (c) standard absorption costing, and (d) standard variable costing. Match each of these methods with the appropriate income statement, A, B, C, or D above, and briefly explain the basis of your selection.
2. During the year, did inventory quantities increase, decrease, or remain the same? Explain briefly.
3. During the year, was the volume of production higher than, lower than, or equal to the company's denominator level of volume? Explain briefly.
4. During the year, was the variable manufacturing overhead incurred more than, less than, or equal to the budget? Explain briefly.

8-35 ***Review of absorption costing, variable costing, and analysis of variances.*** On December 30, 19_1, a bomb blast destroyed the bulk of the accounting records of the Horne Division, a small one-product manufacturing division that uses standard costs and flexible budgets. All variances are written off as additions to (or deductions from) income; none are prorated to inventories. In addition, the chief accountant mysteriously disappeared. You have the task of reconstructing the records for the year 19_1. The general manager has said that the accountant had been experimenting with both absorption costing and direct costing.

The records are a mess, but you have gathered the following data for 19_1:

a. Cash on hand, December 31, 19_1	$ 10
b. Sales	128,000
c. Actual fixed indirect manufacturing costs	21,000
d. Accounts receivable, December 31, 19_1	20,000
e. Standard variable manufacturing costs per unit	1
f. Variances from standard of all variable manufacturing costs	5,000 U
g. Operating income, absorption-costing basis	14,400
h. Accounts payable, December 31, 19_1	18,000
i. Gross profit, absorption costing at standard (before deducting variances)	22,400
j. Total liabilities	100,000
k. Unfavorable budget variance, fixed manufacturing costs	1,000
l. Notes receivable from chief accountant	4,000
m. Contribution margin, at standard (before deducting variances)	48,000
n. Direct-material purchases, at standard prices	50,000
o. Actual selling and administrative costs (all fixed)	6,000

REQUIRED

These do not necessarily have to be solved in any particular order. Ignore income taxes.

1. Operating income on a variable-costing basis.
2. Number of units sold.
3. Number of units produced.
4. Number of units used as the denominator to obtain fixed indirect cost application rate per unit on absorption-costing basis.
5. Did inventory (in units) increase or decrease? Explain.
6. By how much in dollars did the inventory level change (a) under absorption costing, (b) under variable costing?
7. Variable manufacturing cost of goods sold, at standard prices.
8. Manufacturing cost of goods sold at standard prices, absorption costing.

8-36 ***Normal and standard systems, variance analysis.*** (J. Patell) This is not easy.

As a member of the board of directors of Advanced Resource Technology, you have been attempting to track down rumors of cost overruns at the Bio-Tech Division. Bio-Tech produces a single product (a liquid protein supplement), and you have just returned from a brief inspection of the production facilities. While there, you picked up various pieces of possibly relevant information. The first is the published version of the division's 19_6 income statement, based on *standard absorption* costing, and the second is an internal reconstruction of the same statement, based on *normal direct* costing. Both are reproduced below, and on both statements all production variances have been carried to the Cost of Goods Sold."

Income Statement—Published Version

Standard Absorption Costing (in dollars)

Sales		2,240,000
Cost of goods sold		
Beginning inventory	0	
+ Goods produced	2,200,000	
− Ending inventory	440,000	
Standard cost of goods sold	1,760,000	
Correction for *all* variances	44,500	
Cost of goods sold		1,804,500
Gross margin		435,500
Selling and administrative expenses		150,000
Net income		285,500

Income Statement—For Internal Use Only

Normal Direct Costing (in dollars)

Sales		2,240,000
Cost of goods sold		
Beginning inventory	0	
+ Goods produced	1,900,500	
− Ending inventory	380,100	
Normal cost of goods sold	1,520,400	
Correction for overapplied* overhead	21,000	
Cost of goods sold		1,499,400
Selling expenses		80,000
Contribution margin		660,600
Factory overhead	365,000	
Selling and administrative expenses	70,000	435,000
Net income		225,600

**Applied on the basis of* actual *hours of input.*

In addition, while touring the finished-goods storage area, you noted the following information on a stock card attached to a bottle (unit) of protein supplement:

	STANDARD		ACTUAL	
	quantity	**cost**	**quantity**	**cost**
Materials	2 quarts	$2.00 per quart	1.9 quarts	$2.10 per quart
Labor	2 hours	$6.00 per hour	2.1 hours	$6.15 per hour
Total overhead	2 hours	$3.00 per hour		

Your final piece of information emerged from a casual conversation with the production foreman. When asked how the 19_6 production level had compared with its original estimates, he promptly replied that the targeted output level had been exceeded by 10,000 units.

Based on the assumption that the single unit of output that you examined is representative of production activity for the year, construct a complete variance analysis, including price, efficiency, production volume, and flexible-budget variances for all input categories, including variable and fixed overhead. For ease of computation, assume that raw-material inventories are insignificant.

8-37 ***Comprehensive review of flexible budgets and standard product costs.*** (W. Warrick, adapted) "It's darn tough for an old dog like me to have to keep learning new tricks!" exclaimed Walter Warrick with some exasperation. Mr. Warrick, president of Kowloon

Manufacturing Co., explained that he had given his son full responsibility for the operations of one branch of the business a few months previously. "Since then," he said, "it's been one dad-blamed thing after another!"

The most recent cause for complaint was the latest monthly income statement received from the plant run by his son:

Income for Month Ending April 30, 19_1

Sales:			
14,000 X frames @ $15	$210,000		
12,000 H frames @ $16	192,000		$402,000
Standard cost of goods sold:			
26,000 × $9			234,000
Standard gross profit			$168,000
	LOSS	GAIN	
Material variance		$ 3,000	
Labor variance	$6,200		
Burden and overhead variance		7,400	
	$6,200	$10,400	4,200
Gross profit			$172,200
Selling and administrative expenses			80,000
Income before income tax			$ 92,200

Mr. Warrick explained that at the beginning of the year his son had prepared a "Profit-Graph" (Exhibit 8-13), which showed for various levels of volume what his plant sales, various categories of expense, and profit should be. "As nearly as I can figure out that thing, he should have shown a profit of just under $100,000 even at our regular price of $15 per frame. Since it looks as if he got a better rate on his H frames this month, doesn't it look to you as if he should have cleared almost $112,000?" demanded Mr. Warrick.

Further investigation disclosed that the plant under consideration made two types of metal frames that were used in the construction industry. The X frame, although larger than the H frame, was less complex and required less welding than did the H frame. At the beginning of the year when standards were set, it so happened that the extra material cost of the X frame was exactly offset by the extra labor cost of the H frame, so that the prime cost (direct labor plus materials) of each frame was $6. This greatly facilitated the preparation of volume-cost-profit estimates such as the Profit-Graph.

At that time, it was estimated that each X frame required two units of metal stripping and one unit of welding supplies. The H frame, on the other hand, required one unit of metal stripping and two units of welding supplies. Metal stripping normally cost $2.00 per unit and the welding supplies cost $1.20 per unit.

The direct-labor requirement was the opposite of that for the raw materials. The X frame required approximately half the time to fabricate than the H frame did. It was estimated that under normal working conditions, 20 H frames per man-hour could be assembled and one welder could keep up with two assemblers. That is, H frames could be welded at the rate of 40 per welder-hour. Assemblers normally received $20 per hour and welders $24 per hour. Failure to schedule work properly and failure to provide adequately for absenteeism sometimes resulted in overtime or night work, which, of course, was paid for at premium rates. For purposes of variance computation, such extra pay was shown as a labor cost, not a burden cost, since it was felt that this placed the responsibility more nearly where it belonged.

The term "plant overhead" was used to describe a series of costs actually incurred at the plant where the frames were manufactured. Indirect labor consisted mainly of the wages paid to several material handlers employed at the plant. At the time the standards were set, power was purchased at the rate of 16¢ per kwh. Since that time, the rate had gone up to 18¢, although no change had been made in the standards. For control purposes it was assumed that the power requirements would vary directly with the total number of frames produced.

EXHIBIT 8-13

Monthly "Profit-Graph"
(Based on January 19_1 estimates)

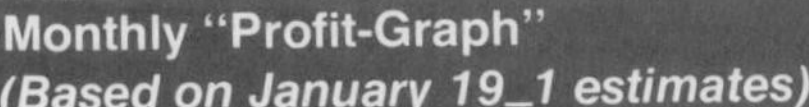

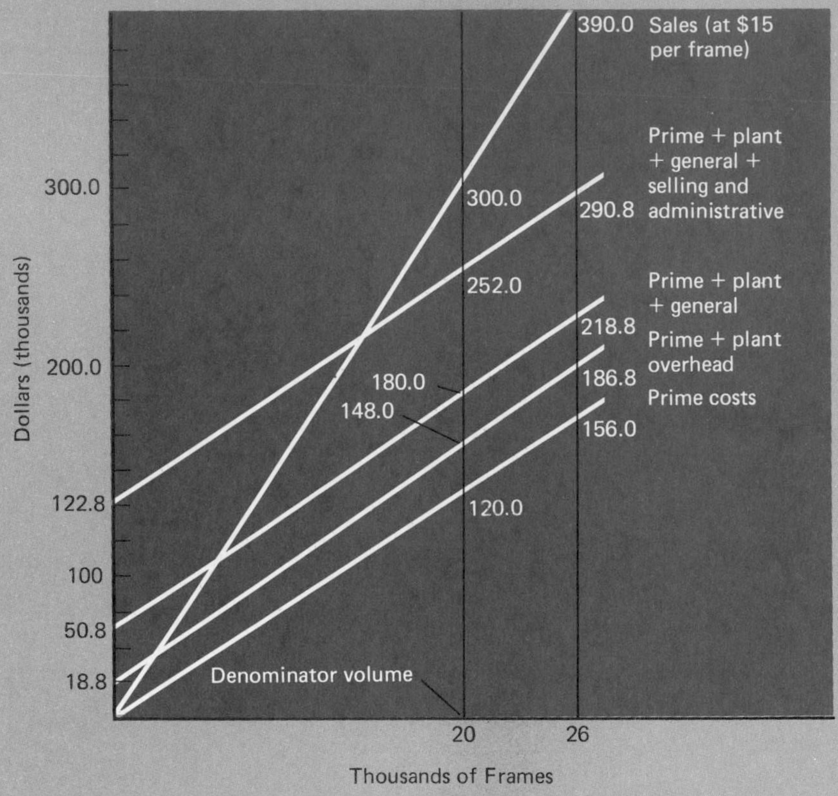

STANDARD COSTS AT DENOMINATOR VOLUME OF 10,000 UNITS OF EACH FRAME:

Prime costs at standard		*$6.00*
Plant overhead:		
Indirect labor	*$.16*	
Power	*.30*	
Supervision and inspection	*.54*	
Depreciation	*.40*	
Subtotal plant overhead		*1.40*
General burden:		*1.60*
Total standard cost per frame		*$9.00*

Supervision and inspection made up a fairly expensive item that tended to be reasonably constant over quite a wide range of output. Depreciation was computed on a straight-line basis and naturally depended upon the cost of the production facilities of the part of the firm under consideration.

An examination of the general burden revealed that this cost was an assigned cost. It was the practice of Kowloon Manufacturing Co. to assign the general administration burden (the cost of such departments as accounting and engineering, which were grouped at a central location) to the various operating branches of the firm. It was the policy of the company to anticipate this category of expense and assign a fixed sum monthly to each of the operating plants. However, when, as occasionally happened, the expenses of these central departments exceeded the amount anticipated, larger sums were assigned to the operating branches in order that such costs might be fully allocated by the end of the year.

Selling and administrative expense was budgeted at a fixed sum per month, since this expense was regarded as a direct result of management decision making and did not vary in direct relation with any of the standard parameters by which business activity might be judged.

Mr. Warrick pointed out that in general, apart from the change in power rate noted above, only one change from standard had been made in the base rate paid for any input to the plant. He explained that the plant was now paying less than formerly for its supply of welding rod. "I'm really tickled at the interest the boy has taken in every part of the operation," he confided. "As you can see, he has managed to raise the price we are getting for H frames. Not only that, he looked around until he found a fellow who would sell us welding rod at a lower price. Rod that used to cost us $1.20 we are now getting for only $1.00. I guess we have to burn a little more, but you can see from that material variance that we are money ahead in the long run."

"Not only that," he continued, "a couple of months ago he talked me into buying some portable conveyors, which he put in the plant and which cut the cost of material handling quite a bit. They were not cheap, but they will last ten years and I expect they will pay for themselves several times over before that."

"Still and all," Mr. Warrick grumbled, resuming the earlier trend of his conversation, "I wish I could get a little more accurate estimate of how well he is doing. When I got lost on that income statement, I asked for a little more dope; here are the actual figures for his April operations."

Raw materials consumed:		
Metal stripping	36,300 units	$ 72,600
Welding supplies	39,600 units	39,600
Direct labor:		
Assemblers	862.5 hours	18,000
Welders	540 hours	17,000
Plant overhead:		
Supervision and inspection		10,800
Power		7,800
Depreciation		14,000
Indirect labor		2,000
General burden		30,000
Total		$211,800

Production: 12,000 X frames; 12,000 H frames

"In spite of the fact that his income statement does not show him making as much as he ought to from the Profit-Graph, it looks to me as if the actual cost for the average frame he has turned out this month is only $8.83—about 17¢ less than standard. It is all pretty confusing," concluded Mr. Warrick. "I would like you to explain a few things to me in plain English. First of all, how come the income statement does not agree with the Profit-Graph? Is it only because of the rate changes from standard? Is there some less-confusing (and not too expensive) way of reporting on how well he's making out? Second, how well is he doing? Is he making progress or is he just making changes? Third, he says because of the changes he has made, some of our standards should be changed. What does he mean by that?"

REQUIRED

Answer Mr. Warrick's questions as completely and simply as possible. Include your supporting computations.

More on Control

SECTION THREE

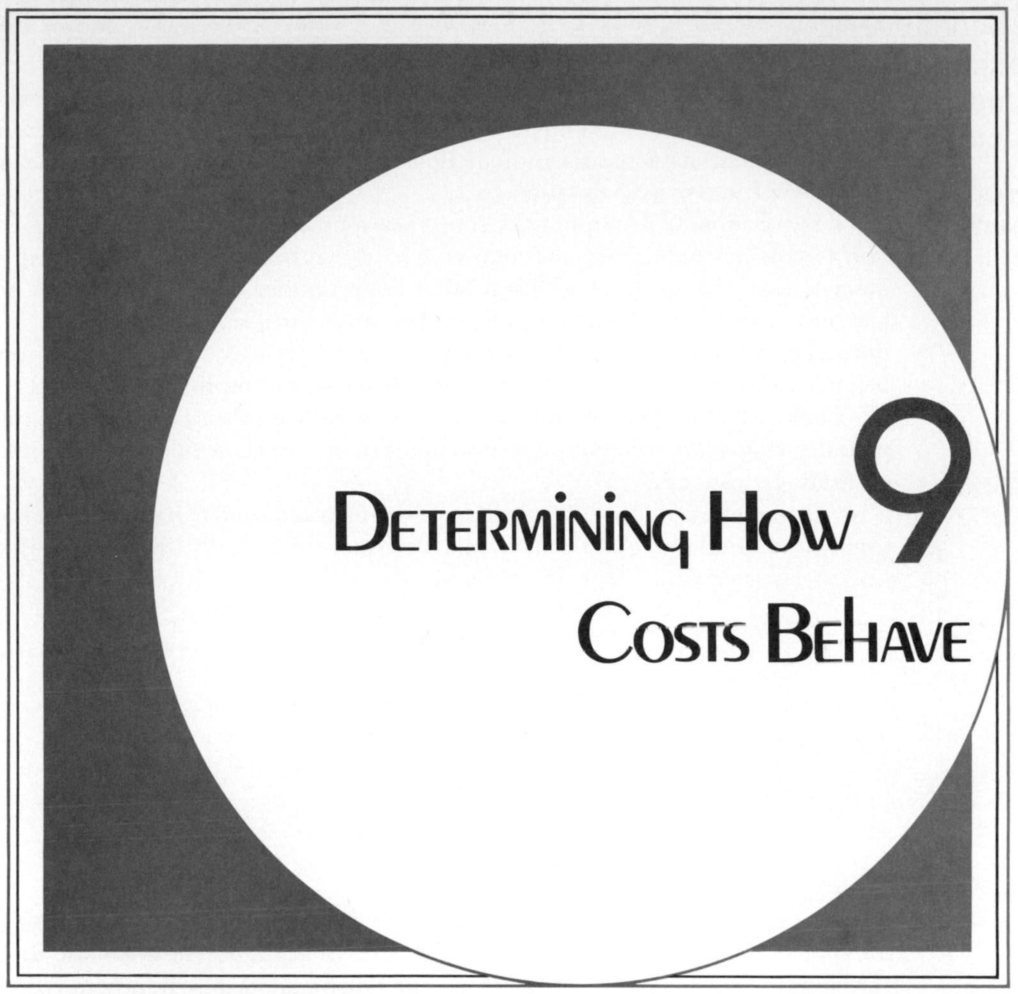

9 Determining How Costs Behave

Know your costs. Throughout this book, again and again we see that knowledge of how costs fluctuate can frequently mean the difference between wise and unwise decisions. Unfortunately for managers and analysts, the world of costs cannot always be neatly divided between variable and fixed costs. This chapter will explore how to identify cost behavior patterns (cost functions) so that predictions are as accurate as feasible.

The choice of a cost function is a decision concerning the cost and value of information. The job of cost analysis is quickly complicated in the real world by a variety of causal factors that underlie any particular result. Modern cost accounting offers useful techniques, although they sometimes seem too crude for the task at hand. Measurement frequently seems to be performed with a yardstick rather than with a micrometer. But a yardstick is sufficient for many measurement problems for which a micrometer is too expensive.

General approach to approximating cost functions

basic terms and assumptions

Accountants and statisticians often distinguish between **cost estimation** and **cost prediction.** The former denotes the attempt to measure historical costs; the latter, future costs. This distinction is not universal; many managers often use *estimated cost* and *cost estimation* to describe forecasts or predictions. Consequently, be sure of the meaning of *cost estimation* in a specific situation.

Two common assumptions or simplifications are widely used in the determination of cost behavior. First, the total cost level can be sufficiently explained by one independent variable (such as direct-labor hours) rather than by more than one (for instance, direct-labor hours, machine-hours, and dimensions of materials). Second, linear approximations to cost functions are "good enough," even though nonlinear behavior may be more likely. We will study these two assumptions later in this chapter. Of course, whether these simplifications provide sufficiently accurate approximations of underlying relationships is a question that can be answered only in actual situations, on a case-by-case basis.

Given the assumptions of one independent variable and of linearity, each cost has some "true" underlying cost behavior pattern, more technically described as a *cost function.* Its expected value, $E(y)$, has the form

$$E(y) = A + Bx$$

where A and B are the true (but unknown) parameters. (A *parameter* is a constant, such as A, or a coefficient, such as B, in a model or system of equations.)

Working with historical data, the cost analyst usually develops a linear formula to approximate the underlying relationship:

$$y' = a + bx$$

where y' is the calculated value as distinguished from the observed value y, and a and b are the approximations of the true A and B. The constant a is the **intercept,** defined as the value of y when x is zero; b is the **slope coefficient,** defined as the amount of increase in y for each unit increase in x.

independent and dependent variables

In determing cost behavior patterns, the manager must make three basic decisions. First, choose the cost to be predicted, which is the **dependent variable,** usually called y. Second, choose an **independent variable,** usually called x. The latter is sometimes termed the **controllable** or **decision** or **explanatory variable,** because the choice—for example, to travel a particular number of miles—is within the specific influence of the decision maker. The dependent variable—say, cost of gasoline—may be expressed as a function of the independent variable. That is, $y = f(x)$. Third, choose a relevant range of activity, the range where the relationship expressed by the cost function is valid.

Which of the possible independent variables should be chosen? Among the typical possibilities are:

units of product	direct-labor dollars
weight of materials	length of materials
dollar sales volume	machine-hours
direct-labor hours	miles driven

The analyst tries to select the independent variable that is likely to have the most influence on total cost incurred (the dependent variable), which is typically some type of material, labor, power, supplies, or other overhead cost.

Exhibit 9-1 illustrates variations of the basic formula, $y' = a + bx$:

EXHIBIT 9-1

Examples of Cost Functions

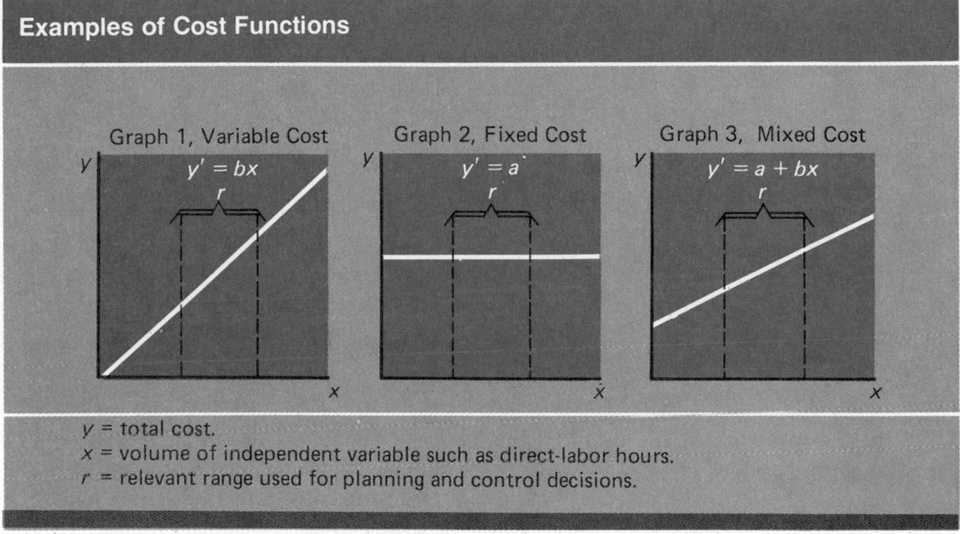

y = total cost.
x = volume of independent variable such as direct-labor hours.
r = relevant range used for planning and control decisions.

examples of cost functions

Graph 1 presents the familiar *variable cost,* which is often referred to as being *proportionately variable, strictly variable,* or *directly variable.* Its total fluctuates in direct proportion to changes in x because the intercept (a) is zero.

Graph 2 presents the familiar *fixed cost.* Its total does not fluctuate within the relevant range because b is zero.

Graph 3 presents a **mixed cost,** sometimes called a **semivariable cost.** As the name implies, a mixed cost has both fixed and variable elements. Its total fluctuates as x changes within the relevant range, but not in direct proportion. Its behavior conforms with the basic formula, $y' = a + bx$.

plausibility and fit

To approximate a cost function, plausible relationships are sought between the activity (volume) and the total costs incurred. The preferable cost function is one that facilitates the prediction of changes in costs, that accurately depicts persistent relationships, regardless of whether particular causes and effects can be established with assurance. The cost function is developed on the basis of some theory that supports the relationships between the dependent and independent variables—not on the basis of observed statistical relationships only.

In choosing a cost function, the analyst should retain the following perspective:

1. *Economic Plausibility.* The relationships between the dependent and independent variables must be credible. That is, they must be logical and appeal to common sense. When possible, physical observation, such as an engineering study, provides the best evidence of a valid relationship.
2. *Goodness of Fit.* The cost analyst tests past data to see which of the plausible cost functions provides the most accurate estimations. Sometimes these tests employ some complicated statistical techniques.

The role of the tests of goodness of fit should be kept in perspective. Begin with logic, intuition, and physical observation. Then formulate a mathematical model without using any data. Finally, use the numbers. Thus, the tests of the data provide confirming evidence.

Economic plausibility and goodness of fit serve as checks on one another. For example, data may show that a clerical overhead cost is more closely related (correlated) to fluctuations in the price of beer than to the number of bills processed. But there may be no logical cause-and-effect relationship that buttresses such closeness of fit. Therefore, a manager should be reluctant to use a cost function based on beer prices to predict how clerical costs will behave.

Mixed or semivariable costs

nature of mixed costs

The fixed element of a mixed cost represents the minimum cost of supplying a good or service. The variable element is that portion of the mixed cost that is influenced by changes in activity. Examples of mixed costs are the rentals of delivery trucks and photocopying machines for a fixed cost per month plus a variable cost based on the volume of usage.

Ideally, there should be no ledger accounts for mixed costs. All such costs should be subdivided into two accounts, one for the variable portion and one for the fixed portion. In practice, these distinctions are rarely made in the recording process because of the difficulty of analyzing day-to-day cost data into variable and fixed portions. Costs such as power, indirect labor, repairs, maintenance, and clerical labor are generally accounted for in total. It is typically very difficult to decide, as such costs are incurred, whether a particular invoice or work ticket represents a variable or fixed item. Moreover, even if it were possible to make such distinctions, the advantages might not be worth the additional clerical effort and costs. Whenever cost classifications are too refined, the perpetual problem of getting accurate source douments is intensified.

In sum, mixed costs are merely a blend of two unlike cost behavior patterns; they do not entail new conceptual approaches. Anybody who obtains a working knowledge of the planning and controlling of variable and fixed costs, separately, can adapt to a mixed-cost situation when necessary.

data for illustration

Direct labor is often regarded as being a classic example of a variable cost. However, many companies do not refine their direct-labor cost accounts for each job or batch of product to distinguish between the time for original setup, the time for intervening adjustment of machinery during a production run, and the time for actually producing the units sought.

Suppose a manufacturer is troubled by apparent fluctuations in efficiency and wants to determine how direct-labor costs are related to volume (various sizes of batches of output). The workers in question set up their own jobs on complex machinery. The data on page 289 show the results of a random sample of ten batches of a given kind.

Note that the data are paired. For example, the next-to-last sample consists of a batch size (independent variable) of 18 with an *associated* direct-labor cost (dependent variable) of $240.

Much more data should be accumulated before deciding how costs behave. However, we will use these data to illustrate some major points.

BATCH SIZE	DIRECT-LABOR COSTS
x	y
15	$180
12	140
20	230
17	190
12	160
25	300
22	270
9	110
18	240
30	320

industrial engineering approach

Five ways of approximating cost functions are: (a) industrial engineering approach, (b) account analysis, (c) visual fit, (d) statistical regression analysis, and (e) high-low points. These ways are not mutually exclusive. In many organizations, each is used in succession or simultaneously over the years as the desire for more accurate estimates becomes apparent.

The *industrial engineering approach*, often called the *engineering* or *analytic* or *work measurement* approach, is used widely by companies having standard-cost systems. The relationships between inputs and outputs are analyzed and quantified in physical terms—hours of direct labor, kilograms of material, gallons of fuel, number of records processed, and so forth. Time and motion studies may be employed. Then the physical measures are transformed into standard or budgeted costs. The engineering approach is costly, but its benefits are often dramatic. It is being increasingly used in nonmanufacturing as well as manufacturing activities.

In our example, management could have industrial engineers study the direct labor and carefully specify the amounts of time for setup and for individual operations regarding various levels of output. But suppose management is unwilling to invest in an engineering approach. The latter may be confined to materials and to only certain types of direct-labor activities. It may be deemed too costly to use for controlling the particular direct labor in question. Moreover, the engineering approach is often not feasible for planning and controlling many types of overhead costs. Physical relationships between inputs and outputs may be difficult or impossible to specify for a host of individual overhead items.

account analysis approach

The *account analysis* or *account classification* approach entails proceeding through ledger accounts and classifying each account into one of three categories: variable, fixed, or mixed. Such classifications may be based on superficial feelings ("I just know how these costs act!") or on inspection of cost behavior for at least a few past periods. In any event, account analysis conducted in such a slipshod manner is clearly a shaky way to prepare cost estimates. For example, in our illustration many managers might automatically classify direct labor as variable without undertaking further analysis.

An examination of the accounts is a necessary first step in a serious study of estimating how costs behave. The analyst must be satisfied that the cost records comply with the relationships necessary for accurate predictions. **An obvious requirement is the systematic use of accounting on the accrual basis rather than the cash basis.** For example, suppose factory supplies are purchased sporadically and stored in a manufacturing department for later use. If the factory supplies used are then not accounted for on the accrual basis, any cost study showing relationships between supplies and manufacturing volume could be misleading.

The analyst should also see that additional criteria are fulfilled. The balances in the ledger accounts should be applicable to the relevant time periods, reasonably free of clerical errors, affected by sufficient variability in volume, unaffected by costs outside the responsibility center under study, and adjusted for the effects of price changes. (See Chapter 24 for additional discussion.)

visual fit

When the analyst is satisfied that the ledger accounts abide by the forgoing criteria, the next step is to plot the data. The first graph in Exhibit 9-2 demonstrates this initial step in determining cost behavior in our example. Such plotting of the data on a scatter diagram should never be skipped. Inspection of the scatter of points will indicate the degree of relationship between cost and volume (often called **correlation**). The scatter diagram is a key to deciding whether the relationship can be estimated by a linear approximation. In this illustration the answer is yes. A straight line could indeed be fitted through the dots.

To avoid the use of more formal procedures, sometimes a visual fit is achieved by drawing a straight line through the points on a scatter diagram. An advantage of visual fit is that all sample points are used in determining the cost function. This procedure may provide more accurate estimates than using a casual summary or only two observations. Nevertheless, a visual fit has no objective tests to ensure that the line is the most accurate representation of the underlying data. Furthermore, visual fit ignores information that may be valuable about the quality of the fit.

regression analysis

Regression analysis uses a statistical model to measure the average amount of change in one variable (e.g., direct-labor cost in our example) that is associated with unit increases in the amounts of one or more other variables (e.g., batch size in our example). When specified assumptions hold, it has measures of probable error. The most widely used regression model is *ordinary least squares*. Regression is discussed at length in Chapter 24, which may be studied now if desired without breaking continuity.

Using least squares, the second graph in Exhibit 9-2 shows the best possible fit. Placing the amounts for a and b in the equation, we have

$$y' = \$24.43 + \$10.53x$$

where y' is the estimated direct-labor cost for any given batch size (x).

This equation may be used for budgeting direct-labor costs. For instance, a lot size of 20 would be expected to have direct-labor costs on the average of $\$24.43 + \$10.53(20) = \$235$ (rounded to nearest dollar).

relevant range and budgeting

The line in the second graph in Exhibit 9-2 is extended backward from the relevant range to intersect the y-axis at $24.43 The extension is deliberately shown as a dashed line to emphasize the focus on the relevant range. The manager is typically interested in cost levels *within the relevant range,* not with the cost level at zero volume. Therefore, keep the $24.43 intercept in perspective. It is not a fixed cost per se. **Instead, it is a fixed or constant component of the formula that provides the best available linear approximation of how a cost behaves within the relevant range.**

EXHIBIT 9-2

Scatter Diagram and Possible Linearity

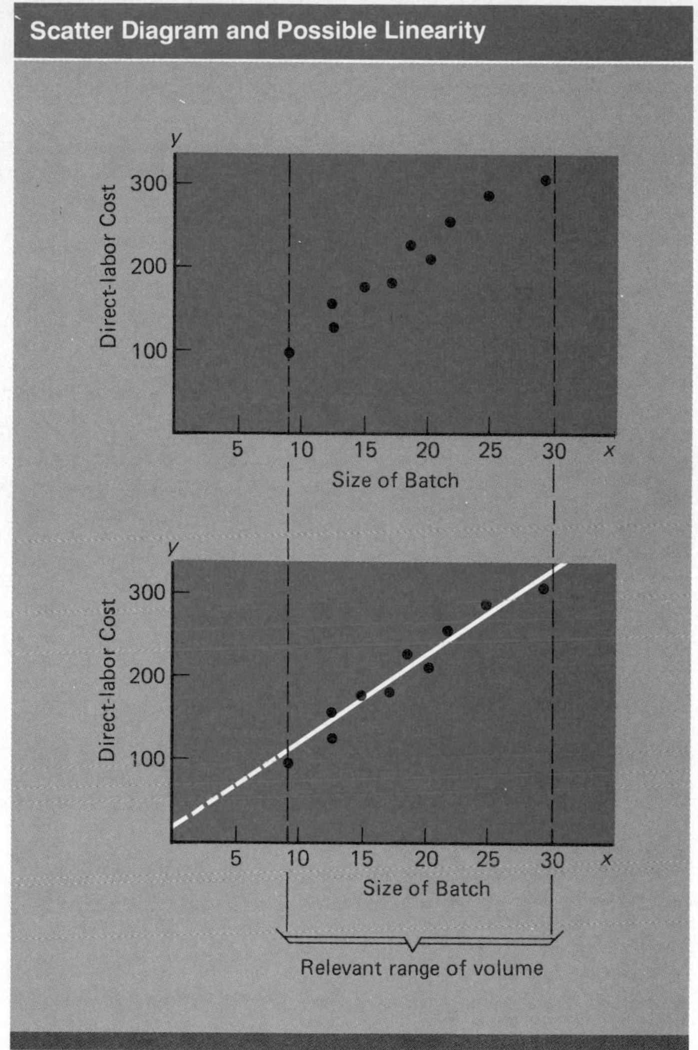

Another limitation of the study of past cost behavior should be familiar by now. Elaborate statistical studies sometimes overemphasize the past and ignore other important factors such as changes in workers, equipment, and price levels. Concern with the past is justified only insofar as it helps prediction. Managers want to plan what costs should be, not merely determine what costs have been.

A practical way to test the predictive power of the cost equation is to compare the predictions of the chosen equation with other possible equations. There is usually a time lapse between the collection of the original data and the computation of the final set of cost estimates. Therefore, a few more new historical observations can be compared with what would have been predicted by using the intercept and slope coefficient.[1]

[1] Robert S. Kaplan, *Advanced Management Accounting* (Englewood Cliffs, N.J.: Prentice-Hall, 1982). Chap. 4, has many suggestions on testing the accuracy of a proposed equation or model.

high-low method Exhibit 9-2 shows a straight line fitted through a mass of dots as a result of using least squares. As a less attractive alternative to least squares, the **high-low method** is used occasionally. It is a relatively crude procedure because it entails choosing only two points, one a *representative* highest cost and one a *representative* lowest cost, within the relevant range. (Note that the haphazard choice of highest and lowest points is avoided.) The line connecting these two representative highest and lowest costs becomes the estimate of the cost behavior.

Using the data in our illustration:

	BATCH SIZE (x)	DIRECT-LABOR COST (y)
High (h)	30	$320
Low (l)	9	110
Difference	21	$210

$$\textbf{Variable rate} = \frac{y_h - y_l}{x_h - x_l} = \frac{\$210}{21} = \$10 \textbf{ per unit}$$

If

$$y = a + bx$$

then

$$a = y - bx$$

or

Fixed-cost component = Total mixed cost less variable-cost component

at

$$x_h = \$320 - \$10(30) = \$20 \text{ fixed-cost component}$$

at

$$x_l = \$110 - \$10(9) = \$20 \text{ fixed-cost component}$$

Therefore:

Mixed-cost formula = $20.00 fixed-cost component + $10.00 per batch variable-cost component

Compare the high-low formula with the least-squares formula, which was $24.43 + $10.53 per batch. At a 20-unit level of volume, cost predictions would be:

Least squares: $24.43 + $10.53(20) = $235

High-low: $20.00 + $10.00(20) = $220

In this illustration, the difference of $235 − $220 = $15 is 6.4 percent of the least-squares estimate. This may not be significant to any decisions. Nevertheless, there is an obvious danger of relying on only two points. They may not be representative of all the points. Hence, the high-low method is not recommended.

Always plot all the representative data. The graph in Exhibit 9-3 illustrates a different situation. It shows why picking the highest and lowest cost can be foolish. In this case, the high-low method understates the fixed-cost component and overstates the variable-cost component of the total cost function.

EXHIBIT 9-3

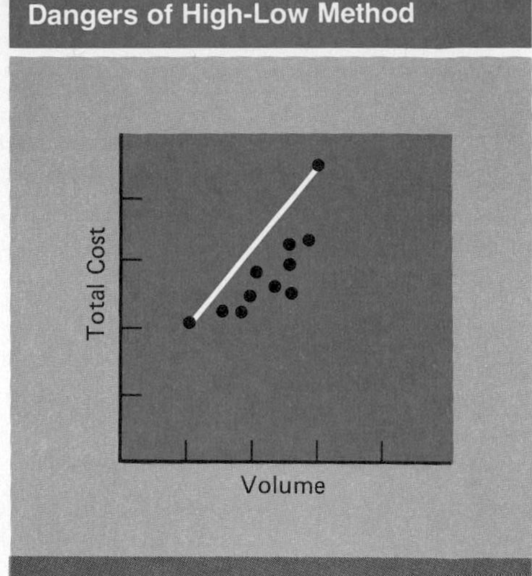

Nonlinearity and cost functions

limits of linearity

Almost without exception, accountants and managers use linear cost functions to approximate the relationships of total costs to a given range of inputs or outputs. There are several assumptions that are sufficient conditions for linearity to exist when total costs are related to output:

1. The technological relationships between inputs and outputs must be linear; for example, each unit of finished product must contain the same amount of raw materials.
2. The inputs acquired must equal the inputs used; for example, each worker hired must be fully utilized.
3. The cost of acquiring each input must be a linear function of the quantity acquired; for example, the unit price of raw materials must be identical regardless of the amount purchased.

EXHIBIT 9-4

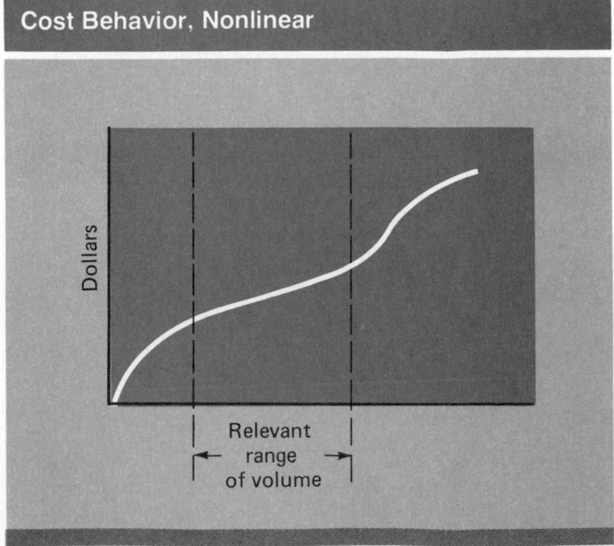

As Exhibit 9-4 shows, **the relevant range of output under consideration may permit a linearity assumption within specified limits of output.** Outside this range the cost of production may increase much faster or slower than the assumed linear rate.

examples of nonlinearity

Nonlinear cost behavior can be caused by a variety of circumstances, for example, economies or diseconomies of scale. Even direct-material costs are not always linear variable costs. For example, consider the upward-sloping supply curve for a raw material, where the purchase price soars as the desired quantity increases, as in Exhibit 9-5. Another example is the availability of quantity discounts, as in Exhibit 9-6, where the cost per unit falls as each price break is reached.

The graph in Exhibit 9-6 shows how *total* cost increases at a decreasing rate. A graph of the *unit* cost (not shown) would show a stair-step pattern with three steps going downward from the y-axis.

step-function costs

Few costs are variable in the strict sense of fluctuating in direct proportion to changes in volume. As already mentioned, many raw-material costs provide examples of this proportionately variable cost behavior, as shown in the first graph in Exhibit 9-7.

The second graph in Exhibit 9-7 exemplifies a **step-function cost,** whereby the cost of the input is constant over various small ranges of output, but it increases by discrete amounts (that is, in steps) as activity moves from one range to the next. This step-like behavior occurs when the input is acquired in discrete quantities but is used in fractional quantities. For example, labor costs of all sorts—direct or indirect, manufacturing or administrative—often represent step-variable costs. These increase or decrease abruptly at intervals of activity because their acquisition comes in indivisible chunks. Labor services cannot be stored for future use; they are either utilized or lost as the workday ebbs away. They cannot be turned on or off like a faucet.

The popular objective in the planning and control of step costs is usually to attain activity or utilization at the highest volume for any given step. This will maximize returns for each dollar spent, because the services involved will be fully utilized and their unit cost will be least. That is why a "linear approximation" of the step-variable cost behavior often takes the form of a proportionately variable cost for budgetary-control purposes, as the second graph in Exhibit 9-7 shows.

EXHIBIT 9-5

Effects of Upward-Sloping Supply Curve

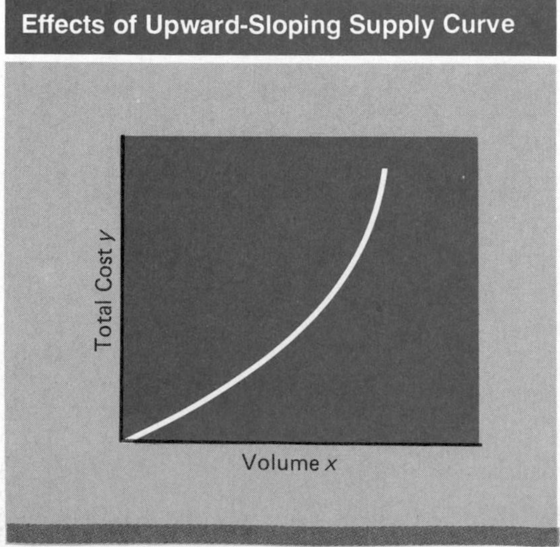

EXHIBIT 9-6

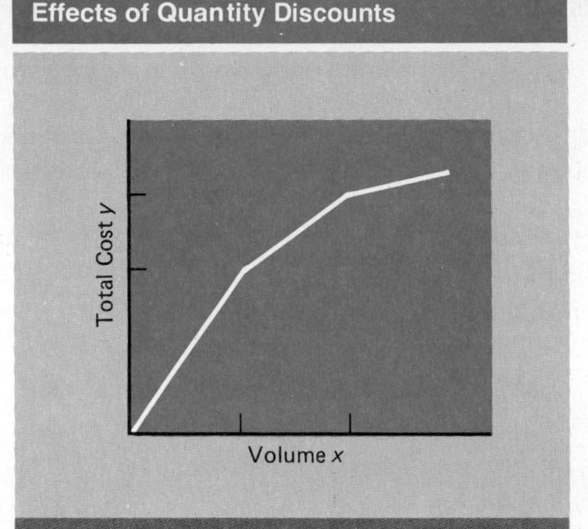

- Total cost increasing at a decreasing rate.

width of steps The problems of measurement are much more difficult for step-variable costs than for proportionately variable costs. The need for a unit of raw material is easy to determine, but the measurement of direct labor, indirect labor, administrative labor, and selling labor becomes progressively more difficult. In practice, secretaries, stock clerks, file clerks, and others are frequently subject to uneven work pressures. They may be able to work intensively or leisurely for various spurts of time.

The width and height of the steps may vary among the types of labor services. For instance, the number of hours worked by each direct laborer may be closely geared to production. The use of overtime, part-time help, or short workweeks may cause the direct-labor-cost steps to be very narrow and very small, so that they approximate a proportionately variable cost behavior pattern. On the other hand, failures to use part-time help, to gear the workweek to current needs, and to use overtime tend to widen and heighten the labor-cost steps.

EXHIBIT 9-7

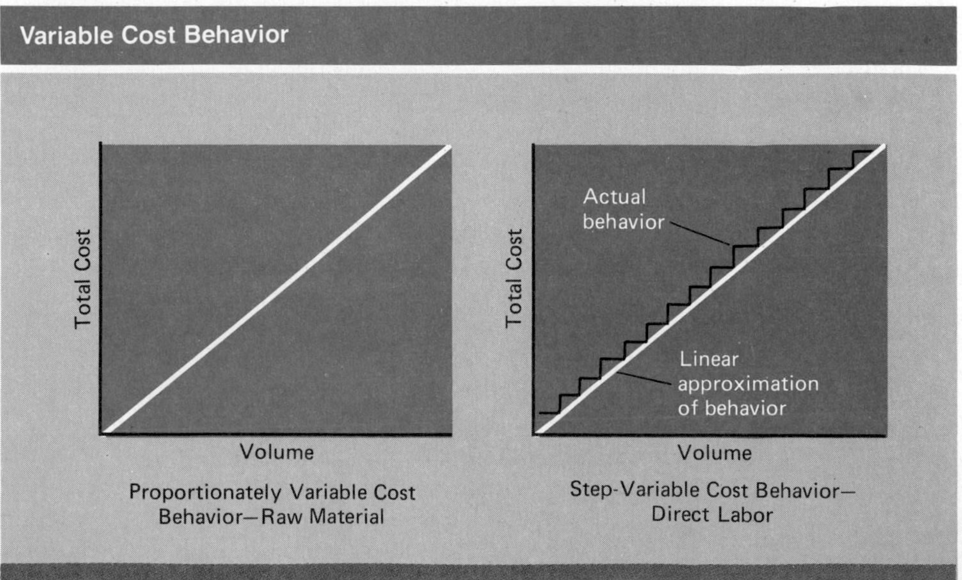

296-299 omitted

Of course, as the steps widen, a so-called step-variable cost may become a "step-fixed" or even a "fixed" cost. Exhibit 9-7 shows how direct labor may be regarded as a variable cost, because only a small error is caused by using a straight line instead of a step function. On the other hand, Exhibit 9-8 demonstrates how supervision costs may have wider steps, so that a fixed-cost approximation would be more accurate than a variable-cost approximation for the bulk of the relevant range under consideration.

EXHIBIT 9-8

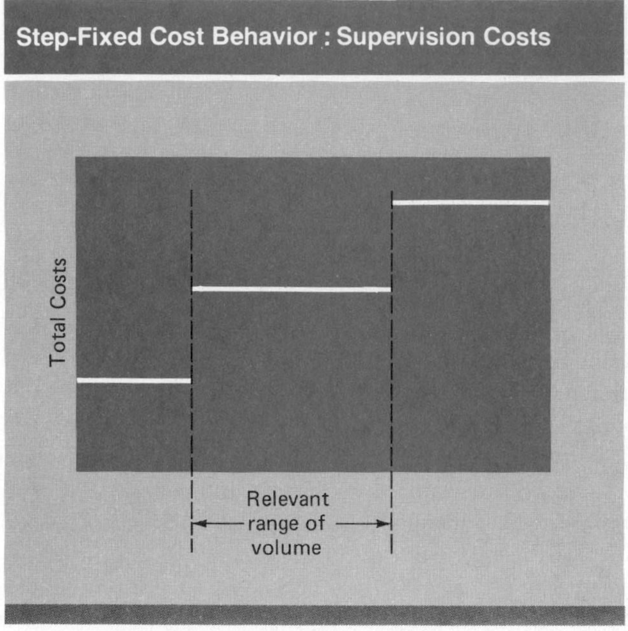

Learning curves and accounting

There are many ways to improve productivity. For example, the Animal Optics Company sells red-tinted contact lenses for 20 cents per pair. The company claims that the lenses make chickens see all the world in a red hue. This reduces their tendency to peck at one another. The death-loss rate from the latter can be as high as 25 percent of the flock. The lenses supposedly reduce the death rate to 5 percent and save farmers a penny per dozen eggs. We now examine the learning curve, a popular tool for measuring the effect of experience on efficiency.

effects of learning on productivity

"Practice makes perfect" is a familiar saying. But it is rarely true. Perfection is seldom attainable. "Practice increases efficiency" is an unfamiliar saying. But it is frequently true. When new products or processes are begun, learning also begins. Efficiency gradually improves in a nonlinear manner.

The effect of learning on output per labor-hour or machine-hour is usually depicted by a learning curve, which helps managers to predict how costs will change as the process matures. A **learning curve** is a cost function whereby average costs per unit of output decline systematically as cumulative production rises. Case studies have shown that the time needed per unit of product should be progressively smaller at some constant percentage rate as experience is gained. The applicable percentage of the previous time usually varies from 60 to 85 percent, but 80 percent is common. For example, as cumulative quantities of production double, average time per unit may fall to only 80 percent of the previous time. Exhibit 9-9 demonstrates an 80 percent learning curve where the first lot of 10 units is produced in a total of 300 minutes:

CUMULATIVE PRODUCTION		TIME IN MINUTES	
number of lots	number of units (lot size = 10)	cumulative average per unit	cumulative
1	10 (10 × 1)	30.0*	300
2	20 (10 × 2)	24.0 (30.0 × 80%)	480 (24.0 × 20)
4	40 (10 × 4)	19.2 (24.0 × 80%)	768 (19.2 × 40)
8	80 (10 × 8)	15.4 (19.2 × 80%)	1,232 (15.4 × 80)
16	160 (10 × 16)	12.3 (15.4 × 80%)	1,968 (12.3 × 160)

**300 minutes ÷ 10 units in first lot.*

As Exhibit 9-9 indicates, as production quantities increase, the average time per unit starts to level off; so if total production were large enough, the time per unit would become quite stable.

EXHIBIT 9-9

Eighty Percent Learning Curve*

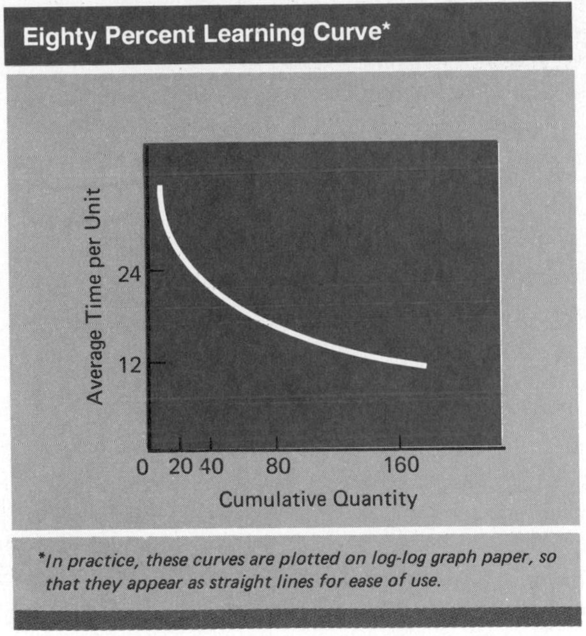

**In practice, these curves are plotted on log-log graph paper, so that they appear as straight lines for ease of use.*

The learning curve is applicable only to setting standards during the learning or startup phases of production.[2] If the production life is sufficiently long, or if the operations are relatively routine, a steady-state phase eventually occurs whereby no increases

---

[2]For an expanded discussion, see E. L. Summers and G. A. Welsch, "How Learning Curve Models Can Be Applied to Profit Planning," *Management Services,* 7 No. 2, pp. 45–50; and N. Baloff and J. W. Kennelly, "Accounting Implications of Product and Process Startups," *Journal of Accounting Research,* 5, No. 2, pp. 131–43. The learning-curve model is a power function:

$$y = ax^b$$

where y = productivity measure
x = cumulative output measure
a = parameter value, the productivity during the first unit of output
b = parameter value, the index of the rate of increase in productivity during learning

in efficiency (often called *productivity* in this context) are predicted. Indexes of efficiency may be expressed, depending on the industry, as tons per machine-hour or finished units per labor-hour, or some other measure.

setting budgets or standards

Predictions of costs should allow for the effects of learning. The costs most likely to be affected include direct labor and related overhead. Costs that may be unaffected typically include many materials, supplies, packing, selling, and nearly all fixed costs. Learning effects are more pronounced when the production process entails dexterity, sequential manual steps, and physical and mental adaptabilities of workers; learning has little application to automated or push-button operations.

The data in our example can be used for predicting costs and setting standards. Suppose the variable costs subject to learning effects consisted of direct labor and related overhead of $120 per hour, or $2 per minute. Then, using the data in the preceding table, the following costs could be predetermined:

CUMULATIVE PRODUCTION				
number of lots	**number of units (lot size = 10)**	CUMULATIVE AVERAGE COST PER UNIT	CUMULATIVE COSTS†	ADDITIONS TO CUMULATIVE COSTS
1	10 (10 × 1)	30 min. × $2 = $60.00	$ 600	$ 600
2	20 (10 × 2)	24 × $2 = $48.00*	960	360
4	40 (10 × 4)	19.2 × $2 = $38.40	1,536	576
8	80 (10 × 8)	15.4 × $2 = $30.80	2,464	928
16	160 (10 × 16)	12.3 × $2 = $24.60	3.936	1,472

**Note that the percentage decrease in cumulative average cost with each lot is 20%.*
†Cumulative quantity in units × Cumulative average cost per unit.

These data on the effects of the learning curve could be used for many different purposes. The data can have a large influence on decisions. For example, a company might set a deliberately low price in order to generate sufficiently high demand to "ride the product down the learning curve" and establish a high share of the market. Moreover, if it is legal, the company might set a low price on the final 80 units. After all, their labor and related cost per unit is only $1,472 ÷ 80 = $18.40, which is much lower than the cost per unit of the first lot produced: $600 ÷ 10 = $60.00

uses and limitations

Standards during the learning phase are often erroneously based on stable or steady-state conditions. That is, anticipated standards are being applied from the start. Using these standards to plan and to judge performance may have undesirable consequences. Among the dangers are faulty cash planning and production scheduling because of failure to allow for the unusually high costs and time consumption of startups.

In addition, the inapplicable standards may have an unfavorable motivational impact. If the unfavorable discrepancy between the steady-state standard and actual performance is large and persistent, the goal may be rejected as unattainable.

Of course, the opposite effect may also occur. That is, the learning curve might be ignored, resulting eventually in outdated standards that are not stringent enough.

The learning curve has many ramifications for business strategies. For example, competitive bidding in defense contracting would be affected by the predicted learning effects. The expected volume could have a dramatic influence on the unit price.[3] The cost per airplane is typically much less if 500 are manufactured than if 50 are manufactured.

The phenomenon of the learning curve will not necessarily occur if the cumulative buildup in output comes too quickly or the work force changes. For example, orders for the Lockheed L-1011 TriStar went from a total of ten in three years to twenty-five per year in 1980 and 1981. Lockheed had to boost division employment to 25,000 from 14,000 in two years:

> Inevitably, green workers have wreaked havoc with the TriStar's learning curve, dramatically boosting the man-hours required to build each airplane. . . . efficiency fell by 50%.[4]

Independent variable for budgeting

In practice, the choice and measurement of volume, the independent variable, is not easy. The exception occurs when a department performs only a single operation or produces a single product. The following guidelines are helpful:

1. *Cause of Cost Fluctuation.* The independent variable should have explanatory power concerning why a cost is at a particular level. An individual cost should be related to some activity that causes that cost to vary. Common measures include hours of direct labor, machine-hours, weight of materials handled, miles traveled, number of calls made by salespeople, number of beds in a hospital, number of lines billed, number of credit investigations, and so forth.
2. *Independence of Activity Unit.* The activity unit should not be greatly affected by variable factors other than output volume. For example, the use of total direct-labor dollars or total dollar sales as a measure of volume is subject to the basic weakness of being changeable by labor-rate or price fluctuations. The use of machine-hours or direct-labor hours eliminates the unwanted influence of fluctuations in the purchasing power of the dollar. Then, if physical volume is unaltered, a change in wage rates does not necessarily mean a change in other costs. The effects of price changes should not affect the unit by which volume is budgeted; this is usually accomplished by using standard wage rates or uniform sales prices.

---

[3]Some observers maintain that learning effects apply to all costs. The Boston Consulting Group has detected a widely applicable *experience curve,* which shows that overall unit costs decline in constant dollars by 20 to 30 percent with each doubling of experience. *Experience* is defined as the combined effects of learning, specialization, investment, and scale, If such an experience curve exists for any given company, it has enormous implications for strategic decisions regarding cost control, make or buy, pricing, growth, and so on. See *Business Week,* September 8, 1973, and "The Decline of the Experience Curve," *Fortune,* October 5, 1981, pp. 139–46.

William J. Abernathy and Kenneth Wayne, "Limits of the Learning Curve," *Harvard Business Review,* 52, No. 5 (September-October 1974), 109–19, maintain that the pursuit of the learning curve can reap great benefits. They state that total costs decline by a constant and predictable percentage in terms of constant dollars each time volume doubles. But there is a practical limit. This limit is not reached because the manager has exhausted means of cutting costs; rather, it is determined by the market's demand for product change, the rate of technological innovation in the industry, and competitors' ability to segment the market via a superior product or customized options. Then the company on the learning curve must either "abandon the all-important volume bases of scale or introduce a major product improvement. Either step, or both, ends the cost-reduction sequence."

[4]"The TriStar's Trail of Red Ink," *Business Week,* July 28, 1980, p. 88. In addition to hiring new personnel, Lockheed was faced with material shortages and the necessity of paying premium prices to suppliers and subcontractors.

3. *Ease of Understanding.* Units for budgeted volume should be easily understandable and should be obtainable at a minimum clerical expense. Complicated indexes are undesirable.
4. *Adequacy of Control over Volume Unit.* The common denominator that serves as a measure of budgeted volume must be under adequate control. *Because it is not affected by variations in performance, the standard direct-labor hours allowed (or machine-hours allowed) for units produced is a better basis for performance evaluation than actual direct-labor hours of input. A department head should not enjoy a more generous overhead budget allowance because of inefficiency.* The latter can occur when the budget is based on actual hours of inputs instead of standard hours allowed for outputs achieved.

If standard allowances are developed for all the factors of production, one factor may be tied to another so that all factors may be related to a common base. For example, if it takes one pound of direct materials, one grinding wheel, one machine-hour, and one direct-labor hour to produce one finished unit, usage may be related to the standard direct-labor hour as follows: If 1,000 standard direct-labor hours are used, the use of 1,000 units of each of the other factors may be anticipated. These relationships may be expedient and meaningful even though use of grinding wheels, repairs, and the like is more closely related than direct-labor hours to finished units produced or even to an assortment of causal factors. It is because of the latter phenomenon that we have stressed the need for an item-by-item analysis of variances.

To summarize, an index of volume based on *actual* hours of input fluctuates with efficiency; it is a measure of inputs, not outputs. The use of *standard hours allowed* or of some base built on standard hours allowed (for example, standard direct-labor dollars) is a measure of outputs. *Flexible budgets based on such measures of outputs permit the inefficient usage of inputs to appear as efficiency variances instead of becoming additional budgetary allowances.*

Costs and benefits

The subject of determining cost functions should be viewed from the perspective of the sensitivity of the results to the decision. Ideally, the decision maker wants to know the "real" or "exact" impact of a variety of actions and events on costs. In the majority of instances, that impact cannot be known with certainty. Instead, the statistician or accountant provides some cost function (for example, $y = bx$) that is a simplification of the underlying relationships. The discussion in cost accounting books is often couched in terms of obtaining more accuracy, as if more accuracy were always desirable. But obtaining more accuracy is often too expensive.

The central question is whether the resulting approximation, which is nearly always a linear function, is good enough for the purpose at hand. The answer to that question is often difficult to establish with much confidence. Nevertheless, it is a cost-and-value-of-information question that cannot be avoided. By the very act of using the cost function, the manager has made an information decision. He or she may have faced the decision squarely and explicitly by saying, "Yes, I can use this cost function for my prediction rather than a simpler or more complicated cost function." Or the manager may have reached the same conclusion implicitly, by proceeding with the given function with no questions asked. For example, when a manager uses an overhead rate of $2 per direct-labor hour as a part of the accumulation of costs for a pricing decision—even though this manager knows that overhead is affected by labor-hours, machine-hours, weight of materials, dimensions of materials, and weather conditions—he or she has made an information decision. The manager has decided that the simple $2 cost function is good enough for a specific purpose. In the manager's mind, the pricing decision would not be sufficiently affected by a more complicated cost function to justify its added cost.

SUMMARY

Predictions of how costs will behave in response to various actions usually have an important bearing on a wide number of decisions. The cost function used to make these predictions is usually a simplification of underlying relationships.

Two common assumptions are widely used in cost analysis. First, cost behavior can be sufficiently explained by one independent variable. Second, linear approximations to cost functions are "good enough" for most purposes.

The engineering approach, which may be expensive and which concentrates directly on the future, is recommended as the best practical and philosophical approach to approximating cost functions. This approach may encompass all kinds of techniques, from time and motion studies to statistical regression. However, in all cases the techniques should serve as checks on one another. The following guides for cost estimation and prediction should be used:

1. ***Economic Plausibility.*** **The relationships between the dependent and independent variables must be believable.**
2. ***Goodness of Fit.*** **The chosen cost function should provide as accurate approximations as feasible. Chapter 24 provides additional discussion.**

Budgeting and the setting of standards should recognize that many costs are nonlinear. The learning curve provides an excellent illustration.

problem for self-study

problem

Suppose a linear approximation is used for flexible budgeting as shown in the accompanying graph. The "true" cost function is the nonlinear function as shown.

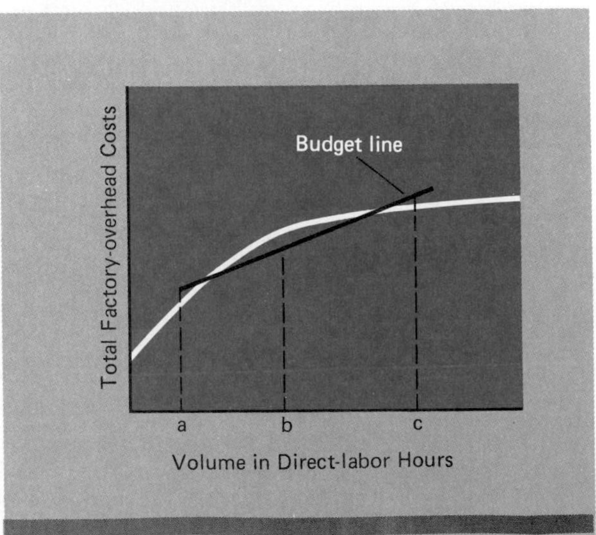

REQUIRED

Will the flexible budget be higher or lower than what the budgeted "true" costs would be at *a*, *b*, and *c*? What are the decision implications of using the linear approximations at each point?

solution

Budgeted factory-overhead costs will be higher at *a*, and *c* and lower at *b*. The decision implications depend heavily on the particular situation and organization. The linear approximation may be good enough in the vast majority of cases in the sense that, for example, the more accurate approximation will not result in changing any decisions regarding pricing or choice of product lines. In terms of the credibility of budgets and their motivational effects, the use of linear approximations may influence the attitudes and beliefs of managers regarding this part of the accounting system or the system as a whole. In other words, a little inaccuracy, by itself, may be unimportant in one decision situation or with respect to one class of costs. But more accuracy may be preferable to less when the system as a whole is judged in relation to a host of decisions and attitudes that might be affected.

Terms to Learn

controllable variable ***correlation*** ***cost estimation*** ***cost prediction*** ***decision variable*** ***dependent variable*** ***explanatory variable*** ***high-low method*** ***independent variable*** ***intercept*** ***learning curve*** ***mixed cost*** ***regression analysis*** ***semivariable cost*** ***slope coefficient*** ***step-function cost***

Special Points and Pitfalls

Five ways of approximating cost functions are: (a) industrial engineering approach, (b) account analysis, (c) visual fit, (d) statistical regression analysis, and (e) high-low points. An obvious requirement is the systematic use of the accrual basis rather than the cash basis of accounting.

The major concern in the analysis of cost behavior should be about how a cost fluctuates within the relevant range. In a linear approximation, the focus should be on the accuracy of the slope of the line.

Where feasible, volume should be measured for budgeting in terms of outputs achieved. In this way, the inefficient use of inputs will appear as efficiency variances. Budgets based solely on volume expressed as inputs fail to measure efficiency.

QUESTIONS, PROBLEMS, AND CASES

9-1 "For practical purposes, curvilinear variable costs may almost always be treated as if they had straight-line behavior." Why?

9-2 What factors must management consider in the year-to-year planning of fixed costs?

9-3 Give two examples of a mixed cost.

9-4 "If only one budget base is to be used for appraising performance, *standard* direct-labor hours is a better base than *actual* direct-labor hours." Do you agree? Why?

9-5 List four criteria for selecting a volume base.

9-6 List six factors besides volume that can cause costs to vary.

9-7 Describe three assumptions that are sufficient conditions for linearity.

9-8 Define *learning curve.* Name four of its uses.

9-9 ***Division of mixed costs into variable and fixed components.*** The controller of the Ijiri Co. wants you to approximate the fundamental variable- and fixed-cost behavior of an account called Maintenance from the following:

MONTHLY ACTIVITY IN MACHINE-HOURS	MONTHLY MAINTENANCE COSTS INCURRED
4,000	$3,000
7,000	3,900

9-10 ***Nonlinear behavior.*** (J. Demski, adapted) Ralph Thurow is manager of logistics for the Cortex Pharmaceutical Company. He has become increasingly uneasy about his cost predictions with respect to the transportation of assorted vaccines. Ordinarily, a transportation cost factor is added to the overall cost of the vaccines by a predetermined formula based on "average" transportation costs for all products. No attempt has ever been made to identify particular transportation costs with particular product lines. Transportation costs depend on units shipped, weight, whether company-owned equipment or outside shippers are used, and so on.

Top management has launched a three-year "profit-search" plan whereby all managers have been urged to "rethink your methods and costs to enhance profitability." Thurow has conducted a fine-toothed investigation of cost behavior; he has uncovered the following nonlinear cost curve, where x denotes thousands of units of vaccine shipped an average of 50 miles:

$$TC(x) = \tfrac{1}{3}x^3 - 8x^2 + 65x + 260$$

REQUIRED

1. Plot $TC(x)$ for $0 \leq x \leq 10$.
2. Determine Ralph's fixed and marginal cost.
3. Consider the range $4 \leq x \leq 8$. Determine Ralph's cost at $x = 4$ and $x = 8$, and then construct a linear approximation to $TC(x)$ by drawing a line between these two points. [Specifically, the *slope* will be $TC(8) - TC(4)/(8 - 4)$.]
   a. Plot this approximation on your graph in requirement 1 above.
   b. Determine, using this "local linear approximation," Ralph's fixed and variable cost.
   c. Can you think of another method of approximating $TC(x)$?

9-11 ***Linear approximations.*** Suppose that the following situation existed:

VOLUME LEVEL IN DIRECT-LABOR HOURS	TOTAL ACTUAL OVERHEAD COST BEHAVIOR
30,000	$340,000
40,000	400,000
50,000	435,000
60,000	477,000
70,000	529,000
80,000	587,000

REQUIRED

1. Compute the formula for the flexible-budget line, using only two "representative" volumes of 40,000 hours and 70,000 hours, respectively.
2. What would be the predicted cost for 50,000 labor-hours using the flexible budget developed in requirement one? Using a nonlinear flexible budget equal to the "actual cost behavior" curve? For 80,000 hours? Plot the points and draw the flexible-budget line and the "actual cost behavior" curve.
3. The manager had a chance to accept a special order that would have boosted production from 40,000 to 50,000 hours of activity. Suppose the manager, guided by the linear flexible-budget formula, rejected a sales order that would have brought a total increase in contribution of $38,000 less the predicted increase in total overhead cost. What is the total contribution forgone?
4. If you were an operating manager responsible for budgetary control of overhead, would you regard the linear budget allowances at 50,000 hours and at 80,000 hours as too tight or too loose as compared with the nonlinear budget? Why?
5. Does the intercept of the flexible-budget line represent the fixed-overhead costs? Why?
6. In your own words, summarize the major lessons of this problem.

9-12 ***Nonlinear cost behavior.*** The MNO Company has assumed that its total manufacturing overhead cost is most heavily affected by only one variable, direct-labor hours. The company used a linear approximation, as shown in the following graph, as a basis for determining its flexible-budget allowances for variable factory overhead at various volumes:

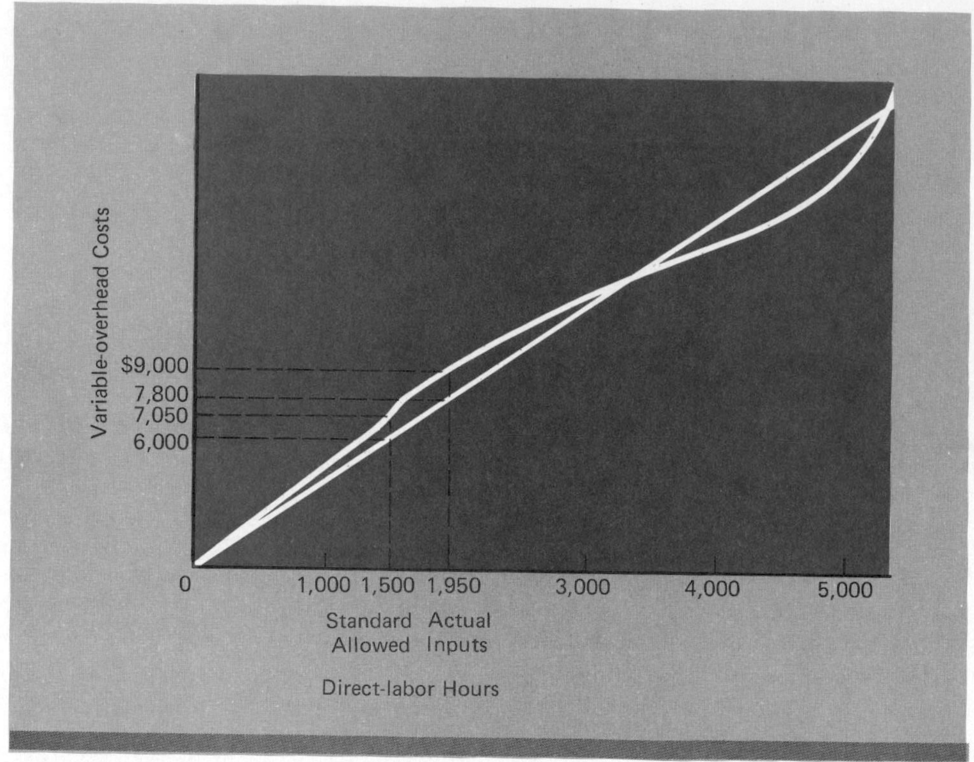

The actual cost behavior pattern is the nonlinear function represented by the curve in the graph.

Suppose that manager Charles is responsible for the whole plant, manager Baker for overhead spending variances, and manager Abel for overhead efficiency variances. At the end of the period, actual hours of input are 1,950 and standard hours allowed are 1,500. Actual overhead is $9,000.

REQUIRED

1. Suppose that the flexible budget was based on the linear approximation. Use the graph to measure the amount of the spending variance, the efficiency variance, and the flexible-budget variance.
2. Suppose the budget was based on the curve. How would your answers in requirement 1 be different? Be specific.
3. Compare your answers in requirements 1 and 2. If the linear approximation in requirement 1 is used as a basis for flexible budgeting, what are the likely effects on the attitudes of each of the three managers?

9-13 ***Two independent variables.*** Suppose the cost behavior pattern of overhead is linear but two-dimensional That is, cost incurrence depends on two independent variables, direct-labor hours, x_1, and machine-hours, x_2. For example, there may be two subdepartments, one heavily automated and one extremely labor-intensive. Therefore, the actual cost behavior pattern is:

$$\textbf{Total overhead} = a + bx_1 + cx_2$$

where a = fixed costs, b = rate per direct-labor hour, and c = rate per machine-hour.

Using the traditional approach, the controller has examined the cost behavior of total overhead in relation to x_1 and x_2. He has decided to compute a budgeted-overhead function that is based on direct-labor hours:

$$\textbf{Budgeted total overhead} = a + bx$$

The results for the most recent reporting period appear on the following graph:

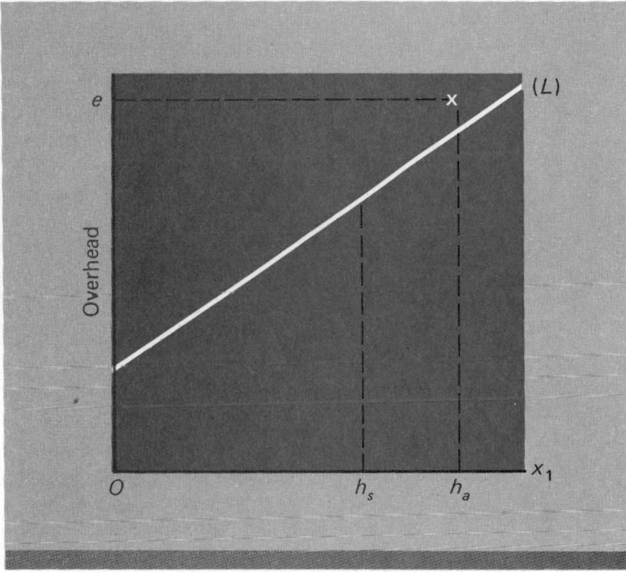

The budget is based on line (L). At the end of the period, actual hours are Oh_a, the standard hours allowed for the work done are OH_s, and actual overhead is Oe. Smith controls direct labor, James controls machine-hours, and Johnson is responsible for total overhead.

REQUIRED

1. Use the graph to measure the amount of the spending variance (call it *ge*), the efficiency variance (call it *gh*), and the budget variance (*he*). Which of the three managers is ordinarily held responsible for each variance?
2. What are the likely effects on the attitudes of the three managers if line (L) is used as a basis for budgeting?

9-14 ***Various cost behavior patterns.*** (CPA, adapted) Select the graph below that matches the numbered factory-cost or expense data. You are to indicate by letter which of the graphs best fits each of the situations or items described.

The vertical axes of the graphs represent *total* dollars of expense, and the horizontal axes represent production during a calendar year. In each case the zero point is at the intersection of the two axes. The graphs may be used more than once.

1. Depreciation of equipment, where the amount of depreciation charged is computed by the machine-hours method.
2. Electricity bill—a flat fixed charge, plus a variable cost after a certain number of kilowatt hours are used.
3. City water bill, which is computed as follows:

First 1,000,000 gallons or less	$1,000 flat fee
Next 10,000 gallons	.003 per gallon used
Next 10,000 gallons	.006 per gallon used
Next 10,000 gallons	.009 per gallon used
etc.	etc.

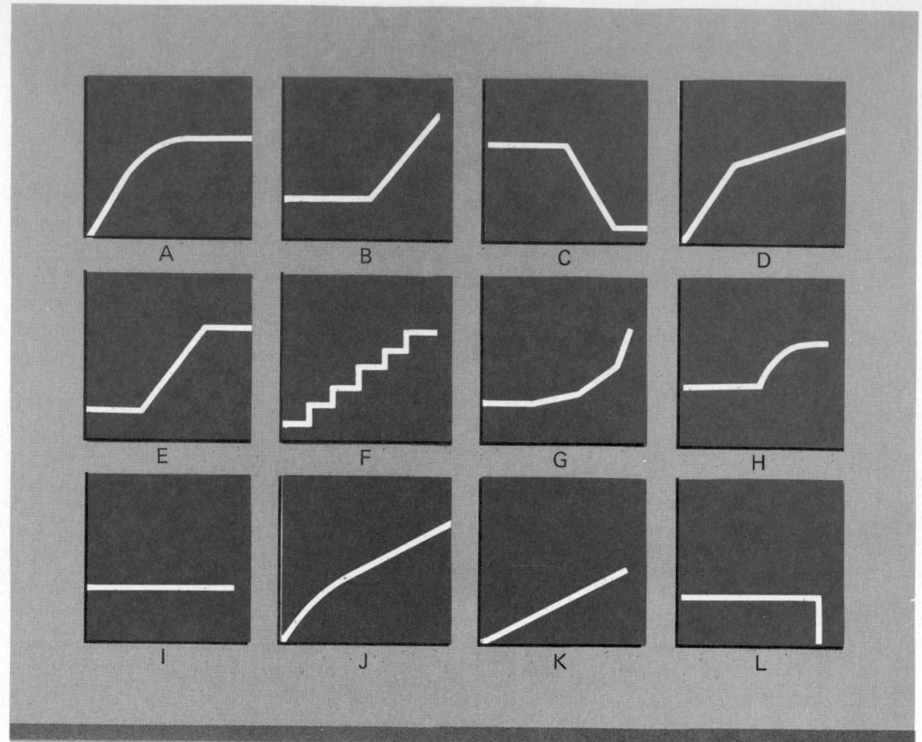

4. Cost of lubricant for machines, where cost per unit decreases with each pound of lubricant used (for example, if one pound is used, the cost is $10; if two pounds are used, the cost is $19.98; if three pounds are used, the cost is $29.94) with a minimum cost per pound of $9.25.
5. Depreciation of equipment, where the amount is computed by the straight-line method. When the depreciation rate was established, it was anticipated that the obsolescence factor would be greater than the wear-and-tear factor.
6. Rent on a factory building donated by the city, where the agreement calls for a fixed-fee payment unless 200,000 man-hours are worked, in which case no rent need be paid.
7. Salaries of repairmen, where one repairman is needed for every 1,000 machine-hours or less (that is, 0 to 1,000 hours requires one repairman, 1,001 to 2,000 hours requires two repairmen, and so forth).
8. Federal unemployment compensation taxes for the year, where labor force is constant in number throughout the year (average annual salary is $6,000 per worker). Maximum salary subject to tax is $4,200 per employee.
9. Cost of raw materials used.
10. Rent on a factory building donated by county, where agreement calls for rent of $100,000 less $1 for each direct-labor hour worked in excess of 200,000 hours, but minimum rental payment of $20,000 must be paid.

9-15 ***Matching graphs with descriptions of cost behavior.*** (D. Green) Given below are a number of charts, each indicating some relationship between cost and another variable. No attempt has been made to draw these charts to any particular scale; the absolute numbers on each axis may be closely or widely spaced.

You are to indicate by number which of the charts best fits each of the situations or items described. Each situation or item is independent of all the others; all factors not stated are assumed to be irrelevant. Only one answer will be counted for any item. Some charts will be used more than once; some may not apply to any of the situations. Note that category 14, "No relationship," is not the same as 15, "Some other pattern."

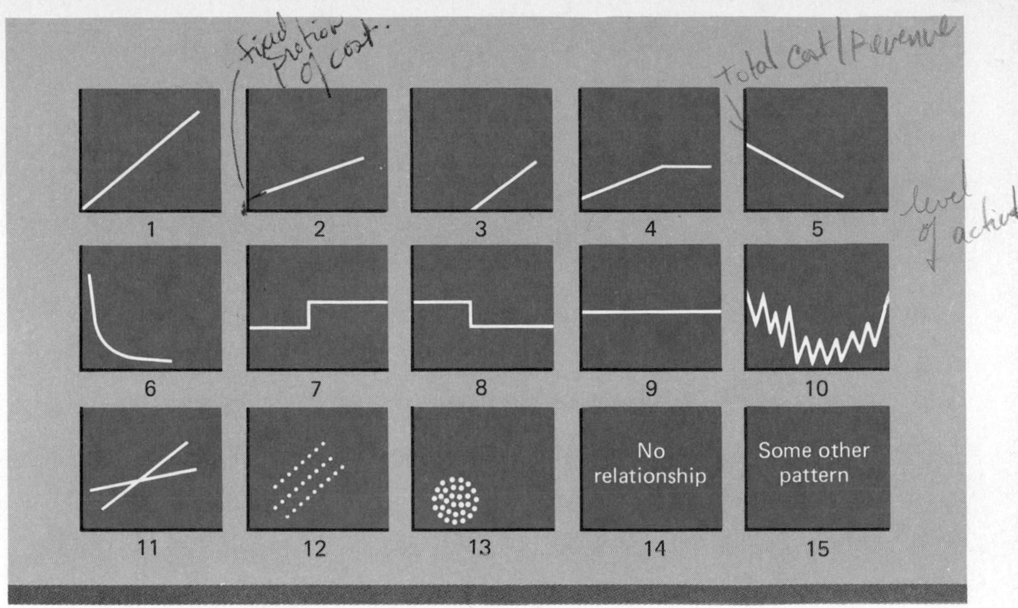

A. Taking the horizontal axis as rate of activity over the year and the vertical axis as *total cost* or *revenue,* indicate the pattern or relationship for each of the following items:
   1. Direct-material cost.
   2. Federal Social Security tax, as legally assessed, per worker, with workers earning over $35,300 per year, which is the maximum subject to tax.
   3. Foremen's salaries.
   4. A breakeven chart.
   5. Total average unit cost.
   6. Mixed costs—for example, electric power *demand charge* plus usage rate.
   7. Average versus marginal cost.
   8. Depreciation of plant, computed on a straight-line, time basis.
   9. Data supporting the use of a variable-cost rate, such as $2 per direct-labor hour.
   10. Vacation pay accrued for all workers in a department or plant.
   11. Data indicating that an indirect-cost rate based on the given activity measure is spurious.
   12. Variable costs *per unit* of output.
   13. Incentive bonus plan, operating only above some level of activity.
   14. Interest charges on money borrowed to finance acquisition of plant, before any payments on principal.

B. Taking the horizontal axis to represent a time series of weeks during a year and the vertical axis as representing *total cost per week,* match the following items with the relationship shown by the charts:
   15. Direct-labor cost under stable production.
   16. Direct materials purchased in small quantities during a period of widely fluctuating prices (inventory held at zero).
   17. Effect of declining production volume over the year.
   18. Result of a shutdown because of vacations, a serious casualty, or complete failure of demand. The shutdown continues to the end of the year.
   19. Underapplied or overapplied factory overhead, taken weekly over the year, when a volume varies widely and the cost rate is assumed to be correct.
   20. Seasonal fluctuation in the use of fuel for heating the plant building over the year.

C. Taking the horizontal axis to represent a time series of weeks or months during a year, but the vertical axis to represent *unit-product cost* as determined by conventional methods, that is, by using indirect-cost rates, match the charts with each of the following items:
   21. Upward revision during the year of the variable indirect-cost rate, because of changes in price, or other factors, expected to be permanent.
   22. Indirect materials acquired for immediate use in small quantities at fluctuating prices.
   23. Unusual repair charges caused by careless operation of the machinery.
   24. A downward revision of the fixed indirect-cost rate because of greater volume than was anticipated; the higher volume is expected to continue over the rest of the year.

9-16 ***Cost behavior and budgets.*** (M. Strecker) The president of Shuz, Inc., called together the vice-presidents in charge of sales and of production. Together they constructed two budgets—one optimistic, one pessimistic. These are shown in columns 1 and 2 below. The actual results are shown in column 3. The company's cost accountant was perplexed as to how to present an analysis. Consequently, he produced variances of actual against both the optimistic projection and the pessimistic projection, columns 4 and 5. Favorable variances are in parentheses.

	(1) OPTIMISTIC	(2) PESSIMISTIC	(3) ACTUAL	(4) OPTIMISTIC VARIANCE	(5) PESSIMISTIC VARIANCE
Units	200,000	75,000	135,000	65,000 U	(60,000)
Sales	$2,000,000	$750,000	$1,350,000	$650,000 U	$(600,000)
Direct material	$ 200,000	$ 75,000	$ 140,000	$ (60,000)	$ 65,000
Direct labor	400,000	150,000	285,000	(115,000)	135,000
Indirect labor	106,000	43,500	72,000	(34,000)	28,500
Maintenance	20,000	20,000	22,000	2,000	2,000
Supplies	28,000	15,500	21,000	(7,000)	5,500
Power	160,000	60,000	108,000	(52,000)	48,000
Heat	50,000	50,000	53,000	3,000	3,000
Light	7,000	4,500	5,900	(1,100)	1,400
Rent	80,000	80,000	80,000	-0-	-0-
Insurance	20,000	13,750	17,000	(3,000)	3,250

The company president is baffled by the analysis. He has asked you for a more understandable performance report. In the columns below, in clear and orderly fashion, prepare a new report. Explain your work to the president. Show computations as needed.

BUDGET ITEM	BUDGET ITEM FORMULA	BUDGET REVISION	ACTUAL PERFORMANCE	VARIANCES
Units			135,000	
Sales			$1,350,000	
Direct materials			$ 140,000	
Direct labor			285,000	
(and so forth)			(and so forth)	

9-17 ***Flexible budget and the special order.*** Although the company had planned for production and sales of 60,000 units per month, results for the first month of this fiscal year showed production of 50,000 units and sales of only 40,000 units. The outlook for the near future makes it doubtful whether additional sales can be made at present prices; indeed, the level of 40,000 units per month seems to be a maximum at the present price of $3.50 per unit. Operating charges for the first month (which agree precisely with the flexible-budget figures) and the budget for 60,000 units of production and sales are as follows:

	MANUFACTURING COSTS LAST MONTH	MASTER BUDGET
Units produced	50,000	60,000
Costs of manufacturing		
Direct materials	$60,000	$72,000
Direct labor	45,000	54,000
Other payroll costs (indirect labor, supervision, payroll taxes, etc.)	12,000	13,200
Power	8,000	9,600
Depreciation and maintenance	2,000	2,000
Miscellaneous	5,000	5,000

	SELLING AND OTHER COSTS LAST MONTH	MASTER BUDGET
Units sold	40,000	60,000
Costs of selling and administration:		
Salesmen's commissions	$ 6,000	$ 9,000
Packing costs	9,000	12,000
Shipping costs	4,000	6,000
Advertising	1,000	1,200
Miscellaneous payrolls (office)	2,000	2,400
Other miscellaneous costs	3,000	3,000

The management of this company is considering an offer from a well-known chain to contract for 10,000 units of this product per month at a price of $3.00 each, terms net, f.o.b. the company's plant. This contract would have no effect upon the company's other sales, although commissions will have to be paid at regular rates (percent of sales dollar) to the company's salesmen on deliveries to the chain. The firm's policy is to carry no finished-goods inventory beyond the 10,000 units now on hand; it schedules its production to fit customer demand. All cost behaviors are continuous and linear.

REQUIRED

From the data given, show your calculations to support or refute the desirability of accepting the offer.

9-18 ***Planned variances, changes in labor mix.*** (CMA) The Lenco Co. employs a standard-cost system as part of its cost-control program. The standard cost per unit is established at the beginning of each year. Standards are not revised during the year for any changes in material or labor inputs or in the manufacturing processes. Any revisions in standards are deferred until the beginning of the next fiscal year. However, in order to recognize such changes in the current year, the company includes planned variances in the monthly budgets prepared after such changes have been introduced.

The following labor standard was set for one of Lenco's products effective July 1, 19_1, the beginning of the fiscal year:

Class I labor	4 hrs.	@ $ 6.00	$24.00
Class II labor	3 hrs.	@ 7.50	22.50
Class V labor	1 hr.	@ 11.50	11.50
Standard labor cost per 100 units			$58.00

The standard was based upon the quality of material that had been used in prior years and what was expected to be available for the 19_1–_2 fiscal year. The labor activity is performed by a team consisting of four persons with Class I skills, three persons with Class II skills, and one person with Class V skills. This is the most economical combination for the company's processing system.

The manufacturing operations occurred as expected during the first five months of the year. The standard costs contributed to effective cost control during this period. However, there were indications that changes in the operations would be required in the last half of the year. The company had received a significant increase in orders for delivery in the spring. There were an inadequate number of skilled workers available to meet the increased production. As a result, the production teams, beginning in January, would be made up of more Class I labor and less Class II labor than the standard required. The teams would consist of six Class I persons, two Class II persons, and one Class V person. This labor team would be less efficient than the normal team. The reorganized teams work more slowly, so that only 90 units are produced in the same time period that 100 units would normally be produced. No raw materials will be lost as a result of the change in the labor mix. Completed units have never been rejected in the final inspection process as a consequence of faulty work; this is expected to continue.

In addition, Lenco was notified by its material supplier that a lower-quality material would be supplied after January 1. One unit of raw material normally is required for each good unit produced. Lenco and its supplier estimated that 5 percent of the units manufactured would be rejected upon final inspection due to defective material. Normally, no units are lost due to defective material.

REQUIRED

1. How much of the lower-quality material must be entered into production in order to produce 42,750 units of good production in January with the new labor teams? Show your calculations.
2. How many hours of each class of labor will be needed to produce 42,750 good units from the material input? Show your calculations.
3. What amount should be included in the January budget for the planned labor variance due to the labor team and material changes? What amount of this planned labor variance can be associated with (1) the material change and (2) the team change? Show your calculations. *Hint:* Planned or budgeted variances are discussed on page 181.

9-19 ***Guaranteed minimum wages and cost behavior patterns.*** (Prepared by the author and adapted for use in a CPA examination). The Lavin Company had a contract with a labor union that guaranteed a minimum wage of $2,000 payable monthly to direct laborers with at least 12 years' service. One hundred workers currently qualified for such coverage. All direct-labor employees are paid $20 per hour.

The budget for 19_1 was based on the usage of 400,000 hours of direct labor, a total of $8,000,000. Of this amount, $2,400,000 (100 workers × $2,000 × 12 months) was regarded as fixed.

Data on performance for the first three months of 19_1 follow:

	JANUARY	FEBRUARY	MARCH
Direct-labor hours actually worked	22,000	32,000	42,000
Standard direct-labor hours allowed*	22,000	32,000	42,000
Direct-labor costs budgeted	$508,000	$648,000	$788,000
Direct-labor costs incurred	440,000	640,000	840,000
Variance (U = unfavorable; F = favorable)	68,000 F	8,000 F	52,000 U

**Note that perfect efficiency is being assumed.*

The factory manager was perplexed by the results, which showed favorable variances when production was low and unfavorable variances when production was high. He felt that his control over labor costs was consistently good.

REQUIRED

1. Why did the variances arise? Use amounts and diagrams, as necessary, to explain.
2. Assume that only 5,000 standard and actual hours were utilized in a given month and that all of the most senior workers were used. Does this direct-labor budget provide a basis for evaluating direct-labor performance? What variances would arise under the approach used in requirement 1? What variances would arise under the approach you recommend?
3. Suppose that 5,500 actual hours of input were used, but that only 5,000 standard hours were allowed for the work accomplished. What variances would arise under the approach used in requirement 1? Under the approach you recommend?

9-20 ***Budgeting indirect labor; mixed cost.*** A certain foreign unionized company hires indirect laborers to support direct laborers by performing a variety of unskilled tasks, such as machine cleanup and material handling and trucking. The direct laborers usually run two machines simultaneously. The relationships that have prevailed in the past three years are as follows:

	19_6			19_7		
	direct labor	**machine-hours**	**auxiliary labor**	**direct labor**	**machine-hours**	**auxiliary labor**
First quarter	$150,000	100,000	$20,000	$162,000	90,000	$22,800
Second quarter	182,000	120,000	22,000	183,000	100,000	24,000
Third quarter	163,000	110,000	21,000	200,000	110,000	25,200
Fourth quarter	158,000	105,000	20,500	205,000	115,000	25,800

	19_8		
	direct labor	**machine-hours**	**auxiliary labor**
First quarter	$238,000	120,000	$29,040
Second quarter	199,000	100,000	26,400
Third quarter	206,000	105,000	27,060
Fourth quarter	189,000	95,000	25,740

The company is installing a budgetary system. You have been asked to prepare an estimate of the quarterly costs of auxiliary labor for 19_9, given the data above and the following. The union contract for auxiliary labor has not been negotiated for 19_9 as yet.

	19_9	
	direct labor	**machine-hours**
First quarter	$231,000	110,000
Second quarter	189,000	90,000
Third quarter	199,500	95,000
Fourth quarter	210,000	100,000

Thoroughly justify your estimate with computations and words that can be understood by the president, a nasty sort who despises technical jargon but admires clear reasoning.

9-21 ***Operation costing and setup costs.*** Variances may be computed in various levels of detail. The following is an excerpt from a real company's cost accounting manual:

> Setup costs as an element of the standard product costs are to be separated from the other costs. Standard setup times are to be established for each part and a standard setup cost based on applicable cost rates for labor and overhead calculated.
>
> Recognizing setup costs on a per-piece basis requires a standard lot size (the number of pieces that are expected to run through the machine before the setup is changed). The standard lot sizes are to be established by the production control department. The standard setup cost per piece will be calculated by dividing the standard lot size into the applicable standard setup costs.
>
> Production runs varying from the standard lot size will create a lot size variance, as follows:
>
> $$\textbf{Lot size variance} = \textbf{Standard setup cost} \times \left(\frac{\textbf{Actual run size} - \textbf{Standard lot size}}{\textbf{Standard lot size}}\right)$$
>
> Lot size variance is to be calculated only in the primary cost centers. If an alternating routing is used, lot size variance will not be calculated but will create an alternate routing variance. The following example illustrates the lot size variance calculation.

Part number:	0109306
Actual run size:	500 pieces
Standard lot size:	1,000 pieces

COST CENTER	OPERATION DESCRIPTION	STANDARD DIRECT-LABOR HOURS ALLOWED PER SETUP	STANDARD RATES PER SETUP HOUR			STANDARD OPERATION COST PER PIECE		
			direct labor	**factory burden**	**total**	**direct labor**	**factory burden**	**total**
411	MAM Lathe	24.00	$20.88	$19.12	$40.00	$.125	$.115	$.24

REQUIRED

Compute the lot size variance. Construct an appropriate journal entry that would identify the lot size variance. *Hint:* Setup costs are discussed on page 185.

9-22 ***Make or buy, learning curve.*** (CMA) The Xyon Company has purchased 80,000 pumps annually from Kobec Inc. The price has increased each year and reached $68.00 per unit last year. Because the purchase price has increased significantly, Xyon management has asked that an estimate be made of the cost to manufacture it in its own facilities. Xyon's products consist of stamping and castings. The company has had little experience with products requiring assembly.

The engineering, manufacturing, and accounting departments have prepared a report for management which included the estimate shown below for an assembly run of 10,000 units. Additional production employees would be hired to manufacture the subassembly. However, no additional equipment, space, or supervision would be needed.

The report states that total costs for 10,000 units are estimated at $957,000, or $95.70 a unit. The current purchase price is $68.00 a unit, so the report recommends a continued purchase of the product.

Components (outside purchases)	$120,000
Assembly labor*	300,000
Factory overhead†	450,000
General and administrative overhead‡	87,000
Total Costs	$957,000

**Assembly labor consists of hourly production workers.*

†Factory overhead is applied to products on a direct-labor dollar basis. Variable overhead costs vary closely with direct-labor dollars.

Fixed overhead	*50% of direct-labor dollars*
Variable overhead	*100% of direct-labor dollars*
Factory overhead rate	*150% of direct-labor dollars*

‡General and administrative overhead is applied at 10 percent of the total cost of material (or components), assembly labor, and factory overhead.

REQUIRED

1. Was the analysis prepared by the engineering, manufacturing, and accounting departments of Xyon Company and the recommendation to continue purchasing the pumps which followed from the analysis correct? Explain your answer and include any supportive calculations you consider necessary.
2. Assume Xyon Company could experience labor cost improvements on the pump assembly consistent with an 80 percent learning curve. An assembly run of 10,000 units represents the initial lot or batch for measurement purposes. Should Xyon produce the 80,000 pumps in this situation? Explain your answer.

9-23 ***Learning curve and cost estimation.*** The Smyth Company, a subcontractor for the aircraft and missile industry, has been asked to bid on a prospective contract for 900 units of a precision missile part. Two months ago, the Smyth Company had produced 300 of these parts at the following total costs:

Direct materials	$ 12,000
Direct labor (6,000 hours @ $20.00)	120,000
Tooling cost*	3,000
Variable overhead†	15,000
Other overhead‡	30,000
Total costs	$180,000

**Tooling can be reused, even though all of its cost was assigned to the original order of 300 parts.*

†Variable-overhead incurrence is directly affected by direct-labor hours.

‡Other overhead is assigned at a flat rate of 25 percent of direct-labor cost for purposes of bidding on contracts.

The Smyth Company uses an 80 percent learning curve as a basis for forecasting what pertinent costs should be.

REQUIRED | Prepare a prediction of the total expected costs for bidding on a contract of 900 units.

9-24 ***Learning curve, cost predictions, and pricing.*** The Boeheed Corporation is a large, multidivision company with annual sales in excess of one billion dollars. One of Boeheed's divisions, the Spriggs Division, manufactures aircraft. The division is currently developing a new type of aircraft that will determine the success of the division for the next few years.

Spriggs has already spent $200 million on developing and testing the new technology that the aircraft will utilize. It is also constructing a new $20 million specialized-production facility, which would become totally obsolete after production of the planes was completed. The engineering department has predicted that an additional $20 million will have to be spent on further development and testing before the aircraft is ready for production. Boeheed's accounting policy was to capitalize all development and equipment costs until production actually started.

The division is now attempting to determine a price for the aircraft. A price is necessary now because of the long production-schedule lead time of about twelve months, which results from the limited production capacity of ten aircraft per month.

Orders will be made on the basis of this established price, even though deliveries will not be made for one or two years.

The marketing department has forecast that demand for the aircraft will range between 200 and 300 units. The actual demand will be determined by both the ultimate aircraft characteristics and, more important, the aircraft price.

The division has made detailed predictions of the aircraft's production costs. These predictions have proven to be extremely accurate on previous projects of this type. All the aircraft parts requirements are subcontracted for fabrication. Spriggs has already contracted for parts for 200 aircraft, which will cost $3 million per aircraft. These contracts have a provision for parts for an additional 100 aircraft but at a 10 percent decrease in cost per aircraft.

Direct labor is the most significant element of the production costs. Labor costs are substantial in an absolute sense. However, a form of "learning curve" is applicable to new aircraft based on ten-unit production lots. There are many varieties of learning curves. In this case, the labor costs are properly calculated using the equation $80X^{-.322}$:

LOT X	$80X^{-.322}$	LOT X	$80X^{-.322}$	LOT X	$80X^{-.322}$
1	80.00	11	36.96	21	30.01
2	64.00	12	35.94	22	29.57
3	56.17	13	35.03	23	29.15
4	51.20	14	34.20	24	28.75
5	47.65	15	33.45	25	28.38*
6	44.93	16	32.76	26	28.02
7	42.76	17	32.13	27	27.68
8	40.95	18	31.54	28	27.36
9	39.44	19	31.00	29	27.05
10	38.12	20	30.49	30	26.76†
	505.22		333.50		282.73

**145.86 = sum of lots 21–25.* *†136.87 = sum of lots 26–30.*

For example, the labor costs of Lot 1 are $80 million, or $8 million per plane. The cumulative labor costs for Lots 1 and 2 are $80 million + $64 million = $144 million, or $7.2 million per each of twenty planes.

The general manager and the controller use these data as a basis for predicting costs and setting unit selling prices for the aircraft.

Combined applicable general, administrative, and indirect production costs are estimated at $50 million annually. Historically, these costs have been applied on the basis of direct-labor costs.

They decided that the fixed costs applicable to the program that must be recovered included $240 million plus whatever indirect production costs and general and administrative costs were incurred. Their prediction of the latter was $100 million if 200 units were produced and sold (2 years × $50 million), and $150 million if 300 units were produced and sold (3 years × $50 million).

REQUIRED

1. What price must be set to break even, assuming 200 units are sold? Assuming 300 units are sold?
2. Suppose that Spriggs sets a price of $8.6 million. This price has produced orders for 250 planes. The marketing department now reports that a potential new customer will purchase 50 planes, but only if the price is $8.1 million or less. This price reduction would have to be made retroactive and applied to all customers. Should Spriggs accept the new order?

9-25 ***Standards in hospital.*** Some management consultants have developed standards for the clerical work force in a large local hospital. Some estimates of overhead behavior also were developed. The standard variable-overhead rate per billing in the billing department was $.12. Five bills per hour is regarded as standard productivity per billing clerk. The actual total overhead incurred was $97,000, of which $70,000 was fixed. There were no variances for fixed overhead. The variable-overhead spending variance was $3,000, favorable. The variable-overhead budget variance was $600, favorable. Compute (1) variable-overhead efficiency variance, (2) actual hours of input, and (3) standard hours allowed for output achieved.

9-26 ***Nonlinear costs.*** See the preceding problem. Suppose that cost studies had developed the following approximation for relating overhead to labor hours (L):

$$\textbf{Total overhead} = \$68{,}000 + \$.40L + \$30\sqrt{L}$$

If this cost function was used as a flexible-budget formula (instead of the linear budget used in the preceding problem), what would be the efficiency variance in this case? (Round your square root to the nearest hour.)

9-27 ***Reformulating a performance report.*** The Touche Manufacturing Company produces and sells instruments for the aircraft industry. Material and labor standards and overhead budgets have been developed for each of the departments. The assembly department budget for 19_4 appears in Exhibit 9-10.

Monthly reports are prepared comparing actual department costs with budgeted department costs. The June report for the assembly department is shown in Exhibit 9-11.

"You're trying to tell me I spent too much," the department foreman shouted when he saw the report, "and I deny it! I've got control over my costs. Look at Fringe Benefits. How can I spend too much? It's a fixed percent of the wages. And direct-labor wages are set by the union contract, so the only way I can spend too much is to work overtime. There were 320 hours of overtime, but that only costs $800, not $2,300.

"I'm being charged for costs I can't control," he complained again. "You know those rush orders Sales keeps bringing us? When we complain we don't have time to do them, they argue that we will be responsible for losing business. So we do them. And they run up the costs.

"There were two special orders this month. One was for #720 thermostats, and the other for #4 altimeters. We usually do up to 1,000 thermostats at a time, and we're allowed 1,100 hours. That 1,100 includes 20 hours of setup time and 20 hours of tear-down time. We need that much time no matter how many we do. They wanted only 500 thermostats. I had to spend 590 hours to complete it and only 50 hours were overtime.

"We usually do 1,000 altimeters and have 1,500 hours[5] to complete them, including 30 hours each of setup time and tear-down time. They wanted 400 altimeters, and it took us 636 hours to do them. We had to work 40 hours overtime on that one. Then, we wasted another 40 hours sitting around waiting for materials that Purchasing should have had in the plant. And that preventive maintenance didn't prevent one of the machines from breaking down. We sat around for 100 hours waiting for that to be fixed.

EXHIBIT 9-10

Touche Manufacturing Company Assembly Department 19_4 Conversion-Cost Budget

Expected Volume—40,000 Direct-Labor Hours

	FIXED COSTS	VARIABLE COSTS	TOTAL COSTS	VARIABLE RATE PER STANDARD DIRECT-LABOR DOLLAR
Standard direct-labor cost	$ —	$200,000	$200,000	—
Overhead:				
Indirect labor	$24,000	$ 32,000	$ 56,000	.160
Supplies	1,800	6,000	7,800	.030
Tools	5,400	5,200	10,600	.026
Power	4,800	8,000	12,800	.040
Maintenance	13,200	15,000	28,200	.075
Fringe benefits	12,000	32,000	44,000	.160
Scrap	—	24,000	24,000	.120
Depreciation and taxes	36,000	—	36,000	—
Total overhead	$97,200	$122,200	$219,400	.611
Total conversion costs	$97,200	$322,200	$419,400	

EXHIBIT 9-11

Touche Manufacturing Company Assembly Department Performance

June, 19_4

	BUDGET	ACTUAL	VARIANCE: FAVORABLE (UNFAVORABLE)
Standard direct-labor cost	$15,500	$17,800*	$(2,300)
Overhead:			
Indirect labor	$ 4,480†	$ 4,735	$ (255)
Supplies	615	660	(45)
Tools	853	904	(51)
Power	1,020	1,087	(67)
Maintenance	2,263	2,382	(119)
Fringe benefits	3,480	3,848	(368)
Scrap	1,860	2,042	(182)
Depreciation and taxes	3,000	3,000	—
Total overhead	$17,571	$18,658	$(1,087)
Total conversion costs	$33,071	$36,458	$(3,387)

**There were no deviations from standard labor rates.*

†The basic cost behavior pattern is revealed in Exhibit 9-10: $2,000 per month + .16($15,500) = $4,480.

[5]Therefore apparently the original allowed hours included in the budget in Exhibit 9-11 for the smaller runs were 110% × 500 and 150% × 400, respectively.

"How do you expect me to keep my costs down when all of this is going on? Just tell me that!"

The production manager told the controller about the foreman's complaint and asked for a different report, which would be more meaningful to the foreman.

REQUIRED

1. Prepare the revised report to show how the foreman is really doing. Use the June 19_4 data. (*Hint:* One way to approach a solution to requirement 1 would be to expand Exhibit 9-11 by adding two rows. Insert a row at the top for "Direct-labor hours." Change the line "Standard direct-labor cost" to "Standard direct-labor cost of hours above." Add another row labeled "Overtime premium," removing that amount from the total now in the "Standard direct-labor cost" row. Then add seven columns with the overall label "Analysis of Variances," including two columns for special orders, two for unavoidable wait time, one for "Balance to Be Explained," one for spending, and one for efficiency. This problem is more detailed than any in this chapter, but careful study will pay off in added understanding of standards and budgets.)
2. For which of these costs can the foreman really be held accountable? Comment.

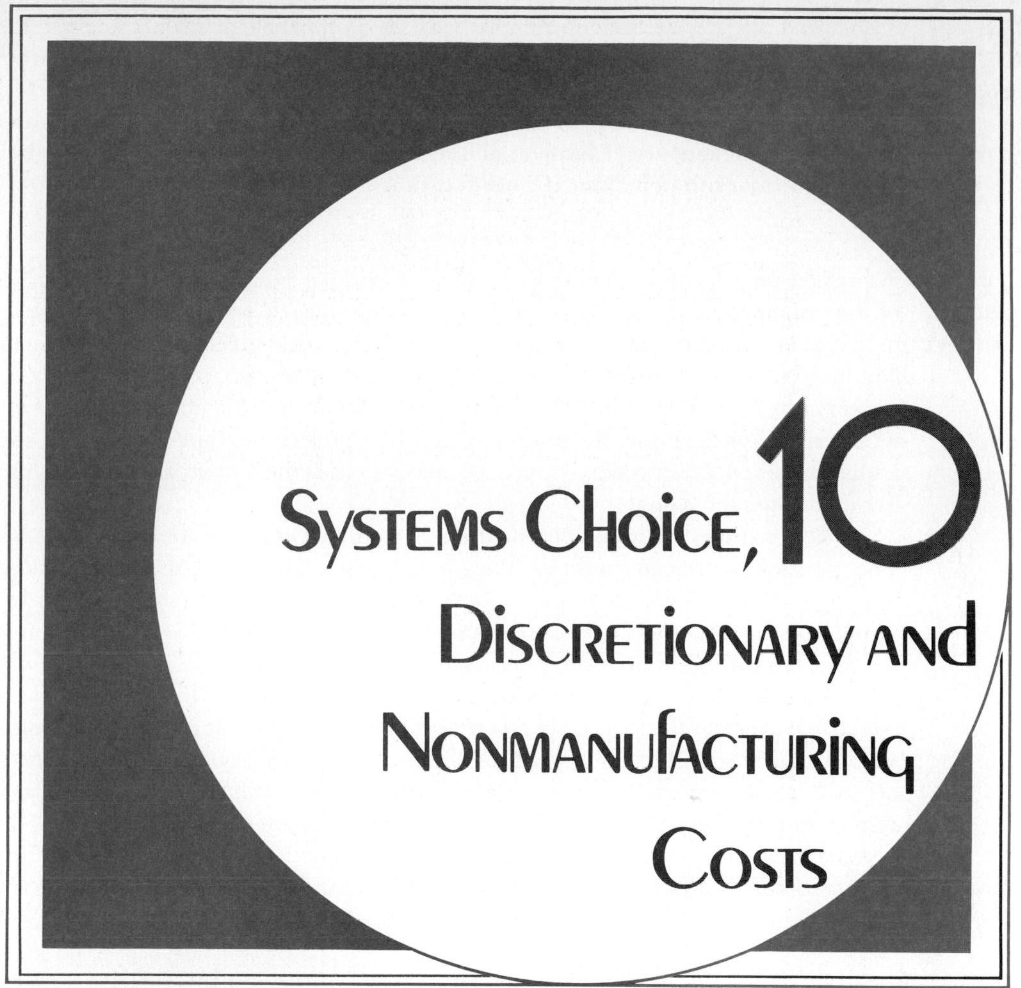

10 Systems Choice, Discretionary and Nonmanufacturing Costs

This chapter begins with an overview of how management control systems should be chosen. Then it compares various budgetary techniques, including zero-base budgeting. Special attention is given to discretionary and nonmanufacturing costs, particularly those costs that are significant in service industries and not-for-profit organizations.

The behavioral problems raised in this chapter are absolutely central to cost or management accounting. The choice of a particular system is not made in the abstract. Sooner or later, behavioral problems must be identified and confronted, although there are no pat answers or even a systematic method for solving the problems.

The first section, Criteria for Judging Systems, suggests an approach that has proven useful to professional accountants and operating executives. It provides a perspective that is applicable to all forms of control systems and all types of activities. Management control systems are not confined solely to factory activities. This section should be reviewed when Chapters 19 and 20 are studied.

Criteria for judging systems

Management control systems are often judged using factors such as characteristics of data processing and vulnerability to fraud. However, a broader focus is preferable. **Systems exist primarily to improve the collective decisions within an organization. Because decisions entail human behavior, our emphasis rightly belongs on human rather than technical considerations.**

cost, congruence, effort

What is a useful starting point for judging a control system? **Obtain a specification of top management's goals for the organization as a whole.** To keep our focus manageable, assume that organizational goals are either given or can be determined. An observer may disagree with the goals specified by top management, but a control system should be judged in light of how well it facilitates the achievement of a given set of goals. For example, the main goal might be maximization of short-run income, a goal regarded as unworthy by many; nevertheless, the system should be appraised in relation to such a goal.

The primary criterion for judging System A versus System B is cost-benefit. That is, systems are commodities. They cost money. They benefit an organization by helping collective decision making. Suppose Systems A and B cost approximately the same. Top managers will buy System A if it is more likely than System B to engender a more desirable set of operating decisions.

To make the primary criterion more concrete, consider the secondary criteria: goal congruence and effort. **Goal congruence is the alignment of organizational goals with the personal and group goals of subordinates and superiors.** Other terms may be used to denote congruence, such as *alignment, coordination,* and *synchronization.* A system can also be judged by how well it promotes effort. **Managerial effort** is defined here as exertion toward a goal. Effort is not confined to its common meaning of a worker producing faster; it embraces all conscientious actions (such as watching or waiting) that result in the optimal relationships of inputs to outputs.

motivation, congruence, effort

Considered together, congruence and effort are really subparts of **motivation:**

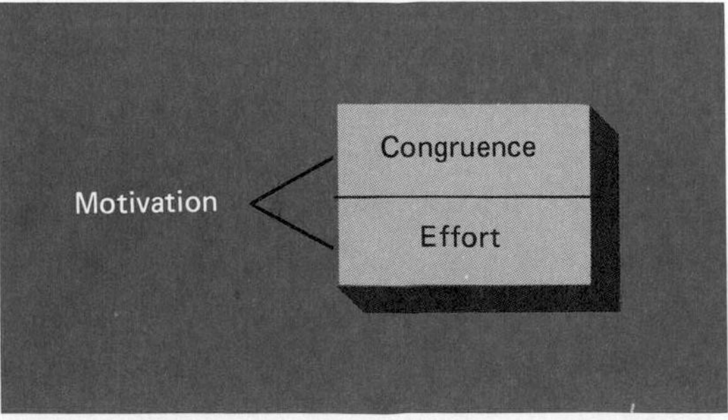

Motivation is the desire for a selected goal (the congruence aspect) together with the resulting drive or pursuit (the effort aspect) toward that goal.

Congruence and effort are often reinforcing aspects of motivation, but each can exist without the other. Thus, a manager can share an organization goal of reaching a target sales level or a product quality level. But the manager may pursue such goals in an unenthusiastic way. Similarly, a manager may pursue a personal goal, such as playing golf instead of working, with great effort that is incongruent.

In sum, the major criterion is cost-benefit. To apply that criterion, the motivational effects of System A versus System B deserve front and center attention. Thus, control systems may have a host of assorted measurements and reports; but to judge how well they are really working, the focus must be on motivation. Therefore, the task of the systems designer is more ill-structured, more complex, and more affected by human aspects than many people believe. **There is a strong link between the seemingly foreign ideas of motivation and the design of accounting systems, even though the relationship may initially appear farfetched.**

three types of control

Various authors[1] have identified three major types of control: **organization, informal group, and individual.** These are compared in Exhibit 10-1.

The organization controls usually consist of formal rules and standard operating procedures plus the informal procedures that are also communicated throughout the organization. The informal group controls "emerge from the shared values and the mutual commitments of members of a group to one another."[2] Individual controls are described in the next section.

These three types of controls are obviously interdependent. The challenge to accountants and managers is to (a) recognize their existence, (b) assess their potential conflicts, and (c) aim at increasing the acceptance of organization controls by the affected groups and individuals. For example, the organization controls may be designed to reward increases in productivity, but they may have little influence if the employees have developed their own group controls that restrict productivity improvements. The ultimate influence of budgets and performance measurements depends on how they affect and, in turn, are affected by the informal group controls and individual controls of managers and employees.[3] At this stage, the dimensions of the problem

EXHIBIT 10-1

Three Types of Interdependent Control

				INCENTIVES	
TYPE	GOALS	PERFORMANCE CRITERIA	FEEDBACK	**rewards or reinforcements**	**punishments or sanctions**
Organization	Profits, share of market, quality of service	Budgets, standard costs, past performance	Quantitative variances	Commendation, promotions, salary raises	Condemnation, dismissal, salary cuts
Informal group	Mutual commitment, group ideals	Group norms	Deviant behavior	Peer approval, membership, leadership	Kidding, hostility, ostracism
Individual	Personal goals aspirations	Expectations, interim targets	Reaching or missing targets	Self-satisfaction, elation	Disappointment, self-hatred

SOURCE: *Adapted from G. W. Dalton and P. R. Lawrence, eds.,* Motivation and Control in Organizations *(Homewood, Ill.: Richard D. Irwin, 1971), p. 15.*

[1] G. W. Dalton and P. R. Lawrence, eds., *Motivation and Control in Organizations* (Homewood, Ill.: Richard D. Irwin, 1971), pp. 1–35; and A. Hopwood, *Accounting and Human Behavior* (Englewood Cliffs, N.J.: Prentice-Hall, 1976), pp. 21–37.

[2] Hopwood, op. cit., p. 30.

[3] Ibid., pp. 35 and 37.

are reasonably clear, but no pat answers or sweeping generalizations are available.

system goals and individual goals

Clearly, it is not enough for the control system simply to specify subgoals so that they harmonize with top-management goals. Ideally, management should also design the system to lead the individual managers toward *acceptance* of those subgoals as their own personal goals. For example, how important is conformance to a budget prediction? If conformance is accepted by the manager as being important, and the accounting feedback is regarded as the most important source of information regarding his or her own appraisal of self-worth (for example, it says, "I am competent"), then the budget will be a crucial part of the control system.

Of course the accounting system is only one of many control systems that influence an individual's behavior. Society as a whole can be viewed as a control system, and various institutions can impinge on an individual's values and reactions. For example, a person can be affected by family, religion, profession, company, department, and so forth. This point may be obvious, but it is not trivial.

importance of informal systems

Even if personal and group goals agree with organization goals, the formal management control system may be dominated by an informal system. There is widespread use of little black books and special memorandums. In addition, many executives, including top managers, rely on rules of thumb and accumulated experience rather than on the output of formal systems such as accounting reports. This method often proves satisfactory because such executives are evaluating the information wisely and making decisions that keep their companies competitive.

As companies grow, however, managers become more dependent on formal rather than informal information systems. Professor Richard Vancil has observed that the formal system provides a crutch for the orderly succession of management. Large companies, with mobile executives who typically move frequently, must have such a system; after all, most managers do not have thirty years of experience on which to base their decisions. The introduction of formal decision models in business is an example of the response to the need for more crutches. For instance, the blending of various ingredients in sausage was once the task of some wise individual with a good feel for the critical variables. Now the blending decision is made by a computer program that resulted from the formalization of a previously informal process.

A prime challenge for systems designers is to discover whether some or all of the informal information system is leading to successful decisions. If so, the designer should attempt to formalize those parts of the informal system. For example, the formal system should aim at incorporating the key numbers or events that a manager may be keeping informally. Consider the pricing decision. The data compiled by the formal system may be ignored by the manager when setting prices because his or her experience and readings of industry or economic data are the keys to decisions. The designer should then try to crystallize the manager's decision model explicitly, so that the critical data may be supplied by the formal system. In this way, the formal system can become the key information system, can engender sincere management support, and can ease the tasks of management succession as managers are promoted or transferred. Hence, collective decisions are likely to be improved.

behavior and risk congruence

Many designers of systems complain that top managements are reluctant to identify a set of organizational goals beyond an overall earnings goal. Such designers prefer to work in terms of **behavior congruence,** concentrating on questions to the superior, such as the following: "In various sets of operating situations, how do you want your subordinates to behave? What actions do you want the subordinate to take? Will System A be more prone to induce the preferred behaviors?"[4]

Risk congruence is the sharing of the same attitudes toward risk taking on the part of superior and subordinates. It is akin to behavior congruence because in the face of uncertainty, subordinates essentially are supposed to make the same decisions as those desired by their superiors.[5]

Clearly, the bearing of risk changes behavior. For instance, Professor Joel Demski has asked, Do you drive more cautiously if your auto insurance expired yesterday and you suddenly realize you forgot to pay your annual premium? Have you ever checked the oil level in a rented car? A marketing consultant has commented, "Marketers are afraid to stick their necks out . . . and for good reason. They get fired a lot."

The entire subject of the sharing of risk is receiving considerable attention from academic researchers in accounting and economics. These researchers tend to perceive the design of management control systems to be largely a problem of how risks should be assigned between superiors (principals) and subordinates (agents).[6] To illustrate, the executive committee of a national public accounting firm might decide that its best long-run interests call for aggressively seeking banking industry clients. Suppose a Milwaukee bank seeks competitive bids for its audit. A local managing partner of the accounting firm may agree with the goal but may be unwilling to exert much effort. He or she may not bid sufficiently low because getting the client at a low price will hurt the office's short-run profits. In short, the partner is too "risk-averse" in the minds of top management, principally because the management control system fails to encourage risk taking.

The top management of the accounting firm (in New York) might encourage its Milwaukee partner to enter a low bid by promising "insurance" against any resulting bad performance. For instance, a bookkeeping entry might award the Milwaukee office a subsidy of full billing rates even though the actual billing rates to the client are much less. **This procedure shifts risk from the subordinate to the superior.** Indeed, the costs of subsidies could be accumulated for later comparison with the long-range profits from attaining bank clients. The key in design is assigning risks. That is, subunit performance is measured so that the managers accept or avoid the risks as desired by top management.

---

[4]Thomas Dyckman, "A Critique" in *Management Accounting and Control,* Proceedings of Beyer Symposium (Madison: University of Wisconsin, School of Business, 1975), p. 40. Also see Arthur Thomas, *A Behavioural Analysis of Joint-Cost Allocation and Transfer Pricing* (Urbana, Ill.' Stipes Publishing Co., 1980), p. 11.

[5]Hiroyuki Itami, "Evaluation Measures and Goal Congruence under Uncertainty," *Journal of Accounting Research,* 13, No. 1 (Spring 1975), 73–96.

[6]Milton Harris and Artur Raviv, "Some Results on Incentive Contracts with Applications to Education and Employment, Health Insurance, and Law Enforcement," *American Economic Review,* March 1978, pp. 20–30; and Joel S. Demski and Gerald A. Feltham, "Economic Incentives in Budgetary Control Systems," *Accounting Review,* April 1978, pp. 336–59.

extrinsic and intrinsic motivation

Congruence is only one aspect of motivation; the other is effort. Typically, efforts are spurred if a connection can be drawn between the efforts and the rewards.

Motivation may be extrinsic or intrinsic. The systems designer must realize that motivation to engage in a particular behavior is determined by

1. People's expectations or beliefs about probable outcomes:
   Effort → Performance (evaluation)
2. The attractiveness assigned to those outcomes by people as a result of the outcomes' ability to satisfy their needs:
   Performance (evaluation) → Rewards

There are two sets of outcomes, that from performance and that from rewards. **Extrinsic motivation** is the effect of extrinsic rewards (e.g., salary increase, bonus) on behavior. **Intrinsic motivation** is the effect of intrinsic rewards (e.g., self-satisfaction). *Extrinsic motivation is small if the individual cannot see the connection between performance and rewards.* Intrinsic motivation is given to an individual by himself or herself; it is the satisfaction of a job well done or of an excellent golf shot. "Organizations can probably best assure that valued outcomes are tied to performance by first determining which rewards are important and then tying them to performance."[7]

There is no single reward plan (e.g., bonus plan) that meets all the criteria for being a good extrinsic motivator. Moreover, organizations have little control over how important different rewards are to different individuals (e.g., some people may not be motivated by money). Nevertheless, organizations also determine the nature of the relationships of Effort → Performance and Performance → Rewards.

general guidelines

A favorite pastime of students, professors, accountants, and managers regarding management control systems is faultfinding. But the heart of judging a system is not in assessing its degree of imperfection. The central questions usually is, **How can the existing system, with all its imperfections, be improved?** A system exists to help managers in their collective making of decisions in organizations. **Using a cost-benefit philosophy, top managers should predict how System A will affect the collective actions of managers in comparison with System B. To make such predictions, managers must be conscious of the likely motivational effects (goal congruence and managerial effort) of systems.**

Many influential variables, such as organizational structure and management style, affect a system. Hence, the most desirable system highly depends on the *specific organization.* What is good for Organization X may be bad for Organization Y.

The influential variables are dynamic. Therefore, many aspects of a system should be changed through *time.* What is good in 1982 may be bad in 1987.

Chapters 19 and 20 contain additional discussions of how influential variables can affect the choice of management control systems.

design choices

The choices in designing the system are almost limitless. A useful classification follows:

1. *Responsibility centers.* What subparts of the organization will be basic reporting units? Should they be cost centers? Profit centers? Some other type of unit of accountability?

---

[7]E. Lawler and J. Rhode, *Information and Control in Organizations* (Pacific Palisades, Calif.: Goodyear, 1976), p. 64.

2. *Performance evaluation.*

a. What general measures should be used to represent organization goals? Net income? Rate of return on investment? Sales? There may be several of these measures capturing several subgoals. For example, there may be measures of defective work or share of the market.

b. How should the measures be defined? What is net income? What is investment? What is defective work? What is share of the market? Should measures of managers' performance be distinguished from the performance of a segment as an economic investment?

c. How should the measures be quantified? Historical cost? Replacement cost? Cost allocations? Transfer prices?

d. What standards or expectations should be used? Differ by type of activity? Tight or loose?

e. What timing and form of feedback is desirable? Who should get reports? When? In what format? Summarized or detailed?

3. *Rewards.* Psychologists and others have depicted the following relationships:

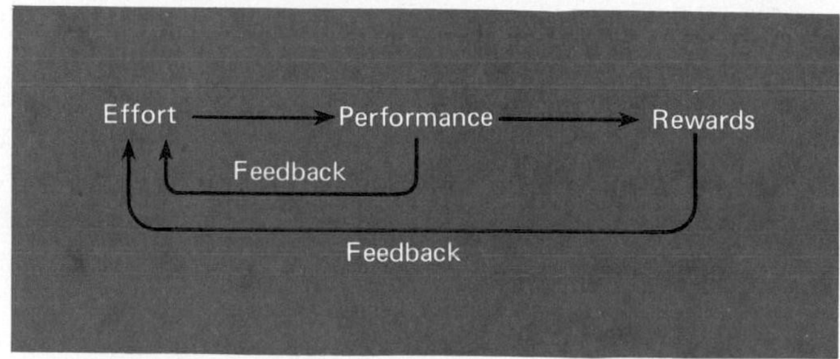

Research reveals a basic principle that is simple and important: Individuals are motivated to perform in a way that leads to rewards. Managers tend to concentrate their efforts in areas where their performance *is measured* and where their performance influences their rewards. Rewards take both pecuniary and nonpecuniary forms: bonuses, promotion, praise, pay raises, fancy offices, self-satisfaction, and so forth. (There are also punishments. For our purposes, punishments are negative rewards.)

Research shows that the more objective the measures of performance, the more likely the managers will provide effort. That is why accounting systems are important. They provide relatively objective evaluations of performance. Research also shows that unless individuals feel that their behavior influences the performance measure, they will not see the connection between performance and rewards.[8]

Committed, engineered, and discretionary costs

Equipped with the general guidelines of cost-benefit, congruence, and effort, management can make intelligent choices among systems. We now explore some major alternatives for exercising control.

The first column in the table on the next page has three cost categories that highlight management's approaches to control:

[8]For a summary of this research, see Lawler and Rhode, op. cit., especially Chaps. 4 and 5.

TYPE OF COST	HORIZON FOR PLANNING AND FEEDBACK	MAJOR ACCOUNTING TECHNIQUES FOR CONTROL
1. Committed	Longest	Capital expenditure budgets
2. Engineered	Short	Flexible budgets and standards
3. Discretionary	Longer	Negotiated static budgets

committed costs

Committed costs are those fixed costs that arise from having property, plant, equipment, and a basic organization. The capital expenditure budget is the principal accounting technique for control. The planning horizon is long, as is the feedback time. Examples of such costs are depreciation, property taxes, insurance, and long-term lease rentals. The uncertainty about many of the accompanying predictions is high, and the magnitudes are large. Therefore, much attention has been devoted to using formal decision models (such as discounted cash flow, which is discussed in Chapter 12) to assist managers' choices. Committed costs are relatively difficult to influence by short-run actions. These costs are affected primarily by long-run sales forecasts that, in turn, indicate the long-run capacity targets. Hence, careful long-range planning rather than day-to-day control is the key to managing committed costs.

The behavior of committed fixed costs may best be viewed by assuming a zero volume of activity in an organization that fully expects to resume normal activity (for example, during a strike or a shortage of materials that forces a complete shutdown of activity). **The committed fixed costs are all those organization and plant costs that continue to be incurred and that cannot be reduced without injuring the organization's competence to meet long-range goals.** Committed fixed costs are the least responsive of the fixed costs, because they tend to be less affected by month-to-month and year-to-year decisions.

In planning, the focus is on the impact of these costs over a number of years. Such planning usually requires tailoring the capacity to future demand for the organization's products in the most economical manner. For example, should the store size be 50,000 square feet, or 80,000, or 100,000? Should the gasoline station have one, or two, or more bays for servicing automobiles? Such decisions usually involve selecting the point of optimal trade-off between present and future operating costs. That is, constructing excess capacity now may save costs in the long run, because construction costs per square foot may be much higher later. On the other hand, if the forecasted demand never develops, the organization may own facilities that remain idle.

Once buildings are erected and equipment is installed, little can be done in day-to-day operations to affect the *total level* of committed costs. From a control standpoint, the objective is usually to increase current utilization of facilities, because this will ordinarily increase net income.

There is another aspect to the control problem, however. A follow-up, or audit, is needed to find out how well the ensuing utilization harmonizes with the decision that authorized the facilities in the first place. The latter approach helps management to evaluate the wisdom of its past long-range decisions and, in turn, should improve the quality of future decisions.

engineered costs

Chapter 7 introduced the distinctions between effectiveness and efficiency. Recall that *effectiveness* is the degree to which a predetermined goal such as a revenue target is attained. *Efficiency* is the degree to which an optimum relationship between inputs and outputs is achieved. **Hence, an engineered cost is any cost that has an explicit, specified relationship with a selected measure of activity.** This relationship is usually physically observable and is established by work measurement. Examples are direct material, fuel, and many labor costs.

The major accounting techniques for control are flexible budgets and standards. The feedback time is short. Indeed, direct-material waste may be monitored as each unit is produced.

nature of discretionary costs

Discretionary costs (sometimes called *managed* or *programmed costs*) are those fixed costs (1) that arise from periodic (usually yearly) appropriation decisions regarding the maximum amounts to be incurred and (2) that do not have a demonstrable optimum relationship between inputs (as measured by the costs) and outputs (as measured by revenue or other objectives such as students' knowledge or patients' health). Examples include much advertising, public relations, executive training, research, and management consulting services. In addition, much compensation paid for personnel, accounting, and legal services is in the discretionary category. Conceivably, these costs could be reduced almost entirely for a given year in dire times, whereas the committed costs would be much more difficult to reduce. Like committed costs, the discretionary resources acquired should be carefully planned and fully utilized if net income is to be maximized.

The major accounting techniques for control are negotiated static budgets, which are determined in various ways discussed in a later section. The feedback time tends to be longer than for engineered costs but shorter than for committed costs.

The most noteworthy aspect of discretionary costs is that we are seldom confident that the "correct" amount is being spent. We are unsure of how much is enough. Discretionary costs are not subject to ordinary engineering input-output relationships.

comparison with engineered costs

Exhibit 10-2 compares engineered costs with discretionary costs. The exhibit focuses on the following characteristics:

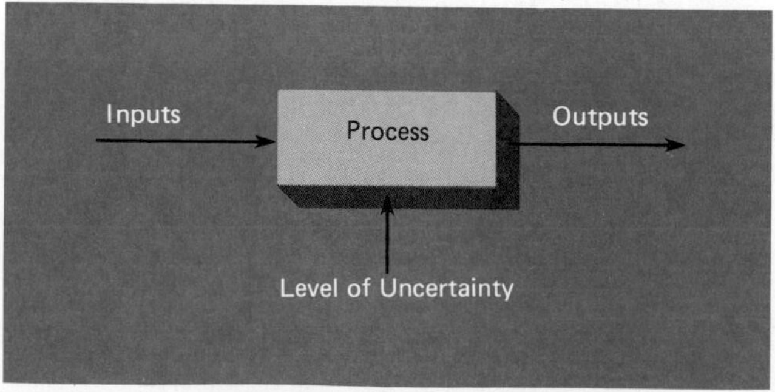

EXHIBIT 10-2

Comparison of Engineered and Discretionary Costs*

CHARACTERISTICS	ENGINEERED COST	DISCRETIONARY COST
1. Primary inputs	Physical and human resources	Human resources
2. Process	a. Detailed and physically observable	a. Black box (because knowledge of process is sketchy or unavailable)
	b. Repetitive	b. Often nonrepetitive or nonroutine
3. Primary outputs	a. Products or quantifiable services	a. Information
	b. Value easy to determine	b. Value difficult to determine
	c. Quality easy to ascertain	c. Quality difficult to ascertain
4. Level of uncertainty	Moderate or small (e.g., production setting)	Great (e.g., marketing, lawsuit, research settings)

**This exhibit is a modification of one suggested by H. Itami.*

As Exhibit 10-2 indicates, the primary inputs that affect engineered costs are both physical and human resources. Examples are materials and labor. In contrast, the primary inputs that affect discretionary costs are human resources. Examples are salaries and fees paid for professional services rendered by people inside or outside the organization.

Exhibit 10-2 shows how processes that are detailed, repetitive, and physically observable are main candidates for using engineered-cost techniques. In contrast, discretionary costs are associated with processes that are sometimes labeled as *black boxes.* The latter may be defined as processes that are not easily understood. Knowledge of the precise process may be sketchy, unmeasurable, or unavailable. Examples include activities like executive education, industrial relations, and public relations.

The contrast between engineered and discretionary costs is also evident when outputs are considered. **In particular, Exhibit 10-2 highlights the fact that the outputs linked with discretionary costs typically are types of information.** Examples are oral or written reports or advice from various accounting, legal, research, and marketing staffs. Value and quality are much more difficult to ascertain for discretionary costs than for engineered costs.

The level of uncertainty also helps determine whether a cost may be engineered or discretionary. *Uncertainty* is defined here as the likelihood that an actual event will deviate from an expected event. The degree of uncertainty may be small or large, depending on whether inputs, process, and outputs are highly predictable. Therefore, engineered costs are more likely to be found in manufacturing settings than in marketing settings. It is much easier to specify that three kilograms of material will be necessary to produce a finished product than to specify that a twelve-hour training program in communications skills will be necessary to produce a quality supervisor.

Engineered costs typically have credible measures of output quantity and quality. Therefore, as Kaplan observes, producing a given amount of output for below-budgeted costs is a favorable indication. In contrast, a favorable discretionary-cost variance "may only imply that less output or output of a lower quality is being delivered."[9]

moving between cost categories

Return to the original table in this section. A hallmark of the evolution of control is the attempt to shift engineered-cost techniques to costs that were formerly subjected to discretionary-cost techniques. The first candidates for this shift were manufacturing costs, obviously because the process is observable and repetitive, the inputs and outputs measurable, and the uncertainty (the factory) relatively controllable. The next candidates have been those nonmanufacturing costs that are subject to credible measurements of the relation between inputs and outputs. Examples are the stocking of shelves, the loading of trucks, and the transportation of mail.

There is nothing hallowed about the distinctions in the table. Many costs are neither innately engineered nor discretionary. **Whether they become one or the other often depends on management's policies of planning and control.** The history of cost accounting reveals a steady march from the discretionary category to the engineered category. Indeed, the management consulting arms of public accounting firms and many industrial engineering firms have flourished by replacing discretionary systems with engineered systems. Examples include transportation and banking functions as well as assorted clerical functions.

Congruence, motivation, and empire building

Many government activities and corporate staff activities provide illustrations of discretionary costs. Examples include health, safety, and inspection activities of government units and corporate staff activities such as labor relations, public relations, product research, legal research, and market research. The managers of these activities tend to be professionals such as physicians, professors, attorneys, and scientists.

An oft-heard criticism is that managers of service departments and nonprofit organizations have personal goals that do not necessarily coincide with top-management goals of running a cost-effective organization. Instead, the managers obtain the most personal satisfaction from getting bigger and bigger budgets. The higher their budget, the greater their number of professionals and workers supervised; more services can be rendered, and higher prestige and salary may be attained.

Top management often has a difficult time contending with the natural desires of managers to build individual empires that can provide a wide variety of services almost instantly. Furthermore, these services rarely must meet the tests of a competitive market. Thus, many service managers attempt to please *all* markets within the organization, so their goals are diffused and not congruent with organization goals.[10]

---

[9]R. Kaplan, *Advanced Management Accounting* (Englewood Cliffs, N.J.: Prentice-Hall, 1982), Chap. 13.

[10]John L. Neuman, "Make Overhead Cuts That Last," *Harvard Business Review,* 53, No. 3 (May–June 1975), 118, points out that professionals "perform their services at a quality level out of proportion to actual need, and they tend to encourage requesters of these services to demand more of the same." Later, p. 122, he comments, "A reduction in service is almost never in the receivers' interests, particularly if they are not charged for the services. Nor will the suppliers normally be happy to see demand for their services reduced."

How should top management decide on the size of budgets for the legal, personnel, accounting, and similar departments? Top managers often lack sufficient specialized knowledge to make informed judgments. Moreover, the top executives frequently have little time or inclination to gather enough information to make such judgments. Furthermore, they may have received sterling departmental services throughout the year that may or may not be representative of general quality. The easy way out, at least in the short run, is perhaps to concede too readily to the manager requesting approval of his or her budget.

Some organizations have at least partially solved this dilemma by creating a new position, vice-president for administration or vice-president for staff services such as legal or accounting. His or her major responsibilities include trying to find the optimal amount of services, including the mix of internal and external services. In any event, contending with the problem of goal congruence is a particularly troublesome challenge in the area of discretionary costs.

The problem of congruence is also accompanied by the problem of "effort." If managers' natural desires are to increase budgets, ways must be found to encourage managers to reduce costs. There is often scant inclination for managers to cut back if there are no opportunities to gain prestige, bonuses, salary increases, or some form of sharing in the fruits of the cost savings. For example, federal government managers gain more status and salary if they supervise more employees and manage more programs.

The U.S. General Accounting Office has recommended to Congress that incentives be given, such as (1) returning to a manager's program part of a budget cut that was recommended by him or her and accepted, (2) releasing a program or activity from an in-depth annual review, and (3) linking pay to performance, including performance regarding the least-wasteful way of conducting operations.[11]

Control of discretionary costs

negotiated static budgets

The most common accounting technique for controlling discretionary costs is the use of **negotiated static budgets:** Discretionary fixed costs are decided upon by management at the start of the budget period. Goals are selected, the means for their attainment are chosen, the maximum expense to be incurred is specified, and the total amount to be spent is appropriated. For example, the U.S. Department of Agriculture requested $1.4 million for pest control of grasshoppers for fiscal 1980, and that was the amount appropriated by Congress. Similarly, a company may appropriate $5 million for an advertising campaign. The company's advertising agency is unlikely to exceed that amount, nor is it likely to spend much less than $5 million in trying to attain the company goals.

The relation of some discretionary fixed costs to volume of activity is easy to delineate. Advertising, research, donations, and training programs, for example, are usually formulated with certain objectives in mind. The execution of such projects is measured by comparing total expenditures with the appropriation. Because the tendency is to spend the entire appropriation, the resulting dollar variances are generally trivial. *But planning is far more important than this kind of day-to-day control.* The perfect execution of an advertising program—in the sense that the full amount

[11]*Streamlining Zero-Base Budgeting Will Benefit Decision-Making,* Report to the Congress of the United States, Comptroller General, PAD-79-45, September 25, 1979, p. 49.

authorized was spent in the specified media at the predetermined times—will be fruitless if the advertisements are unimaginative and lifeless or if they reach the wrong audience.

role of negotiation

No matter how detailed, and no matter how "scientifically" prepared, the final amounts of budgeted discretionary costs are typically lump-sum ceilings. They are inevitably the culmination of a negotiating or bargaining process. Although the latter give-and-take process is beyond the boundaries of this book, discretionary costs, more than other costs, are subject to approval as a result of persuasion rather than cold-blooded analysis. So individual skills of negotiation must be recognized as a key part of the budgeting process.

Given the lack of knowledge of the relationship between inputs and outputs, discretionary costs are prime candidates for cutbacks when the going gets tough. In times of recession, the sizes of corporate staffs get scrutinized and management consulting firms find that fewer engagements become available. In times of taxpayer revolts, government services get reduced.

physical observation and tradition

Salaries and assorted fees for outside services tend to make up the bulk of discretionary costs. Because of the difficulties of establishing a convincing relationship between inputs and outputs, most organizations rely on appropriate hiring and supervision as a means of controlling internal costs. **Therefore, physical observation tends to be the key to planning and control.** There is a pronounced reluctance to overhire.

For many discretionary costs (such as employee training, marketing, research, and donations to charities), industry tradition and management rules of thumb prominently influence the periodic appropriation. For instance, managers comment as follows: "We budget sales promotion or research costs at *x* percent of expected revenue primarily because our competitors spend at about the same rate (or primarily because we have always done it that way)." In essence, this reasoning states: "We don't know what the 'correct' amount is, so our approach is regarded as satisfactory until proven otherwise."

The above reasoning also is frequently influenced by the criterion of affordability. That is, we spend *x* percent of revenue because it is within the limits of what we can afford.

relationship to variable and fixed costs

Engineered costs are usually regarded as variable; discretionary and committed costs, as fixed. Nevertheless, a few discretionary costs do indeed behave as variable costs. For example, a brewery may grant a regional distributor an advertising allowance of 20 cents per case of beer sold. Thus, this advertising cost would have a pattern of variability, but not for the same reasons as engineered costs like direct materials or direct labor. The fluctuations in these total costs are caused by authorization to spend in accordance with a formula determined by management policy. There may be no technical cause-and-effect relationship between such costs and sales.

Incremental budgets

Negotiated static budgets may be classified as incremental and zero-base. Each will be discussed in turn.

Ordinary incremental budgets are by far the most popular. They usually consider the previous period's budget and actual results as givens. The budget amount is then changed in accordance with experience during the previous period and expectations for the next period. For instance, a budget for a research department might be increased because of salary increases, the introduction of a new project, or both.

Priority incremental budgets are similar to incremental budgets but with a noteworthy twist. The budget request must be accompanied by a statement of what incremental activities or changes would occur, first, if the budget were increased by, say, 10 percent and, second, if the budget were decreased by a similar percentage. In this way, superiors can better ensure goal congruence because they can check their own priorities against those of subordinates. Furthermore, the act of establishing some priorities forces the manager to think more carefully and concretely about operations. In a way, priority budgeting may be considered a happy and simple compromise between ordinary incremental budgeting and zero-base budgeting.

zero-base budgets

Zero-base budgeting (ZBB) is an elaborate practice of having a manager justify activities from the ground up as though they were being launched for the first time. ZBB gets at bedrock questions by requiring managers to take and document the following major steps:

1. Determine objectives, operations, and costs of all activities under the manager's jurisdiction.
2. Explore alternative means of conducting each activity.
3. Evaluate alternative budget levels for various levels of effort for each activity.
4. Establish measures of workload and performance.
5. Rank all activities in order of their importance to the organization.

Zero-base budgeting became highly fashionable during the late 1970s. Jimmy Carter had adopted ZBB when he was governor of Georgia and was pleased with its use there. When Carter became president, he directed that all federal government agencies adopt ZBB. More details regarding ZBB are in Appendix 10A.

lessons and conclusions

What major conclusions should we draw about ZBB in relation to other forms of budgeting? Consider the following:

1. The cost-benefit test will probably not be met if ZBB is conducted by all departments annually. However, ZBR (or zero-based "review" as distinguished from "budgeting") deserves serious consideration if it is conducted for all departments sequentially every five years or so. Meanwhile, incremental priority budgeting deserves annual use.
2. Unlike incremental budgeting, ZBB forces managers systematically to consider alternative ways of accomplishing objectives (e.g., use inside or outside services). This is a desirable attribute of any budgeting system for discretionary costs.
3. Although ZBB might be applied to all kinds of costs, its major potential contribution is in the area of discretionary costs. ZBB has received the most attention from nonprofit organizations because they tend to have higher proportions of discretionary costs.
4. The biggest benefit of the notoriety of ZBB will probably be indirect. That is, if ZBB acquires a bad name and fades away, it will have made a major single contribution. Today, more than ever, there has been a decided increase in the prominence of budgeting in general. Inasmuch as intelligent budgeting is a help rather than a hindrance to management, almost any increase in attention to budgeting is a worthwhile contribution.

As discretionary costs have soared, many organizations have taken closer looks at how to achieve a given task. For example, many American companies have increased their legal departments significantly. Their aim is to reduce overall legal costs by reducing dependence on outside law firms. For example, in 1980 Ford Motor Company increased its own law staff by 32 percent to 210 attorneys. BankAmerica handles virtually all litigation, securities, and antitrust matters in-house.

In sum, the control of discretionary costs varies. Most organizations rely on careful hiring and physical observation. The most sophisticated accounting techniques entail (1) transforming as many discretionary costs as possible into engineered costs via work measurement and (2) applying ZBB to the remainder. Note too that work measurement, that is, the attempt to quantify or otherwise specify the relationships between inputs and outputs, is often a prominent feature of ZBB. As always, the choice of budgeting method, if any, depends on particular circumstances in particular organizations.

Nonmanufacturing work measurement

measurement is needed for control

There are two general approaches to cost control. The first, most widespread, approach is informal and is heavily dependent on human supervision. The second approach is more formal and is dependent on work measurement as well as on human supervision; it is getting more attention from organizations as they seek to improve their efficiency. For example, ZBB incorporates measurements of inputs and outputs where feasible. This approach is based on a fundamental premise: *Permanent improvement in any performance is impossible unless the work is measured.*

To portray cost behavior as it responds to volume, we must measure volume (the horizontal axis) as well as cost (the vertical axis). *Industrial engineers and others concerned with cost control steadfastly maintain that control is impossible without careful measures of workloads and capability.* Work measurement began in the factory but has extended into other areas in recent years.

Work measurement is the careful analysis of a task, its size, the methods used in its performance, and its efficiency. Its objective is to determine the workload in an operation and the number of workers needed to perform that work efficiently. The techniques used include time and motion study, observation of a random sample of the work (that is, work sampling), and the estimation, by a work-measurement analyst and a line supervisor, of the amount of time required for the work (that is, time analysis). The workload is expressed in *control-factor units,* which are used in formulating the budget.

For example, the control-factor units in a payroll department might include operations performed on time cards, on notices of change in labor rate, on notices of employee promotion, on new employment and termination reports, and on routine weekly and monthly reports. All of these would be weighed. The estimated workload would then be used to determine the required labor force and budgetary allowance.

other examples of measurement

The activity measure used as a budget base may be sales dollars, product units, cases, tons, or some other unit that best reflects cost influence:

OPERATION	UNIT OF MEASURE (CONTROL-FACTOR UNIT)
Billing	Lines per hour
Warehouse labor	Pounds or cases handled per day
Packing	Pieces packed per hour
Posting accounts receivable	Postings per hour
Mailing	Pieces mailed per hour

Standards for certain order-filling activities, such as packing or driving a truck, may necessarily be less refined than for such manufacturing activities as assembly work, but they still provide the best available formal tool for planning and control. For example, short-interval scheduling has been attempted; this technique routes all work through a supervisor, who batches the work in hourly lots. Such scheduling develops standards, controls backlogs, and provides close follow-up[12]

The measurement of work often spurs controversy, because employees do not usually welcome more stringent monitoring of their productivity. Despite some delicate problems of human relations, there is an increasing tendency for work measurement to be applied in office, transportation, selling, and other nonmanufacturing activities.

Note that all of these examples entail nonmanufacturing activities. The long-held belief is slowly fading that it is somehow acceptable to subject manufacturing activities to work measurement while exempting nonmanufacturing activities. The most obvious candidates for work measurement are high-volume, repetitive tasks. For example, Citibank's Operating Group uses assembly-line tactics for bookkeeping, clearing and filing checks, and preparing bank statements for customers. Each job has a standard.[13] Forecasts are made and performance is measured—annually, monthly, and, in many instances, daily or hourly. A 2 percent variance is considered significant.

The Citibank experience with work measurement was highly successful. In a span of five years, work-force turnover dropped from 50 to 10 percent annually, employment fell from 10,000 to 6,500, and costs per unit processed fell remarkably.

budgeting of nonmanufacturing costs

There is much disagreement about how some nonmanufacturing costs should be controlled. Advocates of work measurement favor a more rigorous approach, which essentially regards these costs as engineered variable costs. In contrast, a discretionary-cost approach, which basically regards these costs as fixed, is more often found in practice.

Assume that five payroll clerks are employed, and that each clerk's operating efficiency *should be* the processing of the pay records of 1,000 employees per month. In the month of June, 4,700 individuals' pay records were processed by these clerks. Each clerk earns $1,200 per month. The variances shown by the engineered-cost approach and the discretionary-cost approach are tabulated below and graphed in Exhibit 10-3.

THE ENGINEERED VARIABLE-COST APPROACH: PERFECTION STANDARDS □ The engineered-cost approach to this situation is to base the budget formula on the unit cost of the individual pay record processed, $1,200 ÷ 1,000 records, or $1.20. Therefore, the budget allowance for payroll-clerk labor would be $1.20 × 4,700, or $5,640. Assume that the five employees worked throughout the month. The following performance report would be prepared:

	ACTUAL COST	FLEXIBLE BUDGET: TOTAL STANDARD COST ALLOWED FOR GOOD UNITS PRODUCED	FLEXIBLE-BUDGET VARIANCE
Payroll-clerk labor	$6,000 (5 × $1,200)	$5,640 (4,700 × $1.20)	$360 U

[12]Vincent Melore, "Cutting Payroll Costs in Manufacturing Staffs," *Management Service,* 1, No. 3, p. 24. Also see "Boosting Productivity at American Express," *Business Week,* October 5, 1981, pp. 62–66.

[13]*Wall Street Journal,* June 6, 1975, p. 1.

EXHIBIT 10-3

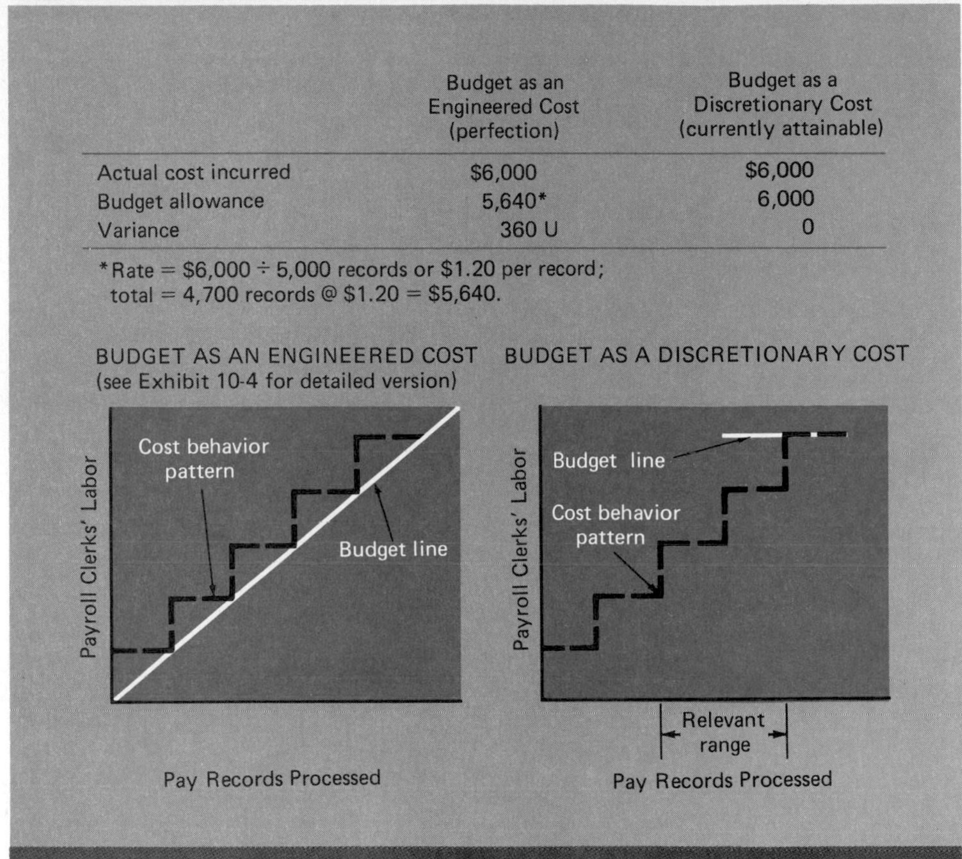

Engineered and Discretionary Costs

	Budget as an Engineered Cost (perfection)	Budget as a Discretionary Cost (currently attainable)
Actual cost incurred	$6,000	$6,000
Budget allowance	5,640*	6,000
Variance	360 U	0

*Rate = $6,000 ÷ 5,000 records or $1.20 per record; total = 4,700 records @ $1.20 = $5,640.

A graphic representation of what has occurred (Exhibit 10-4) may yield insight. For simplicity, price and efficiency variances are not computed here.

Essentially, two decisions must be made in this operation. The first is a policy decision. How many clerks do we desire? How flexible should we be? How divisible is the task? Should we use part-time help? Should we hire and fire as the volume of work fluctuates? The implication of these questions is that once the hiring decision is made, the total costs incurred can be predicted easily—$6,000 in our example.

The second decision concentrates on day-to-day control, on how efficiently and effectively the given resources are being utilized. The work-measurement approach is an explicit and formal attempt to measure the utilization of resources by:

1. Assuming a proportionately variable-cost budget and the complete divisibility of the workload into small units. Note that the *budget line* on the graph in Exhibit 10-4 is variable, despite the fact that the costs are really incurred in steps.
2. Generating a budget variance that assumes a comparison of actual costs with a perfection standard—the cost that would be incurred if payroll-clerk labor could be turned on and off like a faucet. In this case, the variance of $360 informs management that there was overstaffing (that is, the tenth step was only partially utilized). The workload capability was 5,000 pay records, not the 4,700 actually processed. $360 is the extra

EXHIBIT 10-4

Step-Variable Costs and Variances

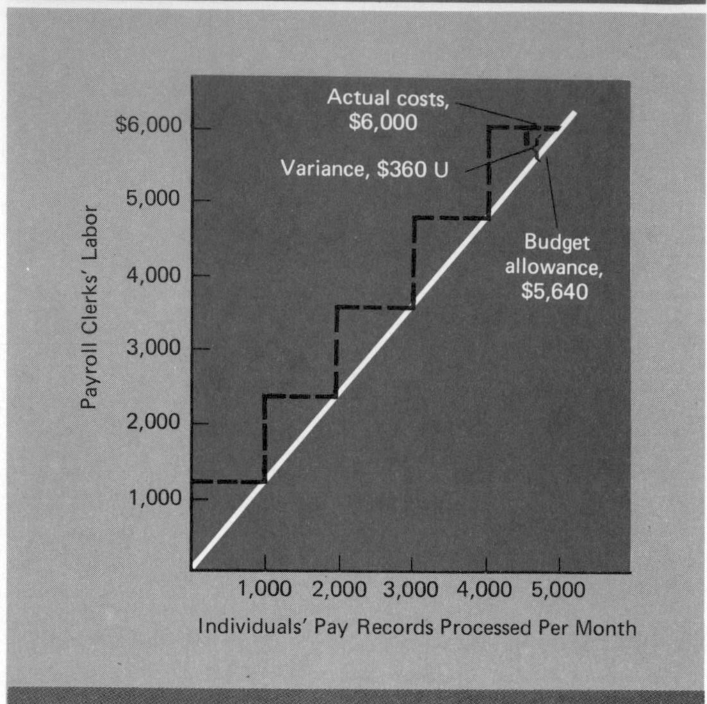

cost that resulted from operating in a way that does not attain the lowest possible cost, even though this may not be the result of a conscious decision but merely the effect of producing the volume that satisfies the total monthly demand. Advocates of work measurement maintain that such a variance shows where the managers should be alert for cost reduction opportunities, because options may be available. Such an approach provides a measure ($360) of the amount that management is currently investing to provide stability in the work force.

The use of a tight budget based on perfection standards generates variances that upon investigation will reveal either or both of the following: (a) inefficient use or underutilization of available personnel (for instance, perhaps 5,000 individual payroll records had to be processed, and other clerks or supervisors had to pitch in to get all the work done); (b) the cost of a management policy of deliberately retaining personnel to service long-run needs even though the volume of the current workload is insufficient (for instance, the maximum work available for payroll clerical labor may be 4,700 individual payroll records and the individual work may have been performed with complete efficiency).

THE DISCRETIONARY FIXED-COST APPROACH: CURRENTLY ATTAINABLE STANDARDS □ Work-measurement techniques are not used in the vast majority of organizations. Consequently, the tendency is to rely on the experience of the department head and superior for judging the size of the work force needed to carry out the department's functions. There is a genuine reluctance to overhire because there is a corresponding reluctance to discharge or lay off people when volume slackens. As a result, temporary peak loads are often met by hiring temporary workers or by having the regular employees work overtime.

In most cases, the relevant range of activity during the budget period can be predicted with assurance, and the work force needed for the marketing and administrative functions can be readily determined. If management refuses, consciously or unconsciously, to control costs rigidly in accordance with short-run fluctuations in activity, these costs become discretionary. That is, their total amount is relatively fixed and unresponsive to short-run variations in volume.

Hence, there is a conflict between common practice and the objective of work measurement, which is to treat most costs as engineered and so subject them to short-range management control. **The moral is that management's attitudes and its planning and controlling decisions often determine whether a cost is fixed or variable. A change in policy can transform a fixed cost into a variable cost and vice versa.**

Moreover, management may regard a cost as a discretionary fixed cost for *cash-planning purposes* in the preparation of the master budget but may use the variable-cost approach for *control purposes* in the preparation of flexible budgets for performance evaluation. These two views may be reconciled within the same overall system. In our example, a master budget conceivably could include the following items:

Payroll-clerk labor:	
Flexible-budget allowance for control	$5,640
Expected flexible-budget variance (due to deliberate overstaffing)	360
Total budget allowance for cash planning	$6,000

FOLLOW-UP ANALYSIS UNDER DISCRETIONARY FIXED COSTS □ Thus, we see that control may be exercised (a) in the commonly accepted sense of the day-to-day follow-up that is associated with engineered costs; and (b) in the special sense of periodically evaluating an expenditure, relating it to the objectives sought, and carefully planning the total amount of the cost for the ensuing period. The latter approach does not mean that day-to-day follow-up is neglected; follow-up is necessary to see that the resources made available are being used fully and efficiently. It does mean that perceptive planning is stressed and that daily control *via a formal measurement system* is de-emphasized. Reliance is placed more on hiring capable people and less on frequent checking up on them.

The practical effects of the discretionary fixed-cost approach are that the budgeted costs and the actual costs tend to be very close, so that resulting budget variances are small. Follow-ups to see that the available resources are being fully and efficiently utilized are regarded as the managers' responsibility, a duty that can be achieved by face-to-face control and by records of physical quantities (for example, pounds handled per day in a warehouse, pieces mailed per hour in a mailing room) that do not have to be formally integrated into the accounting records in dollar terms. However, some benchmarks are still utilized even if such "standards" are not explicit.

difficulties in applying work measurement

The success of the work-measurement, engineered variable-cost approach to some nonmanufacturing costs is limited by the nature of the work being performed. Attempts have been made to measure the work of legal personnel and claims adjusters in insurance companies, of economists in a Federal Reserve Bank, and of stock clerks in retail stores. Such attempts have achieved only limited success because of (a) the inability to develop a satisfactory control-factor unit, or (b) the diversity of tasks and objectives of such personnel, or (c) the difficulty of measuring the output of lawyers or economists.

For example, consider the attempt to measure the work of clerks and stock helpers in a food store. Their tasks are routine and repetitive, but they are often fragmented. Attempts at measuring employee work have shown volatile results. The trouble is that each employee usually performs a variety of tasks on a variety of items. The worker may unpack, price-mark, stock shelves, operate a cash register, bag groceries, cart groceries to automobiles, sweep floors, and watch for shoplifters.

To recapitulate, work measurement has proven helpful in both nonmanufacturing and manufacturing. Its use is becoming more widespread. However, please keep this textbook presentation in perspective. It is not a sales pitch for work measurement. Instead, it has merely described two general approaches to a problem. Whether the engineered-cost approach is "better" than the discretionary-cost approach must be decided on a case-by-case basis, ***using a cost-benefit approach that focuses on how much operating decisions will be improved.*** Of course, the consultants who want to install work-measurement systems will typically try to demonstrate that their more costly formal systems will generate net benefits in the form of cost savings and better customer service.

Program budgeting

A distinction is often made in the management literature between the planning process and the budgeting process, whereby the latter becomes the final step of formalization of the former. **Program budgeting** is an outgrowth of a concept known as Planning, Programming, and Budgeting (PPB), which was experimented with extensively in the U.S. Federal Government during the 1960s. The secretary of defense and other high officers used PPB to analyze military activities in strategic terms. Programs (such as defending the continental United States or obtaining a first-strike capability) were framed to enable the comparison of alternatives based on explicit criteria and assumptions and incorporating expected costs and benefits. A highlight of the approach was the focus on explicit, long-range program decisions, in contrast to the previous procedure of annually deciding how much of the overall appropriation should be allocated to the army, navy, and air force.

PPB was implemented successfully in the Defense Department because (1) outputs were definable and measurable (e.g., the probabilities of U.S. weapons' penetrating enemy defenses); (2) top-management support for PPB was heavy and visible; and (3) competent PPB staff was available to top management.

PPB is more a state of mind than a system. It has become widely used, particularly at state and local governmental levels, where it is often called program budgeting rather than PPB.[14] Its central characteristics were described by a former director of the budget:

> As the first step, PPB calls for a careful specification and analysis of basic program objectives . . . . What are they really trying to accomplish? The objective of our intercity highway program, for example, is *not* to build highways. Highways are useful only as they serve a higher objective, namely transporting people and goods. . . .
>
> The *second* step is to analyze the output of a given program in terms of the objectives . . . .
>
> The *third* step is to measure the *total costs* of the program, not just for one year, but over at least several years ahead . . . not on the basis of the first year costs alone . . . .

[14]For fuller descriptions, see R. Anthony and R. Herzlinger, *Management Control in Nonprofit Organizations,* rev. ed. (Homewood, Ill.: Richard D. Irwin, 1980), Chaps. 8 and 9.

The *fourth* and crucial step is to analyze alternatives . . . . It is competition among alternatives which is crucial . . . .

The *fifth* step is establishing PPB as an integral part of the budgetary decisions. The programming concept is the crucial link that relates planning to budgeting, converting planning from paper exercise to an important part of the decision process.[15]

SUMMARY

Management accounting systems exist primarily to improve the collective decisions within an organization. All systems are imperfect. The central question usually is, How can a system, with all its defects, be improved? Using a cost-benefit philosophy, top managers must be conscious of the motivational effects of a chosen system. That is, how does System A affect goal congruence and managerial effort in comparison with System B?

For budgetary-control purposes, costs are frequently divided into three categories: committed, engineered, and discretionary. Different accounting techniques are used in each category.

Discretionary costs are especially difficult to control with accounting techniques because, by definition, no satisfactory relationships between inputs and outputs can be specified. The most highly developed approach to control is to use work measurement and reclassify some discretionary costs as engineered costs. The remainder of the discretionary costs are then subjected to techniques of zero-base budgeting.

SUGGESTED READINGS

In addition to the items footnoted in the chapter, the following references provide an overview of behavioral research in accounting. Much current attention is being given to the areas of human information processing and contingency theories of organizational behavior. Most of these books contain extensive bibliographies:

BURNS, THOMAS J., ed., **The Behavioral Aspects of Accounting Data for Performance Evaluation.** Columbus, O.: College of Administrative Science, Ohio State University, 1970. This is a collection of six papers, seven critiques, and proceedings of an accounting symposium.

BURNS, THOMAS J., ed., **Behavioral Experiments in Accounting II.** Columbus, O.: College of Administrative Science, Ohio State University, 1979.

CAPLAN, EDWIN H., **Management Accounting and Behavioral Science,** 2nd ed. Reading, Mass.: Addison-Wesley, 1981.

CAPLAN, EDWIN H., and JOSEPH CHAMPOUX, **Cases in Management Accounting: Context and Behavior.** New York: National Association of Accountants, 1978.

CHENHALL, R., G. HARRISON, and D. WATSON, ed., **Organizational Context of Management Accounting.** Boston: Pitman, 1981.

CRESS, W., **A Study of the Relationship between Budget-related Planning and Control Policies and Procedures and Firm Performance and Selected Firm Characteristics** (Ann Arbor, Mich.: University Microfilms International, 1980). A survey of budget practices of American manufacturing firms.

[15]Charles Shultze, U.S. Congress, Senate Committee on Government Operations, *Planning-Programming-Budgeting.* Hearings, 90th Cong., 1st sess. (Washington, D.C.: Government Printing Office). For a description of designing and installing a PPB system, see Robert J. Mowitz, *The Design and Implementation of Pennsylvania's Planning, Program and Budgeting System* (University Park: Pennsylvania State University, 1970).

GALBRAITH, JAY R., **Organization Design: An Information Processing View.** Reading, Mass.: Addison-Wesley, 1973.

HOFSTEDE, G. H., **The Game of Budget Control.** New York: Van Nostrand-Wiley, 1967.

HOPWOOD, A., **Accounting and Human Behavior.** Englewood Cliffs, N.J.: Prentice-Hall, 1976.

LAWLER, E., and J. RHODE, **Information and Control in Organizations.** Pacific Palisades, Calif.: Goodyear, 1976.

LIBBY, R., **Accounting and Human Information Processing.** Englewood Cliffs, N.J.: Prentice-Hall, 1981.

LIKERT, RENSIS, **The Human Organization, Its Management and Value.** New York: McGraw-Hill, 1967.

LIVINGSTONE, J. L., ed., **Managerial Accounting: The Behavioral Foundations.** Columbus, O.: Grid, 1975.

PFEFFER, J., **Power in Organizations.** Marshfield, Ma.: Pitman, 1981.

SCHIFF, M., and Y. LEWIN, eds., **Behavioral Aspects of Accounting.** Englewood Cliffs, N.J.: Prentice-Hall, 1974.

SIMON, H. A., H. GUETZKOW, G. KOSMETSKY, and G. TYNDALL, **Centralization vs. Decentralization in Organizing the Controller's Department.** New York: Controllership Foundation, 1954. This book is incisive and readable. Its title is deceiving because the book covers the entire range of management accounting. Unfortunately, it is out of print, so you may have difficulty in getting a copy.

problem for self-study

problem

The Alic Co. has many small accounts receivable. Work measurement of billing labor has shown that a billing clerk can process 2,000 customers' accounts per month. The company employs 30 billing clerks at an annual salary of $9,600 each. The outlook for next year is for a decline in the number of customers, from 59,900 to 56,300 per month.

REQUIRED

1. Assume that management has decided to continue to employ the 30 clerks despite the expected drop in billings. Show two approaches, the engineered-cost approach and the discretionary fixed-cost approach, to the budgeting of billing labor. Show how the *performance report* for the year would appear under each approach.
2. Some managers favor using tight budgets as motivating devices for controlling operations. In these cases, the managers really expect an unfavorable variance and must allow, in cash planning, for such a variance so that adequate cash will be available as needed. What would be the budgeted variance, also sometimes called expected variance, in this instance?
3. Assume that the workers are reasonably efficient. (a) Interpret the budget variances under the engineered-cost approach and the discretionary fixed-cost approach. (b) What should management do to exert better control over clerical costs?

solution

1. Engineered-cost approach:

Standard unit rate = $9,600 ÷ 2,000 = $4.80 per customer per year
or = $ .40 per customer per month

	ACTUAL COST	FLEXIBLE BUDGET: TOTAL STANDARD INPUTS ALLOWED FOR GOOD UNITS PRODUCED × STANDARD UNIT PRICE	FLEXIBLE-BUDGET VARIANCE
	(30 × $9,600)	(56,300 × $.40 × 12 months)	
Billing-clerk labor	$288,000	$270,240	$17,760 U

Discretionary fixed-cost approach:

	ACTUAL COST	FLEXIBLE BUDGET: A LUMP SUM	FLEXIBLE-BUDGET VARIANCE
Billing-clerk labor	$288,000	$288,000	0

2. The budgeted variance would be $17,760, unfavorable. The master budget for financial planning must provide for labor costs of $288,000; therefore, if the engineered-cost approach were being used for control, the master budget might specify:

Billing-clerk labor:	
Flexible-budget allowance	$270,240
Expected flexible-budget variance	17,760
Total budget allowance for cash planning	$288,000

3. As the chapter explains, management decisions and policies are often of determining importance in categorizing a cost as fixed or variable. If management refuses, as in this case, to control costs rigidly in accordance with short-run fluctuations in activity, these costs are discretionary. The $17,760 variance represents the price that management, consciously or unconsciously, is willing to pay currently in order to maintain a stable work force geared to management's ideas of "normal needs."

   Management should be given an approximation of such an extra cost. There is no single "right way" to keep management informed on such matters. Two approaches were demonstrated in the previous parts of this problem. The important point is that clerical workloads and capability must be measured before effective control may be exerted. Such measures may be formal or informal. The latter is often achieved through a supervisor's regular observation of how efficiently work is being performed.

Terms to Learn

behavior congruence ***committed cost*** ***congruence*** ***discretionary cost*** ***engineered cost*** ***extrinsic motivation*** ***goal congruence*** ***intrinsic motivation*** ***managerial effort*** ***motivation*** ***negotiated static budget*** ***ordinary incremental budget*** ***PPB*** ***priority incremental budget*** ***program budgeting*** ***risk congruence*** ***work measurement*** ***zero base budgeting*** ***ZBB***

Special Points and Pitfalls

The choice of a management accounting system for control is as closely related to the behavioral sciences as it is to economics and quantitative methods. The task of the formal control system is to help attain goal congruence and effort. Behavioral considerations deserve front and center attention.

The accountant and the senior managers must try to harmonize three types of control: organization, group, and individual. Top-management support is a key to getting groups and individuals to accept organization goals as their own.

Appendix 10a: more on zero-base budgets

This Appendix explores zero-base budgets (ZBB) in more depth than in the body of the chapter. Recall that ZBB is an elaborate practice of having a manager justify activities from the ground up as though they were being launched for the first time. The origin of ZBB goes back to at least 1924. As early as 1962, the Department of

Agriculture used a form of ZBB. A successful and widely publicized application of ZBB was used at Texas Instruments in the late 1960s.[16]

basic description

As Exhibit 10-5 displays, ZBB typically begins with decision units, which are the lowest levels in an organization for which a budget is prepared. A set of *decision packages* is prepared for each unit, which basically describes various levels of service that may be rendered by the decision unit. The set must usually include one package below the current level of operations.

Exhibit 10-6 summarizes the ZBB documentation by the manager of the Stanford Internal Audit Group. Note the specification of the objective, the description of the alternative means of accomplishing objectives, and the financial effects of four decision packages (called *decision unit increments* at Stanford). Also note the tremendous magnitude of the costs of compensation in comparison with other costs, which is a typical phenomenon of discretionary costs.

Exhibit 10-7 shows the first decision package, called increment 1 of 4. It represents two levels of service below that being currently rendered, as described in Exhibit 10-6.

Exhibit 10-7 also indicates how an evaluation of the alternative budget levels is conducted. The manager believes this is a bare-bones service level. In addition, note that workload and performance measures are established. For example, the final line enumerates the recommendations made by the internal audit group to various operating managers in comparison with the recommendations implemented.

strengths and weaknesses

Ordinary incremental budgeting usually provides top managers the choices of making a single accept or reject decision, or ordering arbitrary cutbacks (e.g., 5 percent across the board), or redoing the entire budget process. ZBB offers more information on a wider variety of choices, particularly concerning competing alternatives.

ZBB has its boosters and its detractors. The strengths of ZBB are relatively common among its users. The Stanford experience with ZBB has been relatively successful:

1. Goals have been more sharply established and alternative means have been explicitly considered.
2. Managers have become more heavily involved in a well-structured budget process that fosters communication and consensus.
3. Priorities among activities have been better pinpointed.
4. Knowledge and understanding of inputs and outputs have been enhanced. The budget process is generally more rational and less political than most.
5. Resources have been reallocated more efficiently and effectively.

There are many critics of ZBB. Common complaints include the following:

1. The time and cost of preparing the budget are much higher than less-elaborate budgeting processes. Indeed, in some organizations the heavy paperwork has led ZBB to be renamed as Zerox-Base Budgeting.
2. The determination of performance measures (See Exhibit 10-7) is difficult.

---

[16] *Streamlining Zero-Base Budgeting Will Benefit Decision-Making,* op. cit., p. 3. Also see Peter A. Phyrr, *Zero-Base Budgeting* (New York: John Wiley, 1972); and James W. Patillo, *Zero-Base Budgeting* (New York: National Association of Accountants, 1977). For an illustration in a not-for-profit organization, see K. Bennett, L. Owen, and T. Warner, "Implementing ZBB at Stanford University," *Business Officer,* May 1980, pp. 21–27.

EXHIBIT 10-5

Illustration of Zero-Base Budgeting

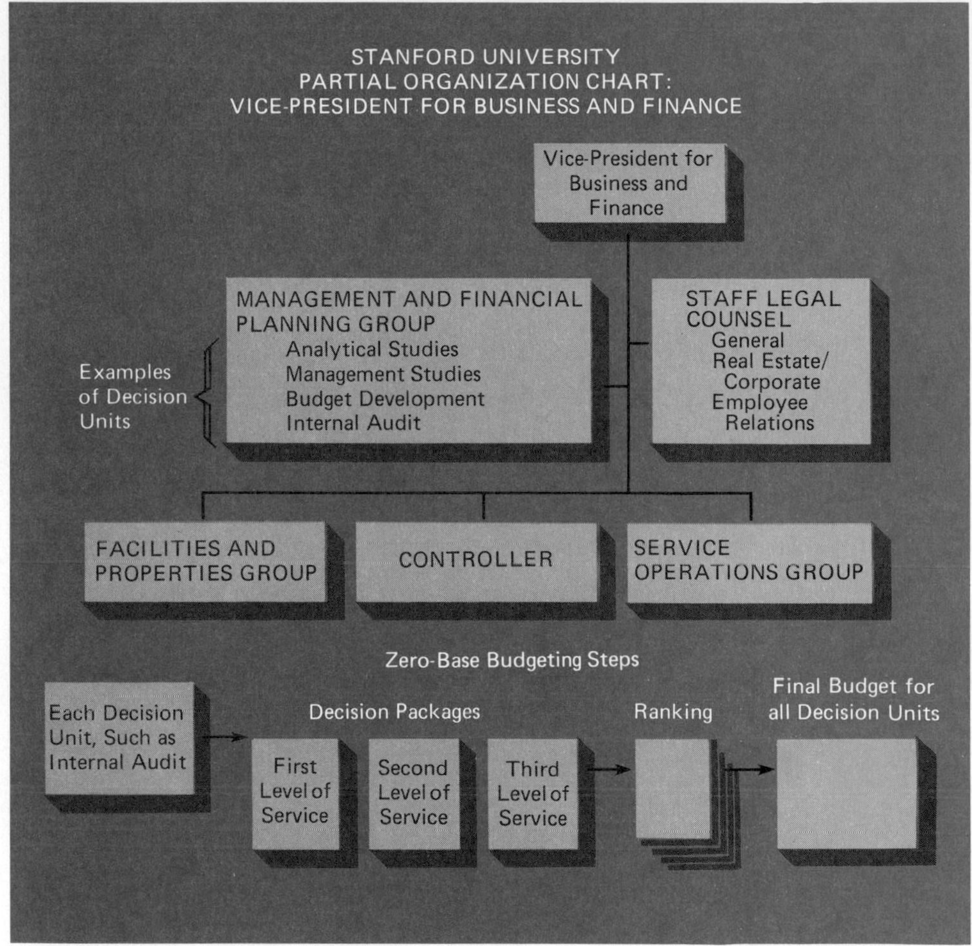

3. The specification of service levels, especially the minimum levels of service, is threatening to many managers.
4. Top managers fail to follow through and use the ZBB information in making choices. In short, they do not really support the process.

Note that most of these weaknesses or problems may be the result of a rigid application of ZBB without tailoring the technique to the peculiarities of a specific organization. Criticisms of budgeting are often misdirected. They are aimed at a budget *technique* or *process* (such as ZBB), when instead they should be aimed at the *administration* of the technique.

example of results

Supporters of ZBB cite the advantages enumerated earlier. To maximize the benefits of ZBB, measurements of inputs and outputs are necessary. For instance, an analysis of overtime costs for the Controller's Office at Stanford showed that the number of transactions processed there grew more than 22 percent in five years (from 564,684 to 689,495). This analysis helped explain pressure for positions in the office. It also gave additional impetus to a pending review of the entire accounting system.

EXHIBIT 10-6

Decision Unit Summary

(1) DECISION UNIT NAME	(2) ORGANIZATION NAME, NUMBER	(3) DECISION UNIT MANAGER	(4) DATE
Internal Audit	Business and Finance	Betty Kercher	10/25/_9

(5) OBJECTIVE OF DECISION UNIT

To promote and perpetuate an effective and responsive management control system by assisting managers and officers in discharging their responsibilities effectively and efficiently.

(6) CURRENT PERSONNEL, ACTIVITIES, SERVICES

One director, 12.5 auditors, and one secretary provide information on internal controls, compliance, economy, efficiency and effectiveness at all levels of the University, Medical Center, and SLAC through the performance of financial, compliance, EDP, and operational audits. In addition, special investigations and studies are conducted. The unit is responsible for reporting to management that policies and procedures, state and federal laws, contractual obligations, and good business practices are being followed. Total full-time equivalent personnel = 14.5.

(7) ALTERNATIVE MEANS OF ACCOMPLISHING OBJECTIVES; REASONS FOR ACCEPTANCE OR REJECTION

a) Engage external auditors and consultants. This alternative would increase external audit fees and cost more in the long-term than maintaining an in-house capability. (Assuming outside salaries stay higher than internal salaries.)

b) Internal auditing performed by people responsible for other business and financial duties (e.g., Controller and Management and Financial Planning) or by GSB students under direction of a University officer. Auditor objectivity and independence would be questionable and use of students would probably be on special projects rather than the overall evaluation of internal control.

(8) CRITICAL LINKAGES TO OTHER DECISION UNITS

This decision unit is a staff function that serves management at all levels of the University, Medical Center, and SLAC. This unit serves as a liaison between institutional administration and all operating departments. (SLAC is the Stanford Linear Accelerator Center.)

(9) DECISION UNIT INCREMENTS (Indicate current level with *)		INCREMENTAL				CUMULATIVE				CURRENT YEAR BUDGETED			
TITLE	Number	FTE	Compen-sation $	OTHER $	TOTAL $	FTE	Compen-sation $	OTHER $	TOTAL $	FTE	Compen-sation $	OTHER $	TOTAL $
Base Requirements	1 of 4	12.5	364.5	42.1	406.6	12.5	364.5	42.1	406.6	14	406.7	38.1	444.8
SLAC Audits	2 of 4	1.5	15.2	1.0	16.2	15.0	379.7	43.1	422.8				
External Audit Assistance*	3 of 4	1.5	37.6	3.1	40.7	15.5	417.3	46.2	463.5				
Increased Operational Aud.	4 of 4	1.5	40.4	3.5	43.9	17.0	457.7	49.7	507.4				
	of												
	of												
	of												

EXHIBIT 10-7

Decision Package

(1) DECISION UNIT NAME Internal Audit	(2) ORGANIZATION NAME Business and Finance				(3) DECISION UNIT MANAGER Betty Kercher				(4) DATE 10/31/_9			
(5) INCREMENT 1 OF 4	PROPOSED INCREMENTAL				PROPOSED CUMULATIVE				CURRENT YEAR BUDGETED			
(6) INCREMENTAL TITLE Base Requirements	FTE	COMP $	OTHER $	TOTAL $	FTE	COMP $	OTHER $	TOTAL $	FTE	COMP $	OTHER $	TOTAL $
(7) RESOURCES	12.5	364.5	42.1	406.6	12.5	364.5	42.1	406.6	14	406.7	38.1	444.8

(8) PERSONNEL, ACTIVITIES, SERVICES PROVIDED BY THIS INCREMENT ONLY: IMPACT ON OTHER UNITS (IF ANY)

Director develops and administers audit policies and procedures and directs the work of 10.5 auditors by assigning projects and reviewing accomplishments. Secretary provides secretarial and administrative support. 10.5 auditors perform financial, compliance, EDP, and operational reviews of University (5 FTE), Medical Center (5 FTE), and SLAC (.5 FTE) administrative departments and functions. This increment strengthens internal accounting and operating controls and provides management with unbiased and useful information on operations to enable changes to conform with prescribed or desired standards.

(9) INTERNAL AND EXTERNAL PROBLEMS RESULTING FROM NOT FUNDING THIS INCREMENT. (IF THIS IS INCREMENT #1, WHY IS IT A MINIMUM?)

This increment meets the minimum needs of an independent appraisal activity within the institution and meets minimum external requirements. Without this increment, SLAC audit coverage would be reduced to a level unacceptable to DOE; severe penalties could result to the institution through noncompliance with guidelines; and operating costs could increase through ineffective management and inefficient operating procedures.

(10) WORKLOAD/PERFORMANCE MEASUREMENTS		INCREMENTAL	CUMULATIVE	CURRENT YR. PROJECT
Productivity:	Number of hours/minor audit	46	46	40
	Number of hours/major audit	302	302	280
	Number of minor/major audits	14/31	14/31	10/45
Efficiency:	Cost of minor audits	$.7K/audit	$.7K/audit	$.6K/audit
	Cost of major audits	$4.7K/audit	$4.7K/audit	$4.0K/audit
Quality/Effectiveness: Number of request audits		26	26	20
Number of 'significant' mgmt. letter items from external auditors				
Recommendations made and implemented for minor/major audits		6:6/93:69	6:6/93:69	5:5/180:162

Prior to ZBB, many Stanford managers thought primarily in terms of the staff time (inputs) necessary to perform a specific function, rather than in terms of results (outputs). To help shift the focus, a variety of measurements were developed, recognizing that no single performance measure could adequately calibrate the quality of service provided. Nevertheless, taken as an aggregate, these measurements could provide strong indications of the volume, type, and quality of work performed.

By decreasing the delays in response time to correspondence, inquiries, or fire alarms, and/or by increasing the number of reports, 'audits, or employment interviews, a level of service could be deemed useful, critical, or merely nice to have.

In the Stanford personnel office, for instance, analysis of the volume of interviews given job applicants—and whether their length or number could be reduced—led to a decision to shift certain types of interviews from the central office to individual departments. Thus, duplication of effort was decreased and resources saved.

In other decision units, such as admissions and funds accounting, there is no discretion in decreasing the volume of work, only in determining the number of tasks supporting the main activity. Examples are the number of folder reviews and the number of days taken to reconcile funds to the general ledger. ZBB required a process of trying to measure tasks and justify the methods used to perform necessary functions.

Overall, Stanford considered 330 decision packages within the Business and Finance organization alone. Top management's ranking the options provided by ZBB was similar to the university admissions process itself. Some options clearly had to be encompassed in the budget, some not. A third group was composed of "swimmers": those whose inclusion depended on financial constraints.

Among the changes stemming from Stanford's use of ZBB, in whole or in part, were decreases in subsidies for public services (e.g., slide projector rentals, public address systems), decreases in the number of community service officers (e.g., for bicycle licensing, police office operations), and elimination of an executive assistant's position. In addition, the Planning Office was reorganized; twelve employees were released.

ZBB also resulted in increases in budgets. The process supplied persuasive evidence that Stanford must correct a growing backlog of building-maintenance work.

general experience

Exhibit 10-8 contains some generalizations concerning ZBB uses. The general experience with ZBB is similar to the strengths and weaknesses and the Stanford experience described earlier.

The U.S. General Accounting Office (GAO) conducted research on experience with ZBB in both the private and public sectors. It concluded that the federal government moved too quickly and too mechanically in trying to implement ZBB. Nevertheless, the GAO concluded:

> We believe that ZBB can work and should be integrated into the Federal budget process. This conclusion reflects our belief that ZBB concepts are valid but that they have been overshadowed by the mechanical process. These concepts—analyzing alternative approaches to programs, establishing alternative funding levels, evaluating program effectiveness, and determining managers' program priorities—were successfully incorporated into some organizations' budget systems. They did not make the mistake of considering ZBB little more than a process. They looked at themselves and they

EXHIBIT 10-8

Some Generalizations Concerning ZBB Experiences

While it is difficult to conclude on the appropriateness and effectiveness of this technique in different organizational settings, the following comparative outline represents an attempt to integrate some of these experiences.

	PRIVATE SECTOR	PUBLIC SECTOR
1. Extent of use:	The use of ZBB has spread rapidly in both sectors since the early 1970s. Furthermore, there is no indication that there is a levelling off of interest in ZBB or its use.	
2. Where and how it is primarily being used:	As a management tool in planning for and controlling the staff and support functions. A ZBB review is normally conducted for a relatively small portion of a corporation's total budget.	As the main system of budget justification (and, in most cases, presentation) for all functions within an organization.
3. Perceived effectiveness of ZBB as a tool in reducing costs/personnel and shifting resource allocations:	There have been some examples of cost/personnel savings and shifts in resource allocation resulting from the use of ZBB, but these have not been widespread.	To date, there have been no substantive examples of savings or shifts in resources allocation which resulted from the use of ZBB.
4. Most frequently mentioned benefit and problem associated with the use of ZBB:	*Benefit*—Increased participation of managers in the budget preparation process. *Problem*—Time and effort required to develop, implement, and operate the system.	
5. Incidence of post audits of ZBB:	Many user organizations in both sectors have conducted a review of the process at various stages in its implementation and use. However, these reviews tend to be informal, providing limited insight into the "real" cost-effectiveness of the process.	

The extent to which these observations are valid is still open to debate, and the test-of-time. Due to the "newness" of the technique the above comments are based on the short-run experiences of users.

Source: *Scott S. Cowen, "Experiences with Zero Base Budgeting in the Private and Public Sectors: An Overview," Proceedings of Annual Meeting, American Accounting Association, 1978. Also in A. Rappaport (ed.),* Information for Decision Making, *3rd ed. (Englewood Cliffs, N.J.: Prentice-Hall, 1982).*

looked at the concepts, and only then did they devise a process—a process to suit their special needs. This spelled success. It can be successful in the Federal Government too.[17]

variations of ZBB

ZBB does not have to be rigidly applied. Consider Alcan Aluminum, which originally used ZBB in its departments of sales, research, and administration. Alcan then adopted the following guidelines for their environment:

[17]*Streamlining Zero-Base Budgeting,* op. cit., p. 47. For a detailed description of experience with ZBB in controlling spending for departments of sales, research, and administration of the Alcan Aluminum Corp., see J. Connell, "ZBB at Its Best," *Management Focus,* November–December 1980, pp. 26–33.

1. Only those departments that have experienced major changes in activities (such as from reorganization or changes in management personnel) or that identify viable activity alternatives will use the full-blown ZBB process, resulting in the preparation of decision packages for a minimum level, status quo, and any incremental increases considered appropriate.
2. Those departments without major changes in activities or viable alternatives will proceed directly to the preparation of decision packages at the status quo level and any incremental increases considered appropriate.[18]

Many activities in both the private and public sectors are legally required. Hence, they are probably doubly misnamed. They are hardly "discretionary" and surely not "zero-base." Hence, the budgeting by decision units encompassing such activities might better be described as *60 percent base* or *80 percent base* budgeting. For example, accounting and personnel departments are required by law to file a multitude of reports to various government agencies. Similarly, many government agencies are required by law to render services to the aged, the poor, and the sick. To illustrate, San Mateo County in California uses 80 percent of its current budget as a minimum and uses ZBB processes to evaluate increments of 4 percent.

Appendix 10b: more on systems choice and human behavior

This Appendix covers additional matters regarding management accounting systems and human behavior. Most of these topics are "soft" in the sense that they are descriptions of commonly encountered problems that do not have numerical solutions. Nevertheless, accountants and managers should be on the alert for the presence of these and similar problems. After all, identification of the central problems must precede any solution, whether numerical or not. Major problems include top-management support, overemphasis on the short-run, slack, or budget padding, competition among managers, and accurate recordkeeping.

alternative views of organizations

A "rationalistic" model of organizations has been advocated *as a point of departure* here, whereby organizational objectives or goals are specified, alternatives systematically identified, consequences weighed, and actions chosen. Of course, in real life things are messier. For instance, some authors have maintained that a "garbage-can" model is more descriptive: ". . . organizations can be viewed for some purposes as collections of choices looking for problems, issues and feelings looking for decision situations in which they might be aired, solutions looking for issues to which they might be an answer, and decision makers looking for workers."[19]

This is not a book on organizations or on behavioral science, so we will not study alternative behavioral models here. Nevertheless, some cautionary words are warranted. For example, many researchers stress that there is no dominant organi-

---

[18]Connell, "ZBB at Its Best," p. 33. Note how the Alcan approach is a combination of incremental and ZBB budget processes. Also see R. Brown, "Beyond Zero-base Budgeting," *Journal of Accountancy* (March 1981), pp. 44–52.

[19]Michael D. Cohen, James G. March, and Johan P. Olsen, "A Garbage Can Model of Organizational Choice," *Administrative Science Quarterly,* Vol. 17, No. 1 (March 1972). For good discussions of alternative models, see A. Hopwood, *Accounting and Human Behavior;* and Edwin H. Caplan, *Management Accounting and Behavioral Science,* 2nd ed. (Reading, Mass.: Addison-Wesley, 1981). For a fascinating description of how different models lead to different conceptions and interpretations of the same phenomena, see Graham T. Allison, *Essence of Decision* (Boston: Little, Brown, 1971), a description of the Cuban missile crisis.

zational goal such as profit maximization. Instead of conducting exhaustive searches for alternatives, managers aim at "satisfactory" profits and focus on individual or group goals that frequently conflict with organization goals.

top-management support

Budgets and standards are major facets of a formal management control system. The motivational influence of a formal system varies from organization to organization and from individual manager to individual manager. For example, some professional personnel, such as research scientists, are often most affected by their personal or group goals. The scientist's feedback sources are more likely to be informal than formal. The opinions of colleagues and external critics may count heavily.

Personal goals, to the extent that acceptance of goals (such as budget goals) can be affected by formal systems within the organization, are likely to be heavily influenced by how higher executives support the system. Without massive top-management backing, the goals specified by the system, which should aim at goal congruence, are less likely to gain acceptance as group goals or as personal goals. Note too that acceptance is the key; acceptance may be best achieved in some cases by participatory processes and in other cases by authoritative processes.[20]

emphasis on short run

The accounting system is still dominant as a means for setting goals and influencing management behavior in most organizations. Goals outside the accounting system, even though meritorious, are regarded as supplementary unless top management follows through and acts as if they are indeed as important as short-run financial performance.

» *EXAMPLE*

The Soviet Union provides many cases where overstress on one or two aspects of the measurement system may lead to uneconomical behavior that focuses on a subgoal without considering overall organizational goals. To illustrate, taxi drivers were put on a bonus system based on mileage. Soon the Moscow suburbs were full of empty taxis barreling down the boulevards to fatten their bonuses. In response to bonuses based on tonnage norms, a Moscow chandelier factory produced heavier and heavier chandeliers until they started pulling ceilings down.

---

[20]Two polar types of management processes are *authoritative* and *participative.* For example, an authoritative way to prepare a budget is to have top management impose it on all managers without consulting them. In contrast, a participative way to prepare a budget is to have all responsible executives hammer out budget goals in a democratic fashion. R. J. Swieringa and R. H. Moncur, *Some Effects of Participative Budgeting on Managerial Behavior* (New York: National Association of Accountants, 1975), studied the use of participative budgeting in four production companies and examined the reactions of a sample of 137 managers. As might be expected, they found no magic guidelines. Instead, they concluded (p. 103) that "different variables may be important for predicting different aspects of how managers use budgeting." Many writers maintain that participative budgeting is better than authoritative budgeting. They also stress that budget-goal setting is highly individualistic. For example, a difficult budget may be perceived by a high achiever, to whom it represents an acceptable aspiration level, as a challenge, or by the low achiever as impossible. A. Buckley and E. McKenna, "Budgeting Control and Business Behavior," *Accounting and Business Research,* Spring 1972, p. 149, conclude that "managers like to achieve budget, since in doing so they fulfill esteem and achievement needs." For appraisals of the implications of behavioral science on accounting, see T. Hofstedt, "Behavioral Accounting Research: Pathologies, Paradigms and Prescriptions," *Accounting, Organizations and Society,* Vol. 1, No. 1 (1976); and T. Dyckman, M. Gibbins, and R. Swieringa, "Experimental and Survey Research in Financial Accounting: A Review and Evaluation" (Durham, N.C.: Duke University Graduate School of Business, 1978).

The most common instance of overemphasis is the short-run maximization of net income or sales that hurts long-run results. There are many questionable ways to improve short-run performance—stinting, for example, on repairs, quality control, advertising, research, or training. A manager may successfully exert pressure on employees for more productivity for short spurts of time. This may have some unfavorable long-run overtones.

As we explore various facets of systems design and techniques, we will see the importance of goal congruence in example after example. Top management must explicitly face the job of goal setting and coordination; it should not be a product of chance or a byproduct of the day-to-day extinguishing of business brush fires. Financial-planning models and master budgets plus feedback reporting are probably the most widely used techniques for coordinating goals.[21]

slack: a universal behavioral problem

The budgetary process entails the setting of goals. If the budget is overemphasized or viewed as a rigid monitor of performance, managers and employees are induced toward behavior that is not usually consonant with the typical goals of the organization as a whole. For example, budgets in not-for-profit organizations usually stipulate a top spending limit. This reinforces a philosophy of "We'd better spend it or we'll lose it," which does not lead to long-range cost reduction. Similarly, managers in industry are often disinclined to reduce costs because this leads to cuts in budget allowances for future periods. In other words, cost-cutting performance now may generate temporary praise or rewards but will make the job tougher later because the future budget will not be as easy to attain.

The personal goals of managers (personal income, size of staff, esteem, power) will often lead to a "bargained" budget, whereby managers intentionally create *slack* as a protective device.[22] *Slack* can be defined in a cost context as the difference between the minimum necessary costs and the actual costs of the firm. (Slack may be called *padding* in some organizations.) This seeking of slack permeates all budgeting in every conceivable sort of organization. Little has been done to counteract it.

An example of the attempt to reduce slack is the widespread use of lump-sum rewards to managers and other employees for "permanent" cost-savings. Another example is allowing the manager to "keep" the saving, in the form of not tightening the budget for a specified subsequent span of one to three years. Therefore, even though the old cost budget of $100,000 should be decreased to $90,000 because of the discovery of a new production method, the cut may be postponed for a year or more. Despite these attempts at counteraction, slack remains as one of the major unsolved problems in budgetary control.

cooperation versus competition

A fragile balance must be struck between careful delineation of responsibility, on the one hand, and a too-rigid separation of responsibility, on the other hand. Buck passing is a pervasive tendency that is supposedly minimized when responsibility is fixed unequivocally.

---

[21]Market share as a goal has been receiving increasing general attention because it frequently goes hand-in-hand with increased profitability. A study of 57 companies revealed that "on the average, a difference of 10 percentage points in market share is accompanied by a difference of about 5 points in pretax return on investment." See R. D. Buzzell, B. T. Gale, and R. G. M. Sultan, "Market Share—A Key to Profitability," *Harvard Business Review*, 53, No. 1 (January–February 1975), 97.

[22]M Schiff and A. Lewin, "Where Traditional Budgeting Fails," *Financial Executive*, XXXVI, No. 5, pp. 51–62; and "The Impact of People on Budgets," *Accounting Review*, XLV, No. 2 (April 1970), 259–69.

» **EXAMPLE**

A large utility used to hire college graduates and rotate them among all departments in the company during a two-year training program. Their salaries were not assigned to the departments, and individual managers took little interest in the trainees. But now it assigns the trainee to a definite department that fits his or her primary interest, where the trainee is given direct responsibility as soon as possible. Both the trainees and the managers are much more satisfied with the new responsibility arrangement.

But often the motivational impact boomerangs; too much falls between the chairs. Managers often wear blinders and concentrate more than ever on their individual worlds. Family cooperation is replaced by intracompany competition. When departments are truly interdependent in many of their important decisions, serious consideration is often given to merging them into a single department for responsibility-accounting purposes.

accurate recordkeeping

Textbooks do not devote much space to the problems of obtaining accurate source documents. Yet this is easily one of the most pervasive, everlasting problems in collecting information. An accounting system cannot help managers predict and make decisions if its recordkeeping is haphazard.

Pressures may spur managers to encourage their subordinates to record time erroneously or to tinker with scrap or usage reports.

» **EXAMPLE**

The maintenance crews of one telephone company regularly performed recurring short-term maintenance and repair work on various projects. At other times, the same crews would be concerned with huge construction projects—installing or building plant and equipment. The company had weekly reports on performance of the regular maintenance work but had only loose control over the construction projects. An investigation disclosed that the foremen were encouraging the workmen to boost the time on the construction projects and to understate the time on the regular maintenance projects. Thus the foremen's performance on the latter always looked good. The situation was corrected when the emphases on maintenance and on construction were balanced so that both were currently budgeted and controlled.

Hopwood[23] takes a dim view of what he calls a *budget-constrained style* of performance evaluation, which appraises managers primarily on the basis of whether they meet the short-term budget. Such a style induces undesirable filtering and falsifying of records. Thus, when a manager chooses to overemphasize a short-run budget, or when a manager misuses data when analyzing subordinates' performance, there are costly implications for accounting systems. For example, there is a higher probability of falsifying source documents. Either the costs of internal audits and other internal controls will rise, or the reliability of the accounting system will fall.

Accurate recordkeeping is essentially a problem of motivation. The accountant and manager should be more sensitive to possible errors, more aware of the futility of trying to get usage of time and materials reported accurately in small increments, and more conscious of the natural tendency of individuals to report their activities so as to minimize their personal bother and maximize their own showing.[24] The hazard of trying to get extremely detailed reports extends not only to lack of confidence in individual reports themselves but to the likelihood of generating monumental contempt for the entire system.

[23]A. Hopwood, "Leadership Climate and the Use of Accounting Data in Performance Evaluation," *Accounting Review,* Vol. XLIX, No. 3 (July 1974).

[24]For more examples, see E. Caplan and J. Champoux, *Cases in Management Accounting: Context and Behavior* (New York: National Association of Accountants, 1978), pp. 37–38.

Top managers can induce accurate scorekeeping if they can persuade subordinates that the documents are important for decision making. Again we see the desirability of active management support.

» ***EXAMPLE***

A firm of civil engineers has surveying jobs throughout California that are largely obtained by firm price quotations. A key to profitability is the ability to predict how much time will be required for the various subtasks on the job. The president of the firm feels so strongly about the need for feedback that his field crew managers must mail daily time reports to the central office. If they are not received on the day expected, the president immediately phones to find out why.

QUESTIONS, PROBLEMS, AND CASES

10-1 "Considered together, congruence and effort are really subparts of motivation." Do you agree? Explain.

10-2 What are the three major types of control?

10-3 "Clearly, the bearing of risk changes behavior." Give an example.

10-4 Give three examples of committed costs.

10-5 Give three examples of discretionary costs.

10-6 Give three examples of engineered costs.

10-7 What are two synonyms for *discretionary costs?*

10-8 What are the most common outputs linked with discretionary costs?

10-9 "A few discretionary costs do indeed behave as variable costs." Explain.

10-10 What are the most obvious candidates for work measurement?

10-11 "The central purpose of a management accounting system is to improve the collective decisions within an organization." Do you agree? Explain.

10-12 Give an example of how a control system can motivate a manager to behave against the best interests of the company as a whole.

10-13 "I'm majoring in accounting. This study of human relations is fruitless. You've got to be born with a flair for getting along with others. You can't learn it!" Do you agree? Why?

10-14 "Interpretation is essential for understanding accounting reports." Suggest how the accounting function may be organized to emphasize interpretation.

10-15 ***Budgets as motivators.*** "Budgets and responsibility accounting and other modern accounting techniques foster a policed, departmental orientation rather than a positive, overall organizational orientation." Do you agree? Explain.

10-16 ***Budgets as pressure devices.*** Sord and Welsch have stated: "It should be recognized that pressure on supervisors need not come from control techniques, assuming that standards of performance are not unfair or too high. Pressure on supervisors comes from the responsibilities inherent in the supervisor's job." Do you agree? Why?

10-17 ***Budgets as motivators.*** "To accept budgets as motivators is to imply that supervisors do not have adequate interest in their job. This is seen as an insult to a person's integrity, and the factory supervisors resent it strongly." Do you agree? Why?

10-18 ***Attitudes toward the accountant.*** A prominent financial analyst, who became very successful with his Wall Street investments, once commented:

"My experience with the accountant is that for him everything has equal importance. He is like the Lord in the Bible, where it is written that 'a thousand years are in His sight as yesterday' when it is past—except that it is just the other way around with the accountant: 10 cents in the balance sheet is just as important as a million dollars. The main thing for him is that every figure should be correct."

Elbert Hubbard, a philosopher popular early in the twentieth century, made the following remarks:

"The typical auditor is a man past middle age, spare, wrinkled, intelligent, cold, passive, non-committal, with eyes like a codfish, polite in contact, but at the same time unresponsive, cold; calm and damnably composed as a concrete post or a plaster-of-Paris cast; a human petrification with a heart of feldspar and without charm of the friendly germ, minus bowels, passion, or a sense of humour. Happily, they never reproduce and all of them finally go to Hell."

In general, do you agree with the remarks above? Why?

10-19 ***Governmental and business budgets.*** (CMA) The term *budget* and the concept of budgeting can have different connotations depending upon the use and situation. A fundamental difference between governmental and business budgets lies in the appropriation nature of the governmental budget. However, a business organization could choose to base its budgeting process on a basis similar to the governmental approach.

REQUIRED

1. Describe the characteristics that exist in the governmental sector that encourage or require the use of appropriation budgeting.
2. If a business were to adopt an appropriation basis for its budgeting process:
   a. Describe the probable effect on a manager's behavior, and
   b. Explain why a manager would behave in this manner.
3. Explain how governmental budgeting could be modified in order to be more effective for managerial control purposes.

10-20 ***Goals of public accounting firm.*** All personnel, including partners, of public accounting firms must usually turn in biweekly time reports, showing how many hours were devoted to their various duties. These firms have traditionally looked unfavorably on idle or unassigned staff time. They have looked favorably on heavy percentages of chargeable (billable) time because this maximizes revenue. What effect is such a policy likely to have on the behavior of the firm's personnel? Can you relate this practice to the problem of harmony of goals that was discussed in the chapter? How?

10-21 ***Goals and recordkeeping.*** (CMA, adapted) A department manager performs the timekeeping function for a manufacturing department. From time to time analysis of overhead and direct-labor variances have shown that the department manager has deliberately misclassified labor hours (e.g., listed direct-labor hours as indirect-labor hours and vice versa) so that only one of the two labor variances is unfavorable. It is not feasible economically to hire a separate timekeeper. What should the company do, if anything, to resolve this problem?

10-22 ***Performance evaluation.*** Consider the following excerpt from a company employee newsletter. It announces the creation of a Perpetual Trophy that will be awarded to the branch with the most outstanding performance during a fiscal year:

> The Trophy will be several feet high and will be designed to be moved from branch to branch each year. Additionally, a small replica of the trophy will be awarded to the manager of the winning branch.
>
> The Trophy will be awarded to the branch with the best combination of sales percentage increase and net operating percentage increase. The actual calculation will be to take the sales percentage increase, plus the net operating profit percentage increase, and divide those two numbers by two, giving equal weight to both sales and profit growth. Only independent branches achieving a minimum 15 percent sales increase will be eligible.

REQUIRED What is your personal evaluation of the way outstanding performance is measured?

10-23 ***Commission plan for new-car sales personnel.*** As an automobile dealer, you are faced with the problem of formulating a commission plan for new-car sales personnel. You have listed the following alternatives:

a. Commissions based on a flat percentage of dollar sales.
b. Commissions based on varying percentages of dollar sales. The higher the sales price of a deal, the higher the commission rate. Also, commissions will vary depending on the accessories sold.
c. Commissions based on net profit after allocation of a fair share of all operating expenses.

REQUIRED Evaluate these alternatives. Are there other methods that deserve consideration?

10-24 ***Budgets and motivation.*** You are working as a supervisor in a manufacturing department that has substantial amounts of personnel and equipment. You are paid a "base" salary that is actually low for this type of work. The firm has a very liberal bonus plan, which pays you another $1,000 each time you "make the budget" and 2 percent of the amount you are able to save.

Your past experiences have been as follows:

MONTHLY PERIOD	1	2	3	4	5	6
Budget	$40,000	$40,000	$39,000	$36,000	$36,000	$36,250
Actual	41,000	39,500	37,000	37,000	36,500	36,000
Variance	$ 1,000 U	$ 500 F	$ 2,000 F	$ 1,000 U	$ 500 U	$ 250 F

REQUIRED

1. What would you do as a "rational person" if you were starting the job all over again from period 1 with the above information?
2. What would you recommend, if anything, be done to the system if you are now promoted to a higher job in management and required to handle the "bonus system" in this department?

10-25 ***Budgets and motivation.*** Christine Everette operates a chain of health centers. One of the largest is in the heart of Chicago. Everette used the services of three managers, Dave, Nick, and Sid. Each had charge of a group of exercise and apparatus rooms similar in all regards. She offered three methods of weekly payment to the men:

Method X. A base rate of $6 per hour and 30 percent of all reductions in expenses below a "norm" of $600 per week

Method Y. A flat wage of $7 per hour

Method Z. No base rate, but a bonus of $300 for meeting the "norm," plus 10 percent of all reductions in expenses below the norm

The men chose their method of compensation before starting employment. Assume a 40-hour week. The record for the past six weeks for the three areas follows (all data are in dollars):

	WEEKS					
	1	2	3	4	5	6
Dave:						
Utilities	250	250	250	250	250	250
Supplies	180	20	20	260	100	20
Repairs & misc.	305	250	220	265	260	200
Total	735	520	490	775	610	470
Nick:						
Utilities	250	250	250	250	250	250
Supplies	100	100	100	100	100	100
Repairs & misc.	250	200	265	220	260	305
Total	600	550	615	570	610	655
Sid:						
Utilities	250	250	250	250	250	250
Supplies	100	100	100	100	100	100
Repairs & misc.	250	250	250	250	250	250
Total	600	600	600	600	600	600

REQUIRED

Which payment methods were most likely chosen by Dave, Nick, and Sid? Base your answer on an analysis of cost behavior patterns. Assume that each man picked a different plan. (Giving your final answer is not enough; briefly explain your choices.)

10-26 ***Budgeting time and judging performance for professional services.*** Henry Johnson, an affable young accounting major, went to work for White, Green, Black & Co., a large

CPA firm, shortly after graduation from college. He became an assistant to Fritz Wilcox, an auditing "senior" who was twenty-six years old and had just become a CPA. Henry had had no auditing courses in college, so he spent the first two weeks of work reading auditing textbooks and doing menial tasks around the office. He finally got his first assignment during the third week. Fritz Wilcox and he went to the office of a client and started to trace paid checks to their invoices. Although the work was tedious, Henry was pleased because he could now start to "earn his pay" by doing actual work instead of studying.

Fritz told Henry that the job had been budgeted for thirty-two hours (two days' work for the two men) by the partner in charge of the engagement. Early in the afternoon of the second day, however, it became obvious that the job would be completed sooner than expected. They finished at 4:00 P.M., an hour early, so the actual time spent was thirty hours instead of the budgeted thirty-two. Henry, very conscientious about his new job, quickly gathered his papers together in order to return to the office. Fritz said, "Whoa, Henry. There's no need to hurry. The job was supposed to take us two days, so the boss won't be expecting us back at the office this afternoon. We might as well just leave early and charge the whole two days to the client on our time sheets. Anyway, if we go back to the office, by the time we get there, we won't have time left to get any work done."

That evening Henry was puzzled over the statement Fritz had made. Henry was glad to charge the whole two days to the client because it gave his firm more revenue. But on the other hand, Henry remembered that when he had been going through orientation, one of the partners had instructed him never to charge time to a client unless the time so charged was actually spent on the client's audit. This made sense to Henry; he realized that the firm might lose clients if billings were too high. The partner had also said that time not spent on a client's audit should be allocated to "available time" (nonchargeable time) on Henry's time sheet.

Henry finally decided that the idea Fritz had had to charge the thirty-first and thirty-second hours to the client was really the best course because it increased Henry's chargeable-time-to-total-time ratio on his time sheet. He felt this would please the partners, because he had learned through the grapevine that the partners had complimented employees in the past who had high chargeable-time-to-total-time ratios. This last point was crucial to Henry, since he was anxious to log as much chargeable time as possible so that the firm could recover the wages it had paid him for the first two weeks of his employ.

REQUIRED Is it "healthy," from the viewpoint of White, Green, Black & Co., for Henry to be puzzled about this? Why?

10-27 ***Motivation and control of costs.*** The Sharp Company develops, manufactures, and markets several product lines of low-cost consumer goods. Top management of the company is attempting to evaluate the present method and a new method of charging the different production departments for the services they receive from one of the engineering departments, which is called Manufacturing Engineering Services (MES).

The function of MES, which consists of about thirty engineers and ten draftsmen, is to reduce the costs of producing the different products of the company by improving machine and manufacturing process design while maintaining the required level of quality. The MES manager reports to the engineering supervisor, who reports to the vice-president, manufacturing. The MES manager, George Amershi, may increase or decrease the number of engineers under him. He is evaluated on the basis of several variables, one of which is the annual incremental savings to the company brought about by his department in excess of the costs of operating his department. These costs consist of actual salaries, a share of corporate overhead, the cost of office supplies used by his department, and a cost of capital charge. An individual engineer is evaluated on the basis of the ratio of the annual savings he or she accomplishes in relation to the engineer's annual salary. The salary range of an engineer is defined by personnel classification; there are four classifications, and promotion from one classification to another depends on the approval of a panel that includes both production and engineering personnel.

Production department managers report to a production supervisor, who reports to the vice-president, manufacturing. The production department for each product line is treated as a profit center, and engineering services are provided at a cost, according to the following plan. When a production department manager and an engineer agree on a possible project to improve production efficiency, they sign a contract that specifies the scope of the project, the estimated savings to be realized, the probability of success, and the number of engineering hours of each personnel classification required. The charge to the particular production department is determined by the product of the number of hours required times the "classification rate" for each personnel classification. This rate depends on the average salary for the classification involved and a share of the engineering department's other costs. An engineer is expected to spend at least 85 percent of his time on specific, contracted projects; the remainder may be used for preliminary investigations of potential cost-saving projects or self-improving study. A recent survey showed that production managers have a high degree of confidence in the MES engineers.

A new plan has been proposed to top management, in which no charge will be made to production departments for engineering services. In all other respects the new system will be identical to the present. Production managers will continue to request engineering services as under the present plan. Proponents of the new plan say that under it, production managers will take a greater advantage of existing engineering talent. Regardless of how engineering services are accounted for, the company is committed to the idea of production departments being profit centers.

REQUIRED

Evaluate the strong and weak points of the present and proposed plans. Will the company tend to hire the optimal quantity of engineering talent? Will this engineering talent be used as effectively as possible?

10-28 ***Control of discretionary costs.*** The manager of a warehouse for a mail-order firm is concerned with the control of her fixed costs. She has recently applied work-measurement techniques and an engineered-cost approach to the staff of order clerks and is wondering if a similar technique could be applied to the workers who collect merchandise in the warehouse and bring it to the area where orders are assembled for shipment.

The warehouse foreman contends that this should not be done, because the present work force of twenty persons should be viewed as a fixed cost necessary to handle the usual volume of orders with a minimum of delay. These employees work a forty-hour week at $15 per hour.

Preliminary studies show that it takes an average of twelve minutes for a worker to locate an article and take it to the order-assembly area, and that the average order is for two different articles. At present the volume of orders to be processed is 1,800 per week.

REQUIRED

1. For the present volume of orders, develop a discretionary-cost and an engineered-cost approach for the weekly performance report.
2. Repeat requirement 1 for volume levels of 1,600 and 1,400 orders per week.
3. What other factors should be compared with the budget variances found in requirements 1 and 2 in order to make a decision on the size of the work force?

10-29 ***Work measurement.*** The Hayward Company has installed a work-measurement program for its billing operations. A standard billing cost of $2 per bill has been used, based on hourly labor rates of $16 and an average processing rate of 8 bills of 10 lines each per hour. Each clerk has a $7\frac{1}{2}$-hour workday and a 5-day workweek.

The supervisor has received the following report of performance from his superior—the office manager, Ann Davis—for a recent 4-week period regarding his clerks:

			VARIANCE	
	ACTUAL	BUDGET	amount	equivalent persons
Billing labor (5 clerks)	$12,000	$7,400 (3,700 bills × $2.00)	$4,600 U	1.9

The supervisor knows that he must explain the unfavorable variance and offer suggestions regarding how to avoid such an unfavorable variance in the future. Because of a recession, the office manager is under severe pressure to cut staff. In fact, she had penciled a question on the report: "Looks as if we can get along with two less clerks?"

Anticipating the pressures, the supervisor had taken a random sample of 400 of the 3,700 bills that were prepared during the period under review. His count of the lines in the sample totaled 5,200.

REQUIRED As the supervisor, prepare a one-page explanation of the $4,600 unfavorable variance, together with your remedial suggestions.

10-30 ***Ford Motor Company's flexible-budget control over clerical costs through work measurement.*** This case illustrates a method by which flexible-budget controls have been adapted to a nonmanufacturing operation to control costs that might normally be classed as fixed labor and operating expense. It is possible and practical to control many expenses of this nature by the use of "standard" processing rates for work performed.

The following information is presented as background material to outline the control approach followed by this company:

The parts and accessories division of the Ford Motor Company controls and evaluates the performance of its branch-warehouse operations by the use of "flexible labor and expense budgets." These budgetary controls are in use in both the warehousing and the accounting activities of these operations and are used for both weekly and monthly analysis.

Primarily, variable-labor functions and controllable-expense classifications are supervised in this manner. Fixed costs that are not controllable by local management, such as supervision, taxes, and depreciation, are administered by the use of fixed (static) budget allowances.

All variable functions of the warehousing and accounting activities have been analyzed and standardized and related to some measurable work output. By maintaining daily control of these functional productivities and related daily labor charges, the required operating reports are prepared and submitted to the general office for analysis, consolidation, and comparison with national operating-budget levels.

A primary source of output statistics is obtained from a record of actual daily shipments made by the warehouse, as many accounting-function statistics are based on this measurement. The determinable output measurements are compared with the predetermined functional-budget rate to calculate "budget hours generated" during the budget period under review. The operating variances are determined by comparing generated budget hours with actual functional-labor charges during the same period. These variances are expressed both in hours of variance and equivalent-persons variance. The latter variance is calculated by comparing the hourly variance amounts with the forty shift-hours available in the budget period under review.

For a recent normal workweek of five operating days, the following labor-distribution detail and output information have been accumulated for certain selected accounting-department functions. The complete budget review is actually applied to approximately fifty separate and distinct activities in this operation.

Functional Budget Rates and Labor Distribution

FUNCTION	BUDGET RATE PER HOUR	ACTUAL HOURS WORKED
Invoice scheduling	135 orders shipped	68.0
Keypunch†	680 line items processed	142.0
Keyverification†	1,360 line items processed	71.0
IBM machine operator†	1,020 line items printed	108.0
Proofreading†	510 line items proofread	208.0
Accounts payable:		125.0‡
Invoice matching	80 line items received	
Check auditing	70 payments made	
Credit adjustments	15 adjustments issued	69.0
Budgeted hourly labor rate—$20.00 per hour		
Actual labor costs —$16,400		

†*To determine the output allowance, the 2,720 line items backordered should be added to the 99,280 items shipped.*

‡*The 125.0 represents the combined actual hours worked on accounts payable; no subdivision is available for invoice matching and check auditing.*

Output Statistics

1. Number of orders shipped	8,640
2. Number of line items* shipped	99,280
3. Number of line items backordered in warehouse	2,720
4. Number of checks written for merchandise received	3,290
5. Number of line items on shipments received	4,960
6. Number of credit adjustments approved	975

**Represents a single part number shipped or received, regardless of quantity.*

REQUIRED

1. Determine labor variance by function. Express variance in both hours and equivalent persons.
2. Calculate the flexible-budget labor variance in dollars.
3. Analyze the flexible-budget variance as determined in requirement 2. What portion of this variance was attributable to a labor-price variance and a labor-efficiency variance?

10-31 ***Work measurement.*** The administrator of the Singapore Hotel has established a budget for the laundry department. The department's equipment consists of a washer that can process 500 pounds an hour. For every 100 pounds of linen processed, soap costs of 15¢ and water costs of 5¢ are incurred. One man operates the laundry. He works eight hours daily, six days per week, at $2 per hour, a good wage in Singapore. There is no premium paid for overtime.

The depreciation on the machine is $1,950 per year. The budget drawn by the administrator calls for $100 of overhead to be charged to the laundry for every four-week period. When the budget was established, the administrator thought that the expenses for the normal volume of linen would be $802 for a four-week period, including fixed expenses.

During the last four weeks, the laundry processed 72,000 pounds of linen and incurred $814 in expenses, of which $145 was for soap, and $35 was for water. The man in charge of the laundry says he is doing a good job, because the budget calls for expenses of $802, and he incurred only $814.

REQUIRED:

1. What volume of laundry did the administrator use for his $802 budget for the four-week period?
2. Prepare a performance report that will give the administrator a method for evaluating the laundry.

10-32 ***Control of purchasing, variances, motivation.*** Henry Evers, controller at Able Manufacturing Co., was delighted with his newest management tool. By adding a few programs and a list of standard material costs to his IBX minicomputer, he enabled the old Accounts Payable program to produce a weekly purchase-price variance report. The standard cost of each item was multiplied by the quantity specified on an invoice. That extended standard cost was then compared with the actual amount billed by the vendor. The difference was the purchase-price variance. Thus a dozen metal caps should have cost $198.00, or $16.50 each. Able Manufacturing Co. paid $216.02 for them, for an unfavorable variance of $18.02. See Exhibit 10-9.)

Evers saw this report as the answer to three major control problems. First, it gave him the total material-price variance figure for his costing reports. Previously this had been done by hand, very slowly, for the work center and project managers. Second, it would give the purchasing department a measure of its performance. Third, it would aid Jack Hill, the newly hired cost accountant, in setting good material-cost standards.

The firm was currently producing in two shifts, with much expediting, rush-order shipping, and overtime. It was also producing three new products and was preparing to make a fourth new product very shortly.

A. In reviewing the first report, Evers was alarmed at the number of extremely large variances, including purchased items for which there was no standard cost at all.

EXHIBIT 10-9

Sample Page from a Purchase-Price Variance Report

ITEM #	DESCRIP.	PROJ/ DEPT #	BUYER	VENDOR	QTY	STD. COST	EXTND COST	INVOICE AMT.	VAR. AMT.	(+) (−)	VAR. %
00103	Metal Cap	644	2	12	12	16.500	198.00	216.02	18.02	−	9.1
00104	Dust Cvr	x89	2	21	2	12.500	25.00	22.00	3.00	+	12.0
00107	Reel	644	3	69	30	6.250	187.50	196.88	9.38	−	5.0
00108	Bracket	644	2	67	30	.420	12.60	15.00	2.40	−	19.0
00109	Base	661	2	21	1	12.750	12.75	14.25	1.50	−	11.8
00113		No Standard for this Item									
00124	R1 Shaft	644	2	32	30	1.200	36.00	39.60	3.60	−	10.0
00125	Washer	644	1	24	100	1.250	125.00	125.00	0.00		00.0
00127	Mic. Swtch	x89	3	21	60	82.100	4926.00	4433.40	492.60	+	10.0
00128	R1 Shaft	661	1	69	30	1.600	48.00	48.00	0.00		00.0
00130	Plate	644	2	67	5	9.600	48.00	59.00	11.00	−	22.0
00133	Vacuum Can	x89	2	12	1	108.500	108.50	108.50	0.00		00.0
00135	Tray	x89	3	5	2	65.000	130.00	130.00	0.00		00.0
00142	Hex Nut	x89	2	21	400	.026	10.40	10.80	.40	−	3.8
00182	Hold Bar	661	2	21	1	.900	.90	1.50	.60	−	40.0
00187	Handle	644	1	67	6	.065	.39	1.50	1.11		245.0
00188	Handle	644	1	67	2	.065	13	1.50	1.37		−1053.0
00189	Handle	644	3	67	50	.065	32.50	32.50	0.00		00.0

Before approaching Purchasing, he asked Jack Hill for an explanation. Hill said that key-punching errors were probably at fault. Item numbers had to match on the invoice and the standards list or the program gave a "No Standard Cost" message, or it used the wrong standard cost for comparison. Evers suspected other causes for the variances and missing standards.

1. Examine the purchasing-department paperwork flow (Exhibit 10-10) and comment on other possible reasons for missing standards and large variances.

B. The purchasing department proved to be very suspicious of Evers's new management report. Ed Hughes, head of the purchasing department, pointed out that because of expediting, he was really not in control of quantities shipped or special handling charges. Thus, he might order too few for a bulk-order price deal and be charged a

EXHIBIT 10-10

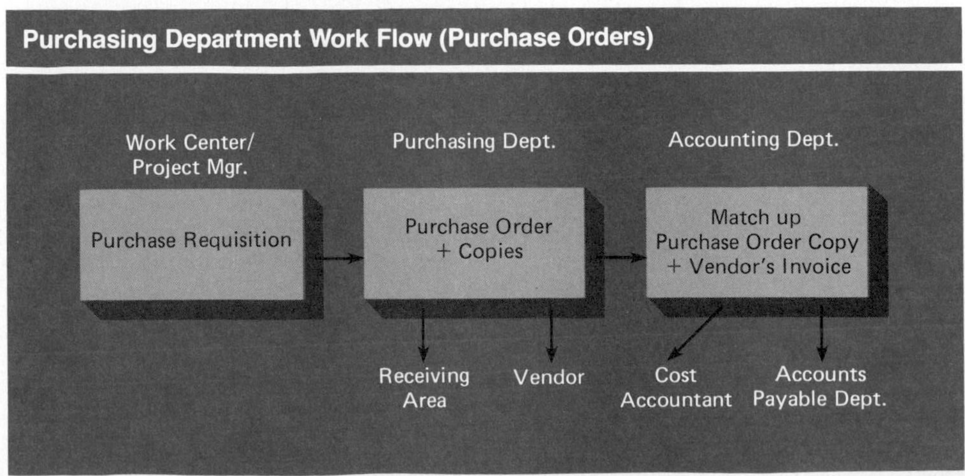

special delivery fee as well. Hughes felt the Price Variance Report did not really reflect what the purchasing department could do under "normal" conditions.

1. In view of Hughes's comment, is the report appropriate?
2. What does the report really measure now?
3. How might Evers change the report to make it more useful to Hughes?
4. Would the additional benefit justify the additional costs?

C. The overall net purchase-price variance for the week ending June 30 was $8,000 (unfavorable) for $200,000 purchased material. Hughes claimed that the 4 percent unfavorable variance was extremely good performance, in view of the expediting pressure.

1. Analyze the sample report page in Exhibit 10-9. Make your own decision about the purchasing department's performance, according to the information there.

D. Jack Hill complained that the number of new products was growing fast and that he was unable to keep up with the job of assigning new cost standards. He asked Evers to have the program changed to allow the first price paid for an item to become the standard cost.

1. Would you approve this change?
2. How else might Able Manufacturing Co. get material standards assigned more quickly?

10-33 ***Practical work measurement.*** A team of job analysts has been studying a U.S. Air Force maintenance base in Ohio. The aim is to apply flexible budgeting to determine how many workers are required.

A repair parts stockroom has been under study. The stockroom has used a perpetual inventory system. The stockroom has a foreman plus two clerks. A second clerk had been added in the middle of the preceding year at the foreman's request.

During the month of March, a job analyst spent several days reviewing and timing the tasks of the stockroom personnel. She classified all workloads as either tasks that vary with the volume of activity or tasks that are necessary regardless of volume.

Variable operations in the stockroom depend upon receipts and issuances of repair parts. The job analyst established the following five operations and time allowances. All time allowances have been adjusted for personal time and fatigue:

OPERATION NUMBER	DESCRIPTION	STANDARD TIME ALLOWANCE IN MINUTES
1	Issuing repair parts	15
2	Recording issues on stores ledger cards and pricing	9
3	Checking parts received and preparing receiving reports	5
4	Recording receipts on stores ledger cards	3
5	Placing parts in stock	10

The analyst also computed time allowances for "standby" activities, which were defined as those activities independent of fluctuations in volume. They were attributed solely to the foreman for a four-week period:

	MINUTES
Testing, expediting, supervising	3,000
Inventory control problems	1,800
Physical counts and comparisons with records	900
Total	5,700

Each four-week period normally had 20 working days of 8 hours each. Therefore, each worker would have $20 \times 8 \times 60 = 9{,}600$ minutes of available work time. Records of actual time spent performing stockroom operations during a recent four-week period showed:

	VARIABLE OPERATION NUMBER						
employee	**1**	**2**	**3**	**4**	**5**	OTHER	TOTAL
Foreman	600		700			8,300	9,600
Clerk #1		3,800		1,000		4,800	9,600
Clerk #2	5,600		1,000		3,000		9,600
Total	6,200	3,800	1,700	1,000	3,000	13,100	28,800

The "other" time consisted of:

	MINUTES
Foreman:	
Testing, expediting, and supervising	5,000
Inventory control problems	3,300
Clerk #1:	
Rearranging items in stock	3,800
Physical inventory counts	1,000

The volume of activity consisted of 350 requisitions filled and processed for parts issued. In addition, 250 receiving reports were prepared and recorded for parts received and placed in stock.

REQUIRED

1. Based upon the level of activity during the period, prepare a performance report in minutes. For each operation, including standby operations, present the appropriate total standard time allowance, the actual time recorded, and the variance.
2. Fill in the blanks:

Total available work time	?
Deduct: total standby workload time allowance	?
Variable workload time available	?
Deduct: total variable workload time allowance	?
Excess time available	?

3. How many excess employees are working in the stockroom?
4. Suppose management decides to reduce the stockroom personnel to two persons, the foreman plus one clerk. What activities offer the best opportunities for improving efficiency?
5. Assume that the foreman earns a salary of $26,000 per year and each clerk is paid $10 per hour. Prepare a budget for the next operating year for compensation. Use (a) a discretionary-cost approach and (b) a work-measurement approach. Show how you arrived at your numbers.
6. Describe at least two "useful generalizations" about work measurement that are illustrated by this situation.

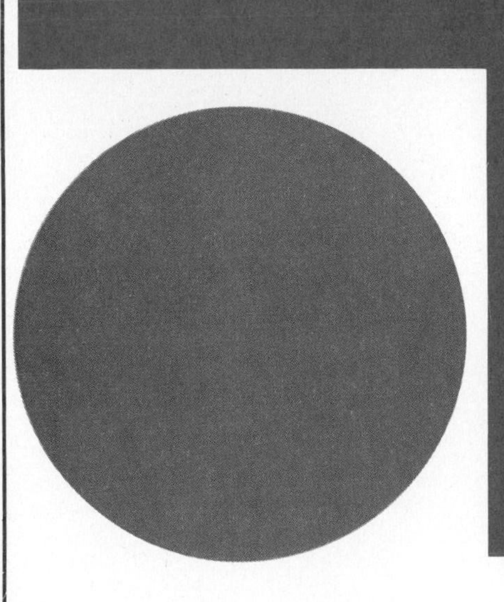

Relevant Costs for Nonroutine Decisions

SECTION FOUR

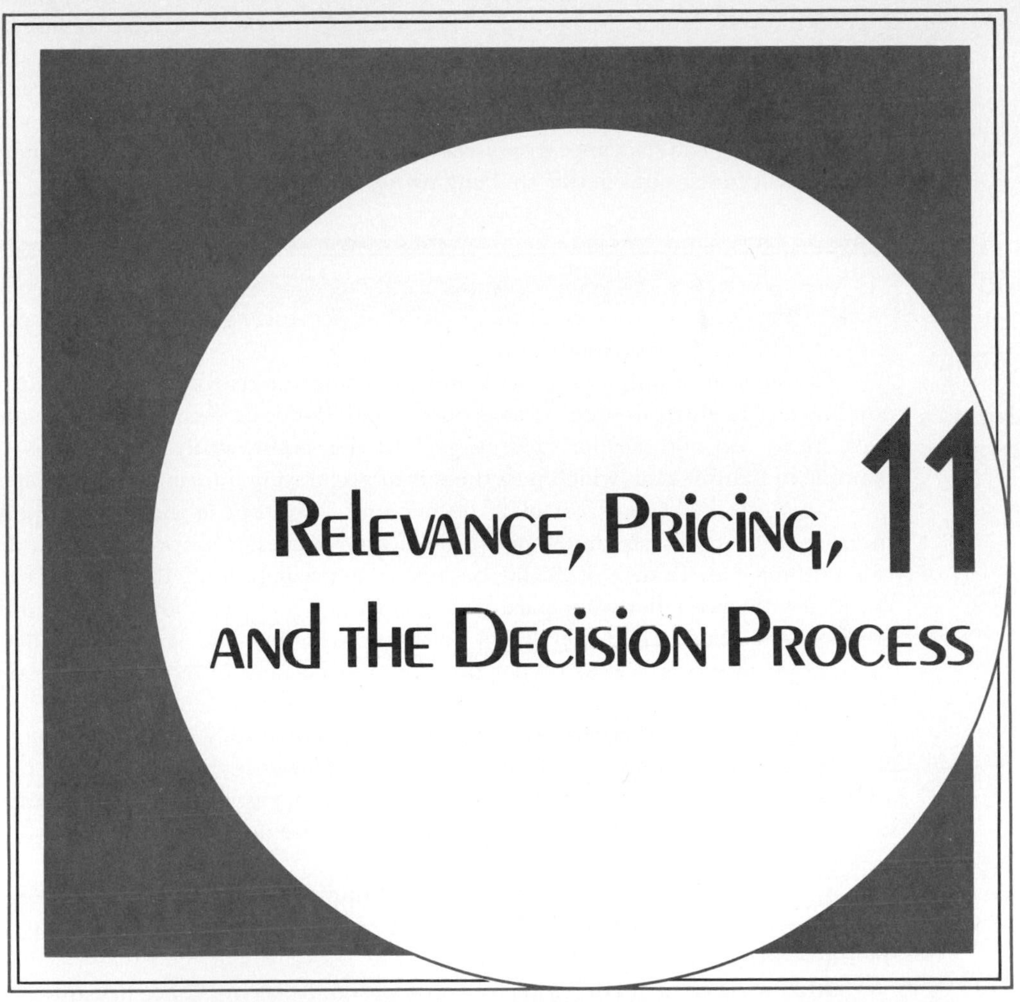

11 Relevance, Pricing, and the Decision Process

We have already seen how the contribution approach, with its emphasis on cost behavior patterns, helps cost analysis and the evaluation of performance. Our study has focused on two purposes: product costing and costing for routine control of operations. In this chapter we turn to a third purpose: costing for special nonroutine decisions, such as the addition or deletion of a product line, the manufacture or purchase of direct materials (make or buy), the acceptance or rejection of a special order, the replacement of equipment, and many others. Teamwork among executives is commonly used in reaching these decisions, which are often fusions of the thinking of engineers, economists, production managers, sales managers, mathematicians, and accountants. Cost analysis is nearly always helpful, and that is why the cost accountant plays an important role in these special decisions.

Years ago the word *relevant* was not overused. Now it seems to be applied in every context imaginable. Nevertheless, *relevant* is particularly apt for our purposes, so we will stress the word in this chapter. When is an item relevant to a particular management decision? When is it irrelevant? These distinctions are crucial to the making of intelligent decisions. The contribution approach, combined with the ability to distinguish relevance from irrelevance, enables accountants and managers to reach correct conclusions in this challenging area.

Information and the decision process

The manager has a method for deciding among courses of action, often called a **decision model.** For now, let us focus on what accounting information to provide, *given* any form of decision model.

predictions and models

Consider an example of a decision concerning the rearrangement of a production line and facilities in order to save operating labor costs. Assume the only alternatives are to "do nothing" or "rearrange." At this point, study the analysis of this example in Exhibit 11-1, which puts the role of accounting information in perspective.

The historical labor cost of $2.00 per unit of output is the starting point for *predicting* the labor costs under both of the alternatives. The prediction under the "do nothing" alternative is $2.00 because the prediction method, used here for simplicity, assumes that the past will exactly repeat itself, although a different prediction method might well have been appropriate. The labor cost under the "rearrange" alternative is $1.80 per product unit because of expected reductions in labor usage.

The specific predictions are fed forward as inputs to a decision model, which might consist of a comparison of the total predicted labor savings against the required additional investment, if any. If the total predicted labor savings were sufficiently high to warrant the investment, the rearrangement would be implemented.

models and feedback

Suppose the decision model specifies a goal of minimizing operating costs. The total labor costs would be compared. The preferred choice would be the alternative with the least cost.

After a choice is made, implementation (action) occurs. The subsequent evaluation of actual performance provides feedback. In turn, the feedback might affect the future predictions, the prediction method itself, the decision model itself, or the implementation.

In our illustration, the actual results of the plant rearrangement may show that the new labor costs are $2.50 per product unit rather than the $1.80 originally predicted. This feedback may lead to better implementation (step 4 in Exhibit 11-1), such as a change in supervisory behavior, in employee training, or in personnel, so that the $1.80 target is achieved. On the other hand, the feedback may convince the decision maker that the prediction method, rather than the implementation, was faulty. Perhaps the prediction method for similar decisions in the future should be modified to allow for worker training or learning time.

Meaning of relevance

historical costs and predictions

Exhibit 11-1 shows that every decision deals with the future—whether it be ten seconds ahead (the decision to adjust a dial) or eighty years ahead (the decision of where to locate a factory). A decision always involves a prediction. Therefore, the function of decision making is to select courses of action for the future. There is no opportunity to alter the past.

EXHIBIT 11-1

(Place a clip on this page for easy reference.)

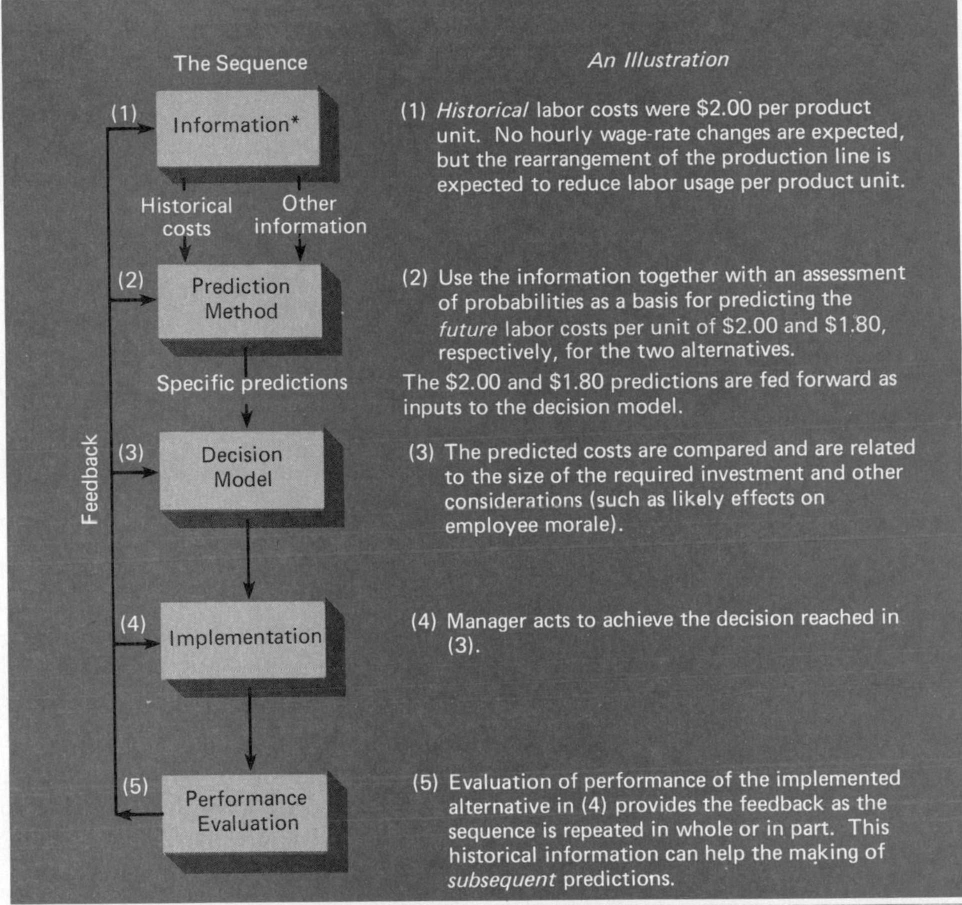

The decision model in Exhibit 11-1 concentrated on a comparison of *expected future* costs that will *differ* among alternatives.[1] If all other considerations are a standoff, and the objective is to minimize costs, then rearrangement is the more desirable alternative. The $2 predicted direct-labor charge may be the same as in the past, and the past records may have been extremely helpful in preparing the $2 forecast. Most accountants and managers view the $2 past cost as the future cost. However, the crucial point is that the $2 is an expected future cost, not a past cost. *Historical costs in themselves are irrelevant to the decision, although they may be the best available basis for predicting future costs.*

Now suppose that past direct-materials costs of $5 per unit should not change under either alternative. Thus, our prediction becomes $5 per unit. Yet these future

[1]The time value of money is discussed in the next chapter. When interest factors are introduced, expected future costs and revenues with the same magnitude but different timing can be relevant.

costs are irrelevant, because they will not differ under alternatives. Of course, there is no harm in preparing a comparative analysis that includes both the relevant direct-labor-cost forecast and the irrelevant direct-material-cost forecast:

COST COMPARISON PER UNIT		
	do not rearrange	**rearrange**
Direct materials	~~$5.00~~	~~$5.00~~
Direct labor	2.00	1.80

However, as the above cancellation marks show, we can safely ignore the direct-material cost, because it is not an element of difference between the alternatives. Concentrating solely on relevant costs may eliminate bothersome irrelevancies and may sharpen both the accountant's and the manager's thinking regarding costs for decision making. A key question in determining relevance is, What difference will it make? (Of course, irrelevant costs may be included in cost comparisons for decisions, provided that they are included properly and do not mislead the decision maker.)

In summary, **relevant costs** for decisions are expected future costs that will differ under alternatives. Historical costs, although helpful in predicting relevant costs, are always irrelevant costs per se.

The definition of relevance is the major conceptual lesson in this chapter. This idea of relevance, coupled with the contribution approach, arms the manager and the accountant with a powerful general weapon for making nonroutine decisions. The rest of this chapter will show how to apply these notions to some commonly encountered decisions. Note particularly that the analytical approach is consistent regardless of the particular decision encountered.

qualitative and quantitative factors

The consequences of each alternative may be divided into two broad categories, *qualitative* and *quantitative.* Qualitative factors are those that can be measured in money only with much difficulty and imprecision. Yet a qualitative factor may easily be given more weight than the measurable cost savings. For example, a militant union that opposes the introduction of some labor-saving machinery may cause an executive to defer or to reject completely the contemplated installation. Or the chance to manufacture some product components at a cost below supplier quotations may be rejected because of a long-run dependency on the supplier for other important subassemblies. Quantitative factors are those that may more easily be expressed in money, such as projected alternative costs of direct materials, direct labor, and factory overhead. The accountant, statistician, and mathematician increasingly try to express as many decision factors as possible in quantitative terms. This approach tends to reduce the number of qualitative factors to be judged.

Illustration of relevance: choosing activity levels

Decisions that affect activity levels are made under a given set of conditions, including existing plant capacity, equipment, and basic operating conditions. Such decisions are essentially short run in nature; but they have long-run overtones that should never be overlooked.

danger of full costs

The accounting system should produce information that leads managers toward correct decisions regarding either evaluation of performance or selection among courses of action. Intelligent analysis of costs is often dependent on explicit distinctions between cost behavior patterns, which is more likely to be achieved via the contribution approach than via traditional methods. The general tendency toward indiscriminate full-cost allocations raises analytical dangers.

» *EXAMPLE*

A bakery distributed its products through route salesmen, each of whom loaded a truck with an assortment of products in the morning and spent the day calling on customers in an assigned territory. Believing that some items were more profitable than others, management asked for an analysis of product costs and sales. The accountants to whom the task was assigned allocated all manufacturing and marketing costs to products to obtain a net profit for each product. The resulting figures indicated that some of the products were being sold at a loss, and management discontinued these products. However, when this change was put into effect, the company's overall profit declined. It was thus seen that, by dropping some products, sales revenues had been reduced without commensurate reduction in costs because the joint manufacturing costs and route-sales costs had to be continued in order to make and sell remaining products.[2]

the special order

Management is sometimes faced with the problem of price quotations on special orders when there is idle capacity.

» *EXAMPLE*

X Company manufactures house slippers. The current operating level, which is below full capacity of 110,000 pairs per year, will probably show the results for the year as contained in Exhibit 11-2. (Note that these are predictions.)

A mail-order chain offers to buy 20,000 pairs at $7.50, for a total of $150,000. The buyer will pay for the shipping expenses. The acceptance of this special order will not affect regular sales. The president is reluctant to accept that order because the $7.50 price is below the $8.125 manufacturing unit cost. Should the offer be accepted?

Exhibit 11-2 is based on an absorption-costing format. In contrast, Exhibit 11-3 shows a report based on the contribution approach that might be presented as a guide for decision making. **The relevant costs are those that will be affected by taking the special order—the variable *manufacturing* costs.** The fixed manufacturing costs and all of the selling expenses are irrelevant because they will not change in total if the

EXHIBIT 11-2

Predicted Income Statement for the Year
Absorption Format

		PER UNIT‡
Sales—80,000 pairs @ $10.00	$800,000	$10.000
Manufacturing cost of goods sold*	650,000	8.125
Gross profit or gross margin	$150,000	$ 1.875
Selling expenses†	120,000	1.500
Operating income	$ 30,000	$ .375

**Includes fixed costs of $250,000. The remaining $400,000 is for variable costs of $5.00 per pair.*
†Includes fixed costs of $80,000. The remaining $40,000 consists only of shipping expenses of $.50 per pair.
‡One pair equals one unit.

[2]Walter B. McFarland, "The Field of Management Accounting," *NAA Bulletin,* XLV, No. 10, Sec. 3, p. 19.

EXHIBIT 11-3

Comparative Predicted Income Statements for the Year
Contribution Format, Two Decision Alternatives

	WITHOUT SPECIAL ORDER, 80,000 UNITS		WITH SPECIAL ORDER, 100,000 UNITS	
	per unit	**total**	**total**	**difference**
Sales	$10.000	$800,000	$950,000	$150,000*
Variable costs:				
Manufacturing	$ 5.000	$400,000	$500,000	$100,000†
Selling	.500	40,000	40,000	—
Total variable costs	$ 5.500	$440,000	$540,000	$100,000
Contribution margin	$ 4.500	$360,000	$410,000	$ 50,000
Fixed costs:				
Manufacturing	$ 3.125	$250,000	$250,000	—
Selling	1.000	80,000	80,000	—
Total fixed costs	$ 4.125	$330,000	$330,000	—
Operating income	$ .375	$ 30,000	$ 80,000	$ 50,000

**20,000 @ $7.50.*
†20,000 @ $5.00.

order is accepted. Therefore, the only relevant items here are sales and variable manufacturing costs.

fixed expenses and unit costs

Exhibit 11-3 also illustrates the frequent irrelevance of fixed costs in a decision of this kind. If the fixed costs remain the same under each alternative (acceptance or rejection), then the $330,000 is irrelevant. You may substitute $1 or $1,000,000 wherever the $330,000 fixed-cost amount is shown without changing the net difference in result.

Note also that the absorption unit cost at the 80,000-unit activity level is $8.125. If such a cost were used as a guide in deciding, the offer might be unwisely rejected, on the grounds that the $7.50 prospective selling price is well below the $8.125 unit cost. **In most cases (as demonstrated here), it is safer to compare *total* costs and revenues rather than the *unit* amounts.** The spreading of the $250,000 fixed manufacturing cost over 100,000 units instead of 80,000 units will lower the average *unit cost* for all units produced. **But how fixed costs are applied to units of product has no bearing on this decision because the *total* fixed costs are unaffected.**

reports for decision making

Frequently, the decision alternatives are compared as in Exhibit 11-3 by preparing a separate income statement for each alternative, as well as by showing the differences. But shortcut reports may emphasize *differences* in order to spotlight only the relevant factors that influence the final results. A shortcut analysis would be confined to the "difference" column in Exhibit 11-3.

Concentration on the revenues and costs that make a difference in analyzing data does not necessarily mean that the final reports submitted to the decision-making executives should contain only these **differential** items. The final reports should be tailored to managerial quirks and wants. There is no single way to present reports. However, the contribution approach tends to facilitate understanding.

confusing terminology

Many different terms are used to describe the costs of specific products and services. For instance, the major distinction between variable costing and absorption costing was described in several earlier chapters (for example, see page 52): Variable costing regards *fixed* indirect *manufacturing* costs as expenses immediately and not as costs of the product.

In a specific situation, be sure to get the exact meaning of the terms used. A particularly troublesome term is **full cost** or **fully distributed cost** or **fully allocated cost.** These are sometimes used as synonyms for absorption cost. In pricing situations, however, "full cost" per unit usually means absorption cost *plus* an allocation of selling and administrative cost. For example, using the amounts in Exhibit 11-3, three different unit costs can be computed:

	COST PER UNIT		
Variable manufacturing cost	$5.000	$5.000	$5.000
Variable selling cost	.500		.500
Total variable costs	$5.500		
Fixed manufacturing cost		3.125	3.125
Absorption cost		$8.125*	
Fixed selling cost			1.000
Full cost (also called fully allocated or distributed cost)			$9.625

***The amount that must be used by U.S. companies for inventory valuation in reports to shareholders and income tax authorities. Also, selling costs are not inventoriable under any inventory method.**

short run and long run

Do not jump to the conclusion that all variable costs are relevant and all fixed costs are irrelevant. This preconceived attack may be handy, but it is far from being foolproof. For instance, in this special-order example, although the selling costs are variable, they are irrelevant because the buyer will bear them. Moreover, fixed costs are often affected by a decision. For example, plans to buy a second car for family use should be most heavily influenced by the new set of fixed costs that would be encountered. **Moreover, if the total family mileage were unaffected, the variable costs could conceivably be wholly irrelevant.**

Economists and accountants agree that if the length of time under consideration is long enough, no type of cost is fixed. However, as Lord Keynes once remarked, "In the long run, we will all be dead." Yet, as a practical matter, management is faced with the task of making decisions when the length of time under consideration is short enough so that many conditions and costs are fixed. What role should fixed costs play in decision making? No categorical answer can be given to this question. **About the most useful generalization is that fixed costs should be considered when they are expected to be altered, either immediately or in the future, by the decision at hand.** If activity levels change so that additional supervision, plant, equipment, insurance, and property taxes are needed, these new fixed costs are relevant. For example, sales or production may expand to the point where a new delivery truck must be bought.

Contribution approach to pricing

The special-order decision is merely one example of a pervasive difficulty that confronts managers: the pricing decision. This decision is the subject of an extensive literature in economics, so we will concentrate on only a few aspects here. Our major purpose is to put the role of costs in perspective with regard to the pricing decision.

superiority of the contribution approach

When used intelligently, the contribution approach offers help that is equal to or better than the absorption-costing approach to guiding a pricing decision.

First, the contribution approach offers more detailed information than the absorption-costing approach, because variable- and fixed-cost behavior patterns are delineated. Because the contribution approach is sensitive to cost-volume-profit relationships, it is a better, easier basis for developing pricing formulas.

Second, a "normal" or "target" pricing formula can be as easily developed under the contribution approach as under absorption costing for the "usual" or "nonincremental" situations. Consider the data in the absorption format of Exhibit 11-2. The target markup percentage is often expressed as a percentage of absorption cost: $1.875 ÷ $8.125 = 23.1 percent. In contrast, consider the data in the contribution format of Exhibit 11-3. The target markup percentage might be expressed as a percentage of variable costs: $4.50 ÷ $5.50 = 81.8 percent. Under *either* approach, the pricing-decision maker will have a formula that will lead toward the *same* target price. Unless such a price is obtained consistently, the company will not achieve its $30,000 income objective or its desired operating-income percentage of sales.

Third, as the preceding example shows, the contribution approach offers insight into short-run versus long-run effects of cutting prices on special orders. Generally, a manager can weigh such decisions by asking whether the expected long-run benefits of not cutting the price are worth a present "investment" equal to the immediate contribution to operating income ($50,000 in Exhibit 11-3) that would otherwise be sacrificed. Under absorption costing, the manager must conduct a special study to find the immediate effects; under the contribution approach, he or she has a system that will routinely provide such information.

the contribution approach or absorption costing?

A major criticism leveled at the contribution approach is that it will result in underpricing and ultimate company disaster. Such a criticism implies that full manufacturing cost is a safer guide because it does not ignore fixed factory overhead and will therefore lead to better long-run pricing decisions.

There are at least four basic weaknesses in that argument. First, full manufacturing cost also ignores some costs—the selling and administrative costs, which are often substantial. Under absorption costing, pricing decisions are often guided by unit gross profit rather than by unit net profit.[3] Second, even when absorption costing is used, there is no single unit cost that may be used as a guide as long as volume is a variable. Third, cost accountants and businesspeople give excessive emphasis to costs as a guide to pricing. That is, they say and perhaps think that costs influence pricing decisions, but their actions show that *customer demand* and *competitor behavior* greatly overshadow costs as price-influencing factors.[4] Fourth, a National Association of Accountants survey (*Report No. 37,* p. 55) of thirty-eight companies that use variable (direct) costing reported:

[3] *Current Application of Direct Costing, N.A.A. Research Report No. 37,* p. 43.

[4] For an expanded discussion, see the second appendix to this chapter.

No instance of unprofitable pricing attributable to direct costing was reported, but, on the contrary, opinion was frequently expressed to the effect that direct costing had contributed to better pricing decisions. However, companies restrict product cost and margin data to individuals qualified to interpret such data and responsible for pricing policy decisions.

Our general theme of different costs for different purposes also extends into the area of pricing. To say that either variable costing or absorption costing provides the best guide to pricing decisions is a dangerous oversimplification of one of the most perplexing problems in business. Lack of understanding and judgment can lead to unprofitable pricing regardless of the kind of cost data available or cost accounting system used.

need for clear information

Consider what managers of airlines are confronted with when they make decisions concerning when, where, and how to compete. *Forbes* (September 1, 1980, p. 37) reported on competition concerning transcontinental routes:

> Last year, it cost between $3,600 and $4,512 an hour to fly a 747. But you could cover the cash operating cost on a coast-to-coast route with perhaps 155 customers paying $129 each, and then contribute to overhead with only a few more customers. . . . The catch is that eventually you have to replace them. You can get trapped into doing everything for the short-term . . . until one day you have to replace your fleet.

Pricing decisions almost inevitably have long-run implications and thus require acute ability for proper weighting of short-run and long-run impacts. Because of the bewildering number of influencing factors, many managers are content with "satisfactory" returns rather than "maximum" returns—primarily because they are rarely sure of what the latter amounts may be. The contribution-margin approach will help clarify some factors that are not easily brought out by the conventional approach. *N.A.A. Research Report No. 37* (p. 55) cited the following cases, which took place before the contribution approach was adopted:

> Instances were cited in which management had unknowingly continued selling products below out-of-pocket cost or had decided to withdraw from the market when a substantial portion of the [fixed] costs could have been recovered. . . .
>
> In one interview . . . when direct costing was introduced, analysis demonstrated that contracts which would have contributed to [fixed] costs had often been refused at times when the company had a large amount of idle capacity.

impact on behavior

The examples in this chapter also relate to the various potential impacts of alternative cost analyses on human motivation and decisions. For example, in pricing decisions, managers face the difficult task of predicting how total costs will be affected. These predictions will obviously affect decisions.

The dilemma is often to choose between (1) and (3) as a guide to pricing:

(1) Total "incremental" or variable costs	xxx
(2) Add: allocation of fixed costs	xxx
(3) Total "full" or absorption cost	xxx

In practice, most managers maintain that variable costs provide understatements of the "real" additions to costs caused by a decision alternative in question. At the same time, most managers will admit that "full" cost is also an inaccurate approximation. **Still, the latter tends to be regarded as a safer basis for an ongoing pricing policy. In short, in coping with uncertainty, managers tend to be more comfortable with the "full-cost" simplification than the "variable-cost" simplification as a routine approximation of the unknown "real-cost" functions that might measure additions to costs.** In this way, managers contend with a fact of life: As more activities are undertaken, costs inevitably creep upward at a rate higher than indicated by the variable or **incremental costs** identified with particular decisions, analyzed one at a time.

costs as substitutes for the market

Market prices frequently do not exist or are unobtainable in any feasible way. The defense-contracting industry offers numerous examples. In these cases, costs become *the* means for establishing a "fair" price—that is, a price that is regarded as mutually acceptable by both buyer (the government) and seller.

When costs are used for determining a "fair," "equitable," or "satisfactory" price, keep in mind that the resulting price may or may not coincide with the "true" underlying costs. For instance, in government contracting some costs are deemed allowable for recovery in the price and some are unallowable (for example, the premium paid for first-class airfare).

Thus, when costs are viewed as substitutes for the market in government contracting, or in allocating costs to service departments, or elsewhere, disputes may arise about how underlying costs "truly" behave. Settling such arguments on the basis of probable cost behaviors is sometimes hopeless. In these cases, certainty is a dream. It may be helpful to recognize that cost allocations are being used to obtain a mutually acceptable price and not necessarily to portray cause-and-effect relationships of cost incurrence. (For additional discussion, see Chapter 15.)

Effects of antitrust laws on pricing

To comply with American antitrust laws, does the computation of "cost" require absorption costing? Will prices above variable costs suffice? The answers are unclear. Comparatively few law cases have discussed the proper method or methods of determining costs for purposes of these statutes.

Pricing in the United States must not be predatory. That is, according to various sections of the Sherman Act, Clayton Act, and Robinson-Patman Act, prices should not be unreasonably low where the purpose is to lessen or eliminate competition.

There is no federal antitrust statute that expressly prohibits sales below cost as such. The significance of the price-cost relationship focuses on whether a seller's conduct is "predatory." The basic question is intent or purpose; it is not one of choosing the proper accounting method. Thus, price cutting in good faith to meet competition is often a persuasive defense in court cases, even if the prices are below "full" or "absorption" costs.

Until the mid-1970s, decisions of regulatory agencies and the courts had been based on absorption costing and fully allocated costs rather than variable costing. However, recent court decisions have been heavily influenced by an article by Areeda and Turner, which concluded that:

a. A price at or above reasonably anticipated average variable cost should be conclusively presumed lawful.

b. A price below reasonably anticipated average variable cost should be conclusively presumed unlawful.[5]

For example, a plaintiff alleged a violation of the Robinson-Patman Act, claiming that the defendant had sold air-conditioner cooler pads in the El Paso market at lower prices than it had sold them elsewhere. The Fifth Circuit Court declared:

> Even if a monopolist is price discriminating, we will not infer damage to competition as a matter of law if the firm is charging a short-run, profit-maximizing price (above average variable cost) in the market in which it faces competition. And even if its price is below this level, we will not infer damage to competition if the firm's price discrimination has beneficial effects or insignificant effects in the competitive market.[6]

The Supreme Court has not reviewed the recent court decisions favoring variable costing as a justification for pricing. Pending such definitive guidance, managers and cost accountants who are concerned with antitrust matters would be prudent to have a system with the following characteristics:

1. Collect data in such a manner as to permit relatively easy compilation of variable costs, absorption costs, and "fully allocated" costs.
2. Review all proposed prices below fully allocated costs, in advance, on a case-by-case basis for indications of possible claims of predatory intent.
3. Review all proposed prices below average variable costs, in advance, with a presumption of claims of predatory intent.
4. Keep as detailed a set of records as feasible, not only of manufacturing costs but also of distribution costs such as advertising, warehousing, and transportation. In this way, a company will be prepared for inquiries by regulatory agencies. Moreover, managers will be better informed. They will be able to predict the impacts on operating income of various pricing and other competitive strategies.

Other illustrations of relevance and the contribution approach

contribution per unit of constraining factor

When a multiproduct plant is being operated at capacity, decisions must often be made as to which orders to accept. The contribution approach supplies the data for a proper decision, because the latter is determined by the product that makes the largest *total* contribution to profits. This does not necessarily mean that the products to be pushed are those with the biggest contribution margin per unit of product or biggest contribution-margin ratios per sales dollar. The objective is to maximize total profits, which depends on getting the highest contribution margin per unit of the *constraining* (that is, *scarce, limiting,* or *critical*) *factor.* The following example may clarify the point. Assume that a company has two products:

[5]P. Areeda and D. Turner, "Predatory Pricing and Related Practices under Section 2 of the Sherman Act," *Harvard Law Review,* 88 (1975), 733. Also see F. M. Scherer's critical comments, 89 (1976), 869–90. Antitrust cases often involve triple damages.

[6]International Air Industries, Inc. *v.* American Excelsior Co., 517 F.2d (5th Cir. 1975) (per Morgan, J.), *cert. denied,* 424 U.S. 943 (1976). Also see the "Legal Developments" sections of the *Journal of Marketing* for summaries of court cases. Also see Janich Bros. Inc. *v.* American Distilling Co., 570 F.2d (9th Cir. 1977) and Hanson *v.* Shell Oil Co., 541 F.2d (9th Cir. 1976).

	PRODUCT (PER UNIT)	
	A	B
Selling price	$10	$15
Variable expenses	7	9
Contribution margin	$ 3	$ 6
Contribution-margin ratio	30%	40%

At first glance, B looks more profitable than A. However, if you were the division manager, had 1,000 hours of capacity available, and knew that you could turn out 3 units of A per hour and only 1 unit of B per hour, your choice should be A because it contributes the most margin *per hour,* the constraining factor in this example:

	A	B
Units per hour	3	1
Contribution margin per hour	$ 9	$ 6
Total contribution for 1,000 hours	$9,000	$6,000

The constraining factor is the item that restricts or limits the production or sale of a given product. Thus, *the criterion for maximum profits, for a given capacity, is the greatest possible contribution to profit per unit of the constraining factor.* The constraining factor in the example above may be machine-hours or direct-labor hours. It also may be cubic feet of display space. The success of the suburban discount department stores illustrates the concept of the contribution to profit per unit of constraining factor. These stores have been satisfied with subnormal markups because they have been able to increase turnover and thus increase the contribution to profit per unit of space. Exhibit 11-4 demonstrates this point and assumes that the same total selling space is used in each store.

EXHIBIT 11-4

	REGULAR DEPARTMENT STORE	DISCOUNT DEPARTMENT STORE
Retail price	$4.00	$3.50
Cost of merchandise	3.00	3.00
Contribution to profit per unit	$1.00(25%)	$ .50(14+%)
Units sold per year	20,000	44,000
Total contribution to profit	$20,000	$22,000

As you can imagine, in most cases there will be many constraining factors that must be utilized by each of a variety of products. The problem of formulating the most profitable production schedules and the mixes of raw materials is essentially that of maximizing the contribution in the face of *many* constraints. These complications are solved by linear-programming techniques, which are discussed in Chapter 23.

make or buy, and idle facilities

Manufacturers are often confronted with the question of whether to make or buy a product—whether, that is, to manufacture their own parts and subassemblies or to buy them from suppliers. The qualitative factors may be of paramount importance. Sometimes the manufacture of parts requires special know-how, unusually skilled labor, rare materials, and the like. The desire to control the quality of parts is often the determining factor in the decision to make them. On the other hand, companies hesitate to destroy mutually advantageous long-run relationships by the erratic order-giving that results from making parts during slack times and buying them during prosperous times. They may have difficulty in obtaining any parts during boom times, when there are shortages of materials and workers and no shortage of sales orders.

What are the quantitative factors relevant to the decision of whether to make or buy? The answer, again, depends on the context. A key factor is whether there are idle facilities. Many companies make parts only when their facilities cannot be used to better advantage.

Assume that the following costs are reported by B Company:

COST OF MAKING PART NO. 300		
	total costs for 10,000 units	**costs per unit**
Direct materials	$ 10,000	$ 1
Direct labor	80,000	8
Variable overhead	40,000	4
Fixed overhead applied	50,000	5
Total costs	$180,000	$18

Another manufacturer offers to sell B Company the same part for $16. Should B Company make or buy the part?

Although the figures above seemingly indicate that the company should buy, the answer is rarely obvious. The key question is the difference in future costs between the alternatives. Consider the fixed overhead. The total applied to the part is $50,000. Perhaps $30,000 of this fixed overhead represents those costs (for example, depreciation, property taxes, insurance, and allocated executive salaries) that will continue regardless of the decision. If so, the entire $30,000 becomes irrelevant, which is $3 per unit for a 10,000-unit volume.

Again it is risky to say categorically that only the variable costs are relevant. Perhaps, as we assume here, $20,000 of the fixed costs will be saved if the parts are bought instead of made. In other words, fixed costs that may be avoided in the future are relevant.

For the moment, let us assume that the capacity now used to make parts will become idle if the parts are purchased. The computations of relevant costs follow:

	TOTAL COSTS			PER-UNIT COSTS		
	make		**buy**	**make**		**buy**
Direct materials	$ 10,000			$ 1		
Direct labor	80,000			8		
Variable overhead	40,000			4		
Fixed overhead that can be avoided by not making	20,000			2		
Total relevant costs	$150,000		$160,000	$15		$16
Difference in favor of making		$10,000			$1	

essence of make or buy: utilization of facilities

The choice in our example is not really whether to make or buy; it is how best to utilize available facilities. Although the data above indicate that making the part is the better choice, the figures are not conclusive—primarily because we have no idea of what can be done with the manufacturing facilities if the component is bought. Only if the released facilities are to remain idle are the figures above valid.

If the released facilities can be used advantageously in some other manufacturing activity or can be rented out, these alternatives also may merit consideration. Suppose the released facilities either can be used to manufacture other products with a contribution of $19,000 or can be rented out for $5,000. The two courses of action have become four (figures are in thousands):

	MAKE	BUY AND LEAVE FACILITIES IDLE	BUY AND USE FACILITIES FOR OTHER PRODUCTS	BUY AND RENT
Rent revenue	$ —	$ —	$ —	$ 5
Contribution from other products	—	—	19	—
Obtaining of parts	(150)	(160)	(160)	(160)
Net relevant costs	$(150)	$(160)	$(141)	$(155)

The analysis indicates that buying the parts and using the vacated facilities for the production of other products should yield best results.

beware of unit costs Unit costs should be analyzed with care in decision making. There are two major ways to go wrong: (a) the inclusion of irrelevant costs, such as the $3 per-unit allocation of fixed costs in the make-or-buy comparison, which would result in a unit of $18 instead of the relevant unit cost of $15; and (b) comparisons of unit costs not computed on the same volume. Generally, it is advisable to use total costs rather than unit costs. Then, if desired, the total may be unitized. Machinery salesmen, for example, often brag about the low unit costs of using their new machines. Sometimes they neglect to point out that the unit costs are based on outputs far in excess of the volume of activity of their prospective customer. The unitization of fixed costs in this manner can be particularly misleading. The lesson here is to use total costs, not unit costs, in relevant cost analysis when possible. This approach has been called "McNamara's First Law of Analysis: always start by looking at the grand total. Whatever problem you are studying, back off and look at it in the large."[7]

Irrelevance of past costs

As defined earlier, a relevant cost is (a) an expected future cost that (b) will differ among alternatives. The contribution aspect of relevant-cost analysis has shown that those expected future costs that will not differ among alternatives are irrelevant. Now we return to the idea that all past costs are also irrelevant.

obsolete inventory A company has 100 obsolete missile parts that are carried in inventory at a manufacturing cost of $100,000. The parts can be (a) remachined for $30,000, and then sold for $50,000; or (b) scrapped for $5,000. Which alternative is preferable?

This is an unfortunate situation because sale of the missile parts will result in a loss. Nevertheless, the $100,000 cost is irrelevant to the decision to remachine or scrap. The only relevant factors are the expected future revenue and costs:

[7] A. Enthoven and K. Wayne Smith, *How Much Is Enough? Shaping the Defense Program 1961–1969*, (New York: Harper & Row, 1971), p. 54, referring to Robert S. McNamara, former U.S. secretary of defense.

	REMACHINE		SCRAP
Expected future revenue	$ 50,000		$ 5,000
Expected future costs	30,000		—
Relevant excess of revenue over costs	$ 20,000		$ 5,000
Accumulated historical inventory costs*	100,000		100,000
Loss on disposal	$(80,000)		$(95,000)
Difference in favor of remachining		$15,000	

**Irrelevant because it is not an element of difference as between the alternatives.*

We could completely ignore the historical cost and still arrive at the $15,000 difference, the key figure in the analysis.

regular inventory

Note another important point. Although the above example dealt with obsolete parts, the idea that past costs are irrelevant per se applies to the historical cost of *any* inventory, whether obsolete or fully merchantable. The replacement cost of additional units of inventory is a future cash outflow that is likely to be common to nearly all alternatives under consideration. However, it is a separate outflow; it should not be confused with the question of what to do with the units on hand. This point can be clarified by an example.

Suppose a company uses copper as an input to four products. At the beginning of the period, there are 1,000 units in copper inventory that were acquired for $110 per unit. Assume further that if the company decides not to use the 1,000 units on hand, it is possible to sell them to a salvage yard for $95 per unit. Another salvage yard has offered $90. There are many alternative end-product uses for the copper. Another alternative would be to throw the units in the city dump. A "total-alternatives" approach to the analysis follows (in thousands of dollars):

	CHOICES						
	use copper in product				salvage		throw away
	A	B	C	D	1	2	
Expected future revenue	220	204	186	170	95	90	—
Expected future costs:							
Labor and overhead	90	70	60	100	—	—	—
Relevant excess of revenue over costs	130	134	126	70	95	90	—
		Best					

opportunity cost

Note that all alternatives are listed and analyzed in the same systematic way under the total-alternatives approach. Ideally, the decision maker should be able to make an exhaustive list of alternatives and then compute the expected results under each, giving full consideration to interdependent and long-run effects. Practically, the decision maker sifts among the possible alternatives, discards many out of hand as being obviously unattractive, undoubtedly overlooks some attractive possibilities, and concentrates on a limited number.

The idea of an **opportunity cost** has arisen because some alternatives are excluded from formal consideration. For example, suppose that the total alternatives under formal consideration are limited to choices A through D above but that the salvage and throwaway alternatives will not be analyzed in the same format. Then an opportunity approach is desirable. **Opportunity cost is the *maximum* contribution that is forgone by using limited resources for a particular purpose.** The use of opportunity cost is a practical means of reducing the number of alternatives under consideration; the solution reached is still the same as that given by a more complete "total-alternatives" approach. The decision maker says, "There are many alternatives that I want to reject without conducting a thorough analysis. Therefore, I shall take the *best* of these, compute its contribution [sell for salvage of $95 in this example], and use that as the cost of the scarce resource [copper in this example] when I explicitly analyze the remaining alternatives." Under the opportunity-cost approach, the decision maker would then organize the analysis of the remaining alternatives as follows (in thousands of dollars):

	CHOICES			
	use copper in product			
	A	B	C	D
Revenue	220	204	186	170
Relevant costs:				
Opportunity cost of copper	95	95	95	95
Outlay costs: Labor and overhead	90	70	60	100
Total relevant costs	185	165	155	195
Net advantage	35	39	31	(25)

Note that the *best* of the alternatives excluded from the previous analysis is included in the formal comparison as an opportunity cost. The other two (or more) excluded alternatives are not in this analysis. The possible uses of the copper in Products A, C, and D may also eventually become excluded alternatives, but they are excluded after formal consideration in the decision model used.

Note that an opportunity cost is not ordinarily incorporated in formal accounting reports to shareholders.[8] Such costs represent contributions *forgone* by rejecting the next-best alternative; therefore, opportunity costs do not entail cash receipts or disbursements. Accountants usually confine their systematic recording of costs to the *outlay costs* requiring exchanges of assets. Accountants confine their history to alternatives selected rather than those rejected, primarily because of the infeasibility of accumulating meaningful data on what might have been.

Many managers fail to consider opportunity costs. For example, the following extract is from a news story about a San Francisco automobile dealer:

> Geary Ford is in the favorable position of owning outright all but a few of the fifteen cars it has available for sale. The owner of the business said, "If we had to pay a point over the prime interest rate on those cars, we'd lose money on every car we sold."

---

[8]However, an argument can be made that the issuance of capital stock by a corporation for noncash assets is accounted for on the basis of opportunity costs. That is, such assets may be recorded at the market value of the stock under the reasoning that the company's best forgone opportunity was the issuance of the stock for cash. This is one of a few applications of the opportunity-cost idea to external accounting.

The owner is mistaken. Any wholly owned asset (whether it be a house, land, or an inventory of cars) has an opportunity cost. "Cost" is not confined to outlays for interest.

book value of old equipment

Assume that there is a machine, with a cost of $120,000, two-thirds depreciated on a straight-line basis, with a **book value** (original cost less accumulated depreciation) of $40,000, and with a remaining useful life of four years. The old machine has a $4,000 disposal value now; in four years, its disposal value will be zero. A new machine is available that will dramatically reduce operating costs. Annual revenue of $100,000 will not change regardless of the decision. The new machine will cost $60,000 and have zero disposal value at the end of its four-year life. The new machine promises to slash variable operating costs from $80,000 per year to $56,000 per year. Many managers and accountants would not replace the old machine because it would entail recognizing a $36,000 "loss on disposal," whereas retention would allow spreading the $40,000 over four years in the form of "depreciation expense" (a more appealing term than "loss on disposal"). See Exhibit 11-5.

Under our definition of relevant costs, book value of old fixed assets is always irrelevant to making decisions. This proposition is very difficult for managers and accountants alike to accept. The real concept of importance here is that *all* historical costs are irrelevant. At one time or another, we all like to think that we can soothe our wounded pride arising from having made a bad purchase decision by using the item instead of replacing it. **The fallacy here is in erroneously thinking that a current or**

EXHIBIT 11-5

Cost Comparison—Replacement of Machine, Including Relevant and Irrelevant Items
(In Thousands of Dollars)

	FOUR YEARS TOGETHER		
	keep	**replace**	**difference**
Sales	$400	$400	$ —
Expenses:			
Variable	320	224	96
Old machine (book value):			
Periodic write-off as depreciation	40		—
or			
Lump-sum write-off		40*	
Disposal value		−4*	4
New machine, written off periodically as depreciation	—	60	−60
Total expenses	$360	$320	$ 40
Operating income	$ 40	$ 80	$ 40

The advantage of replacement is $40,000 for the four years together.

In a formal income statement, these two items would be combined as "loss on disposal" of $36,000.

future action can influence the long-run impact of a past outlay. All past costs are down the drain. *Nothing* can change what has already happened.

We can apply our definition of relevance to four commonly encountered items:

1. *Book value of old equipment.* Irrelevant, because it is a past (historical) cost.
2. *Disposal value of old equipment.* Relevant, because it is an expected future inflow that usually differs between alternatives.
3. *Gain or loss on disposal.* This is the algebraic difference between items 1 and 2. It is therefore a meaningless combination of book value, which is always irrelevant, and disposal value, which is relevant. The combination form, *loss* (or *gain*) *on disposal,* blurs the distinction between the irrelevant book value and the relevant disposal value. Consequently, it is best to think of each separately.
4. *Cost of new equipment.* Relevant, because it is an expected future outflow that will differ between alternatives.

Exhibit 11-5 should clarify the above assertions. Book value of old equipment is irrelevant regardless of the decision-making technique used. The Difference column in Exhibit 11-5 shows that book value of old equipment is not an element of difference between alternatives and could be completely ignored for decision-making purposes. **No matter what the *timing* of the charge against revenue, the *amount* charged is still $40,000 regardless of any available alternative.** In either event, the undepreciated cost will be written off with the same ultimate effect on profit. The $40,000 creeps into the income statement either as a $40,000 offset against the $4,000 proceeds to obtain the $36,000 *loss on disposal* in the current year or as $10,000 depreciation in each of four years. But how it appears is irrelevant to the replacement decision. **In contrast, the $15,000 annual depreciation on the new equipment *is* relevant because the total $60,000 depreciation may be avoided by not replacing.**

EXHIBIT 11-6

Cost Comparison—Replacement of Machine: Relevant Items Only

(In Thousands of Dollars)

	FOUR YEARS TOGETHER		
	keep	**replace**	**difference**
Variable expenses	$320	$224	$ 96
Disposal value of old equipment	—	−4	4
Depreciation—new equipment	—	60	−60
Total relevant expenses	$320	$280	$ 40

Exhibit 11-6 concentrates on relevant items only. Note that the same answer (the $40,000 net difference) will be produced even though the book value is completely omitted from the calculations. The only relevant items are the variable operating costs, the disposal value of the old equipment, and the depreciation on the new equipment.

Role of income taxes

For simplicity, we ignore income-tax considerations and the effects of the time value of money in this chapter. But book value is irrelevant even if income taxes are considered, because the relevant item is then the income-tax cash flow, not the book value. Using the approach in Exhibit 11-1, the book value is essential information for the *prediction method*, but the expected future income-tax cash outflows are the relevant information for the *decision model*. The prediction method would be: Disposal value, \$4,000 − Book value, \$40,000 = Loss on disposal, \$36,000. If the income-tax rate is 40 percent, the income-tax cash saving would be .40 × \$36,000 = \$14,400. This \$14,400 would be the expected future cash flow that is a relevant input to the decision model.

If income taxes are considered, the *timing* of the writing off of fixed-asset costs may influence income-tax payments. In our machine example, there will be a small real difference: the present value of \$40,000 as a tax reduction now versus the present value of a \$10,000 tax deduction each year for four years. But this difference in *future* income-tax flows is the *relevant* item—not the book value of the old fixed asset per se. For elaboration, see Chapter 13, pp. 445–46, Clarification of role of depreciation.

How managers behave

Consider our replacement example in light of the sequence in Exhibit 11-1, page 365:

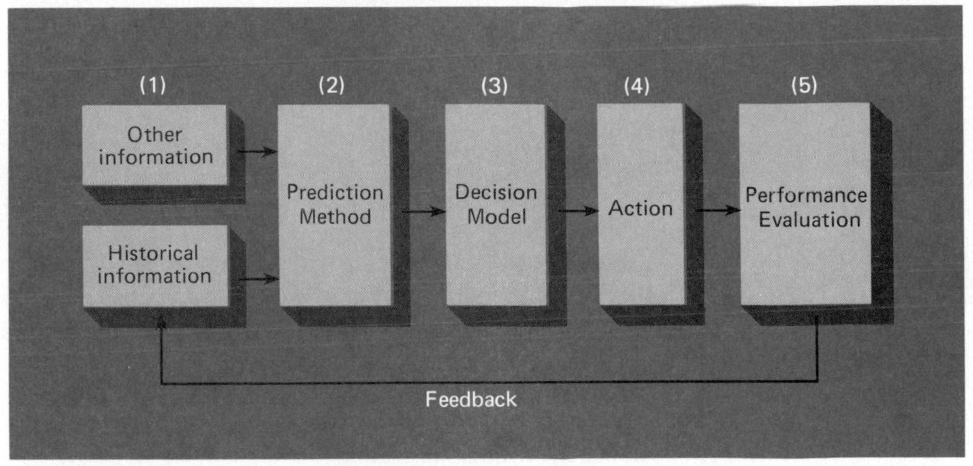

impact of loss

Suppose the *decision model* (box 3) says to choose the alternative that will minimize total costs over the life span of the equipment. The analysis in Exhibit 11-5 favors replacing rather than keeping. In the "real world" would the manager replace? The answer often depends on the manager's perceptions of whether the decision model is consistent with the performance evaluation model (box 5).

Managers tend to favor the alternative that improves the measures used in the performance evaluation model. If there is an inconsistency between the decision model and the performance model, the latter inevitably wins. For example, top management may *say* it favors the decision model in Exhibit 11-5. But the subordinate manager may believe otherwise. That is, if the subordinate's promotion or bonus is perceived to hinge on short-run performance, the temptation to not replace will be overwhelming. Why? Because the ordinary accrual accounting model for measuring performance will show a first-year operating loss if the old machine is replaced:

	FIRST YEAR	
	keep	**replace**
Sales	$100	$100
Expenses:		
Variable	80	56
Depreciation	10	15
Loss on disposal	—	36
Total charges against sales	90	107
Operating income	$ 10	$ (7)

Faced with this performance evaluation model, what might go through the manager's mind?

Among the possibilities:

1. If I keep the equipment, my performance will very likely be in accord with my original predictions. I'll look much better in the first year by keeping than by replacing and showing a loss.
2. Even if top management's goals try to pinpoint long-run considerations, I'll probably be transferred next year anyway. So my concern is naturally with the short run.

synchronizing the models

The conflict between the possible decision models and performance evaluation models just described is frequently a baffling problem in practice. In theory, solving the difficulty seems obvious: Merely design consistent models. Consider our replacement example. Year-by-year income effects can be budgeted over the planning horizon of four years. The first year would be expected to be poor, the next three years much better.

The practical difficulty is basically that systems rarely track each decision in this fashion, one at a time. Performance evaluation focuses on responsibility centers for a specific period, not projects or individual items of equipment for their entire useful lives. Therefore, the impacts of many assorted decisions are combined in a single performance report. In such instances, the manager may predict the first-year effects and be less inclined to take the longer view that may be preferred by top management. Top management, through the reporting system, is rarely made aware of particular desirable alternatives *not* chosen by subordinates.

mingling decisions

Managers and accountants often have fuzzy ideas about how decisions interrelate. The watchwords are to separate decision from decision. Our replacement decision illustrates this perspective. Decision 1 was whether to acquire the first machine. Decision 2 is whether to replace the first machine with a second machine. As our boxes above indicate, feedback about the performance and useful life of the first machine is gathered:

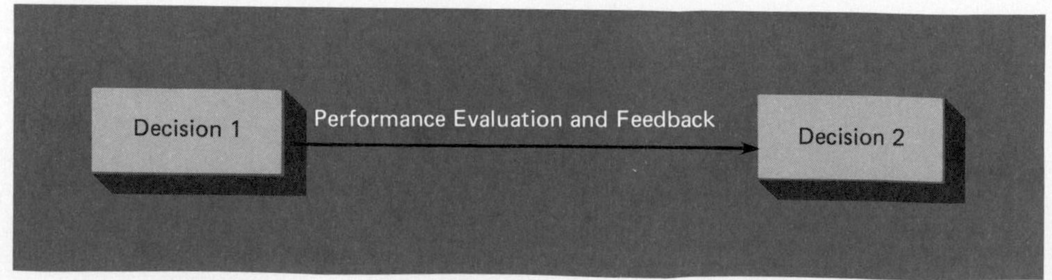

In our illustration, the feedback informs the manager that the original old machine must be eight years old. It is two-thirds depreciated and has a remaining useful life of four years. Therefore, it was originally predicted to have a useful life of twelve years. However, if a superior machine is at hand, then the useful life of the old machine has turned out to be eight rather than twelve years. Given this feedback, top management may wonder about the accuracy of the prediction of a four-year life for the new machine. Who knows, perhaps another new machine may be available a year hence that will make the current "new" machine obsolete!

In short, Decisions 1 and 2 should be analyzed separately. The audit of Decision 1 may provide feedback that may lead to wiser *predictions* concerning Decision 2. **But the financial impact of the past decision should be sharply separated from the current decision.** The danger in these cases is to have Decision 2 bear the burden of Decision 1. That is, the remaining book value or the loss on disposal of the old equipment, by themselves, should not be a part of the relevant analysis of the future financial impact of Decision 2, either in the next year or any future year.

The problem of uncertainty

It is vitally important to recognize that throughout this chapter and the next, dollar amounts of future sales and operating costs are assumed to be certain in order to highlight and to simplify various important points. In practice, the forecasting of these key figures is generally the most difficult aspect of decision analysis. For elaboration, see Chapter 21.

SUMMARY

The accountant's role in special decisions is basically that of a technical expert on cost analysis. His or her responsibility is to see that the manager is supplied with relevant data for guiding decisions.

The ability to distinguish relevant from irrelevant items and the use of the contribution approach to cost analysis are twin foundations for tackling many decisions.

To be relevant to a particular decision, a cost must meet two criteria: (a) it must be an expected *future* cost; and (b) it must be an element of *difference* between alternatives. The key question is, What difference does it make? If the objective of the decision maker is to maximize long-run net income, all *past* (*historical*) costs are irrelevant to any *decision* about the future.

The role that past costs play in decision making is an auxiliary one; the distinction here should be definitive, not fuzzy. Past (irrelevant) costs are useful because they provide empirical evidence that often helps sharpen *predictions* of future relevant costs. But the expected future costs are the *only* cost ingredients in any decision model per se.

For a given set of facilities or resources, the key to maximizing net income is to obtain the largest possible contribution per unit of constraining factor.

Generally, in cost analysis it is advisable to use total costs, not unit costs, because unitized fixed costs are often erroneously interpreted as if they behaved like variable costs. A common activity or volume level must underlie the comparison of equipment.

The book value of old equipment is always irrelevant to replacement decisions. Disposal value, however, is relevant when it differs among alternatives.

Incremental or differential costs are the differences in total costs under each alternative.

Cost reports for special decisions may concentrate on relevant items only (Exhibit 11-6), or they may encompass both relevant and irrelevant items (Exhibit 11-5). The best format depends on individual preferences. The shortcut approach concentrates only on the Difference column, because it summarizes the relevant items. The problem of uncertainty, which is discussed in Chapter 21, complicates prediction and is easily the gravest practical difficulty.

problem for self-study

problem

The San Carlos Company is an electronics company having eight product lines. Income data for one of the products for the year just ended follow (in millions):

Sales—200,000 units @ average price of $100		$20
Variable costs:		
Direct materials @ $35	$7	
Direct labor @ $10	2	
Variable factory overhead @ $5	1	
Sales commissions @ 15 percent of selling price	3	
Other variable costs @ $5	1	
Total variable costs @ $70		14
Contribution margin		$ 6
Fixed costs:		
Discretionary (see Chapter 10) @ $15	$3	
Committed (see Chapter 10) @ $10	2	
Total fixed costs		5
Operating income		$ 1

REQUIRED

1. The electronics industry had severe price competition throughout the year. Near the end of the year, Abrams Co., which was experimenting with various components in its regular product line, offered $80 each for 3,000 units. The latter would have been in addition to the 200,000 units actually sold. The acceptance of this special order by San Carlos would not affect regular sales. The salesman hoped that the order might provide entrance into a new application, so he told George Holtz, the product manager, that he would accept a flat commission of $6,000 if the order were accepted. If Holtz had accepted the offer, what would operating income have been?
2. Holtz pondered for a day, but he was afraid of the precedent that might be set by cutting the price. He said, "The price is below our full costs of $95 per unit. I think we should quote a full price, or Abrams Co. will expect favored treatment again and again if we continue to do business with them." Do you agree with Holtz? Explain.
3. The Gregorio Company had offered to supply San Carlos Company with a key part (M-I-A) for $20 each. One M-I-A is used in every finished unit. The San Carlos Company had made these parts for variable costs of $18 plus some additional fixed costs of $200,000 for supervision and other items. What would operating income have been if San Carlos purchased rather than made the parts? Assume that the discretionary costs for supervision and other items would have been avoided if the parts were purchased.

4. The company could have purchased the M-I-A parts for $20 each and used the vacated space for the manufacture of a different electronics component on a subcontracting basis for Hewlett-Packard, a much larger company. Assume that 40,000 special components could have been made for Hewlett-Packard (and sold in addition to the 200,000 regular units through regular channels) at a unit variable cost of $150, exclusive of parts. Part M-I-A would be needed for these components as well as the the regular production. No sales commission would have to be paid. All the fixed costs pertaining to the M-I-A parts would have continued, including the supervisory costs, because they related mainly to the facilities used. What would operating income have been if San Carlos had made and sold the components to Hewlett-Packard for $170 per unit and bought the M-I-A parts?

solution

1. Analysis of special order:

Additional sales of 3,000 units @ $80		$240,000
Direct materials—3,000 units @ $35	$105,000	
Direct labor—3,000 units @ $10	30,000	
Variable factory overhead—3,000 units @ $5	15,000	
Other variable costs—3,000 units @ $5	15,000	
Sales commission	6,000	
Total variable costs		171,000
Contribution margin		$ 69,000

Note that the variable costs, except for commissions, are affected by physical units of volume, not dollar revenue.

Operating income would have been $1,000,000 plus $69,000, or $1,069,000.

2. Whether Holtz is making a correct decision depends on many factors. He is incorrect if the capacity would otherwise be idle and if his objective is to increase operating income in the short run. If the offer is rejected, San Carlos is willing to invest $69,000 in immediate gains forgone (an opportunity cost) to preserve the long-run selling-price structure. Holtz is correct if he thinks future competition or future price concessions to customers will hurt San Carlos's operating income by more than $69,000.

3.

	MAKE	PURCHASE
Purchase cost @ $20		$4,000,000
Variable costs @ $18	$3,600,000	
Avoidable discretionary costs	200,000	
Total relevant costs	$3,800,000	$4,000,000

Operating income would have fallen by $200,000, or from $1,000,000 to $800,000, if San Carlos had purchased the parts.

4.

Sales would increase by 40,000 units @ $170			$6,800,000
Additional costs to the company as a whole:			
Variable costs exclusive of M-I-A parts would increase by 40,000 units @ $150		$6,000,000	
Effects on overall costs of M-I-A parts:			
Cost of 240,000 parts purchased @ $20	$4,800,000		
Less cost of making 200,000 parts @ $18 (only the variable costs are relevant because fixed costs continue)	3,600,000		
Additional cost of parts		1,200,000	7,200,000
Disadvantage of making components			$ (400,000)

Operating income would decline by $400,000, from $1,000,000 to $600,000.

Terms to Learn

book value ***decision model*** ***differential cost*** ***full cost***
fully allocated cost ***fully distributed cost*** ***incremental cost***
opportunity cost ***relevant cost***

Special Points and Pitfalls

Exhibit 11-1, page 365, is important because it provides an overview of the role of accounting data in management decisions. The first step, the gathering of information, entails examination of historical data, such as feedback in the form of performance reports. In addition, this step entails enough search to assure the manager that central problems and their probable alternative solutions are correctly identified. For example, if machinery seems obsolete because of the appearance of a superior machine, the manager should search sufficiently to be sure of what other machines or methods are available now or in the near future. Of course, search is costly, so managers tend to concentrate on obvious alternatives.

The gathering of information is succeeded by several additional steps. An example of a prediction method is the use of a learning curve to forecast the cost of specified factory operations. An example of a decision model is the comparison of operating costs under each of two alternatives and the choice of the alternative having the lesser cost. An example of a performance evaluation model is a report that compares actual results with expected (budgeted) results. The latter model provides the feedback information that is a major basis for improving future predictions and decisions.

Top management faces a persistent challenge: making sure that the performance evaluation model is consistent with the decision model. A common inconsistency in the United States is (a) to tell subordinates to take a multiple-year view in making decisions, but (b) to judge performance based only on the first year.

Appendix 11a: cost terms used for different purposes

Because costs must be tailored to the decision at hand, many terms (too many!) have arisen to describe different types of cost. The author believes that the variety of terms is more confusing than illuminating; yet the varying usage of such terms necessitates a familiarity with them. Whenever you are confronted by these terms in practice, you will save much confusion and wasted time if you find out their exact meaning in the given case. For that matter, this word of caution applies to all the weird accounting terms used from company to company. Individual companies frequently develop their own extensive and distinctive accounting language. This language is not readily understood by accountants outside the company. The following terms will be related to other terms used previously in this book.

An *imputed cost* is the result of a process that recognizes a cost as it pertains to a particular situation, although the cost may not be routinely recognized by ordinary accounting procedures. Imputed costs attempt to make accounting better dovetail with economic reality.

Imputed costs may be either opportunity costs or outlay costs. A common example of the opportunity cost is the inclusion among divisional or departmental expenses of "interest expense" on ownership equity. Some outlay costs are also imputed costs, but not all outlay costs are imputed costs. For example, if $3,000 is paid for labor, it is an outlay cost but not an imputed cost, because it would be routinely recognized by ordinary accounting processes. By itself, the $3,000 measures the economic impact of that particular event.

On the other hand, suppose $100,000 is loaned to a supplier at simple interest of 2 percent when loans of comparable risk in the free market are being made at 16 percent. Such a loan may be partial consideration under a purchase contract for supplier products at lower than the prevailing market prices. An accurate accounting would require recognizing that a part of the $100,000 loan is really an additional cost of the products purchased during the contract term. This would create an initial loan discount, which would be amortized as interest income over the life of the note. Thus, this transaction illustrates the imputation of part of an outlay of $100,000 as a cost of product.

To illustrate, consider a one-year loan of $100,000 to a supplier. The note has a face amount of $100,000 with a stated interest rate of 2 percent. The note could be sold outright to a bank for $86,000 at the beginning of the year. These facts would require imputation and the following journal entries:

Note receivable	100,000	
Direct-materials inventory (stores)	14,000	
Discount on note receivable		14,000
Cash		100,000
To record the loan to a supplier of $100,000, bearing a nominal interest rate of 2 percent. The current value of the note is $86,000. Therefore, the $14,000 difference has been imputed as an additional cost of materials acquired or to be acquired.		

Discount on note receivable	14,000	
Cash	102,000	
Note receivable		100,000
Interest income		16,000
To record the collection of a note.		

In sum, imputation applies to both outlay costs and opportunity costs. The aim is to get better recognition of the economic impact of a particular event or decision and not to take things at face value.

Out-of-pocket costs, a short-run concept, are those costs that entail current or near-future outlays for the decision at hand. For example, the acceptance of an order so that otherwise idle facilities may be used would entail a compilation of the out-of-pocket costs that could otherwise be avoided by not accepting the order; the depreciation on the machinery and equipment used for production would be irrelevant because it does not entail out-of-pocket outlays as a result of the decision.

Joint cost is that term most often applied to the costs of two or more kinds of manufactured goods that are produced simultaneously by a single process and are not identifiable as individual types of products until a certain stage of production known as the *split-off point* (point of separation) is reached. Examples of such products are soap and glycerin, kerosene and gasoline, chemicals, and lumber. Joint costs are total costs incurred up to the point of separation. Inasmuch as joint costs by their very nature cannot be directly traced to units worked on, any method of apportioning such costs to various units produced is essentially arbitrary. The usefulness of joint-cost apportionment is limited to purposes of inventory costing and income measurement. Such apportionment is generally regarded as useless for cost-planning and control purposes. For elaboration, see Chapter 16.

Viewed broadly, joint costs plague accountants throughout their work. Few costs are not joint in relation to some other factor, such as time or facilities. The entire problem of allocating the costs of fixed assets to months, years, departments, and products is essentially that of joint costing. Sometimes the term *common cost* is used instead of *joint cost* to describe another aspect of joint costing, such as the problem of determining unit cost of such services as bank accounts. Any allocation method is arbitrary, because many facilities and services are shared by many revenue-producing activities. The entire problem of reapportioning service-department costs among producing departments is really one of joint cost. For elaboration, see Chapters 14 and 15.

Postponable costs are those that may be shifted to the future with little or no effect on the efficiency of current operations. The best example of these is maintenance and repairs. Railroads sometimes go on an economy binge and cut their sizable maintenance budgets. But it is really a matter of deferral and not avoidance. Eventually some overhauls must be made and tracks must be repaired.

Avoidable costs are those that may be saved by not adopting a given alternative. For example, by not adopting a new product line, additional direct-material, direct-labor, and overhead costs could be avoided. The criterion here is the question, Which costs can be saved by not adopting a given alternative?

Sunk cost is another term for a past cost that is unavoidable because it cannot be changed no matter what action is taken. The author dislikes this term because it often beclouds the distinction between historical and future costs. However, *sunk cost* is discussed here because it is one of the most widely used terms in special-decision making.

To illustrate, if old equipment has a book value of $600,000 and a scrap value of $70,000, what is the sunk cost? There are two ways of looking at the $600,000 book value of old equipment. This author agrees with a minority view maintaining that the entire $600,000 is sunk because it represents an outlay made in the past that cannot be changed; the $70,000 scrap value is a future factor, to be considered apart from the $600,000 sunk cost. The majority view maintains that $530,000 of the $600,000 is sunk, whereas $70,000 is not sunk because it is immediately recoverable through scrapping; thus, the sunk part of a historical cost is what is irrecoverable in a given situation. This majority view is that the two factors (book value and present scrap value) are complementary in replacement decisions; that is, book value minus scrap value equals sunk cost.

In the author's opinion, the term *sunk cost* should not be used at all. It muddles the task of collecting proper costs for decision making. Because all past costs are irrelevant, it is fruitless to introduce unnecessary terms to describe past costs. The issue of what part of past cost is sunk need not arise. The essence of the distinction between costs, past and future, irrelevant and relevant, was described earlier in this chapter. These distinctions are all that are needed for approaching special decisions. The term *sunk cost* is often more befuddling than enlightening. If it is going to be used, *sunk cost* should have the same meaning as *past cost.*

Appendix 11b: cost-plus for setting prices

Professional economists, self-styled economists, and managers have been arguing for centuries about the cause-and-effect relationships between costs and prices. The problems here are intricate because of the interplay of long-run and short-run factors.

major influences on pricing

Many managers maintain that they use cost-plus pricing. They say that they figure their average unit costs and tack on a "fair" margin that will yield an adequate return on investment. This calculation entails circular reasoning because price, which influences sales, depends upon full cost, which in turn is partly determined by the *volume* of sales. Also, this "plus" in cost-plus is bothersome. It is rarely a rigid "plus."

Instead, it is flexible, depending on the behavior of customers and competitors. Thus, there are at least three major influences on pricing decisions: customers, competitors, and costs.

CUSTOMERS □ The manager must always examine his pricing problems through the eyes of customers. He (or she) cannot point a shotgun at customers and say, "Buy, or else!" Customers can reject a company's product and turn to competitors' products or, perhaps, to a completely different industry for a substitute product. When coffee prices are high, many people drink one cup instead of two; others switch to tea. If a company's prices get too high, the immediate reaction of the customer is to check with competitors, who welcome such inquiries. Perhaps customers make their own products or try to find themselves different products that will serve just as well (aluminum instead of copper). For example, buyers of welding equipment are often most heavily influenced by the way the product affects their costs. The buyers not only have alternative sources of supply within the welding-equipment industry but may not buy at all—they may keep using their existing equipment. They may substitute some other kind of equipment to accomplish their tasks; or they may manufacture the needed equipment themselves.

COMPETITORS □ Rivals' reactions or lack of reactions will influence pricing decisions. In guessing a competitor's reactions, one must speculate on what the competitor's costs are, rather than be concerned with one's own costs. Of course, one's own costs may be helpful in guessing, but it is the rival's costs that are relevant. Knowledge of the rival's technology, plant size, and operating policies help sharpen estimates of one's costs. Companies within industries that loathe price competition have been known to swap detailed cost information for mutual benefit. Where there is no collusion, rivals' reactions and price quotations must be guessed when pricing decisions are made.

COSTS □ The maximum price that may be charged is the one that does not drive the customer away. The minimum price is zero. Companies occasionally will give or virtually give their products away in order to enter a market or to obtain a profitable long-run relationship with a customer. A more practical guide is gleaned from our study of cost-volume-profit relationships. In the short run, the minimum price to be quoted should be the additional costs from accepting the order or segment of available business. Any amount in excess of those additional costs directly increases income.

Where a company has some discretion in price setting, customer demand at various price levels determines the sales volume. In these situations, study must be given to differential cost-volume-profit relationships; in turn, these relationships are dependent on market conditions, elasticity of industry demand, concentration of capacity, and rivals' reactions.

Where a company has little discretion, it accepts the price that competition has set. Then, under given economic conditions, the company ordinarily selects the level of production and sales that maximizes profits.

example of contribution approach to pricing

Exhibit 11-7 shows an actual price-quote format used by the president and sales manager of a small job shop that bids on special machinery orders under highly competitive conditions. This approach is a tool for flexible pricing. Note that the *maximum* price is not a matter of cost at all; the *minimum* price is set by the total variable costs.

EXHIBIT 11-7

Quote Sheet
(Data Assumed)

Direct materials (materials only, at cost)	$ 75,000
Direct labor and variable overhead (3,000 direct-labor hrs. × $20) =	60,000
Commission (varies with job)	6,000
Total variable costs—minimum price	141,000
Add fixed costs applied (3,000 direct-labor hrs. × $15) =	45,000
Total costs (including share of fixed costs)	186,000
Add desired profit	27,000
Selling price (what you think you can get—maximum price)	$213,000

This quote sheet shows two prices, maximum and minimum. Any amount you can get over the minimum price is a contribution margin.

Note also in Exhibit 11-7 that the costs are classified and tailored especially for the pricing task. Pricing duties may be in the hands of a number of different executives. Often it is a joint effort on the part of the sales manager, production manager, and general manager, with the last-named having the final authority. The accountant's task is to supply a format that not only is understandable but involves a minimum of computations. That is why direct labor and variable overhead are lumped together in one overall rate; all fixed costs, whether factory, engineering, selling, or administrative, are lumped together for the same reason.

QUESTIONS, PROBLEMS, AND CASES

11-1 Distinguish between *full cost* and *absorption cost*.

11-2 Distinguish briefly between *quantitative* and *qualitative* factors in decision making.

11-3 Define *relevant cost* as the term is used in this chapter. Why are historical costs irrelevant?

11-4 What is a *differential cost?* Distinguish it from a relevant cost.

11-5 "All future costs are relevant." Do you agree? Why?

11-6 Theater prices are usually lower for matinees than for evening performances. Why? As a movie-theater manager, what factors would influence your decision as to conducting matinees? To what degree are operating costs affected by the size of the audience?

11-7 ***Questions on disposal of assets.***

1. A company has an inventory of 1,000 assorted missile parts for a line of missiles that has been junked. The inventory cost $100,000. The parts can be either (a) remachined at total additional costs of $30,000 and then sold for a total of $35,000 or (b) scrapped for $2,000. What should be done?

2. A truck, costing $10,000 and uninsured, is wrecked the first day in use. It can be either (a) disposed of for $1,000 cash and replaced with a similar truck costing $10,200 or (b) rebuilt for $8,500 and be brand-new as far as operating characteristics and looks are concerned. What should be done?

11-8 ***The careening bookkeeping machine.*** (From W. A. Paton, "Restoration of Fixed Asset Values to the Balance Sheet," *Accounting Review,* XXII, No. 2, pp. 194–210.) A young lady in the accounting department of a certain business was moving a bookkeeping machine from one room to another. As she came alongside an open stairway, she carelessly slipped and let the machine get away from her. It went careening down the stairs with a great racket and wound up at the bottom in some thousands of pieces, completely wrecked. Hearing the crash, the office manager came rushing out, and turned rather white when he saw what had happened. "Someone tell me quickly," he yelled, "if that is one of our fully amortized units." A check of the equipment cards showed that the smashed machine was, indeed, one of those which had been written off. "Thank God!" said the manager.

REQUIRED | Explain and comment on the point of Professor Paton's anecdote.

11-9 ***Reconsideration of Exhibit 11-1.*** Reexamine the plant-rearrangement decision in Exhibit 11-1, page 365.

1. Give an example of (a) a prediction method for direct-labor costs under the "do nothing" alternative that is more specific than using the historical costs indicated in the exhibit; and (b) a decision model that is more specific than described in the exhibit.

2. What steps in Exhibit 11-1 are often described as planning? As control?

11-10 ***Reconsideration of Exhibit 11-1.*** Consider the sequence in Exhibit 11-1. Suppose the labor costs for the year just ended were $2.00 per unit. However, during the preceding year the labor costs had been $2.50 per unit. Continued productivity increases at the most recent percentage rate per year were anticipated if the rearrangement is not made. If the rearrangement occurs, the predicted unit costs would be $1.40 throughout the coming year.

REQUIRED

1. What is the predicted labor cost per unit if the facilities are not rearranged?
2. Suppose no labor-cost records had been kept. As the decision maker, would you be more confident or less confident about choosing whether to rearrange? Why? How would you compute the maximum amount that you would be willing to pay for the historical-cost information?
3. Suppose you chose rearrangement. The first year's results show a labor cost per unit of $2.40. What does this feedback indicate? Be specific.

11-11 ***Multiple choice.*** (CPA) Choose the best answer:

1. Woody Company, which manufactures sneakers, has enough idle capacity available to accept a special order of 20,000 pairs of sneakers at $6.00 a pair. The normal selling price is $10.00 a pair. Variable manufacturing costs are $4.50 a pair, and fixed manufacturing costs are $1.50 a pair. Woody will not incur any selling expenses as a result of the special order. What would the effect on operating income be if the special order could be accepted without affecting normal sales? (a) $0, (b) $30,000 increase, (c) $90,000 increase, (d) $120,000 increase.

2. The Reno Company manufactures Part No. 498 for use in its production cycle. The cost per unit for 20,000 units of Part No. 498 are as follows:

Direct materials	$ 6
Direct labor	30
Variable overhead	12
Fixed overhead applied	16
	$64

The Tray Company has offered to sell 20,000 units of Part No. 498 to Reno for $60 per unit. Reno will make the decision to buy the part from Tray if there is a savings of $25,000 for Reno. If Reno accepts Tray's offer, $9 per unit of the fixed overhead applied would be totally eliminated. Furthermore, Reno has determined that the released facilities could be used to save relevant costs in the manufacture of Part No. 575. In order to have a savings of $25,000, the amount of relevant costs that would be saved by using the released facilities in the manufacture of Part No. 575 would have to be (a) $80,000, (b) $85,000, (c) $125,000, (d) $140,000.

11-12 ***Relevance of equipment costs.*** The Auto Wash Company has just installed a special machine for polishing cars at one of its several outlets. It is the first day of the company's fiscal year. The machine costs $20,000. Its annual operating costs total $15,000, exclusive of depreciation. The machine will have a four-year useful life and no residual value.

After the machine has been used one day, a machine salesman offers a different machine that promises to do the same job at a yearly operating cost of $9,000, exclusive of depreciation. The new machine will cost $24,000 cash, installed. The "old" machine is unique and can be sold outright for only $10,000, less $2,000 removal cost. The new machine, like the old one, will have a four-year useful life and no residual value.

Sales, all in cash, will be $150,000 annually and other cash expenses will be $110,000 annually, regardless of this decision.

For simplicity, assume there is a world of no income taxes and no interest. (The interest implications of this problem are covered in Problem 12-12.)

REQUIRED

1. Prepare a statement of cash receipts and disbursements for each of the four years under both alternatives. What is the cumulative difference in cash for the four years taken together?
2. Prepare statements of income for each of the four years under both alternatives. Assume straight-line depreciation. What is the cumulative difference in net income for the four years taken together?
3. What are the irrelevant items in each of your presentations in requirements 1 and 2? Why are they irrelevant?
4. Suppose that the cost of the "old" machine was $1 million rather than $20,000. Nevertheless, the old machine can be sold outright for only $10,000, less $2,000 removal cost. Would the net differences in requirements 1 and 2 change? Explain.
5. "To avoid a loss, we should keep the old equipment." What is the role of book value in decisions about replacement of equipment?
6. You are the mayor of a small town. You purchased some new lawn-mowing equipment yesterday. Assume the same facts as in requirements 1 and 2; however, no operating revenues exist. Would any of your answers to requirements 1 through 5 change? How? Why?

11-13 ***Relevance of inventory costs to a business investment decision.*** Assume that a wealthy investor is contemplating buying a paper-manufacturing company. Certain inventory of the paper company is carried at $100,000, including $40,000 of variable production costs and $60,000 of fixed factory overhead.

REQUIRED

How much should the investor pay for the inventory? Why?

11-14 ***An argument about pricing.*** A column in a newspaper contained the following:

Dear Miss Lovelorn: My husband and I are in constant disagreement because he drives 10 miles to work every day and drives a mile in the opposite direction to pick up and deliver the man who rides with him. Therefore, the total daily mileage is 24 for the round trip. For this service the man pays $6 every other week toward gas. Bus fare would cost $16 each week. I say this fellow should pay at least $8 each week, which would be one-half the cost for the week's gas. But my husband says he can't just ask him for the money, so he settles for this arrangement month after month. We have three children and are in debt for several hundred dollars, and even this $8 a week would really help, as we live on a very tight budget. Am I reasonable to think the gas expense should be split 50-50?

REQUIRED

As Miss Lovelorn, write a reply.

11-15 ***Contribution approach to pricing.*** Ben Suppan, the president of the Suppan Manufacturing Company, has just attended an executive education program. He observed a demonstration of the virtues of the contribution approach to cost accounting (variable or direct costing). But Suppan said, "I'm unconvinced. My reluctance is based primarily on the probable misuse of the recasted data. There will be lower costs of products. The marketing people will be too tempted to shave prices, a practice that is too prevalent anyway. Therefore, I'll stick to absorption costing."

REQUIRED

Under what circumstances would you tend to agree with Suppan? Disagree?

11-16 ***Contribution approach to pricing.*** The Dill Company had the following operating characteristics in 19_4:

Basic production data at standard cost:	
Direct materials	$1.30
Direct labor	1.50
Variable overhead	.20
Fixed overhead ($150,000 ÷ 150,000 units of denominator volume)	1.00
Total factory cost at standard	$4.00

Sales price, $5.00 per unit.
Selling and administrative expense is assumed for simplicity as being all fixed at $65,000 yearly, except for sales commissions at 5% of dollar sales.

In 19_4, a Dill Company salesman had asked the president for permission to sell 1,000 units to a particular customer for $3.80 per unit. The president refused, stating that the price was below factory cost. Based solely on the information given, compute the effect of the president's decision on 19_4 net income. Specifically, what would be the reasoning of the contribution approach to such a decision?

11-17 ***Contribution approach to pricing.*** A company has a budget for 19_2; the absorption-costing approach follows (figures assumed):

Sales	$100,000	100%
Factory cost of goods sold, including $20,000 fixed costs	60,000	60
Gross profit	$ 40,000	40%
Operating expenses, including $20,000 fixed costs	30,000	30
Net income target	$ 10,000	10%

Normal or target markup percentage:
$40,000 ÷ $60,000 = 66.7% of absorption cost

REQUIRED

1. Recast the income statement in a contribution format. Indicate the normal or target markup percentage based on total variable costs.
2. Assume the same cost behavior patterns as above. Assume further that a customer offers $540 for some units that have a factory cost of goods manufactured of $600 and total variable costs of $500. Should the offer be accepted? Explain.
3. Under what circumstances would you adopt a contribution approach to pricing as a part of your usual accounting system? That is, the system would routinely provide data using the contribution format.

11-18 ***Considering three alternatives.*** (CMA) Auer Company had received an order for a piece of special machinery from Jay Company. Just as Auer Company completed the machine, Jay Company declared bankruptcy, defaulted on the order, and forfeited the 10 percent deposit paid on the selling price of $72,500.

Auer's manufacturing manager identified the costs already incurred in the production of the special machinery for Jay as follows:

Direct materials used		$16,600
Direct labor incurred		21,400
Overhead applied:		
Manufacturing:		
Variable	$10,700	
Fixed	5,350	16,050
Fixed selling and administrative		5,405
Total cost		$59,455

Another company, Kaytell Corp., would be interested in buying the special machinery if it is reworked to Kaytell's specifications. Auer offered to sell the reworked special machinery to Kaytell as a special order for a net price of $68,400. Kaytell has agreed to pay the net price when it takes delivery in two months. The additional identifiable costs to rework the machinery to the specifications of Kaytell are as follows:

Direct materials	$ 6,200
Direct labor	4,200
	$10,400

A second alternative available to Auer is to convert the special machinery to the standard model. The standard model lists for $62,500. The additional identifiable costs to convert the special machinery to the standard model are:

Direct materials	$ 2,850
Direct labor	3,300
	$ 6,150

A third alternative for the Auer Company is to sell, as a special order, the machine as is (i.e., without modification) for a net price of $52,000. However, the potential buyer of the unmodified machine does not want it for 60 days. The buyer offers a $7,000 down payment with final payment upon delivery.

The following additional information is available regarding Auer's operations:

Sales commission rate on sales of standard models is 2 percent while the sales commission rate on special orders is 3 percent. All sales commissions are calculated on net sales price (i.e., list price less cash discount, if any).

Normal credit terms for sales of standard models are 2/10, net/30. Customers take the discounts except in rare instances. Credit terms for special orders are negotiated with the customer.

The application rates for manufacturing overhead and the fixed selling and administrative costs are as follows:

Manufacturing	
Variable	50% of direct-labor cost
Fixed	25% of direct-labor cost
Selling and administrative	
Fixed	10% of the total of direct-material, direct-labor and manufacturing-overhead costs

Normal time required for rework is one month.

A surcharge of 5 percent of the sales price is placed on all customer requests for minor modifications of standard models.

Auer normally sells a sufficient number of standard models for the company to operate at a volume in excess of the breakeven point.

Auer does not consider the time value of money in analyses of special orders and projects whenever the time period is less than one year because the effect is not significant.

REQUIRED

1. Determine the dollar contribution each of the three alternatives will add to the Auer Company's before-tax profits.
2. If Kaytell makes Auer a counteroffer, what is the lowest price Auer Co. should accept for the reworked machinery from Kaytell? Explain your answer.
3. Discuss the influence that fixed-factory-overhead cost should have on the sales prices quoted by Auer Company for special orders when (a) a firm is operating at or below the breakeven point; (b) a firm's special orders constitute efficient utilization of unused capacity above the breakeven volume.

11-19 ***Costs of operating an automobile.*** Here are typical costs of operating a salesman's car for 30,000 miles in a year:

Gasoline—1,500 gallons @ $2	$3,000
Oil changes and lubrication—10 @ $21	210
Tire wear (based on life of 20,000 miles; a new set of 4 costs $300)	450
Regular maintenance and repair	540
Auto insurance	500
Washing and waxing	200
Licenses	200
Garage rent and parking fees	800
Depreciation—($8,800 − $4,400) ÷ 2-year life	2,200
	$8,100

Unit cost is $8,100 ÷ 30,000 miles, or 27¢ per mile.

REQUIRED

1. If the salesman drove 20,000 miles per year, what would be the average unit cost per mile? If he drove 40,000 miles?
2. He takes his car on a 200-mile journey with a friend who agrees to share the cost of the trip. How much should the friend pay?
3. The salesman's wife wants a similar car for shopping and other errands that the husband now performs. If he buys the second car, it will be driven 4,000 miles per year; but suppose the total mileage of the two cars taken together will still be 30,000 miles. What will the annual cost of operating the second car be? The average unit cost? What costs are relevant? Why?
4. List other possible costs of car ownership that are not included in the tabulation above.
5. What costs are relevant to the question of selling the car at the end of one year (market value, $6,000) and using other means of transportation?
6. Assume that the salesman has no car. What costs are relevant to the question of buying the car described versus using other means of transportation?

11-20 ***Different cost terms.*** (CPA) Read Appendix 11A. *Instructions:* You are to match each of the nine numbered "items" that follow with the *one* term listed immediately below (A through R) that *most specifically* identifies the cost concept indicated parenthetically. (*Caution:* An item of cost may be classified in several ways, depending on the purpose of the classification. For example, the commissions on sales of a proposed new product line might be classified as *direct, variable,* and *marginal,* among others. However, if such costs are being considered specifically as to the amount of *cash outlay* required in making a decision concerning adoption of the new line, the commissions are *out-of-pocket costs.* That would be the *most* appropriate answer in the context.) The same term may be used more than once.

Indicate your choice of answer for each item by printing beside the item numbers the capital letter that identifies the term you select.

Terms

A. Byproduct cost	J. Indirect cost
B. Common or joint cost	K. Opportunity cost
C. Controllable cost	L. Original cost
D. Direct cost	M. Out-of-pocket cost
E. Estimated cost	N. Prime cost
F. Fixed cost	O. Replacement cost
G. Historical cost	P. Standard cost
H. Imputed cost	Q. Sunk cost
I. Differential cost	R. Variable cost

Items

1. The management of a corporation is considering replacing a machine that is operating satisfactorily with a more efficient new model. Depreciation on the cost of the existing machine is omitted from the data used in judging the proposal, because it has little or no significance with respect to such a decision. (*The omitted cost.*)

2. One of the problems encountered by a bank in attempting to establish the cost of a commercial-deposit account is the fact that many facilities and services are shared by many revenue-producing activities. (*Costs of the shared facilities and services.*)

3. A company declined an offer received to rent one of its warehouses and elected to use the warehouse for storage of extra raw materials to ensure uninterrupted production. Storage cost has been charged with *the monthly amount of the rental offered.* (*This cost is known as?*)

4. A manufacturing company excludes all "fixed" costs from its valuation of inventories, assigning to inventory only *applicable portions of costs that vary with changes in volume of product.* (*The term employed for the variable costs in this context by advocates of this costing procedure.*)

5. The sales department urges an increase in production of a product and, as part of the data presented in support of its proposal, indicates the total additional cost involved for the volume level it proposes. (*The increase in total cost.*)

6. A CPA takes exception to his client's inclusion, in the cost of a fixed asset, of an "interest" charge based on the client's own funds invested in the asset. The client states that the charge was intended to obtain a cost comparable to what would have been the case if funds had been borrowed to finance the acquisition. (*The term that describes such interest charges.*)

7. The "direct" production cost of a unit includes those portions of factory overhead, *labor,* and *materials* that are obviously traceable directly to the unit. (*The term used to specify the last two of the named components.*)

8. Calling upon the special facilities of the production, planning, personnel, and other departments, a firm estimated its future unit cost of production and used this cost (analyzed by cost elements) in its accounts. (*The term used to specify this scientifically predetermined estimate.*)

9. A chemical-manufacturing company produces three products originating in a common initial material mix. Each product gains a separate identity partway through processing and requires additional processing after the "split." Each contributes a significant share of revenue. The company plans to spread the costs up to the "split" among the three products by the use of relative market values. (*The term used to specify the costs accumulated up to the point of the split.*)

11-21 ***Selection of most profitable product.*** The Reductio Co. produces two basic types of reducing equipment, G and H. Pertinent data follow:

	PER UNIT	
	G	H
Sales price	$100.00	$70.00
Expenses:		
Direct materials	$ 28.00	$13.00
Direct labor	15.00	25.00
Variable factory overhead*	25.00	12.50
Fixed factory overhead*	10.00	5.00
Selling expenses (all variable)	14.00	10.00
	$ 92.00	$65.50
Net margin	$ 8.00	$ 4.50

**Applied on the basis of machine-hours.*

The reducing craze is such that enough of either G or H can be sold to keep the plant operating at full capacity. Both products are processed through the same production centers.

REQUIRED

Which product should be produced? If more than one should be produced, indicate the proportions of each. Briefly explain your answer.

11-22 ***Order-filling costs and minimum order size.*** The Real Vitamin Company has made a time study of the cost of filling orders, with the following results:

SIZE OF ORDERS IN DOLLARS	AVERAGE TIME REQUIRED
.00 to 5.00	.10 hour
5.01 to 15.00	.12 hour
15.01 to 25.00	.16 hour
25.01 to 35.00	.20 hour
Over 35.00	.25 hour

Order-filling costs totaled $12,000 for the month in which the study was made, and 1,600 labor-hours were worked in the order-filling department. During the same period, the costs of receiving orders and of billing and posting the customers' accounts were calculated at a minimum of 40¢ per order. Gross margin (profit) on the company's merchandise averages 20 percent.

Ignoring all considerations other than these cost data, should the company adopt a rule that it will accept orders only above some minimum size? If so, what minimum order size would you recommend?

11-23 ***Opportunity cost.*** (H. Schaefer) Wolverine Corp. is working at full production capacity producing 10,000 units of a unique product, Rosebo. Standard costs per unit for Rosebo are:

Direct material	$ 2
Direct labor	3
Factory overhead	5
	$10

The unit overhead cost is based on a variable cost per unit of $2 and fixed costs of $30,000 (at full capacity of 10,000 units). The nonmanufacturing costs, all variable, are $4 per unit and the sales pricc is $20 per unit.

A customer, the Miami Co., has asked Wolverine to produce 2,000 units of a modification of Rosebo to be called Orangebo. Orangebo would require the same manufacturing processes as Rosebo, and the Miami Co. has offered to share equally the nonmanufacturing costs with Wolverine. It is expected that Orangebo will have a sales price of $15 per unit.

REQUIRED

1. What is the opportunity cost to Wolverine of producing the 2,000 units of Orangebo? (Assume no overtime is worked.)
2. The Buckeye Corp. has offered to produce 2,000 units of Rosebo for Wolverine so that Wolverine may accept the Orangebo offer. Buckeye would charge Wolverine $14 per unit for the Rosebo. Should Wolverine accept the Buckeye offer? (Support with specific analysis.)
3. Suppose Wolverine had been working at less than full capacity producing 8,000 units of Rosebo at the time the Orangebo offer was made. What is the *minimum* price Wolverine should accept for Orangebo under these conditions? (Ignore the $15 price above.)

11-24 ***Relationship of disposal value, book value, and net loss on old equipment.*** Scott Harshaw is the president of a small plastics company. He wants to replace an old special-purpose molding machine (original cost, $18,700; eight years old; book value, $9,100; straight-line depreciation, $1,200 per year; residual value at end of useful life, $700) with a new, more efficient machine. The new machine has an expected useful life of only seven years, but it promises savings in cash-operating costs of $2,257 per year. Operating costs with the new machine are $30,000; with the old machine, $32,257. The cost of the new machine is $8,800. The old machine can be sold outright for $2,300, less $200 removal cost. It is estimated that the old machine would have a net disposal value of $700 seven years from now; the new machine, a value of $750 seven years from now.

Vladimir Galoot, controller, opposes replacement because no advantage is apparent. His analysis shows:

Cost of new investment:	
Outlay	$ 8,800
Loss on old machine ($9,100 minus $2,100)	7,000
Total cost	$15,800
Savings: $2,257 per year × 7 years	15,800 (rounded)
Net advantage of replacement	$ 0

He also adds, "I can't ever see disposing of fixed assets at a loss before their useful life expires. Plant and equipment are bought and depreciated with some useful life in mind. We are in business to maximize income (or minimize loss). It seems to me that the alternatives are clear: (a) disposal of a fixed asset before it diminishes to zero or residual book value often results in a loss; (b) keeping and *using* the same fixed asset avoids such a loss. Now, any sensible person will have brains enough to avoid a loss when his other alternative is recognizing a loss. It makes sense to use a fixed asset till you get your money out of it."

Yearly sales are $90,000, and cash expenses, excluding the data given above, are $50,000.

REQUIRED

(Ignore income tax effects.)

1. How will net income be affected if the old machine is scrapped and the new machine is purchased? Show computations for the seven years taken together.
2. Prepare columnar income statements for years 1 through 7 under both alternatives, as follows:

YEAR 1	EACH YEAR, 2–7	7 YEARS TOGETHER

3. Generalize as to the role of disposal value on old equipment in these decisions.
4. Generalize as to the role of (a) book value in these decisions and (b) net loss on disposal of old fixed assets.
5. Criticize Galoot's schedule and his comments.
6. What important cost factor has been ignored in your answers to requirements 1 and 2?

11-25 ***Production scheduling.*** (R. Jaedicke) A paperboard manufacturing company has two plants, one in Washington and one in California, producing equivalent grades of "cardboard." The Washington plant has been operating at 75 percent of plant capacity, producing 2,700 tons of cardboard per month. The California plant has been operating at 60 percent of plant capacity, producing 3,600 tons per month.

The major raw material used in producing the cardboard is wastepaper. For each 100 tons of product, 80 tons of wastepaper are required. At the Washington plant the local wastepaper costs are $18.75 per tons of wastepaper, but the supply is limited to 1,440 tons per month. At the California plant local wastepaper costs $20.00 per ton and is limited to 4,000 tons. Additional wastepaper must be purchased through brokers at $27.50 per ton (delivered at either plant).

The cost schedules for a typical month's production are as follows:

Washington Plant	
Raw materials (2,160 tons input)	$ 46,800
Fixed cost (per month)	59,400
Variable cost	102,600*
Total cost ($77.33 per ton output)	$208,800

California Plant	
Raw materials (2,880 tons input)	$ 57,600
Fixed cost	108,000
Variable cost	140,400*
Total cost ($85.00 per ton output)	$306,000

**Variable costs are constant per ton of output.*

REQUIRED

(Disregard any marketing costs in your answer to the questions.)

1. If the total combined production of both plants is to be continued at the present rate of 6,300 tons per month, would there be any apparent advantage to shifting part of the scheduled production from one of the plants to the other? If so, which plant's production should be increased and by how much? What is the amount of the cost savings as a result of this switch?
2. If production requirements increased to 9,100 tons per month, how much would you recommend be produced at each plant? (Show calculations.)

11-26 ***Choosing profitable products.*** The subsidiary of a multinational drug company was the largest firm in a developing nation's pharmaceutical industry (comprising some 30 manufacturers), with sales in the vicinity of $20 million. The manufacturing operation consisted primarily of processing and packing imported bulk materials into finished products. The 98 finished products were made from some 50 different kinds of raw (bulk) materials, almost all of which were imported. The firm had its own well-trained "detail" sales force and distribution network.

The subsidiary had grown rapidly after commencing operations in the mid-1960s and became the largest company in terms of sales in 1982 after overtaking its British rival. Although sales had grown phenomenally, the profit performance of the subsidiary had been relatively poor as measured by profits as a percentage of sales. The first president of the company had stressed sales and volume and had provided the sales force with all the financial benefits and assistance possible. His successor, in an effort to improve profitability, had concentrated on reducing costs.

The country in which the subsidiary was located was typical of many developing nations, in that it suffered from severe foreign-exchange problems. Some 80 percent of the foreign exchange available was devoted to the import of food and defense equipment, the remainder being made available for all other imports, including drugs. The amount of foreign exchange available was rationed by industry and by company on a six-month basis. Firms then received permits of $\$X$ of foreign exchange, which they could use to import materials not available in the country in any quantities and in any combination. The permitted amount for each company could vary by significant amounts, but planning beyond a six-month period was almost impossible.

The foreign-exchange limitation made the market for drugs in the country a seller's market. The government kept a close watch on prices, and the pharmaceutical industry was extremely sensitive to arousing public hostility due to pricing, as had been the case in some other developing countries. The task, therefore, was to find a straightforward technique—not requiring sophisticated quantitative skills—that could be used as a guide to maximizing profits.

There are practically, no constraints in manufacturing, and a wide range in production quantities of the 98 different products is possible. For the purpose of this problem, assume that any product can be dropped if necessary.

The following information was chosen at random. It demonstrates how management has been determining the relative priorities for choosing products:

	PER UNIT OF PRODUCT		
	A	B	C
Selling price (in dollar equivalents)	$10.50	$12.00	$ 8.00
Variable costs of production and selling (excluding the cost of imported materials)	2.50	5.00	2.00
Contribution to cost of imported materials and fixed costs	$ 8.00	$ 7.00	$ 6.00
Contribution ratio	76%	58%	75%
Ranking	First	Third	Second
Cost of imported materials	$ 2.00	$ 1.00	$ 1.00

REQUIRED

Will management's ranking maximize profits? Rank the products in the order of desired production and sales effort. Explain your ranking.

11-27 ***Discontinuing a department; make or buy.*** The Trump Publishing Company is in the business of publishing and printing sales catalogs and instruction booklets. The board of directors has engaged you to make a cost study to determine whether the company is economically justified in continuing to print, as well as publish, its catalogs and booklets. You obtain the following information from the company's cost-accounting records for the preceding fiscal year:

	DEPARTMENTS			
	publishing	printing	shipping	total
Salaries and wages	$275,000	$180,000	$35,000	$ 490,000
Telephone and telegraph	12,000	3,700	300	16,000
Materials and supplies	50,000	250,000	10,000	310,000
Occupancy costs	75,000	80,000	10,000	165,000
General and administrative	40,000	40,000	4,000	84,000
Depreciation	5,000	40,000	5,000	50,000
	$457,000	$593,700	$64,300	$1,115,000

ADDITIONAL DATA

1. A review of personnel requirements indicates that if printing is discontinued, the publishing department will need one additional clerk at $14,000 per year to handle correspondence with the printer. Two layout men and a proofreader must be retained from the personnel of the printing department at an aggregate annual cost of $57,000; other personnel in the printing department can be released. One mailing clerk, at $13,000, will be retained by the shipping department; others in the shipping department can be released. Employees whose employment was being terminated would immediately receive, on the average, three months' termination pay. The termination pay would be amortized over a five-year period.
2. Long-distance telephone and telegraph charges are identified and distributed to the responsible department. The remainder of the telephone bill, representing basic service at a cost of $4,000, is allocated in the ratio of 10 to publishing, 5 to printing, and 1 to shipping. The discontinuance of printing is not expected to have a material effect on the basic service cost.
3. Shipping supplies consist of cartons, envelopes, and stamps. It is estimated that the only cost of materials and supplies for the shipping department would be for the envelopes and stamps used for mailing material to an outside printer, $5,000 per year.
4. If printing were discontinued, the company would retain its present building but would sublet a portion of the space at an annual rental of $50,000. Taxes, insurance, heat, light, and other occupancy costs would not be significantly affected.
5. One cost clerk would not be required ($15,000 per year) if printing is discontinued. Other general and administrative personnel would be retained.
6. Included in administrative expense is interest expense on a 12 percent mortgage loan of $500,000.
7. Printing and shipping-room machinery and equipment having a net book value of $300,000 can be sold without gain or loss. These funds in excess of termination pay would be invested in marketable securities earning 12 percent.
8. The company has received a proposal for a five-year contract from an outside printer, under which the volume of work done last year would be printed at a cost of $498,000 per year.
9. Assume continued volume and prices at last year's level.

REQUIRED

Prepare a statement setting forth in comparative form the costs of operation of the printing and shipping departments under the present arrangement and under an arrangement in which inside printing is discontinued. Summarize the net saving or extra cost in case printing is discontinued.

11-28 ***Make or buy and use of capacity.*** (SMA, adapted) North Star Guns is a high-technology enterprise making sophisticated products for the armaments market. North Star is made up of two independent profit centers—North Star Armour and North Star Engineering.

North Star Armour makes two types of tanks—Light and Heavy. Light is a lightweight tank that has a potentially unlimited market and sells for $25,000 per unit. Heavy is a highly sophisticated main-battle tank that uses a special type of radar equipment, imported from West Germany at a cost of $10,000 per unit.

North Star Engineering manufactures two types of electronic guidance units—Standard and Deluxe. These units require a high degree of skill in manufacturing. However, because of a shortage of trained engineers, North Star Engineering has only 100 skilled employees, whose total labor capacity (allowing for sickness, leaves, and so on) is expected to be 100,000 hours per year.

The data for the two divisions are as follows:

North Star Armour

	LIGHT	HEAVY
Materials (parts)	$10,000	$50,000
Labor	100 hrs. @ $10	200 hrs. @ $10
Machine-hours	100 hrs. (1 hr. per labor hr.)	200 hrs. (1 hr. per labor hr.)
Variable overhead per machine hour	$40	$40
Market price	$25,000	$100,000
Fixed overhead: $1,000,000		

North Star Engineering

	STANDARD	DELUXE
Material (parts)	$1,000	$4,000
Labor	10 hrs. @ $20	100 hrs. @ $20
Variable overhead per labor-hour	$10	$10
Market price	$1,500	$10,000
Fixed overhead: $1,000,000		

Standard has a potentially unlimited market, but Deluxe has only the army as a customer. North Star Engineering has a standing order for 500 Deluxe units per year from the army.

It has been known for some time at the Research Center at headquarters that Deluxe could be used to replace the West German radar in Heavy. The modifications would cost only $200 per unit for the additional labor at North Star Armour. However, the complete modifications required have only been recently specified, and these data plus the labor cost have been conveyed to North Star Armour.

REQUIRED

North Star Armour has a current order for 100 Heavy tanks. From the overall company (North Star Guns) viewpoint, should the company use Deluxe units or continue to buy the West German radar? Show your supporting calculations.

11-29 ***Multiple choice; comprehensive problem on relevant costs.*** The following are the Class Company's *unit* costs of making and selling a given item at a level of 20,000 units per month:

Manufacturing:	
Direct materials	$1.00
Direct labor	1.20
Variable indirect cost	.80
Fixed indirect cost	.50
Selling and other:	
Variable	1.50
Fixed	.90

The following situations refer only to the data given above—there is *no connection* between the situations. Unless stated otherwise, assume a regular selling price of $6 per unit.

Choose the answer corresponding to the most nearly acceptable or correct answer in each of the nine items. Support each answer with summarized computations.

1. In presenting an inventory of 10,000 items on the balance sheet, the unit cost conventionally to be used is (a) $3.00, (b) $3.50, (c) $5.00, (d) $2.20, (e) $5.90.

2. The unit cost relevant to setting a *normal* price for this product, assuming that the implied level of operations is to be maintained, is (a) $5.00, (b) $4.50, (c) $3.50, (d) $5.90, (e) $3.00.

3. This product is usually sold at the rate of 240,000 units per year (an average of 20,000 per month). At a sales price of $6.00 per unit, this yields total sales of $1,440,000, total costs of $1,416,000, and a net margin of $24,000, or 10¢ per unit. It is estimated by market research that volume could be increased by 10 percent if prices were cut to $5.80. Assuming the implied cost behavior patterns to be correct, this action, if taken, would (a) decrease profits by a net of $7,200; (b) decrease profits by 20¢ per unit, $48,000, but increase profits by 10 percent of sales, $144,000; net, $86,000 increase; (c) decrease unit fixed costs by 10 percent or 14¢ per unit and thus decrease profits by 20¢ − 14¢, or 6¢ per unit; (d) increase sales volume to 264,000 units, which at the $5.80 price would give total sales of $1,531,200; costs of $5.90 per unit for 264,000 units would be $1,557,600, and a loss of $26,400 would result; (e) none of these.

4. A cost contract with the government (for 5,000 units of product) calls for the reimbursement of all costs of production plus a fixed fee of $1,000. This production is part of the regular 20,000 units of production per month. The delivery of these 5,000 units of product increases profits from what they would have been, were these units not sold, by (a) $1,000, (b) $2,500 (c) $3,500, (d) $300, (e) none of these.

5. Assume the same data as in 4 above, except that the 5,000 units will displace 5,000 other units from production. The latter 5,000 units would have been sold through regular channels for $30,000 had they been made. The delivery to the government increases (or decreases) net profits from what they would have been, were the other 5,000 units sold by (a) $4,000 decrease, (b) $3,000 increase, (c) $6,500 decrease, (d) $500 increase, (e) none of these.

6. The company desires to enter a foreign market, in which price competition is keen. An order for 10,000 units of this product is being sought on a minimum unit-price basis. It is expected that shipping costs for this order will amount to only 75¢ per unit, but the fixed costs of obtaining the contract will be $4,000. Domestic business will be unaffected. The minimum basis for breakeven price is (a) $3.50, (b) $4.15, (c) $4.25, (d) $3.00, (e) $5.00.

7. The company has an inventory of 1,000 units of this item left over from last year's model. These must be sold through regular channels at reduced prices. The inventory will be valueless unless sold this way. The unit cost that is relevant for establishing the minimum selling price would be (a) $4.50, (b) $4.00, (c) $3.00, (d) $5.90, (e) $1.50.

8. A proposal is received from an outside supplier who will make and ship this item directly to the Class Company's customers as sales orders are forwarded from Class's sales staff. Class's fixed selling costs will be unaffected, but its variable selling costs will be slashed 20 percent. Class's plant will be idle, but its fixed factory overhead would continue at 50 percent of present levels. To compare with the quotation received from the supplier, the company should use a unit cost of (a) $4.75, (b) $3.95, (c) $2.95, (d) $5.35, (e) none of these.

9. Assume the same facts as in 8 above, except that if the supplier's offer is accepted, the present plant facilities will be used to make a product whose unit costs will be:

Variable manufacturing costs	$5.00
Fixed manufacturing costs	1.00
Variable selling costs	2.00
Fixed selling costs (new increment)	.50

Total fixed factory overhead will be unchanged, while fixed selling costs will increase as indicated. The new product will sell for $9. This minimum desired net profit on the two products taken together is $50,000 per year. What is the maximum purchase cost per unit that the Class Company should be willing to pay for subcontracting the old production? (There are no multiple-choice answers supplied.)

Capital Budgeting and Cost Analysis 12

Should we add more student housing, hotels, hospitals, warehouses, factories? Buy the new photocopying machine? Add the new product or service? Accounting data often help managers to make these long-range decisions, which are frequently called *capital-budgeting* decisions. The financial stakes, time spans, and risks are often awesome, so the use of an appropriate decision model is especially important. This chapter examines the role of accounting data in the popular decision models for capital budgeting. We also study the relationship of the decision models to the performance evaluation models that help judge the results of the capital-budgeting decisions.

At this stage we again focus on purpose. Income determination and the planning and controlling of operations primarily have a *current time-period* orientation. Special decisions and long-range planning primarily have a *project* or *program* orientation with a far-reaching time span.

EXHIBIT 12-1

The Project Orientation of Capital Budgeting

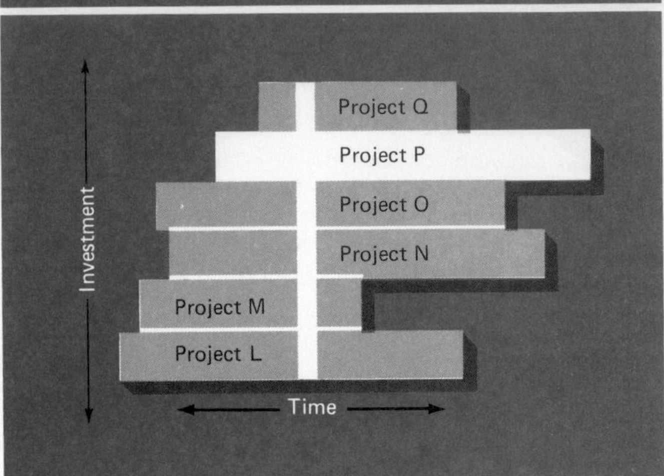

Contrasts in purposes of cost analysis

The project and time-period orientations of Exhibit 12-1 represent two distinct cross sections of the total corporate assets. The vertical dimension signifies the total investment (assets) of the company, which is a portfolio, a collection of resources, that may be subdivided into divisions, product lines, departments, buildings, a fleet of trucks or machines. These parts of an organization's resources are individual *projects* or *programs* that result from investment decisions. The horizontal dimension represents successive years in a company's life.

The distinct horizontal rectangle shows that a project can entail commitments over a prolonged span of time, not just one year. The focus is on a single cross section, a lone investment venture, throughout its life. The interest or other income that can be earned over a period of time (that is, the time value of money) often looms large in special decisions and in long-range planning.

The distinct vertical rectangle illustrates the focus of income determination and current planning and control. The cross-sectional emphasis is upon the company's overall performance and status for a year or less. The time period is relatively short, and the time value of money is usually not directly involved.

The point of all this is that our ordinary accounting systems and techniques have been designed to determine the cost and income of products for current planning and control. There is a great danger of using the existing general-purpose accounting system incorrectly—that is, of using data indiscriminately for solving special, nonroutine problems.

So in this chapter, we shift gears. We shall take a fresh look at the purpose of the nonroutine decision, and then we shall decide what models seem best for achieving that purpose.

Definition of capital budgeting

Capital budgeting is the making of long-term planning decisions for investments and their financing. The profitability of an investment decision depends on two vital factors: (a) future net increases in cash inflows or net savings in cash outflows, and (b) required investment. Thus, a chance to receive an annual return of $5,000 for a given number of years on a bond or stock can be judged only in relationship to how much money need be committed to obtain the $5,000. Depending on risk and available alternatives, individuals and corporate investors usually have some notion of a minimum rate of return that would make various projects desirable investments.

The quantitative approach to the selection of projects generally compares the predicted cash flows with the required investments. Thus, all projects having rates of return in excess of the minimum rate of return would be desirable, and vice versa. The problem of choosing the minimum acceptable rate of return (more a problem of finance than of accounting) is extremely complex.

There are several different models for the capital-budgeting decision. Although we shall discuss (a) urgency and persuasion, (b) discounted cash flow (DCF),[1] (c) payback, and (d) the accrual accounting rate of return, we shall concentrate on discounted cash flow because it is conceptually superior to the others.[2]

Urgency and persuasion

Many phases of business operations are managed in the same manner in which many individuals care for their cars. How many of us keep cars going until that bald tire becomes suddenly useless, the old battery refuses to perform, or the sticky valves keep the car from starting in cold weather? Then what happens? Stopgap action may be taken so that the car can be put back in service quickly. When a machine part fails, a belt breaks, or a generator wears out, routine replacements are made to avoid disruption in production. If the old machine on the assembly line suddenly disintegrates, there may be a fast but uneconomic replacement so that downtime is minimized. Ideally, all repairs, maintenance, and replacements should be implementations of an overall equipment policy that considers future-cost comparisons and timing.

Often the urgent action taken is correct on logical grounds. But it is correct by coincidence rather than by methodical analysis. The pressures of the moment lead to quick remedial action. When a contemplated outlay is large and farreaching in its effects, urgency should not be a convincing influence.

The individual manager's power of persuasion also is often a key factor in influencing the spending decisions of top management. The managers who are best at selling their own projects to the decision maker get the lion's portion of the available money, whereas the rest of the managers either get nothing or wait, and then wait some more. Economic considerations become secondary as individual

[1]Although discounted cash-flow models were used in financial markets for many years, the models did not come into wide use by business managers until the 1950s. As might be expected, the companies making large capital expenditures were the first to search for improved decision models. The leaders in adopting discounted cash-flow models were petroleum companies and public utilities. Keep in mind that the switching to "better" decision models is a cost-benefit decision. Many companies have viewed discounted cash-flow models as too costly to use (in particular, costly in the sense of educating personnel) in relation to the expected benefits of more profitable decisions. But the trend toward wider use of such models is unmistakable.

[2]Surveys of company practices reveal a steadily increasing use of discounted cash-flow models. For example, a survey of 424 firms indicated that 86 percent use DCF methods, most of them in combination with a payback or accounting rate-of-return model. See L. Schall, G. Sundem, and W. Geijsbeek, "Survey and Analysis of Capital Budgeting Methods," *Journal of Finance,* 33 (March 1978), 281–87, S. Kim and E. Farragher, "Current Capital Budgeting Practices," *Management Accounting* (June, 1981), pp. 26–32.

managers war with words and with impressive operating performance that may or may not be relevant to the capital-budgeting problem at hand.

Discounted cash flow

time value of money

The **discounted cash-flow** model for capital-budgeting decisions recognizes that the use of money has a cost (interest), just as the use of a building or an automobile may have a cost (rent). A dollar in the hand today is worth more than a dollar to be received (or spent) five years from today. For instance, in the interim a dollar can be invested in a savings institution; the dollar would grow markedly during a five-year span because of the interest it would earn. **Because the discounted cash-flow model explicitly and routinely weighs the time value of money, it is usually the best model to use for long-range decisions.**

Another major aspect of **DCF** is its focus on *cash* inflows and outflows rather than on *net income* as computed in the conventional accounting sense. Cash is invested now with the hope of receiving cash in a greater amount in the future. As we shall see, the student without a strong accounting background has an advantage here. He or she will not inject accrual concepts of accounting into DCF analysis, as an accounting student may wrongfully do.

There are two main variations of DCF: (a) **net present value (NPV)** and (b) **internal rate of return (IRR),** also often called **time-adjusted rate of return.** A summary of the tables and formulas used is included in Appendix B at the end of this book. **BEFORE READING ON, BE SURE YOU UNDERSTAND THIS APPENDIX.**

» EXAMPLE

The following situation will be used to illustrate the various decision models. A manager of a not-for-profit entity, a hospital, is considering buying a new machine that will aid productivity in the X-ray department. The machine will cost $3,791 now, is expected to have a five-year useful life and a zero disposal value, and will result in cash-operating savings of $1,000 annually. The hospital is not subject to income taxes.

In other words, Alternative A is to continue to operate the X-ray department without change (i.e., do nothing). Alternative B is to buy the new machine, which will reduce hand processing. Because no change in revenue is indicated, the cash savings is the difference between the cash-operating costs under both alternatives.

REQUIRED

1. Compute the project's expected net present value. Assume that the required rate of return (often referred to as RRR or the minimum desired rate of return or *hurdle rate*) is 8 percent. The relatively low interest rate is not unusual for a not-for-profit institution.
2. Compute the expected internal rate of return on the project.

---

net present-value model

The net present-value model entails the following steps:

1. Draw a sketch of relevant cash flows, including the outflow at time zero, the date of acquisition. The right-hand side of Exhibit 12-2 shows how these cash flows are portrayed. Outflows are placed in parentheses. Although such a sketch is not absolutely necessary, it clarifies relationships.
2. Choose the correct compound interest table. Find the discount factor from the appropriate row and column. To obtain the present value, multiply the discount factors by the cash amounts in the sketch.
3. Sum the present values. If the total is zero or positive, the project should be accepted because its rate of return equals or exceeds the desired minimum. If the total is negative, the project is undesirable because its return is below the hurdle rate.

Exhibit 12-2 indicates a net present value of $202, assuming a hurdle rate of 8 percent; therefore, the investment is desirable. The manager would be able to invest

EXHIBIT 12-2

Net Present-Value Model

Original investment	$3,791
Useful life	5 years
Annual cash savings from operations	$1,000
Hurdle rate of return, which is the discount rate	8%

*Approach 1: Discounting each year's cash inflow separately**

	PRESENT VALUE OF $1, DISCOUNTED @ 8%	TOTAL PRESENT VALUE	SKETCH OF RELEVANT CASH FLOWS: 0	1	2	3	4	5
End of Year			0	1	2	3	4	5
Cash flows:								
Annual cash savings	.926	$ 926	←	$1,000				
	.857	857	←		$1,000			
	.794	794	←			$1,000		
	.735	735	←				$1,000	
	.681	681	←					$1,000
Present value of relevant inflows	3.993	$3,993						
Initial outlay	1.000	(3,791)	$(3,791)					
Net present value		$ 202‡						

Approach 2; Using Annuity Table†

			0	1	2	3	4	5
Annual cash savings	3.993	$3,993	←	$1,000	$1,000	$1,000	$1,000	$1,000
Initial outlay	1.000	(3,791)	$(3,791)					
Net present value		$ 202‡						

*Present values from Table 2, Appendix B.

†Present annuity values from Table 4.

‡Rounded.

Note: *Throughout these exhibits regarding discounted cash-flow models, parentheses or negative signs will denote relevant cash outflows.*

$202 more, or a total of $3,993 (that is, $3,791 + $202), and still earn 8 percent on the project.

The higher the hurdle rate, the less the manager would be willing to invest in this project. At a rate of 12 percent, the net present value would be $−186 (that is, $1,000 × 3.605, the present-value factor from annuity Table 4, = $3,605, which is $186 less than the required investment of $3,791). When the hurdle rate is 12 percent, rather than 8 percent, the machine is undesirable at its selling price of $3,791.

assumptions of model

Before reading on, reflect on the meaning of the net present-value model. First, the model assumes a world of certainty. That is, you are absolutely sure that the predicted cash flows will be forthcoming in the amounts and at the times indicated. Second, the model assumes that the original amount of investment funds can be viewed as either borrowed by you or loaned by you at the specified minimum desired interest rate.

EXHIBIT 12-3

Rationale Underlying Net Present-Value Model
(Same Data as in Exhibit 12-2)

Alternative One: Invest and Hold the project.

	(1)	(2)	(3)	(4)	(5)
YEAR	LOAN BALANCE AT BEGINNING OF YEAR	INTEREST AT 8% PER YEAR	(1) + (2) ACCUMULATED AMOUNT AT END OF YEAR	CASH FOR REPAYMENT OF LOAN	(3) − (4) LOAN BALANCE AT END OF YEAR
1	$3,791	$303	$4,094	$1,000	$3,094
2	3,094	248	3,342	1,000	2,342
3	2,342	187	2,529	1,000	1,529
4	1,529	122	1,651	1,000	651
5	651	52	703	1,000	(297)*

**After repayment of the final $703 loan installment, the investor would have $297 left over from the $1,000 cash provided by the project at the end of the fifth year; she would be $297 wealthier at the end of five years.*

Alternative Two: Invest, Sell the Project for $202 an Instant Later, and Deposit the $202 in a Bank.

	(1)	(2)	(3)
YEAR	INVESTMENT BALANCE AT BEGINNING OF YEAR	INTEREST AT 8% PER YEAR	(1) + (2) ACCUMULATED AMOUNT AT END OF YEAR
1	$202	$16	$218
2	218	17	235
3	235	19	254
4	254	20	274
5	274	22	296†

†The investor would have the same amount of wealth at the end of five years as in Alternative One. (The $1 difference between the $296 and the $297 in Alternative One is because of rounding.) Note that stating the net present value at $202 at time zero is equivalent to stating the future amount at $296; the investor is indifferent to whether she has $202 today or $296 five years hence.

Thus, the net present value of $202 in Exhibit 12-2 tells you that if you borrowed $3,791 from a bank at 8 percent per annum, invested in the project, and repaid the loan with the project cash flows, you would accumulate the same net amount of money as if you deposited $202 in a bank at 8 percent interest. Exhibit 12-3 demonstrates these relationships. Suppose somebody approached you at time zero and offered you $202 for the project that you had invested in ten seconds before. Also suppose that she would assume the obligation to repay the bank loan. You accept and invest the $202 in the bank at an interest rate of 8 percent. In our assumed world of certainty, you would be completely indifferent regarding whether you (a) kept the original investment or (b) accepted the person's offer and invested the $202 in the bank.

***Caution:* Do not proceed until you thoroughly understand Exhibits 12-2 and 12-3. Furthermore, compare Approach 1 with Approach 2 in Exhibit 12-2 to see how the two compound interest tables relate to one another. Note how Table 4 is merely a compilation of the present-value factors of Table 2. That is, the fundamental table is Table 2; Table 4 exists merely to reduce hand calculations when there is a *series* of equal cash flows.**

EXHIBIT 12-4

Two Proofs of Internal Rate of Return

Original investment	$3,791
Useful life	5 years
Annual cash inflow from operations	$1,000
Internal rate of return	10%*

Proof 1: Discounting Each Year's Cash Inflow Separately†

	PRESENT VALUE OF $1 DISCOUNTED AT 10%	TOTAL PRESENT VALUE	SKETCH OF RELEVANT CASH FLOWS
End of Year			0 1 2 3 4 5
Cash flows:			
Annual cash savings	.909	$ 909	←-----$1,000 (year 1)
	.826	826	←----------$1,000 (year 2)
	.751	751	←---------------$1,000 (year 3)
	.683	683	←--------------------$1,000 (year 4)
	.621	621	←-------------------------$1,000 (year 5)
Present value of relevant inflows	3.791‡	$3,791‡	
Initial outlay	1.000	(3,791)	$(3,791)
Net present value (the zero difference proves that the rate of return is 10%)		$ 0	

Proof 2: Using Annuity Table§

Annual cash savings	3.791	$3,791	←-----$1,000 $1,000 $1,000 $1,000 $1,000
Initial outlay	1.000	(3,791)	$(3,791)
Net present value		$ 0	

**The rate of return would be computed by methods explained later in the chapter.*
†Present values from Table 2, Appendix B at the end of the book.
‡Sum is really $3,790, but is rounded.
§Present values of annuity from Table 4, Appendix B at the end of the book.

internal rate-of-return model Requirement 2 of our basic example calls for computation of the *internal rate of return.* It is defined as the discount rate that makes the net present value of a project equal to zero, as Exhibit 12-4 shows.

Expressed in other ways, the internal rate can be described as

1. The interest rate that makes the present value of the cash inflows or savings of the project, $3,791, equal to the initial cash outflow, $3,791.
2. The maximum rate of interest that could be paid to a financial institution for borrowing the money invested over the life of the project and exactly break even.
3. The internal rate corresponds to the so-called *yield rate* or *effective rate* that is so widely quoted in the markets for bonds and other forms of long-term debt.

The step-by-step computations of an internal rate of return are not too difficult when the cash inflows are equal. In Exhibit 12-4, the following equation is used:

$3,791 = Present value of annuity of $1,000 at *X* percent for 5 years, or what factor *F* in Table 4 (end of the book) will satisfy the following equation:

$3,791 = $1,000*F*

***F* = 3.791**

On the period-5 line of Table 4, find the percentage column that is closest to 3.791. It happens to be exactly 10 percent. If the factor (F) fell between the columns, straight-line interpolation would be used to approximate the internal rate of return. For an illustration, see Problem 1 of the Problems for Self-Study, page 421.

Note in Exhibit 12-4 that $3,791 is the present value, at a rate of return of 10 percent, of a five-year stream of inflows of $1,000 in cash per year. Ten percent is the rate that equates the amount invested ($3,791) with the present value of the cash inflows ($1,000 per year for five years). In other words, *if* money were borrowed at an effective interest rate of 10 percent, the cash inflow produced by the project would exactly repay the hypothetical loan plus interest over the five years.[3] If the minimum desired rate of return is less than 10 percent, the project will be profitable. If the minimum desired return exceeds 10 percent, the cash inflow will be insufficient to pay interest and repay the principal of the hypothetical loan. Therefore, 10 percent is the internal rate of return for this project.

explanation of compound interest

The internal rate of return is computed on the basis of the investment tied up in the project from period to period instead of solely the original investment. See Exhibit 12-5. The internal rate of return in that exhibit is 10 percent **of the capital invested during each year.** The $1,000 inflow is composed of two parts, as analyzed in columns 3 and 4. Consider year 1. Column 3 shows the interest on the $3,791 invested capital as .10 × $3,791 = $379. Column 4 shows that $1,000 − $379, or $621, is the amount of investment recovered at the end of the year. In this example, the five-year cash inflow exactly recovers the original investment plus annual interest at a rate of 10 percent on the as yet unrecovered capital.

Exhibit 12-5 can be interpreted from both the borrower's and lender's viewpoints. Assume the hospital borrowed $3,791 from a bank at an interest rate of 10 percent per annum, invested in the project, and repaid the loan with relevant cash savings of $1,000 per year. The lender would earn exactly 10 percent per year. The borrower would end up with an accumulated wealth of zero. Obviously, if the hospital could borrow at 10 percent, and the project could generate cash of greater than $1,000 annually, the hospital could keep some cash. Then the internal rate of return, *by definition*, would exceed 10 percent.

depreciation and discounted cash flow

Students are often perplexed by the seeming exclusion of depreciation from DCF computations. A common homework error is to discount cash flows less depreciation. This tendency betrays a lack of understanding of a basic idea of the internal rate of return. Because the DCF approach is fundamentally based on inflows and outflows of *cash* and not on the *accrual* concepts of revenues and expenses, no adjustments should be made to the cash flows for the periodic allocation of the asset cost called depreciation expense (which is not a cash flow). In the DCF approach, the initial cost of an asset is usually regarded as a *lump-sum* outflow of cash at time zero. **There-**

[3] *Research Report 35, Return on Capital as a Guide to Managerial Decisions,* National Association of Accountants, p. 57.

EXHIBIT 12-5

Rationale Underlying Internal Rate-of-Return Model

(Same data as in Exhibit 12-4)

Original investment	$3,791
Annual cash savings from operations	1,000
Useful life	5 years
Internal rate of return	10%

	(1)	(2)	(3)	(4)	(5)
YEAR	UNRECOVERED INVESTMENT AT BEGINNING OF YEAR	ANNUAL CASH SAVINGS	INTEREST AT 10% PER YEAR (1) × 10%	AMOUNT OF INVESTMENT RECOVERED AT END OF YEAR (2) − (3)	UNRECOVERED INVESTMENT AT END OF YEAR (1) − (4)
1	$3,791	$1,000	$ 379	$ 621	$3,170
2	3,170	1,000	317	683	2,487
3	2,487	1,000	249	751	1,736
4	1,736	1,000	173	827	909
5	909	1,000	91	909	0
		$5,000	$1,209	$3,791	

Assumptions: Unrecovered investment at beginning of each year earns interest for whole year. Annual cash inflows are received at the end of each year. For simplicity in the use of tables, all operating cash inflows are assumed to take place at the end of the years in question. This is unrealistic because such cash flows ordinarily occur uniformly throughout the given year, rather than in lump sums at the end of the year. Compound interest tables especially tailored for these more stringent conditions are available, but we shall not consider them here. See J. Bracken and C. Christenson, Tables for Use in Analyzing Business Decisions *(Homewood, Ill.: Richard D. Irwin).*

fore, it is wrong to deduct depreciation from operating cash inflows before consulting present-value tables. To deduct periodic depreciation would be a double-counting of a cost that has already been considered as a lump-sum outflow. (See the next chapter for a discussion of how depreciation affects income-tax cash flows, as distinguished from operating cash flows.)

Comparison of net present value and internal rate-of-return models

We can summarize the decision rules offered by the two discounted cash-flow models as follows:

INTERNAL RATE OF RETURN	NET PRESENT VALUE
1. Using present-value tables, compute the internal rate of return by interpolation.	**1. Calculate the net present value, using the hurdle rate of return as the discount rate.**
2. If this rate equals or exceeds the hurdle rate, accept the project; if not, reject the project.	**2. If the net present value is zero or positive, accept the project; if negative, reject the project.**

We emphasize the net present-value model in this text because it has distinct advantages over the internal rate-of-return model. The net present-value approach does not entail scouring tables and solving for the "true" rate of return. It can be applied to any situation, regardless of whether there is uniform cash flow (present value of annuity) or some uneven cash flows. The internal rate-of-return model is more tedious, as the self-study problem will demonstrate, because it calls for taking the future cash flows for *each* year separately in the contemplated project and discounting them to the present.

In practice, the internal rate of return is used more widely than the net present-value measure. Most accountants and managers seem to be able to interpret the internal rate more easily; moreover, with this method they are not forced to specify a hurdle rate as a prerequisite to discounted cash-flow computations. Awkward trial-and-error calculations of the internal rate, which students must frequently perform by hand, can be performed swiftly by electronic computers. Canned computer programs are commonly available for such computations. Moreover, many hand-held calculators have programs that quickly provide internal rates of return.

Required rate of return

There are two major aspects of capital budgeting: investment decisions and financing decisions. Investment decisions focus on whether to acquire an asset, a project, a product line, and so forth. Financing decisions focus on whether to raise the necessary capital via some form of debt or equity or both. This textbook focuses on the investment decision. Finance textbooks provide ample discussions of financing decisions.[4]

Our approach assumes that the minimum desired rate of return is given. It is specified by management. The minimum desired rate of return is also called the **hurdle rate, cutoff rate, cost of capital, discount rate,** and **required rate of return (RRR).** In general, the riskier the project, the higher the required rate. **The required rate should be an opportunity-cost rate.** That is, it should be determined by what can be earned by alternative investments of similar risk.

Avoid two widely held misconceptions about required rates:

Misconception 1: The rate should be the interest expense on any money borrowed in conjunction with a project. Wrong! The required rate should be unaffected by whether the specific project is financed by all debt, all ownership capital, or some of both. Such a piecemeal approach is nearsighted. For example, suppose a project is judged as being desirable because it has an internal rate of 14 percent and a borrowing rate of 12 percent. The trouble here is that a series of such decisions will lead to an enormous debt that will cause the borrowing rate to jump or will result in a total inability to borrow. Conceivably, during the next year or two, some other project might have an expected internal rate of 18 percent and will have to be rejected because heavy existing debt prohibits additional borrowing. Thus, the most profitable project in the series would be rejected.

Misconception 2: Ownership capital is costless. Wrong again! Investments in projects that are financed by ownership equity should still meet a required rate of return. For example, a mortgage-free house is an investment of ownership capital. If the house were sold, the proceeds could generate earnings elsewhere.

[4]The distinction between *investment aspects* and *financing aspects* is often critical. A good illustration is the financial lease for such items as aircraft and grocery stores. The decision is often described erroneously as being whether to buy or to lease. But it is really a twofold one: (a) whether to acquire or not to acquire an asset—the investment decision, and (b) whether to lease or make some other borrowing arrangement—the financing decision.

The next chapter discusses the required rate in more detail, including the effects of inflation.

Sensitivity analysis

To highlight the basic differences among various decision models, this chapter deals only with the expected values of cash flows as though they will definitely occur. Obviously, managers know that such predictions are inevitably imperfect. Chapter 21 describes how to contend with uncertainty in these and other situations. For now, we concentrate on *sensitivity analysis,* which was originally introduced in Chapter 3. In the realm of capital budgeting, sensitivity analysis answers the question, How will my rate of return or net present value be affected if the predictions of cash flows or useful lives are wrong?

Of course, sensitivity analysis may take various forms. For instance, management may want to know how far annual cash savings will have to fall to break even on the investment. Here "break even" means arrive at the point of indifference, the point where the net present value is zero. Using the data in Exhibit 12-2:

Let X = annual cash inflows and let net present value = 0. Then

$$3.993(X) - \$3{,}791 = 0$$
$$3.993(X) = \$3{,}791$$
$$X = \$3{,}791 \div 3.993 = \$950$$

Thus, the amount by which annual cash savings can drop before they reach the point of indifference regarding the investment is \$1,000 − \$950 = \$50.

Another critical factor is useful life. If useful life were only four years, the gross present value would be \$1,000 times 3.312 (from the period-4 line in Table 4), or \$3,312, producing a negative net present value, \$3,312 − \$3,791, or −\$479.

These calculations are also applicable to testing the sensitivity of rates of return. A fall in the annual cash savings from \$1,000 to \$900 reduces the internal rate of return from 10 percent (which was determined in Exhibit 12-5) to 6 percent:

Investment = P.V. of annuity of \$900 at X percent for 5 years, or what factor (F) in Table 4 will satisfy the following equation:

$$\$3{,}791 = \$900(F)$$
$$F = 4.212$$

Examine the five-year line in Table 4. Find the percentage column closest to 4.212. In this instance, you do not have to interpolate; the rate is exactly 6 percent.

Of course, sensitivity analysis works both ways. It can measure the potential increases in net present value or internal rate of return as well as the decreases. The major contribution of sensitivity analysis is that it provides an immediate financial measure of the possible errors in forecasting. Therefore, it can be very useful because it helps focus on those decisions that may be very sensitive indeed, and it eases the manager's mind about those decisions that are not so sensitive.[5]

In addition, sensitivity analysis is applicable to the comparison of various capital-budgeting decision models. That is, the results under the DCF models may be

[5]For a fuller discussion, see Appendix 21A. Also see Alfred Rappaport, "Sensitivity Analysis in Decision Making." *Accounting Review,* XLII, No. 3, pp. 441–56.

compared with the results, using the same basic data, generated under simpler models such as payback and accounting rate of return.

Analysis of typical items under discounted cash flow

The following is a summary of how some common items are analyzed in DCF models:

1. WIDE APPLICABILITY □ Most of the literature on capital budgeting deals mainly with investments in plant and equipment. But capital-budgeting models may be used regarding a variety of investment projects. Examples include plant rearrangements, advertising programs, research and development, and computer software packages.

2. FUTURE DISPOSAL VALUES □ **The disposal value at the date of termination of a project is an increase in the cash inflow in the year of disposal.** Errors in forecasting disposal value are normally not crucial because the present value is usually small.

3. CURRENT ASSETS □ Additional investments in plant and equipment or in sales promotions of product lines are invariably accompanied by additional investments in the cash, receivables, and inventories required to support these new activities. In the discounted cash-flow model, *all* investments at time zero are alike, regardless of how they may be accounted for by the accrual accounting model. That is, the initial outlays are entered in the sketch of cash flows at time zero. At the end of the useful life of the project, the original outlays for machines may not be recouped at all or may be partially recouped in the amount of the disposed values. In contrast, the entire original investments in receivables and inventories are usually recouped when the project is terminated. **Therefore, except for their expected "disposal" values being different from the initial outlays, all investments at time zero are typically regarded as outflows at time zero, and their terminal disposal values are regarded as inflows at the end of the project's useful life.**

To illustrate, suppose a company buys some new equipment to make a new product. The required investment would also necessitate additional working capital in the form of cash, receivables, and inventories. Such investments would be shown in the format of Exhibit 12-2 as follows (numbers and lives assumed, investments in millions of dollars):

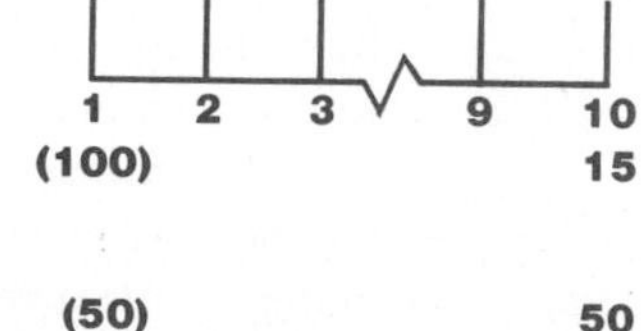

End of year	**1**	**2**	**3**	**9**	**10**
Investment in equipment	**(100)**				**15**
Investment in working capital (cash, receivables and inventories)	**(50)**				**50**

As the sketch shows, the disposed value of the equipment might be relatively small. However, the entire investment in working capital would ordinarily be recovered when the product is no longer manufactured. The difference between the initial outlay for working capital and the present value of its recovery is the present value of the cost of using working capital in the project.

4. PLANNING HORIZON □ Projections should be made as far into the future as feasible. However, many companies do not actually extend the planning horizon

beyond ten years. They justify this practice chiefly on the grounds that predictions beyond that time are subject to enormous error. Furthermore, studies have shown that errors in predictions beyond ten years do not have a major impact on the net present values anyway.

5. CURRENT DISPOSAL VALUES AND REQUIRED INVESTMENT ☐ In a replacement decision, how should the current disposal value affect the computations? For example, suppose that the current disposal value of old equipment is $5,000 and that new equipment is available at $40,000. There are a number of correct ways to analyze these items, all of which will have the same ultimate effect on the decision. Generally, the required investment is most easily measured by offsetting the current disposal value of the old assets against the gross cost of the new assets ($40,000) and by showing the net cash outflow at $35,000.

6. BOOK VALUE AND DEPRECIATION ☐ Depreciation is a phenomenon of accrual accounting that entails an allocation of cost, not a specific cash outlay. Depreciation and book value are ignored in DCF approaches to cash flows from operations for the reasons mentioned earlier in this chapter.

7. INCOME TAXES ☐ In practice, comparison between alternatives is best made after considering tax effects, because the tax impact may alter the picture. (The effects of income taxes are considered in the next chapter.)

8. OVERHEAD ANALYSIS ☐ In the relevant cost analysis of overhead, only the overhead that will differ between alternatives is pertinent. There is need for careful study of how much, if any, fixed overhead is relevant under the available alternatives. In practice, this is an extremely difficult phase of cost analysis, because it is hard to relate the individual costs to any single project.

9. A WORD OF CAUTION. ☐ The foregoing material has been an *introduction* to the area of capital budgeting, which is, in practice, complicated by a variety of factors: unequal lives; mutually exclusive investments; major differences in the size of alternative investments; pecularities in internal rate-of-return computations; various ways of allowing for uncertainty (see Chapter 21); changes over time, in required rates of return; the indivisibility of projects in relation to a fixed overall capital-budget appropriation; inflation; and more. These niceties are beyond the scope of this introductory chapter, but the next chapter will help you pursue them in more depth.

Payback

fundamental model

Payback, sometimes called **payout** or **payoff,** is a rough-and-ready model that is looked upon with disdain by many academic theorists. Yet payback is a widely used decision model, and it certainly is an improvement over the criterion of urgency or postponability. Furthermore, it is a handy device (a) where precision in estimates of profitability is not crucial and preliminary screening of many proposals is necessary; (b) where a weak cash-and-credit position has a heavy bearing on the selection of investment possibilities; and (c) where the contemplated project is extremely risky.

Recall in our example that $3,791 was spent for a machine having a five-year expected useful life and a $1,000 annual cash inflow from operations. The payback calculations follow:

$$\text{Payback time} = \frac{\text{Initial incremental amount invested}}{\text{Uniform annual incremental } \textit{cash} \text{ inflow from operations}}$$

$$P = I/O_c$$

$$P = \$3{,}791/\$1{,}000 = 3.8 \text{ years}$$

Essentially, payback is a measure of the *time* it will take to recoup in the form of cash from operations only the original dollars invested. Given the useful life of an asset and *uniform cash flows,* the shorter the payout period, the greater the profitability; or, given the payback period, the greater the useful life of the asset, the greater the profitability.

Although the payback method may often yield clues to profitability, it should not be used blindly. Note that payback does *not* measure profitability; it does measure how quickly investment dollars may be recouped. An investment's main objective is profitability, not recapturing the original outlay. If a company wants to recover its investment outlay rapidly, it need not bother spending in the first place. Then the payback time is zero; no waiting time is needed.

The major weakness of the payback model is its neglect of profitability. The mere fact that a project has a satisfactory payback does not mean that it should be selected in preference to an alternative project with a longer payback time. To illustrate, consider an alternative to the \$3,791 machine mentioned earlier. Assume that this other machine requires only a \$3,000 investment and will also result in cash savings of \$1,000 per year before depreciation. Compare the two payback periods:

$$P_1 = \$3{,}791/\$1{,}000 = 3.8 \text{ years}$$

$$P_2 = \$3{,}000/\$1{,}000 = 3.0 \text{ years}$$

The payback criterion would favor buying the \$3,000 machine. However, one fact about this machine has been purposely withheld. Its useful life is only three years. Ignoring the complexities of compound interest for the moment, one finds that the \$3,000 machine results in zero profits, whereas the \$3,791 machine (which has a useful life of 5 years) yields profits for 1.2 years beyond its payback period.

nonuniform cash inflows

The payback formula is designed for uniform cash inflows. When cash inflows are not uniform, the payback computation takes a cumulative form. That is, each year's net cash inflows are accumulated until the initial investment is recovered. For example, assume that a \$4,500 machine produces a total cash savings of \$10,000 over ten years, but not at a rate of \$1,000 annually. Instead, the inflows are as follows:

YEAR	CASH SAVINGS	ACCUMULATED	YEAR	CASH SAVINGS	ACCUMULATED
1	\$2,000	\$2,000	6	\$800	\$ 8,300
2	1,800	3,800	7	600	8,900
3	1,500	5,300	8	400	9,300
4	1,200	6,500	9	400	9,700
5	1,000	7,500	10	300	10,000

The payback time is slightly beyond the second year. Straight-line interpolation within the third year reveals that the final \$700 (that is, \$4,500 − \$3,800) needed to recover the investment would be forthcoming in 2.47 years—that is,

$$2 \text{ years} + \left(\frac{\$700}{\$1,500} \times 1 \text{ year}\right) = 2.47 \text{ years}$$

the bailout factor: a better approach to payback

The typical payback computation tries to answer the question, How soon will it be before I can recoup my investment *if operations proceed as planned?* However, a more fundamental question is, Which of the competing projects has the best bailout protection if things go wrong? In other words, Which has the least risk? To answer such a question, we must consider the salvage value of the equipment throughout its life, an item that is ignored in the usual payback computations.

For instance, salvage values of general-purpose equipment far exceed those of special-purpose equipment. These salvage values can be incorporated in a bailout approach to payback as follows:

Assume that Equipment A (general-purpose) costs $100,000 and that Equipment B (special-purpose) costs $150,000. Each has a ten-year life. A is expected to produce uniform annual cash savings of $20,000; B, of $40,000. A's salvage value is expected to be $70,000 at the end of year 1; it is expected to decline at a rate of $10,000 annually thereafter. B's salvage value is expected to be $80,000 at the end of year 1; it is expected to decline at a rate of $20,000 annually. Note the difference in results under the traditional payback and the bailout payback methods. The "bailout payback time" is reached when the cumulative cash operating savings plus the salvage value at the end of a particular year equal the original investment:

TRADITIONAL PAYBACK

If operations go as expected:

$$A: P = \frac{I}{O_c} = \frac{\$100,000}{\$20,000} = 5 \text{ years}$$

$$B: P = \frac{I}{O_c} = \frac{\$150,000}{\$40,000} = 3.75 \text{ years}$$

BAILOUT PAYBACK

If the project fails to meet expectations:

	AT END OF	CUMULATIVE CASH OPERATING SAVINGS		SALVAGE VALUE		CUMULATIVE TOTAL
A:	Year 1	$ 20,000	+	$70,000	=	$ 90,000
	Year 2	40,000	+	60,000	=	100,000
Therefore, payback is 2 years.						
B:	Year 1	$ 40,000	+	$80,000	=	$120,000
	Year 2	80,000	+	60,000	=	140,000
	Year 3	120,000	+	40,000	=	160,000

Therefore, payback is between 2 and 3 years. The exact time depends on assumptions regarding cash flows during the third year.

The analysis above demonstrates how different interpretations of the payback method can produce different results. If the objective is to measure risk (in the sense of how to avoid loss), the bailout method is better than the traditional method.

annuity formula and payback reciprocal

The much-maligned traditional payback method has received increasing attention[6] and approval as being useful for a wide number of situations.

The major argument in favor of payback is based on the equation for the present value of an annuity.

[6]Myron Gordon, "Payoff Period and Rate of Profit," *Journal of Business,* XXVIII, No. 4, pp. 253–60. Also see Alfred Rappaport, "The Discounted Payback Period," *Management Services,* 2, No. 4, pp. 30–35.

General formula for present value of annuity:

$$P_N = O_c\left(\frac{1 - \frac{1}{(1+R)^N}}{R}\right) \quad (1)$$

Restated:

$$P_N = \frac{O_c}{R} - \frac{O_c}{R}\left(\frac{1}{(1+R)^N}\right) \quad (2)$$

Multiply by R:

$$RP_N = O_c - O_c\left(\frac{1}{(1+R)^N}\right) \quad (3)$$

Solve for R:

$$R = \frac{O_c}{P_N} - \frac{O_c}{P_N}\left(\frac{1}{(1+R)^N}\right) \quad (4)$$

P_N = **Investment**
O_c = **annual *cash* savings or cash inflow from operations**
R = **internal rate of return**
N = **life of investment in years.**

Note in equation (4) that the first right-hand term is the reciprocal of the payback period. The second right-hand term is the same reciprocal multiplied by $1/(1 + R)^N$. Now, if either R or N is large, this second term becomes small; therefore, *in these cases,* the rate of return will be closely approximated by the payback reciprocal. (Will the payout reciprocal be larger or smaller than the true rate of return?)

Accrual accounting rate-of-return model

fundamental model

Discounted cash-flow approaches to business decisions are being increasingly used. However, there are other techniques with which the accountant and manager should be at least somewhat familiar, because they are entrenched in many businesses.

Because the technique we are about to discuss is conceptually inferior to DCF approaches, why do we bother studying it? Changes in business practice occur slowly. If older models, such as payback or the accounting rate, are used despite the availability of better tools, they should be used correctly. Many managers use the accounting rate because they regard it as satisfactory for their particular decisions. In other words, the costs (including the costs of educating managers) of more sophisticated models would exceed the benefit from making a sufficient number of more profitable decisions. In such cases, care should be taken so that the cruder tool is used properly. The situation is similar to using a pocket knife instead of a scalpel for removing a person's appendix. If the pocket knife is used by a knowledgeable and skilled surgeon, the chances for success are much better than if it is used by a bungling layperson.

The label for the *accrual accounting model* is not uniform. It is also known as the *financial-statement method,* the *book-value method,* the *rate-of-return-on-assets method,* the *approximate rate-of-return method,* and the *unadjusted rate-of-return method.* Its computations supposedly dovetail most closely with conventional accounting models of calculating income and required investment. However, the dovetailing objective is not easily attained, because the purposes of the computations differ. The most troublesome aspects are depreciation and decisions concerning capitalization versus expense. For example, advertising and research are usually expensed, even though they may often be viewed as long-range investments.

In its simplest form, the **accrual accounting rate of return** is:

$$\text{Accrual accounting rate} = \frac{\text{Increase in expected average annual operating income}}{\text{Initial increase in required investment}}$$

Sometimes the denominator is the average increase in investment, rather than the initial increase.

The facts in our payback illustration would yield the following accounting rate of return (depreciation is $3,791 ÷ 5 = $758):

$$R = \frac{\$1{,}000 - \$758 \text{ average depreciation}}{\$3{,}791} = 6.4\%$$

If the denominator is the "average" investment, which is often assumed for equipment as being the average book value over the useful life, or $3,791 ÷ 2, the rate would be doubled.[7]

computing the investment base

Practice is not uniform as to whether initial investment or average investment in fixed assets should be used in the denominator. Companies defend the use of the initial-investment base because it does not change over the life of the investment; therefore, follow-up and comparison of actual rate of return against predicted rate of return is facilitated. This follow-up is crucial for control and for improving future capital planning and comparison on a year-to-year, plant-to-plant, and division-to-division basis. The initial base is not affected by depreciation methods.

In most cases, the rankings of competing projects will not differ regardless of whether the initial or average investment base is used. Of course, using the average base will show substantially higher rates of return; however, the desirable rate of return used as a cutoff for accepting projects should also be higher.

Current assets, such as cash, receivables, and inventories, often are expanded in order to sustain higher volume levels. In our example, if a $1,000 increase in current assets is required, the denominator will be $3,791 plus $1,000, or $4,791. This $1,000 increase in current assets will be fully committed for the life of the project; so, under the average-investment method, the average base would be $2,896 ($1,896 average investment in equipment plus $1,000 average investment in current assets).

dangers of understating investment and averaging

The gross or initial investment in the project should include the following: all additional required current assets, fixed assets, research costs, engineering costs, market-testing costs, startup costs, initial costs of sales promotion, and so forth. The omission of any of these items from the base can give misleading results.

Although the *accrual accounting model* for investment decisions tries to approximate the figures as they will eventually appear in financial statements, there is not always an exact agreement between figures on conventional statements and figures used for decision making. The tendency in accounting practice is to write costs off to expense quickly. Thus, the assembly of figures for special decisions requires care to see that investment is not understated. Often the investment base for decision making should include items, such as research and sales-promotion costs, that the accountant ordinarily writes off immediately as expenses.

Note that the **accounting rate of return** is based on the familiar financial statements prepared under accrual accounting. **Unlike the payback model, the accounting-rate-of-return model at least has profitability as an objective. However, its most**

[7]The measure of funds recovered in the example above is $758 a year, the amount of the annual depreciation. Consequently, the average funds committed to the project would decline at a rate of $758 per year from $3,791 to zero; hence the average investment would be the beginning balance plus the ending balance ($3,791 + 0) divided by 2, or $1,896.

serious drawback is its ignoring of the time value of money. Expected future dollars are unrealistically and erroneously regarded as equal to present dollars. The discounted cash-flow model explicitly allows for the force of interest and the exact timing of cash flows. In contrast, the accounting model is based on *annual averages.*

evaluation of performance

As the last part of the preceding chapter emphasized, the use of the conventional accrual accounting models for evaluating performance is a stumbling block to the implementation of DCF models for capital-budgeting decisions. To illustrate, John Doe, the manager of a division of a huge company, took a course in management accounting in an executive program. He learned about discounted cash flow. He was convinced that such a model would lead to decisions that would better achieve the long-range profit goals of the company.

When he returned to his company, he was more frustrated than ever. Top management used the overall rate of return of his division to judge his performance. That is, each year divisional net income was divided by average divisional assets to obtain his rate of return on investment (ROI). Such a measure usually inhibits investments in plant and equipment that might be clearly attractive using the DCF models. Why? Because a huge investment often boosts depreciation inordinately in the early years under accelerated-depreciation methods, thus reducing the numerator in the ROI computation. Also, the denominator is increased substantially by the initial cost of the new assets. As one manager said, "Top management is always giving me hell about my new flour mill, even though I know it is the most efficient we've got regardless of what the figures say."

Another illustration of the potential conflict between the decision model and the performance evaluation model is provided by the first example in this chapter. Recall that the internal rate of return is 10 percent, but the accounting rate of return on the initial investment of $3,791 as computed in the immediately preceding section is only 6.4 percent.

Obviously, there is an inconsistency between citing DCF models as being best for capital-budgeting decisions and then using quite different concepts for evaluating subsequent performance. **As long as such practices continue, managers will frequently be tempted to make decisions that may be suboptimal under the present-value criterion but optimal, at least over short or intermediate spans of time, under accrual accounting models of evaluating operating performance.** Such temptations become more pronounced when managers are subject to transfers and promotions.

SUMMARY

Capital budgeting is long-term planning for proposed capital outlays and their financing. Projects are accepted if their internal rates of return exceed a required rate of return.

Because discounted cash-flow (DCF) models explicitly and automatically weigh the time value of money, they are the best models to use for long-range decisions. The overriding goal is maximum long-run net cash inflows.

The DCF model has two variations: internal rate of return and net present value. Both approaches take into account the timing of cash flows and are thus superior to other methods.

The payback model is a widely used approach to capital-spending decisions. It is simple and easily understood, but it neglects profitability.

The accrual accounting rate-of-return model is also widely used, although it is much cruder than DCF models. It fails to recognize explicitly the time value of money. Instead, the accrual accounting model depends on averaging techniques that may yield inaccurate answers, particularly when cash flows are not uniform through the life of a project. The accounting rate-of-return model is adequate where the return plainly far exceeds the required rate or where projects are not subject to close competition for funds from other projects.

A serious practical impediment to the adoption of DCF models is the widespread use of accrual accounting models for evaluating performance. Frequently, the optimal decision under DCF will not produce a good showing in the early years, when performance is computed under accrual accounting methods. For example, heavy depreciation charges and the expensing rather than capitalizing of initial development costs will hurt reported income for the first year.

The difficult forecasting problem makes capital budgeting one of the most imposing tasks of management. Although judgment and attitudes are important ingredients of capital budgeting, the correct application of the models described here should crystallize the relevant factors and help management toward intelligent decision making.

The prediction of cost savings (different cash flows) is the key measurement for capital budgeting. Factors that must be considered in these calculations include income taxes and different capacities of plant and equipment, as well as the usual recurring operating costs. The use of sensitivity analysis and probability theory can help approach and measure the uncertainty that plagues this work. Special difficulties in relevant costs and capital budgeting, including income-tax factors and inflation, are discussed in Chapter 13. A suggested reading list appears at the end of Chapter 13.

problems for self-study

problem 1

Refer to Exhibit 12-2. Suppose the expected cash savings were $1,300 instead of $1,000. All other facts are unchanged: a $3,791 original investment, a five-year useful life, a zero terminal disposal value, and an 8 percent required rate of return. Compute the following:

1. Net present value
2. Internal rate of return
3. Payback period
4. Accounting rate of return on initial investment

solution 1

1. N.P.V. = ($1,300 × 3.993) − $3,791
   = $5,191 − $3,791 = $1,400
2. $3,791 = $1,300$F$

$$F = \frac{\$3{,}791}{1{,}300} = 2.916$$

On the period-5 line of Table 4, the column closest to 2.916 is 22 percent. This may be close enough for most purposes. To obtain a more accurate rate, interpolation is needed:

	PRESENT-VALUE FACTORS	
20%	2.991	2.991
True rate		2.916
22%	2.864	
Difference	.127	.075

$$\textbf{True rate} = \textbf{20\%} + \frac{\textbf{.075}}{\textbf{.127}}\textbf{(2\%)} = \textbf{21.2\%}$$

3. $P = I/O_c = \$3{,}791/\$1{,}300 = 2.9$ years

4. $$R = \frac{\text{Increase in expected average annual operating income}}{\text{Initial increase in required investment}}$$

$$= \frac{\$1{,}300 - \text{Average depreciation}}{\$3{,}791}$$

$$= \frac{\$1{,}300 - (\$3{,}791 \div 5)}{\$3{,}791} = 14.3\%$$

problem 2

A company owns a packaging machine that was purchased three years ago for $56,000. The machine has a remaining useful life of five years but will require a major overhaul at the end of two more years of life, at a cost of $10,000. Its disposal value now is $20,000; in five years its disposal value is expected to be $8,000, assuming that the $10,000 major overhaul will be done on schedule. The cash operating costs of this machine are expected to be $40,000 annually.

A salesman has offered a substitute machine for $51,000, or for $31,000 plus the old machine. The new machine will slash annual cash-operating costs by $10,000, will not require any overhauls, will have a useful life of five years, and will have a terminal disposal value of $3,000.

REQUIRED

Assume that the required rate of return is 14 percent. Using the net present-value model, show whether the new machine should be purchased. Try to solve before examining the solution.

solution 2

A difficult part of long-range decision making is the structuring of the data. We want to see the effects of each alternative on future cash flows. The focus here is on *cash* transactions, not on opportunity costs. Using an opportunity-cost approach may yield the same answers, but repeated classroom experimentation with various analytical methods have convinced the author that the following steps are likely to be the clearest:

Step 1. Arrange the relevant cash flows by project, so that a sharp distinction is made between total-project flows and incremental flows. The top part of Exhibit 12-6 is labeled as the *total-project* approach because the cash flows for *each* alternative are sketched. In contrast, the bottom part of the exhibit is called the *incremental* approach. The incremental flows are merely algebraic differences between two alternatives. (There are always at least two alternatives. One is the status quo, the alternative of continuing with the present mode of operating.)

Step 2. Discount the expected cash flows and choose the project with the least cost or the greatest benefit. Whether you use the total-project approach or the incremental approach is a matter of preference. However, to develop confidence in this area, work with both at the start. In this example, the $8,425 net difference in favor of replacement is the ultimate result under either approach.[8]

[8]The internal rate of return on the investment of $31,000 is 26 percent. See Appendix 12 for the computations, using trial-and-error methods.

EXHIBIT 12-6 *(Place a clip on this page for easy reference.)*

Total-Project versus Incremental Approach to Net Present Value

(Data from Self-study Problem)

	PRESENT-VALUE DISCOUNT FACTOR, @ 14%	TOTAL PRESENT VALUE	SKETCH OF RELEVANT CASH FLOWS					
END OF YEAR			0	1	2	3	4	5
TOTAL-PROJECT APPROACH								
A. *Replace*								
Recurring cash operating costs, using an annuity table*	3.433	$(102,990)	← - - - -	($30,000)	($30,000)	($30,000)	($30,000)	($30,000)
Disposal value, end of year 5	.519	1,557	← - - - -	- - - -	- - - -	- - - -	- - - -	3,000
Initial required investment	1.000	(31,000)	($31,000)					
Present value of net cash outflows		$(132,433)						
B. *Keep*								
Recurring cash operating costs, using an annuity table*	3.433	$(137,320)	← - - - -	($40,000)	($40,000)	($40,000)	($40,000)	($40,000)
Overhaul, end of year 2	.769	(7,690)	← - - - -	- - - -	(10,000)			
Disposal value, end of year 5	.519	4,152	← - - - -	- - - -	- - - -	- - - -	- - - -	8,000
Present value of net cash outflows		$(140,858)						
Difference in favor of replacement		$ 8,425						
INCREMENTAL APPROACH								
A–B *Analysis Confined to Differences*								
Recurring cash operating savings, using an annuity table*	3.433	$ 34,330	← - - - -	$10,000	$10,000	$10,000	$10,000	$10,000
Overhaul avoided, end of year 2	.769	7,690	← - - - -	- - - -	10,000			
Difference in disposal values, end of year 5; $8,000 − $3,000	.519	(2,595)	← - - - -	- - - -	- - - -	- - - -	- - - -	(5,000)
Incremental initial investment	1.000	(31,000)	($31,000)					
Net present value of replacement		$ 8,425						

*Table 4, Appendix B, at the end of the book.

Terms to Learn

accounting rate of return ***accrual accounting rate of return***
capital budgeting ***cost of capital*** ***cutoff rate*** ***DCF***
discounted cash flow ***discount rate*** ***hurdle rate***
internal rate of return ***IRR*** ***net present value*** ***NPV***
payback ***payoff*** ***payout*** ***required rate of return*** ***RRR***
time-adjusted rate of return

Special Points and Pitfalls

If managers are interested in maximizing profits, they should use the best feasible decisión model for capital budgeting. DCF models are preferable to payback models or accrual accounting rate-of-return models.

Common errors in DCF analysis include the deduction of depreciation from operating cash flows and the use of the wrong present-value table. Moreover, any necessary investment in working capital should not be neglected.

Appendix 12: internal rate of return using trial-and-error methods

Reconsider the data from Exhibit 12-6, the incremental approach. Trial-and-error methods must be used to calculate the rate of return that will equate future cash flows with the incremental initial investment of $31,000. If there were only an annuity of $10,000 per year, the factor for the true rate would be $31,000 ÷ 10,000 = 3.100, which is between 18 and 20 percent on the 5-year line of Table 4 in Appendix B at the end of the book. Because there is an additional benefit at the end of year 2, you may want to try a higher rate, say 20 percent. Apply this rate to all flows, year by year; use Table 2, because the flows are not uniform:

		FIRST TRIAL: 20 PERCENT		SECOND TRIAL: 22 PERCENT	
YEAR	NET CASH INFLOWS	**present-value factor**	**total present value**	**present-value factor**	**total present value**
1	$10,000	.833	$ 8,330	.820	$ 8,200
2	20,000	.694	13,880	.672	13,440
3	10,000	.579	5,790	.551	5,510
4	10,000	.482	4,820	.451	4,510
5	5,000	.402	2,010	.370	1,850
			$34,830		$33,510

At 20 percent, the total present value of the future cash flows *exceeds* the initial investment. This means that the "true" rate must be higher than 20 percent. You are trying to find a rate that will make the total present value exactly *equal* to $31,000. A second trial shows that 22 percent is also too low. The third trial, at 26 percent, produces an answer so close that interpolation is not needed. The internal rate is approximately 26 percent:

YEAR	NET CASH INFLOWS	THIRD TRIAL: 26 PERCENT present-value factor	total present value
1	$10,000	.794	$ 7,940
2	20,000	.630	12,600
3	10,000	.500	5,000
4	10,000	.397	3,970
5	5,000	.315	1,575
			$31,085

QUESTIONS, PROBLEMS, AND CASES

Special note: ***For all problems, ignore income taxes and inflation; these factors are considered in the next chapter. Remember that required rate of return, minimum desired rate of return,*** **and** ***hurdle rate*** **are synonyms.**

12-1 Define *capital budgeting.*

12-2 What is the payback method? What is its main weakness?

12-3 Define *internal rate of return.*

12-4 "The payback reciprocal has wide applicability as a meaningful approximation of the internal rate of return. But it has two major limitations." What are the two limitations?

12-5 "The trouble with discounted cash-flow techniques is that their use ignores depreciation costs." Do you agree? Why?

12-6 "Cost of capital is the out-of-pocket interest charge on any debt arising from an undertaking." Do you agree? Why?

12-7 The short-run, marginal approach considers each financing as a separate problem. What is the principal objection to the short-run approach?

12-8 "A project with a useful life of sixty years would have an internal rate of return practically exactly equal to its payback reciprocal." Why?

12-9 ***Exercises in compound interest.*** To be sure that you understand how to use the tables in Appendix B at the end of this book, solve the following exercises. Do the exercises on your own before checking your answers. The correct answers rounded to the nearest dollar are printed after the last problem in this chapter.

1. You have just won $5,000. How much money will you have at the end of ten years if you invest it at 6 percent compounded annually? At 14 percent? Ignore income taxes in this and other parts of this problem.

2. Ten years from now, the unpaid principal of the mortgage on your house will be $8,955. How much do you have to invest today at 6 percent interest compounded annually just to accumulate the $8,955 in ten years?

3. You plan to save $500 of your earnings each year for the next ten years. How much money will you have at the end of the tenth year if you invest your savings compounded at 12 percent per year?

4. If the unpaid mortgage on your house in ten years will be $8,955, how much money do you have to invest annually at 6 percent to have just this amount on hand at the end of the tenth year?

5. You hold an endowment insurance policy that will pay you a lump sum of $20,000 at age 65. If you invest the sum at 6 percent, how much money can you withdraw from your account in equal amounts each year so that at the end of ten years there will be nothing left?

6. You have estimated that for the first ten years after you retire, you will need an annual income of $50,000. How much money must you invest at 6 percent at your retirement age to just realize this annual income? At 20 percent?

7. The following table shows two schedules of prospective operating cash inflows, each of which requires the same initial investment:

YEAR		ANNUAL CASH INFLOWS	
		plan a	**plan b**
0		$ 1,000	$ 5,000
1		2,000	4,000
2		3,000	3,000
3		4,000	2,000
4		5,000	1,000
	Total	$15,000	$15,000

The minimum desired rate of return is 6 percent compounded annually. In terms of present values, which plan is more desirable? Show computations.

12-10 ***Basic nature of present value.*** A company is considering investing in a project with a two-year life and no residual value. Cash inflow will be equal payments of $4,000 at the end of each of the two years. How much would the company be willing to invest to earn an internal rate of return of 8 percent? Use Table 2 at the end of the book to get your answer. Then prepare a tabular analysis of each payment. The column headings should be year, investment at beginning of year, operating cash inflow, return @ 8 percent per year, amount of investment received at end of year, and unrecovered investment at end of year.

12-11 ***Comparison of decison models.*** The Block Company is thinking of buying, at a cost of $22,000, some new material-handling equipment that is expected to save $5,000 in cash operating costs per year. Its estimated useful life is ten years, and it will have zero disposal value. Compute:

1. Internal rate of return
2. Net present value if the required rate is 16 percent
3. Payback period
4. Accrual accounting rate of return based on initial investment and based on average investment

12-12 ***Comparison of approaches to capital budgeting.*** Refer to Problem 11-12, page 391. Use the pertinent data there.

1. Compute the net present value of the proposed investment in new equipment, assuming that the required rate of return is 18 percent. Compute the solution in the two ways illustrated in the second Problem for Self-Study in the chapter, the "incremental" way and the "total-project" way.

2. Compute the internal rate of return and the payback period on the incremental investment.

(The income tax implications of this problem are covered in Problem 13-12.)

12-13 ***Comparison of approaches to capital budgeting.*** City Hospital estimates that it can save $2,800 a year in cash operating costs for the next ten years if it buys a special-purpose machine at a cost of $11,000. No residual value is expected. The company's minimum desired rate of return is 14 percent.

REQUIRED

(Round all computations to the nearest dollar. Ignore income taxes.) Compute:

1. Payback period
2. Using discounted cash flow: (a) internal rate of return, (b) net present value.
3. Compute the accrual accounting rate of return based on (a) average investment, (b) initial investment.

12-14 ***Golf course*** (W. Crum) Gotrocks offers you a chance to buy a miniature golf course he has built near a resort area. It would cost you $50,000 cash. For this you would get an operating golf course built on leased property at a cost of $30,000, with lease payments of $10,000 per year, payable at end of the year. Assume a salvage value of $5,000 for the equipment on the course at end of the lease. Operating costs per year for the golf course are $40,000, disregarding depreciation. Income per year, all in cash, is $60,000. You wish to use a 10 percent interest rate in your evaluation. The lease expires in ten years.

REQUIRED

1. Does this appear to be a good investment for you? Show all figures.
2. Compute the payback period for this investment.

12-15 ***Capital budgeting with uneven cash flows.*** The Braddock Corporation is considering the purchase of a special-purpose machine for $28,000. It is expected to have a useful life of seven years with no terminal salvage value. The corporation's controller estimates the following savings in cash operating costs:

YEAR	AMOUNT
1	$10,000
2	8,000
3	6,000
4	5,000
5	4,000
6	3,000
7	3,000
Total	$39,000

REQUIRED

Compute:

1. Payback period
2. Net present value if the required rate of return is 16 percent
3. Internal rate of return
4. Accrual accounting rate of return (a) on the initial investment, and (b) on the "average" investment.

12-16 ***Salvage value, current assets, and evaluation of performance.*** Hammerlink Company has been offered a special-purpose machine for $110,000. It is expected to have a useful life of eight years with a terminal salvage value of $30,000. Savings in cash operating costs are expected to be $25,000 per year. However, additional current assets are needed to keep the machine running efficiently and without any stoppages. These assets include such items as filters, lubricants, bearings, abrasives, flexible exhaust pipes, and endless belts. These must be continually replaced, so that an investment of about $8,000 must be maintained at all times in these items, but this investment is fully recoverable (will be "cashed in") at the end of the useful life.

REQUIRED

1. Compute the net present value if the required rate of return is 14 percent.
2. Compute the internal rate of return.
3. Compute the accrual accounting rate of return (a) on the initial investment, and (b) on the "average" investment.
4. You have the authority to make the purchase decision. Why might you be reluctant to base your decision on the DCF model?

12-17 ***Current assets, residual values, and choice of models.*** The manager of a local department store, one of a national company's two hundred stores, is considering whether to renovate some space in order to increase sales volume. New display fixtures and equipment will be needed. They will cost $70,000 and are expected to be useful for six years with a terminal salvage value of $4,000. Additional cash operating inflows are expected to be $25,000 per year.

However, experience has shown that, in order to sustain the higher sales volume, similar renovations have required additional investments in current assets, such as merchandise inventories and accounts receivable from customers. An initial investment of $40,000 is needed to finance or "carry" these current assets, and this level must be maintained continuously. If and when it may be decided to terminate this plan or to use the store space for other purposes, the inventories and receivables can soon be liquidated or "cashed in."

REQUIRED

1. Compute (a) net present value, using a required rate of 12 percent; (b) internal rate of return; (c) accrual accounting rate of return on the initial investment; and (d) accrual accounting rate of return on the "average" investment.
2. As the store manager, which type of model would you prefer for the purposes of making this decision and for evaluating subsequent performance? Give reasons and compare the principal types of models.

12-18 ***Sensitivity analysis, payback reciprocal.*** Yale University is considering the replacement of some old research equipment with some new equipment that should save $5,000 per year in net cash operating costs.

The old equipment has zero disposal value, but it could be used indefinitely. The estimated useful life of the new equipment is twelve years and it will cost $20,000.

REQUIRED

1. Payback time.
2. Internal rate of return.
3. Management is unsure about the useful life. What would be the internal rate of return if the useful life were (a) six years instead of twelve, and (b) twenty years instead of twelve?
4. Suppose the life will be twelve years, but the savings will be $3,000 per year instead of $5,000. What would be the rate of return?
5. Suppose the annual savings will be $4,000 for six years. What would be the rate of return?
6. Professor Myron Gordon has pointed out that the payback reciprocal can be a crude approximation of the true rate of return where (a) the project life is at least twice the payback period, and (b) the cash earnings or savings are uniformly received in equal amounts throughout the investment's life. The payback reciprocal, using the original data, will be $5,000 ÷ $20,000, or 25 percent.
   a. How close is this to the internal rate of return?
   b. Compute the payback reciprocals for requirements 3a and 3b. How close are they to the internal rates of return?
   c. Compute the payback reciprocals for requirements 4 and 5. How close are they to the internal rates of return?

12-19 ***Compare two projects.*** (SMA, adapted) The management of Dilex Diversified must decide between two proposals. The following information is available:

PROPOSAL	INVESTMENT NOW	NET CASH INFLOWS		
		period 1	**period 2**	**period 3**
A	$ 80,000	$95,400	$39,000	$12,000
B	100,000	35,000	57,500	80,000

Assuming that the company can earn 12 percent on projects of this type and that the cash inflows are received at the end of each period, advise management regarding the proposal that should be selected. Submit computations of net present values. Ignore income-tax considerations.

12-20 ***Payback period.*** A manager is considering three mutually exclusive investment projects, A, B, and C, each promising a cash flow of $20,000 per year for an initial investment of $100,000. Useful lives are as follows:

PROJECT	YEARS
A	5
B	6
C	7

REQUIRED

1. Compute the payback period for each project. If payback time is the sole criterion for the decision, which project is the most desirable?
2. Which project offers the highest rate of return?

12-21 ***Compute minimum desired rate of return.*** The Strubel Company has used the net present-value method in making capital-investment decisions. The company rejected an offer from a machinery salesman who had convincing evidence that his $12,500 lifting equipment would save the company $3,000 in cash operating costs per year for ten years. The disposal value of the machine was $2,000 at the end of ten years. In applying the net present-value method, the company computed a negative net present value of $457. What was the minimum desired rate of return? Show computations.

12-22 ***Multiple choice.*** (CPA) Choose the best answer. Prepare supporting computations.

1. The Polar Company is planning to purchase a new machine for $30,000. The payback period is expected to be five years. The new machine is expected to produce cash flow from operations of $7,000 a year in each of the next three years and $5,500 in the fourth year. Depreciation of $5,000 a year will be charged to income for each of the five years of the payback period. What is the amount of cash flow from operations that the new machine is expected to produce in the last (fifth) year of the payback period?
(a) $1,000, (b) $3,500, (c) $5,000, (d) $8,500.

2. The Fudge Company is planning to purchase a new machine which it will depreciate on a straight-line basis over a ten-year period with no salvage value and a full year's depreciation taken in the year of acquisition. The new machine is expected to produce cash flow from operations of $66,000 a year in each of the next ten years. The accounting (book value) rate of return on the initial investment is expected to be 12 percent. How much will the new machine cost?
(a) $300,000, (b) $550,000, (c) $660,000, (d) $792,000.

3. Heap Company invested in a two-year project. Heap's expected rate of return is 10 percent. The present value of $1 for one period at 10 percent is .909 and for two periods at 10 percent is .826. The machine is expected to produce cash flow from operations of $40,000 in the first year and $50,000 in the second year. How much will the project cost?
(a) $74,340, (b) $77,660, (c) $81,810, (d) $90,000.

12-23 ***Equipment replacement, sensitivity analysis.*** A toy manufacturer who specializes in making fad items has just developed a $50,000 molding machine for automatically producing a special toy. The machine has been used to produce only one unit so far. It is planned to depreciate the $50,000 original cost evenly over four years, after which time production of the toy will be stopped.

Suddenly a machine salesman appears. He has a new machine that is ideally suited for producing this toy. His automatic machine is distinctly superior. It reduces the cost of materials by 10 percent and produces twice as many units per hour. It will cost $44,000 and will have zero disposal value at the end of four years.

Production and sales would continue to be at a rate of 25,000 per year for four years; annual sales will be $90,000. The scrap value of the toy company's machine is now $5,000 and will be $2,600 four years from now. Both machines will be useless after the 100,000-unit total market potential is exhausted.

With its present equipment, the company's annual expenses will be: direct materials, $10,000; direct labor, $20,000; and variable factory overhead, $15,000. Fixed factory overhead, exclusive of depreciation, is $7,500 annually, and fixed selling and administrative expenses are $12,000 annually.

REQUIRED

1. Assume that the hurdle rate of return is 18 percent. Using discounted cash-flow techniques, show whether the new equipment should be purchased. Use a total-project approach and an incremental approach. What is the role of the book value of the old equipment in the analysis?
2. What is the payback period for the new equipment?
3. As the manager who developed the $50,000 molding machine, you are trying to justify not buying the new $44,000 machine. You question the accuracy of the expected cash operating savings. By how much must these cash savings fall before the point of indifference, the point where net present value of the project is zero, is reached?

12-24 ***Three alternatives, effects on inventory investments.*** The Dull Company has a very stable operation that is not marked by detectable variations in production or sales.

The Dull Company has an old machine with a net disposal value of $5,000 now and $1,000 five years from now. A new Rapido machine is offered for $25,000 cash or $20,000 with a trade-in. The new machine promises annual operating cash outflows of $2,000 as compared with the old machine's annual outflow of $10,000. A third machine, the Quicko, is offered for $45,000 cash or $40,000 with a trade-in; it promises annual operating cash outflows of $1,000. The disposal values of the new machines five years hence will be $1,000 each.

Because the new machines will produce output more swiftly, the average investment in inventories will be as follows:

Old machine	$100,000
Rapido	80,000
Quicko	50,000

The minimum desired rate of return is 20 percent. The company uses discounted cash-flow techniques to evaluate decisions.

REQUIRED

Which of the three alternatives is the most desirable? Show calculations. This company uses discounted cash-flow techniques for evaluating decisions. When more than two machines are being considered, the company favors computing the present value of the future costs of each alternative. The most desirable alternative is the one with the least cost.

P.V. of $1 at 20% for 5 years = .40
P.V. of annuity of $1 at 20% for 5 years = 3.00
Amount of $1 at 20% for 5 years = 2.20
Amount of annuity of $1 at 20% for 5 years = 8.00

12-25 ***Capital budgeting and relevant costs.*** The City of Los Angeles has been operating a *cafeteria* for its employees, but it is considering a conversion from this form of food service to a completely automated set of *coin vending machines,* in which case the old equipment would be sold now for whatever cash it might bring.

The vending machines would be purchased immediately for cash. A catering firm would take complete responsibility for servicing and replenishing the vending machines and would simply pay the city a predetermined percentage of the gross vending receipts.

The following data are available (in thousands of dollars):

Cafeteria cash revenues per year	$120
Cafeteria cash expenses per year	$124
Present cafeteria equipment (10-year remaining life):	
Net book value	$ 84
Annual depreciation expense	$ 6
Current cash value (zero value in 10 years)	$ 4
New vending machines:	
Purchase price	$ 64
Estimated useful life (yrs.)	10
Forecasted terminal scrap value	$ 5
Expected annual gross receipts	$ 80
City's percentage share of receipts	10%
Expected annual cash expenses (negligible)	
Present values at 14%:	
$1 due in 10 years	$0.27
Annuity of $1 a year for 10 years	$5.20

REQUIRED

(Concerning the vending alternative compared with the cafeteria plan.)

1. Expected increase in net annual operating cash inflow
2. Payback period
3. Net present value
4. Point of indifference (zero N.P.V.) in terms of annual gross vending machine receipts

12-26 ***Replacement of machine and uncertainty.*** The Field Co. manufactures a basic auto part, which it markets together with several related parts. Each year the basic part is adapted or a new one produced to meet market trends. The following alternatives are being considered.

First, modify an existing machine at a cost of $12,000. This machine was bought a year ago for $45,000. It could be used for another two years and would then be worthless. The contribution margin of 40 percent will not be affected if this machine is modified.

Second, buy a new machine for $50,000 and sell the old one for $4,000 cash. The new machine could be used for two years and would then have a scrap value of $4,000. The contribution margin will be raised to 60 percent if this machine is used.

It is fairly certain that revenue for the first year will be $200,000. A foreign manufacturer, who has not yet entered the domestic market, is expected to be in competition within a year. The outlook for the second year is uncertain. The feeling of the planning committee is that demand may decline by 25 percent in the second year.

Under either alternative and given either outcome, $100,000 is expected to be tied up in working capital over the two years. The required rate of return is about 30 percent before taxes. Ignore the calculation of tax liability arising from this project. For simplicity, assume that the present value of $1 payable at the end of one and two years, respectively, is 0.80 and 0.60.

REQUIRED The net present value of each alternative for both the best and worst outcomes, treating cash inflows as being received at the end of each year.

12-27 ***When to cut a tree.*** Del Doller, a wealthy capitalist, bought land and put it in the conservation reserve. He was told that if he planted trees on the land, he would get a yearly check, and the government would not come to inspect for twenty years.

A large industrial firm that needs lumber has approached Del. The firm's employees will plant and care for trees on Del's land. In return for the use of the land, they will pay 10¢ a board foot for the lumber they cut. They will cut at Del's discretion.

The number of board feet of lumber in a tree depends upon the age of the tree in years. Assuming an average growth, the growth function for trees is $f(n) = 300\sqrt{n} - 900$, where n is years and $f(n)$ is the number of board feet.

REQUIRED Del wants to know the most profitable time for cutting the trees. Del uses a 20 percent minimum desired rate of return.

n	$\sqrt{n}$	n	$\sqrt{n}$
10	3.162	16	4.000
11	3.317	17	4.123
12	3.464	18	4.243
13	3.606	19	4.359
14	3.742	20	4.472
15	3.873		

12-28 ***Choice of machines; comparison of discounted cash-flow and accounting models.*** The India Manufacturing Company is considering the purchase of a machine for its factory. Two courses are available:

a. Machine A is being offered at a special price of $50,000 with an estimated life of seven years and a disposal value estimated at $1,000. The cash operating expenses would amount to $30,000 annually. The machine would require major repairs every two years at a cost of $5,000.
b. Machine B is available for a price of $75,000 with an estimated life of seven years and a disposal value of $5,000. The cash operating expenses with this machine would amount to $26,000 annually. Major repairs cost $3,500 every third year.

Assume the same revenue flow in all years for both alternatives. Assume that the minimum desired rate of return is 10 percent.

REQUIRED

1. Compute the average annual return on the extra $25,000 needed to buy Machine B, using the accrual accounting model and an "initial" investment base.

2. Using discounted cash flow, compute the present value of all future costs under both alternatives. Also compare the alternatives on an incremental basis.

12-29 ***Stadium turf.*** Ten years ago, Grand State University installed a synthetic turf for its football stadium. Many complaints have been received recently about the dangerously worn playing surface. The athletic director must now make a recommendation regarding the turf's replacement with a new synthetic surface or with grass.

The manufacturer of Tuff Turf has bid $830,000 for the removal of the old surface and the installation of a new playing surface. Maintenance is estimated at $75,000 annually over the expected useful life of seven years. The only alternative to Tuff Turf is bulldozing the present base at a cost of $50,000 and planting a grass cover at a cost of $460,000. Maintenance of the grass is estimated annually at $135,000 plus the cost of water, which, at current rates, would be about $10,000 per year.

REQUIRED

1. A recommendation that ignores the time value of money. Use a seven-year time horizon. Compare the total costs for the seven years under each alternative.
2. A recommendation that reflects a 14 percent discount rate. Use a seven-year time horizon and a net present-value model.
3. A list of other factors that might be relevant to this decision.

12-30 ***Cost-volume-profit analysis and discounted cash flow.*** The Student Center of Great State University wants to make doughnuts to supply all of its food operations. Two machines are proposed for the production of the doughnuts: semiautomatic and automatic. The Center now buys doughnuts from an outside supplier at $.25 each. Manufacturing costs would be:

	SEMIAUTOMATIC	AUTOMATIC
Variable costs per doughnut	$.21	$.20
Fixed costs:		
Annual cash operating outlays	$ 4,500	$ 6,500
Initial cost of machines	$10,000	$28,000
Useful life of machines in years	4	4
Salvage value at the end of 4 years	—	$ 4,000

REQUIRED

1. The manager wants to know how many doughnuts must be sold in order to have total average annual costs equal to outside purchase costs for the (a) semiautomatic machine and (b) automatic machine.
2. At what annual volume of doughnuts would the total annual costs be the same for both machines? Which machine is preferable if the volume exceeds the volume you computed? Why?
3. Assume that the sales forecast over the next four years is 600,000 doughnuts per year. The minimum desired rate of return is 20 percent. Should the automatic machine be purchased? Why? Show calculations. Ignore income taxes.

P.V. of $1.00 at 20% for 4 periods is	.5
P.V. of annuity of $1.00 at 20% for 4 periods is	2.6

Compare your answer with that in requirement 2. Do the answers differ? How? Why?

12-31 ***Capital investment in a baseball player.*** William Brenner, president of the Chicago Chartreuse Sox, is currently considering a player deal in which he will acquire Ian Winfield, a great gate attraction, from the New York Confederates in exchange for $3,800,000 cash plus George Bumble, a regular Sox outfielder who is currently receiving a salary of $60,000 a year. Winfield is to be Bumble's replacement in the regular outfield. Brenner and his fellow executives have assembled the following data:

Estimated useful life of Winfield	5 years
Estimated residual value of Winfield	$80,000
Estimated useful life of Bumble	5 years
Estimated residual value of Bumble	None
Current cash offer for Bumble received from the Atlanta Carpetbaggers Baseball Club	$160,000
Applicable minimum desired rate of return	20%

Other data:

YEAR	WINFIELD'S SALARY	ADDITIONAL CLUB GATE RECEIPTS BECAUSE OF WINFIELD	ADDITIONAL EXPENSES OF HANDLING HIGHER VOLUME
1	$600,000	$3,200,000	$320,000
2	700,000	3,000,000	300,000
3	800,000	2,000,000	200,000
4	800,000	1,000,000	100,000
5	700,000	400,000	40,000

REQUIRED

(Ignore income taxes.)

1. Based on the data as given, should the Sox buy Winfield? Use the following present-value factors for $1 at 20 percent:

	FOR END OF YEAR				
	1	2	3	4	5
Factor	.83	.69	.58	.48	.40

2. What other factors should be considered before making the decision? How much confidence do you have in the available data?

12-32 ***Two sizes of machines; uneven revenue stream; price-level change.*** The Kubek Company has developed a new product for which a growing demand is anticipated. During the first year, sales are expected to be 20,000 units; the second year, 30,000 units; the third year, 50,000 units; the fourth year and each year thereafter, 80,000 units.

The Kubek Company must choose between two alternative production arrangements:

1. Buy a big, heavy-duty machine with a capacity of 90,000 units and an estimated useful life of six years. This machine costs $250,000.

2. Buy a smaller machine with a capacity of 50,000 units and an estimated useful life of three years. Three years from today buy two such machines to replace the one that will be worn out. The smaller machines now cost $100,000 each.

Property taxes and insurance per year are expected to be $8,000 on the big machine and 4 percent of original cost of equipment in use on the small machines. Maintenance cost is expected to be $2,000 per year on the big machine and $1,200 per year on each of the smaller machines. Variable production costs per unit will be $3.00 with the big machine and $3.10 with the smaller machines. Both machines will have zero disposal values at the end of their respective useful lives.

Prices on this type of machinery have been increasing at the rate of 4 percent compounded annually. Which alternative is more attractive? Show all computations clearly, using the total present values of all outlays for each alternative. The minimum desired rate of return is 10 percent. Assume that all outlays take place at the end of the accounting periods. Round off present-value factors to two decimal places.

12-33 ***Decision to sell a business.*** Mr. H. Closet is the sole proprietor of a medium-sized plumbing and heating business. Owing to the increasing amount of government-contract work in his business territory and the fact that the federal government requires that union-scale wages be paid on all government work, Closet is being pressured to unionize his shop.

Sensing Closet's distaste for unions and knowing that he is near the age of retirement, a syndicate promoter, the Ulm Company, has extended a $230,000 cash offer for his business.

Closet, however, sees a large amount of business coming his way if he unionizes and receives the government contracts. He decides that if he does stay in business, he will definitely sell out in eight years. His investment in current assets (cash, inventory, accounts receivable) will be expanded by $24,000 because of the increased volume of business. His equipment will not be in very good condition eight years hence. He therefore expects to sell the business at the end of the eighth year for $40,000.

Closet estimates that the government-contract work will result in a $200,000 increase in yearly sales. Nongovernment sales will remain constant at $400,000 a year. Direct-material costs are proportional to sales. His direct-labor costs are proportional to sales but will increase by 20 percent for all labor because of higher unionized wages. Variable overhead is assumed to vary with sales, and annual fixed overhead will total $60,000, including depreciation. Straight-line depreciation will increase from $8,000 per year to $10,000 per year, because new equipment must be purchased for $16,000. All fixed assets will be fully depreciated at the end of eight years. Selling and administrative expenses will remain at $60,000. Disregard any tax effects.

Keystone Plumbing & Heating Works
Income Statement
(Last Year)

Sales		$400,000
Cost of goods sold:		
Direct materials	$100,000	
Direct labor	150,000	
Variable overhead	30,000	
Fixed overhead	54,000	334,000
Gross margin		$ 66,000
Selling and administrative expense, fixed		60,000*
Net income		$ 6,000

**Includes a $40,000 salary paid to Closet.*

REQUIRED

1. Prepare an income statement, assuming that there will be $200,000 of government contract work and that all costs will vary as stated above. This statement will be applicable to any of the next eight years.
2. Assume that his minimum desired rate of return is 16 percent and that Closet considers his annual net cash flow as his $40,000 salary plus any cash flow from operations. Should Closet sell his business now, or continue in business for another eight years as a union shop? If he sold out, Closet would retire and not work elsewhere. Assume that all additional investments in the business by Closet will be made immediately.
3. Discuss the limitations of the analysis that influenced your recommendation.

12-34 ***A study of the potential economic usefulness of an invention.*** A store manager of a large grocery chain has invented a labor-saving machine. It is designed to automatically cut the tops and bottoms from cases of grocery merchandise. These tops and bottoms, with their one and one-half-inch edges, are used as trays to hold 12 and 24 cans each. These filled trays are then stacked directly onto the shelves. Production time is improved as a result of handling 12 or perhaps 24 in one motion as opposed to hand-stacking the same number of cans in from three to six separate motions.

This "tray-pack" method of shelf stocking and display building is not new to the grocery business. Up until now, however, the trays had to be cut by hand, which is difficult, tedious work that often has unsightly results. The electric tray-cutter is fastened to the roller conveyor in the back room and adjusts itself automatically to any size case. It cuts trays just about as quickly as stock can be pulled by two persons in a grocery back room, simply slicing off the trays as the merchandise rolls by on the conveyor.

Some elementary time-study work was necessary to verify that the machine was indeed a timesaver and to give comparative production figures for the job. The following estimates were made of the annual depreciation and maintenance expenses:

Machine cost	$7,000
Depreciation (annual, straight-line)	1,600
Installation cost	1,000
Annual repair and electricity expense	1,200
Scrap value	0

The weekly savings experienced in an average store, cutting about 1,000 cases of tray-pack merchandise each week, are as follows:

Manual-cutting rate	2 cases per minute
Machine-cutting rate	10 cases per minute

The current labor cost is $12 per hour plus $3 in fringe benefits.

Assume an 18 percent minimum desired rate of return. Also assume that the labor savings are real—that is, that the labor costs under investigation are variable costs.

REQUIRED

1. Compute payback time and the net present value for the average store.
2. What is the lowest volume of cases per week that could be handled and still make the installation desirable? Show computations.

12-35 ***Review of chapters 11 and 12.*** (D. Solomons, adapted) The Rainier Company sells a range of high-grade chemical products that calls for careful packaging. The company has always made a feature of the special properties of the containers used. They had a special patented lining made from a material known as GHJ, and the firm operated a department especially to maintain its containers in good condition and to make new ones to replace those past repair.

Ms. Wood, the general manager, had for some time suspected that the firm might save money and get equally good service by buying its containers outside. After careful inquiries, she approached a firm specializing in container production, Closure Inc., and obtained quotations from them. At the same time she asked Mr. Wrend, the controller, for an up-to-date statement of the cost of operating the container department.

Within a few days the quotation from Closure came in. They were prepared to supply all the new containers required—at that time running at the rate of 15,000 a year—for $300,000 per annum, the contract to run for a term of five years certain and thereafter to be renewable from year to year. If the number of containers required decreased, Rainier would still pay $300,000 per annum. If the number of containers required increased, the contract price would be increased proportionately. Additionally, irrespective of whether the above contract was concluded, Closure undertook to carry out purely maintenance work on containers, short of replacement, for a sum of $70,000 per annum on the same contract terms.

Ms. Wood compared these figures with the following cost figures prepared by Wrend covering a year's operations of the container department:

Materials		$100,000
Direct labor		175,000
Departmental overhead:		
Supervision	$50,000	
Rent	6,000	
Depreciation of machinery	30,000	
Maintenance of machinery	7,000	
Other expenses	31,000	124,000
		$399,000
Proportion of general administrative overhead		33,000
Total cost of department for year		$432,000

Wood leaned toward eliminating the department and entering into the contracts offered by Closure. However, before proceeding, she asked for the observations of the manager of the department, Mr. Spencer; at the same time, she made it clear that Spencer's own employment was not in jeopardy. Even if his department were abolished, there was another managerial position shortly becoming vacant to which Spencer could move without loss of pay or prospects.

Spencer raised a number of considerations. "For instance," he said, "what will you do with the machinery? It cost $240,000 four years ago, but you'd be lucky if you got $40,000 for it now, even though it's good for another five years at least. And then there's the stock of GHJ we bought a year ago. That cost us $120,000 and at the rate we're using it now, it will last us another three years or so. We used up a quarter of it last year. Wrend's figure of $100,000 for materials probably includes about $30,000 for GHJ. But it will be tricky stuff to handle if we don't use it up. We bought cheaply—$150 a ton we paid for it—and you couldn't buy it today for less than $180. But you wouldn't have more than $120 a ton left if you sold it, net of all handling expenses."

Wrend was present during this discussion. He said, "I don't much like all this conjecture. My figures are pretty conclusive. Besides, if we are going to have all this talk about 'what will happen if,' don't forget our problem of space. We're paying $10,000 a year in rent for a warehouse two miles away. If we closed Spencer's department, we'd have all the warehouse space we need without renting."

"That's a good point," said Wood. "Though we should not forget that the total termination costs for the oldest employees released will amount to $14,000 annually for five years." Spencer said, "What about this $33,000 for general administrative overhead? You surely don't expect to fire anyone in the general office if I'm closed down, do you?" "Probably not," said Wrend, "but someone has to pay for these costs. We can't ignore them when we look at an individual department. If we do that with each department in turn, we shall finish by convincing ourselves that general managers, accountants, typists, stationery, and the like, don't have to be paid for. And they do, believe me."

"Well, I think we've thrashed this out pretty fully," said Wood, "but I've been turning over in my mind the possibility of perhaps keeping on the maintenance work ourselves. What are your views on that, Spencer?" "I don't know," said Spencer, "but it's worth looking into. We won't need any machinery for that, and the supervision could be handled by a foreman. You'd save $30,000 a year there, say. You'd only need about one-fifth of the workers, but you could retain the oldest. You wouldn't save any space, so I suppose the rent would be the same. I don't think the other expenses would be more than $13,000 a year." "What about materials?" asked Wood. "We use about 10 percent of the total on maintenance," Spencer replied. "That is, we use about $10,000 per year on maintenance—no GHJ is required."

"Well, I've told Closure that I'd let them know my decision within a week," said Wood. "I'll let you know what I decide to do before I write to them."

REQUIRED

1. Assume that the time value of money is 10 percent. Ignore income taxes. What action should be taken? Show your analysis. Prepare a clear-cut quantitative analysis. Specify your assumptions.
2. Describe any sensitivity analysis that seems particularly advisable. Without doing calculations, predict the effect of the sensitivity analysis on your final computations. For example, what would happen to your two best alternatives if the time value of money were 20 percent instead of 10 percent? State the possible influence of the nonquantified factors on the decision.

answers to exercises in compound interest (problem 12-9)

The general approach to these problems centers on a key question: Which of the four basic tables am I dealing with? No computations should be made until after this basic question is answered with confidence.

1. From Table 1. The $5,000 is a present value. The value ten years hence is an *amount* or *future worth.*

$$S = P(1 + r)^n\text{; the conversion factor, } (1 + r)^n\text{, is on line 10 of Table 1.}$$

$$\text{Substituting at 6 percent:} \quad S = 5{,}000\ (1.791) = \$8{,}955$$

$$\text{Substituting at 14 percent:} \quad S = 5{,}000\ (3.707) = \$18{,}535$$

2. From Table 2. The $8,955 is an *amount* or *future worth.* You want the present value of that amount.

$$P = S/(1 + r)^n\text{; the conversion factor, } 1/(1 + r)^n\text{, is on line 10 of Table 2.}$$

$$\text{Substituting:} \quad P = \$8{,}955(.558) = \$4{,}997.$$

3. From Table 3. You are seeking the *amount* or *future worth* of an annuity of $500 per year.

$$S_n = \$500\ F\text{, where } F \text{ is the conversion factor}$$

$$S_n = \$500(17.549) = \$8{,}775$$

4. From Table 3. The $8,955 is a future worth. You are seeking the uniform amount (annuity) to set aside annually.

$$S_n = \text{Annual deposit } (F)$$

$$\$8{,}955 = \text{Annual deposit } (13.181)$$

$$\text{Annual deposit} = \frac{\$8{,}955}{13.181} = \$679$$

5. From Table 4. When you reach age 65, you will get $20,000. This is a present value at that time. You must find the annuity that will just exhaust the invested principal in ten years.

$$P_n = \text{Annual withdrawal } (F)$$

$$\$20{,}000 = \text{Annual withdrawal } (7.360)$$

$$\text{Annual withdrawal} = \frac{\$20{,}000}{7.360} = \$2{,}717$$

6. From Table 4. You need to find the present value of an annuity for ten years.

$$\text{At 6 percent} \begin{cases} P_n = \text{Annual withdrawal } (F) \\ P_n = \$50{,}000 \ (7.360) \\ P_n = \$368{,}000 \end{cases}$$

$$\text{At 20 percent} \begin{cases} P_n = \$50{,}000 \ (4.192) \\ P_n = \$209{,}600, \text{ a much lower figure} \end{cases}$$

7. Plan B is preferable. Its present value exceeds that of Plan A by $1,038:

YEAR	P.V. FACTORS AT 6% FROM TABLE 2	P.V. OF PLAN A	P.V. OF PLAN B
0	1.000	$ 1,000	$ 5,000
1	.943	1,886	3,772
2	.890	2,670	2,670
3	.840	3,360	1,680
4	.792	3,960	792
		$12,876	$13,914

This chapter continues the discussion of the preceding chapter. Some readers may prefer to study only one or two of its major sections: income-tax factors, clarification of role of depreciation, capital budgeting and inflation, required rate of return (cost of capital), applicability to non-profit organizations, administration of capital budgets, net present value or internal rate of return, and applications of net present value.

The uncertainty about long-run events makes capital budgeting a difficult but challenging area. The imprecision of prediction should overhang any analyst's tendency to split hairs concerning controversial aspects. However, there are a few guideposts that should help toward intelligent decisions. Some were summarized at the end of Chapters 11 and 12. Others are discussed in this chapter.

Income-tax factors almost always play an important role in decision making. It is dangerous to assume that income taxes are irrelevant or insignificant.

Income tax factors

importance of income taxes

Income taxes are major disbursements that often have a tremendous influence on decisions. Even where tax rates and timing are the same for all alternatives, the before-tax differences between alternatives are usually heavily slashed by application of current income-tax rates, so that after-tax differences become narrower. This reduction of differences often results in rejection of alternatives that are seemingly attractive on a pretax basis.

The role of taxes in capital budgeting is no different from that of any other cash disbursement. **There are two major impacts of income taxes: (1) on the *amount* of cash inflow or outflow, and (b) on the *timing* of cash flows.**

The intricacies of the income-tax laws are often bewildering. This chapter will concentrate on a few pertinent provisions of the law in order to highlight a general approach to the problem. Our discussion will be confined to corporations rather than partnerships or individuals.

The applicable tax rate to be used in predicting cash flows is dependent on the income-tax bracket of the taxpayer and on the type of income in question. For example, the federal rate on ordinary corporate net income in the early 1980s was 46 percent on taxable income over $100,000. But most states also levy income taxes, with rates that vary considerably. Thus, the combined tax effect on ordinary income in excess of $100,000 may easily exceed 50 percent.

timing and different depreciation methods

Exhibit 13-1 shows the relationship between depreciation, income taxes, and net income. Assume that a company has a single fixed asset, purchased for $90,000 cash, which has a five-year life and zero terminal disposal value. The purchase cost, less any predicted disposal value, is tax-deductible in the form of yearly depreciation. This deduction has been aptly called a **tax shield**, because it protects that amount of income from taxation. Study this exhibit thoroughly.

As Exhibit 13-2 shows, the cost of a depreciable asset represents a valuable future tax deduction of $90,000. The present value of this deduction depends directly on its specific yearly effects on future income-tax payments. Therefore, the present value is influenced by the depreciation method selected, the applicable tax rates, and the rate used for discounting future cash flows.

the best depreciation method

The three most widely used depreciation methods are **straight-line, sum-of-the-years'-digits (SYD),** and **double-declining balance (DDB).** Their effects are shown in Exhibit 13-2. Note that the present value of the tax savings is greater if the straight-line depreciation is *not* used. The accelerated depreciation methods will generally maximize present values as compared with the straight-line method. The cumulative dollar tax bills may not change, but the early write-offs defer tax outlays to future periods. The measure of the latter advantage depends on the rate of return that can be gained from funds that would otherwise have been paid as income taxes. **The general rule in shrewd income-tax planning is: When there is a legal choice, take the deduction sooner rather than later.**

Should a taxpayer use DDB or SYD? The answer depends on the combination of the depreciation method, the useful life, and the discount rate. As compared with SYD, DDB produces the larger depreciation charges in the first few years of an asset's life and lesser charges in later years. At a rate of 10 percent, DDB is more advantageous if the useful life is five years or less. Using the data in Exhibit 13-2, the present values of the tax savings are $29,013 for SYD and $29,141 for DDB.

EXHIBIT 13-1

Basic Analysis of Income Statement, Income Taxes, and Cash Flows
(Data Assumed)

TRADITIONAL INCOME STATEMENT

(S)	Sales	$100,000
(E)	Less: Expenses, excluding depreciation	$ 62,000
(D)	Depreciation (straight-line of $90,000 ÷ 5 years)	18,000
	Total expenses	$ 80,000
	Income before income taxes	$ 20,000
(T)	Income taxes at 40 percent	8,000
(I)	Net income	$ 12,000

Total after-tax effect on cash inflow from operations is either

$$S - E - T = \$100{,}000 - \$62{,}000 - \$8{,}000 = \$30{,}000$$

or

$$I + D = \$12{,}000 + \$18{,}000 = \$30{,}000$$

ANALYSIS FOR CAPITAL BUDGETING

	Cash Effects of Operations	
(S − E)	Cash inflow from operations: $100,000 − $62,000 =	$38,000
	Income-tax outflow, at 40 percent	15,200*
	After-tax effects of operations (excluding depreciation)	$22,800
	Effect of depreciation	
(D)	Straight-line depreciation: $90,000 ÷ 5 = $18,000	
	Income-tax savings, at 40 percent	7,200*
	Total after-tax effect on cash	$30,000†

**Net cash outflow from income taxes, $15,200 − $7,200 = $8,000.*
†Letting t equal the income-tax rate, this can also be expressed as

$$(S - E)(1 - t) + Dt = (\$100{,}000 - \$62{,}000)(1 - .4) + \$18{,}000(.4) = \$22{,}800 + \$7{,}200 = \$30{,}000$$

shortcut present value You can readily imagine how computations of the present values in conjunction with accelerated depreciation can be cumbersome. To ease calculations, Table 5 in Appendix B at the end of the book provides a shortcut approach to the present value of the income-tax savings from SYD depreciation. For the $90,000 depreciable investment at 10 percent in Exhibit 13-2, use the factor from the period-5 line in Table 5:

$$\text{Present value of SYD depreciation} = \$90{,}000(.806) = \$72{,}540$$

$$\text{Present value of income-tax savings} = \$72{,}540 \times \text{applicable 40\% tax rate} = \$29{,}016$$

Except for rounding, this shortcut result is equal to the $29,013 sum of the individual year-by-year computations in Exhibit 13-2.

				10% DISCOUNT FACTOR	PRESENT VALUE AT 10%	SKETCH OF RELEVANT CASH FLOWS YEAR 1	2	3	4	5
STRAIGHT-LINE DEPRECIATION, CASH EFFECTS:										
Annual depreciation $90,000 ÷ 5 = $18,000										
Cash effects: savings in income taxes @ 40%			= $7,200	3.791	$27,295	←$ 7,200	$7,200	$7,200	$7,200	$7,200

SUM-OF-THE-YEARS'-DIGITS DEPRECIATION, CASH EFFECTS:

year	multiplier*	income-tax deduction	income-tax savings @ 40%	10% DISCOUNT FACTOR	PRESENT VALUE AT 10%	1	2	3	4	5
1	5/15	$30,000	$12,000	.909	$10,908	←$12,000				
2	4/15	24,000	9,600	.826	7,930	←	$9,600			
3	3/15	18,000	7,200	.751	5,407	←		$7,200		
4	2/15	12,000	4,800	.683	3,278	←			$4,800	
5	1/15	6,000	2,400	.621	1,490	←				$2,400
Cash effects: savings in income taxes			$36,000		$29,013					

DOUBLE-DECLINING BALANCE DEPRECIATION, CASH EFFECTS:

year	income-tax deduction = DDB rate × beg.-of-year book value†	income-tax savings @ 40%	10% DISCOUNT FACTOR	PRESENT VALUE AT 10%	1	2	3	4	5
1	40% × $90,000 = $36,000	$14,400	.909	$13,090	←$14,400				
2	40% × $54,000 = $21,600	8,640	.826	7,137	←	$8,640			
3	40% × $32,400 = $12,960	5,184	.751	3,893	←		$5,184		
4	40% × $19,440 = $ 7,776	3,110	.683	2,124	←			$3,110	
5	Remainder, $11,664	4,666	.621	2,897	←				$4,666
Cash effects: savings in income taxes				$29,141					

**The general formula for obtaining the denominator of the multiplier under the sum-of-the-years'-digits method is:*

$S = n\left(\frac{n+1}{2}\right)$ **where** S = **sum-of-the-years'-digits**; n = **number of years of estimated useful life**

$S = 5\left(\frac{5+1}{2}\right) = 5 \times 3 = 15$

†Double-declining balance depreciation (DDB) is computed as follows:
a. Compute the rate (ignoring the terminal value) by dividing 100% by the years of useful life. Then double the rate. In our example, 100% ÷ 5 years = 20%. The DDB rate would be 2 × 20%, or 40%.
b. To compute the depreciation for any year, multiply the beginning book value by the DDB rate: 40% × $90,000 = $36,000 for the first year; 40% × ($90,000 − $36,000) = $21,600 for the second year; etc. Unmodified, this method would never fully depreciate the existing book value. Therefore, in the later years of an asset's life, companies are permitted to switch to a straight-line method. For instance, in this example the taxpayers could switch to straight-line depreciation for the fourth and fifth years. The income-tax deduction would then be $9,720 and $9,720 instead of the $7,776 and $11,664 shown here.

EXHIBIT 13-3 *(Place a clip on this page for easy reference.)*

Lindo Company, After-Tax Analysis of Equipment Replacement: Total-Project Approach

	YEAR	MULTIPLIED BY $15,000	INCOME-TAX DEDUCTION	CASH EFFECTS: INCOME-TAX SAVINGS @ 40%		PRESENT-VALUE DISCOUNT FACTORS @ 10%	TOTAL PRESENT VALUE	SKETCH OF RELEVANT CASH FLOWS: 0	1	2	3	4	5
End of Year								0	1	2	3	4	5
(A) *REPLACE*													
Recurring cash operating costs					$46,000								
Income-tax savings, @ 40 percent					18,400								
After-tax effect on cash					$27,600	3.791	($104,631)		($27,600)	($27,600)	($27,600)	($27,600)	($27,600)
Depreciation deductions (sum of years' digits):													
	1	5/15	$ 5,000	$2,000		.910	1,820*		$2,000				
	2	4/15	4,000	1,600		.830	1,328			$1,600			
	3	3/15	3,000	1,200		.750	900				$1,200		
	4	2/15	2,000	800		.680	544					$800	
	5	1/15	1,000	400		.620	248						$400
			$15,000	$6,000									
Residual value, all subject to tax because book value will be zero and gain equals proceeds					$ 700								
Less: 40% tax on gain					280								
Total after-tax effect on cash					$ 420	.620	260						$420
Cost of a new machine:					$15,000	1.000	(15,000)	($15,000)					
Disposal of old equipment:													
Book value now ($22,000 − $12,000)				$10,000									
Selling price				4,000	$ 4,000								
Net loss				$ 6,000									
Tax savings				×.40	2,400								
Total after-tax effect on cash					$ 6,400	1.000	6,400	$6,400					
Total present value of all cash flows							($108,131)						
(B) *KEEP*													
Recurring cash operating costs					$50,000								
Income-tax savings, @ 40%					20,000								
After-tax effect on cash					$30,000	3.791	($113,730)		($30,000)	($30,000)	($30,000)	($30,000)	($30,000)
Depreciation deductions ($10,000 ÷ 5)				$ 2,000									
Income-tax savings, @ 40%				×.40	$ 800	3.791	3,033		800	800	800	800	800
Residual value, gain equals proceeds					$ 600								
Less: 40% tax on gain					240								
Total after-tax effect on cash					$ 360	.620	223						360
Total present value of all cash flows							($110,474)						
Difference in favor of replacement							$ 2,343						

*Table 5 in Appendix B at the end of the book provides a shortcut approach to computing the present value of the income-tax savings from the sum-of-the-years'-digits (SYD) depreciation

EXHIBIT 13-4

Lindo Company, After-Tax Analysis of Equipment Replacement: Incremental Approach

					PRESENT-VALUE DISCOUNT FACTORS @ 10%	TOTAL PRESENT VALUES	SKETCH OF RELEVANT CASH FLOWS 0	1	2	3	4	5
End of Year							0	1	2	3	4	5
Analysis confined to differences between (A) and (B) in Exhibit 13-3:												
Recurring operating savings, $50,000 − $46,000	$4,000											
Income tax, @ 40%	1,600											
After-tax effect on cash	$2,400				3.791	$9,098	←	$2,400	$2,400	$2,400	$2,400	$2,400
Differences in depreciation:												
YEAR	REPLACE	KEEP	DIFFERENCE	INCOME-TAX CASH EFFECT @ 40%								
1	$5,000	$2,000	$3,000	$1,200	.910	1,092	←	$1,200				
2	4,000	2,000	2,000	800	.830	664	←		$800			
3	3,000	2,000	1,000	400	.750	300	←			$400		
4	2,000	2,000	—	—	.680	—					—	
5	1,000	2,000	(1,000)	(400)	.620	(248)	←					$(400)
Difference in disposal value, end of year 5 (see Exhibit 13-3 for details): $420 − $360 = $60					.620	37	←					$60
Incremental initial investment (see Exhibit 13-3 for details): $15,000 − $6,400 = ($8,600)					1.000	(8,600)	($8,600)					
Net present value of replacement						$2,343						

effects of income taxes on cash flow The effect of income taxes on cash flow may best be visualized by a step-by-step analysis of a simple example. The following example is similar to those in Chapter 12. However, all income-tax effects will now be considered and an *after-tax* hurdle rate is used.

» EXAMPLE

The Lindo Company is considering replacing an old packaging machine with a new, more efficient machine. The old machine originally cost $22,000. Accumulated straight-line depreciation is $12,000 and the remaining useful life is five years. The old machine can be sold outright now for $4,000. The predicted residual value at the end of five years is $600; however, the company has not used a residual value in allocating depreciation for tax purposes. Annual cash operating costs are $50,000 per year.

Company engineers are convinced that the new machine, which costs $15,000, will have annual cash operating costs of only $46,000 per year. The new machine will have a useful life of five years, with an estimated residual value of $700. Sum-of-the-years'-digits depreciation would be used for tax purposes, with no provision for residual value. Assume that the required rate of return, after taxes, is 10 percent. Using the net present-value technique, demonstrate which action is more profitable. Use two ways to get your answer, a total-project approach and an incremental approach, as described in the preceding chapter on page 422. Assume that the zero residual values are acceptable for tax purposes. Assume a 40 percent tax rate.[1]

» SOLUTION

See Exhibits 13-3 and 13-4 for the complete solution. The following steps are recommended. The pertinent income-tax aspects are considered for each step.

Step 1. General Approach. The inclusion of tax considerations does not change the general approach to these decisions. Review Chapter 12, pages 406–409.

Step 2. Cash Operating Costs and Depreciation. Cash operating costs and their income-tax effects are separated from the tax effects of depreciation. **These could be combined if preferred. However, the treatment illustrated facilitates comparisons of alternative depreciation effects and allows the use of annuity tables for the cash operating costs if they are equal per year.**

In this illustration we assume that any cash receipts or disbursements and their related tax effects occur in the same period. For simplicity, we are neglecting the possibility that some tax payments related to the pretax operating cash inflows of year 1 may not actually occur until sometime in year 2. **The analysis could be refined to account for any possible lags. For simplicity, we are ignoring this possibility.**

Step 3. Disposal of Equipment. In general, gains and losses on disposal of equipment are taxed in the same way as ordinary gains and losses.[2]

---

[1]For computing depreciation, the *Internal Revenue Code* allows a taxpayer to ignore the expected terminal residual value as long as it is not expected to exceed 10 percent of the original cost. Even if intervening inflation increases the residual amount, it will not affect the original depreciation schedule after it is set.

[2]In this case, the old equipment was sold outright. Where the old equipment is traded in on new equipment of like kind, no gain or loss can be recognized for tax purposes in the year of the transaction. Rather, the new equipment is capitalized at the book value of the old equipment plus the cash payment. Any gain or loss is then spread over the life of the new equipment through the new depreciation charges.

Many gains on the sale of specified assets qualify for taxation at the *capital-gains* tax rate, which has a ceiling of 28 percent for corporations. A *capital gain* is the profit on the sale of an asset that is typically not held for resale in the ordinary course of business. Examples of such assets are investments in stocks and bonds, land, and equipment.

Before 1962, gains from disposal of equipment were taxed at the capital-gains rate, 25-percent. Since then, the gain on sale of equipment is not considered a capital gain except in special circumstances. This complication frequently results in having part of the gain taxed at ordinary income-tax rates and part at capital-gains rates. For simplicity, this chapter does not introduce the latter complication. We assume that gains on disposal are taxed at ordinary rates.

Exhibit 13-3 shows an analysis of the alternative dispositions of the old equipment. Disposal at the end of year 5 results in a taxable gain, the excess of the selling price over book value (zero in this case). The cash effect is the selling price less the 40 percent tax on the gain.

Immediate disposal of the old equipment results in a loss that is fully deductible from current income. The net loss must be computed to isolate its effect on current income tax, but the total cash inflow is the selling price plus the current income-tax benefit.

Step 4. Total-Project or Incremental Approach? Exhibits 13-3 and 13-4 demonstrate these approaches. Both result in the same net present value in favor of replacement. Where there are only two alternatives, the incremental approach is faster. However, the incremental approach rapidly becomes unwieldy when there are more than two alternatives or when computations become intricate.

investment tax credit

Managers have a responsibility to avoid income taxes. ***Avoidance* is not *evasion.*** Avoidance is the use of legal means to minimize tax payments; evasion is the use of illegal means. Because income-tax planning is exceedingly complex, professional tax counsel should be sought whenever the slightest doubt exists.

The foregoing illustration deliberately excluded many possible complications. Income taxes are affected by many factors, including progressive tax rates, loss carrybacks and carryforwards, many depreciation options, state income taxes, short- and long-term gains, distinctions between capital assets and other assets, offsets of losses against related gains, exchanges of property of like kind, and exempt income. Special tax incentives should also be considered. These come and go as various legislation is enacted and repealed. For example, most equipment purchases in the United States qualify for an **investment tax credit,** which is an immediate reduction in *income taxes,* typically 10 percent of the initial cost; furthermore, the full original cost, less the predicted disposal value, is nevertheless deductible as yearly depreciation over the useful life.

Consider applying an investment tax credit of 10 percent for our Lindo Company illustration. The effect would be an immediate (ignoring any short time lags) reduction of income taxes of 10 percent of $15,000; therefore, the net present value in favor of replacement would increase by $1,500, from $2,343 to $3,843.[3]

Clarification of role of depreciation

Consider the impact of depreciation on various decision models for capital budgeting, as illustrated by the old equipment in Exhibit 13-3. Study the chart on the next page. Note that the inputs to the decision model are confined to the predicted *income-tax* effects on cash. Book values and depreciation amounts may be necessary for making *predictions.* By themselves, however, they are not inputs to DCF *decision models.*

The following points summarize the role of depreciation regarding the replacement of equipment:

1. *Accrual accounting rate-of-return model.* As Chapter 11 explained, depreciation on old equipment is irrelevant. The total book value is ultimately written off regardless of whether

[3]If equipment is replaced before completing its tax credit life, the government "recaptures" a part of the investment credit. Any expected recapture would decrease the net present value of an asset. The 1981 Act established a new Accelerated Cost Recovery System; it totally abandons the concept of useful life. Five classes of capital assets were created, bearing prescribed short lives of 3 to 15 years. The 3-year class has a 6 percent investment tax credit; other classes, the full 10 percent credit.

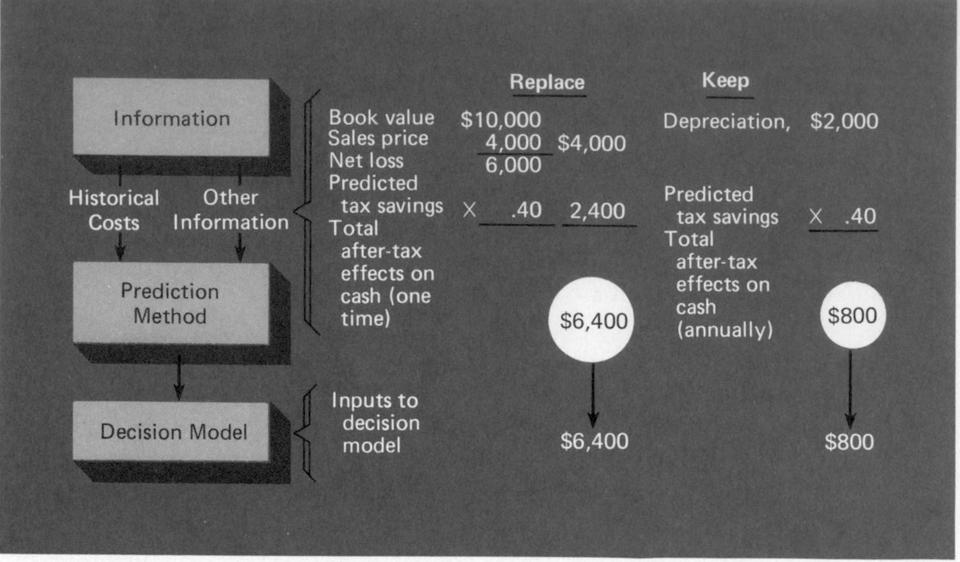

it takes the form of annual depreciation or a lump-sum charge against the proceeds from disposal. In contrast, depreciation on new equipment is relevant because it is an expected future cost that will differ between the alternatives of replacement or no replacement.

2. *Discounted cash-flow model.* Depreciation on the old equipment is irrelevant because it is not a future cash outflow. Depreciation on the new equipment is irrelevant because otherwise the investment would be double-counted. The investment is usually a one-time outlay at time zero, so it should not be deducted again in the form of depreciation.
3. *Relation to income-tax cash flows.* Given the definition of relevance in Chapter 11, book values and past depreciation are irrelevant in all capital-budgeting models. The relevant item is the *income-tax cash effect,* not the book value. Using the approach in Exhibit 11-1 (page 365), the book value and any depreciation charges are essential data for the *prediction method,* but the impacts on expected future income-tax cash disbursements are the relevant data for the *decision model.*

Capital budgeting and inflation

use consistent model

Inflation may be defined as the decline in the general purchasing power of the monetary unit. The degree and volatility of inflation have surged in recent years. Consequently, decision makers face greater uncertainty regarding their predictions of demand, prices, and related factors. Discounted cash-flow models should be correctly adjusted for inflationary effects.

To understand the analysis of inflation, focus on the makeup of the required rate of return, the hurdle rate. The rate can be portrayed as having three elements:

(1) Risk-free element—the "pure" rate of interest that is paid on long-term government bonds

(2) Business-risk element—the "risk" premium above the pure rate that is demanded for undertaking greater risks[4]

(1) + (2) Often called the "real rate"

[4]For example, *Business Week,* February 23, 1981, p. 120, reports that Amfac, Inc., has a "6.9% risk premium investors presumably expect to receive for owning Amfac stock."

(3) Inflation element—the premium demanded because of the anticipated deterioration of the general purchasing power of the monetary unit

(1) + (2) + (3) Often called the "nominal rate" or "money rate"

Reconsider the facts in the example in Exhibit 13-1: purchase cost of equipment, $90,000; useful life, five years; pretax operating cash savings per year, $38,000 (in 19_0 dollars); income-tax rate, 40 percent. For simplicity, assume straight-line depreciation. Also assume an after-tax hurdle rate of 22 percent, which includes a 12 percent element attributable to inflation.

Exhibit 13-5 shows correct and incorrect ways to analyze the effects of inflation. The watchwords are *internal consistency.* Therefore, the correct analysis (a) uses a required rate of return that includes an element attributable to anticipated inflation *and* (b) specifically adjusts the predicted operating cash flows for the effects of inflation.

The incorrect analysis in Exhibit 13-5 is internally inconsistent. It fails to adjust *predicted cash inflows* for inflation. Instead, the predicted cash flows are stated in 19_0 dollars. At the same time, the *discount rate* includes an element attributable to inflation. Note how this analytical flaw may lead to a different decision. The incorrect analysis indicates that the equipment should not be purchased, which is evidently an unwise economic decision.

role of depreciation

Compare the effects of depreciation in the two analyses in Exhibit 13-5. The correct analysis *adjusts* operating cash inflows for inflation, including their income-tax effects. Thus, the taxes are levied on 19_3, 19_4, or 19_5 nominal dollars. However, the correct analysis does *not adjust* the tax effects of depreciation. Why? Because income-tax laws permit a deduction based on unadjusted 19_0 dollars, nothing else.

Critics of income-tax laws point out that capital investment is inhibited by this failure to adjust the depreciation deductions for inflationary effects.[5] For example, the net present value in Exhibit 13-5 would be larger if the depreciation were not restricted to the $18,000 amount per year, which produces a $7,200 saving in 19_1 dollars, then $7,200 in 19_2 dollars, and so forth. In rebuttal, defenders of existing U.S. tax laws claim that capital investment is already encouraged by other means. Examples are permission to use accelerated depreciation (see Exhibit 13-2 in the text), the investment tax credit, and relatively short useful lives.

inflation and feedback

In inflationary times, the ability to predict and cope with changing prices is a valuable management trait, often more valuable than the attainment of sheer operating efficiency. Put another way, inflation tends to boost the importance of price variances, as distinguished from efficiency variances. Auditing and feedback should help monitor management's predictive skills.

The adjustment of the operating cash flows in Exhibit 13-5 is made by using a general price-level increase of 12 percent per annum. Where feasible, however, use specific indexes or other predictions for price changes in materials, labor, and other items. These predictions may bear different percentage changes from year to year.

[5] See C. Nelson "Inflation and Capital Budgeting," *Journal of Finance,* 31 (June 1976), 923–31; and J. Van Horne, *Financial Management and Policy,* 5th ed. (Englewood Cliffs, N.J.: Prentice-Hall, 1980), 130–31. Also see D. Raiborn and T. Ratcliffe, "Are You Accounting for Inflation in Your Capital Budgeting Process?" *Management Accounting,* September 1979, pp. 19–22.

EXHIBIT 13-5 *(Place a clip on this page for easy reference.)*

Inflation and Capital Budgeting

DESCRIPTION		AT 22 PERCENT p.v. factor	AT 22 PERCENT present value	SKETCH OF RELEVANT CASH FLOWS (IN DOLLARS) 0	1	2	3	4	5
End of Year				0	1	2	3	4	5
Correct Analysis (Be sure the discount rate includes an element attributable to inflation and adjust the predicted cash flows for inflationary effects.)									
Cash operating inflows:									
Pretax inflow in 19_0 dollars	$38,000								
Income-tax effect at 40 percent	15,200								
After-tax effect on cash	$22,800								
		.820	$20,931		$25,536*				
		.672	19,213			$28,591			
		.551	17,651				$32,034		
		.451	16,185					$35,887	
		.370	14,864						$40,174
Subtotal			88,844						
Annual depreciation $90,000 ÷ 5 = $18,000									
Cash effect of depreciation: savings in income taxes @ 40% = $7,200		2.864	20,621		$7,200†	$7,200	$7,200	$7,200	$7,200
Investment in equipment		1.000	(90,000)	($90,000)					
Net present value			$19,465						
Incorrect Analysis (A common error is to adjust the discount rate as above, but *not* adjust the predicted cash inflows.)									
Cash operating inflows after taxes		2.864	$65,299		$22,800	$22,800	$22,800	$22,800	$22,800
Tax effect of depreciation		2.864	20,621		7,200	7,200	7,200	7,200	7,200
Investment in equipment		1.000	(90,000)	($90,000)					
Net present value			$ (4,080)						

**Each year is adjusted for anticipated inflation: $22,800 × 1.12, $22,800 × 1.12², $22,800 × 1.12³, etc. Factors are from Table 1 at the end of the book: $22,800 × 1.120, 1.254, 1.405, 1.574, and 1.762. Discrepancies occur because of rounding. For instance, ($22,800 × 1.12) ÷ 1.22 = $20,931, the figure used here; in contrast, $25,536 × .820 is $20,940. The difference is $9.*

†The annual savings in income taxes from depreciation will be unaffected by inflation. Why? Because the income-tax deduction must be based on original cost of the asset in 19_0 dollars.

The correct analysis advocated here expresses predictions in the monetary units (say, 1984, 1985, and similar then-current nominal dollars). This approach is more easily understood because the accounting system routinely generates operating numbers in then-current dollars. In this way, subsequent auditing of capital-budgeting decisions is less cumbersome.[6]

---

[6]Another correct analysis of inflation is to think in terms of "real" monetary units exclusively. To be internally consistent, the DCF model would use an inflation-free hurdle rate plus inflation-free operating cash flows. Using the numbers in Exhibit 13-5, the 22 percent hurdle rate would be lowered to exclude the expected inflation rate, and the $22,800 cash operating inflows of 19_0 would be regarded as the "real" dollars. The latter would be unadjusted in 19_1, 19_2, and so forth.

Provided that the correct discount rate is used, the net present value would be the same under either correct analysis. If continuous price level and interest functions were used, the correct discount rate in this illustration would be 22 − 12 = 10 percent. That is, merely reduce the total discount rate by the rate attributable to inflation.

A continuous function assumes that operating cash inflows occur steadily throughout the fiscal period and that interest is compounded in the same manner.

However, the tables used in this and most textbooks do not use continuous functions. For example, the operating cash flows are assumed to occur at the end of the individual periods. The form of the correct analysis in Exhibit 13-5 for year 1 is:

$$\text{Year 1:} \quad \frac{1.12}{1.22}(\$22{,}800) = \$20{,}931$$

$$\text{Year 2:} \quad \frac{1.12^2}{1.22^2}(\$22{,}800) = \$19{,}213$$

Etc.

Thus, in Exhibit 13-5 the effective discount rate (r) after correction for inflation (the real return on capital) is:

$$\begin{aligned}
1 + \text{Nominal rate} &= (1 + \text{Real rate})(1 + \text{Inflation rate}) \\
1 + .22 &= 1 + \text{Real rate}\ (1 + .12) \\
1 + \text{Real rate} &= \frac{1.22}{1.12} \\
\text{Real rate} &= \frac{1.22}{1.12} - 1 \\
\text{Real rate} &= 1.0892857 - 1 = .0892857 \\
\text{In general:} \quad \text{Real rate} &= \frac{1 + \text{Nominal rate}}{1 + \text{Inflation rate}} - 1
\end{aligned}$$

The correct analysis of real monetary units would be:

P.V. of $22,800 @ 8.92857% for 5 years is	$88,844
P.V. of depreciation is same as before because its future tax effects are unaffected by inflation	20,621
Investment in equipment	(90,000)
Net present value (same as answer in Exhibit 13-5)	$19,465

Also see H. Bierman and S. Smidt, *The Capital Budgeting Decision,* 5th ed. (New York: Macmillan, 1980), pp. 426–33.

This author prefers the 22 percent analysis in Exhibit 13-5 because it is easier to understand and because it provides a planning basis that can be audited in the future in terms of the future monetary units rather than in terms of "real" flows. In this way, the managers may feel more compelled to worry more carefully about predicted inflation rates.

Required rate of return (cost of capital)

focus on risk

The required rate of return (RRR) was discussed briefly in the preceding chapter. You may wish to review that section (page 412) before proceeding. The RRR plays a crucial role in determining the acceptability of an investment proposal. The problem of choosing the RRR is complex and is really more of a central problem in finance than in accounting.

For our purpose, *required rate of return* and *cost of capital* are synonyms. Most theorists in finance agree with the following:

> In effect, each investment opportunity has its own individual cost of capital depending on its risk. So for purposes of evaluating investment opportunities, the *cost of capital* must be interpreted as a set of market-determined opportunity rates that vary with risk. . . . the *cost of capital* . . . and the *market required rate of return* are one and the same.[7]

Capital budgeting would be simplified if all projects bore the same degree of risk. The most frequently encountered approach is to boost the RRR as the risk increases. For example, a petroleum company may use after-tax rates of 6 percent for extending credit to customers, 10 percent for marketing facilities, 16 percent for refining facilities, and 22 percent or higher for exploration and development.

As was discussed in the preceding section, "Capital Budgeting and Inflation," the RRR is the sum of the risk-free rate of interest plus a risk premium. The latter includes all additional risks, including the risk of anticipated inflation.

Of all the methods for dealing with risk, the direct use of probability distributions is likely to grow most rapidly in future practice. This method, which is discussed in Chapter 21, provides managers a straightforward way to evaluate the dispersion of possible outcomes. The RRR is the compensation for taking risks; it will be affected by the nature of the probability distributions.[8]

role of markets

In assessing investment projects, managers should act as agents of the shareholders. Required rates of return are fundamentally related to the maximum rates available in the financial markets. Required rates are the same for all investors. The higher the risk, the higher the required rate.

Above all, managers should avoid the use of a single RRR (unless other means, such as probability analysis, are used to evaluate risks). For example, a chemical company during the 1960s used a single RRR of 12 percent. At the time, the rate on long-term government bonds (the risk-free rate) was 4 percent. The company considered building a chlorine plant, a low-risk venture. The anticipated rate of return was 8 to 10 percent, which was below the RRR of 12 percent. However, the rate was well above returns the stockholders could have earned outside the company at comparable risk. The project was not undertaken:

> The chlorine plant was one of many low-risk reduction projects with returns in the 7 to 10 percent range that were being screened out by the company's 12 percent

[7]E. Solomon and J. Pringle, *An Introduction to Financial Management,* 2nd ed. (Santa Monica, Calif.: Goodyear, 1980), p. 388.

[8]David B. Hertz, "Risk Analysis in Capital Investment," *Harvard Business Review,* 42, No. 1, pp. 95–106; and his "Investment Policies That Pay Off," *Harvard Business Review,* 46, No. 1, pp. 96–108.

cutoff rate. Because these projects were not undertaken, the company experienced over a period of years a drop in its rate of capital investment and a decline in its earnings growth.[9]

The use of a uniform rate for all divisions may lead a company to take larger risks over time without commensurate increases in expected return. Risk-taking divisions may accept projects with expected returns higher than the uniform rate, but lower than they should earn, given the greater risk involved.[10] In contrast, the problem is that some "safe" projects with smaller risks are rejected because they fail to provide a return above the company's uniform stated goal, as shown by the chlorine example above. But some of these projects may produce expected returns greater than the "true" divisional required rate.

divisional rates of return The most extensive survey of company practice concerning RRR indicates an overwhelming tendency to use different rates among divisions or other subunits.[11] A survey question was, How do you set an investment center's target or budgeted return-on-investment (ROI) percentage? The responses follow:

	NUMBER	PERCENTAGE
All investment centers are expected to earn the same ROI	30	7%
Each investment center is assigned its own target ROI based on its profit potential	294	64
Investment centers are not given target ROIs	105	23
No answer or not applicable	30	7
Total	495	101%*

**Because of rounding.*

The majority practice is roughly consistent with modern financial theory. Note also how a budgeted ROI can be adjusted to allow for special circumstances facing a division. In developing target rates within a division, top management would be consistent with modern financial theory by using different rates for different divisional assets. For example, one rate may be used for investments in current assets and another rate for plant assets.

Although the use of uniform companywide rates may be favored in terms of their impact on managers' morale, more and more top managements are recognizing

---

[9]Solomon and Pringle, op. cit., p. 396.

Also see "High Rates Hit Amfac's Planning," *Business Week,* February 23, 1981, p. 120: "But many companies have been slow to adjust their rates. . . . Amfac's reluctance to adjust hurdle rates in 1980 resulted in spending on a department store and a hotel whose returns are now marginal."

[10]James Van Horne, *Financial Management and Policy,* 5th ed. (Englewood Cliffs, N.J.: Prentice-Hall, 1980), Chap. 8, gives a detailed discussion of the finance issues summarized here.

[11]James S. Reece and William R. Cool, "Measuring Investment Center Performance," *Harvard Business Review,* May-June 1978, p. 28. For additional discussion of divisional performance, see Chapters 19 and 20 of this textbook.

that the uniform approach may induce undesirable economic decisions. The firm should be viewed as a collection of different classes of assets whose cash-inflow streams bear different risks.

How should a rate be chosen for a given division? Van Horne[12] suggests trying to identify publicly traded companies that are engaged solely in the line of business of the division. For example, an electrical products division would be matched with a company engaged solely in the manufacture and sale of electrical products. Then the company's cost of capital can be regarded as an approximation of the division's appropriate cost of capital. Frequently, the matching can only be approximate.

Applicability to nonprofit organizations

Discounted cash-flow is applicable to both profit-seeking and nonprofit-seeking organizations. For example, almost all organizations must decide which fixed assets will accomplish various tasks at the least cost. Moreover, all organizations, including governments, have to bear costs of money.[13]

As practiced in the U.S. Department of Defense, uncertainties in quantitative analyses have often been contended with by using sensitivity analysis. In addition, in many analyses three estimates have been used in a procedure called "bop" estimates (for *b*est or most likely estimate, *o*ptimistic, and *p*essimistic). Bop estimates are also frequently used in profit-seeking organizations.

Although DCF models are often used by federal agencies, capital budgeting has been severely criticized. In 1981, the General Accounting Office (GAO) published an accurately titled report: *Federal Capital Budgeting: A Collection of Haphazard Practices.*[14] This report assessed capital budgeting as a tool for analysis and decision making, and it concluded that:

1. Capital items are often the first to be cut when there is a strong push to balance public-sector budgets. Such cuts usually go unnoticed by the public because their effects are not immediately felt by changes in the level of services delivered.
2. Some sections of the nation's physical capital are badly deteriorated. Low priority has been given to major repairs, rehabilitation, and new capital projects.

The GAO studied twenty-four organizations, including four corporations, four cities, four counties, four states, one regional authority, and seven federal agencies. The corporations were American Telephone and Telegraph, General Motors, Boeing, and Republic Steel. Successful capital budgeting was deemed to have several common elements:

---

[12]Van Horne, op. cit., p. 239.

[13]A discussion of the appropriate interest rate to use as a hurdle rate is beyond the scope of this book. Nearly all U.S. Departments must by law use 10 percent; it is a crude approximation of the opportunity cost to the economy of having investments made by public agencies instead of by private organizations. See Bierman and Smidt, op. cit., Chap. 24. Also see R. Anthony and R. Herzlinger, *Management Control in Nonprofit Organizations,* rev. ed. (Homewood, Ill.: Richard D. Irwin, 1980), pp. 292–94.

[14]GAO, P.O. Box 6015, Gaithersburg, Md., PAD-81-19, February 26, 1981. Also see *Business Week,* February 19, 1979, p. 96, which criticized the U.S. Army Corps of Engineers:

> The corps projects unrealistically high traffic volume on proposed new waterways. It also counts as a benefit all the money that shippers save in diverting cargoes from rail to barge. Much of this is not a true economic saving in the cost of transporting goods.

1. Ability to acquire and maintain physical capital even when conditions are adverse
2. Strong link between planning and budgeting
3. Awareness of long-term effects of decisions
4. Incorporation of up-to-date information on the condition of physical capital

The GAO cited the U.S. Postal Service (USPS) as being the best of the federal agencies studied regarding capital budgeting (p. 67):

> Among the analyses USPS uses are return on investment, internal rate of return, and discounted cash flow. The Postal Service also performs a sensitivity analysis. . . . Only the Postal Service conducts follow-up studies to find out if a completed project accomplished its objectives. . . . USPS uses its postaudits to determine the continuing applicability of previous conclusions, to highlight any continuing undesirable trends that warrant management action, to project cost changes through the life of the project, and to compare the results of the project's original economic evaluation.

Administration of capital budgets

The first feature of effective capital-budgeting administration is the awareness on the part of all managers that long-run expenditures are generators of long-run profits. This engenders a constant search for new methods, processes, and products.

Approval of overall capital budgets is usually the responsibility of the board of directors. Depending on the amounts involved, individual projects receive approval at various managerial levels. Requests are usually made semiannually or annually. They are reviewed as they pass upward through managerial levels until they reach a committee that examines capital-budget requests and submits recommendations to the president. In turn, the president submits final recommendations to the board of directors.

Of course, most companies will have a set of forms and a timetabled, uniform routine for processing capital budgets.

When projects are authorized, there is a need for follow-up on two counts. First, control is needed to see that spending and specifications conform to the plan as approved. Second, the very existence of such follow-up will cause capital-spending requests to be sharply conceived and honestly estimated.

Systematic procedures are needed not only to implement capital budgets but to audit the profitability performance of projects. This is *vital* to a successful capital-budgeting program. The comparison of performance with original estimates not only better ensures careful forecasts but also helps sharpen the tools for improving future forecasts.[15]

Net present value or internal rate of return?

Generally, the net present-value and the internal rate-of-return techniques lead to the same decisions regarding the relative desirability of competing proposals. However, some crucial differences in the assumptions underlying the methods may occasionally lead to conflicting rankings of mutually exclusive investment proposals. Exhibit 13-6

[15]For discussions of administrative procedures and audits of performance, see E. Carter, "Designing the Capital Budgeting Process," *TIMS Studies in the Management Sciences,* 5 (1977), 25–42; and J. Schnell and R. Nicolosi, "Capital Expenditure Feedback: Project Reappraisal," *Engineering Economist,* 19 (Summer 1974), 253–61.

EXHIBIT 13-6

				RANKING BY INTERNAL RATE OF RETURN		RANKING BY NET PRESENT VALUE		
							net present value	
PROJECT	LIFE	INVESTMENT	ANNUAL NET CASH EARNINGS	rate of return	ranking	present value of earnings at 10% hurdle rate	amount	rank
A	5	$2,864	$1,000	22%	1	$3,791	$ 927	3
B	10	4,192	1,000	20%	2	6,145	1,953	2
C	15	5,092	1,000	18%	3	7,606	2,514	1

conflict of ranking techniques

illustrates this conflict. (Use tables to check your understanding of the computations in Exhibit 13-6.)

What is the essential difference between these two variations of the discounted cash-flow method? Essentially, differing assumptions are made with respect to the *rate of return on the reinvestment* of the cash proceeds at the end of the shorter investment's life. The two methods make different implicit assumptions as to the reinvestment rate of return.

The internal rate-of-return approach implicitly assumes that the reinvestment rate is equal to the indicated rate of return for the shorter-lived project. The net present-value approach assumes that the funds obtainable from competing projects can be reinvested only at the rate of the company's required rate of return.

unequal lives and reinvestment

As shown in Exhibit 13-6, where mutually exclusive projects have unequal lives, the two methods indicate different rankings.[16] The ranking by internal rate of return favors Project A, but Project C is favored by the net present-value model.

Let us see how these contradictory results occur by visualizing the amount of wealth that will be accumulated at the end of fifteen years. The original investment in Project A will accumulate to more than that in Project C under the internal rate-of-return method, because it is assumed that the *Project A amount at the end of the fifth year can be reinvested to earn a 22 percent rate of return:*

Project A, \$1,000 per year for five years @ 22% will accumulate to 1,000 × 7.740*	\$7,740	
\$7,740 invested @ 22% from the 6th through the 15th year is \$7,740 × 7.305		\$56,541

The 7.740 would be the factor for the 5-period line and the 22 percent column in an expanded Table 3, the amount of an annuity. The 7.305 would be the factor for the 10-period line and the 22 percent column in an expanded Table 1. These lines and columns for the 22 percent rate are not contained in those tables in this book.

On the other hand, the net present-value method assumes that the Project A amount at the end of the fifth year can be reinvested to earn only the *10 percent required rate of return:*

[16]Also, similar conflicting results can occur when the terminal dates are the same but the sizes of the investment outlays differ.

Project A, $1,000 per year for 5 years @ 22% will accumulate to 1,000 × 7.740, as above	$7,740
$7,740 invested @ 10% from the 6th through the 15th year is $7,740 × 2.594 (the factor from Table 1)	$20,078

As long as projects under consideration promise internal rates of return in excess of the required rate, the rate-of-return method has a built-in assumption in favor of short-lived projects such as Project A, whereas the net present-value method has a built-in minimum rate of return that would favor longer-lived projects. If and when we look upon the required rate of return as an approximation of the opportunity rate for reinvestment, the net present-value method should be used rather than the internal rate-of-return method.

How may we reconcile these two approaches? Ideally, the answer is to reject both assumptions as to the reinvestment rate of return and predict a tailor-made rate of return for the time between the termination of the shorter-lived project and the termination of the longer-lived project. In other words, there is a need for a common terminal date and for explicit assumptions as to the appropriate reinvestment rates of funds. Solomon comments:

1. The valid comparison is not simply between two projects but between two alternative courses of action. The ultimate criterion is the total wealth that the investor can expect from each alternative by the terminal date of the longer-lived project. . . .
2. *If the rate of return* is to be used as an index of profitability, then the relevant rate is the per annum yield promised by each alternative course of action from its inception to a common terminal date in the future (usually the terminal date of the longer-lived project).
3. *If the present value* is to be used as an index of relative profitability, the expected reinvestment rate or set of rates should be used as the discounting factor. These rates will be equal to the company's present cost of capital only by coincidence.[17]

The practical difficulties of predicting future profitability on *reinvestment* are greater than those of predicting profitability of immediate projects. But reinvestment opportunities should be considered where they may be foreseen and measured.

equipment replacement

Equipment-replacement decisions are often complicated by unequal lives of competing equipment. One way of approaching the problem of unequal lives is to estimate the disposal value of the new equipment at the end of the remaining useful life of the old equipment. Then a comparison is made only over the remaining life of the old equipment.

Another approach is to compare over the longer time span, including a prediction of replacement cost for the old machine at a later date. In essence, this is the approach described by Solomon above.

Of course, the crux of the problem in replacement decisions is the lack of a realistic common terminal date for both proposals. Thus, some estimate of residual value is necessary, whether the comparison is made over the remaining life of old equipment or the useful life of the new equipment. If new equipment is to last eight

[17]Ezra Solomon, "Arithmetic of Capital Budgeting Decisions," *Journal of Business,* XXIX, No. 2, p. 127.

years and old equipment five years, a decision to retain old equipment implies that replacement will be made in five years. Therefore, if a comparison is to be made over eight years, the future replacement cost (five years hence) of the old equipment has to be predicted and also the terminal value of that replacement at the end of the eight-year span under review. This difficulty goes on and on;[18] the practical answer is to make realistic assumptions regarding residual values at a common terminal date. The common date should be as distant as can be considered with confidence.

reinvestment outlook Capital-budgeting decisions in one year have chain reactions that may affect investment opportunities and availability of capital in future years. Such diverse factors as price-level changes, technological changes, and future investment choices may strongly influence current capital-spending decisions.

For example, in Exhibit 13-6, if investment opportunities five years hence are expected to return less than 15 percent, Project C, which promises a return of 18 percent for fifteen years, may be preferable to Project A, which promises a return of 22 percent for five years. In constrast, if opportunities to invest at 22 percent or more are anticipated in five years but are not available now, the shorter-lived Project A might be more desirable than Project C, even if Project A promised only, say, a 16 percent rate of return. In the latter case, Project C would require a much bigger investment than one would want committed for a prolonged period.

Applications of net present value

Chapter 12 and the preceding section indicated that the attractiveness of a capital project is best measured by discounting at the required rate of return; *any* project with a positive net present value should be undertaken. This is a general rule. Like all general rules, this is subject to qualifications. We shall now see how this rule is applied in various situations.

rationing capital Many companies specify an overall limit on the total budget for capital spending. However, there is no conceptual justification for such a budget ceiling, because all projects that enhance long-run profitability should be accepted. This is the only decision rule that makes economic sense. To the extent that capital rationing exists, it should be a "short-run phenomenon, limiting expenditures only to the current year or two."[19]

There are no hard-and-fast rules to be found in practice regarding the selection of an overall constraint. The net present values (or some similar measure, such as internal rate of return) may strongly influence the overall budget amount. For example, a group of available projects with huge net present values would probably result in a much higher overall budget than would a group of projects with net present values that all slightly exceeded zero.

Other interrelated factors that influence the amount of total funds to be committed in a single year include:

[18]Some writers favor handling this problem by assuming an infinitely continuous replacement cycle. Thus, alternatives are compared by using perpetuity formulas. Although this is conceptually most appealing, it is probably too unrealistic to serve as a practical technique.

[19]H. Martin Weingartner, "The Excess Present Value Index—A Theoretical Basis and Critique," *Journal of Accounting Research,* 1, No. 2, p. 214.

1. Top management's philosophy toward capital spending. (Some managements are highly growth-minded, whereas others are very conservative.)
2. The outlook for future investment opportunities that may not be feasible if extensive current commitments are undertaken.
3. The funds provided by current operations less dividends.
4. The feasibility of acquiring additional capital through borrowing or sale of additional stock. Lead times and costs of financial market transactions can influence spending.
5. Period of impending change in management personnel, when the status quo is maintained.
6. Management attitudes toward risk.

excess present-value index or net present value?

The **excess present-value index** (also sometimes called the profitability index) is the ratio of the total present value of future net cash flows over the initial cash outflow. This index has been proposed by some writers as a means of ranking projects in descending order of attractiveness. If capital rationing does not exist, and if there are no mutually exclusive or indivisible projects, the rankings by index and by net present value will produce the same answers. That is, there is no conflict because all projects will be accepted that have an index of 100 percent or above; these will also have a net present value of zero or above.

However, as we shall now see, conflicts in decisions may be generated if proposals are mutually exclusive, or if certain conditions of capital rationing exist.

mutually exclusive alternatives and budget constraints

Assume that a company is considering two projects that are mutually exclusive—that is, where the acceptance of one alternative automatically results in the rejection of the other. The company can invest in either special-purpose equipment or general-purpose equipment, as follows:

	(1) COST	(2) PRESENT VALUE AT 10% HURDLE RATE	(2) ÷ (1) EXCESS PRESENT-VALUE INDEX	(2) − (1) NET PRESENT VALUE
GP equipment	$1,000,000	$1,400,000	140%	$400,000
SP equipment	3,000,000	3,900,000	130%	900,000

The GP equipment promises a higher return per dollar invested; if all other things, such as risk and alternative uses of funds, were equal, the GP equipment seems an obvious choice. But "all other things" are rarely equal.

Assume that $5,000,000 is the total capital budget for the coming year and that the allocation of resources, using GP equipment for Project A, is as shown under Alternative One in Exhibit 13-7.

Note that the rationing used in Alternative Two is superior to Alternative One, despite the greater profitability per dollar invested of GP equipment compared with SP equipment. Why? Because the $2,000,000 incremental investment in SP equipment has an incremental net present value of $500,000, whereas the $2,000,000 would otherwise be invested in Projects E and B, which have a lower combined incremental net present value of $256,000:

	COST	PRESENT VALUE	INCREASE IN NET PRESENT VALUE
SP equipment	$3,000,000	$3,900,000	
GP equipment	1,000,000	1,400,000	
Increment	$2,000,000	$2,500,000	$500,000
Project E	$ 800,000	$ 912,000	
Project B	1,200,000	1,344,000	
Total	$2,000,000	$2,256,000	$256,000

EXHIBIT 13-7

Allocation of Capital Budget: Comparison of Two Alternatives

ALLOCATION OF $5,000,000 BUDGET								
	alternative one				**alternative two**			
PROJECT*	**investment required**	**excess present-value index**	**total present value at 10%**	PROJECT*	**investment required**	**excess present-value index**	**total present value at 10%**
C	$ 600,000	167%	$1,000,000	C	$ 600,000	167%	$1,000,000
A(GP)	1,000,000	140%	1,400,000				
D	400,000	132%	528,000	D	400,000	132%	528,000
				A(SP)	3,000,000	130%	3,900,000
F	1,000,000	115%	1,150,000	F	1,000,000	115%	1,150,000
					$5,000,000†		$6,578,000§
E	800,000	114%	912,000	E	$ 800,000	114%	Reject
B	1,200,000	112%	1,344,000	B	1,200,000	112%	Reject
	$5,000,000†		$6,334,000‡				
H	$ 550,000	105%	Reject	H	550,000	105%	Reject
G	450,000	101%	Reject	G	450,000	101%	Reject
I	1,000,000	90%	Reject	I	1,000,000	90%	Reject

**Each of the specific plans for the projects listed may have been selected from alternative mutually exclusive proposals. For example, Project D may be for new Ford trucks, selected after considering competing brands. Thus, the capital budget is the crystallization of many "subcapital-budgeting" decisions.*

†Total budget constraint.

‡Net present value, $1,334,000.

§Net present value, $1,578,000.

The example above illustrates that decisions involving mutually exclusive investments of different sizes cannot be based on the excess present-value index (or the internal rate of return, for that matter). The net present-value method is the best general guide.

investment indivisibilities

In general, any ranking procedure by excess present-value indexes or internal rates of return or net present value is an approximation because of investment indivisibilities. For example, assume that five projects are available, as follows:

(1) PROJECT	(2) COST	(3) TOTAL PRESENT VALUE	(3) ÷ (2) EXCESS PRESENT-VALUE INDEX	(3) − (2) NET PRESENT VALUE
V	$6,000	$8,400	140%	$2,400
W	3,000	4,050	135%	1,050
X	2,000	2,600	130%	600
Y	2,000	2,560	128%	560
Z	1,000	1,000	100%	—

Now, if $10,000 is available for capital spending, there are two likely combinations. There might be a tendency to select V, W, and Z and reject X and Y. But this would not yield the optimum answer (see below). Given a budget constraint, it may be wisest to accept smaller, even though less attractive, projects to use the limited funds completely in order to maximize total returns. In our example, the optimum solution rejected Projects W and Z, whose combined excess present-value index and whose combined net present values were less than those of both X and Y:[20]

		ALLOCATION OF $10,000 BUDGET					
		alternative one			alternative two		
PROJECT	COST	cost	present value	index	cost	present value	index
V	$6,000	$ 6,000	$ 8,400		$ 6,000	$ 8,400	
W	3,000	3,000	4,050				
X	2,000				2,000	2,600	
Y	2,000				2,000	2,560	
Z	1,000	1,000	1,000				
Total available funds		$10,000	$13,450	134.5%	$10,000	$13,560	135.6%
Net present value			$ 3,450			$ 3,560	

recapitulation The examples above have demonstrated the weaknesses of the internal rate of return[21] (see Exhibit 13-6) and the excess present-value index (see Exhibit 13-7, for instance).

[20]Integer programming would be the best attack on these difficulties. See Weingartner, "Excess Present Value Index," p. 215. Linear-programming techniques are also helpful in reaching an optimum solution when there are many variables and many constraints. See Charnes, Cooper, and Miller, "Application of Linear Programming to Financial Budgeting and the Costing of Funds," *Journal of Business,* XXXII, No. 1, pp. 20–46.

[21]James H. Lorie and Leonard J. Savage, in "Three Problems in Rationing Capital," *Journal of Business,* Vol. XXVIII, No. 4, have demonstrated a number of weaknesses of the internal rate of return. Of special interest is the phenomenon where *two* rates of return can be calculated for *one* project; this can occur when a project, such as an oil well, may entail heavy outlays at termination date or periodically throughout the life of a project.

The net present-value criterion is the best general rule[22] for choosing projects, whether the complexity involves an overall budget limit, different sizes of outlays, different terminal dates, or mutually exclusive investments. This general rule should be used on an increment-by-increment basis and should be modified where there are investment indivisibilities in relation to a fixed overall capital-budget appropriation.[23]

However, despite the conceptual appeal of the net present-value model, the internal rate-of-return model is widely used in practice. Why? Probably because managers find it easier to understand and because in most instances their decisions would be unaffected by using one model or the other.

The guides above still do not provide answers to some fundamental questions. How do you consider uncertainty? How do you grapple with changes over time in required rates of return? How do you decide on the appropriate required rate of return? These difficulties were considered in an earlier section, but there are no fully satisfying answers. These are subjects of controversy.

SUMMARY

Decisions on types of production equipment are often only remotely identifiable with cash receipts, if at all. Thus, the decision becomes one of cost minimization. A logical approach, especially if there are income-tax complications and several alternative investments available, is to compare all projects, discounting each to the present and choosing the project with the least cost.

The correct analysis in capital budgeting (a) uses a required rate of return that includes an element attributable to anticipated inflation and (b) specifically adjusts the predicted operating cash flows for the effects of inflation.

The required rate of return should vary according to the riskiness of assets, projects, and divisions. The higher the risk, the higher the required return.

Discounted cash-flow models are applicable to both profit-seeking and nonprofit-seeking organizations. The United States government makes extensive use of DCF.

Comparisons of projects with unequal lives necessitate predictions of reinvestment of proceeds of shorter-lived projects and a comparison to the terminal date of the longer-lived project.

Two interrelated constraints for rationing capital are overall funds available and a required rate(s) of return. Capital rationing has no conceptual justi-

[22]Simon M. Keane, "Let's Scrap IRR Once for All," *Accountancy,* February 1974, pp. 78–82, maintains that the internal rate-of-return model is never correct in principle. It is invalid not because of any implicit reinvestment assumption or because of the possibility of producing multiple yields but because a percentage is inappropriate for discriminating between projects of different sizes. And by a series of examples, Keane shows that all projects have different sizes unless they have identical intial outlays *and* cash flows. Keane criticizes the oft-used unequal-lives example because the reinvestment opportunities for the terminal cash flows of the shorter project could be financed independently; thus, they are no more relevant to selection than are the opportunities for reinvesting the intervening cash flows of either project.

[23]For a full discussion, see H. Martin Weingartner, *Mathematical Programming and the Analysis of Capital Budgeting Problems* (Englewood Cliffs, N.J.: Prentice-Hall, 1963).

fication; that is, all desirable projects should be undertaken and the required funds obtained if possible. Under capital budgeting, investment indivisibilities often necessitate juggling project selections to obtain optimum overall results.

Incremental approaches are very useful in checking among multiple alternatives to be certain that each separable investment is earning the required rate of return and that overall funds available are earning a maximum amount.

SUGGESTED READINGS

BIERMAN, H., and T. R. DYCKMAN, **Managerial Cost Accounting,** 2nd ed. New York: Macmillan, 1976.

BIERMAN, H., and S. SMIDT, **The Capital Budgeting Decision,** 5th ed. New York: Macmillan, 1980.

BOWER, J., **Managing the Resource Allocation Process.** Boston: Harvard Business School, 1970.

CLARK, J., T. HINDELANG, and R. PRITCHARD, **Capital Budgeting.** Englewood Cliffs, N.J.: Prentice-Hall, 1979.

GRANT, E. L., W. G. IRESON, and R. S. LEAVENWORTH, **Principles of Engineering Economy,** 6th ed. Salt Lake City, Utah: John Wiley, 1976.

HIRSHLEIFER, JACK, **Investment, Interest, and Capital.** Englewood Cliffs, N.J.: Prentice-Hall, 1970.

SOLOMON, E., and J. PRINGLE, **An Introduction to Financial Management.** Santa Monica, Calif.: Goodyear, 1980.

VAN HORNE, J. C., **Financial Management and Policy,** 5th ed. Englewood Cliffs, N.J.: Prentice-Hall, 1980.

PROBLEMS FOR SELF-STUDY

problem 1

Examine Exhibit 13-2. How would you change the exhibit to accommodate an expected inflation rate of 14 percent?

solution 1

Exhibit 13-2 would not be changed. The tax effects of depreciation are unaffected by inflation. American income-tax laws permit a deduction based on unadjusted 19_0 dollars, nothing else.

problem 2

Examine Exhibit 13-3. Suppose the disposal value of the old equipment was $13,000 rather than $4,000. What would have been the total after-tax effect on cash upon disposal?

solution 2

Selling price	$13,000	$13,000
Book value	10,000	
Taxable gain	3,000	
Taxes paid	× .40	1,200
Total after-tax cash effect		$11,800

problem 3

Examine the correct analysis in Exhibit 13-5, page 448. Suppose the cash operating inflows persisted for an extra year. Compute the present value of the inflow for the sixth year. Ignore depreciation.

solution 3

The cash operating inflow would be $40,174 × 1.12, or $22,800 × 1.12^6, or $22,800 × 1.974, the factor from Table 1 at the end of the book, or $45,007. Its present value would be $45,007 × .303, the factor from Table 2 (22% column, period-6 line), or $13,637.

Terms to Learn

double-declining balance depreciation (DDB)
excess present-value index ***investment tax credit***
straight-line depreciation ***sum-of-the-years'-digits depreciation (SYD)***
tax shield

Special Points and Pitfalls

The role of depreciation in capital-budgeting models is often misunderstood. Be sure to review the chapter section "Clarification of Role of Depreciation."

When interest rates are high, the attractiveness of immediate tax deductions heightens. Therefore, accelerated depreciation should generally be used by taxpayers even if they expect tax rates to increase in future years.

Inflation can easily be explicitly accounted for in a capital-budgeting model. However, expected tax effects of depreciation should not be adjusted for inflation because they are not changed despite inflation.

When dealing with inflation, feedback may highlight management's ability at prediction. For example, if management forecasts a 12 percent inflation rate, the future cash effects can be adjusted accordingly. Later, the results can be compared with such predictions by using the future monetary units rather than the monetary units of earlier years.

QUESTIONS, PROBLEMS, AND CASES

Note: ***Compound interest tables are at the end of the book.***

13-1 "Accelerated depreciation provides higher cash flows in early years." Do you agree? Why?

13-2 What are the two major aspects of the role of income taxes in decision making?

13-3 "It doesn't matter what depreciation method is used. The total dollar tax bills are the same." Do you agree? Why?

13-4 In general, what is the impact of the income tax on disposals of fixed assets?

13-5 "In the case of mutually exclusive investments, smaller profitability indexes may enhance overall economic returns." How?

13-6 "The crux of the problem in replacement decisions is the lack of a realistic common terminal date for both proposals." Briefly describe two practical approaches to the problem.

13-7 "In practice there is no single rate that is used as a guide for sifting among all projects." Why? Explain.

13-8 ***Recapitulation of role of depreciation in chapters 11, 12, and 13.*** A president of a large steel company remarked, "I've read three successive chapters that have included discussions of depreciation in relation to decisions regarding the replacement of equipment. I'm confused. The first chapter said that depreciation on old equipment is irrelevant, but that depreciation on the new equipment is relevant. The second chapter said that depreciation was irrelevant in relation to discounted cash-flow models, but the third chapter indicated that depreciation was indeed relevant."

REQUIRED Prepare a clear explanation for the president that would minimize his or her confusion.

13-9 ***Mining property.*** (W. Crum.) Balek Company develops a mine with expected output of $5,000,000 in sales per year; expected out-of-pocket operating costs of $2,400,000 per year; planned straight-line depreciation and depletion per year of $800,000; income taxes of 50 percent per year. Original cost of the mine and improvements is expected to be $10,200,000. Compute the payback period in years. What does this mean? Compute the payback reciprocal. What does this mean?

13-10 ***Tax impact of depreciation policies.*** The Mayo Corporation estimates that it can save $35,000 a year in cash operating costs for the next five years if it buys a special-purpose machine at a cost of $75,000. No terminal salvage value is expected. Assume an overall income-tax rate of 40 percent and a minimum desired rate of return of 12 percent after taxes.

REQUIRED

1. Assume straight-line depreciation and compute (a) payback period, (b) net present value, (c) internal rate of return.
2. Assume sum-of-years'-digits depreciation and solve for the same three items in requirement 1.

13-11 ***Taxes and depreciation methods.*** Forehand Company has just acquired some specialized machinery for $56,000. This machinery is estimated to have a useful life of seven years and no terminal salvage value. The minimum rate of return desired is 12 percent after income taxes.

The company has always used straight-line depreciation, but its public accounting firm has suggested a shift to accelerated depreciation. However, the company's economist predicts that the overall income-tax rate will probably increase because of a combination of two factors: (1) imminent enactment of a state income-tax law and (2) expected profit increases that will place taxable income in higher federal-tax brackets. The economist fears that accelerated depreciation would waste large amounts of the deduction in the earlier years when the tax rates would be substantially lower.

In order that an enlightened decision may be made in choosing the depreciation method, you have been requested to prepare a comparative analysis of the financial benefits of using the sum-of-the-years'-digits method instead of the straight-line method under each of the following assumptions of average expected overall income tax rates: (a) 30 percent for each of the coming seven years; (b) 30 percent for each of the first three years and 60 percent for each of the following four years.

13-12 ***Review of earlier problem.*** Refer to Problem 11-12. Compute the net present value of replacement, assuming a tax rate of 33⅓ percent and a minimum desired rate of return of 12 percent. Assume straight-line depreciation. (Problem 11-12 is on page 391.)

13-13 ***Approach to income taxes and discounted cash flow.*** The Dudley Company is trying to decide whether to launch a new household product. Through the years, the company has found that its products have a useful life of six years, after which the product is dropped and replaced by other new products. Available data follow:

1. The new product will require new special-purpose equipment costing $900,000. The useful life of the equipment is six years, with a $140,000 estimated disposal value at that time. However, the Internal Revenue Service will not allow a write-off based on a life shorter than nine years. Therefore, the new equipment would be written off over nine years for tax purposes, using the sum-of-the-years'-digits depreciation and no salvage value.

2. The new product will be produced in an old plant already owned. The old plant has a book value of $30,000 and is being depreciated on a straight-line basis at $3,000 annually. The plant is currently being leased to another company. This lease has six years remaining at an annual rental of $9,000. The lease contains a cancellation clause whereby the landlord can obtain immediate possession of the premises upon payment of $6,000 cash (fully deductible for tax purposes). The estimated sales value of the building is $80,000; this price should remain stable over the next six years. The plant is likely to be kept for at least ten more years.

3. Certain nonrecurring market-research studies and sales-promotion activities will amount to a cost of $500,000 during year 1. The entire amount is deductible in full for income-tax purposes in the year of expenditure.

4. Additions to working capital will require $200,000 at the outset and an additional $200,000 at the end of two years. This total is fully recoverable at the end of six years.

5. Net cash inflow from operations before depreciation and income taxes will be $400,000 in years 1 and 2, $600,000 in years 3 through 5, and $100,000 in year 6.

The company uses discounted cash-flow techniques for evaluating decisions. For example, in this case tabulations of differential cash flows would be made from year 0 through year

6. Yearly cash flows are estimated for all items, including capital outlays or recoveries. An applicable discount rate is used to bring all outlays from year 1 through year 6 back to year 0. If the summation in year 0 is positive, the project is desirable, and vice versa.

The minimum desired after-tax rate of return is 12 percent. income-tax rates are 60 percent for ordinary income.

REQUIRED

I. Using an answer sheet, show how you would handle the data listed above for purposes of the decision. Note that you are *not* being asked to apply discount rates. You are being asked for the detailed impact of each of items 1 through 5 on years 0 through 6.

Note, too, that each item is to be considered separately, including its tax ramifications. *Do not combine your answers to cover more than one item.*

Assume that all cash flows take place at the end of each period. Assume that income taxes are due or refundable at the end of the period to which they relate.

Sample Answer Sheet for Problem 13-13

		CASH FLOWS IN YEAR						
ITEM	EXPLANATION	0	1	2	3	4	5	6
1.	*[Allow ample*							
2.	*space between*							
3.	*items]*							
4.								
5.								

II. Total each column. Compute the net present value of the project.

III. Assume an investment tax credit of 10 percent. Compute the net present value of the project.

13-14 ***Multiple choice.*** (CPA, adapted) Choose the best answer for each question. The Apex Company is evaluating a capital-budgeting proposal for the current year. The relevant data follow:

YEAR	PRESENT VALUE OF AN ANNUITY IN ARREARS OF $1 AT 15%
1	$ .870
2	1.626
3	2.284
4	2.856
5	3.353
6	3.785

The initial investment would be $30,000. It would be depreciated on a straight-line basis over six years with no salvage. The before-tax annual cash inflow due to this investment is $10,000, and the income-tax rate is 40 percent paid the same year as incurred. The desired rate of return is 15 percent. All cash flows occur at year-end.

1. What is the after-tax accounting rate of return on Apex's capital-budgeting proposal? (a) 10%, (b) $16\frac{2}{3}$%, (c) $26\frac{2}{3}$%, (d) $33\frac{1}{3}$%.

2. What is the after-tax payback time (in years) for Apex's capital-budgeting proposal? (a) 5, (b) 3.75, (c) 3, (d) 2.

3. What is the net present value of Apex's capital-budgeting proposal? (a) $(7,290), (b) $280, (c) $7,850, (d) $11,760.

4. How much would Apex have had to invest five years ago at 15 percent compounded annually to have $30,000 now? (a) $12,960, (b) $14,910, (c) $17,160, (d) cannot be determined from the information given.

13-15 ***Sensitivity of capital budgeting to depreciation.*** The president of San Juan University, Ms. Martinez, is considering whether to invest $230,000 in some power equipment that will last ten years, have zero residual value, and generate cash operating savings (mostly labor) of $40,000 annually. The minimum desired rate of return is 10 percent per year after taxes.

REQUIRED

1. Compute the net present value of the project, assuming a zero income-tax rate.
2. Assume that Martinez will use the equipment on her farm, income from which is taxable. Compute the net present value (a) assuming a 40 percent tax rate and straight-line depreciation, and (b) assuming a 40 percent tax rate, straight-line depreciation, and an investment tax credit of 10 percent.
3. Repeat requirement 2, assuming sum-of-the-years'-digits depreciation. Use Table 5 at the end of the book.

13-16 ***Replacement of machine.*** (CMA, adapted) The WRL Company makes cookies for its chain of snack food stores. On January 2, 19_1, WRL Company purchased a special cookie-cutting machine; this machine has been utilized for three years. WRL Company is considering the purchase of a newer, more efficient machine. If purchased, the new machine would be acquired on January 2, 19_4. WRL Company expects to sell 300,000 dozen cookies in each of the next four years. The selling price of the cookies is expected to average $.50 per dozen.

WRL Company has two options: (1) continue to operate the old machine, or (2) sell the old machine and purchase the new machine. No trade-in was offered by the seller of the new machine. The following information has been assembled to help decide which option is more desirable.

	OLD MACHINE	NEW MACHINE
Original cost of machine at acquisition	$80,000	$120,000
Salvage value at the end of useful life for depreciation purposes	$10,000	$ 20,000
Useful life from date of acquisition	7 years	4 years
Expected annual cash operating expenses:		
Variable cost per dozen	$.20	$.14
Total fixed costs	$15,000	$ 14,000
Depreciation method used for tax purposes:	Straight-line	Sum-of-years'-digits
Estimated cash value of machines:		
January 2, 19_4	$40,000	$120,000
December 31, 19_7	$ 7,000	$ 20,000

WRL Company is subject to an overall income-tax rate of 40 percent. Assume that all operating revenues and expenses occur at the end of the year. Assume that any gain or loss on the sale of machinery is treated as an ordinary tax item and will affect the taxes paid by WRL Company at the end of the year in which it occurred.

REQUIRED

1. Use the net present-value method to determine whether WRL Company should retain the old machine or acquire the new machine. WRL requires an after-tax return of 16 percent. Round your discount factor to two decimal places before using them.
2. Without prejudice to your answer to requirement 1, assume that the quantitative differences are so slight between the two alternatives that WRL Company is indifferent to the two proposals. Identify and discuss the nonquantitative factors that are important to this decision that WRL Company should consider.

13-17 ***Trade or sell for cash, use of algebra.*** (D. Green) The Kimbark Company has determined that one of its assets is now obsolete. The asset was acquired three years ago at a cost of $550,000. At acquisition, the expected life was ten years, salvage value was set at zero, and SYD depreciation method has been used. Thus, the book value of the asset now stands at $280,000 [$550,000 − ($100,000 + $90,000 + $80,000)].

The new asset is offered for sale at a price of $580,000. Its manufacturer, who deals in both new and used machinery of this type throughout the world, has offered $130,000 trade-in allowance. This is a generous and bona fide offer occasioned by the fact that the manufacturer has a foreign order for an asset of this description.

As the controller of Kimbark points out, the loss on disposition of the asset is not deductible under present tax regulations when it is *traded in* on a new asset. Rather, the unamortized cost of the trade-in plus the additional cash required becomes the tax basis for depreciation of the new asset.

REQUIRED

What is the immediate lowest cash price that Kimbark can take from some other buyer and not be worse off than by trading in? Assume:

1. The depreciable life of the new asset will be five years. There is zero expected salvage value, and SYD depreciation.
2. The relevant income-tax rate is 40 percent.
3. The required rate of return is 12 percent. Round your discount factors to two decimal places before using them.
4. Provisions for recapture of the investment tax credit are not applicable.
5. All cash flows take place at the end of a period.

13-18 ***Inflation and nonprofit institution.*** A university is considering the purchase of a photocopying machine for $3,791 on December 31, 19_0, useful life five years, and no residual value. The cash operating savings are expected to be $1,000 annually, measured in 19_0 dollars. The hurdle rate is 20 percent, which includes an element attributable to anticipated inflation of 12 percent.

REQUIRED

Use the 20 percent hurdle rate for requirements 1 and 2:

1. Compute the net present value of the project without adjusting the operating cash savings for inflation.
2. Repeat requirement 1, adjusting the cash operating savings upward in accordance with the 12 percent inflation rate.
3. Compare your results in requirements 1 and 2. What generalizations seem applicable about the analysis of inflation in capital budgeting?

13-19 ***Sensitivity of capital budgeting to inflation.*** W. Hoverling, the president of a Liverpool trucking company, is considering whether to invest £110,000 in new semiautomatic loading equipment that will last five years, have zero scrap value, and generate cash operating savings in labor usage of £30,000 annually, using 19_0 prices and wage rates. It is December 31, 19_0.

The minimum desired rate of return is 18 percent per year after taxes.

REQUIRED

1. Compute the net present value of the project. Assume a 40 percent tax rate and straight-line depreciation.
2. Hoverling is wondering if the model in requirement 1 provides a correct analysis of the effects of inflation. She maintains that the 18 percent rate embodies an element attributable to anticipated inflation. For purposes of this analysis, she assumes that the existing rate of inflation, 10 percent annually, will persist over the next five years. Repeat requirement 1, adjusting the cash operating savings upward in accordance with the 10 percent inflation rate.
3. What generalizations about the effects of inflation on capital budgeting models and decisions seem warranted?

13-20 ***Inflation and real monetary units.*** As footnote 6 in the chapter explains, an alternate method of analyzing inflation is to think in terms of "real" monetary units. Refer to the data on cash operating savings (only) in the preceding problem. Compute the effective discount rate (r) after correction for inflation, that is, the "real" required return on capital.

13-21 ***Capital budgeting in real monetary units.*** (J. Fellingham) George is considering buying a machine that costs $10,000. The machine will last five years and George estimates that the incremental pretax cash savings from using the machine will be $3,000 annually. The $3,000 is measured at current prices and will be received at the end of each year. For tax purposes, George will depreciate the machine straight-line with no salvage value. George requires a 10 percent *real* rate of return, that is, the rate of return when all cash flows are denominated in 19_0 dollars.

Treat each of the following cases separately.

1. George lives in a world without taxes and without inflation. What is the net present value of the machine in this world?

2. George lives in a world without inflation, but there is a tax rate of 40 percent. What is the net present value of the machine in this world?

3. There are no taxes, but the annual inflation rate is 10 percent. What is the net present value of the machine? The cash savings each year will be increased to reflect the inflation rate, i.e., the cash flow from the machine remains $3,000 per year in terms of 19_0 dollars.

4. The annual inflation rate is 10 percent, and the tax rate is 40 percent. What is the net present value of the machine? *Hint:* See footnote 6 in the chapter. Prepare your analysis in terms of 19_0 dollars. This means that the tax effects of depreciation should be restated for each of the five years. See page 449.

13-22 ***Comparison of projects with unequal lives.*** The manager of the Robin Hood Company is considering two investment projects, which happen to be mutually exclusive.

The cost of capital to this company is 10 percent, and the anticipated cash flows are as follows:

PROJECT NO.	INVESTMENT REQUIRED NOW	CASH FLOWS (INCOME) year 1	year 2	year 3	year 4
1	$10,000	$12,000	0	0	0
2	$10,000	0	0	0	$17,500

REQUIRED

1. Calculate the internal rate of return of both projects.
2. Calculate the net present value of both projects.
3. Comment briefly on the results in requirements 1 and 2. Be specific in your comparisons.

13-23 ***Ranking projects.*** (Adapted from *N.A.A. Research Report No. 35,* pp. 83–85) Assume that six projects in the table that follows have been submitted for inclusion in the coming year's budget for capital expenditures:

	YEAR	A	B	C	D	E	F
Investment	0	$(100,000)	$(100,000)	$(200,000)	$(200,000)	$(200,000)	$(50,000)
	1	0	20,000	70,000	0	5,000	23,000
	2	10,000	20,000	70,000	0	15,000	20,000
	3	20,000	20,000	70,000	0	30,000	10,000
	4	20,000	20,000	70,000	0	50,000	10,000
	5	20,000	20,000	70,000	0	50,000	
Per year	6–9	20,000	20,000		200,000	50,000	
	10	20,000	20,000			50,000	
Per year	11–15	20,000					
Internal rate of return		14%	?	?	?	12.6%	12.0%

REQUIRED

1. Rates of return (to the nearest half percent) for Projects B, C, and D and a ranking of all projects in descending order. Show computations. What approximations of rates of return for Projects B and C do you get by using payback reciprocals?
2. Based on your answer in requirement 1, which projects would you select, assuming a 10 percent hurdle rate:
   a. If $500,000 is the limit to be spent?
   b. If $550,000?
   c. If $650,000?
3. Assuming a 16 percent minimum desired rate of return, and using the net present-value method, compute the net present values and rank all the projects. Which project is more desirable, C or D? Compare your answer with your ranking in requirement 2. If Projects C and D are mutually exclusive proposals, which would you choose? Why?

4. What factors other than those considered in requirements 1 through 3 would influence your project rankings? Be specific.

13-24 ***Choosing among sizes of machines.*** As production manager at the Acme Screw Company, you have been investigating the opportunities for installing a new automatic screw-making machine. An assistant has found that four manufacturers have acceptable equipment, and he has estimated the following data on each. Assume that you can obtain the required funds for any of the proposed machines. Also assume that investment opportunities of comparable risk are available at 12 percent. Which machine, if any, should be purchased? Each machine is mutually exclusive, has a ten-year life, and has zero salvage value.

PROJECT	A	B	C	D
Total investment	$120,000	$190,000	$135,000	$110,000
Estimated annual receipts	45,800	60,500	50,300	41,100
Estimated annual disbursements	21,400	27,000	23,000	18,300

13-25 ***Review: comprehensive, basic problem on equipment replacement.*** A manufacturer of automobile parts acquired a special-purpose shaping machine for automatically producing a special part. The machine has been utilized for one year; it is expected to be useless after three more years. The machine is being depreciated on a straight-line basis for income-tax purposes. It cost $88,000, has a current disposal value of only $29,000, and has an expected terminal value of $6,000. However, no terminal value was provided for in computing straight-line depreciation for tax purposes.

A new machine has become available and is far more efficient than the present machine. It will cost $63,000, will cut annual cash operating costs from $60,000 to $50,000, and will have no terminal value at the end of its useful life of three years. Sum-of-the-years'-digits depreciation would be used for tax purposes.

REQUIRED

1. The applicable income-tax rate is 60 percent. The required rate of return is 14 percent. Using the net present-value model, show whether the new machine should be purchased (a) under a total project approach and (b) under an incremental approach.
2. Assume that a 10 percent investment tax credit is available on the new machine. Recompute your answer in requirement 1. Ignore potential recapture of the credit.

13-26 ***Sale of business, review of chapters 11–13.*** George Weber controls 100 percent of the stock of a company whose sole business is the operation of a huge apartment building on leased land. The lease will expire, and the building will become fully depreciated, in four years. The building is in excellent condition and is fully occupied at favorable rental rates. There has been considerable appreciation in the value of the property. Because depreciation is based on costs of thirty-six years ago—the date of construction of the building—the corporation's taxable income is unusually large. Weber believes that the building and the balance of the leasehold could be sold to Ivan Milgrom's corporation, which is similar to Weber's company. The price would effect a substantial tax advantage to the Weber corporation while still leaving a profitable operation to the buyer for the balance of the four years, when title to the building will revert to the University of Minnesota, the owner of the land. There has been only slight variation in profits for each of the past six years. (Because of a special tax provision, gains on the sale of buildings and leaseholds held more than ten years are subject to income taxes at the capital-gains rate of 25 percent rather than at the ordinary income-tax rate of 52 percent.)

REQUIRED

You are to indicate a proper range of bargaining as to price, based on the averages of the income statements, assuming no change in income, expenses, or tax rates. The sale, if made, would be a cash sale. Ignore any possible relationship between buyer and seller and any residual value of furnishings at the expiration of the lease. Round your discount factors to two decimal places before using them.

1. In this requirement, ignore interest or discount, alternative uses of the funds by either the buyer or the seller, and any other variables.
   a. What is the most the buyer should pay?
   b. What is the least the seller should take?

2. In this requirement, assume that the minimum desired rate of return (the cost of capital) for both buyer and seller is 10 percent per annum.
   a. What is the most the buyer should pay?
   b. What is the least the seller should take?

Average of Income Statements for the Past Six Years

Rental revenue		$1,200,000
Expenses		
Operations	$500,000	
Administration	50,000	
Property taxes	133,333	
Depreciation (straight-line)	100,000	783,333
Income before taxes		$ 416,667
Federal and state taxes at 52%		216,667
Net income		$ 200,000

13-27 ***Review: capital budgeting and inventory changes.*** (M. Wolfson) The Fellingwood Co. is thinking about introducing a new line of jogging shorts. A special machine costing $12,000 must be purchased immediately. The machine would last for four years and would be sold at the end of the fourth year for $1,000. The new product line would also be dropped at that time. The firm's experience with the new product line is expected to be as follows:

	PRODUCTION VOLUME	SALES VOLUME	SELLING PRICE	VARIABLE PRODUCTION COSTS PER UNIT
First year	6,500 units	5,000 units	$5.00	$3.00
Second year	6,500 units	6,000 units	5.00	3.25
Third year	7,000 units	8,000 units	5.00	3.50
Fourth year	3,000 units	4,000 units	5.00	3.75

The selling price is expected to remain at $5.00. Variable production costs are expected to increase at a rate of $0.25 per year due primarily to large increases in the contracted labor rate. Variable selling costs are $1.00 per unit and are not expected to change over the four-year period.

Fellingwood will use straight-line depreciation with no allowance for salvage value for income-tax purposes. Manufacturing costs are deductible for tax purposes only when the finished goods are sold. The firm uses the first-in, first-out inventory method on its tax return. Assume a 40 percent tax rate. Further assume that all operating cash flows, including tax payments, occur at the end of the year. Ignore investment tax credit in your computations. Minimum desired after-tax rate of return is 12 percent.

Absorption costing must be used for income-tax purposes. Therefore, depreciation is applied to the units manufactured by means of a fixed-overhead rate based on the expected production volume, year by year.

REQUIRED

1. Lay out a detailed diagram indicating the relevant cash flows in each period.
2. Compute the net present value to Fellingwood Co. of undertaking the jogging shorts project.

13-28 ***Review: new product; sensitivity analysis.*** (S. Buchin, adapted) As controller of the Buchin Company, John Northrup has just presented the president with his analysis of the proposed addition of a new product, code-named Zim. Northrup summarized his opposition as follows:

Zim should be rejected because it will not earn the minimum desired rate of return of 10 percent after taxes. We cannot sell enough units to break even, even though our marketing people insist that the product can be sold without increasing our sales force.

Zim is expected to be a highly salable product for the next ten years. Our market research department has predicted a sales volume of 45,000 units per year at a selling price of $12. But my computations indicate a breakeven volume of 50,000 units per year:

	PER UNIT
Variable costs:	
Direct material	$ 5.00
Direct labor	2.00
Variable factory overhead at 25% of direct labor	.50
Other costs (using companywide rates):	
General factory overhead at 25% of direct labor	.50
Selling and administrative costs at 1/6 selling price	2.00
Total costs per unit	$10.00

Zim will occupy space that is being vacated by our old product, Yim, which is now obsolete. The new Zim department will incur fixed costs of $100,000 annually. This sum includes $50,000 of annual straight-line depreciation on $500,000 of contemplated new equipment. The equipment is expected to have a ten-year life and zero scrap value. The other $50,000 is composed of supervision, property taxes, heat, and also a generous estimate of various incremental indirect general factory-overhead and selling and administrative expenses.

The breakeven volume is $100,000 divided by $2 contribution per unit, or 50,000 units.

My computation of the breakeven point is conservative in the sense that direct labor could be looked at as being a fixed cost. A special work force will have to be trained. These personnel will not be transferable to other departments and vice versa.

An additional $110,000 will be spent to (a) clean up the area where the new Zim department will go and (b) cover startup and learning costs. This sum can probably be written off immediately for book and tax purposes. Because the $110,000 represents a one-shot expenditure, it has been excluded from the breakeven analysis.

Our total working capital investment will *immediately* increase by about 25 percent of Zim's sales. Because this is fully recoverable as a lump sum whenever we drop Zim from our product line, it too has been excluded from the breakeven analysis.

Last year we spent $300,000 on product development and market research for Zim. Although we have written this off immediately for both book and tax purposes, I think it should be amortized over the first five years of Zim sales. Of course, this would make the picture look even gloomier.

The after-tax effects of the above analysis would decrease Zim's attractiveness. The applicable income-tax rate is 50 percent. As you know, our chairman has insisted that we use the same depreciation method for book, tax, and decision purposes because he feels it is somehow dishonest to "keep more than one set of books."

REQUIRED

1. Appraise Northrup's analysis. Be specific by citing all his points with which you disagree.
2. Prepare your analysis of the attractiveness of the proposal based on an annual volume of 45,000 units. Use discounted cash flow.
3. What volume must be sold to make Zim a desirable investment?
4. Suppose that an investment tax credit of 10 percent of the original cost of new equipment was available at time zero. What would be your answer to requirement 3?
5. Suppose that sum-of-the-years'-digits (SYD) depreciation were used rather than straight-line depreciation. See Table 5 at the end of this book. What would be your answer to requirement 3? Assume that (a) no investment tax credit is available and (b) a tax credit of 10 percent is available.

13-29 ***Conflict of models for decisions and evaluation of performance.*** Refer to the preceding problem, requirement 5. Assume that sum-of-years' depreciation was used for preparing income statements for the performance evaluation of all products. Prepare a condensed income statement for the first year's performance of Zim, assuming that 45,000 units are sold. As the president, would you favor adding Zim to the product line? Why?

13-30 ***Review: capital budgeting and inflation.*** (M. Wolfson) Edwards Corporation is a manufacturing firm that produces and sells a wide range of products. The company not only mass-produces a number of household consumer products but also is capable of producing special-purpose manufacturing equipment to customer specifications.

The firm is adding a new stapler to one of its product lines and is considering building the special equipment that will be required to produce the new stapler.

The special-purpose equipment can be constructed by the firm's own contract equipment department. While the department is currently operating at a level that is normal for the time of year, it is below full capacity. The department could produce the equipment without interfering with its regular revenue-producing activities or incurring any other special setup costs.

The estimated departmental costs for the construction of the special purpose equipment are:

Materials and parts	$ 75,000
Direct labor	60,000
Variable overhead (50% of direct-labor dollars)	30,000
Fixed overhead (25% of direct-labor dollars)	15,000
	$180,000

This $180,000 figure is the tax basis for depreciation. If the equipment is not built, all the fixed overhead would be tax deductible at the end of the current period.

The company feels that the market for the new stapler would last five years. Based on present prices and without adjusting for inflation, the company's estimates of the annual revenue and expenses (excluding depreciation) for producing the new stapler are as follows:

Selling price per stapler	$ 5.00
Variable production costs per stapler:	
Materials	1.70
Variable conversion costs	1.40
	3.10
Unit contribution margin	1.90
Estimated unit volume per year	40,000
Estimated total contribution margin per year	$76,000

Other incremental costs:

Supervision	$18,000
Insurance	5,000
Maintenance	2,000
	$25,000

The special-purpose machine will be depreciated over five years on the sum-of-years'-digits method. Its salvage value at the end of five years is negligible. The company uses an after-tax cost of capital of 18 percent. Its marginal tax rate is 40 percent, and refunds are allowed on negative taxable income. All staplers produced are sold in the same period. Assume that all cash flows occur at the end of the year.

REQUIRED

1. Prepare a detailed table or diagram indicating the relevant cash flows in each period.
2. Compute the net present value to Edwards Corporation of constructing the special-purpose equipment.
3. Edwards feels that inflation will persist over the next five years at a rate of 10 percent per annum. However, the 18 percent minimum desired rate of return already includes an element attributable to anticipated inflation. Repeat requirement 2, taking inflationary effects into consideration.

Cost Allocation in a Variety of Roles

SECTION FIVE

14 Cost Allocation: An Introduction

Cost allocation is an inescapable problem in nearly every organization and in nearly every facet of accounting. How should the costs of fixed assets be allocated to months, years, departments, and products? Accounting for depreciation is essentially a problem of cost allocation. Or, how should the costs of shared services be allocated among departments? How should university costs be split among undergraduate programs, graduate programs, and research? How should the costs of expensive medical equipment, facilities, and staff be allocated in a hospital?

These are inevitably tough questions, so the answers often are not clearly right or clearly wrong. Nevertheless, we shall try to obtain some insights into the pervasive problem of cost allocation—at least to understand the dimensions of the problem, even if the answers seem illusory. The chances are great that you will be directly faced with this problem sometime during your career.

Terminology and general purposes

The terms relating to cost allocation vary throughout the literature and among organizations, so be sure to get mutual agreement on definitions when you deal with allocation problems in practice. **This book uses cost allocation in a *general* sense: the assignment and reassignment of a cost or group of costs to one or more cost objectives. *Allocation* encompasses the assignment of *both* direct and indirect costs.** For example, direct materials may be *allocated* to a department and then to various jobs worked on within that department. Similarly, heating oil may be allocated to the power department and then allocated (reallocated) to production departments. There are other terms that may be used with assorted shades of meaning: **cost assignment** and **reassignment, cost apportionment** and **reapportionment, cost distribution** and **redistribution,** and **cost tracing** and **retracing.**

You are already familiar with the terms *cost application* and *cost absorption,* which have a fairly uniform usage. They are confined to a *special type* of cost allocation, the final tracing of costs to *products,* as distinguished from departments, divisions, territories, or cost centers.

A given cost allocation may be performed for one or more reasons, including the following:

PURPOSES	ILLUSTRATIONS
1. Economic decisions	To decide how to allocate available capacity among products. To decide whether to add a new airline flight.
2. Motivation	To evaluate a manager's performance. To encourage or discourage use of services such as computers, accounting, market research, legal.
3. Income and asset measurement for external parties	To cost products for shareholder and income-tax reporting. These costs may not necessarily coincide with amounts in purpose 1 above; for example, to guide pricing decisions or product promotion decisions, sales commissions may be allocated to specific products.
4. Cost justification or reimbursement	To cost products or services as a basis for establishing a "fair" price. Used in defense contracting, health care, and public utility rate regulations to obtain cost reimbursements.

Ideally, a single cost allocation would satisfy all purposes simultaneously. An example would be the acquisition cost of a direct material such as an airplane engine by an airplane manufacturer. However, the salary of a scientist in a central corporate research department of IBM may be allocated to satisfy purpose 1, may or may not be allocated to satisfy purpose 2, cannot be allocated to inventory to satisfy purpose 3, and, depending on the laws or regulations, may or may not be allocated to a government contract to satisfy purpose 4.

When all four purposes are unattainable simultaneously, the accountant and manager should initially tackle the problem by identifying the purpose that should dominate in the specific situation faced.

The general process of allocation

There are essentially three facets of cost allocation:

1. Choosing the cost objective (the independent variable), which is essentially an *action.*[1] Examples are products, services, processes, contracts, or departments, all of which represent various actions.

2. Choosing and accumulating (pooling) the *costs* (the dependent variable) that relate to the cost objective. Examples are the material, labor, and overhead costs of making a product, as well as the nonmanufacturing expenses of selling and administration.
3. Choosing an *allocation base,* which is a method for specifically linking 2 with 1. For example, direct-labor cost or direct-labor hours are often used as allocation bases for applying factory overhead.

The allocation base is often the key means for developing a cost function that specifically links total costs with cost objectives. The ideal criterion for choosing an allocation base is a cause-and-effect relationship. In other words, the existence of the cost objective should be the dominant factor in causing the incurrence of the costs in question. This relationship is usually easy to establish for direct manufacturing costs such as material and labor. For example, the production of a chair, the cost objective, may be considered the cause of incurring the cost of direct material such as lumber.

Unfortunately, specific causes and effects of factory overhead and nonmanufacturing costs are difficult to pinpoint with assurance.[2] As a practical matter, *relationships* are sought between the cost objective and the cost incurred. The preferable relationship or cost function is one that facilitates the prediction of changes in total costs.

To summarize, there is a "basic principle" of cost allocation for the purpose of economic decisions such as adding or deleting products or choosing volume levels. When economically feasible, allocate costs to cost objectives by using some **cause-and-effect logic** or by using some convincing basis that permits **accurate predictions** of how underlying total costs change in relation to changes in cost objectives.[3]

cost pools and objectives

This and the next chapter will concentrate mainly on the question of how to allocate an **indirect cost pool,** which may be defined as any grouping of individual costs that are not each identified specifically with a cost objective.[4] Costs are most often pooled by departments, but they may also be pooled by natural categories (for example, materials-related or people-related) or by behavior pattern (for example, variable or fixed costs).

---

[1]See Chapter 2 for introductory coverage of cost objectives. For a discussion of the theory of cost allocation, see J. Demski and G. Feltham, *Cost Determination: A Conceptual Approach* (Ames: Iowa State University Press, 1976), especially Chaps. 5 and 6. Also see Y. Ijiri, *Theory of Accounting Measurement* (Sarasota, Fla.: American Accounting Association, 1975), pp. 183–86. A. Thomas, *The Allocation Problem: Part Two* (Sarasota, Fla.: American Accounting Association, 1974) is a comprehensive work on the subject. Also see R. Kaplan, *Advanced Management Accounting,* (Englewood Cliffs, N.J.: Prentice Hall, Inc., 1982) and J. Zimmerman "The Costs and Benefits of Cost Allocations," *The Accounting Review* LIV, No. 3 (July, 1979).

[2]It is an oversimplification to say that there is a single cause-and-effect relationship between cost incurrence and the application base used. William J. Vatter, in "Limitations of Overhead Allocation," *Accounting Review,* XX, No. 2, pp. 164–65, observed: "Every cause has a number of effects; every event arises from many causes; all incidents and observations are bound together by many ties. All costs are more or less interwoven in a complex fabric; in large measure, costs are joint as to their incurrence, as well as to their associations with various costing units."

[3]For a description of how these cost functions might be chosen, see Chapter 24.

[4]Also see Cost Accounting Standard 418, *Allocation of Direct and Indirect Costs,* Paragraph 418.30.

Sometimes cost objectives are divided into "intermediate" and "final" categories. For example, the final cost objective may be a job order. It is "final" in the sense that the accumulated costs are not allocated further except perhaps to the units of product within the job. That is, a job may cost $1,000 for 1,000 units; if 400 are sold and 600 are still held in stock, then $600 of the $1,000 would be allocated to inventory.

The overhead allocated to that job order may arrive there through a circuitous route involving many cost objectives. Consider the salary of the supervisor of the factory building maintenance department. That person's salary may be charged *directly* to the building maintenance department, which is only an intermediate cost objective as far as product costing is concerned. The salary usually becomes a part of a larger grouping of overhead costs—often called an *overhead pool*—that are allocated to two or more subsequent cost objectives:

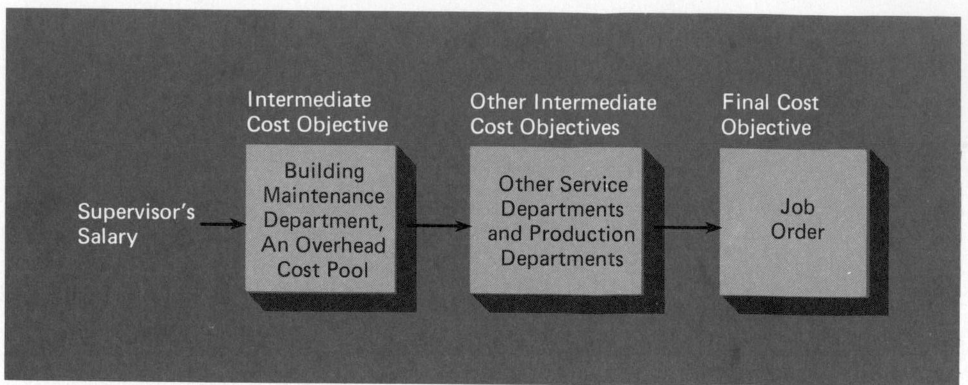

Note that an individual cost usually qualifies initially as a *direct* cost to at least one cost objective, because it can be identified specifically therewith. But the allocation process then proceeds so that costs lose their individuality. They become a part of indirect cost groups, so that subsequent allocations are made of cost pools, not *individual* costs. Thus, the supervisor's salary is not allocated separately to other service and production departments. Instead, the aggregated building maintenance costs are allocated as a group or pool.

cost-allocation base

Given a cost objective and a total cost or cost pool, the problem is to choose a method or function that links the objectives and the costs. Reconsider the boxes illustrated above. How are we to allocate the building maintenance cost pool to other departments that consume the services represented by the pool? In turn, how are we to link the cost pools of other service departments to production departments and finally to products?

The key to the various linkages is the idea of the cost-allocation base, which is a systematic means of relating a given cost or cost pool with a cost objective.[5] The allocation base is easier to explain by example than by clear-cut definition. Direct-labor time is a commonly used cost-allocation base for linking *direct*-labor

[5]An argument could be made that the cost-allocation base, by itself, is an intermediate cost objective. However, *allocation base* is heavily used and generally understood in our literature, although it is rarely defined. For example, the Cost Accounting Standards Board (CASB) has defined many terms, including *accumulate, allocate, cost objective,* and *final cost objective.* The board uses *cost-allocation base* in its pronouncements frequently, but the term is undefined. See CASB Standard 400. If you want to pursue the subject of cost allocation in more depth, begin with the CASB Standards.

costs with cost objectives like departments or jobs as well as for linking *indirect* costs with cost objectives. The cost to be allocated is related to an allocation base that is a common denominator identifiable with the cost objectives in question. To illustrate, the total direct-labor cost and many indirect costs are frequently expressed in terms of the unit of the allocation base as direct-labor cost per hour or overhead cost per direct-labor hour. Then, direct-labor costs and indirect costs are allocated to departments and jobs based on the number of hours (the allocation base) identified therewith.

The next chapter has additional discussion of allocation bases and how to choose among them.

plantwide rate versus departmental rates

Most factories produce more than one product. The variety of products commands varying attention and effort, different material usages, and different production routings. These situations call for refinement of overhead application by departments or cost centers so that different products may bear their related share of factory overhead.

Assume that one job is routed through two departments: machining and finishing. The machining department is heavily mechanized with costly semiautomatic and automatic equipment. The finishing department contains a few simple tools and is dependent on painstaking skilled workmanship. Overhead costs would be relatively large in machining and small in finishing.

Now consider two jobs. The first requires one hour of machining time and ten hours of finishing time. The second requires nine hours of machining time and two hours of finishing time. If a single, plantwide overhead rate based on labor-hours is used, each job would receive the same total-overhead application. But this would probably not be a sufficiently accurate measurement of the underlying relationship, because Job No. 1 made light use of overhead-incurring factors while Job No. 2 made heavy use of such services. Departmental rates, as shown in Exhibit 14-1,

EXHIBIT 14-1

Plantwide Overhead Rate versus Departmental Overhead Rates

	PLANTWIDE RATE		DEPARTMENTAL RATES		
	machining	**finishing**	**machining**	**finishing**	
Budgeted annual overhead	$100,000	$ 8,000	$100,000	$ 8,000	
Direct-labor hours	10,000	10,000	10,000	10,000	
Plantwide rate per DLH:					
$108,000 ÷ 20,000	$ 5.40				
Departmental rates per DLH			$ 10.00	$ .80	
Overhead application:					
Job No. 1					
Labor time, 11 hours @ $5.40	$59.40				
or					
Labor time:					TOTAL
Machining, 1 hour @ $10.00			$ 10.00		
Finishing, 10 hours @ $.80				$ 8.00	$18.00
Job No. 2					
Labor time, 11 hours @ $5.40	$59.40				
or					
Labor time:					
Machining, 9 hours @ $10.00			$ 90.00		
Finishing, 2 hours @ $.80				$ 1.60	$91.60

result in a more accurate linking of overhead with specific jobs when products do not move uniformly through the plant. The plantwide rate in Exhibit 14-1 may mislead managers. They would be inclined to misjudge relative product profitabilities.

Allocation for economic decisions and motivation

some general guidelines

Guidelines should help in deciding how to allocate costs from one department to another. *When feasible:*

1. **Use flexible budgets and standards in all departments, including service departments. In addition, distinctions should be maintained between variable costs and fixed costs.**
2. **Allocate variable and fixed costs separately.**
3. **Establish part or all of the details regarding cost allocation in advance rather than after the fact. For example, use budgeted or standard prices and budgeted or standard hours allowed, not actual prices and actual hours of input.**

applying the guides

Consider a simplified illustration of how to apply these general guides. Suppose there is one service department (electric power) and two production departments in a factory. Here we focus on two major purposes for allocating the service costs: (a) economic decisions concerning the use of electric power and (b) motivation toward optimal usage. The ideal steps for allocation would be the following.

1. Analyze the costs of the service department in detail. Determine which costs can feasibly be regarded as specifically identifiable with the production departments. The most obvious candidates are relatively significant service materials, parts, and some types of labor. But here we concentrate on the allocation of those indirect costs that may be grouped in a variable cost pool and in a fixed cost pool. Suppose the flexible-budget formula for these pooled costs for the next fiscal year is $6,000 monthly plus $.40 per machine hour in the production departments.

2. Allocate the variable cost pool and the fixed cost pool separately.

These main relationships in these first two steps can be depicted as follows:

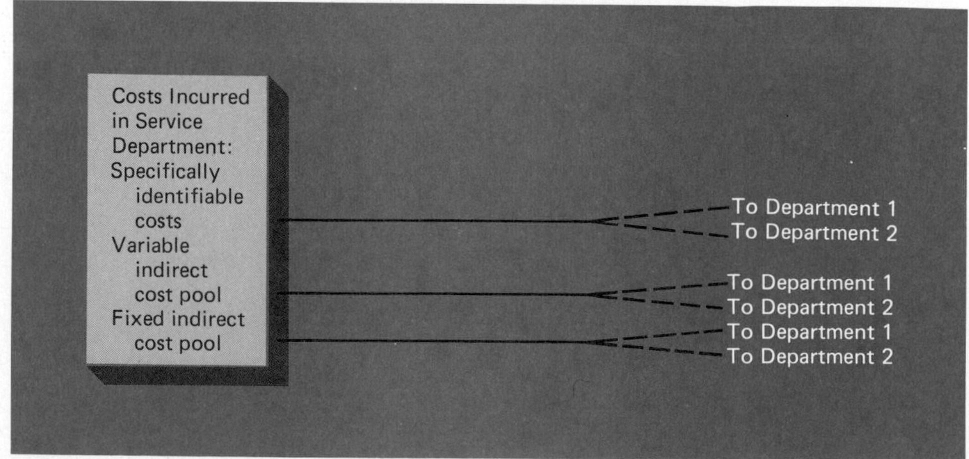

3. Establish allocation procedures in advance.

Steps 2 and 3 will be discussed simultaneously in the following sections on variable cost pools and fixed cost pools.

variable cost pool The preferred way to allocate a variable cost pool is to establish a total amount in advance:

$$\textbf{Total allocated cost} = \textbf{(Budgeted unit price)} \times \left(\begin{array}{c}\textbf{Budgeted or standard quantities}\\ \textbf{allowed for services rendered}\end{array}\right)$$

An allocated cost for a normal repair to machinery might be a flat sum based on the type of work ordered.

In contrast, there may be no standards available for irregular repairs. Such costs might be allocated on the basis of service inputs rendered:

$$\textbf{Total allocated cost} = \textbf{(Budgeted unit price)} \times \left(\begin{array}{c}\textbf{Actual quantities of inputs}\\ \textbf{for services rendered}\end{array}\right)$$

The cause-effect relationship is clear-cut: The greater the quantity of services used, the greater the total variable costs.

Users tend to be tolerant of changes in service material prices and labor rates. However, users frequently lament about the inefficiency of the service department: "If I were managing that service, we'd get improved quality and quantity for each dollar spent!"

To reduce the latter complaints, and to motivate the service manager, services should be rendered so that the consumer (the user) knows the total cost in advance. This practice is especially applicable to routine service. For example, consider the repair of an automobile. The customer is usually given an advance total price based on the repair manager's prediction of the parts and labor to be used. In this way, the customer is responsible for the overall output ordered, but not for variances in unit prices and efficiency. Similarly, in a factory, the total cost allocation can often be based on standard allowed inputs for the outputs achieved multiplied by standard unit prices.

The use of flexible budgets and standards usually helps motivate the manager of the service department to improve efficiency. At the same time, the consuming departments are often protected, at least during the budget period, from intervening price fluctuations and inefficiencies. In our example, the allocation rate would be 40 cents per hour. Wasteful use of coal or oil by the power department would appear as a service-department efficiency variance and would not be passed along to the consuming departments.

Should intervening unit *price* or labor *rate* changes be allocated to departments? If changes are significant and unusually difficult to predict, the answer is probably yes. But the consuming managers hate surprises. They should be informed in advance that such price variances, sooner or later, will affect the final cost allocations.[6]

fixed cost pool **The preferred way to allocate a fixed cost pool is again to establish a total amount in advance:**

$$\textbf{Allocated cost} = \left(\begin{array}{c}\textbf{Budgeted fraction of capacity}\\ \textbf{available for use}\end{array}\right) \times \left(\begin{array}{c}\textbf{Total budgeted}\\ \textbf{fixed costs}\end{array}\right)$$

---

[6]If actual costs are allocated from service departments, some overhead variances in production departments may contain variances of service departments. If desired, detailed variance analyses can disentangle variances caused by service departments and by production departments. See W. Burke, E. Smyth, and J. Macmullen, *Accounting for Management,* 3rd ed. (Sydney: Law Book Company Ltd., 1980), pp. 459–61.

Suppose in our example that the total service-department capacity was originally acquired with the expected "long-run" monthly usage of 60 percent by Department 1 and 40 percent by Department 2. The fixed cost pool would be allocated as follows:

	DEPARTMENT	
	1	2
Fixed costs per month:		
60% of $6,000	$3,600	
40% of $6,000		$2,400

This predetermined lump-sum approach is based on the capacity *available* to the user, regardless of actual usage from month to month. The justification is that the level of fixed costs is affected by long-range planning concerning the overall level of service and the *relative expected* usage, not by *short-run* fluctuations in service levels and relative usage.

Why allocate on the basis of capacity *available* rather than capacity *used?* A noteworthy reason is that short-run charges to a given user are unaffected by the *actual* usage of *other* users. The allocation via budgeted lump sums is more likely to have the desired motivational effects with regard to the ordering of service in both the short run and the long run.

troubles with actual usage

In practice, capacity available is seldom adopted as an allocation base. Instead, actual usage is more popular. In our example, suppose the service department incurred $6,000 of fixed costs in a given month. Suppose also that fixed costs are allocated in proportion to the actual hours used by the consuming departments.

Compare the allocations if the departments vary their usage from month to month:

	ALLOCATION BASE	
	capacity available	**capacity used**
If 10,000 hours are used:		
Department 1, use 6,000 hrs.	$3,600	$3,600
Department 2, use 4,000 hrs.	2,400	2,400
Department 1, use 5,000 hrs.	3,600	3,000*
Department 2, use 5,000 hrs.	2,400	3,000
If 8,000 hours are used:		
Department 1, use 5,000 hrs.	3,600	3,750†
Department 2, use 3,000 hrs.	2,400	2,250

**$6,000 ÷ 10,000 hrs. = $.60 per hour.*
†$6,000 ÷ 8,000 hrs. = $.75 per hour.

The three tabulations demonstrate that allocations based on capacity available result in the same total charges for fixed costs month after month. In contrast, volatility in charges may easily arise if allocations are based on capacity used.

In effect, the fixed costs become variable costs to the user department. Moreover, the rate charged per hour is difficult to predict.

In particular, consider the final two tabulations. Department 1 has done nothing differently. It has used 5,000 hours in each case, but it must bear higher costs of \$3,750 − \$3,000 = \$750, an increase of 25 percent. **Its short-run costs are dependent on what *other* consumers have used, as well as its own actions.**

The allocation of fixed costs based on actual usage can have undesirable motivational effects and can induce erroneous economic decisions regarding the utilization of idle capacity. For example, if uncertain about possible boosts in fixed-costs allocations, the manager of Department 1 might be less likely to accept marginally profitable short-run business.

getting accurate predictions

If fixed costs are allocated on the basis of long-run commitments or plans, some managers will be tempted to underestimate their planned usage. In this way, they will be allocated a lower fraction of the total costs. Top management can counteract these tendencies by systematically comparing actual usage with planned usage. Such feedback is likely to keep future predictions more honest.

In some organizations there are clear-cut rewards in the form of salary increases and promotions for managers who are accurate forecasters. In addition, some cost-allocation methods include penalties for underpredictions. For instance, suppose the manager of Department 2 predicts the usage of 4,000 hours and then demands 6,000 hours. The manager either may not get the power at all or may have to pay a premium price for every hour beyond 4,000.

Allocations to outputs

application to goods and services

Until this point, we have focused on cost allocations from one department to another department. The next step is to allocate (apply) department costs to the final outputs, however defined. Outputs may be products, such as desks and chairs, or they may be services, such as health care:

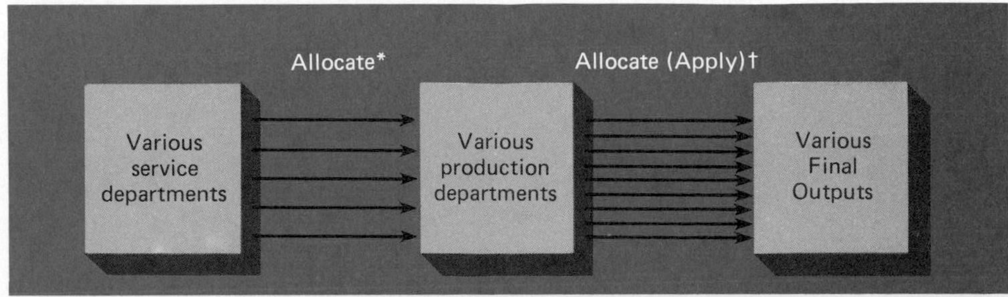

*Might also be called reallocate because costs might have been previously allocated.
†"Apply" usually means allocation to a "final" cost objective, such as a product or service generally destined for customers.

The arrows in the diagram could go in assorted directions. **Service departments support one another plus a few or all production departments.** For example, an accounting department usually serves a personnel department, and vice versa. Some service departments may sell a few services directly to outsiders. For example, a university building and grounds department may bill outsiders for setting up tables for a luncheon held on the campus but sponsored by an outside group.

Allocations to outputs often satisfy all four purposes simultaneously: economic decisions, motivation, income and inventory determination, and cost justification. For example, regulatory agencies routinely specify how hospitals must allocate costs to justify reimbursement. These allocations, rightly or wrongly, then affect decisions, motivation, and income measurement.

service-department allocations

The costs of service departments ultimately find their way to production departments. Assume, for example, that a company has four departments. The two service departments are general factory administration and repair. The two production departments are machining and assembly. Overhead costs are budgeted on a flexible basis and are accumulated by department responsibility for control purposes. For product-costing purposes, the service department costs are sooner or later allocated to those production departments. **The allocation base is the common denominator that best measures the services rendered to the other service and production departments.** The data for our example follow:

	SERVICE DEPARTMENTS		PRODUCTION DEPARTMENTS		
	general factory administration	**repair**	**machining**	**assembly**	TOTAL
Predicted overhead costs before allocation of service-department costs to production departments	$600,000	$116,000	$400,000	$200,000	$1,316,000
Proportions of service furnished:					
By General Factory Administration: (based on total labor-hours):					
Total labor-hours		24,000	12,000	36,000	72,000
Proportion		2/6	1/6	3/6	6/6
By Repair: (based on repair-hours worked for each department):					
Repair-hours	2,000		16,000	2,000	20,000
Proportion	1/10		8/10	1/10	10/10

To keep the illustrations manageable, no distinctions will be made between variable and fixed costs. Instead, total costs will be allocated, using one allocation base for each service department. **Three allocation methods will be shown: *direct, step-down,* and *reciprocal.*** These methods have the following four common phases:

1. Prepare budgets for each department.
2. Choose allocation bases.
3. Allocate (reallocate) service-department costs.
4. Allocate (apply) the total production-department costs to the final products or services.

EXHIBIT 14-2

Direct Method of Allocation

	DEPARTMENT				
	general factory administration	**repair**	**machining**	**assembly**	TOTAL
Predicted overhead costs before allocation of service-department costs to production departments	$600,000	$116,000	$400,000	$200,000	$1,316,000
Allocation:					
General Factory Administration (¼, ¾)*	($600,000)		150,000	450,000	
Repair (8/9, 1/9)†		($116,000)	103,111	12,889	
Total overhead of producing departments			$653,111	$662,889	$1,316,000
Computation of predetermined overhead rates for product-costing purposes:					
Divide by machine-hours			40,000		
Divide by direct-labor hours				30,000	
Rate			$ 16.328	$ 22.096	

**Base is (12,000 + 36,000), or 48,000 hours; 12,000 ÷ 48,000 = ¼; 36,000 ÷ 48,000 = ¾.*
†Base is (16,000 + 2,000), or 18,000 hours; 16,000 ÷ 18,000 = 8/9; 2,000 ÷ 18,000 = 1/9.

direct allocation method **Direct allocation, or some similar method, is the most widely used method for allocation of service-department costs.** This method ignores any service rendered by one service department to another; it allocates each service department's total costs directly to the producing departments. Note in Exhibit 14-2 that this method ignores the service rendered by the general factory administration department to the repair department and also the service rendered by repair to general factory administration. The base used for allocation of general factory administration costs is the 48,000 total labor-hours worked in the producing departments. Distinguish between *total* labor-hours (which includes indirect hours, such as the 24,000 hours of service provided to repair by general factory administration) and *direct*-labor hours. Total labor-hours might be used as the base for allocations of service-department costs, whereas direct-labor hours are often used as the base for developing predetermined overhead rates in producing departments for product-costing purposes.

step-down allocation method Many companies use the **step-down method** (sometimes called the **step** or **sequential** method) of allocation, which recognizes services rendered by service departments to other service departments. Indeed, hospitals *must* use the step-down method to justify reimbursement from health-care agencies. This method is more complicated because a sequence of allocations must be chosen. **The sequence typically begins with the department that renders service to the greatest number of other service departments;[7] the sequence continues in step-by-step fashion and ends with the allocation**

[7] If there is a tie, the department with the greater total cost becomes next in the sequence.

of costs of the service department that renders service to the least number of other departments. Thus, departments such as building and grounds or personnel, would be allocated earlier than would production control or repair.

Exhibit 14-3 shows the step-down method. Note that General Factory Administration costs are allocated to the other service department as well as to the producing departments. Note also that, after the first department's costs are allocated, repair costs include a share of such costs. The new total for repair is then allocated to *subsequent* departments only. **Once a service department's costs have been allocated, no subsequent service-department costs are recirculated back to it.**

Note further that *in this case* the overhead rates for product-costing purposes are significantly different under the two methods. For example, the machine-hour rate is $16.328 under the direct method and $19.522 under the step-down method. Note also that Machining's rate is higher under the step-down method while Assembly's rate is lower. If the data-processing costs are not too different between allocation methods, the step-down method would be preferable in a case like this, because it recognizes the service rendered to Repair by General Factory Administration, whereas the direct method ignores this relationship. However, as always, the choice of an allocation method is a cost-benefit decision. The illustrated discrepancy in product costs may have infinitesimal decision consequences in some situations, but it may have substantial consequences in situations involving pricing or product choice. Also, cost-reimbursement contracts such as those for defense industries, universities, and hospitals would obviously be affected.

reciprocal allocation method

The reciprocal method allocates costs by explicitly including the mutual services rendered among all departments. The reciprocal method is also called the **cross-allocation** method, the **matrix method,** and the **double-distribution method.** The

EXHIBIT 14-3

Step-Down Method of Allocation

	DEPARTMENT				
	general factory administration	**repair**	**machining**	**assembly**	TOTAL
Predicted overhead costs before allocation of service-department costs to production departments	$600,000	$116,000	$400,000	$200,000	$1,316,000
Allocation:					
General Factory Administration (2/6, 1/6, 3/6)	($600,000)	200,000	100,000	300,000	
Repair (8/9, 1/9)		($316,000)	280,889	35,111	
Total overhead of producing departments			$780,889	$535,111	$1,316,000
Computation of predetermined overhead rates for product-costing purposes:					
Divide by machine-hours			40,000		
Divide by direct-labor hours				30,000	
Rate			$ 19.522	$ 17.837	

direct method and the step-down method are not theoretically accurate if service departments render services to one another reciprocally. For example, the factory administration department serves the employees of the building and grounds department, while the factory administration department occupies some floor space and has janitorial attention. If reciprocal services between service departments are significant, elaborate schemes of allocation involving simultaneous equations may be adopted. Ordinarily, however, the step-down method (a simpler model) will yield final charges to the producing departments that are acceptable approximations of the results that would come from the more complex model. But digital computers now facilitate the computations, so we may expect an increasing use of the reciprocal method.

The use of linear algebra may occasionally make a difference in decisions. For example, suppose that the conditions in Exhibit 14-4 exist. The repair department serves the power department and vice versa. Note that a step-down method of allocation may produce answers significantly different from those by the linear algebra method, using the simultaneous equations at the bottom of the exhibit. Linear algebra is the most theoretically defensible method. For example, suppose the company had the opportunity to buy its power outside for $16,500. The step-down method used in Exhibit 14-4 shows a power cost of $16,000, but the linear algebra method shows a power cost of $17,391. In this make-or-buy decision, the cost-allocation method may indeed be an influential difference.

When should the reciprocal method be used? If management is using the results of allocations to make decisions on pricing products, on internal or external purchasing of services, on setting levels of output, and on related activities, the results of step-down allocations should be periodically tested against the results obtained by the reciprocal method. If the decisions are not sensitive to the results of the algebraic computations, then the simpler methods are adequate.

The example in Exhibit 14-4 used only two service departments and two production departments. This required the use of two simultaneous equations.[8] Of course, in practice, many more simultaneous equations may be required. A generalized approach for solving large systems of equations is provided by matrix algebra.[9]

---

[8]Several alternative explanations of reciprocal allocations are possible, although there is always some confusion regarding why the equations in Exhibit 14-4 produce results for R and P ($36,957 + $17,391 = $54,348) that exceed the total of $30,000 + $10,000 = $40,000 to be allocated. This phenomenon occurs because the allocations are *simultaneous.* The *final* total allocation to the production departments is $40,000, not $54,348. Some observers prefer to label the $36,957 and the $17,391 as "artificial" rather than "total" costs of R and P. R. Kaplan, *Advanced Management Accounting,* Chapter 11, says, "While not obvious, it does work out that the sum of allocated costs to production departments equals the sum of traceable service department costs."

Kaplan pursues this topic in more depth. He points out that a service department also often provides service to itself. For example, a personnel department has to hire and supervise its own personnel. Kaplan maintains that it is important that self-service costs be explicitly recognized and included in the analysis.

[9]See Neil C. Churchill, "Linear Algebra and Cost Allocations: Some Examples," *Accounting Review,* XXXIV, No. 4, pp. 894–904; and Rene P. Manes, "Comment on Matrix Theory and Cost Allocation," *Accounting Review,* XL, No. 3, pp. 640–43. Robert S. Kaplan, "Variables and Self-Service Costs in Reciprocal Allocation Models," *Accounting Review,* XLVIII, No. 4 (October 1973), 738–48, stresses the decision-making implications of reciprocal services and evaluates various approaches to allocation. Also see John K. Shank, *Matrix Methods in Accounting* (Reading, Mass.: Addison-Wesley, 1972), pp. 35–40.

EXHIBIT 14-4

(Place a clip on this page for easy reference.)

Comparison of Step-Down Method and Method Using Linear Algebra
(Data Assumed)

	SERVICE DEPARTMENTS		PRODUCTION DEPARTMENTS	
	repair	**power**	**machining**	**assembly***
Hours of repair service used		1,000	3,000	1,000
Percentage of service		20%	60%	20%
Units of power consumed	4,000		2,000	4,000
Percentage of service	40%		20%	40%
Allocation using step-down method:				
Total relevant department costs before allocation of service department costs to production departments	$30,000	$10,000	$ —§	$ —§
Repairs (allocated first†)	(30,000)	6,000	18,000	6,000
Power department		(16,000)	5,333	10,667
Relevant costs after allocation	$ 0	$ 0	$23,333	$16,667
Allocation using reciprocal method‡:				
Relevant costs before allocation	$30,000	$10,000	$ —	$ —
Repairs	(36,957)	7,391	22,174	7,392
Power	6,957	(17,391)	3,477	6,957
Relevant costs after allocation	$ 0	$ 0	$25,651	$14,349

**Heavily automated with modern equipment.*

†Some companies might prefer to allocate power first. You may wish on your own to allocate power first to see how the results compare with the "ideal" results under the reciprocal method. More repair money is spent in the power department than vice versa ($6,000 vs. $4,000).

‡The following equations represent the essence of the linear algebra method. In this case, two simultaneous equations are used to find the value of two unknowns:

Let R = total costs of repair department
P = total costs of power department
(1) $R = \$30,000 + .4P$
(2) $P = \$10,000 + .2R$
Substituting in (1): $R = \$30,000 + .4(\$10,000 + .2R)$
$R = \$30,000 + \$4,000 + .08R$
$.92R = \$34,000$
$R = \$36,957$[a]
Substituting in (2): $P = \$10,000 + .2(\$36,957) = \$17,391$[a]

§The production departments have other costs not shown here. In this way, we focus on the allocation of service-department costs only.

[a]Instead of using equations, we could obtain the same results by using successive rounds of reducing-amount computations.

Amounts before allocation of service department costs	*$30,000.00*	*$10,000.00*
20% of $30,000		*6,000.00*
Total		*$16,000.00*
40% of $16,000	*6,400.00*	
20% of $6,400		*1,280.00*
40% of $1,280	*512.00*	
20% of $512		*102.40*
40% of $102.40	*40.96*	
20% of $40.96		*8.19*
40% of $8.19	*3.28*	
20% of $3.28		*.66*
Totals as above	*$36,956.24*	*$17,391.25*

further illustration of allocation

A more comprehensive illustration is displayed in Exhibit 14-5. Although it contains more detail, Exhibit 14-5 provides a useful overview of cost allocation:

1. Prepare departmental budgets. (Lines 1–12)
2. Choose allocation bases. (Lines 19–23)
3. Allocate (reallocate) service-department costs to production departments, using the step-down method (or the direct method or the reciprocal method). (Lines 13–16)
4. Allocate (apply) the total costs to products. (Lines 17–18)

Lines 1–11 provide the details of the department-overhead budgets, including the cost-allocation bases. The total overhead on line 12 is then allocated, using the step-down method. Repair and Maintenance Department costs are allocated first because they render more service to Building and Grounds than the latter renders to Repair and Maintenance.

Lines 20–22 of Exhibit 14-5 show two computation techniques for allocation. Building and Grounds is allocated on the basis of the departmental percentage of total square footage. An alternative method would be to develop a rate per square foot, as shown on line 21. Then the square footage in each department would be multiplied by the rate. The two calculations are logically identical, and they give the same results. Personal preference determines the arithmetical method used in a specific case.

Besides demonstrating how service-department costs are allocated, Exhibit 14-5 also illustrates how predetermined overhead application rates for the production departments are developed. The bases used in this illustration are standard direct-labor hours in each department. Note that product-costing rates are used only for production departments because products flow only through those departments.

SUMMARY

Costs are allocated for four major purposes: (1) predicting the economic effects of decisions, (2) motivation, (3) income and asset measurement for external parties, and (4) cost justification or reimbursement. When issues arise, a good place to begin is with the question, What is the dominant purpose of the cost allocation in this particular instance?

There are essentially three facets of cost allocation: (1) choosing the cost objective (some action or activity), (2) choosing how to accumulate or pool costs, and (3) choosing the allocation base that relates the two. These three choices should be made simultaneously because they are interdependent.

For purposes of guiding economic decisions and motivation, where feasible, variable costs should be allocated by using predetermined rates for the services *used.* Fixed costs should be allocated by using predetermined lump sums for providing a basic *capacity to serve.* Beware of allocating fixed costs on the basis of actual usage.

Three major methods are used to allocate service-department costs to other departments: direct, step-down, and reciprocal. The last is the most defensible, but the step-down method is widely approved for cost reimbursement by regulatory agencies.

EXHIBIT 14-5

Sample Company

Factory-Overhead Budget: Step-Down Method of Allocation for Application to Product for the Year Ended December 31, 19_1 (Lines 1–17 are in thousands)

	SERVICE DEPARTMENTS			PRODUCTION DEPARTMENTS			
LINE	repair and maintenance	building and grounds	factory administration	machining	assembly	finishing	total
1 Indirect labor (direct to departments [payroll analysis or work tickets])	$ 400	$ 960	$2,200	$ 4,900	$1,000	$ 360	$ 9,820
2 Supplies (direct to departments [requisitions])	640	700	240	3,500	400	1,400	6,880
3 Power (meters or horsepower ratings)	130	1,600	25	1,800	200	500	4,255
4 Payroll taxes (department payrolls)	200	50	200	1,300	300	100	2,150
5 Overtime premium (department payrolls)	100	—	60	600	140	50	950
6 Rework (direct to responsible department)	—	—	—	300	150	40	490
7 Fuel	—	100	—	—	—	—	100
8 Total variable overhead	$1,470	$3,410	$2,725	$12,400	$2,190	$2,450	$24,645
9 Property taxes and insurance	140	770	760	600	100	100	2,470
10 Depreciation	150	700	300	2,300	400	300	4,150
11 Supervision and miscellaneous	700	220	4,015	1,800	1,010	550	8,295
12 Total department-overhead budgets before allocation of service-department costs to production departments	$2,460	$5,100	$7,800	$17,100	$3,700	$3,400	$39,560

Allocation of service-department costs (see Note A):							
13 Repair and maintenance (maintenance service, current month)	$2,460	492	25	1,476	246	221	
14 Building and grounds (square footage occupied)		$5,592	559	3,355	1,119	559	
15 Factory administration (direct-labor hours)*			$8,384	6,708	838	838	
16 Total production-department overhead				$28,639	$5,903	$5,018	$39,560
17 Application bases—budgeted standard direct-labor hours				2,400	300	300	
18 Predetermined overhead rate per standard direct-labor hour				$11,933	$19,677	$16,727	
Note A: Allocation bases:							
19 Repair and maintenance, based on specific maintenance service	100%	20%	1%	60%	10%	9%	
20 Building and grounds, based on square footage in each department			100,000	600,000	200,000	100,000	1,000,000
21 Using rate method, $5,592,000 ÷ 1,000,000 sq. ft. = $5.592 per sq. ft. or (5.592 × 100,000), (5.592 × 600,000), (5.592 × 200,000), (5.592 × 1,000,000)							
22 Percentages based on square footage		100%	10%	60%	20%	10%	
23. Factory administration, based on direct-labor hours			100%	80%	10%	10%	

**Other possible bases might be number of employees or total labor-hours, or total costs excluding factory administration, or any measure that best represents the activity being managed.*

PROBLEM FOR SELF-STUDY

problem

Review the example in the section "Allocation for Economic Decisions and Motivation." Recall that the service department has a flexible-budget formula of $6,000 monthly plus $.40 per machine-hour. Moreover, fixed costs are allocated on a lump-sum basis, 60 percent to Department 1 and 40 percent to Department 2. Variable costs are allocated at the budgeted unit rate of $.40 per machine-hour.

1. Assume that the actual costs coincided exactly with the flexible-budgeted amount. Departments 1 and 2 each worked at 4,000-hour levels. Tabulate the allocations of all costs.
2. Assume the same facts as in part 1 except that the fixed costs were allocated on the basis of actual hours rather than capacity available. Tabulate the allocations of all costs. As the manager of Department 2, would you prefer the method in part 1 or in part 2? Why?
3. Suppose the service department had inefficiencies at an 8,000-hour level, incurring costs that exceeded budget by $800. How would this change your answers in parts 1 and 2? Be specific.

solution

1.

	DEPARTMENT 1	DEPARTMENT 2
Variable costs at $.40 per hour		
4,000 × $.40	$1,600	
4,000 × $.40		$1,600
Fixed costs:		
60% of $6,000	3,600	
40% of $6,000		2,400
Total costs, $9,200*	$5,200	$4,000

**Check: $6,000 per month plus $.40(8,000) = $9,200.*

2.

	1	2
Variable costs, as in part 1	$1,600	$1,600
Fixed costs, 4,000 hours each at $.75†	3,000	3,000
Total costs, $9,200	$4,600	$4,600

†Fixed-cost allocation rate: $6,000 ÷ 8,000 = $.75 per hour

The manager of Department 2 would prefer method 1 in part 1 because it insulates Department 2 from short-run fluctuations in costs caused by other users. The department had operated exactly in accordance with the long-range plan of 4,000 hours. Still, Department 2 is bearing an extra $600 (25 percent more fixed costs than in part 1) because of what *another* consumer is using.

3. If the extra $800 is allocated, the answers in parts 1 and 2 would be increased by $400 in each department. If not allocated, the answers would be unaffected. The justification for not allocating is found in responsibility accounting: The costs of inefficiency should remain charged to the manager who is in the best position to influence them.

Terms to Learn

cost allocation ***cost-allocation base*** ***cost apportionment***
cost assignment ***cost distribution*** ***cost pool*** ***cost reallocation***
cost reapportionment ***cost reassignment*** ***cost redistribution***
cost retracing ***cost tracing*** ***cross-allocation method***
direct allocation method ***double-distribution allocation method***

indirect cost pool   ***matrix allocation method***
reciprocal allocation method   ***sequential allocation method***
step allocation method   ***step-down allocation method***

Special Points and Pitfalls

The problem of cost allocation is closely tied to the problems discussed in Chapters 9 and 24, which concentrate on various patterns of cost behavior such as variable, fixed, and mixed. Management invests in a cost-allocation system. Such a system may be helpful or harmful, depending on how alert managers and accountants are to the basic concepts regarding choices of cost objectives, cost pools, and cost-allocation bases.

Again and again, this book has stressed that erroneous decisions are likely to occur if costs are assumed to be variable when they are really fixed. Managers should be especially on guard regarding cost allocations that transform fixed costs in one department into variable costs in a succeeding department.

QUESTIONS, PROBLEMS, AND CASES

14-1 "A given cost allocation may be performed for one or more purposes." List at least three purposes.

14-2 "There are essentially three facets of cost allocation." What are they?

14-3 What is a cost pool? Give an example.

14-4 Give four examples of cost objectives.

14-5 What is the major reason for having a cost-allocation base?

14-6 What is the most important criterion for selecting an overhead base?

14-7 Why are departmental overhead rates generally preferable to plantwide rates?

14-8 "Service-department costs shouldn't be allocated." Do you agree? Why?

14-9 What are the criteria for selecting allocation bases for service-department costs?

14-10 What is the theoretically most accurate method for allocating service-department costs?

14-11 "Reciprocal cost-allocation schemes are always preferable." Do you agree? Why?

14-12 ***Allocation of advertising.*** (SMA) The H Company allocates national magazine advertising cost to territories on the basis of circulation, weighted by an index that measures relative buying power in the territories. Does this method give cost and profit figures appropriate for the following decisions? Indicate clearly why or why not.

1. For deciding whether or not to close an unprofitable territory

2. For deciding whether or not a territorial manager has obtained sufficient sales volume

3. For determining how efficiently the territorial manager has operated his territory

4. For determining whether or not advertising costs are being satisfactorily controlled

14-13 ***Retailing and costs for decision making.*** (CPA) You have a client who operates a large retail self-service grocery store that has a full range of departments. The management has encountered difficulty in using accounting data as a basis for decisions as to possible changes in departments operated, products, marketing methods, and so forth. List several overhead costs, or costs not applicable to a particular department, and explain how the existence of such costs (sometimes called *common costs* or *joint costs*) complicates and limits the use of accounting data in making decisions in such a store.

14-14 ***Cost of servicing a bank account.*** (CPA) A bank stated that the service charge it makes on accounts is based upon the cost of handling each account. A customer states that he does not see how it is possible to determine the cost of handling his account. Do you agree?

Discuss fully the problems involved in determining cost for such a service, including the limitations of the cost figures obtained.

14-15 ***Allocation of personnel department costs.*** The costs of operating the personnel department of the Kuffle Transportation Company are allocated to three operating departments on the basis of total labor-hours. The results for 19_1 were:

	PERSONNEL	1	2	3
Personnel-department costs	$(300,000)	$100,000	$100,000	$100,000
Total labor-hours		500,000	500,000	500,000

In 19_2, the activity of Department 1 was severely restricted between March and October, requiring many layoffs, much employee counseling, and the hiring of many new employees in October. Operations returned to normal in November and December.

The costs of the personnel department in 19_2 were $300,000. The total labor-hours worked in the operating departments were 250,000, 500,000 and 500,000, respectively.

REQUIRED

1. Allocate the costs for 19_2 using total labor-hours as a base.
2. As the manager of Department 2, what comments would you make about the charges. What would be a better base for allocation?

14-16 ***Cost allocation.*** The power plant that services all factory departments has a budget for the forthcoming year. This budget has been expressed in the following terms, for a normal month:

	KILOWATT HOURS	
FACTORY DEPARTMENTS	**needed at practical capacity production volume***	**average expected monthly usage**
A	10,000	8,000
B	20,000	9,000
X	12,000	7,000
Y	8,000	6,000
Totals	50,000	30,000

**This was the most influential factor in planning the size of the power plant.*

The expected monthly costs for operating the department during the budget year are $15,000: $6,000 variable and $9,000 fixed.

What dollar amounts should be allocated to each department? Show three different sets of answers. Which method do you prefer? Why?

14-17 ***Three allocation methods.*** (W. Crum) Kona Company has a power plant designed and built to serve its three factories. Data for 19_1 follow:

	USAGE IN KILOWATT HOURS	
FACTORY NUMBER	**budget**	**actual**
1	100,000	80,000
2	60,000	120,000
3	40,000	40,000

Actual fixed costs of the power plant were $1,000,000 in 19_1; actual variable costs, $2,000,000.

REQUIRED

Using three different methods, compute the amount of power cost that should be allocated to Factory No. 2. One method must distinguish between variable and fixed costs.

14-18 ***Allocation of service-department costs.*** For simplicity, suppose there is one service department (maintenance) plus two production departments. The flexible budget of the service department is $24,000 monthly plus $1 per machine-hour. Assume that the total service-department capacity was originally acquired with the expected "long-run" usage of 75 percent by Department M and 25 percent by Department N.

REQUIRED

1. Indicate the dual rates for allocating the service department's costs to each production department.
2. Assume that actual costs coincided exactly with the flexible-budgeted amount. Departments M and N each worked at 8,000-hour levels. Tabulate the allocation of all costs.
3. Assume the same facts as in requirement 2 except that the fixed costs were allocated on the basis of actual hours worked by each department rather than on the basis of long-run usage. Tabulate the allocation of all costs. As the manager of Department N, would you prefer the method in requirement 2 or in requirement 3? Why?
4. Suppose the service department had inefficiencies at a 16,000-hour level, incurring costs that exceeded budget by $6,000. How would this change your answers in requirements 2 and 3? Be specific.

14-19 ***Allocation using step-down method and dual rates.*** (R. Garrison) Brigitta Manufacturing Company has two producing departments, Department A and Department B, and three service departments. The service departments, and the bases on which their costs are allocated to using departments, are as follows:

DEPARTMENT	COST	ALLOCATION BASE
Building and grounds	Fixed	Square footage occupied
Medical services	Variable	Number of employees budgeted
	Fixed	Employees needed at full capacity
Equipment maintenance	Variable	Machine-hours
	Fixed	40% to Department A
		60% to Department B

Service-department costs are allocated to using departments by the step-down method, in the order shown above. The company has developed the cost and operating data given in the following table, for purposes of preparing predetermined overhead rates in the two producing departments:

	BUILDING AND GROUNDS	MEDICAL SERVICES	EQUIPMENT MAINTENANCE	DEPT. A	DEPT. B	TOTAL
Variable costs	$ -0-	$22,200	$ 2,850	$146,000	$320,000	$ 491,050
Fixed costs	88,200	60,000	24,000	420,000	490,000	1,082,200
Total	$88,200	$82,200	$26,850	$566,000	$810,000	$1,573,250
Budgeted employees	6	4	30	400	680	1,120
Employees needed at capacity	8	4	45	600	855	1,512
Square footage of space occupied	600	500	1,400	13,000	14,500	30,000
Budgeted machine-hours	—	—	—	16,000	18,500	34,500

REQUIRED

1. How much of the Building and Grounds Department costs would be allocated to the (a) Medical Services Department? (b) Department A?
2. How much of the variable costs would be allocated to Department A from the Medical Services Department?
3. How much of the fixed costs would be allocated to Department A from the Medical Services Department?

14-20 ***Approaches to allocation.*** A computer service department of a large university serves two major users, the School of Engineering and the School of Humanities and Sciences (H&S).

REQUIRED

1. When the computer equipment was initially installed, the procedure for cost allocation was straightforward. The actual monthly costs were compiled and were

divided between the two schools on the basis of the time used by each. In October the costs were $100,000. H&S used 100 hours and Engineering used 100 hours. How much cost would be allocated to each school? Suppose that costs were $110,000 because of various inefficiencies in the operation of the computer department. How much cost would be allocated? Does such allocation seem justified? If not, what improvement would you suggest?

2. Use the same approach as in requirement 1. The actual cost behavior pattern of the computer department was $80,000 per month plus $100 per hour used. In November, H&S used 50 hours and Engineering used 100 hours. How much cost would be allocated to each school?
3. As the computer service department developed, the size and composition of the equipment was affected by a committee that included representatives of H&S and Engineering. They agreed that planning should be based on long-run average utilization of 180 hours monthly by H&S and 120 hours monthly by Engineering. In requirement 2, suppose fixed costs are allocated via a predetermined monthly lump sum based on long-run average utilization; variable costs are allocated via a predetermined standard unit rate per hour. How much cost would be allocated to each school? What are the advantages of this method over other methods?
4. What are the likely behavioral effects of lump-sum allocations of fixed costs? For example, if you were the representative of H&S on the facility planning committee, what would your biases be in predicting long-run usage? How would top management counteract the bias?

14-21 ***Evaluating an allocation method.*** The Medford Company has a service department that provides production departments with power. The budget for the power department was based on its normal anticipated monthly activity of providing power for 17,000 machine-hours at a total cost of $8,500, or $.50 per hour. The consuming departments had the following characteristics:

	PRODUCTION DEPARTMENT			
	A	B	C	TOTAL
Practical capacity in machine-hours	7,000	10,000	3,000	20,000
Normal activity in machine-hours	6,000	8,500	2,500	17,000
Actual activity in October—machine-hours actually used	6,000	5,000	2,700	13,700
Standard machine-hours allowed for the output produced in October	5,500	5,000	2,800	13,300

The *budget* allowance for the production departments was based on the 50-cent rate times the standard machine-hours allowed for the output produced. However, the *actual* costs incurred by the service department were fully allocated monthly to each production department on the basis of the actual hours consumed by the production departments.

The service department incurred actual costs of $8,220 in October.

REQUIRED

1. Using the company's method of cost allocation, prepare a performance report for each production department, showing the amounts budgeted, the actual amounts incurred, and the variances. Use *U* or *F* to indicate whether each variance is unfavorable or favorable. Explain the meaning of the variance as reported by dividing each variance into two or more subparts in columnar fashion and commenting on the significance of your variance analysis.
2. This information should *not* be used in answering requirement 1. A study of the power costs showed that efficient operation of the service department should result in total costs of $8,900 at a level of 19,000 machine-hours. Using this as well as the previous information, show how you would improve on the way the Medford Company allocates its power costs to its production departments. Give a complete illustration of how the allocations would be made for October, including a presentation of budgeted costs, actual costs, and variances by department. Explain fully why your suggested method is better.

14-22 ***Service-department costs.*** (CPA) The Parker Manufacturing Company has two production departments (fabrication and assembly) and three service departments (general factory administration, factory maintenance, and factory cafeteria). A summary of costs and other data for each department prior to allocation of service-department costs for the year ended June 30, 19_3, appears below.

	FABRICATION	ASSEMBLY	GENERAL FACTORY ADMINISTRATION	FACTORY MAINTENANCE	FACTORY CAFETERIA
Direct-labor costs	$1,950,000	$2,050,000	$90,000	$82,100	$87,000
Direct-material costs	$3,130,000	$ 950,000	—	$65,000	$91,000
Manufacturing-overhead costs	$1,650,000	$1,850,000	$70,000	$56,100	$62,000
Direct-labor hours	562,500	437,500	31,000	27,000	42,000
Number of employees	280	200	12	8	20
Square footage occupied	88,000	72,000	1,750	2,000	4,800

The costs of the general-factory-administration department, factory-maintenance department, and factory cafeteria are allocated on the basis of direct-labor hours, square footage occupied, and number of employees, respectively. There are no manufacturing-overhead variances. *Round all final calculations to the nearest dollar.* Choose the best answer:

1. Assuming that Parker elects to distribute service-department costs directly to production departments without interservice-department cost allocation, the amount of factory-maintenance-department costs that would be allocated to the fabrication department would be (a) $0, (b) $111,760, (c) $106,091, (d) $91,440.

2. Assuming the same method of allocation as in requirement 1, the amount of general-factory-administration department costs that would be allocated to the assembly department would be (a) $0, (b) $63,636, (c) $70,000, (d) $90,000.

3. Assuming that Parker elects to distribute service-department costs to other service departments (starting with the service department with the greatest total costs) as well as the production departments, the amount of factory-cafeteria-department costs that would be allocated to the factory-maintenance department would be (*Note:* Once a service department's costs have been allocated, no subsequent service-department costs are recirculated back to it.) (a) $0, (b) $96,000, (c) $3,840, (d) $6,124.

4. Assuming the same method of allocation as in requirement 3, the amount of factory-maintenance-department costs that would be allocated to the factory cafeteria would be (a) $0, (b) $5,787, (c) $5,856, (d) $148,910.

14-23 ***Comparison of departmental and plantwide overhead rates.*** (CGAA) The Sayther Company manufactured two products, A and B, during the first year of its operations. For purposes of product costing, an overhead rate of application of $1.70 per direct-labor hour was used, based on budgeted factory overhead of $340,000 and 200,000 budgeted direct-labor hours, as follows:

	BUDGETED OVERHEAD	BUDGETED HOURS
Department 1	$240,000	100,000
Department 2	100,000	100,000
Total	$340,000	200,000

The number of labor hours required to manufacture each of these products was:

	PRODUCT A	PRODUCT B
In Department 1	4	1
In Department 2	1	4
Total	5	5

At the end of the year, there was no work in process and there were 2,000 and 6,000 finished units, respectively, of products A and B on hand. Assume that budgeted activity was attained.

REQUIRED

1. What was the effect on the company's income of using a plantwide overhead rate instead of departmental overhead rates?

2. Assume that material and labor costs per unit of Product A are $10 and that the selling price is established by adding 40 percent to factory-overhead costs to cover profit and selling and administrative expenses. What difference in selling price would result from the use of departmental overhead rates?
3. Explain briefly but clearly why departmental overhead rates are generally preferable to plantwide rates.

14-24 ***Departmental versus plantwide applications.*** The following are pertinent data for the Alou Company:

	(S1)	(S2)	(P1)	(P2)
budget data for 19_7	**factory personnel**	**production planning and control**	**machining**	**assembly**
Predicted overhead	$51,000	$198,500	$2,235,500	$755,000
Machine-hours			300,000	—
Direct-labor hours			40,000	500,000
Orders to be processed			8,000	2,000
Number of employees		10	30	300

Factory personnel-department costs are to be allocated on the basis of number of employees; production planning and control, on the basis of orders processed. The step-down method is used for allocation.

This company produces a wide variety of products on a job-order basis. Management has always used a single, plantwide overhead application rate based on direct-labor hours.

Recently, however, customer complaints on price quotations, plus the outside auditor's criticism of the plantwide rate, have prompted management to ask you, the controller, to restudy the situation before setting rates for 19_7.

You decide that departmental overhead rates should be developed, at least as a method of attack. You think that a machine-hour rate should be used for the machining department, which contains costly automatic and semiautomatic equipment manned by a few workers who tend and control many machines simultaneously.

The workers may operate a couple of machines at a time on certain jobs, and as many as six machines or more on other jobs. Because the assembly department requires painstaking workmanship but little equipment, you think that direct-labor hours is the most proper overhead base there.

The budget data for 19_7 are little different from those for 19_6, so you pick five representative jobs worked on during December 19_6 as a basis for comparing the plantwide rate with departmental rates. You keep careful records of machine-hours as well as of the direct-labor hours. The results follow:

	MACHINING		ASSEMBLY
job number	**machine-hours**	**DLH**	**DLH**
300	5	2	10
301	40	4	40
302	10	2	30
303	7	1	5
304	15	11	30

REQUIRED

(Show and label computations.)

1. Departmental overhead rates.
2. Plantwide rate.
3. A detailed summary by jobs of (a) total overhead applied, using departmental rates; (b) total overhead applied, using a plantwide rate; (c) difference between (a) and (b).
4. What is the total difference for the jobs taken together?
5. What overhead application base would you recommend? Why?

14-25 ***Allocate service-department costs.*** The X Company has prepared departmental overhead budgets for normal activity levels before allocations, as follows:

Building and grounds	$ 10,000
Personnel	1,000
General factory administration*	26,090
Cafeteria—operating loss	1,640
Storeroom	2,670
Machining	34,700
Assembly	48,900
	$125,000

**To be allocated before cafeteria.*

Management has decided that the most sensible product costs are achieved by using departmental overhead rates. These rates are developed after appropriate service-department costs are allocated to production departments.

Bases for allocation are to be selected from the following:

DEPARTMENT	DIRECT-LABOR HOURS	NUMBER OF EMPLOYEES	SQUARE FEET OF FLOOR SPACE OCCUPIED	TOTAL LABOR-HOURS	NUMBER OF REQUISITIONS
Building & grounds		—	—	—	
Personnel*		—	2,000	—	
General factory administration		35	7,000	—	
Cafeteria—operating loss		10	4,000	1,000	
Storeroom		5	7,000	1,000	
Machining	5,000	50	30,000	8,000	2,000
Assembly	15,000	100	50,000	17,000	1,000
	20,000	200	100,000	27,000	3,000

**Basis used is number of employees.*

REQUIRED

1. Using a worksheet, allocate service-department costs by the step-down method. Develop overhead rates per direct-labor hour for machining and assembly.
2. Same as in requirement 1, using the direct method.
3. What would be the blanket plantwide factory-overhead application rate, assuming that direct-labor hours are used as a base?
4. Using the following information about two jobs, prepare three different total-overhead costs for each job, using rates developed in requirements 1, 2, and 3 above.

	DIRECT-LABOR HOURS	
	machining	**assembly**
Job 88	18	2
Job 89	3	17

14-26 ***Reciprocal allocations.*** Computer Complex, Inc., has two main services: (1) time on a time-shared computer system, and (2) proprietary computer programs. Computer time is provided by the operations department (Op), and programs are written by the programming department (P). Both services are sold by the marketing department (M).

The percentage of each service used by each department for a typical period are:

	SUPPLIER	
USER	**Op**	**P**
Op	—	30%
P	50%	—
Sold to customers	50	70
	100%	100%

In a typical period, the revenues and costs are:

	Op	P	M
Revenue—computer time	—	—	$5,000
Revenue—program use	—	—	5,000
Total costs	$3,000	$3,000	2,000

The marketing manager estimates that 60 percent of the department's efforts go toward selling the use of programs, and 40 percent toward selling computer time.

Computer Complex would like to compute the profitability of each of its two lines of business. The vice-president of finance has stated that the reciprocal method should not be used because it would be too difficult to explain to the line managers. He would like you to tell him which other method to use.

REQUIRED

1. Compute the operating income or loss for each line of business using the reciprocal method.
2. Compute the operating income or loss for each line of business using the direct method and two different sequences of the step-down method. Which of these methods should Computer Complex use?
3. What do you think of the decision not to use the reciprocal method?

14-27 ***Reciprocal cost allocations.*** (D. Green) The Prairie State Paper Company located a plant near one of its forests. At the time of construction, there were no utility companies equipped to provide this plant with water, power, or fuel. Therefore, included in the original facilities were (1) a water plant, which pumped water from a nearby lake and filtered it; (2) a coal-fired boiler room that produced steam, part of which was used for the manufacturing process and the balance for producing electricity; and (3) an electric plant.

An analysis of these activities has revealed that 60 percent of the water is used for the production of steam and 40 percent is used in manufacturing. Half of the steam produced is used for the production of electric power and half for manufacturing. Twenty percent of the electric power is used by the water plant and 80 percent goes to manufacturing.

For the year 19_9, the costs charged to these departments were:

	VARIABLE	FIXED	TOTAL
Water plant	$ 2,000	$ 8,000	$10,000
Steam room	18,000	12,000	30,000
Electric plant	6,000	9,000	15,000
			$55,000

REQUIRED

1. How would you allocate these costs in an absorption product-cost determination situation? Use the reciprocal method.
2. A new power company has offered to sell electricity to Prairie State for two cents a kilowatt-hour. In 19_9, the electric plant generated 600,000 kilowatt-hours. The manager of the electric plant has advised that the offer be rejected, since (he says) "our variable costs were only one cent per kilowatt-hour in 19_9." Was this the right answer? Show computations.

14-28 ***Reciprocal cost allocations and sensitivity of results.*** The Manes Company has two main products, X and Y, each of which is produced in a separate department. In order to produce X and Y, the Manes Company has two major service departments, A and B (for the sake of discussion, a material-handling department and a power-generating department, respectively).

An analysis of the work done by Departments A and B in a typical period follows:

	USER				TOTAL UNITS
SOURCE	A	B	X	Y	OF WORK DONE
Material handling (Dept. A)	0	20	50	30	100
Power (Dept. B)	50	0	10	40	100

The cost of departments during this typical period are as follows:

	A	B
Variable labor and material costs	$ 7,000	$1,000
Supervision	1,000	1,000
Depreciation	2,000	2,000
	$10,000	$4,000
	+ Power costs	+ Material-handling costs

Supervisory costs represent salary costs. Depreciation in B represents the straight-line depreciation of power-generation equipment in its nineteenth year of an estimated twenty-five-year life; it is old but well-maintained equipment.

REQUIRED

1. What are the allocations of costs of Departments, A and B to X and Y using the direct method, two different sequences of the step-down method, and the reciprocal method of reallocation?
2. The power company has offered to supply all the power needed by the Manes Company and to provide all the services of the present power department. The cost of this will be $40 per unit. Should Manes accept?

Cost Allocation: A Closer look

15

This chapter will consider a variety of cost accounting topics, including the contribution approach to cost allocation, costs of central services, more on economic decisions and motivation, cost justification and reimbursement, homogeneous cost pools, and choosing allocation bases. Some of you may not want to cover all of these topics. For example, the first section may be studied alone.

Two major lessons are emphasized in this chapter. First, choices of how to allocate costs may have an important impact on managers' behavior. Second, cost allocations often substitute for market prices as a way of obtaining mutually satisfactory selling prices.

The chapter begins with the contribution approach to making cost allocations. Various subparts of operating income are computed for different purposes. The contribution approach distinguishes sharply between various degrees of objectivity in cost allocations.

The contribution approach to cost allocation

In general, the *contribution approach* means financial reporting and analysis that distinguishes between variable and fixed costs and includes the contribution margin that was described in Chapter 3. The contribution approach may be employed for nonroutine decisions and for performance evaluation.

The contribution approach to cost allocation attempts to respond simultaneously to the purposes of economic decisions and motivation. Exhibit 15-1 is an unusually important exhibit. It stresses cost behavior patterns in relation to individuals and subunits of an organization. Failure to distinguish cost behavior patterns is a big roadblock to clarity in cost analysis.

revenues, variable costs, and contribution margins

The allocation of revenue and of variable costs is usually straightforward, because each item is directly and specifically identifiable with a given segment of activity. The Contribution Margin, item (1) in Exhibit 15-1, is particularly helpful for predicting the impact on income of short-run changes in volume. Changes in income may be quickly calculated by multiplying the change in units by the unit contribution margin or by multiplying the increment in dollar sales by the contribution-margin ratio. For example, the contribution-margin ratio of Product 1 is $120 ÷ $300 = 40 percent. The increase in pretax income resulting from a $20,000 increase in total sales volume can be readily computed as .40 × $20,000, or $8,000. Of course, this calculation assumes no changes in selling prices or operating efficiency.

contributions by managers and subunits

Items (2) and (3) in Exhibit 15-1 distinguish between the performance of the manager as a professional executive and the subunit as an economic investment. For our purposes, **segments** and **subunits** are synonyms. **A *segment* or *subunit* is any line of activity or part of an organization for which separate determinations of costs or revenues or both are desired.**

Controllability is the degree of influence that a specific manager has over the costs or revenues in question. Distinctions between controllable and uncontrollable items are helpful when feasible. They aid motivation and the analysis of performance. For example, unless discrimination is made between the manager and the responsibility center as an economic entity, the skillful executive will be reluctant to accept troublesome responsibilities. Sometimes it takes a miracle worker to get a limping subunit up to a minimally acceptable level of income.

The controllable contribution, keyed as item (2) in Exhibit 15-1, should be interpreted in conjunction with the contribution margin. **Many managers can influence many fixed costs, particularly discretionary fixed costs.** (Examples of these costs are given in Exhibit 15-1.) The incurrence of discretionary costs may have interacting effects on variable costs. For example, heavier outlays for maintenance, engineering, or management consulting may reduce repairs, increase machine speeds, heighten labor productivity, and so forth. Also, decisions on advertising, research, and sales-promotion budgets are necessarily related to expected impacts on sales volumes.

The distinction between controllable and uncontrollable costs must be drawn on a company-by-company basis. For example, some managements may prefer to have depreciation on some classes of plant and equipment deducted when the controllable contribution, item (2), is computed. Getting agreement as to these classifications may be bothersome, but it is not a herculean task.

EXHIBIT 15-1 *(Place a clip on this page for easy reference.)*

The Contribution Approach: Model Income Statement by Segments*

(In Thousands of Dollars)

	COMPANY AS A WHOLE	COMPANY BREAKDOWN INTO TWO DIVISIONS		POSSIBLE BREAKDOWN OF DIVISION B ONLY				
		division A	**division B**	**not allocated**	**product 1**	**product 2**	**product 3**	**product 4**
Net revenues	1,500	500	1,000		300	200	100	400
Variable manufacturing cost of goods sold	780	200	580		120	155	45	260
Manufacturing contribution margin	720	300	420		180	45	55	140
Variable selling and administrative costs	220	100	120		60	15	25	20
(1) Contribution margin	500	200	300		120	30	30	120
Fixed costs controllable by segment managers (certain advertising, sales promotion, salespersons' salaries, engineering, research, management consulting, and supervision costs)	190	110	80	45†	10	6	4	15
(2) Contribution controllable by segment managers	310	90	220	(45)	110	24	26	105
Fixed costs controllable by others (such as depreciation, property taxes, insurance, and perhaps the division manager's salary)	70	20	50	20	3	15	4	8
(3) Contribution by segments	240	70	170	(65)	107	9	22	97
Unallocated costs (not clearly or practically allocable to any segment except by some questionable allocation base)	135							
(4) Income before income taxes	105							

There are two different types of segments illustrated here: divisions and products. As you read across, note that the focus becomes narrower; from the company as a whole, to Divisions A and B, to Division B only.

†*Only those costs clearly identifiable with a product line should be allocated.*

The income statement in Exhibit 15-1 has four measures of performance, ranging from contribution margin to income before income taxes. There is nothing hallowed about these four illustrative measures; some organizations may want to use only two or three such measures. For instance, Reckett & Colman, a large British manufacturer and seller of housewares, has a classification of sales, contribution before marketing costs, marketing costs, contribution after marketing costs, fixed costs, and trading profit.

The distinction between item (2) and item (3) in Exhibit 15-1 is seldom found in practice. Why? Because it is difficult to draw fine distinctions in identifying which fixed costs are controlled by which managers. Nevertheless, distinctions between the performances of the manager and the subunit are still accomplished via intelligent budgeting. For example, the manager's objective for the forthcoming year may be agreed upon: "I'll improve this division's loss from $5 to $3 million." If this objective is attained, the *manager* may subsequently be judged as successful. However, the *subunit* may continue to be regarded as a miserable investment.

allocations to segments

There may be a limit to the allocation of a given cost in a given income statement. Although many discretionary costs may easily be traced to divisions, they may not all be directly traceable to products. Some advertising expenses for Division B may be common to all products. For example, Products 1, 2, and 3 may be consumer items that all benefit from the same advertisements, while Product 4 may be an item sold to manufacturers by a separate sales force with its own fixed costs.

Discretionary and committed costs may or may not be allocated, *depending on the segments in question.* For example, a salesman's salary may easily be identified with a particular territory. However, if he is selling a large number of products, the allocation of his salary among such products is questionable. Consequently, there may be a limit to the allocation of a given cost in a given income statement. For instance, the divisions in Exhibit 15-1 could be territories. The salary of the salesman just described could readily be allocated to Division A or B (a territory), but it could not be allocated convincingly among the products. **A given cost may be allocated with respect to one segment of the organization and unallocated with respect to another.**

If motivation is the dominant purpose regarding whether to allocate, there is merit in not allocating costs that are subject to minimal influence by segment managers.

unallocated costs

Consider the next-to-last line in Exhibit 15-1. An unallocated cost is common to all the segments in question and is not clearly or practically assignable except on some questionable basis. Examples of unallocated costs may be the salaries of the president and other top officers, basic research and development, and some central corporate costs like public relations or corporate-image advertising. Unless the general company costs are clearly traceable to segments, allocation often serves no useful purpose. Therefore, pretax income is not computed by segments in Exhibit 15-1.

Income before taxes, item (4) in Exhibit 15-1, may sometimes be a helpful gauge of the long-run earning power of a whole company. However, it may be misleading to refine this ultimate measure by breaking it into segments (and still have the whole equal the sum of the parts).

This refusal to allocate some costs is the most controversial aspect of the contribution approach to the income statement. Accountants and managers are accustomed to the whole being completely broken down into neat parts that can be added up again to equal the whole. In *traditional* segment income statements, all costs are fully allocated, so that the segments show final net incomes that can be summed to equal the net income for the company as a whole.

Of course, if for some reason management prefers a whole-equals-the-sum-of-its-parts net-income statement, the unallocated costs may be allocated so that the segments show income figures that will cross-add to equal the income for the company as a whole. **The important point is that the contribution approach distinguishes between various degrees of objectivity in cost allocations.** As you read downward in Exhibit 15-1, you become less and less confident about the cost allocations. A dozen independent accountants would be most likely to agree on how the variable costs should be allocated and least likely to agree on whether and how the unallocated costs should be accounted for.

Costs of central services

At first glance, the allocation of central administrative services may appear to be an insignificant problem. However, the income or total costs of a subunit may be very sensitive to the allocations of common costs, even though such costs may be insignificant in relation to sales.[1]

company practices

As we just saw, a convincing basis must exist before costs are allocated under the contribution approach. Surveys of company practices indicate wide divergence on whether central costs should be allocated. A major survey by Reece and Cool indicated that 40 percent of 594 companies calculated income in a manner consistent with the way calculated for shareholder reports. Such companies adhere to the widespread belief that managers should see a direct correspondence between how overall corporate income is measured and how subunit income is measured.

The other 60 percent (359 companies) made various modifications:[2]

	YES	NO
Allocate income taxes to profit centers?	29%	71%
Allocate corporate administrative expenses?	51	49
Allocate interest charges on corporate debt?	36	64
Depreciation calculation differs?	7	93

In particular, note that the interest charges are on corporate debt. They should not be confused with any imputed interest on invested capital, whether that capital be in the form of debt or equity.

[1]George J. Benston, "The Baffling New Numbers Game at the FTC," *Fortune,* October 1975, summarized a survey of 227 companies that showed 40 percent did not allocate common general and administrative costs to lines of business. Benston added, "The survey also showed that, on the average, common costs (excluding income taxes) equal 124 percent of net profits. . . . Most accountants and economists agree that common costs are, by their nature, not allocable at all." Also see R. K. Mautz, *Financial Reporting by Diversified Companies* (New York: Financial Executives Research Foundation), pp. 30–33 and 222–27; and H. Greer, "The Chop Suey Caper," *Journal of Accountancy,* 125, No. 4, pp. 27–34.

[2]Reece and Cool, "Measuring Investment Center Performance," *Harvard Business Review,* (May-June 1978), p. 36. Comparable data in a separate survey can be found in R. Vancil, *Decentralization: Managerial Ambiguity by Design* (New York: Financial Executives Research Foundation, 1979), Exhibit D-9, p. 235.

which allocation base?

The most logical allocation base for central administrative services is usage, either actual or estimated. Many organizations, however, think such measurement is infeasible. **If they still insist on allocation, then most organizations tend to favor sales revenue as a base.** For example, 60 percent of the companies in the Vancil survey use sales revenue as an allocation base.[3] **Other popular bases are the total costs (before allocation) or the total assets of a subunit.**

Not all central services are allocated in the same way. The costs of such services as public relations, top-corporate-management overhead, real estate department, and corporate-planning department are the least likely to be allocated on the basis of usage; the most likely are electronic data processing, advertising, and operations research.[4]

sales revenues as a base

When cause-effect relationships are infeasible or impossible to establish, actual sales revenues (or, rarely, gross profits or contributions to profit) or total costs are chosen as an allocation base. These are sometimes described as "ability-to-bear" allocation bases. Sales revenues and total costs may have a most tenuous causal relationship to the costs being allocated. Moreover, the level of many central costs is determined by budgeted sales. They are discretionary costs that are determined by management policies, not sales results.

Make no mistake. Sales revenues may be the best practical representation of the underlying activities that cause the costs. However, there should always be a serious examination of whether a more logical base is available, or whether *any* allocation is indeed warranted.

The use of *budgeted sales* is preferable to *actual sales* as an allocation base. **This avoids the short-run costs of a user department being affected by the fluctuations in actual sales of the *other* user departments.**

For example, assume that central corporate costs were allocated on the basis of budgeted sales in three product divisions (figures are in millions of dollars):

	PRODUCT				
YEAR 1	A	B	C	TOTAL	
Budgeted sales	$100	$100	$100	$300	(100%)
Costs allocated by dollar sales	$ 10	$ 10	$ 10	$ 30	(10%)

Compare the possible differences in allocations when the actual sales are known:

	PRODUCT			
	A	B	C	TOTAL
Actual sales	$137.5	$137.5	$100.0	$375.0
Costs allocated:				
1. Based on budgeted sales	10.0	10.0	10.0	30.0
or				
2. Based on actual sales	11.0	11.0	8.0	30.0

[3]Vancil, *Decentralization,* p. 235.

[4]Ibid., p. 250. Also see J. Fremgen and S. Liao, *The Allocation of Corporate Indirect Costs* (New York: National Association of Accountants, 1981).

Compare the two sets of allocations. The first is preferable. It indicates a higher ratio of costs to actual sales (10 ÷ 100 = 10%) for C than for A or B (10 ÷ 137.5 = 7.3%). It aims attention at where it is deserved.

In contrast, the second set soaks A and B with more costs because of achieved sales results and relieves C because it had lesser sales success. So C, which did the worst in comparison to budget, is relieved of costs without any reference to underlying cause-effect relationships. C's costs as a percentage of sales fell from 10 percent to 8 percent (8 ÷ 100 = 8%). This is another example of the analytical confusion that may arise when cost allocations to one consuming department are dependent on the activities of *other* consuming departments.

Central advertising, such as that on national television, is a prime example of a cost that is often allocated on the basis of sales revenues. It is better to allocate such a cost on the basis of *potential* sales rather than *actual* sales. Weight may be given to the purchasing power in a particular territory and to local competitive conditions. For example, there would be a consistent relationship between the advertising costs and the sales volume in each territory if all territories were equally efficient. If, however, a manager has poor outlets or a weak sales staff, one of the indicators would be a high ratio of advertising to sales. The usual dangers of budgetary gamesmanship also apply here; that is, there may be a temptation to underbudget sales in order to get a lighter cost allocation.

More on economic decisions and motivation

Two major objectives of cost allocation—economic decisions and motivation—obviously overlap. Anthony has indicated the key question, "What cost constructions are most likely to induce people to take the action that management desires?"[5] This is a motivation objective. A general answer could be, **"The cost construction that best measures cause-and-effect relationships is most likely to provide information that will lead to optimum decisions."** This is an economic decision objective. This section explores how organizations cope with the interrelationships between these objectives.

partial or full allocation

Suppose you are a lone manager. You make all the decisions. Therefore, you are not concerned with how particular cost allocations affect other managers. Nevertheless, you may still want to invest in a cost accounting system that provides careful cost allocations. For example, as was briefly indicated in Chapter 11 (page 371), in deciding what products to produce, you may face the difficult task of predicting how total costs will be affected. The dilemma is often to choose between (1) and (3) as a guide:

(1) Total "incremental" or variable costs	xxx
(2) Add: allocation of fixed costs	xxx
(3) Total "full" costs	xxx

Is (1) or (3) the more accurate approximation of the "real" additions to costs caused by the decision at hand? Generally, all that managers know for sure is that *both* (1) and (3) are inaccurate. Still, managers must buy a cost accounting system that routinely approximates additions to costs.

[5]*Accounting Review,* Vol XXXII, No. 2.

In practice, most managers cope with uncertainty by regarding some version of full cost allocation as yielding a better approximation of the "true" or "real" underlying addition to costs. Why? **Because it is a simple way to allow for the inevitable increases in "fixed" costs that accompany increases in volume.** The exact amounts of such increases may be unknown, but most managers fear that a variable cost approach often provides an underestimate.

Whether one manager or many managers are involved, if costs are fully allocated, managers are less likely to cut prices, to underbid, to be inefficient, to overexpand, and so on. The widespread advocacy of full cost allocations is indicative that such assertions are widely believed. In sum, most top managers and systems designers apparently feel that a collection of managers will make fewer erroneous decisions if full allocations of costs are employed.[6] But we have little systematic evidence to support either side of the argument.

cause-and-effect framework

When a top manager is concerned with obtaining the "true" costs of assorted departments and products, most allocation methods reach only a limited distance with assurance. The cause-effect logic can be carried further with variable costs than with fixed costs. Decisions pertaining to fixed costs often occur at high levels in an organization and affect many subunits. Moreover, fixed costs are incurred in large chunks and are often affected by long-range decisions.

The cause-and-effect logic offers a frame of reference for choosing among cost-allocation methods. Wanting to know the impact of decisions on costs, and faced with few obvious cause-effect relationships, the manager is forced to rely on substitutes as approximations of these causal relationships. Hence, the fully allocated cost rather than a variable cost is often used as an approximation of "the real long-run" incremental cost.

A decision to produce a given batch of goods or services may not, by itself, be causing an increase in overhead at its given moment of production. But its cumulative, indirect effects indeed cause increases in costs. Indirect costs somehow creep upward, often unobtrusively. These "creep" effects are approximated by allocating average unit costs to products and services. The unanswered question is, How accurate are such approximations? Only specific evidence, often too costly or impossible to gather, can answer such a question.

illustration of allocation difficulties

The imposing difficulties of allocation are illustrated by a firm that leases a WATS (Wide Area Telephone Service) line from the telephone company for $3,800 per month. Maximum permitted usage is 100 hours. The service provides toll-free long-distance calls within the United States. Although individual calls are not billed by

---

[6]The allocation of fixed overhead serves as a substitute or proxy for the real but unknown opportunity costs related to fixed facilities. Devine's words are over thirty years old, but they remain pertinent "The businessman's traditional tendency to quote prices on the basis of total costs . . . measures more or less imperfectly the relative usage of the firm's scarce factor of production. The obvious shortcoming of this procedure is that the fixed overhead rate is not an accurate measure of the contribution to profit made by an hour's use of the factory." He concludes: ". . . the usual markup procedure based on total unit cost may provide a simple rule for pricing for high profits at full capacity." See C. Devine, "Cost Acounting and Pricing Policies," *Accounting Review,* October 1950, p. 389.

the phone company, only one call at a time can be placed. The $3,800 is a fixed cost. Should the firm allocate the $3,800 internally among the users?[7]

The question must ultimately be resolved in terms of how the allocation *influences management behavior* in a particular organization. In one organization, allocation may be desirable because it induces the desired behavior. In another organization, the same allocation method may cause an opposite behavioral effect.

Possible answers to the WATS question include the following:

1. Do not allocate. The marginal (variable) cost is zero. Any charge will discourage use, and the value of the resource will not be maximized.
2. Allocate. The correct marginal (variable) cost is not zero. Instead, a cost is imposed on those who either (a) wait until the WATS line is not in use or (b) place a regular toll call when the WATS line is in use. This cost fluctuates between zero, when no one is delayed, and the cost of a regular toll call. It changes from instant to instant. Exact measurement is difficult and costly.
3. Allocate. Because measurement in alternative 2 is difficult, charge $3,800 ÷ 100 = $38 per hour. "A side benefit of such a full-cost allocation is that information is generated regarding the value of the service."[8]

This illustration underscores the cost-benefit theme of this book. That is, obtaining accurate cost data is frequently costly and nearly impossible. Routine cost allocations, which are often straightforward allocations of fixed overhead, are widely used as substitutes or approximations of "true" costs. The true costs take different forms, including the following:

1. One user's utilization of a resource causes others to wait, hence causing delay costs. Examples are maintenance shops, typing pools, and batch-operated computer systems.
2. Degradation of service to other users can often result when a fixed resource is shared. That is, turnaround time or quality may suffer. Supervision is an example. For each supervisor, as the number of workers increases each worker's average productivity is likely to decrease. Degradation costs are frequently found in time-share computer systems.
3. As degradation increases, waiting also increases. Users seek alternatives, including purchasing from outsiders. For instance, if a backlog at a central computer facility becomes too large, users may install a minicomputer or acquire time from an outside source.

arbitrary allocations

Top managers may resort to arbitrary cost allocations, ranging from zero to a high price above full cost. Why? Because the allocation is used as a major means of getting subordinates to behave as desired by top managers. An example is charging the operating divisions for central costs such as basic research even though cause-and-effect justifications are weak. Some top managers will insist that such allocation practices get division managers to take a desired interest in, say, central research activities. Thus, an "arbitrary" cost-allocation scheme may be chosen because the formal accounting system provides the best way to get the desired actions. This practice may be desirable to the extent that this objective is reached without causing confusion in cost analysis and resentment about the methods of cost allocation.

Are there any service departments whose costs should not be allocated even though they are clearly necessitated by the other parts of the organization? Consider

---

[7]J. Zimmerman, "The Costs and Benefits of Cost Allocations," *Accounting Review,* LIV, No. 3 (July 1979), 510–11. The answers here are also based on Zimmerman's presentation.

[8]Ibid., p. 511.

the internal-auditing department or the legal department as examples. Ordinarily, where the other department managers have no discretion over their consumption of such services, the argument in favor of allocation rests on the assumption that the costs should be allocated anyway, and that managers generally do not get too concerned about such allocations as long as all departments are subject to a uniform cost-allocation procedure. The argument against the allocation of such costs rests on the assumption that no costs should be allocated to a manager unless he or she has some direct influence over their amount.

In some organizations, however, operating managers may have much leeway over their usage of such services. Charging for the internal auditing or legal services on the basis of the amount provided may discourage their use, even though such use may be very desirable from the standpoint of the organization as a whole. In such instances, either no charge may be made or a flat annual fee may be charged regardless of the quantity of services consumed. For instance, a large automobile-manufacturing company does not charge for its internal-auditing services because it wants to encourage its managers to utilize such services.

As a general rule, the same objective will be attained by allocating a flat sum to the various departments regardless of actual use. It reminds the managers that the costs do exist. A possible advantage of this procedure is its retainer-fee effect, where the user feels that he is paying for the service in any event, so he had better take advantage of its availability. Of course, there is always the danger that a few managers may demand too much of what they would then regard as a "free" service. Then some priority system must be instituted, and a method of charging on the basis of services consumed may be finally adopted.

Some managers maintain that the morale effects of allocation procedures on the production departments are given too much attention. There are also important effects on the morale of the service-department employees. That is, if the other departments are not charged with service-department costs, the service-department staff is likely to feel that it lacks the status of first-class citizenship as an integral part of the organization.

Cost justification and reimbursement

Cost allocations are frequently performed as justifications for selling prices. For example, Chapter 11 (page 372) has a section on the role of costs in relation to antitrust laws. In addition, in the United States *hundreds of billions (that's right, billions) of dollars* of the revenues of health-care organizations and of suppliers of goods and services to government agencies are directly affected by how costs are allocated. This section will examine cost reimbursement as a major purpose of cost allocations, particularly in relation to government contracts.[9]

cost accounting standards board

The late 1960s and early 1970s were marked by many widely publicized disputes about the high costs of various defense contracts. In 1970, the **Cost Accounting Standards Board (CASB)** was formed by the U.S. Congress to establish uniform cost accounting standards, which must be used by defense contractors and nearly all federal agencies

[9]See D. Neuman, "Defense Contract Audits: The CPA's Role," *Journal of Accountancy*, April 1981, pp. 42–48. Also see J. Burton, R. Palmer, and R. Kay (eds.), *Handbook of Accounting and Auditing* (Boston: Warren, Gorham & Lamont, 1981), Chapter 42. For an overview of cost reimbursement for health care, see *Social Security and Medicare Explained* (Chicago: Commerce Clearing House, periodically updated), Paragraphs 678–82.

in the pricing of negotiated contracts. "Negotiated" means that the price is tied to costs rather than to competitive bidding. One of the problems that led to the formation of this board was that of how costs should be allocated among contracts and among commercial and defense products.

The CASB was terminated in 1980 because its major mission had been accomplished. However, the CASB's rules, regulations, and standards have been included in the major federal government procurement regulations and will continue to have the full force and effect of law.

The titles of the following CASB standards indicate the breadth of coverage. The standards are largely concerned with definitions, uniformity, and consistency. The standards begin with Number 400:

400 Definitions.
401 Cost accounting standard—consistency in estimating, accumulating and reporting costs.
402 Cost accounting standard—consistency in allocating costs incurred for the same purpose.
403 Allocation of home office expenses to segments.
404 Capitalization of tangible assets.
405 Accounting for unallowable costs.
406 Cost accounting standard—cost accounting period.
407 Use of standard costs for direct material and direct labor.
408 Accounting for costs of compensated personal absence.
409 Depreciation of tangible capital assets.
410 Allocation of general and administrative expenses.
411 Accounting for acquisition costs of material.
412 Composition and measurement of pension cost.
413 Adjustment of historical depreciation costs for inflation (withdrawn).
414 Cost of money as an element of the cost of facilities capital.
415 Deferred compensation costs.
416 Accounting for insurance costs.
417 Cost of money as an element of the cost of capital assets under construction.
418 Allocation of direct and indirect costs.
419 Withdrawn.
420 Accounting for independent research and development and bid and proposal costs.

Above all, the purpose of the standards is to obtain a "fair" price for both buyer and seller. **That is, the standards focus on ways of using a "cost accounting pricing system" as a substitute for the "free market pricing system."** Therefore, the applicability of the standards for other purposes, such as external reporting, is subject to challenge. For example, Standard #414 provides for allocating imputed interest on contractors' investments. Contractors are to use the "Renegotiation Board Rate," which is based on the interest rate on new private commercial loans maturing in five years. This rate is applied to the average investment in tangible capital assets and amortizable intangible capital assets. Nevertheless, the imputing of interest on ownership capital is not a generally accepted accounting principle for reports to stockholders.

CASB approach to allocation

The CASB has published a series of standards on cost allocation. Illustrations of the board's approach to cost allocation of home office costs are found in Exhibit 15-2, which is taken from CASB Standard #403, Paragraph 403.50 (b)(1), "Allocation of Home Office Expenses to Segments." The CASB describes its approach as follows:

> The allocation of centralized service functions shall be governed by a hierarchy of preferable allocation techniques which represent beneficial or causal relationships. The

EXHIBIT 15-2

Illustrative Allocation Bases for Centralized Home Office Costs

SERVICE RENDERED	COST-ALLOCATION BASES
1. Personnel administration	1. Number of personnel, labor-hours, payroll, number of hires
2. Data-processing services	2. Machine time, number of reports
3. Centralized purchasing and subcontracting	3. Number of purchase orders, value of purchases, number of items
4. Centralized warehousing	4. Square footage, value of material, volume
5. Company aircraft service	5. Actual or standard rate per hour, mile, passenger mile, or similar unit
6. Central telephone service	6. Usage costs, number of telephones

> preferred representation of such relationships is a measure of the activity of the organization performing the function. Supporting functions are usually labor-oriented, machine-oriented, or space-oriented. Measures of the activities of such functions ordinarily can be expressed in terms of labor hours, machine hours, or square footage.

CASB Standard #418 delineated some criteria for cost allocation. Paragraph 418.40(c) states that the pooled cost shall be allocated "by means of one of the following allocation bases: (i) a resource consumption measure [that is, usage], (ii) an output measure, or (iii) a surrogate [substitute, proxy] that is representative of resources consumed." An example of a consumption measure (i) would be kilowatt hours used, and of an output measure (ii) would be units of finished goods produced.

Paragraph 418.60(f) offers the following example of a surrogate (iii):

> Business Unit F has an indirect cost pool containing a significant amount of material-related costs. The contractor allocates these costs between his machining overhead cost pool and his assembly overhead cost pool. The business unit finds it impractical to use an allocation measure based on either consumption or output. The business unit selects a dollars of material-issued base which varies in proportion to the services rendered. The dollars of material-issued base is a surrogate base which conforms to the provisions.

equity, fairness, benefits received

Although this book has emphasized cause and effect as the preferable criterion for cost allocation, much of the literature in cost accounting has tended to favor equity or fairness or benefits received as preferable criteria.

The trouble with equity or fairness as a possible criterion is that it is so broad that other criteria must be devised to ensure the existence of fairness. Equity and fairness are ethical standards that should be avoided in the building of concepts for a measurement system. In short, they are lofty objectives rather than criteria. To say that cost allocations must be fair or equitable is not an operational statement. Without specific criteria, we cannot judge how fairness conforms to overall tests of truth, justice, equity, and candor.

The CASB provisions frequently state that costs should be allocated on the basis of cause and effect *or* benefits received. But the benefits-received criterion seems to introduce second-best logic when cause-and-effect arguments are available. For example, if the sales price is raised on a particular product line, there is little cause-effect justification for soaking that product line with a higher dose of some cost that is being allocated to products in proportion to sales dollars. If all other things are equal, the costs of the product line would be unaffected by a mere rise in selling price; yet the product line's proportionate share of central overhead costs would rise while other product lines' proportionate shares would fall—results that are hardly "fair" or "equitable."

fairness for pricing

The entire field of negotiated government contracts is marked by the attempt to use *cost* allocations as a means for establishing a mutually satisfactory *price.* There is a subtle but important distinction here. A *cost* allocation, as a *cost* allocation, may be difficult to defend on the basis of any cause-effect reasoning. However, an allocation may be a "reasonable" or "fair" *means of establishing a selling price* in the minds of the affected parties. Various costs become "allowable," whereas others are "unallowable." For example, elaborate rules promulgated by the CASB are used to help determine how costs are allocated to contracts. If cost allocations are to be used in lieu of market-based pricing, much argument and litigation are avoided when the allocation rules are made as explicit as is feasible in advance.

In the context of finding a substitute for a market price, equity becomes the dominant criterion for cost allocation.

> This is a concept which is easy to talk about, harder to write about except in generalities, and very difficult to apply because equity is in the mind of each individual. Yet equity is what this game is all about. Negotiations of contract price are intended to substitute for the automatic equity arising from the arm's length bargaining of the market place. The use of accounting in negotiations and settlements should ease the path to an equitable price or settlement. Accounting (or bookkeeping) form should never be permitted to get in the way of an equitable amount.[10]

Homogeneous cost pools

To simplify the allocation process, costs are pooled (grouped, aggregated) and few allocation bases are used. For example, CASB regulations require **homogeneous cost pools.** Paragraph #418.50(b) states:

> An indirect cost pool is homogeneous if each significant activity whose costs are included therein has the same or a similar beneficial or causal relationship to cost objectives as the other activities whose costs are included in the cost pool. It is also homogeneous if the allocation of the . . . cost pool . . . is not materially different from the allocation that would result if the costs of the activities were allocated separately.

The concept of homogeneity springs from the aggregation process. If elemental individual costs were allocated, no test for homogeneity would be needed. The preceding chapter contained a discussion of why departmental overhead rates are often preferable to plantwide rates. In these situations, the departmental rates may be described as being more homogeneous than the plantwide rates. The following general guidelines concerning homogeneity seem applicable:

1. Begin with the most detailed cost data that are economically feasible to collect. Start to form cost pools only if they are justified by the savings in clerical and other costs.
2. To obtain higher homogeneity, have more rather than fewer cost pools.

[10] Howard W. Wright, "Uniform Cost Accounting Standards: Past, Present and Future," *Financial Executive,* May 1971. Also see H. Wright and J. Bedingfield, *Government Contract Accounting* (Washington, D.C.: Federal Publications, 1979).

3. Cost pools may be formed in any combination by responsibility center, cost behavior pattern, and natural category. The natural category classification is illustrated by the following:[11]

TYPES OF COSTS	EXAMPLES	SUGGESTED USUAL ALLOCATION BASE
People-oriented	Personnel department	Number of employees
Payroll-oriented	Vacation pay, payroll taxes	Payroll dollars
Materials-oriented	Storeroom costs, internal transport	Units of material, weight, size
Machine-oriented	Variable costs of power, supplies, routine maintenance	Machine-hours

Choosing allocation bases

Despite the logical attractions of using various overhead pools and various **cost allocation bases,** the general practice is to use few pools and few bases. The most widely used bases are chosen after considering (a) the factors obviously associated with the individual products or jobs (for example, direct materials and direct labor), (b) necessary clerical costs and effort in application, and (c) differences in final results. Where results do not differ significantly, the easier method is used.

The logic is to relate the final cost objective to various bases and, in turn, to relate the overhead pool to the bases. Consider the data in Exhibit 15-3. The final cost objective is the product. The potential allocation bases are direct materials, direct-labor hours, direct-labor cost, and machine-hours; all these bases can be physically traced to the product. Which of the bases is best for predicting fluctuations in total overhead costs? The answer may be derived arbitrarily or by statistical regression analysis. As long as all the possible causal factors are used in the same proportions on individual jobs, each job will get the same amount of overhead.

Exhibit 15-3 illustrates the following important points:

1. Either direct-labor dollars or direct-labor time may be used as a basis for overhead application to product, as long as the direct-labor dollars and hours vary in direct proportion—that is, as long as labor rates are uniform across all jobs.

2. Where costs related to machines are the predominant overhead factor, machine-hours should be used instead of labor-hours if both do not fluctuate in direct proportion. In other words, if one operator runs one machine for a certain job and three similar machines for another job, other things being equal, the machine-hour base is more rational than a labor base.

3. If labor time has a directly proportionate relationship to machine time, it is unnecessary to use machine-hours because the final costs of a job will not differ.

4. Easy availability of data for a job, a department, or other cost objective is very influential. The base that is easiest and cheapest to apply is often selected, as long

[11] *Standards for Cost Analysis,* a research report prepared by William J. Vatter for the Comptroller General of the United States, August 1969, pp. 56–59.

EXHIBIT 15-3

Comparison of Overhead Application to Product When Bases Are Used Proportionately

ANNUAL OVERHEAD BUDGET DATA:		TOTAL	POSSIBLE RATES
Total overhead		$100,000	
Direct-labor cost		$200,000	50% of direct-labor cost
Direct-labor hours		100,000	$1.00 per DLH
Direct-material usage		$400,000	25% of direct materials
Machine-hours		20,000	$5.00 per machine-hour

JOB DATA:

			POSSIBLE OVERHEAD APPLICATION USING FOLLOWING BASES			
			direct materials	**direct-labor hours**	**direct-labor cost**	**machine-hours**
Job No. 1						
Direct-labor hours		5				
Machine-hours		1				
Direct materials	$ 20					
Direct-labor cost	10					
Prime cost	$ 30					
Overhead	5		.25($20) = $5	$1.00(5 hr.) = $5	.50($10) = $5	1 hr.($5) = $5
Total job cost	$ 35					
Job No. 2						
Direct-labor hours		25				
Machine-hours		5				
Direct materials	$100					
Direct-labor cost	50					
Prime cost	$150					
Overhead	25		.25($100) = $25	$1.00(25 hr.) = $25	.50($50) = $25	5 hr.($5) = $25
Total job cost	$175					

as individual job costs are not significantly affected. Note in Exhibit 15-3 that the final results are the same on a specific job because all bases are used *proportionately*. But if the possible bases are not used proportionately on individual jobs, certain jobs may receive relatively inaccurate amounts of overhead. This latter point is not illustrated specifically in the exhibit. However, the point can readily be seen by changing the number of machine-hours on Job No. 2 from five to six. This would change the overhead application, using a machine-hour rate, from $25 to $30.

Chapter 24 explores some general approaches to choosing allocation bases (independent variable) for aid in predicting how total costs (dependent variable) will fluctuate. A general discussion of the relative merits of some commonly used bases follows:

1. DIRECT-LABOR HOURS ☐ Most overhead costs are more closely related to time expiration than to any other factor. Fixed costs such as depreciation, rent, taxes, and insurance relate to a given time period. Indirect labor and supplies usage are most closely related to the input of hours of effort. That is why time devoted to specific products is often used for correlating overhead with products. Time is traced to specific products by using work tickets for direct labor. Predetermined overhead rates are developed by dividing predicted total overhead by predicted total direct hours.

Thus, the amount of overhead applied to any given product is dependent on the amount of time devoted thereto.

2. MACHINE-HOURS ☐ In these days of mechanized production, machine time is often a better predictor of overhead-cost incurrence than direct-labor time. Depreciation, property taxes, supplies usage, and indirect labor are frequently more closely related to machinery utilization than to direct-labor usage. In theory, then, machine time may be the most accurate base for overhead application.

In practice, however, machine time is rarely used because of the added clerical cost and the difficulty of computing machine time on individual jobs. Machine time may be ignored where the relationship of labor time or labor costs to machine time is unchanging between jobs; that is, the final overhead application to a given type of job would not differ (for example, one direct laborer may always run two similar machines).

3. DIRECT-LABOR COST ☐ If labor rates are nearly uniform for every operation, the use of a labor-*dollar* base for overhead application yields the same results as using direct-labor *hours.* Otherwise, in theory direct-labor *hours* is better in most instances, particularly where the senior and junior workers are equally efficient and therefore use the same amounts of overhead services per hour. For example, a senior worker may earn $16 per hour while a junior worker may earn $15 per hour. If a 200-percent-of-direct-labor-cost rate is in effect, the overhead cost of a given job requiring one hour of direct labor would be $32 if the senior worker were used and $30 if the junior worker were used. Standard or average labor rates generally prevent such ridiculous results.

Direct-labor *dollars* as an overhead base may be conceptually better than labor-*hours* where many overhead items represent fringe labor costs, which are primarily tied to direct-labor *cost* or where high-cost laborers make the greatest use of high-cost facilities and complex machinery.[12]

4. DIRECT MATERIAL ☐ Unless the labor and equipment needed for material handling are a major part of overhead, the use of direct-material dollars or weights is seldom a valid base for overhead application. Again, materials may be used where the final results are the same regardless of the base adopted. Sometimes storeroom and material-handling overhead is separated from other factory overhead and is applied to jobs on the basis of direct-material weight or bulk. The remaining overhead items would be applied by using some other base.

SUMMARY

The contribution approach to the income statement and to the problems of cost allocations is accounting's most effective method for helping management to evaluate performance and make decisions. Allocations are made with thoughtful regard for the purpose of the information being compiled.

[12]The CASB has summarized the use of various allocation bases used by companies under its jurisdiction. Direct-labor dollars is by far the most widely used allocation base, and direct-labor hours is second. For example, their 1979 data bank indicated that of those operating units (405) with a manufacturing overhead pool, 289 (71 percent) use the direct-labor dollars base, 63 (16 percent) use the direct-labor hours base, and 13 percent use a variety of other bases. *Progress Report to the Congress,* published annually through 1981.

The most logical allocation base for central administrative services is usage, either actual or estimated. Many companies, however, use a questionable ability-to-bear criterion such as sales revenues. Other companies do not allocate such central costs if no cause-effect allocation base is available.

For decision making and motivating, questions of cost allocation should be resolved in terms of how the allocation influences behavior.

For almost all purposes, most managers prefer to use fully allocated costs rather than variable or partially allocated costs. These managers feel that the collective decisions and motivation throughout an organization will be better served by full allocations.

Cost accounting is frequently used, especially in health-care and defense contracting, as a substitute for the free market pricing system. Cost allocations are used as a means of establishing a mutually satisfactory price.

Pools of indirect costs are formed as a practical step in accumulating and allocating costs. They may be formed in any combination by responsibility center, cost behavior pattern, and natural category.

Homogeneity is a frequently cited guide for deciding how many cost pools are warranted. The essence of the matter is whether final results in the form of costs and decisions will differ from the optimum as different allocation bases, cost pools, and cost objectives are chosen.

problems for self-study

problem 1

Review the section on the contribution approach to cost allocation, especially Exhibit 15-1.

solution 1

See Exhibit 15-1, page 504.

problem 2

Consider the following case, adapted from a CPA examination:

You have been engaged to install a cost system for the Martin Company. Your investigation of the manufacturing operations of the business discloses these facts:

1. The company makes a line of lighting fixtures and lamps. The material cost of any particular item ranks from 15 percent to 60 percent of total factory cost, depending on the kind of metal and fabric used in making it.
2. The business is subject to wide cyclical fluctuations, for the sales volume follows new-housing construction.
3. About 60 percent of the manufacturing is normally done in the first quarter of the year.
4. For the whole plant, the wage rates range from $12.75 to $25.85 an hour. However, within each of the eight individual departments, the spread between the high and low wage rates is less than 5 percent.
5. Each of the products made uses all eight of the manufacturing departments but not proportionately.
6. Within the individual manufacturing departments, factory overhead ranges from 30 percent to 80 percent of conversion cost.

Based on the information above, you are to prepare a statement or letter for the president of the company, explaining whether in its cost system Martin Company should use:

a. A denominator volume tied to normal volume or master-budget volume (see Chapter 8);
b. A plantwide overhead rate or a departmental overhead rate;
c. A method of factory-overhead application based on direct-labor hours, direct-labor cost, or prime cost.

Include the reasons supporting *each* of your three recommendations.

solution 2

Dear Sir:

From a study of the manufacturing operations of the Martin Company, it is my recommendation that, in applying its manufacturing overhead, the company use normal departmental overhead rates applied as percentages of the *direct-labor cost.*

The company should use normal rather than master-budget volume because of the wide seasonal and cyclical fluctuations in its business. Master-budget rates would, owing to the large fixed-overhead costs, make the per-unit overhead costs high in the low-production periods and low in the high-production periods. The use of normal rates would apply per-unit overhead costs that would be less sensitive to year-to-year fluctuations. Both for quoting prices and for pricing inventories, it is best to use per-unit costs neither inflated by the costs of available but unused factory facilities nor deflated by the gains of better-than-normal use of the factory facilities.

The company should use departmental overhead rates because the rates obviously vary so markedly among the departments. If a plantwide rate were used as an average rate, it would not be correct for any department. Because the company's overhead is a large part of the factory cost, the inaccuracy in the per-unit costs caused by the use of a plantwide rate would be substantial. If all the products made used all the departments proportionately, a plantwide rate would result in substantially accurate total (but not departmental) unit-overhead costs. In the Martin Company, however, the products do not use all the departments proportionately.

As the wage rates are substantially uniform within the separate departments, the labor costs in each department are closely proportionate to the labor time. Therefore, the percent-of-direct-labor-cost method of applying the factory overhead would in this case effect about as accurate an application as would the rate-per-direct-labor-hour method. The clerical expense of the percent-of-direct-labor-cost method would be low, because the method does not require accumulation of the number of direct-labor hours applicable to each job.

The percent-of-prime-cost method of overhead application is not recommended because of the wide differences in the costs of the materials that may be used to make a given lamp or fixture. Factory overhead is primarily the cost of using labor and factory facilities. The factory facilities applied to make a lamp of silver are not more than those used to make the same lamp of copper. For this reason, the use of prime cost (because it includes material cost) would result in an excessive charge to lamps using expensive materials.

Very truly yours,

Terms to Learn

controllability ***Cost Accounting Standards Board (CASB)***
cost-allocation base ***discretionary fixed costs*** ***homogeneous cost pool***
segment ***subunit***

Special Points and Pitfalls

Two important lessons received major attention in this chapter. First, choices of how to allocate costs may affect how managers behave. For example, a manager's use of department services, such as legal or public relations services, depends on whether charges will be forthcoming. Second, cost allocations often substitute for market prices as a way of setting selling prices. For example, amounts paid for special weapons by the U.S. Department of Defense are often directly dependent on a manufacturer's costs.

Accountants and managers should know the assumptions underlying the allocations of costs in their organizations. Then they will be better able to judge the relevance of costs for particular classes of decisions. In short, knowledgeable skepticism is helpful, especially when somebody adamantly maintains that "the cost of this product or service is exactly $48.57."

QUESTIONS, PROBLEMS, AND CASES

15-1 List at least three subtotals that might be highlighted in a contribution income statement by segments.

15-2 For what purpose of cost allocation does equity or fairness become a dominant criterion?

15-3 "Central corporate costs should never be allocated because no cause-and-effect relationships can be established." Do you agree? Explain.

15-4 "In order to save time and effort, we use a single allocation plan to fulfill both product-costing and control purposes." Discuss.

15-5 A prominent economist once said, "Not even Almighty God can tell a railroad the cost of moving a hundred tons of freight from Boston to New York." Do you agree? Why?

15-6 How is homogeneity in cost allocation measured?

15-7 What is the most frequently used cost-allocation base?

15-8 "To obtain higher homogeneity, have more rather than fewer cost pools." Do you agree? Why?

15-9 "In these days of highly mechanized production, more overhead rates should be based on machine-hours." Do you agree? Why?

15-10 ***Allocation of travel costs.*** John Ernst, a graduating senior at a university near Denver, received an invitation to visit a prospective employer in Omaha. A few days later he received a similar invitation to visit North Platte, Nebraska. He decided to combine his visits, traveling from Denver to Omaha to North Platte to Denver.

John received job offers from both locations. Upon his return, he decided to accept the Omaha offer. He was puzzled about how to allocate his travel costs between the two prospective employers. He gathered the following data:

Roundtrip sedan service, dormitory to Denver airport	$ 26
Regular roundtrip fares from Denver to:	
Omaha	348
North Platte	294
Actual airfare paid	396

REQUIRED How much should each employer pay for Ernst's travel costs? Why? Explain. Show computations.

15-11 ***Allocation of central costs.*** TennisAmerica, Inc., had several tennis camps. All the camps were run at fifteen geographically dispersed tennis clubs owned by outside parties. TennisAmerica contracted with each club (hereafter called owner) to pay a rental that was close to 50 percent of the profits accruing to that particular camp.

Central headquarters in Palo Alto was responsible for many functions, including camp reservations and camp advertising. To arrive at a profit figure for each camp, it was necessary to allocate the costs of a central reservation system and advertising. In the past the allocation of these costs was based on gross revenues. The advertising was on a national level; the name of each camp was mentioned in every ad. Some of the owners of camps with higher gross revenue were pushing for an allocation of these costs on an equal basis, that is, one-fifteenth of the costs to each camp. TennisAmerica had refused.

REQUIRED Who is correct? Why? Are there other ways to allocate the expenses? Are they better? Explain.

15-12 ***Using revenue as a basis for allocating costs.*** The Mideastern Transportation Company has had a long-standing policy of fully allocating all costs to its various divisions. Among the costs allocated were general and administrative costs in central headquarters, consisting of office salaries, executive salaries, travel expense, accounting costs, office supplies, donations, rents, depreciation, postage, and similar items.

All these costs were difficult to trace directly to the individual divisions benefited, so they were allocated on the basis of the total revenue of each of the divisions. The same basis was used for allocating general advertising and miscellaneous selling costs. For example, in 19_3 the following allocations were made:

	DIVISIONS			
	A	B	C	TOTAL
Revenue (in millions)	$50.0	$40.0	$10.0	$100.0
Costs allocated on the basis of revenue	6.0	4.8	1.2	12.0

In 19_4, Division A's revenue was expected to rise. But the division encountered severe competitive conditions; its revenue remained at $50 million. In contrast, Division C enjoyed explosive growth in traffic because of the completion of several huge factories in its area; its revenue rose to $30 million. Division B's revenue remained unchanged. Careful supervision kept the total costs allocated on the basis of revenue at $12 million.

REQUIRED

1. What costs will be allocated to each division in 19_4?
2. Using the results in requirement 1, comment on the limitations of using revenue as a basis for cost allocation.

15-13 ***Allocating telephone costs.***[13] A firm leases from a telephone company a WATS (Wide Area Telephone Service) line for $3,800 per month, which provides use of the line for 100 hours per month. This service allows the firm toll-free long-distance calls within the United States. Although each individual long-distance call is not billed by the phone company, only one call at a time can be placed. The $3,800 is a "fixed" cost; the "variable" cost of a call is zero. Should the firm allocate the $3,800 internally among the users?

15-14 ***Contribution approach to cost allocation: income statement by segments.*** Stuart Philatelic Sales, Inc., is engaged in the business of selling postage stamps and supplies to collectors on a retail basis. Stuart also makes up packets of inexpensive stamps that it sells on a wholesale basis to stamp departments of various stores.

Stuart's retail division has two stores, A and B, each of which has a stamp department and an albums and supplies department. Stuart had total net sales in 19_4 of $960,000; cost of merchandise sold was $490,000; and variable operating expenses were $120,000. The company's nonvariable costs, which it fully allocated to its two divisions, were $105,000 of advertising expense and $120,000 of various committed costs. Stuart's joint discretionary and committed costs were $35,000.

The costs of merchandise sold and variable operating expenses allocated to the retail division were $190,000 and $50,000, respectively. Net sales of Retail were $390,000, two-thirds of which were Store A's net sales. Sixty percent of Retail's merchandise costs and 54 percent of its variable operating expenses were allocated to Store A. Advertising costs of $40,000 were allocated to Retail, which in turn allocated 45 percent directly to Store A and 5 percent to Store B; the rest of the $40,000 was unallocated. Of the $120,000 separable committed costs, 50 percent were allocated to Retail, which in turn allocated 50 percent of its committed costs to Store A, had $25,000 of unallocated costs, and allocated the rest to Store B.

OTHER INFORMATION:

1. Allocations to Store B—stamp department

Net sales	$100,000
Cost of merchandise sold	$ 58,000
Variable operating expenses	$ 17,000

Allocations to Store B—albums and supplies department:

Net sales	$ 30,000
Cost of merchandise sold	$ 18,000
Variable operating expenses	$ 6,000

[13] J. L. Zimmerman, "The Costs and Benefits of Cost Allocations," *Accounting Review,* LIV, No. 3 (July 1979), 510.

2. One-half of Store B's allocated advertising expenses could not be further allocated either to the stamp department or to the albums and supplies department; the other half of B's allocated advertising expenses was equally divided between the two departments.

3. Sixty percent of Store B's committed costs were unallocated; three-fourths of the rest was allocated to the stamp department and one-fourth to the albums and supplies department.

REQUIRED

1. What was operating income before taxes for the company as a whole?
2. Determine the contribution margin, contribution controllable by division managers, and contribution by segments for each of the following:
   a. Company as a whole
   b. Wholesale division
   c. Retail division
   d. Store A of the retail division
   e. Store B of the retail division
   f. Stamps department of Store B
   g. Albums and supplies department of Store B

15-15 ***Product-line and territorial income statements.*** The Delvin Company shows the following results for the year 19_1:

Sales	$1,000,000	100.0%
Manufacturing costs of goods sold	$ 675,000	67.5%
Selling and advertising*	220,000	22.0%
Administrative (all nonvariable)	35,000	3.5%
Total expenses	$ 930,000	93.0%
Net income before income taxes	$ 70,000	7.0%

**All nonvariable, except for $40,000 freight-out cost.*

The sales manager has asked you to prepare statements that will help him assess the company efforts by product line and by territories. You have gathered the following information:

	PRODUCT			TERRITORY		
	A	B	C	north	central	eastern
Sales*	25%	40%	35%			
Product *A*				50%	20%	30%
Product *B*				15%	70%	15%
Product *C*				14/35	8/35	13/35
Variable manufacturing and packaging costs†	68%	55%	60%			
Nonvariable separable costs:						
Manufacturing	15,000	14,000	21,000		(not allocated)	
Selling and advertising	40,000	18,000	42,000	48,000	32,000	40,000
Freight out		(not allocated)		13,000	9,000	18,000

Note. *All items not directly allocated were considered common costs.*
**Percent of company sales.*
†Percent of product sales.

REQUIRED

1. Prepare a product-line income statement, showing the results for the company as a whole in the first column and the results for the three products in adjoining columns. Show a contribution margin and a product margin, as well as net income.
2. Repeat requirement 1 on a territorial basis. Show a contribution margin and a territory margin.

3. Should salespeople's commissions be based on contribution margins, product margins, territorial margins, net income, or dollar sales? Explain.

15-16 ***Should we allocate?*** Solve Problem 10-27, which could logically have been placed here.

15-17 ***Allocation of computer costs.*** Salquist, Inc., is an international ethical pharmaceutical manufacturer that specializes in hormone research and the development and marketing of hormone-base products. The 22 different wholly owned subsidiaries and separate divisions that constitute the organization are highly decentralized, but they receive overall direction from a small corporate staff at parent-corporation headquarters in Palo Alto. The laboratories division, research division, and all corporate offices are located at the home-office site. Each of the divisional functional areas operates as a cost center. That is, labs accounting, labs production, labs sales, research accounting, and research operations are separate cost centers. Corporate purchasing, employee relations, office services, and computer (EDP) systems also function as individual cost centers, and they provide their services to Research, Labs, and the other divisions as necessary.

Until recently, no costs of the corporate service cost centers were allocated to the divisional cost centers; they were simply lumped together as central corporate overhead. Recently, however, it was decided to start charging the operating units (that is, the cost centers) for their EDP usage. Prior to this time, EDP services were simply requested as desired by the cost centers; priorities were determined by negotiations, with ultimate recourse to an EDP control committee (each cost center was represented); and all charges were absorbed as corporate overhead.

EDP systems contain both systems programming services and computer operations. In the current "charge-back" system, the EDP director prepares a budget at the start of each quarter based upon his estimates of user demand. Using full absorption costing, he then computes an hourly charge rate, which he promulgates to the user cost centers. The users prepare their budgets utilizing his charge rate and their estimates of the services they think they will be needing. When a user desires to undertake any specific project or use EDP services, he negotiates an agreement with EDP on the hours (thus cost) that he will be charged. The user is free to reject the EDP "bid" and obtain outside services if he does not feel the EDP job estimates are reasonable. Also, since many projects last a year or more but service agreements are arranged on a quarterly basis, the user can drop a project in midstream at the end of a quarter if his overall budget should become too tight. If the actual hours needed to complete a given job exceed those contracted for, the EDP center must absorb the extra cost as an unfavorable overhead variance.

The performance of all cost centers is evaluated on the basis of how closely their actual results match budget. Thus the EDP director must not only ensure that his actual expenditures coincide with those that were budgeted, but that he is able to bill other centers for all his actual charges. He must be sure that he contracts for enough projects from the users to absorb his budget.

The shift to the charge-back method was imposed by the corporate financial vice-president for the "purpose of putting control and responsibility for expenditures where the benefits are received." The VP also felt the move was necessary to avoid a "mushrooming of the EDP group" and to make users more aware of the costs they were incurring. An additional factor mentioned was an almost irresistible tide of "allocationism" prevalent in local industry because of the overpowering influence of government contracting there. He does feel he will resist allocating the other services, however, with the possible exception of printing and reproduction, which has grown to be quite costly in the last few years. The major rationale for not allocating the other services is that they are all uniform, predictable functions, whereas the EDP services are more spasmodic and project-oriented.

The head of the EDP group is strongly opposed to the new system. He believes that there is "too much lip service paid to the specialized nature of computers" and that the new system is reducing the effectiveness of the EDP group to the corporation as a whole. He and several of the user-directors believe the shift was simply a political maneuver on the part of the VP to consolidate the EDP empire under the aegis of the corporate staff. The head of the EDP group believes a nonchargeable system administered by the EDP control committee would yield better results.

REQUIRED

1. What are the motivational and operational effects of this change on users, EDP group, and corporation?
2. Evaluate the impact of having coexistence of allocated and nonallocated services.
3. Evaluate the operation of this particular allocation system.

15-18 ***Cost allocation, equity and motivation.*** (R. Troxel, adapted)[14] A task force of Marwick Corporation has assembled the following information concerning the company's electronic data-processing (EDP) operations:

Present centralized EDP operations per year:

Total actual costs	$1,000,000
Lines of print produced:	
Division A	4,000,000
Division B	4,000,000
Division C	2,000,000
Total	10,000,000
Total estimated costs of EDP operations per year if Division D operations were consolidated with centralized operations	$1,030,000
Total estimated costs of EDP operations per year if all four divisions were to conduct their operations separately:	
Division A	$ 500,000
Division B	500,000
Division C	250,000
Division D (actual)	50,000
Total	$1,300,000

The task force has recommended that the EDP operations of Division D be consolidated with the present centralized EDP operations.

REQUIRED

1. Compute the expected annual total cost savings to the company if Division D data-processing operations were combined with the present centralized EDP operations.
2. You are the manager of the D Division. Assume that you would be satisfied with the quantity and quality of the services your division would receive if its EDP operations were combined with the present centralized operations. Upon inquiry, you discover that the task force has proposed that, after consolidation, the total annual EDP costs be allocated to divisions on the basis of their lines of print. Your division's present annual requirement is 800,000 lines. Compute this cost allocation and explain your reaction to this method. Give specific reasons to support the position you take.
3. Compute the cost allocation by another method that you believe would be more equitable. Explain why you would propose the use of this method instead of the method described above. Be specific.

15-19 ***Choosing allocation bases and denominator volumes.*** (SMA) Concord Ltd. manufactures a variety of metal products sold under its own trade name. Although manufacturing continues throughout the year, the volume of production varies significantly during the year. The manufacturing process comprises two departments. In the machining department, the products are roughly fashioned by metal lathes (all lathes are similar and incur approximately equal costs to operate); while in the finishing department, the products are finished by hand tool operation. The union agreement sets a single wage rate for employees in the finishing department.

[14] *Management Focus,* January-February 1981.

The following additional information is provided:

	MACHINING DEPARTMENT		FINISHING DEPARTMENT	
	at 100% capacity	**actual (month of april)**	**at 100% capacity**	**actual (month of april)**
Direct-labor hours	2,500	2,500	20,000	18,000
Machine-hours	25,000	20,000		
Number of machine operators employed	30	27		
Number of machines used	60	60		
Variable costs:				
Direct labor	$12,500	$11,700	$ 80,000	$ 75,600
Direct material	35,000	27,500	10,000	9,000
Indirect labor	4,500	3,200	10,000	8,100
Supplies, etc.	3,000	2,600	8,000	8,300
	$55,000	$45,000	$108,000	$101,000
Semifixed costs (vary 50% with production)	$ 5,000	$ 4,000	$ 8,000	$ 7,500
Fixed costs:				
Depreciation	$50,000	$49,000	$ 1,000	$ 1,100
Other	6,500	6,400	5,000	5,100
	$56,500	$55,400	$ 6,000	$ 6,200

The costs of unused factory facilities are not considered as manufacturing costs. A standard-cost system is not considered desirable.

REQUIRED

1. Describe, *with reasons,* the method most suited for applying Concord Ltd.'s overhead costs to production. The method described should be selected primarily for theoretical accuracy, with costs for clerical and other accounting work being a secondary consideration.
2. Calculate (a) the overhead application rate(s) to be used, and (b) the amount of overhead applied in the month of April.
3. Under what circumstances would a separate rate be applied for each machine in the machining department? Explain.

15-20 ***Revision of cost allocations.*** (SMA) Zantevan Limited produces heavy industrial machinery for customers' orders. The following income statement was prepared by the company's bookkeeper for the fiscal year ended on March 31, 19_8.

	CONTRACT 1	CONTRACT 2	TOTAL
Contract revenue	$250,000	$340,000	$590,000
Contract costs:			
Direct materials	30,000	40,000	70,000
Direct labor	56,000	140,000	196,000
Manufacturing overhead	79,200	174,900	254,100
Total contract costs	165,200	354,900	520,100
Gross margin on contracts	$ 84,800	$(14,900)	69,900
Administrative and general expenses			20,500
Income before income taxes			$ 49,400

It is the belief of management that the above statement does not reflect their opinion that both contracts were, in fact, profitable because of the method of overhead allocation.

From questioning of company officials and from an analysis of the accounts and records, you have determined that

a. Revenues, direct materials, and direct-labor costs were properly credited or charged to the appropriate contracts.

b. The company has two production departments—A and B. In Department A, there are several large automatic machines that are operated by two attendants. In Department B, there are many small machines, each of which is operated by an individual employee who is paid on a piecework basis. This is because the work in Department B involves considerable skill, and experienced operators are much faster than new operators.

c. The total manufacturing overhead costs allocated to the two contracts ($254,100) consisted of the following:

	DEPT. A	DEPT. B	BUILDING OPERATION COSTS	REPAIR COSTS	TOTAL
Supervision and indirect labor	$ 10,000	$ 20,100	$12,000	$ 7,000	$ 49,100
Supplies, power, and spoilage	8,000	5,000	1,500	—	14,500
Building depreciation	—	—	4,000	—	4,000
Machinery depreciation	96,000	86,000	500	3,000	$185,500
Property taxes	—	—	1,000	—	1,000
	$114,000	$111,100	$19,000	$10,000	$254,100

d. The time required to complete each contract was:

	CONTRACT 1	CONTRACT 2	TOTAL
Direct-labor hours:			
Department A	2,000	1,500	3,500
Department B	10,000	25,000	35,000
	12,000	26,500	38,500
Machine-hours:			
Department A	10,000	4,000	14,000
Department B	9,100	22,750	31,850
	19,100	26,750	45,850

e. There was no work in process at either April 1, 19_7 or March 31, 19_8.

f. Of the total repairs, 10 percent were made to the building, 70 percent to machinery in Department A, and 20 percent to machinery in Department B.

g. Building space is used 75 percent by Department A and 25 percent by Department B.

h. Contract 1 required 50 percent more supervision and indirect labor than Contract 2.

REQUIRED

Prepare a revised income statement showing what you believe to be the results of each contract, together with supporting schedules showing the appropriate allocation of overhead.

15-21 ***Cost allocation and contribution margin.***[15] In discussing the costs incident to various types of operations, the analogy was drawn of the restaurant that adds a rack of peanuts to the counter, intending to pick up a little additional profit in the usual course of business. This analogy was attacked as an oversimplification. However, the accuracy of the analogy is evident when one considers the actual problem faced by the Restaurateur (Joe) as revealed by his Accountant–Efficiency-Expert.

EFF EX: Joe, you said you put in these peanuts because some people ask for them, but do you realize what this rack of peanuts is *costing* you?

[15]Original source unknown. Versions of this situation have been printed and reprinted throughout this century.

JOE: It ain't gonna cost. 'Sgonna be a profit. Sure, I hadda pay $25 for a fancy rack to hold bags, but the peanuts cost 6¢ a bag and I sell 'em for 10¢. Figger I sell 50 bags a week to start. It'll take 12½ weeks to cover the cost of the rack. After that I gotta clear profit of 4¢ a bag. The more I sell, the more I make.

EFF EX: That is an antiquated and completely unrealistic approach, Joe. Fortunately, modern accounting procedures permit a more accurate picture which reveals the complexities involved.

JOE: Huh?

EFF EX: To be precise, those peanuts must be integrated into your entire operation and be allocated their appropriate share of business overhead. They must share a proportionate part of your expenditure for rent, heat, light, equipment depreciation, decorating, salaries for your waitresses, cook . . .

JOE: The *cook?* What's he gotta do wit'a peanuts? He don' even know I got 'em!

EFF EX: Look Joe, the cook is in the kitchen, the kitchen prepares the food, the food is what brings people in here, and the people ask to buy peanuts. That's why you must charge a portion of the cook's wages, as well as a part of your own salary to peanut sales. This sheet contains a carefully calculated cost analysis which indicates the peanut operation should pay exactly $1,278 per year toward these general overhead costs.

JOE: The peanuts? $1,278 a year for overhead? The nuts?

EFF EX: It's really a little more than that. You also spend money each week to have the windows washed, to have the place swept out in the mornings, keep soap in the washroom, and provide free cokes to the police. That raises the total to $1,313 per year.

JOE: [Thoughtfully] But the peanut salesman said I'd make money . . . put 'em on the end of the counter, he said . . . and get 4¢ a bag profit . . .

EFF EX: [With a sniff] He's not an accountant. Do you actually know what the portion of the counter occupied by the peanut rack is worth to you?

JOE: Ain't worth nothing—no stool there . . . Just a dead spot at the end.

EFF EX: The modern cost picture permits no dead spots. Your counter contains 60 square feet and your counter business grosses $15,000 a year. Consequently, the square foot of space occupied by the peanut rack is worth $250 per year. Since you have taken that area away from general counter use, you must charge the value of the space to the occupant.

JOE: You mean I gotta add $250 a year more to the peanuts?

EFF EX: Right. That raises their share of the general operating costs to a grand total of $1,563 per year. Now then, if you sell 50 bags of peanuts per week, these allocated costs will amount to 60¢ per bag.

JOE: *What?*

EFF EX: Obviously, to that must be added your purchase price of 6¢ per bag, which brings the total to 66¢. So you see by selling peanuts at 10¢ per bag, you are losing 56¢ on every sale.

JOE: Somethin's crazy!

EFF EX: Not at all! Here are the *figures.* They *prove* your peanuts operation cannot stand on its own feet.

JOE: [Brightening] Suppose I sell *lotsa* peanuts . . . thousand bags a week 'stead of fifty.

EFF EX: [Tolerantly] Joe, you don't understand the problem. If the volume of peanuts sales increases, our operating costs will go up . . . you'll have to handle more bags with more time, more depreciation, more everything. The basic principle of accounting is firm on that subject: "The Bigger the Operation, the More General Overhead Costs That Must Be Allocated." No, increasing the volume of sales won't help.

JOE: Okay, you so smart, *you* tell *me* what I gotta do.

EFF EX: [Condescendingly] Well . . . you could first reduce operating expenses.

JOE: How?

EFF EX: Move to a building with cheaper rent. Cut salaries. Wash the windows biweekly. Have the floor swept only on Thursday. Remove the soap from the washrooms. Decrease the square-foot value of your counter. For example, if you can cut your expenses 50 percent, that will reduce the amount allocated to peanuts from $1,563 to $781.50 per year, reducing the cost to 36¢ per bag.

JOE: [Slowly] That's better?

EFF EX: Much, much better. However, even then you would lose 26¢ per bag if you only charge 10¢. Therefore, you must also raise your selling price. If you want a net profit of 4¢ per bag you would have to charge 40¢.

JOE: [Flabbergasted] You mean even after I cut operating costs 50 percent I still gotta charge 40¢ for a 10¢ bag of peanuts? Nobody's that nuts about nuts! Who'd buy 'em?

EFF EX: That's a secondary consideration. The point is, at 40¢ you'd be selling at a price based upon a true and proper evaluation of your then reduced costs.

JOE: [Eagerly] Look! I gotta better idea. Why don't I just throw the nuts out . . . put 'em in the ashcan?

EFF EX: Can you afford it?

JOE: Sure. All I got is about 50 bags of peanuts . . . cost about three bucks . . . so I lose $25 on the rack, but I'm outa this nutsy business and no more grief.

EFF EX: [Shaking head] Joe it isn't that simple .You are *in* the peanut business! The minute you throw those peanuts out you are adding $1,563 of annual overhead to the rest of your operation. Joe . . . be realistic . . . *can you afford to do that?*

JOE: [Completely crushed] It's unbelievable! Last week I was making money. Now I'm in trouble . . . just because I think peanuts on a counter is gonna bring me some extra profit . . . just because I believe 50 bags of peanuts a week is easy.

EFF EX: [With raised eyebrow] That is the object of modern cost studies, Joe . . . to dispel those false illusions.

REQUIRED

1. Is Joe losing 56¢ on every sale of peanuts? Explain.
2. Do you agree that if the volume of peanut sales is increased, operating losses will increase? Explain.
3. Do you agree with the "Efficiency Expert" that, in order to make the peanut operation profitable, the operating costs in the restaurant should be decreased and the selling price of the peanuts should be increased? Give reasons.
4. Do you think that Joe can afford to get out of the peanut business? Give reasons.
5. Do you think that Joe should eliminate his peanut operations? Why or why not?

15-22 ***Allocating fixed overhead.*** You have recently been hired as an assistant to the vice-president of planning and analysis, Mr. Jackson, of the Thornhill Towing Company. Thornhill Towing owns and operates a large fleet of harbor and ocean-going tugboats. Founded in Galveston in 1923, the company now has ongoing operations in the Gulf of Mexico and the Caribbean, the North Sea, the Far East, and the Pacific Northwest.

During your second week on the job you have lunch with Jackson and the executive vice-president of finance, Alex Thomson. Thomson mentions that at an upcoming staff meeting the internal accounting group is going to make a presentation highlighting the top ten most profitable operations from the previous month.

Later that day Jackson calls you into his office. He has an internal operating statement of one of the profit centers in his hand. He says, "I feel fairly comfortable with these reports down through 'revenue after variable operating expenses,' but past that I'm just not too sure. We have had this system for about a year, and I know some of our operating managers have been complaining about how fixed vessel costs are allocated. If we are going to start giving corporate recognition to the top ten profit centers, I think we need to be on firmer ground about the allocated fixed vessel costs. Please investigate how we are allocating fixed vessel costs."

You begin to piece together how the current system works. Usually several boats will be stationed at one location, which is the operating base for several functions such as assisting and docking ships, towing inland oil barges, and offshore contract towing. Each of the functions has an operating manager who is responsible for his function as a profit center. The boats stationed at a location are likely to work in any of the functions based at the location for which they are suited. The annual dollar amount of fixed cost is accumulated for each boat and divided into twelve increments to correspond with the monthly accounting periods. This monthly fixed cost is then allocated to each function in which the boat worked during the month as a percentage of the total revenue-producing hours that the boat worked during the month.

REQUIRED

1. Suppose the tug Sam Houston had $3,000 in fixed costs each month. Prepare a tabulation for January, February, and March showing the vessel fixed costs per revenue-hour and the allocated fixed costs to functions A and B if revenue-hours were as follows:

	A	B
January	300	300
February	200	300
March	400	300

2. Comment on the tabulation in requirement 1. What is causing the puzzling results?
3. What cost-allocation system would you recommend? For this requirement, assume that the annual revenue-hours for A is 3,600 and for B is 3,600.

15-23 ***Overhead disputes.*** (Suggested by Howard Wright) The Azure Ship Company works on U.S. Navy vessels and commercial vessels. General yard overhead (for example, the cost of the purchasing department) is allocated to the jobs on the basis of direct-labor costs.

In 19_3 Azure's total $150 million of direct-labor cost consisted of $50 million navy and $100 million commercial. The general yard overhead was $30 million.

Navy auditors periodically examine the records of defense contractors. The auditors investigated a nuclear submarine contract, which was based on cost-plus-fixed-fee pricing. The auditors later claimed that the navy was entitled to a refund because of double-counting of overhead in 19_3.

The government contract included the following provision:

> Par. 15-202. Direct Costs.
> (a) A direct cost is any cost which can be identified specifically with a particular cost objective. Direct costs are not limited to items which are incorporated in the end product as material or labor. Costs identified specifically with the contract are direct costs of the contract and are to be charged directly thereto. Costs identified specifically with other work of the contractor are direct costs of that work and are not to be charged to the contract directly or indirectly. When items ordinarily chargeable as indirect costs are charged to the contract as direct costs, the cost of like items applicable to other work must be eliminated from indirect costs allocated to the contract.

A special expediting purchasing group, the SE group, had been formed to do work (in addition to that rendered by the central purchasing group) on obtaining materials for the nuclear submarine only. Their direct costs, $5 million, had been included as direct labor of the nuclear work. Accordingly, overhead was applied to the contracts in the usual manner. The SE costs of $5 million were not included in the yard overhead costs. The auditors claimed that no overhead should have been applied to these SE costs.

REQUIRED

1. Compute the amount of the refund that the navy would claim.
2. Suppose that later the navy also discovered that $4 million of general yard overhead was devoted exclusively to commercial engine-room purchasing activities. Compute the additional refund that the navy would probably claim. (*Note:* This $4 million was never classified as "direct labor." Furthermore, the navy would claim that it should be reclassified as a "direct cost" but not as "direct labor.")

15-24 ***Dispute about variance allocation.*** G Manufacturing Company has been buying $\frac{1}{4}$-horsepower motors from L Manufacturing Company for several years. L Manufacturing Company has supplied such motors to several large customers. Each customer pays a predetermined price per motor, which is changed annually. The procedure is in the table on the next page (data simplified to ease calculations).

REQUIRED

1. Suppose that Customers F, G, and H each bought 75 motors for the year. Compute the additional charge to each customer.
2. Suppose that Customers F and G each bought 75 motors, but H bought 150. Compute the additional charge to each customer.

3. Refer to requirement 2. In 19_8 L Company changed its method of computing the production volume variance after its top executive commented: "We're not playing fair with our customers by computing the volume variance in such an aggregate way. Instead, we should compute individual volume variances." Compute the charges or rebates under this new allocation method. As an impartial observer, do you favor using the aggregated method or the disaggregated method? Why?

	CUSTOMER			
	F	G	H	TOTAL
Three customers predict their annual volume	100	100	100	300
Standard costs:				
Direct material	$10	$10	$10	
Direct labor	10	10	10	
Variable overhead	5	5	5	
Fixed overhead $3,000 ÷ 300	10	10	10	
Absorption cost per unit	$35	$35	$35	
Add a margin	7	7	7	
Predetermined price	$42	$42	$42	

Each year L Manufacturing also allocates any year-end "unabsorbed overhead production volume variance" as an additional charge or rebate to its customers.

15-25 ***Medicare, cost reimbursement, and pricing.*** The Valley Hospital has two departments (for simplicity here). In its budgeting and pricing, the hospital tries to obtain a modest income. Physicians share in the revenue of both departments. For example, the radiologists obtain 10 percent of the nongovernment revenue from X-rays. There are two basic sources of revenue for various services: (1) nongovernment, that is, individuals who are responsible for paying at predetermined selling prices and (2) government agencies who are responsible for paying under some scheme of "cost reimbursement" regardless of what the selling prices may be.

The hospital's results for 19_7 included (in millions of dollars):

	DEPARTMENT	
	A	B
Revenue	$10	$10
Revenue generated by cost reimbursement plans	50%	75%
Physicians' share of nongovernment revenue	10%	25%
Bad debts related solely to individuals, expressed as a percentage of gross revenue from individuals	10%	20%

Because of various increases in budgeted costs, the hospital's trustees are contemplating announcing a price increase for individual services for 19_8. The trustees have been extremely sensitive to the community's criticisms of price increases in recent years. At the same time, the trustees believe they must be sure that the "bottom line" takes the form of a small profit.

Net revenue is defined as revenue minus the physicians' share and minus bad debts. The physicians' share is not affected by bad debts.

REQUIRED

1. Compute the total *change* in net revenue from a uniform increase in prices of 10 percent for individuals, assuming that the *physical* volume of 19_7 services would not change.
2. Suppose no prices were increased in Department B. By what percentage would prices have to be increased in Department A in order to obtain the same total change in net revenue computed in requirement 1?
3. What implications for pricing strategies arise from the above analysis?

This chapter examines (a) the methods of allocating joint costs to products, (b) the role of joint costs in decision making, and (c) accounting for byproducts.

Viewed broadly, joint costs plague the accountant's work. The preceding two chapters emphasized the difficulties of *one-to-many* allocations. These allocations assign a single cost or cost pool to two or more cost objectives.[1] They are sometimes described simply as *cost allocations,* sometimes as *common cost allocations,* and sometimes as *joint cost allocations.* Examples abound: (1) allocating the cost of equipment to months, years, departments, and products; (2) allocating **common costs,** which are defined as the cost of facilities and services shared by user departments; (3) allocating **joint costs,** which in this book will be restricted to the narrower meaning of **joint-product costs.**

[1]A. L. Thomas, *A Behavioural Analysis of Joint-Cost Allocation and Transfer Pricing* (Urbana, Ill.: Stipes Publishing, 1980), p. 2. Contains an exhaustive analysis of the issues and an extensive bibliography. Regarding joint costs, Thomas observes (p. 111): "It's obvious that no individual allocation method even approaches being reliably behaviour-congruent with respect to all decisions and circumstances."

Meaning of terms

***Joint-product costs* are the costs of manufactured goods of relatively significant sales values that are simultaneously produced by a process or series of processes; the products are not identifiable as different individual products until after a certain stage of production known as the split-off point.** A distinguishing characteristic is the fact that no one of the products may be produced without an accompanying appearance of the other products in the joint group, although perhaps in variable proportions. Examples include lumber, petroleum products, flour milling, copper mining, meat packing, chemicals, leather tanning, soap making, gas manufacturing, canneries, and tobacco manufacturing. A meat-packing company cannot kill a pork chop; it has to slaughter a hog, which supplies various cuts of dressed meat, hides, and trimmings.

The *split-off point* is that juncture of production where the joint products become individually identifiable. Any costs beyond that stage are called **separable costs** because they are not part of the joint production process and can be identified with individual products.

Nearly every manufacturing operation produces two or more products. But ordinarily, all the manufacturing costs of these multiple products are applied to a single product. For example, as cloth or metal is being cut or formed, the excess is regarded as waste or scrap. The minor cost that might be applied to the waste or scrap is usually ignored, and all the production cost is applied to, say, the coat or the lamp that is eventually manufactured. The relative revenue-producing power of multiple products determines whether and how costs are allocated.

The term **byproducts** is usually confined to those multiple products that have minor sales value as compared with that of the major or chief product(s).

Methods of allocating joint costs to products

Any method of allocating truly joint costs to various units produced is useful mainly for purposes of inventory costing, which, of course, will affect the income statement and balance sheet. **Such allocation is useless for cost-planning and control purposes.** This section explores various ways of allocating joint costs to products for inventory-valuation and income-determination purposes. The next section underscores the fact that all these cost allocations are inherently arbitrary and are of no help in making decisions about product mix or whether to sell at the split-off point or process beyond split-off.

nature of joint-product cost

Joint-product costs are total costs incurred up to the point of separation of the different products. Consider Example 1:

» ***EXAMPLE 1***

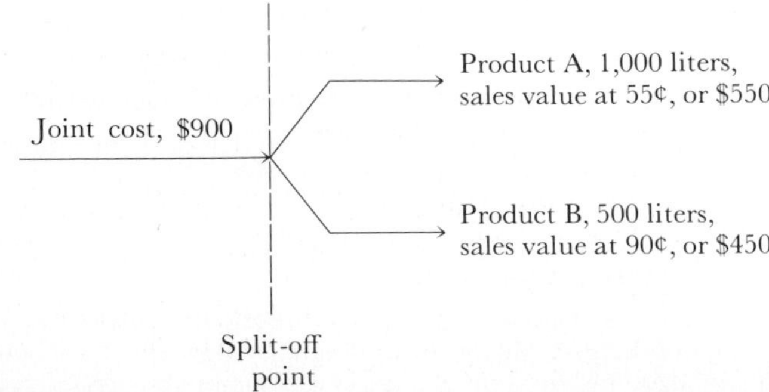

Example 1 uses simple numbers and shows the joint costs of a chemical process that produces Products A and B; both become finished goods at the split-off point. How much of the $900 joint cost is allocable to A? How much to B? The $900 cannot be physically identified or traced to either individual product, because the products themselves were not separated before the split-off point. Yet the accountant chooses to select some systematic means of splitting the $900 between the two products so that ending inventories may be costed and income determined. **Two basic approaches are commonly used, although there are many variations of both: (a) physical measures and (b) net realizable values.**

physical measures

In Example 1, the $900 cost produced 1,500 liters of product on a physical-quantity basis; therefore, the unit cost is $900 ÷ 1,500, or 60¢ per liter. Costs are allocated as follows: 1,000 at 60¢, or $600, to A; and 500 at 60¢, or $300, to B. These computations may be shown in a different manner as follows:

	PRODUCTION	WEIGHTING	JOINT COSTS ALLOCATED
A	1,000 liters	1,000/1,500 × $900	$600
B	500 liters	500/1,500 × $900	300
	1,500 liters		$900

Assume that one-tenth of the output is unsold at the end of the month. A product-line income statement would appear as follows:

Income Statement for Joint Products
For the Month Ended ______

	A		B		TOTAL
Sales	900 liters	$495	450 liters	$405	$900
Joint costs:					
Production costs	1,000 liters	$600	500 liters	$300	$900
Less ending inventory	100 liters	60	50 liters	30	90
Cost of goods sold	900 liters	$540	450 liters	$270	$810
Gross margin		($ 45)		$135	$ 90
Gross-margin percentages		(9.1%)		33.3%	10%

Note that the use of physical weighting for allocation of joint costs may have no relationship to the revenue-producing power of the individual products. Thus, if the joint cost of a hog were assigned to its various products on the basis of weight,[2] center-cut pork chops would have the same unit cost as pigs' feet, lard, bacon, ham, and so forth. Fabulous profits would be shown for some cuts, although losses would consistently be shown for other cuts.

[2]Sometimes one joint product is a liquid while another is a solid. This situation necessitates converting all physical measures into common terms, such as kilograms, liters, and cubic feet.

Although they fail to recognize revenue-generating power, physical measures are often employed. For example, consider Financial Accounting Standards Board Statement No. 19, Paragraph 38, which requires the use of physical measures for amortizing the costs relating to oil and gas reserves produced jointly: "In those cases, the oil and gas produced shall be converted to a common unit of measure on the basis of their approximate relative energy content (without considering their relative sales values)."

net realizable value

How do you choose the "best" method for allocating joint costs to products for inventory purposes? First, you should choose the purpose of the inventory measure. Unfortunately, there is no consensus about the purpose. For example, a few accountants will contend that the purpose is merely to spread the cost in proportion to the physical units produced, as was just illustrated. The majority of accountants, however, support allocation in proportion to some measure of the relative revenue-generating power identifiable with the individual products. **The most popular measure that results in a cost indicative of revenue-generating power is some approximation of net realizable value, which is commonly defined as the predicted selling price in the ordinary course of business less reasonably predictable costs of completion and disposal.**

In Example 1, there are zero costs of completion and disposal, because all products are sold upon split-off at no incremental costs. Therefore, net realizable value is equal to sales value at split-off:

	SALES VALUE AT SPLIT-OFF	WEIGHTING	JOINT COSTS ALLOCATED
A	$ 550	550/1,000 × $900	$495
B	450	450/1,000 × $900	405
	$1,000		$900

Income Statement for Joint Products
For the Month Ended ______

	A	B	TOTAL
Sales	$495.0	$405.0	$900.0
Production costs	$495.0	$405.0	$900.0
Less ending inventory (10%)	49.5	40.5	90.0
Cost of goods sold	$445.5	$364.5	$810.0
Gross margin	$ 49.5	$ 40.5	$ 90.0
Gross-margin percentage	10%	10%	10%

Compare this income statement with the previous one; note that the gross-margin percentage is now the same for both products under the relative-sales-value method.

costs beyond split-off

The **net realizable-value method** becomes more intricate when joint products are processed individually beyond the split-off point and have no ordinary markets at the split-off point. Consider Example 2 (all costs are processing costs):

» ***EXAMPLE 2***

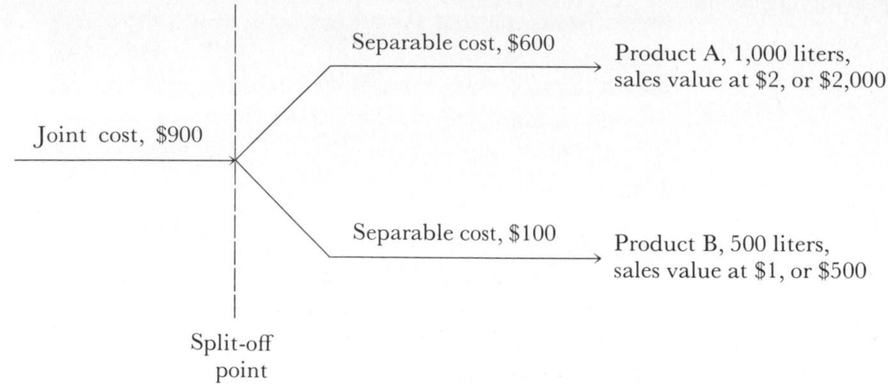

The joint costs are the same as in Example 1, but assume that the products are unsalable in their stage of completion at the split-off point. Further processing costs are needed to put the products into salable form.

If the purpose is to show relative abilities to generate revenue, the best approach to assigning joint costs is the relative sales values at the split-off point. **When sales-price quotations (or replacement prices) at the split-off point are known or can be determined, they should be used as a basis for splitting joint costs in the way illustrated in Example 1.** However, if these values are not explicitly available because there is no market for Products A and B at the split-off point or because the products cannot be purchased from outsiders, the *next best* alternative—for product-costing purposes only—is to take the ultimate relative sales values at the point of sale and work backward to obtain relative *net realizable values* at the split-off point. The conventional way of doing this is as follows:

	PRODUCTION IN TERMS OF ULTIMATE SALES VALUES	LESS COSTS BEYOND SPLIT-OFF POINT	NET REALIZABLE VALUES AT SPLIT-OFF POINT	WEIGHTING	JOINT COSTS ALLOCATED
A (1,000 liters at $2.00)	$2,000	$600	$1,400	1,400/1,800 × $900	$700
B (500 liters at $1.00)	500	100	400	400/1,800 × $900	200
	$2,500	$700	$1,800		$900

Exhibit 16-1 shows a product-line income statement as prepared under this net realizable-value method,[3] assuming no ending inventories. See the top of page 536.

costing joint products at realizable values

The foregoing examples concentrated on allocations. Because the various schemes for joint-cost allocations are subject to numerous valid criticisms, many companies refrain from the attempt entirely. Instead, they carry all inventories resulting from joint processing at sales values at split-off or at net realizable values (ultimate sales values less estimated separable costs to complete and sell). The meat-packing industry is the primary example, but the canning and mining industries provide other examples. This realizable-value approach ignores joint production costs altogether. It is difficult

[3]A variation of this method is described in Appendix 16a.

EXHIBIT 16-1

Income Statement
For the Month Ended ______

		PRODUCT	
	TOTAL	A	B
Sales	$2,500	$2,000	$500
Cost of goods sold:			
Joint costs	$ 900	$ 700	$200
Separable costs	700	600	100
Total cost of goods sold	$1,600	$1,300	$300
Gross margin	$ 900	$ 700	$200
Gross-margin percentage	36%	35%	40%

to criticize this approach when one compares it with the pitfalls of trying to allocate joint costs to products.

However, note that accountants ordinarily frown on carrying inventories at net realizable values, because in this way profit is recognized *before* sales are made. When compared with generally accepted inventory-costing methods, the realizable-value approach results in higher profits as inventory is increased and lower profits as inventory is decreased. Using selling prices or variations thereof as bases for inventory valuation is more justifiable where differences between costs and selling prices are small and where turnover is high (for example, in the meat-packing and other food-product industries).

Probably the most sensible method is followed by the many companies that carry their inventories at *net realizable values less a normal profit margin* to counteract the criticism that the net realizable-value method recognizes profits before goods are sold.

no allocation

Recall that in Chapter 14 (page 477) the cause-effect criterion was cited as being the most defensible logic for cost allocation. Joint-product costing illustrates that such logic has limits. For example, using cause-effect logic, the joint costs may be allocated to Products A and B *together* because their combined production causes the $900 level of costs. However, allocating the joint costs to A and B *individually* goes beyond cause and effect and relies on other criteria. Exhibit 16-2 demonstrates these limits by not allocating the joint costs at all. Only the separable costs are allocated, using cause-effect logic.

To highlight cause and effect, Exhibit 16-2 allocates the separable costs first. Furthermore, the contribution line in the exhibit reminds managers that their product choices at and beyond split-off must focus on additional revenue in comparison to separable costs. Finally, the joint costs are not allocated to A and B as individual products. The next section explores how product choices should be made.

Irrelevance of joint costs in decision making

No technique for allocating joint-product costs should be used for judging the performance of product lines or for managerial decisions regarding whether a product should be sold at the split-off point or processed beyond split-off. When a

EXHIBIT 16-2

(No Allocation of Joint Costs)
Income Statement
For the Month Ended ______

	TOTAL	PRODUCT A	PRODUCT B
Sales	$2,500	$2,000	500
Separable costs	700	600	100
Contribution to joint costs and profits	1,800	$1,400	$400
Joint costs	900		
Gross margin	$ 900		
Gross-margin percentage	36%		

sell or process further

product is an inherent result of a joint process, the decision to process further is not influenced by either the size of the total joint costs or the portion of the joint costs allocated to particular products.

The decision to incur added costs beyond split-off is a matter of determining the differential income attainable beyond the split-off point. Example 2 assumed that zero revenue was available at the split-off point. Therefore, differential revenue for Product A would be $2,000 − 0 = $2,000. Subtracting $600 of differential costs (costs beyond split-off) yields a differential income of $1,400. See Exhibit 16-2. In other words, if Product A is processed beyond split-off, the company is better off by $1,400, the income that would be forgone if Product A were legally dumped in the river upon split-off. Similarly, if Product B were processed beyond the split-off point, the company would be better off by $500 − $100 = $400. The amount of joint costs ($900) and how they are allocated are completely irrelevant with respect to these decisions.

Many manufacturing companies constantly face the decision of whether to process a joint product further. Meat products may be sold as cut or may be smoked, cured, frozen, canned, and so forth. Petroleum refiners are perpetually trying to adjust to the most profitable product mix. The refining process necessitates separating all products from crude oil, even though only one or two may be desired. The refiner must decide what combination of processes to use to get the most profitable quantities of gasoline, lubricants, kerosene, naphtha, fuel oil, and the like. In addition, at times the manager may find it profitable to purchase distillates from some other refiner and process them further. Profitability depends on producing the proper product in the proper quantities at the proper time.

In serving management for these decisions, the accountant must concentrate on opportunity costs rather than on how historical joint costs are to be split among various products. The only relevant costs are the incremental costs (including the "cost" of capital) as compared with incremental revenue. In turn, these must be compared with the revenue forgone by rejecting other alternatives.

To illustrate the importance of the incremental-cost viewpoint, consider another example:

» ***EXAMPLE 3***

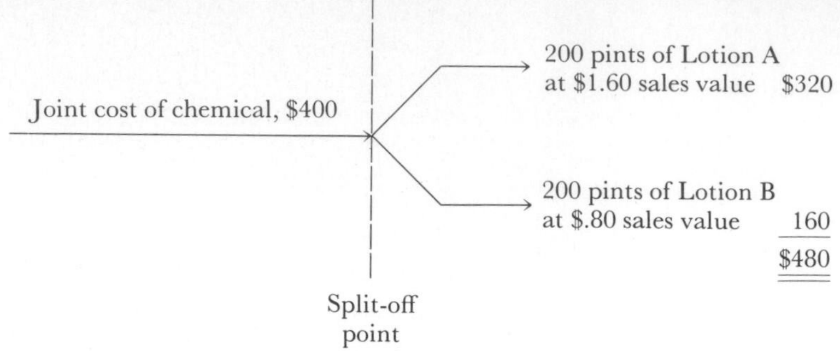

Conventional joint-cost allocations would be:

	BY WEIGHT			BY SALES VALUE		
	pints	**weighting**	**joint cost**	**sales value**	**weighting**	**joint cost**
Lotion A	200	2/4 × $400	$200	$320	32/48 × $400	$267
Lotion B	200	2/4 × $400	200	160	16/48 × $400	133
	400		$400	$480		$400

The manager is faced with the choice of selling the 200 pints of Lotion B at 80¢ ($160) or bottling and perfuming the lotion as 200 bottles of Lotion C. The total additional costs of converting Lotion B into Lotion C would be $50, while the sales price per bottle would be $1.20 (total revenue, $240). The question is whether B should be converted to C.

Not only are conventional methods of joint-cost allocation irrelevant here, but allowing joint-cost allocations to influence the decision will yield inconsistent results. For example, the weight method would show a loss for Lotion C (to be converted from Lotion B), whereas the net realizable-value method would show a profit:

	BY WEIGHT		BY NET REALIZABLE VALUE	
Sales of C, 200 pints, @ $1.20		$240		$240
Joint cost of B	$200		$133	
Incremental costs of C	50	250	50	183
Profit (loss)		$(10)		$ 57

The only approach that will give valid results is to compare the incremental revenue with incremental costs. In this case:

Incremental revenue of C, ($1.20 − $.80) × 200 bottles	$80
Incremental costs of C, added processing	50
Additional income from converting B to C	$30

Another way of looking at the same problem:

Lotion C revenue, 200 pints @ $1.20		$240
Costs:		
Added processing of C	$ 50	
Opportunity cost, forgoing of Lotion B sales (200 × 80¢)	160	210
Difference in favor of further processing of C		$ 30

The validity of this approach may be proven as follows:

TOTAL INCOME COMPUTATIONS					
	sell lotion A and B		sell lotion A and C		DIFFERENCE
Sales	($320 + $160)	$480	($320 + $240)	$560	$80
Total costs		400	($400 + $ 50)	450	50
Effects on income		$ 80		$110	$30

In summary, it is profitable to extend processing or to incur additional distribution costs on a joint product as long as the incremental revenue exceeds incremental explicit costs (and incremental opportunity costs of required additional capital, if any).

pricing decisions

Similarly, pricing decisions generally should not be influenced by allocations of joint costs.[4] The circular reasoning is particularly obvious under the relative net realizable-value method (prices used to set costs and costs then used to set prices). Nevertheless, regulated firms have been subjected to this reasoning as a justification for not permitting them to increase their prices. For example, many critics have claimed that shortages of natural gas have been caused by the Federal Power Commission's (FPC) approach to regulating gas prices. The FPC based prices on old competitive gas prices. Meanwhile, unregulated oil prices rose, resulting in lower and lower proportions of joint costs being allocated to gas, thus restricting gas prices and providing lesser incentives for finding natural gas.

Accounting for byproducts

problems of definition

The distinction among joint products, byproducts, and scrap is largely influenced by the relative sales values of the products in question. However, these distinctions are not firm; the variety of terminology and accounting practice is bewildering. For example, valuable brass turnings may be called *scrap* in one company and *byproducts* in another. Glycerin, which is ordinarily a *byproduct* of soap manufacture, may become a *joint product* during wartime production. Many sewage plants that regarded their products as waste have developed the waste into joint-product stature as valuable fertilizer. Kerosene was once a major petroleum product; now it is a byproduct.

[4]An exception would be a government contract for a joint product that lacks competitive markets. Negotiations for a mutually acceptable price may be based on the allocation of joint-product costs. In such instances, the cost allocation is a means of substituting for market prices.

The Kroehler Company, manufacturer of furniture, provides an example of the impact of technological change on importance of products. Traditionally, there has been 40 percent wastage of wood in a furniture factory. Kroehler now compresses almost all these wood scraps into cultured wood, which is used for bottoms and backs of drawers and other purposes. Previously, two-thirds of the scraps were incinerated at a cost of $2 per ton while the other third was used to fire steam boilers!

Another example of the effects of technology is provided by a brochure given to visitors at a Dole Company packing plant:

> There is practically no waste in pineapple packing. Our exchange plant recovers sugar in the form of pure syrup from surplus juices. The shells of the fruit are chopped, pressed and dried in the pineapple bran department for beef and dairy cattle feed.
>
> We recover, purify and pack bromelain, an important proteolytic enzyme, from the stumps of pineapple plants at this plant. Bromelain is used in a number of pharmaceuticals, has important applications in food processing and is a superior meat tenderizing agent.

Byproducts are products of joint processes that have minor sales value as compared with that of the major or chief product(s). Examples are mill ends of cloth and carpets; cotton meal and cotton hulls in processing of cotton oil; tar, naphtha, and kerosene in gasoline production; minor chemicals, gas, and tar from coke manufacture. The distinction between scrap and byproducts is often difficult to establish. A view that is sometimes helpful is that byproducts (a) have relatively more sales value than scrap, and (b) are often subject to additional costs beyond the split-off point, whereas scrap is usually sold outright. The basic accounting for scrap and for byproducts is the same. **The net realizable values of both are best treated as deductions from the cost of the main product.** The rest of this discussion will be confined to accounting for byproducts.

accounting methods for byproducts

The two basic methods of accounting for byproducts initially recognize the byproduct (1) at time of sale and (2) at time of production. Exhibit 16-3 shows one version of each of the basic methods:

METHOD ONE □ Net revenue from byproduct *sold* is calculated: gross revenue from byproduct sold less separable costs *incurred,* such as additional manufacturing and marketing costs. This net revenue is deducted from the cost of the major product(s) *sold.*

METHOD TWO □ Net realizable value of the byproduct *produced* is calculated: sales value of byproduct produced less separable costs *applicable,* whether already incurred or to be incurred. This net realizable value is deducted from the cost of the major product(s) *produced.*

Of course, many variations and combinations of these two approaches are used. Exhibit 16-4 presents journal entries based on the data in Exhibit 16-3 that may clarify the distinctions between the two methods.

Essentially, the first method has practical appeal, but conceptually it fails to match the value of the byproduct with the cost of the major related products. For example, byproduct income (that is, byproduct revenue less separable costs of disposal incurred) is sometimes shown as "other income" and (a) grouped with other sales

EXHIBIT 16-3

(Place a clip on this page for easy reference.)

Two Accounting Methods for Byproducts

DATA FOR ILLUSTRATION

	MAJOR PRODUCT		BYPRODUCT	
	19_1	**19_2**	**19_1**	**19_2**
Beginning inventory in units	0	1,000	0	300
Production in units	10,000	0	1,000	0
Sales in units	9,000	1,000	700	300
Ending inventory in units	1,000	0	300	0
Sales revenue @ $15.00 and @ $1.50	$135,000	$15,000	$1,050	$450
Disposal costs @ $.30	—	—	210	90
Net revenue from byproduct sold	—	—	840	360
Net realizable value of byproduct produced: 1,000 units @ ($1.50 − $.30)	—	—	1,200	—

PARTIAL INCOME STATEMENTS (IN DOLLARS)

	METHOD (SEE TEXT FOR DESCRIPTION)			
	one		**two**	
	19_1	**19_2**	**19_1**	**19_2**
Sales revenues from major product	$135,000	$15,000	$135,000	$15,000
Cost of major product sold:				
Beginning inventory of major product		$10,000		$ 9,880
Total production costs (assumed)	$100,000		$100,000	
Net realizable value of byproduct produced			1,200	
Net production costs	$100,000		$ 98,800	
Ending inventory of major product (10%)	10,000		9,880	
Cost of major product sold (gross)	$ 90,000	$10,000	$ 88,920	$ 9,880
Net revenue from sale of byproduct	840	360		
Cost of major product sold (net)	$ 89,160	$ 9,640	$ 88,920	$ 9,880
Gross margin	$ 45,840	$ 5,360	$ 46,080	$ 5,120
Gross margin for two years	$51,200		$51,200	

at the top of the income statement, or (b) grouped with other miscellaneous income near the bottom of the income statement, or (c) deducted from the cost of major products *sold,* as is illustrated by Method One in Exhibit 16-3. These methods (and variations thereof) are justified on the grounds that byproducts are incidental and do not warrant costly accounting procedures. Unsold byproduct is inventoried at zero value, although procedures may be adopted for control of physical quantities.

The second general approach tries to relate the net realizable value[5] of the

[5]A variation of Method Two would use net realizable value *less normal profit margin* of byproducts produced (plus separable manufacturing costs incurred, if any). This method is more conservative because the byproduct would be valued lower than its net realizable value. Thus, the costs of major product would be higher, and a "normal profit" would be shown on the byproduct as it is sold. This would shift income to a future period to the extent that the byproduct in question is not sold in the current period. (For exploration of the details, solve Problem 16-20.) This method has conceptual appeal, but it implies that the byproduct is important enough to warrant treatment as a separate product line. In short, the product is now a major product rather than a byproduct.

EXHIBIT 16-4

Journal Entries for Byproducts

	19_1 debit	19_1 credit	19_2 debit	19_2 credit
METHOD ONE				
At time of production:				
No entry				
At time of sale:				
Disposal costs	210		90	
Cash		210		90
Cash	1,050		450	
Revenue from sale of byproduct		1,050		450
Net revenue from sale of byproduct	($1,050 − $210 = $840)		($450 − $90 = $360)	
Note that the valuation (cost) of the byproduct inventory is always zero				
METHOD TWO				
At time of production:				
Byproduct inventory	1,200			
Work in process		1,200		
At time of sale:				
Disposal costs	210		90	
Cash		210		90
Cash	1,050		450	
Revenue from sale of byproduct		1,050		450
Cost of byproduct sold (700 × $1.20)	840		360	
Byproduct inventory		840		360
Valuation (cost) of the ending byproduct inventory	($1,200 − $840 = $360)		($360 − $360 = 0)	
Note that net revenue from the sale of byproduct is not recognized; for example, net revenue in 19_1 = $1,050 − $210 − $840 = 0				

byproducts *produced* to the costs of the major products *produced,* as is illustrated by Method Two in Exhibit 16-3. This method eliminates the effect of lag between production and sales and directly matches the cost-reduction power of byproducts against the production costs of the main product. The byproduct inventory is carried forward at net realizable value (plus separable manufacturing costs incurred, if any).

comparison of the methods

Both methods in Exhibit 16-3 recognize that byproducts somehow reduce the costs of the major products. Method Two is more precise about the timing of such cost reductions. The two periods taken together show the same income by the two methods (there being no beginning inventories for the first period and no ending inventories for the second period). The variations in methods raise some provocative theoretical problems concerning the matching of revenues and expenses. But cost-benefit comparisons in choosing among the accounting alternatives usually lead to whatever alternative seems expedient. By definition, byproducts should be minor and thus immaterial.

The illustration in Exhibit 16-3 assumes that the separable costs of the byproduct are confined to disposal costs (marketing costs). If any significant separable manufacturing costs were incurred, they would be deducted from the byproduct revenue under Method One. This would be an obvious mismatching if all the separable manufacturing costs incurred were applicable to the 1,000 units produced rather than to only the 700 units sold. Under Method Two, the separable manufacturing costs applicable would be deducted in computing the net realizable value of the byproduct produced. For an illustration, see Appendix 16B.

byproducts used internally

Sometimes byproducts are used internally as fuel or even as a component of a new batch of raw materials for the main product. For example, steel companies will often remelt scrap and byproducts along with purchased scrap metal as a part of producing new steel ingots. In these cases, the byproducts are frequently accounted for at net realizable values or replacement values; in turn, the cost of the major product is reduced by the same amount. For instance, scrap metal would be valued at replacement cost, and byproducts such as gas and tar derivatives would be valued at the cost of fuel oil that would otherwise be used to yield equivalent heat units.

byproducts in petroleum

The line of demarcation between joint products and byproducts is fuzzy. In the petroleum industry, byproduct accounting methods are often used even though the products being accounted for as byproducts are important enough to warrant being called joint products. The petroleum industry uses the byproduct approach for product-mix decisions even if a byproduct method is not followed for inventory costing. This byproduct approach views gasoline as the sole major product. The byproduct proportion of production should be increased until overall profit no longer increases. In effect, this approach (which is implemented via linear-programming models) computes the total incremental costs of obtaining a set of all products; the net realizable values of byproducts are computed and deducted. The remainder is the cost of gasoline. For a given gasoline volume, the linear-programming model increases the proportion of byproduct output until profit no longer increases. Any profit increases from byproducts are constantly being traded off against profits from the additional yield of gasoline that could otherwise be obtained. The model produces an optimal solution when the byproducts literally break even.

Again, note that for planning and control the emphasis is on profit opportunities and comparisons of incremental profits and incremental costs. How any joint-product *costs* are allocated among the products is irrelevant, regardless of whether the products are called joint products, byproducts, or scrap.

SUMMARY

Joint costs permeate accounting. Costs are joint with respect to time, facilities, and products. Accountants attempt to split joint costs among products having relatively important sales values. Where the joint product is valueless (for example, waste), all costs are applied to the major product. Where the joint product has minor value, it is often called a *byproduct;* its net realizable value or income from sales is frequently deducted from the cost of the major product.

No matter what the joint-production situation, any allocation of a joint cost is useless for purposes of product-combination decisions. The major use for allocating joint-product costs is for purposes of "reasonable" inventory valuations and income determinations. The *net realizable-value method* is the technique most frequently used for assigning joint costs to products.

Only opportunity costs and incremental costs and revenues are relevant to the decisions on whether to incur additional separable costs beyond the split-off point. As long as the incremental revenue exceeds the incremental costs (including the opportunity costs and the appropriate required rate of return), additional cost incurrence will be warranted.

SUGGESTED READINGS

BIERMAN, H., and T. DYCKMAN, **Managerial Cost Accounting,** 2nd ed. New York: Macmillan, 1976, Chap. 8.

KAPLAN, R., **Advanced Management Accounting.** Englewood Cliffs, N.J.: Prentice-Hall, 1982, Chap. 12.

NURNBERG, H., "Joint and By-Product Costs," in **Handbook of Cost Accounting,** ed. S. Davidson and R. Weil. New York: McGraw-Hill, 1978.

THOMAS, A. L., **A Behavioural Analysis of Joint-Cost Allocation and Transfer Pricing.** Urbana, Ill.; Stipes Publishing, 1980. Thoroughly analyzes alternatives for allocating joint costs. Contains an extensive bibliography.

PROBLEM FOR SELF-STUDY

problem

The Alden Oil Company buys crude vegetable oil. The refining of this oil results in four products, A, B, and C, which are liquids, and D, which is a heavy grease. The cost of the oil refined in 19_9 was $27,600, and the refining department had total processing costs of $70,000. The output and sales for the four products in 19_9 were as follows:

PRODUCT	OUTPUT	SALES	ADDITIONAL PROCESSING COST
A	500,000 gal.	$115,000	$30,000
B	10,000 gal.	10,000	6,000
C	5,000 gal.	4,000	—
D	9,000 gal.	30,000	1,000

REQUIRED

1. Assume that the net realizable value of allocating joint costs is used. What is the net income for Products A, B, C, and D? Joint costs total $97,600.
2. The company had been tempted to sell at split-off directly to other processors. If that alternative had been selected, sales per gallon would have been: A, 15¢,; B, 50¢; C, 80¢; and D, $3. What would the net income have been for each product under this alternative?
3. The company expects to operate at the same level of production and sales in the forthcoming year. Could the company increase net income by altering its processing decisions? If so, what would be the expected overall net income? Which products should be processed further and which should be sold at split-off? Assume that all costs incurred after split-off are variable.

solution 1.

SELL BEYOND SPLIT-OFF

	(A) sales value	(B) separable costs	net realizable value at split-off	(C) allocation of joint costs	A − (B + C) net profit
A	$115,000	$30,000	$ 85,000	85/122 × $97,600 = $68,000	$17,000
B	10,000	6,000	4,000	4/122 × 97,600 = 3,200	800
C	4,000	—	4,000	4/122 × 97,600 = 3,200	800
D	30,000	1,000	29,000	29/122 × 97,600 = 23,200	5,800
	$159,000	$37,000	$122,000	$97,600	$24,400

2.

SELL AT SPLIT-OFF

	(A) relative sales value at split-off	(B) allocation of joint costs	(A) − (B) net profit
A	500,000($ .15) = $ 75,000	75/111 × $97,600 = $65,947	$ 9,053
B	10,000($ .50) = 5,000	5/111 × 97,600 = 4,396	604
C	5,000($ .80) = 4,000	4/111 × 97,600 = 3,517	483
D	9,000($3.00) = 27,000	27/111 × 97,600 = 23,740	3,260
	$111,000	$97,600	$13,400

3. Note that comparing 1 and 2 in the manner computed above is irrelevant. For example, Product C's profit above is $483 or $800, despite the fact that the same amount is sold at the same price in either case. The only proper way to compare is to use an incremental approach:

	SALES BEYOND SPLIT-OFF	SALES AT SPLIT-OFF	INCREMENTAL SALES	SEPARABLE COSTS BEYOND SPLIT-OFF	INCREMENTAL GAIN (OR LOSS)
A	$115,000	$75,000	$40,000	$30,000	$10,000
B	10,000	5,000	5,000	6,000	(−1,000)
D	30,000	27,000	3,000	1,000	2,000
Increase in profit from further processing					$11,000

Based on the given data, the company income, before considering cost of capital for further processing, could be further improved by $1,000 by selling Product B at the split-off point instead of processing it further. That is, B's current incremental loss of $1,000 would be avoided by selling B at the split-off point; the overall net profit would not be otherwise affected.

Terms to Learn

byproducts ***common costs*** ***joint costs*** ***joint-product costs***
net realizable value ***net realizable-value method***
relative sales value method ***separable costs*** ***split-off point***

Special Points and Pitfalls

Joint-product costs provide a splendid illustration of why there is no "true" cost of a product that may be used for all purposes. That is, a cost that is suitable for inventory valuation may be unsuitable for decisions of which products to manufacture and which processes to use.

Appendix 16a: alternative to net realizable value

Speculation about the "best" method for allocating a joint-product cost is a frustrating endeavor because any method is based on shaky assumptions. For example, the net realizable-value method contains the implicit assumption that *all* the markup or margin is attributable to the joint process and *none* of the markup is attributable to the separable costs. This is a vulnerable assumption because profit is frequently thought to be attributable to all phases of the production and marketing functions, not just the joint process.

The *net realizable-value less overall profit-margin* method has been suggested as a way to attribute profit to the separable as well as to the joint processes. The method entails (a) deducting an *overall profit margin* from the sales values, obtaining the total costs that each product line should bear; and (b) deducting the separable costs from the total costs to obtain the joint-cost assignment. The data from Example 2 and Exhibit 16-1 would yield the following results under this *overall margin* method:

	TOTAL		A		B
Sales value	$2,500	1,000 @ $2.00,	$2,000	500 @ $1.00,	$500
Overall gross-margin percentage (from Exhibit 16-1) (36%)	900	(36%)	720	(36%)	180
Total cost	$1,600		$1,280		$320
Separable processing cost	700		600		100
Joint cost	$ 900		$ 680		$220

A favorable aspect of the overall profit-margin technique is cited as follows: "Uniform markup on all products is desirable for inventory purposes. Regardless of the composition of finished goods, equal inventory values (costs) will indicate equal sales possibilities."[6]

Once this approach is understood, it is slightly easier to use than the net realizable-value method. Both techniques rest on arbitrary basic assumptions.

The vulnerability of the *overall-margin* method is the flimsy assumption that there is a uniform relationship between cost and sales value. Few companies have products bearing equal margin percentages. Clearly, accountants and managers are faced with some uncomfortable choices for allocating joint-product costs because they are fundamentally indivisible.

Appendix 16b: byproducts and separable costs

This appendix illustrates the effects of separable manufacturing costs on Method Two in Exhibit 16-3. The accounting becomes slightly more intricate because the separable manufacturing costs incurred are inventoried. Suppose the separable manufacturing costs were $1.00 per unit and the selling price were $2.50 instead of $1.50 per unit. Then the final results in Exhibit 16-3, Method Two, would be unaffected.

[6]Carl Thomas Devine, *Cost Accounting and Analysis* (New York: Macmillan), p. 116.

Some journal entries might clarify the procedure:

	Debit	Credit
1. Byproduct inventory	**1,000**	
Cash		**1,000**
To record separable manufacturing outlays of $1.00 per unit for 1,000 units produced in 19_1.		
2. Disposal costs	**210**	
Cash		**210**
To record disposal outlays of $.30 per unit for 700 units sold in 19_1.		
3. Byproduct inventory	**1,200**	
Work in process		**1,200**
Net realizable value per unit, $2.50 − ($1.00 + $.30) = $1.20 for 1,000 units produced in 19_1.		
4. Cash	**1,750**	
Revenue from sale of byproduct		**1,750**
To record 19_1 sales of 700 units at $2.50 each.		
5. Cost of byproduct sold	**1,540**	
Byproduct inventory		**1,540**
To record cost of 19_1 byproduct sold, 700 units at $2.20 each.		
6. Disposal costs	**90**	
Cash		**90**
To record disposal outlays of $.30 per unit for 300 units sold in 19_2.		
7. Cash	**750**	
Revenue from sale of byproduct		**750**
To record 19_2 sales of 300 units at $2.50 each.		
8. Cost of byproduct sold	**660**	
Byproduct inventory		**660**
To record cost of byproduct sold in 19_2, 300 units at $2.20 each.		

The T-account follows:

BYPRODUCT INVENTORY

1. 1,000 @ $1.00	**1,000**	**5. 700 @ $2.20**	**1,540**
3. 1,000 @ $1.20	**1,200**	**To bal. 300 @ $2.20**	**660**
	2,200		**2,200**
Inventory end of 19_1: 300 @ $2.20	**660**	**8. 300 @ $2.20**	**660**

Note that the ending byproduct inventory is carried at $2.20 per unit, which consists of $1.00 separable manufacturing costs plus $1.20 net realizable value at split-off.

QUESTIONS, PROBLEMS, AND CASES

Note: When the term "net realizable value" is used, it refers to the conventional method of allocating joint costs that is reflected by Exhibit 16-1.

16-1 "The problem of accounting for depreciation is one of joint costs." Do you agree? Why?

16-2 "Nearly every manufacturing operation produces two or more products." Do you agree? Why?

16-3 Briefly describe the two basic methods of accounting for byproducts.

16-4 What is the main weakness of the relative-sales-value method of joint-cost allocation?

16-5 Define *net realizable value.*

16-6 "The relative-sales-value method of joint-cost allocation is the best method for managerial decisions regarding whether a product should be sold or processed further." Do you agree? Why?

16-7 ***Difference between joint products and byproducts.*** (CPA)

1. Explain the basic difference between the method of accounting for joint products and that for byproducts.

2. State the conditions under which an item should be treated as a byproduct rather than as a joint product.

3. Explain the two principal methods of assigning joint costs to the joint products, and state the circumstances under which each would be appropriate.

16-8 ***Net realizable-value method.*** A company produces two joint products, A and B. The joint cost is $24,000. Added processing costs: A, $30,000; B, $7,500. A sells for $50 per unit; B sells for $25 per unit.

If the company produces 1,000 units of A and 500 units of B, what is the proper amount of joint cost that should be allocated to B, assuming that the net realizable-value method of allocation of joint costs is used?

16-9 ***Joint products and further process decision.*** (W. Crum) Tuscania Company crushes and refines mineral ore into three products in a joint cost operation. Costs and production for 19_8 were as follows:

Department 1: Initial joint costs $420,000, producing 20,000 pounds of Alco, 60,000 pounds of Devo, 100,000 pounds of Holo
Department 2: Processes Alco further at a cost of $100,000
Department 3: Processes Devo further at a cost of $200,000

Results for 19_8:

Alco: 20,000 pounds completed; 19,000 pounds sold for $20 per pound; final inventory, 1,000 pounds
Devo: 60,000 pounds completed; 59,000 pounds sold for $6 per pound; final inventory, 1,000 pounds
Holo: 100,000 pounds completed; 99,000 pounds sold for $1 per pound; final inventory, 1,000 pounds; Holo required no further processing.

REQUIRED

1. Use the net realizable-value method to allocate the joint costs of the three products.
2. Compute the total costs and unit costs of ending inventories.
3. Suppose Tuscania had an offer to sell all of its Devo product at the split-off before going through Department 3 for a price of $2 per pound, just as it comes off the line in Department 1, F.O.B. Tuscania plant. Would Tuscania have been better off by selling Devo that way last year rather than by processing it through Department 3 and selling it as it did? Show computations to support your answer. Disregard all other factors not mentioned in the problem.

16-10 ***Joint-product costs: ending inventories.*** The Darl Company operates a simple chemical process to reduce a single basic material into three separate items, here referred to as X, Y, and Z (all three end products being separated simultaneously at a single split-off point).

Products Y and Z are ready for sale immediately upon split-off without further processing or any other additional cost. Product X, however, is processed further before being sold.

The selling prices quoted below have not changed for three years, and no future changes are foreseen.

During 19_3, the selling prices of the items and the total number sold were as follows:

X—120 tons sold for $1,600 per ton
Y—340 tons sold for $1,000 per ton
Z—175 tons sold for $800 per ton

There were no beginning inventories whatsoever of X, Y, or Z.

The total joint manufacturing costs for the year were $505,000. An additional $30,000 was spent in order to finish Product X.

At the end of the year, the following inventories of completed units were on hand: X, 180 tons; Y, 60 tons; Z, 25 tons. There was no ending work in process.

REQUIRED

Prepare a computation of the "cost" of inventories of X, Y, and Z for balance-sheet purposes as of December 31, 19_3. Include in your presentation a summary of the cost of goods sold by product line. (The Darl Company uses the "net realizable-value" method of allocating joint costs to end products.)

16-11 ***Joint cost allocations, process further.*** (A.I.C.P.A.) The Mikumi Manufacturing Company produces three products by a joint production process. Raw material is put into production in Department A, and at the end of processing in this department three products appear. Product X is immediately sold at the split-off point, with no further processing. Products Y and Z require further processing before they are sold. Product Y is processed in Department B, and Product Z is processed in Department C. The Company uses the net realizable-value method of allocating joint production costs. Following is a summary of costs and other data for the year ended September 30, 19_2:

There were no inventories on hand at September 30, 19_1, and there was no raw material on hand at September 30, 19_2. All of the units of product on hand at September 30, 19_2, were fully complete as to processing:

	PRODUCTS		
	X	Y	Z
Pounds sold	10,000	30,000	40,000
Pounds on hand at September 30, 19_2	20,000	-0-	20,000
Sales revenues	$15,000	$81,000	$141,750

	DEPARTMENTS		
	A	B	C
Raw-material cost	$56,000	-0-	-0-
Direct-labor cost	24,000	$40,450	$101,000
Manufacturing overhead	10,000	10,550	36,625

REQUIRED

1. Determine the following amounts for each product:
   (a) Net realizable value as used for allocating joint costs
   (b) Joint costs allocated
   (c) Cost of goods sold
   (d) Finished-goods inventory costs, September 30, 19_2.
2. Assume that the entire output of Product X could be processed further at an additional cost of $2.00 per pound and then sold at a price of $4.30 per pound. What is the effect on operating income if all of the Product X output for the year ended September 30, 19_2, had been processed further and sold, rather than all being sold at the split-off point?

16-12 ***Markups and appendix 16a.***

1. Refer to Appendix 16a. Suppose that market prices were available at split-off of 70¢ for Product A and 40¢ for Product B. What is the joint cost applicable to A? To B? To what would you attribute the gross margin: the joint process or the separable process?

2. Suppose that market prices were available at split-off of 68¢ for Product A and 44¢ for Product B. What is the joint cost applicable to A? To B? To what would you attribute the gross margin: the joint process or the separable process? What is the role of bona fide market prices at split-off in management planning and control? Of computed approximate market prices?

16-13 ***Introduction to joint-costing techniques.*** The Wood Spirits Company produces two products, turpentine and methanol (wood alcohol), by a joint process. Joint costs amount to $12,000 per batch of output. Each batch totals 10,000 gallons, being 25 percent methanol and 75 percent turpentine. Both products are processed further without gain or loss in volume. Added processing costs: methanol, 30¢ per gallon; turpentine, 20¢ per gallon. Methanol sells for $2.10 per gallon; turpentine sells for $1.40 per gallon.

REQUIRED

1. What joint costs per batch should be assigned to the turpentine and methanol, assuming that joint costs are assigned on a physical-volume basis?
2. If joint costs are to be assigned on a net realizable-value basis, what amounts of joint cost should be assigned to the turpentine and to the methanol?
3. Prepare product-line income statements per batch for requirements 1 and 2.
4. The company has discovered an additional process by which the methanol (wood alcohol) can be made consumable and into a pleasant-tasting alcoholic beverage. The new selling price would be $6 a gallon. Additional processing would increase separable costs 90¢ a gallon, and the company would have to pay taxes of 20 percent on the new selling price. Assuming no other changes in cost, what is the joint cost applicable to the wood alcohol (using the net realizable-value basis)? Should the company use the new process?

16-14 ***Joint costs and byproducts.*** (W. Crum) Caldwell Company processes an ore in Department 1, out of which come three products, L, W, and X. Product L is processed further through Department 2; Product W is sold without further processing. X is considered a byproduct and is processed further through Department 3. Costs in Department 1 are $800,000 in total; Department 2 costs are $100,000; Department 3 costs are $50,000. Processing 600,000 pounds in Department 1 results in 50,000 pounds of Product L being produced, with 300,000 pounds of Product W and 100,000 pounds of Product X.

Product L sells for $10 per pound; Product W sells for $2 per pound; Product X sells for $3 per pound. It is desired to make a profit of 10 percent on Product X and also allow 25 percent for selling and administrative expenses. Use the net realizable-value method in handling the byproduct credit for Product X.

REQUIRED

1. Compute unit costs per pound for Products L, W, and X, using X as a byproduct. Use the net realizable-value method for allocating joint costs.
2. Compute unit costs per pound for Products L, W, and X, using all three as joint products and allocating cost by the net realizable-value method.

16-15 ***Joint products and byproducts.***[7] X and Y are two products that, due to the characteristics of the production process, are inevitably produced together; for every unit of X produced, two units of Y are also produced. During 19_2, 20,000 units of X and 40,000 units of Y are produced at a total cost up to the split-off point of $30,000; there are no additional costs for either product beyond the split-off point. The selling price of X is $5.00 per unit; the selling price of Y is $0.20 per unit. There is no inventory of either X or Y at January 1, 19_2.

REQUIRED

1. Assume that X and Y are considered major products, and that the inventory at December 31, 19_2, consists of 10,000 units of X and 20,000 units of Y. Compute the gross margin for 19_2 and the December 31, 19_2 inventory valuation for each product, X and Y, allocating joint costs according to (a) units of output, and (b) relative sales value of output.
2. Continue to assume that X and Y are considered major products, but now assume that the inventory at December 31, 19_2 consists of 10,000 units of X and 10,000 units of Y. Compute the gross margin for 19_2 and the December 30, 19_2, inventory valuation for each product, X and Y, allocating joint costs according to (a) units of output, and (b) relative sales value of output.
3. Assume that X is considered the major product and Y is considered the minor product, and that the inventory at December 31, 19_2, consists of 10,000 units of X

[7] A problem from the third edition, expanded by H. Nurnberg.

and 10,000 units of Y. Compute the gross margin for 19_2 and the December 31, 19_2, inventory valuation for each product, X and Y, where applicable, consistent with each of the following:

a. Byproduct revenues are reported as miscellaneous revenue (near the bottom of the income statement) at the time the byproduct is produced.
b. Byproduct revenues are reported as miscellaneous revenue (near the bottom of the income statement) at the time the byproduct is sold.
c. Byproduct revenues are reported as reductions of the cost of the major product at the time the byproduct is produced.
d. Byproduct revenues are reported as reductions of the cost of the major product at the time the byproduct is sold.

4. Now assume that $6,000 of additional processing costs must be incurred beyond the split-off point in order to convert the 40,000 units of Y into a salable product having the $0.20 per unit selling price indicated above; otherwise, all 40,000 units of Y must be junked as waste, at no disposal cost to the producer. Should this $6,000 separable processing cost be incurred? How does the method of accounting for Y affect this decision?

16-16 ***Net realizable-value of joint products.*** (CPA) Miller Manufacturing Company buys zeon for $.80 a gallon. At the end of processing in Department 1, zeon splits off into Products A, B, and C. Product A is sold at the split-off point, with no further processing. Products B and C require further processing before they can be sold; Product B is processed in Department 2 and Product C is processed in Department 3. Following is a summary of costs and other related data for the year ended June 30, 19_3.

	DEPARTMENT		
	1	2	3
Cost of zeon	$96,000	—	—
Direct labor	$14,000	$45,000	$65,000
Manufacturing overhead	$10,000	$21,000	$49,000

	PRODUCTS		
	A	B	C
Gallons sold	20,000	30,000	45,000
Gallons on hand at June 30, 19_3	10,000	—	15,000
Sales in dollars	$30,000	$96,000	$141,750

There were no inventories on hand at July 1, 19_2, and there was no zeon on hand at June 30, 19_3. All gallons on hand at June 30, 19_3, were complete as to processing. There were no manufacturing-overhead variances. Miller uses the net realizable-value method of allocating joint costs.

1. For allocating joint costs, the net realizable value of Product A for the year ended June 30, 19_3, would be (a) $30,000, (b) $45,000, (c) $21,000, (d) $6,000.

2. The joint costs for the year ended June 30, 19_3, to be allocated are (a) $300,000, (b) $95,000, (c) $120,000, (d) $96,000.

3. The cost of Product B sold for the year ended June 30, 19_3, is (a) $90,000, (b) $66,000, (c) $88,857, (d) $96,000.

4. The value of the ending inventory for Product A is (a) $24,000, (b) $12,000, (c) $8,000, (d) $13,333.

16-17 ***Christmas trees; allocating joint costs.*** S. Claus is a retired gentleman who has rented a lot in the center of a busy city for the month of December 19_0 at a cost of $5,000. On this lot he sells Christmas trees and wreaths. He buys his trees by the bundle for $20 each. A bundle is made up of two big trees (average height, seven feet), four regular-sized trees (average height, five feet), and broken branches. The shipper puts in the broken branches merely to make all the bundles of uniform size for shipping advantages. The amount of branches varies from bundle to bundle.

Mr. Claus gets $2 a foot for the trees. He takes home the broken branches. He and Mrs. Claus, Donner, Blitzen, and the rest sit around the fire in the evenings and make wreaths, which Mr. Claus sells for $8 each. Except for Christmas Eve, these evenings are a time when there is nothing else to do; therefore, their labor is not a cost.

During the course of the season, Mr. Claus buys 1,000 bundles of trees and makes 2,000 wreaths. In addition to the broken branches, the wreaths contain pine cones (100 pounds, total cost $200), twine (4,000 yards @ 10¢ a yard), and miscellaneous items amounting to $400.

In 19_0 Claus sold 1,800 of the seven-foot trees, all the regular-sized ones, and half the wreaths (the local Boy Scouts were also selling wreaths). The department store next door says that it will buy the rest of the wreaths, if Claus will preserve them, for $3 each. The preservative spray costs $2,000 for enough to do the job.

REQUIRED

1. What unit cost should Claus assign to each of his items?
2. What is the inventory cost on January 1, 19_1, if he doesn't sell to the department store?
3. Should he sell to the department store?

16-18 ***Computation of breakeven point for joint processes.*** (J. March) The March-I Company processes soybeans to obtain oil, meal, and chaff. There are three processes. In the cleaning process, the chaff and foreign materials are separated from the beans. In the pressing process, soybean oil and soybean cake are produced. The oil is stored in tanks and later pumped into tank cars for shipment. In the grinding process, the soybean cake is dried and then ground into meal.

The standard yield from a ton (2,000 lbs.) of beans is 100 pounds of chaff, 800 pounds of meal, and 100 gallons of oil. The following selling prices have been chosen for the purpose of calculations: beans delivered to plant, $120 a ton; chaff, $10 a ton; oil, $1.20 a gallon; and meal, $200 a ton. Budgeted costs of processing are:

	VARIABLE COSTS PER UNIT	FIXED COSTS PER MONTH
Cleaning	10¢ per ton of beans	$ 500
Pressing	$2 per ton of cleaned beans	2,000
Grinding	$2 per ton of meal	1,500

Assume that there are no work-in-process inventories and that selling and administrative expenses are: fixed costs of $1,800 monthly; variable costs of 10 percent of dollar sales in the case of oil sales and meal sales and zero in the case of chaff sales.

REQUIRED

1. Chart of physical flow.
2. How many tons of beans must be processed monthly in order to break even? Show computations clearly.
3. Assuming that 200 tons of beans are processed each month, (a) determine the total joint costs of the main products (the sales value of chaff is to be treated as a reduction of joint costs), and (b) compute the inventoriable cost of a fully processed gallon of oil and a fully processed pound of meal under the net realizable-value method.

16-19 ***Alternative accounting methods for byproducts.*** Reconsider the facts in Exhibit 16-3. Prepare a specific description of how the partial income statements for both years would be changed and how net income would be affected if the following accounting methods were used.

a. Net revenue from sale of byproduct, shown as additional revenue.

b. Net revenue from sale of byproduct, shown as other income near the bottom of an income statement.

c. Gross revenue from sale of byproduct, shown as reduction of cost of major product produced.

d. Net revenue from sale of byproduct, shown as deduction from cost of major product produced.

For methods *c* and *d* prepare a tabular comparison that is similar to Exhibit 16-3.

16-20 ***Role of normal margins and byproducts.*** Refer to Problem 16-19 and to Appendix 16b of the chapter. Add the following method:

e. Net realizable value less normal profit margin of byproduct produced deducted from cost of major product produced.

Assume that the normal profit margin on the sale of the byproduct is 12 percent of selling price, or $.18 per unit. Show the effects of method e by adding it to the tabular comparison of c and d. How does method d differ from Method Two in Exhibit 16-3?

16-21 ***Joint and byproducts.*** (CPA) The Harrison Corporation produces three products—Alpha, Beta, and Gamma. Alpha and Gamma are joint products while Beta is a byproduct of Alpha. No joint cost is to be allocated to the byproduct. The production processes for a given year are as follows:

A. In Department One, 110,000 pounds of raw material, Rho, are processed at a total cost of $120,000. After processing in Department One, 60 percent of the units are transferred to Department Two, and 40 percent of the units (now Gamma) are transferred to Department Three.

B. In Department Two, the material is further processed at a total additional cost of $38,000. Seventy percent of the units (now Alpha) are transferred to Department Four and 30 percent emerge as Beta, the byproduct, to be sold at $1.20 per pound. Selling expenses related to disposing of Beta are $8,100.

C. In Department Four, Alpha is processed at a total additional cost of $23,660. After this processing, Alpha is ready for sale at $5 per pound.

D. In Department Three, Gamma is processed at a total additional cost of $165,000. In this department, a normal loss of units of Gamma occurs which equals 10 percent of the good output of Gamma. The remaining good output of Gamma is then sold for $12 per pound.

REQUIRED

1. Prepare a schedule showing the allocation of the $120,000 joint cost between Alpha and Gamma using the net-realizable-value approach. The net realizable value of Beta should be treated as an addition to the sales value of Alpha.
2. Independent of your answer to requirement 1, assume that $102,000 of total joint costs were appropriately allocated to Alpha. Assume also that there were 48,000 pounds of Alpha and 20,000 pounds of Beta available to sell. Prepare a statement of gross margin for Alpha using the following facts:
   a. During the year, sales of Alpha were 80 percent of the pounds available for sale. There was no beginning inventory.
   b. The net realizable value of Beta available for sale is to be deducted from the cost of producing Alpha. The ending inventory of Alpha is to be based on the net cost of production.
   c. All other cost, selling-price, and selling-expense data are those listed in A through D above.

16-22 ***Joints costs and discounted cash flow.*** The Faia Company manufactures Products A, B, and C. These products all derive from the same basic raw material and are then processed into final products. Current operating data are displayed below:

Joint Costs of Production:
$200,000 for 100,000 Gallons

	PER UNIT	
	selling price	**cost past split-off**
A	$15	$10
B	10	4
C	6	2

Every 10 gallons of raw material produce 2 gallons of A, 5 gallons of B, and 3 gallons of C.

The Shrewd Co. has offered to lease a patented device to the Faia Company that will increase the yield from the common raw material by 50 percent for an initial fee of $100,000 plus a royalty of 20¢ per gallon of yield. In addition, Shrewd Co. wants an exclusive contract as a term of the license to purchase all of the firm's final output of A at a price of $8 for the next six years. At the end of this time, Shrewd Co. would grant the Faia Company a rebate of $10,000. If the offer were accepted, the Faia Company could scrap existing equipment with a disposal value of $10,000, a remaining useful life of six years, and an expected disposal value of zero at the end of the six years.

The Faia Company expects that it will be able to market all the additional output at existing prices. The president of the Faia Company has indicated that he will turn down the offer, as it involves selling Product A to Shrewd Co. at a price below out-of-pocket costs.

The Faia Company's minimum desired rate of return is 10 percent.

REQUIRED

Ignoring income taxes and using discounted cash flow, prepare data that will aid the president in making a correct decision. Include your recommendations as to the proper course of action.

16-23 ***Joint costs; change in product mix.*** The Laissez Faire Perfume Company processes a secret blend of flower petals into three products. The process works in such a way that the petals are broken down into a high-grade perfume, Charm, and a low-grade flower oil. The flower oil is then processed into a low-grade perfume, Wild Scent, and a cologne, Personally.

The company used 10,000 pounds of petals last month. The costs involved in reducing the petals into Charm and flower oil were:

Direct materials	$150,000
Direct labor	90,000
Indirect costs	60,000
	$300,000

The cost of producing Wild Scent and Personally from the flower oil were:

Direct materials	$15,000
Direct labor	35,000
Indirect costs	20,000
	$70,000

Total production for the month, with no ending work-in-process inventory, was:

Charm	10,000 ounces
Wild Scent	20,000 ounces
Personally	50,000 ounces

The sales price of Charm is $40 an ounce; of Wild Scent, $10 an ounce; and of Personally, $1 an ounce.

Additional costs, entirely separate for each product, of processing and selling are:

Charm	$ 20,000
Wild Scent	160,000
Personally	40,000
	$220,000

REQUIRED

1. Joint cost of Charm, Wild Scent, and Personally, using the net realizable-value method.
2. Product-line income statement, assuming no beginning or ending inventories.
3. The management, completely ignorant of cost accounting, is considering the possibility of increasing the quality of Wild Scent, at an increase in final processing

cost of $2 per ounce. The selling price would increase to $12 per ounce. This would result in a different product mix of Wild Scent and Personally. Every 10,000 pounds of petals would then result in 10,000 ounces of Charm, 18,000 ounces of Wild Scent, and 60,000 ounces of Personally. The separable costs of Personally and Wild Scent are completely variable. All prices and costs not specifically mentioned will remain unchanged. Should this alternative be selected?

16-24 ***Sell or process further.*** The Mow Company produced three joint products at a joint cost of $100,000. Two of these products were processed further.

Production and sales were:

	WEIGHT	SALES	ADDITIONAL PROCESSING COSTS
A	300,000 lbs.	$245,000	$200,000
B	100,000 lbs.	30,000	None
C	100,000 lbs.	175,000	100,000

REQUIRED

1. Assume that the net realizable value of allocating joint costs is used. What is the net income for Products A, B, and C?
2. The company had been tempted to sell at split-off directly to other processors. If that alternative had been selected, sales would have been: A, $50,000; B, $30,000; and C, $60,000. What would the net income have been for each product under this alternative?
3. The company expects to operate at the same level of production and sales in the forthcoming year. Could the company increase net income by altering its processing decisions? If so, what would be the expected overall net income? Which products should be processed further and which should be sold at split-off? Assume that all costs incurred after split-off are variable.

16-25 ***Adding a department.*** (CMA) The management of Bay Company is considering a proposal to install a third production department within its existing factory building. With the company's present production setup, raw material is passed through Department I to produce materials A and B in equal proportions. Material A is then passed through Department II to yield Product C. Material B is now being sold "as is" at a price of $20.25 per pound. Product C has a selling price of $100.00 per pound.

The per-pound standard costs currently being used by the Bay Company are as follows:

	DEPARTMENT I (MATERIALS A & B)	DEPARTMENT II (PRODUCT C)	(MATERIAL B)
Prior department costs	—	$53.03	$13.47
Direct material	20.00	—	—
Direct labor	7.00	12.00	—
Variable overhead	3.00	5.00	—
Fixed overhead:			
Attributable	2.25	2.25	—
Allocated (2/3, 1/3)	1.00	1.00	—
	$33.25	$73.28	$13.47

These standard costs were developed by using an estimated production volume of 200,000 pounds of raw material as the denominator volume. The company assigns Department I costs to materials A and B in proportion to their net sales values at the point of separation, computed by deducting subsequent standard production costs from sales prices. The $300,000 of common fixed overhead costs are allocated to the two producing departments on the basis of the space used by the departments.

"Attributable overhead" is that amount of fixed overhead that could be avoided if a given product or activity were discontinued.

The proposed Department III would be used to process material B into Product D. It is expected that any quantity of Product D can be sold for $30.00 per pound. Standard costs per pound under this proposal were developed by using 200,000 pounds of raw material as the denominator volume and are as follows:

	DEPARTMENT I (MATERIALS A & B)	DEPARTMENT II (PRODUCT C)	DEPARTMENT III (PRODUCT D)
Prior department costs	—	$52.80	$13.20
Direct material	$20.00	—	—
Direct labor	7.00	12.00	5.50
Variable overhead	3.00	5.00	2.00
Fixed overhead:			
Attributable	2.25	2.25	1.75
Allocated (1/2, 1/4, 1/4)	.75	.75	.75
	$33.00	$72.80	$23.20

REQUIRED

1. If (a) sales and production levels are expected to remain constant in the foreseeable future, and (b) there are no foreseeable alternative uses for the available factory space, should the Bay Company install Department III and thereby produce Product D? Show calculations to support your answer.
2. Instead of constant sales and production levels, suppose that under the present production setup $1,000,000 additions to the factory building must be made every 10 years to accommodate growth. Suppose also that proper maintenance gives these factory additions an infinite life and that all such maintenance costs are included in the standard costs set forth in the text of the problem. How would the analysis that you performed in requirement 1 be changed if the installation of Department III shortened the interval at which the $1,000,000 factory additions are made from 10 years to 6 years? Be as specific as possible in your answer.

16-26 ***Allocating joint costs; sales decision.***

1. The ABC Electronics Company manufactures a line of semiconductor diodes. The diodes are produced in batches, and when they are completed, several of their electrical parameters are tested. On the basis of these tests, some diodes are scrapped, and the rest are classified according to particular combinations of electrical parameters (the production process cannot be controlled to the extent that the parameters of all the diodes are the same). In a recent batch of 1,000 diodes for which production costs of $3,750 were incurred, 750 of the diodes were estimated to have a net realizable value of $5 apiece (on the basis of their parameters), and the remaining 250, $10 apiece. These estimates were based on competitors' prices for diodes with roughly similar parameters. How should production costs be assigned to the diodes? Show computations. What are the limitations of such a method?

2. The batch described is such that the $10 diodes meet all the electrical specifications of the cheaper $5 diodes. Assume that all the $5 diodes have been sold, but that 100 of the $10 diodes remain in inventory. Should the $10 diodes be sold at a net realizable value of $5 to meet additional demand for the cheaper diodes, given that the production cost assigned to them was $6 apiece? Explain.

16-27 ***Deciding on a product mix.*** The Barry Company, a major international chemical company, refines and markets five products worldwide. The raw chemical can be refined into the following products at these costs:

1. At a joint cost of 75¢ per barrel (which includes the cost of the raw chemical), the chemical is first refined to yield equal parts of Products A and B.

2. Any amount of B can be further processed to yield the same quantity of C at an additional cost of 40¢/bbl.

3. Finally, C can be refined into equal amounts of D and E. Two barrels of C will yield one barrel each of D and E at a cost of 50¢ per barrel of C refined.

REQUIRED

Ten million barrels of the raw chemical are available for the relevant planning period. The following prices per barrel are expected to prevail during that period: A, $1.45; B, $1.05; C, $1.40; D, $1.60; and E, $2.40. How much of which products should the company refine? What is the expected contribution to fixed charges with this mix? Ignore any selling, shipping, and handling costs. Assume that the required refining facilities are available.

16-28 ***Sell or process further; allocation of fixed costs.*** The Space Parts Co. receives cold-worked steel in sheet form from a nearby steel mill. The company has a special patented machine that takes the sheet steel and produces three missile parts simultaneously. Part A is taken from the machine and further processed to make it available for sale at $3.50; the additional processing cost for part A is $495. Parts B and C are run through a vat containing a secret "dip" developed by one of the company engineers to make them heat-resistant. This dip costs 20¢ per cubic foot of product. Part B sells for $5 and part C for $8.25.

ADDITIONAL INFORMATION

Materials	$ 8,000
Direct labor	1,600
Maintenance and depreciation	1,200
	$10,800 cost of running special machine for month

Month's production and sales (which is the typical product mix):

Part A	600 units
Part B	800 units
Part C	1,000 units

Part B has a volume of .50 cu. ft.
Part C has a volume of .75 cu. ft.

The vat is being depreciated at the rate of $60 per month, requires two persons for its operation at a total salary of $1,500 per month, and necessitates other operating expenses of $165 per month. All these costs are fixed.

REQUIRED

1. Joint costs assignable to each part for the month's operations. Use the net realizable-value method.
2. The company has a chance to sell part B undipped at split-off at $4.70 each on a long-run basis. Should the company adopt this alternative?

16-29 ***Joint product allocation and byproduct.*** (E. Imhoff) The Harrison Corporation produces three products: Alpha, Beta, and Gamma. Alpha and Gamma are joint products; Beta is a byproduct. The production processes for a given year are as follows:

In Department I, 110,000 pounds of raw material, Rho, are processed at a total cost of $120,000. After processing in Department I, 60 percent of the units (now Delta) are transferred to Department II and 40 percent of the units (now Gamma) are transferred to Department III.

In Department II, Delta is further processed at a total additional cost of $38,000. Seventy percent of the units (now Alpha) are transferred to Department IV and 30 percent emerge as Beta, the byproduct, to be sold at $1.20 per pound. Selling expenses related to disposing of Beta are $8,100.

In Department IV, Alpha is processed at a total additional cost of $23,660. After this processing, Alpha is ready for sale at $5 per pound.

In Department III, Gamma is processed at a total additional cost of $165,000. In this department, a normal loss of units of Gamma occurs, which equals 10 percent of the good output of Gamma. The remaining good output of Gamma is then sold for $12 per pound.

REQUIRED

1. Using the net realizable-value approach, allocate the $120,000 of joint cost from Department I to product Alpha and product Gamma.
2. You believe that there may be a profitable market for Beta as a joint product if it is processed further. Additional processing costs of $35,000 and additional selling costs of $3,000 would enable you to sell Beta for $3.00 per unit. What would be the total manufacturing cost per unit of Beta if it were treated as a joint product instead of a byproduct using the net-realizable-value allocation method? Assume that there are no selling expenses associated with Alpha and Gamma.
3. Given no other information (making no additional assumptions) you must decide

whether to continue to sell Beta as a byproduct, or to process it further and sell it for $3.00 per unit. What is your decision? Support your answer.

16-30 ***Joint costs and relevant costs.*** The Curling Chemical Company begins all production in Department A. At the end of processing in Department A, Products X and Y appear. Both can be sold immediately, but X can also be processed further in Department B, where Products X-1 and X-2 appear at the end of processing. X-1 is then immediately sold; X-2 can be (a) sold in bulk to another processor, (b) packaged and sold as a consumer good, or (c) aged for one year and reintroduced as a raw material, Mysto, in Department A. One unit of aged X-2 is equal to one unit of Mysto.

Production and sales have been stable for the past few years, and the basic demand for all products does not look as though it will change for quite a few more years.

Data for the past year include the following:

Processing costs—Department A:	
Variable	$ 75,000
Fixed	45,000
Processing costs—Department B (not including transferred-in costs):	
Variable	$ 58,000
Fixed	150,000
Unit data:	

	IN UNITS	
	production	**ending inventories**
X	220,000	20,000
Y	200,000	5,000
X-1	70,000	1,000
X-2	30,000	2,000

Selling prices per unit (unchanged throughout this year):	
X (net of separable selling expenses)	$ .20
Y (net of separable selling expenses)	.44
X-1 (after deducting $.10 variable packaging costs)	2.00
X-2 in bulk	4.30
X-2 as consumer good	5.00
Purchase costs:	
Mysto:	$4.00 per unit

5,500 units of Mysto were needed last year for production operations in Department A.
Selling costs of X-2, all variable, 10% of selling price.
Packaging costs of X-2 for consumer sales, 50¢ per unit.
The company's minimum desired rate of return is 10%.
Packaging costs are considered as manufacturing costs by this company.

Unless otherwise stated, consider each situation below independently. State any special assumptions that you make.

REQUIRED

1. The company uses "market value at split-off point" as a basis for allocating joint-production costs to products. What are the appropriate total ending-inventory values for Products X, Y, X-1 and X-2? Show computations *clearly.* For Products X-1 and X-2, show a breakdown in total inventory costs between the Department A portion and the Department B portion.
2. Assume that the outside purchase cost of Mysto is going to rise. Based on the given information, how high will the price of Mysto have to go before the Curling Chemical Company should seriously consider aging X-2 and using it in Department A? Explain.
3. The company is considering adding another material at a cost of $1.00 per unit to Product X-1, packaging the resulting product at a variable cost of 42¢ per unit, and selling it through manufacturer's agents at a straight commission of 10 percent of selling price. The prospective selling price will be $3.80 per finished unit. Should the company adopt this plan? Why? Show computations.

4. The company has been offered some new processing equipment for Department A. The salesman says that the new equipment will slash unit costs by 3.5¢. The new equipment will replace old equipment that has a remaining useful life of seven years, has zero disposal value now, and is being depreciated on a straight-line basis at $10,000 per year. The new equipment's straight-line depreciation would be $25,000 per year. It would last seven years and have no disposal value. The salesman pointed out that the overall unit costs now are slightly over 28.5¢ per unit of product in Department A, whereas the new equipment is being used by one of Curling's competitors at a unit cost of production of only 25¢ per unit of product, computed as follows:

Variable costs	$ 60,060
Fixed costs	76,440*
Total costs	$136,500
Divide by total units of X and Y produced	546,000
Cost per unit	25¢

**The $76,440 includes $25,000 depreciation on the new equipment in question. Curling's supervisory payroll is $6,000 less than this competitor's.*

The salesman went on to point out that a saving of $3\frac{1}{2}$¢ per unit would add $14,700 to Curling's annual profits.

a. Show *specifically* how the salesman made his computations of Department A unit costs.

b. As adviser to Curling's management, evaluate the salesman's contentions and prepare a quantitative summary to support your recommendations for Curling's best course of action.

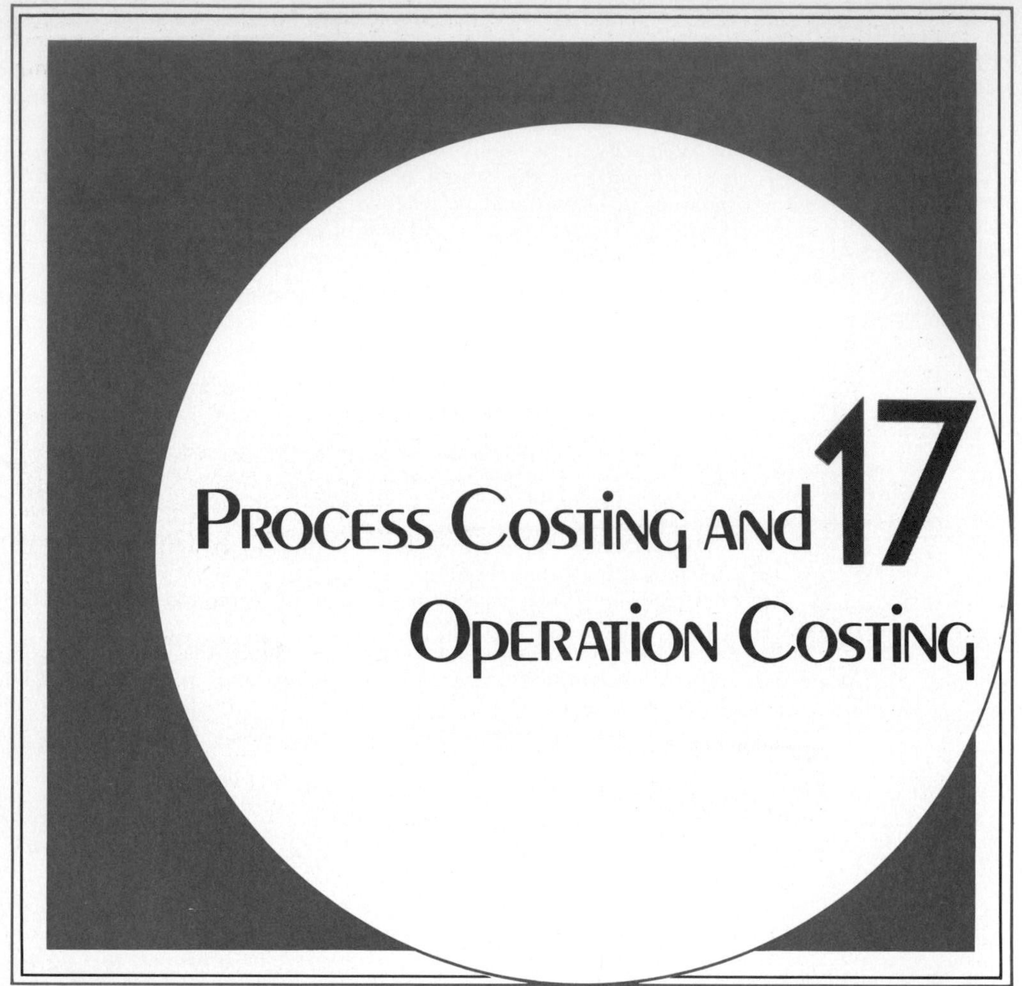

17 Process Costing and Operation Costing

Process-costing systems are used for inventory costing when there is continuous mass production of like units, in contrast to the production of tailor-made or unique goods produced under job-order systems. This chapter will cover the major *product-costing* methods that may be used in process-cost systems. It will be concerned only incidentally with *planning* and *control* because the latter techniques are discussed in other chapters and are applicable to *all* product-costing systems regardless of whether process costing or job-order costing or some hybrid system is used.

This chapter will also cover **operation costing,** a hybrid of process and job costing that is employed in practice to a far greater degree than the process costing usually described in textbooks on cost accounting.

A basic description of process costing and operation costing, including the key concept of equivalent units, appears in Chapter 4 (pages 97–99). **Please review that material before proceeding.** This chapter concentrates on how the presence of beginning inventories affects product costing.

Five major steps

The easiest way to learn process cost accounting is probably by example. The data in Example 1 will be used. **For the time being, concentrate on the data for Department A only.**

» *EXAMPLE 1*

A company has two processes. Material is introduced at the *beginning* of the process in Department A, and additional material is added at the *end* of the process in Department B. Conversion costs are applied uniformly throughout both processes. As the process in Department A is completed, goods are immediately transferred to Department B; as goods are completed in Department B, they are transferred to Finished Goods.

Data for the month of March 19_1 include the following:

	DEPARTMENT A	DEPARTMENT B
Work in process, beginning inventory	10,000 units 40% converted,* $7,500 (materials, $6,000; conversion costs, $1,500)	12,000 units 66⅔% converted,* $21,000 (transferred-in costs, $9,800; conversion costs, $11,200)
Units completed during March	48,000	44,000
Units started during March	40,000	?
Work in process, ending inventory	2,000, 50% converted*	16,000, 37½% converted*
Material cost added during March	$22,000	$13,200
Conversion costs added during March	$18,000	$63,000

**This means that each unit in process is regarded as being fractionally complete with respect to the conversion costs of the present department only, at the dates of the work-in-process inventories.*

REQUIRED

Compute the cost of goods transferred out of each department. Compute ending-inventory costs for goods remaining in each department. Assume (a) first-in, first-out (FIFO) product costing and (b) weighted-average product costing. Show journal entries for the transfers to Department B.

Five major steps in accounting for process costs will be described:

Step 1: Summarize physical units
Step 2: Compute output in terms of equivalent units
Step 3: Summarize the total costs to account for, which are the total debits in Work in Process
Step 4: Compute unit costs
Step 5: Compute total costs of work completed and in process

Although shortcuts are sometimes taken, the methodical procession through each of the five steps minimizes error. The first two steps concentrate on what is occurring in physical or engineering terms. The dollar impact of the production process is measured in the final three steps.

step 1: summarize physical units

Step 1 traces the physical units of production. (Where did units come from? Where did they go?) In other words, (a) what are the units to account for? and (b) how are they accounted for? Draw flow charts as a preliminary step, if necessary. Exhibit 17-1 shows these relationships, which may also be expressed as an equation:

Beginning inventories + Units started = Units transferred + Ending inventories

The total of the left side of the equation is shown as the units to account for: 10,000 + 40,000 = 50,000 in Exhibit 17-1. The total of the right side is shown as the units accounted for: 10,000 + 38,000 + 2,000 = 50,000 in Exhibit 17-1.

EXHIBIT 17-1

Step 1: Summarize Physical Units

Work in process, beginning inventory	10,000 (40%)*
Started	40,000
To account for	50,000
Completed and transferred out during current period:†	
From beginning inventory	10,000
Started and completed currently	38,000
Work in process, ending inventory	2,000 (50%)*
Accounted for	50,000

**Degrees of completion, for conversion costs of this department only, at the dates of the work-in-process inventories.*

†"Current period" is used as a general term. In this example, the current period is one month, March.

There are 10,000 physical units in process at the start of the period. In addition, 40,000 units were begun during the current period. Of the total of 10,000 + 40,000 = 50,000 units to account for, 2,000 units remained in process at the end of the period. Therefore, 48,000 units were completed during the period, consisting of the 10,000 units from the beginning work in process plus 38,000 units from the 40,000 units started.

step 2: compute output in equivalent units

Express the physical units in terms of work done. Because materials and conversion costs are applied differently, the equivalent output is usually divided into material and conversion-cost categories. For example, instead of thinking of output in terms of physical units, think of output in terms of material doses of work and conversion-cost doses of work. **Disregard dollar amounts until equivalent units are computed.**

Step 2 is illustrated in Exhibit 17-2. Concentrate on the work done in the current period regarding materials. In Department A, all the materials are introduced as production begins. Consequently, the material component of work in process is "fully completed" as soon as work is started because all doses of material are used at the initial stage of the process. The work done in the current period *includes* the following material in the physical units:

Started and completed currently, 38,000 × 100% =	38,000
Started and still in process at the end, 2,000 × 100% =	2,000
Work done in current period in terms of equivalent units of material	40,000

Note that this total *excludes* the 10,000 units of material added in the *preceding* period to the beginning inventory of the current period.

EXHIBIT 17-2

Step 2: Compute Output in Equivalent Units

FLOW OF PRODUCTION	(STEP 1) PHYSICAL UNITS	(STEP 2) EQUIVALENT UNITS materials	conversion costs
Work in process, beginning inventory	10,000(40%)*		
Started	40,000		
To account for	50,000		
Completed and transferred out during current period:			
From beginning inventory	10,000		6,000
Started and completed currently	38,000	38,000	38,000
Work in process, ending inventory	2,000(50%)*	2,000	1,000
Accounted for	50,000		
Work done in current period only		40,000	45,000

**Degrees of completion, for conversion costs of this department only, at the dates of the work-in-process inventories.*

The equivalent units for conversion costs for the current period are computed as follows. The 48,000 units completed and transferred out consist of the 10,000 units from the beginning inventory plus 38,000 units started and completed in March. The total work done in March on the physical units transferred out plus the ending inventory would be:

To complete the units in beginning inventory, 10,000 × (100% − 40%) =	6,000
To entirely process the units started and completed during current period, 38,000 × 100%	38,000
Equivalent units on goods transferred	44,000
To do the first part of processing on the ending inventory, 2,000 × 50%	1,000
Equivalent units for current period (work done in current period)	45,000

Note that the 45,000 total *excludes* the beginning inventory of 10,000 × 40% = 4,000 equivalent units of conversion costs added in the *preceding* period to the *beginning inventory* of the *current* period.

As shown in Exhibit 17-2, step 2 ends with the "work done in current period only." **Such measurements are the keys to judging performance during the current period, March in this illustration.** They also provide the basis for inventory valuation using standard costing (which will be described later in this chapter) and first-in, first-out costing (FIFO).

The sketch that is at the top of p. 564 recapitulates the analysis in Exhibits 17-1 and 17-2.

step 3: summarize total costs to account for

Exhibit 17-3 summarizes the total costs to account for, that is, the total debits in Work in Process. The debits consist of the beginning balance, $7,500, plus the current costs, $40,000, added during March. The amounts of materials and conversion costs are also shown because they are frequently necessary for step 4.

	Beginning Inventory	Started and Completed during the Current Period	Ending Inventory	Equivalent Units*
Physical Units	10,000	40,000 (Started during the Current Period)		
	10,000	38,000	2,000	
	Transferred Out			
	Work Done in Current Period			
Material*	0% × 10,000	100% × 38,000	100% × 2,000	40,000
Conversion Costs*	60% × 10,000	100% × 38,000	50% × 2,000	45,000

**Expressed in terms of work done in current period only.*

EXHIBIT 17-3

Step 3: Summarize Total Costs to Account For
(The Total Debits in Work in Process)

	TOTAL COSTS	MATERIALS	CONVERSION COSTS
Work in process, beginning	$ 7,500	$ 6,000	$ 1,500
Current costs	40,000	22,000	18,000
Total costs to account for	$47,500	$28,000	$19,500

First-in, first-out (FIFO) method

The two most-discussed methods of accounting for process-cost inventories are first-in, first-out (FIFO) and weighted-average. We examine each in turn. FIFO will be used to illustrate steps 4 and 5.

step 4: compute unit costs

The FIFO method rests on a specific assumption regarding the flow of costs. The beginning inventory is regarded as if it were a batch of goods separate and distinct from the goods started *and* completed by a process during the current period. Therefore, the

EXHIBIT 17-4

Step 4: Compute Unit Costs
First-in, First-out Method

	MATERIALS	CONVERSION COSTS
Current costs only	$22,000	$18,000
Divided by equivalent units for work done in current period only (see step 2)	÷ 40,000	÷ 45,000
Unit costs	$ .55	$ .40

unit costs are confined to the work done during the current period. That is, as Exhibit 17-4 demonstrates, the *current* costs (only) are divided by the equivalent units for work done in the current period (only).

Note especially that the beginning inventory costs and equivalent units for work done in the preceding period are *excluded* from the calculations in Exhibit 17-4.

step 5: compute total costs of work completed and in process

Exhibit 17-5 shows how the costs are finally summarized. The unit costs computed in step 4 are used to determine the total costs of goods completed and work in process. The units completed are composed of 10,000 physical units of beginning inventory, which is accounted for as if it were a separate batch. The beginning inventory costs of $7,500 have 6,000 equivalent units × $.40 = $2,400 of conversion costs *added* thereto in the current period. Moreover, 38,000 physical units were started and completed during the current period. Therefore, they are allocated costs of $.55 + $.40 = $.95 per equivalent whole unit.

The 2,000 physical units of ending work in process have a full 2,000 equivalent units of materials @ $.55, but only 50 percent of 2,000, or 1,000 equivalent units of conversion costs @ $.40.

As a final check, the costs are totaled to see if they have been fully accounted for.

EXHIBIT 17-5

Step 5: Total Costs of Work Completed and in Process
First-in, First-out Method

		DETAILS		
COSTS	TOTALS	materials	conversion costs	equivalent whole unit
Units completed (48,000)				
From beginning inventory (10,000) (see step 3)	$ 7,500			
Current costs added:				
Materials, none	—			
Conversion costs	2,400		6,000($.40)	
Total completed from beginning inventory	$ 9,900			
Started and completed this period (38,000)	36,100			38,000($.95)
Total costs transferred out	$46,000			
Work in process, ending inventory (2,000)				
Materials	$ 1,100	2,000($.55)		
Conversion costs	400		1,000($.40)	
Total work in process	$ 1,500			
Total costs accounted for	$47,500			

Taken together, the five steps provide all the ingredients of a *production cost report,* which is shown in Exhibit 17-6. The format includes many details that some managers may deem unnecessary. For example, the report could be confined to the first column only and omit the data regarding equivalent units and unit costs.

Weighted-average method

The weighted-average method is another popular way of obtaining product costs. As in the FIFO method, five steps are recommended.

EXHIBIT 17-6 *(Place a clip on this page for easy reference.)*

Department A
Production Cost Report
First-in, First-out Method
For the Month Ended March 31, 19_1

FLOW OF PRODUCTION	(STEP 1) PHYSICAL UNITS	(STEP 2) EQUIVALENT UNITS materials	conversion costs
Work in process, beginning inventory	10,000(40%)*		
Started	40,000		
To account for	50,000		
Completed and transferred out:			
From beginning inventory	10,000	—	6,000
Started and completed currently	38,000	38,000	38,000
Work in process, ending inventory	2,000(50%)*	2,000	1,000
Accounted for	50,000	40,000	45,000

	COSTS	TOTALS	DETAILS materials	conversion costs	equivalent whole unit
	Work in process, beginning inventory	$ 7,500	—	—	
	Current costs	40,000	$22,000	$18,000	
(Step 3)	Total costs to account for	$47,500			
	Divide by equivalent units†		÷40,000	÷45,000	
(Step 4)	Cost per equivalent unit		$ .55	$ .40	$ .95
(Step 5)	Total costs of work completed and in process:				
	Units completed and transferred out (48,000):				
	From beginning inventory (10,000)	$ 7,500			
	Current costs added:				
	Materials, none	—			
	Conversion costs	2,400		6,000($.40)	
	Total completed from beginning inventory	$ 9,900			
	Started and completed this period (38,000)	36,100			38,000($.95)
	Total costs transferred out	$46,000			
	Work in process, ending inventory (2,000):				
	Materials	$ 1,100	2,000($.55)		
	Conversion costs	400		1,000($.40)	
	Total work in process	$ 1,500			
	Total costs accounted for	$47,500			

*Degree of completion on conversion costs of this department.
†For work done in current period only.

steps 1 and 2 Step 1 is the same for both FIFO and weighted-average. Summarize the physical units as shown in Exhibit 17-1, p. 562.

Step 2, the computation of equivalent units, is identical to that shown for FIFO in Exhibit 17-2—except for the necessary addition of the final two line items. As the final lines in Exhibit 17-7 show, the weighted-average method mingles the work done in the current period with the work done in the preceding period on the beginning work in process. The final line represents the *work done to date,* which becomes the basis for computing unit costs in step 3. This contrasts with the *work done in the current period,* which is used in the FIFO method.

EXHIBIT 17-7

Step 2: Compute Output in Equivalent Units, Weighted-Average Method

FLOW OF PRODUCTION	(STEP 1) PHYSICAL UNITS	(STEP 2) EQUIVALENT UNITS materials	conversion costs
Work in process, beginning inventory	10,000(40%)*		
Started	40,000		
To account for	50,000		
Completed and transferred out during current period:			
From beginning inventory	10,000		6,000
Started and completed currently	38,000	38,000	38,000
Work in process, ending inventory	2,000(50%)*	2,000	1,000
Accounted for	50,000		
Work done in current period only†		40,000	45,000
Work done in previous period on the beginning inventory		10,000	4,000
Work done to date (that is, done in the current and previous periods)		50,000	49,000

**Degree of completion on conversion costs of this department.*
†Note that all computations through this line are identical to those in Exhibit 17-2, p. 563.

The sketch in Exhibit 17-8 compares the FIFO and weighted-average computations of equivalent units. The key difference is:

FIFO—Equivalent units are the work done in the current period only.

Weighted-average—Equivalent units are the work done to date, which includes all work done in the current period plus work done in the preceding period on the current period's beginning inventory of work in process.

steps 3, 4, and 5 Step 3, summarizing the total debits in Work in Process, is the same as shown earlier in Exhibit 17-3. The unit costs are calculated in step 4, as shown in Exhibit 17-9.

The weighted-average method has been called a "roll-back" method because the averaging of costs includes the work done in the preceding period on the current period's beginning inventory of work in process. Thus, the total costs and the equivalent units mingle the applicable work begun in the preceding period with the work started during the current period. The total costs include the beginning inventories.

EXHIBIT 17-8

Comparison of Underlying Computations of Equivalent Units

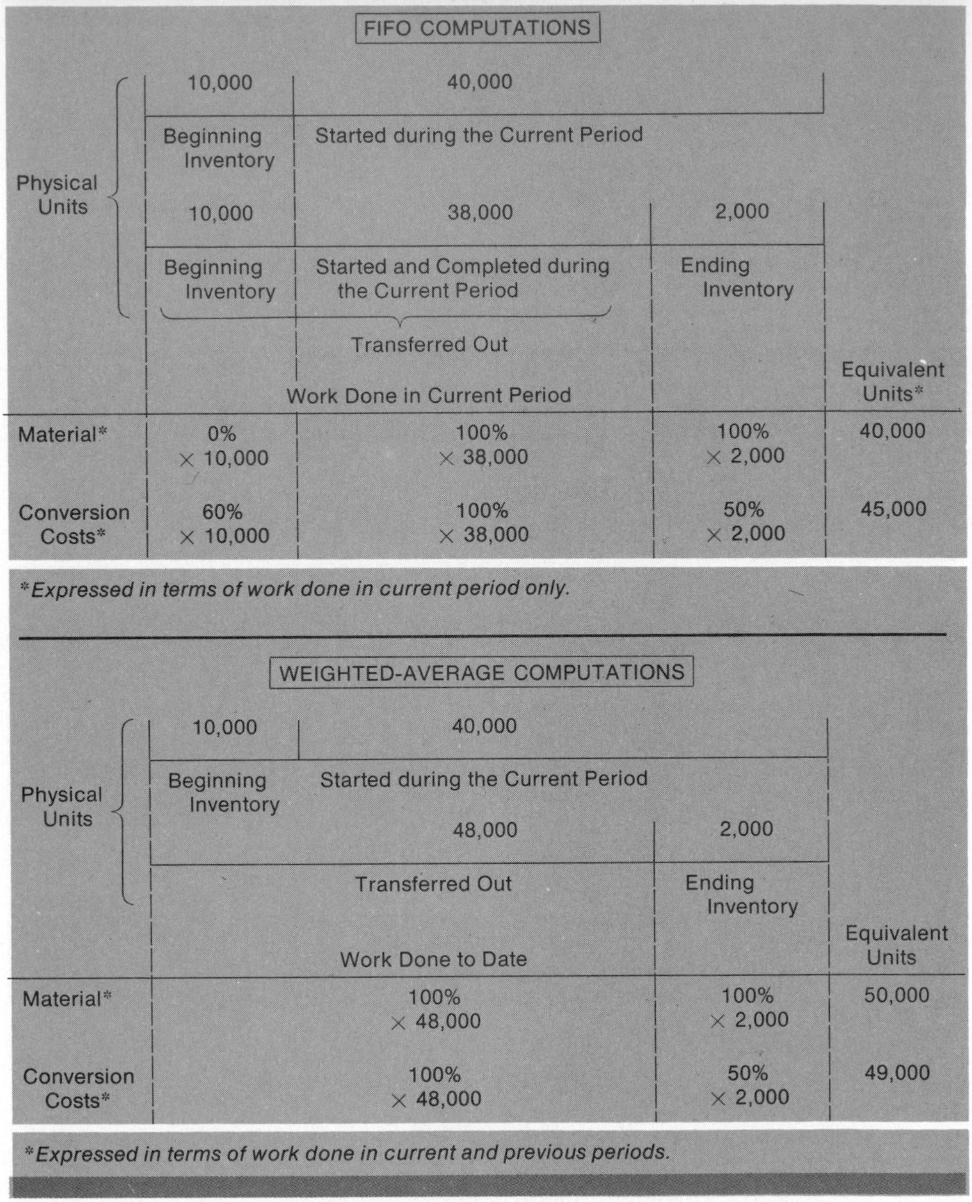

FIFO COMPUTATIONS

Physical Units:

10,000	40,000	
Beginning Inventory	Started during the Current Period	
10,000	38,000	2,000
Beginning Inventory	Started and Completed during the Current Period	Ending Inventory

Beginning Inventory + Started and Completed during the Current Period = Transferred Out

	Work Done in Current Period			Equivalent Units*
Material*	0% × 10,000	100% × 38,000	100% × 2,000	40,000
Conversion Costs*	60% × 10,000	100% × 38,000	50% × 2,000	45,000

**Expressed in terms of work done in current period only.*

WEIGHTED-AVERAGE COMPUTATIONS

Physical Units:

10,000	40,000
Beginning Inventory	Started during the Current Period
48,000	2,000
Transferred Out	Ending Inventory

	Work Done to Date		Equivalent Units
Material*	100% × 48,000	100% × 2,000	50,000
Conversion Costs*	100% × 48,000	50% × 2,000	49,000

**Expressed in terms of work done in current and previous periods.*

The equivalent units include all work done to date on the current month's production, including the beginning inventory of work in process.

Step 5 compiles the total costs of work completed and in process, as shown in the bottom half of Exhibit 17-9.

The computations here are simpler than the comparable FIFO computations in Exhibit 17-5. Why? Because Exhibit 17-5 separately calculated the current costs added to the beginning inventory. No such distinctions are necessary here. Instead, all the units completed are multiplied by a single unit cost, $.958.

Exhibit 17-10 recapitulates the five steps for the weighted-average method. Com-

EXHIBIT 17-9

Step 4: Compute Unit Costs, Weighted-Average Method

	MATERIALS	CONVERSION COSTS	EQUIVALENT WHOLE UNIT
Total costs to account for (step 3)	$28,000	$19,500	
Divide by equivalent units for work done to date (step 2)	÷50,000	÷49,000	
Unit costs	$ .56	$ .398	$ .958

Step 5: Compile Total Cost of Work Completed and in Process

	TOTALS	DETAILS: materials	DETAILS: conversion costs	DETAILS: equivalent whole unit
Units completed and transferred out, (48,000)	$45,984			48,000($.958)
Work in process, end (2,000)				
Materials	$ 1,120	2,000($.56)		
Conversion costs	398		1,000($.398)	
Total cost of work in process	$ 1,518			
Total costs accounted for	$47,500*			

**Rounded from $47,502 for decimal discrepancy. (Decimals carried out to three places.)*

pare the recapitulation in the exhibit with the FIFO recapitulation in Exhibit 17-6. The key difference is the choice of equivalent units for computing unit costs:

Weighted average—work done to date

FIFO—work done in current period only

Another difference is the mingling of beginning inventory costs with current costs in the weighted-average method and the separate handling of beginning inventory costs in the FIFO method.

Operation costing

role of operations

Obviously, a product-costing system should be tailored to the specific conditions that differ from organization to organization. Many of these systems are a blend of ideas from both job-order costing and process costing. The most popular hybrid is called **operation costing** (or **specification costing**), which is often used in the manufacture of goods that have some common characteristics plus some individual characteristics. Examples include products of textile, shoe, clothing, and repetitive woodworking and metal-working industries. Such products are specifically identified by batches or jobs or production runs. They often are variations of a single design and require a sequence of standardized operations. For example, depending on quality or other specifications, a suit of clothes may contain different materials and require different hand operations.

Operation may be defined as a standardized method or technique that is repetitively performed regardless of the distinguishing features of the finished product. For example, a machining department may perform one or more of the following opera-

EXHIBIT 17-10

Department A
Production Cost Report
Weighted-Average Method
For the Month Ended March 31, 19_1

FLOW OF PRODUCTION	(STEP 1) PHYSICAL UNITS	(STEP 2) EQUIVALENT UNITS materials	conversion costs
Work in process, beginning inventory	10,000(40%)*		
Started	40,000		
To account for	50,000		
Completed and transferred out	48,000	48,000	48,000
Work in process, ending inventory	2,000(50%)*	2,000	1,000
Accounted for	50,000	50,000	49,000

	COSTS	TOTALS	DETAILS materials	conversion costs	equivalent whole unit
	Work in process, beginning inventory	$ 7,500	$ 6,000	$ 1,500	
	Current costs	40,000	22,000	18,000	
(Step 3)	Total costs to account for	$47,500	$28,000	$19,500	
	Divide by equivalent units†		÷50,000	÷49,000	
(Step 4)	Cost per equivalent unit		$ .56	$ .398	$ .958
(Step 5)	Total costs of work completed and in process:				
	Units completed and transferred out (48,000)	$45,984			48,000($.958)
	Work in process, ending inventory (2,000):				
	Materials	$ 1,120	2,000($.56)		
	Conversion costs	398		1,000($.398)	
	Total work in process	$ 1,518			
	Total costs accounted for	$47,500‡			

**Degree of completion on conversion costs of this department.*
†For work done to date.
‡Rounded from $47,502 for decimal discrepancy. (Decimals carried out to three places.)

tions: milling, cleaning, grinding, and facing. As a term, *operation* is used loosely to describe assorted activities. An operation is most often one of several activities within a department. However, sometimes an operation may be another name for an entire department or process. For instance, some companies have a finishing department that may instead be called a finishing process or finishing operation.

comparison with other systems

An *operation cost system* collects cost of direct labor and factory overhead by operations. These conversion costs are then applied to all physical units passing through the operation by using a single average unit conversion cost for the operation. The direct-material costs are traced specifically to the product in the same manner as a job-cost system. Exhibit 17-11 compares job order, process, and operation costing.

EXHIBIT 17-11

Comparison of Job-Order, Process, and Operation Costing

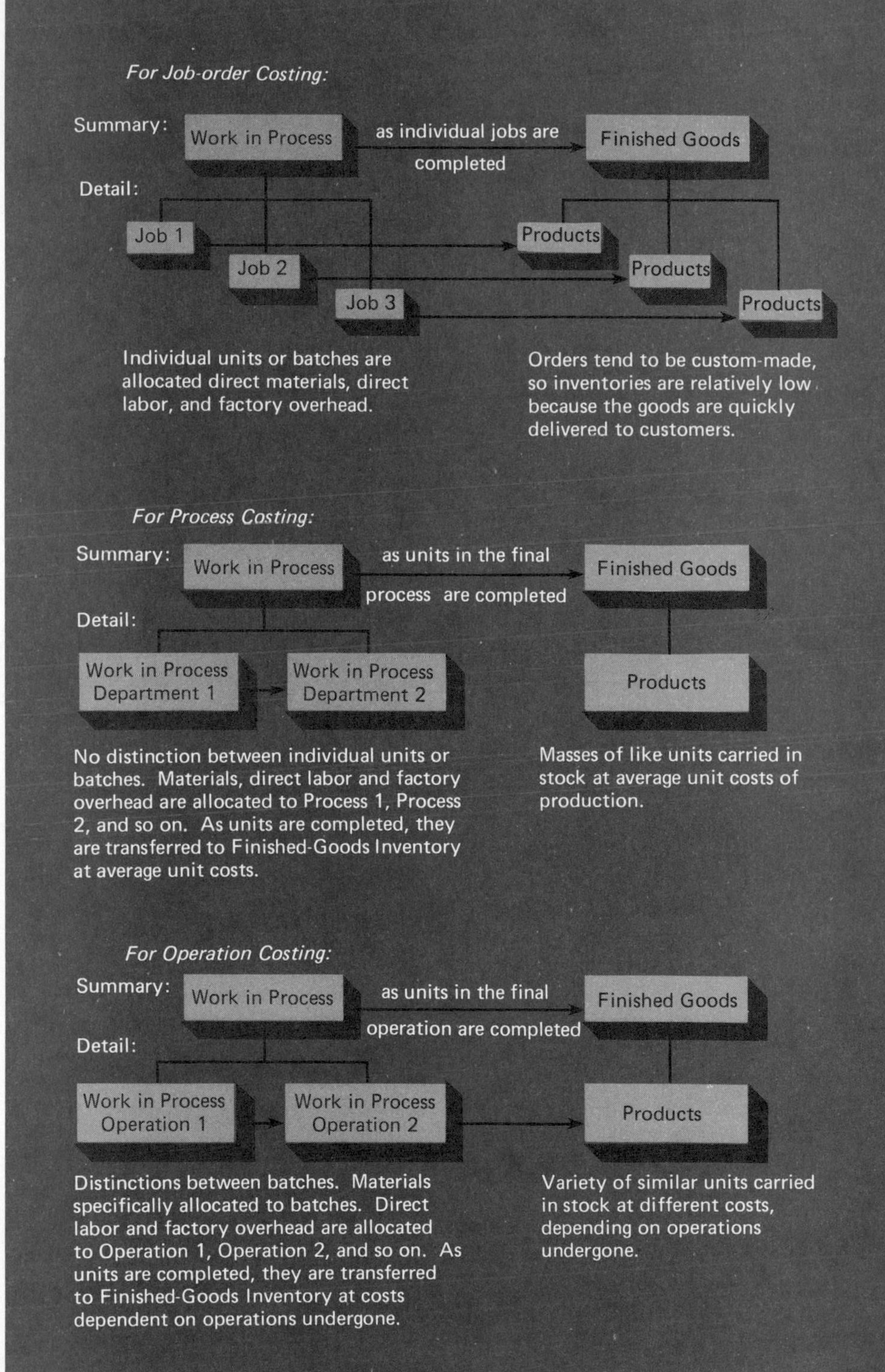

To illustrate, if a company produces lamp bases, the shape of the base may not vary, but the operations needed may differ, depending on the type of metal or finish used. Some metals must be annealed before being worked. Some lamp bases may be plated or painted while others may not. Cutting, stamping, or shaping operations may be identical regardless of the type of metal or finish. Thus, the costs of a given lamp model will consist of direct material used plus only the conversion costs applied by the operations used. Essentially, this system requires collecting conversion costs by operations and applying an average operation cost to those physical units that pass through the operations.

As another illustration, a radio may have the same basic chassis but different cabinets, knobs, and colors; yet the sequence of operations performed on all models may be the same. The cost of the different models would be determined by considering differences in material costs, but the conversion costs would be the same.

The operation-cost system normally requires more detailed records than a process-cost system because there are usually more operations and a greater number of products involved. The operation-cost system meets the need for a costing technique that blends job-order techniques for direct-material application and process-cost techniques for conversion-cost application. A company that has refined its cost-collecting techniques by operations within departments (or processes) has a sound foundation on which to build standard costs.

Exhibit 17-12 compares some major characteristics of job, process, and operation-

EXHIBIT 17-12

Comparison of Job, Process, and Operation System Characteristics

	JOB SYSTEM	OPERATION SYSTEM	PROCESS SYSTEM
Production is scheduled, performed, and charges made to jobs, lots, or batches.	Yes	Yes	No
Charges are made to processes and time periods.	No	Yes	Yes
Homogeneous product.	No	No	Yes
A better system for a diverse product line.	Yes	Yes	No
Performance reporting is by job, and sometimes also by department or operation.	Yes	Yes	No
Performance reporting is by process with respect to time.	No	Yes	Yes
Product-profitability determinations are possible by comparing actual cost with planned cost.	Yes	Yes	Yes
Routings or process sheets are available.	No	Yes	Yes
Generally end product produced for stock.	No	Yes	Yes
Higher investment in equipment; lower labor cost.	No	Yes	Yes
Feasibility for using standard costs.	Yes	Yes	Yes

Source: *Adapted from S. Goodman and J. Reece, eds.,* Controller's Handbook *(Homewood, Ill.: Dow Jones-Irwin, 1978), p. 176. The operation-cost column and the continuum format have been added here, as well as the final line, feasibility for using standard costs. Although a "yes" is designated on the final line for the job system, standard costs are most widely used in process systems.*

cost systems. Exceptions may be taken to the yes-no answers tabulated there. The long underscore (dashed lines) is drawn for each answer to emphasize that the job and process systems are the ends of a continuum with the job system on one end and the process system on the opposite end.

Incidentally, the cost accounting literature often erroneously distinguishes among process costing, job-order costing, and standard costing as though they were mutually exclusive categories of product costing. Actually, standard costing can be used in job, operation, or process systems.

simultaneous use of different systems

The plastics industry provides an excellent illustration of how job, operation, and process-costing systems blur together as cost systems are tailored for an organization. As Exhibit 17-13 shows, at first glance a plastics company appears to have a process-cost system. Plastics, Inc., manufactures extruded plastic sheet and formed products such as buckets, covers, and automotive interior components. The company has an extrusion *process* and subsequent *job operations* to form, trim, grind, and finish parts:

> The trimmed edges and uneven sheets from the extrusion process and trim scrap from forming are broken up and reground. Bad pieces are reported as scrap upon inspection and are reclaimed in regrind for use as raw material. A scrap credit is allowed for scrap pieces and trim in costing the final product. Production counts or weights are taken before all operations and as finished units are transferred to finished goods inventory. Note that

EXHIBIT 17-13

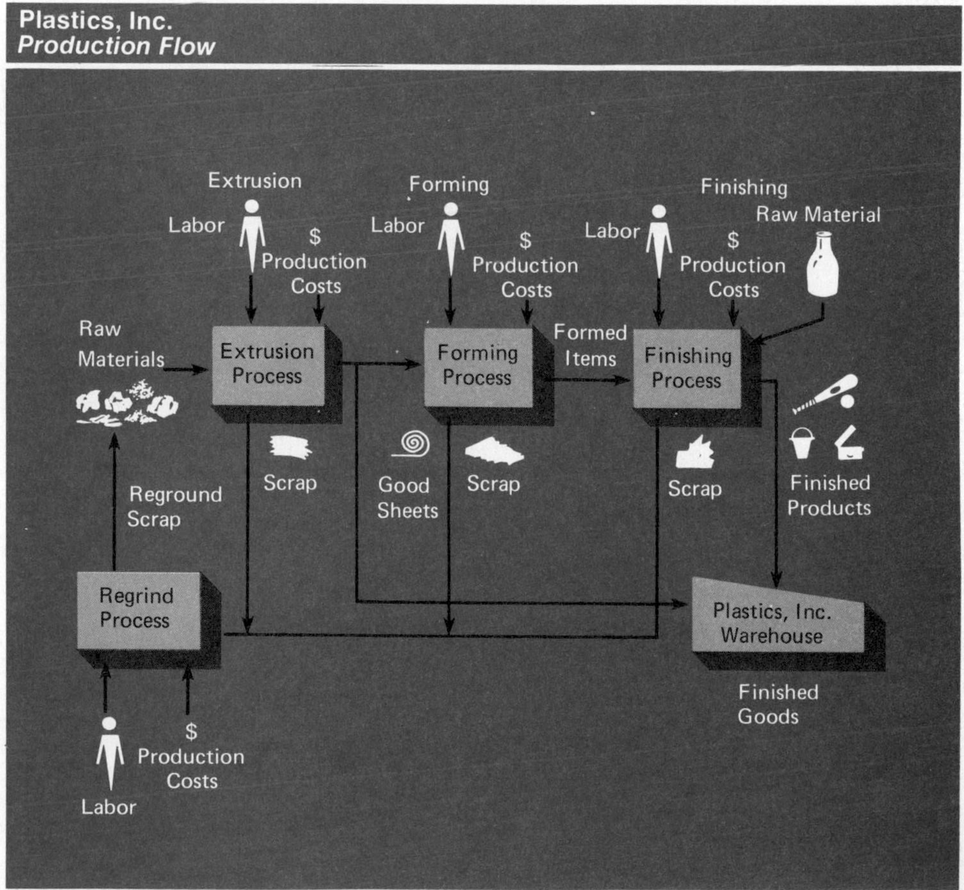

not all of the finished products go through all processes. Some sheet is taken from the extrusion process directly to finished goods. Also, additional raw materials (chemicals and coloring) are added in the finishing process.[1]

As Exhibit 17-13 indicates, the finished-goods warehouse can contain sheets and buckets (the costs of which are accumulated under a process-cost system). But the warehouse can also contain auto parts or specialty items (the costs of which are accumulated under a process-cost system plus perhaps an operation-cost or job-cost system).

Standard costs and process costs

This section assumes that you have already studied Chapters 6, 7, and 8. If you have not studied these chapters, proceed to the next major section, "Additional Aspects of Process Costing."

standards are useful

Previous chapters demonstrated that the use of standard costing is completely general; that is, it can be used in job-order situations, operation-costing situations or process-costing situations, and with absorption costing or variable costing. However, standard-cost procedures tend to be most effective when they are adapted to process-costing and operation-costing situations. Mass, continuous, and repetitive production conditions lend themselves rather easily to setting meaningful physical standards. Price tags may then be applied to the physical standards to develop standard costs. Such standard costs would allow for normal shrinkage, waste, evaporation, or spoilage.

The intricacies and conflicts between weighted-average and FIFO costing methods are eliminated by using standard costs. Further, weighted-average and FIFO methods become very complicated when used in industries that produce a variety of products. Many observers have stressed that standard costing is especially useful where there are various combinations of materials, operations, and product sizes. For example, a steel-rolling mill uses various steel alloys and produces sheets of various sizes and of various finishes. The items of raw material are not numerous; neither are the operations performed. But used in various combinations, they yield too great a variety of products to permit the averaging procedure of historical process-cost accounting. Elsewhere, similar conditions are frequently found—as, for example, in plants manufacturing rubber goods, textiles, ceramics, paints, and packaged food products.

Standard costing is growing in importance in process-costing industries. Therefore, because of its conceptual and practical appeal, standard costing deserves our study. Because we have already seen how standard costing aids planning and control, we shall concentrate on its product-costing aspects.

---

[1]S. Goodman and J. Reece, *Controller's Handbook* (Homewood, Ill.: Dow Jones-Irwin, 1978), p. 175. Interested readers should note that this handbook used the plastics industry as an example of process costing. In contrast, the *Accountants' Cost Handbook,* Section 7, used the plastics industry as an example of job costing. This illustration shows that in practice both types of systems can be combined. For additional discussion of process costing and operation costing, see articles in *Abacus,* December 1978, June 1979, and June 1980 by R. Skinner and G. Partington. Skinner's 1978 article prompted the inclusion of this section on operation costing in this textbook. Operation costing was also described in this book's first edition, pp. 105–6.

computations under standard costing

» *EXAMPLE 2*

The facts are basically the same as those for Department A in Example 1, except that standard costs have been developed for the process as follows:

	PER UNIT
Direct materials, introduced at start of process	$ .53
Conversion costs, incurred uniformly throughout process	.37
Standard cost per unit	$ .90
Work in process, beginning, 10,000 units, 40% completed (materials, $5,300; conversion costs, $1,480)	$ 6,780
Units completed during March	48,000
Units started during March	40,000
Work in process, end	2,000, 50% completed

REQUIRED

1. Compute the standard cost of goods completed and of work in process at end.
2. "Actual" material costs added during the month were $22,000. Conversion costs were $18,000. Show a summary schedule of total materials variance and total conversion-cost variance.

The formal solution is shown in Exhibit 17-14. Requirement 2 appears at the bottom of the exhibit. Careful study of Exhibit 17-14 will readily reveal that a standard-cost system greatly simplifies process-cost computations. A standard-cost system not only eliminates the intricacies of weighted-average versus FIFO inventory methods but also erases the need for burdensome computations of costs per equivalent unit. The standard cost *is* the cost per equivalent unit. In addition, a standard-cost approach facilitates control.

Note how the equivalent units for the current period provide the key measures of the work accomplished during March. Again we see that the analysis of the physical units and equivalent units in Exhibit 17-2 is vital for evaluating current performance. The equivalent units are used to value inventories and to measure variances.

There is a similarity between the FIFO and standard-cost methods in one important respect. Both use the "work done in current period only" in Exhibit 17-2 as the basis for computing equivalent units.

In particular, the standard-cost method compiles the current costs of $21,200 and $16,650 by multiplying the standard cost per equivalent unit times the total equivalent units for the current period. Thus, the approach differs from the weighted-average and FIFO methods, where the totals for current costs are compiled separately and then divided by equivalent units to obtain costs per unit.

Additional aspects of process costing

This chapter's illustrations plus almost all process-cost problems blithely mention various degrees of completion for inventories in process. The accuracy of these estimates depends on the care and skill of the estimator and the nature of the process. Estimating the degree of completion is usually easier for materials than for conversion

EXHIBIT 17-14

Standard Costs in a Process-Cost System
For the Month Ended March 31, 19_1

	TOTALS	DETAILS materials	DETAILS conversion costs
Standard cost per equivalent unit (given)		$.53	$.37
Work done in current period only (Exhibit 17-2, p. 563)		× 40,000	× 45,000
Current costs applied at standard prices	$37,850	$21,200	$16,650
Work in process, beginning inventory	6,780	$ 5,300	$ 1,480
Total costs to account for	$44,630		
Summary of costs:			
Units completed and transferred out 48,000 × ($.53 + $.37)	$43,200*		
Work in process, ending inventory (2,000):			
Materials	$ 1,060	2,000 × $.53	
Conversion costs (half-converted)	370		1,000 × $.37
Total work in process	$ 1,430		
Total costs accounted for	$44,630		
Summary of variances for current performance:			
Current output in equivalent units		40,000	45,000
Current output at standard costs applied		$21,200	$16,650
Actual costs		$22,000	$18,000
Total variance (which could be subdivided if more data were available)		$ 800 U	$ 1,350 U

**Additional details could be provided:*

Work in process, beginning inventory, which is transferred out first	$ 6,780
Additional costs to complete: (10,000)(1 − ⅖)($.37)	2,220
Cost of units started and completed this month: (48,000 − 10,000)($.90)	34,200
Total cost of goods completed and transferred out	$43,200

estimating degree of completion

costs. The conversion sequence usually consists of a number of standard operations or a standard number of hours, days, weeks, or months for mixing, heating, cooling, aging, curing, and so forth. Thus, the degree of completion for conversion costs depends on what proportion of the total effort needed to complete one unit or one batch has been devoted to units still in process. In industries where no exact estimate is possible, or, as in textiles, where vast quantities in process prohibit costly physical estimates, all work in process in every department is assumed to be ⅓ or ½ or ⅔ complete. In other cases, continuous processing entails little change of work-in-process levels from month to month. Consequently, in such cases, work in process is safely ignored and monthly production costs are assigned solely to goods completed.

This is another example of cost-benefit analysis, whereby a simplified system is used because management decisions will be unaffected by a more elaborate cost accounting system. Surveys of practice have shown that work-in-process inventories, as distinguished from completed goods, are typically ignored in process-costing systems. Moreover, FIFO process costing is virtually nonexistent.[2] (The latter is covered in this textbook because it highlights some basic concepts and procedures and because the topic persists in professional accounting examinations.)[3] Standard costing is used with process costing more than either historical weighted-average or FIFO.

overhead and predetermined rates

Direct labor and factory overhead tend to be lumped together as conversion costs for process-costing purposes. In many process-cost industries, continuous, uniform production results in little fluctuation of total factory overhead from month to month. In such cases, there is no need to use predetermined overhead rates. Of course, where overhead costs and production vary from period to period, predetermined overhead rates are used in order to get representative unit costs.

overhead and cost flow

In general, factory overhead is applied on a predetermined basis in the same manner as was introduced in Chapter 4. The assumption that all conversion costs are incurred uniformly in proportion to the degree of product completion is difficult to justify on theoretical grounds. For example, this implies that a wide variety of factory-overhead cost incurrence is directly related to direct-labor cost incurrence. Although such a direct cause-and-effect relationship may not exist, refinements of overhead application beyond this assumption are usually deemed too costly. When more precision is attempted, it is usually confined to developing a predetermined overhead rate to be loaded on material cost to cover such indirect costs as purchasing, receiving, storing, issuing, and transferring materials. In such cases, one overhead rate would be applied along with material costs while a separate overhead rate would be applied along with direct-labor costs.

Transfers in process costing

nature of transferred-in units and costs

Many process-cost situations have two or more departments or processes in the production cycle. Ordinarily, as goods move from department to department, related costs are also transferred. If standard costs are used, the accounting for such transfers is relatively simple. However, if FIFO or weighted-average is used, the accounting can become more complex.

To make the ideas concrete, return to the data in Example 1, which is reproduced here for your convenient reference.

» ***EXAMPLE 1***

A company has two processes. Material is introduced at the *beginning* of the process in Department A, and additional material is added at the *end* of the process in Department B. Conversion costs are applied uniformly throughout both processes. As the process in Department A is completed, goods are immediately transferred to Department B; as goods are completed in Department B, they are transferred to Finished Goods.

Data for the month of March 19_1 are shown on the top of the next page.

REQUIRED

Compute the cost of goods transferred out of each department. Compute ending-inventory costs for goods remaining in each department. Assume (a) first-in, first-out (FIFO) product costing and (b) weighted-average product costing. Show journal entries for the transfers to Department B.

[2]See R. Skinner, "Process Costing," *Abacus,* December 1978; and C. Horngren, "Process Costing in Perspective: Forget FIFO," *Accounting Review,* July 1967.

[3]See the supplement to this textbook: John K. Harris, *Professional Examination Questions and Answers: A Self-Study Approach* (Englewood Cliffs, N.J.: Prentice-Hall, 1982).

	DEPARTMENT A	DEPARTMENT B
Work in process, beginning inventory	10,000 units 40% converted,* $7,500 (materials, $6,000; conversion costs, $1,500)	12,000 units 66⅔% converted,* $21,000 (transferred-in costs, $9,800; conversion costs, $11,200)
Units completed during March	48,000	44,000
Units started during March	40,000	?
Work in process, ending inventory	2,000, 50% converted*	16,000, 37½% converted*
Material cost added during March	$22,000	$13,200
Conversion costs added during March	$18,000	$63,000

**This means that each unit in process is regarded as being fractionally complete with respect to the conversion costs of the present department only, at the dates of the work-in-process inventories.*

The five-step procedure described earlier is still pertinent. Exhibit 17-15 shows for Department B the initial two steps that analyze physical flows and compute equivalent units. Note that material costs pertaining to work in process have no degree of completion regarding the beginning or ending work in process. Why? Because materials are introduced at the *end* of the process in Department B. However, the equivalent units for transferred-in costs are, of course, fully completed at each of the inventory dates, because they are introduced at the *beginning* of the process.

Transferred-in costs tend to give students much trouble, so special study is needed here. As far as Department B is concerned, units coming in from Department A may be viewed as if they were the raw materials of Department B introduced at the beginning of the process. However, they are distinguished from materials and are called **transferred-in costs** (or **previous-department costs**), not material costs. That is, one might visualize the situation as if Department B had bought these goods from an outside supplier. Thus, Department B's computations must provide for transferred-in costs, as well as for any new material costs added in Department B, and for conversion costs added in Department B.

transfers and FIFO method

Exhibit 17-16 displays the FIFO application of costs to products in Department B. The application is similar to the FIFO application in Department A (Exhibit 17-6, page 566) except that transferred-in costs must now be considered. **Before reading on, study Exhibit 17-16 carefully. Concentrate on the bottom half of the exhibit. Note how the divisor equivalent units are based on the steps 1 and 2 shown in Exhibit 17-15.** That is, the current costs are divided by equivalent units for the "total work done in current period only." For example, the divisor for conversion costs is 42,000 equivalent units.

In a series of interdepartmental transfers, each department is regarded as a distinct accounting entity. All transferred-in costs during a given period are carried at one unit cost, regardless of whether weighted-average or FIFO methods were used by previous departments.

In summary, although the so-called FIFO method is sometimes used in process-costing situations, only rarely is an application of strict FIFO ever encountered. It should really be called a *modified* or *departmental* FIFO method. Why? Because, while FIFO is applied within a department to compile the cost of goods transferred *out,* the

EXHIBIT 17-15

Department B

Computation of Output in Equivalent Units
For the Month Ended March 31, 19_1

FLOW OF PRODUCTION	(STEP 1) PHYSICAL UNITS	(STEP 2) EQUIVALENT UNITS		
		transferred-in costs	**materials**	**conversion costs**
Work in process, beginning inventory	12,000($66\frac{2}{3}$%)*			
Transferred in	48,000			
To account for	60,000			
Completed and transferred out during current period:				
From beginning inventory	12,000	—	12,000	4,000
Started and completed currently	32,000	32,000	32,000	32,000
Work in process, ending inventory:	16,000($37\frac{1}{2}$%)*			
Transferred-in costs:				
16,000 × 100%		16,000		
Materials: none			—	
Conversion costs:				
16,000 × $37\frac{1}{2}$%				6,000
Accounted for	60,000			
Total work done in current period only†		48,000	44,000	42,000
Work done in the preceding period on the beginning inventory		12,000	—	8,000
Work done to date (that is, done in the current and preceding periods)‡		60,000	44,000	50,000

**Degrees of completion on conversion costs in this department only, at the dates of the work-in-process inventories. Note that material costs pertaining to work in process have no completion at each of these dates because, in this department, materials are introduced at the end of the process. Note also that transferred-in costs are, of course, fully completed at each of the inventory dates.*

†USED FOR FIFO AND STANDARD COST METHODS.

‡USED FOR WEIGHTED-AVERAGE COST METHOD.

goods transferred *in* during a given period usually bear a single average unit cost as a matter of convenience[4]

[4]Thus, although the FIFO method as used by Department A may show batches of goods accumulated and transferred at different unit costs, these goods are typically "costed in" by Department B at *one* average unit cost, as Exhibit 17-16 demonstrates ($46,000 ÷ 48,000 = $.95833). In other words, a departmental FIFO method may be used, but in practice the strict FIFO method is modified to the extent that subsequent departments use weighted-average methods for cost transferred in during a given period. If this were not done, the attempt to trace costs on a strict FIFO basis throughout a series of processes would become too burdensome and complicated. For example, a four-department process-cost system could have at least eight or more batches, which would need separate costing by the time costs are transferred to and out of the final department. However, as goods are transferred from the last process to Finished Goods, the records of finished stock could be kept on a strict first-in, first-out method if desired. The clerical burden alone is enough to cause most process-cost industries to reject strict FIFO as a costing method. More will be said about the weakness of FIFO in the next chapter concerning spoilage.

EXHIBIT 17-16 *(Place a clip on this page for easy reference.)*

Department B
Production Cost Report
First-in, First-out Method
For the Month Ended March 31, 19_1

FLOW OF PRODUCTION	(STEP 1) PHYSICAL UNITS	(STEP 2) EQUIVALENT UNITS		
		transferred-in costs	**materials**	**conversion costs**
Work in process, beginning inventory	12,000(66⅔%)*			
Transferred in	48,000			
To account for	60,000			
Completed and transferred out:				
From beginning inventory	12,000	—	12,000	4,000
Started and completed currently	32,000	32,000	32,000	32,000
Work in process, ending inventory	16,000(37½%)*	16,000	—	6,000
Accounted for	60,000	48,000	44,000	42,000

	COSTS	TOTALS	DETAILS		
			transferred-in costs	**materials**	**conversion costs**
	Work in process, beginning inventory	$ 21,000	—	—	—
	Current costs	122,200	$46,000	$13,200	$63,000
(Step 3)	Total costs to account for	$143,200			
	Divide by equivalent units†		÷48,000	÷44,000	÷42,000
(Step 4)	Cost per equivalent unit	$2.75833‡	$.95833	$ .30	$ 1.50
(Step 5)	Total costs of work completed and in process:				
	Units completed and transferred out (44,000):				
	From beginning inventory (12,000)	$ 21,000			
	Current costs added:				
	Materials	3,600		12,000($.30)	
	Conversion costs	6,000			4,000($1.50)
	Total completed from beginning inventory	$ 30,600			
	Started and completed (32,000) ($2.75833)	88,267			
	Total costs transferred out	$118,867			
	Work in process, ending inventory (16,000):				
	Transferred-in costs	$ 15,333	16,000($.95833)		
	Materials	—		—	
	Conversion costs	9,000			6,000($1.50)
	Total work in process	$ 24,333			
	Total costs accounted for	$143,200			

**Degree of completion on conversion costs in this department.*
†For work done in current period only.
‡This $2.75833 is the unit cost only for work started and completed this month. However, the unit cost of all units transferred out of this process this month is $118,667 ÷ 44,000 = $2.70152. This average unit cost would be used in charging finished goods.

EXHIBIT 17-17

Department B
Production Cost Report
Weighted-Average Method
For the Month Ended March 31, 19_1

FLOW OF PRODUCTION	(STEP 1) PHYSICAL UNITS	(STEP 2) EQUIVALENT UNITS: transferred-in costs	materials	conversion costs
Work in process, beginning inventory	12,000(66⅔%)*			
Transferred in	48,000			
To account for	60,000			
Completed and transferred out	44,000	44,000	44,000	44,000
Work in process, ending inventory	16,000(37½%)*	16,000	—	6,000
Accounted for	60,000	60,000	44,000	50,000

	COSTS	TOTALS	DETAILS: transferred-in costs	materials	conversion costs
	Work in process, beginning inventory	$ 21,000	$ 9,800	$ —	$11,200
	Current costs	122,184	45,984	13,200	63,000
(Step 3)	Total costs to account for	$143,184	$55,784	$13,200	$74,200
	Divide by equivalent units†		÷60,000	÷44,000	÷50,000
(Step 4)	Cost per equivalent unit	$ 2.714	$ .930	$ .30	$ 1.484
	Total costs of work completed and in process:				
	Units completed and transferred out (44,000)($2.714)	$119,416			
	Work in process, ending inventory (16,000):				
	Transferred-in costs	$ 14,880	16,000($.930)		
	Materials	—			
	Conversion costs	8,904			6,000($1.484)
	Total work in process	$ 23,784			
	Total costs accounted for	$143,184‡			

**Degree of completion on conversion costs of this department.*
†For work done to date.
‡Rounded from $143,200 for decimal discrepancy. (Decimals carried out to three places.)

transfers and weighted-average method The only essential difference between the weighted-average method as applied to Departments A (Exhibit 17-10, page 570) and B (Exhibit 17-17) is the accounting for transferred-in costs in Department B. Concentrate on the bottom half of Exhibit 17-17. Pause again, particularly to see the link between the equivalent units in Exhibit 17-15 and the divisor equivalent units in Exhibit 17-17. The total costs to account for are divided by the equivalent units for the "work done to date." For example, the divisor for conversion costs is 50,000 equivalent units.

journal entries for transfers The journal entries are:

	FIFO METHOD		WEIGHTED-AVERAGE METHOD	
	debit	credit	debit	credit
Department B—Work-in-process control	46,000		45,984	
Department A—Work-in-process control		46,000		45,984
To transfer costs from Department A. For detailed computations, see Exhibits 17-5 and 17-9				
Finished-goods control	118,867		119,416	
Department B—Work-in-process control		118,867		119,416
To transfer costs of goods finished. See Exhibits 17-16 and 17-17.				

Sometimes a problem requires that the Work-in-Process account be split into Work in Process—Materials, Work in Process—Direct Labor, and Work in Process—Factory Overhead. In these cases, the journal entries would contain this greater detail, even though the underlying reasoning and techniques would be unaffected.

Appendix 17A presents a complete set of sample entries for a process-costing system.

common mistakes Students should try to avoid some common pitfalls when accounting for transferred costs:

1. Remember to include transferred-in costs from previous departments in your calculations. Such costs should be treated as if they were another kind of material cost, because each department is treated as a separate entity. In other words, when successive departments are involved, transferred goods from one department become all or a part of the raw materials of the next department, although they are called *transferred-in costs,* not raw materials.
2. In calculating costs to be transferred on a first-in, first-out basis, do not overlook the costs attached at the beginning of the period to goods that were in process but are now included in the goods transferred. For example, do not overlook the $7,500 in Exhibit 17-3.
3. Unit costs may fluctuate between periods. Therefore, transferred goods may contain batches accumulated at different unit costs (see point 2). These goods, when transferred to the next department, are typically valued by that next department at *one* average unit cost.
4. Units may be expressed in terms of kilograms in one department and liters in the next. Consider each department separately. Unit costs would be based on kilogram measures in the first department and liters in the second. As goods are received by the second department, they may be converted to the liter unit of measure.

SUMMARY

Process costing is used for inventory costing when there is continuous, mass production of like units. The key concept in process costing is that of equivalent units, the expression of output during a given period in terms of doses or amounts of work applied thereto.

Five basic steps may be used in solving process-cost problems. Process costing is complicated by varying amounts of cost factors, by the presence of beginning inventories, and by the presence of costs transferred in from prior departments.

Two widely advocated process-costing techniques are known as the *weighted-average* and *first-in, first-out* methods. However, standard costs are the most widely used; they are simpler and more useful than other techniques for both product-costing and control purposes.

Operation costing is a widely used hybrid of job costing and process costing. Direct-material costs are traced specifically to the product in the manner as in a job-cost system. Conversion costs are applied to all physical units passing through a given operation by using a single average or standard unit conversion cost for the operation.

problems for self-study

Review each example in this chapter and obtain the solutions on your own. Then check your work against the solutions, which appear in the various exhibits.

Terms to Learn

equivalent units ***operation*** ***operation costing*** ***previous-department costs*** ***specification costing*** ***transferred-in costs***

Special Points and Pitfalls

In practice, operation costing is more widely used than process costing. In turn, standard costs (rather than FIFO or weighted-average costs) are used frequently in conjunction with both operation costing and process costing. FIFO provides a fine illustration of how costs may logically be applied to inventories and goods completed and transferred. FIFO also highlights the work done during the current period. For these reasons, professional examinations on cost accounting topics have frequently contained questions on FIFO process costing. However, it is not used much in the real world.

The five-step technique is not the only or the fastest way to solve process-cost problems. Nevertheless, it is logical and has self-checks. By applying the five-step approach, you will develop confidence and comprehension. Armed with this approach, you should be able to handle any process-cost situation adequately. Shortcuts should be applied wherever feasible. But it is difficult to generalize on shortcut methods, because they differ depending upon the specific problem and the student's ability to use them.

Appendix 17a: sample entries for process costing

The appendix to Chapter 4 presented a set of entries for a job-order system. In parallel fashion, Exhibit 17-18 presents some typical process-costing transactions, general-ledger effects, subsidiary ledgers, and source documents. To demonstrate the variety of accounting practices that may be encountered, an *actual* rather than a *normal* cost system is illustrated. That is, all actual costs are charged to Work in Process as incurred; no predetermined overhead rates are used, as entry 5 indicates. The use of actual rather than normal overhead is more likely to be used by companies that have steady production levels from month to month.

Note also that all costs are charged to a department account that simultaneously serves as an inventory account, Department A—Work in Process. As goods are completed and transferred, costs are shifted from one department to the next, as entry 6 indicates.

EXHIBIT 17-18

Process Cost System—Sample Entries
Where Predetermined Overhead Rates Are Not Used

TRANSACTION	GENERAL-LEDGER EFFECT*	SUBSIDIARY LEDGERS†	SOURCE DOCUMENTS
1. Purchases of materials and supplies	Stores control Accounts payable	Dr. Stores card, "Received" column	Approved invoice
2. Issuance of materials and supplies	Department A—Work-in-process control Stores control	Dr. Department A cost sheet—appropriate columns Cr. Stores card, "Issued" column	Stores requisition
3. Payroll costs	Department A—Work-in-process control Accrued payroll	Dr. Department A cost sheet—appropriate labor cost columns	Clock cards that are summarized and classified by natural classification (for example, supervision, inspection, mixers). This summary is sometimes called *payroll recapitulation*, a *labor distribution*, or a *payroll summary*.
4. Payroll payments	Accrued payroll Cash		Clock cards that are summarized on payroll sheets each pay period to compute individual payouts.
5. Other costs, such as utilities, insurance, and depreciation	Department A—Work-in-process control Accounts payable Unexpired insurance Allowance for depreciation—equipment	Dr. Department A cost sheet—appropriate columns for utilities, insurance, and depreciation	Approved invoices, insurance registers, and depreciation schedules. Accruals, write-offs, and other charges may be authorized by a top accounting executive.
6. Transfer of completed goods to next department	Department B—Work-in-process control Department A—Work-in-process control	Dr. Department B cost sheet—"Costs Transferred-In" column Cr. Department A cost sheet—"Costs Transferred-Out" column	Production cost report
7. Operating costs of Department B	Same entries as (2)–(5)		
8. Transfer of completed goods to finished stock	Finished goods Department B—Work-in-process control	Dr. Finished stock card, "Received" column Cr. Department B cost sheet—"Costs Transferred-Out" column	Production cost report
9. Sales	Accounts receivable Sales Cost of Sales Finished goods	Dr. Customers ledger Cr. Sales ledgers (if any) Dr. Cost of sales ledger (if any) Cr. Finished stock card, "Issued" column	Sales invoices

These entries are in summary form and are usually posted monthly.

†*Subsidiary ledgers are not necessarily kept for every general-ledger account. That is why there are no entries in subsidiary ledgers for some transactions.*

Appendix 17b: alternative format for process costing

The exhibits in the body of the chapter, such as Exhibit 17-10, stressed the five-step, no-shortcut approach to process costing. Some accountants prefer a more tightly knit format, as shown in Exhibit 17-19. Such a production-cost report does not contain the detailed computations of physical units and equivalent units.

EXHIBIT 17-19

Department A

Application of Costs to Products, Weighted-Average Method
For the Month Ended March 31, 19_1

		(STEP 3)*			(STEP 4)	
		work in process, beginning	current costs	total costs	equivalent units†	average unit costs
	Materials	$6,000	$22,000	$28,000	50,000	$.560
	Conversion costs	1,500	18,000	19,500	49,000	.398
		$7,500	$40,000	$47,500		$.958
(Step 5)	Goods completed: 48,000 units × $.958			45,984		
(Step 5)	Work in process, end, 2,000 units			$ 1,518‡		

See Exhibit 17-7 for Steps 1 and 2, p. 567.

†The divisor for computing unit costs depends on the cost-flow assumption. For the weighted-average method, this is the total work done to date as computed in Exhibit 17-7. The equivalent units include the work completed before March on the beginning inventory as well as the work completed during March. Therefore, the beginning inventory costs are mingled with current costs as shown in the tabulation above.

‡Rounding to three decimal places causes minor discrepancies. The subtraction here would show $1,516. However, $1,518 is used for consistency with Exhibit 17-10.

In particular, note that the cost of the goods completed is simply deducted from the total costs (the total debits to work in process) to obtain the cost of the ending work in process. Nevertheless, it is advisable to check the accuracy of these computations by the following proof:

Materials (2,000 × $.560)	$1,120
Conversion costs (2,000 × .5 × $.398)	398
Total	$1,518

QUESTIONS, PROBLEMS, AND CASES

17-1 "Operation costing is a hybrid." Explain.

17-2 "Previous-department costs are those incurred in the preceding fiscal period." Do you agree? Explain.

17-3 "Standard-cost procedures are particularly applicable to process-costing situations." Do you agree? Why?

17-4 What are some virtues of standard costs as used in process costing?

17-5 "There is no need for using predetermined overhead rates for product costing in process-cost industries." Do you agree? Why?

17-6 Why should the accountant distinguish between *transferred-in costs* and *new raw-material* costs for a particular department?

17-7 What feature of the first two steps of the five-step uniform technique distinguishes them from the final three steps?

17-8 ***Compute equivalent units.*** Consider the following data for May:

	PHYSICAL UNITS
Started in May	50,000
Completed in May	46,000
Ending inventory, work in process	12,000
Beginning inventory, work in process	8,000

The beginning inventory was 90 percent complete regarding materials and 40 percent complete regarding conversion costs. The ending inventory was 60 percent complete regarding materials and 20 percent complete regarding conversion costs.

REQUIRED

Prepare a schedule of equivalent units for the work done during May only and the work done to date.

17-9 ***FIFO and unit material costs.*** The Hiram Company uses the FIFO process-cost method. Consider the following for March:

Beginning inventory, 20,000 units, 60 percent completed regarding materials, which cost $90,000
Units completed, 70,000
Cost of materials placed in process during March, $350,000
Ending inventory, 10,000 units, 20 percent completed regarding materials

REQUIRED

Compute the material cost per equivalent unit for the work done in March only. No units were lost or spoiled.

17-10 ***Counting equivalent production units.*** (CPA) The Felix Manufacturing Company uses a process-cost system to account for the costs of its only product, known as Nino. Production begins in the fabrication department where units of raw material are molded into various connecting parts. After fabrication is complete, the units are transferred to the assembly department. There is no material added in the assembly department. After assembly is complete, the units are transferred to the packaging department where the units are packaged for shipment. At the completion of this process, the units are complete and they are transferred to the shipping department.

At year-end, December 31, 19_7, the following inventory of Ninos is on hand:
No unused raw material or packing material
Fabrication department: 6,000 units, 25 percent complete as to raw material and 40 percent complete as to direct labor
Assembly department: 10,000 units, 75 percent complete as to direct labor
Packaging department: 3,000 units, 60 percent complete as to packing material and 75 percent complete as to direct labor
Shipping department: 8,000 units

REQUIRED

Prepare in proper form schedules showing the following at December 31, 19_7:

1. The number of equivalent units of raw material in all inventories.
2. The number of equivalent units of fabrication-department direct labor in all inventories.
3. The number of equivalent units of packaging-department material and direct labor in the packaging-department inventory.

17-11 ***Equivalent units.*** (CPA) The Jorcano Manufacturing Company uses a process-cost system to account for the costs of its only product, Product D. Production begins in the fabrication department where units of raw material are molded into various connecting parts. After fabrication is complete, the units are transferred to the assembly department. There is no material added in the assembly department. After assembly is complete, the units are transferred to a packaging department where packing material is placed around the units. After the units are ready for shipping, they are sent to a shipping area.

At year-end, June 30, 19_3, the following inventory of Product D is on hand:

No unused raw material or packing material
Fabrication department: 300 units, ⅓ complete as to raw material and ½ complete as to direct labor
Assembly department: 1,000 units, ⅖ complete as to direct labor
Packaging department: 100 units, ¾ complete as to packing material and ¼ complete as to direct labor
Shipping area: 400 units

1. The number of equivalent units of raw material in all inventories at June 30, 19_3, is (a) 100, (b) 1,600, (c) 925, (d) 300.

2. The number of equivalent units of fabrication-department direct labor in all inventories at June 30, 19_3, is (a) 150, (b) 300, (c) 975, (d) 1,650.

3. The number of equivalent units of packing material in all inventories at June 30, 19_3, is (a) 475, (b) 100, (c) 425, (d) 75.

17-12 ***Multiple choice, weighted average.*** (CPA) On April 1, 19_7, the Collins Company had 6,000 units of work in process in Department B, the second and last stage of their production cycle. The costs attached to these 6,000 units were $12,000 of costs transferred in from Department A, $2,500 of material costs added in Department B and $2,000 of conversion costs added in Department B. Materials are added in the beginning of the process in Department B. Conversion was 50 percent complete on April 1, 19_7. During April, 14,000 units were transferred in from Department A at a cost of $27,000; and material costs of $3,500 and conversion costs of $3,000 were added in Department B. On April 30, 19_7, Department B had 5,000 units of work in process 60 percent complete as to conversion costs. The costs attached to these 5,000 units were $10,500 of costs transferred in from Department A, $1,800 of material costs added in Department B and $800 of conversion costs added in Department B.

Choose the best answer for each question:

1. Using the weighted-average method, what were the equivalent units for the month of April?

	TRANSFERRED IN FROM DEPARTMENT A	MATERIALS	CONVERSION
a.	15,000	15,000	15,000
b.	19,000	19,000	20,000
c.	20,000	20,000	18,000
d.	25,000	25,000	20,000

2. Using the weighted-average method, what was the cost per equivalent unit for conversion costs? (a) $4,200 ÷ 15,000, (b) $5,800 ÷ 18,000, (c) $5,800 ÷ 20,000, (d) $5,000 ÷ 18,000.

17-13 ***Multiple choice, FIFO.*** (SMA) Choose the best answer for each of the following three multiple-choice questions. Show your supporting computations. The company uses FIFO.

1. With an opening inventory consisting of 1,000 units 80 percent complete as to materials and 30 percent complete as to conversion work; 11,000 units completed and transferred; no lost units; and a closing inventory of 900 units, 40 percent complete as to materials and 20 percent complete as to conversion; the total cost of the opening inventory before completion was $8,000; and current unit costs being $2 for materials and $8 for conversion; the total current materials costs amounted to (a) $21,120, (b) $21,800, (c) $22,200, (d) $22,720, (e) $23,400.

2. Total current conversion costs amounted to (a) $86,390, (b) $86,680, (c) $87,040, (d) $89,380, (e) $89,440.

3. Costs allocated to the goods transferred out amounted to (a) $6,000, (b) $14,000, (c) $110,000, (d) $114,000, (e) $120,000.

17-14 ***FIFO method, conversion cost.*** (W. Crum) Given the following information, compute the unit conversion cost for the month of June 19_0 for the Molokai Company, using the FIFO process-cost method. Show details of your calculation.

Units completed, 20,000
Conversion cost in beginning inventory, $7,500
Beginning inventory, 3,000 units with 80 percent of conversion cost
Ending inventory, 7,000 units with 60 percent of conversion cost
Conversion costs put into production in June, $65,400

17-15 ***Weighted-average process costing.*** The following information relates to one department operating under a process-cost system: Work in process, December 1, 19_1, 1,000 units, 40 percent complete, consisting of $8,703 of materials and $5,036 of conversion costs. Production completed for December, 8,200 units; work in process, December 31, 19_1, 800 units, 20 percent complete.

All materials are introduced at the start of the process, while conversion costs are incurred uniformly throughout the process. Materials added during December were $72,000; conversion costs were $83,580.

REQUIRED | Using weighted averages, show a schedule of equivalent performance, unit costs, and summary of costs. Also prepare a summary entry for the transfer of completed goods to finished stock.

17-16 ***Standard process costs.*** Refer to the preceding problem. Assume standard costs per finished unit as follows: Direct materials, $8.50; Conversion costs, $10.00.

1. Compute standard costs of goods transferred and still in process.

2. Give the total variances for current performance on direct materials and conversion costs.

17-17 ***Basic operation costing.*** Werke Company manufactures a variety of tool boxes. The company's manufacturing operations and their cost for November were:

	CUTTING	ASSEMBLY	FINISHING
Direct labor	$2,600	$16,500	$4,800
Factory overhead	3,000	2,900	3,300

Three styles of boxes were produced in November. The quantities and direct-material costs were:

STYLE	QUANTITY	MATERIALS
Standard	1,200	$18,000
Home	600	6,660
Industrial	200	5,400

The industrial style requires no finishing operations.

REQUIRED | Compute the total cost and unit cost of each style produced.

17-18 ***Operation costing with ending work-in-process inventory.*** Gilhooley Products uses three operations in sequence to manufacture an assortment of picnic baskets. In each operation, the same procedures, time, and costs are used to perform that operation for a given quantity of baskets, regardless of the basket style being produced.

During April, a batch of materials for 1,100 baskets of Style X was put through the first operation. This was followed in turn by separate batches of materials for 400 baskets of Style Y and 1,300 of Style Z. All the materials for a batch are introduced at the beginning of the operation for that batch. The costs as shown on the top of the next page were incurred in April for the first operation.

All of the units started in April were completed during the month and transferred out to the next operation except 350 units of Style Z, which were only partially completed at

April 30. These were 40 percent completed as to conversion costs and 100 percent completed as to material costs. There were no work-in-process inventories at the beginning of the month.

Direct labor	$29,600
Factory overhead	13,135
Materials:	
Style X	18,700
Style Y	8,000
Style Z	13,000

REQUIRED

1. For each basket style, compute the total cost of work completed and transferred out to the second operation.
2. Compute the total cost of the ending inventory in process.

17-19 ***Standard costing with beginning and ending work in process.*** The Victoria Corporation uses a standard-costing system for its manufacturing operations. Standard costs for the Cooking Process are $2 per unit for materials and $3 per unit for conversion costs. All materials are introduced at the beginning of the process, but conversion costs are incurred uniformly throughout the process. The operating summary for May included the following data for the Cooking Process:

Work-in-process inventories:
May 1, 3,000 units, 60 percent completed
May 31, 5,000 units, 50 percent completed
New units started in May, 20,000
Units completed and transferred out of Cooking in May, 18,000
Additional ("actual") costs incurred for Cooking during May:
Materials, $41,500
Conversion costs, $57,000

REQUIRED

1. Compute the total standard cost of units transferred out in May and the total standard cost of the May 31 inventory of work in process.
2. Compute the total May variances for material cost and conversion cost.

17-20 ***Weighted averages.*** The Dyer Processing Company had work in process at the beginning and end of 19_1 as follows:

	PERCENTAGE OF COMPLETION	
	materials	**conversion costs**
January 1, 19_1—3,000 units	40%	10%
December 31, 19_1—2,000 units	80%	40%

The company completed 40,000 units of finished goods during 19_1. Manufacturing costs incurred during 19_1 were: materials, $242,600; conversion costs, $445,200. Inventory at January 1, 19_1, was carried at a cost of $10,600 (materials, $7,000; conversion costs, $3,600).

Assuming weighted average:

1. Compute new equivalent production for 19_1 for (a) materials and (b) conversion costs.

2. What is the proper cost of ending goods in process?

17-21 ***Standard process costs.*** Refer to the preceding problem. If the standard cost for materials is $5 per finished unit and the standard cost for conversion costs is $10 per finished unit, what would be the total standard cost of work performed during 19_1?

17-22 ***Weighted-average process-costing method.*** The Bright Paint Co. uses a process-cost system. Materials are added at the beginning of a particular process and conversion costs are incurred uniformly. Work in process at the beginning and end is assumed 50 percent complete. One gallon of material makes one gallon of product.

Data:

Beginning inventory	900 gallons
Materials added	9,900 gallons
Ending inventory	450 gallons
Conversion costs incurred	$18,000
Cost of materials added	$20,000
Conversion costs, beginning inventory	$ 800
Cost of materials, beginning inventory	$ 1,600

Use the weighted-average method. Prepare a schedule of output in equivalent units and a schedule of application of costs to products. Show the cost of goods completed and of ending work in process.

17-23 ***Two departments; two months.*** (W. Vatter) One of the products of this company is manufactured by passing it through two processes. The materials are started into production at the beginning of Process 1 and are passed directly from Process 1 to Process 2 without inventory between the processes. Operating data for two months are as follows:

January

Process 1. No initial work in process. During the month, 800 units were put into process and $8,000 was charged to this account for direct materials. Conversion costs incurred during the month were $2,800. Six hundred units were finished and passed on to Process 2. The work in process at January 31 was one-half finished.

Process 2. No work in process on January 1. The work transferred from Process 1 was received and conversion costs of $2,000 were incurred in operations to complete 300 units. At the end of the month, 300 units one-third finished remained in process.

February

Process 1. Six hundred units of material were put into process at a total price of $6,000 for direct materials. Conversion costs incurred were $2,550. At the end of the month, there were 300 units still within the process, two-thirds finished.

Process 2. Conversion costs charged to operations in this process for February were $2,640. On February 28, there were 300 units still within the process, two-thirds finished.

There is no spoilage or shrinkage in either of the processes; all units unfinished at the beginning of the month are completed within that month.

REQUIRED Calculations of production costs for each process for each month on a weighted-average basis.

17-24 ***Alternative format.*** (W. Crum) Study Appendix 17b. The Doral Company has the following data for the month of October:

	DEPARTMENT A	DEPARTMENT B
Beginning inventory in process:	2,000 units	2,000 units
Prior department cost*	0	$4,600
Materials added last month	$2,000 (100%)	$3,200 (80%)
Conversion costs added last month	$900 (60%)	$800 (40%)
Units put in process this month	30,000	29,000
Materials added this month	$30,968	$56,580
Conversion costs added this month	$41,800	$29,803
Units completed and transferred	29,000	30,000
Ending inventory in process:	3,000 units	1,000 units
Material content	90%	50%
Conversion costs	50%	30%

**These are transferred-in costs.*

REQUIRED Using weighted-average costing, prepare a production report for each department. Show the cost of goods completed and transferred and also show the cost of the ending work in process.

17-25 ***FIFO costing.*** Refer to the preceding problem. Using FIFO costing, repeat the requirements.

17-26 ***FIFO computations.*** Repeat Problem 17-15, using the first-in, first-out method.

17-27 ***FIFO computations.*** Repeat Problem 17-22, using the first-in, first-out method.

17-28 ***FIFO computations.*** Repeat Problem 17-23, using the first-in, first-out method.

17-29 ***Weighted-average process costing.*** (CGAA, adapted) The B Lunder Co. Ltd. manufactures a product that requires processing in three departments. In Department C, materials are added at the very beginning of the Department C processing. Conversion costs are added continuously throughout the process. Manufacturing overhead is applied to units in process in Department C at the rate of 125 percent of direct-labor costs.

The following data pertain to the operations of Department C for the month of July: In process, July 1: 4,000 units, 60 percent converted costs:

Dept. B costs	$15,340
Dept. C materials	2,273
Dept. C direct labor	2,764
Dept. C applied overhead	?

During the month, 12,000 units were received from Department B at a cost of $45,460.

Costs incurred by Department C during July included:

Direct materials requisitioned	$ 8,975
Direct labor	11,124

On July 31, there were 6,000 units left in process, 40 percent converted. No units were spoiled or lost in processing.

REQUIRED

Using the weighted-average method of costing, prepare a production-cost report for July.

17-30 ***Weighted-average process costing.*** (CPA) You are engaged in the audit of the December 31, 19_8, financial statements of Spirit Corporation, a manufacturer of a digital watch. You are attempting to verify the costing of the ending inventory of work in process and finished goods, which was recorded on Spirit's books as follows:

	UNITS	COST
Work in process (50% complete as to labor and overhead)	300,000	$ 660,960
Finished goods	200,000	$1,009,800

Materials are added to production at the beginning of the manufacturing process, and overhead is applied to each product at the rate of 60 percent of direct-labor costs. There was no finished-goods inventory on January 1, 19_8. A review of Spirit's inventory-cost records disclosed the following information:

		COSTS	
	UNITS	**materials**	**labor**
Work in process, January 1, 19_8 (80% complete as to labor and overhead)	200,000	$ 200,000	$ 315,000
Units started in production	1,000,000		
Material costs, current period		$1,300,000	
Labor costs, current period			$1,995,000
Units completed	900,000		

REQUIRED

1. Prepare schedules as of December 31, 19_8, to compute the following:
   a. Equivalent units of production using the weighted-average method.
   b. Unit costs of production of materials, labor, and overhead.
   c. Costing of the finished-goods inventory and work-in-process inventory.

2. Prepare the necessary journal entry to correctly state the inventory of finished goods and work in process, assuming the books have not been closed. (Ignore income-tax considerations.)

17-31 ***Weighted-average method.*** (CPA) Lakeview Corporation is a manufacturer that uses the weighted-average process-cost method to account for costs of production. Lakeview manufactures a product that is produced in three separate departments: molding, assembling, and finishing. The following information was obtained for the assembling department for the month of June 19_0.

Work in process, June 1—2,000 units composed of the following:

	AMOUNT	DEGREE OF COMPLETION
Transferred in from the molding department	$32,000	100%
Costs added by the assembling department:		
Direct materials	$20,000	100%
Direct labor	7,200	60%
Factory overhead applied	5,500	50%
	32,700	
Work in process, June 1	$64,700	

The following activity occurred during the month of June:
10,000 units were transferred in from the molding department at a cost of $160,000.
$150,000 of costs were added by the assembling department:

Direct materials	$ 96,000
Direct labor	36,000
Factory overhead applied	18,000
	$150,000

8,000 units were completed and transferred to the finishing department.

At June 30, 4,000 units were still in work in process. The degree of completion of work in process at June 30, was as follows:

Direct materials	90%
Direct labor	70%
Factory overhead applied	35%

REQUIRED

Prepare in good form a cost of production report for the assembling department for the month of June. Show supporting computations in good form. The report should incude (a) equivalent units of production, (b) total manufacturing costs, (c) cost per equivalent unit, (d) dollar amount of ending work in process, (e) dollar amount of inventory cost transferred out.

17-32 ***Process costing, FIFO, and standard-cost methods.*** (CPA, adapted) The Melody Corporation manufactures a single product, known as Jupiter. Melody uses the first-in, first-out (FIFO) process-costing method for both financial statement and internal management reporting.

In analyzing production results, standard costs are used, whereas actual costs are used for financial statement reporting. The standards, which are based upon equivalent units of production, are as follows:

Raw material per unit	1 pound at $10 per pound
Direct labor per unit	.5 hours at $16 per hour
Factory overhead per unit	.5 hours at $5 per hour

Budgeted factory overhead for standard hours allowed for April production is $30,000. Data for the month of April 19_7 are as follows:

The beginning inventory consisted of 2,500 units which were 100 percent complete as to raw material and 40 percent complete as to direct labor and factory overhead.

An additional 10,000 units were started during the month.

The ending inventory consisted of 2,000 units which were 100 percent complete as to raw material and 40 percent complete as to direct labor and factory overhead.

Costs applicable to April production are as follows:

	ACTUAL COST	STANDARD COST
Raw material used (11,000 pounds)	$121,000	$100,000
Direct labor (6,250 hours actually worked)	105,575	82,400
Factory overhead	31,930	25,750

REQUIRED

1. For each element of production for April (raw material, direct labor, and factory overhead), compute (a) equivalent units of production, and (b) cost per equivalent unit of production at actual cost and at standard cost. Show supporting computations in good form.
2. Prepare a schedule analyzing for April production the following variances as either favorable or unfavorable: (a) total materials, (b) materials price, (c) materials usage, (d) total labor, (e) labor rate, (f) labor efficiency, (g) total factory overhead, (h) factory-overhead production volume, (i) factory-overhead budget. Show supporting computations in good form.

17-33 ***Standard process costs and review of Chapters 7 and 8.*** (CPA) Norwood Corporation is considering changing its method of inventory valuation from absorption costing to direct costing and has engaged you to determine the effect of the proposed change on the 19_8 financial statements.

The corporation manufactures Gink, which is sold for $20 per unit. Marsh is added before processing starts, and labor and overhead are added evenly during the manufacturing process. Production capacity is budgeted at 110,000 units of Gink annually. The standard costs per unit of Gink are:

Marsh, 2 pounds	$3.00
Labor	6.00
Variable manufacturing overhead	1.00
Fixed manufacturing overhead	1.10

A process-cost system is used employing standard costs. Variances from standard costs are now charged or credited to cost of goods sold. If direct costing were adopted, only variances resulting from variable costs would be charged or credited to cost of goods sold.

Inventory data for 19_8 follow:

	UNITS	
	January 1	**December 31**
Marsh (pounds)	50,000	40,000
Work in process		
2/5 processed	10,000	
1/3 processed		15,000
Finished goods	20,000	12,000

During 19_8 220,000 pounds of Marsh were purchased and 230,000 pounds were transferred to work in process. Also, 110,000 units of Gink were transferred to finished goods. Actual fixed manufacturing overhead during the year was $121,000. There were no variances between standard variable costs and actual variable costs during the year.

REQUIRED

1. Prepare schedules that present the computation of (a) equivalent units of production for material and conversion costs, (b) number of units sold, (c) standard unit costs under direct costing and absorption costing, (d) amount, if any, of overapplied or underapplied fixed manufacturing overhead.

2. Prepare a comparative statement of cost of goods sold using standard variable costing and standard absorption costing.

17-34 ***Reconciliation of variable and absorption costing.*** Refer to the preceding problem.

REQUIRED

1. Compute the difference in net income between variable and absorption costing.
2. Explain the difference numerically in terms of the changes in the level of the beginning and ending inventories.

17-35 ***Joint costs and process costs; first-in, first-out; sell or process further.*** The Chemo Company manufactures two principal products, known as Gummo and Yummo. The company has three producing departments A, B, and C. Raw material is started in process in Department A. Upon completion of joint processing in that department, two distinct chemicals are produced. One-fourth of the output goes to Department B, where it is made into Gummo; the other three-fourths goes to Department C, where it becomes Yummo. As Gummo and Yummo are completed, they are immediately transferred to finished stock.

The company assigns Department A costs to Gummo and Yummo in proportion to their net realizable values at point of separation, computed by deducting costs to be incurred in subsequent processes from the sales value of the products.

The following information concerns the operations during May 19_1:

Inventories

	APRIL 30		MAY 31
	units	**cost**	**units**
Department A	None		None
Department B	500*	$10,000	700†
Department C	1,000*	11,300	700†
Finished goods—Gummo	800	19,200	500
Finished goods—Yummo	600	13,200	800

**Each unit is 1/5 completed.*
†Each unit is 3/5 completed.

Twelve thousand units of output were produced in Department A.

	COSTS INCURRED IN MAY	
	materials used	**conversion costs**
Department A	$72,000	$72,000
Department B	—	$15,600
Department C	—	$12.00 per equivalent unit

	SALES PRICES
Gummo	$25.00 per unit
Yummo	$22.00 per unit

Prices as of May 31 are unchanged from those in effect during the month.

The company uses first-in, first-out to cost out production.

REQUIRED

1. For May production, conversion cost per equivalent unit in Department B.
2. Conversion cost per equivalent unit in Department A.
3. Total costs transferred to Department B.
4. Costs transferred from Department B to finished stock.
5. The company is considering a chance to sell the product that now goes into Department C at the split-off point, instead of processing it into Yummo. (Gummo would continue to be processed as usual.) If the long-run selling price at split-off point will be $10, should the company close down Department C and sell at split-off? Why? Answer in seventy words or less.

17-36 ***Review of chapters 16 and 17.*** (SMA) Baker Manufacturing Company Ltd. follows process-costing procedures, attaching costs to its inventories using the weighted-average method. The company produces two joint products–Biko and Selludin–and a byproduct–Clinmar. All of these products originate from the mixing department.

Until recently, none of these three products has been processed further, for technological reasons. Moreover, there has been a ready market for all three. It has been possible to sell Biko at $6.00 per unit, Selludin at $8.00 per unit, and Clinmar at $0.80 per unit. In the case of Clinmar, it is necessary to pay a sales commission of 25 percent on units sold. It has been company practice to set up the net realizable value of Clinmar as a reduction of the cost of the completed units of the two joint products, and to allocate the joint costs remaining on the basis of the two products' sales value.

During the current fiscal year technological improvements in the manufacturing process made it possible to process the two joint products further so that unit selling prices of $25 for Biko and $40 for Selludin could be obtained. None of these units was sold at the split-off point during the year. It has been decided to treat the byproduct costs as before and to allocate joint-product costs to the new Biko finishing department and Selludin finishing department, on the basis of sales value less added costs.

At the beginning of the current fiscal year, there were 6,000 units in process in the mixing department. Costs of these units were:

Materials	$15,600
Conversion	12,200
	$27,800

During the current year 68,000 units were started in production in the mixing department, with 2,000 units remaining in process at the end of the year. This work in process was 78 percent complete as to materials and 62 percent complete as to conversion. At the split-off point it was determined that the breakdown of the 72,000 completed units was as follows:

Biko	40,000
Selludin	20,000
Clinmar	12,000
	72,000

Costs of the mixing department during the current year, charged to work in process for the department, were:

Materials	$205,080
Conversion	134,280
	$339,360

Conversion costs on account of the further processing of the joint products were:

Biko	$250,000
Selludin	200,000
	$450,000

All further processing of the 40,000 units of Biko and of the 20,000 units of Selludin was completed during the year, and sales of all three products were as follows:

Clinmar–9,060 units at $0.80	$ 7,248
Biko–33,500 units at $25.00	837,500
Selludin–15,600 units at $40.00	624,000
	$1,468,748

REQUIRED

Compute the cost of the closing inventory of *Selludin* as of the end of the fiscal year. Your solution should include in supporting schedules the determination of equivalent production, unit costs, and the determination and allocation of joint costs.

18 Spoilage, Waste, Defective Units, and Scrap

Problems of spoilage, waste, defective units, or scrap are found in nearly all manufacturing businesses, regardless of the specific production techniques used. Because there is a general approach to this entire area, this chapter views the problem as a whole before considering the peculiar difficulties in process-costing and job-costing situations.

The conceptual ideas of accounting for spoilage center primarily on distinguishing between abnormal and normal spoilage. Abnormal spoilage is often controllable by first-line supervision, whereas normal spoilage is controllable only by those managers who determine the nature of products and processes. Accounting for spoilage, defective units, and the like varies considerably in practice.

This chapter will consider these matters from both product-costing and control viewpoints. Managerial cost accounting must distinguish between normal and abnormal spoilage, primarily for keeping management informed, but also for proper product costing.

Terminology

Terminology and accounting in this area are not at all precise or uniform. This chapter distinguishes between the various terms as follows:

SPOILAGE Production that does not meet dimensional or quality standards and that is junked and sold for disposal value. Net spoilage cost is the total of the costs accumulated to point of rejection less disposal value (sometimes called *salvage value*).

DEFECTIVE UNITS Production that does not meet dimensional or quality standards and that is subsequently reworked and sold through regular channels as firsts or seconds, depending on the characteristics of the product and on available alternatives.

WASTE Material that is lost or evaporates or shrinks in a manufacturing process, or is a residue that has no measurable recovery value; for example, gases, dust, smoke, and unsalable residues. Sometimes waste disposal entails additional costs; for example, atomic waste.

SCRAP Material residue from certain manufacturing operations that has measurable but relatively minor recovery value. For example, outlined metal from a stamping operation, shavings, filings, turnings, borings, and short lengths from woodworking operations, and sprues, ingates, and flash from the casting operation in a foundry. Scrap may be either sold or reused.

Spoilage in general[1]

management implications and factor combination

Most production processes generate some bad units, along with the good ones, as an unavoidable result of the most economical combination of the factors of production. **Although it may be technically possible to eliminate spoilage altogether in many instances, it may be uneconomical to do so because the costs of lowering spoilage rates are greater than the costs of the present spoilage.** Thus, beer bottles sometimes explode, defective castings inevitably appear, and impure as well as pure chemicals and food arise. The problem of spoilage is important from many aspects, the most important being that of managerial planning and control. Managers must first select the most economical production method or process. Then they must see that spoilage is controlled within chosen predetermined limits, so that excessive spoilage does not occur.

normal spoilage

Working within the selected set of production conditions, management must establish the rate of spoilage that is to be regarded as *normal*. **Normal spoilage is what arises under efficient operating conditions; it is an inherent result of the particular process and is thus uncontrollable in the short run.** Costs of normal spoilage are typically viewed as a part of the costs of *good* production, because the attaining of good units necessitates the simultaneous appearance of spoiled units. In other words, normal spoilage is planned spoilage, in the sense that the choice of a given combination of factors of production entails a spoilage rate that management is willing to accept.

[1]The writer acknowledges the helpful suggestions of Samuel Laimon, University of Saskatchewan.

abnormal spoilage **Abnormal spoilage is spoilage that is not expected to arise under efficient operating conditions; it is not an inherent part of the selected production process.** Most of this spoilage is usually regarded as controllable, in the sense that the first-line supervisor can exert influence over inefficiency. Such causes as machinery breakdowns, accidents, and inferior materials are typically regarded as being subject to some manager's influence. Costs of abnormal spoilage are the costs of inferior products that should be written off directly as losses for the period in which it is detected. For the most informative feedback, the Loss from Abnormal Spoilage account should appear on a detailed income statement as a separate line item and not be buried as an indistinguishable part of the cost of goods manufactured.

general accounting procedures for spoilage Before discussing debits and credits for spoiled goods, let us try to relate spoiled goods to two major purposes of cost accounting: control and product costing. Accounting for control is primarily concerned with charging responsibility centers for costs *as incurred.* Product costing is concerned with *applying* to inventory or other appropriate accounts the costs *already incurred.* Where does costing for spoiled goods fit into this framework? First, it must be made clear that the costs of both normal and abnormal spoiled goods are, at least in concept, *product costs.* But abnormal spoilage is a cost of bad product. So it really is not regarded as an inventoriable cost. Instead, abnormal spoilage is written off as a loss immediately when it is detected:

	GOOD-PRODUCT COSTS—INVENTORIABLE	BAD-PRODUCT COSTS—CHARGED OFF AS A LOSS IMMEDIATELY
Cost of spoiled goods—normal	Yes	No
Cost of spoiled goods—abnormal	No	Yes

The existence of spoiled goods does not involve any additional cost beyond the amount already incurred.[2] Therefore, in accounting for spoiled goods, we are dealing with cost application and reallocation rather than new cost incurrence. Our objectives are

1. To accumulate data to spotlight the cost of spoilage so that management is made aware of its magnitude.
2. To identify the *nature* of the spoilage and distinguish between costs of normal spoilage (which should be added to the cost of good units) and of abnormal spoilage (which should be written off as a loss).

Depending on the product(s) or departments involved, there is a bewildering mass of treatments in practice, which vary from the inexcusable to the highly informative. This chapter cannot possibly cover all the theoretical and practical ramifications. It will try to contrast conceptual treatments with some methods used in practice.

A study of the entries in the conceptual treatment in Exhibit 18-1 will show that when a product is spoiled, some debit must be made to balance the necessary credit to

[2]Where spoilage is not detected until completion of goods, spoiled units require the same effort as good units. In other words, a laborer can be performing with equal efficiency on all goods and yet turn out some spoiled units because of inferior materials, worn cutting tools, and the like. So labor efficiency may be very satisfactory, but spoilage may nevertheless be a major problem. Thus, a worker can efficiently turn out spoiled goods.

EXHIBIT 18-1

General Accounting for Spoilage

Assume: Units worked on		1,100
Good units completed	1,000	
Normal spoilage	30	
Abnormal spoilage	70	1,100

Assume a unit cost $10, not including any spoilage allowance. Total costs to account for are 1,100 × $10, or $11,000.

CONCEPTUAL TREATMENT

	debit	credit
1. Work in process	**11,000**	
Stores, accrued payroll, applied overhead		**11,000**
1,100 units worked on.		
2. Cost of spoiled goods	**1,000**	
Work in process		**1,000**
100 units spoiled.		
3. Finished goods	**10,000**	
Work in process		**10,000**
1,000 good units completed.		
4. Finished goods	**300**	
Cost of spoiled goods		**300**
Normal-spoilage allowance, 30 units.		
5. Loss from abnormal spoilage	**700**	
Cost of spoiled goods		**700**
Abnormal spoilage, 70 units.		

PRACTICAL TREATMENT

	debit	credit
1. (Same.)		
2,3,4. Finished goods	**10,300**	
Work in process		**10,300**
1,000 good units completed @ $10 plus normal spoilage of 30 units @ $10. Total costs of 1,000 good units is thus $10,300.		
5. Loss from abnormal spoilage*	**700**	
Work in process		**700**
Abnormal spoilage, 70 units.		

**In practice, abnormal spoilage is often not isolated at all. Instead, the $700 cost is erroneously lumped with the other costs to show a total cost of $11,000 and a unit cost of $11 for the 1,000 good units produced. The $700 abnormal spoilage should not be concealed as a part of the cost of the good product.*

Work in Process. Further, some means must be found to charge normal spoilage to good inventory and abnormal spoilage to a loss account. The entries in the conceptual treatment use a Cost of Spoiled Goods account to highlight the nature of the problem and to stress the notion that the costs applied to Work in Process are initially product costs that are then transferred either to Finished Goods or to a loss account. In practice, Cost of Spoiled Goods is not used, and the second set of entries in Exhibit 18-1 is more likely to be found.

Process-cost accounting procedures and spoilage[3]

Although this discussion of process costing will emphasize accounting for spoilage, the ideas here are equally applicable to waste (shrinkage, evaporation, or lost units). Again we must distinguish between control and product costing. For control, most companies use some version of estimated or standard costs that incorporates an allowance for normal spoilage, shrinkage, or waste in the estimate or standard. This section emphasizes product costing in so-called actual or normal process-costing systems.

[3]This section assumes that you have studied Chapter 17.

distinguish between normal and abnormal spoilage

As a general rule, accumulate the costs of spoilage separately. Then allocate normal spoilage costs to Finished Goods or Work in Process, depending on where in the production cycle the spoilage is assumed to take place. Spoilage is typically assumed to occur at the stage of completion where inspection takes place, because spoilage is not detected until this point. **Normal spoilage need not be allocated to units that have failed to reach this point in the production process, because the spoiled units are related solely to the units that have passed the inspection point.**

Many writers on process costing advocate ignoring the computation of equivalent units for spoilage, shrinkage, or waste. The reason cited in favor of this short-cut technique is that it automatically spreads normal-spoilage costs over good units

EXHIBIT 18-2

Comparison of Accounting for Spoilage

	ACCURATE METHOD: COUNT SPOILAGE			LESS ACCURATE METHOD: IGNORE SPOILAGE		
		EQUIVALENT UNITS			EQUIVALENT UNITS	
FLOW OF PRODUCTION	**physical units**	**materials**	**conversion costs**	**physical units**	**materials**	**conversion costs**
Completed	500	500	500	500	500	500
Normal spoilage	100	100	100	100	—	—
In process, ending inventory	400(50%)*	400	200	400	400	200
Accounted for	1,000	1,000	800	1,000	900	700

		DETAILS			DETAILS	
COSTS	TOTALS	**materials**	**conversion costs**	TOTALS	**materials**	**conversion costs**
Current costs	$3,200	$1,800	$1,400	$3,200	$1,800	$1,400
Divide by equivalent units		1,000	800		900	700
Cost per equivalent unit		$1.80	$1.75		$2.00	$2.00
TOTAL COSTS OF WORK COMPLETED AND IN PROCESS						
Units completed (500):						
Costs before spoilage	$1,775	500($1.80)	500($1.75)			
Add normal spoilage	355	100($1.80)	100($1.75)			
Total costs transferred out	$2,130			$2,000	500($2.00)	500($2.00)
Work in process, ending inventory (400):						
Materials	$ 720	400($1.80)		$ 800	400($2.00)	
Conversion costs	350		200($1.75)	400		200($2.00)
Total work in process	$1,070			$1,200		
Total costs accounted for	$3,200			$3,200		

**Degree of completion on conversion costs of this department.*

through the use of higher equivalent unit costs. However, the results of this shortcut are inaccurate unless (a) no work-in-process inventories exist, or (b) material, conversion, *and* spoilage costs are all incurred *uniformly* throughout the production cycle. To illustrate, assume that a department has no beginning inventory. It starts 1,000 units; 500 are completed, 400 are in process, half-completed, and 100 are spoiled. The 100 units represent normal spoilage. Spoilage is detected upon completion. Material costs are $1,800 and conversion costs are $1,400. All material is introduced at the start of the process.

The solution in Exhibit 18-2 shows that ignoring spoilage lowers total equivalent units; when the latter is divided into the production costs, a higher *unit cost* results. The effective result is to load higher unit costs on work in process that has not reached the inspection point. At the same time, total charges to completed units are too low. Therefore, ending work in process contains costs of spoilage ($130 in this example) that do not pertain to such units and that should properly be charged to completed goods. Further, ending work in process that has not reached inspection undoubtedly contains some units that will not properly be recognized as spoiled until a subsequent period. Thus, work in process is being loaded now with spoilage ($130) that should instead be charged to goods later as they are completed. In effect, work in process is being doubly charged, because it is being charged with spoilage both now and also later when inspection occurs.

base for computing normal spoilage

Normal spoilage should be computed from the good output, or from the *normal* input—not from the total input. Total input includes the abnormal as well as the normal spoilage and is therefore inferior as a basis for computing normal spoilage. For example, if the normal rate of spoilage of polio vaccine is sloppily stated as 5 percent, an input of 100,000 cubic centimeters would be expected to produce 5,000 cubic centimeters of spoilage. Now, if 85,500 cubic centimeters of good units are produced, normal spoilage is not 5,000 centimeters (5 percent of 100,000), because it should have taken only 90,000 cubic centimeters of input to get 85,500 cubic centimeters of good vaccine. If normal spoilage is expressed as 5 percent of input, the good output should be 95 percent of normal input. In this case, abnormal spoilage would be 10,000 cubic centimeters and normal spoilage would be 4,500 cubic centimeters. These relationships may be clarified by the following:

			RELATIONSHIPS	
Input	100,000 c.c.			
Output:				
Good units	85,500 c.c.		95%	
Normal spoilage	4,500 c.c.	90,000 c.c.*	5%	100%
Abnormal spoilage		10,000 c.c.		
		100,000 c.c.		

*Normal input.

Thus, in this case we could express the normal-spoilage rate more accurately either as 5 percent of *normal input* or as 5/95 of good output.

weighted-average and FIFO

» *EXAMPLE 1*

The costs of producing one of the B Company's products are accumulated on a process-cost basis. Materials for this product are put in at the beginning of the production cycle; conversion costs are assumed to be incurred evenly over the cycle. Some units of this product are spoiled as a result of defects not ascertainable before inspection of finished units.[4] Normally the spoiled units are one-tenth of the good output.

At January 1, the inventory of work in process on this product was $29,600, representing 2,000 pounds of material ($15,000) and conversion cost of $14,600 representing four-fifths completion. During January, 8,000 pounds of material ($61,000) were put into production. Direct labor of $40,200 was charged to the process. Factory overhead is assigned at the rate of 100 percent of direct-labor cost. Therefore, the total conversion costs for January were $40,200 + $40,200 = $80,400. The inventory at January 31 consisted of 1,500 pounds, two-thirds finished. Seventy-two hundred pounds of good product were transferred to finished-goods after inspection.

Spoiled units were 2,000 + 8,000 − 1,500 − 7,200 = 1,300. Normal spoilage was 10 percent of the 7,200 completed units, or 720. Thus, abnormal spoilage was 1,300 − 720 = 580 units.

REQUIRED

Using FIFO and then weighted-average, show calculations of

1. Equivalent units of production for January
2. The dollar and unit amount of the abnormal spoilage during January
3. Total product costs transferred to finished goods inventory
4. The cost of work-in-process inventory at January 31
5. Journal entries for transfers out of work-in-process inventory

spoilage and the five basic steps

The answers to requirements 1 through 4 under the FIFO and weighted-average methods are shown in Exhibits 18-3 and 18-4, respectively. Careful study of these exhibits will reveal that the basic five-step procedure introduced in the preceding chapter needs only slight modification to handle spoilage:

Step 1: Summarize physical units. Identify both normal and abnormal spoilage. In both exhibits, there are 580 units of abnormal spoilage and 720 units of normal spoilage.

Step 2: Compute output in equivalent units. Compute equivalent units for spoilage in the same way as for good units. Because inspection occurs upon completion, both exhibits show that the same amount of work was done on each spoiled unit and each completed good unit.

Step 3: Summarize total costs to account for. The details of this step do not differ from those in the preceding chapter.

Step 4: Compute unit costs. The details of this step do not differ from those in the preceding chapter. However, the divisor includes the work applicable to the spoiled units. That is, as shown in step 2, equivalent units do not ignore spoilage.

Step 5: Compute total costs of work completed and in process. This step now includes computation of the cost of spoiled goods in the same manner as the cost of good units and work in process. As shown in Exhibit 18-4, the costs of abnormal spoilage are allocated to a loss account, 580 units × $17.60 = $10,208. The costs of normal spoilage, $12,672, are added to the costs of their related good units.

[4]This illustration assumes inspection upon completion. In contrast, inspection may take place at some other stage—say, at the halfway point in the production cycle. In such a case, normal-spoilage costs would be reallocated to completed goods and to the units in process that are more than half completed. For a computer application to solving this process-cost problem, see Werner Frank, "A Computer Application to Process Cost Accounting," *Accounting Review,* XL, No. 4, pp. 854–62.

Using the information from the final sections of the exhibits, the journal entries (the answers to requirement 5) follow:

	FIFO		WEIGHTED-AVERAGE	
	debit	credit	debit	credit
Finished goods	139,060		139,392	
Processing department—work in process		139,060		139,392
To transfer good units completed in January.				
Loss from abnormal spoilage	10,325		10,208	
Processing department—work in process		10,325		10,208
To recognize abnormal spoilage in January.				

assumptions for allocating normal spoilage

Physical spoilage might actually *occur* at various points or stages of the production process, but spoilage is typically not *detected* until one or more specific points of inspection. The cost of spoiled units is assumed to be all cost incurred prior to inspection. The unit costs of abnormal and normal spoilage are usually the same because both are detected simultaneously. However, situations might arise where abnormal spoilage is detected at a different point than normal spoilage. In such cases, the unit cost of abnormal spoilage would differ from the unit cost of normal spoilage.

Various assumptions prevail regarding how to allocate the cost of normal spoilage between completed units and the ending inventory of work in process. A popular approach follows.

When normal spoilage is presumed to occur at a specific point in the production process, allocate its cost (e.g., a unit cost of $17.60 in Exhibit 18-4) over all units that have passed this point. In our example, spoilage is presumed to occur upon completion, so no cost of normal spoilage is allocated to the ending work in process.

Whether the cost of normal spoilage is allocated to the units in ending work in process strictly depends on whether they have passed the point of inspection. For example, if the inspection point is presumed to be the halfway stage of conversion, work in process that is 70 percent converted would be allocated a full measure of normal-spoilage cost. But work in process that is 40 percent converted would not be allocated any normal-spoilage cost.

Appendix 18A contains additional discussion concerning various assumptions about spoilage.

FIFO process costing and spoilage

A comparison of the methods used in Exhibits 18-3 and 18-4 will show that the FIFO method necessitates an arbitrary assumption in order to split normal-spoilage costs between those goods completed from current production during a given period and those completed from beginning work in process. The most widely used assumption is to load spoilage on all good units at current unit costs. But to do this is inconsistent with the FIFO assumption; examine the last footnote to Exhibit 18-3 for an illustration of the inconsistencies that arise.

In contrast, the weighted-average method does not necessitate splitting normal-spoilage costs between two batches of good units completed, because the initial inventory is merged with the current costs to determine unit costs. The more one examines process costing, the more one becomes convinced that weighted-average costing is

EXHIBIT 18-3 *(Place a clip on this page for easy reference.)*

B Company
Production-Cost Report
FIFO Method
For the Month Ended January 31, 19_1

FLOW OF PRODUCTION	(STEP 1) PHYSICAL UNITS	(STEP 2) EQUIVALENT UNITS	
		materials	conversion costs
Work in process, beginning inventory	2,000(80%)*		
Started	8,000		
To account for	10,000		
Abnormal spoilage	580	580	580
Normal spoilage	720	720	720
Good units completed:			
From beginning inventory	2,000	—	400†
Started and completed	5,200	5,200	5,200
Work in process, ending inventory	1,500($66\frac{2}{3}$%)*	1,500	1,000
Accounted for	10,000	8,000	7,900

	COSTS	TOTALS	DETAILS		
			materials	conversion costs	equivalent whole unit
	Work in process, beginning inventory	$ 29,600			
	Current costs	141,400	$61,000	$ 80,400	
(Step 3)	Total costs to account for	$171,000			
	Divide by equivalent units		÷8,000	÷7,900	
(Step 4)	Cost per equivalent unit		$ 7.625	$10.1772	$17.8022

(Step 5) TOTAL COSTS OF WORK COMPLETED AND IN PROCESS				
(A) Abnormal spoilage (580)	$ 10,325.28			580($17.8022)
Units completed and transferred out (7,200):				
From beginning inventory (2,000)	$ 29,600.00			
Current costs added	4,070.88		400($10.1772)	
Total cost from beginning inventory before spoilage	$ 33,670.88			
Started and completed before spoilage (5,200)	92,571.56			5,200($17.8022)
Normal spoilage‡	12,817.58			720($17.8022)
(B) Total costs transferred out	$139,060.02			
Work in process, ending inventory (1,500):				
Materials	$ 11,437.50	1,500($7.625)		
Conversion costs	10,177.20		1,000($10.1772)	
(C) Total cost of work in process	$ 21,614.70			
(A) + (B) + (C) Total costs accounted for	$171,000.00			

**Degree of completion for conversion costs of this department at the dates of the work-in-process inventories. Note that material costs are fully completed at each of these dates, because in this department materials are introduced at the beginning of the process.*

†Based on work done during the current period only. Note that 2,000 equivalent units of materials and 1,600 equivalent units of conversion costs had been performed on the beginning work in process during a preceding period. Hence, 2,000 − 1,600 = 400 equivalent units of conversion cost were added to the beginning inventory during January.

‡Note that normal spoilage should really be split between the two batches of good units completed if FIFO is to be followed thoroughly. But to split spoilage costs on a pro rata basis implies that all spoilage traceable to beginning inventory is costed on the basis of full current costs, not past costs. This is inconsistent with the FIFO assumption, which states that past costs should be kept separate from current costs. In effect, using current costs for attaching normal-spoilage costs to beginning inventory assumes that all spoilage traceable thereto was begun and completed during the current period—an obvious contradiction of the FIFO concept.

EXHIBIT 18-4

B Company
Production-Cost Report
Weighted-Average Method
For the Month Ended January 31, 19_1

FLOW OF PRODUCTION	(STEP 1) PHYSICAL UNITS	(STEP 2) EQUIVALENT UNITS materials	conversion costs
Work in process, beginning inventory	2,000(80%)*		
Started	8,000		
To account for	10,000		
Abnormal spoilage	580	580	580
Normal spoilage	720	720	720
Good units completed and transferred out	7,200	7,200	7,200
Work in process, ending inventory	1,500(66⅔%)*	1,500	1,000
Accounted for	10,000	10,000	9,500

	COSTS	TOTALS	DETAILS materials	conversion costs	equivalent whole unit
	Work in process, beginning inventory	$ 29,600	$15,000	$14,600	
	Current costs	141,400	61,000	80,400	
(Step 3)	Total costs to account for	$171,000	$76,000	$95,000	
	Divide by equivalent units		÷10,000	÷9,500	
(Step 4)	Cost per equivalent unit		$ 7.60	$ 10.00	$17.60
(Step 5)	TOTAL COSTS OF WORK COMPLETED AND IN PROCESS				
	Abnormal spoilage (580)	$ 10,208			580($17.60)
	Units completed and transferred out (7,200):				
	Costs before adding spoilage	$126,720			7,200($17.60)
	Normal spoilage	12,672			720($17.60)
	Total cost transferred out	$139,392			
	Work in process, ending inventory (1,500):				
	Materials	$ 11,400	1,500($7.60)		
	Conversion costs	10,000		1,000($10.00)	
	Total work in process	$ 21,400			
	Total costs accounted for	$171,000			

**Degree of completion for conversion costs of this department at the dates of the work-in-process inventories. Note that material costs are fully completed at each of these dates, because in this department materials are introduced at the beginning of the process.*

generally superior to first-in, first-out costing for *product-costing* purposes. Moreover, standard costing is superior to either weighted-average costing or first-in, first-out, costing for both *product-costing* and *control* purposes.

Job costing and spoilage

Job-cost accounting for spoilage in practice varies considerably. Where spoiled goods have a disposal value,[5] the net cost of spoilage is computed by deducting disposal value from the costs of the spoiled goods accumulated to the point of rejection.

Where spoilage is considered to be a normal characteristic of a given production cycle, and where causes of spoilage are attributable to work done on all jobs, net spoilage cost is budgeted in practice as a part of factory overhead, so that the predetermined overhead rate includes a provision for normal-spoilage cost. Therefore, spoilage cost is spread, through overhead application, over all jobs rather than being loaded on particular jobs only. The rationale is thus provided for the debit, to the overhead-control account, of the net spoilage cost in the following journal entry made when spoilage is considered to be normal in character:[6]

Stores control (spoiled goods at disposal value)	**150**	
Department factory overhead control (normal spoilage)	**350**	
Work in process		**500**

Assume that 5 pieces out of a lot of 50 were spoiled. Costs accumulated to point where spoilage was detected were $100 per unit. Salvage value is estimated at $30 per unit. Items in parentheses indicate subsidiary postings.

Another method used, where management finds it helpful for control or for pricing, is to credit specific jobs with only the resale value of spoiled units, thus forcing the

[5]In practice, the words *scrap* and *spoilage* are sometimes used indiscriminately. Thus, *spoilage cost* may be thought of as total accumulated cost of spoiled work. Yet the spoiled goods may be "scrapped" (that is, sold for whatever can be recovered—"scrap" value). Thus, *net spoilage cost* is total spoilage cost less scrap recovery.

[6]Conceptually, the prevailing treatments just described can be criticized primarily because *product costs* are being charged back to Department Factory Overhead Control, which logically should accumulate only *costs incurred,* rather than both cost incurrence and product costs. If this distinction is not maintained, Department Factory Overhead Control will include duplicate charges for overhead. For example, as both good units and those units that will eventually be spoiled are worked on, the various production costs (including applied overhead) are charged to the departmental work-in-process account. Then, when the normal spoilage is detected, the conventional treatment results in charging back these same product costs (including applied overhead), in an amount equal to the actual net spoilage cost, to the departmental overhead-control account. For an extended criticism of the duplication of charges to Department Factory Overhead Control, see Alfred P. Koch, "A Fallacy in Accounting for Spoiled Goods," *Accounting Review,* XXXV, No. 3, pp. 501–2.

A student, M. Schley, has suggested using a separate account, Cost of Spoiled Goods—Normal. All debits to it would be allocations of costs already applied to Work in Process; all credits to it would reapply the costs to good units produced by using a predetermined application rate similar to the factory overhead application rate. (This application rate would be exactly the difference between the overhead rate used that incorporates normal spoilage and the rate that excludes normal spoilage rate.) For product-costing purposes, no difference would result. But for control purposes, Department Factory Overhead would consist only of historical costs with no duplicated charges; management would have a separate record of normal spoilage and would be reminded of the burden of normal spoilage borne by good production. (A similar line of reasoning applies to the defective units discussed in the next section.)

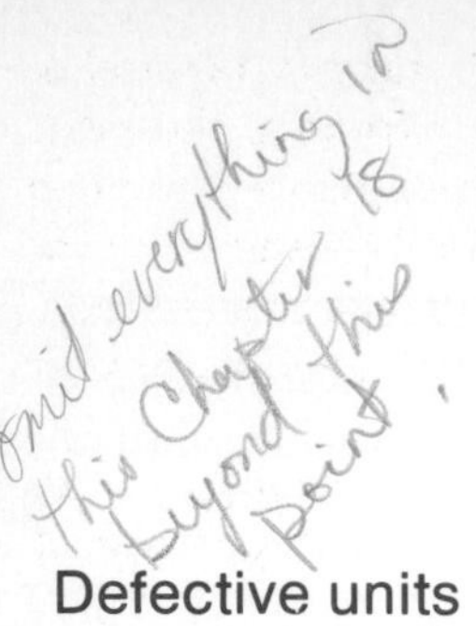

remaining good units in the job to bear net normal-spoilage costs. Under this method, the predetermined overhead rate would not include a provision for normal-spoilage cost because the spoilage would be viewed as being directly attributable to the nature of particular jobs instead of being attributable to general factory conditions or processes. The journal entry, with the same data as were just used, follows:

Stores control (spoiled goods at disposal value)	**150**	
Work in process		**150**

Defective units

Defective units are subsequently reworked and transformed into units to be sold as "firsts" or "seconds." Management needs effective control over such actions, because supervisors are tempted to rework rather than to junk spoiled units. If control is not exercised, supervisors may rework many bad units instead of having them sold for salvage at a greater economic advantage. Rework should be undertaken only if incremental revenue is expected to exceed incremental costs.

Unless there are special reasons for charging rework to the jobs or batches that contained the bad units, the cost of the extra materials, labor, and so on, are in practice usually charged to factory overhead.[7] Thus, once again we see that rework is usually spread over all jobs or batches as a part of a predetermined overhead rate. Assume that the five spoiled pieces used in our prior illustration are reworked and sold as firsts through regular channels. Entries follow:

Original cost accumulations:	**Work-in-process control**	**500**	
	Stores control		**200**
	Accrued payroll		**200**
	Factory overhead applied		**100**
Rework (figures assumed):	**Departmental factory-overhead control (rework)**	**190**	
	Stores control		**40**
	Accrued payroll		**100**
	Factory overhead applied		**50**
Transfer to finished stock:	**Finished-goods control**	**500**	
	Work-in-process control		**500**

Accounting for scrap

Scrap is residue from manufacturing operations that has measurable but relatively minor recovery value. There are two major aspects of accounting for scrap: control and costing. Items like metal chips, turnings, filings, and borings should be quantified

[7]The criticisms of the practical treatment for spoiled goods are also applicable to the treatment described here. The overhead-incurred and applied accounts may be padded for amounts that in themselves did not necessitate overhead incurrence. In other words, the extra materials, labor, and variable overhead may represent extra cost incurrence, but fixed overhead will not be affected. Also, any accounting entry that simultaneously involves a debit to department overhead and a credit to overhead applied tends to blur the primary purpose of the overhead-control account—that of only accumulating overhead costs *as incurred.*

Like spoiled units, defective units can be abnormal as well as normal. Applying the reasoning of the preceding footnote, rework on normally defective units should be charged to a special allocation account and rework on abnormally defective units should be charged off as a special loss. The special allocation account would also have its own application rate.

by weighing, counting, or some other expedient means. Norms or standards should be determined because excessive scrap indicates inefficiency. *Scrap tickets* are prepared as source documents for periodic scrap reports that summarize the amount of scrap and compare it with predetermined norms or standards. Scrap should be returned to the storeroom to be held for sale or for reuse. Scrap should be accounted for in some manner, not only from the point of view of efficiency but because scrap is often a tempting source for theft or manipulation.

There are many methods of accounting for scrap. Typically, scrap is not assigned any cost; instead, its sales value is regarded as an offset to factory overhead, as follows:

Scrap returned to storeroom:	**No journal entry.**		
	(Memo of quantity received is entered on the perpetual record.)		
Sale of scrap:	**Cash or Accounts receivable**	**xx**	
	Department factory overhead control		**xx**
	Posting made to subsidiary record—"Sale of Scrap" column on departmental cost sheet.		

This method is both simple and accurate enough in theory to justify its wide use. A normal amount of scrap is an inevitable result of production operations. Basically, this method does not link scrap with any particular physical product; instead, because of practical difficulties, all products bear regular production costs without any particular credit for scrap sales except in an indirect manner. What really happens in such situations is that sales of scrap are considered when predetermined overhead rates are being set. Thus, the predetermined overhead rate is lower than it would be if no credit for scrap sales were allowed in the overhead budget.

An alternative method in a job-cost situation would be to trace sales of scrap to the jobs that yielded the scrap. This method is used only when it is feasible and economically desirable. For example, there may be agreements between the company and particular customers that provide for charging specific, difficult jobs with all scrap or spoilage costs and crediting such jobs with all scrap sales arising therefrom. Entries follow:

Scrap returned to storeroom:	**No journal entry.**		
	(Memo of quantity received and related job is entered on the perpetual record.)		
Sale of scrap:	**Cash or Accounts receivable**	**xx**	
	Work in process		**xx**
	Posting made to specific job order.		

The illustrations above assume that no inventory value is assigned to scrap as it is returned to the storeroom. However, when the dollar value is material and there is a significant time lag between storing scrap and selling it, there is justification for inventorying scrap at some conservative estimate of net realizable value so that production costs and related scrap recovery may be recognized in the same period.

Some companies tend to delay sales of scrap until the price is most attractive. Volatile price fluctuations are typical for scrap metal. In these cases, if scrap inventory becomes significant, it should be inventoried at some "reasonable" value—a difficult task in the face of volatile market prices.

Comparison of accounting for spoilage, defective work, and scrap

The basic approach to the accounting for spoilage, defective work, and scrap should distinguish among the normal amount that is common to all jobs, the normal amount that is attributable to specific jobs, and abnormal amounts. The following entries recapitulate the preceding examples. Note the parallel approach to the three categories:

spoilage cost (net $350)

Normal (common to all jobs)	Stores	150	
	Departmental factory overhead control	350	
	Work in process		500
Normal (peculiar to specific jobs)	Stores	150	
	Work in process		150
Abnormal	Stores	150	
	Special loss account	350	
	Work in process		500

defective work cost (rework costs of $190)

Normal (common to all jobs)	Department factory overhead control	190	
	Stores		40
	Accrued payroll		100
	Factory overhead applied		50
Normal (peculiar to specific jobs)	Same as preceding entry except that the debit of $190 would be to Work in Process		
Abnormal	Same as preceding entry except that the debit of $190 would be to Special Loss account		

scrap value recovered ($100)

Normal (common to all jobs)	Stores or Cash or Accounts receivable	100	
	Department factory overhead control		100
Abnormal (peculiar to specific jobs)	Same as preceding entry, except that the credit would be to Work in Process		

Some applications to standard costs

shrinkage and waste

When standard-cost systems are used, allowance is made in the standard product costs for a standard shrinkage. Actual shrinkage is usually computed by working back from product output. Shrinkage in excess of standard is a material-efficiency (usage) variance. Unlike spoilage and scrap, shrinkage cannot be tagged and traced by physical identification.

Examples of waste that are not traced and specifically costed include paint or varnish adhering to the sides of its container, mill ends, shavings, evaporation, and so forth. Excess-material consumption is usually revealed through excess-material requisitions or through standard-yield percentages for such materials as lumber, chemicals, and ores. Thus, where 15,000 gallons of raw chemicals ordinarily produce 12,000 gallons of good finished product, the standard-yield percentage could be expressed as 80 percent of normal input. On the other hand, the waste percentage could be expressed as 20 percent of normal input or as 25 percent of good output.

Note that these percentages provide a physical standard that may be used without worrying about price changes. Further, such a standard is easily understood and can readily be used as a timely index of efficiency—on an hourly or batch basis if desired.

scrap Material-efficiency standards usually include allowances for scrap. Although the allowance may be computed in various ways, standards are based on a careful study of the operation(s), not on historical data alone or on wild guesses. The standard cost of direct materials thus becomes (a) standard unit price times the standard input per finished unit, less (b) standard scrap price per unit times standard scrap weight loss per finished unit.

To illustrate, assume that a metal rod is fed into an automatic screw machine. About five inches (ten ounces) at one end of each 105-inch rod (210 ounces) are clutched by the chuck and cannot be used. This results in a "crop loss." It takes five ounces of metal to produce a finished unit that weighs four ounces. Thus, each rod, after the crop loss of ten ounces, weighs 200 ounces and can produce 200 ÷ 5 = 40 units. The standard starting lot size is 4,040 units, but the first 40 units are scrapped in setting up the run. Therefore, the standard *finished* lot size is only 4,000 units, and the scrap piece loss is 40 ÷ 4,000 = 1 percent of good output. Standard-cost computations follow:

	OUNCES	ASSUMED PRICE PER OUNCE	UNIT COST
Standard cost per unit:			
Finished piece	4.00		
Turnings	1.00		
Crop loss (10 oz. ÷ 40 units per rod)	0.25		
Subtotal, before scrap piece loss	5.25*		
Add 1% scrap piece loss	0.0525		
Total	5.3025	$.12	$.6363
Less credit for scrap (1.00 + 0.25 + 0.0525)	1.3025	.04	.0521
Standard cost per finished unit	4.00		$.5842

**Or 210 ÷ 40 = 5.25 ounces, including turnings and crop loss.*

Although standards for direct materials are built in this way for each operation, it is usually inexpedient to trace scrap to specific lots or operations. Comparisons are usually limited to monthly, or sometimes weekly, comparisons of standard costs of good units produced with the total "actual" charges to the department.

spoilage In practice, allowances for net spoilage cost and for rework are often incorporated into the flexible budget for overhead. Spoiled units are removed from Work in Process at standard costs and charged to Factory Overhead. Periodic comparisons of budget allowances with actual spoilage provide summary information for managerial control. If no spoilage is allowed, the budget provided may be zero. Rework is controlled in a similar manner. Day-to-day control is aided by spoilage tags prepared at the point of inspection. These tags, or a summary thereof, are promptly shown to the supervisor and other interested parties.

This procedure really spotlights spoilage and rework as special managerial problems, as opposed to, say, material-efficiency variances that are related to good units. For example, assume that the standard cost for a particular product is as follows:

Direct materials, 1 pound	$ 5.00
Direct labor, .1 hour	3.00
Factory overhead—variable	1.50
Factory overhead—fixed	1.50
Standard cost per unit	$11.00

Assume that no spoilage occurs, but that it takes 1,150 pounds of material to produce 1,000 good units:

Direct materials:	
Actual, 1,150 pounds @ $5.00	$5,750
Standard, 1,000 pounds @ $5.00	5,000
Efficiency variance	$ 750

Assume, instead, that 1,100 units were produced, but that 100 were spoiled because of careless machine operation. There would be two alternatives for analyzing such a variance. First consider the figures presented in the following table:

	COSTS INCURRED	STANDARD COSTS—GOOD OUTPUT	TOTAL VARIANCE
*Direct materials, 1,150 lbs.	$ 5,750	$ 5,000	$ 750 U
Direct labor, 110 hours	3,300	3,000	300 U
Factory overhead—variable	1,650	1,500	150 U
Factory overhead—fixed	1,650	1,500	150 U
	$12,350	$11,000	$1,350 U

**Standard materials allowed for good units*	*1,000 lbs.*
Standard materials allowed for spoiled units, which were spoiled by careless labor	*100 lbs.*
Excess materials used in producing 1,100 units	*50 lbs.*
Total	*1,150 lbs.*

ANALYSIS ONE □ Analyze variances on the basis of good output only. This is the familiar way:

Direct-material efficiency variance	$5,750 – $5,000	$ 750
Direct-labor efficiency variance	$3,300 – $3,000	300
Variable-overhead total variance	$1,650 – $1,500	150
Fixed-overhead total variance	$1,650 – $1,500	150
Total variance explained		$1,350

ANALYSIS TWO □ Isolate a separate variance for spoilage, $1,100, consisting of the four elements shown above. This would entail setting up a special Spoilage Variance account in the ledger. This account would represent the standard cost of spoiled work. Thus, the other variance accounts would not reflect any spoilage effects:

	SPOILAGE VARIANCE	OTHER VARIANCES		TOTAL VARIANCE EXPLAINED
Direct materials	$ 500	Efficiency	$250 U	$ 750
Direct labor	300		—	300
Variable overhead	150		—	150
Fixed overhead	150		—	150
	$1,100		$250	$1,350

Recall that Chapter 6 provided an overview of variance analysis, pointing out that desired levels of detail may vary from organization to organization. Analysis One stops at one level, whereas Analysis Two pushes one step further. Consider the direct materials:

	ACTUAL COSTS INCURRED	ACTUAL INPUTS × STANDARD PRICES	STANDARD COSTS ALLOWED FOR GOOD AND SPOILED OUTPUT	STANDARD COSTS ALLOWED FOR GOOD OUTPUT
	1,150 lbs. × $5 $5,750	1,150 lbs. × $5 $5,750	1,100 lbs. × $5 $5,500	1,000 lbs. × $5 $5,000
ANALYSIS ONE	↑ Price variance, $0 ↑		Efficiency variance, $750 U ↑ (150 lbs. × $5)	
ANALYSIS TWO	↑ Price variance, $0 ↑	Nonspoilage-related efficiency variance $250 U ↑ (50 lbs. × $5)	Spoilage variance, $500 U ↑ (100 lbs. × $5)	

The key difference between the two analyses is centered on how output is measured. Analysis One measures output in terms of good units only. Analysis Two measures output in terms of good units and good units plus spoiled units. This permits the breakdown of the efficiency variance into a spoilage variance and another variance, here called a "nonspoilage-related efficiency" variance. The journal entry would be:

Work in process	**5,000**	
Material spoilage variance (or Cost of spoiled goods)	**500**	
Material nonspoilage-related efficiency variance	**250**	
Stores		**5,750**
To record material usage and isolate the cost of spoiled goods.		

SUMMARY

Nearly every manufacturing company has some problems of spoilage, waste, defective units, or scrap as a consequence of management's choice of those factors of production that will render the most economic benefit. Hence, some of these problems are a normal result of efficient production. Yet there is a

need to distinguish between, for example, normal and abnormal spoilage. Standards or norms must be computed so that performance may be judged and costs properly accounted for. Normal spoilage, then, is spoilage that is unavoidable under a given set of efficient production conditions; abnormal spoilage is spoilage that is not expected to arise under efficient conditions. Laxity in setting currently attainable standards often results in too liberal allowances for normal spoilage.

Accounting for spoilage, defective units, and the like varies considerably. Practically, most of these net costs are allowed for in predetermined overhead rates; or, where standard costs are employed, scrap and spoilage allowances are often incorporated in the standard costs for direct materials, direct labor, and overhead.

Conceptually, some practical treatments are faulty because they muddle the distinction between product costs and costs for control by charging product costs back to Department Factory Overhead Control.

problems for self-study

Review each example in this chapter and obtain the solutions on your own. Then check your work against the solutions, which appear in the text.

Terms to Learn

abnormal spoilage ***defective units*** ***normal spoilage*** ***scrap*** ***spoilage*** ***waste***

Special Points and Pitfalls

When spoilage occurs, trace the units spoiled as well as the units finished and in process. Compute both normal and abnormal spoiled units. Build separate costs of spoiled units. Then allocate normal-spoilage cost to good units produced; charge off abnormal-spoilage costs as a loss. Even if no abnormal spoilage exists, it is helpful to compute normal-spoilage costs separately before allocation. In this way, management will be constantly reminded of the normal-spoilage cost of a given process.

The allocation of the cost of normal spoilage usually depends on where spoilage is detected. If spoilage is detected at the final stage of completion, then no cost of normal spoilage is allocated to ending work in process. This was the assumption in Exhibits 18-3 and 18-4. In contrast, inspection may take place at some other stage—say, at the halfway point in the production cycle. In such a case, some normal-spoilage cost would also be allocated to the units in process that are more than half completed.

Appendix 18a: a closer look at spoilage under process costing[8]

This appendix extends the discussion in the body of the chapter regarding spoilage assumptions and computations. Consider the following illustrative data:

[8]This Appendix was suggested by Professor W. L. Stephens.

	PHYSICAL UNITS
Work in process, beginning inventory	10,000(25%)*
Started	74,000
To account for	84,000
Completed during current period:	
From beginning inventory	10,000
Started and completed	50,000
Good units completed	60,000
Spoiled units	7,000
Work in process, ending inventory	17,000(75%)*
Accounted for	84,000

**Degree of completion for conversion costs of this department at the dates of the work-in-process inventories. Materials are assumed to be introduced at the start of production.*

When distinctions are made between abnormal and normal spoilage, the calculation of the good units passing inspection during the current period is critical. The number of units inspected depends on the amount of conversion work done on them during the current period. Consider three different independent situations:

	POINT OF INSPECTION		
ANALYSIS OF PHYSICAL UNITS SPOILED	**at end**	**at 50% converted**	**at 10% converted**
Work in process, beginning inventory	10,000	10,000	—
Started and completed	50,000	50,000	50,000
Work in process, ending inventory	—	17,000	17,000
Goods units passing inspection during the current period	60,000	77,000	67,000
Spoiled units:			
Total	7,000	7,000	7,000
Normal, 10% of good units passing inspection	6,000	7,700	6,700
Difference, if positive, is abnormal spoilage	1,000	0	300

The calculation of equivalent units of work done on the spoiled units depends on how much material and conversion costs were incurred to get the units to the point of inspection. In the illustration, the 7,000 spoiled units would have 7,000 equivalent units of materials plus 7,000, 50 percent of 7,000, and 10 percent of 7,000 units of conversion costs, respectively. In particular, note that no information concerning the units in the ending work in process is needed for the computation of equivalent units of work done on the spoiled units.

Appendix 18b: interim fluctuations in spoilage rates

There is a tendency among accountants to seize a single figure or a single rate as the standard or index of normal efficiency when in reality the standard or norm is in the middle of a range. Thus, normal spoilage may average 10 percent of good output, but random influences may cause deviations from the 10 percent norm in a range of, say, 0 percent to 14 percent. Over an extended period—say, a year—the rate should center around 10 percent.

This situation, as shown in Example 2, calls for using a predetermined 10 percent normal-spoilage cost rate for charging spoilage costs to good units produced throughout the year, regardless of actual month-to-month fluctuations within the normal range. The differences between normal-spoilage costs charged to production and those actually incurred within the normal range would rest in a temporary general-ledger account called Spoilage Random Fluctuations. It should have a zero balance by the end of a year. If a balance tends to build up, it would indicate that an erroneous normal rate of spoilage was being used.

» *EXAMPLE 2*

Let us assume that a single department process produces 1,000 good units per month, but that spoilage fluctuates. Normal spoilage averages 10 percent of good output, with the normal range considered to be from 0 percent to 14 percent of good output. The company's cost behavior is such that all units are produced at an equivalent unit cost of $10. All spoilage is detected upon completion. The company uses a Spoilage Random Fluctuations account and costs completed units as if they were all accompanied by a 10 percent normal-spoilage factor. Possible situations and general-ledger entries are as follows:

	CASE			
	1	2	3	4
Total units completed	1,100	1,130	1,170	1,060
Goods units completed	1,000	1,000	1,000	1,000
Actual spoilage in units	100	130	170	60
Normal spoilage in units	100	100	100	100
General-ledger entries:				
Finished goods	$11,000 dr.	$11,000 dr.	$11,000 dr.	$11,000 dr.
Spoilage random fluctuations	—	300 dr.	400 dr.	400 cr.
Loss from abnormal spoilage	—	—	300 dr.	—
Department—work in process	11,000 cr.	11,300 cr.	11,700 cr.	10,600 cr.

dr. = debit; cr = credit.

The actual and normal spoilage were equal in Case 1; hence, the charge is to Finished Goods, and the corresponding credit is to Work in Process. Since Case 2 fluctuations did not exceed 14 percent of good units completed, the difference between normal and actual spoilage of 30 units, valued at $10 per unit, results in the $300 debit to Spoilage Random Fluctuations. In contrast, Case 3 shows 170 units, which exceeds 14 percent of 1,000 units, or 170 minus 140 equals 30 units of abnormal spoilage. Thus 30 × $10 equals the $300 debit Loss from Abnormal Spoilage. The latter account is written off as an immediate loss. Finally, Case 4 provides an instance where subnormal spoilage will result in a credit to Spoilage Random Fluctuations based on 100 − 60, or 40 units less than normal.

If a Spoilage Random Fluctuations account were used, abnormal spoilage would usually be recognized only when actual spoilage exceeded the top of the normal range (14 percent in this example; see Case 3 in Example 2).

The handling of subnormal spoilage is shown in Case 4 of Example 2.

SPOILAGE RANDOM FLUCTUATIONS

(2)	300	(4)	400
(3)	400		

This account should balance out to zero over a period of, say, twelve months. If it does not, the process may not be performing in accordance with expectations.

QUESTIONS, PROBLEMS, AND CASES

18-1 "Management has two major planning and control problems regarding spoilage." What are the two problems?

18-2 "Normal spoilage is planned spoilage." Discuss.

18-3 "Costs of abnormal spoilage are lost costs." Explain.

18-4 "In accounting for spoiled goods, we are dealing with cost application and allocation rather than cost incurrence." Explain.

18-5 "Total input includes the abnormal as well as the normal spoilage and is therefore irrational as a basis for computing normal spoilage." Do you agree? Why?

18-6 Explain the operation of a Spoilage Random Fluctuations account.

18-7 "The practical treatments of spoilage in job-order costing can be criticized on conceptual grounds." What is the major criticism?

18-8 Describe the general accounting for scrap where no inventory value is assigned to scrap.

18-9 How is scrap usually accounted for under standard costing?

18-10 ***Two ways of accounting for spoilage.*** (CPA) In manufacturing activities, a portion of the units placed in process is sometimes spoiled and becomes practically worthless. Discuss two ways in which the cost of such spoiled units could be treated in the accounts, and describe the circumstances under which each method might be used.

18-11 ***Different ways of accounting for spoilage.*** (CPA) The D. Hayes Cramer Company manufactures Product C, whose cost per unit is $1 of materials, $2 of labor, and $3 of overhead costs. During the month of May, 1,000 units of Product C were spoiled. These units could be sold for 60¢ each.

The accountant said that the entry to be made for these 1,000 lost or spoiled units could be one of the following four:

entry no. 1

Spoiled goods	600	
Work in process—materials		100
Work in process—labor		200
Work in process—overhead		300

entry no. 2

Spoiled goods	600	
Manufacturing expenses	5,400	
Work in process—materials		1,000
Work in process—labor		2,000
Work in process—overhead		3,000

entry no. 3		
Spoiled goods	600	
Loss on spoiled goods	5,400	
Work in process—materials		1,000
Work in process—labor		2,000
Work in process—overhead		3,000

entry no. 4		
Spoiled goods	600	
Receivable	5,400	
Work in process—materials		1,000
Work in process—labor		2,000
Work in process—overhead		3,000

REQUIRED

Indicate the circumstance under which each of the four solutions above would be appropriate.

18-12 ***Job-cost spoilage and scrap.*** (F. Mayne) Santa Cruz Metal Fabricators, Inc., has a large job, No. 2734, which calls for producing various ore bins, chutes, and metal boxes for enlarging a copper concentrator. The following charges were made to the job in November 19_9:

Materials	$26,951
Direct labor	15,076
Factory overhead	7,538

The contract with the customer called for the price to be based on a cost-plus approach. The contract defined *cost* to include direct materials, direct labor, and overhead to be applied at 50 percent of labor. The contract also provided that the total costs of all work spoiled were to be removed from the billable cost of the job, and that the benefits from scrap sales were to reduce the billable cost of the job.

REQUIRED

1. In accordance with the stated terms of the contract, record the following two items in general journal form:
   a. A cutting error was made in production. The up-to-date job-cost sheet for the batch of work involved showed materials of $650, direct labor of $500, and applied overhead of $250. Since fairly large pieces of metal were recoverable, it was estimated that the salvage value was $600 and that the materials recovered would be used on other jobs. The spoiled work was sent to the warehouse.
   b. Small pieces of metal cuttings and scrap in November 19_9 amounted to $1,250, which was the price quoted by a scrap dealer. You may assume that there were no entries made with regard to the scrap until the price was quoted by the scrap dealer. The scrap dealer's offer was immediately accepted.
2. Consider the issue of normal versus abnormal spoilage that was discussed in the chapter. Suppose that the contract described above had instead contained the clause "a normal spoilage allowance of 1 percent of the job cost will be included in the billable cost of the job."
   a. Is this clause really specific enough to define exactly how much spoilage is normal and how much is abnormal? *Hint:* Consider the inputs versus outputs distinction that was presented in the material on the bottom of p. 610.
   b. Repeat requirement 1a with this "normal spoilage of 1 percent" clause in mind. You should be able to provide two slightly different entries.

18-13 ***Allocating spoilage.*** The ABC Company operates under a process-cost system for one of its products. During the period in question for this product, 3,850 units were put into production. During the period, 3,000 finished units were turned out. Inspection of this product occurs at the halfway point in the process. Normally, rejects amount to 10 percent of the good units passed. The inspection department informs us that the process did in fact function normally during this period. The department supervisor estimates that units still in process are on the average two-thirds complete. All, however, are at least one-half done.

Costs for the period were:

Materials	$38,500—Applied at the beginning of the process
Conversion cost	35,080—Applied uniformly during the process
	$73,580

REQUIRED Determine the cost of goods completed and the cost of the ending inventory of work in process. Assume that there were no beginning inventories.

18-14 ***Normal and abnormal spoilage.*** The Van Brocklin Company manufactures one style of long, tapered wax candle, which is used on festive occasions. Each candle requires a two-foot-long wick and one pound of a specially prepared wax. Wick and melted wax are placed in molds and allowed to harden for twenty-four hours. Upon removal from the molds, the candles are immediately dipped in a special coloring mixture that gives them a glossy lacquer finish. Dried candles are inspected, and all defective ones are pulled out. Because the coloring mixture penetrates into the wax itself, the defective candles cannot be salvaged for reuse. They are destroyed in an incinerator. Normal spoilage is reckoned as 3 percent of the number of candles that pass inspection.

Cost and production statistics for a certain week were as follows:

Raw materials requisitioned (including wicks and wax)	$3,340.00
Direct labor and indirect costs (applied at a constant rate during the hardening process)	1,219.50
Total cost incurred	$4,559.50

During the week, 7,800 candles were completed; 7,500 passed inspection, and the remainder were defective. At the end of the week, 550 candles were still in the molds; they were considered 60 percent complete. There was no beginning inventory. Show computations.

1. Which of the following is the normal cost of the 7,500 candles that passed inspection? (a) $4,333.73, (b) $4,125.00, (c) $4,217.85, (d) $4,248.75, (e) $4,290.00.

2. Which of the following is the normal cost of the candles still in the molds at the end of the week? (a) $393.25, (b) $185.13, (c) $269.50, (d) $274.72, (e) $300.30.

18-15 ***Weighted average and spoilage.*** The Alston Company operates under a process-cost system. It has two departments, cleaning and milling. For both departments, conversion costs are applied in proportion to the stage of completion. But materials are applied at the *beginning* of the process in the cleaning department, and additional materials are added at the *end* of the milling process. Following are the costs and unit production statistics for May. All unfinished work at the *end* of May is one-fourth completed. All beginning inventories (May 1) were four-fifths completed as of May 1. All completed work is transferred to the next department.

BEGINNING INVENTORIES:	CLEANING	MILLING
Cleaning: $1,000 materials, $800 conv. costs	$1,800	
Milling: $6,450 previous dept. cost (transferred-in cost) and $2,450 conv. costs		$8,900
CURRENT COSTS		
Materials	$9,000	$ 640
Conversion costs	$8,000	$4,950
PHYSICAL UNITS		
Units in beginning inventory	1,000	3,000
Units *started* this month	9,000	7,400
Total units finished and transferred	7,400	6,000
Normal spoilage	500	400
Abnormal spoilage	500	0

ADDITIONAL FACTORS

1. Spoilage is assumed to occur at the *end* of *each* of the two processes when the units are inspected.

2. Assume that there is no other waste, shrinkage, evaporation, or abnormal spoilage than that indicated in the tabulation above.

3. Carry unit-cost calculations to three decimal places where necessary. Calculate final totals to the nearest dollar.

REQUIRED

Using the weighted-average method, show for *each* department:

1. Analysis of physical flows and an analysis of equivalent performance
2. Calculations of *unit* costs
3. *Detailed* presentation of the *total* values assigned to goods transferred out and the total values assigned to ending work in process

18-16 Redo Problem 18-15, using FIFO.

18-17 ***FIFO process costing, normal and abnormal spoilage.*** (D. Kleespie) The CeeKay Company uses actual costs in a FIFO process cost accounting system. Materials are added at the beginning of processing in the mixing department; inspection takes place at the end of the process. Operating data for August include:

	POUNDS
Beginning inventory of work in process, 30% complete as to conversion costs ($13,500 conversion cost)	500
Normal spoilage	60
Abnormal spoilage	40
Good units transferred out	2,000
Ending inventory of work in process, 60% complete as to conversion costs	600
Conversion cost per equivalent pound, $100	

REQUIRED

1. How many units were started in production in the mixing department during August?
2. How many equivalent units were used in determining the unit cost for conversion efforts?
3. What is the total dollar amount of the conversion-cost portion of the ending work-in-process inventory?
4. What is the total dollar amount of the conversion-cost portion being transferred out to the next department?
5. What is the total amount of conversion cost charged to the mixing department this period?
6. Assume instead that the CeeKay Company had used the weighted-average method. How many divisor equivalent units would have been used to determine the average unit cost for conversion efforts?
7. Assume as in requirement 6 that the CeeKay Company had used the weighted-average method. What is the total amount of conversion cost charged to the mixing department this period?

18-18 ***Process costs; weighted-average; abnormal spoilage.*** (SMA) The Quebec Manufacturing Company produces a single product. There are two producing departments, Departments 1 and 2, and the product passes through the plant in that order.

There were no work-in-process inventories at the beginning of the year.

In January, materials for 1,000 units were issued to production in Department 1 at a cost of $5,000. Direct-labor and factory-overhead costs for the month were $2,700. During the month, 800 units were completed and transferred to Department 2. The work-in-process inventory at the end of the month contained 200 units, complete in materials and one-half complete in labor and overhead.

Direct labor and factory overhead in Department 2 amounted to $6,250 in January. During the month, 500 units were completed and transferred to finished stock. At the end of the month, 200 units remained in process, one-quarter complete. Ordinarily, in Department 2, spoilage is recognized upon inspection at the end of the process, but in January there was an abnormal loss of 50 units when one-half complete. The effect of abnormal loss is not to be included in inventory.

REQUIRED | Prepare a detailed cost-of-production report for the month of January. Use the weighted-average method.

18-19 ***Process costs; weighted-average.*** (CGAA) The H Co. Ltd. manufactures a single product that is processed in three departments. The process-cost procedure in use bases inventory values on the weighted-average cost method. The following cost and production data are available for Department 2 for the month of April:

Opening work-in-process inventory—1,500 units:	
Cost from preceding department	$12,000
Department 2 material (added at the beginning of the process)	2,041
Department 2 labor and applied overhead	4,168
(These units were 40% complete as to conversion costs.)	
Transferred in during April from Department 1: 6,000 units	46,800
Department 2 costs for April:	
Materials	8,459
Labor and applied overhead	41,727

Production Data: 5,900 units were completed and transferred to Department 3; 1,000 units were still in process (20 percent complete) at the end of April; the balance were spoiled units, detected at the end of the Department 2 processing. One-half the spoilage is abnormal and is to be charged to an Abnormal Spoilage Loss Account.

REQUIRED | Prepare a cost-of-production report for April.

18-20 ***Process costs; weighted-average; spoilage.*** (CMA) Ranka Company manufactures high-quality leather products. The company's profits have declined during the past nine months. Ranka has used unit-cost data that were developed eighteen months ago in planning and controlling its operations. In an attempt to isolate the causes of poor profit performance, management is investigating the manufacturing operations of each of its products.

One of Ranka's main products is fine leather belts. The belts are produced in a single, continuous process in the Bluett Plant. During the process leather strips are sewn, punched, and dyed. Buckles are attached by rivets when the belts are 70 percent complete as to direct labor and overhead (conversion costs). The belts then enter a final finishing stage to conclude the process. Labor and overhead are applied continuously during the process.

The leather belts are inspected twice during the process: (1) right before the buckles are attached (70 percent point in the process), and (2) at the conclusion of the finishing stage (100 percent point in the process). Ranka uses the weighted-average method to calculate its unit costs.

The leather belts produced at the Bluett Plant wholesale for $9.95 each. Management wants to compare the current manufacturing costs per unit with the prices that exist on the market for leather belts. Top management has asked the Bluett Plant to submit data on the cost of manufacturing the leather belts for the month of October. This cost data will be used to evaluate whether modifications in the production process should be initiated or whether an increase in the selling price of the belts is justified. The cost per equivalent unit which is being used for planning and controlling purposes is $5.35 per unit.

The work-in-process inventory consisted of 400 partially completed units on October 1. The belts were 25 percent complete as to conversion costs. The costs included in the inventory on October 1 were as follows:

Leather strips	$1,000
Conversion costs	300
	$1,300

During October 7,600 leather strips were placed in production. A total of 6,800 good leather belts were completed. A total of 300 belts were identified as defective at the two inspection points—100 at the first inspection point (before buckle is attached) and 200 at the final inspection point (after finishing). This quantity of defective belts was considered normal. In addition, 200 belts were removed from the production line when the process was 40 percent complete as to conversion costs because they had been damaged as a result of a malfunction during the sewing operation. This malfunction was considered an unusual occurrence, and consequently, the spoilage was classified as abnormal. Spoiled units are not reprocessed and have zero salvage value. The work-in-process inventory on October 31 consisted of 700 belts which were 50 percent complete as to conversion costs.

The costs charged to production during October were as follows:

Leather strips	$20,600
Buckles	4,550
Conversion costs	20,700
	$45,850

REQUIRED

1. In order to provide cost data regarding the manufacture of leather belts in the Bluett Plant to the top management of Ranka Company, determine for the month of October (a) the equivalent units for each factor of production; (b) the cost per equivalent whole unit for each factor of production; (c) the assignment of total production costs to the work-in-process inventory and to goods transferred out; (d) the average unit cost of the 6,800 good leather belts completed and transferred to finished goods.
2. If Ranka Company decided to repair (rework) the 300 belts that were considered normal spoilage, explain how the company would account for the rework costs.

18-21 ***FIFO process costing, spoilage.*** (SMA) The following information for a recent fiscal period pertains to a producing department of a company that uses process-costing procedures:

Opening work in process (materials 100% complete, conversion 40%)	100,000 units
Materials cost	$ 150,600
Conversion cost	68,100
	$ 218,700
Started in production	420,000 units
Materials cost	$ 567,000
Conversion cost	675,324
	$1,242,324
Spoiled units—detected at final completion stage (includes 15,000 units normal spoilage)	30,000 units
Closing work in process (materials 100% complete, conversion 60%)	90,000 units

REQUIRED

Prepare a report showing the cost of production for the period, using FIFO. The report should include equivalent production, unit costs, and a summary of total costs of goods transferred, spoilage (normal and abnormal) and work in process, showing the disposition of these items.

18-22 ***First-in, first-out process costing; multiple choice.*** The Meara Company uses a process-cost system (first-in, first-out) in costing its sole product. Materials for the product are added at the beginning of the operating cycle; conversion costs are assumed to accrue evenly over the cycle. Spoilage is detected by inspection upon completion of the product. Normally, the spoiled units are equal to one-tenth of the good output.

At January 1, the inventory of work in process was 2,000 units of product, representing an average of three-fourths complete. The cost of these units was $32,200, including $17,000 for raw materials and $15,200 for conversion cost (direct labor and indirect cost). During January, 8,000 additional units of product were begun. During January, material cost of $64,000 was requisitioned from stores and charged to operations. Direct-labor costs for the month were $38,000. Indirect costs are assigned at the rate of 100 percent of direct-labor cost.

At January 31, the work in process consisted of 1,500 units of product, two-thirds complete. During the month, 7,200 units of good product were transferred to finished-goods stock after inspection.

Select the answer that correctly completes each of the following statements (identify your answer by letter). Support your overall answer with a production-cost report.

1. Units of normal spoilage amounted to (a) 580, (b) 1,000, (c) 950, (d) 800, (e) 720.

2. Units of abnormal spoilage amounted to (a) 950, (b) 580, (c) 1,000, (d) 720, (e) 800.

3. The total equivalent units for work done in January only for material cost were (a) 10,000, (b) 8,500, (c) 9,500, (d) 9,000, (e) 8,000.

4. The total equivalent units for work done in January only for conversion cost were (a) 8,000, (b) 9,000, (c) 8,500, (d) 7,000, (e) 7,500.

5. The total equivalent unit cost for materials was (a) \$8.00, (b) \$8.50, (c) \$6.40, (d) \$8.10, (e) \$8.25.

6. The cost of products transferred to finished goods was (a) \$140,184, (b) \$138,550, (c) \$127,950, (d) \$108,350, (e) \$140,550.

18-23 ***FIFO process costs; lost units.*** (CPA) The Biltimar Company manufactures gewgaws in three steps or departments. The finishing department is the third and last step before the product is transferred to finished-goods inventory.

All materials needed to complete the gewgaws are added at the beginning of the process in the finishing department, and lost units, if any, occur only at this point. The company uses the FIFO cost method in its accounting system and has accumulated the following data for July for the finishing department:

1. Production of gewgaws (in units):

In process, July 1 (labor and manufacturing expense three-fourths complete)	10,000
Transferred from preceding departments during July	40,000
Finished and transferred to finished-goods inventory during July	35,000
In process, July 31 (labor and manufacturing expense one-half complete)	10,000

2. Cost of work-in-process inventory, July 1:

Cost from preceding departments	\$ 38,000
Costs added in finished department prior to July 1:	
Materials	21,500
Labor	39,000
Manufacturing expense	42,000
Cost of work-in-process inventory, July 1	\$140,500

3. Gewgaws transferred to the finishing department during July had costs of \$140,000 assigned from preceding departments.

4. During July, the finishing department incurred the following production costs:

Materials	\$ 70,000
Labor	162,500
Manufacturing expense	130,000
Total	\$362,500

REQUIRED

1. The cost of the gewgaws lost in production during July. (Regard these as abnormal spoilage. Also assume that lost units occur after material is added.)
2. The cost of the gewgaws transferred to finished-goods inventory in July.
3. The cost of the work-in-process inventory at July 31.

18-24 ***FIFO, spoiled and lost units.*** (D. Grinnell) The Murphy Manufacturing Company manufactures a single product that is processed in five departments. The following cost data are available for Department 3 for the month of July 19_5:

Opening work-in-process inventory:

Cost transferred in from Department 2	$ 19,000
Department 3 labor cost	3,000

Current costs:

Cost transferred in during July from Department 2	$105,000
Department 3 material cost during July	36,800
Department 3 labor cost during July	42,800

Material used in Department 3 is added to the product at the end of the Department 3 process. Department 3 conversion costs are assumed to be incurred uniformly throughout the Department 3 process; manufacturing overhead is applied to product on the basis of 50 percent of labor cost.

The following represents production data for Department 3 for the month of July 19_5:

Work in process (July 1)	18,000 units (⅓ completed)
Units transferred in during July from Department 2	111,000 units
Good units completed during July	80,000 units
Spoiled units	12,000 units
Work in process (July 31)	28,000 units (¾ completed)

Spoiled units: Spoilage is detected by inspection upon completion of the product by Department 3. Normal spoilage is considered to be 10 percent of the good output. Further, normal spoilage is considered a cost of the good units completed while abnormal spoilage is written off as a loss.

Normal lost units: Units lost during processing are considered to be a normal occurrence *unless* the number of lost units exceeds 5 percent of total units accounted for (total units accounted for is equal to the sum of good units completed plus spoiled units plus units in ending inventory of work in process). The cost of normal lost units is considered a cost of total units accounted for; company accountants make no attempt to specifically determine or separately identify the cost of normal lost units (that is, the method of neglect is used in accounting for normal lost units).

Abnormal lost units: Lost units in excess of 5 percent are considered abnormal. The cost of abnormal lost units is separately identified and written off as a loss. The company accountants follow the policy of assigning only transferred-in costs to abnormal lost units.

REQUIRED

1. Consistent with the *FIFO method* for treating product costs and consistent with the company's treatment of spoilage and lost units, determine the following concerning Department 3 operations for the month of July:
   a. Total loss (in dollars) due to abnormal spoilage
   b. Total loss (in dollars) due to abnormal lost units
   c. Total cost assigned to good units completed during July that is transferred out to Department 4
   d. Total cost assigned to the ending (July 31) work-in-process inventory
2. How would your answers to requirement 1 above be influenced (indicate the total dollar effect) if the spoiled units could be sold for 25¢ each?

18-25 ***Weighted average.*** Repeat requirement 1 of the preceding problem consistent with the *weighted-average* method for treating product costs and consistent with the company's treatment of spoilage and lost units.

18-26 ***Material-spoilage variance.*** Moline Structural Metal Company uses a standard-costing system. One of its products requires 60 pounds of material at $3 per pound, a standard material cost of $180 per product unit. During a recent week, 90 units were produced, of which 12 were spoiled. Total materials purchased and used were 5,550 pounds at $3.20 per pound.

REQUIRED

1. Compute all material variances.
2. Prepare a journal entry to recognize these variances. Assume that the perpetual inventory of materials is carried in the accounts on an actual cost basis.

18-27 ***Standard process costing; spoilage.*** (S. Laimon) The Sharbill Company uses standard process costing in accounting for its cost of production at its factory in Singapore. Only one product is manufactured, with standard costs *per thousand units* as follows:

Material A	15 lbs. @ 80¢		$12.00
Material B	4 lbs. @ $2.25		9.00
Direct labor	5 hours @ $3.60		18.00
Variable overhead	5 hours @ $2.00		10.00
Fixed overhead	5 hours @ $1.60		8.00
Normal spoilage	10% of Material A	$1.20	
	5% of Conversion costs	1.80	3.00
Total standard cost per 1,000 units			$60.00

The standards for materials and conversion costs are exclusive of spoilage costs. The latter costs are allowed for separately in the standard. Material A is added at the beginning of the process. Labor and overhead are added evenly throughout thc process. Inspection at the 50 percent stage of completion removes all spoiled units. Normal spoilage amounts to 10 percent of all *good* units passing the inspection point. Immediately after the removal of spoiled units, Material B is added to the rcmaining good units, and the processing of these units is then completcd.

Production data for April 19_1 were as follows:

Beginning work-in-process inventory	400,000 units	—40% complete
Put into process during April	500,000	
Transferred to finished goods	600,000	
Spoiled units	100,000	
Ending work-in-process inventory	200,000	—60% complete

COST DATA

1. Materials: All price variances on materials are recognized at the time of purchase.

a. Material A: Beginning inventory, 2,000 pounds
Purchased, 10,000 lbs. @ 84¢ = $8,400
Issued to production, 8,000 pounds

b. Material B: Beginning inventory, 1,000 pounds
Purchased, 4,000 lbs. @ $2.00 = $8,000
Issued to production, 3,100 pounds

2. Direct-labor payroll: 3,100 hours @ $3.50 = $10,850.

3. Overhead costs incurred:

a. Variable, $6,500

b. Fixed, $5,610

4. Budget data: Planned production for the month was 675,000 units.

5. Variance disposition: All variances are charged to the period of their incurrence.

REQUIRED

1. Presentation at standard cost of
(a) abnormal spoilage, (b) units transferred, (c) ending work in process.
2. Summary analysis of all variances, including detailed breakdown of direct-labor and overhead variances.

Decentralization and Management Control

SECTION SIX

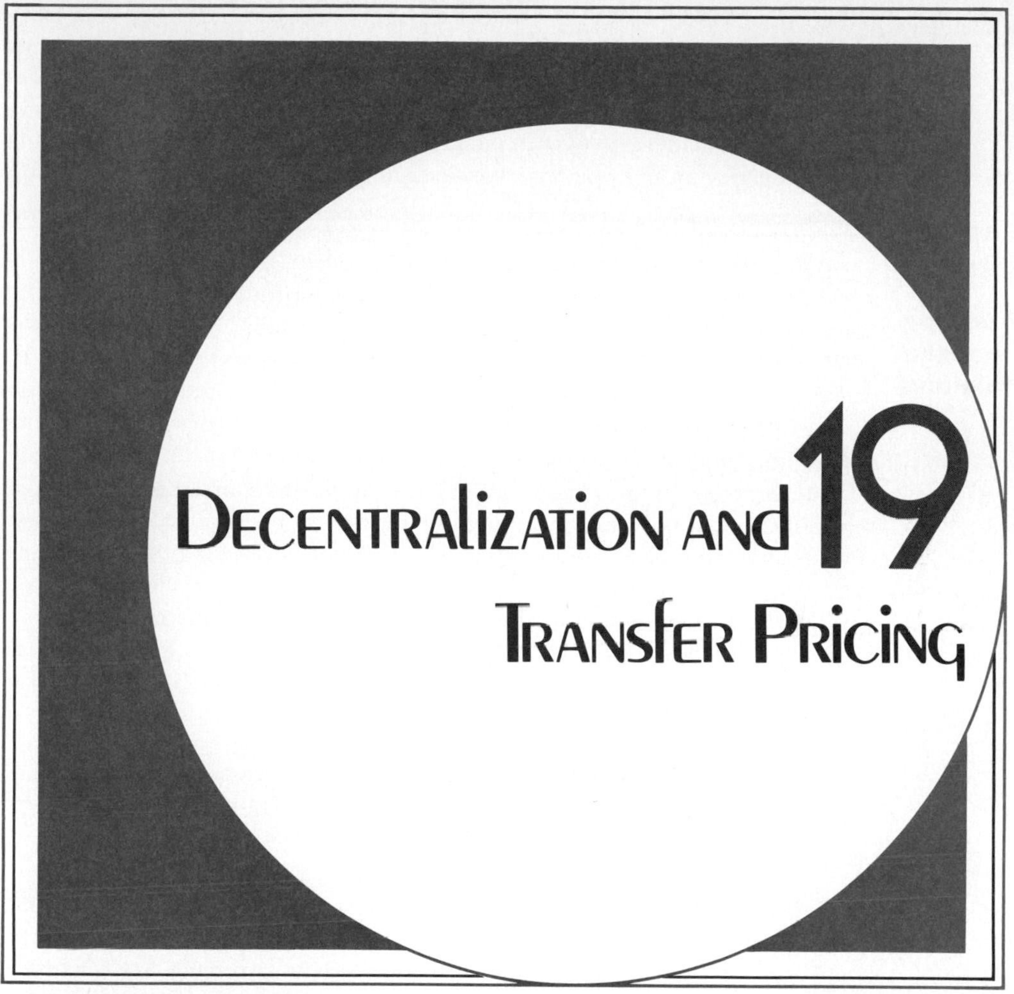

This chapter and the next focus on the role of accounting systems in decentralized organizations. In this chapter we examine the nature of decentralization, profit centers, and transfer pricing. The succeeding chapter concentrates on investment centers, whereby profits are related to the investments in subunits of an organization. The problems described here extend to all types of organizations, including many parts of not-for-profit organizations.

The subject matter of these two chapters is a blend of cost accounting (as narrowly conceived), general management, economics, and organizational behavior. Now is the time to develop a perspective regarding how to judge the quality of any given management accounting system. We quickly see that motivational criteria are vital for reaching such judgments.

These two chapters and Chapter 10 provide "softer" material than the other chapters. As used here, *softer* means that many issues raised cannot be resolved by merely crunching some numbers. Management accountants often must help operating managers grapple with such issues. For example, how should a divisional manager's performance be measured? Both accountants and managers should step back occasionally and try to attain perspective. These two chapters try to help achieve an overall picture of the general role of imperfect management accounting systems in imperfect organizations.

Nature of decentralization

relative freedom to make decisions

As organizations grow, top managers face two continuing problems: (a) how to divide activities and responsibilities, and (b) how to coordinate subunits. Inevitably, the power to make decisions is distributed among various managers. **The essence of decentralization is the freedom to make decisions.** Decentralization is a matter of degree. Total decentralization means minimum constraints and maximum freedom for managers to make decisions, even at the lowest levels. At the other extreme of the continuum, total centralization means maximum constraints and minimum freedom.

In practice, organizations are seldom totally centralized or decentralized. Full centralization is not economic in most instances, because of the impossibility of administering the unavoidable massive volume of decisions at the top-management level. On the other hand, full decentralization implies a collection of completely separate businesses. Solomons has pointed out that subunits should be more than investments.[1] They should contribute not only to the success of the corporation but to the success of each other. They may use a common raw material and therefore permit its purchase more cheaply in bulk. They may provide complementary products (like cameras and film), so that each division's products help to create a demand for the others'. They may share technical information about manufacturing processes or market information about various channels of distribution.

benefits of decentralization

How should top managers decide on how much decentralization is optimal? Conceptually, top managers try to choose a degree of decentralization that maximizes the excess of benefits over costs. Practically, top managers cannot quantify either the benefits or the costs. Nevertheless, this cost-benefit approach helps us identify the central issues.

The claimed benefits of decentralization include the following:

1. **Optimal decisions are more likely, because the manager of the subunit has more information.** He or she is in a better position to react to information about local conditions in a timely way.
2. The burden of decision making is distributed, so that the managers' collective decisions are optimized. Top managers are also likely to have more time for strategic planning than if they had to control day-to-day operations.
3. Greater freedom heightens the managers' motivation, because they have more control over the factors that affect the measures of their performance.
4. Greater freedom induces managers to check outside markets for both raw materials and finished goods more frequently. Intracompany transfers of goods or services are often based on these market prices instead of on costs. Where market-based prices are used as a part of the information system, there is a routine check on market forces that is otherwise not available. This built-in check on market prices often focuses on uneconomic activities that would not be as readily detected in a centralized system.
5. More decision making on a wide spectrum provides better training for managers as they rise in the organization.

---

[1] David Solomons, *Divisional Performance: Measurement and Control* (Homewood, Ill.: Richard D. Irwin, 1968), p. 10. His Chapter 1 is a good summary of the organization of divisionalized businesses.

6. Decentralization is often accompanied by the use of profit or investment centers. The management of a profit center is somehow viewed as a higher-status position than that of a cost center and therefore may provide the psychological benefits of first-class citizenship. In other words, the profit-center structure has a more desirable motivational effect.

costs of decentralization

The largest cost of decentralization is probably **dysfunctional decision making—that is, decision making where the benefit to one subunit is more than offset by the costs or loss of benefit to other subunits.** This may be caused by (a) a lack of harmony or congruence between the overall organizational goals, the subunit goals, and the individual goals of decision makers, and (b) a lack of information for guiding the individual manager concerning the effects of his or her decisions on other parts of the organization. Moreover, the costs of gathering and processing information often increase. Decentralization is usually accompanied by more elaborate information systems, which become more important to top managers in obtaining goal congruence and monitoring a collection of more independent managers. In addition, some central corporate assets, services, and administrative talent tend to be duplicated.

Dysfunctional decision making is most likely where the subunits in the organization are highly interdependent—that is, where the decisions affecting one part of the organization influence the decisions and performance of another part. If interdependence is great, coordination is needed to obtain optimum decisions for the organization as a whole. Subunits can rarely be completely autonomous or self-contained, so interdependence is the biggest inhibiting factor in decentralization. There are countless examples of interdependence where the performance of the receiving unit depends on the quality of the work done by the supplying unit. For instance, parts and raw materials must meet schedules and specifications; two segments of the organization may share or compete for computer services, management skills, or raw materials; they may sell in a common market (for example, Buick and Oldsmobile) in such a way that an action beneficial to one subunit may be harmful to another and to the corporation as a whole.

comparison of benefits and costs

The foregoing benefits and costs must be compared by top managers, often on a function-by-function basis. For example, the controller's function may be heavily decentralized for many attention-directing and problem-solving purposes (such as operating budgets and performance reports), but heavily centralized for other purposes (such as accounts-receivable processing and income-tax planning).

The general patterns of benefits and costs of decentralization are shown in Exhibit 19-1. The graph hypothesizes that, as the degree of decentralization increases, the benefits (B) of decentralization will increase at a decreasing rate and the costs (C) will increase slowly at middle degrees of decentralization but soar quickly at either extreme.

The degree of decentralization (D) varies from zero to one. D is essentially a gauge of the freedom to make decisions. For example, it could be measured by the percentage of equipment acquisition decisions that a division manager can make without needing top-management consent. Various attempts have been made to obtain a measure of D that might be used for comparing various organizations.[2]

---

[2]See T. L. Whisler, H. Meyer, B. H. Baum, and P. F. Sorenson, "Centralization of Organization Control: An Empirical Study of Its Meaning and Measurement," *Journal of Business,* 40, No. 1, pp. 10–26. They develop a Gini ratio of concentration, which is applied to the distribution of individual compensation within each department studied. Their rationale assumes that the way in which executive compensation is distributed reflects rather closely the way in which responsibility and control are distributed.

Decentralization is likely to be most beneficial and least costly when the organizational units are entirely independent of each other. Then there is minimal likelihood of dysfunctional decisions. In general, a subunit is independent (self-contained) to the extent that it

1. Does not compete with other subunits within the organization for the use of limited resources, such as capital, research services, or management skill
2. Does not compete in the same market or buy from the same sources as other subdivisions
3. Does not provide goods to other subunits or depend upon them for its own inputs
4. Can make decisions and obtain goal congruence without coordination with other subunits and without explicitly considering the objectives of the other subunits or of the organization[3]

Of course *B, C,* and *D* in Exhibit 19-1 are impossible to determine with precision. There are indications that top managers perceive the optimum decentralization in practice as being somewhere in the middle. The extent of decentralization in a particular organization is obviously affected by numerous factors.

EXHIBIT 19-1

Benefits and Costs of Decentralization

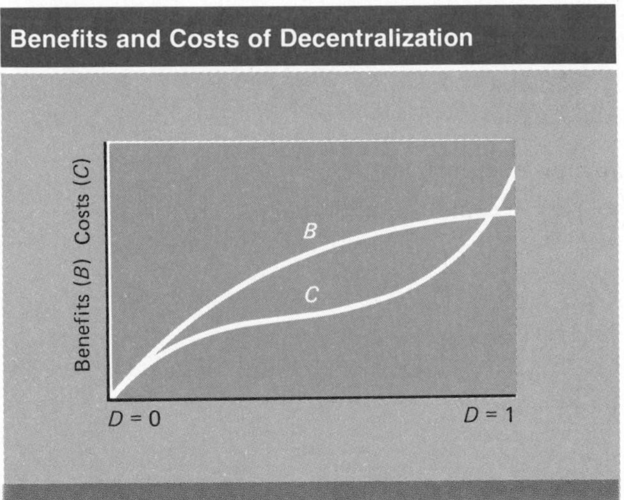

Profit centers

confusion of terms

A **profit center** is any subunit or segment of an organization that is assigned both revenues and expenses. This is a simple, straightforward definition. Note that it does not contain one word about *decentralization,* which was previously defined as the relative freedom to make decisions. **There is enormous confusion in the accounting literature and management literature because the term *profit center* is often erroneously viewed as a synonym for *decentralized subunit.* Usually this confusion is harmless, but occasionally it leads to incorrect analysis.**

[3]See William T. Morris, *Decentralization in Management Systems* (Columbus: Ohio State University Press, 1968), p. 15.

Although it may seem strange at first glance, profit centers could be coupled with a highly centralized organization, and cost centers could be coupled with a highly decentralized organization. Normally, however, the profit center is the major organizational device used to implement decentralization. Still, the existence of profit centers does not necessarily mean that heavy decentralization exists. For example, a company may have many divisions called profit centers, but their managers may have little leeway in making decisions. A manager may be unable to buy or sell outside his or her company, may have to obtain approval from corporate headquarters for every capital expenditure over $200, and may be forced to accept central-staff "advice." In another company, which has only cost centers, managers may have great latitude on capital outlays and on where to purchase materials and services. **In short, the labels of *profit center* and *cost center* are sometimes deceptive as clues to the degree of decentralization.**

size and number of centers Ideas of decentralization and profit center are universal; they are not confined to large organizations. A small medical center or retail store can have several profit centers and may be either heavily decentralized or heavily centralized.

There is a tendency to jump to fallacious conclusions about the extent of decentralization in a particular company. For example, the *number* of profit centers is not a valid index of decentralization. Consider General Electric, which has over two hundred subunit managers with profit responsibility. Some of these subunits have annual sales of over $300 million. Is GE a heavily decentralized company? The answer depends on whether these individual subunits are, in turn, managed on a decentralized basis. A $300-million subdivision that is subject to autocratic rule by the division manager is surely less decentralized than a $200-million outside competitor in the same product lines that has several nearly independent subunits. Taken as a whole, General Electric may appear decentralized; however, each division may be heavily centralized when compared with its outside competitors.

Three motivational criteria

Recall that Chapter 10 (page 318) stressed the importance of motivation as a criterion in judging management control systems. A distinction was made between **goal congruence** and **managerial effort** as separate aspects of motivation.

After considering costs and benefits, top management may decide that heavy decentralization is desirable. By definition, this means that top management will rarely interfere with the decisions of subordinates. Therefore, the preservation of the **autonomy** of subunit managers becomes an additional criterion in the design of a management control system:[4]

1. *Goal congruence.* The sharing of the same objectives by subordinate managers and top managers
2. *Managerial effort.* The degree of striving toward a goal
3. *Autonomy.* The degree of freedom to make decisions

These three motivational criteria are helpful in judging how a management control system might be designed or improved. All three criteria will be used in the discussion that follows in this and the next chapter.

---

[4]Joshua Ronen and George McKinney, "Transfer Pricing for Divisional Autonomy," *Journal of Accounting Research,* Spring 1970, pp. 100–101.

Objectives of transfer pricing

Goods and services are often exchanged between various departments and divisions of a company. What monetary values (transfer prices) should be assigned to these exchanges or transfers? Historical cost? Market price? Some version of either? The transfer-pricing question is often the most troublesome aspect of a control system.

nature of transfer prices

A **transfer price** is the price charged by one segment of an organization for a product or service that it supplies to another segment of the same organization. **In a most fundamental sense, all cost allocation is a form of transfer pricing.** For example, although it is rarely thought of in this way, the allocation of service-department costs to production departments is essentially a form of transfer pricing. In practice, however, the term *transfer price* is usually associated with charges between profit centers.

Why do transfer-pricing systems exist? The main reason is to communicate information that leads to optimal decisions for the organization as a whole.[5] However, transfer prices often cannot satisfy our three motivational criteria simultaneously. For example, a transfer price equal to variable cost may be pertinent for a short-run decision to make or buy, thereby meeting the goal congruence criterion. However, the supplier division manager may have no inclination to sell to a consuming division at variable cost. Why? Because the manager's performance measure—divisional profit—will not be improved. Thus, the managerial effort criterion would not be met. **The measures chosen for performance evaluation are often the keys to whether managerial effort is being encouraged.** Furthermore, suppose a superior instructs the supplier division manager to transfer at variable cost. Then the manager's independence is undermined, and the autonomy criterion would not be met.

company practices

There are few pat answers to the more imposing transfer-pricing situations. Consequently, transfer-pricing policies tend to vary for different types of products and services within the same organization. A survey of 291 companies revealed that 85 percent transferred goods among profit centers. The average value of such transfers accounted for 13 percent of total corporate cost of goods sold. The following observations are revealing:

> It is interesting to note that variable costs are used for establishing transfer prices in only about 5 percent of the companies. From a business perspective, this is not surprising because the profit center managers of supplying divisions would have little incentive to produce if their output were to be transferred on the basis of variable costs. Full costs are used by nearly a quarter of the companies. Thus, about 70 percent of the companies specify transfer prices on the basis of cost plus, negotiation, and market price. These methods obviously require more time and effort than methods equating transfer prices to variable or full costs. The fact that over two thirds of the companies use the more cumbersome methods of transfer pricing perhaps indicates the care with which such prices are arrived at and their importance in motivating profit center managers.[6]

---

[5]See Kenneth J. Arrow, "Control in Large Organizations," *Management Science,* 10, No. 3, pp. 397–408, for a sweeping view of decentralization, and pp. 405–6 for an assessment of the difficulties in applying a price system to the control of an organization. He sees these difficulties as four mutually interacting types: (a) the choice of enforcement rules, (b) the complexity of the operating rules, (c) the limits on the theoretical validity of the price system, and (d) the presence of uncertainty.

[6]R. Vancil, *Decentralization: Managerial Ambiguity by Design* (New York: Financial Executives Research Foundation, 1979), p. 173.

An extensive study of the transfer-pricing literature reinforced the difficulties of transfer pricing by concluding:

> Finally, one's orientation in transfer pricing should always be behavioral. The relevant question is never "What's the correct approach?" There *is* no correct approach, for "correct" implies exactly the sort of theory that is unobtainable here. Instead, the appropriate question is the opportunistic (even slightly cynical) one: "What's apt to produce the sorts of dysfunctional behavior that we best can live with?"[7]

Market prices

appeal of market prices

For day-in, day-out use where the intermediate market is competitive and where interdependencies of subunits are minimal, market price is the most desirable transfer price because it generally leads to optimal decisions. There are no inherent conflicts in abiding by all three criteria (goal congruence, managerial effort, and autonomy). The guidelines are these: (a) a market or negotiated market price should be used; (b) the seller should have the option of not selling internally;[8] and (c) an arbitration procedure should be available for settling disputes.[9] These guidelines assume that the managers of the divisions have access to perfectly competitive outside markets. Where market prices are relevant for making economic decisions, and if the costs of maintaining such a system are justifiable, they are also relevant to the preservation of subunit autonomy and the maintenance of managerial effort.

When the market-price approach is used, the attempt is to transfer goods at a price no higher than that prevailing in an outside market at the time of transfer—that is, at the price that the receiving division would have to pay outsiders. Put another way, the market-price approach is an attempt to approximate an arm's-length, bargained, open-market price.

In most cases, internal procurement is expected where the selling division's products and services are equal to or more attractive than those of outsiders in terms of quality and price. The buying division often obtains benefits such as better quality, assurance of supply, and dependable delivery.

The usefulness of a market-price method is contingent on the availability of dependable market-price quotations of other manufacturers. It is these prices that would be taken into account by parties dealing at arm's length as they establish the competitive price levels.

In sum, if a company's participation in a market has no effect on price, market prices typically establish the ceiling for transfer pricing. In many instances a lower price may easily be justified, particularly when large purchases are made, when selling costs are less, or when an advantage is obtained through an exclusive supplier contract or through a cost-plus arrangement, ensuring profits in all cases. These situations lead to the notion of negotiated market prices, whereby the cost savings to the firm as a whole are split between the selling and buying divisions through bargaining.

Arbitrating or umpiring is sometimes necessary. However, if arbitration is used frequently, it indicates a step toward centralization. Why? Because it usually elevates

[7]A. Thomas, *A Behavioural Analysis of Joint-Cost Allocation and Transfer Pricing* (Urbana, Ill.: Stipes Publishing, 1980), pp. 222–23.

[8]The reason for this option is that the seller might have more profitable alternative opportunities for using facilities to sell other products.

[9]R. N. Anthony and J. Dearden, *Management Control Systems,* 4th ed. (Homewood, Ill.: Richard D. Irwin, 1980).

the decision to a representative of the organization as a whole. Consequently, too much reliance on arbitration indicates the inability of the division managers to operate smoothly on a decentralized basis.

pitfalls in market prices

The use of market prices wherever possible has innate appeal for purposes of both inducing goal congruence and generating managerial effort. **Without routine checks on market prices, managers often obtain critical information only in a haphazard or tardy fashion.** A frequently cited advantage of profit centers is that they compel an approximation of what revenue might be if a division were operated as a completely independent entity; in this way, the managers become more sensitive to market conditions than otherwise.

The trouble with the use of market price is either that few markets are perfectly competitive or that no intermediate market exists for the exact product or service in question. A quoted price for a product or service is strictly comparable only if the credit terms, grade, quality, delivery terms, and auxiliary considerations are precisely the same. Moreover, isolated price quotations are sometimes temporary distress or dumping prices for excess inventories that must be quickly liquidated in financial emergencies. Such prices can seldom be used as a basis for long-range planning, although they may be appropriate for monitoring short-term performance. In nearly all cases, however, temporary market prices are not applicable to repetitive, high-volume transactions, and they hurt the credibility of the so-called market transfer prices.

Many product parts are unique, a situation that causes considerable costs for preparing bids. If an outside supplier prepares a few bids and discovers that the internal supplier division always wins, the so-called resulting market prices either will not be forthcoming in the future or will be unreliable (and perhaps artificially high; after all, the bidder may submit a high price with little effort). Some companies deliberately purchase from outside suppliers to maintain alternative sources of supply and to provide a valid check on market prices.

distress prices

When an industry has idle capacity, sometimes unusually low prices occur. These prices are occasionally called "distress prices" because they are regarded as being caused by temporary unfortunate conditions. What transfer-pricing scheme should be used for judging performance if distress prices prevail? Some companies use these distress transfer prices, but others use long-run average or "normal" market prices. The decision as to which transfer-pricing basis is preferable depends on subjective judgments regarding the costs and benefits of each alternative.

If distress pricing is used, in the short run the manager of the supplier division will meet the price as long as it exceeds his or her additional cost. In the long run, the manager must decide whether disposal of some manufacturing facilities would be desirable by predicting its effect on the price in question. The danger is that managers may not take the long-range, global view and may constrict facilities to boost a short-run divisional rate of return. The resulting cut in the total industry supply may lead to a higher outside future price that may be disadvantageous to the company as a whole in the long run.

On the other hand, transfers may be based on the long-run average price. But this has the weakness of not incorporating current market prices in the information system; to the extent that transfers are forced at above-current-market prices, the short-run performance of the buying division will be hurt and that manager will be unhappy about both his performance measure and his partial loss of autonomy.

However, unless the selling division's incremental costs exceed the market price, the company as a whole would benefit by an internal transfer.

If the danger of precipitous disposal of facilities is given appropriate consideration when analysis is conducted, the use of current market prices (even distress prices) is generally preferable to the use of some long-run average price. In this way, two evaluations are made. The first is a comparison of long-run predictions and current prices; this gives insights on past capital-budgeting decisions. The second entails assessing the current performance of both the buying and supplying divisions in relation to existing opportunities in the form of current prices.

General rule for transfer pricing?

outlay cost and opportunity cost

The preceding section demonstrated that market price was not a cure-all answer to the problem of setting transfer prices. The most obvious example is the nonexistence of an intermediate market for a highly specialized product component.

Is there an all-pervasive rule for transfer pricing that will lead toward optimal economic decisions? The answer is negative because the three criteria of goal congruence, managerial effort, and autonomy must all be considered simultaneously. If an optimal economic decision is wanted in a particular situation, the following general rule serves as a helpful *first step* in the analysis. **The minimum transfer price should be (*a*) the additional outlay costs incurred to the point of transfer (sometimes approximated by variable costs), plus (*b*) opportunity costs to the firm as a whole. This is the price that would ordinarily make the supplying division indifferent as to whether the output were sold inside or outside; the supplying division's contribution would be the same under either choice.**

The term **outlay cost** in this context represents the cash outflows that are directly associated with the production and transfer of the goods or services. Of course, these cash outflows do not necessarily have to be made at a particular instant, but the action of production and transfer will result sooner or later in some cash outflows that will be termed outlay costs.[10] *Opportunity costs* are defined here as the maximum contribution to profits forgone by the firm as a whole **if the goods are transferred internally.** These may be forgone contribution margins in some instances and even forgone net proceeds from the sale of facilities in other instances.

The distinction between outlay and opportunity costs is made here because the accounting records ordinarily record the outlay costs of the alternative selected but fail to record the opportunity costs.[11] If a perfect intermediate market exists, the

---

[10]Other terms, including *incremental costs, additional costs, direct costs,* and *variable costs,* were rejected as not being as sharply descriptive as is the term *outlay cost.* As used here, the term *outlay cost* implies reasonably efficient operations. Also see R. Benke, Jr., and J. Edwards, *Transfer Pricing: Techniques and Uses* (New York: National Association of Accountants, 1980), p. 7.

[11]The jungle of terminology in this area is too dense to dwell on at length here. The "general rule" has been expressed here with the hope that it will ease the understanding of those who are more comfortable with the terminology of accountants than with that of economists. For example, some economists would examine this general rule and say that *both* (a) and (b) together are opportunity cost. That is, the outlay cost is also an opportunity cost because it measures what the firm would have saved had the outlay *not* been incurred. For an excellent discussion of cost as it is used in economics, see George Stigler, *Theory of Price,* 3rd ed. (New York: Macmillan, 1966).

Other economists would say that both (a) and (b) together are the *marginal cost,* because transfer prices are usually expressed on a per-unit basis. The term *marginal cost* is avoided here because it is ambiguous in the literature. That is, some economists in some situations will use it, at any given point of production, to embrace both (a) and (b) for the last unit produced. In

opportunity cost is market price less outlay cost (i.e., the cost of the opportunity forgone by the internal supplier). A *perfect market* is defined as a market where the maximum available output may be sold at unchanging prices. For example, if the outlay cost is $1 and the market price is $4, the transfer price is $1 + ($4 − $1) = $4, which happens to be the market price. However, if no market exists for the intermediate product or alternative products that might utilize the same supplying division's facilities, the opportunity cost may be zero. In the latter case, outlay cost (perhaps approximated by variable cost) may be the correct transfer price.

To recapitulate:

Minimum transfer price	= **(Outlay cost)**	+ **(Opportunity cost to company as a whole if internal transfer is made.)**	
If idle capacity exists:	= **$1**	+ **Possibly 0**	= **$1**
If no idle capacity exists:	= **$1**	+ **(Market price − Outlay cost)**	
	= **$1**	+ **($4 − $1)**	= **$4**

imperfect markets

The problems in transfer pricing would be trivial if the intermediate market were perfect. But too often the intermediate markets are nonexistent, ill structured, or imperfect. *Imperfect competition* exists when one seller or buyer, *acting alone,* can exert an influence on the market price. If the intermediate market is imperfectly competitive, additional volume can be obtained only if selling prices are lowered. This means that the existing market price at a particular volume level is no longer applicable to the decision regarding how much to produce and sell. The additions to revenue will be less than the sales of the additional units at the new selling price because the new lower price will apply to the entire volume. For example, suppose the current selling price is $1 per unit and 80,000 units are being sold. The revenue is $80,000. A cut in price from $1 to $.90 may increase unit sales to 90,000. The increase in revenue is $1,000 (which is 90,000 × $.90, minus $80,000). In these situations the analyses can become exceedingly complex. The optimal transfer price from the viewpoint of the corporation as a whole is different for each situation, depending on the existence of cost interdependencies and demand interdependencies. An example of a cost interdependency is the case where the price of a certain raw material may be dependent on the total purchases by two or more divisions. An example of a demand interdependency is any vertically integrated operation where there is no intermediate market for a unique component part of a finished product. Then the total number of finished products sold is dependent on the total number of components available, and vice versa.[12]

---

other situations, they will use it to represent (a) only. For example, the loss of external profits is not included in the usual economic description of marginal costs, but it must be included in one way or another for marginal cost to be appropriate as a transfer price for the cases of demand or cost dependencies. Moreover, many accountants will use *variable cost* and *marginal cost* as if they were synonymous terms.

The economist would be inclined to express the general rule slightly differently. Solomons, in *Divisional Performance,* p. 181, points out: "Transfer prices should be set equal to the marginal cost of supply, not at just any output, but at one particular equilibrium output." This requires the matching of the outlay costs of the supplying division at different levels of output with the summation of quantities demanded at each level of additional revenue for all demands. Therefore, a general, unchanging transfer price may be appropriate only in the case of a perfect intermediate market or in the case of constant marginal costs.

[12]See Thomas, *Behavioural Analysis,* for numerous examples of cost interdependencies and demand interdependencies.

As we have just seen, market price is a special case rather than a universal guide. The key computation is the (b) part of the general rule above. It is easy to say, "Measure the forgone contribution from transferring goods internally." However, it is not easy to make such a measurement. For example, consider a supplier division with idle capacity and an imperfect demand in the intermediate market. Is its opportunity cost zero? Probably not. One alternative may be to cut price so as to increase demand and hope to increase overall revenue. But measuring the probable effect is difficult, so measuring the opportunity cost is also difficult. **Clearly, the transfer price must be determined in relation to constantly changing levels of supply and demand. There is not *a* transfer price; rather, there is a schedule of transfer prices (a transfer-price function) for various quantities supplied and demanded.**

The proposed "general rule" provides a springboard for analysis because it often provides the solution to the problem of goal-congruent decisions under the assumption that total centralization exists. That is, the most desirable economic decision for the organization as a whole would be dictated centrally. But in situations where some degree of decentralization persists, the optimal transfer price dictated by economic analysis may be variable cost. Then, the manager of the supplying division must be offered some motivation above that minimal transfer price in order to ensure that the desired transfers do indeed occur.

How do you design a performance-evaluation (motivation) scheme that induces goal congruence when heavy interdependencies exist? Obviously, if management control systems were costless, the ideal solution would be to have a flexible (though necessarily complex) transfer-pricing policy that would ensure congruent decisions. But control systems are not costless, so simple rules tend to be used for various classes of transactions. For example, market prices may be used for some transfers and cost prices for others.

Unusual cases tend to be negotiated or settled by central management. The more opportunities and interdependencies, the more likely is the desire for central control. As transfer-pricing rules become more constraining, they represent a move toward more centralization. This move is an attempt to find some intermediate point on the graph (Exhibit 19-1) that may decrease some benefits of decentralization (those arising from giving a manager more freedom of action) but that, it is hoped, will decrease to a greater extent some costs of dysfunctional decisions until the optimal point is reached.

Alternatives to market prices

Sometimes market prices are unavailable or inappropriate or too costly to be used for transfer pricing. Let us explore other ways to set transfer prices. Nearly every version of a transfer price has some drawbacks.

full-cost bases

The use of full cost or full cost-plus is widespread. If the transfers are based on *actual* costs, the performance of the receiving divisions will bear the accumulated efficiencies or inefficiencies of other divisions not subject to their control. Transfer prices that ensure recovery of the selling division's actual costs often fail to provide an incentive to control costs; therefore, some version of *standard* or *budgeted* costs is better than actual costs.

Full or absorption standard costs may minimize the problem of inefficiency but may still lead to suboptimal decisions. For example, Division A may supply parts to Division B at a standard cost of $5 per product unit, including a charge of $3 per unit for fixed costs based on some normal activity level. (There may also be some "plus" added in a cost-plus transfer-pricing system.) Suppose A has idle capacity and B has additional processing and selling costs of $4 per unit. B can obtain additional revenue of only $8 per unit from sales to outside customers. B will refuse to buy, because its performance would worsen at the rate of $1 per unit:

		DIVISION B PERFORMANCE
Additional revenue		$8
Additional costs:		
Transfer price from A	$5	
Additional costs in B	4	9
Decrease in profit		−$1

This full-cost pricing induces goal incongruence. The entity as a whole would benefit from the transfer in the short run:

		ENTIRE COMPANY PERFORMANCE
Additional revenue		$8
Additional costs:		
A ($5 − $3)	$2	
B	4	6
Increase in profit		$2

This is a clear example of goal incongruence that is induced by a transfer price based on so-called full or average total costs. **The transfer-pricing scheme has led B to regard the fixed costs in A as variable costs.** From the viewpoint of the firm as a whole, this may lead to dysfunctional decisions in the short run.[13]

cost-plus as a synthetic market price

Despite the obvious limitations of the approach, transfer prices based on full cost, or on full cost plus some markup, are in common use. A major reason for the wide use of cost-based transfer pricing is its clarity and convenience. Moreover, the transferred product or service in question is often slightly different in quality or other characteristics from that available from outside sources. As a result, cost-plus pricing is often viewed as yielding a "satisfactory" approximation of an outside market price. Therefore, the resulting synthetic market price is regarded as a good practical substitute. The alternative—getting "actual" market prices—is perceived as being too costly for incorporating into a routine management control system.

When market prices are not available, full cost plus some markup is a defensible way to administer transfer prices that are "reasonable" in the eyes of the affected parties. For example, the Internal Revenue Service proposed using the gross profit percentage on domestic sales as the suitable gross profit percentage for international

[13]Of course, the usual caution about the "relevant" cost for pricing—whether it should be based on the short run or long run, and whether it should be variable, absorption, or some other cost—is also applicable to transfer-pricing decisions. See Chapter 11 for a discussion.

sales: "This process was accepted by the court, even though it was somewhat arbitrary, because it was not considered to have reached unreasonable results."[14]

variable cost plus lump sum

Top management often wants the buyer-division manager to make month-to-month purchasing decisions based on the variable costs of the supplier division. Otherwise, as the example in the preceding section showed, the buyer division may be led toward the wrong decision. One way to satisfy the needs of the two divisions and the company as a whole is to transfer at a standard variable cost. A separate predetermined lump-sum charge is made for fixed costs plus a lump-sum profit; this charge may be made annually or monthly. It is based on an *annual expectation,* not on actual purchases. **In any event, the buyer's month-to-month decisions are not influenced by the supplier's fixed costs or the supplier's profit.** Note that, except for the profit, this was the approach recommended in Chapter 14 for the allocation of service-department costs to production departments.

prorating the overall contribution

Recall the idle-capacity example in the earlier section "Pitfalls in Market Prices." The variable cost is $1 per unit, absorption cost is $1.50 per unit, and Division A has an average markup of 60 percent of absorption cost. Suppose that Division B can use the component in a finished product that will sell for $5 and that will entail incurring other variable costs of $3 per unit. How are goal congruence and managerial effort encouraged?

The interdependence of the two divisions regarding this product may be overtly recognized by making a centralized decision and imposing the $1 transfer price. In effect, this approach jettisons decentralization, at least for transactions in this product. Because most organizations are hybrids of centralization and decentralization anyway, this approach deserves serious consideration where such transfers are significant.

One popular solution is to impose a variable-cost transfer price but credit each division for a prorated share of the overall contribution to corporate profit. Suppose that 100,000 units were in question:

Sales of finished product @ $5		$500,000
Variable costs:		
Division A @ $1	$100,000	
Division B @ $3	300,000	400,000
Contribution to corporate profit		$100,000

The proration of the contribution would probably be negotiated in any number of ways. Suppose that it were in proportion to the standard variable costs incurred by each division. Then Division A would get credited for $25,000 and Division B for $75,000. In this way, Division A would be willing to transfer at $1, knowing that the transfers would somehow improve its showing as a profit center. Essentially, this is a standard-variable-cost-plus transfer-pricing system; the "plus" is a function of the overall contribution to corporate profit.

dual pricing

Alternatively, the seeming harshness of the foregoing authoritarian approach can be modified if organizations recognize that there is no necessity to have a *single* transfer

[14]Benke and Edwards, *Transfer Pricing,* p. 128, describing the case of *Eli Lilly and Co.* v. *U.S.,* 372 F.2d 520 (9th Cir.).

price. Decentralization can be preserved more easily if one transfer price is used for one purpose (obtaining goal congruence) and another for a second purpose (spurring managerial effort). In our example, such a dual-pricing scheme could result in the transfer price to Division B being $1, while Division A is given credit for a synthetic market price of perhaps $2.40 ($1.50 plus 60 percent). Under this scheme, each division's performance would be enhanced by the transfer, and the $1 transfer price to Division B would induce the Division B manager to make the correct economic decisions from the viewpoint of the organization as a whole. Note that this dual-pricing plan essentially gives Division A a corporate subsidy. The profit for the company as a whole will be less than the sum of the divisional profits. Suppose that 100,000 units are transferred:

DIVISION A		DIVISION B		
Sales to B @ $2.40	$240,000	Sales of finished product @ $5		$500,000
Variable costs @ $1.00	100,000	Variable costs:		
Contribution	$140,000	Division A @ $1	$100,000	
		Division B @ $3	300,000	400,000
		Contribution		$100,000

Note: as computed previously, the contribution to the corporation as a whole is only $100,000.

At first glance, dual pricing seems to be the solution to our dilemma. But it has a major weakness that may explain why it has not been used widely in practice. **The trouble is that all managers in the subunits win, but the organization as a whole may lose.** The supplier-division manager gets a high price, and the buyer-division manager gets a low price. The danger here is that both managers may tend to get too sloppy regarding cost controls within their subunits. Thus, the looseness of dual pricing may gradually induce undesirable attitudes and practices.

taxes and tariffs

Previous sections have pointed out that there is seldom a single transfer price that will meet the three motivational criteria and thus induce the desired decisions. The "correct" transfer price depends on the economic and legal circumstances and the decision at hand. We may want one transfer price for obtaining goal congruence and a second for generating managerial effort. Furthermore, the optimal price for either may differ from that employed for tax reporting or for other external requirements.

Income taxes, property taxes, and tariffs often influence the setting of transfer prices so that the firm as a whole will benefit, even though the performance of a subunit may suffer under this set of prices. To minimize tariffs and domestic income taxes, a company may want to set an unusually low selling price for a domestic division that ships goods to foreign subsidiaries in countries where the prevailing tax rates are lower. To maximize tax deductions for percentage depletion allowances (which are based on revenue), a petroleum company may want to transfer crude oil to other subunits at as high a price as possible.

Transfer pricing is also influenced in some situations because of state fair-trade laws and national antitrust acts. Because of the differences in national tax structures around the world or because of the differences in the incomes of various divisions and subsidiaries, the firm may wish to shift profits and "dump" goods if legally possible. These considerations are additional illustrations of the limits of decentralization where heavy interdependencies exist and of why the same company may use different transfer prices for different purposes. They are also illustrations of practices that have been criticized, sometimes justly and sometimes unjustly, on legal or moral grounds.

All countries, no matter how backward, are aware of companies' inclination to administer transfer prices to maximize overall corporate net income. Hence, where feasible, tax and customs authorities try to enforce transfer prices that are geared to comparable arm's-length market prices. Obviously, there is much room for dispute between companies and government authorities.[15]

Why profit centers?

In Chapter 5 the evolution of control systems in many organizations from physical observation to historical records to static budgets to flexible budgets was described as being based on an attempt to solve control problems in a cost-effective way. All of these systems are imperfect. **Given the objectives of top management, control systems are changed in a world of uncertainty with the aim of improving congruence and effort in an economically feasible way in a specific organization.**

At this point, after studying all the weaknesses of profit centers and transfer prices, readers often jump to the conclusion that organizations should stay heavily centralized and use nothing fancier than flexible budgets. However, the managerial effort criterion is a major justification for taking the step from a flexible budget to some kind of profit center. Cost centers with flexible budgets and standards have sometimes been found wanting. For instance, some cost-center managers have focused on meeting a budget and on keeping costs under control—and nothing more. When the cost centers are transformed into profit centers, managers may continue to care about costs, but they may give new attention to production schedules and important marketing factors. Top managers have sometimes found that pep talks and cajoling do not get subordinates to accept top-management goals. Instead, giving profit responsibility works better because it crystallizes goals and encourages more effort. **That is, goal congruence may exist in a vague, halfhearted fashion, but profit centers provide the formal system that is so often the most persuasive means of communicating top management's goals and boosting effort.**

Professors and managers can spend hours delineating the weaknesses of profit centers and transfer-pricing schemes, especially when the managers have little local autonomy. Nevertheless, despite their many defects, profit centers may often be the most cost-effective way to obtain the desired goal congruence and managerial effort.

Accounting entries for transfers

Transfer pricing is governed by managerial goals, including measuring divisional performance, minimizing taxes, and controlling the rate of return. These objectives often lead to transfers at prices in excess of the conventional inventory costs used for external reporting.

Accounting for market-based transfer prices provides another illustration of how current accounting systems are being designed primarily to aid managerial planning and control rather than to serve the need for external financial reports. After all, from the viewpoint of the consolidated enterprise, any goods or services transferred within the enterprise and not yet sold to outsiders should be carried at cost. Thus,

---

[15]For expanded discussions, see Benke and Edwards, *Transfer Pricing,* Chap. 6; and Anthony and Dearden, *Management Control Systems,* Chap. 14.

although intracompany transfers may be accounted for and reported in any manner that helps achieve managerial goals, intracompany margins must be eliminated periodically when consolidated financial statements are prepared.

The basic approach may be illustrated as follows:

Whole Company has two divisions, A and B. Goods having a manufacturing cost of $100 are transferred from A to B at a price of $135. Entries follow:

on books of supplier division A		
Accounts receivable—Division B	135	
Sales to Division B		135
Cost of goods sold (transferred)	100	
Inventory—Division A		100

on books of receiving division B		
Inventory—Division B	135	
Accounts payable—Division A		135

An examination of the entries above shows that essentially the two divisions operate as separate companies. However, if the Whole Company had to prepare consolidated financial statements immediately after the transaction, the following eliminating entries would be needed:

Accounts payable—Division A	135	
Accounts receivable—Division B		135
To eliminate intracompany receivable and payable.		
Sales to Division B	135	
Cost of goods sold (transferred)		100
Intracompany gross profit—A		35
To close and recognize Division A's intracompany gross profit.		
Intracompany gross profit—A	35	
Inventory—Division B		35
To eliminate intracompany gross profit.		

These eliminating entries result in the Whole Company showing no accounts receivable, no sales, and the inventory of transferred goods at its manufacturing cost. The entries remind us that transfer pricing fundamentally is nothing more than a means for allocating costs among the subparts of an entity.

SUMMARY

Transfer-pricing systems deserve careful attention if decentralization is to be established in companies whose divisions exchange goods and services. A transfer-pricing system must be judged in relation to its impact on (a) goal congruence, (b) managerial effort (evaluation of performance is the key), and (c) autonomy. Some version of market price as a transfer price will usually best motivate managers toward optimal economic decisions; moreover, the evaluation of performance will then be consistent with the ideas of decentralization.

There is rarely a single transfer price that will serve all needs. Instead, there may be one transfer price for making a particular production decision, another for evaluating performance, and another for minimizing tariffs or income taxes.

Economic analysis can demonstrate that market price is not always the best guide to optimal decisions. In such instances, some centralization of control may be desired to prevent dysfunctional decisions. If so, serious thought should be given to whether profit centers and decentralization provide the optimum organizational design. Above all, the perceived costs and benefits at alternative levels of decentralization should be explicitly considered when choosing a transfer-pricing scheme.

Profit centers usually accompany decentralization, but one can exist without the other. The desirability of a profit center versus a cost center should be judged by their predicted relative impacts on collective decisions.

SUGGESTED READINGS

See the end of the next chapter and the footnotes in this chapter.

PROBLEM FOR SELF-STUDY

problem

A transportation equipment manufacturer, the Pillercat Corporation, is heavily decentralized. Each division head has full authority on all decisions regarding sales to internal or external customers. Division P has always acquired a certain equipment component from Division S. However, when informed that Division S was increasing its unit price to $220, Division P's management decided to purchase the component from outside suppliers at a price of $200.

Division S had recently acquired some specialized equipment that was used primarily to make this component. Juan Gomez, the manager, cited the resulting high depreciation charges as the justification for the price boost. He asked the president of the company to instruct Division P to buy from S at the $220 price. He supplied the following information:

P's annual purchases of component, in units	2,000
S's variable costs per unit	$ 190
S's fixed costs per unit	$ 20

1. Suppose there are no alternative uses for the S facilities. Will the company as a whole benefit if P buys from the outside suppliers for $200 per unit? Show computations.
2. Suppose internal facilities of S would not otherwise be idle. The equipment and other facilities would be assigned to other production operations and would result in annual cash-operating savings of $29,000. Should P purchase from outsiders?
3. Suppose there are no alternative uses for S's internal facilities and that the selling price of outsiders drops $15. Should P purchase from outsiders?
4. What rule would you favor for setting transfer prices in the Pillercat Corporation?
5. As the president, how would you respond to the request of the manager of S? Would your response differ according to the specific situations described in parts 1–3 above? Why?

solution

1–3. The analyses of the first three parts are summarized below (in thousands of dollars):

	(1)	(2)	(3)
Total purchase costs from outsider	400	400	370
Total outlay costs if kept inside	380	380	380
Total opportunity costs if kept inside	—	29	—
Total relevant inside costs	380	409	380
Net advantage (disadvantage) to company as a whole from buying inside	20	(9)	(10)

4. Of course, in part 1, if the manager of S understood cost-volume-profit relationships, and if he wanted to maximize his short-run net income, he would probably accept a price of \$200. This would bring a contribution to the divisional profit of 2,000 × (\$200 − \$190), or \$20,000. The information given indicates that the best rule might be a market price with the seller having the option to refuse to sell internally. This would have led to the correct decision from the viewpoint of both the divisions and the company as a whole.

In situation 1, S would obtain a contribution of \$200 − \$190, or \$10 per unit. In 2, S would lose a contribution of \$10 per unit, or \$20,000; but its \$29,000 cost saving on other work would lead to a net saving of \$9,000, or \$4.50 per unit. In 3, S would lose \$5 per unit, or \$10,000, if the business were bought inside.

5. As president, I probably would not want to become immersed in these disputes. If arbitration is necessary, it should probably be conducted by some other officer on the corporate staff. One possibility is to have the immediate line boss of the two managers make a decision.

If decentralization is to be strictly adhered to, the arbitrator should probably do nothing under any of the conditions described. If no forced transfer were made, P would go outside, resulting in an optimal decision for the overall company in parts 2 and 3 but not in part 1.

Suppose in part 1 that S refuses to meet the price of \$200. This means that the company will be \$20,000 worse off in the short run. Should top management interfere and force a transfer at \$200? This would undercut the philosophy of decentralization. Many managers would not interfere because they would view the \$20,000 as the price that has to be paid for mistakes made under decentralization. But how high must this price go before the temptation to interfere would be irresistible? \$30,000? \$40,000? How much?

In sum, the point of this question is that any superstructure that interferes with lower-level decision making weakens decentralization. Of course, such interference may occasionally be necessary to prevent horrendous blunders. But recurring interference and constraints simply transform a decentralized organization into a centralized organization. Indeed, the trade-offs among goal congruence, managerial effort, and autonomy may justify more centralization in many instances.

Despite the intuitive attractions of market price, the chapter contains illustrations where market price will not lead to optimal decisions. For example, sometimes the adherence by a supplying division to a high market price despite having low variable costs may force the consuming division not to buy even though the company as a whole would benefit.

Note that the "general rule" described in the chapter also might be applied, although it frequently might be subject to suspicion because it seems more awkward than the "market-price" rule. Also, as Case 1 below shows, the goal-congruent decision may be obvious at a transfer price of \$190, but the S manager has no particular motivation to favor transfer:

TRANSFER PRICE	=	OUTLAY COST	+	OPPORTUNITY COST		
1.	=	\$190	+	0	=	\$190
2.	=	\$190	+	(\$29,000 ÷ 2,000)	=	\$204.50
3.	=	\$190	+	0	=	\$190

P would buy inside in Case 1 and outside in 2 and 3; these decisions would provide goal congruence for the company as a whole.

Terms to Learn

autonomy ***decentralization*** ***dysfunctional decision making***
goal congruence ***managerial effort*** ***outlay cost*** ***profit center***
transfer price

Special Points and Pitfalls

Transfer prices convey information that often affects many critical decisions concerning the acquisition and allocation of an organization's resources, just as prices in the entire economy affect decisions concerning the allocation of a nation's resources. Ideally, transfer prices should guide managers to choose inputs and outputs in coordination with other subunits so as to maximize the profits of the organization as a whole. The three motivational criteria (goal congruence, managerial effort, and autonomy) provide insights when designing and judging a transfer-pricing system.

Do not confuse *profit center* and *decentralized subunit.* They are not synonyms. For example, a factory may have heavily decentralized management even though it is a cost center rather than a profit center. Similarly, the managers of some profit centers, such as a unit in a chain of grocery stores, may have little latitude in making decisions.

Appendix 19: economic analysis of transfer pricing

Transfer pricing is analyzed in depth in the literature of economics and management science. A long series of individual situations may be analyzed, including various combinations of intermediate and final markets, availabilities of capacity, and interdependencies of costs and demands. This appendix will limit the discussion to two situations as examples of the analysis.

In the first example, suppose a firm has a vertically integrated operation with two divisions, manufacturing and distribution. Assume further that the two divisions are cost-independent, so that the operations of either have no effect on the cost functions of the other. Also assume that there is no market whatsoever for the intermediate product.

To optimize overall firm profits, both divisions must agree on the quantity to be produced of the intermediate product. The optimal output and price will be where firm marginal cost (MC) per unit of intermediate product equals marginal revenue (MR) per unit of intermediate product, as Exhibit 19-2 demonstrates.

MC is the sum of the marginal manufacturing cost (mmc) in the first division and the marginal distribution cost (mdc) in the second division. If the transfer price is p^*, the second-division manager will choose an output level of q_d, so that $MR = p^* + mdc = MC^*$. In turn, the first-division manager would independently choose an output level of q_m, so that $mmc = p^*$. The transfer price p^* should, therefore, be set so that $q_d = q_m$; that is, so the two divisions operate at the same level.

Hirshleifer comments:

> There are a variety of ways in which the optimum solution might be arrived at operationally. Some device like a neutral umpire might be employed to set an initial trial p^*—after which the divisions would respond by declaring tentative outputs q_m and

EXHIBIT 19-2

Best Joint Level of Output

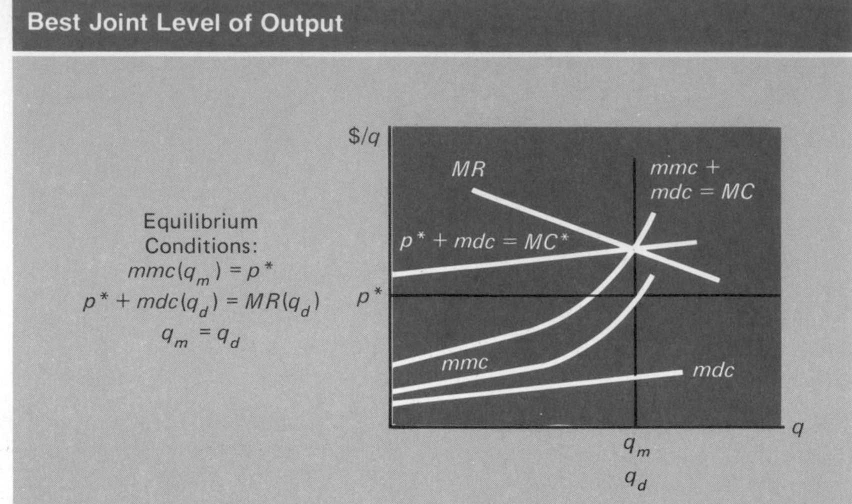

Source: This and the next exhibit are from Jack Hirshleifer, "Internal Pricing and Decentralized Decisions," in C. Bonini, R. Jaedicke, and H. Wagner, eds., Management Controls. New Directions in Basic Research (New York: McGraw-Hill, 1964) pp., 31, 33.

q_d. If q_m exceeds q_d, the p^* should be adjusted downward by the umpire, and the reverse if q_d exceeds q_m—until a p^* is found such that the planned outputs are coordinated.[16]

But coordination cannot be ensured by counting on the independent decisions of the division managers. Each is in a monopolistic position. The first division is inclined to limit supply and generate more profit for itself at the expense of the overall firm. The second division is inclined to behave in the opposite way, but with a similar impact on overall profits.

Note that gamesmanship is likely. Either party may give inaccurate responses to a neutral umpire with the hope of attaining a more favorable price. The forcing of transfers at marginal cost will not be welcomed by the manager of the first division. There is an obvious conflict between the notion of what ordinarily constitutes revenue for profit centers and of what transfer price leads to optimal economic decisions. In this situation, the first division would operate at a loss at all times. Systems of subsidies or taxes have been suggested as remedies for this weakness.[17]

---

[16]Jack Hirshleifer, "Internal Pricing and Decentralized Decisions," in C. Bonini, R. Jaedicke, and H. Wagner, eds., *Management Controls: New Directions in Basic Research* (New York: McGraw-Hill, 1964), p. 30. Hirshleifer's work is the basis for the presentation here. Joshua Ronen and George McKinney, in "Transfer Pricing for Divisional Autonomy," *Journal of Accounting Research,* 8, No. 1 (Spring 1970), 103, suggest an alternative method of supplying information, which might be less restrictive than the Hirshleifer method. Also recommended is Solomons, *Divisional Performance,* pp. 160–232.

[17]Linear programming and decomposition procedures have also been proposed as ways to ensure goal congruence and incentive. Both propose elaborate models that cannot work successfully without exhaustive information about the revenue and cost functions of many divisions. All the necessary conditions lead to the conclusion that centralized decision making may be more cost effective than the use of such models. See W. J. Baumol and Tibor Fabian, "Decomposition, Pricing for Decentralization and External Economics," *Management Science* 11, No. 1, pp. 1–32; and Jerome E. Hass, "Transfer Pricing in a Decentralized Firm," *Management Science: Application,* 14, No. 6, pp. B-310 through B-331.

EXHIBIT 19-3

Imperfectly Competitive Market for Intermediate Product

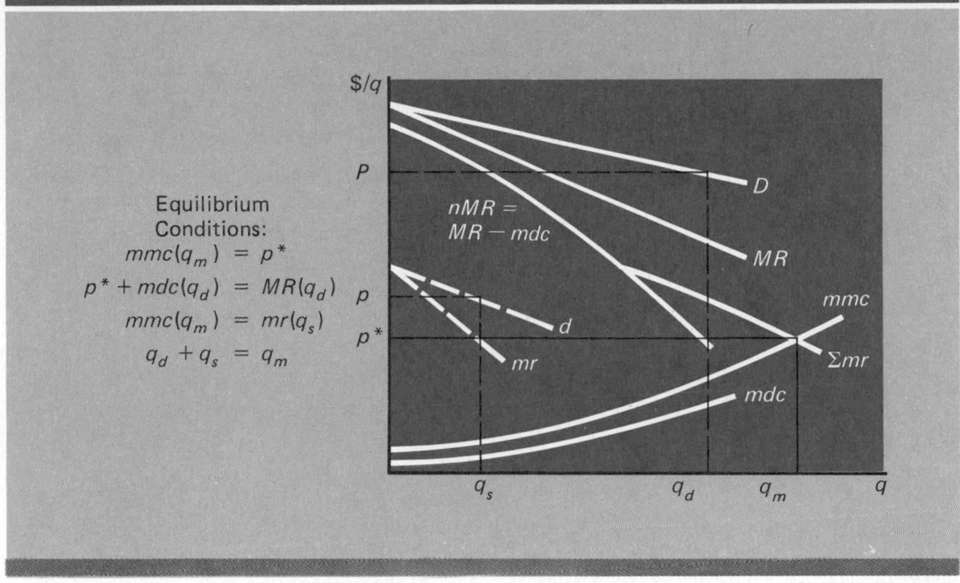

In the second example, assume that there is an imperfectly competitive external market for the intermediate product, so that the marginal cost of Division 1, *mmc,* is less than the prevailing market price, *p*. Therefore, Division 1 is a monopoly. Assume further that there is demand independence; that is, that additional internal sales do not affect external demands. To illustrate, in some cases a refinery selling unbranded gasoline to an affiliated distributor does not expect an adverse effect on the final demand for its branded gasoline. Under these conditions, the overall profit of the firm would be optimized by monopolistic exploitation of outside customers for both the intermediate and final products, but not of the internal intermediate customer.

As Exhibit 19-3 shows, the overall profit of the firm is optimized by having the prices for internal intermediate customers lower than prices for outsiders. In the exhibit, *D* and *d* are demands of outsiders and *P* and *p* are prices to outsiders. The equilibrium value for the internal price $p^* = mmc = mr$, where *mr* is the marginal revenue from selling to the intermediate external market. Note that the external price *p* exceeds p^*. A neutral umpire would set p^* so that q_m, the total intermediate quantity manufactured (which is the sum of q_s, the quantity sold to outside intermediate customers, plus q_d, the quantity incorporated in the product sold to final outside customers), provides optimal profits for the firm as a whole.

Hirshleifer comments on the analysis in Exhibit 19-3 as follows:

> The solution is found analytically by a price discrimination technique—in which *mmc* is equated simultaneously with marginal revenue, *mr*, in the external intermediate market (thus determining external intermediate sales, q_s), and with $MR - mdc$ (which we denote *net marginal revenue, nMR*) for the internal customer, thus making $mmc + mdc = MR$ and determining optimal output q_d in the final external market.[18]

[18]Hirshleifer, "Internal Pricing," p. 34. Later, when discussing the case of interdependent demands for the intermediate and final products, he stresses that internal transfers at marginal cost now entail loss of profitable sales at full price. "So the rule of marginal-cost pricing to internal customers no longer applies—unless marginal cost is redefined to include the loss of external profit."

19-1 What three motivational criteria are applicable to transfer pricing?

19-2 "Transfer pricing is confined to profit centers." Do you agree? Why?

19-3 When does imperfect competition exist?

19-4 Why are intracompany transfer prices often necessary?

19-5 What are two major bases for pricing intracompany transfers?

19-6 What is the major limitation to transfer prices based on cost?

19-7 Where reliable market prices cannot be ascertained for transfer pricing, what is the impact on divisional-performance measurement?

19-8 What is the most common example in transfer pricing of a clash between divisional action and overall company profitability?

19-9 If an optimal economic decision is wanted in a particular situation, what is a general rule for transfer pricing?

19-10 What is outlay cost in the context of transfer pricing?

19-11 Why is market price as a basis for transfer pricing a special case rather than a universal guide?

19-12 ***Transfer pricing in an automobile dealership.*** A large automobile dealership is installing a responsibility-accounting system and three profit centers: parts and service; new vehicles; and used vehicles. Each department manager has been told to run his shop as if he were in business for himself. However, there are interdepartmental dealings. For example:

a. The parts and service department prepares new cars for final delivery and repairs used cars prior to resale.

b. The used-car department's major source of inventory has been cars traded in as part payment for new cars.

The owner of the dealership has asked you to draft a company policy statement on transfer pricing, together with specific rules to be applied to the examples cited. He has told you that clarity is of paramount importance because your statement will be relied upon for settling transfer-pricing disputes.

19-13 ***Variable cost as a transfer price.*** A product's variable cost is $1 and its market value is $2 at a transfer point from Division S to Division P. Division P's variable cost of processing the product further is $1.25, and the selling price of the final product is $2.75.

REQUIRED

1. Prepare a tabulation of the contribution margin per unit for Division P performance and overall performance under the two alternatives of (a) processing further and (b) selling to outsiders at the transfer point.
2. As Division P manager, which alternative would you choose? Explain.

19-14 ***Transfer pricing.*** (D. Kleespie) The Gare Nord Corporation is decentralized in its organizational structure. It uses responsibility accounting and investment centers for performance measurement of its divisional managers. During a recent month the following situation arose in the Lyon Division of the Gare Nord Corporation.

The Lyon Division produces "widgets" that it usually sells to external customers. Current cost and revenue data of the Lyon Division are as follows:

Variable manufacturing cost per widget	$40
Fixed manufacturing cost per widget (based on capacity operations)	$ 5
Selling price per widget to external customers	$60
Plant capacity in units	20,000 widgets

The Midi Division (another division of Gare Nord Corporation) would like to purchase 4,000 widgets from the Lyon Division. Midi Division is currently buying these units from an outside supplier at a cost of $58 per unit and has offered to pay this price to the Lyon Division. The Lyon Division has ample excess capacity to handle all of the Midi Division requirement as well as serve its regular customers.

REQUIRED

Show computations.

1. Assume that the Lyon Division refuses to accept the offer of $58 from the Midi Division. The operating income of Gare Nord Corporation as a whole would be higher (lower) by how much?
2. Assume instead that the Lyon Division is currently selling all of its output (plant capacity of 20,000 units) to external customers. If the Lyon Division is ordered by top management to sell the 4,000 units to the Midi Division, the operating income of Gare Nord Corporation would be higher (lower) by how much?
3. Assuming ample excess capacity is available, what is the minimum price per unit that the Lyon Division should be willing to accept from the Midi Division such that the Gare Nord operating income would be unaffected?

19-15 ***Transfer pricing.*** The Plastics Company has a separate division that produces a special molding powder. For the past three years about two-thirds of the output has been sold to another division within the company. The remainder has been sold to outsiders. Last year's operating data follow:

	TO OTHER DIVISION		TO OUTSIDERS	
Sales	10,000 T. @ $70*	$700,000	5,000 T. @ $100	$500,000
Variable costs @ $50		$500,000		$250,000
Fixed costs		150,000		75,000
Total costs		$650,000		$325,000
Gross margin		$ 50,000		$175,000

**The $70 price is ordinarily determined by the outside sales price less selling and administrative expenses wholly applicable to outside business.*

The buying-division manager has a chance to get a firm contract with an outside supplier at $65 for the ensuing year.

REQUIRED

Assume that the molding-powder division manager says that he cannot sell at $65 because no margin can be earned. As the buying-division manager, write a short reply. Assume that the 10,000 tons cannot be sold by the molding-powder division to other customers.

19-16 ***Transfer-pricing dispute.*** Allison-Chambers Corp., manufacturer of tractors and other heavy farm equipment, is organized along decentralized lines, with each manufacturing division operating as a separate profit center. Each division head has been delegated full authority on all decisions involving the sale of his division's output both to outsiders and to other divisions of Allison-Chambers. Division C has in the past always purchased its requirement of a particular tractor-engine component from Division A. However, when informed that Division A was increasing its price to $150, Division C's management decided to purchase the engine component from outside suppliers.

The component can be purchased by C for $135 on the open market. Division A insists that owing to the recent installation of some highly specialized equipment and the resulting high depreciation charges, A would not be able to make an adequate profit on its investment unless it raised its price. A's management appealed to top management of Allison-Chambers for support in its dispute with C and supplied the following operating data:

C's annual purchases of tractor-engine component	1,000
A's variable costs per unit of tractor-engine component	$120
A's fixed costs per unit of tractor-engine component	$ 20

REQUIRED

1. Assume that there are no alternative uses for internal facilities. Determine whether the company as a whole will benefit if Division C purchases the component from outside suppliers for $135 per unit.
2. Assume that internal facilities of A would not otherwise be idle. By not producing the 1,000 units for C, A's equipment and other facilities would be assigned to other

production operations and would result in annual cash-operating savings of $18,000. Should C purchase from outsiders?

3. Assume that there are no alternative uses for A's internal facilities and that the price of outsiders drops $20. Should C purchase from outsiders?

19-17 ***Transfer-pricing problem.*** Assume in the Allison-Chambers Corp. problem that Division A could sell the 1,000 units to other customers at $155 per unit with variable selling costs of $5 per unit. If this were the case, determine whether Allison-Chambers would benefit if C purchased the 1,000 components from outsiders at $135 per unit.

19-18 ***Pricing and lack of information.*** Company X has more than 100 divisions, including A, B, and H. Division A wants to buy a component for its final product. Two outside bids have been received, one for $200 and one for $212. The supplier who bid $212 will in turn buy some raw materials for $30 from Division H, which has spare capacity, that will increase H's contribution to overall company profits by $20 ($30 revenue minus $10 outlay costs). The supplier who bids $200 will not buy any raw materials from Company X.

REQUIRED

1. Prepare a diagram of the cash flows for both alternatives. Does the use of the external market prices lead to optimal decision for the company as a whole? Explain.
2. Suppose Division B is working at full capacity and can provide the needed part to A or to an outside buyer at the same price of $212. (For convenience, we now assume that $212 is the uniform market price.) If market price were the rule, B would have to meet the $212 bid. Assume that the outlay costs to B of filling the order were $150. Finally, assume that B, unlike the outside supplier, does not buy from H because this conglomerate organization is so large and communications are so bad that the B manager is unaware of this alternative. Will the use of $212 as a transfer price lead to optimal decisions for the firm as a whole? Apply the "general rule" as described in the chapter. Will the resulting transfer price lead to optimal decisions for the firm as a whole?

19-19 ***Conflict of interests of profit centers and company as a whole.*** (This and the next problem are adapted from David Solomons, *Divisional Performance: Measurement and Control* [New York: Richard D. Irwin, 1968, pp. 167–79].) Division A of a company is the only source of supply for an intermediate product that is converted by Division B into a salable final product. Most of A's costs are fixed. For any output up to 1,000 units per day, its total costs are $500 per day. Total costs increase by $100 per day for every additional thousand units made. Division A judges that its own results will be optimized if it sets its price at 40¢ per unit, and it acts accordingly.

Division B incurs additional costs in converting the intermediate product supplied by A into a finished product. These costs are $1,250 for any output up to 1,000 units, and $250 per thousand for outputs in excess of 1,000. On the revenue side, B can increase its revenue only by spending more on sales promotion and by reducing selling prices. Its sales forecast is:

SALES IN UNITS	NET REVENUE PER THOUSAND UNITS
1,000	$1,750.00
2,000	1,325.00
3,000	1,100.00
4,000	925.00
5,000	800.00
6,000	666.67

REQUIRED

1. Prepare a schedule comparing B's costs, including its purchases from A, revenues, and net income at various levels of output.
2. What is B's maximum net income? At that level, what is A's net income? At that level, what is the corporation's aggregate net income?
3. Suppose the company abandons its divisionalized structure. Instead of being two profit centers, A and B are combined into a single profit center with responsibility for the complete production and marketing of the product. Prepare a schedule

similar to that in requirement 1. What volume level will provide the most net income?

4. Evaluate the results in requirement 3. Why did the circumstances in requirement 1 lead to less net income than in requirement 3? How would you adjust the transfer-pricing policy to ensure that overall company net income will be maximized where separate profit centers A and B are maintained?

19-20 ***Transfer prices in an imperfect market.*** Division A is the supplier division and Divisions B and C are the consumer divisions of a large company. After Division B deducts its own processing costs, the total net revenue and the marginal net revenue it derives from various quantities of intermediate product are:

Division B

QUANTITY OF INTERMEDIATE PROCESSED, IN POUNDS	TOTAL NET REVENUE	MARGINAL NET REVENUE
1,000	$ 600	$600
2,000	900	300
3,000	1,100	200
4,000	1,200	100

Similarly, for Division C we have:

Division C

QUANTITY OF INTERMEDIATE PROCESSED, IN POUNDS	TOTAL NET REVENUE	MARGINAL NET REVENUE
2,000	$1,200	$ —
3,000	1,800	600
4,000	2,100	300
5,000	2,300	200
6,000	2,400	100

Division A, the producing division, faces the following cost conditions:

Division A

QUANTITY OF INTERMEDIATE PRODUCED, IN POUNDS	TOTAL COST	MARGINAL COST
4,000	$2,000	$ —
5,000	2,100	100
6,000	2,250	150
7,000	2,425	175
8,000	2,625	200
9,000	2,925	300
10,000	3,325	400

What transfer price should be set for A's output? Why?

19-21 ***The pertinent transfer price.*** The XYZ Company has two divisions, A and B. For one of the company's products, Division A produces a major subassembly and Division B incorporates this subassembly into the final product. There is a market for both the subassembly and the final product, and the divisions have been delegated profit responsibility. The transfer price for the subassembly has been set at long-run average market price.

The following data are available to each division:

Estimated selling price for final product	$300
Long-run average selling price for intermediate product	200
Outlay cost for completion in Division B	150
Outlay cost in Division A	120

The manager of Division B has made the following calculation:

Selling price—final product		$300
Transferred-in cost (market)	$200	
Outlay cost for completion	150	350
Contribution (loss) on product		$ (50)

REQUIRED

1. Should transfers be made to Division B if there is no excess capacity in Division A? Is market price the correct transfer price?
2. Assume that Division A's maximum capacity for this product is 1,000 units per month and sales to the intermediate market are now 800 units. Should 200 units be transferred to Division B? At what relevant transfer price? Assume for a variety of reasons that A will maintain the $200 selling price indefinitely; that is, A is not considering cutting the price to outsiders regardless of the presence of idle capacity.
3. Suppose A quoted a transfer price of $150 for up to 200 units. What would be the contribution to the firm as a whole if the transfer were made? As manager of B, would you be inclined to buy at $150?

19-22 ***Pricing in imperfect markets.*** Refer to Problem 19-21.

1. Suppose the manager of A has the option of (a) cutting the external price to $195 with the certainty that sales will rise to 1,000 units or (b) maintaining the outside price of $200 for the 800 units and transferring the 200 units to B at some price that would produce the same income for A. What transfer price would produce the same income for A? Does that price coincide with that produced by the "general rule" in the chapter, so that the desirable decision for the company as a whole would ensue?

2. Suppose that if the selling price for the intermediate product is dropped to $195, outside sales can be increased to 900 units. Division B wants to acquire as many as 200 units if the transfer price is acceptable. For simplicity assume that there is absolutely no outside market for the final 100 units of Division A capacity.

a. Using the "general rule," what is (are) the relevant transfer price(s) that should lead to the correct economic decision? Ignore performance evaluation (incentive) considerations.

b. Compare the total contributions under the alternatives to show why the transfer price(s) recommended lead(s) to the optimal economic decision.

19-23 ***Market prices and transfers.*** (SMA) The Caplow Company is a multidivisional company, and its managers have been delegated full profit responsibility and complete autonomy to accept or reject transfers from other divisions. Division A produces a subassembly with a ready competitive market. This subassembly is currently used by Division B for a final product that is sold outside at $1,200. Division A charges Division B market price for the subassembly, which is $700 per unit. Variable costs are $520 and $600 for Divisions A and B, respectively.

The manager of Division B feels that Division A should transfer the subassembly at a lower price than market because at this price, Division B is unable to make a profit.

REQUIRED

1. Compute Division B's profit contribution if transfers are made at the market price, and also the total contribution to profit for the company.
2. Assume that Division A can sell all its production in the open market. Should Division A transfer goods to Division B? If so, at what price?
3. Assume that Division A can sell in the open market only 500 units at $700 per unit, out of the 1,000 units that it can produce every month, and that a 20 percent reduction in price is necessary to sell full capacity. Should transfers be made? If so, how many units should it transfer and at what price? Submit a schedule showing comparisons of contribution margins under three different alternatives to support your decision.

19-24 ***Sears transfer pricing.*** Sears, Roebuck & Co. is the world's largest retailer of general merchandise. Until the late 1970s, Sears employed an unusual transfer-pricing practice. It centered on an overbilling account, which was called the 599 account.

A central buyer would purchase an ashtray for $1. In turn, a store manager would be charged $1.20. The extra 20 cents would go into the kitty called the 599 account. The rate of overbilling ranged from 10 to 20 percent, averaging 15 percent.

The 599 account was originally established in the 1930s as a small mechanism to help Sears adjust retail prices and absorb markdowns. In this way, store managers would not bear markdowns on their performance report.

The 599 account began to grow drastically in the 1960s. It soared to $1 billion in the late 1970s, a considerable amount in comparison with annual sales of $15 billion. The account was used for national advertising and a variety of other purposes. Markdowns, however, were the major use of the account.

Sears abandoned the 599 account because it was not helping managers make desirable decisions.

REQUIRED

1. Suppose a store manager routinely doubled the store's cost of ashtrays to set regular selling prices. Prepare a tabulation that would show the store's profit and the company's profit if an ashtray could be sold (a) without a markdown and (b) with a markdown of 40 cents.
2. Describe the likely impact of the 599 account on the behavior of the buyers and the store managers.
3. How would the abandonment of the 599 account affect behavior?

19-25 ***Utilization of capacity.*** (J. Patell) The California Instrument Company (CIC) consists of the semiconductor division and the minicomputer division, each of which operates as an independent profit center. The semiconductor division employs craftsmen who produce two different electronic components, the new high-performance Super-chip and an older product called Okay-chip. These two products have the following cost characteristics:

	SUPER-CHIP		OKAY-CHIP	
Material	Parts	$ 2	Parts	$1
Labor	2 hours @ $14	28	½ hour @ $14	7

Annual overhead in the semiconductor division totals $400,000, all fixed. Owing to the high skill level necessary for the craftsmen, the semiconductor division's capacity is set at 50,000 hours per year.

To date, only one customer has developed a product utilizing Super-chip, and this customer orders a maximum of 15,000 Super-chips per year, at a price of $60 per chip. If CIC cannot meet his entire demand, the customer curtails his own production. The rest of the semiconductor division's capacity is devoted to Okay-chip, for which there is unlimited demand at $12 per chip.

The minicomputer division produces only one product, a process-control unit, which requires a complex circuit board imported from Sweden at a price of $60. The control unit's costs are:

	CONTROL UNIT	
Material	Circuit board	$60
	Other parts	8
Labor	5 hours @ $10	50

The minicomputer division is composed of only a small assembly plant, and all overhead is fixed at a total of $80,000 per year. The current market price for the control unit is $140 per unit.

A joint research project has just revealed that with minor modifications, a single Super-chip could be substituted for the circuit board currently used by the minicomputer division. The modification would require an extra 1 hour of labor by minicomputer's staff, for a new total of 6 hours per control unit. Minicomputer has therefore asked semiconductor to declare a transfer price at which the semiconductor division would sell Super-chip internally.

REQUIRED

1. Minicomputer expects to sell 5,000 control units this year. From the overall viewpoint of California Instruments, how many Super-chips should be transferred to minicomputer to replace circuit boards?

2. If demand for the control unit is sure to be 5,000 units, but its *price is uncertain,* what should the transfer price of Super-chip be to ensure proper decisions? (All other data unchanged.)
3. If demand for the control unit rises to 12,000 units at a price of $140 per unit, how many of the 12,000 units should be built using Super-chip? (All other data unchanged.)

19-26 ***Transfer pricing in banks.*** The Jackson Stone National Bank is a two-branch bank servicing retail and wholesale customers in the greater Big City metropolitan area. The head-office staff consists of the president and the controller. With minor exceptions, the branch managers are permitted to conduct their affairs like the heads of two independent banks. The planning and control system centers on branch income statements prepared by the controller.

The Big City branch, located in the growing downtown area, serves primarily commercial customers. The manager, Mr. Jones, has found in recent years that while he faces a number of vigorous competitors, the principal constraint on his ability to generate new loan business is a lack of supporting deposits. The *only* alternative source of lendable funds is the purchase of Eurodollars, which are dollar deposits held in a bank outside the United States. This option is considered less than acceptable by Jones, as the 22 percent interest he would have to pay for such funds is higher than the rate he is able to charge loan customers, currently 20 percent.

The new Sun City branch, on the other hand, is located outside of town in a large and growing retirement community and is primarily a retail branch. Mr. Smith, the manager, is in his first year with the Stone Bank. In his attempts to sell the bank's services to the Sun City residents, he has found that his only success is in the area of savings deposits. Loan business, on the other hand, is both competitive and scarce. The interest rate he can charge is constrained by the fact that the manager of the local branch of the Behemoth Bank, while not actively soliciting loan business, is apparently charging rates below the prevailing Big City prime rate. Additionally, there seems to be a fundamental resistance on the part of the Sun City residents to the idea of borrowing, even at the 12 percent rates Smith has been offering. In spite of his frequent lectures on the merits of leverage, the best Smith has been able to do is to generate a few golf-cart installment and Social Security check receivable loans. As a result, he finds himself with substantial excess savings deposits on which he is paying 10 percent interest but earning nothing. Aside from the deposits, which he has to keep in the vault to satisfy the government's 20 percent (of deposits) reserve requirement, the vault additionally contains excess lendable funds equal to almost 70 percent of total savings deposits. The controller has suggested that he lend these funds to Jones at the Big City branch. This was acceptable to both managers, although some disagreement arose as to the interest rate appropriate for such a loan. The argument was finally settled by the controller, who indicated that the theoretically correct rate was the rate Smith was paying on savings deposits, 10 percent. It has been further agreed that if Smith could find additional loans, any or all of the funds lent to Jones would be returned.

REQUIRED

1. Evaluate the 10 percent interbranch loan rate, and suggest appropriate changes in relation to the following criteria:
   a. Motivating managers to act in a manner consistent with the best interests of the bank as a whole
   b. Evaluating the performance of individual *branches*
2. Would your answer change if the Sun City loan rate were to rise to 14 percent, while all other rates, as well as the level of loan demand at Sun City, remained the same?
3. Would your answer change if all rates were the same as in requirement 1 except that the cost of Eurodollars dropped to 18 percent?
4. Based on your answers to the questions above, what general statements can you make about the interbranch loan rate appropriate for evaluating individual *managers?*

19-27 ***Paper company.*** (Copyright 1981 by the President and Fellows of Harvard College. Reproduced by permission.) "If I were to price these boxes any lower than $480 a thousand," said Mr. Brunner, manager of Birch Paper Company's Thompson division,

"I'd be countermanding my order of last month for our salesmen to stop shaving their bids and to bid full-cost quotations. I've been trying for weeks to improve the quality of our business, and if I turn around now and accept this job at $430 or $450 or something less than $480 I'll be tearing down this program I've been working so hard to build up. The division can't very well show a profit by putting in bids which don't even cover a fair share of overhead costs, let alone give us a profit."

Birch Paper Company was a medium-sized, partly integrated paper company, producing white and kraft papers and paperboard. A portion of its paperboard output was converted into corrugated boxes by the Thompson division, which also printed and colored the outside surface of the boxes. Including Thompson, the company had four producing divisions and a timberland division which supplied part of the company's pulp requirements.

For several years each division had been judged independently on the basis of its profit and return on investment. Top management had been working to gain effective results from a policy of decentralizing responsibility and authority for all decisions but those relating to overall company policy. The company's top officials felt that in the past few years the concept of decentralization had been successfully applied and that the company's profits and competitive position had definitely improved.

In early 19_7 the Northern division designed a special display box for one of its papers in conjunction with the Thompson division, which was equipped to make the box. Thompson's package design and development staff spent several months perfecting the design, production methods, and materials that were to be used. Because of the unusual color and shape these were far from standard. According to an agreement between the two divisions, the Thompson division was reimbursed by the Northern division for the cost of its design and development work.

When the specifications were all prepared, the Northern division asked for bids on the box from the Thompson division and from two outside companies. Each division manager was normally free to buy from whichever supplier he wished, and even on sales within the company, divisions were expected to meet the going market price if they wanted the business.

In early 19_7 the profit margins of converters such as the Thompson division were being squeezed. Thompson, as did many other similar converters, bought its board, liner, or paper and its function was to print, cut, and shape it into boxes. Though it bought most of its materials from other Birch divisions, most of Thompson's sales were to outside customers. If Thompson got the business, it would probably buy the linerboard and corrugating medium from the Southern division of Birch. The walls of a corrugated box consist of outside and inside sheets of linerboard sandwiching the fluted corrugating medium. About 70 percent of Thompson's out-of-pocket cost of $400 represented the cost of linerboard and corrugating medium. Though Southern had been running below capacity and had excess inventory, it quoted the market price, which had not noticeably weakened as a result of the oversupply. Its out-of-pocket costs on both liner and corrugating medium were about 60 percent of the selling price.

The Northern division received bids on the boxes of $480 a thousand from the Thompson division, $430 a thousand from West Paper Company, and $432 a thousand from Erie Papers, Ltd. Erie Papers offered to buy from Birch the outside linerboard with the special printing already on it, but would supply its own inside liner and corrugating medium. The outside liner would be supplied by the Southern division at a price equivalent of $90 per thousand boxes, and would be printed for $30 a thousand by the Thompson division. Of the $30, about $25 would be out-of-pocket costs.

Since this situation appeared a little unusual, William Kenton, manager of the Northern division, discussed the wide discrepancy of bids with Birch's commercial vice-president. He told the vice-president: "We sell in a very competitive market, where higher costs cannot be passed on. How can we be expected to show a decent profit and return on investment if we have to buy our supplies at more than 10 percent over the going market?"

Knowing that Mr. Brunner had on occasion in the past few months been unable to operate the Thompson division at capacity, the vice-president found it odd that Mr. Brunner would add the full 20 percent overhead and profit charge to his out-of-pocket costs. When asked about this, Mr. Brunner's answer was the statement that appears at the beginning of the case. He went on to say that having done the developmental work on the box, and having received no profit on that, he felt entitled to a good markup on the production of the box itself.

The vice-president explored further the cost structures of the various divisions. He remembered a comment that the controller had made at a meeting the week before to the effect that costs that were variable for one division could be largely fixed for the company as a whole. He knew that in the absence of specific orders from top management, Mr. Kenton would accept the lowest bid, which was that of the West Paper Company for $430. However, it would be possible for top management to order the acceptance of another bid if the situation warranted such action. And though the volume represented by the transactions in question was less than 5 percent of the volume of any of the divisions involved, other transactions could conceivably raise similar problems later.

REQUIRED

1. In the controversy described, how, if at all, is the transfer-price system dysfunctional? Prepare an analysis of the cash flows under each alternative.
2. As the commercial vice-president, what action would you take?

19-28 ***Transfer pricing to Brazil.*** The amplifier division of Cadillac Electronics, Inc., a diversified international company headquartered in New York, sells amplifier kits in the United States and several foreign countries.

The selling price for these kits is $40 in the United States, where the income-tax rate is 50 percent.

The Brazilian market is one of the foreign markets in which the amplifier division is active. Cadillac Electronics has a 60-percent-owned subsidiary in Brazil, which buys the amplifier kits from the amplifier division and sells them to local wholesalers.

The total cost of the kits delivered to the Brazilian port is $30, of which $2 is transportation cost. Brazilian tariffs on amplifiers are 40 percent of declared value. These duties are paid by the Brazilian subsidiary and become part of its cost of inventory. There is a minimum declared value legally allowed of $30 but no upper limit. The applicable income tax rate in Brazil is 35 percent. *There are no other restrictions or taxes affecting the transfer of funds from Brazil to the United States.*

REQUIRED

1. In the past, Cadillac Electronics has transferred the kits to the Brazilian subsidiary at a declared price equal to the United States market price, i.e., $40. Ignoring performance measurement and motivational issues, do you find the $40 declared value a sound economic decision? If not, what declared value would you select? Explain. (For simplicity, ignore the income tax complications caused by such items as the equalization tax paid on remitted earnings.)
2. Does the transfer price you recommend suit the need for good relations with the minority shareholders of the Brazilian subsidiary? Why?

19-29 ***Transfer pricing in different situations.*** The Neumann Company, Ltd., adopted a philosophy of decentralization several years ago. All the company's autonomous manufacturing divisions are located in Great Britain, where the company manufactures a wide range of electronic controls and automated machine tools. Nominally, all divisions of the company are conducted as separate enterprises, which must negotiate all orders independently with prospective purchasers. Each division is then responsible for its own profitability and return on investment. However, all divisions are required to consider purchasing from other Neumann divisions whenever possible.

The machine-products division (MPD), situated in London, manufactures small precision components that can be integrated with other Neumann components in a variety of automated systems. Both the components and the entire systems are generally quite profitable and in high demand by other Neumann divisions, as well as by independent purchasers. The machine-products division is the only Neumann plant with the facilities to produce a very essential component, magnesium balance wheels. The market price for these items is £100, both in Great Britain and in the United States. However, an import duty of 10 percent (of the selling price without the duty) is charged on the import of this type of product into the United States. The MPD income statement for the last twelve months is as follows (in thousands of pounds):

Net sales		£1,100
Direct labor	£250	
Direct materials	300	
Manufacturing overhead	250	800

Gross margin		300
Fixed selling expenses	100	
Fixed administrative expenses	80	180
Divisional profit		£ 120

The cost of a batch of balance wheels has been calculated in the following manner:

Direct labor	£25
Direct materials	30
Manufacturing overhead*	25
Total cost	£80

**100% of direct labor.*

When the company was decentralized, several assembly and marketing divisions were opened in new areas to expand the size of the markets for existing manufacturing divisions. These divisions were expected to be less profitable than other Neumann divisions, especially where import duties might necessitate more burdensome costs. One of these new marketing and assembly divisions (Middle Continental) was headquartered in Chicago under Mr. Gorot. Gorot had previously worked in London under the divisional manager for MPD, Mr. Miller, who was a 35-year veteran of the company. Even though Gorot had been a highly successful department head while in London, Miller had surreptitiously instigated a transfer for Gorot because of a personality conflict. Needless to say, Miller was quite unhappy to hear of Gorot's recent successes as head of Middle Continental while he himself was struggling to eliminate unfavorable capacity variances in the MPD.

Miller has been reluctant in the past to sell MPD components to other divisions at less than the domestic price; he sees no reason why he should make less profit than if he sold them in Great Britain. Furthermore, he has stated categorically, "I will not hurt my own profits to help that upstart in Chicago!"

One of the most important systems sold by Middle Continental requires the use of magnesium balance wheels. In the past, Gorot has been under some pressure to purchase balance wheels from MPD at a base price of £100 plus £10 import duty. This practice has unduly affected his profit performance, and he is necessarily eager to obtain permission to purchase these components from local suppliers.

REQUIRED

1. As the divisional controller at MPD, you are asked by Miller for advice in response to a memorandum from Gorot that he has obtained permission to purchase balance wheels in the United States unless MPD lowers its price. What would you advise Miller to do? Why? For this and the next requirement, assume that the manufacturing overhead is totally variable.
2. After you have given your advice to Miller, he receives a cablegram from Gorot indicating that several manufacturers in the United States have reduced their price on balance wheels to £85. How would you change your advice, if at all? Why?
3. Several days later, you determine that half the manufacturing overhead is fixed cost. Would this cause you to alter any of your previous decisions? In what way? (Use this new information for requirements 4 through 6.)
4. About a year later, MPD is operating at practical capacity. Gorot sends MPD another order for balance wheels at the previously negotiated price in requirement 1. Would you now recommend that this price be accepted? Why?
5. If the Neumann Company were to eliminate its divisions, what company guidelines should be established for transfers of goods between segments of the company?
6. Two years later, you are promoted to the controller's office of the entire Neumann Company. You are then asked to advise your new superior on whether some firm guidelines should be established for the determination of transfer prices between divisions as they were organized in 1–4 above. What would you recommend? Why?

19-30 ***Multinational transfer-pricing policies.*** You are on the corporate controller's staff at Maxchem Co., a profit-maximizing multinational chemical corporation, and you have been asked to consider the transfer-pricing problem that faces a subsidiary company. This subsidiary, Company A, operates a factory in Country A and deals with two other subsidiary companies, B and C. Company B operates the corporation's mines, in Country B; and Company C operates company freighters that can transport the minerals from Country B to Country A. Company C is registered in Country C. The manager of Company A is responsible for buying the necessary minerals for its production runs from Company B (the corporation's only source of raw materials) and for chartering vessels (whether company owned or not) to ensure timely delivery of the minerals to the factory. His compensation is directly linked to Company A's after-tax profit, which is reported to headquarters.

Company A's total cost to convert the materials and to sell the finished product is $3.00 per hundredweight (cwt.). Selling price is $10.50. The income-tax rate in Country A is 50 percent.

Company B's total production cost per cwt. extracted from the ground is $3.20. In addition, royalty payment of 30 percent of gross revenues must be made to the government. Country B has decreed that all of its minerals that are exported must be sold at a price of $6.00. Income is taxed at a rate of 20 percent.

As for Company C, the variable cost per voyage per cwt. is $1.00. Country C does not levy income taxes but instead assesses annual company registration fees. These fees must be paid *regardless* of company ship activity, and they amount to $0.20 per voyage per cwt. at the current volume of production. There are other tanker companies offering identical transportation services available in the market, and the manager of Company A has the choice of using Company C's tankers or of chartering vessels of other firms.

REQUIRED

Assume that no variances are incurred and that the cost figures given above are correct. Answer the following questions on a per-cwt. basis.

1. Company C currently uses a full-cost plus 10 percent profit method to determine the freight charge to Company A. The current open-market charter price for a voyage from Country B to Country A is $1.40 per cwt. Will the manager of Company A charter a freighter from Company C or will he or she obtain a charter on the open market? Why? What is the consolidated profit that the three subsidiary companies will report to headquarters under (a) chartering from Company C, (b) chartering on the free market? Is the manager's decision consistent with corporate objectives?
2. Suppose that the market price for a voyage drops to $1.10. Answer the same questions asked in requirement 1. What is the difference in profit per cwt. if A charters C freighters instead of using the open market?
3. Given the same set of circumstances as in requirement 2, determine what kind of decision would be made by the manager of Company A under a market-price transfer-price scheme. What modifications can be made to ensure that the manager's decision is consistent with corporate objectives?
4. Given the same set of circumstances as in requirement 2, determine what decision would be made by the manager of Company A under a variable-cost transfer-pricing scheme. How do the results differ from those in requirement 3? Why?
5. Under which transfer-pricing method are total profits for the corporation highest: (1) full cost + 10 percent, (2) market price, (3) variable cost? Comment on the general implications of the above problem. Given that the corporate structure is such that a profit-sharing plan among subsidiaries is not practical, which of the three schemes would you recommend and why?

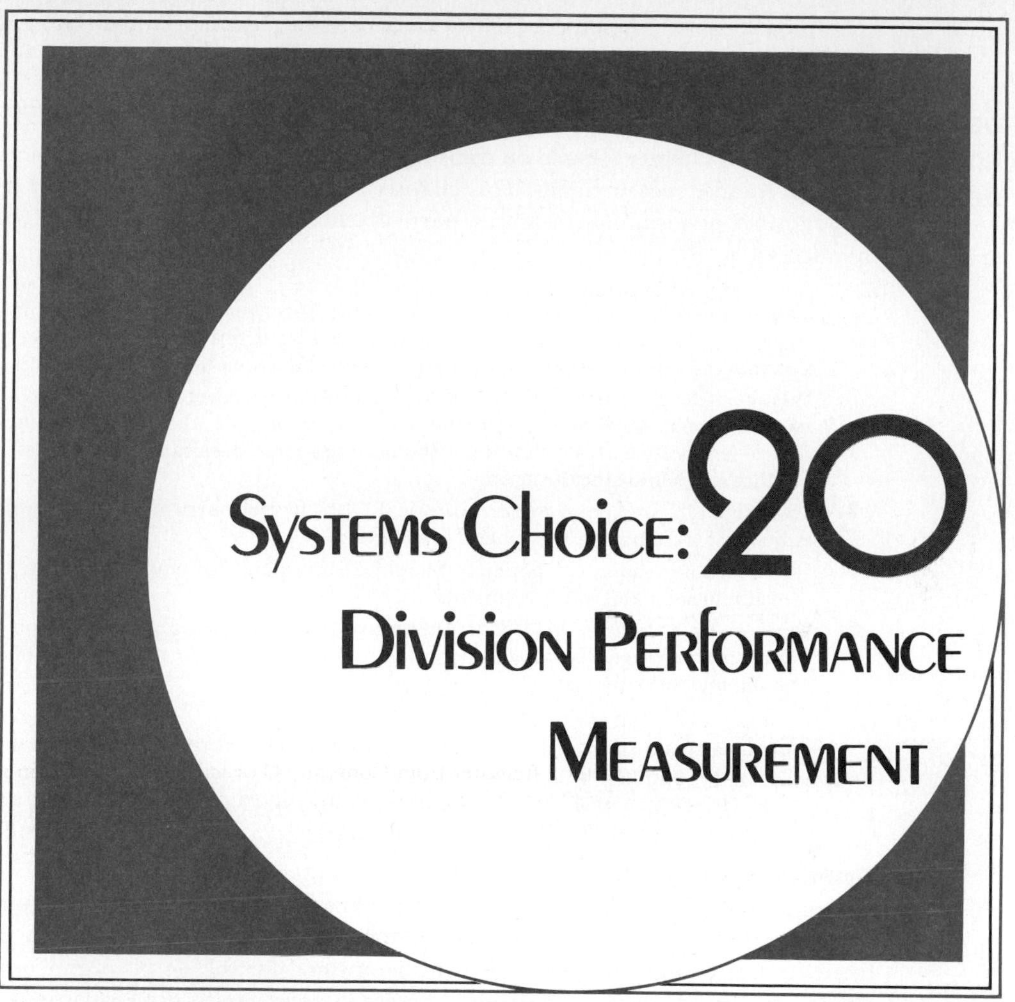

This chapter examines the general problems of designing an accounting system for measuring performance. We will be especially concerned with the difficulties of relating profits to invested capital.

The preceding chapter described a profit center. **An investment center goes a step further; its success is measured not only by its income but also by relating that income to its invested capital.** In practice, the term *investment center* is not widely used. Instead, *profit center* is used indiscriminately to describe segments that are always assigned responsibility for revenue and expenses but may or may not be assigned responsibility for the related invested capital.

Profit centers and investment centers are widely used. For instance, the 1,000 largest U.S. industrial companies were surveyed. Of 620 responses, only 4.2 percent indicated that they used neither profit centers nor investment centers. Investment centers were used by 74.0 percent; profit centers, by 21.8 percent.[1]

Overview of problems of design

The preceding chapter focused on transfer pricing as an example of the choices affecting performance measurement. This chapter explores five general steps for choosing among other performance measures, particularly as they bear on subunits and their managers:

1. Choose a measure of accomplishment that represents *top-management goals.* This provides a conceptual structure. Should it be net income, rate of return on investment, contribution margin, sales, or some other measure? Should the measure be maximized?
2. Whatever measure is chosen, the designer must then select *definitions of such items as income or investment.* Should income be based on variable or absorption costing? Should central corporate costs be allocated? Should investment consist of assets, or assets minus liabilities, or some other grouping?
3. How should items be *measured?* Historical cost? Replacement cost? Realizable value? Adjusted for changes in the general price level?
4. What *standards* should be applied? Should all divisions be required to earn the same rate of return on all their investments?
5. What *timing of feedback* is needed? Quarterly? Annually? Should feedback on the performance of managers be timed differently from feedback on the performance of divisions as economic investments?

The first three steps will be discussed in the next three major sections of this chapter. The fourth step was discussed in Chapter 13 (pages 450–452), where it was pointed out that different required rates of return should be used for different divisions. The fifth step, the timing of feedback, has been discussed in many places in this book. Timing depends largely on the specific level of management.

These five steps are not necessarily taken sequentially. Instead, the answers to these questions are interdependent. Taken together, they produce a *particular* management control system that is supposed to be optimal for the *specific* organization as a whole. In turn, as in the preceding chapter, the answers to these questions depend on predictions of how these information alternatives may fulfill the behavioral criteria of goal congruence, managerial effort, and subunit autonomy in a cost-effective manner. The overlay of cost-benefit analysis is still present. Appendix 20B explores these matters in more detail.

Measure that represents top-management goals

role of investment

What quantitative measure best represents top-management goals? Many managers are preoccupied with the measures of dollar sales, dollar profits (net income), and profit percentages (the ratio of profits to dollar sales). However, the ultimate test of profitability is not the absolute amount of profit or the relationship of profit to sales. The critical test is the relationship of profit to invested capital. The most popular way of expressing this relationship is by means of a rate of return on investment (ROI). The **ROI** approach has been used for centuries by financiers and others. Still, this technique did not become widespread in industry for judging operating performance

[1] J. Reece and W. Cool, "Measuring Investment Center Performance," *Harvard Business Review,* May-June 1978, p. 29. Similar results can be found in R. Vancil, *Decentralization: Managerial Ambiguity by Design* (New York: Financial Executives Research Foundation, 1979).

until the early 1960s. **Conceptually, ROI has innate appeal because it blends in one number all the major ingredients of profitability; the ROI statistic by itself can be compared with opportunities elsewhere, inside or outside the company.** Practically, however, ROI is an imperfect measurement that should be used with skepticism and in conjunction with other performance measurements.

Companies take different approaches to the problem of measuring return on investment, differing mostly with respect to the appropriate measure of invested capital, but also differing in the measure of income.

A useful approach to the problem may be outlined by using the following relationships:

$$\frac{\textbf{Sales}}{\textbf{Invested capital}} \times \frac{\textbf{Net income}}{\textbf{Sales}} = \frac{\textbf{Net income}}{\textbf{Invested capital}}$$

or

Capital turnover × Net income percentage of sales = Return on investment

Consider the components of the relationships. One may make the following obvious generalizations. ROI is increased by any action that (a) boosts sales that produce income, (b) reduces invested capital, or (c) reduces costs—while holding the other two factors constant. **Put another way, there are two basic ingredients in profit making: capital turnovers and profit margins.** An improvement in either without changing the other will enhance return on invested capital.

ROI as a tool for management

Assume that top management decides that a 20 percent return on invested capital is a profit target that will yield adequate rewards and yet not invite entry into the market by new competitors. How can this return be attained? Present performance (in millions of dollars) follows:

	sales / invested capital	×	net income / sales	=	net income / invested capital
Present	$\frac{100}{50}$	×	$\frac{9}{100}$	=	9/50, or 18%
Alternatives:					
A. Increase net income by lowering expenses	$\frac{100}{50}$	×	$\frac{10}{100}$	=	10/50, or 20%
B. Decrease assets	$\frac{100}{45}$	×	$\frac{9}{100}$	=	9/45, or 20%

Alternative A demonstrates a popular way of improving performance. Margins may be increased by reducing expenses, as in this case, or by boosting selling prices, or by increasing sales volume relative to a given amount of fixed expenses.

Alternative B shows that changes of investments in assets may also improve performance. Management has always been very conscious of the need for increasing sales and for controlling costs so that good profit margins may be attained. But control of investment has not always received conscientious managerial attention. Too often, asset balances rise without justification. Not only do operating costs have to be controlled but investment in cash, inventory, receivables, and fixed assets must be kept to the minimum that is consistent with effective performance. This means investing idle cash, determining proper inventory levels, managing credit judiciously, and spending carefully on fixed assets. In other words, increasing asset turnover means getting the maximum amount of sales out of every dollar invested in business resources. For example, having too much inventory is sometimes worse than having too little. Turnover decreases and goods deteriorate or become obsolete, thus dragging the rate of return downward.

ROI or residual income?

Earlier we saw that the ultimate test of profitability is the relationship of profit to invested capital. Until this point, our examples implied that the desired objective of management is the maximization of the rate of return on investment. But an investment center may be judged on what has been labeled **residual income** instead of on its rate of return. **Residual income is the net income of an investment center, less the "imputed" interest on the invested capital used by the center.** The choice of whether to use ROI or residual income as a management goal may induce different decisions.

Compare the calculations for two identical divisions:

	DIVISION A	DIVISION B
(1) Net income (after income taxes)	$ 25,000	$ 25,000
(2) Imputed interest at 16% of invested capital		16,000
(3) Invested capital	100,000	100,000
ROI [(1) ÷ (3)]	25%	
Residual income [(1) − (2)]		9,000

The objective of maximizing residual income assumes that as long as the division earns a rate in excess of the charge for invested capital, the division should expand. The manager of Division B would expand as long as incremental opportunities earned 16 percent or more on incremental assets.

General Electric has favored the residual-income approach because managers will concentrate on maximizing a number (dollars of residual income) rather than a percentage (rate of return).[2] The objective of maximizing ROI, however, may induce managers of highly profitable divisions to reject projects that, from the viewpoint of the corporation as a whole, should be accepted. For example, the manager of Division A would be reluctant to accept a new project with a 20 percent rate even though top management regards 16 percent as a minimum desired rate of return. In contrast, the residual-income approach would charge a division only 16 percent, and its manager would be inclined to accept all projects that exceed that rate.

There is a parallel between the discounted cash-flow methods in capital budgeting and the comparison of ROI and residual income. In Chapter 13 comparisons were made between the internal rate of return and the net present-value methods. The internal rate method is similar to the ROI method, and the net present-value method is similar to the residual-income method. **Residual income changes the goal from "maximize ROI" to "maximize dollar return in excess of minimum desired ROI."** In other words, ROI implies, "Go forth and maximize your *rate* of return." In con-

[2]See Robert W. Lewis, *Planning, Managing, and Measuring the Business* (New York: Financial Executives Research Foundation), p. 32.

trast, residual income implies, "Go forth and maximize your *absolute amount* of income in excess of some desired minimum." As always, the choice depends on top management's preferences in light of how decisions might differ under ROI or residual income.

controllable performance

As Chapters 5 and 15 stressed, a **distinction should be made between the performance of the division manager and the performance of the division as an investment by the corporation.** The manager should be evaluated on the basis of a set of individually tailored budgeted performances. For other decisions, "such as a new investment or a withdrawal of funds from the division, the important thing is the success or failure of the divisional venture, not of the men who run it."[3]

The most skillful division manager is often put in charge of the sickest division in an attempt to change its fortunes. Such an attempt may take years, not months. Furthermore, it may result in merely bringing the division up to a minimum acceptable rate of return. The division may continue to be a poor profit performer in comparison with other divisions. If top management relied solely on the absolute rate of return to judge management, the skillful manager would be foolhardy to accept such trouble-shooting assignments.

distinction between managers and investments

Comparisons of income or rates of return among investment centers should be made with extreme caution because there tend to be too many peculiarities that destroy their validity. Even for similar factories making similar products, local conditions often cause a variety of environments and costs. **Therefore, a manager would usually be more appropriately judged by performance against some budget target rather than against other investment centers.**

Definitions of income and investments

possible investment bases

The base that is used for defining invested capital may appropriately differ among companies and within segments of the same company. The possible alternative bases include:

1. *Total assets available.* This base includes all business assets, regardless of their individual purpose.
2. *Total assets employed.* This base excludes excess or idle assets, such as vacant land or construction in progress.
3. *Working capital plus other assets.* This base is really the same as 1 except that current liabilities are deducted from current assets in determining total assets available. In a sense, this represents an exclusion of that portion of current assets that is supplied by short-term creditors. The main justification for this base is that the manager often does have direct influence over the amount of short-term credit that a division utilizes. An able manager should maximize the use of such credit, within some overall constraints to prevent endangering the company's credit standing.
4. *Stockholders' equity.* This base centers attention on the rate of return that will be earned by the business owners.

comparison of asset and equity bases

Stockholders' equity, as a possible investment base, is important to the owners, but it is not so significant to the operating manager. He or she is usually concerned with the management of assets, not with the long-term sources of assets. **There are two major management functions: operating and financing. To the extent possible, the mea-**

[3]David Solomons, *Divisional Performance Measurement and Control* (Homewood, Ill.: Richard D. Irwin, 1968), p. 84.

surement of operating decisions (the acquisition and utilization of assets) should not be influenced by financing decisions (what long-term sources of assets were chosen).

For example, consider the following companies:

	(1)	(2)	(3)	(4)	(5)	(6)	(4) ÷ (1)	(6) ÷ (3)
		EQUITIES					RETURN ON INVESTMENT*	
	ASSETS	liabilities	stock-holders' equity	INCOME BEFORE INTEREST	12% INTEREST	NET INCOME*	assets	stock-holders' equity
Co. A	$1,000,000	$500,000	$ 500,000	$200,000	$60,000	$140,000	20%	28%
Co. B	1,000,000	—	1,000,000	200,000	—	200,000	20%	20%

*Income taxes ignored here for simplicity.

It would be invalid to use stockholders' equity as a basis for comparing the operating performance of the managers of Company A and Company B. The 28 percent rate of return does not distinguish between the operating and the financing decisions. Company A in effect has paid 12 percent for the use of $500,000, which in turn has earned a return on assets of 20 percent. This is an example of risk taking that is often called *trading on the equity* or *using financial leverage.* It is a financing decision that results in borrowing money at a fixed interest rate with the expectation of earning a higher rate on such funds. Trading on the equity should be viewed as a separate decision and should not affect the measurement of operating performance.

For measuring the performance of division managers, any one of the three other asset bases listed above is almost always superior to stockholders' equity. If the division manager's mission is to utilize all assets as best he or she can without regard to their financing, then base 1 is best. If top-management directives force the division manager to carry extra assets that are not currently productive, then 2 is best. If the manager has direct control over the amount of the division's short-term trade credit and bank loans, then 3 is best. In practice, 1 is used about as much as 3.[4]

variety of incomes

Various definitions of income and investment are possible, and companies have worked out definitions to suit their specific preferences. Almost any approach is subject to criticism, but getting agreement within a company is not an insurmountable task. The contribution approach described in Chapter 15 can help distinguish between the performance of a division and the performance of its manager. Exhibit 15-1, p. 504, shows a sample format of the contribution approach. That exhibit and its accompanying text also deal with the problems of how to allocate costs among company divisions. That discussion will not be repeated here.

[4]Reece and Cool, "Measuring Investment Center Performance," p. 40, analyzed the responses of 459 companies regarding the inclusion of assets and liabilities in the investment base. Virtually all companies include external receivables, inventories, and fixed assets in their investment base. Cash was included by 63 percent and other current assets by 78 percent of the responses. About half of the companies deduct current liabilities in computing the investment center's asset base. Vancil, *Decentralization,* p. 340, conducted a similar survey and analyzed 286 responses, obtaining similar results.

allocating assets to divisions

Chapters 14 and 15 concentrated on the problems of cost allocation.[5] The points made there apply also to the problems of asset allocation. **Again, the aim is to allocate in a manner that will induce the desired behavior.**

Incidentally, as long as the managers feel that they are being treated uniformly, they tend to be more tolerant about the imperfections of the allocation. For example, should cash be included under controllable investment if the balances are strictly controlled by corporate headquarters? Arguments can be made for both sides, but the manager is usually regarded as being responsible for the volume of business generated by the division. In turn, this volume is likely to have a direct effect on the overall cash needs of the corporation. Commonly used bases for allocation, when assets are not directly identifiable with a specific division, include the following:

Asset Class	*Possible Allocation Base*
Corporate cash	Budgeted cash needs
Receivables	Sales weighted by payment terms
Inventories	Budgeted sales or usage
Plant and equipment	Usage of services in terms of long-run forecasts of demand or area occupied

Where the allocation of an asset (such as central corporate facilities) would indeed be arbitrary, many managers feel that it is better not to allocate. Fewer than 50 percent of the Reece and Cool respondents favored including allocations of shared facilities as part of the investment base. Only 30 percent of Vancil's respondents said that assets of central headquarters units were allocated to investment centers.[6] The statistics reveal the following inconsistency: Many companies do not hesitate to allocate *costs* but are reluctant to allocate the corresponding *assets.*

Measurement alternatives for investments

How should we measure the assets that are included in the investment base? Should assets be valued at net book value, replacement cost, realizable value, or some other value? There is a propensity to have one investment measure serve many masters. **Net book value[7] predominates, but its prevalence does not mean that it is necessarily conceptually correct.** Of course, the relevant value depends on the decisions being affected and evaluated. Among the decision purposes are:

[5]An extensive description of allocation of costs to segments can be found in R. K. Mautz, *Financial Reporting by Diversified Companies* (New York: Financial Executives Research Foundation, 1968).

[6]See Reece and Cool "Measuring Investment Center Performance," p. 40; and Vancil, *Decentralization,* p. 341.

[7]Reece and Cool, in "Measuring Investment Center Performance," p. 42, report that plant and equipment are valued at net book value by 85 percent of the respondents; 14 percent use gross book value, that is, original cost before deducting accumulated depreciation. Less than 2 percent used replacement cost. (Percentages are rounded.) Vancil's respondents reported 85, 15, and 0 percent, respectively (p. 351). *Fortune* (September 22, 1980, p. 138) reports that American Standard Corporation's internal accounting system computes "depreciation on a replacement-cost basis rather than on traditional historical cost."

1. Acquisition of a subunit
2. Evaluation of performance for motivating and for improving future decisions
3. Disposal of a subunit

acquisition (expansion) or not

As explained in Chapter 12, the original acquisition (or expansion) of an asset or subunit entails an analysis using a discounted cash flow (DCF) decision model:

Total Present Value
compared with
Required Investment

For example, suppose there is a world of perfect certainty. A $4,212.96 investment in equipment is expected to generate an annual operating cash inflow of $2,000 for three years. The predicted terminal disposal value is zero:

	TOTAL PRESENT VALUE	SKETCH OF RELEVANT CASH FLOWS (IN DOLLARS)			
Year		0	1	2	3
Present value @ 20%: $2,000 × 2.10648, factor from five-place annuity table	$4,212.96		2,000	2,000	2,000
Required investment: $(4,212.96) × 1.00000	(4,212.96)	(4,212.96)			
Net present value	0				

Here we see that the relevant values are the acquisition cost of the *required investment* in comparison with the *total present value* of the future cash inflows. The internal rate of return is exactly 20 percent. If the minimum desired rate of return does not exceed 20 percent, the investment should be made.

evaluation of performance

As was also discussed in Chapter 12, ideally, the decision model used to make a capital-investment decision and the model used to judge subsequent performance would be consistent. **However, in practice we often find DCF models being used for investment decisions and the accrual-accounting models being used for performance evaluation.**

This conflict of models may lead to dysfunctional decisions. Managers are sometimes reluctant to make capital outlays that are justified by DCF methods but lead to poor performance records in the first year or two after the outlay. This is especially likely if the outlay is subject to immediate write-off (for instance, product advertising, engineering development, and process improvement costs) or to accelerated-depreciation methods.

The most obvious way of evaluating performance consistently is to see, year by year, whether the predicted cash flows and the actual cash flows coincide.[8] In other

[8]Yuji Ijiri, "Recovery Rate and Cash Flow Accounting," *Financial Executive,* XLVII (March 1980), 54–60, suggests a cash recovery rate for periodic performance measurement. The rate is defined as the cash flow from operations divided by the gross assets. Also see R. Kaplan, *Advanced Management Accounting* (Englewood Cliffs, N.J.: Prentice-Hall, 1982), Chap. 15.

words, the decision model and the performance measurement model become totally consistent. See Appendix 20a for additional discussion.

disposal of a subunit

As Chapter 12 demonstrated, the DCF model needs two values for either the disposal versus replacement decision or the disposal versus continuance decision:

Total Present Value
compared with
Disposal Value

Reconsider the data in our illustration. Suppose it is the end of year 1. Many changes might occur that would affect our predictions of cash flows for the next two years. Suppose the manager expects annual cash flows of $1,800 instead of the original $2,000. The manager solicits and receives a $2,400 cash offer for the asset (or subunit or division or any identifiable segment of our company):

Total present value of the alternative to continue operations, $1,800 × 1.528, the P. V. of $1.00 at 20% for 2 years	$2,750
Current disposal value, the total present value of the alternative to sell today	$2,400

The analysis favors retention of the asset. **The relevant data consisted of *both* the total present value and the current disposal value[9] in the best alternative use.**

The very act of continuance implies that, as a minimum, the continuance or disposal decision has been made. Often, continuance occurs automatically, simply because disposal is so obviously economically unattractive that formal analysis is unnecessary. The decision is made unconsciously. However, the economic recession of the 1970s in the United States induced many managers to pause and explicitly analyze some activities. These analyses led to decisions to dispose of assets. Managers found that current disposal values were higher than the total present values of continuance in use. This illustrates the need for a periodic monitoring of both total present values and current disposal values, a monitoring that is not ordinarily incorporated in existing management control systems.

To recapitulate, the manager faces acquisition decisions and disposal decisions. The relevant comparisons are:

---

[9]The terms **current value** or **current cost** and **market value** are often used to describe disposal or sales or exit value. These general terms are avoided here because they are ambiguous in the literature and in discussions. Sometimes *current value* or *current cost* is used to represent total present value. At other times it is used to represent replacement cost. At still other times, it is used to represent market value. Similarly, *market value* is sometimes used to describe disposal value, but at other times it means replacement cost. The two values must be compared before an intelligent decision can be made. If the disposal value exceeds the total present value, the asset should be sold, and vice versa. Of course, linking the word "current" with some other descriptive term like "disposal" or "replacement" reduces the ambiguity. Thus, the terms "current disposal value" or "current replacement cost" are better than "current value" or "current cost."

Acquire (Expand)	*Disposal*
Total Present Value compared with Required Investment	Total Present Value of Continuance compared with Current Disposal Value

Note that the total present value depends on a deliberate *subjective* assessment of expected future cash inflows: Current disposal value and required-investment values may be identical for highly marketable securities[10] (ignoring brokerage fees, markups, and income-tax aspects), but they may be quite different for investments in highly specialized assets with no market values. For example, a company may invest $4,213 in new special equipment. An instant after acquisition, the replacement cost is $4,213 but the disposal value in the next best use may be only $2,400 or less. **Note especially that total present value is always relevant to these decisions, whether the alternative is to reduce, continue, or expand.**

evaluation of economic investment

As pointed out earlier, budgets are frequently used to help judge the performance of a manager, as distinguished from the performance of a subunit as an economic investment. Now we turn to the latter. **A fundamental rule for making comparisons of the productivity of assets is that their measurement basis be uniform.** That is, you would expect assets that produce the same net cash inflows with the same risk to have the same value. For example, it would be nonsense to judge economic performance on the holding of 100 shares of General Motors common stock for one year by comparing the increase in the market value of that stock (plus cash dividends) with its historical cost. If one investment manager had bought the stock in 19_1, another in 19_4, and another on December 31, 19_6, the comparisons of performance of the three managers for holding the hundred shares during 19_7 would surely not be related to the historical costs of investments. Instead, they would be related to what the 100 shares would have cost on December 31, 19_6. In short, the relevant investment measure for the routine evaluation of performance is replacement cost, because it provides a common denominator representing the equivalent of what would have been the required investment at the beginning of any given period.

Consider another example. If one subunit acquired plant and equipment in 19_1, and another subunit acquired *identical* plant and equipment on December 31, 19_6 (identical in every way: appearance, technology, and expected cash-inflow productivity), the value of the investment measure for judging 19_7 performance should be identical. In a sense, every economic unit starts a new year afresh;[11] all existing assets are viewed as if they were acquired on New Year's Eve. Thus, **replacement cost** is used as a common denominator to compare current productivity and to help predict the potential for competitive entry.

[10]Both would be measured by quoted market prices. That is why "market value" is cited as being the relevant number for sell, hold, or buy decisions in managing a security portfolio. Historical cost is irrelevant to these decisions except as it bears on income-tax considerations.

[11]Also see Yaaqov Goldschmidt, *Information for Management Decisions* (Ithaca, N.Y., and London: Cornell University Press, 1970), p. 64.

nature of replacement cost When assets are already in use, approximations of replacement market prices often do not exist. Note that the task of approximation is *not* to obtain a price of a new asset that would in fact be used to replace an existing asset. **Instead, the aim is to approximate how much it would cost to obtain similar assets that would produce the *same* expected operating cash inflows as the existing asset.** The essence of the asset is its expected cash flow, not its physical or technological features. Managers rarely replace assets exactly in kind with new assets having identical operating and economic characteristics.

Approximating a replacement cost for the 1982 delivery truck in 1985 may not be too difficult, because active markets exist. But the hunt would be for prices for 1982 models in equivalent condition, not for a new 1985 model—even though in fact a 1985 model would actually be purchased if replacement occurred in 1985.

As equipment becomes more highly specialized and subject to obsolescence, the task of approximating replacement cost becomes trickier. If no market exists, either specific price indexes for similar classes of equipment or appraisal might be used. The use of indexes provides more objectivity but perhaps less relevance, because they may not be exactly applicable to the particular assets in question. On the other hand, if appraisals are used, subjectivity heightens. In many instances, the appraisal value is often obtained by discounting the expected operating cash inflows. In such cases, total present value and replacement cost may be indistinguishable. That is, the total present value is assumed to be the best representation of replacement cost in the absence of an active replacement market. But the distinction, at least in concept, should be kept in mind. **Total present value is a subjective appraisal of expected cash inflows, whereas replacement cost is an approximation of what investment would currently be required to obtain that expected stream.**

total present value Many advocates cite total present value as the ideal investment measure for the evaluation of performance. Of course, the use of such a measure requires a concept of income (an income model) that differs from the conventional accrual-accounting model. *Annual income* is defined as the difference between total present values at the beginning and at the end of a year (assuming no cash dividends or additional investments). This requires an annual computation of a new total present value of the expected cash inflows. The resulting income would be affected by more than just current operating activities. Because it is dependent on a measurement of total present value at the end of the year, it would also be affected by other events (such as new inventions) and by explicit predictions of future events.

The present-value approach to measuring performance has overwhelming practical limitations because of its high degree of subjectivity. It necessitates predictions of cash flows that are uncertain and that are often interdependent with the cash flows of other assets. It also requires choosing a discount rate and perhaps changing that rate through the years. For these reasons, the use of present values for routine judging of performance of managers is rarely feasible. However, periodic attempts should be made to approximate present values in judging the desirability of assets as investments. Otherwise, managers will overlook obsolescence and investment opportunities.

Incidentally, many advocates of replacement cost favor it as an investment measure for routine evaluation of performance because, even though as a concept it is distinct from total present value, it provides answers that are reasonably objective approximations of what would be obtained under a present-value approach. In short, replacement cost is a practical surrogate for the "ideal" present value in the sense that it serves, at least usually, as a somewhat objective approximation of a *minimum* present value.

approximation of replacement cost

If an old asset provides a service that is comparable to a new asset's service, the value of the assets should be based on these services. Suppose a new warehouse will cost $1,000,000 and will provide the same services as an existing warehouse, which yields net rents of $100,000 per year, a return of 10 percent. The old asset should be valued at $1,000,000, the replacement cost of an asset that will provide similar services.

But suppose the old warehouse requires maintenance costs that are $20,000 higher than those of the new warehouse. The net services provided would be $100,000 − $20,000 = $80,000. Therefore, the value of the old warehouse would be $80,000 ÷ .10 = $800,000. All other things being equal, management would be indifferent as to buying a new warehouse for $1,000,000, paying $100,000 in interest charges, and selling it after a year for $1,000,000; or buying an old warehouse for $800,000, paying $80,000 in interest and $20,000 for maintenance, and selling it for $800,000 after one year.[12]

Suppose the old warehouse had a net book value of $60,000 and the new warehouse a net book value of $1,000,000. As a manager, which warehouse would you prefer to supervise? You can readily see why in practice managers often prefer to manage the old assets if ROI computations are based on net book values. In most cases, however, replacement costs (even if crudely approximated) would probably be regarded as providing a more "equitable" or "fair" basis for performance evaluation. As a practical matter, working with historical costs, wise budgeting recognizes that some managers have older equipment than others.

Note too that in this example there is no readily obtainable market price for the old asset per se. The $800,000 approximation of replacement cost is based on a subjective appraisal of the value of expected future cash inflows—total present value. In a practical setting, total present value is often used as an approximation of replacement cost where no market prices are available. This illustrates how present value and replacement-cost values can get blurred together even though they are essentially different concepts.

general price-level adjustments

Some companies are exploring the use of historical cost adjusted for general price-level changes. This entails restating *historical* data in terms of current general purchasing power by use of a general index such as the gross national product implicit price deflator. General Electric has experimented with this approach for its investment centers.

In particular, as is explained more thoroughly in the literature on external reporting, note that the use of *general* price-level adjustments represents restatements of historical costs. Conceptually, restated costs are *not* the same as replacement-cost accounting, which is sometimes approximated via the use of *specific* price indexes. (However, a separate line of reasoning claims that general price-level accounting is a practical, cost-effective way of getting crude approximations of results under replacement-cost accounting.)

---

[12]Adapted from an example in Goldschmidt, *Information for Management Decisions.* For simplicity this example uses rates of return based on infinite useful lives, but the principles are unchanged for finite useful lives.

plant and equipment: gross or net?

Because historical-cost investment measures are used most often in practice, there has been much discussion[13] about the relative merits of using original cost (gross book value) or net book value. Those who favor using gross assets claim that it facilitates comparisons among plants and divisions. **If income decreases as a plant ages, the decline in earning power will be made evident, while the constantly decreasing net book value will reflect a possibly deceptive higher rate of return in later years.** For this reason, du Pont and Monsanto use gross book value as a measure of their fixed assets when they compute rate of return.[14]

One reason often cited for using original cost is that it partially compensates for the impact of the changing price level on historical cost. However, if a company desires to use replacement cost as a base, it should face the problem squarely by using appraisal values or specific price indexes. **Reliance on gross book value is an unreliable means of approximating replacement value.**

Solomons comments on the gross versus net book value debate:

> There is something inherently strange about the view that it is right to include fixed assets in a balance sheet at their depreciated value, but wrong to include them in a computation of capital at that value. The only reason for holding such a view is the irrational behavior of ROI when fixed assets are taken at book value rather than at cost. The proper remedy is to be found in the use of a compound interest method of depreciation, not in the abandonment of book value as a basis for valuing investment. If depreciation were handled in a theoretically correct manner (i.e., by the compound interest method), the decline in the book value of depreciating assets would not of itself disturb the stability of ROI.[15]

The proponents of using net book value as a measure maintain that it is less confusing because (a) it is consistent with the total assets shown on the conventional balance sheet, and (b) it is consistent with net-income computations, which include deductions for depreciation. The major criticism of net book value is not peculiar to its use for ROI purposes. The critics say that historical cost does not represent a current economic sacrifice and is useless for making decisions about allocations of resources. On the other hand, as explained in the appendix on compound-interest depreciation, if net book value is used in a manner that is consistent with the planning model, it can be useful for auditing past decisions and it might suffice for motivation purposes. Also see the next section.

Historical cost or current costs?[16]

Some form of current-value accounting is now required in the shareholder reports of large companies in the United States and elsewhere. Nevertheless, there is no evident rush toward applying current values to the performance measurement of subunits. Almost 99 percent of the responses in the Reece-Cool 1976 survey used historical

---

[13] *Return on Capital as a Guide to Managerial Decisions,* National Association of Accountants, Research Report No. 35; and Solomons, *Divisional Performance,* pp. 134–42.

[14] Reece and Cool, "Measuring Investment Center Performance," p. 42. Fourteen percent of the companies surveyed use gross book value.

[15] Solomons, *Divisional Performance,* p. 135. He discusses these issues at length on pp. 134–42.

[16] Parts of this section are based on C. Horngren, "Budgets, Respect, and Inflation," *Journal of Accountancy,* March 1980, pp. 80–87.

costs for valuing plant and equipment for measuring the performance of subunits.[17] Despite such widespread use, historical costs are often assailed. Consider the following typical example:

> In our opinion, there is not much good to be said for accounting based on historical costs . . . and . . . replacement cost measures are clearly superior to historical cost measurements.[18]

If an accounting method possesses innate superiority, why are few organizations adopting it for internal purposes? Among the possible reasons are (1) ignorance, (2) misstatement of the basic alternatives, (3) the overlooking of the importance of budgets, (4) costs of systems, (5) motivational implications, and (6) external influences. Each of these reasons will be examined briefly.

ignorance of defects

The simplest explanation for ignorance of defects pinpoints the infirmities of historical-cost accounting. The defects of existing systems and the benefits of alternative systems are not seen. Supposedly, if managers only knew better, they would recognize that historical cost is irrelevant for most decisions.

Such an explanation is not persuasive to this author. Managers live in a highly competitive environment. They are always seeking an edge. Managers will invest in a more elaborate accounting system if they think a better set of collective operating decisions will ensue and if they think their personal goals will be achieved more easily.

misstatement of alternatives

Our perspective may be improved if we express the alternatives more precisely. Too often, the critics of historical costs imply that there are two major choices among systems:

System A		System B
(Historical Data)	or	(Nonhistorical Data)

What is the most popular type of management accounting system among well-managed companies today? Is it a historical-cost system? Not really, although it is often described as such. Perhaps a better name would be *budgeting system,* which is not used enough to describe existing systems.

The choices are not nearly as stark as picking either a "historical-cost" or a "current-cost" system. Almost all well-managed companies today do not use a historical-cost system as it is portrayed by critics. Instead, the choices are better expressed as follows:

System A		System B
(Budgeted Data and Historical Data)	or	(Current Value Data)

[17] Reece and Cool, "Measuring Investment Center Performance," p. 42. Also, Chenhall found that 80 percent of 173 companies in Australia reported in 1977 that they used historical cost. See Robert H. Chenhall, "Some Elements of Organisational Control in Australian Divisionalized Firms," *Australian Journal of Management,* Supplement 4, No. 1 (April 1979), pp. 1–36.

[18] Richard F. Vancil and Roman L. Weil, *Replacement Cost Accounting: Readings on Concepts, Uses & Methods* (Glen Ridge, N.J.: Thomas Horton, 1976), p. 8.

In passing, note two characteristics about the above comparisons. First, although it is possible to do so, neither system adjusts its monetary measurements for changes in the general price level. Second, System B could be coupled with budgeted data in the same manner as System A.

importance of budgets

What do we mean when we say *budgeting system?* We mean that projected data heavily influence decisions. Moreover, feedback concentrates on historical results in relation to these projected data. The point here is that the role of budgeting is often strong, but it is overlooked in discussions about whether current-value systems are superior to historical systems.

Budgeting is an extremely pervasive activity. Indeed, in some organizations (e.g., in some service industries such as advertising agencies) one could contemplate budgets being used without any record of "current value" or "current cost." The current-value accounting controversy would be placed in better perspective by giving budgeting more explicit respect and attention as a way of contending with changing prices and inflation and asking whether current value or historical value is more desirable as a part of a budgeting system. **In other words, let us start with a budgeting system as a given factor and then compare historical-cost accounting with current-cost accounting as potential subparts of it.**

Many criticisms of historical-cost accounting involve questionable logic: Historical-cost systems are defective. Therefore, current-value systems are better.

Given a well-administered budgeting system, management accounting systems are closer to using current value than meets the eye. Moreover, if they must choose among ways to improve their systems, managers will often spend their money on systems more wisely by upgrading their budgeting systems than by installing current-value systems.

Many advocates of current-value accounting assert that "bad" decisions are being made because accounting systems are not based on current values. But the evidence is scattered. Consider some decision models in wide use today: cost-volume-profit, inventory planning, production scheduling, pricing, capital budgeting. What types of data are common among those models? Budgeted data! For example, in capital budgeting, expected inflation is built into forecasts.[19] Historical costs are not direct inputs, but they are compiled and compared with budgets so that planning will be improved.[20] The comparisons also help answer at least two questions about the managers: Do you budget accurately? Do you adhere to your plans? Historical records per se are helpful in this feedback loop (which keeps cycling through a series of periods).

cost of systems

A key aspect of the definition of systems is *regularity*. For example, historical data are recorded in an orderly fashion as a part of everyday operations. Continuous compilation tends to be more expensive than occasional compilation. Other data may be gathered irregularly as desired; for example, replacement costs may be sought via special cost studies when specified equipment is being evaluated.

A persuasive reason for not adopting current value is the "good enough" cost-benefit rationale. That is, managers are skeptical that a current-value system will

---

[19]See Chapter 13 (pp. 446–449) for a discussion.

[20]Yuji Ijiri, Studies in Accounting Research No. 10, *Theory of Accounting Measurement* (Sarasota, Fla.: American Accounting Association, 1975), p. 88, observes, "Without historical cost, which is a consequence of a past decision rule, how can we evaluate the quality of past decisions?"

significantly improve the collective operating decisions that are wanted. The existing systems are good enough for *routine* evaluation of performance. Ijiri remarks:

> Although it may be argued that a manager should always keep in mind the disposal value of all his plants even when this alternative is not explicitly considered, a continuous record of such disposal values is just as remotely useful as a continuous record of estimated death tolls at each instance in time should an atomic war occur.[21]

There is a major lesson from the theory of information economics, the empirical studies of the relation of accounting data to security prices, and studies of how managers make decisions: Accounting reports provide only one source of information for decision-making. There are many other sources. Consequently, accountants should never take themselves too seriously. Although their role of measuring income and wealth is valuable and important—indeed, some accountants would maintain that their role is indispensable—the accountant has no monopoly on the provision of information. **Much data is more efficiently and effectively obtained through other sources.**

motivational implications

If astutely designed and administered, the budget can overcome many limitations of measurement that upset many critics of existing management accounting systems. For example, budgets can remedy the oft-cited defects of using historical cost as an asset measure for investment center performance:

> . . . there is no reason why the phenomenon of return on investment or residual income increasing with the passage of time cannot be allowed for when one is budgeting an investment center's *future* performance.[22]

The conceptual impurities of historical costs have been described frequently throughout this book. (For example, see Chapter 11 and the appendix on compound interest for this chapter.) To illustrate, critics of historical costs have indicated how high rates of return on old assets may erroneously induce a manager not to replace assets. However, as was pointed out earlier in this chapter, the manager's mandate is often, "Go forth and attain the budgeted results." And the budget is carefully negotiated with full knowledge of many accounting pitfalls.

The desirability of tailoring a budget to a particular manager cannot be overemphasized. For example, many problems of asset valuation and profit measurement (whether based on historical cost or current cost) can be satisfactorily solved if top management gets everybody to focus on what is attainable in the forthcoming budget periods.

Another explanation of why managers are reluctant to adopt current values is more troublesome. Managers have their own interests, including compensation and job security.[23] They are comfortable with the known (a historical-cost system of performance evaluation), and they regard the unknown (some current-value system of

---

[21] Ibid., p. 87. A survey by C. Casey and M. Sandretto, "Internal Uses of Accounting for Inflation," *Harvard Business Review*, Nov.–Dec. 1981, found increasing uses. However, no definitive findings were provided regarding the *routine* evaluation of performance.

[22] Reece and Cool, "Measuring Investment Center Performance," p. 42.

[23] Alfred Rappaport, "Executive Incentives vs. Corporate Growth," *Harvard Business Review*, July-August 1978. Also see his "Measuring Company Growth Capacity during Inflation," *Harvard Business Review*, January-February 1979.

performance evaluation) as a risk. Whether the latter perception is justified is debatable. Nevertheless, few managers welcome the opportunity to explain to shareholders that the historical-cost profits, when restated, are shriveled numbers.

external influence Inflation will not disappear in the foreseeable future. The greatest hope for the advocates of current-value accounting is the existing requirement that supplementary current-value reports be used for external purposes. If current values are being compiled routinely anyway, their ready accessibility may encourage their use for internal purposes. After all, the costs of tapping an available data bank are much lower than the costs of constructing a data bank from scratch. Moreover, users will become less antagonistic if current-value accounting becomes accepted for external purposes, principally because the long, slow learning process (both through education and through experience) will make the numbers less strange.

The evolution of systems for internal purposes is often affected by external-reporting requirements. For instance, years ago depreciation accounting was almost nonexistent in many companies. Now depreciation expense is routinely recognized for internal purposes. A principal catalyst was having depreciation expense as an allowable deduction for income-tax purposes (or for rate-making decisions).

Finally, note that this section should be interpreted as being neither for nor against current-cost or current-value accounting. Indeed, unless a budget is also used, a strong case can be made for rejecting historical costs as a basis for performance measurement. For management accounting purposes, the main issue for a given organization is whether the costs of a new current-cost system, including all indirect costs of education, will yield a greater benefit than an existing or improved budgeting system.

Problems in current practice

ROI and residual income are subject to the usual criticisms leveled at accounting techniques. Such criticisms include

1. Overemphasis on short-run results.
2. Overemphasis on profit and underemphasis on quality, employee relations, development of subordinates, share of the market, discovery of new products, and so on.
3. Incongruent decisions[24] because of accounting policies regarding measures of investment and policies that tend to exclude the following from the investment base: research, market development, and leased assets. For example, a manager may lease an asset even though economic analysis favors its purchase; the leased asset might be excluded from the manager's investment base, whereas the owned asset is ordinarily included.
4. Unjustifiable comparisons among divisional results, where the economic and accounting differences are significant.

Despite these weaknesses, investment centers are often the most feasible means for promoting goal congruence, managerial effort, and autonomy in a cost-effective way.

[24]For an interesting discussion of various investment bases and depreciation methods plus several examples of how division managers' interest can conflict with the interests of the company as a whole, see John Dearden, "Problem in Decentralized Profit Responsibility," *Harvard Business Review*, 38, No. 3, pp. 79–86.

SUMMARY

Many techniques like ROI or residual income fall far short of helping goal congruence, managerial effort, and autonomy. Nevertheless, in practice their conceptual shortcomings may be unimportant; often they are the best techniques available for obtaining the perceived top-management goals.

Performance reports should distinguish between the performance of the division manager and the performance of the divisional unit as an economic investment.

Although in practice the book values of assets tend to be used for ROI and residual-income purposes, many accountants believe that replacement cost is a preferable multipurpose basis. Despite the theoretical attractiveness of various alternative current-value methods, most managements have apparently decided that a budgeting system coupled with historical costs is good enough for the *routine* evaluation of managers. Apparently, this crude approach provides the desired motivational effects and gives clues as to whether to invest or dispose of a particular division. The investment decision is evidently not routine enough to justify gathering information regarding replacement costs or realizable values except as special occasions arise.

SUGGESTED READINGS

These readings apply to Chapters 19 and 20. However, also see the footnotes in these chapters and the Suggested Readings for Chapter 10, page 337.

ANTHONY, R., and J. DEARDEN, **Management Control Systems,** 4th ed. Homewood, Ill.: Richard D. Irwin, 1980.

ANTHONY, R. and R. HERZLINGER, **Management Control in Nonprofit Organizations,** rev. ed. Homewood, Ill.: Richard D. Irwin, 1980.

BENKE, R., and J. EDWARDS, **Transfer Pricing: Techniques and Uses.** New York: National Association of Accountants, 1980.

CAPLAN, EDWIN H., and J. CHAMPOUX, **Cases in Management Accounting: Context and Behavior.** New York: National Association of Accountants, 1978.

HOPWOOD, A., **Accounting and Human Behavior.** Englewood Cliffs, N.J.: Prentice-Hall, 1976.

KAPLAN, R., **Advanced Management Accounting.** Englewood Cliffs, N.J.: Prentice-Hall, 1982.

LAWLER, E., and J. RHODE, **Information and Control in Organizations.** Pacific Palisades, Calif.: Goodyear, 1976.

LORANGE, P., **Corporate Planning: An Executive Viewpoint.** Englewood Cliffs, N.J.: Prentice-Hall, 1980.

OUCHI, W., **Theory Z.** Reading, Mass.: Addison-Wesley, 1981.

SOLOMONS, D., **Divisional Performance Measurement and Control.** Homewood, Ill.: Richard D. Irwin, 1968.

VANCIL, R., **Decentralization: Management Ambiguity by Design.** New York: Financial Executives Research Foundation, 1979.

WILLIAMSON, O., **Markets and Hierarchies: Analysis and Antitrust Implications.** New York: Free Press, 1975.

PROBLEMS FOR SELF-STUDY

problem 1

Suppose that a division's budgeted data are as follows:

Average available assets:	
Receivables	$ 300,000
Inventories	200,000
Fixed assets, net	500,000
	$1,000,000
Fixed costs	$ 225,000
Variable costs	$5 per unit
Desired rate of return on average available assets	27.5%
Expected volume	200,000 units

a. What average unit sales price is needed to obtain the desired rate of return on average available assets?
b. What would be the expected turnover of assets?
c. What would be the net-income percentage of dollar sales?
d. What rate of return would be earned on assets available if sales volume is 300,000 units, assuming no changes in prices or variable costs per unit?

solution 1

a. 27.5% of $1,000,000 = $275,000 target net income

$$\begin{aligned}
\textbf{Let } X &= \textbf{unit sales price} \\
\textbf{Dollar sales} &= \textbf{Variable costs} + \textbf{Fixed costs} + \textbf{Net income} \\
200{,}000\,X &= 200{,}000\,(\$5) + \$225{,}000 + \$275{,}000 \\
X &= \$1{,}500{,}000 \div 200{,}000 \\
X &= \$7.50
\end{aligned}$$

b. $\text{Expected asset turnover} = \dfrac{200{,}000 \times \$7.50}{\$1{,}000{,}000} = \dfrac{\$1{,}500{,}000}{\$1{,}000{,}000} = 1.5$

c. $\text{Net income as a percentage of dollar sales} = \dfrac{\$275{,}000}{\$1{,}500{,}000} = 18.33\%$

d. At a volume of 300,000 units:

Sales @ $7.50	$2,250,000
Variable costs @ $5.00	1,500,000
Contribution margin	$ 750,000
Fixed costs	225,000
Net income	$ 525,000
Rate of return on $1,000,000 assets	52.5%

Note that an increase of 50 percent in unit volume almost doubles net income. This is so because fixed costs do not increase as volume increases.

problem 2

A division managed by Mario Bonini has assets of $200,000 and net income of $60,000.
a. What is the division's ROI?
b. If interest is imputed at 14 percent, what is the residual income?
c. What effects on Bonini's management behavior can be expected if ROI is used to gauge performance?
d. What effects on Bonini's management behavior can be expected if residual income is used to gauge performance?

solution 2

a. $60,000 ÷ $200,000 = 30%
b. $60,000 − .14($200,000) = $32,000
c. If ROI is used, the manager is prone to reject projects that do not earn an ROI of at least 30 percent. From the viewpoint of the organization as a whole, this may be undesirable because its best investment opportunities may lie in that division at a rate of, say, 22 percent. If a division is enjoying a high ROI, it is less likely to expand if it is judged via ROI than if it is judged via residual income.
d. If residual income is used, the manager is inclined to accept all projects whose expected ROI exceeds the minimum desired rate. His division is more likely to expand, because his goal is to maximize a dollar amount rather than a rate.

Terms to Learn

(Many of these terms are explained in Appendixes 20a and 20b.)

agency theory ***annuity depreciation***
compound-interest method of depreciation
critical economic success factors ***critical success factors***
current cost ***current value*** ***industry economics*** ***investment center***
key result areas ***key variables*** ***managerial style*** ***market value***
matrix organization ***organization goals*** ***organization morality***
organization objectives ***organization structure*** ***profit center***
replacement cost ***residual income*** ***risk averse*** ***risk neutral***
ROI ***strategic planning***

Special Points and Pitfalls

Many organizations measure divisional performance on the basis of profits alone. In general, ROI or residual-income measures are better measures if top-management goals focus on return on investment.

This is a good time for review and reflection. In particular, ponder the behavioral implications of what accountants do. Restudy the first parts of Chapters 10 and 19. For additional study of these issues, see the appendixes to this chapter.

Appendix 20a: compound interest and models for measuring performance

This appendix uses the same example as in the body of the chapter. A $4,212.96 investment in equipment is expected to generate an annual operating cash inflow of $2,000 for three years. The predicted terminal disposal value is zero.

compound-interest depreciation

Suppose management insists on using an accrual-accounting model for measuring performance. Then compatibility with the DCF decision model can be achieved only by using the **compound-interest method of depreciation.** **This method holds the *rate* of return on the investment constant. Depreciation is equal to the cash inflow for the period less the internal rate of return multiplied by the asset's net book value at the start of the period.** When the cash inflows are the same each period, this depreciation method is frequently called the **annuity method of depreciation.**

Study Exhibit 20-1. Suppose subsequent performance adhered to predictions. The income statement that dovetails with the assumptions of the DCF model would be

EXHIBIT 20-1

Depreciation Methods and Rates of Return
(in dollars)

	COMPOUND INTEREST			STRAIGHT LINE			SUM-OF-YEARS'-DIGITS		
Year	1	2	3	1	2	3	1	2	3
Cash operating income	2,000	2,000	2,000	2,000	2,000	2,000	2,000	2,000	2,000
Depreciation	1,157*	1,389*	1,667*	1,404†	1,404	1,405	2,107‡	1,404	702
Net income	843	611	333	596	596	595	(107)	596	1,298
Investment base—beginning balance	4,213	3,056	1,667	4,213	2,809	1,405	4,213	2,106	702
Rate of return on beginning balance	20%	20%	20%	14%	21%	42%	−3%	28%	185%

**See table in adjoining text explanation.*
†$4,212.96 ÷ 3 = $1,404.32 per year.
‡Sum of digits = 1 + 2 + 3 = 6. Therefore, 3/6 × $4,213 for first year, 2/6 for second year, and 1/6 for third year.

shown in the first three columns in Exhibit 20-1. **If cash inflows are equal each year, the compound-interest method results in an increasing charge for depreciation over the useful life of the asset. In contrast, as Exhibit 20-1 shows, straight-line depreciation generates equal charges; sum-of-years'-digits depreciation, decreasing charges.**

As explained in Chapter 12, DCF methods assume a capital-recovery factor that is related to funds in use. Each period's income is *defined* as the internal rate of return on the beginning investment. Each cash payment consists of income (rate of return) plus recovery of principal (depreciation):

YEAR	(1) INVESTMENT AT BEGINNING OF YEAR	(2) OPERATING CASH INFLOW	(3) 20 × (1) INCOME @ 20% PER YEAR	(4) (2) − (3) "DEPRECIATION," INVESTMENT RECOVERED AT END OF YEAR	(5) (1) − (4) NET BOOK VALUE, UNRECOVERED INVESTMENT AT END OF YEAR
1	$4,212.96	$2,000	$842.59	$1,157.41	$3,055.55
2	3,055.55	2,000	611.11	1,388.89	1,666.66
3	1,666.66	2,000	333.34	1,666.66	0

effects on performance Exhibit 20-1 assumes steady cash inflows. Under these conditions, the commonly used depreciation models show increasing profitability as the asset ages.[25] Such varying

[25]A cash-flow pattern could occur that would yield a compound-interest pattern of equal depreciation charges each period. Interested readers could check to see that the following cash inflows will generate compound-interest depreciation of $1,404 yearly: $2,246.92, $1,964.04, and $1,683.18. The beginning book values each year would be $4,212.96, $2,808.64, and $1,404.32. Incidentally, these same cash flows are used in the text illustration in the next section, "Residual Income Effects." Note there that the depreciation pattern is determined by the *predicted* cash flows at the time the asset is acquired, not by the *actual* cash flows.

rates of return have no relation to the DCF planning models.[26] Many critics of straight-line and sum-of-the-years'-digits depreciation worry that managers are motivated against buying new assets because their early rates of return appear worse than they should. However, the critics also worry that managers are motivated to hold on to existing assets too long. Why? Because, as Exhibit 20-1 shows, in the late years the rates of return on old assets appear much better than they should.[27]

residual-income effects

Using the data in Exhibit 20-1, the compound-interest method of depreciation would show the following effects on residual income (in dollars):

Year	1	2	3
Cash operating income	2,000	2,000	2,000
Depreciation (based on original expectations)	1,157	1,389	1,667
Imputed interest (charged against subunit at the 20% required rate of return)	843	611	333
Total expenses	2,000	2,000	2,000
Residual income	0	0	0

Any actual cash flow that deviated from the predicted cash flow would affect residual income. Suppose actual cash flows were as follows (in dollars):

Year	1	2	3
Cash operating income	2,247	1,964	1,683
Depreciation, as above (based on original expectations)	1,157	1,389	1,667
Imputed interest, as above	843	611	333
Total expenses	2,000	2,000	2,000
Residual income (loss)	247	(36)	(317)

This illustration underscores that depreciation methods of all kinds are based on *predicted* cash flows, not *actual* cash flows. Thus, the deviations between budgeted performance and actual performance may be explained by various operating and economic conditions, not by the depreciation pattern.

linking decisions and performance

Industry has rejected the compound-interest method of depreciation primarily because:

1. The conventional depreciation methods have become firmly entrenched in external reporting, and companies cling to using the same depreciation method for internal reporting and shareholder reporting.

[26]For an elaboration of the differences, see Ezra Solomon, "Alternative Rate of Return Concepts and Their Implications for Utility Regulation," *Bell Journal of Economics and Management Science,* 1, No. 1 (Spring 1970), 65–81.

[27]For additional discussion and examples of the effects of compound-interest depreciation and other depreciation methods on performance measurement, see Kaplan, *Advanced Management Accounting,* Chap. 15.

2. If cash flows are equal per year, they produce an increasing charge over the useful life of an asset. Intuitively, however, managers do not see the justification for an increasing charge for depreciation if cash flows remain constant. Moreover, many executives believe that most investments in depreciable assets tend to generate higher cash inflows in earlier years. If so, straight-line depreciation may give approximately the same results as compound-interest depreciation.
3. The compound-interest method works clearly if projected annual operating flows are reasonably equal, but the implicit principal-recovery pattern is more difficult to compute and explain if projected cash flows differ markedly through the years.
4. The market values of particular assets do not coincide with the book values produced by the compound-interest method, particularly in the early years of use.

Until formal attempts are made to reconcile DCF models for planning with accrual-accounting models for control, follow-up of investment decisions must rely on the sampling of projects or on a dual-planning scheme. In sampling, DCF decisions would be audited by gathering data, year by year, to see whether the specific cash flow predictions proved accurate. In dual planning, the DCF decision would simultaneously be cast in the form of an accrual-accounting rate-of-return prediction; then the following-up would be based on the accrual-accounting model. (For additional discussion, see pages 381–83 and 420.)

Appendix 20b: perspective on design of management control systems

Is General Motors' management control system better than Ford's? What criteria should we use to judge whether a system is satisfactory? This subject was introduced in Chapter 10 (page 318–23). Please review that material now. This appendix uses some of those earlier ideas to help suggest a conceptual framework for judging control systems. The framework here is deliberately simplified to highlight the points that are usually the most critical.[28]

organization goals

As shown in Exhibit 20-2, the heaviest influence on systems design should be **organization goals (organization objectives),** that is, goals specified by top management. (The management literature often distinguishes between *goals* and *objectives,* but no such distinction is made here.) A favorite goal is the maximization of stockholder wealth, which many managers believe is achieved by trying to maximize long-run corporate earnings. However, such a goal is frequently regarded as too broad or abstract, so a set of goals or subgoals is sometimes identified.

A primary goal may be the reaching of a budgeted net income of, say, $10 million for a given year. In turn, the company may pinpoint subgoals, also called **key variables, key result areas, critical success factors,** or **critical economic success factors,** as essential to attainment of the primary goal. These subgoals are key or critical because their achievement will virtually ensure success, to the extent that success is controllable by management. Examples are the McDonald's Corporation's emphasis on quality, service, and cleanliness. If the manager of a store does well in these areas, the store's success will be enhanced. Of course, environmental conditions, such as gasoline rationing or the building of a Burger King outlet next door, could upset

[28]Many alternative frameworks are available. For example, see the suggested readings in this chapter. Also see W. Ouchi, *Theory Z* (Reading, Mass.: Addison-Wesley, 1981); R. Waterman, T. Peters, and J. Phillips, "Structure Is Not Organization," *Business Horizons,* June 1980; R. F. Vancil, "Managing the Decentralized Firm," *Financial Executive,* March 1980; and A. Edstrom and J. R. Galbraith, "Transfer of Managers as a Coordination and Control Strategy in Multinational Organizations," *Administrative Science Quarterly,* June 1977.

EXHIBIT 20-2

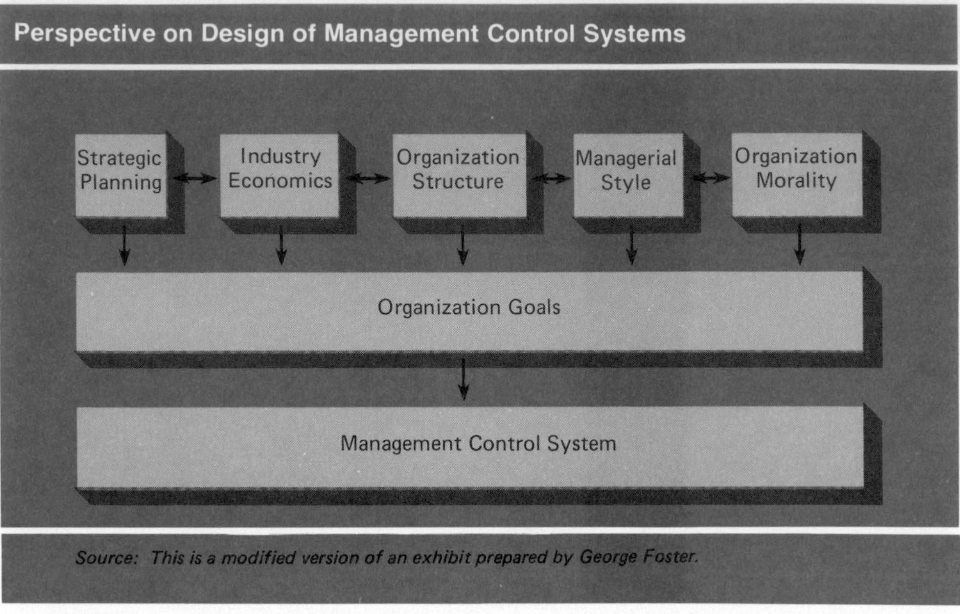

Source: This is a modified version of an exhibit prepared by George Foster.

results. Other examples of subgoals are skillful pricing, manufacturing efficiency, employee training, innovation, and share of the market.

trade-offs between goals

A major aspect of the subgoals is that managers often face trade-off decisions that may improve performance of one goal to the detriment of another goal. Thus, a manager may lower prices. He or she may gain a larger share of the market but hurt short-run profits. Other examples of trade-offs are cutting back on quality-control inspections (thus decreasing costs) to improve short-run earnings, spending more on training and research (thus increasing costs) to improve long-run profitability, or reducing efficiency by paying overtime (thus increasing costs) to meet production targets.

The most common problem in setting organization goals, at least in the United States, is the attaining of a balance between long-run and short-run goals. Unless the strategic-planning goals can be included among the set of organization goals, too much emphasis may be placed on short-run results. For example, innovation, such as the development of new products, may be downplayed by managers if it is not an explicit goal. A television producer, Norman Lear, commented in a speech: "Whether it is in industry, government, or academia, our leaders everywhere seem all too ready to sell the future short for a moment of success."

Chapter 10 emphasized goal congruence as a major criterion for judging control systems. The selections of the subgoals *and* their accompanying measures of performance are keys to obtaining goal congruence. In particular, they should be *complete* in the sense that all subgoals are included in the performance measurements. For example, top management may cite goals of profits, efficiency, share of the market, and product innovation, but the selections are incomplete if performance is measured in relation to only one or two of these goals.

If top management is really serious about getting subordinates to take the long-range view, the organization goals can be specified accordingly. In turn, the management control system can put teeth into long-range thinking by incorporating such measures as the development of new products as a part of performance evaluation and rewards. For example, General Foods and Nabisco use such measures.

In addition to specifying goals and control systems to help a long-run focus, some organization structures are also especially designed with the long run in mind. The most heavily publicized illustration is the organization structure at Texas Instruments. Many managers wear two hats and must meet two sets of goals, one for strategic (long-run) activities and one for operating (short-run) activities.[29]

Organization objectives are enormously important. They deserve serious thought. A prominent management consultant has stated:

> Objectives come before strategy. Strategy comes before structure. Strategy cannot exist without reference to purpose and objectives. . . . Without objectives there can be neither leadership nor an organization. Each person serves himself alone. With unworthy or trivial objectives there can be only weak leadership. Weak objectives result in weak organizations.[30]

influential variables

The top five boxes in Exhibit 20-2 are called *influential variables* because they affect one another and also affect the choice of goals and subgoals. A lengthy discussion of these variables is beyond the scope of this book, but a brief description follows.

Strategic planning is essentially long-run planning concerning products, processes, and the general direction of the organization. It considers the resources of the organization, the behavior of competitors, and the current and projected demands of the *marketplace*. For example, in the early 1970s, Miller Brewing Company decided that it had the competence to produce and market its Lite beer, that competitors had little faith in the demand, and that strong marketing would increase demand. Consequently, Miller advertised its Lite brand heavily and successfully.

Industry economics are factors such as supply, demand, and competition, which affect the goals and subgoals of the organization. For example, the prices in some industries, such as glass or automobile parts, are set almost wholly by market forces. In these cases, price is a given as far as the design of a control system is concerned. Then subgoals such as quality of product and customer service are usually critical. Ideally, all these subgoals are monitored by the control system. In other industries, such as construction or defense contracting, the prices are heavily influenced by management decisions. In these cases, the improvement of pricing skills may be an important subgoal of management.

Organization structure is the way top management has arranged the lines of responsibility within an entity. For example, one company may be organized primarily by *functions,* such as manufacturing and marketing; another company, by *divisions* having heavy decision-making authority concerning both manufacturing and marketing, such as the eastern and western divisions, or the coffee and cereal divisions; another company, by some hybrid arrangement.

An example of a hybrid is the **matrix organization.** Consulting firms, aerospace firms, and construction firms typically use a matrix form, whereby one manager is given responsibility for a project or product that must use services from several functional responsibility centers such as manufacturing plants. In the following illustration,

---

[29]Peter Lorange, *Corporate Planning: An Executive Viewpoint* (Englewood Cliffs, N.J.: Prentice-Hall, 1980), pp. 69–70.

[30]B. Henderson, "Objectives and the Organization" (Boston Consulting Group, Brochure 235, April 1981).

the managers of Product A and Product C share the services of Plant 1; A and B, of Plant 2; B and C, of Plant 3.[31]

Marketing Managers	Manager, Plant 1	Manager, Plant 2	Manager, Plant 3
Manager, Product A	X	X	
Manager, Product B		X	X
Manager, Product C	X		X
	Manufacturing Managers		

Other examples of projects are construction of various buildings or equipment. Examples of functional responsibilities are bricklayers, carpenters, and electricians. Such relationships are often complicated because the goals of the project managers conflict with the goals of the responsibility center managers. That is, the project manager wants primary care for his or her project. In contrast, the functional responsibility center manager must juggle all demands from many project managers.[32]

Managerial style is the way a manager operates from day to day. Some managers are authoritarian; others depend on heavy participation and consensus in reaching decisions. Some managers emphasize written communication; others emphasize oral communication and physical observation. The former managers may desire and strongly support an elaborate formal control system, whereas the latter may not. **Top-management support is absolutely essential for the success of any control system. Without clear and continuous top-management backing, the goals specified by the system are less likely to gain acceptance by subordinates as group goals or as personal goals.** A consultant has observed that "the ability of the leader to remain the leader depends on how well he personifies in his personal behavior those things which are perceived to be the most important with respect to the organization's objectives.[33]

As Chapter 10 points out (page 320), not all control is attained via the formal organization control system. For example, physical observation, oral communication, and non-financial information are often instrumental but informal. The chief executive officer's style usually has the most significant impact on the prominence and

[31] See R. Vancil, "What Kind of Management Control Do You Need?" *Harvard Business Review,* March-April 1973, pp. 75–86. His exhibit on p. 84 is similar to the one used here.

[32] Lorange describes a form of matrix organization at Texas Instruments. A dual operating/strategic structure has been developed. The same manager may wear two hats, having responsibilities for attaining explicit strategic (long-range) goals and tactical (short-range) goals. See P. Lorange, *Corporate Planning: An Executive Viewpoint* (Englewood Cliffs, N.J.: Prentice-Hall, 1980), pp. 69–70.

[33] Henderson, "Objectives and the Organization."

characteristics of the formal control system. Indeed, when a highly influential chief resigns, the existing control system usually deserves changing.[34]

Organization morality refers to legal and top-management constraints on goals, behavior, and control systems. Notable examples are antitrust laws and the Foreign Corrupt Practices Act. As Chapter 27 points out, the act requires the systems to give reasonable assurance that no illegal payments are occurring. In addition, many companies have prepared formal codes of ethics regarding a wide range of operating matters.

The arrows in Exhibit 20-2 indicate interplay between the boxes. Thus, the control system could be influenced by an organization goal, say, to be a setter of low prices. The decision to tend toward low rather than high prices could be influenced by any or all of the following:

1. Strategic planning—Price low, gain market share and economies of scale.
2. Industry economics—Few competitors, infrequent product innovation.
3. Organization structure—Responsibility by product lines.
4. Managerial style—Participative, heavy use of monthly reports.
5. Organization morality—Antitrust laws prohibit collusion among competitors or price discrimination among customers.

Top management would probably want a control system to provide regular feedback as to how managers have abided by the organization's pricing policies.

Designing the system

motivational criteria

The underlying criterion is cost-benefit in relation to what top management seeks from a given system. That is, how well does System A achieve top-management goals in relation to System B? If A and B cost approximately the same, then choose the system that is more likely to engender the desired set of collective operating decisions (behavior). The focus is on predicting whether subordinates will behave as desired by their superiors. Put another way: Does the system communicate the right information to the right people at the right time—under both normal and stress conditions?

Cost-benefit recognizes that there are many ways to control. That is, control systems may have many forms and may use various sources of information. For example, some organizations prosper with little formal control, relying primarily on physical observation, oral communication, and nonfinancial calibrations of performance.

Two additional criteria, the motivational criteria of goal congruence and managerial effort, help make the primary criterion of cost-benefit more concrete. The diagram in Exhibit 20-3 may aid perspective.

choices of responsibility centers

The overall approach to designing systems initially focuses on goal congruence. Goals and subgoals should be identified, giving full recognition to the existence of informal group goals and individual goals. The designer should ask whether sufficient managerial effort exists toward the goals and whether subordinates are achieving the desired coordination and trade-offs among various goals. For example, is the division manager devoting too much effort to manufacturing efficiency and insufficient effort to customer service?

[34]For observations on the management practices of thirty-seven companies that are often used as examples of well-run organizations, see T. Peters, "Putting Excellence into Management," *Business Week*, July 21, 1980, pp. 196–205.

EXHIBIT 20-3

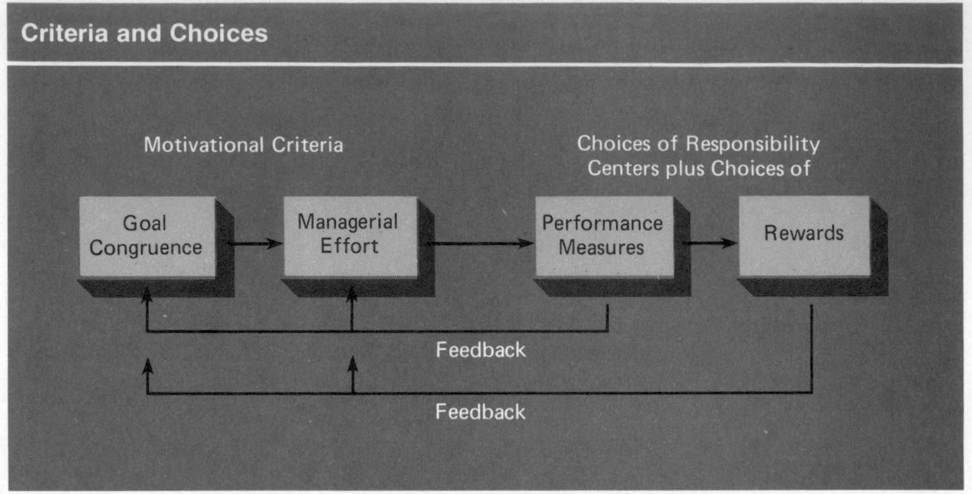

The top-management goals are sometimes difficult to specify and relate to one another. After this step has been carefully taken, the designer chooses responsibility centers, performance measures, and rewards.

The choice of responsibility centers frequently depends on a given organization structure. However, a distinction should be made between the choices of organization structure and the choices of responsibility centers. The former focuses on *who reports to whom,* that is, how does the overall work of the organization get accomplished? For example, should the plant manager report to a division manager or to a central vice-president of manufacturing? The responsibility center question focuses on *how to account* for the work of the various subunits. For example, should a plant be a profit center or a cost center? Our attention in Chapters 19 and 20 has focused on the latter question, and only incidentally on the former.

Sometimes the systems designer may be in a position to persuade top mangement that goals or organization structures or other influential variables warrant change in conjunction with changes in the control system. **However, most changes are piecemeal improvements rather than grandiose replacements. Hence, the designer must work within the constraints of given goals and organization structures.**

performance measures and rewards

Numerous performance measurement choices have been described in this book. Examples are whether to use variable or absorption costing and whether to use tight or loose performance standards.

Rewards were also described on page 323. Recall the major lesson: **In general, managers concentrate on the areas where their performance is measured in a relatively objective way and where their performance clearly affects their rewards.**

The choice of rewards is clearly within the province of management control systems. However, the design of a reward system is mainly the concern of top managers, who often get advice from many sources besides accountants.

agency theory

A large segment of the academic accounting and economics literature during the 1970s began to concentrate on **agency theory.** A superior manager is an example of a principal; a subordinate is an example of an agent. This theory focuses on the design of performance measures and rewards so that subordinates are more likely to act in the interest of the whole organization.

The formal theory of principals and agents generally rests on the following assumptions about individuals as agents:

1. They are rational and wish to maximize their own utilities.
2. They seek both financial and nonfinancial rewards (attractive offices, special privileges).
3. They are generally **risk averse** if stakes are sufficiently large. For example, most individuals would be unwilling to bet $10,000 on a coin toss, double or nothing. If the individuals would be willing to make such a bet, they are called **risk neutral.** Risk aversion is a worldwide phenomenon. Hence, managers tend to play it safe and are reluctant to innovate. (See the next chapter for additional discussion of risk attitudes and utilities.)
4. As agents, subordinates' individual interests will not always coincide with the interests of the principal.
5. They prefer leisure to hard work.

managerial effort

The implications of assumption 5 are enormous and distasteful. Do most managers prefer to exert no effort rather than effort? Do they lie, cheat, shirk? Or are such tendencies overemphasized by the theory? This author believes that managers get satisfaction from exerting effort and being honest. Nevertheless, much of the agency literature is concerned about the existence of "private information." That is, agents often know more about their operating conditions and their actions than their principals know. Consider the following example:

» EXAMPLE

> We are not suggesting that managers are evil or indifferent to the overall performance of the firm. We are suggesting that when managers will be evaluated and promoted based on comparing their performance to some standard, we should not expect that managers will act contrary to their own self-interest in providing information about what an appropriate standard should be.[35]

A more positive view emphasizes mutual trust and takes a long-range view. For example:

» EXAMPLE

> A profit center manager's willingness to take independent action is significantly colored by his relationship with his boss. He is more likely to act independently if he and his superior have worked together for a sufficient length of time to develop a mutual self respect and a trust in each other's capabilities. Self-confidence and trust cannot be mandated in an organization, but corporate managers can seek to create a climate which encourages risk-taking and is tolerant of the inevitable mistakes that will occur. The organizational philosophy of decentralization has a major impact on the profit center manager's sense of his autonomy.[36]

emphasis on attitudes toward risks

Thus, principal-agent theory is concerned with how to achieve a commonality of interest between the principal (top managers) and the agent (subordinate managers). Divergence of interest occurs because of differences in risk attitudes, the existence of private information, and the limited or costly ways of observing agents in action. The principal invests in a management control system that motivates the desired behavior by routine methods of evaluating performance and of issuing rewards. Kaplan observes that agency costs are "the sum of the costs of the incentive compensation plan, the cost of monitoring actions, *and* the remaining cost of actions taken by managers that diverge from the preferences of the owners."[37]

---

[35]Kaplan, *Advanced Management Accounting,* Chap. 13. Also see J. Demski, *Information Analysis,* 2nd ed. (Reading, Mass.: Addison-Wesley), Chap. 6.

[36]Vancil, *Decentralization,* pp. 64–65.

[37]Kaplan, *Advanced Management Accounting,* Chap. 16.

Agency research offers a different perspective on control systems. Nevertheless, there are parallels between its overview and the overview described earlier. For example, the attempt to get commonality of interest (congruence of goals, behaviors, and risk attitudes) is nothing new.

Perhaps the biggest practical contribution of agency theory to date is the emphasis on risk attitudes. For example, a revered tenet of performance measurement and reward has been controllability. That is, managers supposedly should not be given responsibility for costs or revenues beyond their control. Examples can demonstrate that adhering to the controllability criterion is unwise when the principal and agent have identical beliefs about probabilities and have utility functions in the same class. Instead, the principal and agent should have a profit-sharing arrangement. Hence, an uncontrollable outcome affects the manager's compensation, "thereby apparently violating one of the cherished dictums of cost accounting."[38] **Thus, the example implies that the design of the control system should focus on who bears the risks rather than who exerts control.**

Despite the stimulating hypotheses offered by agency theory, the work to date has been confined to highly simplified and abstract situations. Nevertheless, agency theory frequently provides "a more solid conceptual basis for many cost accounting and management control procedures that are now advocated on an intuitive, judgmental basis."[39]

QUESTIONS, PROBLEMS, AND CASES

20-1 Under what circumstances does the gross-asset base make most sense?

20-2 Proponents of net book value as an investment base usually cite two major reasons for their position. What are these reasons?

20-3 How should interest expense and nonrecurring expenses be considered in computing incomes that are related to investment bases?

20-4 "In recent years there has been a tendency toward corporate decentralization, accompanied by a setting of individual rate-of-return targets for corporate segments. This provides incentive because managers can operate their segments as if they were separate companies of their own." Do you agree? Why?

20-5 What income concept is likely to be most realistic for measuring performance of various corporate segments?

20-6 "The rate-of-return tool is so hampered by limitations that we might as well forget it." Do you agree? Why?

20-7 What measures besides rate of return are commonly used to judge managerial performance?

20-8 "Too much stress on rate of return can hurt the corporation." How?

20-9 "Net income divided by sales is the most important single measure of business success." Do you agree? Why?

20-10 List four possible bases for computing the cost of invested capital.

20-11 "The stockholder's-equity base is the best investment base for appraising operating management." Do you agree? Why?

20-12 "The use of undepreciated cost of fixed assets as part of the investment base compensates for the impact of the changing price level on historical cost." Do you agree? Why?

---

[38]Ibid., Chap. 17, p. 13. Also see J. Demski and G. Feltham, "Economic Incentives in Budgetary Control Systems," *Accounting Review,* April, 1978; and J. Demski, "Uncertainty and Evaluation Based on Controllable Performance," *Journal of Accounting Research,* Autumn 1976.

[39]Kaplan, *Advanced Management Accounting,* Chap. 17.

20-13 ***Government contracts and profit margins.*** Spokespersons for many companies that are heavily involved in government-contract work often complain that defense work is not very profitable. They cite low-percentage profit margins as evidence. Are such contentions justified? Why, or why not?

20-14 ***Analysis of return on capital; comparisons of three companies.*** (Adapted from *N.A.A. Research Report No. 35,* pp. 34–35.)

1. Rate of return on capital is often expressed as follows:

$$\frac{\textbf{Income}}{\textbf{Capital}} = \frac{\textbf{Income}}{\textbf{Sales}} \times \frac{\textbf{Sales}}{\textbf{Capital}}$$

What advantages can you see in the breakdown of the computation into two separate components?

2. Fill in the blanks:

	COMPANIES IN SAME INDUSTRY		
	A	**B**	**C**
Sales	$1,000,000	$500,000	$ —
Income	100,000	50,000	—
Capital	500,000	—	5,000,000
Income as a percent of sales	—	—	0.5%
Turnover of capital	—	—	2
Return on investment	—	1%	—

After filling in the blanks, comment on the relative performance of these companies as thoroughly as the data permit.

20-15 ***Auto dealership profit centers.*** Many automobile dealers divide their businesses into two major divisions: (a) parts and service and (b) vehicle sales. The gross profit of the parts and service activity is looked upon as the amount that is supposed to "cover" all parts and service overhead plus all general overhead of the dealership. If this goal can be achieved, the gross profit of the vehicle division can be regarded as "gravy"—as net profit. In other words, the contribution margin of the parts and service activity is looked upon as a cost recovery, whereas the vehicle sales are regarded as the profit-making mechanism.

REQUIRED

Evaluate the merits of this approach. If you were managing an automobile dealership, would you view your operations any differently? How?

20-16 ***Computation of gross profits on car sales.*** Many auto dealers use the "washout" concept. *Washout* is the method for computing gross profits on a series of deals starting with the sale of a new unit and ending with the straight (no trade-in) sale of the last vehicle in the series. The gross profit on the sale of the new unit and used units is totaled and stated in terms of gross profit per new unit retailed.

REQUIRED

Evaluate the washout concept in terms of assigning responsibility to profit centers. How else could gross profit be computed?

20-17 ***ROI and residual income.*** (D. Kleespie) The Gaul Company produces and distributes a wide variety of recreational products. One of its divisions, the Goscinny Division, manufactures and sells "menhirs," which are very popular with cross-country skiers; the demand for these menhirs is relatively insensitive to price changes. The Goscinny Division is considered to be an investment center and in recent years has averaged a return on investment of 20 percent. The following data are available for the Goscinny Division and its product:

Total annual fixed costs	$1,000,000
Variable costs per menhir	$300
Average number of menhirs sold each year	10,000
Average operating assets invested in the division	$1,600,000

REQUIRED

1. What is the minimum per-unit selling price that the Goscinny Division should charge in order to avoid a negative performance rating for Mary Obelix, the division manager? (You may assume that the judgment of Obelix's performance is based on the division's ROI record.)
2. Assume that the Gaul Company's judgment of the performance of its investment center managers is based on the residual income rather than ROI as was assumed in requirement 1 above. The company's minimum acceptable earning rate is considered to be 15 percent. What is the minimum per-unit selling price that the Goscinny Division should charge in order to avoid a negative performance rating for Obelix?

20-18 ***Pricing, rate of return, and measuring efficiency.*** A large motorized bicycle company follows a pricing policy whereby "normal" or "standard" activity is used as a base for pricing. That is, prices are set on the basis of long-run annual-volume predictions. They are then rarely changed except for notable changes in wage rates or material prices.

You are given the following data:

Materials, wages, and other variable costs	$1,320 per unit
Fixed overhead	$300,000,000 per year
Desired rate of return on invested capital	20%
Normal volume	1,000,000 units
Invested capital	$900,000,000

REQUIRED

1. What net-income percentage based on dollar sales is needed to attain the desired rate of return?
2. What rate of return on invested capital will be earned at sales volumes of 1,500,000 and 500,000 units, respectively?
3. The company has a sizable management bonus plan based on yearly divisional performance. Assume that the volume was 1,000,000, 1,500,000, and 500,000 units, respectively, in three successive years. Each of three managers has served as division manager for one year before being killed in an automobile accident. As the major heir of the third manager, comment on the bonus plan.

20-19 ***The General Electric approach.*** (D. Solomons, adapted) Consider the following:

	(000'S OMITTED)	
	Division A	**Division B**
Total assets	$1,000	$5,000
Net annual earnings	$ 200	$ 750
Rate of return on total assets	20%	15%

REQUIRED

1. Which is the more successful division? Why?
2. General Electric Company has used "residual income," the excess of net earnings over the cost of capital, as the measure of management success—the quantity a manager should try to maximize. The cost of capital is deducted from the net annual earnings to obtain residual income. Using this criterion, what is the residual income for each division if the cost of capital is (a) 12 percent, (b) 14 percent, (c) 17½ percent? Which division is more successful under each of these rates?

20-20 ***Various measures of profitability.*** When the Coronet Company formed three divisions a year ago, the president told the division managers that a bonus would be paid to the most profitable division. However, absolute profit as conventionally computed would not be used. Instead, the ranking would be affected by the relative investments in the three divisions. Each manager has now written a memorandum claiming that he is entitled to the bonus. The following data are available:

DIVISION	GROSS BOOK VALUE AT START OF YEAR	NET INCOME AS COMPUTED FOR CONVENTIONAL EXTERNAL ANNUAL REPORT COMPILATION
X	$400,000	$47,500
Y	380,000	46,000
Z	250,000	30,800

All the assets are fixed assets that were purchased ten years ago and have ten years of usefulness remaining. The Coronet cost of capital is 10 percent. All computations of current return should be based on a balance at the start of the year.

Which method for computing profitability did each manager choose? Make your description specific and brief. Show supporting computations. Where applicable, assume straight-line depreciation.

20-21 ***Using gross or net book value of fixed assets.*** Assume that a particular plant acquires $400,000 of fixed assets with a useful life of four years and no residual value. Straight-line depreciation will be used. The plant manager is judged on income in relation to these fixed assets. Annual net income, after deducting depreciation, is $40,000.

Assume that sales, and expenses except depreciation, are on a cash basis. Dividends equal net income. Thus, cash in the amount of the depreciation charge will accumulate each year. The plant manager's performance is judged in relation to fixed assets because all current assets, including cash, are considered under central company control.

1. Prepare a comparative tabulation of the plant's rate of return and the company's overall rate of return based on:

a. Gross (i.e., original cost) assets.

b. Net book value of assets. Assume (unrealistically) that any cash accumulated remains idle.

2. Evaluate the relative merits of gross assets and net book value of assets as investment bases.

20-22 ***ROI for measuring performance.*** (CMA) The Texon Co. is organized into autonomous divisions along regional market lines. Each division manager is responsible for sales, cost of operations, acquisition and financing of divisional assets, and working-capital management.

The vice-president of general operations for the company will retire in September 19_5. A review of the performance, attitudes, and skills of several management employees has been undertaken. Interviews with qualified outside candidates have also been held. The selection committee has narrowed the choice to the managers of Divisions A and F.

Both candidates were appointed division managers in late 19_1. The manager of Division A had been the assistant manager of that division for the prior five years. The manager of Division F had served as assistant division manager of Division B before being appointed to

EXHIBIT 20-4

	DIVISION A			DIVISION F		
	19_2	19_3	19_4	19_2	19_3	19_4
Estimated industry sales			(000 omitted)			
—market area	$10,000	$12,000	$13,000	$5,000	$6,000	$6,500
Division sales	$ 1,000	$ 1,100	$ 1,210	$ 450	$ 600	$ 750
Variable costs	$ 300	$ 320	$ 345	$ 135	$ 175	$ 210
Discretionary costs	400	405	420	170	200	230
Committed costs	275	325	350	140	200	250
Total costs	$ 975	$ 1,050	$ 1,115	$ 445	$ 575	$ 690
Net income	$ 25	$ 50	$ 95	$ 5	$ 25	$ 60
Assets employed	$ 330	$ 340	$ 360	$ 170	$ 240	$ 300
Liabilities	103	105	115	47	100	130
Net investment	227	235	245	123	140	170
Return on investment	11%	21%	39%	4%	18%	35%

his present post. He took over Division F, a division newly formed in 19_0, when its first manager left to join a competitor. The financial results of their performance in the past three years are reported in Exhibit 20-4.

REQUIRED

1. Texon Co. measures the performance of the divisions and the division managers on the basis of their return on investment (ROI). Is this an appropriate measurement for the division managers? Explain.
2. Many believe that a single measure, such as ROI, is inadequate to fully evaluate performance. What additional measure(s) could be used for performance evaluation? Give reasons for each measure listed.
3. On the basis of the information given, which manager would you recommend for vice-president of general operations? Present reasons to support your answer.

20-23 ***Motivation and bonus program.*** (CMA) Study Appendix 20b.

Rimald Corporation is a large decentralized organization with six subsidiary companies operating as individual businesses each having independent manufacturing and marketing operations. Subsidiary performance is measured by return on total assets employed less current liabilities.

The Mospace subsidiary manufactures and markets products for the automotive and aerospace industries. It has accounted for 60 percent of Rimald's total sales for the past four years. Unfortunately Mospace's profits and return on investment have declined in the last four years. Mospace was responsible for about 40 percent of Rimald's total net income before taxes in 19_8, which is considerably lower than in prior years. The decreasing contribution to total corporation profits is causing concern throughout Mospace.

One sales manager commented. "The increases in sales prices, of about 15 percent over the four years, are inadequate to keep pace with increasing manufacturing costs—especially direct-labor costs. The hourly wage rates and employee benefit costs have increased, and the number of workers seems to have increased even though our production levels have not changed during the past four years. We need some kind of incentive program to control labor costs in order to improve profitability."

After further thought the sales manager proposed an incentive program keyed to labor costs. The incentive program would be based on the reduction in the labor-cost ratio (LCR). The LCR would be computed by dividing the cost of labor, including benefits, by the "added value" of Mospace products. The "added value" would be determined by subtracting all costs except labor and benefits from sales. The incentive features of the program are

> The improvement in the LCR over the prior-year ratio multiplied by the labor cost of the prior year will be defined as the gross savings to be shared equally between management employees and the subsidiary.
>
> The management employees' share will be divided equally among the twenty-five employees who are affected.
>
> A report of the results and payments will be made no later than the second month following the end of the year.

Mospace management accumulated the accompanying financial data for the last four fiscal years so that the sales manager's proposal can be evaluated.

REQUIRED

1. How effective would the participation provisions (e.g., share equally with the subsidiary, share equally with other management employees, and the annual payment of share) be in the motivation of managers? Explain your answer.
2. The incentive program, based upon the improvement in the LCR, is designed to motivate managers to be more effective in the control of labor cost.
   a. Does the formula measure only the effect of changes in labor cost? Explain your answer.
   b. Are the factors that affect the changes in the LCR within the control of the subsidiary management? Explain your answer.
3. Did the sales manager identify the primary cause of Mospace's profit decline? Explain your answer.

Mospace Subsidiary
(000 omitted)

	19_8	19_7	19_6	19_5
Sales	$21,500	$20,675	$19,500	$18,750
Expenses				
Raw material	10,360	9,855	8,875	8,450
Labor cost*	7,061	6,649	6,171	5,760
All other expenses	1,900	1,920	1,875	1,850
Total	$19,321	$18,424	$16,921	$16,060
Net income before taxes	$ 2,179	$ 2,251	$ 2,579	$ 2,690
Other data				
Volume data:				
Pounds of raw material (000 omitted)	3,700	3,650	3,550	3,500
Labor hours (000 omitted)	614	610	605	600
Unit data:				
Average cost per pound of raw material	$ 2.80	$ 2.70	$ 2.50	$ 2.41
Average labor rate per hour*	$11.50	$10.90	$10.20	$ 9.60

**Includes employee benefit costs.*

20-24 ***Investment bases in an oil company.*** An oil company is having trouble in deciding whether to continue to use its old gasoline stations and in evaluating the performance of these stations in terms of return on investment. Top management has explored various ways of establishing a value for such stations. Book value, market value, and replacement value are the three alternatives now under consideration.

REQUIRED

1. Which of the three bases is applicable for deciding whether to dispose of an old station? Why?
2. Which of the three bases is applicable for judging the performance of the station and its manager? Why? Why is your answer the same as or different from your answer in requirement 1?

20-25 ***What investment bases should be used?*** The president of a giant corporation has attended miscellaneous management education programs during the past few years. He has a persistent desire to keep abreast of the latest thinking regarding information for decisions and performance measurement. He greets you, a new graduate from a school of management, with the following comments and questions:

"As I read more and more on this subject and as I listen to more and more discussions, I become increasingly bewildered by the nomenclature and the concepts. Oh, I am aware of the infirmities of historical costs. What I am concerned about are such terms and concepts as market value, current value, replacement value, economic value, present value, opportunity value, disposal value, entry value, and countless similar terms.

"Consider our new processing equipment in Division A. It cost $10 million. We could sell it for perhaps $7 million. How should it be valued for measuring performance in year 1? In year 5? In year 10?

"I am not asking you to pick from the existing practices of valuation. I am asking a normative question. That is, first tell me how these assets *should* be valued to assist decisions and to evaluate performance—without regard to the practical difficulties of implementation. After you answer the question on a normative basis, then answer it again on the basis of what might be accomplished now in our organization to implement what is conceptually most desirable."

REQUIRED

Prepare a memorandum in response to the president's requirements. Include definitions of the various cost terms he mentioned. You may wish to use an example to clarify your points.

20-26 ***Responsibility and control of costs.*** Solve Problem 10-27, which could logically have been placed here.

20-27 ***Allocation of computer costs.*** Solve Problem 15-17, which could logically have been placed here.

20-28 ***ROI based on gross and net investment.*** Study Appendix 20a.

Using DCF analysis, the Ezra Company invested $100,000 in plant and equipment having a useful life of six years and generating $22,961 in operating cash inflows each year. At the end of six years, the assets are scrapped at zero salvage value.

1. What is the internal rate of return?

2. Suppose straight-line depreciation is used as a basis for performance evaluation. What is the ROI for the first, fourth, and sixth years if ROI is based on the initial balance (gross investment base)? On net book value at the beginning of the year?

3. How closely do the answers in part 2 approximate the internal rate of return? Why do they differ?

20-29 ***Compound-interest depreciation.*** Study Appendix 20a. A hospital X-ray department is considering investing in a $7,132 machine having an expected useful life of two years and no terminal disposal value. As compared with an existing machine, the new machine will save $4,000 in cash-operating costs.

REQUIRED

1. Compute the internal rate of return.
2. Prepare a tabular comparison of the effect of the investment on operating income, using compound-interest, straight-line, and sum-of-years'-digits depreciation for each of the two years. Also show the yearly rate of return on the beginning balance of the investment.
3. How closely do the answers in requirement 2 approximate the internal rate of return? Why do they differ?
4. Assume that compound-interest depreciation is used. Compute the residual income in each of two years. Assume that the cash-operating savings were (a) $4,000 in each year and (b) $4,500 in the first year and $3,800 in the second year.

20-30 ***Discounted cash flow and evaluation of performance.*** Study Appendix 20a. John Castleman, the general manager of a division of a huge, highly diversified company, recently attended an executive training program. He learned about discounted cash-flow analysis, and he became convinced that it was the best available guide for making long-range investment decisions.

However, upon returning to his company, he became frustrated. He wanted to use the discounted cash-flow technique, but top management had a long-standing policy of evaluating divisional management performance largely on the basis of its rate of return as calculated by dividing divisional net income by the net book value of total divisional assets. Therefore, in his own best interests and in accordance with the specifications of his superiors, he had to make decisions that he felt were not really the most desirable in terms of maximizing what he considered to be the "true" rate of return (that is, the discounted cash-flow rate).

REQUIRED

1. Suppose Mr. Castleman had an opportunity to invest $30,000 in some automated machinery with a useful life of three years and a scrap value of zero. The expected cash savings per year were $12,060. Compute the internal rate of return. Ignore income-tax effects.
2. Show the effect on net income for each of the three years, assuming straight-line depreciation. Also show the rate of return based on the beginning balance of the net book value of the fixed asset for each year.
3. Repeat requirement 2, assuming sum-of-the-years'-digits depreciation.
4. Top management has indicated a minimum desired rate of return of 10 percent. After examining the results above, Mr. Castleman was more baffled than ever. He just could not see why he should invest in the machinery if his net income in the first year would not be at least 10 percent of the investment base. He discussed the matter with a professor at a nearby business school.

   The professor reacted: "The basic trouble is not confined to your company. Many companies now insist that their managers use discounted cash-flow techniques for appraising investment opportunities, but they use conventional accounting techniques for judging operating performance. In short, one model is supposed to be used for planning, but another model is used for control.

"A possible solution is to use the compound-interest method of depreciation for evaluating subsequent performance. The compound-interest method is based on the same model as the discounted cash-flow technique. That is, each receipt ($12,060 in this case) consists of interest on the beginning investment balance plus the recovery of principal. For example, the $12,060 cash savings during the first year would be analyzed as consisting of 'interest' of 10 percent of $30,000, or $3,000, plus a recovery of principal ('depreciation') of $9,060."

Repeat requirement 2, assuming the compound-interest method of depreciation.

5. Contrast the pattern of depreciation in requirement 4 with the other methods. Why is industry reluctant to use the compound-interest method of depreciation? What other means might be used to reconcile the two models described in requirement 4?

20-31 ***Conflict of accrual and DCF models.*** Study Appendix 20a.

1. The Marples Company, a small job shop, has landed a three-year exclusive contract for 10,000 proprietary widgets per year at $2.50 each. Total variable costs, including overhead but exclusive of the machinery required, are estimated at $1.00 per unit. John Marples, the president, is considering some proposals for tooling up to meet this demand.

One of the alternatives is the purchase of a new special-purpose machine. This would cost about $30,000 including installation and setup, and maintenance requirements would be about $310 yearly.

Marples will introduce an entirely new line of widgets in three years. The machine is not adaptable to the new manufacturing process, and the expected salvage value at that time will barely cover removal costs. The company depreciates its tools and equipment investments on a straight-line basis and uses 20 percent as its minimum desired rate of return on new investments.

Ignoring income taxes, compute the internal rate of return on the initial investment. Do you recommend its purchase?

2. Marples invests in the new machine and conducts a project review at the end of one year. He evaluates product profitability on the basis of ROI on the beginning investment for the year. He uses straight-line depreciation. He finds a significant difference between the observed rate and the projected rate of return, despite the fact that all costs were kept to budgeted figures. He asks you to explain the difference, and to recommend a simple system that will eliminate this problem.

What will you tell him?

20-32 ***Performance evaluation, motivation, compound-interest depreciation.*** (G. Foster) Study Appendix 20a.

I. Hobie Leland, Jr., has just been appointed divisional manager for the Goal Congruence Corporation. He must choose between adopting one (or adopting neither) of two projects, both of which are in mining ventures. The cash inflows and outflows of the two projects are predicted to be:

	PROJECT A	PROJECT B
Cash outflow at		
Start of Period 1	$15,000	$15,000
Net cash inflows at		
End of Period 1	$ 6,000	$ 5,000
End of Period 2	$ 6,000	$ 5,000
End of Period 3	$ 6,000	$ 5,000
End of Period 4	$ 3,000	$ 5,000
End of Period 5	$ 2,000	$ 5,000

Hobie's contract with Goal Congruence specifies his bonus to be 10 percent of annual residual income (if positive) of the division. Depletion (depreciation) of the mine is based on the straight-line method, assuming a life of five years and no salvage value. The capital charge for assets employed in the division is calculated as 10 percent of the opening book value of the mine ($15,000 minus accumulated depletion) for each period.

REQUIRED

1. Using the net present-value model, and before considering any bonus to Hobie, which project should Goal Congruence adopt? The minimum desired rate of return is 10 percent.
2. Hobie decides to choose the project that maximizes the net present value of his bonuses, and he uses a 20 percent discount rate in determining the net present value of the bonuses. Which project will he choose?
3. When it came time to submit capital-budgeting proposals to the head office, Hobie made the mistake of sending in his working papers rather than his formal proposal. The working papers were received at the head office by Delilah Jones, assistant to the president of Goal Congruence. Delilah was very upset at the contents of the working papers and showed them to the president. She then made a suggestion—change the depletion rate on the mine from straight-line to sum-of-the-years'-digits method. The new depletion rate would be implemented prior to Hobie's making a final decision between the two projects. How much is Delilah's suggestion worth to Goal Congruence?

II. The president of Goal Congruence is a realist. He knows that Hobie will not always make the convenient mistake of mailing his working papers rather than formal proposals. Moreover, he views Delilah's suggestion as, at best, providing an interim solution. He seeks your advice on what problems may arise with the existing performance measurement and incentive system used for Hobie.

REQUIRED

1. What problems would you mention in a report to the president of Goal Congruence?
2. What proposals would you make to help reduce the problems cited in requirement 1?

III. The president of Goal Congruence receives a suggestion that involves the use of a "compound-interest" depletion method, as explained in Appendix 20a. However, the president is confused as to how this method works when the internal rate of return exceeds the minimum desired rate of return. Delilah suggests he consider two alternatives:

(a) Use the internal rate of return in computing the "depletion" on the mine. The divisional net income would be calculated as:

Cash inflow	x
Less depletion	x
= Divisional net income	x

(b) Increase the "cost" of the investment to the present value of the cash inflows. Then use (i) the revised "cost" figure as the opening investment base for year one and (ii) the cost of capital in computing the "depletion" on the mine. In the year the project is adopted, the net present value is credited to the divisional net income. Thus, the divisional net income would be calculated as:

Cash inflow	x
Less depletion	x
Plus N.P.V. of newly adopted projects	x
= Divisional net income	x

Hobie's bonus would be calculated as 10 percent of divisional net income under either (a) or (b).

REQUIRED

1. Illustrate how each alternative "compound-interest" method would work for Goal Congruence. Would either alternative overcome some (or all) of the problems mentioned in II(1)?
2. What problems may exist in implementing either version of the "compound-interest" depletion method?

20-33 ***Soviet approach to return on investment.*** The Soviet System is a management control and evaluation system (bonus system) that is used in much of the Soviet economy. It is used to evaluate managers and determine their bonuses, and thus (it is hoped) to motivate the individual managers to cut costs and work toward the country's goals as specified by the central planning agency. One of these goals is to modernize the country's production facilities. The stated purpose was to increase the material interest of the management and employees in the economic results of the enterprise. The new management control system was a part of sweeping economy reforms that took effect in January 1966. As stated in Bertrand Horwitz, *Accounting Controls and the Soviet Economic Reforms of 1966* (Sarasota, Fla.: American Accounting Association, 1970), p. 23:

> Prior to January 1966, when the reforms first took effect, the director of a Soviet enterprise was confronted with the requirement of satisfying numerous physical and accounting goals. The enterprise was essentially a cell in a tautly administered system which allowed the director little room for independent action because the number of physical and accounting indexes by which he could be judged highly constrained his economic actions.

The new bonus system was based on the enterprise's increase in profits and the rate of return on assets employed in the enterprise. The exact formula used to compute the total bonuses to be distributed to the enterprise's employees is as follows:

$$\lambda_t = \alpha \frac{P_t - P_{t-1}}{P_{t-1}} + \beta \frac{P_t}{K_t} \tag{1}$$

and the total amount of the bonus for the enterprise is

$$TB_t = W_t \lambda_t \tag{2}$$

where W_t = **the wage fund for time period t, centrally determined**

P_t = **profit in period t that is net of explicit charges for the use of current and fixed gross assets at original cost**

TB_t = **total amount of enterprise bonus for period t**

K_t = **total average gross assets in t at original cost**

α, β = **coefficients that are centrally assigned norms; both are less than one and are nonnegative**

The first term of equation (1) is the rate of increase in earnings over the previous year. The second term is the ROI for the enterprise based on its gross assets. The sum of these two terms gives a factor (λ_t) that, when multiplied by the enterprise's wage fund, determines the total bonus for the enterprise. Thus, the total bonus for the enterprise depends on the enterprise's increase in profit over the previous year and its ROI.

The wage fund (W_t) for the enterprise in a period is centrally determined and therefore is a given amount for purposes of computation of the bonus. The accounting profit (P_t) is the enterprise's net profit before capital charges, minus (a) charges at the rate of 6 percent of gross assets, for the use of fixed assets and normal or planned working capital; (b) fixed (rent) payments; and (c) interest on bank credit. The charge of 6 percent is essentially the enterprise's cost of capital, because the enterprise gets its fixed assets from the government. The charge is also based on gross assets. The rent payments are designed to eliminate the differences between different enterprises because of natural operating conditions. Thus, a firm with very favorable conditions would have to make rent payments, while one operating under less-favorable conditions would not. The interest is for short-term loans from the central bank.

Average gross assets (K_t) is used as the investment base in order to motivate managers to replace their older, less-efficient assets. The purpose is to get managers to modernize their equipment.

The coefficients α and β are centrally assigned and are set so that the resulting bonuses will be reasonable in light of the enterprise's operating conditions. This is essentially another way of equalizing the natural operating conditions of the various enterprises in the economy.

Assume that the enterprise did not have to make any rent payments and had no short-term loans from the central bank. Suppose the enterprise had the following profit (after deductions), gross assets, and wage fund, in thousands of rubles:

$$P_t = 3{,}000 \qquad K_t = 20{,}000$$
$$P_{t-1} = 2{,}800 \qquad W_t = \ \ 4{,}000$$

Also, suppose that the central planners had assigned the firm an $\alpha = .5$ and $\beta = .25$.

REQUIRED

1. Compute the total bonus.
2. Compare the probable motivational effects of the Soviet method with those of ROI and residual income.

20-34 ***Design of management control system; review of chapters 19 and 20.*** Western Pants, Inc., is one of America's oldest clothing firms. Founded in the mid-nineteenth century, the firm weathered lean years and depression largely as the result of the market durability of its dominant, and at times only, product—blue denim jeans. Until as recently as 1950, the firm had never seriously marketed other products or even additional types of trousers. A significant change in marketing strategy in the 1950s altered that course, which had been revered for one hundred years by Western's management. Aggressive new management decided at that time that Western's well-established name could and should be used to market other lines of pants. Initial offerings in a men's casual trouser were well received. Production in different patterns of this basic style continued, and stylish, tailored variations of the same casual motif were introduced almost yearly.

Alert planning in the early 1960s enabled Western to become the first pants manufacturer to establish itself in the revolutionary "wash and wear" field. Further refinement of this process broadened the weave and fabric types that could be tailored into fashionable trousers and still survive enough machine washings and dryings to satisfy Western's rigid quality-control standards.

With the advent of "mod" clothing and the generally casual yet stylish garb that became acceptable attire at semiformal affairs, pants became fashion items, rather than the mere clothing staples they had been in years past. Western quickly gained a foothold in the bell-bottom and flare market, and from there grew with the "leg look" to its present position as the free world's largest clothing manufacturer.

Today Western, in addition to its still remarkably popular blue denim jeans, offers a complete line of casual trousers, an extensive array of "dress and fashion jeans" for both men and boys, and a complete line of pants for women. Last year the firm sold approximately 30 million pairs of pants.

PRODUCTION

For the last twenty years, Western Pants has been in a somewhat unusual and enviable market position. In each of those years it has sold virtually all its production and often had to begin rationing its wares to established customers or refusing orders from new customers as early as six months prior to the close of the production year. Whereas most business ventures face limited demand and, in the long run, excess production, Western, whose sales have doubled each five years during that twenty-year period, has had to face excess and growing demand with limited—although rapidly growing—production.

The firm has developed 25 plants in its 150-year history. These production units vary somewhat in output capacity, but the average is roughly 20,000 pairs of trousers per week. With the exception of two or three plants that usually produce only the blue denim jeans during the entire production year, Western's plants produce various pants types for all of Western's departments.

The firm has for some years augmented its own productive capacity by contractual agreements with independent manufacturers of pants. At the present time, there are nearly 20 such contractors producing all lines of Western's pants (including the blue jeans). Last year contractors produced about one-third of the total volume in units sold by Western.

THE CONTROL SYSTEM

"We treat all our plants pretty much as cost centers" [See Exhibit 20-5], Mr. Wicks the Western vice-president for production and operations, commented. "Of course, we exercise no control whatever over the contractors. We just pay them the agreed price per pair of pants. Our own

EXHIBIT 20-5

Organization Chart: Western Pants Inc.

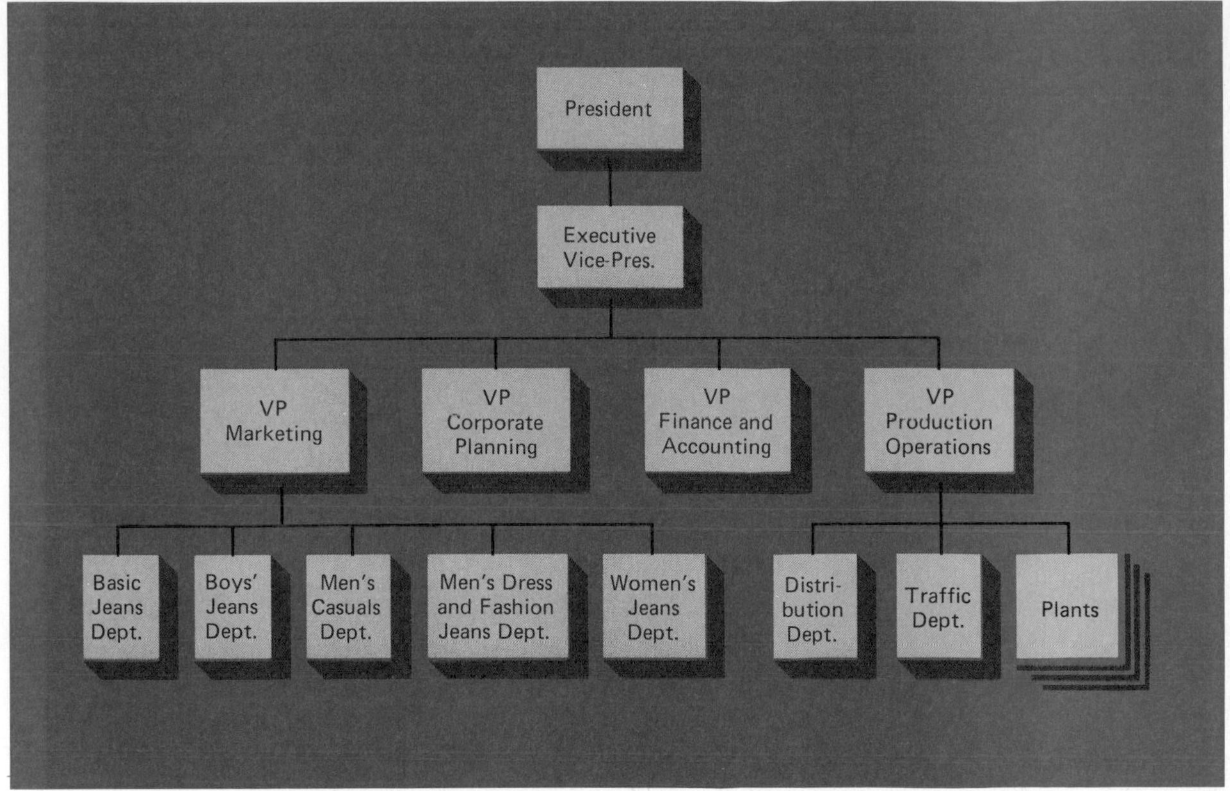

operations at each plant have been examined thoroughly by industrial engineers. You know, time-motion studies and all. We've updated this information consistently for over ten years. I'm quite proud of the way we've been able to tie our standard hours down. We've even been able over the years to develop learning curves that tell us how long it will take production of a given type of pants to reach the standard allowed hours per unit after initial startup or a product switchover. We even know the rate at which total production time per unit reaches standard for every basic style of pants that Western makes!

"We use this information for budgeting a plant's costs. The marketing staff figures out how many pants of each type it wants produced each year and passes that information on to us. We divvy the total production up among plants pretty much by eyeballing the total amounts for each type of pants. We like to put one plant to work for a whole year on one type of pants, if that's possible. It saves time losses from startups and changeovers. We can sell all we make, you know, so we like to keep plants working at peak efficiency. Unfortunately, marketing always manages to come up with a lot of midyear changes, so this objective winds up like a lot of other good intentions in life. You know what they say about the road to Hell! Anyhow, it's still a game plan we like to stick to, and two or three plants making the basic blue jeans accomplish it every year.

"The budgeting operation begins with me and my staff determining what a plant's quota for each month should be for one year ahead of time. We do this mostly by looking at what past performance at a plant has been. Of course, we add a little to this. We expect people to improve around here. These yearly budgets are updated at the end of each month in the light of the previous month's production. Budget figures, incidentally, are in units of production. If a plant manager beats this budget figure, we feel he's done well. If he can't meet the quota, his people haven't been working at what the engineers feel is a very reasonable level of speed and efficiency. Or possibly absenteeism, a big problem in all our plants, has been excessively high. Or turnover, another big problem, has been unacceptably high. At any rate, when the quota hasn't been made, we want to know why, and we want to get the problem corrected as quickly as possible.

"Given the number of pants that a plant actually produces in a month, we can determine, by using the standards I was boasting about earlier, the number of labor hours each operation should have accumulated during the month. We measure this figure against the hours we actually paid for to determine how a plant performed as a cost center. As you might guess, we don't like to see unfavorable variances here any more than in a plant manager's performance against quota.

"We watch the plant performance figures monthly. If a plant manager meets his quota and his cost variances are OK, we let him know that we are pleased. I almost always call them myself and relay my satisfaction, or, if they haven't done well, my concern. I think this kind of prompt feedback is important.

"We also look for other things in evaluating a plant manager. Have his community relations been good? Are his people happy? The family that owns almost all of Western's stock is very concerned about that."

A Christmas bonus constitutes the meat of Western's reward system. Mr. Wicks and his two chief assistants subjectively rate a plant manager's performance for the year on a one-to-five scale. Western's top management at the close of each year determines a bonus base by evaluating the firm's overall performance and profits for the year. That bonus base has recently been as high as $6,000. The performance rating for each member of Western's management cadre is multiplied by this bonus base to determine a given manager's bonus.

Western's management group includes many finance and marketing specialists. The casewriter noted that these personnel, who are located at the corporate headquarters, were consistently awarded higher ratings by their supervisors than were plant managers. This difference consistently approached a full point. Last year the average rating in the corporate headquarters was 3.85; the average for plant managers was 2.92.

EVALUATION OF THE SYSTEM

Mia Packard, a recent valedictorian of a business school, gave some informed opinions regarding Western's production operation and its management control procedures.

"Mr. Wicks is one of the nicest men I've ever met, and a very intelligent businessman. But I really don't think that the system he uses to evaluate his plant managers is good for the firm as a whole. I made a plant visit not long ago as part of my company orientation program, and I accidentally discovered that the plant manager 'hoarded' some of the pants produced over quota in good months to protect himself against future production deficiencies. That plant manager was really upset that I stumbled onto his storehouse. He insisted that all the other managers did the same thing and begged me not to tell Mr. Wicks. This seems like precisely the wrong kind of behavior in a firm that usually has to turn away orders! Yet I believe the quota system that is one of Western's tools for evaluating plant performance encourages this type of behavior. I don't think I could prove this, but I suspect that most plant managers aren't really pushing for maximum production. If they do increase output, their quotas are going to go up, and yet they won't receive any immediate monetary rewards to compensate for the increase in their responsibilities or requirements. If I were a plant manager, I wouldn't want my production exceeding quota until the end of the year.

"Also, Mr. Wicks came up to the vice-presidency through the ranks. He was a plant manager himself—a very good plant manager. But he has a tendency to feel that everyone should run a plant the way he did. For example, in Mr. Wicks' plant there were eleven workers for every supervisor or member of the office and administrative staff. Since then, Mr. Wicks has elevated this supervision ratio of 11:1 to some sort of sacred index of leadership efficiency. All plant managers shoot for it, and as a result, usually understaff their offices. As a result, we can't get timely and accurate reports from plants. There simply aren't enough people in the offices out there to generate the information we desperately need *when we need it!*

"Another thing—some of the plants have been built in the last five years or so and have much newer equipment, yet there's no difference in the standard hours determined in these plants than the older ones. This puts the managers of older plants at a terrific disadvantage. Their sewing machines break down more often, require maintenance, and probably aren't as easy to work with."

REQUIRED

Evaluate the management control system used for Western's plants. What changes should be given serious consideration?

20-35 ***Design of management control system; review of chapters 19 and 20.*** (Copyright © 1981 by the President and Fellows of Harvard College. Reproduced by permission.)

Empire Glass Company was a diversified company organized into several major product divisions, one of which was the glass products division. This division was responsible for manufacturing and selling glass food and beverage bottles. Each division was headed by a divisional vice-president who reported directly to the company's executive vice-president, Landon McGregor.

Mr. McGregor's corporate staff included three men in the financial area—the controller, the chief accountant, and the treasurer. The controller's department consisted of only two men—Mr. Walker and the assistant controller, Allen Newell. The market research and labor relations departments also reported in a staff capacity to Mr. McGregor.

All the product divisions were organized along similar lines. Reporting to each product division vice-president were several staff members in the customer service and product research areas. Reporting in a line capacity to each individual vice-president were also a general manager of manufacturing and a general manager of marketing. The general manager of manufacturing was responsible for all the division's manufacturing activities. Similarly, the general manager of marketing was responsible for all the division's marketing activities. Both these executives were assisted by a small staff of specialists. Exhibit 20-6 presents an organization chart of the glass product division's top-management group. All the corporate and divisional management groups were located in British City, Canada. Exhibit 20-7 shows the typical organization structure of a plant within the glass products division.

EXHIBIT 20-6

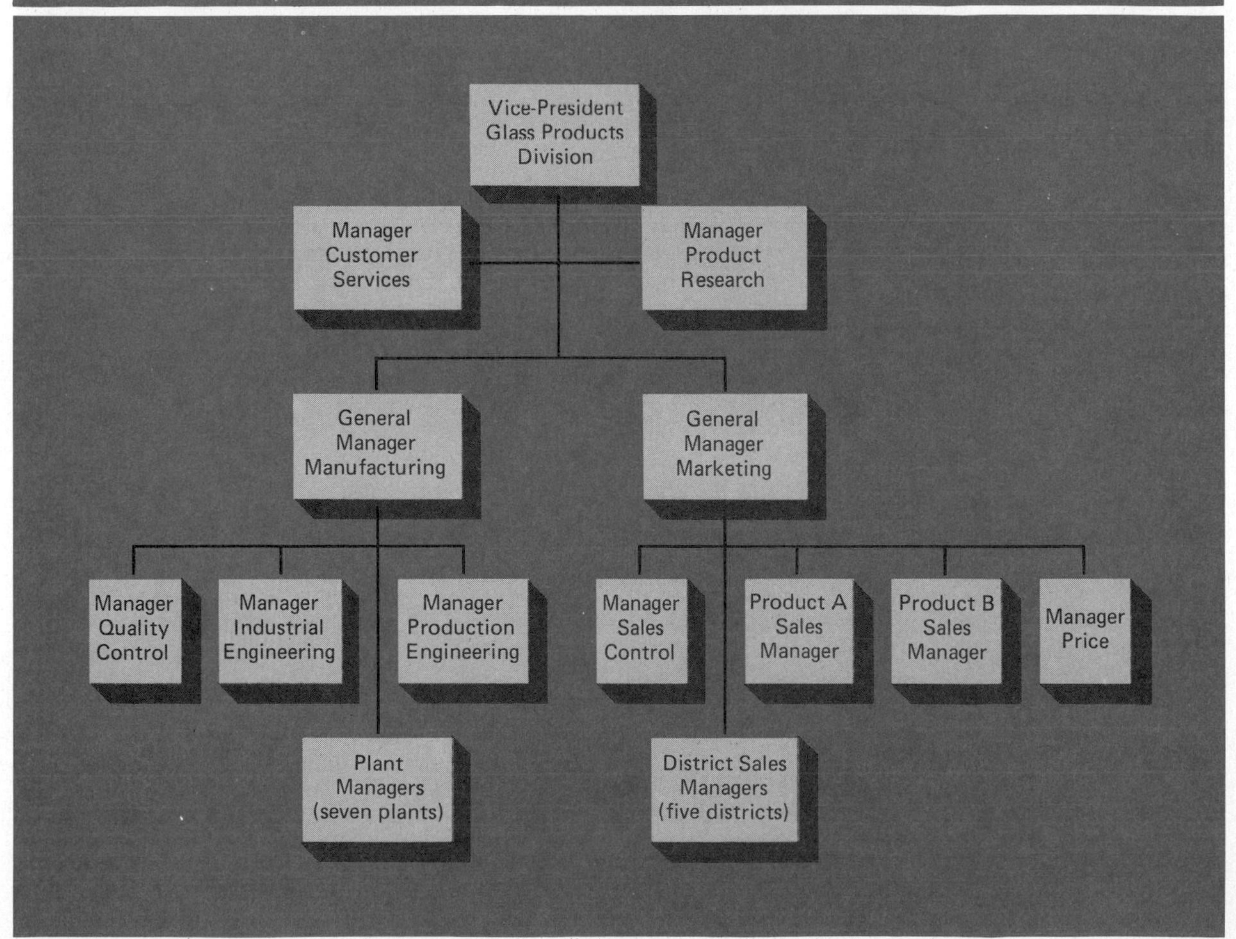

EXHIBIT 20-7

Empire Glass Company
Typical Plant Organization—Glass Products Division

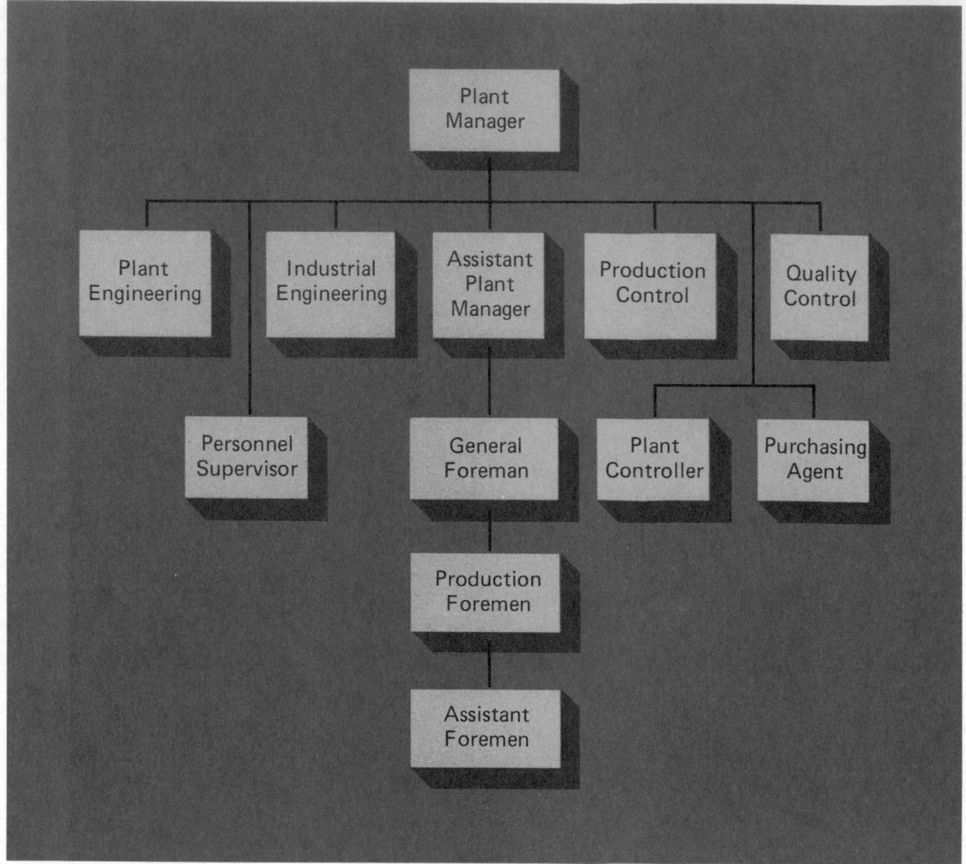

PRODUCTS AND TECHNOLOGY

The glass products division operated a number of plants in Canada producing glass food and beverage bottles. Of these products, food jars constituted the largest group, including jars for products like tomato catsup, mayonnaise, jams and jellies, honey, and soluble coffee. Milk bottles and beer and soft drink bottles were also produced in large quantities. A great variety of shapes and sizes of containers for wines, liquors, drugs, cosmetics, and chemicals were produced in smaller quantities.

Most of the thousands of different products varying in size, shape, color, and decoration were produced to order. According to British City executives, during 19_3 the typical lead time between the customer's order and shipment from the plant was between two and three weeks.

The principal raw materials for container glass were sand, soda ash, and lime. The first step in the manufacturing process was to melt batches of these materials in furnaces or "tanks." The molten mass was then passed into automatic or semiautomatic machines, which filled molds with the molten glass and blew the glass into the desired shape. The ware then went through an automatic annealing oven or lehr, where it was cooled slowly under carefully controlled conditions. If the glass was to be coated on the exterior to increase its resistance to abrasion and scratches, this coating—often a silicone film—was applied at the lehr. Any decorating (such as a trademark or other design) was then added, the product inspected again, and the finished goods packed in corrugated containers (or wooden cases for some bottles).

Quality inspection was critical in the manufacturing process. If the melt in the furnace was not completely free from bubbles and stones (unmelted ingredients or pieces of refinery material), or if the fabricating machinery was slightly out of adjustment, or molds were worn, the rejection rate was very high. Although a number of machines were used in the inspection process, including electric eyes, much of the inspection was still visual.

Although glassmaking was one of the oldest arts, and bottles and jars had been machine molded at relatively high speed for over half a century, the glass products division had spent substantial sums each year to modernize its equipment. These improvements had greatly increased the speed of operations and had substantially reduced the visual inspection and manual handling of glassware.

Most of the jobs were relatively unskilled and highly repetitive, and gave the worker little control over work methods or pace. The moldmakers who made and repaired the molds, the machine repairmen, and those who made the requirement setup changes between different products were considered to be the highest classes of skilled workers. Wages were relatively high in the glass industry. Production employees belonged to two national unions, and for many years bargaining had been conducted on a national basis. Output standards were established for all jobs, but no bonus was paid to hourly plant workers for exceeding standard.

MARKETING Over the years, the sales of the glass products divisions had grown at a slightly faster rate than had the total market for glass containers. Until the late 1950s, the division had charged a premium for most of its products, primarily because they were of better quality than competitive products. In recent years, however, the quality of the competitive products had improved to the point where they now matched the division's quality level. In the meantime, the division's competitors had retained their former price structure. Consequently, the glass products division had been forced to lower its prices to meet its competitor's lower market prices. According to one division executive:

"Currently, price competition is not severe, particularly among the two or three larger companies that dominate the glass bottle industry. Most of our competition is with respect to product quality and customer service. . . . In fact, our biggest competitive threat is from containers other than glass. . . ."

Each of the division's various plants shipped its products throughout Canada to some extent, although transportation costs limited each plant's market primarily to its immediate vicinity. While some of the customers were large and bought in huge quantities, many were relatively small.

BUDGETARY CONTROL SYSTEM In the fall of 19_3, James Walker, Empire Glass Company controller, described the company's budgetary control system to a casewriter. Mr. Walker had been controller for some fifteen years. Excerpts from that interview are reproduced below.

"To understand the role of the budgetary control system, you must first understand our management philosophy. Fundamentally, we have a divisional organization based on broad product categories. These divisional activities are coordinated by the company's executive vice-president, while the head office group provides a policy and review function for him. Within the broad policy limits, we operate on a decentralized basis; each of the decentralized divisions performs the full management job that normally would be inherent in any independent company. The only exceptions to this philosophy are the head office group's sole responsibilities for sources of funds and labor relations with those bargaining units that cross division lines.

"Given this form of organization, the budget is the principal management tool used by head office to direct the efforts of the various segments of the company toward a common goal. Certainly, in our case, the budget is much more than a narrow statistical accounting device."

SALES BUDGET □ "As early as May 15 of the year preceding the budget year, top management of the company asks the various product division vice-presidents to submit preliminary reports stating what they think their division's capital requirements and outlook in terms of sales and income will be during the next budget year. In addition, corporate top management also wants an expression of the division vice-president's general feelings toward the trends in these particular items over the two years following the upcoming budget year. At this stage, head office is not interested in too much detail. Since all divisions plan their capital requirements five years in advance and had made predictions of the forthcoming budget year's market when the budget estimates were prepared last year, these rough estimates of next year's conditions and requirements are far from wild guesses.

"After the opinions of the divisional vice-presidents are in, the market research staff goes to work. They develop a formal statement of the marketing climate in detail for the forthcoming budget year and in general terms for the subsequent two years. Once these general factors have been assessed, a sales forecast is constructed for the company and for each division. Consideration is given to the relationship of the general economic climate to our customers' needs and Empire's share of each market. Explicitly stated are basic assumptions as to price, weather conditions, introduction of new products, gains or losses in particular accounts, forward buying, new manufacturing plants, industry growth trends, packaging trends, inventory carry-overs, and the development of alternative packages to or from glass. This review of all the relevant factors is followed for each of our product lines, regardless of its size and importance. The completed forecasts of the market research group are then forwarded to the appropriate divisions for review, criticism, and adjustments.

"The primary goal of the head office group in developing these sales forecasts is to assure uniformity among the divisions with respect to the basic assumptions on business conditions, pricing, and the treatment of possible emergencies. Also, we provide a yardstick so as to assure us that the company's overall sales forecast will be reasonable and obtainable.

"The product division top management then asks each district manager what he expects to do in the way of sales during the budget year. Head office and the divisional staffs will give the district sales managers as much guidance as they request, but it is the sole responsibility of each district sales manager to come up with his particular forecast.

"After the district sales managers' forecasts are received by the divisional top management, the forecasts are consolidated and reviewed by the division's general manager of marketing. Let me emphasize, however, that nothing is changed in the district sales manager's budget unless the district manager agrees. Then, once the budget is approved, nobody is relieved of his responsibility without top-management approval. Also, no arbitrary changes are made in the approved budgets without the concurrence of all the people responsible for the budget.

"Next, we go through the same process at the division and headquarters levels. We continue to repeat the process until everyone agrees that the sales budgets are sound. Then, each level of management takes responsibility for its particular portion of the budget. These sales budgets then become fixed objectives."

MANUFACTURING BUDGETS □ "Once the vice-presidents, executive vice-president, and company president have given final approval to the sales budgets, we make a sales budget for each plant by breaking down the division sales budgets according to the plants from which the finished goods will be shipped. These plant sales budgets are then further broken down on a monthly basis by price, volume, and end use. With this information available, the plants then budget their gross profit, fixed expenses, and income before taxes.

"The plant manager's primary responsibility extends to profits. The budgeted plant profit is the difference between the fixed sales-dollar budget and the sum of the budgeted variable costs at standard and the fixed-overhead budget. It is the plant manager's responsibility to meet this budget profit figure, even if actual dollar sales drop below the budget level.

"Given his sales budget, it is up to the plant manager to determine the fixed overhead and variable costs—at standard—that he will need to incur so as to meet the demands of the sales budget. In my opinion, requiring the plant managers to make their own plans is one of the most valuable things associated with the budget system. Each plant manager divides the preparation of the overall plant budget among his plant's various departments. First, the departments spell out the programs in terms of the physical requirements, such as tons of raw material, and then the plans are priced at standard cost.

"The plant industrial engineering department is assigned responsibility for developing engineered cost standards and reduced costs. Consequently, the phase of budget preparation covered by the industrial engineers includes budget standards of performance for each operation, cost center, and department within the plant. This phase of the budget also includes budgeted cost reductions, budgeted unfavorable variances from standards, and certain budgeted programmed fixed costs in the manufacturing area, such as service labor. The industrial engineer prepares this phase of the budget in conjunction with departmental line supervision.

"Before each plant sends its budget into British City, a group of us from head office goes out to visit each plant. For example, in the case of the glass products division, Allen Newell, assistant controller, and I, along with representatives of the glass products division manufacturing staffs visit each of the division's plants. Let me stress this point: We do not go on these trips to pass judgment on the plant's proposed budget. Rather, we go with two purposes in mind. First, we wish to acquaint ourselves with the thinking behind the figures that each plant manager will send in to British City. This is helpful, because when we come to review these budgets with the top management—that is, management above our level—we will have to answer questions about the budgets, and we will know the answers. Second, the review is a way of giving guidance to the plant managers in determining whether or not they are in line with what the company needs to make in the way of profits.

"Of course, when we make our field review we do not know about what each of the other plants is doing. Therefore, we explain to the plant managers that while their budget may look good now, when we put all the plants together in a consolidated budget, the plant managers may have to make some changes because the projected profit is not high enough. When this happens, we must tell the plant managers that it is not their programs that are unsound. The problem is that the company cannot afford the programs. I think it is very important that each plant manager has a chance to tell his story. Also, it gives them the feeling that we at headquarters are not living in an ivory tower.

"These plant visits are spread over a three-week period, and we spend an average of half a day at each plant. The plant manager is free to bring to these meetings any of his supervisors he wishes. We ask him not to bring in anybody below the supervisory level. Then, of course, you get into organized labor. During the half day we spend at each plant, we discuss the budget primarily. However, if I have time, I like to wander through the plant and see how things are going. Also, I go over in great detail the property replacement and maintenance budget with the plant manager.

"About September 1, the plant budgets come into British City, and the accounting department consolidates them. Then, the product division vice-presidents review their respective divisional budgets to see if the division budget is reasonable in terms of what the vice-president thinks the corporate management wants. If he is not satisfied with the consolidated plant budgets, he will ask the various plants within the division to trim their budget figures.

"When the division vice-presidents and the executive vice-presidents are happy, they will send their budgets to the company president. He may accept the division budgets at this point. If he doesn't, he will specify the areas to be reexamined by division and, if necessary, by plant management. The final budget is approved at our December board of directors meeting."

COMPARISON OF ACTUAL AND STANDARD PERFORMANCE ☐ "At the end of the sixth business day after the close of the month, each plant wires to the head office certain operating variances, which we put together on what we call the variance analysis sheet. Within a half-hour after the last plant report comes through, variance analysis sheets for the divisions and plants are compiled. On the morning of the seventh business day after the end of the month, these reports are usually on the desks of the interested top management. The variance analysis sheet highlights the variances in what we consider to be critical areas. Receiving this report as soon as we do helps us at the head office to take timely action. Let me emphasize, however, we do not accept the excuse that the plant manager has to go to the end of the month to know what happened during the month. He has to be on top of these particular items daily.

"When the actual results come into the head office, we go over them on the basis of exception; that is, we look only at those figures that are in excess of the budgeted amounts. We believe this has a good effect on morale. The plant managers don't have to explain everything they do. They have to explain only where they go off base. In particular, we pay close attention to the net sales, gross margin, and the plant's ability to meet its standard manufacturing cost. Incidentally, when analyzing the gross sales, we look closely at the price and mix changes.

"All this information is summarized on a form known as the Profit Planning and Control Report No. 1 [see Exhibit 20-8]. This document is backed up by a number of supporting documents [see Exhibit 20-9]. The plant PPCR No. 1 and the month-end trial balance showing both actual and budget figures are received in British City at the close of the eighth business day after the end of the month. These two very important reports, along with the supporting reports (PPCR No. 2, PPCR No. 11) are then consolidated by the accounting department on PPCR-type forms to show the results of operations by division and company. The consolidated reports are distributed the next day.

"In connection with the fixed-cost items, we want to know whether or not the plants carried out the programs they said they would carry out. If they have not, we want to know why they have not. Here, we are looking for sound reasons. Also, we want to know if they have carried out their projected programs at the cost they said they would.

"In addition to these reports, at the beginning of each month the plant managers prepare current estimates for the upcoming month and quarter on forms similar to the variance

EXHIBIT 20-8

Empire Glass Company
Profit Planning and Control Report No. 1

MONTH					YEAR TO DATE		
Income Gain (+) or Loss (−) From		Actual	Ref.		Actual	Income Gain (+) or Loss (−) From	
Prev. Year	Budget					Budget	Prev. Year
			1	Gross Sales to Customers			
			2	Discounts & Allowances			
			3	Net Sales to Customers			
%	%		4	% Gain (+)/Loss (−)		%	%
				DOLLAR VOLUME GAIN (+)/ LOSS (−) DUE TO:			
			5	Sales Price			
			6	Sales Volume			
			6(a)	Trade Mix			
			7	Variable Cost of Sales			
			8	Profit Margin			
				PROFIT MARGIN GAIN (+)/ LOSS (−) DUE TO:			
			9	Profit Volume Ratio (P/V)			
			10	Dollar Volume			
%	%	%	11	Profit Volume Ratio (P/V)	%	%	%
		Income Addition (+)			Income Addition (+)		
			12	Total Fixed Manufacturing Cost			
			13	Fixed Manufacturing Cost — Transfers			
			14	Plant Income (Standard)			
%	%	%	15	% of Net Sales	%	%	%
		Income Addition (+) Income Reduction (−)			Income Addition (+) Income Reduction (−)		
%	%	%	16	% Performance	%	%	%
			17	Manufacturing Efficiency			
		Income Addition (+)			Income Addition (+)		
			18	Methods Improvements			
			19	Other Revisions of Standards			
			20	Material Price Changes			
			21	Division Special Projects			
			22	Company Special Projects			
			23	New Plant Expense			
			24	Other Plant Expenses			
			25	Income on Seconds			
			26				
			27				
			28	Plant Income (Actual)			
%	%		29	% Gain (+)/Loss (−)		%	%
%	%	%	30	% of Net Sales	%	%	%
			36A				
Increase (+) or Decrease (−)				EMPLOYED CAPITAL	Increase (+) or Decrease (−)		
			37	Total Employed Capital			
%	%	%	38	% Return	%	%	%
			39	Turnover Rate			

__________ Plant   __________ Division   __________ Month 19___

analysis sheets. Since our budget is based on known programs, the value of this current estimate is that it gets the plant people to look at their programs. We hope they will realize that they cannot run their plants on a day-to-day basis.

"If we see a sore spot coming up, or if the plant manager draws our attention to a potential trouble area, we may ask that daily reports concerning this item be sent to the particular division top management involved. In addition, the division top management may send a division staff specialist—say, a quality control expert if it is a quality problem—to the plant concerned. The division staff members can make recommendations, but it is up to the plant manager to accept or reject these recommendations. Of course, it is well known throughout the company that we expect the plant managers to accept gracefully the help of the head office and division staffs."

SALES-MANUFACTURING RELATIONS ☐ "If a sales decline occurs during the early part of the year, and if the plant managers can convince us that the change is permanent, we may revise the plant budgets to reflect these new circumstances. However, if toward the end of the year the actual sales volume suddenly drops below the predicted sales volume, we don't have much time to change the budget plans. What we do is ask the plant managers to go back over their budgets with their staffs and see where reduction of expense programs will do the least harm. Specifically, we ask them to consider what they may be able to eliminate this year or delay until next year.

"I believe it was Confucius who said, 'We make plans so we have plans to discard.' Nevertheless, I think it is wise to make plans, even if you have to discard them. Having plans makes it a lot easier to figure out what to do when sales fall off from the budgeted level. The understanding of operations that comes from preparing the budget removes a lot of the potential chaos and confusion that might arise if we were under pressure to meet a stated profit goal and

EXHIBIT 20-9

Empire Glass Company

Brief Description of PPCR No. 2–PPCR No. 11

INDIVIDUAL PLANT REPORTS

report	description
PPCR No. 2	Manufacturing expense: Plant materials, labor, and variable overhead consumed. Detail of actual figures compared with budget and previous year's figures for year to date and current month.
PPCR No. 3	Plant expense: Plant fixed expenses incurred. Details of actual figures compared with budget and previous year's figures for year to date and current month.
PPCR No. 4	Analysis of sales and income: Plant operating gains and losses due to changes in sales revenue, profit margins, and other sources of income. Details of actual figures compared with budget and previous year's figures for year to date and current month.
PPCR No. 5	Plant control statement: Analysis of plant raw material gains and losses, spoilage costs, and cost reduction programs. Actual figures compared with budget figures for current month and year to date.
PPCR No. 6	Comparison of sales by principal and product groups: Plant sales dollars, profit margin, and P/V ratios broken down by end-product use (i.e., soft drinks, beer). Compares actual figures with budgeted figures for year to date and current month.

DIVISION SUMMARY REPORTS

report	description
PPCR No. 7	Comparative plant performance, sales, and income: Gross sales and income figures by plants. Actual figures compared with budget figures for year to date and current month.
PPCR No. 8	Comparative plant performance, total plant expenses: Profit margin, total fixed costs, manufacturing efficiency, other plant expenses, and P/V ratios by plants. Actual figures compared with budgeted and previous year's figures for current month and year to date.
PPCR No. 9	Manufacturing efficiency: Analysis of gains and losses by plant in areas of materials, spoilage, supplies, and labor. Current month and year to date actuals reported in total dollars and as a percentage of budget.
PPCR No. 10	Inventory: Comparison of actual and budget inventory figures by major inventory accounts and plants.
PPCR No. 11	Status of capital expenditures: Analysis of the status of capital expenditures by plants, months, and relative to budget.

sales declined quickly and unexpectedly at year-end, just as they did last year. In these circumstances, we don't try to ram anything down the plant managers' throats. We ask them to tell us where they can reasonably expect to cut costs below the budgeted level.

"Whenever a problem arises at a plant between sales and production, the local people are supposed to solve the problem themselves. For example, a customer's purchasing agent may insist he wants an immediate delivery, and this delivery will disrupt the production department's plans. The production group can make recommendations as to alternative ways to take care of the problem, but it's the sales manager's responsibility to get the product to the customer. The salesmen are supposed to know their customers well enough to judge whether or not the customer really needs the product. If the sales manager says the customer needs the product, that ends the matter. As far as we are concerned, the customer's wants are primary; our company is a case where sales wags the rest of the dog.

"Of course, if the change in the sales program involves a major plant expense that is out of line with the budget, then the matter is passed up to division for decision.

"As I said earlier, the sales department has the sole responsibility for the product price, sales mix, and delivery schedules. They do not have direct responsibility for plant operations or profit. That's the plant management's responsibility. However, it is understood that the sales group will cooperate with the plant people wherever possible."

MOTIVATION □ "There are various ways in which we motivate the plant managers to meet their profit goals. First of all, we promote only capable people. Also, a monetary incentive program has been established that stimulates their efforts to achieve their profit goals. In addition, each month we put together a bar chart that shows, by division and plant, the ranking of the various manufacturing units with respect to manufacturing efficiency.[39] We feel the plant managers are 100 percent responsible for variable manufacturing costs. I believe this is true, since all manufacturing standards have to be approved by plant managers. Most of the plant managers give wide publicity to these bar charts. The efficiency bar chart and efficiency measure itself is perhaps a little unfair in some respects when you are comparing one plant with another. Different kinds of products are run through different plants. These require different setups, etc., which have an important impact on a position of the plant. However, in general, the efficiency rating is a good indication of the quality of the plant manager and his supervisory staff.

"Also, a number of plants run competitions within the plants, which reward department heads or foremen, based on their relative standing with respect to a certain cost item. The plant managers, their staffs, and employees have great pride in their plants.

"The number one item now stressed at the plant level is *quality.* The market situation is such that in order to make sales you have to meet the market price and exceed the market quality. By quality I mean not only the physical characteristics of the product but also such things as delivery schedules. As I read the company employee publications, their message is that if the company is to be profitable, it must produce high-quality items at a reasonable cost. This is necessary so that the plants can meet their obligation to produce the maximum profits for the company in the prevailing circumstances."

THE FUTURE □ "An essential part of the budgetary control system is planning. We have developed a philosophy that we must begin our plans where the work is done—in the line organization and out in the field. Perhaps, in the future, we can avoid or cut back some of the budget preparation steps and start putting together our sales budget later than May 15. However, I doubt if we will change the basic philosophy.

"Frankly, I doubt if the line operators would want any major change in the system; they are very jealous of the management prerogatives the system gives to them.

[39]**Manufacturing efficiency** $= \dfrac{\textbf{Total actual variable manufacturing costs}}{\textbf{Total standard variable manufacturing costs}} \times \textbf{100\%}$

"It is very important that we manage the budget. We have to be continually on guard against its managing us. Sometimes the plants lose sight of this fact. We have to be made conscious daily of the necessity of having the sales volume to make a profit. And when sales fall off and their plant programs are reduced, they do not always appear to see the justification for budget cuts—although I do suspect that they see more of the justification for these cuts than they will admit. It is this human side of the budget to which we have to pay more attention in the future."

REQUIRED

Comment on the strong points and the weak points in the management control system of the Empire Glass Company. What changes, if any, would you suggest? (Assume that sales districts cannot match up perfectly with manufacturing plants.)

Decision Models and Accounting

SECTION SEVEN

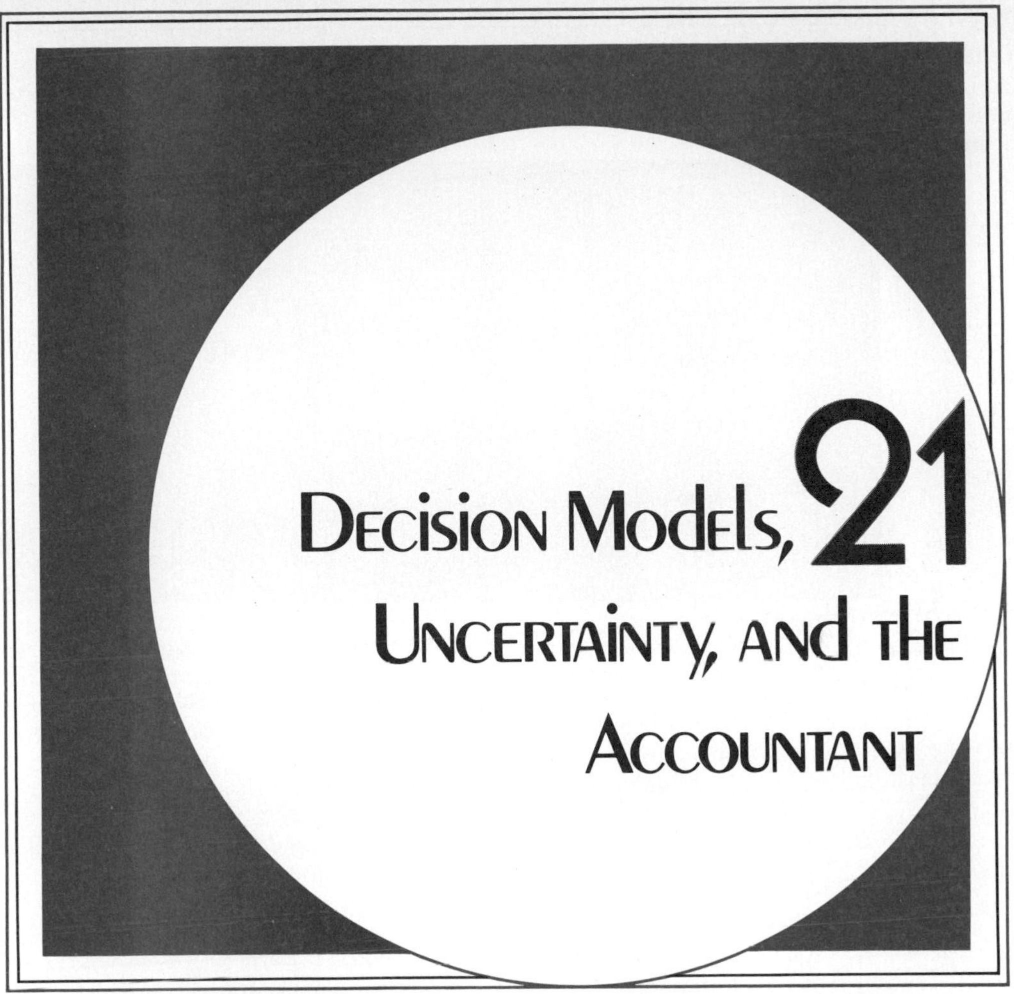

21 Decision Models, Uncertainty, and the Accountant

The first part of Chapter 1 indicated that the results of an operating process, a decision, or a collection of decisions will be affected by the environment. That is, the predictions and decisions of managers and accountants are made in a world of uncertainty. **Uncertainty** is defined as the possibility that an actual amount will deviate from an expected amount. This chapter explores the characteristics of uncertainty and a way of coping with uncertainty that should help both managers and accountants.

Chapter 1 explained how feedback can play an essential role in management control. A major form of feedback is a performance report, which often consists of a comparison of budgeted with actual results. Using this historical information and other information (such as the general state of the economy or industry), the manager makes predictions. In turn, the predictions become inputs to a decision model, action occurs, and performance is evaluated and fed back to management.

Characteristics of uncertainty

role of decision model

The manager has a method for deciding among courses of action, often called a **decision model.** A formal decision model measures the predicted effects of alternative actions; it usually has the following characteristics:

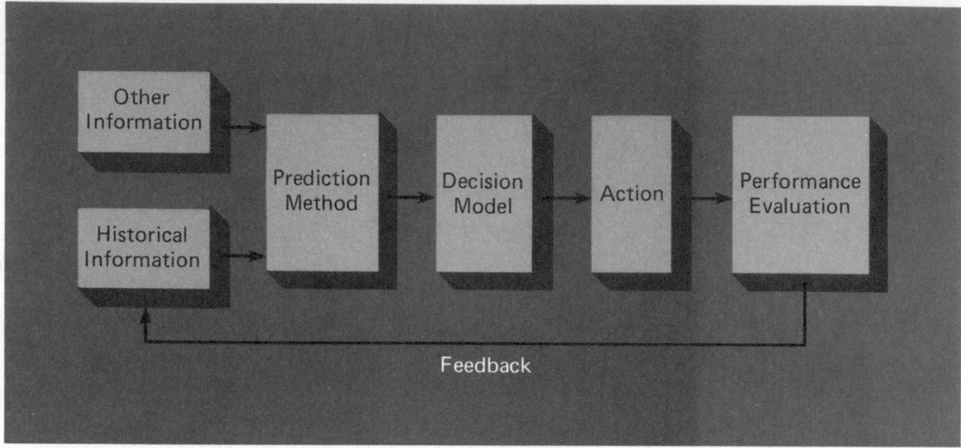

1. An objective that can be quantified. This objective can take many forms. Most often it is expressed as a maximization (or minimization) of some form of profit (or cost). This quantification is often called a **choice criterion** or an **objective function.** This objective function is used to evaluate the courses of action and to provide a basis for choosing the best alternative.
2. A set of the alternative courses of action under explicit consideration. This set of **actions** should be collectively exhaustive and mutually exclusive.
3. A set of all the relevant **events** (sometimes called **states** or **states of nature**) that can occur. Because this set should also be collectively exhaustive and mutually exclusive, only one of the events will actually occur. Examples of events include success or failure, rain or no rain, war or peace, and so on.
4. A set of **probabilities** that shows the likelihood of each event's occurring.
5. A set of **outcomes** (often called **payoffs**) that measure, in terms of the objective function, the predicted consequences of the various possible combinations of actions and events. Each outcome is conditionally dependent on a specific course of action and a specific event.

Several examples in this chapter will clarify these essential ingredients of a formal decision model.

decisions under certainty

Decisions are frequently classified as those made under certainty and those made under uncertainty. **Certainty** exists when there is absolutely no doubt about which event will occur. Hence, there is a single outcome for each possible action. When an event is certain, the prediction is a single point with no dispersion on either side. There is a 100 percent chance of occurrence; the probability of the event is 1.0. For example, the expected cash inflow on a federal Treasury note might be, say, $4,000 for next year, graphed as shown on the top of the next page.

Decisions under certainty are not always obvious. There are often numerous possible actions, each of which may offer certain outcomes. The problem is then finding the best action. For example, the problem of allocating twenty different job orders to twenty different machines, any one of which could do the job, can involve

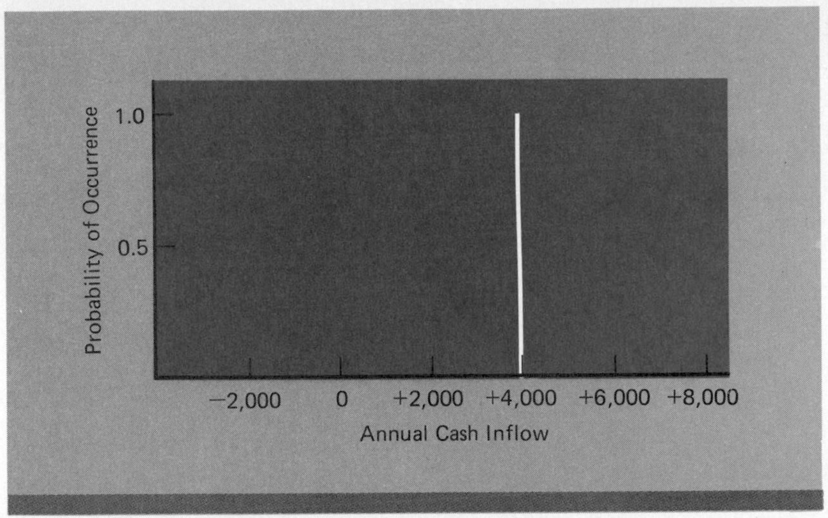

literally *billions* of different combinations. Each way of assigning these jobs is another possible action.

A **decision table** (sometimes called a **payoff table** or **payoff matrix**) is a convenient summary of the contemplated actions, events, probabilities, and outcomes. For allocating the jobs to the machines, the table would appear as follows:

	EVENT: SUCCESSFUL IMPLEMENTATION
probability of event	**1.0**
ACTION:	
Combination 1	Measure of outcome (production costs)
Combination 2	Measure of outcome (production costs)
Combination 3	Measure of outcome (production costs)
(and so forth)	(and so forth)

As the decision table indicates, in a world of certainty, there is a single possible outcome for each action. The decision obviously consists of choosing the action that will produce the most desirable outcome. But the decision is not a trivial problem. The above decision table has only one *column* because the costs of production using the various machines are assumed to be known. In some cases, decision models have been developed to facilitate choice among these many combinations. The linear-programming technique outlined in Chapter 23 is an example of such a decision model.

decisions under uncertainty

Of course, the decision maker must frequently contend with *uncertainty* rather than certainty; he or she faces a number of possible events for each possible action. The distinction among various degrees of uncertainty centers on how probabilities are assigned. The probabilities may be assigned with a high degree of confidence. That is, the decision maker may know the probability of occurrence of each of the events because of mathematical proofs or the compilation of historical evidence. For example, the probability of obtaining a head in the toss of a symmetrical coin is .5; that of drawing a particular playing card from a well-shuffled deck, $\frac{1}{52}$. In a business, the probability of having a specified percentage of defective units may be assigned with great confidence based on production experience with thousands of units.

If the decision maker has no basis in past experience or in mathematical proofs for assigning the probabilities of occurrence of the various events, he or she must resort to the *subjective* assignment of probabilities. For example, the probability of the success or failure of a new product may have to be assessed without the help of any related experience. The assignment is subjective because no two individuals assessing a situation will necessarily assign the same probabilities. Executives may be virtually certain about the *range* of possible events or outcomes, but they may differ about the likelihoods of various possibilities within that range.

The concept of uncertainty can be illustrated by considering two investment proposals on new projects.[1] The manager believes that the following discrete **probability distribution** describes the relative likelihood of flows for the next year (assume that the useful life of the project is one year):

PROPOSAL A		PROPOSAL B	
probability	**cash inflow**	**probability**	**cash inflow**
0.10	$3,000	0.10	$2,000
0.20	3,500	0.25	3,000
0.40	4,000	0.30	4,000
0.20	4,500	0.25	5,000
0.10	5,000	0.10	6,000

expected value and standard deviation

Exhibit 21-1 shows a graphical comparison of the probability distributions. One approach to this problem is to compute an **expected value** for each probability distribution. An *expected value* is an arithmetic mean, a weighted average using the probabilities as weights.

The expected value ($\bar{A}$, called *A bar*) of the cash inflow in Proposal A is[2]

$$\bar{A} = 0.1(3{,}000) + 0.2(3{,}500) + 0.4(4{,}000) + 0.2(4{,}500) + 0.1(5{,}000) = \$4{,}000$$

The expected value for the cash inflow in Proposal B is also $4,000:

$$\bar{A} = 0.1(2{,}000) + 0.25(3{,}000) + 0.3(4{,}000) + 0.25(5{,}000) + 0.1(6{,}000) = \$4{,}000$$

Incidentally, the expected value of the cash inflow in the federal Treasury note mentioned on page 716 is also $4,000:

$$\bar{A} = 1.0(4{,}000) = \$4{,}000$$

---

[1]James C. Van Horne, *Financial Management and Policy,* 5th ed. (Englewood Cliffs, N.J.: Prentice-Hall, 1980), Chap. 2.

[2]The formula is

$$\bar{A} = \sum_{x=1}^{n} A_x P_x$$

where A_x is the outcome or payoff or cost or cash flow for the xth possible event or state of nature, P_x is the probability of occurrence of that outcome, $\bar{A}$ is the expected value of the outcome, x is the identity of each event, and n is the number of events.

EXHIBIT 21-1

Comparison of Probability Distributions

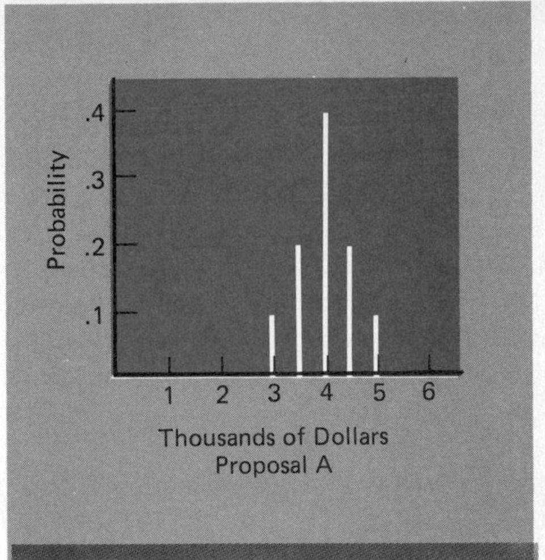

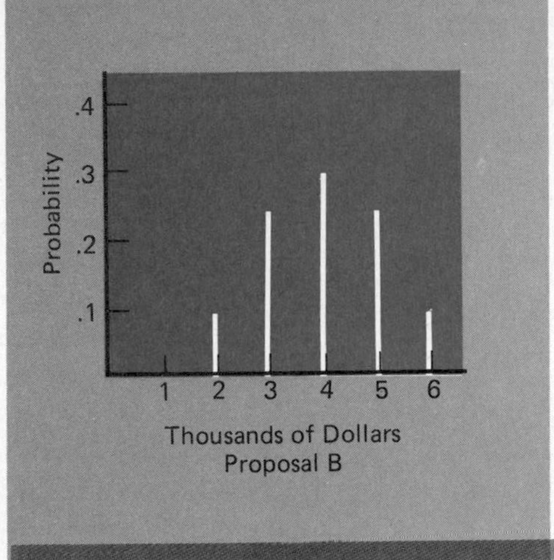

Note that mere comparison of these \$4,000 expected values is an oversimplification. These three single figures are not strictly comparable; one represents certainty, whereas the other two represent the expected values over a range of possible outcomes. The decision maker must explicitly or implicitly (by "feel" or hunch) recognize that he or she is comparing figures that are really representations of probability distributions; otherwise the reporting of the expected value alone may be misleading.[3]

To give the decision maker more information, the accountant could provide the complete probability distribution for each proposal. However, often that course means flooding the manager with too much data for comprehension. Therefore, a summary measure of the underlying dispersion is often supplied. The conventional measure of the dispersion of a probability distribution for a single variable is the standard deviation. The **standard deviation** is the square root of the mean of the squared deviations from the expected value:

$$\sigma = \sqrt{\sum_{x=1}^{n} (A_x - \bar{A})^2 P_x}$$

The standard deviation for Proposal A is smaller than that for Proposal B;

For A: $\sigma = [.1(3{,}000 - 4{,}000)^2 + .2(3{,}500 - 4{,}000)^2 + .4(4{,}000 - 4{,}000)^2 + .2(4{,}500 - 4{,}000)^2 + .1(5{,}000 - 4{,}000)^2]^{1/2}$
$= [300{,}000]^{1/2} = \$548$

For B: $\sigma = [.1(2{,}000 - 4{,}000)^2 + .25(3{,}000 - 4{,}000)^2 + .3(4{,}000 - 4{,}000)^2 + .25(5{,}000 - 4{,}000)^2 + .1(6{,}000 - 4{,}000)^2]^{1/2}$
$= [1{,}300{,}000]^{1/2} = \$1{,}140$

For the Treasury note: $\sigma = \sqrt{1.0(4{,}000 - 4{,}000)^2} = 0$

[3]For example, how would you feel about choosing between the following two investments? First, invest \$10 today with a probability of 1.0 of obtaining \$11 in two days. Second, invest \$10 today with a probability of .5 of obtaining \$22 in two days and .5 of obtaining \$0. The expected value is \$11 in both cases. Also see a later section of this chapter on expected monetary value and utility.

A measure of relative dispersion is the **coefficient of variation,** which is the standard deviation divided by expected value. The coefficient for Proposal B is 1,140 ÷ 4,000 = .29; for A it is 548 ÷ 4,000 = .14; and for the Treasury note it is 0 ÷ 4,000 = 0. Therefore, because the coefficient is a relative measure of **risk** or uncertainty, B is said to have a greater degree of risk.[4]

the accountant and uncertainty

Many accounting practitioners and businesspeople shudder at the notion of using subjective probabilities to quantify things that are supposedly "intangible" or "unmeasurable" or "qualitative" or "unquantifiable." However, this position is weak, simply because decisions *do* have to be made. The attempts by statisticians, mathematicians, and modern accountants to measure the unmeasurable is an old and natural chore that scientists have performed for centuries. The use of subjective probabilities merely formalizes the intuitive judgments and hunches that managers so often use. It forces the decision maker to expose and evaluate what he or she may have done unconsciously for years.

We should distinguish between **cost estimation,** which is an attempt to measure historical costs, and **cost prediction,** which is an attempt to measure expected future costs. Almost all accounting data are subject to uncertainty, whether the data are predictions or are historical. Too often, managers and accountants regard historical accumulations as precise calibrations rather than as approximations. The estimates (the measures of the effects of past events) should be marked by less uncertainty than are the predictions. Still, we must recognize that the accounting process deals with the real world, a world marked by uncertain predictions and uncertain estimates about what really happened.

Many statisticians and accountants favor presenting the entire probability distribution directly to the decision maker. Others first divide the information into a threefold classification of optimistic, middle, and pessimistic categories. Still others provide summary measures of dispersion, such as the standard deviation or the coefficient of variation. In any event, we are likely to see the formal recognition of uncertainty and probability distributions in the accountant's reports. In this way, the information will portray underlying phenomena in a more realistic fashion instead of portraying the data as if they came from a world of certainty.

Coping with uncertainty

illustrative problem

The following problem will be used to demonstrate the general approach to uncertainty. Suppose that a decision maker, a manager named Mark Eastman, must choose between two molding machines, M1 and M2. Each machine will be used to produce a souvenir toy. M2 wastes less material and uses less labor but costs more to acquire and maintain. For simplicity, assume that each machine has a useful life of one year.[5] Comparative operating incomes follow:

[4]As most widely defined, *risk* is the dispersion described above. However, to many individuals risk is not dispersion by itself; rather, it is the possibility of downside deviations from the expected value. As Van Horne and others have pointed out, an investor does not consider upside deviations undesirable. A measure of downside risk may be helpful, but the mathematical complexities are imposing for anything beyond the simplest situations. Moreover, the riskiness of a single investment should be related to its role as a part of a portfolio of investments. Some risk can be diversified away by investments in independent projects. For an expanded discussion, see Van Horne, *Financial Management and Policy,* Chaps. 6–8.

[5]The presentations here and in Appendixes 21b and 21c draw, in part, from teaching notes prepared by Professors George Foster and Robert W. Williamson.

$$A(\text{Buy M1}) = \$20x - \$15{,}000$$
$$A(\text{Buy M2}) = \$24x - \$21{,}000$$

A = **Operating income** x = **Demand in units**

In words, the first equation says that the operating income from M1 will be $20 times the number of units sold minus the cost of acquiring and maintaining M1 ($15,000). If M2 is acquired, the $20 rises to $24 because less material and labor will be used, but the $15,000 cost rises to $21,000 because M2 is a more complex machine.

general approach to uncertainty

The construction of a model for decision making contains five steps, which are keyed to the five characteristics described at the outset of this chapter:

Step 1. Identify the objective of the decision maker. Assume that Eastman's choice criterion or objective function is to maximize operating income.[6]

Step 2. Identify the set of actions under explicit consideration. Eastman has two possible actions:

M1 = Buy M1
M2 = Buy M2

Step 3. Identify the set of relevant events that can occur. Eastman's only uncertainty is the level of future demand:

x_1 = **Demand is 1,200 units**
x_2 = **Demand is 2,000 units**

Step 4. Identify the set of probabilities of the occurrence of each event. Eastman thinks that there is a 40 percent chance that future demand will equal 1,200 units and a 60 percent chance that it will equal 2,000 units. Therefore, he has assessed the following probabilities:

$$Px_1 = .4$$
$$Px_2 = .6$$

Step 5. Identify the set of outcomes that are dependent on specific actions and events. The outcomes in this example take the form of four possible operating incomes (A), which are displayed in a decision table in Exhibit 21-2.

Eastman now has all the necessary quantitative ingredients for making a decision. As shown in Exhibit 21-2, he can compute the expected value ($\overline{A}$) of each action. He would choose M2 because its expected operating income is higher than that of M1 by $19,320 − $18,600, or $720.

---

[6]Throughout most of this chapter we imply that expected monetary values represent the general case. However, decision theory regards the use of expected monetary values as a special application of the general approach, which uses utility values. In particular, the use of expected monetary value ignores aversion to risk. See the discussion at the end of the chapter.

EXHIBIT 21-2
(Place a clip on this page for easy reference.)

Decision Table

	EVENTS	
	$x_1 = 1{,}200$	$x_2 = 2{,}000$
probability of events	.4	.6
ACTION:		
Buy M1	A = \$9,000*	A = \$25,000‡
Buy M2	A = \$7,800†	A = \$27,000§

A = Operating income
$\overline{A}$ = Expected value of operating income
Expected values:
Buy M1, $\overline{A}$ = \$9,000(.4) + \$25,000(.6) = \$18,600
Buy M2, $\overline{A}$ = \$7,800(.4) + \$27,000(.6) = \$19,320

**\$20(1,200) − \$15,000*   *‡\$20(2,000) − \$15,000*
†\$24(1,200) − \$21,000   *§\$24(2,000) − \$21,000*

good decisions and bad outcomes

Always distinguish between a good decision and a good outcome. One can exist without the other. By definition, uncertainty rules out guaranteeing that the best outcome will be obtained. Thus, it is possible that "bad luck" will produce unfavorable consequences even when "good" decisions have occurred.

Consider the following example. Suppose you are offered a gamble for a mere \$1, a fair coin toss where heads you win, tails you lose. You will win \$20 if the event is heads, but you will lose \$1 if the event is tails. As a rational decision maker, you proceed through the logical phases: gathering information, assessing consequences, and making a choice. You accept the bet. The coin is tossed. You lose. From your viewpoint, this was a bad outcome but a good decision. From your opponent's viewpoint, it was a good outcome but a bad decision.

A decision can only be made on the basis of information available at the time of the decision. Hindsight is often flawless, but a bad outcome does not necessarily mean that it flowed from a bad decision. As D. W. North said, "the best protection we have against a bad outcome is a good decision."[7]

buying perfect information

Even though the expected value of the operating income is \$720 higher under M2, Eastman might be nervous. The only uncertainty is what event (demand) will occur. *Eastman's assessments of probabilities are based on his existing information.* The worst possible operating income, \$7,800, can occur if M2 is acquired and demand is 1,200 units. His present cost-analysis staff is overloaded with other work. However, Eastman can hire an expensive consultant, Mary O'Leary, to study the demand situation. Assume that she has a magical ability to predict in these matters. What is the maximum amount Eastman should be willing to pay for the consultant's errorless wisdom? This amount is called the **expected value of perfect information (EVPI).**

The basic decision here is whether to purchase advance revelation (perfect information) *without knowing what the revelation will be.* There are five steps in computing EVPI:

[7]D. W. North, "A Tutorial Introduction to Decision Theory," *IEEE Transactions on Systems Science and Cybernetics,* September 1968, p. 201. Also see Charles A. Holloway, *Decision Making under Uncertainty* (Englewood Cliffs, N.J.: Prentice-Hall, 1979), pp. 7–8.

Step 1. Identify the optimal action conditional on knowing what event will occur. If the consultant tells Eastman that demand will be 1,200, he will buy M1 and obtain an operating income of $9,000; similarly, if 2,000, M2, and $27,000.

Step 2. Identify the probabilities of each event's being revealed after the purchase of advance state revelation. Eastman's best estimates of the two demands being revealed are his current assessments of probabilities, .4 and .6, respectively.

Step 3. Compute the expected value with perfect information. The perfect information in advance of each occurrence of the events will contain only one of the two predictions. Therefore, the expected value of the decision *with* perfect information is the sum of the optimum outcome for each event multiplied by its probability:

$$(.4 \times \$9{,}000) + (.6 \times \$27{,}000) = \$19{,}800$$

Step 4. Compute the expected value with existing information. Using the earlier data in Exhibit 21-2, Eastman computed an expected value for M2 of $19,320, which is the larger of the expected values for the two actions in this example.

Step 5. Compute EVPI. The top price Eastman should be willing to pay for perfect advance information would be the difference between the expected value with *perfect* information and the expected value with *existing* information. This *difference* is the expected value of perfect information:

Expected value *with* perfect information (from step 3)	$19,800
Expected value *with* existing information (from step 4)	19,320
Expected value *of* perfect information (EVPI)	$ 480

time for reflection

Information gathering is costly, so the cost-benefit test must be met. In a general sense, the consultant may be considered as an *accounting system* or *information system.* The decision maker's action will depend on the message or **signal** (the specific prediction) supplied by the system. That is, the decision maker buys the system without being certain as to the forthcoming signal.

Eastman's action will depend on the particular signal. Indeed, if Eastman would choose the same action regardless of the signal, he would be unwilling to pay anything for the information system. Moreover, Eastman will be unwilling to pay for a system unless it is expected to generate an increase in expected value of the action in excess of the increase in cost of the system.

The sequence of analysis is straightforward but crucial. Its ultimate focus is on changes in expected value of the available actions. But the model moves from the *system* to the *signals* to the *actions* induced by the decision maker's *expected value:*

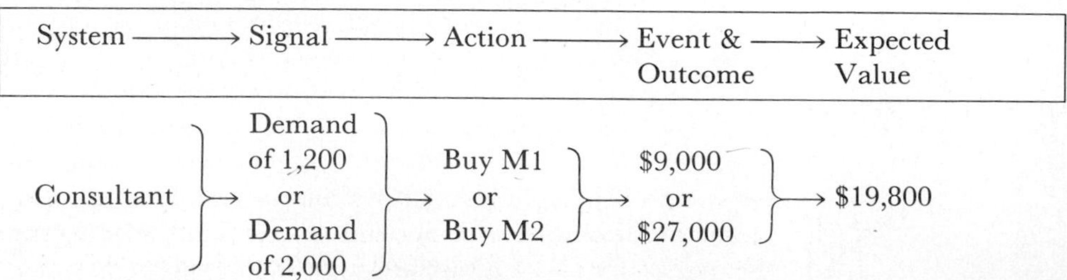

or

No Consultant → {Demand of 1,200 or Demand of 2,000} → Buy M2 → {$ 7,800 or $27,000} → $19,320

Maximum increase in expected value (EVPI):

$19,800 − $19,320 = $ 480

Finally, the choice of an optimal information system is "decision specific." That is, the choice depends on the existing information set (the information system) available to the decision maker, the decision table (the payoff matrix, as in Exhibit 21-2), the cost of the information system, and the objective function of the decision maker.

buying imperfect information

Eastman's only uncertainty is whether x_1 or x_2 will occur. Obviously, perfect information is generally unobtainable (except in textbooks), but imperfect information may still be worth buying. Note that knowledge of EVPI permits outright rejection of any additional information gathering whose cost exceeds EVPI. Thus, if the consultant's fee exceeds $480, Eastman can cease pondering whether to buy more information.

Suppose the consultant's fee will be $300. Should Eastman acquire the imperfect information system offered by the consultant? Again, the answer depends on whether the expected value with the new information system exceeds the expected value with existing information. In turn, expected values depend on what type of report Eastman foresees. See Appendix 21c for additional discussion.

cost-benefit is paramount

Reconsider the preceding example. There were two choice problems: First, should a report be acquired? Second, what machine should be purchased? The first problem is merely an example of possible accounting alternatives, such as what accounting system to employ, what cost estimate to use, and so on. Note that the choice among accounting alternatives is critical only when they are perceived as inducing different economic decisions. Furthermore, the "costs of obtaining the cost estimates" are an ingredient of the decision of how much information to buy.

The second problem, the action choice, affects how the first problem, the accounting system or data choice, is resolved. That is, the preferred accounting system, data, or report is not a single, absolute truth. Rather, it is any of a *set* of several alternatives that helps induce the preferred economic decision (subject to cost of the system or data). For example, when should we care whether an overhead rate is "truly" $2 per labor-hour or $1 per labor-hour? Sometimes we may care a lot, but other times we may be indifferent. Our degree of concern depends strictly on whether the action choice is going to be altered because of that specific cost estimate. That is, to be "useful," accounting data must be capable of altering the recipient's probabilities sufficiently to affect his or her selection of an action.

The cost-benefit approach provides a philosophical overview, but it becomes difficult for us to apply in concrete fashion when choosing among alternative accounting systems. The trouble is that systems must be designed to accommodate a multitude of routine decisions; an appraisal of costs and benefits must be made in light of their collective effect. Therefore, even though given data may have little or no value in a particular decision situation, the system that provides such data may nevertheless be economically justifiable in a collective sense. For example, a discounted cash-flow model may be part of an accounting system that supports capital-budgeting decisions. For any specific decision, a simpler model may be good enough because the data provided by the discounted cash-flow model would not change the action choice. **Therefore, the data or models may be valueless for a particular decision, but the models or systems may still be economically justifiable when their impact on the entire class of decisions is predicted.**

Applications in accounting

sensitivity analysis

To emphasize and simplify various important points throughout this book, we usually work with single-number "best estimates" (sometimes called a **certainty equivalent**) that represent several possible outcomes. For example, our cost-volume-profit models, budget models, and capital-investment models make strong assumptions regarding such critical items as the levels of variable costs, fixed costs, and volume. In other words, for purposes of introducing and using many decision models, we often conveniently assume a world of certainty and use only a single number that represents our best guess of what will occur.

As discussed earlier in this chapter, there are decision models available that deal with uncertainty by formal analysis and computation of expected values in conjunction with probability distributions. However, the application of **sensitivity analysis** to the certainty model is the most widely used approach. *Sensitivity analysis* is a "what-if" technique that measures how the expected values in a decision model will be affected by changes in the critical data inputs. In the context of cost-volume-profit analysis, sensitivity analysis answers such questions as "What will my net income be if the unit variable costs or the sales prices change by some amount from the original prediction?"

The major benefit of sensitivity analysis is its provision of an immediate financial measure of the consequences of possible prediction errors. It helps focus on those aspects that are very sensitive indeed, and it eases the manager's mind regarding those predictions that have little impact on decisions.

The advantages of using certainty models coupled with sensitivity analysis are their relative simplicity and economy. The major disadvantage is the possible overlooking of "better" actions that might be forthcoming if more formal models that include uncertainty were used. See Appendix 21a, "Applications of Cost of Prediction Error," for a discussion of how sensitivity is measured.

use of probabilities

A major objective of this chapter is to increase awareness that accountants and managers generally prepare single-number estimates without conducting formal analysis encompassing probabilities. Given our world of uncertainty, there are potential benefits of explicitly stating probabilities when analyzing alternatives. In this way, a manager is less likely to analyze his or her alternatives too simplistically.

For example, the presentation of three possible outcomes, together with their respective probabilities, may seem warranted for major decisions. Suppose a company is contemplating rearranging some equipment. A typical analysis might show expected operating savings of, say, $23,000. However, a closer examination might indicate the costs and probabilities as shown at the top of the next page. Such a probabilistic analysis provides the decision maker with a more complete financial picture of what is faced in a world of uncertainty.

	EVENTS		
	much success	small success	no success
probability of event	.5	.2	.3
ACTION:			
Do nothing	$200,000	$200,000	$200,000
Rearrange	120,000	180,000	270,000

Expected values of the costs:

Do nothing, $\bar{A}$ = $200,000(.5) + $200,000(.2) + $200,000(.3) = $200,000

Rearrange, $\bar{A}$ = $120,000(.5) + $180,000(.2) + $270,000(.3) = 177,000

Difference, expected operating savings $ 23,000

expected monetary value and utility

In most business cases, expected monetary value is a useful guide to action; that is, the manager chooses the act that will bring the greatest expected financial advantage. However, there are instances where expected monetary profit will not be governing. For psychological reasons—perhaps fear of bankruptcy—managers may have *personal* evaluations that do not coincide with monetary evaluations.

For example, suppose that each of two managers has an opportunity to prepare a proposal at a cost of $10,000. There is a 50-50 chance that the proposal will be accepted, in which case there would be a $25,000 net profit (after deducting all associated costs, including the $10,000 proposal cost). The table and the computation of an expected monetary value of $7,500 for making the proposal follow:

	EVENT	
	get contract	do not get
probability	.5	.5
ACTION:		
Make proposal	$25,000	−$10,000
No proposal	-0-	-0-

$\bar{A}$ (Make proposal) = .5(25,000) + .5(−10,000) = $7,500

$\bar{A}$ (No proposal) = 0

But the two managers may have very different attitudes toward the situation. The attractiveness of the proposal to each may depend on the individual's own financial position. If one of the managers may be easily bankrupted by the loss of the $10,000 proposal cost, he or she may decide to forgo this opportunity. The other manager may have adequate working capital and may make the proposal. What must be decided is simply whether it is worth taking a 50 percent risk of losing $10,000 in order to have an even chance of a $25,000 profit. This decision depends on a direct expression of personal preference.

Thus, where the amounts at stake are large, an expected value of one dollar may not be worth a dollar to the manager; that is, an expected dollar may have an expected **utility value** of only, say, 70 cents (a direct expression of personal preference). Strict money value then will not be a valid guide to action. The approach to the decision will be the same, but in these special cases *monetary values* will no longer coincide with *utility values,* and so the latter will replace dollar values in the evaluation.

Utility value may be defined as the value of a specific outcome, such as a monetary amount, to a decision maker.

risk and utilities A decision maker's utility function depends on attitudes toward risks. There are three basic attitudes: **risk neutral, risk averse,** and **risk seeking.** These attitudes are portrayed in Exhibit 21-3, where monetary amounts (dollars) are plotted on the horizontal axis and **utiles** are plotted on the vertical axis. Utility is arbitrarily measured in *utiles,* which are quantifications of the utility value of given monetary amounts.

RISK NEUTRAL ☐ Utility is directly proportional to monetary amounts. In other words, the utility function is linear; it always bears a constant relationship to monetary amounts.

RISK AVERSE ☐ The individual's utility for monetary amounts increases at a *decreasing* rate. Thus, a risk averter is generally willing to take fair gambles only if the investment is less than the *expected monetary value* of the gambles.

RISK SEEKING ☐ The opposite of risk averse. The individual's utility for monetary amounts increases at an *increasing* rate. Thus, a risk seeker is generally willing to pay more than the *expected monetary value* of the gambles.

Research has shown that most managers and investors are risk averse. For example, few individuals are willing to gamble double-or-nothing on a coin toss at even odds unless the amount of the bet is relatively small.

EXHIBIT 21-3

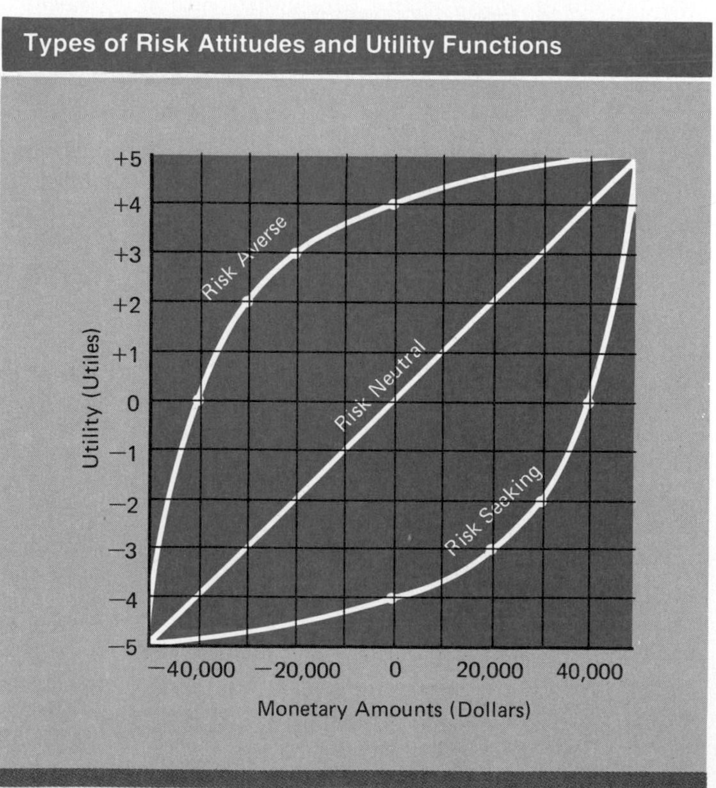

Exhibit 21-3 reveals the nature of the tradeoffs made between risks and returns. Mary Goldman, a risk-neutral decision maker, may be financially secure and will get about as much pleasure from increasing her wealth by $50,000 as pain from decreasing her wealth by $50,000. Her utility varies accordingly from +5 to −5 in linear fashion.

The risk-averse decision maker, Adam Johnson, increases his utility only slightly when the monetary amounts exceed zero. For example, moving from $0 to $50,000 on the horizontal scale increases his value from +4 to +5 on the utility scale. In contrast, moving from $0 to −$20,000 on the horizontal scale moves the risk-averse decision maker from +4 to +3 on the vertical scale. Johnson will avoid situations where high losses will occur.

The risk-seeking decision maker enjoys taking chances. Delores Medina believes that a large loss will not bring as much pain in relation to the enormous pleasure of a large profit. For example, an increase from $40,000 to $50,000 will increase her utiles by 5 (from +0 to +5). In contrast, a decrease from $0 to −$10,000 will decrease her utiles by only .25; the vertical scale shows a decline from −4 to −4.25.[8]

risk and cost-volume-profit model

The cost-volume-profit model provides a simple illustration of why single numbers and expected monetary values are often insufficient for guiding decisions. Assume that a manager, Amy Anton, is going to choose between the production and sale of Product 1 or Product 2. Both products will require the same amounts of manufacturing facilities. The following data are available:

	PRODUCT 1	PRODUCT 2
Contribution margin per unit	$ 4	$ 4
Increment in annual fixed costs	$400,000	$400,000
Breakeven volume	100,000 units	100,000 units

Given these facts, the manager should be indifferent between these two products. Indeed, for any level of sales, both products will have the same total contribution margins. However, consider the additional data:

	PROBABILITY DISTRIBUTION	
UNITS SOLD	**product 1**	**product 2**
50,000	.1	.2
75,000	.2	.3
100,000	.3	.2
125,000	.3	.1
150,000	.1	.1
225,000	.0	.1
	1.0	1.0

The expected values of sales in units are:

[8]See R. Levin and C. Kirkpatrick, *Quantitative Approaches to Management,* 5th ed. (New York: McGraw-Hill, 1981), Chap. 5.

For Product 1: .1(50,000) + .2(75,000) + .3(100,000) + .3(125,000) + .1(150,000) = 102,500

For Product 2: .2(50,000) + .3(75,000) + .2(100,000) + .1(125,000) + .1(150,000) + .1(225,000) = 102,500

Both products have the same expected values for unit sales and hence the same expected values for contribution margins of 102,500 × \$4 = \$410,000. Nevertheless Anton is unlikely to be indifferent. Product 2 is riskier. Why? Because the probability is .2 + .3, or .5, that sales will be less than or equal to only 75,000 units, which is below breakeven. In contrast, the comparable probability for Product 1 is .1 + .2, or .3. Moreover, Product 2 has a probability of .7 of being just at breakeven sales or below, in contrast to Product 1's probability of .6. Product 2 has a higher dispersion around its expected sales and a higher probability of loss. Both products have the same expected profits.

Given the additional information about the probability distributions, which product will Anton select? It depends on her attitude toward risk. If she is risk neutral, she will use expected monetary value and be indifferent. However, if she is risk averse, she will choose Product 1 because it has less probability of loss. Finally, if she is risk seeking, she will choose Product 2 because it has a .1 probability of generating a much larger profit than Product 1. As Kaplan observes, the accountant can help by supplying probability distributions and leaving it "to the manager to apply his own risk attitude toward the different probability distributions when selecting a course of action."[9]

trade-off of risks and returns

Reconsider the initial data that accompany Exhibit 21-1. Recall that the expected value of each project was \$4,000. However, Proposal B had the greater degree of risk as measured by its coefficient of variation. Suppose the manager is risk averse; that is, the manager is willing to give up some expected monetary values in return for bearing less risk.[10] Such a trade-off might be measured in many different ways. Suppose the decision maker's attitude toward risk could be quantified as follows: First, express utility for outcomes by the logarithmic function

$$\textbf{Utility (outcome)} = \textbf{Log}_{10}\ \textbf{(outcome)}$$

Second, compute the expected utility of each project. Third, choose the project with the highest expected utility.

Exhibit 21-4 shows that the mechanics of the calculation of expected utilities are exactly the same as the calculation of expected monetary values. The only difference is that the outcomes are expressed in terms of common logarithms. Proposal A has a higher expected utility than Proposal B.

---

[9]The illustration here is from R. Kaplan, *Advanced Management Accounting* (Englewood Cliffs, N.J.: Prentice-Hall, 1982), Chap. 6. His entire chapter deals with cost-volume-profit analysis under uncertainty.

[10]We assume here that where the manager is not the owner, both have the same attitudes toward risk. It is beyond the scope of this book to discuss the many issues that arise when the manager and the owner have different risk attitudes. Moreover, in corporations with many shareholders, the task of eliciting (let alone aggregating) risk attitudes of the individual owners is awesome. For a discussion of these issues, see J. Demski, *Information Analysis,* 2nd ed. (Reading, Mass.: Addison-Wesley, 1980), Chap. 6; and Kaplan, *Advanced Management Accounting,* Chap. 17.

EXHIBIT 21-4

Computation of Expected Utilities

PROPOSAL A			PROPOSAL B		
probability	**monetary amounts**	**$\log_{10}$ values***	**probability**	**monetary amounts**	**$\log_{10}$ values***
0.10	$3,000	3.477	0.10	$2,000	3.301
0.20	3,500	3.544	0.25	3,000	3.477
0.40	4,000	3.602	0.30	4,000	3.602
0.20	4,500	3.653	0.25	5,000	3.699
0.10	5,000	3.699	0.10	6,000	3.778

**From a table of logarithms not included in this book.*

For A: Expected utility $= 0.10(3.477) + 0.20(3.544) + 0.40(3.602) + 0.20(3.653) + .10(3.699)$
$= .3477 + .7088 + 1.4408 + .7306 + .3699 = 3.5978$

For B: Expected utility $= 0.10(3.301) + 0.25(3.477) + .30(3.602) + .25(3.699) + .10(3.778)$
$= .3301 + .8693 + 1.0806 + .9248 + .3778 = 3.5826$

We now have examined three ways of presenting information relating to the initial project in this chapter:

1. Report the expected monetary value:

	PROPOSAL A	PROPOSAL B
Expected monetary value	$4,000	$4,000

   This presentation of the information omits any details on the potential dispersion of the actual cash flow.

2. Report the expected monetary value and a measure of dispersion of the cash flow:

	PROPOSAL A	PROPOSAL B
Expected monetary value	$4,000	$4,000
Coefficient of variation	.14	.29

3. Report the expected utility of each proposal, using a utility function that captures the decision maker's tradeoff between risk and expected monetary value:

	PROPOSAL A	PROPOSAL B
Expected utility	3.5978 utiles	3.5826 utiles

Note that the decision maker will not necessarily always choose by means of expected monetary values alone. There are situations where expected utility will favor one of two competing proposals, and expected monetary value will favor the other proposal.

SUMMARY

Accountants must be acquainted with the entire decision process. They must focus on decision objectives, prediction methods, decision models, and alternative outcomes.

Formal decision models are used increasingly, because they replace or supplement hunches and implicit rules with explicit assumptions and criteria. The decision maker must choose the decision model to use. Both the choice criterion or objective function and the complexities of the decision situation affect the choice of model. What information is to be compiled depends on the chosen prediction method and the decision model.

Managers and accountants are often prone to regard quantification as precise just because numbers are somehow supposed to be accurate. However, almost all data, whether they depict the past or the future, are subject to uncertainty. Accounting reports for decision making are aimed increasingly toward the formal, explicit recognition of uncertainty. Cognizance of probability distributions is often essential to providing information for decisions, and the use of utility values provides a systematic way for measuring risk-return trade-offs.

SUGGESTED READINGS

The following provide basic coverage of decision theory:

AMERICAN ACCOUNTING ASSOCIATION, **"Report of the Committee on Managerial Decision Models,"** *Accounting Review* (Supplement), Vol. XLIV, 1969. Also see the reports of other committees on related topics in the annual Supplements in succeeding years.

DEMSKI, J. S., **Information Analysis,** 2nd ed. Reading, Mass.: Addison-Wesley, 1980.

DEMSKI, J. S., and G. A. FELTHAM, **Cost Determination: A Conceptual Approach.** Ames: Iowa State University Press, 1976.

FELTHAM, G. A., **Information Evaluation.** Sarasota, Fla.: American Accounting Association, 1973.

HOLLOWAY, C., **Decision Making under Uncertainty.** Englewood Cliffs, N.J.: Prentice-Hall, 1979.

RAIFFA, H., **Decision Analysis: Introductory Lectures on Choices under Uncertainty.** Reading, Mass.: Addison-Wesley, 1968.

Extensions and applications abound in the academic literature. Some examples follow:

HILTON, R., **"The Determinants of Cost Information Value: An Illustrative Analysis,"** *Journal of Accounting Research,* Vol. 17, No. 2, Autumn 1979.

MAGEE, R., **"Equilibria in Budget Participation,"** *Journal of Accounting Research,* Vol. 18, No. 2, Autumn 1980.

SUNDEM, G., **"A Game Theory Model of the Information Evaluator and the Decision Maker,"** *Journal of Accounting Research,* Vol. 17, No. 1, Spring 1979.

PROBLEM FOR SELF-STUDY

problem

Review the Eastman illustration, especially Exhibit 21-2. Suppose Eastman's best current estimates of the two demands being revealed are .3 and .7 instead of .4 and .6, respectively. What is the expected value of perfect information? Why is the EVPI less than the $480 computed in the chapter?

solution

Expected value *with* perfect information, (.3 × $9,000) + (.7 × $27,000)	= $21,600
Expected value *with* existing information, per altered Exhibit 21-2, (.3 × $7,800) + (.7 × $27,000)	= 21,240
Expected value *of* perfect information (EVPI)	$ 360

The EVPI is less than the $480 computed earlier because with existing information there is less uncertainty about M2 being the wiser choice. That is, there is a 70 percent instead of a 60 percent chance that demand will be 2,000.

Terms to Learn

actions ***certainty*** ***certainty equivalent*** ***choice criterion*** ***coefficient of variation*** ***conditional loss*** ***cost estimation*** ***cost of prediction error*** ***cost prediction*** ***decision model*** ***decision table*** ***events*** ***expected value*** ***expected value of perfect information (EVPI)*** ***objective function*** ***opportunity loss*** ***outcomes*** ***parameter*** ***payoff matrix*** ***payoff*** ***payoff table*** ***probabilities*** ***probability distribution*** ***risk*** ***risk averse*** ***risk neutral*** ***risk seeking*** ***sensitivity analysis*** ***signal*** ***standard deviation*** ***states of nature*** ***uncertainty*** ***utiles*** ***utility value***

Special Points and Pitfalls

This chapter underscores some characteristics of uncertainty and shows how the accountant might cope with them. Sensitivity analysis is a widely used way of dealing with uncertainty. However, the formal use of probability distributions is also receiving more attention.

Accountants increasingly recognize that expected *monetary* value ignores risk. If accountants work with expected *utility* value, the risk attitudes of the decision maker are contained in the utility function. Then maximizing expected utility does indeed explicitly make risk-return trade-offs.

The practical problems of developing utility functions are enormous. Therefore, the next-best solution is for the accountant to provide expected monetary values *plus* probability distributions. Then the decision maker can explicitly or implicitly apply his or her own risk attitudes to the different probability distributions when choosing an action.

Appendix 21a: applications of cost of prediction error

What is the cost of an erroneous prediction? The **cost of prediction error** is the cost of failing to forecast a critical **parameter.**[11] Such a cost can be calculated without reference to the probability of various events. It can be a key element in using sensitivity analysis, which can be performed without the probability trappings described in the body of the chapter. **Hence, if desired this appendix can be studied without referring to the earlier parts of this chapter.**

This appendix demonstrates how the cost of prediction error can be utilized in sensitivity analysis. Two illustrations are provided that are extensions of illustrations

[11]A *parameter* is a constant or the coefficient of some variable in a model or system of equations. Examples are the total fixed costs, the demand, the unit variable cost, and the unit selling price.

used in earlier chapters: the cost-volume-profit model (Chapter 3) and the capital-budgeting model (Chapter 12).

cost-volume-profit model

Chapter 3 contained the following example:

> A person plans to sell a toy rocket at the state fair. He may purchase these rockets at 50¢ each with the privilege of returning all unsold rockets. The booth rental is $200, payable in advance. The rockets will be sold at 90¢ each. How many rockets must be sold to break even? (Ignore income taxes.)

Sensitivity analysis can be either a calming influence or a signal to buy more data before reaching a decision. Examples of such buying include getting more samples of how costs have behaved at various levels of volume, or scrapping the linear cost-volume model and replacing it with a more elaborate model.

If formal decision models such as the cost-volume-profit model are used, often it is feasible to measure sensitivity by estimating the *cost of prediction errors.* The procedure follows:

1. Begin with the basic solution, the optimal original decision. Predict the value of the critical parameter and solve the decision problem by computing the expected value, given this original prediction: Critical parameter, predicted sales = 1,000 units Optimal original decision: purchase 1,000 units Expected net income = $200 [(1,000 units × $.40 contribution margin) − $200 fixed costs = $200]	
2. Given an alternative possible value for the critical parameter, re-solve the decision problem. The solution produces a new decision, which may or may not be the same as the decision in step 1: Alternative parameter value, actual sales = 600 units Optimal new decision: purchase 600 units Expected net income = [(600 units × $.40 contribution margin) − $200 fixed costs = $40]	$40
3. Given the original decision in step 1 and the alternative parameter value in step 2, compute the financial result: Expected net income = [(600 units × $.40 contribution margin) − $200 fixed costs + 400 units returned at no cost = $40]	40
4. The cost of prediction error is the financial result in step 2 minus the financial result in step 3.	$ 0

In a complete sensitivity analysis, steps 2 through 4 would be repeated for a range of possible demand values. This would reveal that for an actual demand above 500 units, the decision is insensitive to any predicted sales level above 500 units. If predicted demand is less than 500 units (the breakeven volume), the optimal decision is to avoid renting the booth.

Now assume that the manager did not have the privilege of returning any unsold rockets. Instead, because of their souvenir markings, they became worthless. He had acquired 1,000 units. What was the cost of prediction error?

1. Critical parameter value, predicted sales = 1,000 units
Optimal original decision: purchase 1,000 units
Expected net income = $200

2. Alternative parameter value = 600 units
Optimal new decision: purchase 600 units

Expected net income (as above)	$ 40
3. Results of original decision under alternative parameter value	
Expected net income (loss):	
Revenue (600 units × \$.90) − Cost of rockets (1,000 units × \$.50) − \$200 fixed costs =	(160)
4. Cost of prediction error, step 2 minus step 3	\$200

The cost of prediction error can be used for sensitivity analysis either *before* or *after* the decision to order the rockets. To determine the cost of a prediction error *after the actual outcome* value of the parameter is known, the actual value would be used in steps 2 and 3. In these examples we have the vantage point of knowing the actual value of the parameter, and we can therefore compute how much the poor prediction has cost. Of course, the entire sensitivity analysis could have been conducted for a number of demand values before any decision was made. The decision maker could then appraise the possible magnitude of various potential prediction errors and their effects on decisions. **The focus is on the relationship of data to decisions.**

EXHIBIT 21-5

Net Present-Value Model

Original investment	\$3,791
Useful life	5 years
Annual cash savings from operations	\$1,000
Hurdle rate of return, which is the discount rate	8%

*Approach 1: Discounting each year's cash inflow separately**

	PRESENT VALUE OF \$1, DISCOUNTED @ 8%	TOTAL PRESENT VALUE	SKETCH OF RELEVANT CASH FLOWS 0	1	2	3	4	5
End of Year			0	1	2	3	4	5
Cash flows:								
Annual cash savings	.926	\$ 926	←------	\$1,000				
	.857	857	←------------		\$1,000			
	.794	794	←----------------			\$1,000		
	.735	735	←---------------------				\$1,000	
	.681	681	←---------------------------					\$1,000
Present value of relevant inflows	3.993	\$3,993						
Initial outlay	1.000	(3,791)	\$(3,791)					
Net present value		\$ 202‡						

Approach 2; Using Annuity Table†								
Annual cash savings	3.993	\$3,993	←-------	\$1,000	\$1,000	\$1,000	\$1,000	\$1,000
Initial outlay	1.000	(3,791)	\$(3,791)					
Net present value		\$ 202‡						

**Present value from Table 2, Appendix B.*

†*Present annuity values from Table 4.*

‡*Rounded.*

capital-budgeting model

Refer to Exhibit 21-5, which is a reproduction of the exhibit on page 407, the net present-value model for capital budgeting. In the context of capital budgeting, sensitivity analysis answers the question, "How will the net present value be changed if the computations of the useful life or the cash flows are inaccurate?"

Suppose that in Exhibit 21-5 the cash inflows were $800 annually instead of $1,000. What would be the cost of the prediction error?

1. Critical parameter, predicted annual cash savings, $1,000		
Optimal original decision: invest		
2. Alternative parameter value, cash savings, $800		
Gross present value, $800 × 3.993 (the factor from Exhibit 21-5)	$ 3,194	
Required investment	−3,791	
Net present value	$ −597	
Optimal new decision: do not invest		
Financial results		$ 0
3. Results of original decision and the alternative parameter value, financial result		−597
4. Cost of prediction error, step 2 minus step 3		$ 597

The cost of prediction error represents the difference between the best possible outcome and the outcome of the original decision, given an alternative parameter. It can be zero but never negative. Why? Because step 2 above will always have a financial result at least as attractive as the result in step 3. The literature of decision sciences frequently refers to the cost of prediction error by other names, such as **conditional loss** or **opportunity loss.** Also see Appendix 21b.

Appendix 21b: cost of prediction error and perfect information

This appendix demonstrates how the cost of prediction error is related to the expected value of perfect information.

Review the Eastman illustration in the body of the chapter. For your convenience, Exhibit 21-2 is reproduced here.

EXHIBIT 21-2

Decision Table

	EVENTS	
	$x_1 = 1,200$	$x_2 = 2,000$
probability of events	.4	.6
ACTION:		
Buy M1	A = $9,000*	A = $25,000‡
Buy M2	A = $7,800†	A = $27,000§

A = Operating income

$\bar{A}$ = Expected value of operating income

Expected values:

Buy M1, $\bar{A}$ = $9,000(.4) + $25,000(.6) = $18,600

Buy M2, $\bar{A}$ = $7,800(.4) + $27,000(.6) = $19,320

**$20(1,200) − $15,000* *‡$20(2,000) − $15,000*

†$24(1,200) − $21,000 *§$24(2,000) − $21,000*

The optimal original decision was M2. But suppose $x = 1{,}200$. Then M1 would be preferable. What is the cost of prediction error?

1.	Critical parameter, predicted sales. The approach in Exhibit 21-2 weighed the likelihood of $x = 1{,}200$ and $x = 2{,}000$ and led to an optimal original decision favoring M2.	
2.	Alternative parameter value, $x = 1{,}200$ Optimal new decision: Buy M1 Financial results, operating income (from Exhibit 21-2)	$9,000
3.	Given the original decision in step 1 and the alternative parameter in step 2, compute the financial results, operating income (from Exhibit 21-2)	7,800
4.	Cost of prediction error, step 2 minus step 3	$1,200

Given a particular original decision, there is a nonnegative cost of prediction error for every possible event. These costs can be presented in a prediction error table, as shown in Exhibit 21-6. *Note that these amounts are computed without reference to the probability of various events.*

EXHIBIT 21-6

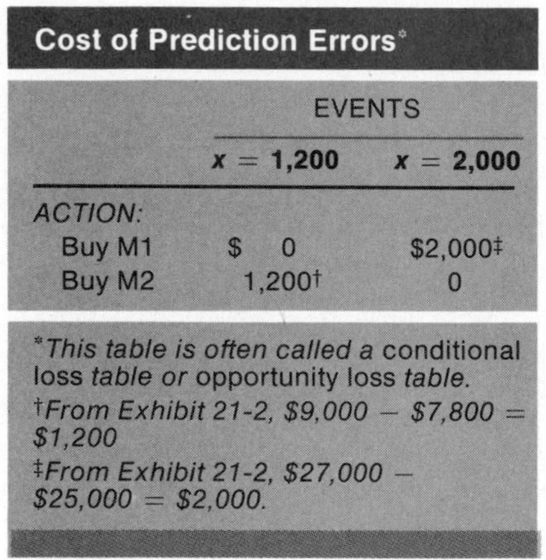

Cost of Prediction Errors*

	EVENTS	
	$x = 1{,}200$	$x = 2{,}000$
ACTION:		
Buy M1	$ 0	$2,000‡
Buy M2	1,200†	0

**This table is often called a* conditional loss *table or* opportunity loss *table.*
†From Exhibit 21-2, $9,000 − $7,800 = $1,200
‡From Exhibit 21-2, $27,000 − $25,000 = $2,000.

Reflect on what Exhibit 21-6 reveals. If you know the demand in advance, you buy M1 if $x = 1{,}200$ and M2 if $x = 2{,}000$. But you are unsure whether a flawless consultant will supply $x = 1{,}200$ or 2,000. That is, the perfect information in advance of an event will contain only one of the two predictions. Therefore, probabilities must be considered.

Note the relationship of EVPI to the cost of prediction error in Exhibit 21-6. Given the original decision of buying M2, the cost of prediction error was $1,200 if $x = 1{,}200$ and $0 if $x = 2{,}000$. But in a world of uncertainty, as a manager, you would be willing to pay $480, not $1,200, for additional information. Why? Because the cost of prediction error does not consider the probability of various events occurring. After all, if there is a 60 percent chance that $x = 2{,}000$, given the buying of M2, there is also a 60 percent chance that your cost of prediction error will be zero. Hence:

EVPI = .4($1,200) + .6($0) = $480

Thus, EVPI is the weighted-average cost of prediction error where the weights are the probabilities of the various events occurring.

Appendix 21c: value of imperfect information

This appendix explores the buying of imperfect information. It explains how probabilities are revised, using Bayes's Theorem.

effects of imperfect information

Review the Eastman illustration (pages 720–24). Recall that the expected value of perfect information (EVPI) was $480. But no consultant has flawless predictive powers. How much should Eastman pay for the imperfect information system (the consultant)? Suppose the consultant has requested $300. Eastman should pay no more than the value of the imperfect information, which we will now compute.

In advance of each occurrence of the events in this illustration, the consultant is expected to produce only one of the two signals (reports). A pessimistic report will be a prediction of $x = 1{,}200$; an optimistic report will be a prediction of $x = 2{,}000$. The original decision table in Exhibit 21-2, page 735, would be changed by each of these reports, as shown in Exhibit 21-7.

Exhibit 21-7 summarizes the expected values with imperfect information. Note that the operating incomes are identical in Exhibits 21-2 and 21-7. The only substantial difference between the exhibits is the **change in probabilities** (and hence the change in expected values) caused by the possibility of additional information. The computation of these probabilities is explained in the next section, but let us obtain some perspective first. The *expected value of imperfect information* (sometimes called the *expected value of sample information*) is defined as the difference between the expected value of the result given the additional information and the expected value of the result given existing information.

In our example, suppose Eastman assesses the probability of getting a pessimistic report as .44; an optimistic report, .56. (The computation of these probabilities is explained in the next section.) Therefore:

Expected value with imperfect information (.44 × $13,368) + (.56 × $24,254) =	$19,464
Expected value with existing information, per Exhibit 21-2	19,320
Expected value of imperfect information	$ 144

Thus, the most that should be paid for the consultant's report is $144, which is considerably less than the $480 EVPI and the $300 fee requested.

Suppose the consultant lowers the fee from $300 to $100. Eastman hires her. The report is pessimistic. What should Eastman do now? Make the relevant computations, as before, using the revised probabilities. As Exhibit 21-7 shows, the expected value is $13,368, considerably lower than the expected value of $19,320 in Exhibit 21-2. Does this mean the decision to engage the consultant was wrong? No. The additional information has revised Eastman's probabilities and resulting expected values. The additional information has made M1 the optimal decision.

computing the value of imperfect information

The Eastman illustration included a revision of probabilities and resulting expected values, as summarized in Exhibit 21-7. There are five steps in computing the expected value of imperfect information.

Step 1. Determine the set of signals that the information system may produce. Assume that the consultant will produce only one of two possible reports, pessimistic or optimistic:

EXHIBIT 21-7

Expected Values with Imperfect Information

	EVENTS	
	x = 1,200	x = 2,000
If a pessimistic report, probability of events	.727*	.273*
If optimistic report, probability of events	.143*	.857*
ACTION:		
Buy M1	A = \$9,000†	A = \$25,000†
Buy M2	A = \$7,800†	A = \$27,000†

Assume pessimistic report:

$\bar{A}$(M1) = .727(\$9,000) + .273(\$25,000) = \$13,368‡

$\bar{A}$(M2) = .727(\$7,800) + .273(\$27,000) = \$13,042

Assume optimistic report:

$\bar{A}$(M1) = .143(\$9,000) + .857(\$25,000) = \$22,712

$\bar{A}$(M2) = .143(\$7,800) + .857(\$27,000) = \$24,254‡

*See the next section for an explanation of how these probabilities are computed.
†As in Exhibit 21-2.
‡Optimal.

$$y_1 = \text{Prediction of } x_1 = 1{,}200$$

$$y_2 = \text{Prediction of } x_2 = 2{,}000$$

where y_k is the kth signal from an information system, the consultant.

Step 2. Determine the probability of receiving each signal. Eastman determines that the consultant's predictions are correct only 80 percent of the time. For example, if the consultant supplies a prediction of 1,200, the actual demand 20 percent of the time will be 2,000. Similarly, a prediction of 2,000 will mean that the actual demand 20 percent of the time will be 1,200.

These probabilities are summarized as follows:

$$P(y_1|x_1) = .8 \qquad P(y_2|x_2) = .8$$

$$P(y_2|x_1) = .2 \qquad P(y_1|x_2) = .2$$

where P = probability; y_1 = pessimistic report; y_2 = optimistic report; x_1 = demand of 1,200; and x_2 = demand of 2,000.

Given that $P(x_1) = .4$ and $P(x_2) = .6$, use the following formula (which is developed in many books on elementary decision theory and statistics) to develop the probabilities of obtaining a pessimistic or optimistic report:

$$P(y_k) = \sum_{i=1}^{n} P(y_k|x_i) \cdot P(x_i)$$

where P = probability; y_k = specific report (or signal); x_i = specific event (demand); and n = number of events.

Then

$$P(y_1) = (.8 \times .4) + (.2 \times .6) = .44$$

$$P(y_2) = (.8 \times .6) + (.2 \times .4) = .56$$

In words, if the consultant is correct 80 percent of the time, and if the probability of $x = 1{,}200$ is 40 percent, then the probability of a pessimistic report is 44 percent. The computation is as follows:

$$\text{Probability of pessimistic report} = \left(\begin{array}{c}\text{Probability of pessimistic}\\ \text{report, given low demand}\\ \times \text{Probability of low demand}\end{array}\right) + \left(\begin{array}{c}\text{Probability of pessimistic}\\ \text{report, given high demand}\\ \times \text{Probability of high demand}\end{array}\right)$$
$$= (.8 \times .4) + (.2 \times .6)$$
$$= .32 + .12 = .44$$

$$\text{Probability of optimistic report} = \left(\begin{array}{c}\text{Probability of optimistic}\\ \text{report, given high demand}\\ \times \text{Probability of high demand}\end{array}\right) + \left(\begin{array}{c}\text{Probability of optimistic}\\ \text{report, given low demand}\\ \times \text{Probability of low demand}\end{array}\right)$$
$$= (.8 \times .6) + (.2 \times .4)$$
$$= .48 + .08 = .56$$

Step 3. Determine the revised probabilities of each event's occurring, conditional upon receiving a particular signal from the information system. Eastman is fundamentally interested in whether additional information will change his initial assessment of probabilities of x_1 and x_2. Bayes's Theorem, which is also developed in textbooks on basic decision theory, permits these *prior probabilities* to be revised as *posterior probabilities.* The revision depends on specification of the prior probabilities and the probabilities of obtaining a specific signal from the information system (that is, a pessimistic or optimistic report). The Bayes formula would be used as follows:

$$P(x_i|y_k) = \frac{P(x_i) \cdot P(y_k|x_i)}{P(y_k)}$$

$$P(x_1|y_1) = \frac{.4 \times .8}{.44} = .727$$

$$P(x_2|y_1) = \frac{.6 \times .2}{.44} = .273$$

$$P(x_1|y_2) = \frac{.4 \times .2}{.56} = .143$$

$$P(x_2|y_2) = \frac{.6 \times .8}{.56} = .857$$

These computations are often tabulated as follows:

	PRIOR			POSTERIOR
	$P(x_i)$	$P(y_k\|x_i)$	$P(y_k \cdot x_i)$	$P(x_i\|y_k)$
If pessimistic report (y_1)				
Demand of 1,200	.4	.8	.32	.727
Demand of 2,000	.6	.2	.12	.273
			.44	
If optimistic report (y_2)				
Demand of 1,200	.4	.2	.08	.143
Demand of 2,000	.6	.8	.48	.857
			.56	

In words, there is a 72.7 percent chance that $x = 1{,}200$ if a pessimistic report is produced and an 85.7 percent chance that $x = 2{,}000$ if an optimistic report is forthcoming. Note especially that "being right 80 percent of the time" does not mean that $P(x_1|y_1) = .8$.

Step 4. Determine the optimal action conditional upon each signal from the information system. Each signal (optimistic report or pessimistic report) will generally cause Eastman's posterior probabilities to differ from his prior probabilities. Thus, the optimal action may change. Therefore, it is necessary to redo the five-step analysis that was originally performed with the prior information for each signal. Exhibit 21-7 shows these computations of expected values, one conditional upon receiving a pessimistic report and one conditional upon receiving an optimistic report.

Step 5. Determine the expected value with the (imperfect) information system. This step was performed earlier in conjunction with the explanation of Exhibit 21-7. The expected value with imperfect information depends on the probabilities of receiving a pessimistic or optimistic report:

$$(.44 \times \$13{,}368) + (.56 \times \$24{,}254) = \$19{,}464$$

As the previous section explained, Eastman should purchase the information system only if its price does not exceed $144, which is $19,464 minus the $19,320 expected value with existing information.

QUESTIONS, PROBLEMS, AND CASES

21-1 "Determining the problem is the key to successful decision making." Comment.

21-2 A fire has destroyed a factory. As the company manager, list as many alternative actions as you can formulate.

21-3 "Taking no action must always be listed among alternative courses of action." Discuss.

21-4 "The management consultant is happy when he finds that his client has wholeheartedly accepted a beautiful decision program that is the consultant's brainchild and the product of weeks of analysis." Later, the consultant's joy often becomes sadness when he finds that the decisions were never transformed into action. What is the probable reason for the apparent failure of the consultant's plans?

21-5 "The wisdom of a decision can never really be measured until the future becomes the past." What are the merits and weaknesses of a postdecision audit?

21-6 What steps should be taken in computing expected value?

21-7 Many businesspeople refuse to accept marginal business at cut prices under any circumstances. They say that acceptance of such orders will hurt the industry price structure and thus boomerang to the detriment of "unmeasurable" future profits. Does the businessperson base such decisions on quantitative, tangible factors? Explain.

21-8 What is the major benefit of using subjective probabilities in forecasting?

21-9 ***Size of inventory.*** Once a day, a retailer stocks bunches of fresh-cut flowers, each of which costs 40¢ and sells for $1. The retailer never cuts his price; leftovers are given to a nearby church. He estimates demand characteristics as follows:

DEMAND	PROBABILITY
0	.05
1	.20
2	.40
3	.25
4	.10
5 or more	.00
	1.00

How many units should he stock in order to maximize profits? Why?

21-10 ***Perfect information.*** Refer to the preceding problem. Compute the most he should be willing to pay for a faultless prediction concerning the number of units to be sold on any given day.

21-11 ***Competitive bidding.*** A road-building company gets contracts by competitive bidding. It has estimated that its costs on a particular project will be $100,000. Based on past experience, the president anticipates the following probabilities of bids:

BID*	PROBABILITY OF BID
$ 90,000	0.05
100,000	0.10
110,000	0.20
120,000	0.30
130,000	0.25
140,000	0.10
150,000	0.00
	1.00

**For simplicity, assume that bids must be in $10,000 units.*

The company's objective is to maximize expected profit. What bid should be made? Show computations.

21-12 ***Marketing a new product; selection of equipment.*** The Ardo Company makes specialty items that are sold through novelty stores. The demand for specific items is difficult to predict. Yet long experience is helpful in predicting the probable range of sales volumes for most items.

The president must decide on whether to manufacture and market a new item that will sell for $2 per unit. If the item is produced, one of the following types of special equipment will be used. The equipment will be scrapped after the selling season is over.

	SPECIAL EQUIPMENT	
	A	B
Cost of equipment	$50,000	$100,000
Variable production cost per unit	$1.39	$.90

No matter which equipment is chosen, batches of production may be closely geared to demand so that no unsold units will be left after the season is over.

The president and other executives have assigned the following probabilities to the range of anticipated sales volume:

SALES VOLUME IN UNITS	PROBABILITY
50,000	0.30
100,000	0.40
150,000	0.20
200,000	0.10
	1.00

REQUIRED

(Show computations.)

1. Assuming that profit maximization is the sole objective, which course of action should be taken?
2. What sales volume in units would show identical profits regardless of the choice of equipment?

21-13 ***Expected-value tables.*** As an appliance dealer, you are deciding how to service your one-year warranty on the 1,000 color television sets you have just sold to a large local hotel.

You have three alternatives:

1. A reputable service firm has offered to service the sets, including all parts and labor, for a flat fee of $18,000.

2. For $15,000, another reputable service firm would furnish all necessary parts and provide up to 1,000 service calls at no charge. Service calls in excess of that number would be $4 each. The number of calls is likely to be:

EVENT	CHANCE OF OCCURRENCE	PROBABILITY OF OCCURRENCE	TOTAL COST
1,000 calls or less	50%	0.5	$15,000
1,500 calls	20	0.2	17,000
2,000 calls	20	0.2	19,000
2,500 calls	10	0.1	21,000
	100%	1.0	

3. You can hire your own labor and buy your own parts. Your past experience with similar work has helped you to formulate the following probabilities and costs:

EVENT	CHANCE OF OCCURRENCE	PROBABILITY OF OCCURRENCE	TOTAL COST
Little trouble	10%	0.1	$ 8,000
Medium trouble	70	0.7	10,000
Much trouble	20	0.2	30,000
	100%	1.0	

Using expected-value tables, compare the three alternatives. Which plan do you favor? Why?

21-14 ***Standard deviation and coefficient of variation.*** Refer to the preceding problem. For each alternative, compute the standard deviation and the coefficient of variation. Which alternative is most risky?

21-15 ***Standard deviation and comparisons.*** Freund, a salesman of industrial chemicals, made sales of $15,000 in April; Williams, a salesman of office supplies, made sales of $6,250. Sales in April by salesmen of industrial chemicals and of office supplies had, respectively, means of $13,000 and $5,000 and standard deviations of $2,000 and $500.

REQUIRED

1. How many standard deviations above the mean were the sales of Freund and Williams? Who rated higher in their respective groups?
2. Which group of sales had higher dispersion?

21-16 ***Setting prices and uncertainty.*** Assume that the unit cost of a product is known with certainty to be $1.60. The top executives are trying to decide whether to set a selling price of $2.00 or of $2.20. The top price has been $2.00 for the past 30 months. Average monthly sales are forecast as follows:

AT A PRICE OF $2.00

units	probability
1,050	.05
1,000	.90
950	.05

AT A PRICE OF $2.20

units	probability
800	.10
750	.60
700	.30

REQUIRED | Which is the optimal price? Show computations.

21-17 ***Measuring dispersion.*** Refer to the preceding problem. Compute, for the two alternative prices, the expected monthly sales in units, their standard deviation, and their coefficient of variation.

21-18 ***Cost-volume-profit under uncertainty.*** (J. Patell) In your recently won position as supervisor of new product introduction, you have to decide on a pricing strategy for a specialty product with the following cost structure.

Variable cost per unit = \$50
Fixed cost of production = \$200,000

The units are assembled upon receipt of orders, so the inventory levels are insignificant. Your market research assistant is very enthusiastic about probability models and has presented the results of his price analysis in the following form.

a. If you set the price at \$100/unit, the probability distribution of total sales dollars is uniform between \$300,000 and \$600,000.

b. If you lower the price to \$70/unit, the distribution remains uniform, but it shifts up to the \$600,000 to \$900,000 range.

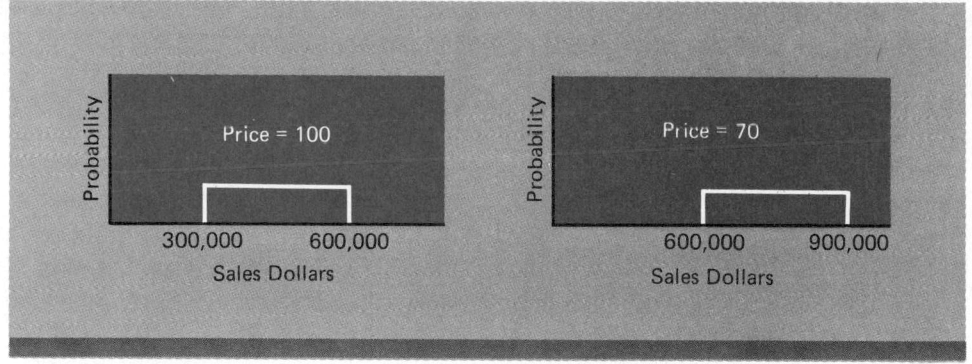

1. This is your first big contract and, above all, you want to show a profit. You decide to select the strategy that maximizes the probability of breaking even or earning a positive profit.

a. What is the probability of at least breaking even with a price of \$100/unit?

b. What is the probability of at least breaking even with a price of \$70/unit?

2. Your assistant suggests that maximum expected profit might be a better goal to pursue. Which pricing strategy yields the higher expected profit?

21-19 ***Expected value.*** (CMA) Jackston Inc. manufactures and distributes a line of Christmas toys. The company had neglected to keep its doll house line current. As a result, sales have decreased to approximately 10,000 units per year from a previous high of 50,000 units. The doll house has been redesigned recently and is considered by company officials to be comparable to its competitors' models. The company plans to redesign the doll house each year in order to compete effectively. Joan Blocke, the sales manager, is not sure how many units can be sold next year, but she is willing to place probabilities on her estimates. Blocke's estimates of the number of units that can be sold during the next year and the related probabilities are as follows:

ESTIMATED SALES IN UNITS	PROBABILITY
20,000	.10
30,000	.40
40,000	.30
50,000	.20

The units would be sold for \$20 each.

The inability to estimate the sales more precisely is a problem for Jackston. The number of units of this product is small enough to schedule the entire year's sales in one production run.

If the demand is greater than the number of units manufactured, then sales will be lost. If demand is below supply, the extra units cannot be carried over to the next season and would be given away to various charitable organizations. The production and distribution cost estimates are as follows:

	UNITS MANUFACTURED			
	20,000	30,000	40,000	50,000
Variable costs	$180,000	$270,000	$360,000	$450,000
Fixed costs	140,000	140,000	160,000	160,000
Total costs	$320,000	$410,000	$520,000	$610,000

The company intends to analyze the data to facilitate making a decision as to the proper size of the production run.

REQUIRED

1. Prepare a payoff table for the different sizes of production runs required to meet the four sales estimates prepared by Joan Blocke for Jackston Inc. If Jackston Inc. relied solely on the expected monetary value approach to make decisions, what size of production run would be selected?
2. Identify the basic steps that are taken in any decision process. Explain each step by reference to the situation presented in the problem and your answer for requirement 1.

21-20 ***Breakeven in executive education.*** (SMA) Management Development Ltd. is deciding which one of two new executive courses to offer. The costs associated with course development would be $5,000 for either course. Administrative facilities are available within the firm for one additional course without additional costs. The course would have a one-year life. Enrollment in either course would be $100 and the variable costs associated with offering the course would be $60 per executive.

To decide which course to offer, the management of M.D.L. has estimated the demand for the courses and utilized subjective probabilities to estimate the likelihood of varying levels of course enrollment. The information derived from this process is as follows:

COURSE ENROLLMENTS	PROBABILITY COURSE A	PROBABILITY COURSE B
50	0.1	0.1
100	0.1	0.2
200	0.2	0.4
300	0.4	0.2
400	0.2	0.1
	1.0	1.0

REQUIRED

1. Calculate the number of course enrollments required to break even for each course.
2. Which course should M.D.L. select? Explain why and show all computations.
3. Suppose instead that M.D.L. were absolutely certain that the enrollment in Course A would be 205. Which course should be offered? Discuss the key factor that would lead to a decision in this situation.

21-21 ***Probabilities and contribution margins.*** (CPA) Part a. The Wing Manufacturing Corporation produces a chemical compound, Product X, which deteriorates and must be discarded if it is not sold by the end of the month during which it is produced. The total variable cost of the manufactured compound, Product X, is $50 per unit and its selling price is $80 per unit. Wing can purchase the same compound from a competing company at $80 per unit plus $10 freight per unit. Management has estimated that failure to fill orders would result in the loss of 80 percent of customers placing orders for the compound. Wing has manufactured and sold Product X for the past 20 months. Demand for Product X has been irregular and at present there is no consistent sales trend. During this period, monthly sales have been as follows:

UNITS SOLD PER MONTH	NUMBER OF MONTHS
8,000	5
9,000	12
10,000	3

REQUIRED

1. Compute the probability of sales of Product X of 8,000, 9,000, or 10,000 units in any month.
2. Compute what the contribution margin would be if 9,000 units of Product X were ordered and either 8,000, 9,000, or 10,000 units were manufactured in that same month (with additional units, if necessary, being purchased).
3. Compute the average monthly contribution margin that Wing can expect if 9,000 units of Product X are manufactured every month and sales orders are filled.

Part b. In the production of Product X, Wing uses a primary ingredient, K-1. This ingredient is purchased from an outside supplier at a cost of $24 per unit of compound. It is estimated that there is a 70 percent chance that the supplier of K-1 may be shut down by a strike for an indefinite period. A substitute ingredient, K-2, is available at $36 per unit of compound, but Wing must contact this alternative source immediately to secure sufficient quantities. A firm purchase contract for either material must now be made for production of the primary ingredient next month. If an order were placed for K-1 and a strike occurred, Wing would be released from the contract and management would purchase the chemical compound from its competitor. Assume that 9,000 units are to be manufactured and all sales orders are to be filled.

REQUIRED

1. Compute the monthly contribution margin from sales of 8,000, 9,000, and 10,000 units if the substitute ingredient, K-2 is ordered.
2. Prepare a schedule computing the average monthly contribution margin that Wing should expect if the primary ingredient, K-1, is ordered with the existing probability of a strike at the supplier. Assume that the expected average monthly contribution margin from manufacturing will be $130,000 using the primary ingredient, and the expected average monthly loss from purchasing Product X from the competitor (in case of a strike) will be $45,000.

21-22 ***Uncertainty and cost-volume-profit analysis.*** (This and the next problem are adapted from Robert K. Jaedicke and Alexander A. Robichek, "Cost-Volume-Profit Analysis under Conditions of Uncertainty," *Accounting Review,* XXXIX, No. 4, pp. 917–26.) The Jaedicke and Robichek Company is considering two new products to introduce. Either can be produced by using present facilities. Each product requires an increase in annual fixed expenses of $400,000. The products have the same selling price and the same variable cost per unit: $10 and $8, respectively.

Management, after studying past experience with similar products, has prepared the following subjective probability distribution:

EVENTS (UNITS DEMANDED)	PROBABILITY— PRODUCT A	PROBABILITY— PRODUCT B
50,000	—	0.1
100,000	0.1	0.1
200,000	0.2	0.1
300,000	0.4	0.2
400,000	0.2	0.4
500,000	0.1	0.1
	1.0	1.0

REQUIRED

1. What is the breakeven point for each product?
2. Which product should be chosen? Why? Show computations.
3. Suppose management was absolutely certain that 300,000 units of Product B would be sold. Which product should be chosen? Why? What benefits are available to management from the provision of the complete probability distribution instead of just a lone expected value?

21-23 ***Uncertainty, choice of product, and cost-volume-profit analysis.*** You are a division manager of the K Company. You have conducted a study of the profit potential of three products:

	PRODUCTS		
	1	2	3
Expected profit	$450,000	$450,000	$ 450,000
Standard deviation of profit	$500,000	$681,500	$1,253,000
The probability of:			
At least breaking even	.816	.745	.641
Profit at least $250,000	.655	.615	.564
Profit at least $600,000	.382	.413	.456
Loss greater than $300,000	.067	.136	.274

The expected contribution per unit for each product is $1,250, and the expected fixed expenses per year are $5,800,000, so each product has the same breakeven quantity, 4,640 units.

REQUIRED

Which product would you choose? Explain fully, including comparisons of the relative riskiness of the three products.

21-24 ***Expected profits on special order.*** (SMA) The Xyrox Company makes low-quality garments on a mass-production basis. The production vice-president knows that there is some idle capacity in the plant. A European importer approached Xyrox and requested it to supply a few thousand dozen of stylish men's shirts at a contract price of $250 per dozen. Management at Xyrox is uncertain as to whether the order should be accepted because the demand can be either for 3,000, 4,500, or 6,000 dozen depending on how well the European importer does the advertising. The shirts can also vary between two different types of materials depending on the ultimate buyer's request. The variable cost per dozen can thus vary between $200 per dozen and $165 per dozen, but the selling price for Xyrox remains firm at $250 per dozen. It is estimated that incremental fixed costs if the order is accepted will amount to $295,000.

The market research department of the European importer has predicted that 75 percent of the consumers will prefer the more expensive material while the remaining 25 percent will prefer the cheaper kind because it requires no ironing. They also report that there is a 90 percent chance that less than 6,000 dozen will be sold, and a 30 percent chance that less than 4,500 dozen will be sold. Assume that consumer preference probabilities are independent of sales value probabilities.

REQUIRED

1. Compute the incremental profit or loss, and the probability of occurrence, for the *six* states of nature that can occur.
2. What is the probability that the project is profitable?
3. Compute the expected value if the order is accepted. Would you accept the order?
4. Assume the answer to requirement 2 remains as computed, and the answer to requirement 3 is $25,000. Discuss briefly whether you would accept.

21-25 ***Risk aversion and utilities.*** Reconsider the initial data of the purchase of M1 or M2 in the chapter. Suppose the decision maker was risk averse, so that the monetary values are reexpressed as utility values or utiles that are not linear:

Monetary values	$7,800	$9,000	$25,000	$27,000
Utiles	0.9	1.0	2.3	2.4

REQUIRED

1. If the decision maker maximizes expected operating income expressed in utiles instead of monetary values, will the decision change? Show calculations.
2. Suppose that the utiles for $9,000 were 1.1 instead of 1.0. Would the decision change? Show calculations.

21-26 ***Risk aversion and utilities.*** A decision maker is considering a plant rearrangement with an expected useful life of one year. The only alternatives are to do nothing (predicted operating costs, $200,000) or rearrange. If the rearrangement occurs, there is a .5 probability of success (predicted operating costs, $100,000) and a .5 probability of failure (predicted operating costs, $260,000).

REQUIRED

1. Compute the expected monetary value of each alternative. The decision maker chooses on the basis of the alternative with the least expected cost. Which alternative would be chosen?
2. Suppose the decision maker was risk averse so that the monetary values are reexpressed as utility values or utiles that are not linear:

MONETARY VALUES	UTILES*
$100,000	− .4623
200,000	−1.1598
260,000	−1.7183

*Derived from an exponential utility function, where the expected value of the cost = $1 - e^{c/260}$, where c represents cost in thousands. Tables of exponential functions are not included in this book.

If the decision maker minimizes expected costs expressed in utiles instead of in monetary values, will the decision change? Show calculations.

3. Suppose that the utiles for $260,000 were −1.90 instead of −1.7183. Would the decision change? Show calculations.

21-27 ***Risk attitudes and utilities.*** (H. Itami, adapted) Assumes knowledge of Chapter 12. A division manager is trying to decide between three projects of varying risks as measured in terms of standard deviations:

Project	*A*	*B*	*C*
Internal rate of return	20	15	30
Standard deviation	8	5	20

The measure of the manager's performance is measured by the following linear equation:

$$w = a + b(y - 15)$$

$$w = 10 + .9(y - 15)$$

where w is compensation based on the excess (shortage) of actual rate of return over the minimum desired rate of return; a is minimum compensation; b is the weighting of the difference between the actual rate and the minimum desired rate; y is the actual rate of return; and 15 percent is the minimum desired rate of return.

Extensive discussions with the manager revealed that her attitude toward risk and compensation could be expressed as

$$f = u_w - 2\sigma_w$$

where f is the utility value of each expected level of compensation; u_w is the expected value of w; and σ_w is the standard deviation of w and is measured by the expression $b^2\sigma_y$.

REQUIRED

Compute the manager's expected utility from each course of action. Which action would she choose?

21-28 ***Relevant costs, probabilities, discounted cash flow and pricing.*** The Vasquez Construction Company is bidding on a construction contract, here called Contract No. 1. If the bid is accepted, work will begin in a few days, on January 1, 19_1. Ten thousand units of material X will be needed at that date. The company currently has 10,000 units of this material in stock, originally costing a total of $10,000. The current purchase cost of material X is $1.20 per unit. The company could sell material X now for $.80 per unit after all selling costs.

If this current contract is not landed, material X could be used on Contract No. 2 to begin in one year, on January 1, 19_2. Then the company would not need to buy a substitute material at $1.02 per unit.

If it is not used in either of these ways, material X would be of no use to the company and would be sold a year hence, probably for $.80 per unit, net. The president estimates that the probability of using material X on Contract No. 2 is .7.

The president of the construction company is puzzled about the appropriate total cost of material X to be used in bidding on Contract No. 1. He has assembled the following data:

	TOTAL COSTS
Miscellaneous materials	$40,000
Material X, 10,000 units	?
Direct labor	60,000
Relevant overhead	30,000
Total relevant costs	$xxx,xxx

Competition is intense and markups are practically zero. He asks you to suggest the appropriate total-cost figure for material X. Show all computations, carefully labeled, and state all assumptions made. The minimum desired rate of return is 10 percent per annum.

21-29 ***Cost of prediction errors.*** Reconsider the toy-rocket illustration in Appendix 21a. Suppose the manager does not have the privilege of returning any unsold rockets. Instead, because of their souvenir markings, they are worthless. He acquired 1,000 units, but unforeseen competition reduced sales to 800 units.

REQUIRED

1. What was the cost of the prediction error?
2. Suppose that demand was unusually heavy. He sold all 1,000 units, but he was sure that he could have sold a total of 1,200 units if he had not run out of stock. What was the cost of the prediction error?

21-30 ***Cost of prediction errors.*** Study Appendix 21a. A company set a price for its product at $20 per unit. Predicted variable costs were $14 per unit. Expected sales were 100,000 units. Fixed costs for the year were expected to be $400,000.

REQUIRED

Compute the cost of the prediction error if:

1. All of the forecasts were accurate except that the actual variable costs were $15 per unit. (Given a $15 variable cost, the $20 price would not be changed.)
2. Actual variable costs were $15 per unit. Sales could have been 110,000 units if enough stock were available. However, only 100,000 units were acquired and sold.

21-31 ***Prediction error, channels of distribution.*** Study Appendix 21a. Through the end of 19_3, Mavis Company, a television manufacturer, had always sold its products through distributors. In 19_3 its sales were $50,000,000 and its net income was 10 percent of sales. Total fixed expenses (manufacturing and selling) were $10,000,000.

During 19_3 a number of Mavis's competitors had begun selling their units through discount houses and huge outlets. Mavis's marketing research group was asked to predict the effects of eliminating distributors from Mavis's channels of distribution and selling directly to retailers. The group was instructed to predict both changes in sales volume and changes in selling expenses, under the provision that the *selling price per unit would remain unchanged.*

The marketing analysis yielded the following predictions. Total sales dollars in 19_4 would *drop* 20 percent from the 19_3 figures, but net income for 19_4 would rise to $5,200,000 owing to savings in selling expenses. This net savings in selling expenses from eliminating the "middleman" was impressive, since total fixed expenses (manufacturing and selling) would *increase* to $10,800,000 because of the additional warehouse and delivery facilities required. If the 19_3 distribution system were continued, however, 19_4 results would replicate 19_3.

REQUIRED

1. What was the breakeven point (in sales dollars) under the original situation prevailing in 19_3?
2. What would be the breakeven point (in sales dollars) under the proposed situation for 19_4?
3. On the basis of this analysis, Mavis adopted the new direct-distribution plan for 19_4, and reduced 19_4 production to the 40,000,000-sales-dollar level. Unfor-

tunately, it became clear by early December 19_4 that sales would reach only \$38,000,000, and Mavis cut back production so that no ending inventory remained. Variable costs *per unit* and total fixed costs were as predicted. Compute the cost of Mavis's prediction error. Assume that sales would have been \$50 million if the 19_3 distribution system had been continued.

21-32 ***Prediction error.*** Study Appendix 21a and Chapter 12. Assume that an original investment was \$3,791, useful life five years, annual cash inflow from operations \$1,000, and internal rate of return 10 percent.

1. Suppose the annual cash flow were \$900 instead of \$1,000. All other parameter predictions are correct. What is the cost of prediction error measured in terms of net present value, assuming a minimum desired rate of return of 10 percent?

2. Repeat part 1, but assume that the annual cash flow was \$1,100.

21-33 ***Prediction error.*** Study Appendix 21a and Chapter 12. The Gehrig Company predicted that it could save \$2,800 per year in cash-operating costs for the next ten years if it bought a special-purpose machine at a cost of \$11,000. No residual value was expected. The company's minimum desired rate of return is 14 percent. The company invested in the machine.

Suppose the annual cash flow were \$3,200 instead of \$2,800. All other parameter predictions are correct. What is the cost of prediction error measured in terms of net present value? What is the cost of prediction error if the annual cash flow of \$2,800 were to last only five years instead of ten, assuming all other parameter predictions are correct?

21-34 ***Sensitivity and prediction error.*** (J. Demski, adapted) Ralph is attempting to decide whether to accept (or reject) a new product proposal. He predicts that development of the project will require an initial outlay of $\$a < 0$ (cash) and will then return an end-of-period contribution of $\$b$ (cash) per unit of product produced and sold in any given period. The demand for the product is predicted to be a constant d units per period for T periods.

Letting ρ denote Ralph's minimum desired rate of return, and assuming a tax-free world, he would accept this new product proposal if and only if

$$\text{NPV}(\rho) = a + \sum_{t=1}^{T} bd(1+\rho)^{-t}$$

$$= a + bx \geq 0$$

where

$$x = \sum_{t=1}^{T} d(1+\rho)^{-t}$$

1. To be a little less abstract, let $a = \$-1000$, $b = 1$, and $x = 1200$. Then $\text{NPV}(\rho) = -1000 + 1(1200) = 200 \geq 0$. In the following graph, plot the maximum net present value associated with this decision as the contribution margin varies between $b = -1$ and $b = 5$ (given $a = -1000$ and $x = 1200$). You should clearly label the accept-reject point on your graph.

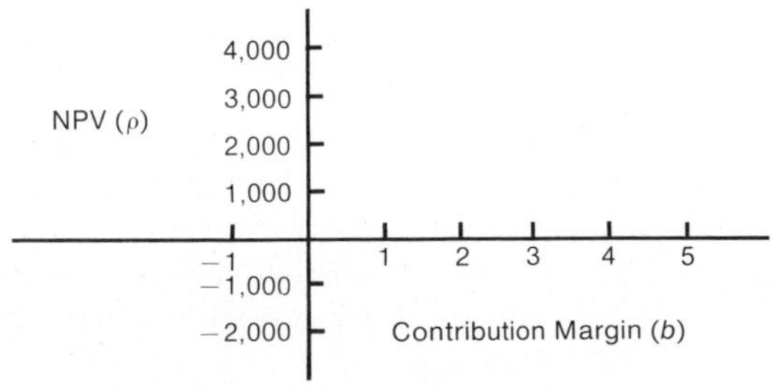

2. Suppose Ralph predicts that $b = 1.7$ given $a = -1000$ and $x = 1200$, and thus implements the project. Further suppose that the a and x parameter predictions are correct, but the contribution prediction, b, is incorrect. Plot, on a second graph, the cost of this prediction for all possible values of b in the range -1 to $+5$.

3. Suppose Ralph rejected the project because he predicted that $b = 0$. How would your graph in part 2 change?

4. Think about your graphs. What is the major lesson of this problem?

21-35 ***Buying perfect information.*** As a manager of a post office, you are trying to decide whether to rearrange a production line and facilities in order to save labor and related costs. Assume that the only alternatives are to "do nothing" or "rearrange." Assume also that the choice criterion is that the expected savings from rearrangement must equal or exceed $11,000.

Based on your experience and currently available information, you predict:

a. The "do nothing" alternative will have operating costs of $200,000.
b. The "rearrange" alternative will have operating costs of $100,000 if it is a success and $260,000 if it is a failure. You think there is a 60 percent chance of success and a 40 percent chance of failure.

REQUIRED

1. Compute the expected value of the costs for each alternative. Compute the difference in expected costs.
2. You can hire a consultant, Joan Zenoff, to study the situation. She would then render a flawless prediction of whether the rearrangement would succeed or fail. Compute the maximum amount you would be willing to pay for the errorless prediction. (The next problem explores imperfect information.)

21-36 ***Buying imperfect information.*** Study Appendix 21c. Refer to the preceding problem. Zenoff's eventual prediction of success or failure will be imperfect. The following analysis is provided:

	EVENTS	
probability of events	**success**	**failure**
If optimistic report	.818	.182
If pessimistic report	.333	.667

REQUIRED

1. Compute the expected costs, assuming an optimistic report.
2. Compute the expected costs, assuming a pessimistic report.
3. The probability of getting an optimistic report is .55; a pessimistic report, .45. (The computation of these probabilities is not necessary for solving this problem. The next problem covers the method, which is explained in Appendix 21c.) Compute the expected value of imperfect information. Compare it with the expected value of perfect information as computed in the preceding problem. The consultant's fee is $1,000. Should she be hired?
4. Suppose you hire the consultant. The report is pessimistic. Should you proceed with the rearrangement?

21-37 ***Revising probabilities.*** Study Appendix 21c. This problem explores how the probabilities in the preceding problem were computed. You determined that Zenoff's predictions were correct only 75 percent of the time. For example, if Zenoff supplies an optimistic prediction of success, a failure will occur 25 percent of the time.

Let P = probability; y_1 = optimistic report; y_2 = pessimistic report; x_1 = success; and x_2 = failure.

Then

$$P(y_1|x_1) = .75 \qquad P(y_2|x_2) = .75$$
$$P(y_2|x_1) = .25 \qquad P(y_1|x_2) = .25$$

REQUIRED

1. Given the existing information, the probability of success is .6 and of failure is .4. Compute the probabilities of obtaining a pessimistic or optimistic report.
2. Compute the revised probabilities of each event's occurring, conditional upon receiving a particular optimistic or pessimistic report. That is, revise your prior probabilities as posterior probabilities.

21-38 ***Imperfect information and special order.*** (J. Demski and C. Horngren) Study Appendix 21c. Consider a decision of whether to accept or reject a special order for 1,000 units of a product that is a unique variation of a firm's regular output. Acceptance of this order will not interfere with regular sales, now or in the future. The incremental revenue will be $20,000, and production will require raw materials costing $5,000 plus 800 direct-labor hours from department A and 200 hours from department B. The special order will be accepted if it has a positive expected contribution margin. Thus, if the expected incremental cost of labor and overhead is less than $15,000 (20,000 − 5,000), the decision maker will accept the offer.

The accounting system currently uses a *plantwide rate* to assign labor and variable overhead costs to production. The rate for the preceding period was $16 per hour, and, without additional information, the decision maker will use this rate to predict the incremental labor and overhead cost for the special order. Hence, in the absence of additional information, he will reject the offer: $20,000 − $5,000 − $16(800 + 200) = −$1,000.

Consider the question of whether this choice can be improved. The accountant is concerned about the quality of the data to be used in the decision. In particular, the $16 rate is based on the regular use of an equal number of hours from the two departments, and the accountant suspects that the rates for the two departments are not identical. A special analysis could be conducted to determine the departmental rates. The question, then, is whether the accountant should conduct this analysis and report the resulting data to the decision maker. The outcome of the analysis is not presently known, but the accountant feels that one of three findings will materialize: The rates for departments A and B will be, respectively, $12 and $20, $14 and $18, or $16 and $16. The respective contribution margins will then be:

	ANALYSIS OUTCOME		
Departmental rates (A and B)	$12 and $20	$14 and $18	$16 and $16
Expected incremental revenue	$20,000	$20,000	$ 20,000
Expected incremental costs			
Raw materials	$ 5,000	$ 5,000	$ 5,000
Labor and variable overhead			
Dept. A (800 hrs.)	9,600	11,200	12,800
Dept. B (200 hrs.)	4,000	3,600	3,200
Total	$18,600	$19,800	$ 21,000
Expected contribution margin	$ 1,400	$ 200	$−1,000

Moreover, the accountant perceives that if he learns and reports the actual rates, the decision maker will employ those rates in his decision. Hence, the offer will be accepted by the decision maker only if the rates of $12 and $20 or $14 and $18 are reported.

The accountant, then, has two alternatives: (1) do not perform the analysis, which guarantees an incremental gain to the firm of $0; (2) perform the analysis, which guarantees an incremental gain to the firm of $1,400, $200, or $0, less the cost of the analysis. Choice between them will, of course, depend on his risk attitudes, his beliefs concerning how likely the three cost figures will be, and how costly the analysis is. Suppose that he is risk neutral and assigns respective probabilities of .2, .2, and .6 to the three events.

REQUIRED

1. Compute the expected contribution margin if the special analysis is conducted (before considering the cost of the special analysis). Compute the most that the accountant or decision maker should be willing to pay for the analysis.
2. Repeat requirement 1, but assume that the decision maker will not accept the special order unless its expected contribution margin is at least $500.
3. The accountant could present all the data in the problem together with the probabilities. If so, what is the expected contribution margin? Why does he not consider this as a feasible alternative presentation to the decision maker at the outset?
4. Suppose the probabilities were .2, .6, and .2. What would be your answers to requirements 1 and 2 above?
5. What is the principal lesson of the above computations?

21-39 ***Cost and value of information; using decision trees.*** (Adapted from "Report of Committee on Managerial Decision Models," *Accounting Review,* Supplement to Vol. XLIV) Study Appendix 21c. An oil well driller, George Davis, is thinking of investing $50,000 in an oil well lease. He estimates the probability of finding a producing well as .4. Such a discovery would result in a net gain of $100,000 ($150,000 revenue − $50,000 cost). There is a .6 probability of not getting any oil, resulting in the complete loss of the $50,000.

EXHIBIT 21-8

Possible Outcomes and Conditional Value

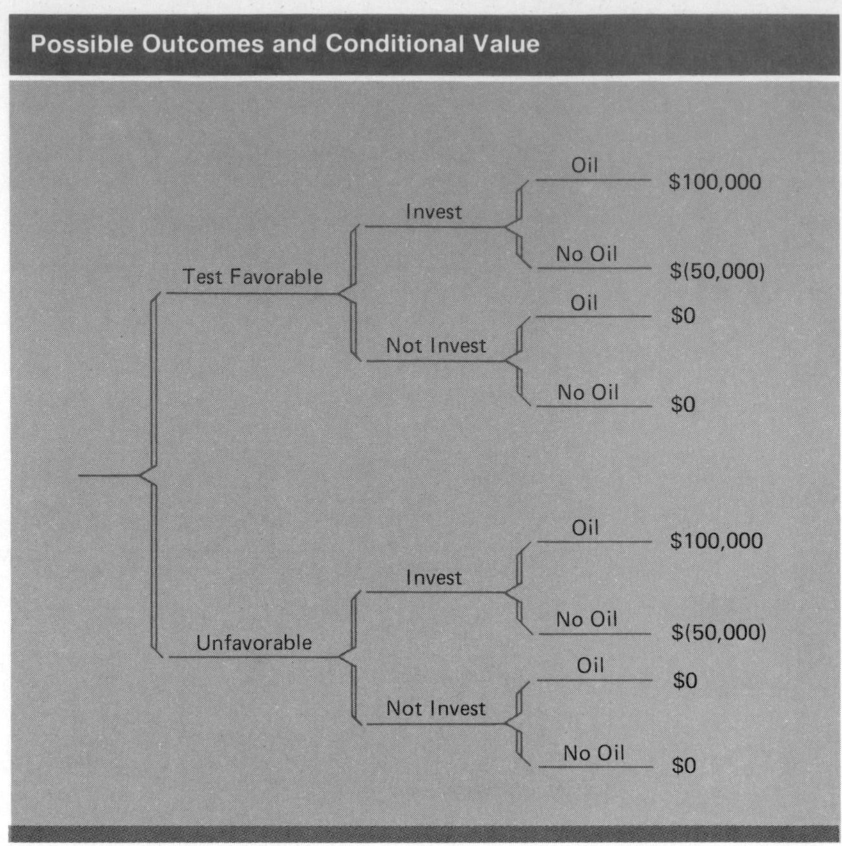

REQUIRED

1. What is the net expected value of investing?
2. Mr. Davis desires more information because of the vast uncertainty and the large costs of making a wrong decision. There will be an unrecoverable $50,000 outlay if no oil is found; there will be a $100,000 opportunity cost if he does not invest and the oil is really there. What is the most he should be willing to pay for perfect information regarding the presence or absence of oil? Explain.
3. Although perfect information is seldom obtainable, some additional information is usually available at some price. Mr. Davis might consider a geological test of the subsurface. His decision tree would then appear as in Exhibit 21-8.

   The geological testing company might advise the wildcatter that if there is oil on the land, the test results will be favorable (positive) three-quarters of the time and unfavorable (negative) one-quarter of the time. In other words, the test is not perfect. Similarly, if there is no oil, the test will give unfavorable results two-thirds of the time but will be (falsely) favorable one-third of the time. (These probabilities will be referred to as conditional probabilities.)

   The wildcatter wants to know the probability of finding oil, given the result of the test. These revised conditional probabilities are found by weighing the prior subjective probabilities by the appropriate likelihoods as shown on the top of p. 753.

   The computations of conditional probabilities show that the probability of finding oil is 0.6, given a *favorable* test. However, if the test is *unfavorable*, the probability of finding oil is only .2. With this knowledge, construct a payoff table for Mr. Davis. How much should he be willing to pay for the test? Explain.

PROBABILITIES OF STATES, GIVEN A FAVORABLE OR UNFAVORABLE TEST RESULT

event (e)	(1) prior p (e)	(2) conditional probabilities of favorable test	(1) × (2) probabilities of test outcome and event	probabilities of events given the test outcomes
If the test is favorable:				
Oil	.4	¾	.3	.3 ÷ .5 = .6
No oil	.6	⅓	.2	.2 ÷ .5 = .4
Probability of favorable test			.5	1.0
If the test is unfavorable:				
Oil	.4	¼	.1	.1 ÷ .5 = .2
No oil	.6	⅔	.4	.4 ÷ .5 = .8
Probability of unfavorable test			.5	1.0

21-40 ***Probability revisions, utilities.*** (G. Foster) Study Appendix 21c.

I. On-the-Move Corp. is a company active in the "takeover game." At present, it is considering acquiring a publicly listed company—XYZ Corp. On-the-Move can acquire XYZ for $2 million. The key issue in the takeover decision is the value of the assets of XYZ. XYZ's latest balance sheet shows cash of $1 million and municipal bonds of $3 million, and no liabilities. The municipal bonds mature in one year, with an interest rate of 20 percent. On-the-Move can invest cash at 10 percent with its bank.

On-the-Move is concerned with the possibility of the municipality's defaulting on the bonds. Indeed, it assesses the probability of such a default at .8. A default would mean On-the-Move would receive nothing for the $3 million in bonds or the accrued interest of $600,000. On-the-Move chooses projects on an expected monetary payoff basis.

REQUIRED

1. Should On-the-Move take over XYZ, or should it invest the $2 million with its bank? (Let State 1 be no default; State 2 be default.)
2. What is the value of perfect information about whether the municipality will default on the bonds?

II. On-the-Move decides to consider purchasing more information about the municipal bonds. It approaches a merchant bank, which offers On-the-Move a variety of alternatives:

Alternative A. For $100,000 (paid at the end of the year), it will use its automated bond-rating program. This program will yield one of two signals:

y_1: **rating ≥ B grade**

y_2: **rating < B grade**

On-the-Move assesses that $\phi(y_1 | s_1) = .6$, and $\phi(y_1 | s_2) = .3$, where ϕ = probability; s_1 = no default; and s_2 = default.

Alternative B. For $200,000 (paid at the end of the year), it will engage its super-consultant, Hobie Leland, Jr., to rate the bonds. Hobie will also report two signals:

y_1: **rating ≥ B grade**

y_2: **rating < B grade**

On-the-Move assesses that $\phi(y_1 | s_1) = .9$, and $\phi(y_1 | s_2) = .25$.

REQUIRED

1. On what basis would On-the-Move make its assessments of $\phi(y_k | s_i)$?
2. Should On-the-Move adopt Alternative A *or* Alternative B *or* neither?

III. On-the-Move decides that it should be risk averse in its takeover decisions. It will still choose projects on an expected utility basis, but its utility for outcomes is now expressed by the following logarithmic function:

$$U(W) = \log_{10}(W)$$

Monetary amounts:	$4,600,000	$4,500,000	$2,100,000	$2,000,000	$1,000,000	$900,000
Log_{10} values:	6.663	6.653	6.322	6.301	6.000	5.954

REQUIRED | Redo requirement II(2) using this utility function.

22 Inventory Planning, Control, and Costing

There is an optimum level of investment for any asset, whether it be cash, physical plant, or inventories. For example, cash balances may be too large or too small. The principal cost of having too much cash is the sacrifice of earnings; idle cash earns nothing. The principal cost of having too little cash may be lost discounts on purchases or harm to one's credit standing. For every asset class, then, there is a conceptual optimum investment that, when considered with optimum levels in other asset classes, helps to maximize long-run profits.

The major goal of "inventory control" is to discover and maintain the optimum level of investment in all types of inventories, from raw materials and supplies to finished goods.[1] Two limits must be imposed in controlling inventory levels, because there are two danger points that management usually wants to avoid. **The first danger, that of inadequate inventories, disrupts production and may lose sales. The second danger,**

[1]Throughout this chapter, the term *inventory control* will refer to both planning inventory investment and implementing the plans.

excessive inventories, introduces unnecessary carrying costs and obsolescence risks. The optimum inventory level lies somewhere between the two danger points. Our major purpose in this chapter will be to see how this optimum inventory level is computed and maintained. The various methods of inventory costing are discussed in the chapter appendix.

Characteristics of inventories

need for inventories

If production and delivery of goods were instantaneous, there would be no need for inventories except as a hedge against price changes. Despite the marvels of computers, automation, and scientific management, the manufacturing and merchandising processes still do not function quickly enough to avoid the need for having inventories. Inventories must be maintained so that the customer may be serviced immediately, or at least quickly enough so that he or she does not turn to another source of supply. In turn, production operations cannot flow smoothly without having inventories of direct materials, work in process, finished parts, and supplies.

Inventories are cushions (a) to absorb planning errors and unforeseen fluctuations in supply and demand, and (b) to facilitate smooth production and marketing operations. Further, inventories help isolate or minimize the interdependence of all parts of the organization (for example, departments or functions) so that each may work effectively. For example, many parts and subassemblies may be purchased or manufactured, stored, and used as needed. This avoids nerve-racking reliance on the pinpoint timing of deliveries from others.

inventory records and control

Inventory records are only a means to the end of inventory control. A company may have thousands of impressive stores cards whose balances are always in precise agreement with physical counts taken in its immaculate storeroom. The requisition, purchasing, receiving, and material-handling duties may be at peak efficiency. But despite errorless paper shuffling and diligent employees, inventory control may still be inadequate. Management's major duty with respect to inventory control is not clerical accuracy. (In many cases, it is possible to attain excellent inventory control through visual inspection rather than through elaborate perpetual-inventory records.) The major inventory-control problem is to maximize profitability by balancing inventory investment costs against what is required to sustain smooth operations. Note that profitability can also take the form of minimizing costs in nonprofit organizations; for instance, problems of inventory management extend to hospitals and the armed forces.

Relevant costs for inventory decisions

In most instances, the total costs of an inventory policy consist of

Total acquisition cost + Total ordering cost + Total carrying cost

The most obvious costs—those of *acquiring* the stock through buying or manufacturing—are usually unaffected by various inventory policies unless quantity discounts are available. For instance, whether total annual requirements of 3,000 units are purchased at $1.00 each in thirty 100-unit lots or in three 1,000-unit lots may affect the costs of ordering or carrying, but the total *acquisition* cost will be $3,000 under each alternative if no quantity discounts are available.

The **ordering costs** usually consist of clerical costs of preparing a purchase order or production order and special processing and receiving costs relating to the number of *orders* processed.

The **carrying costs** usually consist of a desired rate of return on the investment in inventory and costs of storage space, breakage, obsolescence, deterioration, insurance, and personal property taxes.[2]

When acquisition costs are the same for many alternatives, they are irrelevant and are often excluded from the decision model that determines inventory policy. Thus, the relevant costs are most often confined to ordering costs and carrying costs. These two costs behave in opposite ways. For example, if huge inventories are carried, ordering costs will be low and carrying costs will be high. Some of the difficulties of measuring these costs will be discussed later. First, consider the fundamentals of the inventory decision.

Choice of order quantity

The objective of inventory decisions is usually to minimize the total relevant costs. Two central decisions must be faced in designing an inventory control system: (a) *How much* should we buy (or manufacture) at a time? (b) *When* should we buy (or manufacture)? Regardless of their complexity, all inventory planning models focus on the twin problems of size and timing.

how much to order?

A key factor in inventory policy is computing the optimum size of either a normal purchase order for raw materials or a shop order for a production run. The strategy is to order the same amount each time an order is placed. **This optimum size is called the economic order quantity (EOQ), the size that will result in minimum total annual costs of the item in question.**

» EXAMPLE 1

A refrigerator manufacturer buys certain steel shelving in sets from outside suppliers at $4.00 per set. Total annual needs are 5,000 sets at a rate of 20 sets per working day.

The following cost data are available:

Desired annual return on inventory investment, 10% × $4.00	$.40	
Relevant insurance, taxes, breakage per unit per year	.10	
Carrying costs per unit per year		$ .50
Costs per purchase order:		
Clerical costs, stationery, postage, telephone, receiving, etc.		$10.00

What is the economic order quantity?

» SOLUTION

Exhibit 22-1 deserves careful study. It shows a tabulation of total costs under various alternatives. The column with the least cost will indicate the economic order quantity.

Exhibit 22-1 shows minimum costs at two levels, 400 and 500 units. The next step would be to see if costs are lower somewhere between 400 and 500 units—say, at 450 units:

Average inventory (450/2), 225 × $.50	= $113 Carrying costs
Number of orders (5,000/450), 11.1 × $10	= 111 Purchase-order costs
	$224 Total annual relevant costs

[2]Inventory is classified as personal property, as distinguished from real property.

EXHIBIT 22-1

Annualized Relevant Costs of Various Standard Orders
(250 Working Days)

SYMBOLS					LEAST COST	LEAST COST				
E	Order size	50	100	200	400	500	600	800	1,000	5,000
$E/2$	Average inventory in units*	25	50	100	200	250	300	400	500	2,500
A/E	Number of purchase orders†	100	50	25	12.5	10	8.3	6.7	5	1
$S(E/2)$	Annual carrying cost @ $.50	$ 13	$ 25	$ 50	$100	$125	$150	$200	$ 250	$1,250
$P(A/E)$	Annual purchase-order cost @ $10.00	1,000	500	250	125	100	83	67	50	10
C	Total annual relevant costs	$1,013	$525	$300	$225	$225	$233	$267	$ 300	$1,260

E = Order size
A = Annual quantity used in units: 5,000
S = Annual cost of carrying one unit in stock one year: $.50
P = Cost per purchase order: $10.00
C = Total annual relevant costs

**Assume that stock is zero when each order arrives. (Even if a certain minimum inventory were assumed, it has no bearing on the choice here as long as the minimum is the same for each alternative.) Therefore, the average inventory relevant to the problem will be one-half the order quantity. For example, if 600 units are purchased, the inventory on arrival will contain 600. It will gradually diminish at a constant rate until no units are on hand. Therefore, the average inventory would be 300; the carrying cost, $.50 × 300, or $150.*

†Number to meet the total annual need for 5,000 sets.

The dollar differences here are extremely small, but the approach is important. The same approach may be shown in graphic form. See Exhibit 22-2. Note that when costs behave as assumed here, the graph shows that total cost is at a minimum where total purchase-order cost and total carrying cost are equal.

---

order-size formula The graphic approach can be expressed in formula form (derived via calculus).[3] The total annual relevant cost (for any case, not just this example) is differentiated with respect to order size. Where this derivative is zero, the minimum annual cost is

[3]The formula may be derived as follows:

(1) $$C = \frac{AP}{E} + \frac{ES}{2}$$

(2) $$\frac{dC}{dE} = \frac{-AP}{E^2} + \frac{S}{2}$$

(3) $$\text{Set } \frac{dC}{dE} = 0; \frac{S}{2} - \frac{AP}{E^2} = 0$$

(4) $$SE^2 = 2AP$$

(5) $$E^2 = \frac{2AP}{S}$$

(6) $$E = \sqrt{\frac{2AP}{S}}$$

EXHIBIT 22-2

Graphic Solution of Economic Order Quantity

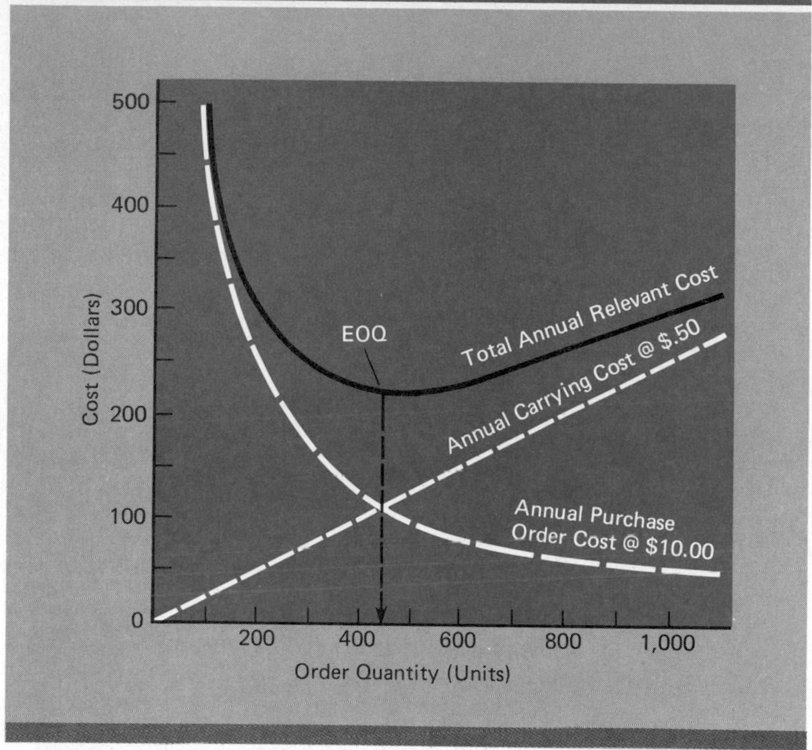

attained. The widely used formula approach to the order-size problem may be expressed in a variety of ways, one of which follows:

$$E = \sqrt{\frac{2AP}{S}}$$

where E = order size; A = annual quantity used in units; P = cost per purchase order; and S = annual cost of carrying one unit in stock for one year.

Substituting:

$$E = \sqrt{\frac{2(5{,}000)(\$10)}{\$.50}} = \sqrt{\frac{\$100{,}000}{\$.50}} = \sqrt{200{,}000}$$
$$= 448, \text{ the economic order quantity}$$

As we may expect, the order size gets larger as A or P gets bigger or as S gets smaller.

Another widely used formula is for computing total relevant costs. As Exhibit 22-1 shows:

$$C = \frac{AP}{E} + \frac{ES}{2}$$

 which attains its minimum value when E is set at the optimal EOQ value:

$$C_{min} = \sqrt{2APS} \qquad \text{(applicable at the EOQ level only)}^{4}$$

Substituting:

$$C_{min} = \sqrt{2(5{,}000)(\$10)(\$.50)} = \sqrt{\$50{,}000} = \$224$$

Implications for accountants

cost of prediction errors

The EOQ model and its variations are obviously affected by the cost predictions used. However, as Exhibit 22-2 shows, the total curve happens to be flat over the range near the minimum. **The square root in the EOQ formula reduces the sensitivity of the model to errors. Therefore, a salient feature of inventory decisions is that they are rarely affected by minor variations in cost predictions.** For example, suppose the carrying cost was erroneously predicted wildly at 50¢ instead of the correct cost of, say, \$1.60. Even then, the cost of the prediction error would be \$70 (calculated below), an error that is less than 18 percent of the optimal financial result of \$400.

As explained in Appendix 21a, p. 732, the cost of prediction error may be computed by using a general approach. Let us apply it to the inventory situation:

1. Begin with the basic solution, the optimal original decision. Predict the value of the critical parameter and solve the decision problem by computing the expected value, given this original prediction:
   Critical parameter, predicted carrying cost = \$.50
   Optimal original decision: order size of 448
2. Given an alternative possible value for the critical parameter, re-solve the decision problem. The solution produces a new decision, which may or may not be the same as the decision in step 1:
   Alternative parameter value, actual carrying cost = \$1.60
   Optimal new decision: order size of 250[5]

---

[4]Derivation:

$$C = \frac{AP}{E} + \frac{ES}{2}$$

Multiply by $2E/2E$ to get common denominator, and combine terms:

$$C = \frac{AP(2E)}{E(2E)} + \frac{ES(2E)}{2(2E)} = \frac{2AP}{2E} + \frac{E^2S}{2E} = \frac{2AP + E^2S}{2E} \qquad (1)$$

Substitute $E = \sqrt{2AP/S}$:

$$C_{min} = \frac{2AP + \frac{2AP}{S}S}{2\sqrt{\frac{2AP}{S}}} = \frac{4AP}{2\sqrt{\frac{2AP}{S}}} = \frac{2AP}{\sqrt{\frac{2AP}{S}}} = 2AP\frac{\sqrt{S}}{\sqrt{2AP}} = \sqrt{2APS} \qquad (2)$$

[5]Or $C = \sqrt{2APS} = \sqrt{2(5{,}000)(\$10)(\$1.60)} = \sqrt{\$160{,}000} = \$400$. Again note that this shortcut formula is valid *only* at the optimum EOQ level. That is why it is not used in step 3. (Negative signs are used in the final calculation to denote *costs,* as distinguished from *revenue.*) Also see J. Demski and G. Feltham, "Forecast Evaluation," *Accounting Review,* July 1972.

Expected financial result:

$$E = \sqrt{\frac{2AP}{S}} = 250$$

$$C = \frac{AP}{E} + \frac{ES}{2}$$

$$= \frac{5{,}000(\$10)}{250} + \frac{250(\$1.60)}{2} = \$200 + \$200 = \$-400$$

3. Given the original decision in step 1 and the alternative parameter value in step 2, compute the financial result:

   Actual cost, given original choice of 11.1 orders of 448 units each, but using alternative cost of \$1.60 rather than \$.50:

$$C = \frac{AP}{E} + \frac{ES}{2}$$

$$= \frac{5{,}000(\$10)}{448} + \frac{448(\$1.60)}{2}$$

$$= \$112 + \$358 = \qquad -470$$

4. The cost of prediction error is the financial result in step 2 minus the financial result in step 3. **\$ 70**

impact on human behavior

A fascinating aspect of inventory management is the possible conflict between what the decision model might indicate as the optimal action and what the manager might perceive as optimal. Managers are frequently governed by how their performance is evaluated, and the formal accounting system may record some inventory-related costs but ignore others, although they may be relevant.

Reconsider Exhibit 22-1. Note that if annual carrying costs were not charged to the manager in any way, there would be no inducement toward larger order sizes, even though they may be uneconomical from the viewpoint of the entire firm. For example, a production manager prefers longer (and fewer) production runs because the lower setup costs will tend to reduce the total annual costs charged, although larger inventories must be carried to bridge the gaps between production runs.

Of course, the answer to this conflict is to design the performance evaluation system so that the carrying costs are charged to the appropriate manager. For example, we frequently see systems where an "imputed interest" charge is levied against managers for the inventories under their responsibility. This practice inhibits managers from overbuying stocks, a common temptation.

The inventory area provides another illustration of why accountants and managers must be alert to the motivational implications of failing to dovetail a performance-evaluation model with the decision model that is favored by top management.[6]

[6]Also see W. Morse and J. Scheiner, "Cost Minimization, Return on Investment, Residual Income: Alternative Criteria for Inventory Models," *Accounting and Business Research,* Autumn 1979, pp. 320–24.

difficulties of cost prediction

Opportunity costs often do not explicitly appear on formal accounting records. Examples are forgone quantity discounts,[7] forgone contributions to profit from sales lost because of inventory shortages, and forgone fortuitous purchases because existing stock inhibits additional acquisitions. Even if these costs were easy to identify, their measurement would often be subject to dispute. Perhaps the clearest example of the difficulty is measuring the impact of being out of stock. What is the financial impact when a disgruntled customer vows to buy elsewhere forevermore?

The size of many relevant costs will differ, depending on the specific alternative uses of resources. For example, if storage space is owned and cannot be used for other profitable purposes, differential space costs are zero. But if the space may be used for other productive activities, or if there is rental cost geared to the space occupied, a pertinent cost of space usage for inventory purposes must be recognized.

To the extent that money is invested in inventories, there is an interest cost of carrying stock. But how is this to be measured? In practice, this rate sometimes is based on current borrowing rates, the long-run average cost of capital, or some "appropriate" rate selected by management. The proper rate should depend on investment opportunities available to management; it may be small or large, depending on the risks.[8]

Other costs that may or may not be relevant to policy decisions include overtime premiums on rush orders that would be unnecessary if bigger inventories were carried, idle time caused by material shortages, emergency expediting, extra transportation costs (for example, air freight), extra physical-count taking, obsolescence risks, and extra moving and handling costs.

As in any policy-making situation, inventory costs that are common to all alternatives are irrelevant and may be ignored. Costs that are often irrelevant because they might not be affected by the inventory decision include salaries of stores record clerks, storekeepers, and material handlers, depreciation on building and equipment, and fixed rent.

In practice, however, for purposes of inventory planning most of the wage costs are unitized on a per-order or a per-unit-handled basis. Thus they are regarded as fully variable costs. Whether this is justified depends on specific circumstances. Surely the cost of processing 4,000 orders per period will be strikingly greater than the cost of processing 1,000 orders. The basic question is often whether in the same situation, the cost of processing 3,400 orders will be notably different from the cost

---

[7]Quantity discounts affect unit prices; in general, the bigger the order, the lower the unit price. The price usually holds over ranges of order sizes; within each range a uniform unit price prevails.

The basic formula used previously can be adapted to such situations, but its complexities will not be described further here. For our purposes the following approach will be easiest to understand.

First, compute annual basic expenses in the manner illustrated in Exhibit 22-1. Then merely add the additional expenses of *forgoing* quantity discounts. The economic order will, of course, be the one that offers the lowest total annual relevant costs.

[8]See Chapter 13 for a discussion of choosing a required rate of return. The only essential difference between an investment in equipment and inventory is that the former usually entails a discrete investment, whereas the latter represents a continuum of possible investments. See J. Van Horne, *Financial Management and Policy,* 5th ed. (Englewood Cliffs, N.J.: Prentice-Hall, 1980), p. 475.

of processing 3,000 orders. This is simply another example of the importance of determining what is relevant to any given decision-making situation.[9]

carrying cost The relevant carrying costs (S) in the EOQ model consist of *outlay costs* for such items as insurance and property taxes, plus the *opportunity cost* of capital. But how is the opportunity cost computed? For example, suppose the required rate of return is 20 percent on invested capital. To what items is the 20 percent applicable?

Many simplifying assumptions underlie the EOQ model. In particular, the opportunity cost of capital is applied only to those costs that **vary with the number of units purchased** and that **are incurred at the time the units are received.** In other words, an "interest" opportunity cost must be charged because of the decision to carry inventory. The theory is that such a cost would not exist if the units could be acquired at the instant of their use or sale.

Apply Opportunity Cost of Capital?	
Yes	*No*
1. Invoiced acquisition cost of materials or variable costs of manufactured goods.	1. Fixed factory overhead, whether expressed as a total or as a cost per unit.
2. Freight in, when variable and identified with units.	2. The costs of ordering, which are identified as P in the EOQ formula. These costs are unaffected by the number of units ordered. Examples include clerical costs, setup costs, and flat freight costs per truck or ship where the total costs are unaffected by the number of units ordered.
3. Unloading, inspection, cleaning, and placing in stock upon receipt or upon start of production.	3. Inspection or cleaning costs while in inventory or upon withdrawal for use or sale.
	4. Insurance costs that depend on number of units in inventory. These are regarded as part of S, the costs of carrying, but not as part of the invested capital.

In particular, note that the components of P are not included in the invested capital, although in theory a case could be made for such inclusion.[10]

For an illustration of these distinctions, see the third of the Problems for Self-Study at the end of this chapter.

---

[9]It is easy to criticize various mathematical approaches to problems of inventory control on the grounds that the relevant costs are impossible to measure. But such criticisms are invalid in nearly all situations. Optimum inventory policies can be achieved without knowledge of "true costs." For an interesting discussion, see D. W. Miller and M. K. Starr, *Executive Decisions and Operations Research,* 2nd ed. (Englewood Cliffs, N.J.: Prentice-Hall), pp. 328–36.

[10]An extreme example highlights the issue. Suppose only one order is placed. The entire annual needs are acquired at the beginning of the year. In theory, a case can be made for regarding the cost of ordering, P, as a part of invested capital. After all, the money is "tied up" from the beginning of the year.

Safety stocks

when to order?

Although we have seen how to compute EOQ, we have not yet considered another key decision: When to order? This question is easy to answer only if we know the **lead time**—**the time interval between placing an order and receiving delivery**—know the EOQ, and are *certain* of demand during lead time. The graph in Exhibit 22-3 will clarify the relationships among the following facts:

Economic order quantity	448 sets of steel shelving
Lead time	2 weeks
Average usage	100 sets per week

Exhibit 22-3, Part A, shows that the **reorder point**—**the quantity level that automatically triggers a new order**—is dependent on expected usage during lead time; that is, if shelving is being used at a rate of 100 sets per week and the lead time is two weeks, a new order would be placed when the inventory level reaches 200 sets.

EXHIBIT 22-3

Demand in Relation to Inventory Levels

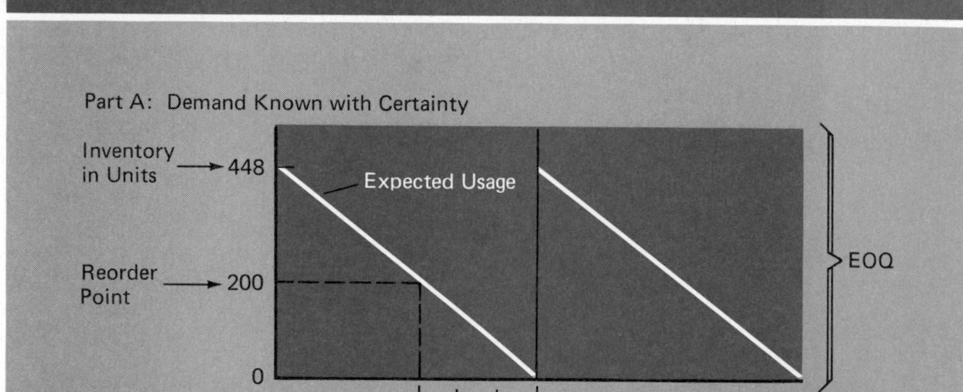

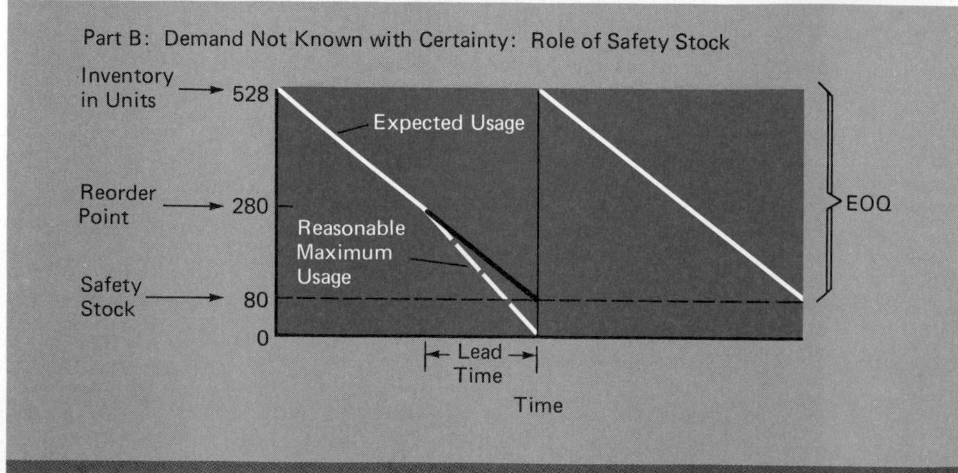

minimum inventory: safety allowance for fluctuations in demand

Our previous example assumed that 100 sets would be used per week—a demand pattern that was known with certainty. Businesses are seldom blessed with such accurate forecasting. Instead, demand may fluctuate from day to day, from week to week, or from month to month. Thus, the company will run out of stock if there are sudden spurts in usage beyond 100 per week, delays in processing orders, or delivery delays. Obviously, then, nearly all companies must provide for some **safety stock**—some minimum or buffer inventory as a cushion against reasonable expected maximum usage. Part B of Exhibit 22-3 is based on the same facts as Part A except that reasonable expected *maximum* usage is 140 sets per week. The safety stock might be, say, 80 sets (excess usage of 40 sets per week × 2 weeks). **The reorder point is commonly computed as safety stock plus the average usage during the lead time.**[11]

computation of safety stock

In our example, we used 80 sets as a safety stock. The computation of safety stocks hinges on demand forecasts. The executive will have some notion—usually based on past experience—of the range of daily demand: what percentage chance (probability) exists for usages of various quantities.

A frequency distribution based on prior daily or weekly levels of demand will offer data for constructing the associated costs of maintaining safety (minimum) stocks. The major relevant costs are the **carrying costs,** which are primarily interest on investment, obsolescence write-offs, and space costs; and the **stockout costs,** which include expensive expediting, loss of contribution margins, and loss of customer goodwill. For example, suppose a customer comes to buy a tire bearing a contribution margin of \$40. The store has none at the moment, so the customer buys elsewhere. The stockout cost is a minimum of \$40; if 4 tires were going to be bought, 4 × \$40 = \$160. These opportunity costs are especially difficult to measure, but statisticians and mathematicians have used statistical probability techniques on this problem with some success.[12] **The optimum safety-stock level exists where the costs of carrying an extra unit are exactly counterbalanced by the expected stockout costs.** This would be the level that minimizes the annual total stockout costs and carrying costs.

For instance, suppose in our earlier example that the total usage during the two-week lead time is expected to be:

								TOTAL PROBABILITY
Total usage	80	120	160	200	240	280	320	
Probability	.04	.06	.20	.40	.20	.06	.04	1.00

[11]This handy but special formula does not apply where the receipt of the standard order fails to increase stocks to the order-point quantity; for example, where the lead time is three months and the standard order is a one-month supply. In these cases, there will be overlapping of orders. The order point will be average usage during lead time plus safety stock *minus orders placed but not yet received.* This is really the general formula for computing the reorder point. In most cases, a simplified version is used because the last term in the general formula is zero. For elaboration, see almost any book on inventory systems.

[12]Inventory theory advances the idea that the rational entrepreneur should attempt to vary inventory levels with the square root of sales rather than with sales. This is based on the relationships expressed in the EOQ formula, discussed earlier, where the optimum order size increased in proportion to the square root of the annual quantity used. See D. Mehta, *Working Capital Management* (Englewood Cliffs, N.J.: Prentice-Hall, 1974), Chaps. 4–5.

Thus, if we decide to use a reorder point equal to 200 units plus a safety stock, we could expect the following stockout results:

Probability of stockout	.20	.06	.04
Total actual usage during lead time	240	280	320
Less expected usage provided for	200	200	200
Stockouts if provision is also made for a safety stock of:			
zero units	40	80	120
40 units	0	40	80
80 units	0	0	40
120 units	0	0	0

Suppose further that a stockout cost is predicted at $.60 per unit per order. Recall that the average carrying cost is $.50 per unit per year. Of the four safety-stock levels considered, Exhibit 22-4 shows that the total costs are minimized at $51 when a safety stock of 80 units is maintained.

The most difficult cost to determine is *stockout cost,* consisting mainly of the forgone present and future contribution to profit from losing an order because of lack of inventory:

> But if there is no demand during the period an item is out of stock, there is no lost profit, and reliable information on unfilled demand is seldom maintained. Where there is unfilled demand, but the customer is willing to wait or accept a substitute, there may be no immediate loss of profit. But there may be loss of future business as a result of dissatisfied customers.[13]

EXHIBIT 22-4

Computation of Safety Stock

SAFETY-STOCK LEVELS IN UNITS	PROBABILITY OF STOCKOUT	STOCKOUT COSTS: stockout in units	stockout cost*	orders per year†	expected stockout cost‡	CARRYING COSTS§	TOTAL COSTS
0	.20	40	$24	11.2	$ 54		
	.06	80	48	11.2	32		
	.04	120	72	11.2	32		
					$118	$ 0	$118
40	.06	40	24	11.2	$ 16		
	.04	80	48	11.2	22		
					$ 38	$20	$ 58
80	.04	40	24	11.2	$ 11	$40	$ 51
120	0	0	0	11.2	$ 0	$60	$ 60

**Stockout units × stockout cost of $.60 per unit.*
†Annual demand 5,000 ÷ 448 EOQ = 11.2 orders per year.
‡Stockout cost × probability × number of orders per year.
§Safety stock × annual carrying cost of 50¢ per unit. Assumptions: Safety stock is on hand at all times and there is no overstocking caused by decreases in expected usage.

[13] N.A.A. Research Report No. 40, *Techniques in Inventory Management,* p. 14.

Instead of estimating a cost of stockouts, some managers may stipulate a maximum allowable probability of being out of stock. In our example, a manager may choose to maintain a safety stock of 80 units, so that there would be a probability of only 4 percent of not meeting all demands.

The forgoing discussion of inventory control revolved around the so-called **two-bin** or **constant order-quantity system:** When inventory levels recede to level *X,* then order quantity *Y.* There is another widely used model in practice, the **constant order-cycle system:** The reorder date is fixed, and the quantity ordered depends on the usage since the previous order and the outlook during the lead time. The minimization of the total associated costs of inventories is still the prime objective, regardless of the system used. For an expanded discussion, see any book on inventory systems.

Emphasis on optimality

Note that the emphasis in this chapter is on the word *optimum,* not *minimum.* Contrast this with the commonly used index of inventory management—inventory turnover, the number of times the average inventory is sold or used in a year. The traditional rule has been, "The higher the turnover, the better the inventory management." Consider the following comments:

> An infinite turnover can be achieved by carrying no inventory whatsoever. But such an inventory policy would not be a good policy because a company with no inventory would be continuously buying, expediting. . . . Turnover is worth improving, yes, but only if there is no substantial increase in ordering cost and only if there is no substantial loss of sales resulting from excessive stockouts.[14]

Control classifications: the ABC method

Sometimes it is difficult to comprehend the enormous number of items that companies must keep in stock—up to 50,000, and often more. An effective inventory-control system will not have all items in the inventory treated in the same manner under the same control techniques. Many companies find it useful to divide materials, parts, supplies, and finished goods into subclassifications for purposes of stock control. For example, Exhibit 22-5 shows direct materials, **which are subclassified in step-by-step fashion by (a) itemizing total annual purchase cost of each item needed and (b) grouping in decreasing order of annual consumption cost.** This technique is often called the **ABC METHOD** although it also has other labels.

The final A, B, C classification in Exhibit 22-5 demonstrates that only 5 percent of the items represent 72 percent of the total cost. In general, the greatest degree of continuous control would be exerted over these A items, which account for high annual consumption costs and correspondingly high investment in inventories. This type of control would mean frequent ordering, low safety stocks, and a willingness to incur expediting costs on A items, because the costs of placing and following up orders are relatively low in comparison with costs of carrying excess inventories. At the other extreme, where the total yearly purchase cost is relatively low, there would be less-frequent ordering, higher safety stocks, and less paper work (C items).

[14]Joseph Buchan and Ernest Koenigsberg, *Scientific Inventory Management* (Englewood Cliffs, N.J.: Prentice-Hall), p. 90.

EXHIBIT 22-5 **ABC Analysis of Material Inventory**

Step 1. Multiply average usage times unit price to obtain total cost:

ITEM	AVERAGE USAGE	UNIT PRICE	TOTAL CONSUMPTION COST (SEE NOTE 1)
H20	1,000	$20.00	$20,000
H21	1,000	.05	50
H22	10,000	.02	200
H23	11,000	1.00	11,000
H24	110,000	.10	11,000

(and so forth for 50,000 inventory items)

Step 2. List the 50,000 items above in descending order of total consumption cost and then divide into three classes (see Note 2):

	ITEMS		DOLLARS	
CLASS	**number of items**	**percent of total**	**total cost**	**percent of total**
A	2,500	5%	$14,400,000	72%
B	12,500	25	3,800,000	19
C	35,000	70	1,800,000	9
	50,000	100%	$20,000,000	100%

Note 1: The total annual cost of raw materials consumed is dependent on two main factors: physical quantity needed and cost per unit. It is the total cost rather than the unit cost that matters. Thus, 11,000 units @ $1.00 requires the same total cost as 110,000 units @ $.10.

Note 2: For example, of the items above, H20 would be the most likely to become a Class A item. It has the highest total consumption cost of $20,000.

Type A and B items are ordered according to budget schedules prepared by a production-planning department.[15] Essentially, sales forecasts are the cornerstone for production scheduling. In turn, these production schedules are "exploded" (a commonly used term for giving detailed breakdowns of data) into the various direct-material, parts, and supply components. These explosions result in purchase schedules for major items. The purchase schedules are adjusted for lead times, planned changes in inventories, and normal waste and spoilage. Purchases are made accordingly, and follow-ups are instituted by the purchasing department as needed. In other words, Type A and B items are budgeted almost on a hand-to-mouth basis, because carrying costs are too high to warrant inventories that are sizable in terms of many days' usage.

[15]The Ford Motor Company uses four inventory classes and keeps two days' supply of A items; five days' supply of B; 10 days' supply of C; and 20 or more days' supply of D items. Many Japanese factories use a Kanban system to reduce inventory requirements. The system focuses on the final production process and then looks to the preceding processes. The earlier processes produce only enough quantities to replace those withdrawn by the subsequent processes. As a result, there are more setups and smaller lot sizes. See Y. Monden, "What Makes the Toyota Production System Really Tick?" *Industrial Engineering* 13, No. 1 (January 1981), pp. 36–46.

Stores cards or similar computer records are usually kept for Type A and B items. Such cards increasingly carry a physical-unit balance only. More managements are becoming doubtful that the added clerical costs of carrying actual unit prices on stores cards are worthwhile.

The U.S. automobile industry has pioneered in sophisticated inventory systems, but it has been stuck with swollen inventories occasionally. *Fortune* has commented: ". . . an inventory management system, however sophisticated, is no better than the sales forecasts on which it is based."[16]

The mechanics of the system

fixing responsibility

As a business becomes more complex, the interdependent problems of production planning and inventory control become imposing enough to warrant appointing an executive to assume sole responsibility for implementing a coordinated inventory-control policy. The scope of this position varies from company to company. In some firms, the manager may be a vice-president in charge of production planning and control. In other firms, the planning and control functions may be separated. Duties of purchasing, receiving, and storing may be the responsibility of a particular executive, although day-to-day duties may be delegated to various officers, such as a purchasing agent, a receiving-room supervisor, and a storeroom supervisor.

An important aspect of inventory and production control systems is that they may be largely dehumanized. For example, when reorder points, economic order quantities, safety stocks, and other technicalities are calculated, the entire system may be automated with the help of a digital computer. The system can then operate with a minimum dependence on human judgment. That is why inventory-control systems are being increasingly computerized. However, human judgment cannot be eradicated altogether. The ingredients (ordering costs, carrying costs, and demand) of the model do frequently change, and a constant surveillance for the sensitivity of the model to such changes is an important, and not too automatic, part of an effective control system.

systematic controls

Just as in production operations, inventory-control procedures should be systematized in order to promote efficiency and reduce errors, fraud, and waste. Commonly followed internal-control rules should be applied in setting up an inventory system. Appendix 27a (page 919) discusses a typical company system in detail, including descriptions of the routing of multicopies of requisitions, purchase orders, vouchers, invoices, and receiving reports.

The purchasing department is responsible for getting favorable prices, following up unusual situations, using approved suppliers, and taking advantage of discounts. Separate, sequential records for each item may be kept by purchase lots, showing dates, source, quantity, unit price, total costs, discounts, and special remarks. Thus, all pertinent data for control are kept on a current basis at the point where control is supposed to be exercised.

Purchasing agents should be free to devote their energies to obtaining optimum prices, investigating sources, and studying market conditions. Their buying should be triggered strictly by purchase requisitions. In general, inventory levels and purchase requisitions are ultimately the responsibility of production planning and control, not of the purchasing department. Obviously, ample communication is desirable. For ex-

[16]E. Meadows, "How Detroit Got Stuck with All Those Cars," *Fortune,* October 22, 1979, p. 54.

ample, purchasing may occasionally want to know if future needs are sufficiently high to warrant taking advantage of unusually low prices.

An effective method of controlling material usage was described in Chapter 6, but we shall summarize it here. Production-planning departments or production managers present standard bills (requisitions) of materials, including allowances for normal spoilage, to the storeroom. If standards are not met, different-colored or coded excess-materials requisitions are used to obtain additional materials. These should be routed to the production manager's superior so that immediate follow-up may be made. Any materials left over are returned to the storeroom by inspectors or production personnel.

SUMMARY

Inventory control is primarily concerned with optimizing inventory balances so that net income is maximized. Recordkeeping in itself is only one of the important phases of inventory control. Top management's task is to formulate inventory policies that will result in optimum inventory investment, will promote efficiency, and will control errors, fraud, and waste.

Associated costs that are affected by various inventory policies are ordering costs and carrying costs. They include opportunity cost of interest on investment, an especially prominent cost, plus other costs such as quantity discounts, contribution margins on lost sales, space costs, overtime premiums, idle time, expediting, transportation, obsolescence, training, learning, setup, order processing, order filling, personal property taxes, insurance, and handling. These costs are often difficult to isolate and measure, especially with regard to their differential behavior between alternatives. However, attempts at sensible measurement at least cast light on a *range* of optimum alternatives.

Different control policies may be applied to different segments of the inventory. Thus, a variety of purchase timing, storing, receiving, and recording techniques may be employed at the same time within the same company.

Modern mathematical methods have been applied on a wide front to the problems of production planning and inventory control. The complexity of inventory control is such that many consulting firms specialize in the area to the extent of studying a business's inventory problems and tailor-making a special formula for computing economic order quantities.

The subject matter of this chapter again shows how the field of managerial accounting spills over and invades allied fields, such as engineering, modern mathematics, and business policies. The complexities of modern business make it increasingly difficult to construct fences around technical specialties.

problems for self-study

problem 1

Review Example 1 in this chapter. Suppose the annual purchase-order cost was $20 per order instead of $10. What is the economic order quantity?

solution 1

$$E = \sqrt{\frac{2(5{,}000)\$20}{\$.50}} = \sqrt{\frac{\$200{,}000}{\$.50}} = \sqrt{400{,}000} = 633$$

Note that the higher the order cost, the higher the economic order quantity. This problem is an example of sensitivity analysis. The accountant or manager may be unsure about the "true" purchase-order cost, but in this case a doubling of the unit cost will only increase the economic order quantity from 448 to 633 units.

problem 2

Review the example that accompanies Exhibit 22-4.

solution 2

See the solution in Exhibit 22-4.

problem 3

Suppose a company has an absorption manufacturing cost of $60 per unit, including $10 of applied fixed factory overhead. Setup costs are $100 per job order. Because they have a tendency to deteriorate, the units are inspected at a cost of $1 per unit when they are removed from the finished-goods inventory for delivery to customers. The insurance premium is $.40 per unit per year; it is based on the average cost of inventory on hand. The required rate of return on investment in inventory is 20 percent. Annual demand is 52,000 units. Compute the economic order quantity.

solution 3

$$\begin{aligned}
A &= \text{annual demand, 52,000 units} \\
P &= \text{setup cost, \$100} \\
S &= \text{outlay cost for insurance} + \text{opportunity cost of invested capital} \\
&= \$.40 + .20(\$60 - \$10 \text{ fixed overhead}) \\
&= \$10.40
\end{aligned}$$

The inspection charge is irrelevant because it is unaffected by the size of the order or the number of orders. (Moreover, the charge is incurred when the items are removed, not when they are acquired.)

The setup cost, or any cost that is ordinarily classified as part of *P*, is not considered to be a part of the invested capital used as a basis for calculating *S*.

$$E = \sqrt{\frac{2AP}{S}} = \sqrt{\frac{(2)(52{,}000)(\$100)}{\$10.40}} = 1{,}000 \text{ units}$$

Terms to Learn

ABC method ***carrying costs*** ***constant order-cycle system*** ***constant order-quantity system*** ***economic order quantity (EOQ)*** ***lead time*** ***ordering costs*** ***reorder point*** ***safety stock*** ***stockout costs*** ***two-bin system***

Special Points and Pitfalls

The EOQ model helps managers to keep inventories at optimum levels. In general, the decisions regarding order quantities are not significantly affected by errors in predicting carrying costs or ordering costs.

The cost-benefit theme of this book is well illustrated by ABC control systems for inventories. That is, some items in inventory may warrant elaborate and costly control systems, whereas other items may warrant scant attention.

The potential conflict between decision models and performance evaluation models is exemplified by the EOQ model. The opportunity cost of the interest on the investment in inventory plays a key role in the EOQ decision model. Still, many organizations measure managerial performance on the basis of total costs or total profits without providing for any opportunity cost of interest.

Appendix 22: inventory-costing methods

purpose of discussion of inventory methods

How should the costs of inventories be computed? Management must decide. These decisions are important because they directly affect the way income will be computed.

We have already seen how price fluctuations in inventories are accounted for under standard costing. The following discussion surveys alternative approaches to the costing of identical materials acquired at various prices. The intention here is to demonstrate methodology rather than to dwell on important theoretical issues of inventory costing that are discussed at length in typical introductory, intermediate, and advanced accounting texts. Also, the influence of income taxes, which is immense, is not discussed at length here.

the question of timing

With few exceptions, the differences between inventory methods are merely ones of timing. In short, when do inventory costs become expenses? Where it is impractical to link inventories with specific usage or sales, some assumption is made for transferring certain costs out of inventory. The most commonly used assumption is one of the following three:

1. *First-in, first-out (FIFO).* The earliest-acquired stock is assumed to be used first; the stock on hand is assumed to be the stock most recently acquired.
2. *Last-in, first-out (LIFO).* The latest-acquired stock is assumed to be used first; the stock on hand is assumed to be the stock least recently acquired. The LIFO method releases the most recent (or last) inventory costs as cost of goods used or sold. It attempts to match the most current cost of obtaining inventory against sales for a period. As compared with FIFO, the use of LIFO will tend to result in less reported net income during periods of rising prices and more income in periods of falling prices.
3. Some version of an *average-inventory method.* An example would be the *moving-average method,* whereby each purchase is lumped with the former inventory balance so that a new average unit price is used to price subsequent issues of inventory. This method may be used with a perpetual-inventory system. A *weighted-average method* is often used with a periodic-inventory system; this average is computed by dividing the total cost of the beginning inventory plus purchases by the total number of units in those two classes. These methods are best understood through illustration.

» EXAMPLE 2

Try to solve the problem yourself before consulting the answers that follow. (Adapted from a CPA examination.) The Saunders Corporation uses raw material A in a manufacturing process. Information as to balances on hand, purchases, and requisitions of material A are given in the accompanying table. You are to answer each question on the basis of this information.

1. If a perpetual-inventory record of material A is operated on a FIFO basis, it will show a *closing inventory* of (a) $150, (b) $152, (c) $159, (d) $162, (e) $170, (f) answer not given.
2. Assume that no perpetual inventory is maintained for material A, and that quantities are obtained by an annual physical count. The accounting records show information as to purchases but not as to issues. On this assumption, the *closing inventory* on a FIFO basis will be (a) $150, (b) $156, (c) $159, (d) $160, (e) $170, (f) answer not given.
3. If a perpetual-inventory record of material A is operated on a LIFO basis, it will show a *closing inventory* of (a) $150, (b) $152, (c) $156, (d) $160, (e) $170, (f) answer not given.

RAW MATERIAL A	QUANTITIES			DOLLARS			
DATE	received	issued	balance	unit price	received	issued	balance
Jan. 1			100	$1.50			$150
Jan. 24	300		400	1.56	$468		
Feb. 8		80	320				
Mar. 16		140	180				
June 11	150		330	1.60	240		
Aug. 18		130	200				
Sept. 6		110	90				
Oct. 15	150		240	1.70	255		
Dec. 29		140	100				

4. Assume that no perpetual inventory is maintained for material A, and that quantities are obtained by an annual physical count. The accounting records show information as to purchases but not as to issues. On this assumption, the *closing inventory* on a LIFO basis will be (a) $150, (b) $152, (c) $156, (d) $160, (e) $170, (f) answer not given.

5. If a perpetual-inventory record of material A is operated on a moving-average basis, it will show a *closing inventory* that is (a) lower than on the LIFO basis, (b) lower than on the FIFO basis, (c) higher than on the FIFO basis, (d) answer not given.

6. The exact closing inventory in question 5 is $______.

7. Assume that no perpetual inventory is maintained, and that quantities are obtained by an annual physical count. The accounting records show information as to purchases but not as to issues. On this assumption, the closing inventory on a weighted-average basis will be $______.

» SOLUTIONS

1. (e) $170. Under FIFO, the ending-inventory valuation may be most easily obtained by first working back from the closing date until the number of units purchased equals the number of units in ending inventory. Then, by applying the appropriate unit purchase costs, the total dollar amount is obtained. In this example, 100 units @ $1.70 is $170.

2. (e) $170. The answer is identical under perpetual and periodic systems. Under a periodic inventory method, files must be combed for recent invoices until 100 units are tallied. In this case, the most recent invoice would suffice. In other cases, more than one invoice may be needed to cover the 100 units in the ending inventory.

3. (b) 90 units @ $1.50 plus 10 units @ $1.70 equals $152. Under LIFO, the ending-inventory valuation may generally be obtained by working forward from the beginning inventory until the total number of units equals the number of units in ending inventory. Then, by applying the appropriate beginning-inventory unit costs and the early current-purchase unit costs, the total dollar amount is obtained.

   However, under a perpetual LIFO method, a temporary reduction (September 6) below the number of units in the beginning inventory calls for the assignment of the base-inventory price to the number of units released from the base inventory.

4. (a) 100 units @ $1.50, or $150. Under a periodic LIFO method, a *temporary* reduction below the number of units in the beginning inventory will have no effect upon the valuation of the ending inventory as long as the number of units in the count of ending inventory for the year as a whole is at least equal to the beginning inventory.

5. (b) FIFO assigns earliest costs to cost of sales and latest costs to inventory. Unit prices have been rising during the period. Therefore, more of the earlier and lower-cost units will be contained in the ending inventory under the moving-average method than under FIFO.

6. $165.125. This technique requires the computation of a new average unit cost after each acquisition; this unit cost is used for all issues until the next purchase is made.

MOVING-AVERAGE PERPETUAL METHOD

DATE	RECEIVED units	price	amount	ISSUED units	price	amount	BALANCE units	price	amount
Jan. 1							100	$1.50	$150.00
Jan. 24	300	$1.56	$468				400	1.545	618.00
Feb. 8				80	$1.545	$123.60	320	1.545	494.40
Mar. 16				140	1.545	216.30	180	1.545	278.10
June 11	150	1.60	240				330	1.57	518.10
Aug. 18				130	1.57	204.10	200	1.57	314.00
Sept. 6				110	1.57	172.70	90	1.57	141.30
Oct. 15	150	1.70	255				240	1.65125	396.30
Dec. 29				140	1.65125	231.175	100	1.65125	165.125

RECAPITULATION

Costs to account for: $150 + $468 + $240 + $255 =	$1,113,000
Deduct: Issues	947,875
Ending balance	$ 165,125

7. $159. (100 units × $1.59.)

WEIGHTED-AVERAGE PERIODIC METHOD

DATE	UNITS	UNIT PRICE	DOLLARS
Jan. 1	100	$1.50	$ 150
Jan. 24	300	1.56	468
June 11	150	1.60	240
Oct. 15	150	1.70	255
To account for	700		$1,113
Weighted unit cost, $1,113 ÷ 700 = $1.59			
Costs released		600 @ $1.59	$ 954
Costs in ending inventory		100 @ $1.59	159
Costs accounted for			$1,113

Note that the assumption of a weighted-average approach is subject to criticism because the October 15 purchase influences the costing of issues throughout the year, even though, strictly speaking, the cost of earlier issues would not have been affected by purchases made later in the year.

LIFO versus FIFO

If unit prices did not fluctuate, all inventory methods would show identical results. Price changes appear in the financial records in different ways, depending on the specific inventory method used. LIFO ordinarily reflects current purchase prices in current operating results, whereas FIFO delays recognition of price effects. If price changes are volatile, year-to-year reported net incomes may differ dramatically between LIFO and FIFO approaches.

Balance-sheet presentations are also affected by the choice of LIFO or FIFO. LIFO usage tends to result in older and older, and hence less meaningful, prices being shown in inventory if stocks are stable or grow through the years, whereas FIFO tends to reflect more nearly current prices on the balance sheet.

If prices are rising, LIFO shows less income than FIFO, and thus it tends to postpone outlays for income taxes. Also, the periodic LIFO method permits immediate influencing of net income by timing of purchases, a feature that has not received the attention it deserves. For example, if prices are rising and a company desires to show less income in a given year because of income-tax or other reasons, all that need be done is to buy a large amount of inventory near the end of the year—thus releasing higher costs to expense than ordinarily.

Neither FIFO nor LIFO isolates and measures the effects of price fluctuations as special managerial problems. For example, when prices rise, FIFO buries price gains in the regular income figure, whereas LIFO excludes the effects of price changes from the income statement:

			LIFO			FIFO
Sales, 5,000 @ 20¢			$1,000			$1,000
Inventory, beginning	1,000 @ $.10 =	$100			$100	
Purchases	5,000 @ $.15 =	750			750	
		$850			$850	
Inventory, ending	1,000 @ $.10 =	100	750	1,000 @ $.15 =	150	700
Gross margin			$ 250			$ 300

Consider the $50 rise in price pertaining to the ending inventory (1,000 units × $.05 = $50). FIFO includes the $50 in income as part of the gross profit of $300. LIFO excludes the $50 from income by showing a gross profit of $250 and ignoring the $50.

Here again we see the benefit of a standard-cost approach. When currently attainable standards are in use, standard costing automatically provides a measure of price "gains" or "losses" that can be reported separately on an income statement. This has two advantages: (a) it prevents price changes from influencing appraisal of efficiency in operations; (b) it spotlights and measures the impact of some price changes on overall company results.

QUESTIONS, PROBLEMS, AND CASES

22-1 "There are two danger points that management usually wants to avoid in controlling inventories." Explain.

22-2 "Inventory records are only a means to the end of inventory control." Explain.

22-3 Certain costs associated with inventory policies do not appear on formal accounting records. Enumerate at least three.

22-4 "Identical space costs for inventory can be zero during some months and sizable during other months." Explain.

22-5 "The practical approach to determining economic order quantity is concerned with locating a minimum cost *range* rather than a minimum cost *point*." Explain.

22-6 What is a *safety stock?* What techniques are used to compute safety stocks?

22-7 Describe a "two-bin" inventory system.

22-8 What are the major responsibilities of the purchasing department?

22-9 Distinguish between the *moving-average* and the *weighted-average* inventory methods.

22-10 "Standard costing is superior to both LIFO and FIFO for isolating and measuring the effects of price fluctuations as special managerial problems." Why?

22-11 ***Comparison of LIFO and FIFO.*** Study Appendix 22. The Dowell Coal Co. does not maintain a perpetual-inventory system. The inventory of coal on June 30 shows 1,000 tons at $6 per ton. The following purchases were made during July:

July 5	2,000 tons @ $7 per ton
July 15	500 tons @ $8 per ton
July 25	600 tons @ $9 per ton

A physical inventory on July 31 shows a total of 1,200 tons on hand. Revenue from sales of coal for July totals $30,000.

REQUIRED

Compute the inventory cost as of July 31, using

1. LIFO—Last in, first out
2. FIFO—First in, first out

22-12 ***Inventory card, moving-average.*** (SMA) Study Appendix 22. Steel Stores Limited is a dealer in steel products.

The company purchases its steel from various mills. Prices are f.o.b. point of shipment. On January 1, freight costs were $5 per ton; but on January 14, they advanced 10 percent. The steel industry uses the standard 2,000-pound ton.

During the month of January, the following transactions in hot rolled sheet, 60″ long and 36″ wide, took place:

Jan. 1	Inventory	10 tons at $6.00 per 100 lbs.
Jan. 2	Purchased	3 tons at $5.50 per 100 lbs.
Jan. 3	Sold	2 tons
Jan. 5	Purchased	2 tons at $5.60 per 100 lbs.
Jan. 6	Sold	3 tons
Jan. 10	Purchased	8 tons at $5.55 per 100 lbs.
Jan. 12	Sold	8 tons
Jan. 15	Purchased	2 tons at $5.55 per 100 lbs.
Jan. 16	Sold	2 tons
Jan. 30	Purchased	5 tons at 05.60 per 100 lbs.
Jan. 31	Sold	7 tons

Sales prices are determined by applying a markup of 30 percent to laid-down costs at the beginning of each month.

REQUIRED

1. Show these transactions as they would appear on a perpetual-inventory card, using the moving-average cost method. Calculations should be made to the nearest cent.
2. Calculate the gross profit for the month.
3. Name two methods other than the moving-average cost method that could have been used in pricing the issue transactions above.

22-13 ***Multiple choice; comparison of inventory methods.*** (CPA) Study Appendix 22. The Berg Corporation began business on January 1, 19_4. Information about its inventories under different valuation methods is shown below. Using this information, you are to choose the phrase that best answers each of the following questions.

INVENTORY

	LIFO COST	FIFO COST	MARKET	LOWER OF COST OR MARKET
Dec. 31, 19_4	$10,200	$10,000	$ 9,600	$ 8,900
Dec. 31, 19_5	9,100	9,000	8,800	8,500
Dec. 31, 19_6	10,300	11,000	12,000	10,900

1. The inventory basis that would show the *highest net income for 19_4* is (a) LIFO cost, (b) FIFO cost, (c) market, (d) lower of cost or market.

2. The inventory basis that would show the *highest net income for 19_5* is (a) LIFO cost, (b) FIFO cost, (c) market, (d) lower of cost or market.

3. The inventory basis that would show the *lowest net income for the three years combined* is (a) LIFO cost, (b) FIFO cost, (c) market, (d) lower of cost or market.

4. For the year 19_5, how much higher or lower would profits be on the *FIFO cost basis* than on the *lower-of-cost-or-market basis?*
(a) $400 higher, (b) $400 lower, (c) $600 higher, (d) $600 lower, (e) $1,000 higher, (f) $1,000 lower, (g) $1,400 higher, (h) $1,400 lower.

5. On the basis of the information given, it appears that *the movement of prices* for items in the inventory was (a) up in 19_4 and down in 19_6, (b) up in both 19_4 and 19_6, (c) down in 19_4 and up in 19_6, (d) down in both 19_4 and 19_6.

22-14 ***Economic order quantity.*** Compute the economic order quantity for an inventory item with the following relevant data: annual requirements, 20,000 units; ordering cost, $16; and inventory carrying cost, $.10 per unit per annum.

22-15 ***Economic order quantity.*** (SMA, adapted) The XYZ Company has revised its procedure to improve control of materials, which represent 75 percent of the finished-product cost. Standard forms have been developed to effectively control the flow of materials throughout the operation.

Calculate the economic order quantity and the number of orders needed per year for the acquisition of blue bag cloth B.P. 12345.

AVAILABLE DATA

Annual requirements of cloth B.P. 12345	7,200 yards
Ordering cost	$12.50 per order
Carrying cost of inventory	20%
Safety-stock requirements	None
Unit cost of blue bag cloth B.P. 12345	$2.50 per yard

22-16 ***Reorder point and economic lot size.*** An automobile manufacturer has a planned usage of 500,000 automobile tires of a certain size during the next year. The incremental cost of placing an order is $8. The cost of storing one tire for one year is $2. Lead time on an order is five days, and the company is going to keep safety stock of two days' usage.

Usage is assumed to be constant over a 250-workday year.

REQUIRED

1. Calculate the reorder point.
2. Calculate the economic order quantity.
3. Graph the inventory level (Y-axis) against time (X-axis) through two complete inventory cycles. Show the reorder points.

22-17 ***Miscellaneous inventory-control computations.*** Lt. Brighteyes, supply officer at a remote radar site, has been informed that the lead time for his supplies will be reduced from the present 180 days to 90 days.

The maximum daily usage of 12AU6 pentodes has been 10 per day; average, 8 per day; minimum, 6 per day. Average inventory during the past two years has been 1,360 tubes. Determine the minimum inventory, reorder point, normal maximum stock level, absolute maximum stock level, and the economic order quantity that Lt. Brighteyes has been submitting.

Do the same for the new 90-day level, *assuming that the economic order size is unchanged.*

22-18 ***Relevant and irrelevant costs of carrying.*** A firm is introducing an inventory-control system designed to minimize inventory costs, subject to required customer service levels that are influenced, but not completely determined, by shortage-cost estimates. A large range of products is carried, but for the purposes of this preliminary study, the following item may be taken as "average" with regard to selling price and cost structure. However, this is not necessarily a high-volume item.

CURRENT DATA FOR ONE (AVERAGE) UNIT

Selling price	$20
Purchase-invoice cost	10
Road freight inward	1
Air freight inward	25

BUDGETS AND ESTIMATES (OTHER THAN DATA ABOVE)

Annual sales	$1.5 million
Advertising budget	5% of sales budget
Administration	$100,000 per year
Property costs (depreciation, etc.)	$50,000 per year
Interest and insurance on inventory	30% per year
Warehouse operating cost	$2,000 per week + $10 per incoming order (bought) + $1 per unit sold. (Note: The warehouse has spare capacity.)
Clerical and other office costs	$1,000 per week + $2 per purchase order processed + $1 per unit sold. (Note: Buying lead time is about 2 weeks by road and 1 day by air freight.)

REQUIRED

Estimate unit carrying and shortage (stockout) costs, and the relevant cost of a purchase order. State the assumptions necessary to support your conclusions; there may be more than one answer in some cases.

22-19 ***Economic order quantity; price discounts.*** A medium-sized manufacturing company uses 50 barrels of soap a year in one of its plants. It costs the company $1 a year to store a barrel, and a purchase order costs $10 to process.

The following discount schedule applies to the purchase price of the soap:

QUANTITY	DISCOUNT
1–9	None
10–49	$0.50 per barrel
50–99	$1.00 per barrel
100–up	$2.00 per barrel

Determine the economic order quantity, and briefly show why it is where it is.

22-20 ***Inventory planning and monthly cost savings.*** Grossman Drug Stores, Inc., buys a large, economy-sized toothpaste package to market under its own brand name. Monthly sales of this product in all of the company's stores are about 60,000 units and quite steady.

The company now purchases this item in lots of 60,000 at a unit price of $1 and delivery of 15 days. An 18,000-unit base inventory is kept at all times, so that the reorder point is 48,000 units.

The supplier has offered to sell Grossman Drug Stores, Inc., this item for 90¢ a unit if the company will increase the order size to 300,000 units and accept 30-day delivery. If it accepts this plan, it will still have to maintain an 18,000-unit minimum inventory.

If the company goes through with the proposed change, it will have to rent extra storage space at a cost of $6,000 per year. Other expenses associated with the increased space will total $4,000 per year.

Also, if the new plan is adopted, handling costs will be increased 83⅓¢ per hundred on units sold.

REQUIRED

1. Calculate the monthly savings (loss) if the new plan is adopted.
2. Grossman Drug Stores, Inc., expects, and can obtain, a return of 12 percent per annum on invested capital elsewhere. The company policy is to impute a 1 percent per month interest charge on average inventory investment in computing the net monthly saving. What is the monthly saving (or loss)? Would you recommend that the new plan be adopted?

22-21 ***EOQ and relevant costs.*** (CMA, adpated) Evans, Inc., is a large wholesale distributor dealing exclusively in baby shoes. Owing to the substantial costs related to ordering and storing the shoes, the company has decided to employ the economic-order-quantity method (EOQ) to help determine the optimum quantities of shoes to order from the different manufacturers.

Before Evans, Inc., can employ the EOQ model, it needs to develop values for two of the cost parameters, which it calls ordering costs (C_o) and storage costs (C_s). As a starting point, management has decided to develop the values for the two cost parameters by using cost data from the most recent fiscal year, 19_5.

The company placed 4,000 purchase orders during 19_5. The largest number of orders placed during any one month was 400 in June and the smallest number was 250 in December. Selected cost data for these two months and the year for the purchasing, accounts payable, and warehousing operations are shown at the top of the next page.

The purchasing department is responsible for placing all orders. The costs listed for the accounts payable department relate only to the processing of purchase orders for payment. The warehouse costs reflect two operations—receiving and shipping. The receiving clerks inspect all incoming shipments and place the orders in storage. The shipping clerks are responsible for processing all sales orders to retailers.

The company leases space in a public warehouse. The rental fee is priced according to the square feet occupied during a month. The annual charges during 19_5 totaled $34,500.

	COSTS FOR HIGH-ACTIVITY MONTH (JUNE; 400 ORDERS)	COSTS FOR LOW-ACTIVITY MONTH (DECEMBER; 250 ORDERS)	ANNUAL COSTS
Purchasing Department			
Purchasing manager	$ 1,750	$ 1,750	$ 21,000
Buyers	2,500	1,900	28,500
Clerks	2,000	1,100	20,600
Supplies	275	150	2,500
Accounts Payable Department			
Clerks	2,000	1,500	21,500
Supplies	125	75	1,100
Data processing	2,600	2,300	30,000
Warehouse			
Foreman	1,250	1,250	15,000
Receiving clerks	2,300	1,800	23,300
Receiving supplies	50	25	500
Shipping clerks	3,800	3,500	44,000
Shipping supplies	1,350	1,200	15,200
Freight out	1,600	1,300	16,800
	$21,600	$17,850	$240,000

Annual insurance and property taxes on the shoes stored in the warehouse amounted to $5,700 and $7,300, respectively. Investments are expected to produce a rate of return of 20 percent before taxes.

The inventory balances tend to fluctuate during the year, depending upon the demand for baby shoes. Selected data on inventory balances follow.

Inventory, January 1, 19_5	$160,000
Inventory, December 31, 19_5	120,000
Highest inventory balance (June)	220,000
Lowest inventory balance (December)	120,000
Average monthly inventory	190,000

The boxes in which the baby shoes are stored are all approximately the same size. Consequently, the shoes all occupy about the same amount of storage space in the warehouse.

REQUIRED

1. Using the 19_5 data, determine estimated values appropriate for
   a. C_o—cost of placing an order
   b. C_s—the annual cost of storage per dollar of investment in inventory
2. Should Evans, Inc., use the cost parameters developed solely from the historical data in the employment of the EOQ model? Explain your answer.

22-22 ***Inventory planning.*** (J. Patell) Acro-Cel Tool and Machine produces gongs under a long-term contract at an average rate of 200 gongs each month. However, the management of Acro-Cel feels that production runs of 200 gongs may not be economical, and it has asked you to determine an optimal production-inventory system. Each gong has a full (absorption) cost of $42, composed of:

Direct material	$20.00
Direct labor (2 hours at $8/hour)	16.00
Applied overhead*	6.00
	$42.00

**Applied overhead = $400 per month + $2 per labor hour.*

Acro-Cel incurs some other costs *not included* above. Each production run requires setup procedures that consume five hours of direct labor as well as variable overhead. Additionally, when the gongs are removed from inventory for delivery, they are inspected for flaws: The inspection crew is paid at the same rate of $8.00 per hour and can process 32 gongs per hour. Acro-Cel fire and theft insurance contains a clause covering the inventory, but the premium rate depends on the average value of inventory on hand: The annual premium is set at $0.20 per unit per year.

To protect against the possibility of missing a delivery, Acro-Cel will maintain a safety stock of 200 gongs. Acro-Cel aims for a return on capital employed in the business of 10 percent (before tax).

REQUIRED

1. What is the optimal production run size?
2. What is the amount of the dollar saving achieved by using the solution to requirement 1, compared with Acro-Cel's present practice of producing 200 gongs per run?

22-23 ***Inventory planning and control.*** (CPA) You have been engaged to install an accounting system for the Kaufman Corporation. Among the inventory-control features Kaufman desires as a part of the system are indicators of *how much* to order *when.* The following information is furnished for one item, called a komtronic, which is carried in inventory:

1. Komtronics are sold by the gross (twelve dozen) at a list price of $800 per gross f.o.b. shipper. Kaufman receives a 40 percent trade discount off list price on purchases in gross lots.

2. Freight cost is $20 per gross from the shipping point to Kaufman's plant.

3. Kaufman uses about 5,000 komtronics during a 259-day production year and must purchase a total of 36 gross per year to allow for normal breakage. Minimum and maximum usages are 12 and 28 komtronics per day, respectively.

4. Normal delivery time to receive an order is 20 working days from the date a purchase request is initiated. A rush order in full gross lots can be received by air freight in five working days at an extra cost of $52 per gross. A stockout (complete exhaustion of the inventory) of komtronics would stop production, and Kaufman would purchase komtronics locally at list price rather than shut down.

5. The cost of placing an order is $10; the cost of receiving an order is $20.

6. Space storage cost is $12 per year per gross stored.

7. Insurance and taxes are approximately 12 percent of the net delivered cost of average inventory, and Kaufman expects a return of at least 8 percent on its average investment (ignore return on order and carrying cost for simplicity).

REQUIRED

1. Prepare a schedule computing the total annual cost of komtronics based on uniform order lot sizes of one, two, three, four, five, and six gross of komtronics. (The schedule should show the total annual cost according to each lot size.) Indicate the economic order quantity (economic lot size to order).
2. Prepare a schedule computing the minimum-stock reorder point for komtronics. This is the point below which the komtronics inventory should not fall without reordering so as to guard against a stockout. Factors to be considered include average lead-period usage and safety-stock requirements.
3. Prepare a schedule computing the cost of a stockout of komtronics. Factors to be considered include the excess costs for local purchases and for rush orders.

22-24 ***Inventory control.*** (SMA, adapted) A large appliance manufacturing company markets its products through a number of sales divisions. Each division is decentralized and accountable for its profit contributions. Warehousing and manufacturing, however, is centralized. Warehousing and stockkeeping costs are charged to the divisions based on average divisional inventory levels. The rate during 19_3 was 20 percent and is not expected to change during 19_4. Only overapplied or underapplied overhead from the manufacturing operation is charged to divisions.

A decline in divisional profits in the residential sales division during 19_3 was caused by allocated charges from warehousing and from manufacturing. Apparently, the major portion of this allocated cost was incurred by one standard household product, "Clean-O-Matic."

Warehousing reported that 19_3 shipments to customers totaled 250,000 units, deliveries from Manufacturing averaged 5,000 units per week, over a 50 workweek period, and that the 19_3 safety stock was 80,000 units. The unit cost is $48, bringing the average inventory value of this product to $3,960,000. Furthermore, the raw-material inventory included a high-value part worth $12, of which two are required to manufacture one Clean-O-Matic. Parts were purchased in lots of 30,000 during 19_3. The safety stock is 90,000 parts.

Manufacturing reported that the underapplication charged to the residential division was caused by high setup costs for production runs of the Clean-O-Matics. One setup, including labor testing and spoilage, amounts to $720, or $36,000 for 50 production runs during 19_3.

The divisional sales manager recommended the following changes for 19_4:

Safety stock of Clean-O-Matics should gradually be reduced to 40,000 units by the end of 19_4.

Production runs should be larger to reduce total annual setup costs.

Safety stock of parts should be reduced to one average month (19_4) usage immediately, and the order size should be equal to the requirement for one production run.

Expected 19_4 sales: 280,000 Clean-O-Matics.

REQUIRED

1. Compute the 19_4 economic production lot size.
2. Assuming that the sales manager's recommendations can be implemented, calculate the divisional savings of warehousing costs in 19_4 over 19_3 for finished-goods and parts inventories. Assume that production runs for 19_4 are 6,000 units each. Show your calculations.

22-25 ***Reorder point, uncertainty, and safety stock.*** (CMA) The Starr Company manufactures several products. One of its main products requires an electric motor. The management of Starr Company uses the economic-order-quantity formula (EOQ) to determine the optimum number of motors to order. Management now wants to determine how much safety stock to order.

Starr Company uses 30,000 electric motors annually (300 working days.) Using the EOQ formula, the company orders 3,000 motors at a time. The lead time for an order is five days. The annual cost of carrying one motor in safety stock is $10. Management has also estimated that the cost of being out of stock is $20 for each motor they are short.

Starr Company has analyzed the usage during past reorder periods by examining the inventory records. The records indicate the following usage patterns:

USAGE DURING LEAD TIME	NUMBER OF TIMES QUANTITY WAS USED
440	6
460	12
480	16
500	130
520	20
540	10
560	6
	200

REQUIRED

1. Using an expected-value approach, determine the level of safety stock for electric motors that Starr Company should maintain in order to minimize costs. *Author's note:* When computing carrying costs, assume that the safety stock is on hand at all times and that there is no overstocking caused by decreases in expected usage.
2. What would be Starr Company's new reorder point?
3. What factors should Starr Company have considered to estimate the out-of-stock costs?

22-26 ***Cost of prediction error.*** Ralph Menard has used the classic economic-lot-size model (with no stockouts) to compute an optimal order quantity for each of his raw materials and acquired parts. He initially predicts an annual demand of 2,000 units. Each unit has a supplier purchase price of $50. The incremental cost of processing an order is $40. The incremental cost of storage is $4 per unit plus 10 percent of supplier purchase price.

REQUIRED

1. The total "relevant" or "associated" costs of this inventory policy.
2. Suppose that Ralph is precisely correct in all his predictions but is wrong about the purchase price. If he had been a faultless predictor, he would have foreseen that the

purchase price would have dropped to $30 at the beginning of the year and would have been unchanged throughout the year. What is the cost of the prediction error?

22-27 ***Prediction error.*** (J. Demski) Ralph Swash, an aggressive entrepreneur, is working on some make-or-buy decisions and a related inventory system. For one such product (and you may assume, for purposes of argument, that all such situations are independent), he decides to use the classic economic-lot-size model with *no* stockouts to determine an optimal order quantity. He initially predicts that annual demand will be 2,000 units, that each unit will cost $45, that the incremental cost of processing each order (and receiving the ordered goods) will be $67 in this case, and that the incremental cost of storage, in this case, will be $6 per physical unit per year.

1. What is the optimal order quantity?

2. What are the total relevant costs of inventory from following your policy in part 1 above?

3. Suppose that Swash is incorrect in his $67 incremental-cost-per-order prediction but is precisely correct in all other predictions. State and solve the equation to predict the maximum amount Swash should pay to discover the true incremental cost per order *if* (a) this true cost is $33 per order and (b) in the absence of any knowledge to the contrary, Swash will implement the solution in part 1 above and will not alter it for *one* full year.

4. What happens to your answer in part 3 above if we admit that Swash has also made errors in predicting demand, price, and the cost of storage?

5. Suppose Swash implements the solution in part 1 above for *two* years. Further suppose that all of his initial predictions were (and are) correct except that the actual incremental cost of storage is $20 per average unit. If it costs Swash a total of $4 to alter his inventory policy, state the equation to determine the cost of prediction error of not changing his inventory policy at the beginning of the second year. *Note:* You may assume that the inventory cycle precisely repeats every year; otherwise you would have to adjust for nonintegral values.

22-28 ***Performance and motivation.*** Refer to Problem 22-27.

1. Assume that Ralph is approached at the beginning of the period and offered 2,000 units at $44 each as a bargain one-shot purchase. The units will be delivered immediately and placed in Ralph's warehouse by the vendor, so Ralph's P = zero. What are the costs of this policy? Use the same approach as in 22-27, part 2.

2. Now assume that you used a "typical" standard costing system to judge performance. Suppose that the *budget* for 19_1 was based on the answer in 22-27, part 2. But on January 1 the purchasing agent chose the one-shot alternative. What variances and amounts would appear on his performance report?

22-29 ***Perfect information and inventory control.*** (J. Demski) This problem assumes that you are familiar with Chapter 21 and Appendixes 21a and 21b. The latter begins on p. 732.

Ralph is a consultant. His client uses the economic-order-quantity model (with no stockouts). A particular raw-material item is now under study. The annual requirement is 40,000 units. The item costs $40 per unit, and delivery costs average $10 per unit. Processing an order requires 3 hours of labor and consumes $5 of miscellaneous materials. Labor costs $8 per hour; in addition, variable overhead averages $7 per hour of labor. No storage costs other than the opportunity cost of 8 percent per year are involved.

1. Determine the optimal order quantity *and* the minimum relevant annual cost associated with the optimal policy.

2. Ralph questions the variable overhead rate. In consultation with the client, he decides that the variable overhead rate is either $5 per labor-hour, $7 per labor-hour, or $9 per labor-hour. Assuming each value to be equally probable, compute the expected value (per annum) of discovering the actual variable overhead (per labor-hour) *before* the policy in part 1 above is implemented.

22-30 ***Relevant costs of inventory planning; sensitivity analysis.*** (G. Feltham) The Super Corporation distributes widgets to the upper delta region of the Sunswop River. The demand for widgets is very constant and Super is able to predict the annual demand with considerable accuracy. The predicted demand for the next couple of years is 200,000 widgets per year.

Super purchases its widgets from a supplier in Calton at a price of $20 per widget. In order to transport the purchases from Calton to the upper delta region, Super must charter a ship. The charter services usually charge $1,000 per trip plus $2 per widget (this includes the cost of loading the ship). The ships have a capacity of 10,000 widgets. The placing of each order, including arranging for the ship, requires about 5 hours of employee time. It takes about a week for an order to arrive at the Super warehouse.

When a ship arrives at the Super warehouse, the widgets can be unloaded at a rate of 25 per hour per employee. The unloading equipment used by each employee is rented from a local supplier at a rate of $5 per hour. Supervisory time for each shipload is about 4 hours.

Super leases a large warehouse for storing the widgets; it has a capacity of 15,000 widgets. The employees working in the warehouse have several tasks:

a. Placing the widgets into storage, after they are unloaded, can be done at the rate of about 40 per hour.

b. Checking, cleaning, etc., of the widgets in inventory requires about one-half hour per widget per year.

c. Removing a widget from inventory and preparing it for shipment to a customer requires about one-eighth hour.

d. Security guards, general maintenance, etc., require about 10,000 hours per year.

The average cost per hour of labor is approximately $10 (including fringe benefits). Super has developed the following prediction equation for its general overhead (excluding shipping materials, fringe benefits, and equipment rental):

Predicted overhead for the year = $1,000,000 + ($8 × Total labor hours)

The materials used to ship one widget to a customer cost $1, and the delivery costs average out to about $2 per widget.

The company requires a before-tax rate of return of 20 percent on its investment.

REQUIRED

1. Super has decided to base its ordering policy on an EOQ model. What amount should it order each time and what should it use as the reorder point? Show all calculations.
2. If the true overhead prediction equation is

   $800,000 + ($12 × Total labor hours)

   what is the cost of the prediction error?

22-31 ***Comprehensive study of inventory planning and control.*** The Ward Company is trying to obtain better means of controlling inventory levels and attendant costs for an expensive part that it has been using for some time. Studies of cost behavior patterns reveal the following information:

Variable costs of placing and following up purchase orders (stationery, postage, telephone, etc.) total $3 per order. Other clerical costs, such as salaries and related office-equipment expenses, have a step cost behavior as follows: For every additional 200 orders processed per week, there is a $70 increase in purchasing costs, a $60 increase in accounting costs, and an $80 increase in receiving costs.

Insurance and taxes on inventory are 4 percent of average inventory value per year.

The factory is rented at a cost of $60,000 per year. It contains 100,000 square feet of floor space, of which 3,000 square feet are reserved for storing this item. Excess storage space is available in the neighborhood at 75¢ per square foot per year. Extra handling costs for using excess storage space will be 2½¢ per inventory unit in excess storage space per year. The article requires storage space, allowing for aisles, of three square feet each and can be stacked six units high.

Breakage, obsolescence, and deterioration amount to about 2 percent of average inventory per year.

The company's average before-tax cost of capital is 10 percent per annum. The company uses this rate for inventory-investment decisions.

The Ward Company works 52 weeks a year, 5 days per week. It uses an average of 100 subassemblies per workday, but usage fluctuates from as low as 50 to as high as 150 per day. Many suppliers are available; but regardless of the source of supply and the size of the order, it will take two weeks from the time a purchase order is placed until delivery. Top management wants to keep an ordinary minimum stock of 1,500 units.

The purchasing agent is anxious to take advantage of savings in unit invoice and freight costs by purchasing in large quantities. Pertinent purchasing data are as follows:

	INVOICE COST		FREIGHT COST	
LOT SIZE	**unit cost**	**total cost**	**unit cost**	**total cost**
1,000	$55.00	$ 55,000.00	$5.00	$ 5,000.00
2,000	55.00	110,000.00	5.00	10,000.00
4,000	55.00	220,000.00	5.00	20,000.00
5,000	54.00	270,000.00	5.00	25,000.00
6,000	54.00	324,000.00	4.40	26,400.00
8,000	54.00	432,000.00	4.00	32,000.00
10,000	54.00	540,000.00	3.80	38,000.00
13,000	53.50	695,500.00	3.80	49,400.00
26,000	52.00	1,352,000.00	3.50	91,000.00

Special note: Assume that the base stock is already on hand and is therefore irrelevant. The average inventory that is relevant is exclusive of the base. Assume, too, that the maximum inventory to be computed for commitments to excess storage space will be the *absolute* maximum, computed as follows: order point less minimum usage + standard order.

REQUIRED

1. What order size should the Ward Company use? Support your answer by tabular analysis of the relevant costs for each lot size given above from 1,000 to 26,000.
2. What considerations other than the quantitative data may influence the decision here?
3. Comment on the cost behavior patterns in the situation. Which costs appear to be the most crucial?

23 Cost Accounting and Linear Programming

As management decisions have become more closely studied, mathematical models have become more widely adopted; examples discussed in other chapters include discounted cash-flow models for capital-budgeting decisions, control models for inventory decisions, and regression models for estimating cost behavior patterns. To avoid groping in the dark, accountants and managers must be able to interpret the inputs, outputs, assumptions, and limitations of these models. The ultimate usefulness of these decision models depends on their key ingredients—which are often accounting data. In particular, users should be conscious of the effects of measurement errors on decisions.

Linear programming (hereafter often referred to as LP) will be the last formal decision model discussed in this book. Our basic approach is not altered. We examine the model and explore its implications for accounting systems and measurements. Our cost-benefit theme persists; the worth of formal models and more elaborate systems ultimately depends on whether decisions will be collectively improved.

The rudiments of LP are discussed, but the focus is on the interpretation of the solutions, not on the procedures for obtaining the solutions. Of course, books on quantitative methods should be consulted if you wish to develop a solid grasp of resource allocation models like LP.

The linear-programming model[1]

Although the **linear-programming** model may be used in a variety of decision contexts, its most widespread use is as a short-run allocation model. **All such short-run models assume that a fixed set of resources is available that generates a specified level of fixed costs. The objective is to decide on what types and amounts of products or services to produce or sell in the face of revenue and cost behavior regarding the given set of resources.** Practical examples of LP applications include blending gasoline, scheduling flights, formulating shipping schedules, and setting production schedules.

previous chapters

The relationships of costs to volume and to profits were introduced in Chapter 3. That chapter dealt mostly with a single product or a combination of products being sold without restriction. The focus was on maximizing contribution margin, given a level of fixed costs.

An example in Chapter 11 (page 373) pointed out that the choice of what product to emphasize is not dependent on contribution margins alone. That is, the most profitable product is not necessarily the product with the highest gross profit or contribution margin per unit of *product.* Instead, the preferable product is that which produces the largest contribution per unit of the scarce resource or constraining factor, such as total available machine-hours.

The basic idea propounded in Chapter 11 still holds, but in practice there is usually more than one constraint. **Therefore, the problem becomes one of maximizing total contribution, given many constraints.** The LP model is designed to provide a solution to such problems.

The focus remains on the contribution margin. Such a focus avoids allocation of fixed costs, which are irrelevant, given the assumptions of the LP model.[2]

building the model

All of us are familiar with linear equations (for example, $X + 3 = 9$). We also know that simultaneous linear equations become progressively more difficult to solve with pencil and paper as the number of equations (and unknowns) increases. LP essentially involves (a) constructing a set of simultaneous linear equations and inequalities, which represent the model of the problem and which include many variables; and (b) solving the equations with the help of the digital computer.

The formulation of the equations—that is, the building of the model—is far more challenging than the mechanics of the solution. The model aims at being a valid

[1]If you are familiar with linear programming, skip these sections and jump to the section "Implications for managers and accountants," page 791.

[2]To be relevant, fixed costs must be clearly *traceable* to the product and be *avoidable* if the product is discontinued. Such situations are beyond the capability of the LP model. A more complex model called the "fixed charge problem" must be used; it is a special case of mixed-integer programming models. The model provides for finding the product mix that maximizes contribution margin less avoidable fixed costs. See R. Kaplan, *Advanced Management Accounting* (Englewood Cliffs, N.J.: Prentice-Hall, 1982), Chap. 5.

and accurate portrayal of the problem. Computer programs can then take the equations and process the solution.

As a minimum, accountants and managers should be able to recognize the types of problems in their organizations that are most susceptible to analysis by linear programming. They should also be able to help in the construction of the model—that is, in specifying the objective, the constraints, and the variables. Ideally, they should understand the mathematics and should be able to communicate effectively with the operations researchers who are attempting to express the problem mathematically. **However, the position taken here is that the accountant and the manager should concentrate on the formulation of the model** and not worry too much about the technical intricacies of the solution. The latter may be delegated to the mathematicians; the feasibility of delegating the former is highly doubtful.

Consider a company that has two departments, machining and finishing. This company makes two products, A and B, each of which requires processing in each of two departments, machining and finishing. There are 200 hours of machining capacity and 120 hours of finishing capacity available per day. Product A requires 1 hour of machining time per unit and 1 hour of finishing time per unit. Therefore, the daily capacities for A are 200 product units for machining and 120 for finishing. However, Product B requires 2 hours of machining time per unit, but only .6 hours of finishing time per unit. Therefore, the daily capacities for B are $200 \div 2 = 100$ product units for machining and $120 \div .6 = 200$ for finishing. These and other relevant data are summarized as follows:

PRODUCTS	CAPACITIES (PER DAY) IN PRODUCT UNITS		CONTRIBUTION MARGIN PER UNIT
	dept. 1 machining	**dept. 2 finishing**	
A	200	120	$2.00
or			
B	100	200	$2.50

Severe material shortages for Product B will limit its production to a maximum of 90 per day. How many units of each product should be produced each day to obtain the maximum profit?

The LP approach has the following basic pattern, although variations and shortcuts are available in particular situations:

1. Determine the objective. Usually this takes the form of either maximization of profit or minimization of cost. Technically, this objective is usually expressed as an **objective function.**
2. Determine basic relationships in the situation, especially the constraints (which specify the available or *feasible* alternatives).
3. Compute the optimum solution. Techniques may vary here. In uncomplicated situations, the graphic approach is easiest to see. However, algebraic approaches are more widely used in practice.

Using our example, let's apply these steps.

1. *Determine the objective.* The objective here will be to find the product combination that maximizes *total* contribution margin. This can be expressed in equation form as follows: $\$2.00A + \$2.50B =$ Total contribution margin, where A equals the number of A

EXHIBIT 23-1

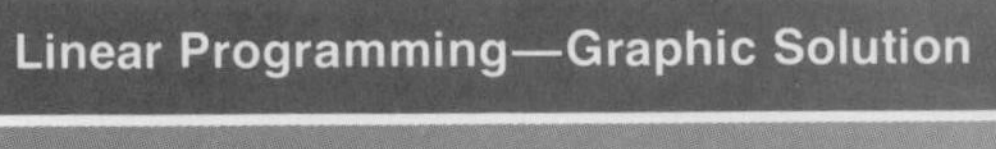

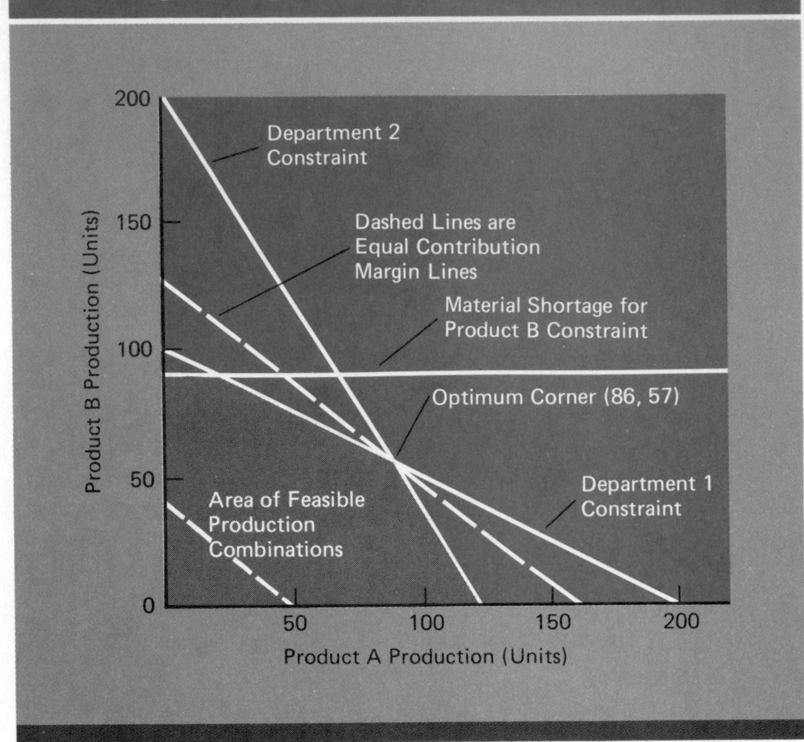

product units and B the number of B product units. We want to maximize this objective function.

2. *Determine the basic relationships.* The relationships here can be depicted by inequalities as follows:

Department 1:	$A + 2B \leq 200$
Department 2:	$A + .6B \leq 120$
Material shortage for Product B:	$B \leq 90$
Because negative production is impossible,	$B \geq 0$ and $A \geq 0$

The three solid lines on the graph in Exhibit 23-1 will aid visualization of the existing constraints for Departments 1 and 2 and of the material shortage.[3] The feasible alternatives are those that are technically possible. We do not want to bother with useless computations for impossible alternatives. The shaded area in Exhibit 23-1 shows the boundaries of those product combinations that are feasible—that is, combinations of quantities of A and B that satisfy all the constraining factors.

3. *Compute optimum solution.* In step 2 we have concentrated on physical relationships alone. Now we return to the economic relationships expressed as the objective in step 1.

graphic solution **In the graphic solution, the optimum solution must lie on one of the corners of the "area of feasible product combinations."** Why must the best solution lie on a corner? Consider all possible combinations that will produce an equal total contribution margin, say, a total contribution margin of \$100 (\$2.00A + \$2.50B = \$100). This is a straight dashed line through (50, 0) and (0, 40). Other equal total contribution margins can be represented by lines parallel to this one. The equal total contribution margins

[3]As an example of how the lines are plotted in Exhibit 23-1, use equal signs instead of inequality signs and assume for Department 1 that $B = 0$; then $A = 200$. Assume that $A = 0$; then $B = 100$. Connect those two points with a straight line.

increase as the lines get farther from the origin. The optimum dashed line is the one farthest from the origin that has a feasible point on it; this happens at a corner (86, 57). This will become apparent if you put a ruler on the graph and move it outward from the origin and parallel with the $100 line. In general, the optimal solution lies at the corner where the dashed line intersects an *extreme point* of the area of feasible combinations.[4]

The slope of the objective function (the dashed line representing the equal total contribution margin, *TCM*) can be computed from the equation

$$TCM = \$2.00A + \$2.50B$$

To find the slope (the rate of change of *B* for one additional unit of *A*),[5] divide by the coefficient of *B* and transfer *B* to the left-hand side of the equation:

$$\frac{TCM}{\$2.50} = \frac{\$2.00}{\$2.50}A + B$$

$$B = \frac{TCM}{\$2.50} - \frac{\$2.00}{\$2.50}A$$

Therefore, the slope of the objective function is a negative $2.00/$2.50, or $-\frac{4}{5}$.

trial and error The same result can be accomplished by trial and error, usually by working with coordinates of the corners of the polygon delineated by the constraints. The steps are simple:

a. Start with any set of corner points and compute the total contribution margin.

b. Move to another corner to see if it will improve the result in *a*. Keep moving from corner to corner until no further improvement is possible.[6]

---

[4]An exception occurs if the dashed line has the same slope as a constraint line. Then any combination along the intersection of the dashed line and constraint line would provide the same maximum total contribution margin.

[5]If desired, the slope can also be expressed in terms of the rate of change of *A* for one additional unit of *B*.

[6]This is a simplified version of the *simplex* method, which is described later in this chapter. Note in this example that the optimum point (86, 57) can be solved algebraically by solving the two pertinent constraint inequalities as simultaneous equations:

(1) $A + 2B = 200$

(2) $A + .6B = 120$

Subtract (2) from (1): $2B - .6B = 200 - 120$

$1.4B = 80$

$B = 80 \div 1.4 = 57$

Substitute for *B* in (1): $A + (2)(57) = 200$

$B = 200 - 114 = 86$

This approach is not recommended. It provides a solution that maximizes the total number of *physical units,* but it ignores the critical role of the *contribution per unit.* However, this approach is useful in locating the exact coordinates of corners that are needed for solving a simple LP problem by trial computations, corner by corner.

These computations, corner by corner, are summarized as follows:

TRIAL	CORNER	COMBINATION product A	product B	TOTAL CONTRIBUTION MARGIN
1	0,0	0	0	\$2.00(0) + \$2.50(0) = \$ 0
2	0,90	0	90	2.00(0) + 2.50(90) = 225.00
3	20,90	20	90	2.00(20) + 2.50(90) = 265.00
4	86,57	86	57	2.00(86) + 2.50(57) = 314.50*
5	120,0	120	0	2.00(120) + 2.50(0) = 240.00

**Optimum*

Substitution of scarce resources

At the outset of this example, the reader may have jumped to the conclusion that production of Product B, which promises the most margin *per unit,* should be maximized. Then any remaining productive capacity should be devoted to Product A. This is fallacious reasoning, because the scarce factor is productive capacity. **The key to the optimum solution rests in the relative rates of substitution and profitability per unit (hour or day) of *productive capacity*.** This point becomes clearer if we examine the graph. Moving from corner (20, 90) to corner (86, 57) implies that the company is transferring the scarce resource (productive capacity) between the products. In Department 1, each productive hour devoted to one unit of Product B may be given (sacrificed or traded) for two units of Product A. Will this exchange add to profitability? Yes, as shown below:

Total contribution margin at corner (20, 90)		\$265.00
Added contribution margin from Product A:		
86-20 or 66 more units @ \$2.00	\$132.00	
Loss contribution margin, Product B:		
57-90 or 33 less units @ \$2.50	82.50	
Net additional contribution		49.50
Total contribution margin at corner (86, 57)		\$314.50

As we move from corner (20, 90) to corner (86, 57), we are contending with the Department 1 constraint. There is a net advantage of trading two units of A for one unit of B; such substitution will add \$1.50 to the total contribution (receive two times \$2.00, or \$4.00, instead of one times \$2.50). The increase in total contribution, as shown above, is \$49.50.

But the advantage of substituting A for B reverses when the Department 2 constraint takes effect. As we move from corner (86, 57) to corner (120, 0), the rate of substitution may be stated as follows: Each productive hour devoted to one unit of Product B may be devoted to .6 of a unit of Product A. This would entail giving up \$2.50 contribution margin in exchange for .6(\$2.00) or \$1.20 contribution margin, a decrease of the total contribution margin of \$1.30 for each unit of Product B given up. Therefore, corner (86, 57) is the optimum solution.

Note again that the heart of the substitutions discussed above is a matter of swapping a given contribution margin per unit of *scarce resource* for some other contribution margin per unit of *scarce resource;* it is not simply a matter of comparing margins per unit of *product.*

Implications for managers and accountants

Like all formal decision models, LP models are subject to measurement errors and other limitations that often have important implications for managers and accountants.

sensitivity analysis

What are the implications of a faulty estimate of the revenue, cost, or **technical coefficients**[7] used in the LP model? **These accounting and engineering measurements inevitably affect the slope of the objective function, the equal-contribution line in our example, and also affect the area of feasible product combinations.** Questions about measurement errors are frequently explored via sensitivity analysis, as we have done in previous chapters.

Errors in approximations of costs and revenues per unit may reduce or increase unit-contribution margins but may not tilt the slope of the equal-contribution line enough to alter the optimal solution. That is, the slope of the equal-contribution line may change, but when the line is pushed outward from the origin, the extreme corner can be the same as before. Thus, the optimal decision about product mix may be unchanged, even though the total contribution margin is affected.

Reconsider the material costs for Product A in our illustration. Management is concerned that its material costs for A will be, say, \$10.00 instead of the \$9.50 used in computing the \$2.00 contribution appearing in the original solution. What is the cost of the prediction error?

The contribution margin for A would become \$1.50 instead of \$2.00. The new optimal solution can be found by either graphic means or by corner computations, as before. The slope of the equal-contribution line, the objective function, would change from the $-4/5$ in Exhibit 23-1 to $-3/5$.[8] The new optimal solution would be unchanged,[9] so the cost of the prediction error would be zero (that is, the decision would be the same regardless of this particular error).

The next obvious question is, How much measurement error can be tolerated before the optimal choice would change? That is, what is the critical value, the value where the (86, 57) combination is no longer optimal? Concentrate on the constraint for Department 1. If the slope of the objective function is the same as that constraint, optimal solutions will be identical all along that constraint as long as it is binding. For example, if the contribution of Product A falls to \$1.25, the objective function will be $\$1.25A + \$2.50B$, which is the same slope as the constraint for Department 1. Then the total contribution would be the same for corners (20, 90) and (86, 57):

CORNER	TOTAL CONTRIBUTION MARGIN
20, 90	\$1.25(20) + \$2.50(90) = \$250
86, 57	1.25(86) + 2.50(57) = 250

---

[7] The coefficients of the constraints are often called *technical coefficients*. For example, in Department 1 the technical coefficient of A is 1 hour and the technical coefficient of B is 2 hours.

[8] The computation of the slope shown earlier would be altered by substituting \$1.50 for the \$2.00 used in the original computation.

[9]

CORNER	TOTAL CONTRIBUTION MARGIN
20, 90	\$1.50(20) + \$2.50(90) = \$255
86, 57	1.50(86) + 2.50(57) = 272*

**Optimum*

Suppose the material cost were $.90 higher than originally expected. Then the contribution margin for A would become $1.10 instead of $2.00. The slope of the objective function would change from $-4/5$ to $-11/25$. The new optimal solution would be different. If you put a ruler on the graph and move it outward from the origin using a $-11/25$ slope, the optimum corner will now be (20, 90), providing a contribution of $247. The cost of the prediction error[10] would be:

(1)	Given the critical parameter, the optimal original decision was (86,57)	
(2)	Alternative parameter, the contribution margin would be $1.10 rather than $2.00 per unit of A:	
	Optimal new decision would be (20,90)	
	Financial results, contribution margin, $1.10(20) + $2.50(90)	$247
(3)	Given the original decision in step 1 and the alternative parameter in step 2, compute the financial results, contribution margin, $1.10(86) + $2.50(57)	237
(4)	Cost of prediction error, step 2 minus step 3	$ 10

effects of other costs

In the illustration above, the original solution is relatively insensitive to errors in predicting material costs. Of course, other complexities could be introduced. For example, the material costs of both A and B might change simultaneously. Moreover, a change in labor productivity would affect both the unit contribution margins and the technical coefficients. You can easily imagine more complicated situations where heavy interdependencies (many constraints and many products) might make the action choices very sensitive.

Regardless of what decision model is used, the impact of sensitivity analysis is usually the same. **If the prediction errors may prove costly, more resources may be spent initially to enhance the accuracy of the predictions before an action choice (decision) is made.** Also, once the choice is made, extra efforts may be made to implement the choice so that the predicted outcomes (for example, costs or production volumes) are achieved. Such endeavors are economically justifiable when the costs of prediction errors are sufficiently alarming. Indeed, when optimal actions are very sensitive to measurement errors, the formal model can be linked to the accounting control system.[11]

shadow prices

The output of computer programs frequently provides **shadow prices,** which are measures of the contributions forgone by failing to have one more unit of scarce capacity in a particular situation. Thus, a shadow price of $1 for machining means that the total contribution margin of the firm would increase by $1 if machining capacity were increased by one unit. Therefore, shadow prices facilitate the computation of the possible changes in total contribution margin from expansion of capacity.

Despite their ready availability, shadow prices should be interpreted cautiously. They are valid quantifications of opportunity costs provided that the basic solution (the chosen types of products and idle facilities) does not change. For example, the shadow prices would not change as long as some A, some B, and some idle facilities were present. But the shadow prices would change if either all A or all B became the optimal solution.

---

[10]Appendix 21a describes how to compute the cost of a prediction error. See page 732.

[11]See J. Demski, "Variance Analysis Using a Constrained Linear Model," in D. Solomons, ed., *Studies in Cost Analysis* (Homewood, Ill.: Richard D. Irwin, 1968), pp. 526–40.

assumptions and limitations Among the major assumptions underlying the LP model are:

1. All relationships are linear. (For a discussion of linearity, see Chapter 9.)
2. All constraints and coefficients are stated with certainty—that is, are known magnitudes. (However, probabilities may be used to forecast the specific magnitudes that are used in the construction of the LP model.)
3. Solutions in fractional units are permissible. (Otherwise, rounding is performed;[12] or integer programming may be desirable, whereby only whole-number solutions are allowed.)

Few actual situations completely satisfy these assumptions. Therefore, the user must be on guard that the approximations of the LP model are simplifications that are tolerable in relation to their impact on the particular decisions faced. The key question is whether some costly blunders may be made as a result of choosing the wrong decision model or as a result of various measurement errors.

Simplex method

The fundamental problem of linear programming is to discover the specific set of variables that satisfies all constraints and maximizes (or minimizes) the objective sought. Although graphical methods aid visualization and are useful for two or possibly three variables, they are impractical where many variables exist. The **simplex method,** a general technique for solving any linear-programming problem, is an iterative, step-by-step process that is very effective, especially when a digitial computer performs the calculations. Basically, the simplex method proceeds by solving sets of simultaneous equations where the number of unknowns in each set is equal to the number of constraints. Although it is much too detailed to be described here, the simplex method essentially starts with a specific feasible alternative and algebraically tests it by substitution to see if the solution can be improved. These substitutions continue until no further improvement is possible, and thus the optimum solution is obtained.

Computer programs can accommodate a large number of variables and constraints. Therefore, users such as accountants or managers should concentrate on the construction of the model and on the validity of its inputs—the statement of the

---

[12]For example, rounding occurred in this chapter's illustration. The original optimum solution was really (85.714, 57.14286). Strictly speaking, the (86,57) rounded solution does not satisfy the second constraint: 86 + .6(57) = 120.2. Similarly, the optimum contribution margin is

$$\$2.00(85.714) + \$2.50(57.14286) = \$314.28515, \text{ not } \$314.50.$$

Finally, using unrounded numbers, the shadow price for one more hour of machining capacity is $0.92914, not $1:

$$\begin{aligned} A + 2B &\leq 201 \\ A + .6B &\leq 120 \\ B &= 57.857142 \\ A &= 85.28572 \end{aligned}$$

Total contribution margin would be:	
$2.00(85.28572) + $2.50(57.857142) =	$315.21429
Compared with original optimum	314.28515
Shadow price	$ 0.92914

objective function, the constraints, the estimation of all magnitudes employed. For example, are plant capacities and unit-contribution margins accurately measured?

SUMMARY

The linear-programming model is a widely used formal decision model for deciding how to optimize the use of a given set of scarce resources in the face of interdependencies and constraints. Accountants and managers should be especially alert to the sensitivity of the LP solution to possible measurement errors of all parameters of the model—the technical coefficients (resource required per unit), constant terms (total capacities) in the constraint equations, and the coefficients (e.g., unit-contribution margin) of the objective function.

SUGGESTED READINGS

BIERMAN, HAROLD, and THOMAS R. DYCKMAN, **Managerial Cost Accounting,** 2nd ed. New York: Macmillan, 1976.

DEMSKI, JOEL S., **Information Analysis,** 2nd ed. Reading, Mass.: Addison-Wesley, 1980.

EPPEN, G., and F. GOULD, **Quantitative Concepts for Management.** Englewood Cliffs, N.J.: Prentice-Hall, 1979.

FELTHAM, GERALD A., **Information Evaluation.** Sarasota, Fla.: American Accounting Association, 1972.

KAPLAN, ROBERT S., **Advanced Management Accounting.** Englewood Cliffs, N.J.: Prentice-Hall, 1982, especially Chapter 5.

WAGNER, HARVEY M. **Principles of Operations Research with Applications to Managerial Decisions,** 2nd ed. Englewood Cliffs, N.J.: Prentice-Hall, 1975.

PROBLEM FOR SELF-STUDY

problem

Reconsider the illustration in the chapter. Suppose the production rate for Product A in Department 1 will be 400 per day instead of 200. The relevant conversion cost (direct labor and overhead) for Department 1 regarding Product A in the original solution was assumed to be $1,600 per day, which was $8.00 per product unit. The total conversion cost of $1,600 per day is unchanged. What is the cost of the prediction error?

solution

The conversion cost for Product A would be reduced from $8.00 per unit to $1,600 ÷ 400 = $4.00 per unit. Thus, the contribution margin for A would be increased from $2.00 to $6.00 per unit. In addition, the machining time for Product A would be reduced to 200 ÷ 400 = .5 hour per product unit. Therefore, the objective function and the constraint for Department 1 would change:

$$\textbf{Total contribution margin} = \$6.00A + \$2.50B$$
$$\textbf{Department 1:} \quad .5A + 2B \leq 200$$

The new relationships are shown in Exhibit 23-2. Note that the new slope of the objective function is −6.00/2.50, or −2.4, which is steeper than the slope of the Department 2 constraint. This means that as you push the equal-total-contribution line outward from the origin, the most extreme feasible point will be (120, 0), providing a total contribution margin of $6 × 120 units, or $720.

EXHIBIT 23-2

Linear Programming—Revised Graphic Solution

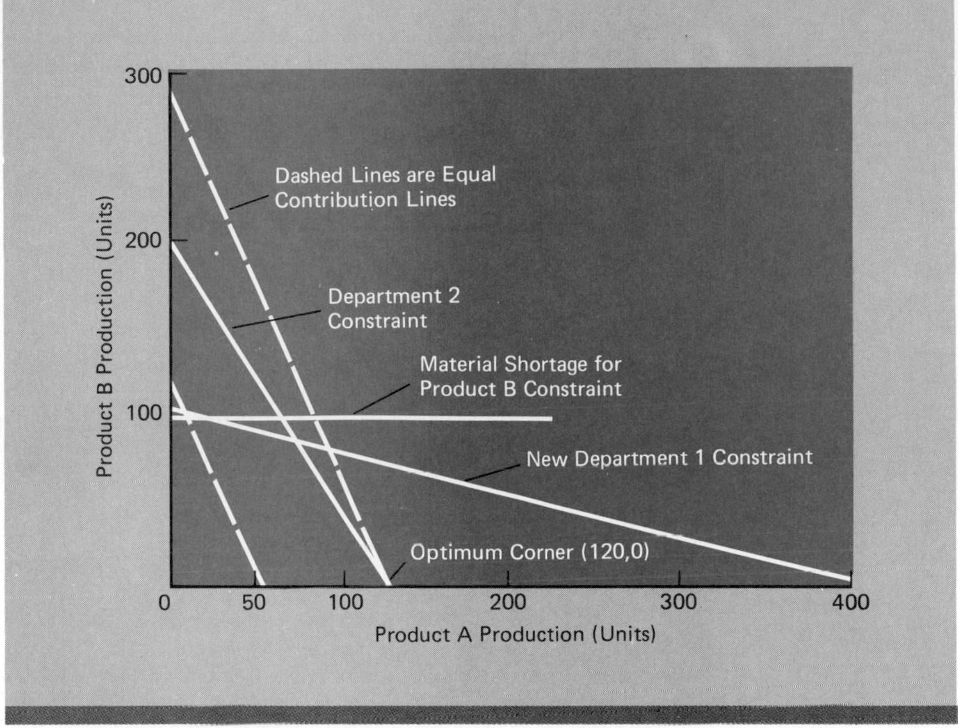

The cost of the prediction error is:

(1) Original decision, given original parameter: (86, 57)	
(2) Results of optimal decision, given alternative parameters	$720
(3) Results of original decision, using alternative parameters: $6.00(86) + $2.50(57) or $516 + $143	659
(4) Cost of prediction error, step 2 minus step 3	$ 61

Terms to Learn

linear programming (LP) ***objective function*** ***shadow prices***
simplex method ***technical coefficients***

Special Points and Pitfalls

The linear-programming model is often regarded as a multiple-product extension of the cost-volume-profit model that was introduced in Chapter 3. In addition, it extends the resource-allocation model that was introduced in Chapter 11, where only one constraint was discussed.

Accountants and managers should periodically remind themselves that LP solutions may be highly sensitive to the measurements of the costs used in the model.

QUESTIONS, PROBLEMS, AND CASES

23-1 Give five examples of business applications of linear programming.

23-2 What are the four basic steps in linear programming?

23-3 List three assumptions underlying the LP model.

23-4 "The objective function in an LP model must be to achieve a maximum contribution margin or similar measure of profit." Do you agree? Explain.

23-5 "Measurement error in an LP model can be tolerated as long as the cost of the prediction error is zero." Do you agree? Explain.

23-6 "Fixed costs are irrelevant in LP models." Do you agree? Explain.

23-7 "The LP model is an extension of the cost-volume-profit model." Do you agree? Explain.

23-8 ***Allocation of machine time.*** Machine 1 has 24 hours available time and Machine 2 has 20 hours for processing the two products. Product X yields a contribution margin of $2 per unit; Product Y, $1 per unit. These products must be sold in proportions such that the quantity of X will be equal to or less than the quantity of Y. X requires 6 hours processing time on Machine 1 and 10 hours' time on Machine 2. Product Y requires 4 hours' time on Machine 1 only.

REQUIRED Using graphic techniques, determine which product combination will maximize profit. Express the relationships in mathematical form.

23-9 ***Finding optimal mixture for box of chocolates.*** (Adapted from D. W. Miller and M. K. Starr, *Executive Decisions and Operations Research,* 2nd ed. (Englewood Cliffs, N.J.: Prentice-Hall, 1975), pp. 217–22.) A candy manufacturer is attempting to find the optimal mixture for a box of chocolates. There are two kinds of candy that he wants in the box, C_1 and C_2. The following are the characteristics of the candy and the box:

	C_1	C_2	BOX
Number of pieces	x	y	35 or greater
Weight per piece (oz.)	1.6	0.8	32 or more
Space per piece (sq. in.)	2.0	1.0	65*
Cost per piece	$.20	$.10	$6.00 maximum

**Maximum. By the use of fillers, the box can range from 40 square inches to 65 square inches.*

REQUIRED Find the optimal mixture (least cost) by graphic means.

23-10 ***Adding another constraint.*** Assume the same facts and requirements as in 23-9 except that at least 10 pieces of C_1 must be in the mixture.

23-11 ***Linear programming and minimum cost.*** The local agricultural center has advised Sam Bowers to spread at least 4,800 pounds of a special nitrogen fertilizer ingredient and at least 5,000 pounds of a special phosphate fertilizer ingredient in order to increase his crops. Neither ingredient is available in pure form.

A dealer has offered 100-pound bags of VIM at $1 each. VIM contains the equivalent of 20 pounds of nitrogen and 80 pounds of phosphate. VOOM is also available in 100-pound bags, at $3 each; it contains the equivalent of 75 pounds of nitrogen and 25 pounds of phosphate.

Express the relationships as inequalities. How many bags of VIM and VOOM should Bowers buy in order to obtain the required fertilizer at minimum cost? Solve graphically.

23-12 ***Formulate objective function.*** (SMA) Z LTD. produces two products, A and B. Product A sells for $50 per unit and requires 3 hours of direct-labor time to produce. Product B sells for $30 per unit and requires 2 hours of direct-labor time. Assume, for simplicity, that direct labor is the only variable production cost. The cost of direct labor is $7 per hour.

Fixed costs of Z LTD. are $500 per period.

Owing to the specialized nature of Z LTD.'s direct-labor requirements, the amount of direct labor available for production cannot be varied in the short run. For next period the maximum number of direct-labor hours available is 120 hours.

Z LTD.'s marketing expert advises that the maximum number of units that could be sold next period is 30 units of A and 45 units of B.

REQUIRED

1. Z LTD. must decide how many units of A and B to produce next period in order to maximize its profit. To assist in this decision problem you are asked to formulate it as a linear-programming problem—i.e., set up the objective function and the constraints. You are not required to solve the problem.
2. A linear-programming problem is an example of a *deterministic* model; i.e., the various numbers and relationships within the model are assumed to be known with certainty. Given, however, that most firms operate in an uncertain environment, do you think that it is wise to ignore uncertainty in decisions such as this? Why?

23-13 ***Formulate objective function.*** (CMA, adapted) The Tripro Company produces and sells three products, hereafter referred to as Products A, B, and C. The company is currently changing its short-range planning approach in an attempt to incorporate some of the newer planning techniques. The controller and some of his staff have been conferring with a consultant on the feasibility of using a linear-programming model for determining the optimum product mix.

Information for short-range planning has been developed in the same format as in prior years. This information includes expected sales prices and expected direct-labor and material costs for each product. In addition, variable-overhead and fixed-overhead costs were assumed to be the same for each product, because approximately equal quantities of the products were produced and sold.

PRICE AND COST INFORMATION (PER UNIT)

	A	B	C
Selling price	$25.00	$30.00	$40.00
Direct labor	7.50	10.00	12.50
Direct materials	9.00	6.00	10.50
Variable overhead	6.00	6.00	6.00
Fixed overhead	6.00	6.00	6.00

All three products use the same type of direct material, which costs $1.50 per pound. Direct labor is paid at the rate of $5.00 per hour. There are 2,000 direct-labor hours and 20,000 pounds of direct materials available in a month.

REQUIRED

1. Formulate and label the linear-programming objective function and constraint functions necessary to maximize Tripro's contribution margin. Use Q_A, Q_B, Q_C to represent units of the three products.
2. What underlying assumptions must be satisfied to justify the use of linear programming?

23-14 ***Multiple choice.*** (CPA) Choose the best answer for each question.

The Random Company manufactures two products, Zeta and Beta. Each product must pass through two processing operations. All materials are introduced at the start of Process No. 1. There are no work-in-process inventories. Random may produce either one product exclusively or various combinations of both products subject to the following constraints:

	PROCESS NO. 1	PROCESS NO. 2	CONTRIBUTION MARGIN PER UNIT
Hours required to produce one unit of:			
Zeta	1 hour	1 hour	\$4.00
Beta	2 hours	3 hours	5.25
Total capacity in hours per day	1,000 hours	1,275 hours	

A shortage of technical labor has limited Beta production to 400 units per day. There are no constraints on the production of Zeta other than the hour constraints in the above schedule. Assume that all relationships between capacity and production are linear, and that all of the above data and relationships are deterministic rather than probabilistic.

1. Given the objective to maximize total contribution margin, what is the production constraint for Process No. 1? (a) Zeta + Beta ≤ 1,000; (b) Zeta + 2Beta ≤ 1,000; (c) Zeta + Beta ≥ 1,000; (d) Zeta + 2Beta ≥ 1,000.

2. Given the objective to maximize total contribution margin, what is the labor constraint for production of Beta? (a) Beta ≤ 400; (b) Beta ≥ 400; (c) Beta ≤ 425; (d) Beta ≥ 425.

3. What is the objective function of the data presented? (a) Zeta + 2Beta = \$9.25; (b) \$4.00 Zeta + 3(\$5.25) Beta = Total contribution margin; (c) \$4.00 Zeta + \$5.25 Beta = Total contribution margin; (d) 2(\$4.00) Zeta + 3(\$5.25) Beta = Total contribution margin.

23-15 ***Multiple choice.*** (CPA) A company markets two products, Alpha and Gamma. The marginal contributions per gallon are \$5 for Alpha and \$4 for Gamma. Both products consist of two ingredients, D and K. Alpha contains 80 percent D and 20 percent K, while the proportions of the same ingredients in Gamma are 40 percent and 60 percent, respectively. The current inventory is 16,000 gallons of D and 6,000 gallons of K. The only company producing D and K is on strike and will neither deliver nor produce them in the foreseeable future. The company wishes to know the numbers of gallons of Alpha and Gamma that it should produce with its present stock of raw materials in order to maximize its total revenue.

1. The objective function for this problem could be expressed as
a. $f_{max} = 0X_1 + 0X_2 + 5X_3 + 5X_4$
b. $f_{min} = 5X_1 + 4X_2 + 0X_3 + 0X_4$
c. $f_{max} = 5X_1 + 4X_2 + 0X_3 + 0X_4$
d. $f_{max} = X_1 + X_2 + 5X_3 + 4X_4$
e. $f_{max} = 4X_1 + 5X_2 + X_3 + X_4$

2. The constraint imposed by the quantity of D on hand could be expressed as
a. $X_1 + X_2 \geq 16{,}000$
b. $X_1 + X_2 \leq 16{,}000$
c. $.4X_1 + .6X_2 \leq 16{,}000$
d. $.8X_1 + .4X_2 \geq 16{,}000$
e. $.8X_1 + .4X_2 \leq 16{,}000$

3. The constraint imposed by the quantity of K on hand could be expressed as
a. $X_1 + X_2 \geq 6{,}000$
b. $X_1 + X_2 \leq 6{,}000$
c. $.8X_1 + .2X_2 \leq 6{,}000$
d. $.8X_1 + .2X_2 \geq 6{,}000$
e. $.2X_1 + .6X_2 \leq 6{,}000$

4. To maximize total revenue, the company should produce and market
a. 106,000 gallons of Alpha only
b. 90,000 gallons of Alpha and 16,000 gallons of Gamma
c. 16,000 gallons of Alpha and 90,000 gallons of Gamma
d. 18,000 gallons of Alpha and 4,000 gallons of Gamma
e. 4,000 gallons of Alpha and 18,000 gallons of Gamma

5. Assuming that the marginal contributions per gallon are $7 for Alpha and $9 for Gamma, the company should produce and market

a. 106,000 gallons of Alpha only
b. 90,000 gallons of Alpha and 16,000 gallons of Gamma
c. 16,000 gallons of Alpha and 90,000 gallons of Gamma
d. 18,000 gallons of Alpha and 4,000 gallons of Gamma
e. 4,000 gallons of Alpha and 18,000 gallons of Gamma

23-16 ***Linear programming.*** (CMA adapted)

PART A

The Witchell Corporation manufactures and sells three grades, *A, B,* and *C,* of a single wood product. Each grade must be processed through three phases—cutting, fitting, and finishing—before they are sold.

The following unit information is provided:

	A	B	C
Selling price	$10.00	$15.00	$20.00
Direct labor	5.00	6.00	9.00
Direct material	.70	.70	1.00
Variable overhead	1.00	1.20	1.80
Fixed overhead	.60	.72	1.08
Materials requirements in board feet	7	7	10
Labor requirements in hours:			
Cutting	3/6	3/6	4/6
Fitting	1/6	1/6	2/6
Finishing	1/6	2/6	3/6

Only 5,000 board feet per week can be obtained.

The cutting department has 180 hours of labor available each week. The fitting and finishing departments each have 120 hours of labor available each week. No overtime is allowed.

Contract commitments require the company to make fifty units of *A* per week. In addition, company policy is to produce at least fifty additional units of *A* and fifty units of *B* and

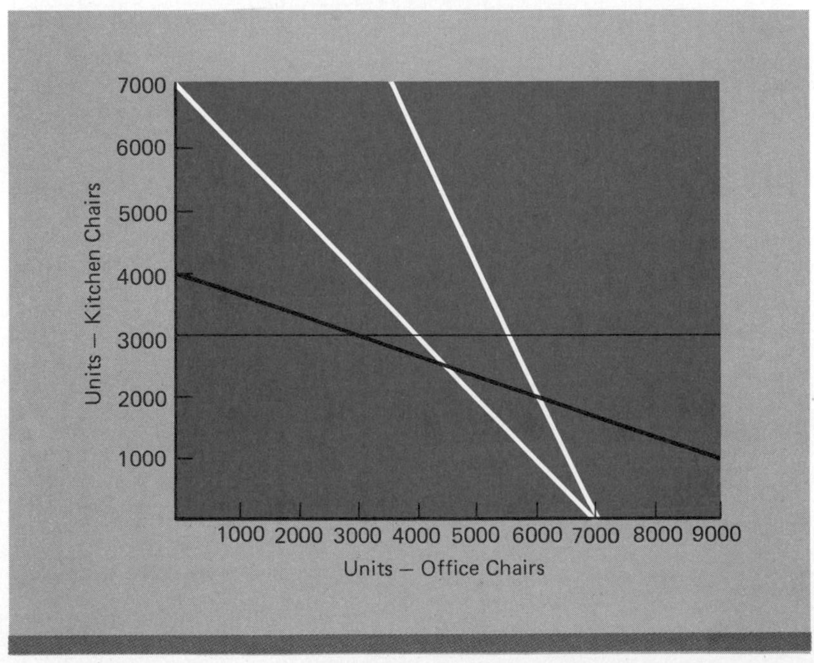

fifty units of C each week to actively remain in each of the three markets. Because of competition, only 130 units of C can be sold each week.

REQUIRED

Formulate and label the linear objective function and all of the constraint functions necessary to maximize the contribution margin.

PART B

The graph on p. 799 presents the constraint functions for a chair manufacturing company whose production problem can be solved by linear programing. The company earns $8 for each kitchen chair sold and $5 for each office chair sold.

REQUIRED

1. What is the profit-maximizing production schedule?
2. How did you select this production shedule?

23-17 ***Formulate LP model.*** (CMA) The Elon Co. manufactures two industrial products: X-10, which sells for $90 a unit, and Y-12, which sells for $85 a unit. Each product is processed through both of the company's manufacturing departments. The limited availability of labor, material, and equipment capacity has restricted the ability of the firm to meet the demand for its products. The production department believes that linear programming can be used to routinize the production schedule for the two products.

The following data are available to the production department.

	AMOUNT REQUIRED PER UNIT	
	X-10	**Y-12**
Direct material—weekly supply limited to 1,800 pounds at $12 per pound	4 lbs.	2 lbs.
Direct labor:		
Department 1—weekly supply limited to 10 people at 40 hours each at an hourly cost of $6	⅔ hour	1 hour
Department 2—weekly supply limited to 15 people at an hourly rate of $8	1¼ hours	1 hour
Machine time:		
Department 1—Weekly capacity limited to 250 hours	½ hour	½ hour
Department 2—Weekly capacity limited to 300 hours	0 hours	1 hour

The overhead costs for Elon are accumulated on a plantwide basis. The overhead is assigned to products on the basis of the number of direct-labor hours required to manufacture the product. This base is appropriate for overhead assignment because most of the variable-overhead costs vary as a function of labor time. The estimated overhead cost per direct-labor hour is:

Variable-overhead cost	$ 6
Fixed-overhead cost	6
Total overhead cost per direct-labor hour	$12

The production department formulated the following equations for the linear-programming statement of the problem.

A = number of units of X-10 to be produced

B = number of units of Y-12 to be produced

Objective function to minimize costs:

$$\text{Minimize } Z = 85A + 62B$$

Constraints:

Material

$4A + 2B \leq 1{,}800$ lbs.

Department 1 labor

$\frac{2}{3}A + 1B \leq 400$ hours

Department 2 labor

$1\frac{1}{4}A + 1B \leq 600$ hours

Nonnegativity

$A \geq 0, B \geq 0.$

REQUIRED

1. The formulation of the linear-programming equations as prepared by Elon Co.'s production department is incorrect. Explain what errors have been made in the formulation prepared by the production department.
2. Formulate and label the proper equations for the linear-programming statement of Elon Co.'s production problem.
3. Explain how linear programming could help Elon Co. determine how large a change in the price of direct materials would have to be to change the optimum production mix of X-10 and Y-12.

23-18 ***Formulate LP model.*** (SMA) Raymond Company manufactures three products: A, B, and C. There is no upper ceiling in demand in the market for these products, as they are all well accepted. Data concerning the three products follow:

	A	B	C
Selling price	\$15	\$19	\$24
Material costs	\$ 5	\$10	\$13
Other variable costs (paid when incurred)	\$ 6	\$ 4	\$ 7
Portion of revenue collected in month of sale	1/3	0	0

Each product requires one unit of its own special raw material, and these materials are not interchangeable. The raw materials at the beginning of the month are:

200 units of material for A
120 units of material for B
50 units of material for C

Additional quantities can be bought immediately when required and are paid in cash.

The products pass through two departments. The maximum machine time in Department 1 during the month is 400 hours; and in Department 2, 800 hours. Machine time for processing a unit in each department is:

	HOURS REQUIRED BY ONE UNIT OF		
DEPARTMENT	**A**	**B**	**C**
1	½	1	¼
2	1	1	4½

Fixed costs will be \$900 during the month for both departments, and this includes \$200 for depreciation. The balance of fixed cost is paid in cash. The beginning cash balance is expected to be \$6,600, and the ending balance cannot be less than \$3,000. The company will have no accounts receivable outstanding at the beginning of the month.

REQUIRED

Since the use of existing materials has a different effect on cash than that of newly purchased materials, let A_1, B_1, and C_1 be the amount of existing materials, and A_2, B_2, and C_2 the amount of newly purchased materials.

1. Formulate an objective function to maximize profits.
2. Identify and formulate all constraints applicable to this function. Do not solve the problem.

23-19 ***LP and probabilities.*** (SMA) The Caldo Company is changing its current short-term planning approach in an attempt to incorporate some newer planning techniques that will permit selection of an optimum production mix. Caldo's controller has developed the following price and cost information per unit of each product:

	PRODUCT		
	A	B	C
Selling price	$50	$60	$80
Direct labor	15	20	25
Direct materials	18	12	21
Variable overhead	12	12	12
Fixed overhead (at total production level of 55,000 units made up of equal amounts of each product)	2	2	2

REQUIRED

(Solve each part independently of the other.)

1. All three products use the same direct material which costs $3 per kilogram, and the direct-labor rate is $10 per hour. Monthly capacities are 2,000 direct-labor hours and 20,000 kilograms of direct materials. Fixed overhead is assumed to be the same for each product.

   Formulate and label, without solving, the linear-programming functions necessary to maximize Caldo's net income.
2. Caldo's management has decided to produce Product C only. Caldo's marketing manager presented the following results of his price analysis for Product C. At a selling price of $80 per unit, the probability distribution of total sales is uniform between $300,000 and $600,000. At a selling price lowered to $70 per unit, the probability distribution of total sales is uniform between $600,000 and $900,000.
   a. What is the probability of at least breaking even at a selling price of $80 per unit? (Review the first parts of Chapter 21.)
   b. Which pricing strategy yields a higher expected profit?

23-20 ***LP and joint process.*** (D. Ng) The Knulf Company produces two products, A and B, by a joint process. One unit of input X processed in Department 1 will yield three units of Product A and two units of Product B. The variable operating costs in Department 1 total $2 per unit of input X processed. Each unit of Product A can either be sold at the split-off point for $8 per unit or processed further in Department 2 to form Product C. One unit of Product A is needed to produce one unit of C. Variable processing costs incurred in Department 2 amount to $6 per unit of A processed, and each unit of C can be sold at a price of $18. Product B can be sold at $7 per unit at the split-off point.

Highly skilled labor is required in each of the two departments, and the total available labor force is limited to 80,000 hours per week. To process one unit of X requires 1.5 direct-labor hours. If A is processed further, three hours per unit of A processed are needed. Furthermore, raw material X can be acquired up to a maximum quantity of 40,000 units per week.

The company's market survey shows that the maximum weekly demand for Product A is 40,000 units and for Product C is 5,000 units. The survey further concludes that virtually any amount of Product B can be sold immediately without difficulty.

Weekly production does not have to be equal to weekly sales for any of the company's products. However, since all three products are perishable, any unsold quantity at the end of the week will be discarded.

REQUIRED

Consider each part independently.

1. Formulate a linear program to determine the optimal weekly production mix for the Knulf Company that maximizes profits subject to the various production, market, and technology constraints. Do not attempt to solve for optimal values. *Define your variables.*
2. Assume that, at the optimum, the marginal values associated with the maximum market demand for A constraint, the maximum market demand for C constraint, and the maximum supply of X constraint are $8, $12, and $12, respectively. Assume

further that all other constraints have zero marginal values. What is the maximum achievable contribution? *Show calculations.*

23-21 ***Choosing a product mix.*** Brian Jones has just received a university degree in management. He has taken the position of assistant to the president of a fairly small company in South Africa that manufactures tungsten carbide drill steels for the gold-mining industry.

Two types of drill steels are manufactured. One has a steel rod of ¾-inch diameter and the other a diameter of 1 inch. The manufacturing takes place in three departments. In the tip-fabricating department, tungsten carbide tips are manufactured from powdered wolfram. In the steel-forging department, the steel rods are slotted and prepared for the insertion of the tips. The assembly department puts the tips and steel rods together in a brazing process.

Each department has severe capacity limits. The first constraint prohibits further capital expenditure because of a very weak liquid position arising from past losses; the second is the labor situation in South Africa, which makes the hiring of more labor or the working of overtime virtually impossible. The capacity of each department is as follows:

Tip fabricating (Dept. A)	240,000 hours
Steel forging (Dept. B)	180,000 hours
Assembly (Dept. C)	180,000 hours

The treasurer has just completed the budget for the forthcoming year. Because of the renewed confidence in gold, the company is expected to produce at full capacity.

The treasurer has produced the following profit analysis of the two products, on which a major production decision was based:

	¾″	1″
Selling price	$5.00	$6.00
Direct materials		
Tungsten carbide	$ .75	$1.00
Steel	1.45	2.05
	$2.20	$3.05
Direct labor		
Department A	$ .60	$ .30
Department B	.20	.30
Department C	.20	.15
	$1.00	$ .75
Prime costs (from above)	$3.20	$3.80
Factory overhead	.80	.60
Selling and administration	.50	.60
Total costs	$4.50	$5.00
Profit	$ .50	$1.00

The market survey performed by the sales manager showed that the company could sell as many of either type of rod as it could produce. However, the sales manager urged that the needs of three of the big gold mines must be satisfied in full, even though this meant producing a large number of the ¾-inch rods that had only half the profit of the 1-inch rods. The quantities required by these three gold mines amounted to 270,000 ¾-inch rods and 540,000 1-inch rods.

As the 1-inch rods have twice the profit of the ¾-inch rods, the treasurer suggested that the remaining capacity be used to produce two 1-inch rods for every ¾-inch rod. This would mean producing an additional 135,000 ¾-inch rods and 270,000 1-inch rods. Department B would then be working at full capacity and would be the constraint on any further production.

The treasurer then produced the accompanying budgeted income statement for the forthcoming year. Sales are expected to occur evenly throughout the year.

Jones, as his first assignment, is asked by the president to comment on the budgeted income statement. Specifically, the president feels that capacity might be better utilized with a different sales mix. He wants to know just how much it is costing the company in lost profits by supplying the full needs of the three big gold-mining customers. He feels it might be more profitable to produce only the 1-inch rods.

	$\frac{3}{4}''$	1''
Sales (in units)	405,000	810,000
Sales (in dollars)	$2,025,000	$4,860,000
Direct materials	891,000	2,470,500
Direct labor	405,000	607,500
Factory overhead	324,000	486,000
Selling and administration	202,500	486,000
Total costs	$1,822,500	$4,050,000
Profit	$ 202,500	$ 810,000

Jones gathers the following additional information before making his recommendations:

Wolfram is purchased at $10 per kilogram (1,000 grams). The $\frac{3}{4}$-inch tips use an average of 75 grams and the 1-inch tips 100 grams. The special alloy steel costs $2,000 per 2,000 pounds. The $\frac{3}{4}$-inch rods use 1.45 pounds and the 1-inch rods 2.05 pounds.

Direct-labor costs per hour follow:

Department A	$2.40
Department B	1.80
Department C	1.50

Tip fabricating (Department A) is a skilled process. The smaller tips require twice as much detailed work. Owing to the nature of the work, most of the labor is considered fixed because it would be difficult to replace. Approximately 200,000 hours per annum in Department A are considered fixed. In the steel-forging process, the bigger rods require more time because of the handling difficulties. In the assembly department, the smaller rods again take more time because of the intricacies of the operations. However, this is not skilled work.

Factory overhead in the budgeted income statement is considered 50 percent fixed. It has been allocated to the products on the basis of direct labor.

Fixed selling and administrative expenses have been allocated on the basis of the number of units sold. Variable selling expenses are predicted to be 10¢ per unit sold of either size.

REQUIRED If you were Jones, what would be your recommendations to the president?

23-22 ***Sensitivity analysis.*** Refer to the basic illustration in the chapter. To what amount must the unit contribution of Product B rise so that the present optimal product combination of (86, 57) no longer applies?

23-23 ***Meaning of total contribution.*** Consider an objective function:

$$\textbf{max.}\quad \$1A + \$2B + \$4C$$

The optimum solution is $A = 100{,}000$, $B = 200{,}000$, $C = 300{,}000$.

$$\begin{aligned}\textbf{Net profit} &= \textbf{Total contribution margin} - \textbf{Other costs}\\ &= \$1{,}700{,}000 - \$400{,}000 = \$1{,}300{,}000\end{aligned}$$

Additional investigation of cost behavior revealed that the unit contributions should have been $1.10, $2.80, and $4.30, respectively. Despite the better cost approximations that provided the more accurate unit contributions, the optimal decision of 100,000, 200,000, and 300,000 units was unchanged.

REQUIRED Would the change in unit contributions affect the net profit? Why? By how much? What is the cost of the prediction error?

23-24 ***General review, prediction error.*** (J. Demski and C. Horngren) Mary Demhorn is the manager of a company that produces two products in two departments. She has great confidence in her cost-accounting data regarding direct material and direct labor, but she is less sure about the manufacturing overhead. She has been using a plantwide total factory overhead prediction equation of:

$9,000 per month + $4 per direct-labor hour

Mary is considering whether to produce either product alone or some combination of the two products. The available alternatives are:

	PRODUCE AND SELL PRODUCT	
ALTERNATIVES	X	Y
a_1	0	0
a_2	200	400
a_3	0	500
a_4	250	0

Mary collects the following price, cost, and technical data:

	PRODUCT	
	X	Y
Selling price per unit	$114	$149
Incremental selling cost per unit sold	$ 4	$ 8
Direct material per unit	$ 20	$ 30
Direct-labor hours per unit:		
Machining	1	2
Finishing	4	3

The wage rate is $7 per hour in machining and $9 per hour in finishing. In addition, miscellaneous (all fixed) nonmanufacturing costs for the company as a whole are $12,000 per month.

REQUIRED

(Show computations)

1. Which action should Mary select?
2. What are the per-unit (a) variable costs and (b) absorption costs that each product would be valued at as finished-goods inventory? Use a "denominator" volume of 3,000 hours.
3. The day after she has made an irrevocable decision in requirement 1, Mary is presented with some impeccable regression analysis of the manufacturing overhead costs in each department:

Machining overhead = $6,000 per month + $3.00 per machining direct-labor hour

Finishing overhead = $3,000 per month + $5.00 per finishing direct-labor hour

She is convinced that these prediction models give a "truer" or "more accurate" picture than the plantwide model that she used. What is the cost of using the wrong model (akin to the cost of prediction error)?

23-25 ***Comprehensive review.*** (J. Demski) Access to a computer is necessary.

In November 19_1 the Bayshore Manufacturing Company in Singapore was in the process of preparing its budget for 19_2. As the first step, it prepared a pro-forma income statement for 19_1 based on the first ten months' operations and revised plans for the last two months. This income statement, in condensed form, was as follows:

Sales		$3,063,000
Materials	$1,105,000	
Direct labor	343,000	
Factory overhead	858,000	
Selling and administrative	459,000	2,765,000
Operating profit		$ 298,000

These results were better than expected and operations were close to capacity, but Bayshore management was not convinced that demand would remain at present levels and hence had not planned any increase in plant capacity. Its equipment was specialized and made to its order; over a year lead time was necessary on all plant additions.

Bayshore produces three products; sales have been broken down by product, as follows:

100,000 of Product A @ $20.63	$2,063,000
40,000 of Product B @ 10.00	400,000
20,000 of Product C @ 30.00	600,000
Total sales	$3,063,000

Management has ordered a profit analysis for each product and has available the following information:

	A	B	C
Material	$ 6.00	$ 4.00	$17.25
Direct labor	2.33	1.00	3.50
Factory overhead	5.83	2.50	8.75
Selling and administrative	3.09	1.50	4.50
Total costs	$17.25	$ 9.00	$34.00
Selling price	20.63	10.00	30.00
Operating profit	$ 3.38	$ 1.00	$(4.00)

Factory overhead has been applied on the basis of direct-labor cost at a rate of 250 percent; management feels that approximately a quarter of the overhead is variable and that it varies primarily with labor cost. Selling and administrative costs have been allocated on the basis of sales at the rate of 15 percent; approximately one-half of these costs are variable, and they vary primarily with sales in dollars.

As the first step in the planning process, the sales department has been asked to make estimates of what it could sell; these estimates have been reviewed by the firm's consulting economist and by top management. They are as follows:

A	130,000 units
B	50,000 units
C	50,000 units

Production of these quantities is impossible. Each product requires the use of machines in each of two departments; Department 1 has a practical capacity of 75,000 hours and Department 2, 60,000 hours. Assume that labor hours are equal to machine hours for each department. The industrial engineering department has concluded that these capacities cannot be increased without the purchase of additional equipment. The production rates for the two departments are:

	PRODUCT		
	A	**B**	**C**
Department 1	2 per hour	4 per hour	4 per hour
Department 2	3 per hour*	8 per hour	⅔ per hour

**Thus, it takes .333 hours to process Product A in Department 2, not .33 or .3333. In this problem your answer is extremely sensitive to rounding, so for uniformity use .333.*

These solutions to the limited-production problem have been rejected: (1) subcontracting the production out to other firms is considered to be unprofitable because of problems of maintaining quality, (2) operating a second shift is impossible because of shortage of labor, (3) operating overtime would create problems because a large number of employees are "moonlighting" and would therefore refuse to work more than the normal 40-hour week. Price increases have also been rejected; although they would result in higher profits this year, the long-run competitive position of the firm would be weakened, resulting in lower profits in the future.

The treasurer then suggested that Product C had been carried at a loss too long and that now was the time to eliminate it from the product line. If all facilities were used to produce A and B, profits would be increased.

The sales manager objected to this solution because of the need to carry a full line. In addition he maintained that there was a group of customers who had provided and would continue to provide a solid base for the firm's activities and these customers' needs must be met. He obtained a list of these customers and their estimated purchases (in units), which totaled as follows:

A	80,000
B	32,000
C	12,000

It was impossible to verify these assertions, but they appeared reasonable, and they served to narrow the bounds of the problem so that the president concurred.

The treasurer reluctantly acquiesced, but maintained that the remaining capacity should be used to produce A and B. Because A produced about 3.4 times as much profit as B, he suggested that the production of A (in excess of the 80,000 minimum set by the sales manager) be 3.4 times that of B (in excess of the 32,000 minimum set by the sales manager).

The production manager made some quick calculations and said that this would result in budgeted production and sales of approximately

A	122,000
B	44,000
C	12,000

The treasurer then made a calculation of what profits would be, as follows:

A	122,000 @ $3.38	$412,360
B	44,000 @ $1.00	44,000
C	12,000 @ ($4.00)	(48,000)
Operating profit		$408,360

As this would represent a substantial increase over the current year, there was a general feeling of self-satisfaction. Before final approval was given, however, the president said he would like to have his new assistant check over the figures. Somewhat piqued, the treasurer agreed, and at that point the group adjourned.

The next day the above information was submitted to you as your first assignment on your new job as the president's assistant. *Prepare an analysis showing the president what he should do.*

Exhibit 23-3 presents additional cost-related data that are available in the accounting records.

EXHIBIT 23-3

Accounting Information for the First Ten Months of 19_1.

	LABOR COST			OVERHEAD				
MONTH	dept. 1	dept. 2	total	dept. 1	dept. 2	total	SALES REVENUE	SELLING & ADMINISTRATIVE EXPENSE
1	14,000	14,600	28,600	31,512	34,638	66,150	275,000	39,900
2	13,500	12,500	26,000	29,825	33,487	63,312	240,000	37,400
3	12,200	11,800	24,000	29,450	33,133	62,583	230,000	36,950
4	13,200	13,800	27,000	31,025	33,854	64,879	260,000	38,800
5	13,800	13,200	27,000	31,437	34,381	65,818	270,000	39,700
6	12,300	11,700	24,000	29,675	32,962	62,637	230,000	37,200
7	11,500	11,500	23,000	29,325	32,321	61,646	220,000	36,200
8	14,500	13,500	28,000	31,400	34,208	65,608	270,000	39,050
9	12,000	13,000	25,000	30,950	33,591	64,541	255,000	38,750
10	11,700	11,300	23,000	29,262	32,485	61,747	220,000	36,300
Total	128,700	126,900	255,600	303,861	335,060	638,921	2,470,000	380,250

23-26 ***Sensitivity analysis.*** (J. Demski) Refer to the preceding problem. The managers of Bayshore are uncertain about some of the predictions they made in arriving at their production plans for 19_2. You are to determine the cost of the following possible prediction errors if they were to occur and if the production plans were based on the predictions in the preceding problem. The errors in each section are to be analyzed separately. You should assume, however, that any production-rate changes systematically affect the respective product's labor cost.

1. The selling price of Product A may actually be $21.63 instead of the predicted magnitude of $20.63.

2. The material cost of producing Product B may actually be $5.00 instead of the predicted magnitude of $4.00.

3. Major repairs to the machinery in Department 2 may reduce its capacity to 55,000 hours.

4. The production rate in Department 1 for Product C may actually be 3 per hour instead of the predicted magnitude of 4 per hour.

5. The production rate in Department 2 for Product C may actually be 2 per hour instead of $\frac{4}{3}$ per hour.

If the planned production is infeasible, Bayshore's production staff usually cuts back the production with smallest profit (*as calculated in the first profit analysis in the preceding problem*) subject to the restriction that the production of any product must be sufficient to satisfy the demands of the customers whose needs must be met.

Special Topics for Further Study

SECTION EIGHT

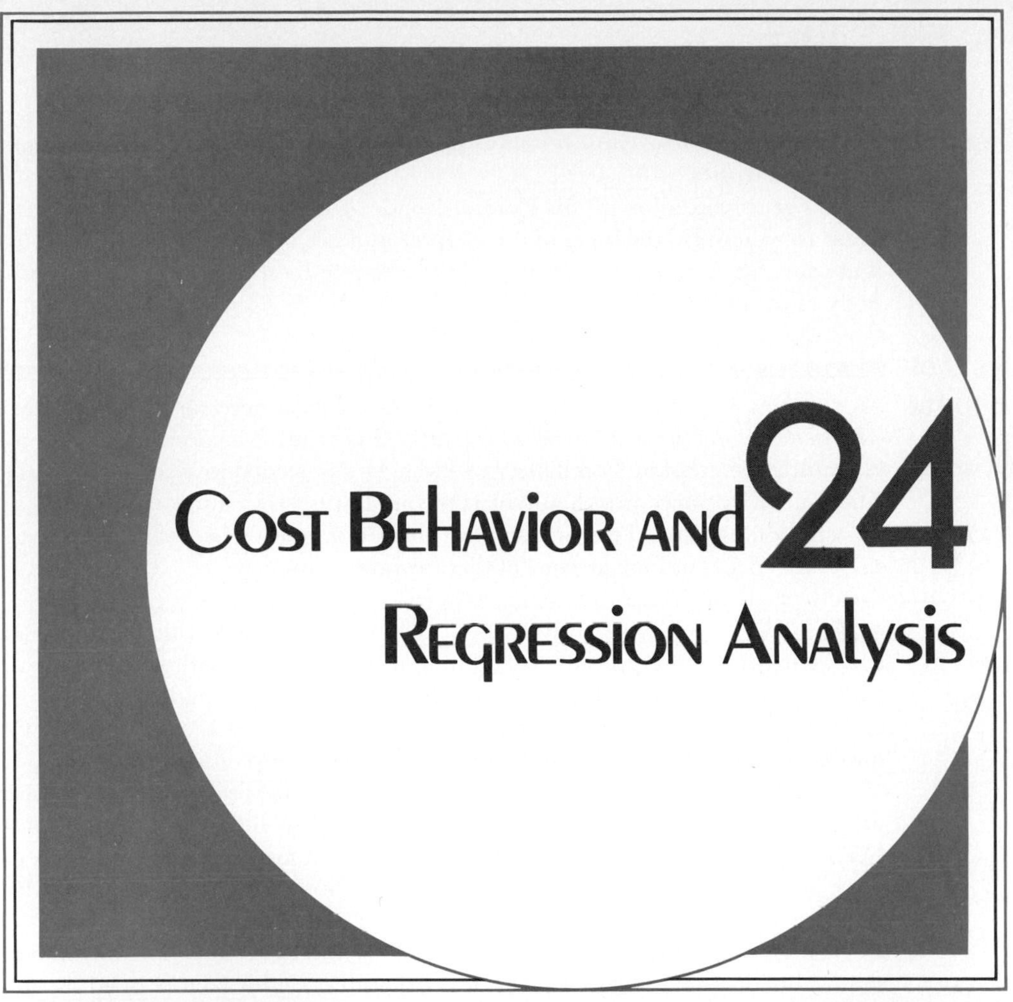

24 Cost Behavior and Regression Analysis

Chapter 9 provided an overview of how to determine cost behavior patterns (cost functions) so that predictions are as accurate as feasible. This chapter extends Chapter 9 by concentrating on the role of regression analysis in the estimation of how costs behave. **Before undertaking this chapter, be sure you are comfortable with the contents of Chapter 9.**

"Regression analysis" uses a formal model to measure the *average* amount of change in one variable that is associated with unit increases in the amounts of one or more other variables. When only two variables are studied, the analysis is called **simple regression;** when more than two variables are studied, it is called **multiple regression.**

When all its assumptions are met, and when *analysis* rather than just mechanical curve fitting is conducted, regression is a powerful technique. Regression analysis is superior to other techniques because it also produces measures of probable error. Moreover, procedures can be performed to test the assumptions, and regression can be applied where there are several independent variables instead of just one.

The remainder of this chapter assumes that you are already familiar with the fundamentals of both simple and multiple regression. **Therefore, before reading on, if you need a review, consult either the Appendix to this chapter or any elementary book on statistics.**

The organization of this chapter is more cohesive than appears at first glance. Suppose you begin the body of the chapter and are puzzled by some of the language and concepts. Stop immediately. Study the Appendix thoroughly. Then return to the body of the chapter.

Analysis of accounts

An examination of the ledger accounts is obviously a necessary first step, no matter whether cost functions are to be approximated via simple inspection of the accounts or via multiple regression. Familiarity with the data is needed to avoid analytical pitfalls. The study of the accounts should alert the analyst to how closely the cost records comply with some technical requirements for the determination of cost functions by statistical methods. Let us look at some of these requirements.

1. LENGTH OF TIME PERIODS □ The time periods should be long enough to permit the recording procedures to link output produced with the cost incurred because of that production. For example, allowance should be made for lags in recording costs.[1] The recording of production in one period and related costs such as supplies or indirect labor in another will obscure the true underlying relationships.

The time periods should be short enough to avoid the averaging of fluctuations in production within a period. Averages also tend to hide the true relationship between cost and output. For example, month-to-month comparisons may overlook some important week-to-week changes in production within particular months.

2. SEPARATE SPECIFICATION OF FACTORS □ All factors that influence costs should be identified separately as far as is feasible. Other factors besides output that influence costs include changes in technology, periods of adjustment to new processes or products (learning time), seasonal differences, inflationary effects, and unusual events. These factors must often be separately specified as independent variables.

3. ERRORS IN MEASUREMENT □ In addition to detecting clerical errors, the analyst must be on guard against the tendency to allocate fixed costs as if they were variable. For example, such costs as depreciation, insurance, or rent may be allocated on a per-unit-of-output basis. The danger is to regard these costs as variable rather than fixed. They may seem to be variable because of the accounting methods used. However, there is no point in including these costs in the dependent variable if they really do not vary with the independent variables.

4. ACCRUAL BASIS □ Mere inspection of the ledger accounts will not suffice for determining cost functions. Above all, this first step should concentrate on whether an accrual basis of accounting is in use. For example, are vacation pay, sick pay, and paid holidays being accrued throughout the year, or are they being recognized as expense

[1]George J. Benston, "Multiple Regression Analysis of Cost Behavior," *Accounting Review*, XLI, No. 4, p. 663.

as the cash is disbursed? To the extent that accrual accounting is not practiced, the analyst must "recognize that estimated relationships will be weaker than they otherwise could be."[2]

5. FOCUS ON RESPONSIBILITY CENTERS □ The effects of costs incurred outside the responsibility center under study should be removed. The inclusion of costs incurred outside the center, or omission of costs incurred because of a center's activity level, will reduce the explanatory power of the estimated relationship.

6. VARIABILITY IN VOLUME □ Select a time period that will contain some variability in activity levels. Obtain as many observations as possible. However, be on the alert for significant changes in the operating process—such as new equipment and new methods.

7. CONCENTRATE ON PHYSICAL MEASURES □ Try to work with physical measures of the inputs rather than their costs. Otherwise, the confounding effects of changes in the price level must be adjusted for via index numbers.

As is indicated by the above points, knowledge of operations *and* cost accounting is required for intelligent regression analysis. For example, consider repair costs. They may occur when output is low because machines may be taken out of service at these times. In this case, regression analysis would indicate that the higher the output, the lower the repair costs. And, if these costs were aggregated with other overhead costs, the estimated variability of cost with output would be understated. Thus, the true extent of the variation of overhead cost would be masked.[3]

In other words, the engineering link of repairs to output can usually be clearly established. There is a cause-and-effect relationship; the higher the volume, the higher the repairs. However, a blind mechanical application of regression analysis would produce just the opposite picture. This example illustrates the following guidelines:

1. To the extent that physical relationships or engineering data are available for establishing cause-and-effect links, use them.
2. To the extent that relationships can be implicitly established via logic and knowledge of operations, use them—preferably in conjunction with number 3.
3. To the extent that the relationships in 1 or 2 can be buttressed by an appropriate statistical analysis of data, use them. Regression analysis is often the best available check on 1 and 2.

Presentation of regression results

Regression analysis fundamentally entails using a *sample* of past cost behavior to formulate an estimation of how the entire *population* of costs truly behaves. The equation of the least-squares line is often presented as follows, where y' is the estimated total cost.

$$y' = a + bx$$

[2]Robert S. Kaplan, *Advanced Management Accounting* (Englewood Cliffs, N.J.: Prentice-Hall, 1982), Chap. 2. Kaplan offers extensive guidance for applying all the methods of cost estimation. The points 4 through 7 listed here are suggested by Kaplan. Kaplan also provides incisive advice in his "Management Accounting in Hospitals: A Case Study," in J. Livingstone and R. Gunn, eds., *Accounting for Social Goals* (New York: Harper and Row, 1974).

[3]Benston, "Multiple Regression Analysis," p. 668.

The following is the result of the simple regression described in the chapter Appendix, where y' is the direct-labor cost and x is batch size:

$$y' = 24.43 + 10.53x$$
$$(15.70) \quad (.81)$$
$$r^2 = .9557$$

The numbers in parentheses are the standard errors of the regression coefficients. The t-values may or may not be presented. **(To reduce clutter, dollar signs are rarely used in this chapter.)**

Alternatively, a digital computer will often present the results of regression analysis in the following format:

VARIABLE	COEFFICIENT	STANDARD ERROR	t-VALUE	
Intercept	24.43			
2	10.53	.81	13.00	
Value of r^2 is				.9557

Choosing among regressions

Often the accountant or the manager is confronted with a choice among various possible regressions that use different independent variables or combinations thereof. For example, one regression may use direct-labor hours as the independent variable, another may use machine-hours, and another some combination thereof. How does the decision maker pick from among these alternatives? My colleague, Joel Demski, has suggested that for regression to be helpful at all, the following three criteria should be met:

1. The regression equation should be plausible. It should make economic sense intuitively to both the accountant and the operating manager.
2. The *goodness of fit* should be acceptable. The r^2 (**coefficient of determination**) should be "high." The ***t*-values** (the regression coefficient of each independent variable divided by its standard error) should be "respectable"—say, at least 2.0.
3. **Specification analysis** should be conducted so that various statistical pitfalls are guarded against or allowed for. This analysis includes tests of the basic assumptions underlying regression analysis. Digital computer programs are widely available for the routine performance of these tests.

If the accountant decides that regression analysis is indeed appropriate, he or she may then use the results to pick one or more independent variables. For instance, in choosing between direct-labor hours and machine-hours as a base for overhead application, the accountant would ordinarily run three regressions using (a) direct-labor-hours, (b) machine-hours, and (c) direct-labor hours *and* machine-hours as independent variables. **The accountant would then pick the regression equation that fitted the data the best.[4] This judgment is often based on the equation having the highest r^2, assum-**

[4]Various tests of goodness of fit may be appropriate, depending on the size of the sample and other characteristics. Some analysts may want to use the coefficient of correlation (r), the standard error of the estimate (s_e), or F distributions. The coefficient of correlation (r), coefficient of determination (r^2), and standard error of the estimate (s_e) are related measures of goodness of fit. They all try to measure the scatter and thus measure how well the independent variable accounts for the variability in the dependent variable.

ing that the t-values of the coefficients were sufficiently high, that both independent variables were logically defensible, and that no specification difficulties were apparent.

Criterion 1: economic plausibility

The first criterion, economic plausibility, places regression analysis in perspective. Does a high correlation between two variables mean that either is a cause of the other? Correlation, by itself, cannot answer that question; x may cause y, y may cause x, x and y may interact on one another, both may be affected by z, or the correlation may be due to chance. High correlation merely indicates that the two variables move together. No conclusions about cause and effect are warranted. For example, church attendance and beer consumption correlate over the years, but this does not mean that attending church makes one thirsty or that drinking beer incites piety; they both simply increased with population growth.[5]

But high correlation coupled with economic plausibility is desirable. Thus, if a factory overhead cost had a high r^2 in relation to advertising space committed, you might doubt the plausibility of the relationship. But if a factory overhead cost had a high r^2 in relation to direct-labor hours worked, you might have greater confidence in the plausibility of the relationship. Our knowledge of cost behavior and the production function confirms the latter relationship; in contrast, there is no theoretical basis to support the former.

The point is that qualitative correlation, which implies causality in a logical sense, should ideally be coupled with quantitative correlation, which uses formal statistical means to determine the extent to which a change in one factor was accompanied by a change in another.

If decision makers cannot resort to physical identification to establish a basis for prediction, they may use regression analysis to help identify a reliable relationship. But first they use their prior knowledge of operations to choose a particular relationship that may be so intuitively satisfying that formal regression is unnecessary (as in allocating power on the basis of related machine-hours). Of course, where it is applicable and feasible, such intuition should be buttressed by regression analysis.

Criterion 2: goodness of fit

use of tests

The accountant and manager use tests of goodness of fit for personal reassurance about their choice of a plausible cost function. They look at r^2 because it is a ready interpretation of the extent to which the independent variable accounts for the variability in the dependent variable. They look at t-values for the slopes—that is, the b's—because they seek reliable slope coefficients for predicting how costs change over a range of volume.

The t-value for a is seldom important, because regression is rarely concerned with ascertaining the value at the y-intercept. Instead, the major objective is to predict how costs behave as activity changes over a relevant range of activity, which seldom encompasses zero activity.

An example may clarify why the t-value of a may be unimportant. Suppose a company had a nonlinear cost function but used a linear approximation over the relevant range of activity, as in Exhibit 24-1.

Note that a has a high t-value, but a is negative! How can a cost be negative at zero activity? It is virtually impossible, but who cares? The cost analyst should be un-

[5]W. Spurr and C. Bonini, *Statistical Analysis for Business Decisions,* rev. ed. (Homewood, Ill.: Richard D. Irwin, 1973), p. 483.

EXHIBIT 24-1

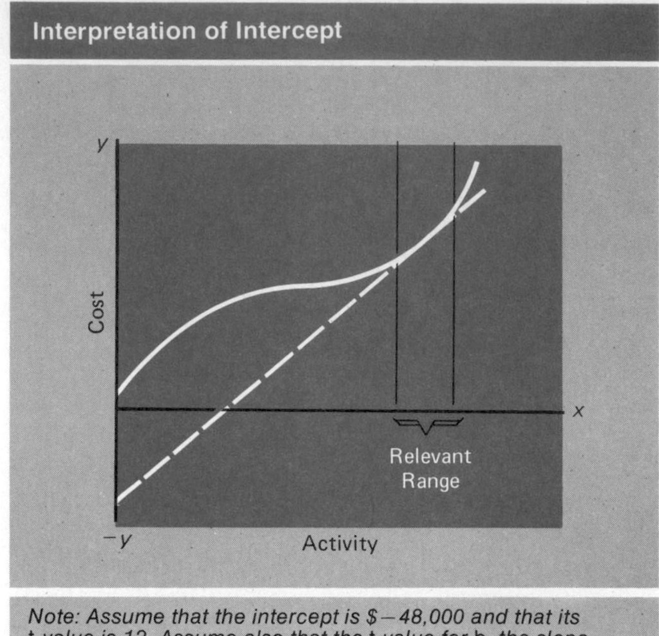

Note: Assume that the intercept is $−48,000 and that its t-value is 12. Assume also that the t-value for b, the slope within the relevant range, is 25.

concerned, because he or she wants a reliable basis for prediction within the relevant range; the t-value for b is critical for this purpose. Its extremely high value of 25 indicates that great confidence can be placed in b as a predictor ***only within the relevant range.*** Thus, in this case of a nonlinear cost function, the cost analyst would find the linear approximation offered by regression analysis very comforting.

Of course, if a cost function is expected to be linear from zero to a very high level of activity, the t-value of a would help in judging goodness of fit. For example, the negative intercept shown in Exhibit 24-1 would (a) lead to the rejection of that cost function because negative costs are not "conceptually" possible or (b) lead to a closer look as to whether linearity indeed exists over such a wide range of activity. Moreover, in cases where a cost function is hypothesized to be wholly variable, an insignificant a coefficient (t-value less than 2) would be expected. To illustrate, direct-material costs would be expected to have an a coefficient of zero.

fixed-cost component

The foregoing example illustrates why the oft-called "fixed-cost" component of a total-cost function should be carefully interpreted and labeled.

As is seen in Exhibits 24-1 and 24-2, which should be examined now, a cost function that is estimated for a mixed (semivariable) cost may yield a good approximation to the actual cost function over the relevant range. However, that relevant range rarely includes zero activity. *Therefore, rather than thinking of the intercept (the fixed component) as a fixed cost, think of it as merely the intercept at $x = 0$.* For example, see Exhibit 24-2. Note that a would be a valid estimate of fixed cost if the actual observations included the point where activity was zero and the relationship between activity and output was linear. If more observations were available, perhaps the dashed curve would be a better approximation and a would be zero. Therefore, the value of the constant term, a, is *not* the expected cost at zero activity; it is only the value that is computed as a result of the regression line calculated from the available data. Too often, cost analysts unjustifiably

EXHIBIT 24-2

Demonstration of Relevant Range

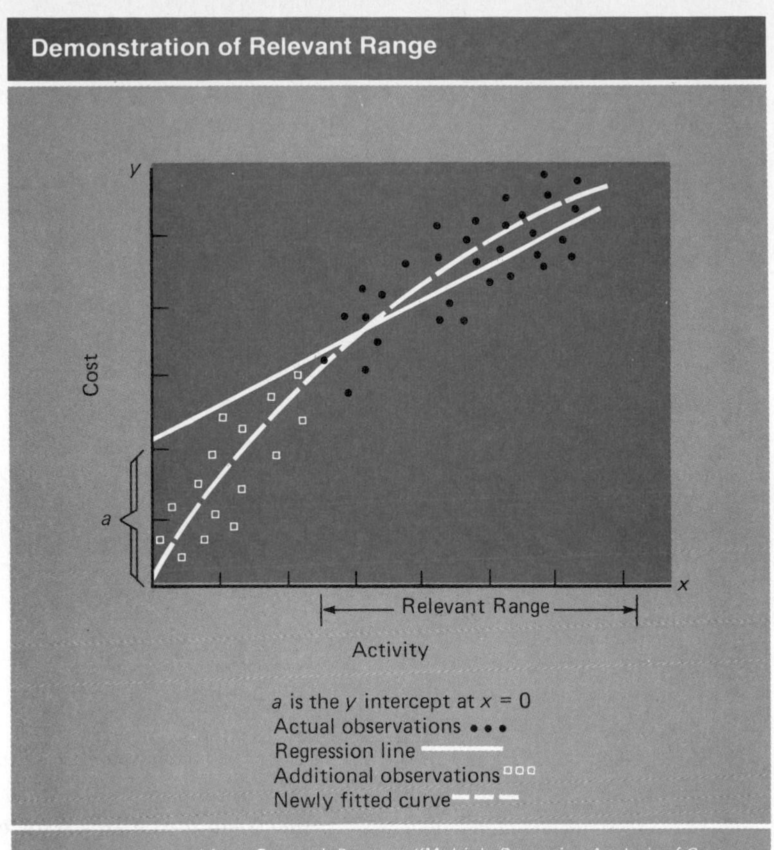

Source: Adapted from George J. Benston, "Multiple Regression Analysis of Cost Behavior," Accounting Review, XLI, No. 4, p. 662.

extrapolate beyond the range of the data upon which the regression equation was estimated.

Criterion 3: specification analysis

Although regression analysis can be a helpful tool for predictions and decisions, it can easily be misused. There is no shortcut or substitute for the scrutiny of a particular situation to ensure that the assumptions of regression analysis are applicable to the data. Too often, regression is conducted mechanically, using canned computer programs and invalid assumptions about the pertinence of the statistical tools to the data being analyzed. The reading of one chapter on regression does not qualify a person to apply regression analysis in practice. Professional help from statisticians is vital for any successful application.

Probably the most important limitation of regression analysis is the assumption that the relationships will persist—that there is an ongoing, stable relationship between cost and the independent variable or variables used to estimate the cost. That is why regression analysis is usually confined to repetitive operations.

To make valid inferences from sample data about population relationships, four assumptions must be satisfied: (1) linearity, (2) constant variance, (3) independence, and (4) normality.[6]

[6]Ibid., pp. 469–70.

The inherent appeal of regression is that computer programs usually have tests that may be systematically applied to see whether these and other assumptions hold. These tests are often referred to as *specification analysis.* When these assumptions are satisfied, the sample values a and b are the best available efficient, unbiased estimates of the population values A and B.[7]

linearity and relevant range First, linearity must exist between x and y in the population. The hypothesized relation is

$$y = A + Bx + u$$

and we assume $E(u) = 0$. This leads to

$$E(y) = A + Bx$$

where A and B are the true (but unknown) parameters of the regression line. The deviation of the *actual* value of y from the true regression line is called the *disturbance term u* (also called the *error term* or *residual term*), which is defined as $y - y'$. The average or expected value of u is zero. When there is one independent variable, the presence of linearity can be checked most easily by studying the data on a scatter diagram—a step that often is unwisely skipped.

The role of the relevant range is paramount in interpreting the scatter diagram. In the present context, the *relevant range* can be defined as the span of activity or volume that encompasses the observed relationships. As Exhibit 24-2 shows, the round dots indicates that a linear relationship exists. A regression line might be calculated from these data that would provide an accurate fit for the relevant range.

But suppose that a new relevant range enveloped all activity from zero to the maximum shown. The additional observations are portrayed by the square dots, and the round dots plus the square dots would be better approximated by the newly fitted curve. In other words, the linearity assumption must hold for the relevant range that the analyst is concerned about. As always, it is risky to extrapolate beyond the relevant range.

constant variance The second assumption is that the standard deviation and variance of the u's, is constant[8] for all x's, that the u's are drawn from the same population. It is the same for all values of x. This indicates that there is a uniform scatter or dispersion of points about the regression line. Again, the scatter diagram is the easiest way to check for **constant variance;** this assumption is valid for the first chart, but not the second chart, that appears at the top of p. 819.

The constant-variance assumption implies that the distribution of the u's is not affected by the size of the independent variables. If the assumption does not hold, the accuracy of the b coefficient is open to question. Violation of this assumption is likely in

[7]One way to appreciate these assumptions is to construct a set of data that are consistent with them. To illustrate, suppose the actual relationship is

$$y = 10{,}000 + 25x + u$$

where u is normally distributed about a mean of zero with a variance of 100. For each value of x in the sample, the corresponding value of y will then be $10{,}000 + 25x$ *plus* a random draw from the indicated normal distribution.

[8]Constant variance is known as *homoscedasticity* (but let us refer to it as constant variance). Violation of this assumption is called *heteroscedasticity.*

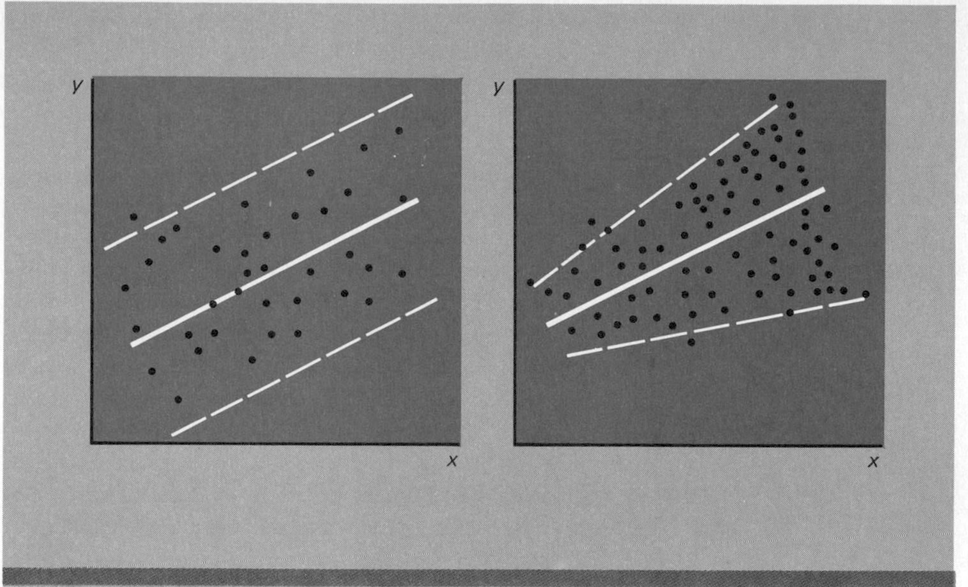

many cost-volume-profit relationships. As the second diagram indicates, the higher the volume, the higher the probability of higher scatter for higher x's than for lower x's.[9]

independence The third assumption is that the u's are independent of each other. That is, the deviation of one point about the line (its u value, where $u = y - y'$) is unrelated to the deviation of any other point. If the u's are not independent, the problem of **serial correlation** (also called **autocorrelation**) is present.

To illustrate, when observations are taken in successive time periods, the disturbances that arose in period t may not be independent of those that arose in previous periods $t - 1, t - 2$, and so on. One cause of serial correlation is the tendency of costs to be "sticky." That is, costs may rise in response to increases in volume over time but may not decline in the same way as volume declines.

When serial correlation exists, (a) the standard errors of the regression coefficients are seriously underestimated, (b) the sampling variances of the coefficients will be very large, and (c) the predictions of cost made from the regression equations will be more variable than is ordinarily anticipated from least-squares estimation.[10] The computation of standard errors is based on n independent observations. If observations are not independent, there simply are not enough observations in the sample. Fortunately, computer programs usually have tests for serial correlation.[11]

---

[9]Spurr and Bonini, *Statistical Analysis,* p. 469, point out that if the scatter tends to be a constant *percentage* of the independent variable X, then the use of log Y makes the deviations about the regression line more uniform. For an expanded discussion of this and similar transformations, particularly when applied to multiple regression, see R. Jensen, "A Multiple Regression Model for Cost-Control—Assumptions and Limitations," *Accounting Review,* XLII, No. 2, pp. 265–73. Also see J. Johnston, *Econometric Methods,* 2nd ed. (New York: McGraw-Hill), p. 216, which shows the effects when the variance of the disturbance term is proportional to the square of x.

[10]Benston, "Multiple Regression Analysis," p. 668.

[11]The degree of first-order serial correlation is tested by the Durbin-Watson statistic (DW), which is a summary measure of the amount of serial correlation in the u's. If the statistic approaches a value of 2, there is no serial correlation. If the u's are highly positively correlated,

normality The fourth assumption is that the points around the regression line are normally distributed. That is, the u values are normally distributed. This assumption is necessary concerning inferences about y', a, and b. For example, the normality assumption is necessary to make probability statements using the standard error of the estimate. In addition, the rule of thumb that the t-values must be equal to or greater than 2 is based on the normality assumption.

no multicollinearity A fifth assumption, the absence of **multicollinearity,** is applicable only to multiple regression, which is discussed in the chapter appendix. In multiple regression there are two or more independent variables—for instance, two or more product lines. Multicollinearity exists when the independent variables are highly correlated with each other. Often the net regression coefficients may be unreliable. For example, when marginal costs are computed, we would prefer to estimate the marginal cost of each class of product manufactured in a multi-product firm. Consider the manufacturer of major home appliances. If the demand for all appliances is highly correlated, the number of refrigerators, dishwashers, and clothes dryers produced will move together. Then it is impossible to use multiple regression to disentangle the marginal cost of making refrigerators from the marginal cost of making dishwashers and clothes dryers. However, the regression equation can provide accurate predictions of *total* costs if the past relationships of production among the different outputs are maintained. Still, the analyst is often concerned about the reliability of the individual coefficients; in other words, the analyst wants to know the separate effects of each independent variable on y. If multicollinearity is present, estimates of coefficients become very sensitive to particular sets of sample data, and the addition of a few more observations can substantially shift some coefficients.[12]

The presence of multicollinearity can be tested by examining the correlation between the independent variables. As a rule of thumb, if a correlation exceeds, say, .8, the less important of the two independent variables should be dropped from the estimating equation.

Kaplan has the following comments on the effect of multicollinearity on accounting applications:

> The collinearity problem is most severe when we are trying to obtain accurate coefficient estimates for product planning, pricing, and a cost-volume-profit analysis. If we are mainly interested in using the regression equation to predict cost behavior in a period (i.e., as a flexible budget), then we are not concerned with the individual coefficient estimates. The standard error of the regression and of the forecasts from the regression are not affected by collinearity among subsets of the independent variables. Therefore, if the analyst feels that the correlated variables are all necessary for predicting overall costs, they can remain in the regression equation.[13]

DW would be less than 1 and could get near zero. If the u's are highly negatively correlated, DW would be greater than 3 and could get near the upper limit of 4. Analysts often search for a new variable that will explain the systematic pattern of the u's. For an excellent discussion, see Kaplan, *Advanced Management Accounting,* Chap. 3.

[12]Johnston, *Econometric Methods,* p. 160. Multicollinearity is also suspected if the model has a high r^2 but insignificant t-values for two or more x's. Also see Benston, "Multiple Regression Analysis."

[13]Kaplan, *Advanced Management Accounting,* Chap. 4.

statistics and bias

Bias in statistics does not mean prejudice because of race or religion. Instead, it means failure of a random sample to represent a population because of some systematic error. Put another way, bias is the failure of an estimate to be a "true" estimate of an underlying coefficient. For example, suppose an estimate shows total overhead as increasing by, say, $8 per direct-labor hour. Suppose also that the *true but unknown* relationship is an increase of $5 per direct-labor hour plus $3 per hundred kilograms of direct materials. Finally, suppose direct materials and direct labor are highly correlated. Ordinarily, 100 kilograms are used per direct-labor hour. Then the $8 rate per direct-labor hour would be described as being biased upward in the sense that the $8 systematically overstates the true underlying relationship between direct labor and overhead.

SUMMARY

The following guidelines for cost estimation should be used:

1. **To the extent that physical relationships or engineering data are available for establishing cause-and-effect links, use them.**
2. **To the extent that relationships can be implicitly established via logic and knowledge of operations, use them—preferably in conjunction with number 3.**
3. **To the extent that the relationships in 1 or 2 can be buttressed by an appropriate statistical analysis of data, use them. Regression analysis is often the best available check on 1 and 2.**

Regression analysis is the most systematic approach to cost estimation. Unlike other approaches, it has measures of probable error and it can be applied when there are several independent variables instead of one. Nevertheless, regression has many assumptions and pitfalls, so professional help should be sought when it is applied.

SUGGESTED READINGS

BENSTON, GEORGE, **"Multiple Regression Analysis of Cost Behavior,"** *Accounting Review,* XLI, No. 4, pp. 657–72.

FREUND, J., and B. PERLES, **Business Statistics: A First Course.** Englewood Cliffs, N.J.: Prentice-Hall, 1974.

JENSEN, ROBERT, **"Multiple Regression Models for Cost Control—Assumptions and Limitations,"** *Accounting Review,* XLII, No. 2, pp. 265–72.

JOHNSTON, J., **Econometric Methods,** 2nd ed. New York: McGraw-Hill, 1972.

________. **Statistical Cost Analysis.** New York: McGraw-Hill, 1960.

KAPLAN, ROBERT, **Advanced Management Accounting.** Englewood Cliffs, N.J.: Prentice-Hall, 1982, especially Chapters 2–4.

________, **"Management Accounting in Hospitals: A Case Study,"** in J. Livingstone and R. Gunn, eds., **Accounting for Social Goals.** New York: Harper and Row, 1974).

LEVIN, RICHARD I., **Statistics for Management,** 2nd ed. Englewood Cliffs, N.J.: Prentice-Hall, 1981.

SPURR, WILLIAM A., and CHARLES P. BONINI, rev. ed. **Statistical Analysis for Business Decisions.** Homewood, Ill.: Richard D. Irwin, 1973.

problems for self-study

problem 1

You are trying to predict the costs of overhead. You have decided to choose one of the following independent variables: direct-labor hours or machine-hours. A computer program has been used to analyze the past behavior of overhead over eighteen months in relation to each independent variable:

VARIABLE	COEFFICIENT	STANDARD ERROR	*t*-VALUE	*r*-SQUARED
Intercept	30,000	5,000	6.00	
2 (Direct-labor hours)	1.50	.30	5.00	
				.907
Intercept	10,000	4,000	2.50	
3 (Machine-hours)	.50	.15	3.33	
				.658

Which base should be used to predict overhead cost incurrence? Why?

solution 1

Both are equally plausible. Labor-hours would be chosen as the basis for the application of overhead, because they explain a higher percentage of the past variations in overhead than did machine-hours (r^2 of .907 versus .658). The t-values are significant in both cases; the higher t-value for labor-hours reinforces the choice of labor-hours in preference to machine-hours.

problem 2

In the preceding problem, you also decided to analyze the overhead in relation to the two independent variables simultaneously:

VARIABLE	COEFFICIENT	STANDARD ERROR	*t*-VALUE	*r*-SQUARED
Intercept	21,000	10,000	2.10	
2	2.00	1.20	1.67	
3	.25	.40	.63	
				.942

CORRELATION COEFFICIENTS

Variable	2	3
2	1.000	.917
3	.917	1.000

Does the use of both independent variables together improve your confidence in your prediction of overhead cost incurrence? Why?

solution 2

If your intent is *solely* to predict overhead cost, then the higher r^2 indicates that the multiple regression gives a better fit—as long as the past relationships of machine-hours and direct-labor hours are maintained. However, note the deterioration of the t-values of the individual coefficients. These lower t-values indicate high multicollinearity. Thus we have much less confidence about the *individual* coefficients; it is risky to pinpoint the effect on overhead costs of adding one more direct-labor hour versus one more machine-hour. The latter is often a central question of cost analysis.

In sum, when two variables have a correlation greater than 0.9, reliable estimates of the separate coefficients are unlikely. Another way of identifying multicollinearity is the presence of a high r^2 together with coefficients bearing low t-values. It is not always preferable to choose a regression on the basis of obtaining the highest r^2. Kaplan observes that standard errors may be "high because of the high correlation among the independent variables. One solution is to drop one of the correlated independent variables from the regression so that more reliable coefficient estimates can be obtained for the remaining variables."[14]

[14]Ibid.

problem 3

In Problem 1, suppose that the regression model had a negative intercept. An industrial engineer informs you that the actual overhead cost in any month of zero activity would be about $14,000. There were no months of zero activity during the previous eighteen months. Does this additional number alter your decision in Problem 1? Why?

solution 3

No data in Problem 1 covered zero activity. The 30,000 or 10,000 intercept in Problem 1 or the possible negative intercept suggested here are *not* estimates of overhead cost when activity is zero. These intercepts are merely the intercept of the estimation model for the *range spanned by the data.* For additional explanation, see the sections in this chapter on goodness of fit and the fixed-cost component.

Terms to Learn

autocorrelation ***bias*** ***coefficient of determination*** ***confidence interval*** ***constant variance*** ***multicollinearity*** ***multiple regression*** ***r^2*** ***r-squared*** ***serial correlation*** ***simple regression*** ***specification analysis*** ***standard error*** ***standard error of estimate*** ***t-value***

Special Points and Pitfalls

Cost estimation and cost prediction should be initiated by a careful analysis of the ledger accounts. In particular, the costs should be placed on the accrual basis.

The regression equation is a final step. The manager must be convinced about the economic plausibility of the relationships between the independent and dependent variables. The goodness of fit must be acceptable. Tests should be conducted regarding the underlying assumptions of linearity, constant variance, independence, and normality.

Linear-regression analysis tends to be highly technical. As a result, it is easy to overlook some highly important points:

1. Several major assumptions underlie the use of the regression model.
2. If these assumptions are incorrect the regression results will be invalid.
3. "Specification errors" exist when any of the underlying assumptions are not satisfied.
4. The names of the different types of specification errors are (a) nonlinearity, (b) inconstant variance (heteroscedasticity), (c) serial correlation (autocorrelation), and (d) abnormal distribution of the disturbance terms. In addition, multicollinearity is a frequent problem in multiple regression.

Appendix 24: regression analysis

least squares

Although an experienced statistician can visually fit a straight line to a scatter diagram with remarkable accuracy, the surest, most exact fit is obtained by two major steps. First, plot the data and inspect the scatter chart to detect any unusual features that warrant further investigation. For example, one or two points may be obviously awry. Investigation may reveal clerical errors that need correction. Perhaps an unusual situation (such as a strike or a storm that disrupted the usual relationships between, say, machine-hours and direct-labor costs) may justify removing isolated or extreme cases from the data.

Second, apply the mathematical method of least squares. This ensures an objective, precise fit, and it can easily be performed with widely available, inexpensive standardized computer programs.

To illustrate regression analysis,[15] suppose that a manufacturer is troubled by fluctuations in labor productivity and wants to determine how direct-labor costs are related to volume (the various sizes of batches of output). The workers in question set up their own jobs on complex machinery. The following data (which were also discussed in Chapter 9) show the results of a random sample of ten batches of a given kind:

BATCH SIZE x	DIRECT-LABOR COSTS y
15	$180
12	140
20	230
17	190
12	160
25	300
22	270
9	110
18	240
30	320

Note that the data are paired. For example, the next-to-last sample consists of a batch size (independent variable) of 18 with an *associated* direct-labor cost (dependent variable) of $240.

The scatter diagram of these ten points in Exhibit 24-3 indicates that a straight line should provide a reasonable approximation of the relationship between direct-labor costs and size of batch that prevailed during the sample history. The least-squares criterion is the most widely used means of judging whether a line drawn through the points provides the best possible fit. That is, the sum of the squares of the vertical devia-

EXHIBIT 24-3

Scatter Diagram and Possible Linearity

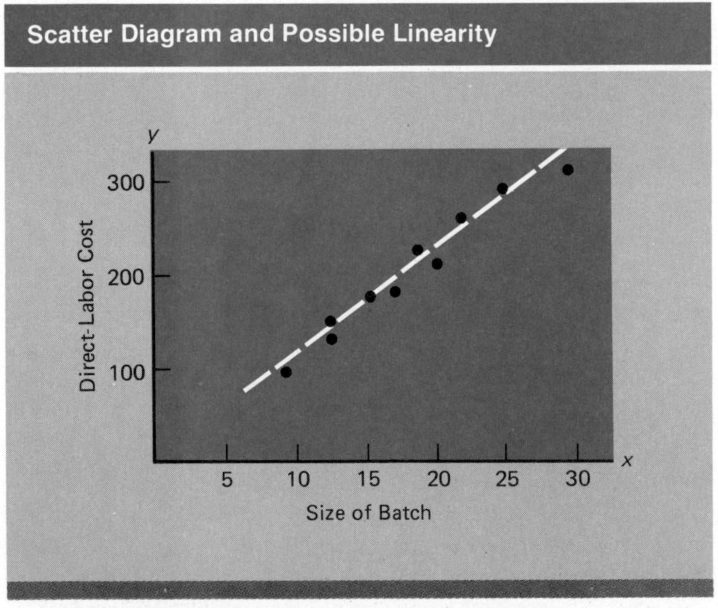

[15]This illustration and analysis is adapted from John E. Freund and Frank J. Williams, *Elementary Business Statistics: The Modern Approach,* 2nd ed. (Englewood Cliffs, N.J.: Prentice-Hall, 1972), pp. 299ff.

EXHIBIT 24-4

Least-Squares Criterion

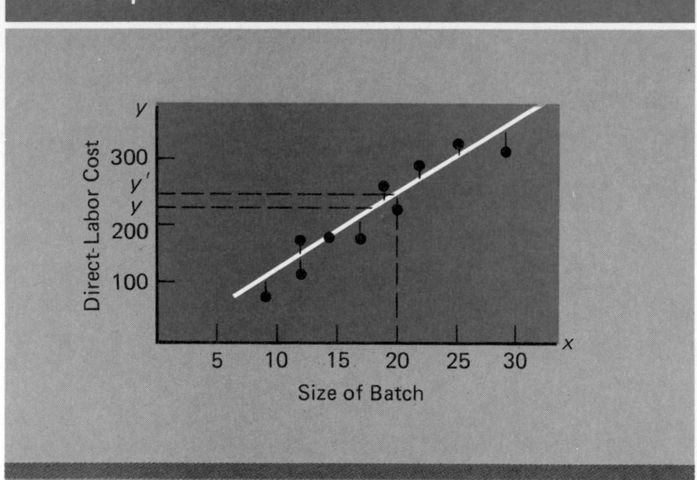

tions (distances) from the points to the line must be smaller than they would be from any other straight line. Note especially that, as the graph in Exhibit 24-4 shows, the deviations are measured vertically. The deviations are *not* perpendicular to the regression line.

The object is to find the values of a and b in the predicting equation $y' = a + bx$, where y' is the calculated value as distinguished from the observed value y. We wish to find the numerical values of the constants a and b that minimize $\Sigma\,(y - y')^2$, the difference between the actual y and the y' value predicted by the equation relating y to changes in x. This is accomplished by using two equations, usually called *normal equations:*[16]

---

[16]These normal equations can be derived through elementary calculus. Let

$$q = \sum_{i=1}^{n} (y_i - a - bx_i)^2$$

where n is the number of paired observations in the sample.

The objective of least squares requires the estimates of a and b to minimize q. Therefore, a and b should be values that make

$$\frac{\partial q}{\partial a} = 0 \quad \text{and} \quad \frac{\partial q}{\partial b} = 0$$

These partial derivatives are

$$\frac{\partial q}{\partial a} = -2 \sum_{i=1}^{n} (y_i - a - bx_i)$$

$$\frac{\partial q}{\partial b} = -2 \sum_{i=1}^{n} x_i(y_i - a - bx_i)$$

The normal equations are then obtained by setting the partial derivatives equal to zero and performing the indicated summations. (The discerning student would check second-order conditions here to ensure that a minimum is being attained.)

$$\Sigma y = na + b(\Sigma x)$$
$$\Sigma xy = a(\Sigma x) + b(\Sigma x^2)$$

where n is the number of pairs of observations, Σx and Σy are, respectively, the sums of the given x's and y's, Σx^2 is the sum of the squares of the x's, and Σxy is the sum of the products obtained by multiplying each of the given x's by the corresponding observed value of y.

Using our numerical illustration, we obtain the ingredients of our normal equations from the table in Exhibit 24-5.

EXHIBIT 24-5

Computations for Least Squares

BATCH SIZE	DIRECT-LABOR COSTS		
x	y	x^2	xy
15	$ 180	225	$ 2,700
12	140	144	1,680
20	230	400	4,600
17	190	289	3,230
12	160	144	1,920
25	300	625	7,500
22	270	484	5,940
9	110	81	990
18	240	324	4,320
30	320	900	9,600
180	$2,140	3,616	$42,480

Substituting into the two simultaneous linear equations, we obtain:

$$2{,}140 = 10a + 180b$$
$$42{,}480 = 180a + 3{,}616b$$

The solution is $a = 24.43$ and $b = 10.53$, which can be obtained by direct substitution if the normal equations are reexpressed symbolically as follows:

$$a = \frac{(\Sigma y)(\Sigma x^2) - (\Sigma x)(\Sigma xy)}{n(\Sigma x^2) - (\Sigma x)^2}$$

$$b = \frac{n(\Sigma xy) - (\Sigma x)(\Sigma y)}{n(\Sigma x^2) - (\Sigma x)^2}$$

and for our illustration we now have[17]

[17] Another way of obtaining the values is often used. First, b is calculated as above. Then its value is substituted into the first of the two normal equations to obtain a:

$$2{,}140 = 10a + 180(10.53)$$
$$a = 24.46$$

$$a = \frac{(2,140)(3,616) - (180)(42,480)}{10(3,616) - (180)^2} = \frac{91,840}{3,760} = 24.43$$

$$b = \frac{10(42,480) - (180)(2,140)}{10(3,616) - (180)^2} = \frac{39,600}{3,760} = 10.53$$

Placing the amounts for a and b in the equation of the least-squares line, we have

$$y' = 24.43 + 10.53x$$

where y' is the predicted direct-labor cost for any given batch size. A prime is placed on the y to distinguish between the value of y that was actually observed for a specified value of x and the corresponding value obtained with the use of the equation of the line.

If we apply the equation, we would predict, for example, that a batch size of 20 would have direct-labor costs on average of \$24.43 + \$10.53(20) = \$235.03. See Exhibit 24-6, an enlarged version of the graph in Exhibit 24-4, for the graph at this batch size.

Because the points in Exhibit 24-3 are somewhat dispersed, we know that our predictions for any given batch size x will be subject to error. The regression line represents an *average* relationship; it is an estimation of the average values of y for different batch sizes.

Correlation

How much of the total variation of the y's can be attributed to chance? How much can be attributed to the relationship between the two variables x and y? The coefficient of correlation (r) is a measure of the extent to which the independent variable

EXHIBIT 24-6

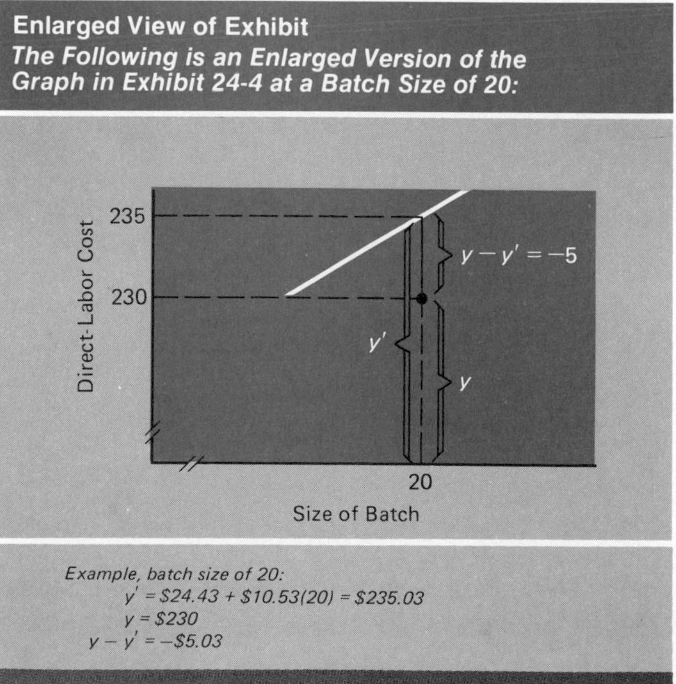

EXHIBIT 24-7

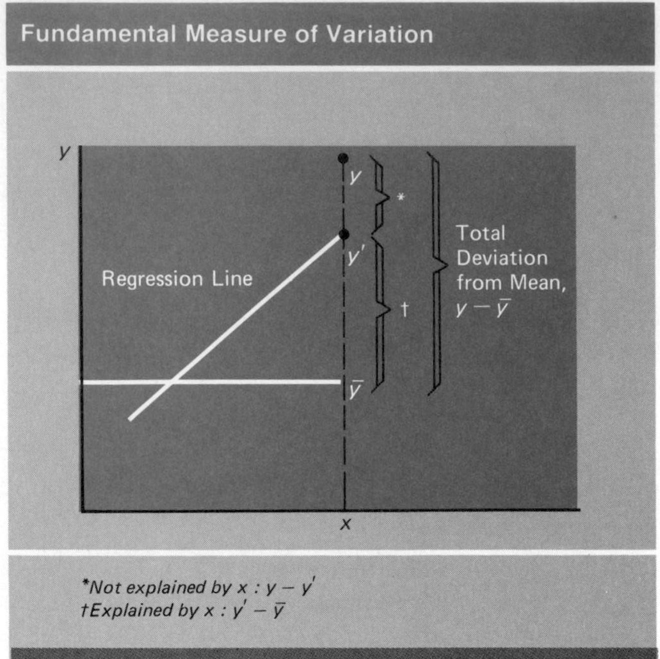

accounts for the variability in the dependent variable. Note in Exhibit 24-7 that the total deviation of the dependent variable y from its mean $\bar{y}$ (that is, $y - \bar{y}$) can be divided into two parts: first, the deviation of the value on the line (y') from the mean $\bar{y}$, or ($y' - \bar{y}$), which is explained by the given value of x; and second, the deviation of y from the regression line ($y - y'$), which is not explained by x.

The measure of the closeness of fit of a regression line is made by comparing $\Sigma\,(y - y')^2$ with the sum of the squares of the deviations of y's from their mean $\Sigma\,(y - \bar{y})^2$. Using our illustration from Exhibit 24-5, $\Sigma\,y = \$2{,}140$ and $\bar{y} = \$2{,}140 \div 10 = \$214$. Therefore,

$$\Sigma\,(\mathbf{y} - \bar{\mathbf{y}})^2 = (180 - 214)^2 + (140 - 214)^2 + \cdots + (240 - 214)^2 + (320 - 214)^2 = 43{,}640$$

Chance variation is measured by the deviations of the points from the regression line, by the quantity $\Sigma\,(y - y')^2$. If all the points actually fell on a straight line, $\Sigma\,(y - y')^2$ would equal zero. To compute this quantity for our illustration, the predicted values y' must be calculated by substituting the given values of x into the least-squares equation

$$\mathbf{y'} = 24.43 + 10.53\mathbf{x}$$

Therefore, we obtain $y' = 24.43 + 10.53(15) = 182.38$ for the first batch, $y' = 24.43 + 10.53(12) = 150.79$ for the second batch, and so on. Substituting these values and the observed y's into $\Sigma\,(y - y')^2$, we get

$$\Sigma\,(\mathbf{y} - \mathbf{y'})^2 = (180 - 182.38)^2 + (140 - 150.79)^2 + \cdots + (320 - 340.33)^2 = 1{,}934$$

Therefore,

$$\frac{\Sigma (y - y')^2}{\Sigma (y - \bar{y})^2} = \frac{1,934}{43,640} = .0443 = 4.43\%$$

of the variation in the cost of the batches can be attributed to random variation (chance) and the effect of other variables not explicitly incorporated in the model. The remaining 95.57 (100 − 4.43) percent of the variation in the costs is accounted for by differences in the size of the batch.

The coefficient of determination is often called ***r*-square (r^2).** It indicates the proportion of the variance, $(y - \bar{y})^2$, that is explained by the independent variable x. The coefficient of determination is also more informatively expressed as 1 minus the proportion of total variance that is not explained:

$$r^2 = 1 - \frac{\Sigma (y - y')^2}{\Sigma (y - \bar{y})^2} = 1 - \frac{\text{Unexplained variance}}{\text{Total variance}}$$

$$= 1 - \frac{1,934}{43,640} = 1 - .0443 = .9557$$

The square root of the proportion .9557 (that is, the proportion of the total variation in costs that is accounted for by differences in the size of the batches) is called the coefficient of correlation, r:

$$r = \pm \sqrt{1 - \frac{\Sigma (y - y')^2}{\Sigma (y - \bar{y})^2}}$$

The sign attached to r is the sign of b in the predicting equation:

$$r^2 = .9557$$
$$r = + \sqrt{.9557} = .978$$

In this illustration, the least-squares line provides an excellent fit, so there is indication of a strong relationship between the direct-labor costs and the size of the batch. The coefficient of correlation is a relative measure of the relationship between two variables, varying from zero (no correlation) to ±1 (perfect correlation).

Note that the coefficient of correlation may indicate a higher degree of explanation than is warranted. For instance, if 60 percent of the variance in y is explained by x, $r^2 = .60$, but $r = \sqrt{.60} = .775$.

Standard error of estimate

How accurate is the regression line as a basis for prediction? We are using a sample of historical events. Obviously, if we duplicated that sample using different data, we would not expect to obtain the same line. The values for a and b would be different for each sample taken. What we really want to know is the true regression line of the entire population,

$$y = A + Bx$$

where A and B are the true coefficients. The values of a and b are estimates based on samples. Therefore, they are subject to chance variation like all sample statistics.

In Chapter 21, we saw that data are often expressed as averages. A standard deviation and a coefficient of variation were computed to help indicate the relative degree of dispersion about the mean. Similarly, the line we obtained with the method of least squares, $y' = 24.43 + 10.53x$, is only an *estimate* of the true regression line.

To judge the accuracy of the regression line, we examine the dispersion of the observed values of y around the regression line. A measure of this dispersion will assist us in judging the probable accuracy of a prediction of the average direct-labor cost of a batch of, say, 20 units. The measure of the scatter of the actual observations about the regression line is termed the **standard error of estimate.** The standard error of estimate for the population may be calculated from a sample in linear regression, as follows:

$$s_e = \sqrt{\frac{\Sigma (y - y')^2}{n - 2}}$$

where n is the size of the sample.[18]

As will be demonstrated in more detail later, the sum of the squared deviations, $\Sigma (y - y')^2$, is that portion of the total variation in y's that can be attributed to chance.

When a linear regression has been fitted by least squares, a simpler computation is

$$s_e = \sqrt{\frac{\Sigma y^2 - a \Sigma y - b \Sigma xy}{n - 2}}$$

Consider our illustration. All the data are from Exhibit 24-5, except for Σy^2, which happens to be \$501,600.

$$s_e = \sqrt{\frac{\$501{,}600 - \$24.43(\$2{,}140) - \$10.53(\$42{,}480)}{10 - 2}}$$

$$s_e = \$15.80$$

Assume the four assumptions underlying regression analysis (linearity, independence, constant variance, and normality, as discussed elsewhere in this chapter) are satisfied. Then we can use the standard error to help gauge our confidence in our predictions. For instance, if no sampling error exists, then approximately two-thirds of the points should lie within the band $\pm$ one standard error:

$$\$235.03 \pm (1.0)(\$15.80)$$

Thus the band is \$219.23 to \$250.83. Management can predict that a batch size of 10

---

[18]The standard error of the estimate for the sample itself is $\sqrt{\Sigma (y - y')^2/n}$. The use of $n - 2$ represents the degrees of freedom around the regression line. It is $n - 2$ because two constants, a and b, had to be computed first on the basis of the original data. Moreover, computer programs will frequently provide for an r^2 that is "adjusted" or "corrected" for the degrees of freedom. The unadjusted r^2 will never decrease as additional explanatory variables are added to a regression, but it is possible for the adjusted r^2 to decline if an additional variable produces too small a reduction in $(1 - r^2)$ to compensate for an increase in $(n - 1)(n - k)$, where k is the number of coefficients (including the constant term, the intercept). See Johnston, *Econometric Methods,* p. 130.

would result in costs between \$219.23 and \$250.83 with two chances out of three that the confidence interval constructed in this manner will contain the true value.[19]

Sampling errors and regression coefficients

testing for significance of a relationship

Does a significant explanatory relationship exist between x and y? For example, the regression coefficient of x of \$10.53 implies a change in cost of \$10.53 for each additional unit in a batch. The regression coefficient \$10.53 is an estimate of a population parameter. A particular sample may indicate a relationship, even when none exists, by pure chance. If there is no relationship, then the slope B of the true regression line would be zero. A hypothesis can be set up that $B = 0$. If the sample value b is significantly different from zero, we would reject the hypothesis and assert that there is a definite relationship between the variables.

To test this hypothesis, we need to calculate the standard error of the b coefficient:

$$s_b = \frac{s_e}{\sqrt{\Sigma (x - \bar{x})^2}}$$

It may also be expressed as

$$s_b = \frac{s_e}{\sqrt{\Sigma x^2 - \bar{x} \Sigma x}}$$

where s_e is the sample standard error of the estimate, and the denominator describes the dispersion of x values around their mean. The value s_b is a measure of the amount of sampling error in b. The s_b for our example is

$$s_b = \frac{\$15.80}{\sqrt{3{,}616 - 18(180)}} = \frac{\$15.80}{\sqrt{3{,}616 - 3{,}240}} = \frac{\$15.80}{\sqrt{376}} = \frac{\$15.80}{19.4} = \$.81$$

The procedure[20] for deciding whether a positive relationship exists between batch size and direct-labor costs is this:

Null hypothesis: $B = 0$ (no relationship)
Alternative hypothesis: $B \neq 0$ (direct-labor costs increase as batch sizes increase)

The value of b is \$10.53. If the null hypothesis is true, $B = 0$, and b is \$10.53 units from B. In terms of its standard error, this is \$10.53 ÷ \$.81 = 13.0. Therefore, b is 13 standard errors from $B = 0$. A deviation of more than two standard errors is usually regarded as significant. Therefore, the chance is infinitesimal that a

[19]See Kaplan, *Advanced Management Accounting,* Chap. 3, for an expanded discussion of the relationships between the standard error of estimate and the standard error of a forecast. He warns that the explanatory power of the model in the prediction period will not be nearly as good as that encountered in the estimation period:

> The r^2 indicates the percentage of variation of a dependent variable, *as measured from the mean of the dependent variable,* that is explained by variation in the independent variable. . . . When attempting to predict future values of the dependent variable, however, we will not know the mean of these future observations.

[20]Spurr and Bonini, *Statistical Analysis,* pp. 566–68.

deviation as large as 13 standard errors could occur by chance. Consequently, we reject the null hypothesis and accept the alternative hypothesis that there is a significant relationship between the variables.

The amount of 13.0 standard errors just computed is called the *t-value* of the regression coefficient:

$$t\text{-value} = \frac{\text{Coefficient}}{\text{Standard error of the coefficient}} = \frac{\$10.53}{\$.81} = 13.0$$

High t-values enhance confidence in the value of the coefficient as a predictor. Low t-values (as a rule of thumb, under 2.00) are indications of low reliability of the predictive power of that coefficient.[21]

confidence intervals and *t*-values

The standard error of the regression coefficient and the table of values of t permit us to assess a probability that the "true" B is between specified limits. These limits are usually called **confidence intervals.** The 95 percent confidence interval is computed with the use of the appropriate t-value from the table in Exhibit 24-8.

For instance, with a sample size of 10, we find the row in Exhibit 24-8 with $n - 2 = 8$ degrees of freedom and the column $t_{.025}$ (for one-tail) to find the confidence interval:

$$b \pm t_{.025}(s_b)$$

This is

$$\$10.53 \pm 2.306(\$.81)$$
$$= \$10.53 \pm \$1.87$$

If all the pertinent assumptions hold, the accountant could assess a probability of .95 that the "true" marginal cost (B) is between \$8.66 and \$12.40.[22] Similarly, if a narrower confidence interval is desired, the accountant could assess a probability of .80 that the interval is between \$9.40 and \$11.66. The latter is computed by using $t_{.100}$ instead of $t_{.025}$: \$10.53 ± 1.397(\$.81) = \$10.53 ± \$1.13.

Multiple regression

In many cases, satisfactory predictions of a cost may be based on only one independent variable, such as direct-labor hours. Nevertheless, there are instances where accuracy

[21]For reasons explained in the body of this chapter, we have concentrated on the t-value of b rather than the t-value of a, which is computed as follows:

$$s_a = s_e \sqrt{\frac{1}{n} + \frac{\bar{x}^2}{\Sigma(x - \bar{x})^2}}$$

$$s_a = 15.8 \sqrt{\frac{1}{10} + \frac{324}{376}} = 15.8\sqrt{.962}$$

$$s_a = 15.8(.981) = 15.70$$

$$t\text{-value}_a = 24.43 \div 15.70 = 1.56$$

[22]Kaplan, *Advanced Management Accounting,* Chap. 3, points out that this interpretation is not precisely correct: "The correct statement is that 95 percent of the confidence intervals constructed in this manner will contain the true value." For any particular confidence interval, such as (\$8.66, \$12.40), the true value is either in the interval or not.

EXHIBIT 24-8

Values of *t*

d.f.	$t_{.100}$	$t_{.050}$	$t_{.025}$	$t_{.010}$	$t_{.005}$	*d.f.*
1	3.078	6.314	12.706	31.821	63.657	1
2	1.886	2.920	4.303	6.965	9.925	2
3	1.638	2.353	3.182	4.541	5.841	3
4	1.533	2.132	2.776	3.747	4.604	4
5	1.476	2.015	2.571	3.365	4.032	5
6	1.440	1.943	2.447	3.143	3.707	6
7	1.415	1.895	2.365	2.998	3.499	7
8	1.397	1.860	2.306	2.896	3.355	8
9	1.383	1.833	2.262	2.821	3.250	9
10	1.372	1.812	2.228	2.764	3.169	10
11	1.363	1.796	2.201	2.718	3.106	11
12	1.356	1.782	2.179	2.681	3.055	12
13	1.350	1.771	2.160	2.650	3.012	13
14	1.345	1.761	2.145	2.624	2.977	14
15	1.341	1.753	2.131	2.602	2.947	15
16	1.337	1.746	2.120	2.583	2.921	16
17	1.333	1.740	2.110	2.567	2.898	17
18	1.330	1.734	2.101	2.552	2.878	18
19	1.328	1.729	2.093	2.539	2.861	19
20	1.325	1.725	2.086	2.528	2.845	20
21	1.323	1.721	2.080	2.518	2.831	21
22	1.321	1.717	2.074	2.508	2.819	22
23	1.319	1.714	2.069	2.500	2.807	23
24	1.318	1.711	2.064	2.492	2.797	24
25	1.316	1.708	2.060	2.485	2.787	25
26	1.315	1.706	2.056	2.479	2.779	26
27	1.314	1.703	2.052	2.473	2.771	27
28	1.313	1.701	2.048	2.467	2.763	28
29	1.311	1.699	2.045	2.462	2.756	29
inf.	1.282	1.645	1.960	2.326	2.576	inf.

The t-value *describes the sampling distribution of a deviation from a population value divided by the standard error.*

Degrees of freedom (d.f.) *are in the first column. The probabilities indicated as subvalues of* t *in the heading refer to the sum of a one-tailed area under the curve that lies outside the point* t.

For example, in the distribution of the means of samples of size n = *10,* d.f. = n − *2 = 8; then .025 of the area under the curve falls in one tail outside the interval* t ± *2.306.*

improving accuracy

can be substantially improved by basing the prediction on more than one independent variable. The most widely used equations to express relationships among a dependent variable and two or more independent variables are linear equations of the form[23]

$$y = a + bx_1 + cx_2 + dx_3 + \cdots + u$$

where y is the variable to be predicted; x_1, x_2, and x_3 are the independent variables on which the prediction is to be based; a, b, c, and d are unknown constants; and u is the "disturbance term" that includes the net effect of other factors. For cost predictions, there may be two, three, or more independent variables such as labor-hours, labor cost, machine-hours, weight or length of materials, temperature, types of machines, and types of labor skill. For example, the weekly cost of labor in a shipping room may be more accurately predicted by the equation:

$$y = \$180 + \$.80 \text{ (units shipped)} + \$.30 \text{ (per hundred pounds of units shipped)}$$

than by basing the prediction on either units shipped or weight of units shipped alone.

The linear coefficients, 80¢ and 30¢, measure the change in the dependent variable, labor cost, associated with a unit change in each independent variable—**assuming that the other independent variable is held constant.** For example, the effect of shipping one more unit will cause labor costs to increase by 80¢ for units of the same weight. Similarly, the effect of shipping 200 more pounds will cause labor costs to increase by 30¢ × 2 = 60¢ for a specified number of units shipped.

The same basic statistical tests, such as interpretations of the standard errors of the coefficients and r^2, are conducted whether simple or multiple regression is employed.

The major difficulty in fitting a linear equation having more than two unknowns to a given set of data is that of finding the constants $a, b, c, d \ldots$, so that the resulting equation will yield the best possible predictions. As in simple regression, this problem is generally solved by using the method of least squares.

Fundamentally, the problem of finding predicting equations of the form $y = a + bx_1 + cx_2 + dx_3 + \cdots$ does not differ from that of fitting lines of the form $y = a + bx$. Moreover, the widespread availability of suitable computer programs makes the use of multiple regression feasible. Least-squares equations having 25 or more variables can be solved in a matter of seconds on a fast digital computer.

---

[23]These equations may be expressed in many alternative forms. For instance:

$$y = b_0 + b_1x_1 + b_2x_2 + b_3x_3 + \cdots$$

A general form is:

$$Y_i = A_0 + \sum_{j=1}^{n} X_{ij}A_i + u_i \qquad i = 1, \ldots, n$$

where the Y_i are the dependent variables, the X_{ij} are the independent variables, and the u_i are the residual (error) terms. The u_i is the sum of the unspecified factors, the disturbances, that are assumed to be normally distributed with a zero mean and a constant variance.

illustration of technique The details of multiple regression are beyond the scope of this text. However, the following example will show how regression may be used for cost analysis.[24] Suppose a firm manufactures electronic circuit boards and other products in which the services of several departments are used. In the assembly department, two types of circuit boards are produced, *nenex* and *denex.* The nenex are assembled in batches, but the denex are assembled singly. Weekly observations on cost and output are taken and punched on cards. Graphs are prepared, and it appears that a linear relationship is present. Furthermore, the cost of producing nenex is not believed to be a function of the production of denex or other explanatory variables. Therefore, the following regression is computed:

$$\begin{aligned} y = {} & 110.3 + 8.21n - 7.83b + 12.32d + 235s + 523w - 136a \\ & (40.8) \quad (.53) \quad (1.69) \quad (2.10) \quad (100) \quad (204) \quad (154) \end{aligned}$$

$r^2 = .892$ (the coefficient of multiple determination)

where the number of observations is 156 and

y = expected cost
n = number of nenex
b = average number of nenex in a batch
d = number of denex
s = summer dummy variable, where $s = 1$ for summer, 0 for other seasons
w = winter dummy variable, where $w = 1$ for winter, 0 for other seasons
a = autumn dummy variable, where $a = 1$ for autumn, 0 for other seasons

As in the body of the chapter, the numbers in parentheses beneath the coefficients are the standard errors of the regression coefficients. For example, the regression coefficient 8.21 is an estimate of the population parameter. The sampling error associated with this estimate is called the *standard error of the regression coefficient.* If the underlying assumptions of regression are satisfied, the standard error of the coefficient, .53, permits us to assess a probability of 0.67 that the "true" marginal cost is between 7.68 and 8.74 [8.21 ± (1 × .53)] and of 0.95 that it is between 7.15 and 9.27 [8.21 ± (2 × .53)] for large *n.*

Moreover, we can use the *t*-value to test whether the presence of the independent variable contributes significantly toward explanation of the movements in the dependent variable. For example, the *t*-value of *n* is $8.21 \div .53 = 15.68$. Such a high *t*-value enhances confidence in the value of the coefficient as a predictor.

The regression might be used for flexible budgeting and the analysis of performance. For example, suppose the following for one week: $n = 532$; $b = 20$; $d = 321$; and s = summer = 1. If this week is like an average of the experience for past weeks, total costs would be

$$110.3 + 8.21(532) - 7.83(20) + 12.32(321) + 235.3(1) = 8{,}501$$

[24]Adapted from Benston, "Multiple Regression Analysis," pp. 670–71. Also see Robert Jensen, "Multiple Regression Models for Cost Control—Assumptions and Limitations," *Accounting Review.* XLI, No. 4, pp. 265–72.

With the help of a computer program, the standard error of the estimate can be computed so that the budget can provide a range of, say, \$8,501 ± the standard error. The actual costs can then be compared with this expected amount. With these figures, management can judge how unusual the actual production costs are in light of past experience.

QUESTIONS, PROBLEMS, AND CASES

24-1 What is the role of the relevant range in interpreting a scatter diagram?

24-2 Give two synonyms for *disturbance term.*

24-3 "Multicollinearity exists when the dependent and the independent variable are highly correlated." Do you agree? Explain.

24-4 To make valid inferences from sample data about population relationships, what four assumptions must be satisfied?

24-5 "High correlation between two variables means that one is the cause and the other is the effect." Do you agree? Why?

24-6 Why does regression analysis offer a means of cost estimation that other methods do not?

24-7 ***Interpretation of regression coefficient.*** A manager learned about linear regression techniques at an evening college course. He decided to apply regression in his study of repair costs in his plant. He plotted 24 points for the past 24 months and fitted a least-squares line:

Total repair cost per month = \$80,000 − \$.50*x*

where x = number of machine-hours worked.

He was baffled because the result was nonsense. Apparently, the more the machines were run, the less the repair costs. He decided that regression was a useless technique.

REQUIRED

Why was the puzzling regression coefficient negative? Do you agree with the manager's conclusion regarding regression? Explain.

24-8 ***Account analysis and cause and effect.*** The costs of maintenance of way and structures (M of W & S) are incurred by a railroad to continue in usable condition the fixed facilities employed in the carrier's railway operations. These costs are usually very material in relation to revenue and net income. A substantial portion of M of W & S costs is incurred on a cyclical program. For example, the costs are influenced by the tonnage that moves over the road for periods of up to or more than ten years. The costs are also influenced by management policy decisions and other nontraffic factors.

REQUIRED

1. What are likely to be heavy influences (the influential independent variables) on the M of W & S costs for any given year? Be as specific as possible.
2. If M of W & S costs were estimated by simple regression using a measure of traffic (such as train-miles or gross ton-miles) as the independent variable, would the variable-cost portion (the b-coefficient) tend to be too high or too low? Why?

24-9 ***Fundamentals of least squares.*** (Adapted from *Separating and Using Costs as Fixed and Variable, N.A.A. Bulletin,* Accounting Practice Report No. 10) Assume that nine monthly observations of power costs are to be used as a basis for developing a budget formula. A scatter diagram indicates a mixed cost behavior in the form $y = a + bx$. The observations are:

MONTH	MACHINE-HOURS	TOTAL MIXED COST
1	22	$ 23
2	23	25
3	19	20
4	12	20
5	12	20
6	9	15
7	7	14
8	11	14
9	14	16
	129	$167

REQUIRED | Using least squares, compute the equation for the budget formula.

24-10 ***Rudiments of least-squares regression analysis.*** (H. Nurnberg) ABC Corporation wishes to set flexible budgets for each of its operating departments. A separate maintenance department performs all routine and major repair work on the corporation's equipment and facilities. It has been determined that maintenance cost is primarily a function of machine-hours worked in the various production departments. The actual machine hours worked and maintenance cost incurred during the first four months of 19_1 are as follows:

	MACHINE-HOURS	MAINTENANCE COST
January	800	$350
February	1,200	350
March	400	150
April	1,600	550

(This example simply illustrates the methods that can be used for determining similar information. If, as in this instance, the number of observations is small, additional analysis should be performed to determine whether the results are reliable.)

REQUIRED

1. Draw a scatter diagram.
2. Compute variable maintenance cost per machine-hour and fixed maintenance cost per month, consistent with the high-low method.
3. Compute variable maintenance cost per machine-hour and fixed maintenance cost per month, consistent with least-squares regression analysis.
4. Compute the coefficient of determination, the r^2.
5. Compute the standard error of estimate, the s_e. Assume that 1,100 machine-hours are budgeted for May. Compute a point estimate and a prediction interval of maintenance cost for May. Use 95 percent confidence coefficient.
6. The maintenance manager of ABC Corporation questions your computation of variable maintenance cost per machine-hour computed as part of requirement 3. He argues that maintenance cost per machine is a discretionary fixed cost. Test the validity of his argument. Use 95 percent confidence coefficient.

24-11 ***Simple regression.*** (Adapted from an illustration in Benjamin Perles and Charles Sullivan, *Freund and Williams' Modern Business Statistics* [Englewood Cliffs, N.J.: Prentice-Hall], pp. 288ff.) A random sample of various batch sizes and of recorded direct-labor costs is on p. 838.

REQUIRED

1. Prepare a scatter diagram.
2. Using least-squares analysis, compute the equation of the line.
3. Compute the coefficient of determination.
4. What is the level of fixed costs at zero activity? Explain fully.

SIZE OF BATCH	DIRECT-LABOR COST
48	$312
32	164
40	280
34	196
30	200
50	288
26	146
50	361
22	149
43	252

24-12 ***Perform least-squares analysis.*** (SMA, adapted) The GH Manufacturing Company makes a product called Z. Some of the manufacturing overhead is easily identified as fixed or directly variable with production. The cost accountant of the company is confronted with the problem of preparing a flexible budget for the coming year and wishes to determine the fixed and variable elements of the semivariable manufacturing overhead.

The following details are provided for the first ten months of the past year:

MONTH	NUMBER OF UNITS PRODUCED	SEMIVARIABLE MANUFACTURING OVERHEAD
1	1,500	$ 800
2	2,000	1,000
3	3,000	1,350
4	2,500	1,250
5	3,000	1,300
6	2,500	1,200
7	3,500	1,400
8	3,000	1,250
9	2,500	1,150
10	1,500	800

REQUIRED

Determine by simple regression the fixed and variable elements of the semivariable manufacturing overhead based on the first ten months of the past year.

24-13 ***Basic regression analysis.*** (SMA, adapted) Q LTD. wishes to study the relationship between the total costs of operating one of its departments and the physical output of that department. It decides to begin with a simple linear probabilistic model relating weekly total operating cost to weekly output, as follows:

$$y = \beta_0 + \beta_1 x + \varepsilon$$

where y is weekly total operating cost, x is weekly unit production, and ε is a random variable assumed to follow a normal probability distribution with mean μ of zero and standard deviation of σ.

REQUIRED

1. Give a brief interpretation of the parameters β_0 and β_1 of the model above, so that an accountant would understand what they stand for.
2. Give a brief outline of the role of ε in the model. In particular, indicate why it is there.
3. Q LTD. obtains the following data on weekly production and costs:

WEEKS AGO	x: UNITS PRODUCED	y: TOTAL OPERATING COST
1	1 (thousands)	$2 (thousands)
2	4	5
3	10	9
4	7	7
5	3	3

Using these data, estimate the coefficient β_0 and β_1 of the model.

4. Explain how you would go about deciding whether or not the model above fits the data reasonably well, i.e., how well it seems to have captured the underlyng process generating the monthly departmental operating costs.
5. If you were told that next week's production was planned as 2,000 units, what would your prediction of next week's operating costs be?

24-14 ***Multiple choice.*** (CMA) The Alpha Company, which produces several different products, is making plans for the introduction of a new product that it will sell for $6 a unit. The following estimates have been made for manufacturing costs on 100,000 units to be produced the first year:

Direct materials	$50,000
Direct labor	$40,000(the labor rate is $4 an hour)

Overhead costs have not yet been estimated for the new product, but monthly data on total production and overhead costs for the past 24 months have been analyzed using simple linear regression. The following results were derived from the simple regression and will provide the basis for overhead cost estimates for the new product.

SIMPLE REGRESSION ANALYSIS RESULTS ($y = a + bx$)

Dependent variable(y)—Factory-overhead costs	
Independent variable (x)—Direct-labor hours	
Computed Values:	
y-intercept	$40,000
Coefficient of independent variable	$2.10
Coefficient of correlation	.953
Standard error of estimate	$2,840
Standard error of regression coefficient	.42
Mean value of independent variable	$18,000
Coefficient of determination	.908

1. What percentage of the variation in overhead costs is explained by the independent variable? (a) 90.8%, (b) 42%, (c) 48.8%, (d) 95.3%, (e) some amount other than those shown above.

2. To determine a confidence interval for the parameter estimated by b in the regression computation, an appropriate t-value would be selected from a table of values from a t distribution corresponding to the desired level of confidence and having (a) 0 degrees of freedom, (b) 2 degrees of freedom, (c) 10 degrees of freedom, (d) 22 degrees of freedom, (e) 24 degrees of freedom.

3. Assuming that the appropriate t-value is 2.07, a 95 percent confidence interval for the b values would be (a) (1.23, 2.97), (b) (.10, 4.10), (c) (2.1, 2.97), (d) (.22, 3.97), (e) some amount other than those shown above.

4. The total overhead cost for an estimated activity level of 20,000 direct-labor hours would be (a) $42,000, (b) $82,000, (c) $122,000, (d) $222,000, (e) some amount other than those shown above.

5. The expected contribution margin per unit to be earned during the first year on 100,000 units of the new product would be (a) $4.49, (b) $4.89, (c) $0.30, (d) $5.10, (e) some amount other than those shown above.

24-15 ***Choosing independent variable.*** (SMA) Small Limited produces two products, A and B, and uses simple regression techniques to determine overhead costs. Both products have to go through two departments: the machining department, where basic raw materials are blended to form major components, and the assembly department, where subcomponents are added on to the major ones. Each unit of A requires six direct-labor hours in assembly and 0.6 machine-hours. Each unit of B requires nine direct-labor hours in assembly and 0.8 machine-hours. The financial and production records in the month of November give the following statistical information:

INDEPENDENT VARIABLE	COEFFICIENT	STANDARD ERROR	t-VALUE	COEFFICIENT OF DETERMINATION
Intercept	10,000	650	25	
Direct-labor hours	8	2	8	.884
Intercept	6,500	6	8	
Machine-hours	15	4	3	.967

1. Which independent variable should the accountant at Small Limited use to predict overhead? Give two reasons for your choice.
2. November is a normal production month. Predict the total annual overhead if the master budget calls for 10,000 units of Product A and 12,000 units of Product B.

24-16 ***Use of regression output.*** (SMA) The accountant in a firm that produces a special electrical gauge wishes to determine the relationship(s) between overhead costs and number of gauges produced. He has the following data from the last five months of operations:

MONTH	GAUGES PRODUCED	OVERHEAD COSTS
January	0	$295
February	150	410
March	125	348
April	110	334
May	175	440

By considering number of gauges as the independent variable x, and overhead as the dependent variable y, the accountant presumes a linear relationship of the type $y = a + bx$.

Various statistical calculations produce the following data:

$$a = 115$$

$$b = 1.9$$

$$r^2 = 0.9727 = \text{correlation (sample) squared}$$

$$\text{Standard error of estimate, } S_e = 11.21$$

$$\text{Standard error of coefficient, } S_b = 0.1835$$

The t-value for 3 degrees of freedom for a one-tail test probability of 0.025 is

$$t_{0.025} = 3.182$$

REQUIRED

1. Is the accountant's assumption of a linear relationship justified? Give two reasons to substantiate it.
2. Given that the accountant is correct, calculate a 95 percent confidence interval for the variable overhead per gauge.
3. The actual overhead costs incurred would fall within what range of values?
4. Predict the value of variable overhead if the number of gauges produced is 180.

24-17 ***Choosing a prediction method.*** (CMA, adapted) The Ramon Co. manufactures a wide range of products at several different plant locations. The Franklin Plant, which manufactures electrical components, has been experiencing some difficulties with fluctuating monthly overhead costs. The fluctuations have made it difficult to estimate the level of overhead that will be incurred for any one month.

Management wants to be able to estimate overhead costs accurately in order to plan its operation and financial needs better. A trade association publication to which Ramon Co. subscribes indicates that, for companies manufacturing electrical components, overhead tends to vary with direct-labor hours.

One member of the accounting staff has proposed that the cost behavior pattern of the overhead costs be determined. Then overhead costs could be predicted from the budgeted direct-labor hours.

Another member of the accounting staff suggested that a good starting place for determining the cost behavior pattern of overhead costs would be an analysis of historical data. The historical cost behavior pattern would provide a basis for estimating future overhead costs. The methods proposed for determining the cost behavior pattern included the high-low method, the scatter-graph method, simple linear regression, and multiple regression. Of these methods Ramon Co. decided to employ the high-low method, the scatter-graph method, and simple linear regression. Data on direct-labor hours and the respective overhead costs incurred were collected for the previous two years. The raw data follow:

	19_3		19_4	
	DIRECT-LABOR HOURS	OVERHEAD COSTS	DIRECT-LABOR HOURS	OVERHEAD COSTS
January	20,000	$84,000	21,000	$86,000
February	25,000	99,000	24,000	93,000
March	22,000	89,500	23,000	93,000
April	23,000	90,000	22,000	87,000
May	20,000	81,500	20,000	80,000
June	19,000	75,500	18,000	76,500
July	14,000	70,500	12,000	67,500
August	10,000	64,500	13,000	71,000
September	12,000	69,000	15,000	73,500
October	17,000	75,000	17,000	72,500
November	16,000	71,500	15,000	71,000
December	19,000	78,000	18,000	75,000

Using linear regression, the following data were obtained:

Coefficient of determination	.9109
Coefficient of correlation	.9544
Coefficients of regression equation:	
Constant	39,859
Independent variable	2.1549
Standard error of the estimate	2,840
Standard error of the regression coefficient for the independent variable	.1437
True *t*-statistic for a 95% confidence interval (22 degrees of freedom)	2.074

REQUIRED

1. Using the high-low method, determine the cost behavior pattern of the overhead costs for the Franklin Plant.
2. Using the results of the regression analysis, calculate the estimate of overhead costs for 22,500 direct-labor hours.
3. Of the three proposed methods (high-low, scatter-graph, linear regression), which one should Ramon Co. employ to determine the historical cost behavior pattern of Franklin Plant's overhead costs? Explain your answer completely, indicating the reasons why the other methods should not be used.

24-18 ***Regression assumptions.*** (CMA) The controller of the Connecticut Electronics Company believes that the identification of the variable and fixed components of the firm's costs will enable the firm to make better planning and control decisions. Among the costs the controller is concerned about is the behavior of indirect supplies expense. He believes there is some correlation between the machine-hours worked and the amount of indirect supplies used.

A member of the controller's staff has suggested that a simple linear-regression model be used to determine the cost behavior of the indirect supplies. The regression equation shown below was developed from 40 pairs of observations using the least-squares method of regression. The regression equation and related measures are as follows:

$$S = \$200 + \$4H$$

where S = total monthly costs of indirect supplies, and H = machine hours per month.

Standard error of estimate: $S_e = 100$
Coefficient of correlation: $r = .87$

REQUIRED

1. When a simple linear-regression model is used to make inferences about a population relationship from sample data, what assumptions must be made before the inferences can be accepted as valid?
2. Assume the assumptions identified in requirement 1 are satisfied for the indirect supplies expense of Connecticut Electronics Company.
   a. Explain the meaning of "200" and "4" in the regression equation $S = \$200 + \$4H$.
   b. Calculate the estimated cost of indirect supplies if 900 machine-hours are to be used during a month.
   c. In addition to the estimate for the cost of indirect supplies, the controller would like the range of values for the estimate if a 95 percent confidence interval is specified. He would use this range to judge whether the estimated costs indicated by the regression analysis was good enough for planning purposes. Calculate, for 900 machine-hours, the range of the estimate for the cost of indirect supplies with a 95 percent confidence interval.
3. Explain briefly what the
   a. Coefficient of correlation measures.
   b. Value of the coefficient of correlation ($r = .87$) indicates in this case if Connecticut Electronics Company wishes to predict the total cost of indirect supplies on the basis of estimated machine-hours.

24-19 ***Choosing one of two regression analyses.*** (CMA) The Alma Plant manufactures the industrial product line of CJS Industries. Plant management wants to be able to get a good, yet quick, estimate of the manufacturing-overhead costs that can be expected to be incurred each month. The easiest and simplest method to accomplish this task appears to be to develop a flexible-budget formula for the manufacturing-overhead costs.

The plant's accounting staff suggested that simple linear regression be used to determine the cost behavior pattern of the overhead costs. The regression data can provide the basis for the flexible-budget formula. Sufficient evidence is available to conclude that manufacturing-overhead costs vary with direct-labor hours. The actual direct-labor hours and the corresponding manufacturing-overhead costs for each month of the last three years were used in the linear-regression analysis.

The three-year period contained various occurrences not uncommon to many businesses. During the first year, production was severely curtailed during two months due to wildcat strikes. In the second year, production was reduced in one month because of material shortages and materially increased (overtime scheduled) during two months to meet the units required for a one-time sales order. At the end of the second year, employee benefits were raised significantly as the result of a labor agreement. Production during the third year was not affected by any special circumstances.

Various members of Alma's accounting staff raised some issues regarding the historical data collected for the regression analysis. These issues were as follows.

1. Some members of the accounting staff believed that the use of data from all 36 months would provide a more accurate portrayal of the cost behavior. While they recognized that any of the monthly data could include efficiencies and inefficiencies, they believed these efficiencies/inefficiencies would tend to balance out over a longer period of time.

2. Other members of the accounting staff suggested that only those months that were considered normal should be used so that the regression would not be distorted.

3. Still other members felt that only the most recent 12 months should be used because they were the most current.

4. Some members questioned whether historical data should be used at all to form the basis for a flexible-budget formula.

The accounting department ran two regression analyses of the data—one using the data from all 36 months and the other using only the data from the last 12 months. The information derived from the two linear regressions is shown on the next page.

REQUIRED

1. From the results of Alma Plant's regression analysis that used the data from all 36 months:
   a. Formulate the flexible-budget equation that can be employed to estimate monthly manufacturing-overhead costs.

Least-Squares Regression Analyses

	DATA FROM ALL 36 MONTHS	DATA FROM MOST RECENT 12 MONTHS
Coefficients of the regression equation:		
Constant	\$123,810	\$109,020
Independent variable (DLH)	\$1.6003	\$4.1977
Coefficient of correlation	.4710	.6891
Standard error of the estimate	13,003	7,473
Standard error of the regression coefficient for the independent variable	.9744	1.3959
Calculated *t*-statistic for the regression coefficient	1.6423	3.0072
t-statistic required for a 95% confidence interval		
34 degrees of freedom (36 − 2)	1.960	
10 degrees of freedom (12 − 2)		2.228

b. Calculate the estimate of overhead costs for a month when 25,000 direct-labor hours are worked.

2. Using only the results of the two regression analyses, explain which of the two results (12 months versus 36 months) you would use as a basis for the flexible-budget formula.
3. How would the four specific issues raised by the members of Alma's accounting staff influence your willingness to use the results of the statistical analyses as the basis for the flexible-budget formula? Explain your answer.

24-20 ***Predicting cash balances.*** (CMA) Jackson Co. is experiencing cash-management problems. In particular, it has been unable to determine its temporary cash needs on a timely basis. This has increased the cost of borrowing, because the company has often been unable to obtain desirable terms. Borrowing in advance would give it better terms at a lower cost. A review of the cash flows indicates that all factors can be adequately predicted except the expenditures for hourly payroll and certain other expenditures. The cash receipts can be accurately determined because Jackson's customers are all reliable and pay on an identifiable schedule within the two calendar months following the sale. The payments for raw materials are similarly predictable because they are all paid in the calendar month subsequent to the purchase. Disbursements for monthly fixed obligations, such as lease payments and salaried personnel, are known well in advance of the payment dates.

In an attempt to better forecast cash changes for the next month, the company conducted a statistical analysis of many possible variables that might be suitable as a basis for forecasting the expenditure for payroll and other items. This analysis revealed a high correlation between the advance sales orders received in a month and those expenditures in the next month. The following relationships useful for cash forecasting have been identified (n = the forecast month):

1. Collections on account:

$$C_n = .9S_{n-1} + .1S_{n-2} \qquad \text{where } S = \text{sales}$$

2. Disbursements for raw-material purchases:

$$D_n = R_{n-1} \qquad \text{where } R = \text{raw-material purchases}$$

3. Monthly fixed obligations:

$$F_n = \$400{,}000$$

4. Payroll and other expenditures:

$$P_n = .25A_{n-1} + \$70{,}000, \quad \text{where } A = \text{advance sales orders}$$

Coefficient of correlation	= .96
Standard error of the estimate	= 10,000
Standard error of the regression coefficient of the independent variable	= .0013
t-statistic for 95% confidence interval	= 2.07

REQUIRED

1. Estimate the change in the cash balance for July 19_5 using the relationships specified above and the following data:

	SALES (S)	RAW-MATERIAL PURCHASES (R)	ADVANCE SALES ORDERS (A)
April	$1,300,000	$300,000	$1,225,000
May	1,200,000	400,000	1,050,000
June	1,000,000	350,000	1,400,000

2. Revise your estimate of the change in cash to recognize the uncertainty associated with the payroll and other expenditures.
3. How could management use this information to study alternative plans to reduce the short-term borrowing costs?

24-21 ***Choosing independent variables.*** A post office department has used a flexible-overhead budget for years:

$$\textbf{Budgeted overhead} = a + bx$$

where a = the intercept; b = rate per direct-labor hour; and x = number of direct-labor hours.

In recent years, much automated machinery has been introduced. The actual (but not measured) cost behavior pattern is

$$\textbf{Budgeted overhead} = a + bx_1 + cx_2$$

where c = rate per machine-hour and x_2 = number of machine-hours.

The department, which is managed by Richard, has two foremen. George is in charge of the machinery area. Harold is in charge of an area where direct laborers work intensively.

For the month of June, actual direct-labor hours of input exceeded the standard hours allowed for the output achieved by 20 percent. Moreover, the actual overhead incurred for the 6,000 actual direct-labor hours of input actually worked was $36,000.

REQUIRED

1. Prepare a graph of the flexible budget being used by the department. Let a = $14,000 and b = $3 per direct-labor hour. Compute and graph the budget, spending, and efficiency variances.
2. Which of the three managers is traditionally held responsible for each variance? What are the likely effects on the attitudes of the three managers under the existing budgeting formula?

24-22 ***Explaining a multiple-regression equation.*** (G. Benston) Assume that a cost recorded in a week is a function of such specified factors as x_1 = units of output, x_2 = number of units in a batch, and x_3 = the ratio of the number of luxury units to total units produced. The expected cost for any given week is $C = 100 + 30x_1 - 20x_2 + 500x_3$.

REQUIRED

1. What is the marginal cost of producing an additional unit of output?
2. The coefficient for x_2 is negative. Why? Explain fully.

24-23 ***Choosing among regressions.*** (SMA) The manager of the McMaster Manufacturing Company is planning production for the 19_2 calendar year. He has reliable estimates of direct-labor and material costs but is uncertain about overhead costs, which seem to fluctuate in response to both direct-labor hours and machine-hours. He asks his controller to determine relationships between overhead costs on direct-labor hours, machine-hours, and both.

As a first step toward solution of the problem, the controller runs three linear regressions, whose results are shown in the following table.

DETAILS	REGRESSION 1	REGRESSION 2	REGRESSION 3
Independent variable (X)	Labor-hours	Machine-hours	Machine-hours
Dependent variable (Y)	Overhead in dollars	Overhead in dollars	Labor hours
a	40,200	47,300	1,200
b	4.90	8.30	1.70
r^2	0.84	0.72	0.89
S_e	3,060	4,350	1,710
S_b	2.31	6.11	2.41

The above figures were arrived at using 12 months of monthly data.

The value of the t-statistic with 0.025 probability in the upper tail (generating a symmetric 95 percent confidence interval) is $t_{0.025} = 2.228$ with 10 degrees of freedom.

REQUIRED

1. What is the overhead budget's formula for 19_1? How did you arrive at your conclusion?
2. Do you think that the manager should run a multiple regression on *both* labor- and machine-hours? Why or why not?

24-24 ***Review of chapters 23 and 24.*** Refer to Problem 23-13. The consultant, upon reviewing the data presented and the linear-programming functions developed, performed further analysis of overhead costs. He used a multiple linear-regression model to analyze the overhead cost behavior. The regression model incorporated observations from the past 48 months of total overhead costs and the direct-labor hours for each product. The following equation was the result:

$$Y = \$5{,}000 + \$2X_A + \$4X_B + \$3X_C$$

where Y = monthly total overhead in dollars

X_A = monthly direct-labor hours for Product A

X_B = monthly direct-labor hours for Product B

X_C = monthly direct-labor hours for Product C

The total regression has been determined to be statistically significant, as has each of the individual regression coefficients.

Reformulate the objective function for Tripro Company using the results of this analysis.

24-25 ***Review of chapters 22 and 24.*** (J. Fellingham) José has an appliance store. He wishes to install an inventory control system and, in particular, calculate and utilize an optimal order quantity using the EOQ model. In pursuit of this goal, he collected some data about inventory item C:

Purchase price	\$25 per unit
Inventory insurance and other variable costs of storage paid at year-end	\$.50 per unit
Annual demand	1,000 units

José's opportunity rate of return is 10 percent. He anticipates no need for a safety stock. José is unsure about the cost behavior associated with ordering inventory. He collected some data about the most recent 20 orders made for inventory item C. He ran a regression using the number of units in each order to predict the total cost of the order (clerical, freight, receiving, and so forth). The results of the regression follow:

$$\widehat{TC} = 55.0 + 2.73\,x \text{ (number of units ordered)}$$
$$(11.0) \quad (.54)$$

$$r^2 = .83$$

The items in parentheses in the second line are the standard errors of the coefficients.

REQUIRED

1. Using only the data given above, what optimal order quantity would you recommend? Label your work.
2. What is the 95 percent confidence interval of the variable ordering cost per unit ordered?
3. Briefly list two regression assumptions that must be maintained in order to answer the preceding question. No more than two sentences.
4. The actual costs of ordering turned out to be $40 per order plus $3.50 per unit ordered. Assuming that the recommendation in requirement 1 was implemented, what was José's cost of prediction error? Label your work.

24-26 ***Analysis of regression results.*** (J. Demski) Ralph's Division (RD) is, for your convenience, a two-product, two-department firm. The two departments are code-named I and II, and the two products are designated A and B. Ralph's first problem is to determine a satisfactory production schedule; in thinking about this problem, he decides to analyze the firm's overhead structure. The accountant tells him that manufacturing overhead averages "about $9 per *direct-labor hour*." The accountant also supplies Ralph with the following data for the ten most recent *quarters*.

RD OVERHEAD AND VOLUME DATA

period	DL hours in dept. I	overhead in dept. I	DL hours in dept. II	overhead in dept. II	total DL hours	total overhead
1	984	$12,600	1,841	$13,200	2,825	$25,800
2	967	11,500	2,143	17,000	3,110	28,500
3	710	9,200	1,980	15,500	2,690	24,700
4	1,040	11,900	1,610	11,200	2,650	23,100
5	1,015	11,650	1,485	10,600	2,500	23,250
6	940	11,200	2,160	17,300	3,100	28,500
7	950	11,000	1,600	11,100	2,550	22,100
8	640	8,400	2,100	16,900	2,740	25,300
9	680	8,600	1,940	15,400	2,620	24,000
10	1,018	11,980	1,567	11,200	2,585	23,180

A computer program has been used to analyze these data. The results are:

DEPENDENT VARIABLE	INDEPENDENT VARIABLE	COEFFICIENT	STANDARD ERROR	*t*-VALUE	ADJUSTED r^2
6	1	8.51	1.40	6.1	
	3	10.09	.83	12.1	
	Intercept	−1,357	2,471	−.6	
					.94
Std. error of estimate,		538			
2	1	9.47	.85	11.1	
	Intercept	2,337	777	3.0	
					.93
Std. error of estimate,		392			
4	3	10.59	.49	21.6	
	Intercept	−5,579	915	−6.1	
					.98
Std. error of estimate,		382			
6	5	10.03	.87	11.5	
	Intercept	−2,617	2,404	−1.1	
					.94
Std. error of estimate,		565			

A correlation matrix shows:

VARIABLE	1	2	3	4	5	6
1	1.00	.97	−.56	.61	.05	−.06
2	.97	1.00	−.47	.54	.13	.03
3	−.56	−.47	1.00	.99	.81	.85
4	−.61	−.54	.99	1.00	.76	.82

VARIABLE	1	2	3	4	5	6
5	.05	.13	.81	.76	1.00	.97
6	−.06	.03	.85	.82	.97	1.00

REQUIRED

1. After surveying these results, Ralph picks the model relating total manufacturing overhead to total direct-labor hours. State (indicating intercept and slope values and independent variable) the model Ralph is proposing to use and give a *one-sentence* interpretation of the coefficients.
2. Ralph, filling with confidence, calls an accounting friend to show him this model. Regardless of your answer to requirement 1, suppose Ralph submits a model having a negative intercept. The friend inquires about the negative intercept, and Ralph (being none too confident) is subsequently shattered when he is informed (by technical personnel) that actual manufacturing cost for any quarter with zero production will be approximately $4,000. How, in *one sentence,* do you reconcile (or compare) the $4,000 datum with the negative regression intercept?
3. Suppose Ralph now obtains relevant data and runs a regression relating the cost of direct material in A to units of Product A. The results are

$$\widehat{(\textbf{DM Cost})}_A = -407.8 + 3.14A$$
$$(98.2) \qquad (1.01) \qquad r^2 = .83$$

Provide Ralph with a *one-sentence* interpretation of the negative intercept.

24-27 ***Analysis of regression results.*** (J. Demski) Ralph's Sauna, Ltd., manufactures custom electronic instruments and analog computer components. All "jobs" are manufactured to customer specification; the firm is, in fact, a classic example of the job shop. The firm has become interested in its cost function and is in the process of attempting to estimate its manufacturing overhead cost. A single manufacturing department was focused on and the following data were obtained (for the most recent 16 months):

TOTAL DEPARTMENTAL OVERHEAD	TOTAL DIRECT-LABOR HOURS	MATERIAL UNITS	ORDERS PROCESSED
$25,835	878 hours	970 Units	88 Orders
27,451	1,088	934	100
28,611	1,281	667	108
32,361	1,340	1,243	110
28,967	1,090	964	90
24,817	1,067	903	67
29,795	1,188	876	88
26,135	928	820	28
31,361	1,319	984	19
26,006	790	933	90
27,812	934	966	93
28,612	871	940	87
22,992	781	518	81
31,836	1,236	1,017	236
26,252	902	881	92
26,977	1,140	751	140

A computer program has been used to analyze these data. The results are:

DEPENDENT VARIABLE	INDEPENDENT VARIABLE	COEFFICIENT	STANDARD ERROR	t-VALUE	ADJUSTED r^2
1	2	8.50	1.93	4.4	
	3	6.95	2.21	3.2	
	4	6.59	7.19	.9	
	Intercept	12,052	2,286	5.3	
					.76
	Std. error of estimate,	1,281			
1	2	8.88	1.87	4.7	
	3	7.06	2.19	3.2	
	Intercept	12,190	2,267	5.4	
					.76
	Std. error of estimate,	1,273			

DEPENDENT VARIABLE	INDEPENDENT VARIABLE	COEFFICIENT	STANDARD ERROR	t-VALUE	ADJUSTED r^2
1	2	10.98	2.27	4.8	
	Intercept	16,310	2,421	6.7	
					.60
Std. error of estimate,		1,646			
1	3	10.68	3.26	3.27	
	Intercept	18,277	2,997	6.14	
					.39
Std. error of estimate,		2,027			

A correlation matrix shows:

	OVERHEAD	LABOR	MATERIAL	ORDERS
OVERHEAD	1.0000			
LABOR	.7913	1.0000		
MATERIAL	.6580	.3489	1.0000	
ORDERS	.3253	.2420	.1324	1.0000

REQUIRED

1. (a) Develop, (b) present, and (c) defend what you think is the most "reasonable" estimate of the recently experienced manufacturing overhead cost function.
2. Interpret the coefficients and independent variable (or variables) in your above answer.
3. Do you think your answer in requirement 1 would also provide a "useful" prediction of the manufacturing overhead that might be experienced next month?
4. For what purposes do you think management might use your answer in requirement 1?

24-28 ***Selecting an order.*** (J. Demski) Z Company has excess production capacity. The manager is trying to decide between two orders, one for 300 units of Product G at $38 each and the second for 200 units of Product H at $54 each. The cost predictions per unit are:

	DIRECT MATERIALS	DIRECT LABOR	FACTORY OVERHEAD	TOTAL
G	$20	$6	$12	$38
H	30	8	16	54

Five hundred machine-hours of capacity are going to be idle next year, so they could be utilized for producing one of these products. Factory overhead is applied at a rate of $8 per machine-hour. Nonmanufacturing costs will not be allocated to either order. Freight costs will be borne by the purchaser.

Further examination of the accounting indicates that the $8 per machine-hour is a firm-wide rate that reflects allocations of central management overhead. Listed below are data relating to actual overhead expenditures for the particular producing facilities concerned. The underlying relationships and levels of expenditures are expected to remain essentially the same during the coming period.

TOTAL FACTORY OVERHEAD EXPENDITURES	PRODUCTION OF G	PRODUCTION OF H	MACHINE-HOURS
$12,935	169 units	41 units	1,279 hrs.
25,918	306 units	366 units	4,559 hrs.
31,821	371 units	453 units	5,947 hrs.
26,367	270 units	480 units	5,045 hrs.
20,513	375 units	166 units	3,486 hrs.
31,736	258 units	513 units	5,737 hrs.

REQUIRED Which order should be accepted? Explain, showing computations.

24-29 ***Special order and breakeven analysis.*** (G. Feltham) The Holman Company manufactures a synthetic fiber that can be sold in its raw state or chemically impregnated and manufactured into cloth. The demand for the cloth has been spotty in the past, but Holman's prime customer (and usually the only one) has offered to sign a contract for 9,000 bolts per month at a price of $160 per bolt. This would be a 12-month contract, and if Holman does not accept it, the customer will go elsewhere. The Holman Company must decide whether to accept this contract and has accumulated the following information:

a. The demand for fiber has been weak during the past year, but the marketing manager believes that the company can sell 20,000 units per month at $80 per unit during the coming year. (A unit of fiber is the amount required to produce one bolt of cloth.)

b. The company has two production facilities, and each has a 10,000-unit capacity. The standard cost of a unit of fiber in each of these facilities is as follows:

	A	B
Materials	$20	$20
Labor	10	12
Overhead (300% of labor)	30	36
Total	$60	$68

c. Facility B may be used to produce cloth instead of fiber. If B is used to produce cloth, the capacity is 10,000 bolts and the standard cost of a bolt of cloth is:

Cost of fiber produced in Facility A	$ 60
Additional materials	10
Additional direct labor	15
Overhead	45
Total	$130

Facility B will be used to produce either fiber or cloth, but not both.

d. The overhead rate is based on the labor costs and overhead incurred during the previous year. The monthly data plus the total production (units of fiber plus bolts of cloth) are as follows:

MONTH	TOTAL OVERHEAD (THOUSANDS)	TOTAL PRODUCTION (THOUSANDS)	LABOR COST (THOUSANDS)
1	$ 585	19	$ 208
2	515	13	160
3	535	15	166
4	590	18	225
5	570	17	215
6	545	14	150
7	585	20	220
8	530	16	200
9	540	16	178
10	495	10	125
11	505	13	138
12	565	17	205
Total	$6,560	188	$2,190

REQUIRED

1. Will acceptance or rejection of the contract yield the highest profits? Present the analysis that supports your answer.
2. What level of sales is required to break even if only fiber can be sold?
3. What level of sales is required to break even if only cloth can be sold?

24-30 ***Predicting how costs will vary.*** (J. Demski) You are to determine a set of equations that will be useful for predicting the manner in which certain costs will vary. Listed below are three costs—production overhead, direct production, and marketing—along with five possible independent variables. Determine a "satisfactory" prediction model for each of the three costs. Determine each one separately, and defend your selection. (Note that labor quantity and production quantity are highly correlated; also, marketing is totally separate from production.)

	(1) OVERHEAD	(2) DIRECT	(3) MARKETING	(4) DIRECT-LABOR INPUT	(5) PRODUCTION QUANTITY	(6) SALES QUANTITY	(7) PRODUCTION LESS PRODUCTION LAST PERIOD	(8) PRODUCTION LESS PRODUCTION LAST PERIOD, THE QUANTITY SQUARED
1	$11,719	$1,035	$604	81.9	76	100	−24	576
2	11,190	1,071	582	85.5	79	95	3	9
3	11,860	871	565	65.1	70	70	−9	81
4	19,225	1,756	735	132.3	136	136	66	4,356
5	12,876	1,618	591	127.9	125	109	−11	121
6	11,922	1,725	387	130.3	128	91	3	9
7	12,261	1,698	622	124.9	125	105	−3	9
8	11,747	1,804	355	143.8	133	83	8	64
9	11,747	1,725	696	135.1	124	122	−9	81
10	12,057	1,699	609	126.6	129	113	5	25
11	12,771	1,477	636	120.1	115	94	−14	196
12	12,575	1,060	748	83.1	84	104	−31	961
13	11,034	1,088	666	90.9	84	92	0	0
14	14,316	1,597	551	122.4	122	91	38	1,444
15	13,380	1,148	537	89.1	90	100	−32	1,024

24-31 ***Choosing from among independent variables.*** (J. Demski) Data relating overhead cost to possible independent variables have been collected for the ten most recent periods and are presented below. Determine an equation that you feel would be useful in predicting the dependent variable (overhead cost) for the coming period. Your answer should contain the equation and the reason you feel it is the most appropriate alternative.

PERIOD	OVERHEAD COST	PRODUCTION (UNITS OF A)	PRODUCTION (UNITS OF B)	PRODUCTION (UNITS OF C)
1	$7,792	8	67	45
2	1,514	0	16	45
3	1,189	12	11	57
4	6,670	5	70	64
5	3,912	12	37	31
6	3,313	12	30	44
7	7,857	5	98	65
8	1,810	6	20	66
9	8,435	1	76	76
10	2,671	13	24	53

24-32 ***Effects of overtime.*** (J. Demski) Ralph Larutan produces a natural food product, consisting mainly of prunes and pig hocks, that is nationally marketed under the tradename Natural (which is Larutan spelled backwards). A highly placed government official has asked Ralph to produce 100 bushels of a special blend of new Natural to be used in a special government program. This extra quantity will not alter Ralph's present demand, and the only issue is whether the offered price of $5,000 is sufficient for Ralph to accept the offer.

Ralph collects the following production-cost data:

Standard material cost per bushel	= $20
Standard labor cost (at $10/hour) per bushel	= $10
Overhead	= $20
Standard cost per bushel	= $50

The overhead standard is based on recent monthly experiences of overhead averaging about $20 per labor-hour (at an average of about 1,000 labor-hours per month). Selling costs average about $10 per bushel, but these will not be incurred if the government's offer is accepted.

Ralph is relatively certain of the material- and labor-cost components but is bothered by the overhead. In particular, he realizes that the $20 datum is but an average that may be far removed from actual incremental shifts. Moreover, he also knows that this particular order, if accepted, will have to be produced on an overtime schedule, necessitating time and one-half labor payments.

One question, then, concerns predicting the cost of processing this order for 100 bushels of new Natural. Ralph feels that a linear approximation to the overhead cost function is sufficiently accurate for analysis of this decision; he also feels that labor-hours is a defensible independent variable. Hence, he collects the monthly data displayed in the accompanying table (from the 15 most recent months) and obtains the following regression result:

$$\widehat{\text{OVHD}} = \underset{(2,902)}{12,475} + \underset{(2.7)}{8.2}\ (\text{DL hrs}) \qquad r^2 \text{ adj} = .38$$

These results are somewhat disappointing because Ralph expected a better fit, and he thought that the actual overhead rate was closer to (a slope of) $10 per DL hour.

RALPH'S RECENT OVERHEAD DATA

total overhead	total DL hours	regular-time DL hours	overtime DL hours
$21,358	976	897	97
18,747	1,038	951	87
22,114	1,194	1,049	145
23,275	1,187	1,091	96
19,416	983	927	56
23,009	1,418	1,320	98
21,229	1,059	950	109
24,664	1,162	1,079	83
20,952	833	781	52
21,445	1,132	1,013	119
21,254	1,107	1,021	86
23,864	1,202	1,138	64
20,397	1,153	1,056	97
20,155	873	735	138
17,617	911	846	65

REQUIRED

1. What is the literal interpretation of the regression coefficients in the above equation?
2. What, using these predictions, is the full absorption cost and the direct (variable) cost per bushel of Natural?
3. What is the literal interpretation of each datum given in requirement 2? A two-sentence answer will suffice.
4. What is the predicted incremental gain to Ralph if he accepts the government's offer?
5. At this point, Ralph begins to stop placing so much faith in his accounting data. In particular, he knows that overtime premiums are generally lumped into overhead. (Check the data again.) Assuming this to be the case, would the 8.2 regression coefficients be biased? If your answer is yes, you should also state the *direction* of the bias.
6. Ralph also feels that other additional costs—besides the labor premium—are incurred by overtime production. Diseconomies in maintenance provide an example. Are the data consistent with Ralph's hypothesis? Give a one-sentence answer in support of your position.
7. Do you think Ralph's hypothesis (in requirement 6 above) is incorrect? Why?

24-33 ***Regression analysis.*** (J. Patell) Mike Mean, controller of Acro-Cel, has hired you as a consultant with data analysis skills to help him construct a flexible budget for overhead costs in 19_7. He has supplied you with the following monthly data from 19_6:

MONTH	DIRECT-LABOR HOURS	MATERIAL COSTS	OVERHEAD COSTS
Jan.	1295	$19,810	$8,900
Feb.	1108	17,001	8,444
Mar.	1330	19,208	8,056
Apr.	1302	22,137	8,209
May	1264	22,793	9,621
June	1340	19,596	8,747
July	830	11,032	6,701
Aug.	766	4,930	6,924
Sept.	1298	20,304	8,474
Oct.	1200	20,393	8,453
Nov.	1135	21,867	8,262
Dec.	1090	19,237	7,596

You have run a number of regression analyses and are now in the process of explaining the output. In all the regressions shown below, the *dependent* variable is overhead costs.

A. Mike initially felt that both labor-hours and material costs might be related to overhead expenditures, but he had no idea of their relative merits. Therefore you ran regression 1.

```
            OVHD        LAB HR    MATL $
OVHD        1.000
LAB HR      0.809       1.000
MATL $      0.787       0.873     1.000


> REGR  1
◆ GIVE NAME OR COL. NO. OF DEPENDENT VARIABLE : OVHD
HOW MANY INDEPENDENT VARIABLES ?2
INDEP. VAR. 1 = ?LAB HR
INDEP. VAR. 2 = ?MATL $


> COEF

VARIABLE     B(STD.V)       B           STD.ERROR(B)        T

 LAB HR      0.5158    2.1826E+00    1.6274E+00        1.341
 MATL $      0.3366    5.2868E-02    6.0396E-02        0.875
CONSTANT      0        4.6984E+03    1.0874E+03        4.321

> SUMM

              MULTIPLE R   R-SQUARE
UNADJUSTED      0.8260       0.6823
 ADJUSTED       0.7821       0.6117
 STD. DEV. OF RESIDUALS =          506.636

> DURB
DURBIN-WATSON STAT. = 2.176
```

1. State in equation form the overhead flexible budget indicated by regression 1.

2. "What do you mean, 'the *t*-statistics indicate that both labor-hours and material costs are insignificant'?" State in no more than two sentences the meaning of the *t*-statistics shown above.

3. "Look, I may not understand 'regression analysis' but I understand this company and I know that when we work more hours and use more material I get higher bills for indirect costs." If Mike is correct, how do you explain (in no more than three data analytic sentences) the *t*-statistics in regression 1?

B. Knowing that Mike was really interested in an inexpensive, easy-to-understand budget system, you also ran regressions 2 and 3.

```
> REGR  2
• GIVE NAME OR COL. NO. OF DEPENDENT VARIABLE : OVHD
HOW MANY INDEPENDENT VARIABLES ?1
INDEP. VAR.  1 = ?LAB HR


> COEF

VARIABLE    B(STD.V)       B          STD.ERROR(B)       T

 LAB HR      0.8095   3.4256E+00   7.8572E-01       4.360
CONSTANT      0       4.2144E+03   9.2529E+02       4.555

> SUMM

               MULTIPLE R   R-SQUARE
UNADJUSTED       0.8095      0.6553
 ADJUSTED        0.7879      0.6208
 STD. DEV. OF RESIDUALS =          500.68


> REGR  3
• GIVE NAME OR COL. NO. OF DEPENDENT VARIABLE : OVHD
HOW MANY INDEPENDENT VARIABLES ?1
INDEP. VAR.  1 = ?MATL $


> COEF

VARIABLE    B(STD.V)       B          STD.ERROR(B)       T

 MATL $      0.7867   1.2354E-01   3.0661E-02       4.029
CONSTANT      0       5.9514E+03   5.7813E+02      10.294

> SUMM

               MULTIPLE R   R-SQUARE
UNADJUSTED       0.7867      0.6188
 ADJUSTED        0.7620      0.5807
 STD. DEV. OF RESIDUALS =          526.477
```

"I'm not sure I follow exactly what's going on, but I'm glad you got both labor-hours and material costs to be 'significant' by doing things separately. Now let's just take the individual labor and material coefficients and plug them into the joint model you went after in the first regression. I think both effects really are important."

4. If Mike is correct about the form of the "true relation" he seeks, will his suggestion give you a good approximation of the coefficients? Explain thoroughly why or why not in no more than four sentences.

5. What is the meaning of the Durbin-Watson Statistic obtained for regression 1, and what does its numerical value of 2.176 indicate?

6. Using a *t*-probability table, construct a "95 percent confidence interval" for the labor-hour coefficient in *regression 2.* In no more than two sentences, what do you mean by a confidence interval?

7. Mike is intrigued by the idea of using labor-hours as a predictor of all costs, including material costs. Estimate the percentage of explained variance you would expect to achieve in a regression in which labor-hours were used to predict material costs.

24-34 ***Standard cost variances and regression analysis*** (M. Wolfson) The Clothworks Company produces embroidered tablecloths. A department store chain has offered to purchase 1,000 tablecloths at a price of $47 each. Clothworks has enough excess capacity to produce the extra 1,000 units without expansion. However, it will need to pay a 20 percent premium on labor costs for overtime, which will be charged to overhead.

Standard specifications for each tablecloth are as follows:

2 hours direct labor @ $8 per hour.
3 yards material @ $5 per yard.
Variable overhead is $4 per direct-labor hour.
Budgeted monthly fixed overhead totals $20,000.
Denominator level of activity is 10,000 standard direct-labor hours per month.

Alice Knight, the person responsible for this decision, would like to compute the variances for the month just ended. The following information is already available:

Number of tablecloths produced: 4,000
Actual overhead: $62,000
Fixed-overhead spending (flexible-budget) variance: 2,000 F
Variable-overhead efficiency variance: $9,000 U

REQUIRED

1. Determine the production-volume variance, variable-overhead spending variance, and labor-efficiency variance.
2. Determine the standard absorption cost of one tablecloth under the present standards.

The standards are used for motivational purposes and may not provide a good guide for such decisions as whether to accept the department store's offer. Clothworks computes the usual material, labor, and overhead variances on a monthly basis. Alice has just finished glancing at the variances for the past thirty months. She has confirmed that the standards are attained (on average) except in the cases of labor efficiency, variable-overhead efficiency, and material price. Three of the many regressions she ran are shown below (a positive variance is *unfavorable*):

```
(1) LABOR-EFFICIENCY VARIANCE = $150 + $4.0 UNITS PRODUCED
    (STANDARD ERRORS)            (300)   (0.5)
          R2 = 0.8          ADJ. R2 = 0.793  DURBIN-WATSON STAT. = 2.01

(2) LABOR-EFFICIENCY VARIANCE = $40 + $1.25 UNITS PRODUCED + $2.90M*
    (STANDARD ERRORS)            (280)   (8.9)                  (15.6)

          R2 = 0.83         ADJ. R2 = 0.817  DURBIN-WATSON STAT. = 2.2

*WHERE M REPRESENTS THE NUMBER OF YARDS OF MATERIAL USED.

(3) MATERIAL-PRICE VARIANCE = -$5000 + $0.0 ACTUAL LABOR WAGE RATE
    (STANDARD ERRORS)            (400)   (6.1)
          R2 = 0.001        DURBIN-WATSON STAT. = 1.85
```

Note: The answer to each of the following questions (except 7) does not depend upon the answers to earlier questions.

3. a. What is the economic interpretation of the negative intercept for the regression of material-price variance on actual labor rate (regression 3)?
   b. The r^2 for regression 3 is 0.001. Can we say anything about the statistical significance of the estimated constant (−5000)?
   c. Assuming the production-volume and material-efficiency variance to be (on average) zero, what is the average price paid for a yard of material? Assume that the material-price variance is determined at the time of usage.

4. Using regression 1 and the standards as your sources of information, what is the average number of labor-hours worked per unit of output?
5. Alice is somewhat perplexed about the second regression equation in which units produced and yards of material used appear on the right-hand side of the regression equation. The parameter estimates seem significantly less precise.
   a. What coefficient has the highest t-value in this regression and what is that value? (You may assume the dependent variable to be normally distributed.)
   b. Is this t-value significant, and what does this mean? (Two-sentence maximum.)
   c. Does this regression explain more sample variation in the labor-efficiency variance than the first regression in which units produced was the only independent variable? Explain. (Three-sentence maximum.)
   d. What is the apparent statistical relationship between the two independent variables used in the second regression? Is this unexpected? (Three-sentence maximum for each part.)
6. What is the meaning of the Durbin-Watson statistic of 2.01 in the first regression equation? (Three-sentence maximum.)
7. What is the apparent incremental cost of producing one tablecloth? Should the department store offer be accepted?

25 Variances: Mix, Yield, and Investigation

A principal function of comparing results with plans is to help explain what has happened. In this way, the user improves his or her comprehension of the impact of key variables on the actual results and acquires some feeling about areas that deserve more investigation. In short, the user may employ variance analysis to decide what additional information, if any, to buy. For example, a large variance may indicate a high probability that there will be a net benefit from conducting an investigation and gathering more data.

This chapter surveys some major areas of the analysis of accounting variances that have been covered only briefly, if at all, in earlier chapters. Three subjects are discussed: (a) the analysis of sales-quantity and sales-mix variances, (b) the analysis of production-yield and production-mix variances, and (c) the problem of when to investigate variances. Each subject can be studied independently, so the chapter is divided into three major parts.

Part one: sales-quantity and sales-mix variances

Most organizations produce more than one product or service. Therefore, overall plans for revenue usually specify some quantity and combination (often called **sales mix**) of products to be sold. Managers often want help in tracing deviations from original plans. From Chapter 6 we are already familiar with how price, efficiency, and sales-volume variances assist in this regard for *individual* products or services. Now we explore the complications that may arise at the individual and aggregate levels when the quantity and mix differ from the original plan.

The accounting literature on variance analysis in multiple-product situations is sizable and bewildering.[1] Every author and every organization seems to have a pet way of attacking the problem. Therefore, the first point is: be on guard whenever you see the terms "quantity variance," "mix variance," or "yield variance." In any situation be sure that all parties discussing such variances agree regarding definitions of all variances involved.

sales-volume variance

Consider an illustration. Suppose Ajax Company makes two types of products, A and B. Ajax has a budgeting system, basing its budget on last year's performance, general economic conditions, and its expected share of predicted industry sales.

Ajax prepared a static (master) budget for a given period, expecting to sell 160,000 units of output:

Budget 160,000

Sales	$1,000,000
Variable costs	600,000
Contribution margin	400,000
Fixed costs	300,000
Operating income	$ 100,000

Flexible budgets and standards were introduced in Chapter 6, which emphasized that managers can evaluate performance by seeking various levels of detail. Exhibit 6-6, page 174, provided an overview of variances. Pause and review that exhibit before reading further. Distinctions among variances were made at various levels of detail. Even in companies having mutiple products, the simplest, most informative analysis usually concentrates on a product-by-product analysis that has three components: *price, efficiency*, and *sales-volume* variances. Chapter 6 dwelled on the price and efficiency variances; we now focus on the sales-volume variance. The **sales-volume variance** is defined as the difference between the flexible-budget amounts and the static (master)-budget amounts. Unit prices are held constant.

Assume that Ajax actually sold 160,000 units during the period. The following table shows an analysis of the results:

---

[1]For an excursion into chaos, see the suggested readings on quantity, mix, and yield variances at the end of this chapter. Note that nearly everyone begins from the same place: Total variance = Actual costs minus some version of budgeted costs, or $v = a - b$. But disagreement arises rapidly when $(a - b)$ is factored so that

$$(a - b) = (a - a') + (a' - b') + (b' - b)$$

Consensus is hard to obtain regarding how and where a' and b' should be defined.

	ACTUAL	FLEXIBLE-BUDGET VARIANCES	FLEXIBLE BUDGET	SALES-VOLUME VARIANCES	STATIC (MASTER) BUDGET
Physical units of output	160,000		160,000		160,000
Revenue	$1,125,000	$75,000 F	$1,050,000	$50,000 F	$1,000,000
Variable costs	620,000	30,000 U	590,000	10,000 F	600,000
Contribution margin	$ 505,000	$45,000 F	$ 460,000	$60,000 F	$ 400,000
Fixed costs	305,000	5,000 U	300,000	—	300,000
Operating income	$ 200,000	$40,000 F	$ 160,000	$60,000 F	$ 100,000

F = Favorable; U = Unfavorable.

effects of more than one product

The table provides a fine overview of the variances, but most managers would seek more detail. In addition, there are puzzling aspects in the final three columns. How can the flexible-budget amounts differ from the static (master) budget if the number of units actually sold is equal to the 160,000 units originally budgeted? If this were a single-product company, there would be less confusion. There would be no divergence between the static budget and the flexible budget if the *total* number of units budgeted equaled the *total* number actually sold. But remember that budgets are summaries of underlying details, as the more detailed analysis will show.

In a multiproduct company, each product will have its own standards and flexible budgets. If the product *mix* changes, the flexible budget is affected because it is merely a *summation* of the flexible budget for the *individual* products sold.

Exhibit 25-1 shows how the original budgeted contribution margin of $400,000 was the sum of the budgeted contribution margins for 120,000 units of A and 40,000 units of B. But 110,000 units of A and 50,000 units of B were actually sold! The applicable flexible budget for 160,000 units would *not* be the same as the static budget *unless* the mix were unaffected.

Exhibit 25-1 provides the details of the volume variance by product. It shows how the flexible budget is really a compilation of individual flexible budgets and how the total flexible-budget amounts could easily differ from the static-budget amounts. The details of the sales-volume variance tell the manager a straightforward story. Consider the sales-volume variance for the contribution margin:

Sales-volume variance = (Flexible-budget units − Static-budget units) × (Budgeted individual product contribution margin per unit)

For A:	= (110,000 − 120,000) × $1	=	$10,000 U
For B:	= (50,000 − 40,000) × $7	=	70,000 F
Total			$60,000 F

Before reading on, study Exhibit 25-1 carefully. Note that *the Flexible-Budget columns are based on the actual units sold.* Some readers may prefer to use "Actual" as a heading, but "Flexible Budget" is a more accurate description because all the numbers are based on *budgeted* unit prices, not *actual* unit prices.

Note also how the sales-volume variance might be better labeled as a "marketing variance." Other things being equal, the failure to sell the originally expected 120,000 units of Product A would cause a decline in operating income of 10,000 units ×

EXHIBIT 25-1

Sales-Volume Variances by Product

	PRODUCT A			PRODUCT B			TOTAL		
	flexible budget*	**static (master) budget**	**sales-volume variance**	**flexible budget***	**static (master) budget**	**sales-volume variance**	**flexible budget***	**static (master) budget**	**sales-volume variance**
Sales in units	110,000	120,000	10,000 U	50,000	40,000	10,000 F	160,000	160,000	—
Sales @ \$5 and @ \$10	\$550,000	\$600,000	\$50,000 U	\$500,000	\$400,000	\$100,000 F	\$1,050,000	\$1,000,000	\$50,000 F
Variable costs @ \$4 and @ \$3	440,000	480,000	40,000 F	150,000	120,000	30,000 U	590,000	600,000	10,000 F
Contribution margin @ \$1 and @ \$7	\$110,000	\$120,000	\$10,000 U	\$350,000	\$280,000	\$ 70,000 F	\$ 460,000	\$ 400,000	\$60,000 F
Fixed costs							300,000	300,000	—
Operating income							\$ 160,000	\$ 100,000	\$60,000 F

**Based on actual units sold during the period.*
F = Favorable; U = Unfavorable)

$1 = $10,000. However, the selling of 10,000 more units of Product B than originally expected would cause an increase in operating income of 10,000 units × $7 = $70,000.

use by managers

Consider the appropriate variance analysis at three levels of management: (1) the individual product manager, (2) the manager of the two-product line consisting of A plus B, (3) higher management in a vast company that markets numerous product lines.

The individual managers of Products A and B in Exhibit 25-1 will be primarily concernied with why their volume levels differed from their individual budgets. We have discussed this type of variance analysis before (Chapter 6, p. 169).

The manager of the A–B product line may concentrate on the "total" columns in Exhibit 25-1. In particular, note that the total columns offer the manager only an analytical beginning. First, note that the budgeted and actual aggregated physical units were equal. So what? Adding physical units together often offers a summed hodgepodge. For example, Product A may be shaving lotion and Product B may be shampoo. The point is that as we move beyond a one-product situation, aggregated physical units fail to provide a common denominator for measuring overall sales volume. Instead, physical units are converted into monetary equivalents such as sales dollars. But we should not lose sight of the fact that the fundamental inputs and outputs of organizations are physical goods or services.

Second, the aggregated dollars give an overall picture of the product line, but decisions typically must focus on individual products. The variances in the total columns are merely the sums of the individual product sales-volume variances.

Third, there is enormous confusion regarding the $50,000, $10,000, and $60,000 total sales-volume variances. Taken together, the **total sales volume in units** was unchanged, but the original proportions or mix changed. That is why this total variance is sometimes called something else, or some of it is called a mix variance while the remainder is called a volume variance. **No matter what the label, the fundamental explanation is that the actual physical volumes of individual products deviated from what was expected.** Obviously, if the original budget in total units is attained, but a larger proportion of higher-margin products are sold than was specified in the original mix, higher profits will ensue.

Fourth, if the product-line manager really wants a full explanation, he or she must buy more information. That is, the manager must get the individual product analyses contained in the other columns. This is not a trivial point. Many accounting systems do not routinely prepare current reports by individual products, so the manager may have to work with only the totals in dollars (not even including the total physical units).

higher managers

Higher managers usually receive summary monetary figures rather than being flooded with too much detail. Occasionally, using the summary signals generated by variance analysis, higher managers will buy more information by requesting the underlying disaggregated analyses. Thus, higher managers would probably receive only the dollar amounts (not the number of physical units) in the total column in Exhibit 25-1.

What does higher management learn from such numbers? All variances are favorable. That is comforting! But why? Did physical volume of each product rise by 5 percent? Or did the sales of higher-margined items soar while the lower-margined items merely met targeted levels? Again, the higher managers will never know unless they obtain a product-by-product breakdown. Of course, higher managers may frequently be satisfied with the aggregated data as shown; they may prefer to have subordinates conduct the detailed follow-up.

quantity and mix variances

Many accountants favor probing the sales-volume variances further. The analysis in Exhibit 25-1 reveals how the overall sales-volume variances can be affected by two major factors, the actual physical quantity of goods sold and the relative proportions of products bearing different contribution margins.

To simplify the computations, focus solely on contribution margins, even though these variances could be separately computed for revenues and variable costs. **Sales-quantity variances** and **sales-mix variances** for the contribution margins may be defined as follows:

Sales-quantity variance = (Actual volume in units − Static-budget volume in units) × Budgeted average contribution margin per unit

For A:	**= (110,000 − 120,000) × $2.50***	**= $25,000 U**
For B:	**= (50,000 − 40,000) × $2.50***	**= 25,000 F**
Total		**$ 0**

**Computed from the total static budget: $400,000 ÷ 160,000 units = $2.50 per unit.*

Sales-mix variance = Difference in units (as above) × (Budgeted individual contribution margin per unit − Budgeted average contribution margin per unit)

For A:	**= (110,000 − 120,000) × ($1.00 − $2.50)**	**= $15,000 F**
For B:	**= (50,000 − 40,000) × ($7.00 − $2.50)**	**= 45,000 F**
Total		**$60,000 F**

Observe that the sales-quantity variance weighs all physical units at a single overall weighted-average budgeted contribution margin per unit. For a given change in physical volume, the total contribution margin would be expected to change at the $2.50 rate of the average unit margin.

Ponder the role of the *average* unit margin. It helps focus on *overall* results, not *individual product* results. By itself, an individual sales-quantity variance for A does not help understanding if it is based on an average margin. However, the total sales-quantity variance can enhance understanding. The manager can see how income should fluctuate if the original product mix is maintained as overall physical volume departs from that originally budgeted.

Incidentally, the initial term in the formula is: actual volume minus static-budget volume. It could also be expressed as: flexible-budget volume minus static-budget volume. Why? Because the actual physical volume and the flexible-budget physical volume are always the same.

The *sales-mix variance* measures the impact of the deviation from the budgeted average contribution margin per unit associated with a change in the quantity of a particular product. The actual mix produced a weighted-average unit contribution of $2.875:

	ACTUAL UNITS SOLD	BUDGETED UNIT CONTRIBUTION MARGIN	ACTUAL CONTRIBUTION AT BUDGETED MARGINS
A	110,000	$1.00	$110,000
B	50,000	7.00	350,000
	160,000		$460,000

Weighted average = $460,000 ÷ 160,000 = $2.875

Therefore, the unit margins attained were \$.375 higher than the \$2.50 budgeted. Thus, the sales-mix variance would be 160,000 units at \$.375 each, the same \$60,000 computed on p. 861.[2]

The sales-mix variance is favorable when either (a) selling more of the products bearing unit contribution margins higher than average (Product B) or (b) selling less of the products bearing unit contribution margins lower than average (Product A).

If the original sales mix were maintained, but physical volume increased by 5 percent, there would be no sales-mix variance, only a sales-quantity variance. The actual sales would be 126,000 units of A and 42,000 of B. The sales-quantity variance would be:

For A:	= (126,000 − 120,000) × \$2.50	=	\$15,000 F
For B:	= (42,000 − 40,000) × \$2.50	=	5,000 F
Total	= (168,000 − 160,000) × \$2.50	=	\$20,000 F

This would be consistent with the idea that, given an unchanging sales mix, a 5 percent increase in physical volume should produce a 5 percent increase in sales dollars and a 5 percent increase in contribution margin. The budgeted contribution margin would increase from \$400,000 to \$420,000, or the \$20,000 increase calculated above.

industry variances

Many companies regard their fate as being heavily affected by (a) overall demand for the products of an industry and (b) a company's ability to maintain its share of the market. Sometimes industry statistics are readily available, so the company's market share can easily be monitored. Examples are automobiles, television sets, housing, and steel. At other times, industry statistics are not easy to obtain, at least in timely fashion.

Suppose our illustrative company had reliable statistics and expected to maintain a 5 percent share of an industry market of 3,200,000 units during the budget period: .05 × 3,200,000 = 160,000 units. Suppose further that the industry market was actually 4,000,000 units, but the company got only a 4 percent share. The sales-quantity variance can be subdivided into the *market-size variance* and the *market-share variance.*[3]

---

[2]Readers who prefer mathematical notation can express these variances as follows:

$$\text{Sales-quantity variance} = \sum_i (\Delta x_i) m^*$$

$$\text{Sales-mix variance} = \sum_i (\Delta x_i)(m_i - m^*)$$

where Δx_i = actual minus budgeted units sold of Product i
m^* = budgeted average contribution margin per unit if all products were sold in proportion to the product mix
m_i = budgeted contribution margin per unit for Product i

See Robert S. Kaplan, *Advanced Management Accounting* (Englewood Cliffs, N.J.: Prentice-Hall, 1982), Chap. 9.

[3]Also see J. Shank and N. Churchill, "Variance Analysis: A Management Oriented Approach," *Accounting Review,* October 1977, p. 955.

Market-size variance = (Budgeted market-share percentage)
× (Actual industry volume in units
− Budgeted industry volume in units)
× (Budgeted average contribution margin per unit)
= .05 × (4,000,000 − 3,200,000) × $2.50
= $100,000 F

Market-share variance = (Actual market-share percentage
− Budgeted market-share percentage)
× (Actual industry volume in units)
× (Budgeted average contribution margin per unit)
= (.04 − .05) × 4,000,000 × $2.50
= $100,000 U

Managers are likely to gain some insights from these variances. They measure the additional contribution margin, $100,000, that would be expected because the market size expanded. Unfortunately, the company attained only 4 percent of the industry market (160,000 ÷ 4,000,000 = .04). This failure to maintain market share caused an equal offsetting variance. (Obviously, the dollar amounts will not always be equally offsetting.)

problem for self-study

problem

Review Exhibit 25-1. Suppose that 100,000 units of Product A and 44,000 units of Product B were sold. Focus on the contribution-margin line. Compute the sales-volume variances for each product and in total. Subdivide the sales-volume variance into sales-quantity and sales-mix variances. Using your numerical results, comment on the meaning of the three types of variance.

solution

Sales-volume variance = Difference in units sold
× Budgeted individual contribution margin per unit

For A:	= (100,000 − 120,000) × $1.00 =	$20,000 U
For B:	= (44,000 − 40,000) × 7.00 =	28,000 F
Total		$ 8,000 F

This variance is straightforward. The manager can see that selling 20,000 fewer units of A hurt the total contribution margin by $20,000. However, selling 4,000 more units of B, which is more profitable per unit, more than offset the unfavorable effects of A.

Sales-quantity variance = Difference in units sold
× Budgeted average contribution margin per unit

For A:	= (100,000 − 120,000) × $2.50 =	$50,000 U
For B:	= (44,000 − 40,000) × $2.50 =	10,000 F
Total	= (144,000 − 160,000) × $2.50 =	$40,000 U

Given an unchanging mix, a failure to attain the budgeted unit quantity of 160,000 units would produce an unfavorable sales-quantity variance of 160,000 − 144,000, or 16,000 units multiplied by the average unit contribution of $2.50, for a total of $40,000.

Sales-mix variance = Difference in units sold
× (Budgeted individual contribution margin per unit
− Budgeted average contribution margin per unit)

For A: = (100,000 − 120,000) × ($1.00 − $2.50) = $30,000 F
For B: = (44,000 − 40,000) × ($7.00 − $2.50) = 18,000 F
Total **$48,000 F**

The weighted-average unit contribution was $2.8333:

	ACTUAL UNITS SOLD	BUDGETED UNIT CONTRIBUTION MARGIN	ACTUAL CONTRIBUTION AT BUDGETED MARGINS
A	100,000	$1.00	$100,000
B	44,000	7.00	308,000
	144,000		$408,000

Weighted average = $408,000 ÷ 144,000 = $2.8333

Therefore, the unit contribution margin attained was $.3333 higher than the $2.50 budgeted. This produced a sales-mix variance of $48,000, which could be computed by multiplying 144,000 units by $.3333.

A summary of these three variances follows:

Sales-quantity variance	$40,000 U
Sales-mix variance	48,000 F
Sales-volume variance	$ 8,000 F

Part two: production-yield and production-mix variances

Manufacturing processes often entail the combination of a number of different materials and a number of different direct-labor skills to obtain a unit of finished product, or the use of a single material or direct-labor skill to produce several joint products. Chemicals, plastics, lumber, fruit, vegetables, rubber, and fabrics, for example, can sometimes be combined in various ways without affecting the specified quality characteristics of a finished product. Similarly, the composition of teams of labor may differ from hour to hour or day to day.

What is usually meant by the terms **material yield** and **material mix?** The meaning of each should be pinpointed at a particular setting. In general, *mix* refers to the relative proportion or combination of the various ingredients of direct materials or of the components of a finished product line. *Yield* refers to the quantity of finished output produced from a predetermined or *standard combination and amount of inputs,* such as direct material. The analysis of production-yield and production-mix variances is similar to the analysis of the sales-mix and sales-quantity variances illustrated in the preceding section.

Material-yield and material-mix variances

When we initially examined material and labor variances in Chapter 6, we saw that managers sometimes make trade-offs between price and efficiency variances. For example, a shoe manufacturer may try some variations in grades of leather if the potential savings exceed the potential costs of waste or rejects.

In addition to considering whether to make deliberate changes, managers must contend with technical characteristics that are frequently uncontrollable, at least in the short run. For example, humidity, temperature, molecular structure, or other physical characteristics can dramatically affect the relationships between inputs and outputs.

the usual analysis Consider a specific example of multiple inputs and a single output. Suppose a chemical company has the following standards:

5 gallons of Material F at	$ .70 =	$3.50
3 gallons of Material G at	1.00 =	3.00
2 gallons of Material H at	.80 =	1.60
10 gallons of standard combination of inputs at	.81	$8.10

which should produce 9 gallons of finished product at a standard cost of $8.10 ÷ 9 = $.90 a gallon.

Suppose, for simplicity, that no inventories of raw materials are kept. Purchases are made as needed, so that all price variances relate to materials used. Actual results show that 100,000 gallons were used during a certain period:

45,000 gallons of F at actual cost of $ .80 =	$36,000
33,000 gallons of G at actual cost of $1.05 =	34,650
22,000 gallons of H at actual cost of $ .85 =	18,700
100,000	$89,350
Good output was 92,070 gallons at standard cost of $.90	82,863
Total variance to be explained	$ 6,487 U

A production manager may seek no more than the usual price and efficiency variances, as explained in Chapter 6. The total variance would be analyzed in the familiar manner:

MATERIAL	ACTUAL INPUTS × ACTUAL PRICES	ACTUAL INPUTS × STANDARD PRICES	STANDARD INPUTS ALLOWED × STANDARD PRICES
F	45,000 × $ .80 = $36,000	45,000 × $ .70 = $31,500	51,150 × $ .70 = $35,805
G	33,000 × $1.05 = 34,650	33,000 × $1.00 = 33,000	30,690 × $1.00 = 30,690
H	22,000 × $ .85 = 18,700	22,000 × $ .80 = 17,600	20,460 × $ .80 = 16,368
Total	100,000 $89,350	100,000 $82,100	102,300* $82,863

Price variance, $7,250 U — Efficiency variance, $763 F

Flexible budget variance, $6,487 U

Note that the budged input must be that standard combination normally needed to produce 92,070 gallons, or 92,070 ÷ .9, or 102,300 gallons. Material F's budgeted share would be .5 × 102,300, or 51,150 gallons; G's, .3 × 102,300, or 30,690; H's, .2 × 102,300, or 20,460.

First, concentrate on the total variance. Note that it is computed in the usual way: (Actual inputs × Actual prices) − [(Good output, or Standard inputs allowed) × Standard prices]. Moreover, the usual way of computing the price and efficiency variances provides a supplementary explanation of where these numbers arose. Consider the price variances:

Price variance = Difference in unit price × Actual product quantity

For F:	**= ($ .70 − $ .80) × 45,000 =**	**$4,500 U**
For G:	**= ($1.00 − $1.05) × 33,000 =**	**1,650 U**
For H:	**= ($ .80 − $ .85) × 22,000 =**	**1,100 U**
		$7,250 U

The efficiency variances may also be computed in the usual manner. The differences in inputs are:

MATERIAL	DETAILED COMPUTATIONS FOR COLUMN (1)	**(1)** BUDGETED OR STANDARD QUANTITY OF INPUTS ALLOWED	**(2)** ACTUAL QUANTITY OF INPUTS USED	**(1) − (2)** DIFFERENCE
F	(.5 × 102,300)	51,150	45,000	+6,150
G	(.3 × 102,300)	30,690	33,000	−2,310
H	(.2 × 102,300)	20,460	22,000	−1,540
Total	(10/9 × 92,070)	102,300	100,000	+2,300

The dollar amounts are:

Efficiency variance = Difference in inputs × Standard price

For F:	**= +6,150 × $ .70 =**	**$4,305 F**
For G:	**= −2,310 × $1.00 =**	**2,310 U**
For H:	**= −1,540 × $ .80 =**	**1,232 U**
Total		**$ 763 F**

The analysis above may suffice where managers control each input on an individual basis and where no discretion is permitted regarding the physical mix of material inputs. For example, there is often a predetermined mix of materials needed for the assembly of radios, automobiles, razors, and dryers. Suppose that all deviations from the engineered input/output relationships are deemed to be attributable to efficiency. In these cases, the price and efficiency variances individually computed for each material typically provide all that is needed for decisions because no deliberate substitutions of inputs are tolerated.

role of yield and mix variances

Should production-yield and production-mix variances be calculated as a routine part of a management accounting system? The answer depends on the insights that managers might obtain. The greater the opportunity for trade-offs or substitutions between materials, the more likely that these variances may aid managers by pinpointing the results of these substitutions.

In our illustration, the efficiency variance of $763 may be subdivided into yield and mix components:

Material-yield variance = Difference in units of input × Budgeted average price per unit of input

For F:	**= +6,150 × $.81**	**=**	**$4,981.50 F**
For G:	**= −2,310 × $.81**	**=**	**1,871.10 U**
For H:	**= −1,540 × $.81**	**=**	**1,247.40 U**
Total	**= +2,300 × $.81**	**=**	**$1,863.00 F**[4]

A distinction must be drawn between complete substitutability of materials and constrained or partial substitutability. For example, shirts may be made of 100 percent cotton or 100 percent dacron or some combination thereof. If the manager has discretion regarding complete substitution, no mix variance is necessary. He or she should pick the material that results in the product with the lowest overall cost. (We are assuming, perhaps foolishly in this example, that the quality of the product is unaffected by this substitution decision.) Where there is complete substitution, there is no mix problem. Only one input should be used. There should be no mix variance because there should be no mix.[5]

Material-mix variance = Difference in units of input
× (Budgeted individual price per unit of input
− Budgeted average price per unit of input)

For F:	**= +6,150 × ($ .70 − $.81) =**	**$ 676.50 U**
For G:	**= −2,310 × ($1.00 − $.81) =**	**438.90 U**
For H:	**= −1,540 × ($ .80 − $.81) =**	**15.40 F**
Total		**$1,100.00 U**

This subdivision of the efficiency variance shows that if the combination of ingredients were held constant and 2,300 units less input were used, the savings would have been $1,863, solely because of improved yield of a given mix of inputs. In effect, the yield variance holds average unit price constant and views all units of input as if they were alike. The mix variance shows that higher usage of more expensive ingredients and lower usage of less expensive ingredients caused higher costs. In short, there was a trade-off among ingredients that boosted yield but caused average budgeted unit costs of the overall inputs to be higher than expected. The trade-off resulted

---

[4]Another way of computing this variance is to compute the difference between the standard cost of the output and the standard cost of a standard combination of input:

Output:	92,070 gallons at $.90 =	$82,863
Input:	100,000 gallons at $.81 =	81,000
Material-yield variance		$ 1,863

Still another way is to compute the standard yield from 100,000 gallons of input, which is 90,000 gallons. The actual production exceeded the standard yield of the input by 2,070 gallons (92,070 − 90,000). At a standard material cost of $.90 per gallon, the favorable yield variance is $1,863.

[5]J. L. Livingstone, ed., *Management Planning and Control: Mathematical Models* (New York: McGraw-Hill, 1970), p. 190.

in a net favorable variance of $763.[6] Thus, the material-yield and material-mix variances provide additional insights for the manager.

Direct-labor yield and direct-labor mix variances

As we have just seen, the standard costs of products are frequently developed by using specified combinations of materials bearing different individual prices. The same approach is often used for direct labor. Pursuing our example, suppose the production process required considerable human attention. The direct-labor rate per gallon of output was computed as follows:

(1) Labor price per hour:	
1 skilled worker @ $20	$20
2 unskilled workers @ $11	22
Total cost of standard combination of labor	$42
Average price per hour, $42 ÷ 3 =	$14
(2) Standard labor price per gallon of output at 10 gallons per hour, $14 ÷ 10 =	$1.40
(3) Standard labor cost of 92,070 gallons of output, $1.40 × 92,070, or $14 × 9,207 hours =	$128,898
(4) Actual inputs, 9,000 hours consisting of:	
3,400 hours of skilled labor @ $21	$ 71,400
5,600 hours of unskilled labor @ $10	56,000
9,000 hours @ $14.1555	$127,400

First, consider the usual direct-labor variances:

DIRECT LABOR	ACTUAL INPUTS FOR ACTUAL OUTPUTS × ACTUAL PRICES		ACTUAL INPUTS × STANDARD PRICES		STANDARD INPUTS ALLOWED × STANDARD PRICES	
Skilled	3,400 × $21 =	$ 71,400	3,400 × $20 =	$ 68,000	3,069* × $20 =	$ 61,380
Unskilled	5,600 × $10 =	56,000	5,600 × $11 =	61,600	6,138* × $11 =	67,518
Total	9,000	$127,400	9,000	$129,600	9,207	$128,898

Price variance, $2,200 F

Efficiency variance, $702 U

Flexible-budget variance, $1,498 F

*1/3 × 9,207 and 2/3 × 9,207.

---

[6] Readers who prefer mathematical notation can express these variances as follows:

$$\textbf{Material-yield variance} = \sum_i (\Delta x_i) p^*$$

$$\textbf{Material-mix variance} = \sum_i (\Delta x_i)(p_i - p^*)$$

where Δx_i = budgeted or standard quantity of inputs of material i allowed minus actual quantity of inputs used

p^* = budgeted average price per unit of the standard combination of inputs

p_i = budgeted price per unit of input of material i

See Kaplan, *Advanced Management Accounting*, Chap. 9.

The labor-efficiency variance may be subdivided into yield and mix variances in the same way that we subdivided material-efficiency variance in the previous section. The differences in inputs are:

LABOR	DETAILED COMPUTATIONS FOR COLUMN (1)	(1) BUDGETED OR STANDARD QUANTITY OF INPUTS ALLOWED	(2) ACTUAL QUANTITY OF INPUTS USED	(1) − (2) DIFFERENCE
Skilled	(1/3 × 9,207)	3,069(33.3%)	3,400(37.8%)	−331
Unskilled	(2/3 × 9,207)	6,138(66.7%)	5,600(62.2%)	+538
		9,207(100.0%)	9,000(100.0%)	+207

Labor-yield variance = Difference in units of input × Budgeted average price per hour of input

For skilled: = −331 × $14 = $4,634 U

For unskilled: = +538 × $14 = 7,532 F

Total = +207 × $14 = $2,898 F

Labor-mix variance = Difference in units of input × (Budgeted individual price per hour of input − Budgeted average price per hour of input)

For skilled: = −331 × ($20 − $14) = $1,986 U

For unskilled: = +538 × ($11 − $14) = 1,614 U

Total = $3,600 U

This illustration highlights the financial impact of the interaction of *all* variances. The manager may have deliberately decided to change the mix of skilled and unskilled labor. The budgeted proportion of skilled labor was 33.3 percent, whereas the actual proportion was 3,400 ÷ 9,000 = 37.8 percent. Moreover, the labor was paid $21 per hour instead of the budgeted rate of $20. As a result, a net advantage ensued. Even though a small efficiency variance of $702 occurred, a price variance of $2,200 was achieved because the unskilled workers were paid a rate of $10 rather than the budgeted rate of $11. Perhaps the manager made the trade-off because many of the unskilled workers were new, earning lower-than-budgeted rates, and were expected to be more inefficient than the usual unskilled workers. By introducing a mix with a higher proportion of skilled workers, the overall budgeted efficiency was almost attained.

The financial effect of substitution on labor efficiency is measured by the yield and mix variances. *In particular, note that all price variances are excluded from these calculations.* The **labor-yield variance** tells the manager that if the mix of labor inputs were held constant and 207 fewer hours of input were used than budgeted for the output achieved, the labor-yield variance would be favorable—assuming other things (mix) are unaffected.

The **labor-mix variance** showed that the higher-than-budgeted proportion (37.8 percent instead of 33.3 percent) of more expensive labor and the lower-than-budgeted proportion (62.2 percent instead of 66.7 percent) of less expensive labor caused higher costs—if other things (yield) are unaffected. In this instance, ignoring price variances, the manager's trade-off was unwise because the higher cost of the more expensive mix, $3,600, exceeded the savings, $2,898, of the improved yield. Thus, the manager may find the mix and yield variances helpful in understanding why the total efficiency variance was $702, unfavorable.

problem for self-study

problem

Review the example on material-yield variances. Suppose that 40,000 gallons of G and 15,000 gallons of H were actually used. Compute the total price and total efficiency variances. Explain why the efficiency variance is no longer $763, favorable. Also compute the material-yield and material-mix variances.

solution

MATERIAL	ACTUAL INPUTS × ACTUAL PRICE	ACTUAL INPUTS × STANDARD PRICE	STANDARD INPUTS ALLOWED × STANDARD PRICE
F	45,000 × $ .80 = $36,000	45,000 × $ .70 = $31,500	51,150 × $ .70 = $35,805
G	40,000 × $1.05 = 42,000	40,000 × $1.00 = 40,000	30,690 × $1.00 = 30,690
H	15,000 × $ .85 = 12,750	15,000 × $ .80 = 12,000	20,460 × $ .80 = 16,368
	$90,750	$83,500	$82,863

↑ Price variance, $7,250 U* ↑ Efficiency variance, $637 U ↑

**Coincidentally, the price variance of $7,250 U is the same as the $7,250 U in the original example. This is because both G and H have unfavorable unit-price variances of $.05, and the same total quantities of these were used in each example (55,000).*

The efficiency variance of $763, favorable, has become $637, unfavorable, a $1,400 move in the wrong direction, because the new actual combination is less economical than the old actual combination:

INPUTS USED

	old combination		new combination		difference
F	45,000 × $ .70 =	$31,500	45,000 × $ .70 =	$31,500	$ 0
G	33,000 × $1.00 =	33,000	40,000 × $1.00 =	40,000	7,000 U
H	22,000 × $ .80 =	17,600	15,000 × $ .80 =	12,000	5,600 F
	100,000	$82,100	100,000	$83,500	$1,400 U

Note that the yield variance would be unaffected; only the combination of inputs has changed, **and yield variances are based on an assumption of no change in the standard combination of inputs.**

Material-yield variance = Difference in units of input × Budgeted average price of input

For F: = (51,150 − 45,000) × $.81 = $4,981.50 F
For G: = (30,690 − 40,000) × $.81 = 7,541.10 U
For H: = (20,460 − 15,000) × $.81 = 4,422.60 F
Total = (102,300 − 100,000) × $.81 = $1,863.00 F

Material-mix variance = Difference in units of input × (Budgeted individual price per unit of input − Budgeted average price per unit of input)

For F: = +6,150 × ($ .70 − $.81) = $ 676.50 U
For G: = −9,310 × ($1.00 − $.81) = 1,768.90 U
For H: = +5,460 × ($ .80 − $.81) = 54.60 U
Total $2,500.00 U

The change in the efficiency variance is solely attributable to the change in the mix of the materials. As compared with the actual materials in the original illustration, the new mix of actual materials contains 7,000 more units of G, which bear a higher unit cost than the 7,000 units of H displaced by G.

This computation of mix and yield variances tells the manager that the trade-off was unwise. That is, yield was better than standard, but the use of higher-cost materials more than offset the advantage of yield.

Part three: the decision to investigate

Given feedback in the form of routine reports of cost variances, when should managers investigate a process where variances occurred? These variances may lead to investigation or no investigation. In turn, investigation may prompt corrective action or no corrective action.

The accounting system often plays a part in these decisions, but it is not an exclusive source of information. Managers obviously do not investigate every variance that arises, line by line. As usual, the decisions are based on layers of simplifications, assumptions, and imperfect knowledge about the relative costs and benefits. This section explores the dimensions of this investigation decision.

types of deviations

Suppose feedback—such as a cost variance—prompts a decision maker to investigate the process. One or more of five separate deviations (that is, sources of variances) might have contributed to this variance between actual and predicted costs: implementation, prediction, measurement, model, and random.[7] These types of deviations are discussed in sequence. Note that each may call for different corrective actions.

1. An *implementation* deviation is a human or mechanical failure to achieve a specific obtainable action. For example, consider the economic-order-quantity inventory model, which was discussed in Chapter 22. Perhaps because of improper motivation or instruction, a clerk or worker may order the wrong quantity or produce the wrong size of batch. The economic order quantity is assumed to be obtainable, given whatever events may have occurred. Consequently, there is a strong likelihood that the deviation can be immediately suppressed once its existence is determined.

The optimal correction requires that we compare the cost of suppression (which is likely to be minimal in this example) with the resultant saving (benefit). If no other deviations are present, this net saving indicates the expected amount of net benefit (per future period, if this deviation is likely to persist) that will be saved by correction.

2. A *prediction* deviation is an error in predicting a parameter value in the decision model. For example, in an economic-order-quantity model, the cost of storage, the cost of a setup, or the total amount of production or materials required in a time period, may be incorrectly predicted. (Another example is a discounted cash-flow model for capital budgeting, where perhaps the useful life or the annual cash inflows may be incorrectly predicted.)

Optimal correction in the economic-order-quantity model again requires that we compare the cost of adjusting the optimal order-quantity with the resultant cost saving per period. Sensitivity analysis will help the manager to decide the potential net benefits from maintaining a routine monitoring of possible prediction deviations.

[7] Joel S. Demski, *Information Analysis* (Reading, Mass.: Addison-Wesley, 1972), Chap. 6. Also see Chapter 4 of his second edition, 1980.

3. A *measurement* deviation is an error in measuring the actual cost of operating a process. For example, a worker may incorrectly count the ending inventory, resulting in an erroneous measure of total costs. Note the distinction made here between the prediction of a future cost and the measurement of a past cost. Improper classification, counting, or recording produces such measurement deviations.

Optimal correction usually centers on the problems of obtaining accurate documentation by individual employees as a part of their everyday work habits. This is an especially troublesome problem of systems design and motivation that permeates all types of organizations. For example, employees are sometimes encouraged to falsify time records so that the true variances from standards on particular operations are masked.

4. A *model* deviation is an erroneous functional representation or formulation in the decision model. That is, the objective function, variables, or constraints may be incorrectly identified. For example, the failure to include a constraint for maximum storage space may be an error in the formulation of an inventory model. Another example would be the failure to provide for salvage value in a capital-budgeting model.

Note that a model error is not the same as a prediction error. The model error pertains to an incorrect functional relationship, while the prediction error pertains to an incorrect parameter prediction.

Deciding to correct a model error usually necessitates a comparison of the cost of correction with the benefits over many future time periods. In contrast, the decision to correct a parameter prediction involves a similar analysis but typically relates to a shorter time period, because these predictions are updated more frequently.

5. A *random* deviation is discussed in the next section.

random deviations

A *random* deviation is a divergence between actual cost and (statistically) expected cost arising from the typical fluctuations of some correctly specified random parameter. For example, the raw-material input per unit of output in a chemical process may fluctuate because of random variations that are inherent in the process. By definition, a random deviation per se calls for no corrective action affecting the existing process. However, as we shall see in later sections, to distinguish random deviations from other types is a helpful step in deciding whether and when to investigate any deviations.

The idea of randomness is rarely formally recognized by accounting systems. Instead, standard costing systems view a standard as a *single* acceptable measure. Practically, the accountant (and everybody else) realizes that the standard is a *band* or *range* of possible acceptable outcomes. In other words, the performance (and costs) ought to be generated by a well-behaved underlying process. If the process is not behaving acceptably, it may be economical to intervene to make it behave better. For example, a foreman may expect a machine operator to produce an average of 100 bearing brackets per hour. If he notices that 105 are being turned out the first hour, 98 the second, 103 the third, and 95 the fourth, he may consider such a variation in performance to be *random*. However, if the performance falls to 85 and then jumps to 120, he may consider the performance *nonrandom* and worth investigating.

The distinctions among the five types of deviations above formalize and make explicit the complexities that decision makers face. The manager should be alert for these five sources of variances because they focus on assumptions about prediction methods, decision models, and implementation. In contrast, the traditional view of a cost variance tends to focus almost wholly on implementation deviations.

difficulties in analysis of variances

Ideally, managers would like to have an information system that pinpoints the deviations just described into five mutually exclusive categories and that indicates a sequence of investigation that will maximize net payoff, the excess of benefit over cost. Unfortunately, the state of the world is complex and the state of the accountant's and the mathematician's art in this area is primitive and simple. The overall problems can be delineated, sometimes with rigor.[8] However, the interdependences are manifold and the difficulties of ascertaining the costs and benefits of investigation are imposing. For example, the five sources of variances described above may not be independent. The time needed for investigation of each source may also not be independent. Furthermore, the net savings associated with each alternative of when, how, and where to investigate a deviation will depend on the state of each process subject to investigation. Neither the processes, investigations, nor time periods are necessarily independent.

When a manager is deciding whether to investigate a deviation, he or she must consider the nature of the search. For instance, the time needed for investigation will differ for each form of deviation. An implementation-deviation search may require interviewing a specific worker or a supervisor. A model-deviation search may focus on discussions with the appropriate engineer or mathematician. Of course, the expected costs of these investigations must be compared with their expected savings before investigation is launched.

comparison of costs and benefits

The essential nature of the decision to investigate is best illustrated by a simple example. Consider the two-state, two-action situation depicted in Exhibit 25-2.[9] Examine the exhibit carefully so that the facts are clear.

Suppose the probability of the process being in control (θ_1) is .82 and the probability of its being out of control (θ_2) is 0.18. Then the expected costs (E) are:

If investigate,[10]

$$E(a_1) = C(1 - p_{\theta_2}) + (C + M)p_{\theta_2}$$
$$E(a_1) = \$2{,}000(.82) + \$5{,}000(.18) = \$2{,}540$$

If do not investigate,

$$E(a_2) = \qquad Lp_{\theta_2}$$
$$E(a_2) = \$0 \qquad + \$15{,}000(.18) = \$2{,}700$$

[8]See Demski, op. cit.; T. R. Dyckman, "The Investigation of Cost Variances," *Journal of Accounting Research,* 7, No. 2, pp. 215–44; and H. Bierman, Jr., and T. R. Dyckman, *Managerial Cost Accounting,* 2nd ed. (New York: Macmillan, 1976), Chap. 2; and R. Kaplan, "The Significance and Investigation of Cost Variance: Survey and Extensions," *Journal of Accounting Research,* Vol. 13, No. 2 (Autumn 1975).

[9]The example is based on one in Bierman and Dyckman, *Managerial Cost Accounting,* pp. 36–40. As they point out (p. 35), there are several implicit assumptions, including the following: The decision maker is willing to act on the basis of expected values; incurred costs are reported on a periodic basis, so a do-not-investigate action implies that an activity is continued at least until the next cost observation is available; and an investigation always detects the cause of an out-of-control situation that can and will be immediately corrected.

[10]This equation may also be expressed as

$$E(a_1) = C + Mp_{\theta_2}$$
$$E(a_1) = \$2{,}000 + \$3{,}000(.18) = \$2{,}540$$

EXHIBIT 25-2 **Decision Table**

ACTIONS: a_i	θ_1: in control	θ_2: out of control
	STATES: θ_j	
a_1: investigate	$C = \$2,000$	$C + M = \$\ 5,000$
a_2: do not investigate	0*	$L = \$15,000$

where

$C = \$2,000$, the cost of investigation; $M = \$3,000$, the cost of correction if an out-of-control process is discovered; $L = \$15,000$, the present value of the extra costs over the planning horizon, which may be either the time until the process is expected to go out of control again or the time until a routine intervention is scheduled. Clearly, the amount of L depends on expected future actions.

**All other amounts in this table are incremental in relation to this action and state.*

Therefore, investigation is the optimal action, because the expected costs are $160 less than the alternative of no investigation.

role of probabilities

The foregoing computation illustrates the critical role of the assessment of probabilities in the decision of whether to investigate. A low probability, say .10, of the process being out of control will change the desirability of conducting an investigation:

If investigate,

$$E = \$2,000(.90) + \$\ 5,000(.10) = \$2,300$$

If do not investigate,

$$E = \$0 \qquad + \$15,000(.10) = \$1,500$$

Of course, the level of the critical probability will depend on the relative costs and benefits in a particular situation. In our example, it can be computed as follows. The point of indifference (sometimes called the breakeven point) is where the expected costs of each action are the same:

$$\text{Let } p_{\theta_2} = \text{level of probability where } E_{a_1} \text{ and } E_{a_2} \text{ are equal}$$
$$E_{a_1} = E_{a_2}$$

Substituting:

$$C(1 - p_{\theta_2}) + (C + M)p_{\theta_2} = Lp_{\theta_2}$$
$$C - Cp_{\theta_2} + Cp_{\theta_2} + Mp_{\theta_2} = Lp_{\theta_2}$$
$$C + Mp_{\theta_2} = Lp_{\theta_2}$$
$$C = Lp_{\theta_2} - Mp_{\theta_2}$$
$$p_{\theta_2} = \frac{C}{L - M}$$
$$p_{\theta_2} = \frac{\$2,000}{\$15,000 - \$3,000} = .17$$

Therefore, in this example, investigation is desirable only if the probability of being out of control exceeds .17.[11]

Note especially that variances provide the information for assessing these critical probabilities. However, the measurements of the costs and benefits are unlikely to be provided by the variances. For example, the table in Exhibit 25-2 does not contain the cost variance itself, but the size of the cost variance may be crucial in assessing the probabilities of .82 and .18.

practical approach

Again and again we have seen that managers use simple decision models in complex situations. In the area of variance analysis, they use judgments that generally grow from the experience and know-how of the executives involved. For some items, any tiny variance from budget or standard may spark scrutiny. For other items, 5, 10, or 25 percent variances from standard may be necessary to spur follow-ups. Rules of thumb are frequently developed that focus either on the absolute size of the variance or on some percentage obtained by dividing the cost variance by the budgeted or standard cost.

Of course, when rules of thumb or intuition are used to decide whether to investigate, the manager has at least implicitly proceeded through the decision process illustrated in our example. He or she has combined costs, benefits, and probabilities in such a way that the rules of thumb are equivalent to go/no-go points of indifference.

statistical quality control

In practice, the standard cost variances are simple signals that do not neatly trace back to one of the five types of deviations described earlier. Nevertheless, because the costs and benefits of investigation differ, depending on the type of suspected deviation, managers are faced with the problem of at least implicitly classifying the likely deviations. As a first step in deciding whether to investigate variances, managers frequently attempt to distinguish random deviations from all other types.

A whole field of **statistical quality control (SQC)** has been developed to pinpoint random deviations in industrial processes and other repetitive operations. Control charts are frequently used, whereby the means of small samples are successively plotted. Statistical tables of the normal distributions are used to formulate upper and lower control limits. Only the observations beyond these limits ordinarily are regarded as nonrandom and worth investigating. These observations have usually been measured in engineering terms (such as times, material usage, rejects) rather than economic terms (such as dollars of cost). The biggest weaknesses of traditional SQC are that (a) its rules for setting the control limits have not explicitly considered costs and benefits, and (b) its monitoring procedures do not allow for prior observations.[12]

Although there are some obvious similarities between traditional SQC and accounting variances, fundamental differences limit the usefulness of traditional SQC procedures in an accounting setting.[13] SQC provides frequent observations (sometimes

---

[11]Prior probabilities, based on past performance, are subject to revision by means of current sample evidence and Bayes's theorem to provide posterior probabilities for use in revising expected costs. See Dyckman, "Investigation of Cost Variances," p. 222ff.

[12]To pursue this subject in more depth, begin with Kaplan, *Advanced Management Accounting.* Also see D. Dittman and P. Prakash, "Cost Variance Investigation: Markovian Control versus Optimal Control," *Accounting Review,* LIV, No. 2 (April 1979), 358–73.

[13]Kaplan, "Significance and Investigation." Incidentally, some accountants favor using statistical regression for developing budgets and standards and then using confidence intervals in conjunction with judgment to make the decision of whether to investigate variances. For

hourly or more frequently), but accounting reports rarely are prepared more often than weekly.

Furthermore, the out-of-control physical processes discovered under SQC can frequently be placed back into control with the manipulation of a dial or a similar procedure. Consequently, the benefit from investigation can be measured by the almost certain return to the in-control state.

In contrast, the investigation of cost variances contains no similar assurance that performance will be restored to its original standard. For instance, prices may have changed or operating procedures developed that may be difficult or impossible to reverse. The underlying processes for which costs are being aggregated are often not as easily indentifiable as those processes for which SQC controls are typically exercised. Thus, the benefits from investigations of cost variances are more uncertain. The difficulty of measuring likely benefits may be the major barrier to the implementation of formal decision models for this purpose.

using control charts

Control charts take many forms. Basically, they are graphical plots of performance. Their upper and lower control limits distinguish between "normal" and "abnormal" performance. They also help detect trends or drifts away from normal operations.

Control charts offer some practical advantages, as described by Kaplan:

> The graphical format of a control chart is an excellent way of communicating trends that can be spotted easier by the human eye than by statistical tests:

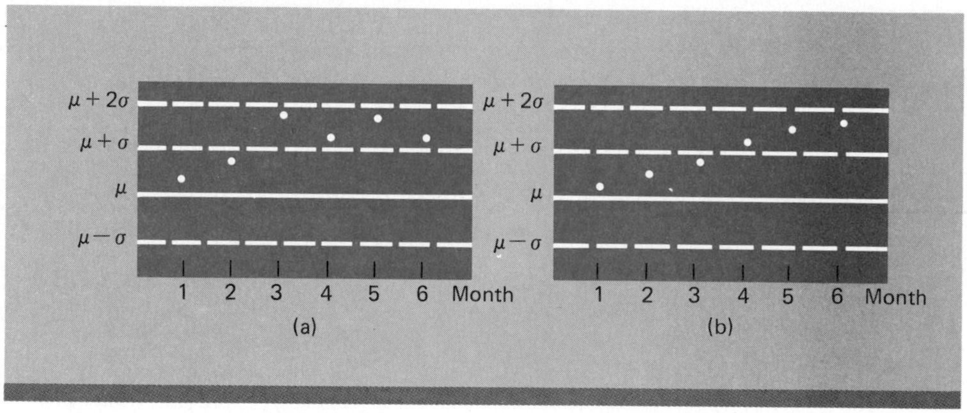

> For example, Figure a plots the actual monthly cost or usage relative to the standard amount, μ, and its expected standard deviation σ. No one of the observations is statistically significant (larger than 2σ from the standard, μ) but the last four observations are well above 1σ from the standard. In Figure b, we can see a pattern of steadily increasing accounting variances without yet hitting a 2σ deviation. Both patterns indicate a highly likely shift away from standard operations but would not be signaled by a mechanical 2σ statistical significance rule applied only to the most recent observation. The control chart presentation enables the manager to use his superior pattern recognition ability in conjunction with the computer's comparative advantage to compute and display numbers. Six or twelve month histories of key accounts could be presented using the

---

discussions of some pros and cons, see W. Ferrara and J. Hayya, "Toward Probabilistic Profit Budgets," *Management Accounting,* October 1970, pp. 23–28; and S. Buzby, "Extending the Applicability of Probabilistic Management Planning and Control Models," *Accounting Review,* XLIX, No. 1 (January 1974), 42–49.

control chart format to enable managers to detect emerging or consistent problems faster than is possible when only one or two months of data are presented in tabular form.[14]

After surveying the accounting, statistics, and management science literature dealing with the significance and investigation of variances, Kaplan offered the following suggestions:

> In practice, therefore, it seems sensible to model the variance investigation decision using some variant of the control chart approach by following this sequence. Attempt to obtain a standard deviation for each standard and, for each observation, compute the probability that an observation came from the in-control distribution. Depending upon the importance of an account, and the cost of an investigation, develop rough rules of thumb to determine whether an investigation is signaled by a probability level, say, of .10, .05, or .01. Over time, refine the probability limits for investigation of an account to balance off false alarms versus the cost of not investigating out-of-control processes. For particularly important processes, it may prove beneficial to introduce a benefit-cost approach as more data on the process, both in-control and out-of-control, become available. But the benefits of starting with complex models seem small compared to the cost of the information requirements and processing algorithms, and the small incremental benefits found from using these models in simulation studies.[15]

PROBLEM FOR SELF-STUDY

problem

Refer to the example in Exhibit 25-2. Suppose that *C*, the expected costs of investigation, were \$4,000 instead of \$2,000, with the probability of being in control unchanged. What would be the expected costs of investigation and of no investigation? What level of probability would exist of the process's being out of control where the expected costs of each action would be the same?

solution

If investigate, $E = \$4{,}000(.82) + \$\ 7{,}000(.18) = \$4{,}540$
If do not investigate, $E = \$0 + \$15{,}000(.18) = \$2{,}700$

Therefore, do not investigate. The level of probability of being out of control where the expected costs would be the same is

$$p_{\theta_2} = \frac{\$4{,}000}{\$15{,}000 - \$3{,}000} = .33$$

Proof:

If investigate, $E = \$4{,}000(.67) + \$\ 7{,}000(.33) = \$5{,}000$ (rounded)
If do not investigate, $E = \$0 + \$15{,}000(.33) = \$5{,}000$

SUMMARY

Accounting variances are a means of communicating what has happened. By this and other means, the manager enhances understanding and decides whether specified areas deserve more investigation.

[14] Kaplan, *Advanced Management Accounting,* Chap. 10.

[15] Ibid.

Quantity, mix, and yield variances sometimes aid comprehension, but they are supplements to the basic price, efficiency, and sales-volume variances that were introduced in Chapter 6.

The decision to investigate variances is often one of minimizing expected costs. It requires consideration of the profitable states of the process, the costs of investigation and correction, and the present value of the net savings. Because these factors are difficult to quantify, rules of thumb are often used in practice for deciding when to investigate.

SUGGESTED READINGS

FOR PARTS ONE AND TWO

CHUMACHENKO, NIKOLAI G., **"Once Again: The Volume-Mix-Price/Cost Budget Variance Analysis,"** *Accounting Review,* XLIII, No. 4, pp. 753–62. This is an exhaustive article by a Soviet author on the alternative ways of analyzing sales-mix variances.

HASSELDINE, C. R., **"Mix and Yield Variances,"** *Accounting Review,* XLII, No. 3, pp. 497–515. This article concentrates on alternative ways of analyzing mix and yield of various combinations of direct materials in a production context.

HOBBS, JAMES R., **"Volume-Mix-Price/Cost Budget Variance Analysis: A Proper Approach,"** *Accounting Review,* XXXIX, No. 4, pp. 905–13.

MALCOM, R. E., **"Sales Variances; A Further Look,"** *Management Advisor,* March-April 1971, pp. 948–53.

MANES, RENE P., **"In a Seminar on Budget Mix Variances,"** *Accounting Review,* XLIII, No. 4, pp. 784–87.

WOLK, H. I., and HILLMAN, A. D., **"Material Mix and Yield Variances—A Suggested Improvement,"** *Accounting Review,* 42, No. 3, pp. 549–53.

FOR PART THREE

BIERMAN, H., and T. R. DYCKMAN, **Managerial Cost Accounting,** 2nd ed., Chap. 2. New York: Macmillan, 1976.

DEMSKI, JOEL S., **Information Analysis,** 2nd ed. Reading, Mass.: Addison-Wesley, 1972.

DITTMAN, D. A., and P. PRAKASH, **"Cost Variance Investigation—Markovian Control of Markov Processes,"** *Journal of Accounting Research,* Spring 1978, pp. 14–25.

———, **"Cost Variance Investigation: Markovian Control versus Optimal Control,"** *Accounting Review,* LIV, No. 2 (April 1979), 358–73.

DUVALL, R. M., **"Rules for Investigating Cost Variances,"** *Management Science,* Vol. 13, No. 10, pp. 631–41.

KAPLAN, R., **Advanced Management Accounting.** Englewood Cliffs, N.J., Prentice-Hall, 1982. His Chapter 9 pertains to Parts One and Two of this chapter; his Chapter 10, to Part Three.

———, **"Optimal Investigation Strategies with Imperfect Information,"** *Journal of Accounting Research,* VII, No. 1 (Spring 1969), 32–43.

———, **"The Significance and Investigation of Cost Variances: Survey and Extensions,"** *Journal of Accounting Research,* Vol. 13, No. 2 (Autumn 1975).

LEV, B., **"An Information Theory Analysis of Budget Variances,"** *Accounting Review,* XLIV, No. 4, pp. 704–10.

LUH, F. S., **"Controlled Cost: An Operational Concept and Statistical Approach to Standard Costing,"** *Accounting Review,* XLIII, No. 1, pp. 123–32.

MAGEE, R. P., **"A Simulation Analysis of Alternative Cost Variance Investigation Models,"** *Accounting Review,* July 1976, pp. 529–44.

OZAN, T., and T. R. DYCKMAN, **"A Normative Model for Investigation Decisions Involving Multi-Origin Cost Variances,"** *Journal of Accounting Research,* Vol. 9., No. 1.

Terms to Learn

control chart ***labor-mix variance*** ***labor-yield variance***
market-share variance ***market-size variance*** ***material mix***
material-mix variance ***material yield*** ***material-yield variance***
sales mix ***sales-mix variance*** ***sales-quantity variance***
sales-volume variance ***statistical quality control (SQC)***

Special Points and Pitfalls

This chapter illustrates the cost-benefit theme of this book. If the perceived benefits exceed the costs, managers will pay for more detailed variance analyses and for formal models of when to investigate variances. Otherwise, managers settle for less detail and rely on their individual experience for judging when variances deserve a closer look.

Many readers get too mired in the details of the variances described in this chapter. Above all, recognize that variances are almost always interdependent. Hence, it is unwise to focus on each in isolation. For example, sales mix is a function of the quantity sold and the prices charged. Another example is the control of direct labor. Decisions on labor mix may depend on the relative prices of labor and the relationships of mix to yield.

In sum, standing alone, a single variance rarely is sufficient for decision making. Five distinct variables can cause actual performance to differ from budgeted performance:

1. Direct substitutions of finished products or factors of production such as materials and labor.
2. Actual *individual* quantities different from budgeted quantities.
3. Actual *total* quantities different from budgeted quantities.
4. Differences between actual and budgeted unit costs.
5. Differences between actual and budgeted unit sales prices.

For example:

1 and 2 can occur without 3.
1 and 2 can occur with 3.
2 and 3 can occur without 1.

Each represents a different decision situation. Moreover, 4 and 5 may not be independent of 1 through 3.

QUESTIONS, PROBLEMS, AND CASES

25-1 Distinguish between the *sales-mix variance* and the *sales-quantity variance* with respect to contribution margins.

25-2 In relation to production variances, distinguish between production-*mix* and production-*yield* variances.

25-3 What are some common difficulties in the analysis of variances?

25-4 Contrast the accountant's and the statistician's concept of the word *standard.*

25-5 Describe the basic approach of statistical quality control.

25-6 What does the word *quality* mean as it is used in *statistical quality control?*

25-7 What is the *state of statistical control?*

25-8 "When a process is in control, it is beyond change or improvement." Comment.

25-9 "The sales-volume variance might be better labeled as a *marketing variance.*" Do you agree? Explain.

25-10 "A company can sell exactly the same number of units as specified in the static budget and still have a flexible budget with numbers that differ from those in the static budget." Do you agree? Explain.

25-11 "Production-mix and production-yield variances should be calculated as a routine part of a management accounting system." Do you agree? Explain.

25-12 "Price variances are excluded from all calculations of mix and yield variances." Do you agree? Explain.

PROBLEMS FOR PART ONE

25-13 ***Sales-volume, sales-mix, and sales-quantity variances.*** Review Exhibit 25-1. Suppose that 114,000 units of Product A and 41,000 units of Product B were sold. Consider the contribution-margin line only. Compute the sales-volume variances for each product and in total. Subdivide the sales-volume variance into quantity variances and mix variances.

25-14 ***Quantity and mix.*** Consider the following budget:

	PRODUCT X			PRODUCT Y			TOTAL		
	units	price	total	units	price	total	units	price	total
Sales	1,000	$10.00	$10,000	9,000	$2.50	$22,500	10,000	$3.25	$32,500
Variable costs	1,000	6.00	6,000	9,000	2.00	18,000	10,000	2.40	24,000
Contribution margin	1,000	$ 4.00	$ 4,000	9,000	$ .50	$ 4,500	10,000	$ .85	$ 8,500
Contribution-margin percentage		40%			20%			26.15%	

Suppose that 7,000 units were actually sold: 2,000 of X and 5,000 of Y:

	PRODUCT X			PRODUCT Y			TOTAL		
	units	price	total	units	price	total	units	price	total
Sales	2,000	$10.25	$20,500	5,000	$2.50	$12,500	7,000	$4.71+	$33,000
Variable costs	2,000	6.00	12,000	5,000	2.00	10,000	7,000	3.14+	22,000
Contribution margin	2,000	$ 4.25	$ 8,500	5,000	$ .50	$ 2,500	7,000	$1.57+	$11,000
Contribution-margin percentage		41.46%			20%			33.33%	

Prepare a complete explanation of why the contribution margin is $2,500 more than originally budgeted. Include a detailed variance analysis of price changes per unit and changes in sales volume. Also subdivide the sales volume variance for the contribution margin into changes in quantities and changes in mix.

25-15 ***Sales-mix variances for motorboats.*** Suppose a motorboat distributor planned on selling only two models, Storms and Thunderheads. He expected to sell the following during a given year:

	STORMS			THUNDERHEADS			TOTAL		
	units	price	total	units	price	total	units	price	total
Sales	4,000	$4,000	$16,000,000	1,000	$6,000	$6,000,000	5,000	$4,400	$22,000,000
Variable costs	4,000	3,200	12,800,000	1,000	4,500	4,500,000	5,000	3,460	17,300,000
Contribution margin	4,000	$ 800	$ 3,200,000	1,000	$1,500	$1,500,000	5,000	$ 940	$ 4,700,000

Suppose that 5,100 units were actually sold:

	STORMS			THUNDERHEADS			TOTAL		
	units	price	total	units	price	total	units	price	total
Sales	3,700	$4,000	$14,800,000	1,400	$6,000	$8,400,000	5,100	$4,550	$23,200,000
Variable costs	3,700	3,200	11,840,000	1,400	4,500	6,300,000	5,100	3,558	18,140,000
Contribution margin	3,700	$ 800	$ 2,960,000	1,400	$1,500	$2,100,000	5,100	$ 992	$ 5,060,000

The dealer is astounded to learn that he reached his target unit selling prices, unit costs, and unit contribution margins. He realizes that his unit sales were not on target, and he has asked you to analyze the figures in more depth so that he may get more insight into his problems.

REQUIRED

1. Prepare an explanation of why the actual total contribution margin differed from the budgeted margin, using (a) only a sales-volume variance and (b) a sales-quantity variance and a sales-mix variance.
2. Which of the two variance analyses in requirement 1 did you prefer? Explain fully.

25-16 ***Sales-mix and sales-quantity variances.*** (SMA) Bright Business Machines Ltd. is marketing two of its latest models of computers, the Quick Speed and the Super Accuracy. Budgeted data for the two models appear as follows:

	QUICK SPEED			SUPER ACCURACY			TOTAL		
	units	price	total	units	price	total	units	price*	total
Sales	4,500	$3,200	$14,400,000	1,200	$6,000	$7,200,000	5,700	$3,789	$21,600,000
Variable costs	4,500	2,800	12,600,000	1,200	4,800	5,760,000	5,700	3,221	18,360,000
Contribution margin	4,500	$ 400	$ 1,800,000	1,200	$1,200	$1,440,000	5,700	$ 568	$ 3,240,000

**Numbers are rounded to the nearest dollar.*

The target unit selling prices, unit costs, and unit contribution margins were all reached, and the actual results appeared as follows:

	QUICK SPEED			SUPER ACCURACY			TOTAL		
	units	price	total	units	price	total	units	price	total
Sales	4,200	$3,200	$13,440,000	1,800	$6,000	$10,800,000	6,000	$4,040	$24,240,000
Variable costs	4,200	2,800	11,760,000	1,800	4,800	8,640,000	6,000	3,400	20,400,000
Contribution margin	4,200	$ 400	$ 1,680,000	1,800	$1,200	$ 2,160,000	6,000	$ 640	$ 3,840,000

REQUIRED

1. Consider the contribution line only. Prepare an analysis for each product and in total showing why the actual total contribution margin differed from the budgeted margin using a sales-volume variance, a sales-quantity variance, and a sales-mix variance.
2. Discuss the circumstances where the use of the sales-volume variance would suffice versus situations where the quantity-mix approach might yield additional insights.

25-17 ***Sales-mix variances vs sales-volume variances.*** The MSD Company produces four products, labeled here as A, B, C, and D. A product manager is responsible for each product and reports to his or her respective line manager. Likewise, a line manager is responsible for each product line. Line AB is composed of Product A and Product B; line CD is composed of Product C and Product D. Finally, a marketing manager, Anthony Amato, is responsible for all four products (ABCD), with the two line managers reporting to him. The following table gives the budgeted and actual results for the year ending 19_1. The budgeted sales are determined by the marketing manager.

PRODUCT	BUDGETED SALES IN UNITS	ACTUAL SALES IN UNITS	CONTRIBUTION MARGIN PER UNIT
A	10,000	10,000	$3.00
B	10,000	12,000	5.00
C	15,000	20,000	2.00
D	15,000	14,000	6.00

All prices and contribution margins per unit were equal to those budgeted. The company was not producing near capacity.

REQUIRED

1. Compute and tabulate the sales-quantity, sales-mix, and sales-volume variances for the total contribution margin of A, B, AB, C, D, CD, and ABCD.
2. If you were a line manager, would you prefer a summary report containing only the total quantity and total mix variances for your line, only the total sales-volume variances, or both sets of total variances? Why?
3. Answer requirement 2 as if you were the marketing manager.
4. Would your answer to requirement 3 change if the company were producing at capacity? Why?
5. How would you change the marketing manager's summary report to improve its information content?

25-18 ***Sales analysis.*** (CMA, adapted) The Arsco Co. makes three grades of indoor-outdoor carpets. The sales volume for the annual budget is determined by estimating the total market volume for indoor-outdoor carpet, and then applying the company's prior-year market share, adjusted for planned changes due to company programs for the coming year. The volume is apportioned between the three grades based upon the prior year's product mix, again adjusted for planned changes due to company programs for the coming year.

Given below are the company budget for 19_3 and the results of operations for 19_3.

BUDGET

	grade 1	grade 2	grade 3	total
Sales—units	1,000 rolls	1,000 rolls	2,000 rolls	4,000 rolls
Sales—dollars (000 omitted)	$1,000	$2,000	$3,000	$6,000
Variable expense	700	1,600	2,300	4,600
Variable margin	$ 300	$ 400	$ 700	$1,400
Traceable fixed expense	200	200	300	700
Traceable margin	$ 100	$ 200	$ 400	$ 700
Selling and administrative expense				250
Net income				$ 450

ACTUAL

	grade 1	grade 2	grade 3	total
Sales—units	800 rolls	1,000 rolls	2,100 rolls	3,900 rolls
Sales—dollars (000 omitted)	$810	$2,000	$3,000	$5,810
Variable expense	560	1,610	2,320	4,490
Variable margin	$250	$ 390	$ 680	$1,320
Traceable fixed expense	210	220	315	745
Traceable margin	$ 40	$ 170	$ 365	$ 575
Selling and administrative expense				275
Net income				$ 300

Industry volume was estimated at 40,000 rolls for budgeting purposes. Actual industry volume for 19_3 was 38,000 rolls.

REQUIRED

1. Prepare a comparison for each product, and for all products in total, of the original budgeted total contribution margin and the actual total contribution margin. Show price variances and sales volume variances.
2. What is the dollar impact on profits (using budgeted variable margins) of the shift in product mix from the budgeted mix? That is, split the sales volume variance in requirement 1 into its quantity and mix components.
3. What portion of the variance, if any, can be attributed to the state of the carpet market?

25-19 ***Material yield and mix.*** A company has the following standards for producing a special gasoline additive:

50 gallons of petroleum concentrate G-101 @ \$.10	= \$ 5.00
50 gallons of petroleum concentrate G-177 @ \$.30	= \$15.00
100 gallons of standard mix @ \$.20	= \$20.00

Every 100 gallons of input should yield 80 gallons of PST, the finished product.

The production manager is supposed to make the largest possible amount of finished product for the least cost. He has some leeway to alter the combination of materials within certain wide limits, as long as the finished product meets specified quality standards.

Actual results showed that 400,000 gallons of PST were produced during the previous week. The raw materials used in this production were 280,000 gallons of G-101 and 240,000 gallons of G-177.

No price variances were experienced during the period.

REQUIRED

Comment on the performance of the manager. Include a presentation of yield and mix variances.

25-20 ***Material-mix and material-yield variances.*** A company has the following standards:

50 pounds of Material C at	\$1.40 =	\$ 70.00
30 pounds of Material D at	2.00 =	60.00
20 pounds of Material E at	1.60 =	32.00
100 pounds of standard mix at	1.62 =	\$162.00 should produce 90 pounds of finished product at a standard cost of \$1.80 per pound (\$162.00 ÷ 90).

No inventories of raw materials are kept. Purchases are made as needed, so that all price variances relate to materials used. Actual results showed that 50,000 pounds were used during a period.

26,000 pounds of C at actual cost of \$1.20 =	\$31,200
16,000 pounds of D at actual cost of 2.10 =	33,600
8,000 pounds of E at actual cost of 1.90 =	15,200
50,000	\$80,000

Good output was

40,000 pounds at standard cost of \$1.80	= 72,000
Total material variance to be explained	= \$ 8,000 U

What are the efficiency, yield, and price variances?

25-21 ***Material-yield and material-mix variances.*** (SMA) The Scent Makers Company Ltd. produces a perfume for men. To make this perfume, three different types of fluids are used. Dycone, Cycone, and Bycone are applied in proportions of 2/5, 3/10, and 3/10, respectively, at standard, and their standard costs are \$6.00, \$3.50, and \$2.50 per gallon, respectively. The chief engineer reported that in the past few months, the standard yield has been at 80 percent on 100 gallons of mix. The company maintains a policy of not carrying any raw materials, as storage space is costly. Current production has been set at 4,160,000 gallons of perfume for the year.

Last week the company produced 75,000 gallons of perfume at a total raw-materials cost of \$449,500. Actual number of gallons used and costs per gallon for the three fluids are as follows:

	GALLONS	COST PER GALLON
Dycone	45,000	\$5.50
Cycone	35,000	4.20
Bycone	20,000	2.75

REQUIRED

1. Compute the price, yield, and mix variances for each of the three fluids. Reconcile these variances with the total material variance.
2. Explain the managerial significance of the price, yield and mix variances in the above situation.

25-22 ***Labor-mix and labor-yield variances.*** A supervisor in a sheet metal operation has the following direct-labor standard:

(a) Labor price per hour:	
2 journeymen @ $22	$44
3 helpers @ $12	36
Total cost of standard combination of labor	$80
Average price per hour, $80 ÷ 5 =	$16
(b) Standard labor price per unit of output at 8 units per hour, $16 ÷ 8 =	$ 2
(c) Standard labor cost of 20,000 units of output, 20,000 × $2, or 2,500 × $16 =	$40,000
(d) Actual inputs, 2,900 hours consisting of:	
900 hours of journeymen @ $23	$20,700
2,000 hours of helpers @ $11	22,000
	$42,700

The supervisor had to pay a higher average wage rate to his journeymen because of the inclusion of some skilled workers who had bargained for a superior rate of pay. As a result, he tried to save some costs by using more helpers per journeyman than usual.

REQUIRED

1. Compute the price and efficiency variances.
2. Divide the efficiency variance into yield and mix components.
3. What would the actual costs probably have been if the standard labor mix had been maintained even though the actual labor prices were incurred?

25-23 ***Labor-mix and labor-yield variances.*** (CMA, adapted) Landeau Manufacturing Company has a process cost accounting system. An analysis that compares the actual results with both a monthly plan and a flexible budget is prepared monthly. The standard direct-labor rates used in the flexible budget are established each year at the time the annual plan is formulated and held constant for the entire year.

The standard direct-labor rates in effect for the fiscal year ending June 30, 19_8, and the standard hours allowed for the output for the month of April are shown in the following schedule:

	STANDARD DIRECT-LABOR RATE PER HOUR	STANDARD DIRECT-LABOR HOURS ALLOWED FOR OUTPUT
Labor class III	$8.00	500
Labor class II	$7.00	500
Labor class I	$5.00	500

The wage rate for each labor class increased on January 1, 19_8, under the terms of a new union contract negotiated in December 19_7. The standard wage rates were not revised to reflect the new contract.

The actual direct-labor hours (DLH) worked and the actual direct-labor rates per hour experienced for the month of April were as follows:

	ACTUAL DIRECT-LABOR RATE PER HOUR	ACTUAL DIRECT-LABOR HOURS
Labor class III	$8.50	550
Labor class II	$7.50	650
Labor class I	$5.40	375

REQUIRED

1. Calculate the dollar amount of the total direct-labor variance for the month of April for the Landeau Manufacturing Company and analyze the total variance into the following components:
   a. Direct-labor price variance
   b. Direct-labor efficiency variance
   c. Direct-labor mix and yield variances
2. Discuss the advantages and disadvantages of a standard-cost system in which the standard direct-labor rates per hour are not changed during the year to reflect such events as a new labor contract.

PROBLEMS FOR PART THREE

25-24 ***Types of deviations.*** The chapter described five possible kinds of deviations as sources of a variance between actual and predicted costs: (a) implementation, (b) prediction, (c) measurement, (d) model, and (e) random. Below are listed some examples of deviations. Use one of the letters (a) through (e) to identify the most likely type of deviation being described.

1. A foreman gets a year-end bonus that is really attributable to overtime that he worked seven months previously. The bonus is charged to overhead at year-end.

2. Costs of supplies are charged to overhead as acquired rather than as used.

3. Costs of setting up printing jobs are consistently pegged too low when bids are made.

4. The salvage value of scrap from production is forecast incorrectly.

5. Normal spoilage in a food-processing plant amounts to 5 percent of good output.

6. The salvage value of scrap from production is ignored completely.

7. A worker is inefficient because of daydreaming.

8. A worker is inefficient because he is new at his job and is just learning how to do the work.

25-25 ***Decision to investigate a variance.*** A semiautomated process is rarely out of control. The cost of investigation is $300. If a process is discovered to be out of control, its cost of correction is $1,000, and gross savings are the equivalent of $2,500 received at the end of each year for three years.

REQUIRED

1. Suppose the minimum desired rate of return is 12 percent per annum. The manager has examined a cost variance that makes him assess a probability of .05 that the process is out of control. Should the process be investigated? Show computations.
2. At what level of probability will the manager be indifferent about whether to investigate?

25-26 ***Decision to investigate a variance.*** When a process is investigated in an automated department, the costs of investigation are $1,000. If an out-of-control process is discovered, the cost of correction is $1,500. The manager is always indifferent about conducting an investigation when there is a probability of .60 that the process is in control.

REQUIRED

How large must the present value of the cost savings be to warrant an investigation?

25-27 ***Statistical-control limits and investigation decision.*** Traditionally, control limits, using the techniques of statistical quality control, have been set at ±2 sigmas in British countries and ±3 sigmas in the United States. Consider the 2-sigma limits, which imply that the probability is .05 of observing a nonrandom deviation when the dollar amount of the variance is within the 2-sigma limits.

REQUIRED

1. Suppose C is $100, M is $800, and L is $5,800. Would you investigate deviations that lie within the 2-sigma limits? Why?

2. In the decision of whether to investigate, what is the role of the size of the variance in relation to the standard cost? In relation to the potential savings?

25-28 ***Decision to investigate a variance.*** You are the manager of a manufacturing process. A variance of $10,000 in excess material usage has been reported for the past week's operations. You are trying to decide whether to investigate. You feel that if you do not investigate and the process is out of control, the present value of the cost savings (L) over the planning horizon is $3,800. The cost to investigate is $500. The cost to correct the process if you discover that it is out of control is $1,000. You assess the probability that the process is out of control at .30.

REQUIRED

1. Should the process be investigated? What are the expected costs of investigation and of no investigation?
2. What level of probability that the process is out of control would exist where the expected costs of each action would be the same?
3. If the cost variance is $10,000, why is L only $3,800?

25-29 ***Decision to investigate.*** (CPA) The folding-department foreman must decide each week whether his department will operate normally the following week. He may order a corrective action if he feels the folding department will operate inefficiently; otherwise he does nothing. The foreman receives a weekly folding-department efficiency-variance report from the accounting department. A week in which the folding department operates inefficiently is usually preceded by a large efficiency variance. The accompanying graph gives the probability that the folding department will operate normally in the following week as a function of the magnitude of the current week's variance reported to the foreman:

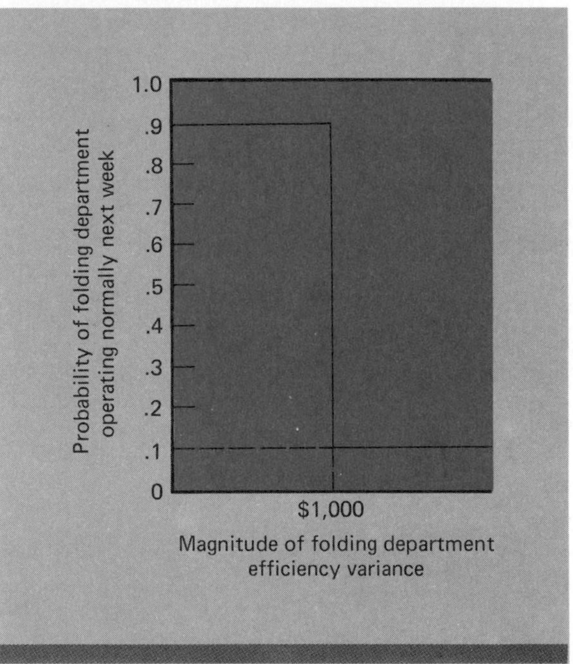

Choose the best answer for each of the following:

1. An efficiency variance of $1,500 this week means the probability of operating normally the following week is (a) 0%, (b) 10%, (c) 90%, (d) 100%.

2. What are the possible relationships between the current efficiency variance and next week's operations?

a. Large variance followed by normal operation, large variance followed by inefficient operation, small variance followed by normal operation, and small variance followed by inefficient operation.

b. Large variance followed by normal operation, small variance followed by inefficient operation, and small variance followed by normal operation.

c. Large variance followed by inefficient operation, small variance followed by normal operation, and small variance followed by inefficient operation.

d. Large variance followed by 90 percent of normal operation, small variance followed by 10 percent of normal operation, large variance followed by inefficient operation, and small variance followed by inefficient operation.

3. If the foreman can determine for certain whether the folding department will operate normally next week, and the cost of corrective action is less than the extra cost of operating the folding department inefficiently, then the best decision rule for the foreman to follow is

a. If normal operations are predicted, do *not* take corrective action; if inefficient operations are predicted, take corrective action.

b. Regardless of the current variance, do *not* take corrective action.

c. If normal operations are predicted, take corrective action; if inefficient operations are predicted, do *not* take corrective action.

d. Regardless of the current variance, take corrective action.

4. The following cost information is relevant to the folding department foreman in deciding whether corrective action is warranted:

\$500 = cost of corrective action that will ensure normal operation of folding department for the following week

\$3,000 = excess cost of operating folding department inefficiently for one week

The foreman receives a report that the folding-department efficiency variance is \$600. The expected cost of *not* taking corrective action is (a) \$0, (b) \$300, (c) \$2,700, (d) \$3,000.

25-30 ***Whether to investigate.*** (SMA) The standard material cost for producing a conventional truck at the Fleetliner Company Limited is \$28,000. Last week several trucks were produced at an average material cost of \$34,000. U. R. Able, a recent college graduate who joined the company as the cost analyst, is asked to decide whether investigation is necessary.

Mr. Able feels that if nothing is done and the process is out of control, the present value of extra costs over the planning horizon is \$2,600. The cost to investigate is \$380. The cost to correct the process if out of control is \$850. He also feels that there is an 80 percent chance that the process is in control.

REQUIRED

1. Submit computations to show whether the process should be investigated.
2. What level of probability that the process is in control would be necessary to make Mr. Able indifferent about investigating the process?
3. If the process is out of control, why is the present value of the extra costs incurred substantially less than the current variance between the standard and actual costs of trucks produced?

25-31 ***When to investigate.*** (SMA) Mr. Able has just joined Hilson Limited as controller. The company manufactures precision instruments. Mr. Able has determined from historical production records that there is a 55 percent chance that the quality will not be up to company standards, and some form of adjustment will be necessary to bring the instruments up to normal specifications. The cost of investigation is \$13,500. If adjustments are required, the incremental revenue (net of adjustment costs, but excluding the cost of investigation) is estimated to be as follows:

ANTICIPATED INCREMENTAL REVENUE	PROBABILITY
\$10,000	.10
25,000	.25
28,000	.35
30,000	.20
32,000	.10

REQUIRED Should Mr. Able investigate? Submit all calculations.

25-32 ***Effects of variability on decisions to analyze operations.*** Review Chapter 21. A plant manager is trying to determine when to analyze operations. He does not have a standard-cost system, but he has accumulated a great deal of data. He finds that the cost of Process A per week per thousand units is $76,000 with a standard deviation of $22,000. Last week the cost was $109,000. Process B has a cost per week per thousand units of $26,000 with a standard deviation of $4,000. Last week the cost was $38,000.

REQUIRED

Suppose the costs of investigation are identical for each process, and the plant manager has decided to investigate only one of the two processes. Which process should be investigated? Which process is more variable?

25-33 ***Buying imperfect information.*** Review Appendix 21c. The following problem (as in many real situations) contains some simple assumptions that are made to underscore some fundamental points:

Linda Knight manages a factory that is in the midst of processing a large order to make thousands of newly designed portable stereo record players. Several serious production problems have been encountered.

Knight is concerned whether the units will be of acceptable quality. If they are acceptable, the factory will have a net gain (revenue less cost) of $800,000. If the units have unacceptable quality, the legal problems, warranty repair outlays, and unfavorable publicity will result in a net loss of $500,000. However, Knight could add an intricate inspection procedure so that all defective units would be discovered and repaired before the product left the factory; alas, the cost of this fail-safe procedure would be $830,000.

REQUIRED

1. Formulate Knight's problem as a "decision table" or "payoff table," showing actions, events, and outcomes.
2. Suppose that both events are equally likely and that Knight bases her decision strictly on expected monetary return. Which action will Knight prefer?
3. Suppose Knight could obtain a consultant's special accounting analysis that would affect her assessments of probabilities of acceptable or unacceptable quality. The consultant is expected to produce one of three possible reports: neutral, optimistic, or pessimistic.

   The neutral report would not change the original decision in requirement 2. The optimistic report would change Knight's assessments of probabilities to .7 acceptable and .3 unacceptable. The pessimistic report would have the reverse effect, changing the probabilities to .3 acceptable and .7 unacceptable.

   Knight assesses probabilities of receiving various reports as follows: .3 that the report will be neutral, .3 optimistic, and .4 pessimistic. What is the top price that Knight should pay for the report?

25-34 ***Navy rework.*** (C. Oleson) The Naval Air Rework Facility (NARF) at Alameda, Calif., is one of several facilities throughout the U.S. that have as their main function the overhaul and repair of naval aviation weapons systems. These include aircraft, missiles, engines, electronics, and other miscellaneous systems.

The NARF operates like civilian organizations that have a profit/loss responsibility. "Sales" are made to project managers in Washington who have overall accountability for the maintenance of specified weapons systems. Because the government is generally nonprofit, the price does not include a "profit" but is based solely on standard absorption costs.

To motivate efficiency, the navy holds each NARF responsible for attaining standards. This is accomplished by measuring the NARF's performance in meeting a zero-profit objective while pricing on the basis of standards, called norms, which are derived from historical data and engineering estimates. If costs exceed norms, the NARF suffers a loss. If costs are less than norms, the NARF derives a profit. Either situation represents a deviation from the desired objective. The first situation is deemed to result from inefficiency; the second, from loose standards.

Norms for any given work are determined immediately prior to the quarter in which the work starts; the price is negotiated accordingly with the Washington project manager. At this time, the exact condition of the units (say aircraft) is unknown. Predictions must be based on known general characteristics such as age, number of flight hours on the unit, and type of work to be done. Although the average cost per unit may be accurately predicted from such characteristics, the cost for a particular unit may vary widely from the average because its exact condition is unknown when the predictions of cost are made. One aircraft, for example, may have excess corrosion from having been outside near the ocean spray. Another may have been abused by a careless crew. Thus, the norm set at the planning conference represents the mean of a distribution with some standard deviation.

Although the resultant profit would be zero over a long period that included many production units where norms were being met on the average, the controller was concerned that for a period as short as a year these random deviations between actual and expected costs might have a significant effect on fiscal-year operating results (profits). He decided to study the problem in more detail.

Data on unit actual and expected (norm) costs were gathered over a three-year period from 19_1 through 19_3. The resulting distribution of actual less expected costs had a small negative mean, indicating that on the average norms had been beaten (or set somewhat loosely). It was then assumed that setting this mean to zero would result in the distribution of random deviations caused by differences in unit condition. This distribution was then used in a model that simulated product flow and the accounting system by quarters throughout a fiscal year. One thousand iterations of this model resulted in a distribution of probable outcomes of fiscal-year profits if norms were met on the average. The distribution was approximately normal with a mean of zero, as expected, and standard deviation of $350,000.

REQUIRED

1. What are the implications of this study for the manager of the NARF? For his superior in Washington?
2. A cost-benefit analysis showed that the cost of investigating a *negative* deviation from zero profit (a loss) was $3,650, the cost of correcting the average out-of-control process was $7,000, and the present value of cost savings over the planning horizon from correcting an out-of-control process was $12,000. Determine the level of loss at which the NARF manager would be indifferent to investigating. (Use Table 1.)

TABLE 1

Normal Distribution with Standard Deviation of $350,000

X ($)	PROBABILITY OF DEVIATION $\leq$ X ($\geq$|X|)
0	.50
−105,000	.38
−210,000	.27
−315,000	.18
−420,000	.12
−525,000	.07
−630,000	.04
−735,000	.02
−840,000	.01
−945,000	.004
−1,050,000	.001

Probability of being in control = Probability of deviation $\leq$X

25-35 ***Review of chapters 12, 21, and 25: whether to investigate variances.*** (G. Foster) From a cost variance analysis report for the previous period, Hobie Leland, Jr., discovered that Department Y had a $4,000 unfavorable material efficiency variance. If the usage process were out of control, the variance would continue for this period and the subsequent two periods. The efficiency variance occurs continuously throughout each period. If the usage process were in control this period, it would remain in control for the subsequent two periods.

Hobie had a decision to make. If he made an investigation, an outlay of $1,000 would be required immediately (start of the current period). If the usage were found to be out of control, correction would be made at the end of the current period (at an additional cost of $2,000) due to the length of time necessary for an investigation. Thus, any out-of-control variances would remain for at least the current period, even if an investigation were made. Hobie had a desired rate of return of 10 percent per period.

REQUIRED

1. Sketch the cash flows for the current period and the two subsequent periods for each of the two actions available to Hobie (investigate/not investigate).
2. What is the probability of the process being in control, at which level Hobie should be indifferent between investigating and not investigating the process? (The present value of $1 received at the end of period 1 is .909; the present value of $1 received continuously during period 1 is .9516.)
3. In requirements 1 and 2 it is assumed that the cost to the firm of the process being out of control is the $4,000 unfavorable materials efficiency variance. Give three reasons why this assumption need not be valid.
4. Hobie had been using the following rule of thumb for investigating cost variances: investigate if an unfavorable variance exceeds the standard by more than 10 percent. Hobie decided that more sophistication was necessary and adopted the 2σ (that is, two standard deviations) rule in deciding whether to investigate a cost variance. Hobie was astounded when his friend from the "Institution of Cost-Benefit Analysis" suggested that further analysis was necessary before changing his current rule of thumb to the 2σ rule. Discuss four specific factors that should be considered in the cost-benefit analysis of which cost-investigation rule to adopt.

25-36 ***Cost of prediction error.*** Refer to the preceding problem. Review Appendix 21a, "Cost of Prediction Error." Assume that the cost of the process being out of control is now assessed to be $3,000 per period. Department Y has a $4,000 unfavorable materials efficiency variance. What is the cost of prediction error using the materials efficiency variance of $4,000 as the period cost of being out of control? Assume that the probability of the process being out of control is .3.

The tasks of accounting for payrolls are complicated by the necessity for withholding specified amounts from employee earnings, measuring costs of employment fringe benefits, and meeting the government requirements for taxation and regulation. There are three major problems: (a) allocating labor costs to functions, departments, and products; (b) accurately computing earnings and promptly paying individual employees; and (c) computing and remitting withholdings and fringe benefits. Many of the aspects of classifying and controlling labor costs—point (a) above—have been covered previously (Chapters 4 and 8). This chapter will concentrate on other facets of payroll.

Individuals who are responsible for payroll accounting agree that, from the viewpoint of employees at least, promptness of payment and pinpoint accuracy are the foremost criteria for judging the merits of any payroll system. Whatever their educational level, be it twenty years of schooling or two, employees are excellent auditors of their own paychecks. Employees demand prompt and accurate payment, and they voice their dissatisfaction with vigor.

Government impact

complexity of payroll accounting

Many years ago, an employee who earned $60 per week received $60 in cash on payday. The bookkeeping problems for payroll were relatively simple. Only two parties (employer and employee) were involved.

Nowadays, the data-processing problems of accounting for payroll are staggering, and the clerical expenses for payroll accounting have soared accordingly. The rash of withholdings, fringe benefits, and incentive pay schemes requires an intricate network of accounts and supporting documents. Accounting for payroll has become so voluminous that new machine or computer installations invariably handle payroll as one of their first routine tasks.

Government requirements regarding payroll records play a big role in systems and forms design. Exhibits 26-1 and 26-2 show some of the government's impact on payroll accounting. **The government has at least two major influences: (a) it requires the employer to be its collecting agent for income taxes from employees, and (b) it levies special payroll taxes on the employer.**

withholding taxes

The employer must withhold ordinary income taxes. As used here, "ordinary" refers to all federal, state, and municipal income taxes. Hereafter, these will simply be called *income taxes*. Employers must also withhold a special income tax, commonly called the *Social Security tax*. Other terms for the Social Security tax are *federal insurance contributions act tax* (F.I.C.A. tax) and *federal old-age benefits tax* (F.O.A.B. tax). The amounts and timing of these tax payments to the government are shown in Exhibits 26-1 and 26-2. The basic journal-entry pattern is as follows:

Work-in-process control	120,000	
Factory-overhead control	30,000	
Selling-expense control	40,000	
Administrative-expense control	10,000	
Accrued payroll (gross)		200,000
Accrued payroll	35,000	
Withheld income taxes payable		29,000
Withheld F.I.C.A. taxes payable		6,000
Withheld income taxes payable	29,000	
Withheld F.I.C.A. taxes payable	6,000	
Cash (or some similar credit that has this ultimate effect on cash)		35,000

The entries above show that the *gross* payroll cost is the measure of the various basic labor costs incurred by the employer. The taxes *on employees* are withheld and remitted (usually monthly) to the government. Somehow this practice tends to make the pain of the tax bite seem less severe to the employee.

EXHIBIT 26-1

U.S.A. Payrolls and Taxes

TAX	BASIS FOR COMPUTATION	RATE	PERIOD COVERED	DATE OF FILING FORM
Federal income tax on employees	Gross earnings paid	Depends on gross earnings and dependents	Calendar quarters supplemented by a reconcilliation at year-end	On or before end of month following close of calendar quarter
F.I.C.A. tax on employees	Limited amount* of gross earnings paid to each employee	6.7%, but increases frequently	Calendar quarters	Same as above—Form 941
F.I.C.A. tax on employers	Limited amount of gross earnings paid to each employee	Same as above	Calendar quarters	Same as above—Form 941
State unemployment insurance tax on employers†	First $6,000 of gross earnings paid to each employee‡	Generally 2.7%, but may vary from .2% to 4%, depending on various state merit-rating systems for employer's labor turnover experience	Calendar quarters	Same as above—Special state form
Federal unemployment insurance tax on employers	Same as above‡	Generally, effective rate is .7% (3.4% nominal rate less 2.7% rate credit for state unemployment tax payments)	Previous calendar year	January 31—Form 940
State workmen's compensation insurance (or tax) on employers	Gross earnings paid	Varies for different occupational classifications	If insured by private company, annual premium is usually paid in advance. If taxed by state, same due-date provisions apply as for state unemployment tax.	

**The current statutory limit is tied to the increments in cost-of-living benefits since 1976, when the maximum taxable wage limit was $15,300. In 1981 the limit was $29,700.*

†A few states also have an employee unemployment tax.

‡Employers are not subject to tax unless they have one or more employees for at least one day a week for 20 weeks in a calendar year or pay at least $1,500 in wages in a quarter.

EXHIBIT 26-2

Calendar of Employer's Obligations Under U.S.A. Federal Law

WHEN HIRING	FORM NUMBER
Have employee fill out withholding exemption certificate, providing his or her Social Security number	W-4
If employee has no Social Security number, he or she should file application on	SS-5
WHEN PAYING	
Withhold both income taxes and F.I.C.A. taxes.	
By end of April, July, October, and January:	
File combined return for all F.I.C.A. taxes and withheld income taxes covering the quarter ending with the prior month. For example, the first calendar quarter's return must be filed by April 30.	941
By January 31 and at termination of employment:	
Give each employee a withholding statement in duplicate showing F.I.C.A. earnings and withholdings, total earnings subject to income-tax withholdings, and income tax withheld.	W-2
By January 31:	
File reconciliation of quarterly returns	W-3
—plus collector's copy of all individual W-2's given to employees for prior year	W-2a
File annual return and pay unemployment tax	940

Thus, the employer does not regard withheld taxes as an employer tax; instead, the employer performs a collection-agent service for the government.[1]

other withholdings

A flock of other withholdings from employees also exists. Withholdings as such are not employer costs. **They are merely portions of the employee's gross earnings that are being funneled via the employer to third parties, primarily for the employee's convenience.** Examples include employee contributions to group life insurance plans, hospitalization insurance, pension funds, employee savings plans, donations, and union dues.

---

[1]Employees who have held jobs with two or more employers during a single year are entitled to a refund if excess F.I.C.A. taxes were withheld. For example, if the F.I.C.A. withholding rate is 7 percent and John Doe earned $20,000 from one employer and $25,000 from another, each employer would legally have to withhold 7 percent of the first, say, $39,000 paid. Therefore, this employee would be entitled to a $420 refund as follows:

Employer 1	.07 × $20,000 =	$1,400
Employer 2	.07 × $25,000 =	1,750
Total withheld		$3,150
Taxable limit for individual:	.07 × $39,000 =	2,730
Excess F.I.C.A. tax withheld		$ 420

His claim would be filed on his own individual income tax return. His W-2 forms would be evidence in support of his claim.

The employer is not entitled to any refund.

Fringe benefits

large size of fringe benefits

The gross earnings of employees are only nominal measures of the payroll costs really borne. The employer not only must pay payroll taxes like Social Security and unemployment levies but must also incur many more fringe costs. The following breakdown of payroll costs illustrates the general pattern:

Gross earnings of employee (Assume $30,000.)	100.00%
Federal old-age tax and hospital insurance on employers (Rate based on average employee earnings of $30,000. Tax would be, say, 6.7%.)	6.70
Federal unemployment tax (.7% of $6,000, or $42. Divide $42 by $30,000.)	.14
State unemployment tax (2.7% of $6,000, or $162. Divide $162 by $30,000.)	.54
Workmen's compensation tax (Rates vary with hazards; average rate shown.)	1.25
Vacations and paid holidays (15 days vacation and 10 holidays. Divide 25 by 235 days' pay.)	10.64
Minimum total for most employers	119.27
Add:	
Employer contributions to pension funds (average rate)	10.00
Employer contributions to dental, life, and other insurance, etc. (average rate)	6.00
Total cost incurred by many employers	135.27%

These figures demonstrate that fringe costs are no longer a dribble; their waterfall proportions have caused an increasing number of companies to recast their account classifications. Instead of treating all fringe costs as overhead, some companies add an average (that is, "equalized" or "leveled") fringe rate to the basic direct-labor rate to bring into focus a better measure of direct-labor costs. This leveled rate is computed as shown in the table above. **However, perhaps because of inertia, most companies continue to treat fringe costs as a part of overhead.**

timing of cost recognition

As in many other phases of accounting, there is often a time lag between incurrence and payment of various payroll fringe costs. For example, the liability for vacation payments really accrues from week to week as each employee accumulates a claim to vacation pay. Thus, many companies use an estimate to spread total vacation costs over a year instead of recognizing such costs as payments are made:

Work-in-process control (direct labor)	19,000	
Factory-overhead control (indirect labor plus $1,000 vacation pay)	7,000	
Estimated liability for vacation pay		1,000
Accrued payroll		25,000
To accrue vacation pay throughout the year because it is related to work done throughout the year. Leveled rate is 4% of Accrued Payroll. Entry here is, say, for January.		
Accrued payroll	25,000	
Estimated liability for vacation pay	300	
Cash		22,000
Withholdings payable (various)		3,300
The liability account for vacation pay is debited as actual vacation payments are made.		

Similar treatment can be given to bonus plans, holiday pay, contributions to pension funds, and contributions to guaranteed annual wage funds. The decision to adopt such leveling arrangements in accounting for fringe costs largely depends on the significance of the amounts involved and on the distortion of month-to-month costs that may arise from failure to spread charges over the year.

Employer payroll taxes: theory and practice

Employers must pay Social Security taxes and unemployment taxes on specified compensation paid to each employee every calendar year—up to maximum statutory taxable-wage limits that are changed by Congress from time to time. In most cases, this means that heavier tax outlays will be made in the earlier months of the calendar year than in the later months, because the employer liability diminishes as wage payments to an increasing number of employees gradually reach and pass the yearly statutory taxable-wage limit.

The problem of timing charges for employer payroll taxes raises some special theoretical questions. The employer's legal liability is ordinarily a function of wages *paid* rather than of wages *accrued.* Yet in practice, employer payroll taxes are usually accrued as wages are *earned.* Furthermore, such payroll tax accrual diminishes as months pass because more and more employees' earnings gradually surpass the maximum taxable limit.[2]

To illustrate, assume that a company has a gross payroll of $25,000 per month, $16,000 of which is direct labor, and $9,000 of which is indirect factory labor. Assume that the tax rate on employers is .7 percent for federal unemployment, 1.6 percent for state unemployment, and 6.7 percent for Social Security benefits, a total payroll tax rate of 9 percent.

Early months:	**Work-in-process control**	**16,000**	
	Factory-overhead control ($9,000 plus $2,250)	**11,250**	
	Accrued payroll		**25,000**
	Employer's payroll taxes payable		**2,250**
	Payroll tax is .09 × $25,000 = $2,250.		
Late months:	**Work-in-process control**	**16,000**	
	Factory-overhead control	**9,000**	
	Accrued payroll		**25,000**
	Payroll is not subject to payroll tax because every employee's salary has passed the maximum taxable limits.		

In theory, employer payroll taxes (a) should be accrued as wages are earned (this practice is widely followed), and (b) should be spread over the year, using a leveled rate. Thus, payroll taxes would be handled in a fashion similar to the previous illustration on vacation pay. The reasoning in support of spreading payroll taxes over the year is that, for a going concern, the commitment to hire employees is made for a year; the payroll tax is an annual tax that is related to the year as a whole. Because it benefits the entire year's operations, such a tax should not be loaded on the early months of the calendar year.[3]

[2]Conceivably, in some companies, if no new workers are hired in the late months of the calendar year, the employer may show no payroll tax costs for these months.

[3]This is also the essential position of FASB Statement 43, *Compensated Absences* (Stamford, Conn.: Financial Accounting Standards Board, 1980).

Illustration of payroll accounting

» EXAMPLE

The Stengal Company has a gross payroll of $1,000 per day, based on a five-day, forty-hour, Monday-through-Friday workweek. Withholdings for income taxes amount to $100 per day. Payrolls for each week are paid on the following Tuesday.

Gross payrolls consist of $600 direct labor, $200 indirect labor, $140 selling expense, and $60 administrative expenses each day. The general-ledger entry to record the total of the payroll cost incurred (including accrued employer payroll fringe costs) is made on the last day of each month. Fringe costs borne by the employer are:

	PERCENT OF GROSS PAYROLL
Vacation pay	4.0%
F.I.C.A. tax	6.7%
Federal unemployment tax	.7%
State unemployment tax	1.6%
	13.0%

For our purposes, assume that the company starts business on March 3.

MARCH						
S	M	T	W	T	F	S
						1
2	3	4	5	6	7	8
9	10	11	12	13	14	15
16	17	18	19	20	21	22
23	24	25	26	27	28	29
30	31					

APRIL						
S	M	T	W	T	F	S
		1	2	3	4	5
6	7	8	9	10	11	12
13	14	15	16	17	18	19
20	21	22	23	24	25	26
27	28	29	30			

Try to solve the following requirements by yourself before examining the solution. (Exhibit 26-1 contains some helpful information.)

REQUIRED

1. All general-journal payroll entries for March 11, 18, 25, and 31, April 1, 8, 15, 22, 29, and 30.
2. All postings to Accrued payroll, Employees' income taxes payable, Employees' F.I.C.A. taxes payable, and Employer's F.I.C.A. taxes payable.

» SOLUTION

1. Journal entries follow:

March 11	**Accrued payroll (5 × $1,000)**	**5,000.00**	
	Cash		**4,165.00**
	Employees' income taxes payable (assume 5 × $100)		**500.00**
	Employees F.I.C.A. taxes payable (.067 × $5,000)		**335.00**
	To pay payroll		

The identical entry would be repeated every Tuesday, March 18 through April 29. Note that payroll settlements are made every *payday,* regardless of when payroll costs are recognized as being incurred.

March 31	**Work-in-process control**		
	(21 days × $600)	**12,600.00**	
	Factory-overhead control		
	(21 × $200) + .13(21 × $200) + .13($12,600)	**6,384.00**	
	Selling-expense control		
	(21 × $140) + .13(21 × $140)	**3,322.20**	
	Administrative-expense control		
	(21 × $60) + .13(21 × $60)	**1,423.80**	
	Accrued payroll (21 days × $1,000)		**21,000.00**
	Estimated liability for vacation pay		
	(.04 × $21,000)		**840.00**
	Employer's F.I.C.A. taxes payable		
	(.067 × $21,000)		**1,407.00**
	Federal unemployment taxes payable		
	(.007 × $21,000)		**147.00**
	State unemployment taxes payable		
	(.016 × $21,000)		**336.00**

Such an entry is usually made and posted monthly. If desired, it could be made weekly, biweekly, or at any other interval. As contrasted with the previous entry, this entry recognizes cost incurrence rather than payment. Its measurements depend on the number of work days in a calendar month.

(Note that the entries on *paydays* are the same for April as for March.)

April 30	**Work-in-process control (22 × $600)**	**13,200.00**	
	Factory-overhead control		
	(22 × $200) + .13(22 × $200) + .13($13,200)	**6,688.00**	
	Selling-expense control		
	(22 × $140) + .13(22 × $140)	**3,480.40**	
	Administrative-expense control		
	(22 × $60) + .13(22 × $60)	**1,491.60**	
	Accrued payroll (22 × $1,000)		**22,000.00**
	Estimated liability for vacation pay		
	(.04 × $22,000)		**880.00**
	Employer's F.I.C.A. taxes payable		
	(.067 × $22,000)		**1,474.00**
	Federal unemployment taxes payable		
	(.007 × $22,000)		**154.00**
	State unemployment taxes payable		
	(.016 × $22,000)		**352.00**

The entry above is based on 22 days of work done in April.

April 30	**Employees' income taxes payable**		
	(3 paydays × $500)	**1,500.00**	
	Employees' F.I.C.A. taxes payable		
	(3 × $335)	**1,005.00**	
	Employer's F.I.C.A. taxes payable		
	(3 × $335)	**1,005.00**	
	Cash		**3,510.00**
	Payment of taxes withheld on *paydays* in March plus employer's matching of F.I.C.A. taxes withheld.		

These taxes are detailed on Form 941, a quarterly return. Legal liability arises as payroll is paid during a calendar quarter rather than as payroll is accrued. Compare, for example, the employer's F.I.C.A. taxes accrued as of March 31 ($1,407) with the amount remitted with this return ($1,005). This ($402) difference represents six days' cost incurred in March ($67 per day × 6 days) that was not *paid* with this quarterly return. It will be paid during a subsequent period.

April 30	**State unemployment taxes payable (.016 × $5,000 × 3 paydays in March)**	**240.00**	
	Cash		**240.00**
	Payment to state for legal liability for first calendar quarter.		

2. Postings to selected accounts for March and April follow:

ACCRUED PAYROLL

March 11	5,000		
March 18	5,000		
March 25	5,000		
To balance	6,000	March 31	21,000
		March 31 balance, six days' gross earnings	6,000
April 1	5,000		
April 8	5,000		
April 15	5,000		
April 22	5,000		
April 29	5,000	April 30	22,000
To balance	3,000		
		April 30 balance, three days' gross earnings	3,000

EMPLOYEES' INCOME TAXES PAYABLE

		March 11, 18, 25	1,500
		April 1, 8, 15, 22, 29	2,500
April 30	1,500		

EMPLOYEES' F.I.C.A. TAXES PAYABLE

		March 11, 18, 25	1,005
		April 1, 8, 15, 22, 29	1,675
April 30	1,005		

EMPLOYER'S F.I.C.A. TAXES PAYABLE

		March 31	1,407
		April 30	1,474
April 30	1,005		

A study of the T-accounts above shows the following:

1. The Accrued Payroll balance at the close of business on March 31 represents the unpaid amount of *gross* earnings of employees applicable to the last six days worked in March.
2. The timing of recognition of liability for employees' and employer's F.I.C.A. taxes differs. Legally, both liabilities arise when payroll is paid. But the employer accrues liability when regular labor-cost incurrence is recognized, because such payroll taxes are basically related to time of *earnings* rather than to time of *payout.*

Payroll bank account

Companies with many employees usually use a separate checking account to keep payroll checks apart from checks for other disbursements. This procedure facilitates control, preparation, and reconciliation of vast numbers of payroll checks. The general working of a payroll bank account is as follows, using the data for March 11 in our illustration:

March 11	**Accrued payroll (5 × $1,000)**	**5,000.00**	
	Cash		**4,165.00**
	Employees' income taxes payable (assume 5 × $100)		**500.00**
	Employees' F.I.C.A. taxes payable (.067 × $5,000)		**335.00**
	To pay payroll.		

A single $4,165 check is drawn against the company's regular checking account to cover the net payroll. The bank would then transfer $4,165 from the regular account to a special payroll bank account. Assume that there are 15 employees. Fifteen payroll checks totaling $4,165 would be prepared and issued. The size, color, and numerical sequence of these checks would differ from those of the regular checks. Note that, as far as this company is concerned, its payroll bank account should always have a zero balance. Any balance in the payroll account as shown by the bank represents outstanding payroll checks.

Incentive plans

pay as a motivational device

Chapter 10 (page 322) described the relationships between:

effort ------→ performance ------→ reward

A major finding of research in this area is that workers are more likely to increase effort if they see a clear link between these three elements. However, this is a complicated area. For instance, rewards such as extra pay or salary increases that are significant to most people are not significant to all.

Exhibit 26-3 summarizes four organizational factors that have been identified as important to the choice of possible incentive plans. Each of the factors may rule out some kinds of pay plans.

1. *Human relations climate.* If an organization tends to have an autocratic management style, pay and similar rewards should be tied to hard criteria such as quantity of output, profits, or sales. Such criteria require a minimum level of trust. They have a much better chance of success than approaches that depend on joint goal setting and soft criteria. Moreover, the same incentive plan that works well in one organization may fail miserably if adopted by a similar organization. In short, beware of any simple answers.
2. *Production type.* Firms that produce individual units, small batches, large batches, or masses of assembled units may justifiably give rewards based on individual performance.

EXHIBIT 26-3

Relevance of Four Organizational Factors to Pay Plans

CLASSIFICATION	SUBCLASSIFICATION	PAY PLAN
1. Human relations climate	Authoritarian	Need objective hard criteria; pay clearly tied to performance
	Democratic	Can use participative goal setting and softer criteria
2. Production type	Mass and unit	Can usually develop hard criteria; rewards on individual or small group basis
	Process	Need to encourage cooperation; individual performance not highly visible or measurable
	Professional organizations (i.e., hospital, school, consulting firm)	Individually based plans; soft criteria; high-individual involvement in own evaluation
3. Size	Large	Organizationwide bonuses poor for all but a few top-level managers
	Small	Organizationwide bonuses possible in some situations
4. Degree of centralization	Centralized	Hard to base performance on subunit (i.e., plant) performance
	Decentralized	Pay can be based on profit center or subunit performance for members of management

Source: *E. Lawler and J. Rhode,* Information and Control in Organizations *(Pacific Palisades, Calif.: Goodyear, 1976). Adapted from p. 63.*

However, such rewards are difficult in continuous process industries subject to plantwide or department control. Group or team incentives are more successful. In professional service organizations, tailor-made incentive plans (such as the management-by-objectives plans described in Chapter 5) are often preferable.

3. *Size.* In large organizations, most employees perceive that their effort is remotely connected with the performance of the organization. Therefore, a plan that rewards on the basis of organizationwide performance is unlikely to motivate performance in large organizations.
4. *Centralization.* If much decision-making power is vested in the central office and local plant management is rewarded on how the plant performs, "the motivational impact on the local management will be minimal."[4]

objective of incentives

Most employees are paid a flat salary or a flat rate per hour, but wage incentive systems are widespread. Incentive plans provide extra compensation for performance that is superior to some predetermined goal or standard. The wide variety of factory incentive systems has a common objective: minimization of total costs for a given volume of production. **In other words, the sweetening of the pay envelope must at least be balanced by reductions in other cost factors or by reductions in labor cost per unit.** For example, assume that Earl Johnson is paid \$12.00 an hour and produces 10 units in that time, resulting in an average labor cost of \$1.20 per unit. He is placed on a strict piece-rate system at a rate of \$1.10 per piece. His productivity may increase to 12 units per hour. His earnings would then be \$13.20 per hour (12 × \$1.10)—higher pay per worker and yet less cost per unit for the employer. A piece rate of

[4]E. Lawler and J. Rhode, *Information and Control in Organizations* (Pacific Palisades, Calif.: Goodyear, 1976), p. 62.

$1.20 or more may even be desirable for the employer if savings in other costs like materials, power, repairs, or other variable-overhead items can offset increased labor costs.

Incentive plans are not panaceas for problems of cost control. They add to clerical costs and may tend to increase spoilage costs and lessen quality. Yet many companies have been pleased with overall results. In any event, no incentive plan can substitute for adequate management as the most effective means of controlling labor costs.

accounting for incentive plans

Incentive plans vary widely in their details and application. The Gantt Task and Bonus Plan awards a higher piece rate, or bonus, for all production in excess of standard. The Taylor Differential Piece-Rate System applies a higher piece rate for *all* production per hour or day as long as the hourly or daily production standard is met. Incentive plans may be arranged to reward individual performance, group performance, assembly-line performance, and even plantwide performance.

A common incentive plan is piecework coupled with a guaranteed minimum hourly rate. Thus, if the standard number of pieces per hour is not produced, pay is provided to "make up" the difference between the guaranteed rate and the piecework earnings. An example of computations follows:

DAILY EARNINGS SUMMARY*

CLOCK NUMBER	NAME	DEPARTMENT	OPERATION	UNITS PRODUCED	PIECE RATE	PIECEWORK EARNINGS	MAKEUP	TOTAL EARNINGS
414	Atwood	4	1004	100	$1.10	$110.00	$ —	$110.00
445	Barnes	4	1004	70	1.10	77.00	19.00	96.00
446	Charnes	4	1004	80	1.10	88.00	8.00	96.00

**Guaranteed rate is $12.00 per hour or $96.00 per day.*

Makeup pay would be charged to the department as an overhead item and would be part of the department's overhead budget. The standard labor cost for the operation would be $1.10 per unit.

SUMMARY

Payroll accounting is overwhelmed with detail, much of which is kept because of legal requirements rather than because of managerial needs.

The data-processing function is often divided between cost allocation and payouts to employees. Although electronic data processing increasingly accomplishes these objectives simultaneously, most companies allocate costs on one time basis (for example, monthly in the general ledger, daily in subsidiary records) and account for payouts on another time basis (for example, weekly).

Organizations use pay as a major means of rewarding employees. Pay and other rewards should be designed by (a) determining which rewards are important and (b) tying the rewards to performance. Incentive pay should be adopted by employers if they predict that the overall costs per unit will decline.

PROBLEM FOR SELF-STUDY

Review the problem used as an illustration in the chapter.

QUESTIONS, PROBLEMS, AND CASES

26-1 "Accounting for payroll embraces plenty of big problems." Name three.

26-2 "The need for accuracy in payroll accounting is paramount." Explain.

26-3 "The government has at least two major influences on payroll accounting." What are they?

26-4 Name the major taxes associated with payrolls.

26-5 Jane Ripon worked for three employers during a year. Her gross earnings were $1,000, $7,800, and $29,000—a total of $37,800. How much of the earnings should each employer regard as subject to F.I.C.A. taxes?

26-6 "The Federal Unemployment Insurance Tax rate is 0.7 percent." Do you agree? Why?

26-7 Identify the following forms: W-4, 941, W-2, W-3, 940.

26-8 "Withheld taxes are taxes on employers." Do you agree? Why?

26-9 Name four common withholdings other than taxes.

26-10 "Payroll fringe costs are large enough these days to justify adding an average fringe rate to the basic direct-labor rate." Do you agree? Why?

26-11 "Leveling or averaging of vacation costs and holiday pay is used to relate them to work done throughout the year." What criteria should affect the decision to adopt such leveling arrangements?

26-12 "Conceivably, in some companies an employer may show no payroll tax costs for the last quarter of the year." Why? Explain.

26-13 Contrast the theoretical and practical accounting treatments of employer payroll taxes.

26-14 If all bookkeeping is up to date, what does the balance in Accrued Payroll represent?

26-15 "The timing of recognition of liability for employees' and employer's F.I.C.A. taxes differs." Explain.

26-16 What are incentive plans? What is their objective?

26-17 What is "makeup"? How is it accounted for?

26-18 A company uses a separate payroll bank account. Weekly wage payments are $10,000. A $1,000 minimum balance is kept to provide for salary advances, separation payments, and so forth. What cash balance should ordinarily be shown on the company balance sheets?

26-19 ***Payroll liability and payments.*** The Arjay Company had the following liabilities, March 31, 19_1:

F.I.C.A. taxes payable	$ 14,000
State unemployment taxes payable	7,000
Federal unemployment taxes payable	3,000
Employees' income taxes payable	100,000

In April the gross payroll was $3,000,000. Income taxes withheld from employees were $660,000. Of the gross payroll, $2,600,000 was subject to a 7 percent F.I.C.A. tax rate, whereas $2,000,000 was subject to a 0.7 percent federal unemployment tax rate and a 1.7 percent state unemployment tax rate.

REQUIRED

Prepare journal entries to record

1. The payment of all March 31 liabilities for taxes.

2. The recognition of the gross payroll liability and related liabilities for the month of April. (Debit Labor Costs)
3. The payment, less withholdings, of the April payroll to employees.

26-20 ***Journal entries for payroll.*** The Stable Company operates the year-round with a gross payroll of $5,000 a day. Withholdings for Social Security taxes and federal income taxes amount to $1,500 a day. The concern works five days a week, and the payroll period covers Monday to Friday, both inclusive. Payrolls for the week are paid on the following Tuesday.

Gross payrolls consist of $3,000 direct labor, $1,000 indirect labor, $700 selling expense, and $300 general and administrative expense each day. The general-ledger entry to record the total of the payroll cost incurred each month is made on the last day of the month. These totals are obtained by summarizing the Payroll Cost Recapitulation sheets. This firm uses a "leveled" percentage of 6 percent to estimate its own contribution to Social Security.

REQUIRED

Using the calendar as a guide, answer the following questions:

APRIL

SU	*M*	*TU*	*W*	*TH*	*F*	*SA*
		1	2	3	4	5
6	7	8	9	10	11	12
13	14	15	16	17	18	19
20	21	22	23	24	25	26
27	28	29	30			

1. What is the balance in Accrued Payroll as of the close of business on March 31?
2. What journal entries should be made on (a) April 1? (b) April 29? (c) April 30?
3. What is the ending balance in Accrued Payroll as of the close of business on April 30?

26-21 ***Journal entries for payroll.*** (J. March) The balance of the Accrued Wages of Kem Industries, Inc., was $12,120 on October 31, 19_1. The company has a job-order cost system. The cost accounts are in the general ledger. Time tickets for pay periods falling wholly or partly in November are summarized as follows:

PAY PERIOD	DIRECT LABOR	FACTORY OVERHEAD	TOTAL
Nov. 1–7	$8,250	$4,510	$12,760
Nov. 8–14	8,450	4,490	12,940
Nov. 15–21	8,570	4,570	13,140
Nov. 22–28	7,920	4,060	11,980
Nov. 29–Dec. 5	8,430	4,470	12,900

Of the wages earned in the pay period ending December 5, one-third is applicable to November.

Payrolls for pay periods ending in November are summarized as follows:

		DEDUCTIONS		
PAY PERIOD ENDING	GROSS EARNINGS	**F.I.C.A.**	**income tax**	NET PAY
Oct. 31	$12,120	$550	$2,200	$ 9,370
Nov. 7	12,760	540	2,250	9,970
Nov. 14	12,940	560	2,280	10,100
Nov. 21	13,140	510	2,300	10,330
Nov. 28	11,980	475	2,200	9,305

The payroll for the period ending November 28 was paid December 2.

REQUIRED

1. Journal entry for labor-cost allocation.
2. Journal entry for payrolls paid in November.
3. Postings in the Accrued Wages account.
4. Journal entry for accrual of employer's payroll taxes for the month of November at a leveled rate of 10 percent of gross earnings.
5. Answer the following questions:
   a. Theoretically, should the accrual of employer's payroll taxes be based on wages earned or on wages paid during the month?
   b. Why is the amount of F.I.C.A. deductions less than 6.7 percent of the gross earnings?
   c. What does the balance of Accrued Wages represent?

Journal explanations in all cases should state clearly how you arrived at your amounts.

26-22 ***Unemployment compensation taxes.*** (CPA) The cost of unemployment compensation taxes to an employer is sometimes reduced as a result of a "good" experience rating. A manufacturer negotiated with the federal government a contract that necessitated the construction of a specific plant and related facilities for the sole purpose of producing the goods called for in the contract. Because the goods were required to meet emergency needs of the government, it was possible that after the plant facilities were constructed, the employees hired, and work on the order begun, the contract would be canceled. The ensuing termination of services of employees hired for this specific job would make the employer's experience rating worse, which in turn would increase the cost of his unemployment compensation taxes. This "possible" cost was recognized as a cost in negotiating the contract.

Describe in order of preference three alternative methods of recording in accounts and/or disclosing on the financial statements the "possible" cost during the course of operations of this emergency plant under the contract. State your reasons.

26-23 ***Accounting for idle time.*** (J. March) The labor distribution of the Dunne Desk Company is made from its payroll, all the wages of its twenty shop employees, except the foreman's, being treated as direct labor. The company pays for idle time of workmen caused by material shortages, and this amounts to a substantial portion of the payroll.

For the year 19_1, the direct labor, according to the ledger, was $400,000 and the overhead $320,000. Accordingly, an overhead rate of 80 percent was used in 19_2 for the purpose of estimating costs of new products. The manager thinks that the estimates are wrong, for his income statement shows a gross margin of only $6 a desk, whereas his selling prices are at least $30 a desk above the estimated costs. He suspects that the idle-time factor is not being included in the cost estimates, and he asks you to investigate the situation.

1. How would you proceed to determine whether the manager's suspicions are correct?

2. Recompute the overhead rate for 19_1 on the assumption that $40,000 was paid for idle time that should be treated as overhead instead of as direct labor.

3. Suggest a change in the method of labor-cost allocation that would result in a more accurate accounting for idle time.

26-24 ***Group incentives.*** (SMA, adapted) The Smart Company of Hong Kong operates with five direct workers in its stamping department. All work is done on a job-order basis. During the week of August 15, each man worked a full 40-hour week, with output as follows:

NAME	GUARANTEED HOURLY MINIMUM	UNITS PRODUCED
Brackett, S. J.	$15.00	1,840
Emery, P. L.	16.00	1,900
Evans, E. C.	15.00	1,960
Forest, T. A.	17.00	2,050
Simmons, F.	15.00	1,650

REQUIRED

1. Compute the gross earnings of each worker, assuming that a group incentive plan is in operation and that the standard output of the department is 7,200 units per week. Each member of the group receives the guaranteed hourly minimum if

production is equal to or less than the standard output. The hourly rate for each worker is increased 1 percent for each 200 units per week in excess of standard production.

2. What effect does excess of "normal" or "standard" output have on the unit cost of production? Explain.
3. Assess the effectiveness of this incentive system for the Smart Company, giving reasons for your answer.

26-25 ***Incentive wage plans.*** (CPA, adapted) During your audit of the accounts of the Gelard Manufacturing Corporation of Singapore, your assistant tells you that he has found errors in the computation of the wages of factory workers and he wants you to verify his work.

Your assistant has extracted from the union contract the following description of the systems for computing wages in various departments of the company. The contract provides that the minimum wage for a worker is his base rate, which is also paid for any "downtime"—time when the worker's machine is under repair or he is without work. The standard workweek is 40 hours. The union contract also provides that workers be paid 150 percent of base rates for overtime production. The company is engaged in interstate commerce.

1. Straight piecework. The worker is paid at the rate of $2.00 per piece produced.

2. Percentage bonus plan. Standard quantities of production per hour are established by the engineering department. The worker's average hourly production, determined from his total hours worked and his production, is divided by the standard quantity of production to determine his efficiency ratio. The efficiency ratio is then applied to his base rate to determine his hourly earnings for the period.

3. Emerson Efficiency System. A minimum wage is paid for production up to 66⅔ percent of standard output or "efficiency." When the worker's production exceeds 66⅔ percent of the standard output, he is paid at a bonus rate. The bonus rate is determined from the following table:

EFFICIENCY	BONUS
Up to 66⅔%	0%
66⅔–79%	10%
80–99%	20%
100–125%	45%

Your assistant has prepared the following schedule of information pertaining to certain workers for a weekly payroll selected for examination:

WORKER	WAGE INCENTIVE PLAN	TOTAL HOURS	DOWN-TIME HOURS	UNITS PRODUCED	STANDARD UNITS	BASE RATE	GROSS WAGES PER BOOKS
Long	Straight piecework	40	5	400	—	$18	$ 820
Loro	Straight piecework	46	—	455*	—	18	910
Huck	Straight piecework	44	4	420†	—	18	840
Nini	Percentage bonus plan	40	—	250	200	22	1,200
Boro	Percentage bonus plan	40	—	180	200	19	670
Wiss	Emerson	40	—	240	300	21	920
Alan	Emerson	40	2	590	600‡	20	1,180

**Includes 45 pieces produced during the 6 overtime hours.*

†Includes 50 pieces produced during the 4 overtime hours. The overtime, which was brought about by the "downtime," was necessary to meet a production deadline.

‡Standard units for 40 hours' production.

REQUIRED

Prepare a schedule comparing each individual's gross wages per books and his gross wages per your calculation. Computations of workers' wages should be in good form and labeled with the workers' names.

The subject of internal control was once regarded as a technical matter that was confined to a course in auditing. However, many secret payments and embezzlements were disclosed during the 1970s. As a result, internal control has become a central responsibility of top management. This idea has recently been reinforced and expanded by the U.S. Foreign Corrupt Practices Act.

The systems and techniques for implementing internal control are aimed mainly at improving the accountability for actions, the accuracy and reliability of records, the safeguarding of assets, and the overall efficiency of operations. A key role in achieving these goals is played today by a company's audit committee.

This chapter explains internal control in general. Appendix 27a illustrates internal control in conjunction with the purchase of merchandise.[1] Appendix 27b describes some additional specialized techniques for

[1]Internal control is covered in other accounting books, such as this author's *Introduction to Financial Accounting* (Englewood Cliffs, N.J.: Prentice-Hall, 1981), Chap. 8. It is included in this text for those readers who have not studied this crucial and pervasive subject elsewhere.

accumulating accounting data, including the use of factory ledgers, which are often used by companies with two or more locations.

Overview of internal control

importance of accounting systems

Regardless of an entity's size or type, and regardless of whether it is held privately or publicly, managers and accountants should be alert to the rudiments of accounting systems and controls. Accounting records are kept for a variety of purposes. **A major purpose is to help managers operate their entities more efficiently and effectively.** Any person who forms a business will soon discover that recordkeeping is absolutely essential. For instance, records of receivables and payables must be created for transactions with customers and creditors, and cash disbursements and receipts must be traced to the individual accounts. Even the simplest of organizations must have some records. The cost-benefit test is easily met. Unless orderly compilation occurs, intolerable chaos results. In short, an accounting system is a wise business investment.

An *accounting system* is a set of records, procedures, and equipment that *routinely* deals with the events affecting the financial performance and position of the entity. The focus of the accounting system is on repetitive, voluminous transactions, which almost always fall into four categories:

1. Cash disbursements
2. Cash receipts
3. Purchases of goods and services, including employee payroll
4. Sales or other rendering of goods and services

The magnitude of the physical handling of records is often staggering. For example, consider the telephone company or the credit-card companies. They must process *millions* of transactions daily. Without computers and photocopying equipment, most modern organizations would be forced to halt operations. Too often, accounting systems are regarded as a necessary evil. But these systems deserve a loftier status. Well-designed and well-run accounting systems are positive contributions to organizations and the economy.

Advances in computer technology continue to be awesome. The description of a specific accounting system is likely to be outdated before it comes off the presses. Consequently, this chapter emphasizes the *general* features of accounting systems that persist regardless of specific computer programs and hardware. The purpose here is not to develop skills as a systems designer; the purpose is to develop an acquaintance with the scope and nature of accounting systems and controls. No manager or would-be manager can afford the risks of not having an awareness of the primary attributes of a suitable internal control system.

definition of internal control

Definitions of internal control vary considerably. In its broadest sense, *internal control* refers to both *administrative* control and *accounting* control:

1. *Administrative control* comprises the plan of organization (for example, the formal organization chart concerning who reports to whom) and all methods and procedures that facilitate management planning and control of operations. Examples are departmental budgeting procedures and reports on performance.
2. *Accounting control* comprises the methods and procedures that are mainly concerned with the authorization of transactions, the safeguarding of assets, and the accuracy of the financial records. Good accounting controls help *maximize* efficiency; they help *minimize* waste, unintentional errors, and fraud.

This chapter focuses on internal accounting controls, as distinguished from internal administrative controls. The latter have been covered in most of the chapters in this book.

management's responsibility

External auditors attest to the financial reports of an entity.[2] **However, management bears the *primary responsibility* for a company's financial statements.** Today the annual reports of publicly held companies generally contain an explicit statement of management responsibility for its financial statements.

These *management statements of responsibilities* usually state that management is responsible for all audited and unaudited information in the annual report, include a statement on the adequacy of internal control, and include a description of the composition and duties of the audit committee as well as the duties of the independent auditor. These features are highlighted in color in Exhibit 27-1, the management statement of General Motors.

Foreign Corrupt Practices Act, a misnomer

The U.S. Congress passed the *Foreign Corrupt Practices Act* in 1977. The title is misleading because the act's provisions pertain to the internal control systems of all publicly held companies, ***even if they do no business outside the United States*. The act contains not only specific prohibitions against bribery and other corrupt practices but also requirements (a) for maintaining accounting records in reasonable detail and accuracy and (b) for maintaining an appropriate system of internal accounting controls.** In general, as a part of intelligent management practices, most organizations already abide by these prohibitions and requirements. However, these responsibilities have now been explicitly codified as part of a federal law.

Public reporting on the adequacy of internal control has become an explicit responsibility of management under the act. Consequently, management in general, not just accountants, has focused on systems of internal control as never before. Boards of directors assure themselves of compliance with the act and with SEC requirements by (a) obtaining far more documentation of a system than previously existed and (b) compiling written evidence of management's evaluation and ongoing review of a system. **The biggest impact of the act has been the mandatory documentation of evaluation of internal control *by management* rather than only by external auditors.**

The documentation should systematically refer to (a) management's cost-benefit choices regarding the system and (b) management's evaluation of how well the system is working. Documentation includes memos, minutes of meetings discussing the act and internal control concepts with all affected individuals, written statements of intention to comply, flow charts, procedure manuals, and the like. Moreover, there should be a written program for ongoing review and evaluation of the system. Finally, there should be letters from external auditors stating that they found no material weaknesses in internal control during their audit, or that necessary improvements have been made.

[2]*External auditors* should be distinguished from *internal auditors,* who are full-time employees of the organization being audited. External auditors are also called *independent auditors* or *outside auditors* because they are certified public accountants hired for a fee to issue their independent opinion regarding financial statements.

EXHIBIT 27-1

Management's Statement of Responsibilities for Financial Statements

Consolidated Financial Statements

General Motors Corporation and Consolidated Subsidiaries

Responsibilities for Financial Statements

The following financial statements of General Motors Corporation and Consolidated Subsidiaries **were prepared by the management which is responsible for their integrity and objectivity.** The statements have been prepared in conformity with generally accepted accounting principles and, as such, include amounts based on judgments of management. Financial information elsewhere in this Annual Report is consistent with that in the financial statements.

Management is further responsible for maintaining a system of internal accounting controls, designed to provide reasonable assurance that the books and records reflect the transactions of the companies and that its established policies and procedures are carefully followed. From a stockholder's point of view, perhaps the most important feature in the system of control is that it is continually reviewed for its effectiveness and is augmented by written policies and guidelines, the careful selection and training of qualified personnel, and a strong program of internal audit.

Deloitte Haskins & Sells, **independent certified public accountants,** are engaged to examine the financial statements of General Motors Corporation and its subsidiaries and issue reports thereon. Their examination is conducted in accordance with generally accepted auditing standards which comprehend a review of internal accounting controls and a test of transactions. The Accountants' Report appears on page 26.

The Board of Directors, through the Audit Committee (composed entirely of non-employe Directors), is responsible for assuring that management fulfills its responsibilities in the preparation of the financial statements. The Committee selects the independent public accountants annually in advance of the Annual Meeting of Stockholders and submits the selection for ratification at the meeting. In addition, the Committee reviews the scope of the audits and the accounting principles to be applied in financial reporting. The independent public accountants, representatives of management, and the internal auditors meet regularly (separately and jointly) with the Committee to review the activities of each and to ensure that each is properly discharging its responsibilities. To ensure complete independence, Deloitte Haskins & Sells have full and free access to meet with the Committee, without management representatives present, to discuss the results of their examination, the adequacy of internal accounting controls, and the quality of the financial reporting.

Chairman

Roger B Smith

Chief Financial Officer

F. Alan Smith

The act specifies that internal accounting controls are supposed to provide reasonable assurance concerning

1. ***Authorization.*** **Transactions are executed in accordance with management's general or specific intentions.**
2. ***Recording.*** **All authorized transactions are recorded in the correct amounts, periods, and accounts. No fictitious transactions are recorded.**
3. ***Safeguarding.*** **Precautions and procedures appropriately restrict access to assets.**
4. ***Reconciliation.*** **Records are compared with other independently kept records and physical counts. Such comparisons help ensure that other control objectives are attained.**
5. ***Valuation.*** **Recorded amounts are periodically reviewed for impairment of values and necessary write-downs.**

The first three general objectives—authorization, recording, and safeguarding—relate to establishing the system of accountability and are aimed at *prevention* of errors and irregularities. The final two objectives—reconciliation and valuation—are aimed at *detection* of errors and irregularities.

In this author's opinion, **a sixth objective of an internal control system should be added: *promoting operating efficiency.* Although the act is not particularly concerned with efficiency, management should recognize that an internal control system's purpose is as much a positive one (promoting efficiency) as a negative one (preventing errors and fraud).**

The audit committee

The first objective of internal accounting control is *authorization;* transactions should be executed in accordance with management's intentions. Moreover, management bears primary responsibility for the entity's financial statements. This authority and responsibility extends upward to the board of directors. The 1970s were marked by the widespread formation of *audit committees* of the board. Indeed, such committees are required of companies whose shares are listed on the New York Stock Exchange. The primary responsibility of the audit committee is fiscal vigilance.

Audit committees are typically composed of three or more "outside" board members. Not being everyday employees of the company, they are usually considered to be more independent than the "inside" directors, who, as employees, also serve as part of the corporation's management. **The objective of the audit committee is to oversee the accounting controls, financial statements, and financial affairs of the corporation. The committee represents the full board and provides personal contact and communication among the board, the external auditors, the internal auditors, the financial executives, and the operating executives.** These relationships are depicted in Exhibit 27-2.

The display in Exhibit 27-2 is only one of many possible arrangements. Above all, note how the audit committee is supposed to be the main pipeline to the board of directors, especially for individuals responsible for the accounting function. Exhibit 27-2 shows that the internal audit manager is directly responsible (solid line) to the accounting executives, who, in turn, are directly responsible to both the audit committee and the executive vice-president. The dashed lines indicate that the audit department should communicate with and gather information directly from the external auditors and the internal auditors.

These relationships are evolving. For example, the internal auditing department sometimes is directly responsible to the executive vice-president, or to the president, or to the audit committee itself. Many observers believe that the internal audit staff should be totally independent of the financial officers.

The audit committee typically meets at least twice annually. The first meeting is to review the annual external audit plan; the second, to review the audited financial statements before their publication. Additional meetings may be held (a) to consider and approve the retention of the external auditors; (b) to review the company's accounting system, particularly the internal controls; and (c) to review any special matters raised by internal audits.

As a minimum, meetings should be attended by the chief financial officer and a representative of the external auditing firm. At least once a year, the committee should discuss with the external auditors their evaluation of corporate management (without the presence of the latter). Similarly, the committee should discuss with management their evaluation of the external auditors.

EXHIBIT 27-2 **Typical Corporate Organization Chart**

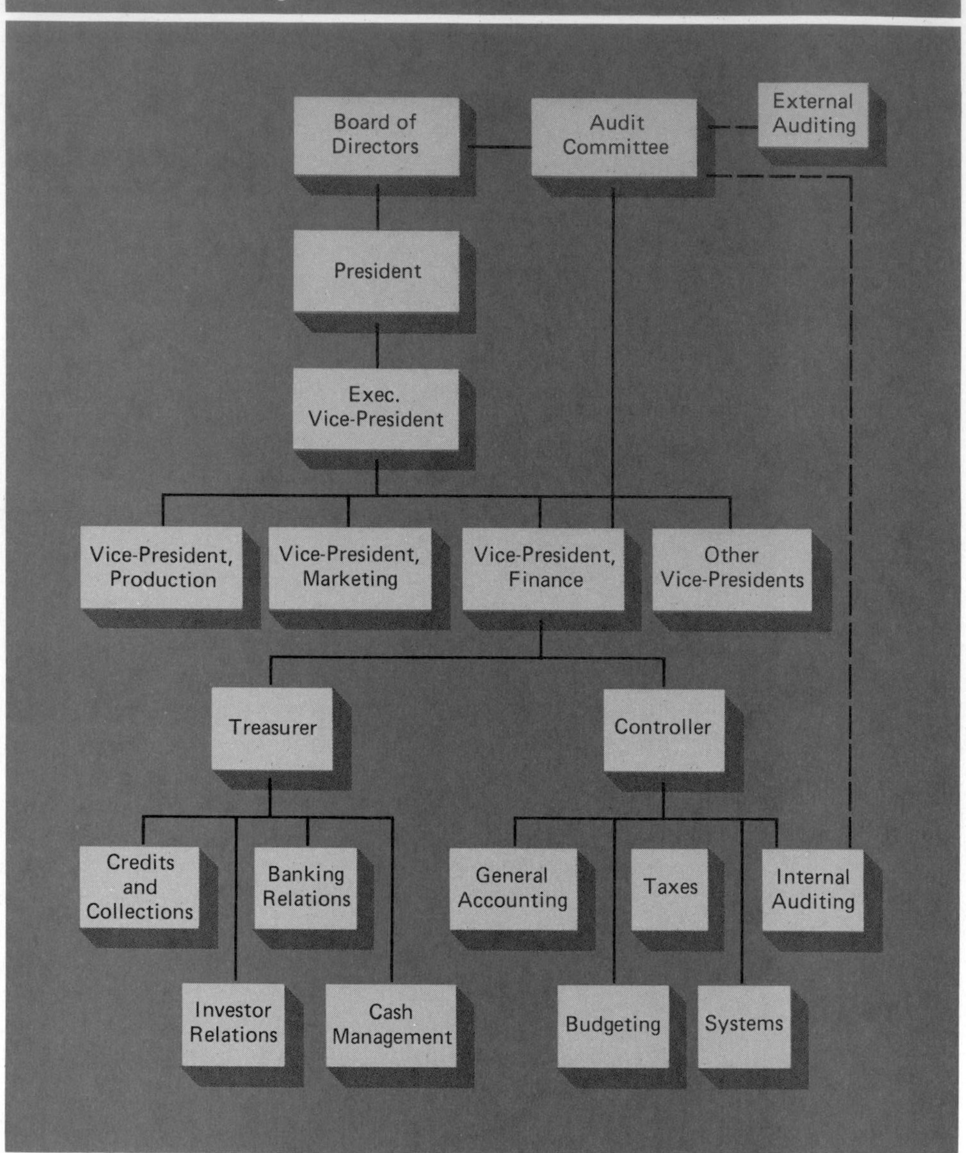

Checklist of internal control

All good systems of internal control have certain features in common. These features can be termed a *checklist of internal control,* which may be used to appraise any specific procedures for cash, purchases, sales, payroll, and the like. This checklist is sometimes called *principles* or *rules* or *concepts* or *characteristics* or *features* or *elements.* The following checklist summarizes the guidance that is found in much of the systems and auditing literature.[3]

[3]For an expanded discussion, see Alvin Arens and James Loebbecke, *Auditing,* 2nd ed. (Englewood Cliffs, N.J.: Prentice-Hall, 1980), Chap. 7.

1. Reliable personnel with clear responsibilities. The most important element of successful control is personnel. Incompetent or dishonest individuals can undermine a system, no matter how well it meets the other items on the checklist. Individuals obviously must be given authority, responsibility, and duties commensurate with their abilities, interests, experience, and reliability. Yet many employers use low-cost talent that may prove exceedingly expensive in the long run, not only because of fraud but because of poor productivity.

Reliability begins at the top of the organization. The entire system deserves surveillance by operating management to see if it is working as prescribed and if changes are warranted. In addition, appropriate overseeing and appraisal of employees are essential. The most streamlined accounting system is deficient if its prescribed procedures are not being conscientiously followed.

Responsibility means tracking actions as far down in the organization as is feasible, so that results may be related to individuals. It means having salesclerks sign sales slips, inspectors initial packing slips, and workers sign time cards and requisitions. The psychological impact of fixing responsibility tends to promote care and efficiency. Employees often perform better when they must explain deviations from required procedures.

2. Separation of duties. This element not only helps ensure accurate compilation of data but also limits the chances for fraud that would require the collusion of two or more persons. This extremely important and often neglected element can be subdivided into four parts:

a. *Separation of operational responsibility from recordkeeping responsibility.* The entire accounting function should be divorced from operating departments so that objective, independent records may be kept either by other operating people or by clerks. For example, product inspectors, not machine operators, should count good units produced; stores record clerks or computers, not storekeepers, should keep perpetual inventory counts.

b. *Separation of the custody of assets from accounting.* This practice reduces temptation and fraud. For example, the bookkeeper should not handle cash, and the cashier should not have access to ledger accounts such as the individual records of customers.

   In a computer system, a person with custody of assets should not have access to programming or any input records. Similarly, an individual who handles programming or input records should not have access to tempting assets.

c. *Separation of the authorization of transactions from the custody of related assets.* To the extent feasible, persons who authorize transactions should not have control over the related asset. For instance, the same individual should not authorize the payment of a supplier's invoice and also sign the check in payment of the bill. Nor should an individual who handles cash receipts have the authority to indicate which accounts receivable should be written off as uncollectible.

d. *Separation of duties within the accounting function.* An employee should not be able to record a transaction from its origin to its ultimate posting in a ledger. Independent performance of various phases will help ensure control over errors.

3. Proper authorization. This element is stressed in the Foreign Corrupt Practices Act. Authorization can be either *general* or *specific.* General authorization is usually found in writing. It often sets definite limits on what costs to charge (whether to fly economy or first class), on what price to charge (whether to offer a sales discount), on what credit limits to grant to customers, and so forth. There may also be complete prohibitions (against paying extra fees or bribes or overtime premiums).

Specific authorization usually means that a superior manager must permit (typically in writing) any particular deviations from the limits set by general authorization. For example, the plant manager, rather than the lathe supervisor, may have to approve overtime. Another example is the need for approval from the board of directors regarding expenditures for capital assets in excess of a specific limit.

4. Adequate documents. Documents and records vary considerably, from source documents like sales invoices and purchase orders to journals and ledgers. Immediate, complete, and tamper-proof recording is the aim. It is encouraged by having all source documents prenumbered and accounted for, by using devices such as cash registers and locked compartments in invoice-writing machines, and by designing forms for ease of recording.

Immediate recording is especially important for handling cash sales. Devices used to ensure immediate recording include cash registers with loud bells and compiling tapes, private detectives, guaranteeing "rewards" to customers if they are not offered a receipt at the time of sale, and forcing clerks to make change by pricing items at $1.99, $2.99, and $3.99 rather than at $2, $3, and $4.[4]

5. Proper procedures. Most organizations have *procedures manuals,* which specify the flow of documents and provide information and instructions to facilitate adequate recordkeeping.

Routine and automatic checks are major ways of attaining proper procedures. In a phrase, this means doing things "by the numbers." Just as manufacturing activities tend to be made more efficient by the division and specialization of repetitive activities, so can recordkeeping activities be made less costly and more accurate. Repetitive procedures may be prescribed for nonmanufacturing activities such as order taking, order filling, collating, and inspecting. The use of general routines permits specialization of effort, division of duties, and automatic checks on previous steps in the routine.

6. Physical safeguards. Obviously, losses of cash, inventories, and records are minimized by safes, locks, watchmen, and limited access.

7. Bonding, vacations, and rotation of duties. Key people may be subject to excessive temptation; top executives, branch managers, and individuals who handle cash or inventories should have understudies, be forced to take vacations, and be bonded.

A facet of this idea is also illustrated by the common practice of having receivables and payables clerks periodically rotated in duties. Thus a receivables clerk may handle customer accounts from A to C for three months and then be rotated to accounts M to P for three months, and so forth.

Incidentally, the act of bonding, that is, buying insurance against embezzlement, is not a substitute for vacations, rotation of duties, and similar precautions. Insurance companies will pay only when a loss is proven; establishing proof is often difficult and costly in itself.

8. Independent check. All phases of the system should be subjected to periodic review by outsiders (for example, by external auditors) and by internal auditors who do not ordinarily have contact with the operation under review.

---

[4]Historically, such pricing was originally adopted to force clerks to make change as well as for its psychological impact on potential customers.

The idea of independent check extends beyond the work performed by professional auditors. For example, bank statements should be reconciled with book balances. The bank provides an independent record of cash. Furthermore, the monthly bank reconciliations should be conducted by some clerk other than the cash, receivables, or payables clerks. Other examples of independent checks include monthly statements sent to credit customers and physical counts of inventory to check against perpetual records.

One of the main jobs of internal auditors and external auditors is to appraise the effectiveness of internal control; such appraisal affects the extent of the sampling of transactions needed to test the validity of account balances.

9. Cost-benefit analysis. Highly complex systems tend to strangle people in red tape, so that the system impedes rather than promotes efficiency. Besides, there is "a cost of keeping the costs" that sometimes get out of hand. Investments in more costly systems must be judged in the light of expected benefits. Unfortunately, such benefits are difficult to measure. It is much easier to relate new lathes or production methods to cost savings in manufacturing than a new computer to cost savings in the form of facilitating new attacks on problems of inventory control, production scheduling, and research. Yet hardheaded efforts, as are used in making other business decisions, must be made to measure alternative costs of various accounting systems.

The relationship of costs to benefits sometimes leads to using sampling procedures. Although many companies implement more complex procedures to improve internal control, a few have taken a reverse course. They have decided that the increased costs of additional scrutiny are not worth the expected savings from finding mistakes or crooks. For example, an aerospace manufacturer routinely pays the invoice amounts without checking supporting documentation except on a random-sampling basis. An aluminum company sends out a blank check with its purchase orders, and then the supplier fills out the check and deposits it.

No framework for internal control is perfect in the sense that it can prevent some shrewd individual from "beating the system" either by outright embezzlement or by producing inaccurate records. The task is not total prevention of fraud, nor is it implementation of operating perfection; rather, the task is the designing of a cost-effective tool that will help achieve efficient operations and reduce temptation.

Effects of computers on internal control

The use of computers has both positive and negative effects on the possibilities of errors, fraud, and waste. New types of errors arise when data must be manually punched into cards or paper tape. Each step that places data into a different form boosts the probability of error. Common blunders include using the wrong magnetic tape, using an obsolete or erroneous program, processing the same data twice, and skipping a batch of data.

Computer systems also are less flexible than manual systems. In a manual system, humans regularly interpret, adjust, and act upon imperfect documents that would automatically be rejected under the tight discipline of computer programs. The computer correction system is necessarily more complicated and more formal and tends to be concentrated on the first run of the data.

Despite frequent horror stories to the contrary, the computer itself has very high reliability. Data are processed in strict accordance with the program, and both manual and programmed internal checks can enhance that reliability.

Although computers have generally tended to increase the efficiency and effectiveness of information systems, they sometimes have an unwarranted constraining effect on overall systems design. The attitude to avoid is "Oh, we can't do that. It won't fit on our data-processing card!"

The checklist of internal control applies to both computer and manual systems. For example, consider the separation of duties. Programmers should not be allowed to operate the computers physically. A computer consultant commented that he had immense stealing opportunities when he ran computer operations for a large bank: "I alone designed the dividend-payment operation, wrote the program for it, and ran the job on the machine. The operation was so big that it had a mistake tolerance of nearly $100,000. I could have paid at least half that much to myself, in small checks, and the money wouldn't even have been missed." **Nobody should have complete control of recording, even in this day of on-line operations.**

Another example of separation of duties is the necessity to keep the check-writing process out of reach of computer operators. Unless these operators have some way to convert their tampered machine records onto checks, they cannot operate successfully.

The rotation of duties is another characteristic of good internal check. Companies should shift operators and programmers unpredictably from machine to machine and project to project. If a tempted individual cannot cover up a theft by machine, he or she is less likely to begin stealing.

Reliability of personnel is a check that applies to all employees, including computer personnel. It is surprising how often embezzlements are repeated by individuals who move from employer to employer. **It is also surprising how often employers fail to investigate the backgrounds of newly hired personnel.**[5]

Control of inventories in retailing

inventory shrinkage

Retail merchants must contend with a major operating problem that is often called inventory shrinkage, a polite term for shoplifting by customers and embezzling by employees. The National Retail Merchandise Association reported that in 1981, shrinkage amounted to 3.1 percent of all general merchandise sales, up from 2.0 percent in 1965. Some department stores suffered shrinkage losses of 4 to 5 percent of their sales volume; compare this with the typical net-profit margin of 5 to 6 percent.

A management consultant firm has demonstrated how widespread shoplifting has become. The firm concentrated on a midtown New York department store. Five hundred shoppers, picked at random, were followed from the moment they entered the store to the time they departed. Forty-two shoppers, or one out of every twelve, stole something. They took $300 worth of merchandise, an average of $7.15 each. Similar experiments were conducted in Boston (1 of 20 shoplifted), Philadelphia (1 of 10), and again in New York (1 of 12).

The experts on controlling inventory shrinkage generally agree that the best deterrent is an alert employee at the point of sale. But other means are also used. Retail stores have gone so far as to use tiny sensitized tags on merchandise; if not detached or neutralized by a salesclerk, these miniature transmitters trip an alarm as the culprit begins to leave the store. Macy's in New York has continuous surveillance with over fifty television cameras. **Retailers must scrutinize their own personnel, because they account for 30 to 40 percent of inventory shortages.**

[5]See "The Spreading Danger of Computer Crime," *Business Week,* April 20, 1981, pp. 86–92, for additional discussion of internal control and computers.

Some stores have hired actors to pose as shoplifters, who are then subjected to fake, calm arrests. If potential thieves see the arrests, they may be deterred. Such ploys have helped reduce thefts by employees at major retail chains.

The problem of stealing is not confined to profit-seeking entities. According to the student newspaper at Northwestern University, $14,000 worth of silverware, glasses, and china is stolen from the university dining halls annually. That amounts to $4.71 for every regular customer. Signs are posted at the end of each school term requesting the return of "borrowed" goods, but they have had little success. The food service director commented, "Two years ago, we put up really nice signs and set out boxes for returns. Kids saw the boxes and stole them for packing."

The imposing magnitude of retail inventory shrinkage demonstrates how management objectives may differ among industries. For example, consider the grocery business, where the net income percentage on sales hovers around 1 percent. **You can readily see why a prime responsibility of the store manager is to control inventory shrinkage rather than boost gross sales volume. The trade-off is clear: If the operating profit on sales is 2 percent, to offset a $1,000 increase in shrinkage requires a $50,000 boost in gross sales.**

retail method of inventory control

A widely used inventory method, known as the *retail method,* is utilized as a control device as well as for obtaining an inventory valuation for financial statement purposes. The wide variety, low unit value, and high volume of most retail merchandise prevent any economical use of a perpetual inventory system as commonly conceived. The following is a general version of how food stores use the retail method to control grocery inventories at the store level. All merchandise is accounted for at retail prices[6] as follows:

		RETAIL PRICES
	Inventory, January 5 (by surprise count by branch auditors)	$ 15,000
	Purchases (shipments to store from branch warehouse)	101,000
	Additional retail price changes:	
	Markups	2,000
	Markdowns	(5,000)
(1)	Total merchandise to account for	$113,000
	Sales (per cash-register records)	$100,000
	Allowable shrinkage (shoplifting, breakage etc., usually a predetermined percentage of sales)	1,000
(2)	Total deductions	$101,000
(1) – (2)	Inventory, February 11, should be	$ 12,000
	Inventory, February 11, by physical count	11,100
	Inventory shortage	$ 900

[6]Of course, an inventory measured at retail prices can be restated in terms of an average cost for financial statement purposes by applying an average-cost ratio. For example, if the average gross profit is 20 percent of sales price, $11,100 inventory (at retail) would be shown at a cost of .8 × $11,100, or $8,880.

If the inventory shortage is not within predetermined limits, the manager usually bears prime responsibility. There are worrisome behavioral implications here. For utmost accuracy, the retail method requires the prompt application of the directed changes in retail prices that are ordered by the branch managers. For example, to help ensure a good performance regarding his or her control of shrinkage, the store manager may be inclined to delay the entering of markdowns on price tags and may be inclined to overstate the retail prices of merchandise if possible. The branch manager typically relies on other means, such as surprise spot checks, to ensure that markup and markdowns directives are being followed.

SUMMARY

The following general characteristics form a checklist that can be used as a starting point for judging the effectiveness of internal control:

1. **Reliable personnel with clear responsibilities**
2. **Separation of duties**
3. **Proper authorization**
4. **Adequate documents**
5. **Proper procedures**
6. **Physical safeguards**
7. **Bonding, vacations, and rotation of duties**
8. **Independent check**
9. **Cost-benefit analysis**

This checklist is equally applicable to both computer and manual systems.

The blizzard of paper work continues to intensify in most organizations. Too frequently, systems and forms and reports tend to "just grow." Periodic appraisals of systems are needed to see whether they are indeed optimal under new conditions. Occasionally, managers overreact to an overwhelming number of reports and documents by ignoring them entirely. The key question involves the cost and value of information: What are the costs and benefits of alternative systems?

Managers at all levels have a major reponsibility for the success of a given system. If they do not insist on accurate documents, separation of duties, and so on, trouble is inevitable. In 1977 the U.S. Congress passed a law that explicitly places the ultimate responsibility for the adequacy of internal controls of publicly held companies on top management (including the audit committee of the board of directors).

problem for self-study

problem

A news story of April 25, 1979, reported:

> A federal grand jury indicted seven former Cenco Inc. officials, accusing them of an inventory overstatement scheme that led the concern to report about $25 million in false profits from 1970 to 1974. The indictment charged that the overstatement was accomplished by increasing the number of products shown on inventory tabulating cards and making up new cards. The inflation of inventory lessened the reported cost of sales and thereby resulted in a greater reported profit figure.

REQUIRED

Given this description, were any assets stolen? What is the major feature in the chapter checklist of internal control that is aimed at preventing such dishonesty? Indicate how such dishonest acts could be accomplished and how the dishonest officials might have expected to benefit from these acts.

solution

Assets in the form of inventories were probably not stolen. The overstatement of ending inventory also causes overstatement of net income in the current period. Major motives were job security (by means of a display of higher net income) and greed (by means of management bonuses and raises in future salaries). Indeed, the manager who began the scheme was hired in May 1969 on a four-year contract with Cenco, giving him an annual base salary of $40,000 plus a bonus that added 1 percent to his salary for every 1 percent increase in the Cenco Medical Health (CMH) Group's net income. Net profits nearly doubled between 1970 and 1973. The manager reaped total compensation of $76,000 that year.

Two subordinate managers had no incentive bonus plans, but they played along with the inventory scheme to please their boss. A variety of ways were used to overstate inventories. For example, three boxes of gauze pads would become twenty-three. The auditors were fooled with the help of fake invoices and lies. The scheme was uncovered when a subordinate informed the company treasurer. Three executives were given prison terms ranging from one to three years.

The major feature that should prevent such dishonesty is *separation of duties*. Collusion makes dishonest acts harder to accomplish. Nevertheless, as the Cenco case illustrates, separation of duties is not enough to detect fictitious inventories.

Reliable personnel with clear responsibilities is an additional feature on the checklist that is illustrated by this case. Personnel not only must be competent and honest but should be adequately instructed and supervised. The lack of top-management surveillance undoubtedly contributed to this unfortunate situation. Immediate supervisors should know enough about underlying operations so that they can sense any significant unauthorized conduct.

Independent check is another feature that helps. That is why outside auditors conduct their own physical counts.

Appendix 27a: internal control of purchases and inventories

Internal accounting controls entail an enormous amount of detail that is beyond the scope of this book. Systems are designed to integrate controls over cash receipts, inventories, and receivables, on the one hand; and cash disbursements, inventories, and payables, on the other hand. Exhibit 27-3 shows how the latter are generally controlled in a wholesale company.

inventory and payables control

Exhibit 27-3 indicates the following steps in internal accounting control:

1. A multicopy purchase requisition is issued by a perpetual inventory clerk (or a computer) when the records indicate that purchases are necessary:

Copy 1—To purchasing department as a formal request and authorization to purchase.

Copy 2—To accounts payable clerk (or computer data bank), who compiles all records centrally before eventual payment is made.

Copy 3—File copy.

2. A multicopy purchase order is issued by the purchasing manager:

Copy 1—To vendor as a formal offer to purchase.

Copy 2—To an "on order" record for follow-up purposes as necessary.

Copy 3—To accounts payable clerk for central compilation before payment.

Copy 4—To receiving department. Frequently, this is called a "blind" copy because it does not disclose the physical or dollar amounts ordered.

EXHIBIT 27-3

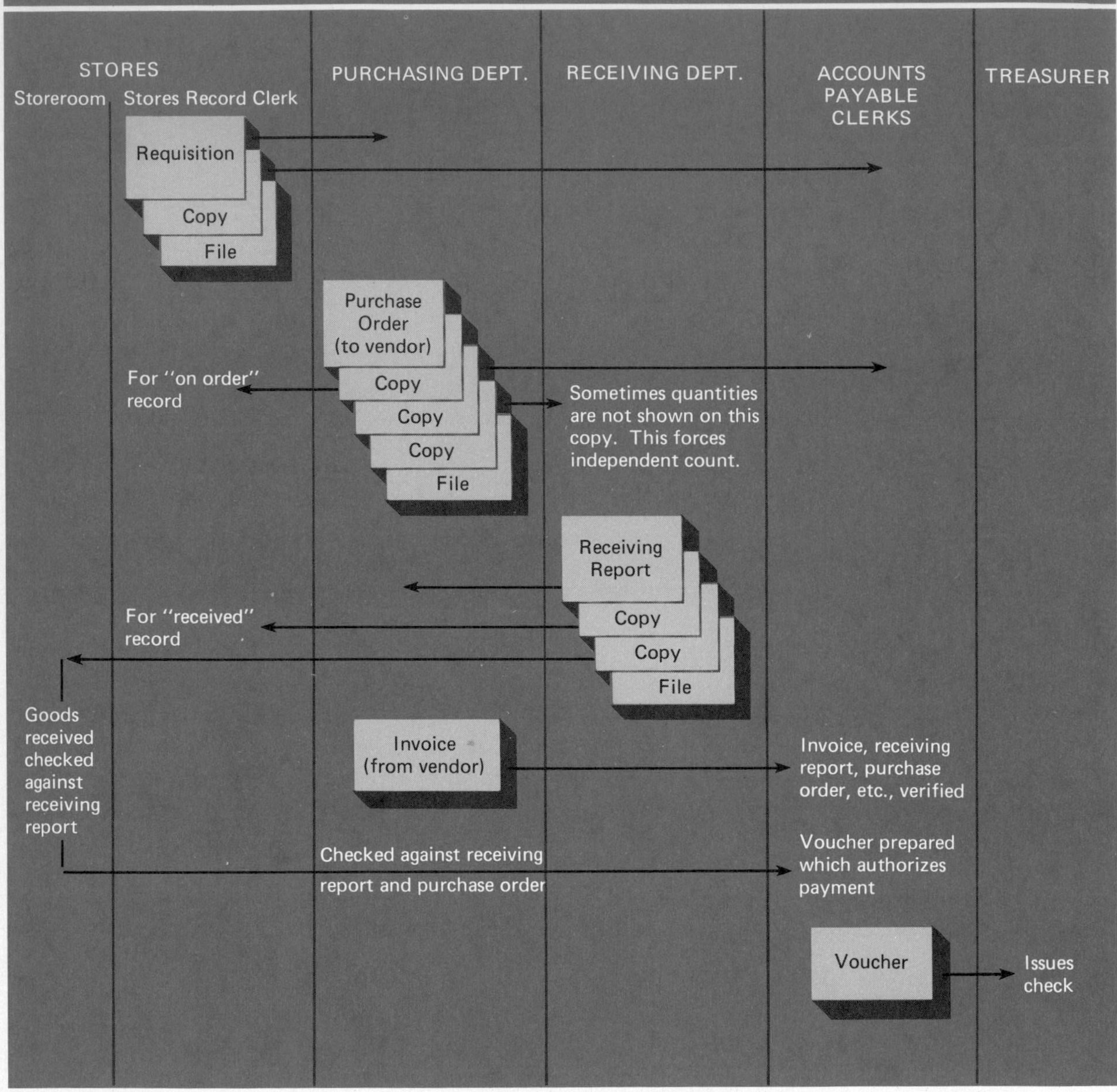

Thus the receiving personnel must count the merchandise as received and enter the amounts independently.

Copy 5—File copy.

3. The blind copy of the purchase order may be in multicopies so that it also serves as a receiving report. Otherwise, an entirely new multicopy receiving report may be prepared:

Copy 1—To inform the purchasing department of the arrival of the merchandise.

Copy 2—To the perpetual inventory clerk for the "received" record.

Copy 3—The warehouse floor or storeroom gets the physical inventory, counts it, and checks it against the receiving report. (Of course, independent counts would be forced again at this stage if desired.) This copy is then forwarded to the accounts payable clerk.

Copy 4—File copy.

4. The accounts payable clerk will get the invoice from the vendor (supplier) after it is initially checked by the purchasing department. The clerk then compares and verifies the validity and accuracy of the requisition, purchase order, and receiving report. The clerk then either stamps an approval for payment on the invoice or prepares a separate *disbursement voucher* (often simply called a *voucher*). A disbursement voucher is a document that formally authorizes the issuance of a check. Frequently, all related documents are attached as supporting evidence of the purchase transaction.

illustration of checklist

The internal controls checklist described earlier in this chapter is illustrated by Exhibit 27-3:

1. **Reliable personnel with clear responsibilities.** If a company is sufficiently large, a separate manager will be placed in exclusive charge of each function indicated in the vertical columns. Duties of purchasing, receiving, and storing may be the responsibility of a single executive (such as a vice-president of purchasing), although day-to-day duties may be delegated to various officers, such as a purchasing agent, a receiving-room supervisor, and an inventory manager.

Competence and honesty are the goals. It is tempting to be penny-wise and pound-foolish when hiring the individuals who perform the duties indicated in Exhibit 27-3. For instance, a crooked or bungling purchase agent can cost an organization dearly. In some companies, the cost of inward transportation is sufficiently large to justify hiring specialists whose sole duties are to find ways of minimizing such costs of "logistics." Space is usually provided for signing or initialing the documents, which can fix responsibilities for various control steps. For instance, the receiving employee must sign the receiving report; the warehouse floor employee must also sign the report when the goods are placed into stock.

2. **Separation of duties.** Note how the receiving department is divorced from the purchasing department. **Purchasing personnel should not have access to physical inventories.** Similarly, the person who finally approves the release of a check should not have access to the accounts payable records. Also, the individual responsible for the inventory recordkeeping should not count the physical inventory.

3. **Proper authorization.** The authorizations for purchasing typically take the form of where to buy, when to buy, how much to buy, and when to pay. Purchasing tends to create conflicts of interest. Most companies prohibit or severely restrict their executives from having relatives or financial interests in the supplier companies.

4. **Adequate documents.** Complete recording is tabulated in two main ways. First, all documents are serially numbered before use. Second, all documents are designed to encourage accurate recording. For example, carbon copies or photocopies avoid the necessity of completely rewriting basic data again and again.

5. **Proper procedures.** This feature is aimed more at promoting specialization, efficiency, and accuracy than at preventing fraud. For example, disbursement-voucher systems are widely used in industry, as Exhibit 27-3 demonstrates. The essential feature of such a system is that no checks may be signed without a disbursement voucher that so authorizes. In turn, the voucher will not be prepared unless all

supporting documents, such as pertinent requisitions, purchase orders, invoices, receiving reports, and freight documents, have been reviewed. Each step in the review serves as a check on previous steps.

Forms are designed so that the absence or incorrectness of key information is automatically uncovered and corrected on the spot. For example, the absence of a receiving clerk's signature on a receiving report would halt preparation of a disbursement voucher, and the omission of a foreman's signature prevents payments of overtime pay.

6. **Physical safeguards.** Warehouses are guarded to various extents, depending on the value of the merchandise. Obviously, precious goods may warrant safes and twenty-four-hour surveillance.

7. **Bonding, vacations, and rotation of duties.** Key managers, such as purchasing agents and the stockroom manager, should be bonded. Moreover, purchasing employees (especially) should be shifted as much as feasible from buying one type of goods (small appliances) to another (hardware). This minimizes the chances of becoming overly friendly with (and less objective about) certain suppliers. It also provides broader training and experience.

8. **Independent check.** Independent checks can occur internally and externally. For instance, Exhibit 27-3 shows how the receiving employee counts items independently to provide a check against the quantities ordered by the purchasing department. Moreover, physical inventories are checked against perpetual records by both internal and external auditors.

9. **Cost-benefit analysis.** Each system must be tailored to the specific characteristics and size of an organization. For example, hand, mechanical, and electronic systems are in use. Exhibit 27-3 shows a routine that is widely followed, but it is not necessarily based on an electronic system. The latter tends to reduce the number of copies of documents and to do many functions in one massive central data file. For instance, the computer would simultaneously update perpetual inventory records, match various documents, and write a check for payment (and produce it for mailing on a predetermined due date).

Purchasing is a high-risk area. Bribery and collusion are sometimes encountered. Auditors sometimes take special precautions. For example, auditors recommend that a responsible independent executive should annually review the volume of business done with suppliers who are not nationally known. **Extra attention should be given to suppliers of services such as rentals of buildings and equipment, advertising, consulting, and public relations.**

Appendix 27b: factory ledgers

In this appendix, we study an example of some specialized techniques for accumulating accounting data. The purpose here is not to dwell on the intricacies of a specific system. Rather, it is to offer an overview of the immense task of effective systems design. Persons without accounting experience often find it difficult to visualize the avalanche of paper work that most companies face. It should be recognized that routine data collection and classification is the most time-consuming task of the controller's department. That is why the expenditure of time, care, and money on planning and shaping an accounting system is nearly always a worthwhile investment.

classification and coding Any sizable company finds it convenient to classify accounts in detail and to number or otherwise code the accounts accordingly. Although an outsider may not know what the code means, accounting employees become so familiar with the code that they think, talk, and write in terms of account numbers instead of account names. Thus, if Cash is account No. 1000 and Accounts Payable is account No. 7000, an external auditor may find payments to creditors journalized as follows:

		MONEY COLUMNS	
#7000		125,000	
	#1000		125,000

A company usually has a chart of accounts that classifies all accounts in the entire company by name and code number. Codes differ from company to company. Each coding system is usually some variation on the following example:

GEOGRAPHIC LOCATION	GENERAL-LEDGER ACCOUNT	DEPARTMENT	SUBSIDIARY CLASSIFICATION
0	00	000	000

This classification may be used by a multiplant company with far-flung operations. It would be too cumbersome for many companies and not detailed enough for giant companies.

Assume that a company has a central plant in Chicago and branch plants in Dallas, Pittsburgh, and San Francisco. Debits for various sample transactions could be coded as shown in Exhibit 27-4.

The numbers used to code debits and credits are obtained from the company chart of accounts. These numbers are originally entered or keypunched on the source documents (requisitions, vouchers, work tickets) that are the basis for ledger entries

EXHIBIT 27-4

Sample Entries Using Account Coding

SAMPLE TRANSACTION	GENERAL-LEDGER ENTRY	NUMBER CODE FOR DEBIT			
		geographic location	**general-ledger account**	**department**	**subsidiary classification**
1. Requisition of supplies by a machining department in Chicago	Factory-overhead control Stores	1	91	011	112
2. Requisition of supplies by a finishing department in Dallas	Factory-overhead control Stores	2	91	015	112
3. Indirect labor incurred by machining department in San Francisco	Factory-overhead control Accrued payroll	4	91	011	202
4. President's salary	Administrative-expenses control Accrued payroll	1	98	060	801

and other analyses. For example, Chicago is coded as 1, Factory Overhead Control as 91, a machining department as 011, and supplies used as 112. The account number for such a transaction would be 1-91-011-112. What would be the complete account number for indirect-labor cost incurred by the finishing department in Chicago? The answer is 1-91-015-202.

branch ledger Many companies have branch plants sprawled all over the country and the world. Cost accumulation and analysis are most often conducted at the various geographic locations, whereas records of receivables, payables, and similar accounts may be centralized in the home office. The division of accounting between central headquarters and a branch plant calls for splitting the accounts between the two locations. At the same time, some set of procedures must be used to ensure the dovetailing of all company accounts so that duplications, omissions, and other errors are minimized. Generally, two *reciprocal accounts* are introduced, one in the home office and one at the factory.

» EXAMPLE

The central offices of the Homeware Company are in Chicago, but the manufacturing operations are located in Richmond, Indiana. The company uses a separate factory ledger that is maintained at Richmond for the benefit of the plant management. The factory is given credit for finished goods at cost when the goods are shipped to the central warehouses. All goods are shipped to customers from the warehouses.

The chart of general-ledger accounts for the company is as follows:

CODE	HOME-OFFICE ACCOUNTS	CODE	FACTORY ACCOUNTS
1	Cash in bank	A	Stores control
2	Accounts-receivable control	B	Work-in-process control
3	Finished-goods control	C	Factory overhead applied
4	Plant and equipment control	D	Factory-overhead control
5	Allowance for depreciation	E	Home-office-ledger control
6	Accounts payable		
7	Accrued payroll		
8	Common stock		
9	Retained earnings		
10	Factory-ledger control		
11	Sales		
12	Cost of goods sold		
13	Selling-cost control		
14	Administrative-cost control		

Below is a summary of some transactions for one month.

PARTIAL LIST OF TRANSACTIONS	
1. Materials purchased on credit	$200,000
2. Direct materials requisitioned	150,000
3. Factory payroll accrued (direct labor, $130,000; other, $70,000)	200,000
4. Miscellaneous factory overhead incurred*	68,000
5. Factory overhead applied	65,000
6. Cost of goods shipped to warehouse	325,000
7. Cost of goods sold	300,000
8. Sales (on credit)	450,000
9. Cash collected on account	340,000

**Credit Accounts Payable except for $5,000 depreciation.*

EXHIBIT 27-5

Sample Journal Entries for Branch Accounting

TRANSACTION	HOME-OFFICE LEDGER			FACTORY LEDGER			ENTRIES THAT WOULD BE MADE IN A REGULAR, UNIFIED LEDGER		
1. Material purchases	Factory-ledger control	200,000		Stores control	200,000		Stores control	200,000	
	Accounts payable		200,000	Home-office-ledger control		200,000	Accounts payable		200,000
2. Requisitions	None			Work-in-process control	150,000		Work-in-process control	150,000	
				Stores control		150,000	Stores control		150,000
3. Factory payroll	Factory-ledger control	200,000		Work-in-process control	130,000		Work-in-process control	130,000	
	Accrued payroll		200,000	Factory-overhead control	70,000		Factory-overhead control	70,000	
				Home-office-ledger control		200,000	Accrued payroll		200,000
4. Miscellaneous overhead	Factory-ledger control	68,000		Factory-overhead control	68,000		Factory-overhead control	68,000	
	Allowance for depreciation		5,000	Home-office-ledger control		68,000	Allowance for depreciation		5,000
	Accounts payable		63,000				Accounts payable		63,000
5. Overhead application	None			Work-in-process control	65,000		Work-in-process control	65,000	
				Factory overhead applied		65,000	Factory overhead applied		65,000
6. Shipments to warehouse	Finished-goods control	325,000		Home-office-ledger control	325,000		Finished-goods control	325,000	
	Factory-ledger control		325,000	Work-in-process control		325,000	Work-in-process control		325,000
7. Cost of goods sold	Cost of goods sold	300,000		None			Cost of goods sold	300,000	
	Finished-goods control		300,000				Finished-goods control		300,000
8. Sales	Accounts-receivable control	450,000		None			Accounts-receivable control	450,000	
	Sales		450,000				Sales		450,000
9. Collections	Cash	340,000		None			Cash	340,000	
	Accounts-receivable control		340,000				Accounts-receivable control		340,000

Postings:

Factory-Ledger Control

	Debit		Credit
(1)	200,000	(6)	325,000
(3)	200,000		
(4)	68,000		
		To bal.	143,000
Bal.	143,000		

Home-Office-Ledger Control

	Debit		Credit
(6)	325,000	(1)	200,000
		(3)	200,000
		(4)	68,000
To bal.	143,000		
		Bal.	143,000

Indicate the accounts debited and credited in the factory ledger and in the home office ledger. Show postings and ending balances in Factory-Ledger Control and Home-Office-Ledger Control. Try to solve this problem yourself before looking at the solution.

» SOLUTION

Remember that this is only an example. The solution is shown in Exhibit 27-5. A general ledger may be split into two or more parts in any manner whatsoever, depending on practical needs. Thus, the ledger in our example could have been designed so that accounts for plant and equipment could be kept at the factory instead of at the home office? If this were done, what journal entry or entries would be changed? Entry 4 would have the Allowance for Depreciation in the factory ledger instead of the home-office ledger. Moreover, the entries to the reciprocal accounts would be for $63,000, not $68,000.

Difficulties in factory-ledger accounting center on lagging or otherwise faulty communications, which result in disagreement in the balances of the reciprocal accounts. Common causes for discrepancies include transfers of inventories and cash that are in transit at the trial-balance cutoff date and failure to recognize nonroutine payments for factory costs by the office on behalf of the branch.

QUESTIONS, PROBLEMS, AND CASES

27-1 Into what four categories can the most repetitive, voluminous transactions in most organizations be divided?

27-2 Distinguish *internal accounting control* from *internal administrative control.*

27-3 "The primary responsibility for internal controls rests with the external auditors." Do you agree? Explain.

27-4 What are the two major ways of ensuring compliance with the Foreign Corrupt Practices Act regarding internal control systems?

27-5 Give three examples of documentation of an internal accounting control system.

27-6 Name five objectives of the Foreign Corrupt Practices Act with respect to internal accounting controls.

27-7 What is the primary responsibility of the audit committee?

27-8 Who should attend meetings of the audit committee?

27-9 What is the essential idea of separation of duties?

27-10 "Business operations would be a hopeless tangle without the paper work that is often regarded with disdain." Explain.

27-11 "There are nine check points that I always use as a framework for judging the effectiveness of an internal control system." Name them.

27-12 "The words *internal control* are commonly misunderstood. They are thought to refer to those facets of the accounting system that are supposed to help prevent embezzling." Do you agree? Why?

27-13 "Internal control systems have both negative and positive objectives." Do you agree? Explain.

27-14 The branch manager of a national retail grocery chain has stated, "My managers are judged more heavily on the basis of their merchandise-shrinkage control than on their overall sales volume." Why? Explain.

27-15 ***Use of credit cards.*** A business-school student used a VISA card for a variety of purchases. When checking his monthly bill, he compared his original copy with a duplicate copy for a gasoline purchase made at a local discount-store shopping center. The original copy showed a purchase of $14.25; the duplicate was raised to $16.25.

REQUIRED

Who obtained the extra $2? How can the system be improved to prevent such thievery?

27-16 ***Appraisal of payroll system.*** (CPA). The Generous Loan Company has one hundred branch loan offices. Each office has a manager and four or five subordinates who are employed by the manager. Branch managers prepare the weekly payroll, including their own salaries, and pay their employees from cash on hand. The employee signs the payroll sheet, signifying receipt of his or her salary. Hours worked by hourly personnel are inserted in the payroll sheet from time cards prepared by the employees and approved by the manager.

The weekly payroll sheets are sent to the home office along with other accounting statements and reports. The home office compiles employee earnings records and prepares all federal and state salary reports from the weekly payroll sheets.

Salaries are established by home-office job-evaluation schedules. Salary adjustments, promotions, and transfers of full-time employees are approved by a home-office salary committee, based upon the recommendations of branch managers and area supervisors. Branch managers advise the salary committee of new full-time employees and of terminations. Part-time and temporary employees are hired without referral to the salary committee.

REQUIRED

Based upon your review of the payroll system, how might payroll funds be embezzled?

27-17 ***Routing of source documents.*** Study Appendix 27a. The purchasing of merchandise usually entails separation of duties. Several copies of various business documents are typically used, including a purchase requisition (three copies), a purchase order (five copies), and a receiving report (four copies).

REQUIRED

1. Indicate the routing of the above documents.
2. Comment on how each of the points in the checklist of internal control applies to the purchasing of merchandise.

27-18 ***Embezzlement and checklist of internal control.*** Cranium Products Company manufactures a variety of sports headgear, which it sells to hundreds of distributors and retailers.

A company "cash clerk" processes all cash received in the mail (mostly checks from customers on account). He opens the mail, sending to the accounting department all accompanying letters and remittance advices that show the amounts received from each customer or other source. The letters and remittance advices are used by the accounting department for appropriate entries in the accounts. The cash clerk sends the currency and checks to another employee, who makes daily bank deposits but has no access to the accounting records. The monthly bank statements are reconciled by the accounting department, which has no access to cash or checks.

The sales manager has the authority for granting credits to customers for sales returns and allowances, and the credit manager has the authority for deciding when uncollectible accounts should be written off. However, a recent audit revealed that the cash clerk had forged the signatures of the sales manager and the credit manager to some forms authorizing sales allowances and bad-debt write-offs for certain accounts. These forms were then sent to the accounting department, which entered them on the books and routinely posted them to customers' accounts.

REQUIRED

1. How could the cash clerk have used these forgeries to cover an embezzlement by him? Assume there was no collusion with other employees. Be specific.
2. See the chapter checklist of internal control. Identify the items that would be relevant to such an embezzlement, and describe briefly any different procedures that should have been followed by Cranium Products.

27-19 ***Audit committee.*** The partial organization chart on p. 928 depicts the place of the audit committee in American Building Maintenance Industries, a large company (revenues of $250 million) whose major business is janitorial service in large office buildings.

REQUIRED

Comment on these relationships. Explain any changes you favor.

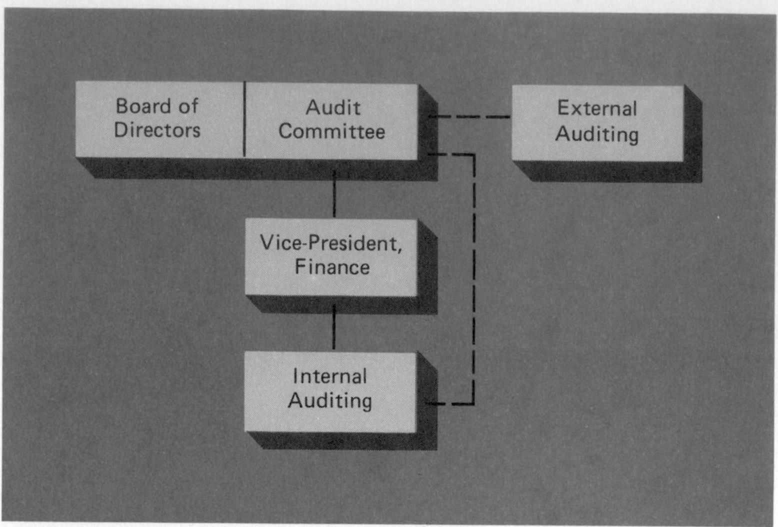

27-20 ***Audit committee role.*** In a recent court decision, an American corporation was required to delegate certain responsibilities to its audit committee, management being required to

1. Consult with its independent auditors before deciding any significant or material accounting question or policy.

2. Retain independent auditors to perform quarterly reviews of all financial statements prior to public issuance.

3. Conduct internal audits, with personnel reporting directly to the audit committee. Internal auditors must report to the audit committee quarterly.

The court also ruled that the audit committee must be composed of at least three outside directors who have no business dealings with the firm other than directors' fees and expense reimbursements. It is authorized to

4. Retain or dismiss independent and internal auditors.

5. Consult with the independent auditors on their quarterly reviews of financial statements.

6. Review all monthly corporate and division financial statements and the auditor's management letter.

7. Receive quarterly reports from independent auditors on internal control deficiencies.

8. Review and approve all reports to shareholders and the SEC before dissemination.

REQUIRED

a. Prepare a partial corporation organization chart to depict these requirements. Use boxes only for Audit Committee, Independent Auditors, Internal Auditing, Finance Vice-President, and Board of Directors. Connect the appropriate boxes with lines: solid lines for direct responsibility, dashed lines for information and communication. Place numbers on these lines to correspond to the eight items specified by the court decision.

b. Identify the main elements of the chapter checklist of internal control that seem most relevant to this system design.

27-21 ***Assignment of duties.*** The Cyclometric Corporation is a distributor of several popular lines of drawing and measuring instruments. It purchases merchandise from several suppliers and sells to hundreds of retail stores. Here is a *partial list* of some of the company's necessary office routines:

1. Daily sorting of incoming mail into items that contain money and items that do not

2. Distributing the above mail: money to cashier, reports of money received to accounting department, and remainder to various appropriate offices

3. Making daily bank deposits

4. Reconciling monthly bank statements

5. Verifying and comparing related purchase documents: purchase orders, purchase invoices, receiving reports, etc.

6. Preparing vouchers for cash disbursements and attaching supporting purchase documents

7. Signing above vouchers to authorize payment (after examining vouchers with attached documents)

8. Preparing checks for above

9. Signing checks (after examining voucher authorization and supporting documents)

10. Mailing checks

The company's chief financial officer has decided that no more than five different people will handle all of these routines, including himself as necessary.

REQUIRED

Prepare a chart to show how these operations should be assigned to the five employees, including the chief financial officer. Use a line for each of the numbered routines and a column for each employee: Financial Officer, A, B, C, D. Place a check mark for each line in one or more of the columns. Observe the rules of the textbook checklist for internal control, especially separation of duties.

27-22 ***Retail method and internal control.*** The following figures pertain to the Zenith Gift Store for the two-month period November and December, 19_8:

Sales	$170,000	Purchases (at sales price)	$ 80,000
Additional markups	10,000	Inventory at November 1, 19_8:	
Markdowns	25,000	At cost price	105,000
Purchases (at cost price)	52,000	At selling price	160,000

REQUIRED

1. What should the inventory amount to at December 31, 19_8, at retail price using the conventional retail inventory method?
2. Suppose the allowable shrinkage is 2 percent of sales. The physical inventory at retail prices at December 31 amounts to $50,000. What is the inventory shortage?

27-23 ***Retail method and internal control.*** (W. Crum) The following data are for a ladies' clothing department in a large department store at retail selling prices:

Net sales	$1,900,000	Transfers in from other branches	$30,000
Discounts granted to employees, churches, etc.	23,500	Transfers out to other branches	12,000
Beginning inventory	900,000	Additional markups	14,000
Net purchases	2,068,000	Markdowns	79,000

REQUIRED

1. What should be the ending inventory at retail prices using the conventional retail inventory method and assuming no allowances for losses (shrinkage)?
2. Suppose the estimated shrinkage is 1 percent of sales. What should be the ending inventory at retail prices? Suppose the cost ratio is 62 percent—that is, the *cost* of the ending inventory is approximated at 62 percent of retail price. What should be the ending inventory at cost? Again, assume 1 percent shrinkage.
3. The actual ending physical inventory at retail is $950,000. What is the total loss at retail? At cost? Prepare a section of the income statement through gross profit on sales. Assume that beginning inventory at cost was $580,000 and that applicable net purchases (including transfer effects) at cost were $1,280,000.

27-24 ***Control of retail clothing inventories.*** Contemporary Clothes, Inc., operates a chain of men's clothing stores. The following data pertain to merchandising operations for the first quarter of a certain year for one of the stores:

Beginning inventory:		Purchases:	
At cost prices	$ 80,000	At cost prices	$ 90,000
At retail prices	130,000	At retail prices	140,000
Sales	200,000	Markdowns	30,000
Additional markups	10,000		

An investigation revealed the theft during this period of a number of suits costing \$2,900 and bearing retail price tags totaling \$5,000. A salesman had attempted to cover his theft by making false markdown entries in the supplementary records he maintained as part of his assigned duties.

REQUIRED

1. Compute the ending inventory at retail price:
   a. Assuming you were unaware of the theft and its cover-up
   b. Assuming the theft had not taken place
2. Assume that the actual physical inventory at retail was \$48,300. Compute the inventory shrinkage due to causes other than this particular theft.
3. Explain briefly how the false markdown entries would mask the theft.
4. See the chapter checklist of internal control. Identify the items that would be relevant to such a theft, and describe briefly any different procedures that should have been followed by Contemporary Clothes.

27-25 ***Reconciliation of inventory records.*** As part of a test of inventory control you examined the perpetual-inventory records of stockroom M. A full set of records (subsidiary and control) is maintained in the factory, while a controlling account is also kept in the accounting department.

You are required to set up a summarizing schedule in money amounts that simultaneously reflects the flow of materials (starting with initial inventory and ending with final inventory) and reconciles the accounting-department records with those of the factory in regard to opening inventory, receipts, withdrawals of materials, and ending inventory.

The items to be considered in preparing this schedule are as follows:

1. An initial inventory, according to factory records, of \$11,000 in stockroom M. Receipts were \$14,000 and withdrawals were \$13,000, according to the records of the accounting department.

2. Receipts of materials in stockroom M, entered properly on factory records but treated by the accounting department as stockroom N, \$240.

3. Correction made by the accounting department of an error in a prior period. The error was the recording of an \$800 withdrawal of materials as \$500. The original item had been correctly entered by the factory record clerk.

4. A shortage of item M-143, amounting to \$45, which was noted and entered during the period on the factory records but information on which had not been transmitted to the accounting department.

27-26 ***Multiple choice; discovering irregularities.*** In questions 1 through 7, you are given a well-recognized procedure of internal control. You are to identify the irregularity *that will be discovered or prevented by each procedure.* Write the numbers 1 through 7 on your answer sheet. Then place the letter of your chosen answer next to your numbers.

1. The general-ledger-control account and the subsidiary ledger of accounts receivable are reconciled monthly. The two bookkeepers are independent.

a. The accounts-receivable subsidiary-ledger bookkeeper charges a customer with \$72 instead of \$74, the correct amount. The error is due to misreading the sales slip. The credit-sales summary for the day has the correct amount of \$74.

b. The accounts-receivable subsidiary-ledger bookkeeper charges a sale to Mr. Smith instead of Mr. Smithe (that is, the wrong customer). The error is due to misreading the sales slip.

c. The employee opening mail abstracts funds without making a record of their receipt. Customer accounts are not credited with their payments.

d. The general-ledger bookkeeper takes funds and covers the loss by charging "Miscellaneous General Expenses."

e. When friends purchase merchandise, the salesclerk allows them an employee discount by using an employee name on the sales slip and deducting the discount on the slip. This is against company policy.

2. The voucher system requires that invoices be compared with receiving reports and express bills before a voucher is prepared and approved for payment.

a. Unrecorded checks appear in the bank statement.

b. The treasurer takes funds by preparing a fictitious voucher charging "Miscellaneous General Expenses."

c. An employee in the purchasing department sends through fictitious invoices and receives payment.

d. A cash shortage is covered by underfooting outstanding checks on the bank reconciliation.

e. A cash shortage is covered by omitting some of the outstanding checks from the bank reconciliation.

3. Both cash and credit customers are educated to expect a sales ticket. Tickets are serially numbered. All numbers are accounted for daily.

a. Customers complain that their monthly bills contain items that have been paid.

b. Some customers have the correct change for the merchandise purchased. They pay and do not wait for a sales ticket.

c. Customers complain that they are billed for goods they did not purchase.

d. Customers complain that goods ordered are not received.

e. Salesclerks destroy duplicate sales tickets for the amount of cash stolen.

4. The storekeeper should sign a receipt for goods received from the receiving and inspection room, and no payment should be made without his signature.

a. Invoices are paid twice.

b. Employees send through fictitious invoices and receive payment.

c. Materials are withdrawn from the storeroom for personal use rather than for business purposes.

d. Employees send through purchase requisitions for materials for personal use. After the materials are received and receiving reports are issued, employees take the merchandise for personal use.

e. The storekeeper takes materials and charges them to company use.

5. At a movie theater box office, all tickets are prenumbered. At the end of each day, the beginning ticket number is subtracted from the ending number to give the number of tickets sold. Cash is counted and compared with the number of tickets sold.

a. The box office gives too much change.

b. The ticket taker admits his friends without a ticket.

c. The manager gives theater passes for personal expenses. This is against company policy.

d. A test check of customers entering the theatre does not reconcile with ticket sales.

e. Tickets from a previous day are discovered in the ticket taker's stub box despite the fact that tickets are stamped "Good on Date of Purchase Only."

6. In Hutchinson Commons Cafeteria, the customers enter at an *IN* door and choose their meals. Before leaving the serving rail, they are billed by a biller for the food taken. After they eat, they present their bills and make payments to a cashier. At the end of the day, cash receipts are reconciled with billings.

a. A friend of the biller and the cashier moves through the lines and takes a free meal without being billed or paying.

b. A customer who has been billed goes out the *IN* entrance without paying.

c. Meat is stolen by an employee.

d. The biller makes an error by billing an order at $1.15 instead of the correct amount, $1.35.

e. A customer sneaks under the serving rail, takes an extra cup of coffee, sneaks back under the rail, and returns to his table.

7. The duties of cashier and accounts-receivable bookkeeper should be separated.

a. There are two cashiers. At the end of a certain day, there is a sizable cash shortage. Each cashier blames the other. It is impossible to fix responsibility.

b. A cash shortage is covered by overfooting (overadding) cash in transit on the bank reconciliation.

c. A cash shortage is covered by charging it to "Miscellaneous General Expenses."

d. Customers who paid their accounts in cash complain that they still receive statements of balances due.

e. The accounts-receivable bookkeeper charges off the accounts of friends to "Allowance for Bad Debts."

27-27 ***Factory-ledger fundamentals.*** Refer to Exhibit 27-4. State the debit number code for (a) requisition of supplies by a finishing department in San Francisco; (b) indirect labor incurred by a machining department in Dallas.

27-28 ***Factory-ledger fundamentals.*** Refer to the chart of general-ledger accounts used in the factory-ledger illustration in Appendix 27b. Indicate the proper journal entries for the following transactions. Set up your solution in a form similar to the one illustrated in Exhibit 27-5.

1. Payments made to creditors on open account	$ 50,000
2. Cash sales	3,000
3. Depreciation on factory equipment	15,000
4. Declaration of dividend	24,000
5. Payment of payroll	105,000
6. Return of materials to vendors	2,000
7. Direct materials requisitioned	40,000
8. Factory overhead applied	30,000
9. Cost of goods shipped to warehouse	50,000
10. Cost of goods sold	25,000

27-29 ***Factory ledger.*** (SMA) Study Appendix 27b. The DEF Company uses both a factory ledger, which includes all transactions up to Cost of Sales, and a general ledger. It records its cost under a job-cost plan.

The following transactions took place during the month of March:

1. Materials purchased and delivered directly to production order No. 305–$200.
2. Depreciation on factory buildings and equipment–$5,000.
3. Finished goods returned for credit–$2,000.
4. Cost of finished goods returned–$1,200.
5. The raw-material book inventory at the end of the month amounted to $354,348. A physical inventory taken at that time showed a value of $354,148.

REQUIRED

Prepare the journal entries necessary to record this information in the general and factory ledgers.

27-30 ***Factory ledger; journal entries.*** Study Appendix 27b. The home offices of the Splitpea Company are in Chicago, but the manufacturing operations are located in Gary. The company uses a separate factory ledger, which is maintained at Gary for the benefit of the plant management. The factory is given credit for finished goods when the goods are shipped to the central warehouses. All goods are shipped to customers from the warehouses.

Some transactions for the month of March 19_6 are summarized below:

1. Miscellaneous manufacturing expenses incurred–$10,000. The invoices for $10,000 were received.
2. Materials received by the factory (proper invoice received)–$75,000.
3. Sales to customers billed during March–$90,000.
4. Factory cost of goods sold–$70,000.
5. Direct materials placed into production–$50,000.

Questions 6–8 refer to certain discrepancies that were found upon auditing the reconciliation accounts. You are to select the entry (or entries) that *would correct* the general-ledger accounts involved.

6. Salesmen's salaries of $2,000 were incorrectly charged to Manufacturing-Expense Control.

7. Machinery of $1,200 purchased by the home office for the branch was taken up in the branch books as a Stores item.

8. The machinery in 7 had been ignored in computing depreciation for one month (rate, 1 percent per month).

CODE	HOME-OFFICE ACCOUNTS	CODE	FACTORY ACCOUNTS
1	Cash in bank	A	Material-stores control
2	Accounts receivable	B	Work-in-process control
3	Finished goods	C	Manufacturing-expense control
4	Accounts payable	D	Manufacturing expense applied
5	Accrued payroll	E	Home-office-ledger control
6	Common stock	F	Direct-labor control
7	Retained earnings		
8	Factory-ledger control		
9	Sales		
10	Factory cost of goods sold		
11	Selling-cost control		
12	Administrative-cost control		
13	Plant and equipment control		
14	Allowance for depreciation		

REQUIRED

For each of the eight transactions, indicate by code the accounts debited and credited in the factory ledger and the home-office ledger. Use the account codes given. More than one account may be debited or credited for each entry.

27-31 ***Internal audit of inventory differences.*** Superfine Supermarkets is the operator of a chain of ninety-five supermarket grocery stores. The individual stores are the familiar supermarket type, located in community shopping centers in the outskirts of a number of large cities in the Middle West. The company makes careful studies of potential locations before establishing a unit, and in general will not give consideration to any location in which the potential first-year volume is under $500,000. The result of this policy is that each of the units is a sizable operation, with volume running from $500,000 to $1,200,000 per year.

Control of packaged grocery items follows the customary pattern of retail inventory value. The majority of products handled in the stores are ordered by the store managers from the central warehouse, where accounting control over the stores is maintained. At the time of shipment, the store inventory account is charged with the retail sales value of the shipment. Perishable products, such as dairy items, are delivered directly to stores by suppliers. These direct deliveries are reported to the warehouse on the store report, where they are compared with billing by suppliers. On the basis of this billing, the store inventory account is charged at selling price.

When a price change is made, the store reports inventory of the products affected by the change to the warehouse, and corresponding adjustment is made in the retail inventory control value.

Fruits and vegetables are handled by a separate produce supervisor, who has authority to order according to his own judgment. Highly perishable items may be purchased locally, while semiperishables, such as potatoes and oranges, are ordered from the warehouse. In this department, the maintenance of a strict monetary control based upon units is not feasible, because much of the product is supplied in bulk for repackaging and there is considerable loss because of waste and spoilage. Consequently, inventory control over the produce department is effected by charging the produce department at cost for all shipments from the warehouse or direct purchases.

The meat department is handled on a basis similar to the produce department. The reason for this is that the large meat items, such as a side of beef, are delivered at a single overall price per pound. The butchers in the meat department then cut the meat, with the value of the final cut depending on the desirability of the meat. There is also considerable waste in bones, fat, and similar unsalable items.

To a considerable degree, the profit of the meat and produce departments will depend on the skill of the managers. The expertness of the butchering will be a most important factor in the meat department, while skill in purchasing and anticipating requirements will be a governing factor in the profitability of the produce operations. Consequently, supervisory control over produce and meat departments is through a watch of gross margin realized from sales.

So far we have been concerned with the charges to inventory controls. To summarize, packaged groceries are charged at retail, while produce and meat are charged at cost. For purposes of this problem, we will assume that all credits will come through sales (disregarding minor adjusting items such as breakage and returnable containers). Sales credits are developed when customers pass by the checking counters. The cashier-checkers, in operating their cash registers, develop separate totals for the three departments. Thus, total sales are developed separately for packaged groceries, produce, and meat. Register totals are taken each day by the store manager and recorded on the daily report to the warehouse accounting office. Entry of these sales in the accounting records has the following results:

1. In the case of packaged groceries, total reported sales should offset original charges at retail selling price.

2. In the case of produce and meats, sales in comparison with cost will result in development of separate gross-margin figures for each of these departments.

Under company policy, internal auditors take inventories of stores every three months. Packaged-grocery inventories are taken at selling prices, so that there should be no difference if all transactions were perfectly handled, and if there had been no losses from theft by customers or for other reasons. Naturally, perfect operation does not exist, and it is usual to develop a shortage, which is written off at the time of inventory. In the produce and meat departments, the physical inventory by auditors is used to adjust the book value, which is arrived at through applying an estimated percentage of markdown to reported sales for each accounting period.

Below are shown final figures developed as the result of three inventories of the Springfield store. In the case of the packaged grocery department, a percentage of loss (shrinkage) in relation to sales for the period is shown; in the case of produce and meat, the percentage of gross margin on sales developed as a result of the inventories is the figure given.

	PACKAGED GROCERIES (SHRINKAGE)	PRODUCE MARGIN	MEAT MARGIN
January	⅔%	20%	23%
April	3% over	10%	32%
July	4% short	15%	24%

One of the control records that is maintained is a comparative record of packaged grocery inventory shrinkage and produce- and meat-department margins at all stores. In checking the January inventory, you find that all the Springfield store figures are comparable with other stores and may therefore be assumed to be correct. A further factor in considering the answer to the questions is the quantity of the average inventory. In packaged groceries, it is three weeks' sales; in produce, two days; and in meat, one week.

REQUIRED

1. In the April inventory, which items merit immediate attention and follow-up? What are the possible explanations for the apparent abnormalities?
2. In the July inventory, which items appear to be out of line? What would be possible explanations?

27-32 ***Analysis of production and shipping control.*** The Cucaracha Coffee Company is a large producer of coffee for the retail market. Each day, 300,000 pounds of green coffee are roasted; this results in finished-goods production of somewhat more than 250,000 pounds, as there is a loss in roasting of from 14 to 15 percent of the original weight of the green coffee. This loss is known as "shrinkage." About one-half the production is in the most expensive coffee, Cuca Special, which is packed in vacuum cans. The remainder is in a cheaper blend that is packed in paper bags.

From the roasting plant, shipment is made by truck to fifty distributing branches, from which sale and delivery are made to 100,000 retail grocery stores.

PART I From an anonymous source, a report comes to the company that the most expensive grade of coffee—the vacuum pack—is being stolen from the roasting plant and sold to retail stores.

Original investigation of this report is assigned to the sales branch in the territory from which the report comes. They find that the company's Cuca brand is being offered for sale in several small stores in poorer neighborhoods at a price that is considerably lower than the usual retail price and that is even somewhat lower than the company's selling price to its smaller outlets. The branch has no record of sales to these stores, so it seems quite possible that the report of stealing is true.

As internal auditor, you are then assigned to checking the entire control plan for finished products at the roasting plant, to the end of finding out where the possibility of leakage exists and who may be responsible. As has been previously mentioned, the production is over 250,000 pounds per day, packed in shipping cases of 24 pounds; this means that over ten thousand cases clear through the production and shipping cycle each day.

You begin by observing the whole production operation, which starts with the dumping of green coffee from the bags in which it is received into mixers. Various grades and types are combined according to formulas prescribed by the coffee blenders, with a total of twenty bags being combined and mixed in a single batch. After mixing, the coffee is stored in hoppers from which it is fed to the roasters. The roasting is done in batches of about 600 pounds; after roasting, the coffee is cooled and conveyed to grinders, and then the ground coffee is fed into hoppers that feed the scales on the automatic packing lines.

The vacuum-can packing lines on which Cuca Special is produced are highly automatic and operate at a speed of about 150 cans per minute for each line. The employees on the line are principally concerned with watching for cans that may not be completely filled, damaged or defective cans, or anything else that may be wrong in the finished product or that may interrupt the operation of the line. At the end of the lines, cans are accumulated in lots of 24, which are put into corrugated cases that run through a machine that seals the cases on top and bottom. The finished cases are then stacked upon platform skids in lots of sixty cases to each skid.

The packing lines for the cheaper grade of coffee, which is packed in bags, are less automatic, because the paper bags cannot be handled in the packing equipment. On these lines, the empty bags are unfolded by hand by a worker who holds them under a scale that is set to "dump" 25 pounds a minute. This speed sets the pace for the line. After filling, the bags move on a conveyor belt past workers who fold over and seal the tops. At the end of the line, bags are packed in cases of 24 pounds each; these cases are sealed in a case sealer and then stacked on skids, also in lots of sixty cases.

To the point that the cases leave the packing line, your observation is that there is no opportunity for abstraction of finished goods. The entire flow is mechanical, down through the filling operation. Once the coffee is in cans, it is under observation by a number of employees until it is packed in cases and the cases are sealed and placed on skids.

Separate packing foremen supervise the vacuum and bag lines. As skids are loaded, the number of skids loaded is tallied before they are moved to the shipping floor. This tally is forwarded to the factory accounting department and serves to establish the original charge to the finished-goods inventory. When skids are moved to the shipping floor, the shipping clerk acknowledges the quantities received, and subsequently accounts for these quantities as shipments to branches or as stock on hand.

Shipping-floor stocks are checked by physical inventory taken by the plant accounting department every few days, and quantities reported shipped (which are the credits to inventory) are reported to the central-office accounting department where they are checked with quantities acknowledged by sales branches. You examine all the reports of production, inventory, and acknowledgement and can find only inconsequential differences for the several months that you check.

Despite the seeming indication that all is in order, you are faced with the fact that the sales-department reports indicate very definitely that coffee is being stolen. You then conclude that the only possibility is collusion within the plant. Again reviewing the established controls, you narrow the field. Your final conclusion is determined to some extent by the fact that the tally sheet of skid loads delivered to the shipping floor is a check sheet, prepared in pencil, that could readily be altered.

What would be your analysis of the situation and of the employees who must be in on any collusion? Pause and formulate your own answer before proceeding to Part II.

Based on your analysis of the employees who may be involved, other plant employees and outside detectives have "broken" the case, with the result that the accounting-department employee who handles the production records has confessed to altering the tally sheets by one skid load (1,440 pounds) each day, and a shipping clerk has confessed to giving this extra skid load to one of the regular truckers, who in turn sold it to outside sources for about one-half the regular selling price.

Your next concern is consideration of further controls to guard against a repetition. You decide that one or two of the following four possibilities would provide greater protective control. (In your recommendation, you are concerned with the cost to the company, with the value to management, and with the capabilities of the employees who must prepare the reports.)

1. To have an additional tally sheet prepared by the operator of the lift truck who moves the filled skids from the packing lines to the shipping floor.

2. To install a cumulative, nonresettable counter on the case-sealing machine and to provide for daily counter readings, which must balance with inventory controls over production.

3. To balance the consumption of vacuum cans with production on a monthly basis, when physical inventory of cans on hand is taken. This would require the keeping of a count of cans spoiled and discarded in packing lines—which has not previously been taken.

4. To check carefully each month and inquire into any unusual variations in "shrinkage" between the weight of green coffee put into process and the weight of roasted coffee produced. As previously mentioned, this figure may vary between 14 and 15 percent normally.

REQUIRED

Two of these plans you discard, and two you recommend. In recommending one of them, a factor in your recommendation is the value that the control figures will have for the plant management.

Tell which plans are discarded and why, and the reasons for recommendation of the remaining two.

27-33 ***Hospital internal control.*** You have been assigned to study various means to help reduce the overall cost of running a hospital.[7] Your first project is in the pharmacy. Upon discussing the issue of drug usage and control, various pharmacists have indicated a suspicion that a significant quantity of drugs is not accounted for. There were three possible sources of loss: (a) breakage, spillage, and wastage; (b) failure to charge patient for drugs actually delivered; and (c) theft.

The chief pharmacist estimates that the revenue value of these losses is about $120,000 per year. The three causes listed earlier probably each account for one-third of this amount. The actual invoice cost of drugs is about one-quarter of the billing price that patients pay. Drugs are ordered in bulk, and large quantities are held in inventory to minimize stockouts. Ordering and handling costs account for another 10 percent of the drug invoice cost. The remaining drug markup covers miscellaneous pharmacy overhead and contribution to hospital overhead.

Under the present system, the source document for billing purposes is the medical record sheet filled out by the nurse each time she administers medication. When the doctor prescribes a specific drug, the request is sent to the pharmacy, where the order is filled and sent up to the floor along with the rest of the drugs for that ward. The medication containers have the patients' names on them and are placed in open bins in the storeroom according to room number. The storeroom is located in the central nursing area, adjacent to the head nurse's office. The storeroom is never locked, since many different nurses and doctors use the room around the clock to prepare medication.

When the pharmacist fills the order, he includes the number of doses that will probably be required during the next three or four days. Unused portions of the order that can be reused (i.e., pills, sealed immunization ampules) are returned to the pharmacy when the patient no longer requires them. The actual number of units in the container is not tallied

[7]Assume that an objective of the hospital is to have total revenue exceed total expenses by 6 percent. Another objective is to minimize hospital cost to the patient in the face of tremendous past price increases.

because it is irrelevant, as billing comes from the medical record sheet. So, if any medication is lost either through accident, neglect, or mischief, no one would really be able to trace the actual amount lost.

Two new systems have been proposed to improve the situation. One involves charging patients for all medication when the orders are filled by the pharmacist and crediting each patient for any usable returns. This "front-end-billing" is commonly used in some other hospitals. With this system, there is no lost revenue; the patient pays for all drugs that theoretically have been allocated to him or her. It is estimated that revenue would increase by $120,000 annually if this system were implemented. A new clerk would be needed to handle credits at a total annual cost of $16,000.

The other system involves installation of three satellite pharmacies in strategic locations in the wards. These would replace the present medication storerooms. Full-time pharmacists would be in charge of these satellites. They would be responsible for all inventory and would place the exact medication needed for each shift in a tray for the nurse. If the pharmacist felt that a particular nurse might be neglectful in recording drug administration, he could compare her medical record sheet with his records. Since the pharmacist would be the only person to have access to the satellite inventory, and since this inventory would be accurately quantified as it left the central pharmacy and had to be completely accounted for, it was felt that losses would be almost entirely eliminated. Rescheduling of personnel and shifting of inventory from the central pharmacy would enable satellite operation at an increased annual cost of $24,000.

REQUIRED

1. What is the actual current loss of net income due to the drug-control problem?
2. Of the systems being considered, which would you recommend? Explain fully.

27-34 ***Manipulation of profits, review of chapters 1, 20, and 27.*** Throughout the 1970s, H. J. Heinz Co. had a publicly stated objective: to seek an increase in earnings at a steady and consistent rate. For example, the Heinz 1978 annual report said: ". . . the annual compound growth rate has been 11.7% for the past 10 years and 14.0% for the past five years, which is consistent with the company's financial objectives for a compound growth rate in earnings per share of 10% to 12% per year."

In 1979, Heinz disclosed that several managers had engaged in "profit-switching" practices since 1972. These practices resulted in the improper transfer of $16.4 million in pretax income to the fiscal 1979 year from prior years. A news story reported that "the intent of the practices was to smooth out earnings increases to create the appearance of consistent, orderly growth."

For your information, "profit-switching" and "improper transfer" refer to keeping records so that profits that appropriately belong in one reporting period are actually reported in a different reporting period.

The report of the Heinz audit committee to the board of directors, May 6, 1980, p. 2, contained the following summary of the effects on consolidated income before tax (000's omitted):

	INCOME TRANSFERRAL PRACTICES					
FY	improper recognition of expenses	improper recognition of sales	other practices	increase (decrease) net income before tax	TOTAL NET INCOME BEFORE TAX AFTER RESTATEMENT	% EFFECTS OF RESTATEMENT
1972	$ (513)	$ —	$ —	$ (513)	$ 75,894	(.7)
1973	$(1,814)	$(1,968)	$ —	$ (3,782)	$ 84,777	(4.5)
1974	$(4,250)	$ (309)	$(1,364)	$ (5,923)	$ 98,173	(6.0)
1975	$ 2,476	$ 1,527	$ (615)	$ 3,388	$113,137	3.0
1976	$ (111)	$(1,815)	$ 877	$ (1,049)	$128,682	(.8)
1977	$(4,139)	$(1,294)	$ 268	$ (5,165)	$160,101	(3.2)
1978	$ 734	$(2,872)	$ 671	$ (1,467)	$170,198	(.9)
1979	$ 8,888	$ 7,085	$ 396	$16,369	$183,178	8.9
1980	$ 76	$ (354)	$ (233)	$ (511)	$ —	—

The report continued: "The accumulated effects of such practices on shareholders' equity and working capital did not exceed 2%."

The audit committee also stated (p. 13): ". . . the effect of these practices was not material to the annual consolidated income. . . . Such practices did, however, have a significant effect on certain quarterly consolidated income statements."

The report said (p. 8):

> During the Investigatory Period, World Headquarters used the conventional tools of business plans, budgets and financial reports to monitor the programs and operations of the various Affiliates.* The financial reports, which were received on a regular basis, compared budget against the results of the current period, as well as the year to date, and furnished an updated estimate of year-end results. If any of the reports showed an unexpected variance, immediate inquiry was made of the Affiliate concerned seeking the reason for such variance. If, however, the reports were as expected, little inquiry was made. About the end of the third fiscal quarter, reviews were conducted by World Headquarters officers with officers of each Affiliate to determine the then current estimates of the fiscal year-end results for each Affiliate. If there was to be any shortfall in the expected results of a particular Affiliate, other Affiliates might be encouraged to show extra profit, which could be accomplished by various means, including the reduction of discretionary expenses. The overall aim was to meet the projected consolidated earnings and goals. Predictability was the watchword, and surprises were to be avoided.
>
> ---
>
> *The Company consists of a World Headquarters and a division which is an operating unit. It also has various subsidiaries which are operating units. The operating units are generally referred to in the Company organization as, and are herein called, "Affiliates."

REQUIRED

1. Given this description, were any assets stolen by management? Identify at least one way to falsely defer profit to a future period. What feature in the chapter checklist of internal control is aimed at preventing the practice you describe?
2. Heinz is a heavily decentralized company. Divisional accounting personnel report directly to the division chief executive. What changes in the control system would you recommend?

Cost Accounting in Professional Examinations 28

This chapter describes the role of cost accounting in United States professional examinations. The suggestions offered are also applicable to professional examinations in other nations. Appendix 28 presents some major alternative approaches in the design of general ledgers and standard costs.

Cost/managerial accounting receives abundant attention in professional examinations. The assignment materials in the previous chapters of this book have included numerous illustrations of the variety and degrees of difficulty that may be encountered. A conscientious reader who has solved a representative sample of the problems at the end of the chapters will be well-prepared for the professional examination questions dealing with cost accounting. The major purposes of this chapter are to provide perspective, instill confidence, and encourage readers to take the examinations.

Types of professional examinations

CPA and CMA designations

Many American readers may eventually take the Certified Public Accountant (CPA) examination or the Certified Management Accountant (CMA) examination. Similar examinations are conducted in other countries. Certification is important to professional accountants for many reasons, such as

1. Recognition of achievement and technical competence by fellow accountants and by users of accounting services
2. Membership in professional bodies having programs of career-long education
3. Enhancement of career opportunities
4. Personal satisfaction

An editorial in *Management Accounting* (January 1973) distinguished between the CPA and the CMA as follows:

> Essentially, the Certificate in Management Accounting is not, and never was, designed to be in "competition" with a CPA certificate. The latter is in effect a license to practice—issued by a state agency: the CMA is intended to be a document which identifies the level of professional attainment of the holder. The two areas—management and public accounting—are compatible; they are not competitive.

A prominent feature of the field of financial accounting is the use of independent (external) auditors to give assurance about the reliability of the financial statements supplied by managers. These auditors are called Certified Public Accountants in the United States and Chartered Accountants in many other English-speaking nations. The major U.S. professional association in the private sector that regulates the quality of external auditors is the American Institute of Certified Public Accountants (AICPA).[1]

The largest association of management accountants in the United States is the National Association of Accountants (NAA). In 1972 the NAA established the Institute of Management Accounting. The Institute administers a program leading to the Certificate in Management Accounting (CMA).[2] The objectives of the program are threefold:

1. To establish management accounting as a recognized profession by identifying the role of the management accountant and the underlying body of knowledge, and by outlining a course of study by which such knowledge can be acquired.
2. To foster higher educational standards in the field of management accounting.
3. To establish an objective measure of an individual's knowledge and competence in the field of management accounting.

---

[1]The AICPA also prepares the Uniform CPA Examination. Information regarding this *examination* may be obtained from the Director of Examinations, AICPA, 1211 Avenue of the Americas, New York, N.Y., 10036. Information regarding *specific requirements* for taking the CPA Examination in a particular state are available from that state's Board of Public Accountancy.

[2]Information regarding the CMA program may be obtained from the Institute, 570 City Center Building, Ann Arbor, Mich., 48104.

The CMA examination has five parts: (1) economics and business finance, (2) organization and behavior, including ethical considerations, (3) public reporting, standards, auditing and taxes, (4) periodic reporting for internal and external purposes, and (5) decision analysis, including modeling and information systems. The CMA designation is gaining increased stature in the business community as a credential parallel to the CPA designation.

taking both examinations

There are good reasons for students to take both the CPA and the CMA examinations. Many more people are employed as management accountants than as public accountants. Many students work in public accounting immediately after graduation but spend most of their careers elsewhere. The material covered in both examinations is comparable in rigor and overlaps considerably. Therefore, candidates should try to prepare for both examinations at about the same time.

Students should take the CMA and CPA examinations as soon as possible after attaining their university degrees in accounting. At that point, if they conduct an appropriate review of their courses, students are likely to be as adequately prepared as they ever will be. The examinations are essentially academic in nature. They are really aimed at determining whether a candidate is a qualified *entrant* into a profession rather than at determining whether a candidate is a full-fledged, highly qualified practitioner.

Review for examinations

Cost/managerial accounting plays a prominent part in both the CPA and the CMA examinations. As Exhibit 28-1 shows, on the average, cost/managerial accounting

EXHIBIT 28-1

Content Comparison of CPA and CMA Examinations

SUBJECT AREAS	CPA†	CMA‡
Cost/managerial accounting including quantitative methods*	9%	40%
Financial reporting	37	14
Auditing		
External	20	4
Internal		4
Taxation		
Individual	4	—
Corporate	4	5
Governmental accounting	6	—
Business law	20	—
Business finance	—	10
Economics	—	11
Management and organization behavior	—	8
Information systems	—	4
	100%	100%

*Essentially material covered in this textbook.

†*Source: AICPA* Content Specification Outlines for the Uniform Certified Public Accountant Examination, 1981.

‡*Source: J. Harris and J. Krogstad, "The MBA—CMA, An Emerging Professional,"* Collegiate News and Views, *Spring 1979, pp. 5–8.*

EXHIBIT 28-2

Competency Levels for Topics Currently Covered in CPA and CMA Examinations, Cost/Management Accounting, Including Quantitative Methods

TOPIC	CPA EXAM	CMA EXAM	CHAPTER REFERENCE IN THIS BOOK
Planning: short-run budgets	2	3	5
Planning: long-run forecasts	2	3	5, 12, 13
Cost accumulation systems—job order and process, absorption and variable	3	3	4–8, 17–18
Cost control— flexible budgets and standard costs	3	3	6–8, 25
Divisional performance and transfer pricing	2	3	19–20
Cost-volume-profit relationships	3	3	3, 8, 21
Tax implications of alternative decisions	2	2	13
Capital budgeting	2	3	12–13
Behavioral science applications in accounting	1	2	5, 10, 19–20
Probability	2	2	21
Regression analysis	2	3	24
Decision models and operations research	2	3	21–24

Levels of competency:

Level 1: Introductory level knowledge, implying an awareness and general understanding of principal topics.

Level 2: Application of knowledge and demonstration of analytical capability in the solution of specific problem situations.

Level 3: An extension of Level 2 capabilities to include interpretation, evaluation, and synthesis of complex situations. Level 3 implies an in-depth understanding of the topic and the ability to communicate conclusions.

Source: *Adapted from the Report of the Committee on Professional Examinations,* Accounting Review, *Supplement to Vol. XLXI, pp. 6–7.*

prominence of cost accounting

represents 9 percent of the content of the CPA examination and 40 percent of the CMA examination. This book includes numerous questions and problems extracted from past CPA and CMA examinations.[3] In addition, a supplement to this book, *Professional Examination Questions and Answers: A Self-Study Approach* (John K. Harris [Englewood Cliffs, N.J.: Prentice Hall, 1982]), contains many more CPA and CMA questions. The organization of the Harris supplement is keyed to the chapters in this textbook.

Exhibit 28-2 classifies the cost accounting on CPA and CMA examinations by topical area, indicating the relative depth of knowledge required. The most popular

[3]These are designated in this book as "(CPA)" and "(CMA)." In addition, the problems designated "(SMA)" in this book are from the set of regular examinations (which are graduated by levels of difficulty) of the Society of Management Accountants of Canada, and the ones designated "(CGAA)" are from the examinations of the Certified General Accountants Association of Canada. Some of the professional examination questions and problems in this book have been adapted to bring out particular points in the chapter for which they were chosen. Note that examinations are also given by the U.S. Institute of Internal Auditors; however, cost accounting is not as important in these examinations.

topics are standard costs, flexible budgets, analyses of variances, cost-volume-profit analysis, variable (direct) costing, relevant costs for special decisions, and discounted cash-flow analysis. Problems on product costing are also covered regularly. They emphasize process costing, including joint costs.

The candidate faces an imposing task of review. In addition to preparing for probable cost accounting topics, he or she must recognize two special characteristics of a professional examination. First, accounting terminology is not uniform. Second, alternative solutions are possible for many accounting problems.

divergent terminology

Variations in terminology will inevitably appear in a professional examination that is drawn from many sources. Likely questions and problems are contributed by individual accounting practitioners, public accountants, accounting teachers, and employees of the relevant professional association. They are stockpiled and used as needed.

Thus, the candidate should be familiar with the variety and interchangeability of many cost terms. For example, *factory overhead* is usually interchangeable with the following terms: *indirect manufacturing costs, manufacturing expenses, factory burden,* and *manufacturing overhead. Cost of goods sold* is often called *cost of sales.*

alternative solutions

Alternative solutions can arise because there are slight variations in practical accounting procedures or techniques. Thus, the candidate must anticipate problem situations that do not exactly coincide with either the text treatments that he or she knows or the cases encountered in practice. The candidate can be confident that the *proper* use of the specific techniques learned will be given full credit. However, in some instances, candidates can strengthen a solution by pointing out important aspects that might receive alternative treatment.

The associations take elaborate steps to ensure equitable grading of examinations. The graders recognize and give full credit to all alternative solutions that are reasonable. Therefore, the candidate should not be discouraged if in the course of the review he or she finds published solutions that do not precisely agree with a favorite approach or the approach learned in a particular cost accounting course. The associations have found it impracticable to publish a large collection of alternative solutions, so they usually confine their "unofficial answers" to one widely accepted approach.

Divergences in practice and terminology creep not only into the examination but also into the "unofficial answers" that are published subsequent to the examination dates. These published answers are neither official nor necessarily the only acceptable solutions. Yet many students and teachers have the mistaken belief that the published solutions are *the* only acceptable answers.

Problems are designed to be straightforward. Requirements should be taken at face value. Special assumptions are rarely necessary. Sometimes a candidate still feels that an assumption must be made. If so, the assumption should be stated, together with the reasons therefor. *Such reasons should include a statement as to why a possible alternative assumption is being rejected.*

In summary, although the candidate does not have to worry about the acceptability of alternative solutions to a given problem, he or she should have an awareness of divergencies in accounting practice and terminology. As a minimum, the candidate's terminology should coincide with that given in the problem. The candidate should also know what areas of cost accounting tend to have alternative treatments. In these areas especially, he or she should take particular pains with the answer so that it will be clear to all graders. These areas are examined further in the appendix to this chapter.

SUMMARY

Cost accounting is an important part of professional examinations. The candidate should be aware of which cost accounting topics are likely to appear on a professional examination. An analysis of the five or six most recent examinations provides the best clues.

Careful study of appropriate topics in this book will fortify the candidate with sufficient background for success in the cost accounting phases of the professional examinations. Chapters 2–9, 11–13, 16–17, and 22 should be particularly helpful for the CPA examination. Chapters 10 and 19–26 should be of additional help for the CMA examination.

SUGGESTED READINGS

GLEIM, I., **CMA Examination Review.** Gainesville, Fla.: Accounting Publications, annually.

———, and P. DELANEY, **CPA Examination Review.** New York: Wiley, annually.

HARRIS, JOHN K., **Professional Examination Questions and Answers: A Self-Study Approach.** Englewood Cliffs, N.J.: Prentice-Hall, 1982. Actual examination materials are aligned with the individual chapters in Horngren, *Cost Accounting,* 5th ed.

HORNGREN, CHARLES T., and J. ARTHUR LEER, **CPA Problems and Approaches to Solutions,** 5th ed. Englewood Cliffs, N.J.: Prentice-Hall, 1979.

MILLER, HERBERT E., and GEORGE MEAD, **eds., CPA Review Manual,** 5th ed. Englewood Cliffs, N.J.: Prentice-Hall, 1979.

NEWTON, G., **Certificate in Management Accounting Review.** New York: Harper & Row, annually.

WILLIAMS, D., and B. NEEDLES, JR., **The CPA Examination: A Complete Review.** Englewood Cliffs, N.J.: Prentice-Hall, annually.

In addition, the *Journal of Accountancy* contains numerous advertisements for CPA review materials.

Appendix 28: alternative general-ledger treatments

The text has generally shown one technique for cost accumulation in the general ledger. Obviously, there are alternative methods, some of which have been briefly described (Chapters 4 and 6). Comparisons of a few alternative techniques are shown in Exhibit 28-3. The first and third columns show the methods used throughout this book; the second and fourth columns show alternative techniques that are preferred by many accountants for reasons of convenience or feasibility. For example, consider the problem of when to isolate a material-efficiency variance. In concept, it should be isolated as quickly as possible for control purposes (see column 3). Yet often the efficiency variance is impossible to calculate until the work is completed. Consequently, in these cases, the method shown in the fourth column is used.

EXHIBIT 28-3

Alternative General-Ledger Designs

	NONSTANDARD COST ACCOUNTING						STANDARD COST ACCOUNTING					
TRANSACTION	**col. 1**			**col. 2**			**col. 3**			**col. 4**		
Direct-material usage	Work in process	xx		Direct material used	xx		Work in process	xx		Work in process	xx	
	Stores		xx	Stores		xx	Efficiency or usage variance	xx		Stores		xx
							Stores		xx			
				Work in process	xx					Finished goods	xx	
				Direct materials used		xx				Efficiency or usage variance	xx	
										Work in process		xx
Payroll accounting	Work in process	xx		Direct labor	xx		Work in process	xx		Direct labor	xx	
	Department overhead	xx		Department overhead	xx		Direct-labor price variance	xx		Department overhead	xx	
	Accrued payroll		xx	Accrued payroll		xx	Direct-labor efficiency variance	xx		Direct-labor price variance	xx	
							Department overhead	xx		Accrued payroll		xx
							Accrued payroll		xx			
				Work in process	xx					Work in process	xx	
				Direct labor		xx				Direct labor		xx
										Finished goods	xx	
										Direct-labor efficiency variance	xx	
										Work in process		xx
Overhead accounting	Department overhead	xx										
	Various accounts		xx	(Similar methods to those shown at the left.)								
	or											
	(a) Depreciation	xx										
	Repairs	xx										
	Supplies used	xx										
	Various accounts		xx									
	(b Department overhead	xx										
	Depreciation		xx									
	Repairs		xx									
	Supplies used		xx									

standard costs Standard costs may be integrated into the general ledger in a number of ways, depending on the preferences of the person who is setting up the standard-cost system. The candidate should be familiar with alternative methods, because the ledger procedure described in a given problem will influence a solution. No computations or entries should be prepared until the given general-ledger procedure (and specific types of variance analysis called for, if any) is fully comprehended. Problems on standard costs usually emphasize general-ledger entries and variance analysis. A key account, Work in Process, could appear in any one of three alternative ways, depending upon the system employed:

(ALTERNATIVE 1) **WORK IN PROCESS**

Debit	Credit
Actual quantities × Actual prices	Standard quantities × Standard prices

(ALTERNATIVE 2) **WORK IN PROCESS**

Debit	Credit
Actual quantities × Standard prices	Standard quantities × Standard prices

(ALTERNATIVE 3) **WORK IN PROCESS**

Debit	Credit
Standard quantities × Standard prices	Standard quantities × Standard prices

computation of overhead variances As explained in Chapter 6, the terminology for variances and the timing of the isolation of material, labor, and overhead variances will be influenced by the specific system employed.

Although the computations of material and labor variances are usually the same regardless of the standard-cost system used, the computations of overhead variances are by no means uniform in practice. The methodology described in Chapter 7 is generally superior to other methods, but published solutions have shown a number of alternative approaches. Moreover, a single overhead application rate, composed of both variable and fixed elements as described in a section of Chapter 7, is often used. These alternative solutions are described below, using the following basic data:

Budget formula for monthly overhead:
$100,000 fixed overhead + ($1.00 × direct-labor hours)
Denominator volume, which is often called normal or standard volume:
400,000 hours
Combined overhead rate for product costing:

$$\frac{\$100{,}000 + (400{,}000 \times \$1.00)}{400{,}000} = \$1.25$$

Month of August:	
Actual direct hours of input	450,000
Standard direct hours allowed for outputs achieved	430,000
Actual overhead, including $103,000 of fixed costs	$570,000
Applied overhead, 430,000 × $1.25	$537,500
Total variance, $570,000 less $537,500	$ 32,500

ALTERNATIVE 1 □ The recommended approach as described in Chapter 7. Budget based on standard hours allowed.

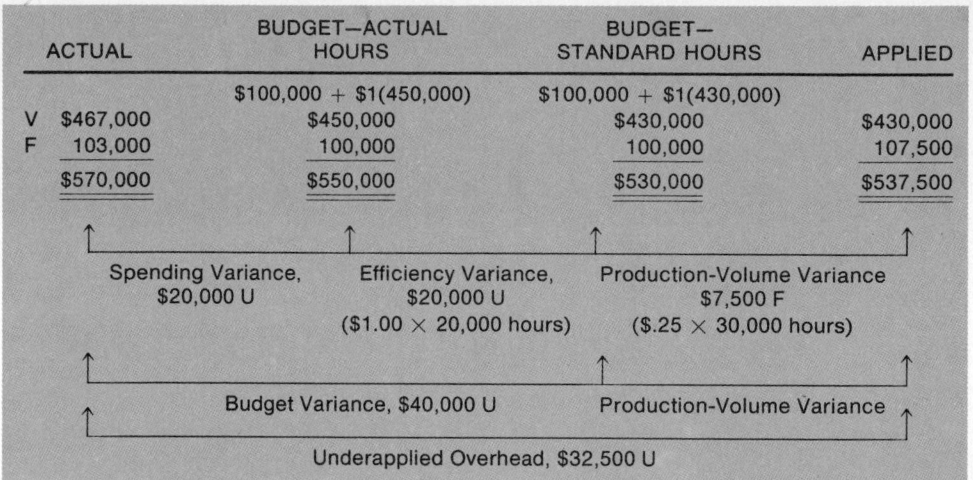

ALTERNATIVE 2 □ The pertinent budget level for measuring the production-volume variance is considered to be actual hours rather than standard hours as in Alternative 1. Also, fixed factory overhead shows an efficiency variance (sometimes called an *effectiveness variance*), measured like other efficiency variances. This supposedly gives a measure of the efficient or inefficient utilization of facilities.

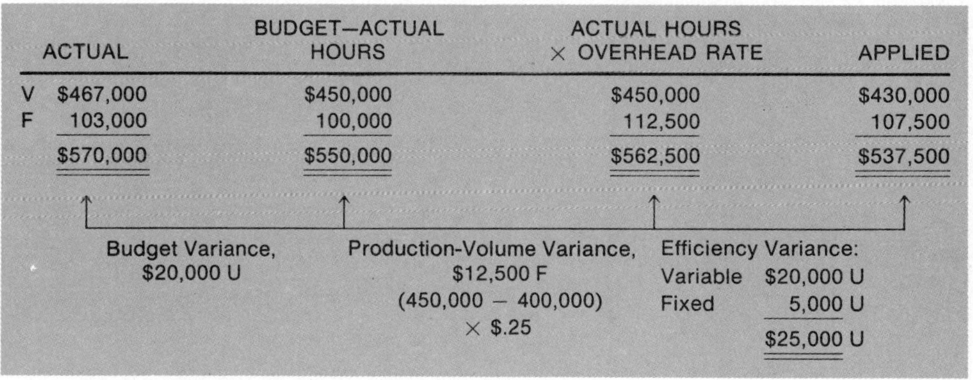

COMPARISON OF ALTERNATIVES 1 AND 2: EFFICIENCY VARIANCE FOR FIXED OVERHEAD? □ Note that the efficiency variance is a subpart of the budget variance under Alternative 1, whereas it could be considered a subpart of the volume variance under Alternative 2. Let us compare these two alternatives more closely.

Alternative 1: Budget variance consists of both spending and efficiency variance.
Alternative 2: Budget variance is the same as the "spending" variance under Alternative 1.

The efficiency variance for variable overhead is the same under both alternatives.

Under Alternative 2, the fixed-overhead analysis differs considerably from that in Alternative 1. Basically, however, all that is done is to take the production-volume variance of $7,500 computed in Alternative 1 and subdivide it further as shown on p. 948.

The efficiency variance for fixed overhead is a misnomer. It should be distinguished sharply from the efficiency variances for materials, labor, and variable

Production-volume variance in Alternative 1		$7,500 F
Breakdown in Alternative 2:		
Fixed-overhead efficiency variance, $.25 × 20,000 hours	$ 5,000 U	
True "volume" variance (actual hours of input minus denominator hours) × rate (50,000 hours × $.25)	12,500 F	$7,500 F

overhead, because efficient usage of these three factors can affect actual cost incurrence, whereas short-run fixed-overhead cost incurrence is not affected by efficiency. Thus, a better label for the fixed-overhead "efficiency" variance would be "effectiveness" variance, a sort of rough-and-ready measure that may have some psychological value as a reminder to the department head that his or her efficiency has an impact on effective utilization of facilities.

This writer sees little merit in this computation except where ineffective utilization of facilities means a loss of sales. For instance, if maximum capacity is 500,000 standard hours, and the sales department can obtain orders in excess of 500,000-hour capacity, the inefficient use of facilities involves an opportunity cost that is properly chargeable to the foreman. The best measure of this cost would often be the lost contribution margins on the orders not filled. In lieu of this measure, the use of the effectiveness variance could be a crude attempt to quantify the foreman's performance. Hence, if an efficiency or effectiveness variance is employed, its weakness should be recognized.

Thus, the production-volume variance in Alternative 1 would be chargeable to someone other than the foreman. It might be traceable to the sales manager, to the head of production control, or to random outside influences. Under Alternative 1, the foreman would not ordinarily be considered explicitly responsible for efficient use of facilities.

QUESTIONS, PROBLEMS, AND CASES

28-1 Why is certification important to professional accountants?

28-2 "It is a good idea for the entry-level accountant to take both the CPA and the CMA examinations." Do you agree? Explain.

28-3 What are the significant differences between the content of the CPA and CMA examinations? Be specific.

28-4 "We should be careful to review the solutions to past professional examinations in accounting so that we learn the official answers." Do you agree? Why?

28-5 ***Two methods of analyzing overhead variances.*** Study Appendix 28. The Signe Company uses a combined-overhead rate of $4 per hour for product costing under a standard-cost system. Denominator activity is 10,000 hours, or 5,000 finished units. At that level the overhead budget is: variable, $30,000; fixed, $10,000.

Actual level of activity: 8,700 hours and 4,400 units produced
Actual overhead incurred: variable, $28,000; fixed, $9,700

REQUIRED | Show two different methods of analyzing overhead variances.

Note: *Additional problems from professional examinations can be found for nearly every chapter in this book, designated as (CPA), (CMA), or (SMA). Also see the supplement to this book by John K. Harris,* Professional Examination Questions and Answers: A Self-Study Approach *(Englewood Cliffs, N.J.: Prentice-Hall, 1982).*

Appendixes

SECTION NINE

The literature in cost accounting and related areas is vast and varied. To pursue particular topics in more depth than is feasible in this book, consult the chapter footnotes and suggested readings. In turn, these readings lead to additional literature.

Individuals have an assortment of reasons for probing beyond this textbook. For example, some readers may concentrate on preparing for professional examinations. In the United States, such individuals may wish to study John K. Harris, *Professional Examination Questions and Answers: A Self-Study Approach.* For a second example, other readers may want to study mathematical models in relation to cost accounting for specific decision making and control. Such individuals will be interested in Robert S. Kaplan, *Advanced Management Accounting.* For a third example, many readers may wish to relate the advances in management sciences, including the behavioral sciences, to the task of designing management accounting systems. These individuals should be helped by a readings book such as that by Alfred Rappaport (editor), *Information for Decision Making,* third edition. These three books were published by Prentice-Hall in 1982.

Readers who are especially interested in the behavioral aspects of management accounting should consult the references at the ends of Chapters 10 and 20. They should also examine the periodical accounting literature since 1980 for the many articles on human information processing. The latter research explores theories and statistical methods from psychology to discover how individuals use information in reaching decisions. Also see Robert Libby, *Accounting and Human Information Processing: Theory and Applications* (Englewood Cliffs, N.J.: Prentice-Hall, 1981).

Agency theory is a very popular topic among academicians who do research in management accounting. The agency literature discusses formal models of relationships between a principal (e.g., a superior) and an agent (e.g., a subordinate) in a world of uncertainty. The emphasis is on choosing performance measures and incentive contracts. For a brief summary, see Appendix 20B in this book. Also see Kaplan, *Advanced Management Accounting,* and L. P. Jennergen, "On the Design of Incentives in Business Firms—A Survey of Some Research," *Management Science,* XXVI (February 1980), 180–201.

The National Association of Accountants, 919 Third Avenue, New York, N.Y., 10022, and the Financial Executives Institute, 633 Third Avenue, New York, N.Y., 10017, have long lists of publications that tend to emphasize management accounting.

The following books on planning and control should also be helpful:

ANTHONY, R. N., and JOHN DEARDEN, **Management Control Systems,** 4th ed. Homewood, Ill.: Richard D. Irwin, 1980.

BARRETT, M., and W. BRUNS, **Case Problems in Management Accounting.** Homewood, Ill.: Richard D. Irwin, 1981.

BEYER, ROBERT, and DONALD TRAWICKI, **Profitability Accounting for Planning and Control,** 2nd ed. New York: Ronald Press, 1972.

DEMSKI, J., **Information Analysis.** Reading, Mass.: Addison-Wesley, 1980. This book is more rigorous than the others in this list.

DERMER, J., **Management Planning and Control Systems.** Homewood, Ill.: Richard D. Irwin, 1977.

LORANGE, P., **Corporate Planning: An Executive Viewpoint.** Englewood Cliffs, N.J.: Prentice-Hall, 1980.

LORANGE, P., and R. VANCIL, **Strategic Planning Systems.** Englewood Cliffs, N.J.: Prentice-Hall, 1977.

ROTCH, W., and B. ALLEN, **Cases in Management Accounting and Control Systems.** Richmond, Va.: Robert F. Dame, 1982.

SHANK, J., **Contemporary Managerial Accounting: A Casebook.** Englewood Cliffs, N.J.: Prentice-Hall, 1981.

SOLOMONS, DAVID, **Divisional Performance: Measurement and Control.** Homewood, Ill.: Richard D. Irwin, 1968. This book has an extensive bibliography. It is especially strong on transfer pricing.

STAUBUS, G., **Activity Costing and Input-Output Accounting.** Homewood, Ill.: Richard D. Irwin, 1971.

VANCIL, RICHARD, **Decentralization: Managerial Ambiguity by Design.** New York: Financial Executives Research Foundation, 1979.

WILLSON, J., and J. CAMPBELL, **Controllership: The Work of the Managerial Accountant,** 3rd ed., New York: John Wiley, 1981.

For a book-length study of management accounting in not-for-profit organizations, see

ANTHONY, R. N., and R. HERZLINGER, **Management Control in Nonprofit Organizations,** rev. ed. Homewood, Ill.: Richard D. Irwin, 1980.

Several books of readings and handbooks are published each year. The following is a list of those published in 1977 and later:

ANTON, HECTOR R., PETER A. FIRMIN, and HUGH D. GROVE, **eds., Contemporary Issues in Cost and Managerial Accounting,** 3rd ed. Boston: Houghton Mifflin, 1978.

BENSTON, GEORGE J., **Contemporary Cost Accounting and Control,** 2nd ed. Encino, Calif.: Dickenson, 1977.

BLACK, H., and J. EDWARDS, **eds., Managerial and Cost Accountant's Handbook.** Homewood, Ill.: Dow Jones-Irwin, 1979.

DAVIDSON, S., and R. L. WEIL, **eds., Handbook of Cost Accounting.** New York: McGraw-Hill, 1978.

DECOSTER, D., K. RAMANTHAN, and G. SUNDEM, **eds., Accounting for Managerial Decision Making,** 2nd ed. Los Angeles: Melville, 1978.

GELLER, L., and J. SHIM, **eds., Readings in Cost and Managerial Accounting.** Dubuque, Iowa: Kendall/Hunt, 1980.

GOODMAN, S., and J. REECE, **eds., Controllers' Handbook.** Homewood, Ill.: Dow Jones-Irwin, 1978.

HOLZER, H. P., **ed., Management Accounting 1980: Proceedings of the University of Illinois Management Accounting Symposium.** Urbana: University of Illinois, 1980.

SCHIFF, J., **ed., Readings in Managerial Accounting.** Princeton, N.J.: Dow Jones/Arno Press, 1980.

THOMAS, W., **ed., Readings in Cost Accounting, Budgeting and Control.** 5th ed. Cincinnati: South-Western Publishing, 1978.

Appendix B: Notes on Compound Interest and Interest Tables

Interest

Interest is the cost of using money. It is the rental charge for funds, just as rental charges are made for the use of buildings and equipment. Whenever a time span is involved, it is necessary to recognize interest as a cost of using invested funds. This requirement applies even if the funds in use represent ownership capital and if the interest does not entail an outlay of cash. The reason why interest must be considered is that the selection of one alternative automatically commits a given amount of invested funds that could otherwise be invested in some other opportunity. The measure of the interest in such cases is the return forgone by rejecting the alternative use.

Interest is rarely unimportant, even when short-term projects are under consideration, and it looms large when long-run plans are being considered. For this reason, the rate of interest is of telling import. The rate used will often influence the ultimate decision. For example, \$100,000 invested now and compounded annually for ten years at 8 percent will accumulate to \$215,900; at 20 percent, to \$619,200.

Interest tables

Four basic tables are used for computations involving interest. Tables 2 and 4 are the most pertinent for our purposes.

table 1— future amount of $1

Table 1 shows how much $1 invested now will accumulate in a given number of periods at a given compounded interest rate per period. The future proceeds (often simply called *amount*) of an investment of $1,000 for three years at 8 percent compound interest could be sketched as follows:

Accumulate →

$\$1{,}000 \times (1.08)^3$ or $\$1{,}000 \times 1.2597$* (from Table 1) $= \$1{,}259.70$

END OF YEAR 0 3

Present Value ← Future Amount

Discount

To minimize discrepancies from rounding, the four-place factor (1.2597) is used here instead of the three-place factor (1.260) shown in Table 1.

Tabular Calculation

YEAR	INTEREST PER YEAR	CUMULATIVE INTEREST, CALLED COMPOUND INTEREST	TOTAL AT END OF PERIOD
0	$ —	$ —	$1,000.00
1	80.00	80.00	1,080.00
2	86.40	166.40	1,166.40
3	93.30	259.70	1,259.70

Note that what is really being done in the tabular presentation is a series of computations that could appear as follows:

$$S_1 = \$1{,}000(1.08)$$
$$S_2 = \$1{,}000(1.08)^2$$
$$S_3 = \$1{,}000(1.08)^3$$

The formula for the "amount of 1," often called the "future value of $1" or "future amount of $1," can be written:

$$S = P(1 + r)^n$$
$$S = 1{,}000(1 + .08)^3 = \$1{,}259.70$$

S is the *amount*, the future value; P is the present value, $1,000 in this case; r is the rate of interest; n is the number of periods.

Fortunately, tables make key computations readily available, so that a facility in selecting the ***proper*** table will minimize computations. Check the accuracy of the answer above against Table 1, page 959.

table 2— present value of $1

In the previous example, if $1,000 compounded at 8 percent per annum will accumulate to $1,259.70 in three years, then $1,000 must be the present value of $1,259.70 due at the end of three years. The formula for the present value can be derived by reversing the process of *accumulation* (finding the future amount) that we just finished. Look at the earlier sketch to see the relationship between accumulating and discounting.

If

$$S = P(1 + r)^n$$

then

$$P = \frac{S}{(1 + r)^n}$$

$$P = \frac{\$1{,}259.70}{(1.08)^3} = \$1{,}000$$

Use Table 2, page 960, to check this calculation.

When accumulating, we advance or roll forward in time. The difference between our original amount and our accumulated amount is called *compound interest.* When discounting, we retreat or roll back in time. The difference between the future amount and the present value is called *compound interest* or *compound discount.* Note the following formulas (where $P = \$1{,}000$):

$$\textbf{Compound interest} = P[(1 + r)^n - 1] = \$259.70$$

$$\textbf{Compound discount} = S\left[1 - \frac{1}{(1 + r)^n}\right] = \$259.70$$

table 3—amount of annuity of $1

An (ordinary) *annuity* is a series of equal payments (receipts) to be paid (or received) at the *end* of successive periods of equal length. Assume that $1,000 is invested at the end of each of three years at 8 percent:

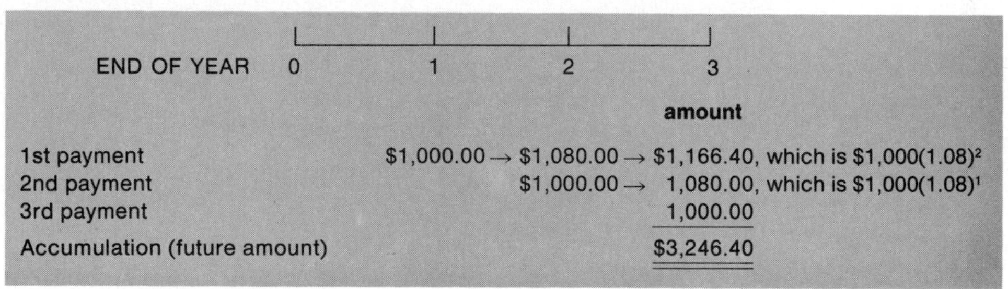

END OF YEAR	0	1	2	3
				amount
1st payment		\$1,000.00 →	\$1,080.00 →	\$1,166.40, which is \$1,000(1.08)²
2nd payment			\$1,000.00 →	1,080.00, which is \$1,000(1.08)¹
3rd payment				1,000.00
Accumulation (future amount)				\$3,246.40

The arithmetic shown above may be expressed algebraically as the amount of an ordinary annuity of \$1,000 for three years $= \$1{,}000(1 + r)^2 + \$1{,}000\ (1 + r)^1 + \$1{,}000$.

We can develop the general formula for S_n, the amount of an ordinary annuity of $1, by using the example above as a basis:

1. $S_n = 1 + (1 + r)^1 + (1 + r)^2$

2. Substitute: $S_n = 1 + (1.08) + (1.08)^2$

3. Multiply (2) by $(1 + r)$: $(1.08)S_n = 1.08 + (1.08)^2 + (1.08)^3$

4. Subtract (2) from (3): Note that all terms on right-hand side are removed except $(1.08)^3$ in equation (3) and 1 in equation (2). $1.08S_n - S_n = (1.08)^3 - 1$

5. Factor (4): $S_n(1.08 - 1) = (1.08)^3 - 1$

6. Divide (5) by (1.08 − 1): $S_n = \frac{(1.08)^3 - 1}{1.08 - 1} = \frac{(1.08)^3 - 1}{.08}$

7. The general formula for the amount of an ordinary annuity of \$1 becomes: $S_n = \frac{(1 + r)^n - 1}{r}$ or $\frac{\text{Compound interest}}{\text{Rate}}$

This formula is the basis for Table 3, page 961. Look at Table 3 or use the formula itself to check the calculations.

table 4—present value of an ordinary annuity of \$1

Using the same example as for Table 3, we can show how the formula of P_n, *the present value of an ordinary annuity*, is developed.

END OF YEAR			0	1	2	3
1st payment	$\frac{1{,}000}{1.08}$ =	\$ 926.14 ←		\$1,000		
2nd payment:	$\frac{1{,}000}{(1.08)^2}$ =	\$ 857.52 ←			\$1,000	
3rd payment:	$\frac{1{,}000}{(1.08)^3}$ =	\$ 794.00 ←				\$1,000
Total present value		\$2,577.66				

For the general case, the present value of an ordinary annuity of \$1 may be expressed:

1. $P_n = \frac{1}{1 + r} + \frac{1}{(1 + r)^2} + \frac{1}{(1 + r)^3}$

2. Substituting, $P_n = \frac{1}{1.08} + \frac{1}{(1.08)^2} + \frac{1}{(1.08)^3}$

3. Multiply by $\frac{1}{1.08}$: $P_n\frac{1}{1.08} = \frac{1}{(1.08)^2} + \frac{1}{(1.08)^3} + \frac{1}{(1.08)^4}$

4. Subtract (3) from (2): $P_n - P_n\frac{1}{1.08} = \frac{1}{1.08} - \frac{1}{(1.08)^4}$

5. Factor: $P_n\left(1 - \frac{1}{1.08}\right) = \frac{1}{1.08}\left[1 - \frac{1}{(1.08)^3}\right]$

6. or $P_n\left(\frac{.08}{1.08}\right) = \frac{1}{1.08}\left[1 - \frac{1}{(1.08)^3}\right]$

7. Multiply by $\frac{1.08}{.08}$: $P_n = \frac{1}{.08}\left[1 - \frac{1}{(1.08)^3}\right]$

The general formula for the present worth of an annuity of \$1.00 is

$$P_n = \frac{1}{r}\left[1 - \frac{1}{(1 + r)^n}\right] = \frac{\text{Compound discount}}{\text{Rate}}$$

Solving,

$$P_n = \frac{.2062}{.08} = 2.577$$

The formula is the basis for Table 4, page 962. Check the answer in the table. The present-value tables, Tables 2 and 4, are used most frequently in capital budgeting.

Note that the tables for annuities are not really essential. That is, with Tables 1 and 2, compound interest and compound discount can be readily computed. Then it is simply a matter of dividing either of these by the rate to get values equivalent to those shown in Tables 3 and 4.

table 5—present value of SYD depreciation

As Chapter 13 explains more fully, depreciation is a deductible item that reduces income-tax cash outflows. Assume that some equipment has an original cost of $6,000, a useful life of three years, and a terminal scrap value of zero. Table 5, the *Present Value of Sum-of-the-Years'-Digits Depreciation (SYD),* on page 963 is developed for $6,000 depreciable investment at 8 percent:

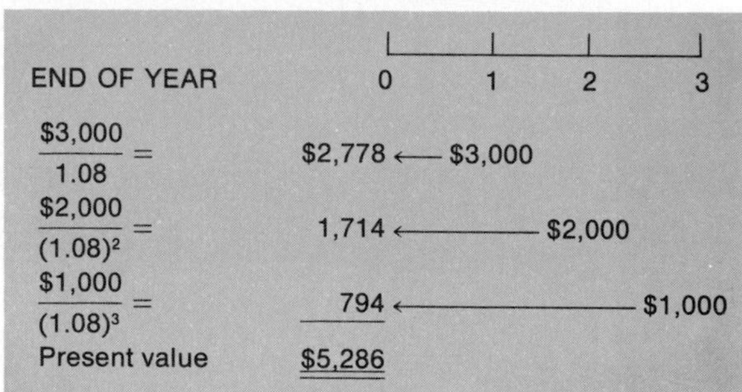

Compare this result with the factor from the third-period row of Table 5: $6,000(.881) = $5,286.

To get the present value of the *income-tax* savings, the present value of SYD depreciation should be multiplied by the applicable tax rate. If the tax rate were 40 percent, the present value of the associated tax savings would be $5,286 × .40, or $2,114.

Consider another example of new equipment having a depreciable cost of $100,000 and being depreciated on an SYD basis for eight years. The present value at 10 percent of the associated tax savings would be $100,000 × (.740) × the income-tax rate. If the tax rate were 40 percent, the present value of the tax savings would be $100,000(.740)(.40) = $29,600.

TABLE 1

Compounded Amount of $1.00 (The Future Value of $1.00)
$S = P(1 + r)^n$. In this table P = $1.00.

PERIODS	4%	6%	8%	10%	12%	14%	20%
1	1.040	1.060	1.080	1.100	1.120	1.140	1.200
2	1.082	1.124	1.166	1.210	1.254	1.300	1.440
3	1.125	1.191	1.260	1.331	1.405	1.482	1.728
4	1.170	1.263	1.361	1.464	1.574	1.689	2.074
5	1.217	1.338	1.469	1.611	1.762	1.925	2.488
6	1.265	1.419	1.587	1.772	1.974	2.195	2.986
7	1.316	1.504	1.714	1.949	2.211	2.502	3.583
8	1.369	1.594	1.851	2.144	2.476	2.853	4.300
9	1.423	1.690	1.999	2.359	2.773	3.252	5.160
10	1.480	1.791	2.159	2.594	3.106	3.707	6.192
11	1.540	1.898	2.332	2.853	3.479	4.226	7.430
12	1.601	2.012	2.518	3.139	3.896	4.818	8.916
13	1.665	2.133	2.720	3.452	4.364	5.492	10.699
14	1.732	2.261	2.937	3.798	4.887	6.261	12.839
15	1.801	2.397	3.172	4.177	5.474	7.138	15.407
16	1.873	2.540	3.426	4.595	6.130	8.137	18.488
17	1.948	2.693	3.700	5.055	6.866	9.277	22.186
18	2.026	2.854	3.996	5.560	7.690	10.575	26.623
19	2.107	3.026	4.316	6.116	8.613	12.056	31.948
20	2.191	3.207	4.661	6.728	9.646	13.743	38.338
30	3.243	5.744	10.063	17.450	29.960	50.950	237.380
40	4.801	10.286	21.725	45.260	93.051	188.880	1469.800

TABLE 2 *(Place a clip on this page for easy reference.)*

Present Value of $1.00.

$P = \frac{S}{(1+r)^n}$. In this table S = $1.00.

PERIODS	4%	6%	8%	10%	12%	14%	16%	18%	20%	22%	24%	26%	28%	30%	40%
1	.962	.943	.926	.909	.893	.877	.862	.847	.833	.820	.806	.794	.781	.769	.714
2	.925	.890	.857	.826	.797	.769	.743	.718	.694	.672	.650	.630	.610	.592	.510
3	.889	.840	.794	.751	.712	.675	.641	.609	.579	.551	.524	.500	.477	.455	.364
4	.855	.792	.735	.683	.636	.592	.552	.516	.482	.451	.423	.397	.373	.350	.260
5	.822	.747	.681	.621	.567	.519	.476	.437	.402	.370	.341	.315	.291	.269	.186
6	.790	.705	.630	.564	.507	.456	.410	.370	.335	.303	.275	.250	.227	.207	.133
7	.760	.665	.583	.513	.452	.400	.354	.314	.279	.249	.222	.198	.178	.159	.095
8	.731	.627	.540	.467	.404	.351	.305	.266	.233	.204	.179	.157	.139	.123	.068
9	.703	.592	.500	.424	.361	.308	.263	.225	.194	.167	.144	.125	.108	.094	.048
10	.676	.558	.463	.386	.322	.270	.227	.191	.162	.137	.116	.099	.085	.073	.035
11	.650	.527	.429	.350	.287	.237	.195	.162	.135	.112	.094	.079	.066	.056	.025
12	.625	.497	.397	.319	.257	.208	.168	.137	.112	.092	.076	.062	.052	.043	.018
13	.601	.469	.368	.290	.229	.182	.145	.116	.093	.075	.061	.050	.040	.033	.013
14	.577	.442	.340	.263	.205	.160	.125	.099	.078	.062	.049	.039	.032	.025	.009
15	.555	.417	.315	.239	.183	.140	.108	.084	.065	.051	.040	.031	.025	.020	.006
16	.534	.394	.292	.218	.163	.123	.093	.071	.054	.042	.032	.025	.019	.015	.005
17	.513	.371	.270	.198	.146	.108	.080	.060	.045	.034	.026	.020	.015	.012	.003
18	.494	.350	.250	.180	.130	.095	.069	.051	.038	.028	.021	.016	.012	.009	.002
19	.475	.331	.232	.164	.116	.083	.060	.043	.031	.023	.017	.012	.009	.007	.002
20	.456	.312	.215	.149	.104	.073	.051	.037	.026	.019	.014	.010	.007	.005	.001
21	.439	.294	.199	.135	.093	.064	.044	.031	.022	.015	.011	.008	.006	.004	.001
22	.422	.278	.184	.123	.083	.056	.038	.026	.018	.013	.009	.006	.004	.003	.001
23	.406	.262	.170	.112	.074	.049	.033	.022	.015	.010	.007	.005	.003	.002	
24	.390	.247	.158	.102	.066	.043	.028	.019	.013	.008	.006	.004	.003	.002	
25	.375	.233	.146	.092	.059	.038	.024	.016	.010	.007	.005	.003	.002	.001	
26	.361	.220	.135	.084	.053	.033	.021	.014	.009	.006	.004	.002	.002	.001	
27	.347	.207	.125	.076	.047	.029	.018	.011	.007	.005	.003	.002	.001	.001	
28	.333	.196	.116	.069	.042	.026	.016	.010	.006	.004	.002	.002	.001	.001	
29	.321	.185	.107	.063	.037	.022	.014	.008	.005	.003	.002	.001	.001	.001	
30	.308	.174	.099	.057	.033	.020	.012	.007	.004	.003	.002	.001	.001		
40	.208	.097	.046	.022	.011	.005	.003	.001	.001						

TABLE 3

Compound Amount of Annuity of $1.00 in Arrears* (Future Value of Annuity)

$$S_n = \frac{(1 + r)^n - 1}{r}$$

PERIODS	4%	6%	8%	10%	12%	14%	20%
1	1.000	1.000	1.000	1.000	1.000	1.000	1.000
2	2.040	2.060	2.080	2.100	2.120	2.140	2.200
3	3.122	3.184	3.246	3.310	3.374	3.440	3.640
4	4.247	4.375	4.506	4.641	4.779	4.921	5.368
5	5.416	5.637	5.867	6.105	6.353	6.610	7.442
6	6.633	6.975	7.336	7.716	8.115	8.536	9.930
7	7.898	8.394	8.923	9.487	10.089	10.730	12.916
8	9.214	9.898	10.637	11.436	12.300	13.233	16.499
9	10.583	11.491	12.488	13.580	14.776	16.085	20.799
10	12.006	13.181	14.487	15.938	17.549	19.337	25.959
11	13.486	14.972	16.646	18.531	20.655	23.045	32.150
12	15.026	16.870	18.977	21.385	24.133	27.271	39.580
13	16.627	18.882	21.495	24.523	28.029	32.089	48.497
14	18.292	21.015	24.215	27.976	32.393	37.581	59.196
15	20.024	23.276	27.152	31.773	37.280	43.842	72.035
16	21.825	25.673	30.324	35.950	42.753	50.980	87.442
17	23.698	28.213	33.750	40.546	48.884	59.118	105.930
18	25.645	30.906	37.450	45.600	55.750	68.394	128.120
19	27.671	33.760	41.446	51.160	63.440	78.969	154.740
20	29.778	36.778	45.762	57.276	75.052	91.025	186.690
30	56.085	79.058	113.283	164.496	241.330	356.790	1181.900
40	95.026	154.762	259.057	442.597	767.090	1342.000	7343.900

**Payments (or receipts) at the end of each period.*

TABLE 4 *(Place a clip on this page for easy reference.)*

Present Value of Annuity of $1.00 in Arrears*

$$P_n = \frac{1}{r}\left[1 - \frac{1}{(1+r)^n}\right]$$

PERIODS	4%	6%	8%	10%	12%	14%	16%	18%	20%	22%	24%	25%	26%	28%	30%	40%
1	0.962	0.943	0.926	0.909	0.893	0.877	0.862	0.847	0.833	0.820	0.806	0.800	0.794	0.781	0.769	0.714
2	1.886	1.833	1.783	1.736	1.690	1.647	1.605	1.566	1.528	1.492	1.457	1.440	1.424	1.392	1.361	1.224
3	2.775	2.673	2.577	2.487	2.402	2.322	2.246	2.174	2.106	2.042	1.981	1.952	1.923	1.868	1.816	1.589
4	3.630	3.465	3.312	3.170	3.037	2.914	2.798	2.690	2.589	2.494	2.404	2.362	2.320	2.241	2.166	1.849
5	4.452	4.212	3.993	3.791	3.605	3.433	3.274	3.127	2.991	2.864	2.745	2.689	2.635	2.532	2.436	2.035
6	5.242	4.917	4.623	4.355	4.111	3.889	3.685	3.498	3.326	3.167	3.020	2.951	2.885	2.759	2.643	2.168
7	6.002	5.582	5.206	4.868	4.564	4.288	4.039	3.812	3.605	3.416	3.242	3.161	3.083	2.937	2.802	2.263
8	6.733	6.210	5.747	5.335	4.968	4.639	4.344	4.078	3.837	3.619	3.421	3,329	3.241	3.076	2.925	2.331
9	7.435	6.802	6.247	5.759	5.328	4.946	4.607	4.303	4.031	3.786	3.566	3.463	3.366	3.184	3.019	2.379
10	8.111	7.360	6.710	6.145	5.650	5.216	4.833	4.494	4.192	3.923	3.682	3.571	3.465	3.269	3.092	2.414
11	8.760	7.887	7.139	6.495	5.938	5.453	5.029	4.656	4.327	4.035	3.776	3.656	3.544	3.335	3.147	2.438
12	9.385	8.384	7.536	6.814	6.194	5.660	5.197	4.793	4.439	4.127	3.851	3.725	3.606	3.387	3.190	2.456
13	9.986	8.853	7.904	7.103	6.424	5.842	5.342	4.910	4.533	4.203	3.912	3.780	3.656	3.427	3.223	2.468
14	10.563	9.295	8.244	7.367	6.628	6.002	5.468	5.008	4.611	4.265	3.962	3.824	3.695	3.459	3.249	2.477
15	11.118	9.712	8.559	7.606	6.811	6.142	5.575	5.092	4.675	4.315	4.001	3.859	3.726	3.483	3.268	2.484
16	11.652	10.106	8.851	7.824	6.974	6.265	5.669	5.162	4.730	4.357	4.033	3.887	3.751	3.503	3.283	2.489
17	12.166	10.477	9.122	8.022	7.120	6.373	5.749	5.222	4.775	4.391	4.059	3.910	3.771	3.518	3.295	2.492
18	12.659	10.828	9.372	8.201	7.250	6.467	5.818	5.273	4.812	4.419	4.080	3.928	3.786	3.529	3.304	2.494
19	13.134	11.158	9.604	8.365	7.366	6.550	5.877	5.316	4.844	4.442	4.097	3.942	3.799	3.539	3.311	2.496
20	13.590	11.470	9.818	8.514	7.469	6.623	5.929	5.353	4.870	4.460	4.110	3.954	3.808	3.546	3.316	2.497
21	14.029	11.764	10.017	8.649	7.562	6.687	5.973	5.384	4.891	4.476	4.121	3.963	3.816	3.551	3.320	2.498
22	14.451	12.042	10.201	8.772	7.645	6.743	6.011	5.410	4.909	4.488	4.130	3.970	3.822	3.556	3.323	2.498
23	14.857	12.303	10.371	8.883	7.718	6.792	6.044	5.432	4.925	4.499	4.137	3.976	3.827	3.559	3.325	2.499
24	15.247	12.550	10.529	8.985	7.784	6.835	6.073	5.451	4.937	4.507	4.143	3.981	3.831	3.562	3.327	2.499
25	15.622	12.783	10.675	9.077	7.843	6.873	6.097	5.467	4.948	4.514	4.147	3.985	3.834	3.564	3.329	2.499
26	15.983	13.003	10.810	9.161	7.896	6.906	6.118	5.480	4.956	4.520	4.151	3.988	3.837	3.566	3.330	2.500
27	16.330	13.221	10.935	9.237	7.943	6.935	6.136	5.492	4.964	4.524	4.154	3.990	3.839	3.567	3.331	2.500
28	16.663	13.406	11.051	9.307	7.984	6.961	6.152	5.502	4.970	4.528	4.157	3.992	3.840	3.568	3.331	2.500
29	16.984	13.591	11.158	9.370	8.022	6.983	6.166	5.510	4.975	4.531	4.159	3.994	3.841	3.569	3.332	2.500
30	17.292	13.765	11.258	9.427	8.055	7.003	6.177	5.517	4.979	4.534	4.160	3.995	3.842	3.569	3.332	2.500
40	19.793	15.046	11.925	9.779	8.244	7.105	6.234	5.548	4.997	4.544	4.166	3.999	3.846	3.571	3.333	2.500

*Payments (or receipts) at the end of each period.

TABLE 5

Present Value of Sum-of-The-Years'-Digits Depreciation on $1.00 of Initial Investment*

PERIODS	8%	10%	12%	14%	16%	20%
3	.881	.855	.831	.808	.786	.745
4	.860	.830	.802	.776	.751	.706
5	.839	.806	.775	.746	.719	.670
6	.820	.783	.749	.718	.689	.637
7	.801	.761	.725	.692	.661	.606
8	.782	.740	.701	.667	.635	.578
9	.765	.720	.680	.643	.610	.552
10	.748	.701	.659	.621	.587	.528
11	.731	.683	.639	.600	.565	.506
12	.715	.665	.620	.581	.545	.485
13	.700	.648	.602	.562	.526	.465
14	.685	.632	.585	.544	.508	.447
15	.671	.616	.569	.527	.491	.430
16	.657	.601	.553	.511	.475	.414
17	.644	.587	.538	.496	.460	.400
18	.631	.573	.524	.482	.445	.386
19	.618	.560	.510	.468	.432	.373
20	.606	.547	.497	.455	.419	.360
30	.504	.442	.393	.353	.320	.269
40	.428	.369	.323	.287	.257	.213

**The quantity tabulated is equal to*

$$\sum_{n=1}^{N} \frac{2(N - n + 1)}{N(N + 1)(1 + r)^n}$$

where n = the number of the individual year

N = number of years of estimated useful life

r = rate of return

Example: Consider the data in the table of Exhibit 13-3, page 442. Assume that the income-tax rate is 40 percent, and the depreciation life is five years.

For a $15,000 depreciable investment at 10 percent, use the factor from the five-period row to obtain the present value of SYD depreciation: $15,000 (.806) = $12,090. To get the present value of the income-tax savings, the present value of $12,090 should be multiplied by the applicable tax rate: $12,090 × .40 = $4,836. When rounded to $4,840, this shortcut result is equal to the sum of the individual year-by-year computations in Exhibit 13-3: $1,820 + $1,328 + $900 + $544 + $248 = $4,840.

The italicized words within the definitions or explanations are themselves defined or described in this glossary. When a term is immediately followed by an italicized term, the latter is typically a synonym explained elsewhere in this glossary. For instance, see *activity accounting*.

ABC METHOD. Stock control technique that divides materials, parts, supplies, and finished goods into subclassifications and uses different control systems for each classification.

ABNORMAL SPOILAGE. Product loss that is not an inherent part of the selected production process. It is not expected to arise under efficient operating conditions and is thus usually controllable in the short run. Contrast with *normal spoilage.*

ABSORPTION COSTING. Method of product costing where fixed manufacturing overhead is included in the inventoriable costs. Contrast with *variable costing.*

ACCOUNTABILITY CENTER. *Responsibility center.*

ACCOUNTING RATE OF RETURN. *Accrual accounting rate of return.*

Accrual Accounting Rate of Return. Method of evaluating performance that divides an accounting measure of income by an accounting measure of investment. Also called *accounting rate of return.*

Actions. Set of the alternative decisions under explicit consideration.

Activity Accounting. *Responsibility accounting.*

Activity Variance. *Production-volume variance.*

Actual Costing. Method of allocating costs to products using actual *direct materials,* actual *direct labor,* and actual *factory overhead.* Contrast with *normal costing* and *standard costing.*

Actual Costs. Amounts determined on the basis of costs incurred (historical costs).

Agency Theory. Conceptual framework in economics that provides a formal model of relationships between a principal (e.g., a superior or owner) and an agent (a subordinate). The theory specifies preferences, risk attitudes, beliefs, and possible *events, actions,* and *outcomes.* The emphasis is on choosing performance measures and incentive contracts.

Allocation. Assigning one or more items of cost or revenue to one or more segments of an organization according to cause, benefits received, responsibilities, or other logical measure of use.

Annuity Depreciation. *Compound interest depreciation.*

Applied Overhead. Factory overhead allocated to products or services, usually by means of some predetermined (budgeted) rate.

Autocorrelation. *Serial correlation.*

Autonomy. Degree of freedom to make decisions.

Average Cost. Computed by dividing some total cost (the numerator) by some denominator.

Avoidable Cost. Costs that will not continue if an ongoing operation is changed or deleted.

Behavior Congruence. Actions by subordinates that are the same as those desired by superiors. Contrast with *goal congruence.*

Bias. Failure of a random sample to represent a population because of some systematic error.

Book Value. Original cost less any accumulated depreciation, depletion, or amortization. Also called *net book value.*

Breakeven Point. Point of activity (sales volume) where total revenues and total expenses are equal.

Budget Appropriation. An authority to spend, usually up to a ceiling amount.

Budget Approximation. Estimate of how a cost truly behaves. The approximation is usually in linear rather than nonlinear form.

Budgets. Formal quantifications of management's predictions. A plan of action expressed in figures.

Budget Variance. Difference between an *actual* amount and a *budget* amount. Also see *control-budget variance.*

Byproducts. Products of joint processes that have minor sales value as compared with that of the major or chief products. Contrast with *joint products.*

Capacity Variance. *Production-volume variance.*

Capital Budgeting. Long-term planning for proposed capital outlays and their financing.

Carrying Costs. Usually consist of a desired rate of return on the investment in inventory and costs of storage space, breakage, obsolescence, deterioration, insurance, and personal property taxes.

CASB. Abbreviation for *Cost Accounting Standards Board.*

Cash Budget. Schedule of expected cash receipts and disbursements. Also see *financial budget.*

CASH CYCLE. *Self-liquidating cycle.*

CERTAINTY. One hundred percent assurance about which *event* will occur.

CERTAINTY EQUIVALENT. Single-number "best estimates" that represent several possible outcomes for a particular *event.*

CERTIFIED MANAGEMENT ACCOUNTANT (CMA). Designation given by the Institute of Management Accounting of the National Association of Accountants to those who pass an examination and meet specified experience and education requirements.

CHOICE CRITERION. Objective that can be quantified, often expressed as a maximization (or minimization) of some form of profit (or cost).

CLOCK CARD. Card used by an employee paid an hourly wage. It is used as a basis for determining an individual's earnings. Contrast with *work ticket.*

CMA. Abbreviation for *Certified Management Accountant.*

COEFFICIENT OF DETERMINATION. Same as r^2.

COEFFICIENT OF VARIATION. *Standard deviation* divided by *expected value.*

COMMITTED COSTS. *Fixed costs* that arise from having property, plant, equipment, and a basic organization.

COMMON COSTS. Costs of facilities and services shared by user departments. Also see *joint costs.*

COMPOUND INTEREST DEPRECIATION. Depreciation method that holds constant the rate of return on the investment. Also called *annuity depreciation.*

COMPREHENSIVE BUDGET. *Master budget.*

COMPTROLLER. *Controller.*

CONDITIONAL LOSS. *Cost of prediction error.*

CONDITIONAL VALUE. Value that will ensue if a particular event occurs.

CONFIDENCE INTERVAL. Upper and lower limits within which the true value is supposed to lie.

CONGRUENCE. *Behavior congruence, goal congruence,* and *risk congruence.*

CONSTANT ORDER-QUANTITY SYSTEM. *Two-bin system.*

CONSTANT VARIANCE. Uniform scatter of points about a regression line. Also known as *homoscedasticity.*

CONTINUOUS BUDGET. A budget that perpetually adds a month in the future as the month just ended is dropped.

CONTRIBUTION APPROACH. Method of preparing income statements that separates variable costs from fixed costs in order to emphasize the importance of cost behavior patterns for purposes of planning and control.

CONTRIBUTION MARGIN. Revenue minus all *variable costs.* May be expressed as a total, per unit, or a ratio.

CONTRIBUTION-MARGIN RATIO. *Contribution margin* divided by revenue.

CONTROL. (a) Action that implements the planning decision and (b) performance evaluation that provides feedback of the results.

CONTROL-BUDGET VARIANCE. Difference between an actual amount incurred and a *budget* amount based on a *flexible budget.*

CONTROL CHART. Graph that plots performance. It distinguishes between abnormal and normal performance, and it helps detect trends.

CONTROL FACTOR UNIT. Measure of workload. Examples are lines typed per hour and pieces mailed per hour.

CONTROLLABLE. *Controllable cost.*

CONTROLLABLE COST. Cost that may be directly regulated at a given level of managerial authority during a given time span.

CONTROLLABLE VARIABLE. *Independent variable.*

CONTROLLABILITY. Degree of influence that a specific manager has over the costs or revenues in question.

Controller. Chief management accounting executive. Also spelled *comptroller.*

Controlling. Obtaining conformity to plans through action and evaluation.

Conversion Cost. *Direct labor* plus *factory overhead.*

Correlation. Relationship between two or more variables.

Cost. Sacrifice made for goods or services. May take the form of an *outlay cost* or an *opportunity cost.* In the most general sense, cost means sacrifice or forgoing.

Cost Accounting. Quantitative method that accumulates, classifies, summarizes, and interprets information for three major purposes: (1) operational planning and control, (2) special decisions, and (3) product costing.

Cost Accounting Standards Board (CASB). Agency formed by the U.S. Congress in 1970 to establish uniform cost accounting standards, which must be used by defense contractors and nearly all federal agencies in the pricing of negotiated contracts.

Cost Accumulation. Collection of cost data in an organized way via an accounting system.

Cost Allocation. Assignment and reassignment of a cost or group of costs to one or more *cost objectives.*

Cost-Allocation Base. Systematic means of relating a given cost or *cost pool* with a *cost objective.*

Cost Apportionment. *Cost allocation.*

Cost Approximation. *Cost estimation.*

Cost Assignment. *Cost allocation.*

Cost Behavior Pattern. *Cost function.*

Cost-Benefit Approach. Primary criterion for choosing among alternative systems or accounting methods. As a system is changed, its expected additional benefits should exceed its expected additional costs.

Cost Center. Smallest *segment* of activity or area of responsibility for which costs are accumulated.

Cost Distribution. *Cost allocation.*

Cost Estimation. Attempt to measure historical costs by specifying some underlying relationship between x and y over a stipulated *relevant range* of x that may be of interest. Contrast with *cost prediction.* Also called *cost approximation.*

Cost Function. Relationship between a cost and one or more variables, such as the total cost of repairs in relation to miles driven. Also called *cost behavior* pattern.

Cost Object. *Cost objective.*

Cost Objective. Any activity for which a separate measurement of costs is desired. Examples include departments, products, and territories.

Cost of Capital. As used in this book, and in many finance books, a synonym for *required rate of return.*

Cost of Prediction Error. Cost of failing to forecast a critical parameter correctly. Also called *conditional loss* and *opportunity loss.*

Cost Pool. *Indirect cost pool.*

Cost Prediction. Attempt to measure future costs. Also called *opportunity loss.*

Cost Reallocation. *Cost allocation.*

Cost Reapportionment. *Cost allocation.*

Cost Redistribution. *Cost allocation.*

Cost Retracing. *Cost allocation.*

Cost Tracing. *Cost allocation.*

CPA. Abbreviation for *Certified Public Accountant.*

Critical Economic Success Factors. *Key variables.*

Critical Success Factors. *Key variables.*

Cross-Allocation Method. *Reciprocal allocation method.*

CURRENTLY ATTAINABLE STANDARDS. Standards expressing a level of economic efficiency that can be reached with skilled, diligent, superior effort.

CURRENT COST. Cost stated in terms of current market prices instead of historical cost.

CURRENT-COST METHOD. *Current cost.*

CURRENT VALUE. Disposal value or sales value or exit value.

CUTOFF RATE. *Required rate of return.*

DCF. Abbreviation for *discounted cash flow.*

DECENTRALIZATION. Relative freedom to make decisions. The lower the level in the organization that decisions are made, the greater the decentralization.

DECISION MODEL. Formal method for making a choice that often involves quantitative analysis.

DECISION TABLE. Convenient summary of the contemplated *actions, events, probabilities,* and *outcomes.* Also called a *payoff table.*

DECISION VARIABLE. *Independent variable.*

DEFECTIVE UNITS. Production that does not meet dimensional or quality standards and is subsequently reworked and sold through regular channels as firsts or seconds, depending on the characteristics of the product and/or available alternatives.

DENOMINATOR LEVEL. Preselected volume level used to set a budgeted fixed-factory-overhead rate.

DENOMINATOR VARIANCE. *Production-volume variance.*

DENOMINATOR VOLUME. The production-volume level used in setting a *factory-overhead* rate for product costing.

DEPENDENT VARIABLE. Cost to be predicted, usually called y.

DIFFERENTIAL COST. *Incremental cost.*

DIRECT ALLOCATION METHOD. Method that allocates each service department's total costs directly to the producing departments, ignoring services to other service departments.

DIRECT COSTING. *Variable costing.*

DIRECT LABOR. All labor that is physically traceable to the finished good in an economically feasible manner.

DIRECT-MATERIAL INVENTORY. Material on hand and awaiting entry into the production process.

DIRECT MATERIALS. All materials that are physically observable as being identified with the finished good and that may be traced to the finished good in an economically feasible manner.

DISCOUNTED CASH FLOW. Method of valuing expected future cash receipts and disbursements in terms of a common date.

DISCOUNT RATE. Minimum desired (required) rate of return.

DISCRETIONARY COSTS. Costs arising from periodic, usually yearly, *budget* appropriation decisions that directly reflect top-management policies. Usually have a *fixed cost* behavior pattern. Also called *managed costs* or *programmed costs.*

DISTURBANCE TERM. Deviation of the actual value of an observation from the true regression line.

DOUBLE-DECLINING-BALANCE DEPRECIATION (DDB). Form of accelerated depreciation that results in first-year depreciation being twice the amount of straight-line depreciation when zero residual value is assumed.

DOUBLE-DISTRIBUTION ALLOCATION METHOD. *Reciprocal allocation method.*

DURBIN-WATSON STATISTIC. Summary measure of the amount of serial correlation in the *disturbance term.*

DYSFUNCTIONAL BEHAVIOR. Actions taken in conflict with top-management goals.

DYSFUNCTIONAL DECISION MAKING. Decisions that may benefit a subpart of an organization but hurt the organization as a whole.

Economic Order Quantity (EOQ). Amount of inventory that should be ordered at one time so that the associated annual costs of the inventory can be minimized.

Effectiveness. Attainment of a predetermined goal.

Efficiency. Relationship between inputs and outputs.

Efficiency Variance. Standard price for a given resource, multiplied by the difference between the actual quantity of inputs used and the standard quantity of inputs allowed for the number of good outputs achieved.

Effort. *Managerial effort.*

Engineered Cost. Any cost that has an explicit, specified relationship with a selected measure of activity.

Environment. Set of uncontrollable factors that affect the success of a process.

EOQ. Abbreviation for *economic order quantity.*

Equivalent Units. Expression of output in terms of doses or amounts of work applied thereto.

Error Term. *Disturbance term.*

Events. Set of all the relevant occurrences that can happen.

EVPI. Abbreviation for *expected value of perfect information.*

Excess-Materials Requisition. Form to be filled out by the production staff to secure any materials needed in excess of the standard amount allotted for output.

Excess Present-Value Index. Ratio of the total present value of future net cash flows of a project to the initial cash outflow of the project.

Expected Annual Activity. *Master-budget volume.*

Expected Annual Capacity. *Master-budget volume.*

Expected Annual Volume. *Master-budget volume.*

Expected Value. Arithmetic mean, a weighted average using the *probabilities* as weights.

Expected Value of Perfect Information (EVPI). Difference between the *expected value* with perfect information and *expected value* with existing information.

Expected Variance. Anticipated variances stipulated in the *budget* for cash planning.

Explanatory Variable. *Independent variable.*

Extrinsic Motivation. Effect of external rewards (e.g., salary increase, bonus) on behavior.

Factory Burden. *Factory overhead.*

Factory Overhead. All costs other than *direct materials* and *direct labor* that are associated with the manufacturing process.

Feedback. In control systems, consists of a comparison of the *budget* with the actual results.

Financial Accounting. Is concerned mainly with how accounting can serve external decision makers, as distinguished from *management accounting.*

Financial Budget. That part of the *master budget* that is composed of the capital budget, cash budget, budgeted balance sheet, and budgeted statement of changes in financial position.

Financial-Planning Model. Mathematical statements of the relationships among all operating and financial activities, as well as other major internal and external factors that may affect decisions. Usually used with a computer.

Finished-Goods Inventory. Goods fully completed but not yet sold.

Fixed Costs. Costs that remain unchanged in total for a given time period despite wide fluctuations in activity.

Flexible Budget. *Master budget* that is adjusted for changes in volume. Also called *variable budget.*

Flexible-Budget Variances. Difference between actual amounts and the *flexible-budget* amounts for the actual output achieved.

FULL COST. Has two commonly used meanings. First, it is often a synonym for *absorption cost.* Second, it often means absorption cost *plus* an allocation of nonmanufacturing costs.

FULLY ALLOCATED COST. *Full cost.*

FULLY DISTRIBUTED COST. *Full cost.*

FUNCTIONAL AUTHORITY. Right to command action laterally and downward with regard to a specific function or specialty.

FUNCTIONAL COSTING. Classifying costs by allocating them to the various functions performed, such as manufacturing, warehousing, delivery, and billing.

GOAL CONGRUENCE. Same goals are shared by top managers and their subordinates.

GOODS IN PROCESS. *Work-in-process inventory.*

GOODS IN PROGRESS. *Work-in-process inventory.*

GROSS MARGIN. Also called *gross profit.* Excess of sales over the cost of goods sold; that is, over the cost of the inventory that is acquired or manufactured and sold.

GROSS PROFIT. *Gross margin.*

HETEROSCEDASTICITY. Violation of the assumption of *constant variance.*

HIGH-LOW METHOD. Method of approximating a *cost function.* The highest and lowest costs are plotted. The slope of the line that connects the two points is regarded as the variable cost per unit of volume. The method is a relatively crude procedure used occasionally as a less-attractive alternative to *regression analysis.*

HOMOGENEITY. An *indirect cost pool* is homogeneous if similar costs are grouped together such that their allocation is not materially different from the allocation that would result if the costs of the activities were allocated separately.

HOMOGENEOUS COST POOL. One approach used to simplify the allocation process by aggregating similar costs and using few allocation bases.

HOMOSCEDASTICITY. Uniform scatter of points about a regression line.

HURDLE RATE. Minimum desired rate of return. Also called *required rate of return.*

IDEAL CAPACITY. *Theoretical capacity.*

IDLE CAPACITY VARIANCE. *Production-volume variance.*

IDLE TIME. Typically represents wages paid for unproductive time caused by machine breakdowns, material shortages, sloppy production scheduling, and the like.

INCENTIVE. *Motivation.*

INCREMENT. *Incremental.*

INCREMENTAL. Change in total results (such as revenue, expenses, or income) under a new condition in comparison to some given or known condition.

INCREMENTAL APPROACH. In capital budgeting, a method of determining which of two alternative courses of action is preferable by calculating the present value of the difference in net cash inflow between one alternative and the other.

INCREMENTAL COST. Difference in total cost between two alternatives.

INDEPENDENT VARIABLE. Usually called x. In cost accounting contexts, usually a measure of volume subject to influence of a decision maker. Also called *controllable variable.*

INDIRECT COST POOL. Any grouping of individual costs that are not identified with a *cost objective.*

INDIRECT LABOR. All factory labor that is not *direct labor.*

INDIRECT MANUFACTURING COSTS. *Factory overhead.*

INDUSTRY ECONOMICS. Factors such as supply, demand, and competition that affect the goals and subgoals of the organization.

INTERCEPT. Value of y when x is zero.

INTERNAL ACCOUNTING. *Management accounting.*

INTERNAL RATE OF RETURN (IRR). Rate of interest at which the present value of expected cash inflows from a project equals the present value of expected cash outflows of the project. Also called *time-adjusted rate of return.*

INTRINSIC MOTIVATION. Effect of internal rewards (e.g., self-satisfaction) on behavior.

INVENTORIABLE COST. *Product cost.*

INVESTMENT CENTER. A *responsibility center* that is accountable for revenues, expenses, and investments.

INVESTMENT TAX CREDIT. Direct reductions of income taxes arising from the acquisition of depreciable assets.

IRR. Abbreviation for *internal rate of return.*

JOB-COST SHEET. Basic document used by a job-order system to accumulate product costs.

JOB ORDER. Document that shows the costs allocated to a specific batch of product.

JOB-ORDER COSTING. Method of allocating costs to products that receive varying attention and effort.

JOINT COSTS. Cost of manufactured goods of relatively significant sales values that are simultaneously produced by a process or series of processes.

JOINT PRODUCT COSTS. *Joint costs.*

JOINT PRODUCTS. Goods that cause *joint costs.*

KEY RESULT AREAS. *Key variables.*

KEY VARIABLES. Subgoals essential to attainment of the primary goal.

LABOR-MIX VARIANCE. Difference in units of input × (Budgeted individual price per hour of input − Budgeted average price per hour of input).

LABOR-YIELD VARIANCE. Difference in units of input × Budgeted average price per hour of input.

LEAD TIME. Time interval between placing an order and receiving delivery.

LEARNING CURVE. *Cost function* such that average costs per unit of output decline systematically as cumulative production rises.

LINEAR PROGRAMMING (LP). Mathematical approach to a group of business problems that contain many interacting variables and that basically involve combining limited resources to maximize profits or minimize costs.

LINE AUTHORITY. Authority that is exerted downward over subordinates.

LP. Abbreviation for *linear programming.*

MANAGED COSTS. *Discretionary costs.*

MANAGEMENT ACCOUNTING. Is concerned mainly with how accounting can serve internal decision makers.

MANAGEMENT AUDIT. Review to determine whether the policies and procedures specified by top management have been implemented.

MANAGEMENT BY EXCEPTION. Practice by the executive of focusing his or her attention mainly on significant deviations from expected results. It might also be called management by variance.

MANAGEMENT CONTROL SYSTEM. Human control in which the major role of the superior is to oversee the work of subordinates.

MANAGERIAL EFFORT. Exertion by a manager toward a goal.

MANAGERIAL STYLE. Way a manager operates from day to day.

MANUFACTURING EXPENSES. *Factory overhead.*

MANUFACTURING OVERHEAD. *Factory overhead.*

MARGINAL COSTING. *Variable costing.*

MARGINAL INCOME. *Contribution margin.*

MARKET-SHARE VARIANCE. (Actual market-share percentage)−(Budgeted market-share percentage) × (Actual industry volume) × (Budgeted average contribution margin). The market-share variance can also be measured in terms of revenues or costs as well as contribution margins.

MARKET-SIZE VARIANCE. (Budgeted market-share percentage) × (Actual industry volume − Budgeted industry volume) × (Budgeted average contribution margin). Can also be measured in terms of revenues or costs.

MARKET VALUE. *Current value.*

Master Budget. *Budget* that summarizes the objectives of all subunits of an organization—sales, production, distribution, and finance. Also called *comprehensive budget.*

Master-Budget Activity. *Master-budget volume.*

Master-Budget Volume. Anticipated level of capacity utilization for the coming *budget* year.

Master Operations List. List compiled for routing and scheduling a variety of products through a series of operations or processes.

Material Mix. Relative proportion or combination of the various ingredients of *direct materials* or of the components of a finished product line.

Material-Mix Variance. Difference in units of input × (Budgeted individual price per unit of material − Budgeted average price per unit).

Material Requisition. *Stores requisition.*

Material Yield. Quantity of finished output produced from a predetermined or standard combination and amount of inputs such as direct material.

Matrix Allocation Method. *Reciprocal allocation method.*

Matrix Organization. Hybrid arrangement whereby one manager is given responsibility for a project that must use services from several functional *responsibility centers.*

Mixed Cost. Has both fixed and variable elements. Its total fluctuates as x changes within the *relevant range,* but not in direct proportion. Its behavior conforms with the basic formula $y = a + bx$.

Model. Depiction of the interrelationships among the recognized factors in a real situation.

Motivation. Desire for a selected goal together with the resulting drive or pursuit toward that goal.

Multicollinearity. Presence of high correlation between the *independent variables* in a *multiple regression.*

Multiple Regression. When more than two *independent variables* are studied by *regression analysis.*

NAA. *National Association of Accountants.*

National Association of Accountants (NAA). Largest U.S. professional organization of accountants whose major interest is *management accounting.*

Negotiated Static Budget. Most common accounting technique for controlling *discretionary costs.*

Net Book Value. *Book value.*

Net Present Value (NPV). Method of calculating the expected utility of a given project by discounting all expected future cash flows to the present, using some predetermined minimum desired *rate of return.*

Net Realizable Value. Estimated selling price of a product in the ordinary course of business, less reasonably predictable costs of completion and disposal.

Net-Realizable-Value Method. Method of *joint-cost* assignment that assigns costs in proportion to a product's ability to generate revenue.

Normal Costing. Method of charging costs to products using actual *direct materials,* actual *direct labor,* and predetermined *factory-overhead* rates.

Normal Cost System. *Normal costing.*

Normal Spoilage. *Spoilage* that is an inherent result of the particular process and is thus uncontrollable in the short run.

Normal Volume. Level of capacity utilization (which is less than 100 percent of *practical capacity*) that will satisfy average consumer demand over a span of time that includes seasonal, cyclical, and trend factors (usually three to five years).

NPV. Abbreviation for *net present value.*

Objective Function. Quantification of a goal to be maximized or minimized in an LP model.

Object of Costing. *Cost objective.*

Operating Budget. *Budget* of the income statement together with supporting schedules.

Operation. Standardized labor or machine method or technique that is repetitively performed regardless of the distinguishing features of the finished product.

Operation Costing. Method where distinctions are made between batches of product. Materials are specifically allocated to the batches, and conversion costs are computed for each operation undergone during production.

Opportunity Cost. The maximum amount that might have been earned if the productive good, service, or capacity had been applied to an alternative use.

Opportunity Loss. *Cost of prediction error.*

Ordering Costs. Usually consist of clerical costs of preparing a purchase order or production order and special processing and receiving costs relating to the number of orders processed.

Ordinary Incremental Budget. *Budget* that usually considers the previous period's *budget* and actual results as given. The budget amount is then changed in accordance with experience during the previous period and expectations for the next period.

Organization Goals. Goals specified by top management.

Organization Morality. Legal and top-management constraints on goals, behavior, and control systems.

Organization Objectives. *Organization goals.*

Organization Structure. Formal relationships among the individuals and *segments* within an organization.

Outcomes. Consequences of the various possible combinations of *actions* and *events.*

Outlay Cost. Cash disbursement, as distinguished from an *opportunity cost.*

Overapplied Factory Overhead. Excess of overhead applied to products over actual overhead incurred.

Overapplied Overhead. *Overapplied factory overhead.*

Overtime Premium. Classification of *indirect labor* costs, consisting of the wages paid to all factory workers in excess of their straight-time wage rates.

Parameter. A constant, such as a, or a coefficient, such as b, in a model or system of equations, such as $y = a + bx$.

Payback. Measure of the time needed to recoup, in the form of cash inflow from operations, the initial dollars invested in a project. Also called *payout.*

Payoffs. *Outcomes.* Distinguish from *payback.*

Payoff Matrix. *Decision table.*

Payoff Table. *Decision table.*

Payout. *Payback.*

Performance Reports. Measurements of actual results, which are often compared with budgeted amounts in a columnar manner.

Period Cost. A noninventoriable cost. Such costs are deducted as expenses during the current period without having been previously classified as costs of inventory.

Periodic-Inventory Method. Method whereby the cost of goods sold is computed periodically by relying solely on physical counts and not keeping day-to-day records of units sold or on hand.

Perpetual-Inventory Method. Requires a continuous record of additions to or reductions in materials, work in process, and cost of goods sold on a day-to-day basis.

Planning. Delineation of goals, predictions of potential results under various ways of achieving goals, and a decision of how to attain the desired results.

P.P.B. *Program budgeting,* which is sometimes referred to as planning or programming and budgeting.

Practical Capacity. Maximum level at which the plant or department can operate efficiently.

Prepaid Expenses. Assets that exist because operating supplies and rights to services have been acquired in advance of use.

Previous-Department Costs. *Transferred-in costs.*

Price Variance. Difference between actual unit prices and budgeted or standard unit prices multiplied by the actual quantity of goods or services in question.

Prime Costs. Consists of *direct materials* plus *direct labor.*

Principal-Agent Paradigm. *Agency theory.*

Priority Incremental Budget. Similar to *ordinary incremental budget.* However, the budget request must be accompanied by a statement of what incremental activities or changes would occur if the *budget* were increased or decreased by a given amount or percentage.

Probabilities. Likelihoods of occurrence of *events.*

Probability Distribution. Describes the relative likelihood of *events.*

Process. Series of *actions* or *operations* leading to a definite end.

Process Costing. System for applying costs to like products that are mass produced in continuous fashion through a series of production steps called *processes.*

Product-Cost. Cost identified with goods acquired or produced for sale.

Production-Volume Variance. Budgeted fixed factory overhead − Applied fixed factory overhead. Also may be expressed as Fixed-factory-overhead rate × (*denominator volume* − Actual volume of output). Also called *activity variance, capacity variance, denominator variance,* and just plain *volume variance.*

Profitability Accounting. *Responsibility accounting.*

Profit Center. *Segment* of a business that is responsible for both revenue and expense.

Pro Forma Statements. Budgeted financial statements.

Program Budgeting. Careful specification and analysis of objectives, outputs, inputs, costs, and alternatives that link plans to budgets.

Programmed Costs. *Discretionary costs.*

Proration. Apportioning of any variances, including *underapplied* or *overapplied overhead,* among various inventories and cost of goods sold.

P/V Chart. Profit-volume graph showing the impact of changes in volume on net income.

Quantity Variance. *Efficiency variance* pertaining to *direct materials* and *direct labor.* Also see *sales-quantity variance.*

r^2. The proportion of the variance that is explained by the independent variable. Also called the *coefficient of determination.*

Rate Variance. *Price variance* for *direct labor.*

Reciprocal Allocation Method. Method that allocates costs by explicitly recognizing the mutual services rendered among all departments.

Regression Analysis. Measurement of the average amount of change in the *dependent variable* (e.g., shipping cost) that is associated with unit increases in the amounts of one or more *independent variables* (e.g., miles traveled).

Relative-Sales-Value Method. *Net-realizable-value method.*

Relevant Cost. Expected future cost that will differ among alternatives.

Relevant Data for Decision Making. Expected future data that will differ among alternatives.

Relevant Information. *Relevant data for decision making.*

Relevant Range. Band of activity in which budgeted sales and expense relationships will be valid.

Reorder Point. Quantity level at which a new order should be placed.

Replacement Cost. Cost to replenish a given amount of an asset.

Required Rate of Return. Minimum desired rate of return.

Residual Income. Net income of a *profit center* or *investment center,* less the "imputed" interest on the net assets used by the center.

Residual Term. *Disturbance term.*

Responsibility Accounting. System of accounting that recognizes various *responsibility centers* throughout the organization and reflects the plans and actions of each of these centers by allocating particular revenues and costs to those having the pertinent responsibilities. Also called *profitability accounting* and *activity accounting.*

Responsibility Center. Part or *segment* of an organization that is accountable for a specified set of activities. Also called *accountability center.*

Risk. Relative dispersion around an *expected value.*

Risk Averse. Individual's utility for monetary amounts increases at a *decreasing* rate. Thus, a risk averter is generally willing to pay less than the expected monetary value of fair gambles.

Risk Congruence. Sharing of the same attitudes toward risk-taking on the part of superior and subordinates.

Risk Neutral. Utility is directly proportional to monetary amounts. In other words, the utility function is linear; it always bears a constant relationship to monetary amounts.

Risk Seeking. Opposite of *risk averse.* The individual's utility for monetary amounts increases at an *increasing* rate. Thus, a risk seeker is generally willing to pay more than the expected monetary value of fair gambles.

ROI. Abbreviation for return on investment.

RRR. Abbreviation for *required rate of return.*

R-Square. Same as r^2. Also called *r-squared.*

Safety Stock. Minimum or buffer inventory used as a cushion against reasonable expected maximum usage.

Sales Mix. Relative combination of the quantities of a variety of company products that compose total sales.

Sales-Mix Variance. Difference in units × (Budgeted individual contribution margin per unit − Budgeted average contribution margin per unit).

Sales-Quantity Variance. (Actual volume − Static budgeted volume in units) × Budgeted average contribution margin per unit.

Sales-Volume Variance. Difference between the *flexible-budget* amounts and the *static (master) budget* amounts. Unit prices are held constant.

Scrap. Material residue from certain manufacturing operations that has measurable but relatively minor recovery value.

Segment. Any line of activity or part of an organization for which separate determinations of costs or revenues or both are desired.

Self-Liquidating Cycle. Movement from cash to inventories to receivables and back to cash. Also called *cash cycle.*

Semivariable Cost. *Mixed cost.*

Sensitivity Analysis. A "what-if" technique that measures how the expected values in a *decision model* will be affected by changes in the critical data inputs.

Separable Costs. Costs beyond the *split-off point* that are not part of the joint process and can be exclusively identified with individual products.

Sequential Allocation Method. *Step-down allocation method.*

Serial Correlation. Relation of the *disturbance terms* to each other. Also called *autocorrelation.*

Setup Time. Time needed to prepare equipment and related resources for producing a specified number of finished units.

Shadow Prices. Measures of the maximum contributions forgone by failing to have one more unit of scarce capacity in a particular situation. A type of *opportunity cost.*

Signal. Message or specific prediction supplied by the system.

Simple Regression. When only one *independent variable* is studied by *regression analysis.*

Simplex Method. General technique for solving any *linear-programming* problem.

Slope Coefficient. Amount of increase in y for each unit increase in x.

Source Documents. Original records of any transaction. An example is a *stores requisition.*

Specification Analysis. Tests of the basic assumptions underlying *regression analysis.*

Specification Costing. *Operation costing.*

Spending Variance. Actual amount of overhead incurred minus the amount expected to be incurred because of the actual inputs used (as contrasted with the outputs achieved).

Split-Off Point. The juncture of production where the *joint products* become individually identifiable.

Spoilage. Production that does not meet dimensional or quality standards and is junked and sold for disposal value. See *abnormal spoilage* and *normal spoilage.*

SQC. Abbreviation for *statistical quality control.*

Staff Authority. Authority to advise but not to command; it may be exerted laterally or upward.

Standard Absorption Costing. That type of product costing in which the cost of the finished unit is calculated as the sum of the costs of the standard allowances for factors of production, *including fixed factory overhead,* without reference to the costs actually incurred.

Standard Bill of Materials. Specifies the physical quantities allowed for manufacturing a specified number of acceptable finished units.

Standard Costing. *Standard absorption costing* and *standard variable costing.*

Standard Costs. Carefully predetermined costs that should be attained, usually expressed per unit.

Standard Deviation. Square root of the mean of the squared deviations from the *expected value.*

Standard Error. Refers to the sampling error of the *slope coefficients.* Obtained by dividing the *standard error of estimate* by the dispersion of the x values around their mean.

Standard Error of Estimate. Measure of the scatter of the actual observations about the regression line.

Standard Hours Allowed. Number of standard hours that should have been used to obtain actual goods produced (actual outputs achieved).

Standard Hours Earned. *Standard hours allowed.*

Standard Hours of Input Allowed for Good Output Produced. *Standard hours allowed.*

Standard Hours Worked. *Standard hours allowed.*

Standard Variable Costing. Same as *standard absorption costing* except that fixed *factory overhead* is excluded.

States. Synonym for *states of nature.*

States of Nature. See *events.*

Static Budget. *Budget* prepared for only one level of activity and, consequently, one that is not adjusted automatically to changes in the level of volume. Contrast with *flexible budget.*

Statistical Quality Control (SQC). Formal means of distinguishing between random (chance) deviations and other deviations from normal expectations in an operating process.

Step Allocation Method. *Step-down allocation method.*

Step-Down Allocation Method. Method that recognizes services rendered by service departments to other service departments.

Step-Function Cost. Cost of the input is constant over various small ranges of output, but it increases by discrete amounts (that is, in steps) as activity moves from one range to the next.

Stockout Costs. Costs that include expensive expediting, loss of contribution margins, and loss of customer goodwill.

Stores Requisition. Form used to charge *job-cost sheets* for *direct materials* used.

Straight-Line Depreciation. A method of allocating the cost of plant assets based on units of time.

Strategic Planning. Long-run planning concerning products, processes, and the general direction of the organization.

Subunit. *Segment.*

Sum-of-the-Years'-Digits Depreciation (SYD). Popular form of accelerated depreciation where the sum of the digits is the total of the numbers representing the years of life.

Sunk Cost. A cost that is already incurred and, therefore, is irrelevant to the decision process.

Tax Shield. Noncash items (e.g., depreciation) charged against revenue, thus protecting that amount of revenue from taxation.

Technical Coefficients. Coefficients of the constraints in an *LP* model.

Theoretical Capacity. Measurement of capacity that assumes the production of output 100 percent of the time.

Time-Adjusted Rate of Return. Same as *internal rate of return.*

Total Project Approach. Method of comparing two or more alternatives by computing the total expected cash flows of each alternative and then converting these flows to their present values.

Transfer Price. Price charged by one *segment* of an organization for a product or service that it supplies to another segment of the same organization.

Transferred-in Costs. In *process costing,* costs incurred in a previous department that have been received by a subsequent department.

Treasurer. Financial executive who is primarily responsible for obtaining investment capital and managing cash.

t-value. Regression coefficient of each *independent variable* divided by its *standard error.*

Two-Bin System. Inventory-control system where two bins are kept, and after the first bin is emptied, a withdrawal from the second bin is used to signal the need for a reorder. Also called *constant order-quantity system.*

Unavoidable Cost. Opposite of *avoidable cost.*

Uncertainty. Possibility that an actual amount will deviate from an expected amount.

Underapplied Factory Overhead. Excess of actual *factory overhead* over the factory overhead applied to products.

Underapplied Overhead. *Underapplied factory overhead.*

Usage Variance. *Efficiency variance* pertaining to *direct materials* or *direct labor.*

Utiles. Quantifications of the *utility values* of a given monetary amount.

Utility Value. Value of a specific *outcome,* such as a monetary amount, to a decision maker. Also see *risk averse.*

Variable Budget. *Flexible budget.*

Variable Cost. Cost that is uniform per unit but fluctuates in total in direct proportion to changes in the related total activity or volume.

Variable Costing. Type of product costing that charges fixed *factory overhead* immediately as incurred against the revenue of the period, without assigning it to specific units produced. Also called *direct costing* or *marginal costing.*

Variable-Cost Ratio. *Variable-expense ratio.*

Variable-Expense Ratio. All variable expenses divided by revenues.

Variances. Deviations of actual results from the expected or budgeted or standard results.

Volume Variance. *Production-volume variance* and *sales-volume variance.*

Waste. Material that is lost or evaporates or shrinks in a manufacturing process, or is a residue that has no measurable recovery value.

Working Capital Cycle. *Self-liquidating cycle.*

Working Capital Provided by Operations. Revenues less all operating expenses requiring working capital.

Work-in-Process Inventory. Goods undergoing the production process but not fully completed.

WORK IN PROGRESS. *Work-in-process inventory.*

WORK MEASUREMENT. Careful analysis of a task, its size, the methods used in its performance, and its efficiency.

WORK TICKET. Indicates the time spent on a specific job. Contrast with *clock card.*

ZBB. *Zero-base budgeting.*

ZERO-BASE BUDGETING. Budgeting from the ground up as though the budget were being initiated for the first time. Also called *zero-based budgeting.*

INDEX